New Learning Solutions

Student Resources

Resources

Online Health Resources

Log on to glencoe.com

Internet resources are just a click away

HEALTH
Making Life Choices

GLENCOE

Teacher Resources

- PuzzleMaker game
- Fitness Zone videos and podcasts
- Health eNewsletter library
- Scope and Sequence
- National Standards correlations charts
- Conference/grant links

Assessment Resources

- Fast Files
- *ExamView® Assessment Suite*

HEALTH
Making Life Choices

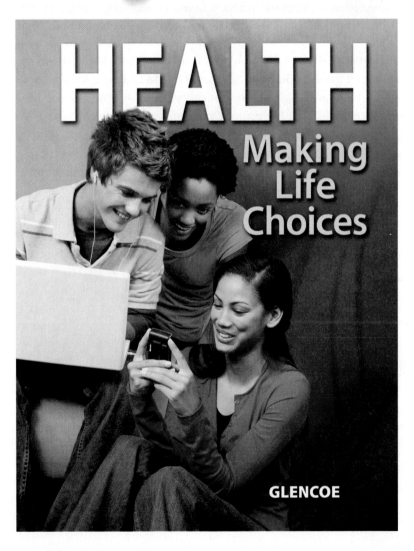

Frances Sizer Webb   **Linda Kelly DeBruyne**

Glencoe

About the Authors

Frances Sizer Webb, MS, RD, FADA, received an Associate of Arts in Nursing from Miami-Dade Community College in 1977; she attended Florida State University's College of Human Sciences where, in 1980, she received her BS, and in 1982, her MS in nutrition. She has counseled clients in the University's stress-reduction clinic and served as consultant to schools and alcoholism programs in Florida. Among her writings are the textbooks *Nutrition: Concepts and Controversies,* now entering its twelfth edition; *Life Choices: Health Concepts and Strategies; Essential Life Choices;* and *The Fitness Triad: Motivation, Training, and Nutrition.* She has published in *Shape* magazine, in the newsletter *Healthline,* and in the *Journal of Chemical Senses.* She is vice-president and a founding member of Nutrition and Health Associates, an information resource center in Tallahassee, Florida, now entering its twenty-fifth year. She now devotes full time to writing and lecturing on topics in health and nutrition. In her free time, she actively supports *ECHO,* a Tallahassee-based resource that provides emergency food, clothing, job readiness training, and other assistance to people in crisis.

Linda Kelly DeBruyne, MS, RD, received her BS in 1980 and her MS in 1982 in nutrition and food science at the Florida State University. She is also a founding member of Nutrition and Health Associates, where her specialty areas are fitness and life-cycle nutrition. Her other textbooks are *Life Span Nutrition: Conception through Life; The Fitness Triad: Motivation, Training, and Nutrition; Nutrition for Health and Healthcare,* and *Nutrition and Diet Therapy.* She also serves as consultant to a group of Tallahassee pediatricians for whom she teaches infant nutrition classes to parents. She is a member of the American Dietetic Association.

 **Glencoe**

The McGraw-Hill Companies

Send all inquiries to:
Glencoe/McGraw-Hill
21600 Oxnard Street, Suite 500
Woodland Hills, CA 91367

ISBN: 978-0-07-880043-6 (Student Edition)
MHID: 0-07-880043-9 (Student Edition)

ISBN: 978-0-07-880735-0 (Teacher Annotated Edition)
MHID: 0-07-880735-2 (Teacher Annotated Edition)

1 2 3 4 5 6 7 8 9 027/043 13 12 11 10 09 08

TAE Table of Contents

Glencoe/McGraw-Hill *Health: Making Life Choices* Program Overview

Health: Making Life Choices provides a comprehensive health education

Health: Making Life Choices covers a broad range of topics, including areas of mental, physical, and social health. The text is divided into the following eight units:

- **I.** Introduction to Health
- **II.** Your Emotional and Mental Health
- **III.** Your Physical Health
- **IV.** Drug Use and Abuse
- **V.** Disease Prevention
- **VI.** The Life Cycle
- **VII.** First Aid and Safety
- **VIII.** Global Issues

Meets the National Health Education Standards

Health: Making Life Choices meets all the National Health Education Standards. The text is correlated to National Health Education Standards. A correlations chart is included as part of the *Health: Making Life Choices* Online Learning Center.

Provides Increased Reading Comprehension

Health: Making Life Choices will help students increase their reading comprehension. Definitions for health terms are written into the text. All vocabulary terms are highlighted and bolded in the text.

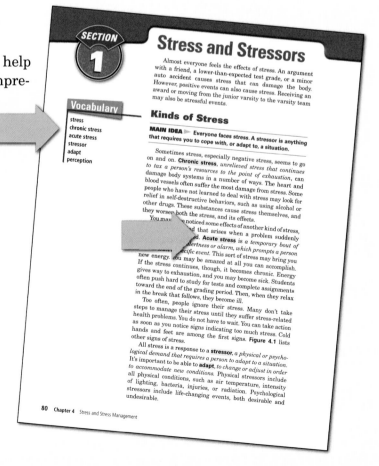

SECTION 1

Stress and Stressors

Almost everyone feels the effects of stress. An argument with a friend, a lower-than-expected test grade, or a minor auto accident causes stress that can damage the body. However, positive events can also cause stress. Receiving an award or moving from the junior varsity to the varsity team may also be stressful events.

Vocabulary

stress
chronic stress
acute stress
stressor
adapt
perception

Kinds of Stress

MAIN IDEA ▶ Everyone faces stress. A stressor is anything that requires you to cope with, or adapt to, a situation.

Sometimes stress, especially negative stress, seems to go on and on. **Chronic stress**, *unrelieved stress that continues to tax a person's resources to the point of exhaustion*, can damage body systems in a number of ways. The heart and blood vessels often suffer the most damage from stress. Some people who have not learned to deal with stress may look for relief in self-destructive behaviors, such as using alcohol or other drugs. These substances cause stress themselves, and they worsen both the stress, and its effects.

You may have noticed some effects of another kind of stress, ...d that arises when a problem suddenly ...d. **Acute stress** *is a temporary bout of* ...lertness or alarm, which prompts a person ...ecific event. This sort of stress may bring you new energy. You may be amazed at all you can accomplish. If the stress continues, though, it becomes chronic. Energy gives way to exhaustion, and you may become sick. Students often push hard to study for tests and complete assignments toward the end of the grading period. Then, when they relax in the break that follows, they become ill.

Too often, people ignore their stress. Many don't take steps to manage their stress until they suffer stress-related health problems. You do not have to wait. You can take action as soon as you notice signs indicating too much stress. Cold hands and feet are among the first signs. **Figure 4.1** lists other signs of stress.

All stress is a response to a **stressor**, *a physical or psychological demand that requires a person to adapt to a situation*. It's important to be able to **adapt**, *to change or adjust in order to accommodate new conditions*. Physical stressors include all physical conditions, such as air temperature, intensity of lighting, bacteria, injuries, or radiation. Psychological stressors include life-changing events, both desirable and undesirable.

80 Chapter 4 Stress and Stress Management

Sexuality Information

Health: Making Life Choices provides sexuality information in two parts: *Understanding Sexuality* and *Preventing Pregnancy and STDs*. The three Sections of *Understanding Sexuality* provide information on sexual activity, sexual myths, and sexual orientation. *Preventing Pregnancy and STDs* deals with the major contraceptive methods, sterilization, and contraceptive failure.

Illustrations and Photographs

Health: Making Life Choices displays colorful graphics, creating high visual appeal for the students and teachers. Illustrations and other graphics are integrated into the text, providing students who are visual learners with another way of understanding the information in the text. Photographs selected for inclusion in *Health: Making Life Choices* also offer students a visual way of understanding the information in the text.

The Stressors of High School

MAIN IDEA ▶ All high school students face many stressors.

During the high school years, teens must adapt to a variety of changes. In fact, high school is often considered one of the most stressful periods of life. Many of the changes high school students face seem positive, and others seem negative. All kinds of change, however, can be stressors.

A group of researchers studied the effects of life changes on high school students. They found that, when students faced more than one change at a time, their grade point averages dropped. So did their scores on a test of self-esteem. Students who handled changes one at a time were less affected by stress. If you are experiencing many changes or stressors listed in **Figure 4.2**, try focusing on them one at a time. That will help reduce your level of stress and protect your self-esteem.

" The greatest weapon against stress is our ability to choose one thought over another."

—William James
(1842–1910)
Psychologist and philosopher

The Perception of a Stressor

MAIN IDEA ▶ An event may be more or less stressful, depending on how you perceive that event.

Your reaction to an experience depends largely on your **perception**, *a meaning given to an event based on an individual's previous experience or understanding of it*. Your perception of any event is not quite like anyone else's, because your life experiences are unique to you. Your life experiences shape your perceptions.

For example, you and a friend might be together during a powerful thunderstorm. Your friend might be afraid while you enjoy watch the rain come down. You and your friend react to the storm based on your perceptions of thunderstorms.

Figure 4.3 demonstrates how your perception affects the way you respond to events.

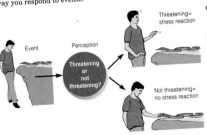

Event

Perception

Threatening or not threatening?

Threatening= stress reaction

Not threatening= no stress reaction

Figure 4.3

Perceptions and Stressors
To produce stress, and event must be perceived as threatening.

Section 1 Stress and Stressors **83**

Health: Making Life Choices Program Overview

Teacher Annotated Edition

The *Health: Making Life Choices* Teacher Annotated Edition (TAE) is designed to help you make the most effective use possible of the student text. The activities suggested in the Teacher Annotated Edition offer ideas for classroom and homework activities.

Health: Making Life Choices also provides activities for students of different ability levels and learning styles. Students are asked to create visual presentations, such as posters and bulletin boards, and to use new technology when completing some of the activities.

Class Activity
Organize: Not having enough time in the day to complete their activities is a common source of stress for teenagers. The best way students can respond to such stress is to develop effective time management strategies.

* Ask students to create a time management chart. In the first column of the chart, have them list their school, home, work, and social activities.
* In the second column they should record the amount of time spent in each of the four activity areas.
* In column three they should write what they can do, if anything, to reduce the amount of time spent on each activity area.
* In the fourth column, have students include what they would do with the free time they have now created for themselves.

■ **Figure 4.9** *It's important to manage your time. How can managing your time benefit you?*

Caption Answer: I can have time to spend with my friends.

Time Management

MAIN IDEA ▶ Wise time management helps control stress.

Efficient time management can also help you to minimize stress. Time is similar to financial income. You receive certain amounts of it at regular intervals. In the case of time, you receive 24 hours each day.

Managing time wisely helps you plan ahead and enjoy the present. When your friends call on a Sunday to invite you out, you don't want to be caught with no money on hand, no clean clothes, and no studying done for the big exam on Monday. That is an avoidable stress. Planning ahead can prevent it.

The best way to manage your time is to make a time budget. Follow these steps to create your own weekly time schedule (see **Figure 4.10**):

* Draw a grid that lists the days of the week across the top. List blocks of time, such as each hour from waking to bedtime, down the left side.
* Fill in your set appointments, such as class meetings.
* Add study time, waking and travel time, time for physical activities, chores, and mealtimes.
* Add times for recreation and relaxation.
* Make a list of special plans for the week.

CHAPTER 1 Planning Guide

CHAPTER 1 Health Choices and Behavior

Objectives	Features
• Explain the relationship between health and wellness.	• *Applying Health Skills:* Decision-Making Skills (page 9)
• Describe how many of the leading diseases are related to lifestyle choices.	• *Consumer Skills Activity:* Understanding Health News (page 12)
• List the lifestyle habits that you can adopt to maximize your wellness.	• *Health Skills:* Reading Health News (page 13)
• Describe how your mental/emotional, physical, and social health are related to wellness.	• *Health Skills:* Steps to Goal Setting (page 18)
• Define the steps in goal setting.	

Introduction
Teaching Support
Fast Files
* *Vocabulary:* Learning Vocabulary, Crossword Puzzle, Fill in the Missing Term
* *Study Outline*
* *Reading Cloze*
* *Reteaching:* Lifestyle Diseases, Motivation, Wellness
* *Enrichment Activities:* What Is Important? Wellness Day, Steps to Goal Setting
* *Career Briefs:* Sociologists
* *Life Choice Inventory:* How Long Will You Live?
* *Section Quizzes:* Sections 1–3
* *Tests:* Chapter 1 Test A, Chapter 1 Test B

Multimedia Support
* *ExamView® Assessment Suite*
* Online Learning Center

Introducing Chapter 1
Chapter Preview Activity
This activity will serve to introduce the chapter and help students begin getting to know each other. Follow these steps:

1. Introduce the definition of life-management skills and the concept of wellness.
2. Divide the class into small discussion groups, or have the students work individually on paper. Ask students:
   a. What do you expect to learn from this course? What information will help you manage your life?
   b. How would you define wellness?
   c. What are two personal wellness goals you would like to achieve by the end of the course?

⏱ Not Enough Time?
Here are some suggestions to ensure that you cover the key topics in this chapter.

DAY 1 Before class, have students read Sections 1 and 2 and the Fact or Fiction (p. 3). Complete activities in Sections 1 and 2 in class. You may also want to assign one of the reteaching activities from the Teacher Classroom Resources

DAY 2 Before class, have students read Section 3 and the Consumer Skills Activity on page 12. Reproducible quizzes and two versions of the Chapter Test are available in the Teacher Classroom Resources.

Bulletin Board Activity
Place two sheets of poster board on the wall. Write the word *wellness* in the center of one poster board. Write the word *health* in the center of the other poster board. Circle each word.

Have students take turns writing definitions of the words on the poster boards outside the circles. Read the definitions aloud to the class.

With a bright marker, write the definitions you will be using in class inside the circles.

Fact or Fiction?

Answers:
1. True.
2. False. Today, most of the leading causes of death are primarily related to lifestyle.
3. True.

 Writing Paragraphs will vary.

SECTION 1 Wellness and Your Choices

Focus
Vocabulary Activity
Vocabulary worksheets are provided in the Teacher Classroom Resources.

Teach and Apply
Group Activity
Apply Divide the class into groups of three or four. Assign each group one of the lifestyle factors listed in the chapter. Have each group discuss and write down their views on the following:

1. What are all possible consequences to individuals who do not follow this lifestyle factor?
2. What consequences may affect others?
3. How do these consequences affect one's quality of life?
   a. Immediate effects (daily)
   b. Long-term effects (if the behavior continues for long periods of time)
4. List ways in which teens can change these behaviors and the benefits received if lifestyle behaviors are changed.

Have the class share and discuss each group's answers. Students should realize that every behavior will have positive and negative impacts on their own lives and the lives of those around them. They should realize that by following these basic lifestyle factors, they are making good decisions that will improve their level of health and their quality of life.

Health: Making Life Choices Online Learning Center

The *Health: Making Life Choices* Online Learning Center (OLC) at **glencoe.com** offers online games and activities to enhance student learning. Many of the online activities help students strengthen their health vocabulary skills. Other games and activities offer students health education beyond the classroom.

Fitness Zone Online is a multimedia resource that helps students find ways to be physically active each day.

Student Edition Overview

Strengthens Student Reading and Writing

Health: Making Life Choices enhances student's reading ability to improve students' health literacy and reading comprehension. In the student edition, features such as the Chapter Preview, Fact or Fiction?, Main Ideas, and Caption Questions improve health literacy and writing skills.

Chapter Preview – Heightens students' interest in the text by providing a thought-provoking introduction to the content they are about to study.

Fact or Fiction? – Teachers can assess prior knowledge of the chapter content by having students answer three True/False questions. Each Fact or Fiction section ends with a writing activity, providing students with the opportunity to strengthen writing skills.

Vocabulary – Health vocabulary is highlighted and bolded in the text. The definition for all vocabulary terms are integrated into the text, appearing immediately after the term.

Main Ideas –The main concepts of a section are summarized in the one- or two-sentence Main Idea, appearing under each main section title.

Caption Questions –The caption that accompanies each photo or figure includes a caption question that evaluates students' understanding of the concept discussed.

Compelling feature activities offer students the opportunity to practice the skills they just learned. These activities also offer teachers with limited class time the opportunity to have students practice using health skills.

APPLYING Health Skills

Stress Management

Objectives
- Identify the relationship between time and stress.
- Demonstrate how to apply time-management tips to reduce stress.

Stressed Out Over Time

Deonte's dad was diagnosed with cancer last month. Deonte is really worried about his dad. He also has more responsibilities around the house now that his dad is sick. He has to make sure his little brother finishes his homework, and has to make sure dinner is ready. Tuesdays and Thursdays he works at a supermarket for three hours after school. Mondays and Wednesdays he picks his little brother up from school.

One of Deonte's teachers just assigned a project that requires group work with a few of his classmates for a project. He's worried that he won't have the time to meet with his group and wonders how he will complete the project. The deadline is two weeks away, but it's already causing him stress.

Identify the Problem
1. What is causing Deonte stress?

Form an Action Plan
2. How could Deonte apply time-management tips to solve his problem?
3. Create and fill in a two-week planner for Deonte. Use the information given above and your own estimates of the time needed for other activities, such as sleeping, eating, and homework. Schedule Deonte's project by breaking it into smaller tasks and adding deadlines to the planner. Do you think Deonte will have enough time to complete his project? If not, how could he gain extra time?

What Did You Learn?
4. If you needed more time to complete a project, what would you do to gain extra time?

Applying Health Skills features help student learn, apply, and practice steps for each of the Health Skills. Each feature provides students with the steps to successfully complete the skill.

The activity of the immune system is lower than normal during times of stress. However, between periods of stress, the immune system recovers quickly. Short periods of stress, followed by periods of relief from stress, can strengthen the immune system. Long periods of unrelieved stress, however, can reduce the number of white blood cells or reduce the effectiveness of white blood cells. This makes a person likely to suffer diseases.

The physical changes that take place in your body during times of stress can take a toll on your body. Some of the physical effects of stress include:
- Headache.
- A weakened immune system.
- High blood pressure.
- Digestive disorders.

SECTION 2 Review

Reviewing the Vocabulary

Review the vocabulary on page 85. Then answer these questions.
1. What is the *nervous system*?
2. What is a *hormone*?
3. Which system protects the body from disease?

Reviewing the Facts
4. **Analyze.** Explain what makes cold weather a stressor.
5. **Synthesize.** What might happen if production of the stress hormones were blocked?
6. **Analyze.** Why can chronic stress increase a person's risk of disease?

Writing Critically
7. **Persuasive.** How would you persuade a person you care about to reduce the stress in his or her life? What reasons would you give? What facts would you explain? Write one persuasive paragraph that might convince your reader to reduce and manage stress.

Go Online

For more information on health careers, visit Career Corner at glencoe.com.

Writing Critically questions in the Section Review provide students with an opportunity to develop critical thinking and writing skills. All Writing Critically features focus on one of five writing styles, including: Descriptive, Narrative, Expository, Persuasive, and Personal writing.

Consumer SKILLS ACTIVITY

Claims for "Stress Vitamins"

People often wonder whether any particular diet can protect against the ill effects of stress. Stress does drain the body of its nutrients. It uses up protein from muscle and other lean tissue, calcium from the skeleton, and vitamins and minerals from every cell of the body. Yet most people cannot eat during crises or cannot digest their food, because the stress response shuts down digestive activity in favor of muscular activity. Going without food and nutrients further stresses the body.

To store the needed nutrients ahead of time, you need to eat foods that contain those nutrients. Proper nutrition can build up your defenses.

However, products advertised as "stress vitamins" are not the best choice. They simply cannot provide all the nutrients and other substances that the body needs. If you cannot eat for a long time, you probably do need vitamins, but you need minerals as well. It may help a little to take a vitamin-mineral preparation that supplies a balanced assortment of nutrients, not in "megadoses" but in the amounts needed daily. Even the best pills can't take the place of nourishing food. It's still important to eat as well as possible. There are no quick-fix pills that will make you strong in a crisis.

Writing

1. In what ways can stress drain the body of its nutrients? Why are stress vitamins popular?
2. Why are stress vitamins not the best choice for supplying the needs of the body under stress?
3. How should a person prepare nutritionally for times of stress?

Consumer Skills Activity helps students learn to analyze health-related products and services before they buy. Students learn to analyze the advertising and other claims associated with health-related products and services and to make a decision on sound judgment.

What Teens THINK

What Causes the Most Stress for Teens?

For me, the most stressful thing is school. Because school is a central part of my life, it can be very hard to balance other things such as after-school activities or hanging out with friends. Some days the homework can take hours to finish, and when I have after-school activities in the way, it takes even longer. This creates another problem that a lot of teens face—lack of sleep. Not getting enough sleep can be very stressful on the body. It seems like I can never catch up, which produces even more stress.

—*Alexandra C., 15, California*

My home environment causes the most stress in my life. This involves my siblings, parents, and after-school activities. It seems the days get shorter and shorter. I never seem to have enough time to do everything. There is much pressure to be mature and responsible at home. When you're with your friends you can relax and be yourself, but at home there is a specific format you feel you must follow. Also, when you're home you have more time to think about your current problems, and they all come together at once.

—*Anand M., 16, New York*

The most stress in teens, I think is the pressure they get from school. The students that have goals in life and try to become something probably have the most stress because they are trying the hardest.

—*Terence M., 15, New Mexico*

I believe that it is peer pressure. Peer pressure is the thing that causes stress for so many other matters. For instance, with school, people try to fit in so they go to a party instead of doing their homework. That causes stress at school. Then at home, they try to be "cool" so they stay out late, come and argue with their parents. That causes stress in the home. Peer pressure causes stress with students themselves, with students and school, and with students and their parents.

—*Saundra D. 16, West Virginia*

I would have to pick violence. My family was raised under violence. We lived in and around the projects. There were drug sellers, drunks, fights, and shooting every week. I would worry where I was and who I was with.

—*Jordan H., 15, Massachusetts*

The thing that causes the most stress for me is my schedule. I have enough trouble keeping up with my homework, after-school sports, and part-time job, finding any time to spend with my friends can be impossible. I am always staying up late studying when my friends are watching TV, playing computer games, or surfing the net.

—*Franklin L., 17, Virginia*

School definitely causes the most stress in my life. Starting high school was so stressful. There are so many rules and things to worry about. Everyone is so concerned about being cool. You have to worry about your clothes, your hair, who likes you, who doesn't. Then there are your grades, getting into college, and your future to worry about. It all makes me so stressed out.

—*Carlotta. J. 15., Texas*

What Teens Think offers students a way of relating to the material presented by providing quotes from real teens who face the same problems as students reading this textbook.

Other features included in the Student Edition of *Health: Making Life Choices* are

- Health Skills provide students with ideas of how they can apply the information in the Section.
- Did You Know? offers short bursts of information that are not included, but are related to the Section content.
- Go Online at **glencoe.com** promps students to access the Glencoe Online Learning Center for more information and to test their skills with the online student quizzes and other activities.

Health: Making Life Choices TAE Offers Teachers Comprehensive Tools to Teach Health

The Teacher Annotated Edition (TAE) offers tools to help the teacher, including supplemental information, cross-references, and more. A Planning Guide helps the teacher map out how they will teach the chapter. Information contained in the Planning Guide includes the four step Focus, Teach and Apply, Assess, and Close format to help teachers plan how they will cover the lesson.

- Focus includes the main learning objectives for the section, and one or two activities to focus students' attention on the topic.

- Teach and Apply provides a variety of activity suggestions. The types of activities that may be included in this section are: interdisciplinary activities, learning with visuals, discussion ideas, comprehension checks, group activities, or role play suggestions.

- Assess activities help the teacher gauge students' comprehension of the material. Some evaluations may be subjective, including essay writing, role playing, or oral presentations.

- Close activities sum up the section's content. In many cases, students will be asked to cite key points. These activities are different from those in the Teach and Apply section.

Annotated Text offers teachers activities and projects to assess and enhance their students' understanding of the content.

Additionally, the Teacher Annotated Edition provides teachers with activities covering a broad range of learning styles. Some of the activity types include:

The Teacher Annotated Edition includes answers to the Fact or Fiction? questions, caption questions, answers to section quizzes, and chapter reviews. Finally, additional activities are included in the margins at point-of-use. These point-of-use activities offer teachers another valuable tool to help students understand the health content.

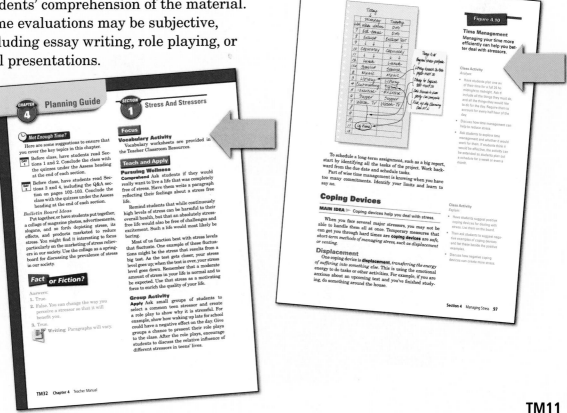

Print Resources

Teacher Classroom Resources—Print

Accompanying the *Health: Making Life Choices* student text and Teacher Annotated Edition is an extensive package of reproducible classroom materials. These materials include one Fast File resource booklet for each chapter. The following provides an example of some Fast File worksheets:

- **Vocabulary Worksheets,** including crossword puzzles and other games based on key terms in the text.
- **Study Outlines** list the main heads of each chapter with space for students to write notes or key points from the text.
- **Reading Clozes** are reading comprehension exercises.
- **Reteaching Worksheets** that offer students an opportunity to relearn the most important concepts of the section.
- **Enrichment Worksheets** that provide students who have mastered the content with an opportunity to expand their knowledge.

Health: Making Life Choices offers teaches and students technology resources designed for the modern classroom.

Visit *Health: Making Life Choices* Online at glencoe.com

Health: Making Life Choices Online provides up-to-date resources and activities that are fully integrated to Glencoe's comprehensive health program.

For Students

Student Center

- Interactive Study Guides, including the following games:
  - eFlashcards
  - Concentration
  - True/False
- Life Choice Inventory
- Health Podcast Activities
- Fitness Zone Online
- Career Corner

For Teachers

Teacher Center

- At glencoe.com click any of the features below to access both student- and teacher-specific resources
- National Health Education Standards Correlations
- Professional Development Articles
- Conference/Grant Links
- National Organizations
- Teaching Today
- Health Podcast Activities
- Fitness Zone Activities
- PuzzleMaker
- *ExamView® Assessment Suite* Instructions
- Scope and Sequence

Fitness Zone Online is a multimedia resource that helps students find ways to be physically active each day.

The Nutrition and Physical Activity Resources include:

- Clipboard Energizer Activities
- Fitness Zone Videos
- Polar Heart Rate Monitor Activities
- Nutrition, Physical Activity, and Injury Prevention Tips
- Links to Nutrition and Physical Activity Resources
- And More!

Create tests from an extensive bank of questions with the latest version of the *ExamView® Assessment Suite* software. Tests can be developed in a variety of formats and customized. All questions are correlated to the National Health Education Standards. With *ExamView®* software, teachers can:

- Create differentiated tests quickly and easily
- Generate progress reports and disaggregate data with Test Manager
- Analyze reports to make sure assessment aligns with instruction!

Pacing Guide

Course Presentation

Health: Making Life Choices is a comprehensive health text with 27 chapters. The study of this text may extend over the course of one semester or one year. Consider the following possible outlines as course outlines.

OUTLINE 1 FULL COURSE
One-year (36 week) course, 27 chapters

UNIT		CHAPTERS	WEEKS
Unit 1	Introduction	Chapter 1	1
Unit 2	Your Social and Emotional Health	Chapters 2, 3, 4, 5	6
Unit 3	Your Physical Health	Chapters 6, 7, 8, 9, 10	6
Unit 4	Drug Use and Abuse	Chapters 11, 12, 13, 14	5
Unit 5	Disease Prevention	Chapters 15, 16, 17	4
Unit 6	The Life Cycle	Chapters 18, 19, 20, 21, 22, 23	8
Unit 7	First Aid and Safety	Chapters 24, 25	3
Unit 8	Global Issues	Chapters 26, 27	3

OUTLINE 2 HEALTH SURVEY COURSE
One-semester (18 week) course, 27 chapters

UNIT		CHAPTERS	WEEKS
Unit 1	Introduction	Chapter 1	1
Unit 2	Your Social and Emotional Health	Chapters 2, 3, 4, 5	3
Unit 3	Your Physical Health	Chapters 6, 7, 8, 9, 10	3
Unit 4	Drug Use and Abuse	Chapters 11, 12, 13, 14	3
Unit 5	Disease Prevention	Chapters 15, 16, 17	2
Unit 6	The Life Cycle	Chapters 18, 19, 20, 21, 22, 23	2
Unit 7	First Aid and Safety	Chapters 24, 25	2
Unit 8	Global Issues	Chapters 26, 27	2

OUTLINE 3 PHYSICAL FITNESS & NUTRITION
One-semester (18 week) course, 17 chapters

UNIT		CHAPTERS	WEEKS
Unit 1	Introduction	Chapter 1	1
Unit 3	Your Physical Health	Chapters 6, 7, 8, 9, 10	6
Unit 4	Drug Use and Abuse	Chapters 11, 12, 13, 14	4
Unit 5	Disease Prevention	Chapters 15, 16, 17	3
Unit 7	First Aid and Safety	Chapters 24, 25	2
Unit 8	Global Issues	Chapters 26, 27	2

OUTLINE 4 MENTAL, EMOTIONAL, & SOCIAL HEALTH
One-semester (18 week) course, 20 chapters

UNIT		CHAPTERS	WEEKS
Unit 1	Introduction	Chapter 1	1
Unit 2	Your Social and Emotional Health	Chapters 2, 3, 4, 5	4
Unit 4	Drug Use and Abuse	Chapters 11, 12, 13, 14	4
Unit 5	Disease Prevention	Chapters 15, 16, 17	3
Unit 6	The Life Cycle	Chapters 18, 19, 20, 21, 22, 23	4
Unit 8	Global Issues	Chapters 26, 27	2

National Health Education Standards

The *Health: Making Life Choices* program meets the National Health Education Standards.

The National Health Education Standard 1

Students will comprehend concepts related to health promotion and disease prevention to enhance health.

1.1 Predict how healthy behaviors can impact health status.

1.2 Describe the interrelationships of emotional, intellectual, physical, and social health.

1.3 Analyze how environment and personal health are interrelated.

1.4 Analyze how genetics and family history can impact personal health.

1.5 Propose ways to reduce or prevent injuries and health problems.

1.6 Analyze the relationship between access to health care and health status.

1.7 Compare and contrast the benefits of and barriers to practicing a variety of healthy behaviors.

1.8 Analyze personal susceptibility to injury, illness, or death if engaging in unhealthy behaviors.

1.9 Analyze the potential severity of injury or illness if engaging in unhealthy behaviors.

The National Health Education Standard 2

Students will analyze the influence of family, peers, culture, media, technology, and other factors on health behaviors.

2.1 Analyze how family influences the health of individuals.

2.2 Analyze how culture supports and challenges health beliefs, practices, and behaviors.

2.3 Analyze how peers influence healthy and unhealthy behaviors.

2.4 Evaluate how the school and community can impact personal health practice and behaviors.

2.5 Evaluate the effect of media on personal and family health.

2.6 Evaluate the impact of technology on personal, family, and community health.

2.7 Analyze how the perceptions of norms influence healthy and unhealthy behaviors.

2.8 Analyze the influence of personal values and beliefs on individual health practices and behaviors.

2.9 Analyze how some health risk behaviors can influence the likelihood of engaging in unhealthy behaviors.

2.10 Analyze how public health policies and government regulations can influence health promotion and disease prevention.

The National Health Education Standard 3

Students will demonstrate the ability to access valid information and products and services to enhance health.

3.1 Evaluate the validity of health information, products, and services.

3.2 Utilize resources from home, school, and community that provide valid health information.

3.3 Determine the accessibility of products and services that enhance health.

3.4 Determine when professional health services may be required.

3.5 Access valid and reliable health products and services.

The National Health Education Standard 4

Students will demonstrate the ability to use interpersonal communication skills to enhance health and avoid or reduce health risks.

4.1 Utilize skills for communicating effectively with family, peers, and others to enhance health.

4.2 Demonstrate refusal, negotiation, and collaboration skills to enhance health and avoid or reduce health risks.

4.3 Demonstrate strategies to prevent, manage, or resolve interpersonal conflicts without harming self or others.

4.4 Demonstrate how to ask for and offer assistance to enhance the health of self and others.

The National Health Education Standard 5

Students will demonstrate the ability to use decision-making skills to enhance health.

5.1 Examine barriers that can hinder healthy decision making.

5.2 Determine the value of applying a thoughtful decision-making process in health-related situations.

5.3 Justify when individual or collaborative decision making is appropriate.

5.4 Generate alternatives to health-related issues or problems.

5.5 Predict the potential short- and long-term impact of each alternative on self and others.

5.6 Defend the healthy choice when making decisions.

5.7 Evaluate the effectiveness of health-related decisions.

The National Health Education Standard 6

Students will demonstrate the ability to use goal-setting skills to enhance health.

6.1 Assess personal health practices and overall health status.

6.2 Develop a plan to attain a personal health goal that addresses strengths, needs, and risks.

6.3 Implement strategies and monitor progress in achieving a personal health goal.

6.4 Formulate an effective long-term personal health plan.

The National Health Education Standard 7

Students will demonstrate the ability to practice health-enhancing behaviors and avoid or reduce risks.

7.1 Analyze the role of individual responsibility for enhancing health.

7.2 Demonstrate a variety of healthy practices and behaviors that will maintain or improve the health of self and others.

7.3 Demonstrate a variety of behaviors to avoid or reduce health risks to self and others.

The National Health Education Standard 8

Students will demonstrate the ability to advocate for personal, family, and community health.

8.1 Utilize accurate peer and societal norms to formulate a health-enhancing message.

8.2 Demonstrate how to influence and support others to make positive health choices.

8.3 Work cooperatively as an advocate for improving personal, family, and community health.

8.4 Adapt health messages and communication techniques to a specific target audience.

CHAPTER 1 Health Choices and Behavior

Objectives

- Explain the relationship between health and wellness.
- Describe how many of the leading diseases are related to lifestyle choices.
- List the lifestyle habits that you can adopt to maximize your wellness.
- Describe how your mental/emotional, physical, and social health are related to wellness.
- Define the steps in goal setting.

Features

- *Applying Health Skills:* Decision-Making Skills (page 9)
- *Consumer Skills Activity:* Understanding Health News (page 12)
- *Health Skills:* Reading Health News (page 13)
- *Health Skills:* Steps to Goal Setting (page 18)

Introduction

Teaching Support

Fast Files

- *Vocabulary:* Learning Vocabulary, Fill in the Missing Term
- *Study Outline*
- *Reading Cloze*
- *Reteaching:* Lifestyle Diseases, Motivation, Wellness
- *Enrichment Activities:* What Is Important? Wellness Day, Steps to Goal Setting
- *Career Briefs:* Sociologists
- *Life Choice Inventory:* How Long Will You Live?
- *Section Quizzes:* Sections 1–3
- *Tests:* Chapter 1 Test A, Chapter 1 Test B

Multimedia Support

- *ExamView® Assessment Suite*
- Online Learning Center

Introducing Chapter 1

Chapter Preview Activity

This activity will serve to introduce the chapter and help students begin getting to know each other. Follow these steps:

1. Introduce the definition of life-management skills and the concept of wellness.

2. Divide the class into small discussion groups, or have the students work individually on paper. Ask students:

    a. What do you expect to learn from this course? What information will help you manage your life?

    b. How would you define wellness?

    c. What are two personal wellness goals you would like to achieve by the end of the course?

Not Enough Time?

Here are some suggestions to ensure that you cover the key topics in this chapter.

 DAY 1 Before class, have students read Sections 1 and 2 and the Fact or Fiction (p. 3). Complete activities in Sections 1 and 2 in class. You may also want to assign one of the reteaching activities from the Teacher Classroom Resources

DAY 2 Before class, have students read Section 3 and the Consumer Skills Activity on page 12. Reproducible quizzes and two versions of the Chapter Test are available in the Teacher Classroom Resources.

Bulletin Board Activity

Place two sheets of poster board on the wall. Write the word *wellness* in the center of one poster board. Write the word *health* in the center of the other poster board. Circle each word.

Have students take turns writing definitions of the words on the poster boards outside the circles. Read the definitions aloud to the class.

With a bright marker, write the definitions you will be using in class inside the circles.

Fact or Fiction?

Answers:
1. True.
2. False. Today, most of the leading causes of death are primarily related to lifestyle.
3. True.

 Writing Paragraphs will vary.

Wellness and Your Choices

Focus

Vocabulary Activity

Vocabulary worksheets are provided in the Teacher Classroom Resources.

Teach and Apply

Group Activity

Apply Divide the class into groups of three or four. Assign each group one of the lifestyle factors listed in the chapter. Have each group discuss and write down their views on the following:

1. What are all possible consequences to individuals who do not follow this lifestyle factor?

2. What consequences may affect others?

3. How do these consequences affect one's quality of life?

   a. Immediate effects (daily)

   b. Long-term effects (if the behavior continues for long periods of time)

4. List ways in which teens can change these behaviors and the benefits received if lifestyle behaviors are changed.

Have the class share and discuss each group's answers. Students should realize that every behavior will have positive and negative impacts on their own lives and the lives of those around them. They should realize that by following these basic lifestyle factors, they are making good decisions that will improve their level of health and their quality of life.

Comprehension Check

Analyze Write two headings on the board. One reading Infectious and the other reading Lifestyle. Ask students to name examples of each disease, and write those names on the board. Then, ask student to analyze the types of diseases that fall under each heading and to tell you what the major difference is between the two diseases. (Infectious diseases can be passed from person to person while lifestyle diseases can not.)

Life Choice Inventory

Ask students to complete the Life Choice Inventory found in the Teacher Classroom Resources or the Online Learning Center.

Assess

Worksheets

A reproducible quiz for Section 1 is provided in the Teacher Classroom Resources.

Close

Have the students write a contract describing how they will change, improve, or maintain a specific lifestyle pattern. Students may volunteer to share some of the changes they are making. You should also make a contract and volunteer some of the changes you will make.

SECTION 2
Portrait of a Well Person

Focus

Vocabulary Activity

Vocabulary worksheets are provided in the Teacher Classroom Resources.

Teach and Apply

Learning with Visuals

Evaluate Draw an equilateral triangle on the board. Label the sides with the components of wellness—physical, social, mental/emotional—one on each side. Ask students if they agree that optimum health needs equal amounts of the three components and that there needs to be balance between the three. Then, ask how a weakness on one side would influence the other sides. (Examples: How would low self-esteem influence a person's social and physical sides? How would constant colds and flu affect a person's mental and social health?) The point should be made that unless all three sides are in a balance, a person cannot be considered as having optimum health.

Class Activity

Discuss Explain that teens need about eight to 10 hours of sleep each night to keep their growing bodies healthy. Add that getting enough sleep helps keep all sides of the health triangle in balance. Ask students how they feel after getting at least eight hours of sleep at night? How do they feel on the mornings when they do not get enough sleep? Prompt students to provide answers other than they feel tiredness. Do they feel like they can play sports as well? Are they as mentally alert as when they get enough sleep? Are they more likely to choose unhealthy foods in order to get a quick boost of energy?

Assess

Worksheets

A reproducible quiz for Section 2 is provided in the Teacher Classroom Resources.

Close

Ask students to list health goals that they would like to work toward in their own lives and to set realistic time limits for accomplishing them.

SECTION 3
Making Behavior Changes

Focus

Vocabulary Activity

Vocabulary worksheets are provided in the Teacher Classroom Resources.

Teach and Apply

Pursuing Wellness

Apply Introduce students to the concept of short-term goals versus long-term goals. Have students write out some short and long term goals that they have. The short-term goals are more specific, more easily obtained goals. They should have dates assigned to some. For example, short-term goals could include training to make the junior varsity track team or getting a good grade in a literature course. An example of a long-term goal could be choosing and applying for admission to a college or university.

Class Activity

Describe Ask students to write a two page essay describing the lifestyle of a fictional adult. The adult is either very healthy or very unhealthy. They should describe the person's sleeping habits, what the person eats, how much physical activity the person gets, and how these habits affect the person in a positive or negative way. In the final paragraph, students should predict the person's health status as a senior. Students should list things the person is doing to maintain good health, or things the person could do to become healthy.

Assess

Worksheets

A reproducible quiz for Section 3 is provided in the Teacher Classroom Resources.

Reproducible Chapter Tests A and B are provided in the Teacher Classroom Resources.

Close

Have students read the Health Skills sidebar "Steps to Goal Setting" on page 18. Then encourage students to think of one health goal they would like to set using the steps. Have students write a short note to themselves explaining how far they expect to be on this goal in three months. Students will place notes into a self-addressed envelope. Explain to the students that these will be given to them in three months for their own self-evaluation.

Go Online

To find supplemental information to suit your individual class, you may want to visit the following Web sites, where you can find additional Internet resources to enhance the study of this chapter. As with all Web sites, you should check the site out first to be sure the information found there is appropriate for your students.

American Medical Association (AMA) Adolescent Health Online

www.ama-assn.org/ama/pub/category/1947.html

This Web site is geared for adolescents ages 11 to 21. The links include Science Update, Adolescent Health Links, American Medical Association Adolescent Health Resources, and others.

CHAPTER 2 Planning Guide

CHAPTER 2 Emotional Health

Objectives

- Discuss the importance of self-acceptance, positive thinking, and values clarification in promoting emotional health.
- Recognize that the acceptance and appropriate expression of feelings are important to emotional health.
- Discuss the advantages of assertive behavior, and identify assertive behavior strategies.
- Describe the role that fear of rejection plays in forming new relationships, and discuss ways to overcome this fear.
- Outline the steps for making a decision.
- Discuss the need for developing a workable relationship with society.

Features

- *Health Skills:* Think Positively (page 27)
- *Applying Health Skills:* Conflict Resolution (page 29)
- *Consumer Skills Activity:* "Added-Value" Advertising (page 31)
- *Health Skills:* How to Resolve Conflicts (page 35)
- *Health Skills:* Making Your Wishes Known (page 39)
- *Q&A:* Teens and Violence (page 46)

Introduction

Teaching Support

Fast Files

- *Vocabulary:* Learning Vocabulary, Matching
- *Study Outline*
- *Reading Cloze*
- *Reteaching Activities:* True or False
- *Enrichment Activities:* Sentence Completion, John's Dilemma, Community Help, Allison's Problem, Describing Yourself
- *Career Briefs:* Recreational Therapists
- *Life Choice Inventory:* Do You Cultivate Emotional Well-Being?
- *Quizzes:* Sections 1–4
- *Tests:* Chapter 2 Test A, Chapter 2 Test B

Multimedia Support

- *ExamView® Assessment Suite*
- Online Learning Center

Introducing Chapter 2

Chapter Preview Activity

Have the students write an "About Me" poem. Write the following format on the board. Have the students write a poem about themselves using this format as a guide.

1. (first name only)
2. (four traits that characterize you)
3. (son, daughter, sister, brother, friend)
4. who loves (three things)
5. who fears (three things)
6. who feels (three things)

7. who would like to see (three things)

8. resident of (town, state, country)

9. (last name only)

Collect the poems, save them, and ask students to share them at the end of the chapter or unit.

 Not Enough Time?

Here are some suggestions to ensure that you cover the key topics in this chapter.

DAY 1 Before class, have students read Chapter 2. Begin the class with the Chapter Preview Activity.

DAY 2 Review the SOFTEN technique on page 40. Have students review steps for making decisions, Section 3.

DAY 3 Have students do the Chapter Review on pages 48–49.

DAY 4 Conclude with the Life Choice Inventory, "Do You Cultivate Emotional Well-Being?" Discuss the inventory with students. At this point, you may want to give students Chapter 2 Test A or Test B, which are provided in your Teacher Classroom Resources.

Bulletin Board Ideas

Have students make collages from pictures depicting various emotions. Have the students title their collages, label each picture with the emotion it depicts, and circle five emotions they have felt. Ask some students to tell about their collages. Display the collages on the bulletin board.

 **Fact or Fiction?**

Answers:

1. False. Emotional health is closely tied to physical health.

2. False. Once a person adopts values, that person continues to test those values and can change them when necessary.

3. False. It is best to face and deal with all feelings as promptly as possible, even those that seem illogical or unpleasant.

 **Writing** Paragraphs will vary.

SECTION 1 Self-Knowledge

Focus

Vocabulary Activity

Vocabulary worksheets are provided in the Teacher Classroom Resources.

Teach and Apply

Class Activity

Apply Arrange the desks in one large circle around the room. Have each student put his or her name at the top of a blank piece of plain paper. Pass the papers one person to the left or right every 20 to 30 seconds (you say "pass") until everyone has written something positive about each person. Remind them not to sign their names. After all the papers have made their way around the circle, allow time for students to silently read what the others have written about them. This lets students know how others perceive them in a positive way. (Comments should include values, personality characteristics, academic ability, and so on.)

Life Choice Inventory

Evaluate Complete the Life Choice Inventory found in the Teacher Classroom Resources or the Online Learning Center.

Pursuing Wellness

Apply Ask students to keep a journal in which they record the emotions they feel throughout the day. Have them write about their response to the emotions they felt. Each student should evaluate how they dealt with their emotions and reflect on how their responses could be more healthful.

Assess

Worksheets

A reproducible quiz for Section 1 is provided in the Teacher Classroom Resources.

Close

Apply Ask students to identify a negative thought they may have had during the day. Remind students to practice replacing negative thoughts with positive ones whenever they occur.

SECTION 2

Relating to Others

Focus

Vocabulary Activity

Vocabulary worksheets are provided in the Teacher Classroom Resources.

Teach and Apply

Class Activity

Recall Review the importance of support systems. List and explain the systems in your school and community (e.g., school support groups).

Pursuing Wellness

Apply Have students reflect on what they learned in the previous section about expressing emotions, specifically anger. Then have pairs of students write a script in which they properly handle a conflict. Make sure students demonstrate assertive, not aggressive, communication styles.

Assess

Worksheets

A reproducible quiz for Section 2 is available in the Teacher Classroom Resources.

Close

Apply Have students practice ways of saying things in an assertive manner. Have volunteers role-play some ways to say things assertively. See page 38 for suggestions.

SECTION 3

Making Decisions and Solving Problems

Focus

Vocabulary Activity

Vocabulary worksheets are provided in the Teacher Classroom Resources.

Teach and Apply

Class Activity

Discuss Write a problem on the board for students to think about. (A local school issue is a good choice.) Ask, "What do you think should be done about this problem?" After getting several ideas, ask how they came up with their solutions. Discuss ways that people decide how to solve problems.

Pursuing Wellness

Evaluate Lead a class discussion that emphasizes the importance of good decision-making skills throughout the lifetime. Have students interview a family member who is at a different stage of life to learn more about the decisions they need to make in their life. Have students compare the decisions they are faced with to those of the family member.

Assess

Worksheets

A reproducible quiz for Section 3 is available in the Teacher Classroom Resources.

Close

Apply Have students identify a current problem in their lives and use the decision-making process to make a plan to solve it.

SECTION 4 · Finding A Place in Society

Focus

Vocabulary Activity

Vocabulary worksheets are provided in the Teacher Classroom Resources.

Teach and Apply

Class Activity

Synthesize Ask students to quietly list, on paper, as many jobs and careers as they can think of in two minutes. Have each student name a career on his or her list. Go around the room two or three times, trying not to duplicate any that have already been said. Conclude that there are many career options available if we become aware of them.

Learning with Visuals

Apply Ask students to research a career that they can identify with. Then have each student create a collage or an informational poster that shows why he or she is interested in that particular career. You may ask the students to include a brief summary describing the career, as well as information regarding educational requirements, and the work environment. Have the students present their posters and their research to their classmates. Display the posters in the class.

Assess

Worksheets

A reproducible quiz for Section 4 is available in the Teacher Classroom Resources.

Reproducible Chapter Tests A and B are provided in the Teacher Classroom Resources.

Close

Apply Discuss with students ways of showing tolerance and acceptance of differences. Ask students if there has ever been a time that they felt alienated or ostracized. Let them reflect on the way it felt and then discuss ways they can ensure that they do not make other people feel that way.

Go Online

To find supplemental information to suit your individual class, you may want to visit the following Web sites, where you can find additional Internet site resources to enhance the study of this chapter. As with all Web sites, you should check the site out first to be sure the information found the site is appropriate for your students.

The International Foundation for Research and Education on Depression Inc.

www.ifred.org

Mayo Clinic www.mayoclinic.com

Both sites offer information about mental illnesses and how to get help. The Mayo Clinic site has vast amounts of information on many different health-related topics.

CHAPTER 3   Your Changing Personality

Objectives	Features
• Discuss the influence change has on an individual's personality. • List and discuss Maslow's hierarchy of needs. • Identify what specific needs are in each of Maslow's major categories. • Discuss the influence that gender roles have on an individual's personality. • Identify ways to promote self-acceptance. • Discuss the importance of peer groups and their influence on an individual's personal growth. • Demonstrate refusal skills in situations involving peer pressure.	• *Health Skills:* Improving Self-Esteem (page 65) • *Applying Health Skills:* Communication Skills (page 66) • *Health Skills:* Making New Friends (page 69) • *What Teens Think:* What Experiences Have You Had with Peer Pressure? (page 71) • *Health Skills:* Practicing Your Refusal Skills (page 72) • *Q&A: Dealing with Peer Pressure* (page 74)

Introduction

Teaching Support

Fast Files

- *Vocabulary:* Learning Vocabulary, Complete the Word(s)
- *Study Outline*
- *Reading Cloze*
- *Reteaching Activities:* Healthy Personality Circle Puzzle; Healthy Personality; Stages, Needs, Gender, and Self Esteem
- *Enrichment Activities:* Healthy Personality Gender Roles, Cooperative Learning
- *Career Briefs:* Counselors
- *Life Choice Inventory:* How Well Do You Speak Up for Yourself? How Sharp Are Your Refusal Skills?
- *Quizzes:* Sections 1–4
- *Tests:* Chapter 3 Test A, Chapter 3 Test B

Multimedia Support

- *ExamView® Assessment Suite*
- Online Learning Center

Introducing Chapter 2

Chapter Preview Activity

Write these words on the board or an overhead:

1. friendly
2. helpful
3. honest
4. funny
5. responsible
6. grateful
7. patient
8. good listener
9. empathic

10. inventive

11. generous

12. sensitive

13. loyal

14. kind.

Now have the students remember a time when they displayed each of these qualities. Have them write their examples of each quality on a piece of paper. Don't let them give up until they have an example for each one. Give them 10 points for each example. Then say, "If you have 140 points, you have a pretty good start on developing self-esteem. If you have fewer than 140 points, think deeper for examples." This activity will show the students that everyone has good qualities, but developing them requires daily practice.

 **Not Enough Time?**

Here are some suggestions to ensure that you cover the key topics in this chapter.

DAY 1 Before class, have students read Sections 1 and 2. Conclude the class with the Section 1 and 2 Reviews. You may want to assign reteaching activities from the resource materials for those students who need extra practice.

DAY 2 Before class, have students read Sections 3 and 4. During class, lead the students in the Focus Activity and the Class Activities.

DAY 3 Use the Section 3 and 4 Reviews for evaluation.

Bulletin Board Ideas

Write the following quote in large letters on a piece of paper, and place it in the center of the bulletin board. "What you do with your problem is far more important than what your problem does to you."—Robert Schuller

Ask students to write a paragraph on what the quote means to them. What is Schuller trying to say? How could they apply this statement to themselves and problems they have had in their lives? Post the student essays around the quote. At the end of the chapter, ask students to reread their paragraph and determine if they still agree with their earlier thoughts.

 **Fact or Fiction?**

Answers:

1. True.

2. False. Human beings first need the essentials for survival—food, clothing, and shelter. Then they become free to notice other needs.

3. False. People who imagine themselves as greater or more successful than they are may be taking an important first step toward a more successful future.

 Writing Paragraphs will vary.

SECTION 1

Life's Stages and Human Needs

Focus

Vocabulary Activity

Vocabulary worksheets are provided in the Teacher Classroom Resources.

Teach and Apply

Class Activity

Apply Explain to students that everyone has strengths that make them unique and different than others.

As a class, place students desks in one large circle facing in. Begin by making a positive comment about the student sitting nearest to you. Then ask each person in the class to make a positive comment about that student. Continue until each person in the class, including you, has received comments from the class. Comments will vary but might include smart, outgoing, funny, athletic, and so on.

Have students record their classmates comments. Ask them to write about how the comments affected their self-esteem, as well as how it felt to give others compliments. Some of the comments may concern things about themselves that they believed to be weaknesses. Students will realize that their self-esteem improves when they compliment others or do something nice for other people.

Learning With Visuals

Synthesize Ask one half of the students to create a poster or graphic representation of Erikson's stages of life and present them to the class explaining the brief details associated with each stage. Have the other half of the class create a poster or graphic representation of Maslow's hierarchy of needs and present them to the class explaining the brief details of each of the needs. Encourage students to incorporate technology through a computer slide show presentation or a computer generated graphic.

Class Activity

Analyze Ask students to list traits that they feel best describe their own personalities. Students will not share these traits with the class. Then read the following list of traits to students and ask them to add any traits they feel may apply to them to their lists. The traits are: aggressive, caring, impulsive, confident, outgoing, cooperative, creative, careless, blunt, courteous, tactful, narrow-minded, pessimistic, realistic, sensitive, optimistic. Then, ask students to review their lists and place a P next to those traits they view as being positive and an N next to those traits they view as being negative. Ask students to write one paragraph describing themselves that focuses on their positive traits.

Assess

Worksheets

A reproducible quiz for Section 1 is available in the Teacher Classroom Resources.

Close

Recall On a sheet of paper, have the students draw a pyramid and divide it into five horizontal sections. Beginning at the bottom, have them label each section in this order: physical needs, safety needs, love needs, esteem needs, and self-actualization needs. Review "Human Needs According to Maslow" on pages 55–57. Have students make a list of their needs and ask them to copy those needs below the pyramid they drew. Now have the students look at each need and label it as a physical need (PN), a safety need (SN), a love need (LN), an esteem need (EN), or a self-actualization need (SA).

Assign a summary paragraph in which students explain why basic needs must be met before higher needs can be met.

SECTION 2 Gender and Personality

Focus

Vocabulary Activity

Vocabulary worksheets are provided in the Teacher Classroom Resources.

Teach and Apply

Class Activity

Evaluate Ask for volunteers to name some stereotypes associated with gender roles. Lead a class discussion geared toward rectifying these ideas. Have students record their feelings toward these issues. Encourage them to move away from stereotypes in their lives and to be accepting of others opinions.

Comprehension Check

Comprehend Tell students the following:

  a. Females increase their strength by about 45 percent during puberty; males by 65 percent.

  b. Males develop greater amounts of oxygen-carrying hemoglobin. This, along with the male's larger heart and lungs, gives him greater endurance.

  c. Males are only slightly stronger than females before puberty. After puberty, the average male can bench press about 1.7 times as much as the average female.

  d. Males secrete about 30 to 200 micrograms of testosterone each day following puberty. Females secrete from 5 to 20 micrograms. Because testosterone stimulates muscle growth, this difference means that females do not develop as much muscle tissue as do males in response to exercise.

Class Activity

Examine Tell students that in some societies, gender roles are different than those in our society. For example, among the Arapish of New Guinea, the men are passive, peaceful, and nurturing. The Mandugumor women of New Guinea were expected to be violent, competitive, and sexually aggressive. Ask students to conduct research at the library or on the Internet to learn about gender roles in the U.S. in the 1900s, 1920s, 1940s, 1960s, and now. Students should pick one time period and write a one page paper describing how gender roles have changed over time.

Assess

Worksheets

A reproducible quiz for Section 2 is available in the Teacher Classroom Resources.

Close

Evaluate Have the class list any people they know—famous or not—who have broken stereotyped roles and become very individualistic. Now have each student write a short paragraph on why it is important for each human being to become an individual, and how the differences in people benefit our society. Have the class members discuss their lists and the positive aspects they noted.

SECTION 3 — Developing Self-Esteem

Focus

Vocabulary Activity

Vocabulary worksheets are provided in the Teacher Classroom Resources.

Teach and Apply

Pursuing Wellness

Apply Provide students with examples of appropriate letters to the editor from a local newspaper. Point out that letters to the editor provide an opportunity for individuals to share their point-of-view with others. Have students write a letter to the editor encouraging teens to take steps to improve their self-esteem. Remind students that their letters should provide a persuasive reason for why teens should work to improve self-esteem, and specific activities teens can participate in that would help. Ask students to share their completed letters with the class. If possible, submit some or all of the letters for publication in a school or local newspaper.

Group Activity

Apply In groups, have students make a list of positive self-talk phrases they can replace negative self-talk with.

Planning Guide

Comprehension Check

Discuss Review the information on positive self-talk with students. Positive self-talk means thinking or making positive statements about yourself to improve your self-esteem. Ask students how positive self-talk can improve self-esteem. Ask students to share some positive self-talk statements. Remind students not to share any personal information.

Assess

Worksheets

A reproducible quiz for Section 3 is available in the Teacher Classroom Resources.

Close

Evaluate Have students read the Applying Health Skills activity. Do you think assertive behavior improves self-esteem? Discuss or debate in class.

SECTION 4
The Importance of Peer Groups

Focus

Vocabulary Activity

Vocabulary worksheets are provided in the Teacher Classroom Resources.

Teach and Apply

Group Activity

Describe Ask students to write a one page script showing the steps a teen would take to resist negative peer pressure. Encourage students with video cameras to tape thier scripts.

Apply Have students create a script in which a teen is faced with one of the following situations and he or she deals with the negative peer pressure healthfully.

1. Cheating during an exam

2. Stealing/shoplifting

3. Cutting class or school

Assess

Worksheets

A reproducible quiz for Section 4 is available in the Teacher Classroom Resources.

Reproducible Chapter Tests A and B are provided in the Teacher Classroom Resources.

Close

Have students evaluate the peer groups they are in now. On a piece of paper, for their eyes only, have them list the peer groups in which they are involved. The students should label each as positive or negative based on its rules, controls, punishments, and outcomes. Have the students evaluate their dependency on the group. Have their choices in peer groups made them more or less independent?

Go Online

To find supplemental information to suit your individual class, you may want to visit the following Web site, where you can find additional Internet site resources to enhance the study of this chapter. As with all Web sites, you should check these out first to be sure the information found there is appropriate for your students.

National Association for Self-Esteem
www.self-esteem-nase.org

The National Association for Self-Esteem site has educational programs, research and references, and a chat room.

CHAPTER 4 Stress and Stress Management

Objectives

- Discuss different types of stress and the influence stressors have on an individual's perception of an event.
- Express understanding of the affects stress has on each of the body's systems.
- Identify stages of the stress response. Understand the body's physical reactions to the stress response.
- Demonstrate understanding of ways to manage stress.
- Identify ways to change perceptions of events that cause stress.

Features

- *Consumer Skills Activity:* Claims for "Stress Vitamins" (page 87)
- *What Teens Think:* What Causes the Most Stress for Teens? (page 92)
- *Health Skills:* Managing Stress (page 95)
- *Applying Health Skills:* Stress Management (page 98)
- *Q&A:* Healing and the Placebo Effect (page 102)

Introduction

Teaching Support

Fast Files

- *Vocabulary:* Learning Vocabulary, Fill in the Blanks
- *Study Outline*
- *Reading Cloze*
- *Reteaching Activities:* Match the Mechanism
- *Enrichment Activities:* Time Management Skills, What Creates Stress in Your Daily Life? Decision-Making Plan: Coping Positively, Stress and Disease: Is There a Relationship?
- *Career Briefs:* Occupational Therapists
- *Life Choice Inventory:* How Well Do You Resist Stress?
- *Handouts:* Medical Signs of Stress, Interventions to Manage Stress, Stress-Reducing Strategies
- *Quizzes:* Sections 1–4

- *Tests:* Chapter 4 Test A, Chapter 4 Test B

Multimedia Support

- *ExamView® Assessment Suite*
- Online Learning Center

Introducing Chapter 4

Chapter Preview Activity

Have the students read the chapter preview section. Ask the students to think of a time of day that is very stressful for them. Is it morning, a certain class at school, homework time? Have the students write all that they can about that stressful time. Who is involved? Why do they feel stressed? What are their feelings? Ask the students to decide what they could do to change the stress. List some changes that they would be willing to make to reduce the stress. List both the factors that they can and cannot control. Ask the students to describe how they feel when the stressful moment has ended.

Planning Guide

 Not Enough Time?

Here are some suggestions to ensure that you cover the key topics in this chapter.

DAY 1 Before class, have students read Sections 1 and 2. Conclude the class with the quizzes under the Assess heading at the end of each section.

DAY 2 Before class, have students read Sections 3 and 4, including the Q&A section on pages 102–103. Conclude the class with the quizzes under the Assess heading at the end of each section.

Bulletin Board Ideas

Put together, or have students put together, a collage of magazine photos, advertisements, slogans, and so forth depicting stress, its effects, and products marketed to reduce stress. You might find it interesting to focus particularly on the marketing of stress relievers in our society. Use the collage as a springboard for discussing the prevalence of stress in our society.

 Fact or Fiction?

Answers:

1. True.

2. False. You can change the way you perceive a stressor so that it will benefit you.

3. True.

Writing Paragraphs will vary.

Stress And Stressors

Focus

Vocabulary Activity

Vocabulary worksheets are provided in the Teacher Classroom Resources.

Teach and Apply

Pursuing Wellness

Comprehend Ask students if they would really want to live a life that was completely free of stress. Have them write a paragraph reflecting their feelings about a stress free life.

Remind students that while continuously high levels of stress can be harmful to their overall health, but that an absolutely stress-free life would also be free of challenges and excitement. Such a life would most likely be boring.

Most of us function best with stress levels that fluctuate. One example of these fluctuations might be the stress that results from a big test. As the test gets closer, your stress level goes up; when the test is over, your stress level goes down. Remember that a moderate amount of stress in your life is normal and to be expected. Use that stress as a motivating force to enrich the quality of your life.

Group Activity

Apply Ask small groups of students to select a common teen stressor and create a role play to show why it is stressful. For example, show how waking up late for school could have a negative effect on the day. Give groups a chance to present their role plays to the class. After the role plays, encourage students to discuss the relative influence of different stressors in teens' lives.

Learning With Visuals

Apply Have students create a personalized illustration of the stressors in their lives. Have them draw a picture of themselves and surround it with stress arrows with the name of a stressor on each arrow.

Assess

Worksheets

A reproducible quiz for Section 1 is available in the Teacher Classroom Resources.

Close

Evaluate Have the students identify the physical and psychological stressors that exist in the classroom. List them on the board. Ask the students to agree or disagree as a group with each item listed. Make some suggestions to reduce or eliminate the stressors within the classroom. Are the suggestions practical? If they are, try as a class to reduce or eliminate the stressors for one week. At the end of the week, decide if the stress in the classroom has lessened.

SECTION 2 Stress and Your Body

Focus

Vocabulary Activity

Vocabulary worksheets are provided in the Teacher Classroom Resources.

Teach and Apply

Group Activity

Apply Review the list of ways for dealing with stress including: physical activity, relaxation, time management, coping devices, defense mechanisms, and changed perception.

Give students specific situations that can cause stress. For example: You walk into your toughest class and written on the board are the words—"Surprise Quiz Today!" Assign each of the ways of dealing with stress to a pair of students. Give them three minutes to discuss it, then ask them to present the reasons why that way is best for dealing with the stressful situation. After all presentations have been made, have the class vote to decide which is actually the best way to handle that particular stress. Is there always one best way?

Other examples you may want to use:

1. Your best friend has a date for a big dance and you don't.

2. You fail your driving test.

3. Your best friend is supposed to drive you home after a party, but has been drinking.

Learning With Visuals

Recall Have students recall the information they have learned about managing stress. Ask them to make a poster to present to the class that reflects healthful ways of dealing with stress.

Class Activity

Discuss Ask each student to think about the last time he or she had a cold, a bout of the flu, or other illness. Then, ask students to think back to that time and try to recall any stressors they were experiencing at that time. Remind students that stress weakens the immune system, making it more likely that they will catch a cold or the flu.

Assess

Worksheets

A reproducible quiz for Section 2 is available in the Teacher Classroom Resources.

Close

Analyze Discuss some career choices that your students are considering. Analyze the stress level of those career choices. Discuss the importance of evaluating job-related stress in choosing a career.

SECTION 3 — The Stress Response

Focus

Vocabulary Activity

Vocabulary worksheets are provided in the Teacher Classroom Resources.

Teach and Apply

Learning With Visuals

Apply Have students do an illustration of the stressors in their lives. Then draw a picture of themselves (or paste in a school picture) and surround it with stress arrows (with the stressor written on the arrow).

Class Activity

Comprehend Lead a class discussion regarding the stress response's affect on physical health. Ask students, When something suddenly startles you, how does your body respond? (my heart races my breathing speeds up, I sweat).

Signs that a person is exposed to severe long term stress include: panic or anxiety attacks, constant feelings of being pressured, allergic reactions, or frequent sadness or feelings of hopelessness. Invite students to seek help if they feel as though they cannot handle their stress.

Assess

Worksheets

A reproducible quiz for Section 3 is available in the Teacher Classroom Resources.

Close

Comprehend Have students name and explain the stages of the stress response.

SECTION 4 — Managing Stress

Focus

Vocabulary Activity

Vocabulary worksheets are provided in the Teacher Classroom Resources.

Teach and Apply

Group Activity

Apply Ask students to identify positive and negative responses to stress. Divide the class into groups of three or four students. Have each group write a list of common stressors. Ask the students to list of all the positive and negative ways to deal with each stressor.

Have groups then list all the benefits of handling stress in a positive way, and the detriments of negative ways. How would the way(s) they handle stress affect their overall health? Have groups share their responses with each other.

Class Activity

Apply Ask the class to brainstorm situations in which using refusal skills could help a teen avoid stress. Call on volunteers to demonstrate how to use refusal skills in one of the situations. Discuss how using refusal skills could help avoid unnecessary stress in that situation.

Comprehension Check

Explain Remind students that they can relieve stress by making sure they don't take on more projects or activities than they can handle. Tell students they need to separate out what they must do, such as homework, tasks for the family, etc., from the things that they may not need to do immediately. Encourage teens to say "no" tasks that are not absolutely necessary if they have too much to handle.

Assess

Worksheets

A reproducible quiz for Section 4 is available in the Teacher Classroom Resources.

Reproducible Chapter Tests A and B are provided in the Teacher Classroom Resources.

Close

Recall Ask students to think of a stressful time of their day (math class, getting home from school, and so on). What creates the stress? What can they do to prepare for this stressful time? Are they willing to do the preparation necessary to help reduce the stress?

Go Online

To find supplemental information to suit your individual class, you may want to visit the following Web site where you can find additional Internet resources to enhance the study of this chapter. As with all Web sites, you should check the site out first to be sure the information found there is appropriate for your students.

KidsHealth
www.kidshealth.org/teen/

This site is an interactive opportunity for teens to learn about stress and ways to cope during difficult times.

CHAPTER 5 Planning Guide

CHAPTER 5   Mental and Emotional Problems

Objectives	Features
• Discuss emotions such as fear, anxiety, sadness, guilt, and how to cope with these difficult emotions. • Identify mental and emotional problems. • Identify and discuss anxiety, mood and other mental or emotional disorders. • Discuss major risk factors for suicide. • Identify ways to prevent suicide. • Discuss reasons for seeking help from therapy. • Identify types of therapy. • Learn how to help others.	• *Health Skills:* Dealing with Anxiety or Fear (page 108) • *Health Skills:* Overcoming Shyness (page 113) • *Health Skills:* Coping with Minor Depression (page 115) • *Q&A:* Dealing with Loss and Grief (page 126)

Introduction

Teaching Support

Fast Files
- *Vocabulary:* Learning Vocabulary, Break the Code
- *Study Outline*
- *Reading Cloze*
- *Reteaching Activities:* Phobia Matching, Reviewing the Chapter
- *Enrichment Activities:* Being a Good Friend, Finding Emotional Health, Angel's Role
- *Career Briefs:* Psychologists
- *Handouts:* Performance During Past Year as Indicator of Severity of Mental Disorders; Negative Rules and Negative Messages Commonly Heard in Alcoholic and Other Troubled Families; Family Roles in Dysfunctional Families; Developing Health Through Recovery

- *Quizzes:* Sections 1–4
- *Tests:* Chapter 5 Test A, Chapter 5 Test B

Multimedia Support
- *ExamView® Assessment Suite*
- Online Learning Center

Introducing Chapter 5

Chapter Preview Activity

Have the students, alone or in small groups, create a list of words or phrases they think of when they hear the word *psychiatrist*. Write this list on the board and follow up with the questions listed under "Fact or Fiction?" Encourage students to share their thoughts and attitudes, both positive and negative, toward the mental health field before you begin the chapter.

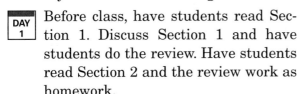

Not Enough Time?

Because it is likely that many of your students will have experienced some of the problems described in this chapter, it is important that you give the chapter as much time as possible. Students who identify with the problems in the chapter will be feeling many confusing emotions and may wish to discuss them if sufficient time is allowed and they feel comfortable doing so.

DAY 1 Before class, have students read Section 1. Discuss Section 1 and have students do the review. Have students read Section 2 and the review work as homework.

DAY 2 Discuss and correct the Section 2 review with students. During class, do the activities listed throughout the section.

DAY 3 Have students complete the activities throughout Section 3. Have the students complete Section 3 review as homework.

DAY 4 Begin class with a discussion of the homework. Have students complete Section 4 review for homework.

DAY 5 Begin class with a review and discussion of Sections 1–4. The quiz can be given the next day or at the end of class. Have the students complete the chapter review.

Bulletin Board Ideas

Write the title of the various health care professionals discussed in the chapter (counselor, psychiatrist, psychoanalyst, psychologist, social worker) on large pieces of paper, one title per paper. Then, on five more pieces of paper, write the description of each professional. On additional papers, write local agencies where such a professional might be found. Post the papers on the bulletin board and use five different colors of string, one per professional, to connect the title to the job description and to local agencies where such professionals might be found.

Answers:
1. False. Emotionally healthy people often benefit from such help, and it is well worth seeking.
2. False. Ordinary anxiety is a normal emotion that everyone experiences from time to time.
3. True.

 Writing Paragraphs will vary.

SECTION 1 — Coping with Difficult Emotions

Focus

Vocabulary Activity

Vocabulary worksheets are provided in the Teacher Classroom Resources.

Teach and Apply

Group Activity

Evaluate Divide the class into 10 different groups, assigning each group one of the following emotional disorders to research and report on. Each report must contain a written portion with their resources cited and a visual aid, and must be presented orally to the class. Visual aids may include a video, poster, or overhead. Each group may also write up a quiz for their classmates to take after the presentation. Allow groups to research their subject areas during class periods. Written reports should be turned in at the same time the oral report is due. Suggested report topics:

Schizophrenia, Depression, Attention-deficit/hyperactivity disorder, Obsessive-compulsive disorder, Post-traumatic stress disorder, anorexia nervosa/bulimia, and phobias.

Planning Guide

Mental and Emotional Disorders

Class Activity

Discuss Lead a class discussion on the stigma associated with mental health disorder. Ask students if they think someone with a mental health disorder is ill, or has a weak will. Ask them why they think what they do. Tell students that mental health disorders are illnesses, just like a cold or the flu. For example, depression can be caused by a chemical imbalance in the brain. Drugs are available to treat many mental health disorders.

Pursuing Wellness

Synthesize Have students create a list of activities that they participate in to relieve them of fear, anxiety, sadness, or grief. Examples might be running, painting, writing, or even discussing the troubling situation with a trusted friend.

Assess

Worksheets

A reproducible quiz for Section 1 is available in the Teacher Classroom Resources.

Close

Apply Discuss with students the differences between guilt and shame, and anxiety and depression. Write the lyrics of the song "Rudolph the Red-Nosed Reindeer" on the board. Use the lyrics of the song as an example of how emotional problems can be increased by peer and family pressures, and decreased or eliminated by the realization of one's own value. Brainstorm ways people can come to realize their own worth. Be sure that seeking help from a qualified professional is on the list. You might encourage students to identify other song lyrics which promote self-esteem.

Focus

Vocabulary Activity

Vocabulary worksheets are provided in the Teacher Classroom Resources.

Teach and Apply

Class Activity

Apply Music is often a daily part of teen life. Some students listen to certain music because that is the music their peer group listens to. Others may make more independent musical choices. In either case, as young people listen repeatedly to a set of songs, they are being subjected to the messages conveyed by the music. They may or may not be aware of the types of messages they are receiving, but research has shown that many teens are deeply affected emotionally by the music they listen to.

Ask students to make a list of five songs they listen to most frequently. Next to each song, ask them to indicate how listening to the song makes them feel. Finally, ask them to write a short summary of the lyrics of the songs. Do the words of the song make a difference in how the song makes them feel, or are they reacting solely to the music?

Pursuing Wellness

Evaluate Have students evaluate their day thus far. Write the following questions on the board and have them answer the questions honestly. The answers are only for themselves and will not be collected or shared with others. What emotions have you felt today? How are you feeling right now? Why do you feel the way they feel. Do you like the way they are feeling? What can you do to improve your present emotional state?

Comprehension Check

Analyze Ask students when someone with a mental health disorder should seek help from a mental health professional. Remind students that any time a person has intense feelings that overwhelm his or her ability and desire to solve problems, he or she should seek help.

Class Activity

Discuss Lead a class discussion on whether being physically active helps emotional health. Ask students how they feel after they have finished a workout. Does working out regularly help students feel happy most of the time? Remind students that physical activity affects all sides of the health triangle, physical, mental/emotional, and social health. It's recommended that teens exercise for at least 60 minutes a day, most days of the week.

Assess

Worksheets

A reproducible quiz for Section 2 is available in the Teacher Classroom Resources.

Close

Comprehend Discuss with students the difference between temporary sadness and major depression. Discuss the warning signs of depression and ways to cope with each.

SECTION 3 Teens and Suicide

Focus

Vocabulary Activity

Vocabulary worksheets are provided in the Teacher Classroom Resources.

Teach and Apply

Class Activity

Synthesize Discuss the most common reasons teens commit suicide. Review the signs students can look for and the ways they can help. Help students understand that they are not responsible for the actions of a friend, but a friend is more likely to turn to them than to an adult.

Group Activity

Apply Have students research suicide hotlines and create a note card containing warning sides of suicide as well as contact information for the hotline. Cards should be business card size so it can easily be kept in a wallet to share with someone in need.

Assess

Worksheets

A reproducible quiz for Section 3 is available in the Teacher Classroom Resources.

Close

Apply Review warning signs for suicide with students. Then review the important ways to help in the event a student observes any of these behaviors in a friend.

SECTION 4 Emotional Healing

Focus

Vocabulary Activity

Vocabulary worksheets are provided in the Teacher Classroom Resources.

Teach and Apply

Pursuing Wellness

Synthesize Have students remember a time that they needed help with something that they could not do on their own. Ask students how they felt when they tried to complete the task all on their own. What lead them to ask for help? How did they feel once they asked for help? How did they feel once they completed the task? Explain that those feelings are similar to the overwhelming feeling of needing emotional support. Express the importance of seeking help because things can't always be resolved on their own.

Class Activity

Evaluate Have students research a mental health profession. These professions may include psychiatrists, psychologists, psychiatric nurses, social workers, and counselors. Have students write a brief report explaining the duties of their chosen profession. In the report also ask students to discuss the training that is required to work in a career in mental health. If possible, invite someone that is currently practicing in a mental health profession to come to class and further explain their work and participate in a question and answer session with the students.

Class Activity

Role Play Divide students into pairs and refer them to the Health Skills feature in this Section. Have students take turns asking their partner for help, using the strategies described in the feature. Each student should get a turn to ask for help and to respond to the request for help.

Class Activity

Discuss Ask students if they have ever given advice to a friend who was having an emotional problem. Ask them if they felt comfortable giving the advice? Did they think they had enough knowledge of the situation or training to provide help? Remind students that sometimes the best advice they can give is to encourage their friend to seek professional help. An untrained person can cause more problems. Talk about the difference between offering caring support and encouragement, and providing advice about actions to take.

Assess

Worksheets

A reproducible quiz for Section 4 is available in the Teacher Classroom Resources.

Reproducible Chapter Tests A and B are provided in the Teacher Classroom Resources.

Close

Apply Have students write a list of questions or concerns about emotional problems. Invite a school counselor to class and allow students to conduct an interview.

Go Online

To find supplemental information to suit your individual class, you may want to visit the following Web sites, where you can find additional Internet resources to enhance the study of this chapter. As with all Web sites, you should check these out first to be sure the information found there is appropriate for your students.

Suicide Awareness/Voices of Education

www.save.org/

This site is devoted to education and awareness of signs of and alternatives to suicide.

For reliable information on a variety of health topics try www.healthfinder.gov

CHAPTER 6 Planning Guide

CHAPTER 6 The Human Body and Its Systems

Objectives

- Identify structures within the body.
- Identify parts of the skeletal system and how it functions.
- Identify parts of the muscular system and how it functions.
- Identify parts of the nervous system and how it functions.
- Identify parts of the digestive system and how it functions.
- Identify parts of the cardiovascular (circulatory) system and how it functions.
- Identify parts of the urinary system and how it functions.
- Identify parts of the respiratory system and how it functions.
- Identify parts of the immune system and how it functions.
- Identify parts of the hormonal system and how it functions.
- Identify parts of the female reproductive system and how it functions.
- Identify parts of the male reproductive system and how it functions.

Introduction

Teaching Support

Fast Files

- *Vocabulary:* Learning Vocabulary, Fill in the Blanks
- *Study Outline*
- *Reading Cloze*
- *Reteaching Activities:* The Skeletal System, The Skeletal System (2), The Muscular System, The Muscular System (2), The Nervous System, The Nervous System (2), The Digestive System, The Digestive System (2), The Cardiovascular System, The Cardiovascular System (2), The Urinary System, The Urinary System (2), The Respiratory System, The Respiratory System (2), The Immune System, The Hormonal System, The Hormonal System (2), The Female Reproductive System, The Female Reproductive System (2), The Male

Reproductive System, The Male Reproductive System (2)

- *Career Briefs:* Chiropractors
- *Quizzes:* Sections 1–12
- *Tests:* Chapter 6 Test A, Chapter 6 Test B

Multimedia Support

- *ExamView® Assessment Suite*
- Online Learning Center

Introducing Chapter 6

Chapter Preview Activity

Have students work in pairs to complete the following activity. Assign one member of each pair to perform a simple task, such as opening a book to a certain page and reading a paragraph, or doing a couple of jumping jacks. (All "performers" should do the same activity.) The second member of the pair should carefully observe the performance.

The pair should then work together to generate a list of the individual movements that occurred during the performance. They should try to match movements to the body system(s) involved in making that movement. Have all pairs participate to help develop a class list on the board.

 Not Enough Time?

You may want to use this chapter periodically throughout your course. If you teach the chapter in its entirety, as a review of the body systems, you may want to use the following plan.

 DAY 1 Before class, have students read Sections 1–6. Have students do the activities listed throughout the sections.

 DAY 2 Before class, have students read Sections 7–12. During class, have students do the activities throughout the sections. If time permits, use a variety of the activities for each section.

Bulletin Board Ideas

Write the names of the various systems of the body covered in this chapter (skeletal, muscular, nervous, digestive, cardiovascular, urinary, respiratory, immune, hormonal, and reproductive) on separate rectangles of construction paper. Then write a description of each system on additional rectangles of construction paper. Arrange the system rectangles down one side of the bulletin board, with the descriptions randomly placed down the other side. Use yarn to match the system to its description.

You might have students create and use the bulletin board as a study aid.

 Fact or Fiction?

Answers:

1. False. Adult bones are continuously breaking down and building up throughout life.

2. True.

3. False. The lungs fill passively with air when the diaphragm contracts and reduces the air pressure in the chest cavity.

Writing Paragraphs will vary.

SECTION 1 The Integrated Body

Focus

Vocabulary Activity

Vocabulary worksheets are provided in the Teacher Classroom Resources.

Teach and Apply

Group Activity

Comprehend Divide the class into groups of three, allowing one student in each group to have a textbook open, one to have paper and a pen or pencil, and one to be the questioner. Have students switch roles in the group after they finish each section. Encourage students to work within their own group and give only positive, cooperative comments to each other.

To help groups study the body systems, have the person with the book read the information in the book about one of the body systems. The person with the paper and pen or pencil is to take notes and record any questions they or the questioner may have. The questioner comes up with as many questions as possible to help stir up debate on the body system for the group to discuss.

The questioner may also facilitate questions that help the group understand how all the body systems relate to each other and work together. After all body systems have been covered, have the groups describe how the body systems work together.

Assess

Worksheets

A reproducible quiz for Section 1 is available in the Teacher Classroom Resources.

Close

Recall Ask students to:

1. Tell what makes up a body system.

2. Discuss what makes each cell different and what cells need in order to function properly.

3. Give an example of a homeostatic process that occurs in the body.

SECTION 2 — The Skeletal System

Focus

Vocabulary Activity

Vocabulary worksheets are provided in the Teacher Classroom Resources.

Teach and Apply

Group Activity

Recall Collect and clean various types of animal bones (chicken, fish, beef/pork ribs, etc.). Divide students into small groups. Ask each group to think about and record everything they know about bones. Hand out bones to each group. Tell students to feel, cut, scrape, and examine the bones. Have each group record any questions they have about the bones and the bones' parts. Have a class discussion about the discoveries and the questions.

Assess

Worksheets

A reproducible quiz for Section 2 is available in the Teacher Classroom Resources.

Close

Comprehend Ask students to:

1. Give an example of the bones that protect, give shape, allow movement, store vitamins, and produce blood cells.

2. Describe the changes that occur in the bones throughout life.

SECTION 3 — The Muscular System

Focus

Vocabulary Activity

Vocabulary worksheets are provided in the Teacher Classroom Resources.

Teach and Apply

Class Activity

Apply Have students, at their desks, do a back push-up. To do this, they should hold onto the edge of their chairs with legs out straight and lower themselves down as far as they can, and then push back up. Have students list the muscles they worked.

Assess

Worksheets

A reproducible quiz for Section 3 is available in the Teacher Classroom Resources.

Close

Recall Ask students to:

1. Give examples of the three muscle types.

2. Identify and locate most major muscles of the body.

SECTION 4

The Nervous System

Focus

Vocabulary Activity

Vocabulary worksheets are provided in the Teacher Classroom Resources.

Teach and Apply

Class Activity

Apply Create a loud noise, without warning, causing students to react. Then ask the students, What kind of reactions did you have? Do you know what these involuntary reactions are called? (reflexes) What inside your body causes these reflexes to occur? (nerves or nerve impulses, nervous system)

Assess

Worksheets

A reproducible quiz for Section 4 is available in the Teacher Classroom Resources.

Close

Comprehend Ask students to:

1. Name the two major parts of the central nervous system.

2. Explain why our brain is the master organ of our body.

Focus

Vocabulary Activity

Vocabulary worksheets are provided in the Teacher Classroom Resources.

Teach and Apply

Comprehension Check

Comprehend Ask students to describe and name the actions of the digestive system.

Class Activity

Analyze Have students research the digestive systems of different animals. What are the similarities between the animal's digestive system and a human digestive system?

Assess

Worksheets

A reproducible quiz for Section 5 is available in the Teacher Classroom Resources.

Close

Comprehend Ask students to:

1. Identify the organs involved in digestion.

2. Name some ways the digestive system protects itself from harmful substances.

SECTION 6

The Cardiovascular System

Focus

Vocabulary Activity

Vocabulary worksheets are provided in the Teacher Classroom Resources.

Teach and Apply

Class Activity

Apply Instruct each student to crumple a scrap piece of paper into a ball and hold it in his or her hand. Then count to 90 out loud in one minute. Have the students squeeze the paper ball each time a number is said. Explain to students that this demonstrates how strong the heart is and how hard it works.

Assess

Worksheets

A reproducible quiz for Section 6 is available in the Teacher Classroom Resources.

Close

Comprehend Ask students to:

1. Describe the function of the cardiovascular system.

2. Explain how blood helps to eliminate cell waste.

3. List the four blood types.

The Urinary System

Focus

Vocabulary Activity

Vocabulary worksheets are provided in the Teacher Classroom Resources.

Teach and Apply

Class Activity

Apply Have students help you list the major organs of the urinary system.

Assess

Worksheets

A reproducible quiz for Section 7 is available in the Teacher Classroom Resources.

Close

Synthesize Have students write a half-page essay that compares the kidneys to a filter or large net that monitors the composition of the blood.

The Respiratory System

Focus

Vocabulary Activity

Vocabulary worksheets are provided in the Teacher Classroom Resources.

Teach and Apply

Group Activity

Apply Have students break into small groups. Supply each group with balloons and a ruler. Instruct each student to breathe normally and then expel that air in a normal fashion into the balloon. Then have them measure the balloon across the broadest part with their ruler and record the measurement. Empty the balloon of any air and then breathe in and out normally and then expel all remaining air into the balloon, exerting as much pressure on the lungs as possible to push out any remaining air. Measure the balloon again. Empty the balloon again and have the students breathe in normally, and then try to expel all the air that is in their lungs into the balloon. Then measure as above. This activity will give the students a hands-on approach to understanding how their lungs function.

Assess

Worksheets

A reproducible quiz for Section 8 is available in the Teacher Classroom Resources.

CHAPTER 6

Planning Guide

 **SECTION 10** The Hormonal System

Close

Comprehend Ask students to:

1. Locate and describe the major parts of the respiratory system.

2. State the functions of the sinuses.

 SECTION 9 The Immune System

Focus

Vocabulary Activity

Vocabulary worksheets are provided in the Teacher Classroom Resources.

Teach and Apply

Comprehension Check

Recall Ask students to explain why their glands swell when they are experiencing an illness.

Assess

Worksheets

A reproducible quiz for Section 9 is available in the Teacher Classroom Resources.

Close

Recall Ask students to:

1. Describe lymph.

2. Explain the actions of the white cells that attack bacteria and infections.

3. Name factors that negatively affect the immune system.

Focus

Vocabulary Activity

Vocabulary worksheets are provided in the Teacher Classroom Resources.

Teach and Apply

Learning with Visuals

Synthesize On a diagram, have students locate the major endocrine glands and discuss the function of each gland.

Assess

Worksheets

A reproducible quiz for Section 10 is available in the Teacher Classroom Resources.

Close

Recall Ask students to:

1. Locate the major hormonal glands of the body.

2. Describe the functions of the body's major hormones.

 **SECTION 11** The Female Reproductive System

Focus

Vocabulary Activity

Vocabulary worksheets are provided in the Teacher Classroom Resources.

Teach and Apply

Pursuing Wellness

Apply Invite a health care practitioner to class who specializes in reproductive health and/or teens and development. Before the speaker comes to class, have students write several questions they have about reproduction, reproductive health, and communicating with doctors about sensitive issues. Review the questions, and then have students practice asking the questions to partners before the speaker comes to class. Encourage each student to ask the speaker a question.

Assess

Worksheets

A reproducible quiz for Section 11 is available in the Teacher Classroom Resources.

Close

Recall Ask students to:

1. Describe the organs that transport the ova from the ovary to the vagina.

2. Relate menstruation to the cycle of time needed for the journey of the ova to the vagina.

SECTION 12 — The Male Reproductive System

Focus

Vocabulary Activity

Vocabulary worksheets are provided in the Teacher Classroom Resources.

Teach and Apply

Pursuing Wellness

Apply Invite a health care practitioner to class who specializes in reproductive health and/or teens and development. Before the speaker comes to class, have students write several questions they have about reproduction, reproductive health, and communicating with doctors about sensitive issues. Review the questions, and then have students practice asking the questions to partners before the speaker comes to class. Encourage each student to ask the speaker a question.

Assess

Worksheets

A reproducible quiz for Section 12 is available in the Teacher Classroom Resources.

Reproducible Chapter 6 Tests A and B are provided in the Teacher Classroom Resources.

Close

Recall Ask students to:

1. Name and describe the organs of the male reproductive system.

2. Identify both differences and similarities between the male and female reproductive systems.

Go Online

You may want to have your students visit the following Web site, where they will find information and additional Internet resources to enhance their study of this chapter. As with all Web sites, you should check this one out first to be sure the information found there is appropriate for your students.

BodyQuest

library.thinkquest.org/10348/

BodyQuest is specifically designed for students and includes lots of good activities. (Body systems are shown in computer-generated art.)

CHAPTER 7 Nutrition: The Nutrients

Objectives

- Discuss why good nutrition promotes health and helps prevent disease.
- Introduce students to the MyPyramid guide.
- Identify the five food groups.
- Discuss how we obtain and store energy from food.
- Discuss carbohydrates' role in processing energy.
- Discuss fat's role as a major source of fuel for the body.
- Discuss good fats and bad fats.
- Demonstrate how to read a food label.
- Identify sources of protein.
- Discuss vitamin safety.
- Identify sources of vitamins.
- Identify sources of minerals.

Features

- *Health Skills:* Dietary Guidelines for Americans (page 162)
- *Applying Health Skills:* Practicing Healthful Behaviors (page 169)
- *Consumer Skills Activity:* Liquid or Solid—They're All Added Sugars (page 177)
- *Health Skills:* Getting the Saturated Fat Out of Your Diet (page 180)
- *Consumer Skills Activity:* How to Read a Food Label (page 182)
- *Q&A:* SOS: Selection of Supplements (page 196)

Introduction

Teaching Support

Fast Files

- *Vocabulary:* Learning Vocabulary, The Scrambler, Using Your Knowledge About Vitamins and Minerals, Vocabulary Relationships
- *Study Outline*
- *Reading Cloze*
- *Reteaching Activities:* Nutrients, Undernutrition vs. Overnutrition, Vitamins and Minerals
- *Enrichment Activities:* Calculations from Labels, Applying the Dietary Guidelines, Vitamin Contracts, Balancing the

Unbalanced, Diet Analysis, Menu Analysis

- *Cooperative Learning Activities:* Nutrient Advertisements
- *Career Briefs:* Dietitians and Nutritionists
- *Life Choice Inventory:* How Well Do You Eat?
- *Handouts:* Fast Foods Low in Fat and Calories, Teacher's Instructions for Handout 7–21, Analyzing Nutrient Labels, Nutrients in Typical Lunches, Selecting Nutritious Foods, U.S. Public Health Service Objectives

- *Quizzes:* Sections 1–8
- *Tests:* Chapter 7 Test A, Chapter 7 Test B

Multimedia Support
- *ExamView® Assessment Suite*
- Online Learning Center

Introducing Chapter 7
Chapter Preview Activity
Write the following statement on the board. "A body must be well nourished to be healthy." Ask students to answer these questions: What kinds of foods do you eat that contribute to a healthy body? What kinds of foods do you eat that do not contribute to a healthy body?

Bulletin Board Ideas
Have students write a report on a diet tip to make a person's diet healthier. The report should focus on something people can do to improve the quality of foods they eat and provide persuasive arguments in favor of adopting this healthy eating lifestyle.

 **Not Enough Time?**

DAY 1 Before class, have students read Sections 1 and 2. During class, do the Chapter Preview Activity and the activities throughout Sections 1 and 2.

DAY 2 Discuss Section 3. Have students write down what they ate the day before. Then review the vocabulary terms for the section. Assign Sections 5 and 6 for homework.

DAY 3 Ask students to name health risks related to being overweight. Lead a class discussion that focuses on food's role in weight management. Focus on ideas to cut unhealthy fats from a diet. Assign Sections 7 and 8 for homework.

DAY 4 Discuss the role of supplements in a person's diet. Focus on the benefits as well as the negative effects it can have on a person. Have students complete the Chapter Review on pages 198–199.

 Fact or Fiction?

Answers:
1. False. True
2. False. Saturated and trans fats can increase the risk for heart disease, while vegetable oils and fish oils may have heart health benefits in small amounts.
3. False. Low intakes of calcium are common, because few foods contain it in large amounts.

 Writing Paragraphs will vary.

SECTION 1 — Benefits of Nutrition

Focus
Vocabulary Activity
Vocabulary worksheets are provided in the Teacher Classroom Resources.

Teach and Apply
Pursuing Wellness
Apply Have students study the Health Skills sidebar "Dietary Guidelines for Americans. Have them think about the last three meals they have eaten. How ask them to evaluate those meals based on these guidelines. Discuss their results.

Comprehension Check
Comprehend You may want to make sure that students understand the several different forms of the word *nutrition*. Write *nutrition*, *nutrients*, *well-nourished*, and *nourishing* on the board. As a class, develop definitions for each word, then have students write sentences using each word.

CHAPTER 7 Planning Guide

Assess

Worksheets

A reproducible worksheet for Section 1 is provided in the Teacher Classroom Resources.

Close

Synthesize Divide the class into five groups; assign each group one of the food groups. Have each group draw a simple picture or symbol to stand for its food group. Have each group share and discuss its picture/symbol. Then have students close their books and name the food group by using the pictures as a guide. Have students name them without the pictures.

SECTION 2 How to Choose Nutritious Foods

Focus

Vocabulary Activity

Vocabulary worksheets are provided in the Teacher Classroom Resources.

Teach and Apply

Learning with Visuals

Comprehend Have students create a poster showing how to substitute healthy food choices for those that are high in fat or do not provide many nutrients. Have them list how many calories they saved by substituting one food for another.

Class Activity

Evaluate Discuss with students the idea of balance and how too little or too much of anything can be unhealthy. Discuss the need for balance in eating to make sure that a variety of foods are eaten to ensure a variety of vitamins and minerals. Also, make sure students understand that sometimes taking a vitamin or mineral supplement can cause an unbalanced state in a person's diet, but that foods are safe sources. Have students identify foods that are a good source of vitamins and minerals.

Assess

Worksheets

A reproducible quiz for section 2 is provided in the Teacher Classroom Resources.

Close

Evaluate Ask students why the diet industry is so successful. Address the fact that poor nutrition choices are sometimes a result of a lack of knowledge, money, or time. Poor nutrition also results from poor choices.

SECTION 3 Energy from Food

Focus

Vocabulary Activity

Vocabulary worksheets are provided in the Teacher Classroom Resources.

Teach and Apply

Learning with Visuals

Synthesize Have students draw a graphic representation of the role of glycogen, glucose, the hypothalamus, the liver, and blood in the body. They might use symbols to represent glucose and glycogen. They may want to refer to illustrations of the body systems in Chapter 6.

Life Choice Inventory

Apply Ask students to complete the Life Choice Inventory found in the Teacher Classroom Resources or the Online Learning Center.

Assess

Worksheets

A reproducible quiz for Section 3 is provided in the Teacher Classroom Resources.

Close

Recall Have students write a definition of a calorie, explain how calories are related to energy for the body, and tell what happens to extra calories.

SECTION 4 The Carbohydrates

Focus

Vocabulary Activity

Vocabulary worksheets are provided in the Teacher Classroom Resources.

Teach and Apply

Learning with Visuals

Apply Have students draw a diagram illustrating the characteristics that starch, fiber, and sugar have in common. Then have them illustrate the differences between each. Have students present their findings to the class, explaining the differences and similarities, and how they chose to represent these on paper.

Class Activity

Apply Bring a teaspoon, sugar, and two glasses to class. Ask students how much sugar they put on their cereal or in a drink. Spoon sugar into the glass, one teaspoon at a time, and have the students tell you when to stop. Then, take the second glass and add 10 to 15 teaspoons of sugar to that glass.

Hold the second glass up, and ask if they would drink something poured into the glass with that much sugar. Explain that this is the amount of sugar in one can of soda.

Assess

Worksheets

A reproducible quiz for Section 4 is provided in the Teacher Classroom Resources.

Close

Recall Have students review the benefits of carbohydrates, fiber, and sugar in a person's diet. Ask for any negative effects associated with having too much or too little of any of these in your diet.

SECTION 5 The Fats

Focus

Vocabulary Activity

Vocabulary worksheets are provided in the Teacher Classroom Resources.

Teach and Apply

Class Activity

Apply Have students bring food and beverage labels to class. Have the class break into teams of two or more students. Have teams choose one or two labels, and answer the following about each item:

1. What constitutes a serving, according to the label?

2. How many servings are in a container?

3. How many calories are in one serving?

4. How many grams of fat are in one serving?

5. What vitamins and minerals does the item supply? (The answer may be "none," if no vitamins or minerals are listed on the label.)

Then ask the teams to discuss the following questions, and present their ideas to the class:

1. Did the serving size on the label surprise you? In what way?

2. What serving size do you typically consume?

3. Are calories in a serving too high, too low, or just right?

4. Is the product high or low in fat? (Read the right-hand column of the label—Percent of Daily Value—to find the percentage of a typical day's fat allowance provided in a serving.)

Group Activity

Evaluate Have each student to bring in samples of food labels from five different foods. Divide the class into small groups so that each group has at least 15 different food labels to work with. Ask students to use the labels to develop two different menus of approximately 2,000 calories each. Each menu must contain at least seven different food items. The first menu should be a nutritious low-fat menu. The second menu, while still containing at least seven different food items totaling around 2,000 calories, should *not* be nutritious, so that students can see the difference between nutritious calories and empty calories.

Have groups share their menus with each other by presenting an oral report and their charted findings. Ask the students to determine the most nutritious menu, the least nutritious menu. Which menu would they most likely follow.

Assess

Worksheets

A reproducible quiz for Section 5 is provided in the Teacher Classroom Resources.

Close

Recall Have students name as many reasons as they can think of to monitor the amount of fats in their diets.

SECTION 6
Protein

Focus

Vocabulary Activity

Vocabulary worksheets are provided in the Teacher Classroom Resources.

Teach and Apply

Class Activity

Analyze Ask students to write down how protein functions in the body. Then have them call out their responses while you list them on the board. Students should write down any correct answers that they do not have on their lists. Then have students read this section. Each time they encounter an item on their lists, they should circle it.

Group Activity

Apply Have students put together a vegetarian menu for a week. Remind them to make sure the necessary amino acids are included. Have students underline sources of protein, circle sources of fiber, and put a check mark beside those that provide carbohydrates. They should put a dot by those that are high in fat. Ask students to share their vegetarian menus with the rest of the class.

Assess

Worksheets

A reproducible quiz for Section 6 is provided in the Teacher Classroom Resources.

Close

Apply Divide the class into two teams. Give each side five seconds to think of a food that is rich in protein. Have students go back and forth until one of the sides is stumped and cannot think of a protein source in time. The team with the highest number of correct answers wins.

SECTION 7 Vitamins

Focus

Vocabulary Activity

Vocabulary worksheets are provided in the Teacher Classroom Resources.

Teach and Apply

Learning with Visuals

Apply Have students draw a picture depicting the lack of a certain vitamin in the body. The picture should make an obvious connection between the vitamin and the related symptoms of the deficiency. It should contain the name of the vitamin and perhaps some depiction of food sources from which the vitamin is derived. Have students present their pictures to the rest of the class. They should be able to answer any questions about their vitamins and the related deficiencies.

Group Activity

Comprehend Divide the class into two teams. Give each side five seconds to think of a food that is rich in vitamins. Have students go back and forth until one of the sides is stumped and cannot think of a vitamin source in time. The team with the highest number of correct answers wins.

Assess

Worksheets

A reproducible quiz for Section 7 is provided in the Teacher Classroom Resources.

Close

Evaluate Have students define the word *vitamin* and name as many vitamins as they can with their books closed. Write the vitamins on the board and have students call out food sources that supply those vitamins. Write these on the board next to the appropriate vitamins.

SECTION 8 Minerals

Focus

Vocabulary Activity

Vocabulary worksheets are provided in the Teacher Classroom Resources.

Teach and Apply

Pursuing Wellness

Analyze Ask students to conduct research on diseases that are prompted by mineral overloads or mineral deficiencies. How can these overloads or deficiencies be avoided? How can an individual incorporate more minerals into their diet?

Learning with Visuals

Synthesize Have students research the role of electrolytes in the body and draw a graphic representation of how electrolytes affect the balance of bodily fluids. Students should research what events might cause a person's electrolytes to become unbalanced and what would happen as a result.

Assess

Worksheets

A reproducible quiz for Section 8 is provided in the Teacher Classroom Resources.

CHAPTER 8 Planning Guide

CHAPTER 8 Nutrition: Healthy Body Weight

Objectives

- Discuss the connection of health risks linked to too much or too little body fat.
- Identify various ways to measure body fat.
- Discuss the balance between food energy taken in and energy spent.
- Determine safe and unsafe weight-management techniques.
- Discuss strategies to use to design a successful and realistic weight-loss plan.
- Identify healthy strategies to promote weight gain.
- Discuss the dangers of eating disorders.

Features

- *What Teens Think:* Do Teens Diet Too Much or Too Little? (page 207)
- *Health Skills:* Identifying Unsound Weight-Loss Programs (page 211)
- *Consumer Skills Activity:* Weight-Loss Schemes (page 212)
- *Applying Health Skills:* Analyzing Influences (page 224)
- *Q&A:* Eating Disorders (pages 226–227)

Introduction

Teaching Support

Fast Files

- *Vocabulary:* Learning Vocabulary and Fill in the Blanks
- *Study Outline*
- *Reading Cloze*
- *Reteaching Activities:* Reviewing the Chapter
- *Enrichment Activities:* Decreasing Impulsive Snacking, Diana's Dilemma, Calorie Quiz
- *Career Briefs:* Medical Record Technicians
- *Life Choice Inventory:* Eating Attitudes Test
- *Handouts:* Tips for Reducing Sodium Intake, Seasoning Without Your Salt Shaker, Evaluating a Weight-Loss Diet
- *Teacher Information Sheet:* Diagnosing Anorexia and Bulimia

- *Quizzes:* Sections 1–6
- *Tests:* Chapter 8 Test A, Chapter 8 Test B

Multimedia Support

- *ExamView®* Assessment Suite
- Online Learning Center

Introducing Chapter 8

Chapter Preview Activity

Students as well as adults are often made to believe false or exaggerated claims for weight-loss diets and products. Billions of dollars are spent on dieting products each year.

To help students evaluate the reliability of advertisers' claims, try this activity. Ask the class if they think the following diet claim could be true: ***Lose 25 pounds in one week!*** Take a vote to see how many believe it is possible and how many don't. Then give the class the following information:

1. To lose one pound of body fat a person must go without 3,500 calories.

2. The imaginary person going on this diet has an energy requirement of 2,500 calories per day.

Ask students to figure out if it would be possible for this person to lose 25 pounds in one week using the following formula. Multiply 7 (days in a week) × 2,500 (daily calorie requirement) = 17,500 calories (normally eaten in one week). Multiply 25 pounds × 3,500 calories (calories to lose one pound) = 87,500 calories (must be burned to lose 25 pounds). Ask students for their answers.

Even if a person ate nothing all week, which would not be advised, the person would still have 70,000 calories to burn to lose the 25 pounds. What about exercise? To burn 70,000 calories in one week a person would have to run at a fast rate of speed, 24 hours a day, for all seven days.

This exercise will help students to see through some of the outrageous claims diet advertisers make.

 Not Enough Time?

Here are some suggestions to ensure that you cover the key topics in this chapter.

DAY 1 Before class, have the students complete the "Fact or Fiction" questions on page 201 and give their answers in class. Read the Chapter Preview.

DAY 2 During class, complete the activities listed throughout the chapter.

DAY 3 Discuss the Q&A section on 226–227.

Bulletin Board Ideas

Make a collage of diet advertisements, including both written and photographic claims. Have students determine if the claims in the advertisements are reliable. Post more examples of reliable healthy eating strategies than unrealistic diet advertisements.

 **Fact** *or Fiction?*

Answers:

1. True.

2. False. Weight loss may reflect loss of water or lean tissue rather than loss of fat.

3. False. It is as hard for a person who tends to be thin to gain a pound as it is for a person who tends to be fat to lose one.

 Writing Paragraphs will vary.

SECTION 1 **Body Fat Risks**

Focus

Vocabulary Activity

Vocabulary worksheets are provided in the Teacher Classroom Resources.

Teach and Apply

Class Activity

Evaluate Have students close their books and take out a piece of paper. Tell the class to write down four problems associated with being underweight, four with being overweight, and four benefits of maintaining ideal weight. Discuss the students' answers.

Class Discussion

Discuss Ask students what they feel is the most important reason ideal weight should be maintained. Write the different responses on the board. This will help students understand the many reasons why weight management and nutrition are so important to overall health.

Planning Guide

Assess

Worksheets

A reproducible quiz for Section 1 is provided in the Teacher Classroom Resources.

Close

Evaluate Lead a class discussion on problems students have had with weight control.

SECTION 2 — The Right Weight for You

Focus

Vocabulary Activity

Vocabulary worksheets are provided in the Teacher Classroom Resources.

Teach and Apply

Pursuing Wellness

Comprehend There are a number of health concerns associated with obesity. Heart disease, high blood pressure, atherosclerosis, diabetes and stroke are more common in obese persons. The burden of extra fat puts a strain on the skeletal system. Arthritis is more common, particularly in the hips, knees, and lower spine. The more weight a person carries, the greater the wear and tear on the joints. This wear and tear can cause pain that results in even less physical activity and the risk of additional weight gain. Low-back pain is also more common in people who are obese.

Surgical procedures on obese people involve an increased risk, as well as an increase in the potential for post-surgical complications such as infection. In addition, being obese also increases anesthetic risk.

Overweight mothers tend to have a higher infant and maternal mortality rate. Finally, cancer is more prevalent in obese people. Males who are obese tend to have a higher incidence of cancer in the colon, rectum, and prostate. In women who are obese, there is a higher incidence of cancer of the ovaries, uterus, cervix, and breasts.

Class Discussion

Evaluate Have students write anonymously on a piece of paper how they determine if their own weights are at a healthy level. Collect the papers in a small box and read the responses. Discuss the responses with the class. Ask the following questions:

1. Do these responses refer to appearance, energy, or health?

2. How much should we be concerned with appearance if we have energy and are healthy?

3. Why is a scale not necessarily an accurate measure of how much one should weigh?

Assess

Worksheets

A reproducible quiz for Section 2 is provided in the Teacher Classroom Resources.

Close

Evaluate Ask students to write a paragraph on what criteria they use in determining their ideal weights.

SECTION 3 — Energy Balance

Vocabulary Activity

Vocabulary worksheets are provided in the Teacher Classroom Resources.

Class Activity

Synthesize Give students the Calorie Quiz from the Teacher Classroom Resources with these directions. "Number your paper 1 through 15. I will name two foods. By the number, write the food that you think has the most calories, or if you believe they are the same, write same." After the quiz, give the students the correct answers and discuss students' reactions to the calories.

Class Activity

Apply Explain to students that over time, small changes in diet may result in large gains or losses in weight. For example, if a person consumes 2,000 calories a day, but increases physical activity by walking an additional ten minutes a day, five pounds would be lost in a year. Have students share examples of other small changes they can make now that could result in weight gains or losses.

Assess

Worksheets

A reproducible quiz for Section 3 is provided in the Teacher Classroom Resources.

Close

Evaluate Ask students to imagine they have gained 10 pounds of unnecessary weight. Ask students how they would try to lose this weight. What would be the healthiest and most sensible approach to take?

SECTION 4
Weight Gain and Weight Loss

Vocabulary Activity

Vocabulary worksheets are provided in the Teacher Classroom Resources.

Group Activity

Analyze Explain to students that there are safe and unsafe ways of losing and gaining weight. A number of diet programs offer quick results that can lead to a rapid return of the weight when the dieter quits the program. A diet that doesn't change a person's long-term behavior usually will not be successful. Diets that have quick results may also be hazardous, whether they are designed to help a person lose or gain weight.

Divide your class into groups of three or four. Instruct students to bring advertisements for diet programs to class. In their groups, have students analyze at least two advertisements by answering the following questions about each one.

1. Does the advertisement promise quick results?

2. How much weight loss or gain is promised per week?

3. Does the advertisement warn of any health risks?

4. What is the total cost of the program?

Have students share their findings with the class. Remind the class that successful programs are those that include physical activity and loss or gain of only one or two pounds per week. In order to lose weight, people need to burn more calories than they consume and to gain weight they need to consume more calories than they burn.

Assess

Worksheets

A reproducible quiz for Section 4 is provided in the Teacher Classroom Resources.

Close

Recall Have students write, without using their books, five of the eight clues to identifying unsound weight-loss programs. They are listed in the Health Skills sidebar entitled "Identifying Unsound Weight-Loss Programs" on page 211.

SECTION 5 Smart Weight-Loss Strategies

Vocabulary Activity

Vocabulary worksheets are provided in the Teacher Classroom Resources.

Teach and Apply

Pursuing Wellness

Analyze Have students keep a health diary for an entire week. Ask them to keep track of what they eat and drink, including quantities, and where and when they eat. They should also include physical activity, including walking to and from school, and so on.

Help students analyze their own health habits. Ask them to look for patterns in their diets and physical activity habits. They probably have some good patterns as well as some that have a negative effect on their overall health. To conclude, help students find places where they can make any needed changes in their eating habits and physical activity.

Class Activity

Synthesize It is estimated that between 95 and 98 percent of people who lose weight gain it all back, plus a few more pounds. Ask students why they think this happens. Explain to students that the body, as a survival tactic, lowers its metabolism when it is being starved. If a female eats less than 1,000 calories per day or a male eats less than 1,200 calories, it is considered starvation-level calories. For each pound of fat lost while eating less than these limits, energy

requirements may drop permanently by ten calories. These permanent changes in metabolism may occur in as little as 72 hours. Ask students, "If a person loses 10 pounds on a 'starvation' diet, what happens after the diet is over?" (The weight is gained back because calorie expenditure has dropped 100 calories.) Ask students how this might affect someone who was constantly dieting.

Assess

Worksheets

A reproducible quiz for Section 5 is provided in the Teacher Classroom Resources.

Close

Apply Give students the following scenario. A friend who is overweight asks your advice about going on a diet. What would you tell your friend? Question students as to what their responses would be, and discuss their ideas.

SECTION 6 Smart Weight-Gain Strategies

Vocabulary Activity

Vocabulary worksheets are provided in the Teacher Classroom Resources.

Teach and Apply

Class Activity

Evaluate Ask students to consider the following scenario. Imagine there are two identical twins; one regularly eats 2,600 calories, with 50 percent of those calories coming from fat, while the other also eats 2,600 calories, with only 30 percent of calories coming from fat. All other aspects of their lives—exercise, metabolism, and so on—are the same. Ask the class if the twins would have the same body composition (the same amount of fat and lean muscle mass). Take a class vote.

The answer is that the twin with the higher fat content in the diet would have a higher percentage of body fat. Why? Our bodies use the energy nutrients differently. Dietary fat is changed to body fat with little effort. Carbohydrates, on the other hand, require a larger energy expenditure to be changed to body fat.

To give an example of this, Japanese people eat 20 percent more calories than Americans, but 33 percent less fat. The Japanese as a group of people are generally leaner than Americans. However, as Japanese people adopt Western eating habits, their body fat usually increases.

Pursuing Wellness

Apply We have learned that weight loss or gain happens when the number of calories we eat does not equal the number of calories we burn. One method of determining calorie requirements for the day is to use the following formula: Multiply your ideal healthy weight by the number below that best describes your activity level. The answer you get will represent your calorie needs for the day:

13 —very sedentary person, inactive.

14 —sedentary, does light housework, moves slowly.

15 —average, activities such as doing errands and light yard work, moves at a normal pace.

16 —above average, does hard work involving heavy lifting and moving at a brisk pace, exercises regularly for fun.

17 —strenuous, has a demanding exercise program and works hard physically, moving at a fast pace the major portion of the day.

If an individual's weight is above a desired level, try exercising more. About five calories are burned for every minute walked. Remind students that small changes in behavior add up.

Assess

Worksheets

A reproducible quiz for Section 6 is provided in the Teacher Classroom Resources.

Reproducible Chapter Tests A and B are provided in the Teacher Classroom Resources.

Close

Recall Have students design a list of behavior modification strategies for underweight people. Give students 15 minutes and then discuss their findings.

Go Online

To find supplemental information to suit your individual class, you may want to visit the following Web sites, where you can find additional Internet resources to enhance the study of this chapter. As with all Web sites, you should check these out first to be sure the information found there is appropriate for your students.

Healthy People 2010:
 www.healthypeople.gov
American Dietetic Association:
 www.eatright.org
Shape Up America:
 www.shapeup.org

These sites deal with understanding weight control and offer strategies for diet and exercise for a healthy balance.

CHAPTER 9 Planning Guide

CHAPTER 9   Fitness

Objectives

- Identify benefits of physical fitness.
- Identify the components of fitness.
- Understand the importance of both a warm-up and a cool-down.
- Identify aerobic activities.
- Identify stretching techniques
- Identify techniques to gaining muscle strength and endurance.
- Identify risks of steroid use.
- Demonstrate injury prevention.

Features

- *Applying Health Skills:* Goal Setting (page 238)
- *Consumer Skills Activity:* Nutritional Supplements (page 253)
- *Q&A:* Food for Sports Competition (pages 260–261)

Introduction

Teaching Support

Fast Files

- *Vocabulary:* Learning Vocabulary, Break the Code
- *Study Outline*
- *Reading Cloze*
- *Reteaching Activities:* Word Choice, Understanding Fitness, Stretches and Exercises Chart, Understanding How Oxygen is Delivered to the Muscles
- *Enrichment Activities:* Exploring Fitness Centers, Designing a Personal Fitness Program, Honoring Your Commitment to Exercise
- *Cooperative Learning Activity:* Design a Fitness Course
- *Career Briefs:* Physical Therapists
- *Life Choice Inventory:* How Physically Active Are You?
- *Handouts:* Strategies for Overcoming Fitness Obstacles, The Pre-competition Meal

- *Teacher Information Sheet:* More on the Effects of Steroid Hormones on the Body, Vitamins and Minerals, Excerpts from the Surgeon General's Report on Physical Activity and Health, Can You Meet the President's Challenge?
- *Quizzes:* Sections 1–6
- *Tests:* Chapter 9 Test A, Chapter 9 Test B

Multimedia Support

- *ExamView® Assessment Suite*
- Online Learning Center

Introducing Chapter 9

Chapter Preview Activity

Ask students to complete the fitness test of the President's Council on Physical Fitness before teaching the chapter so that students will have a comparative personal learning experience. Ask students to write down their personal fitness levels and set goals for themselves to maintain or improve their fitness level.

Not Enough Time?

Here are some suggestions to ensure that you cover the key topics in this chapter.

DAY 1 Assign Sections 1 and 2 ahead of time. In class, complete the Preview Activity. Do the activities listed throughout the chapter. Have students read Sections 3 and 4 before the next class.

DAY 2 Continue with the activities listed throughout the chapter. Assign Sections 5 and 6 as reading before the next class.

DAY 3 Complete the activities and have students complete the Chapter Review.

Bulletin Board Ideas

Reproduce **Figure 9.2**, "Fitness Contributes to All Aspects of Health and Wellness" found on page 233, on a bulletin board. Show how the three areas overlap. Ask students to contribute pictures of people involved in physical activity found in magazines or drawn by hand.

Answers:

1. True.
2. False. You should stop to avoid serious injury.
3. False. It's best to rehydrate as you go.

 Writing Paragraphs will vary.

SECTION 1 Benefits of Fitness

Focus

Vocabulary Activity

Vocabulary worksheets are provided in the Teacher Classroom Resources.

Teach and Apply

Group Activity

Apply Refer students to **Figure 9.2** on page 233. Divide students into three groups. Assign each group one of the three health categories (physical health; mental/emotional and spiritual health; social health). Ask each group to write descriptions giving examples of ways in which the benefits of fitness contribute to health. Encourage the groups to do research or interview friends to provide "proof" that the two benefits are real. Finally, ask all the students to explain in writing why "a fit person benefits in all areas of life."

Assess

Worksheets

A reproducible quiz for Section 1 is provided in the Teacher Classroom Resources.

Close

Recall Students should be able to list the benefits of fitness. Give students 30 seconds to list as many benefits of fitness as possible. When time is up, collect the lists. Give credit for correct responses.

SECTION 2 The Path to Fitness: Conditioning

Focus

Vocabulary Activity

Vocabulary worksheets are provided in the Teacher Classroom Resources.

Teach and Apply

Learning With Visuals

Apply Have students create a podcast or video script to explain the importance of conditioning and what activities can be performed to increase physical fitness. If students have a video camera or tape recorder, have them record their scripts and invite

the groups to share their podcast or video with the class.

Learning With Visuals

Apply Organize students into five small groups. Give each group poster paper and a marker. Assign one component of fitness to each group (cardiovascular endurance, flexibility, muscle strength, muscle endurance, and body composition). Ask one member to write down their responses. Then, give the groups one minute to write as many exercises as possible that fit that component. Have the groups trade papers, but keep the same color markers. Then, ask each group to list the injuries that could occur if the exercise technique is not done correctly. Have each group trade papers again. For the next minute, have students list the results of not meeting this component. Have each group trade papers again. Have each group list positive results for that component. Hang the posters and lead a class discussion on the results.

Group Activity

Apply Have students design an advertisement listing the benefits of physical activity. Explain to students that advertising can be used as a method to promote fitness, the same way it is used to promote products. You might also want to bring in examples of popular advertising campaigns to help give the students ideas.

Comprehension Check

Comprehend Write the words *warm-up* and *cool-down* on the board. Have students list on their own papers as many activities as they can for each heading. Emphasize that it is necessary to warm up and cool down all of the major muscle groups. Examples may include: Warm-up: 15 arm circles, touch toes, and jogging one lap. Cool-down: 10 arm circles, jog two laps, touch toes. Challenge students to think of new exercises for the warm-up and cool-down.

Assess

Worksheets

A reproducible quiz for Section 2 is provided in the Teacher Classroom Resources.

Close

Apply Have students describe in writing one physical activity goal for the week. Tell students that their goal must list the types of activities, number of repetitions, when and if each will be increased. Encourage students to include physical activities for each muscle group.

SECTION 3
Gaining Cardiovascular Endurance

Focus

Vocabulary Activity

Vocabulary worksheets are provided in the Teacher Classroom Resources.

Teach and Apply

Class Activity

Synthesize Hang two posters on the board, one labeled "Aerobic" and one labeled "Anaerobic." Give each student an index card and a piece of tape. Have students list a favorite activity on the card. Then, ask students to tape their index cards on the correct posterboard. When all have placed their cards, ask the class if they would move any activities to the other category, and to explain why.

Comprehension Check

Comprehend Have students determine their resting heart rate. Then, have students stand by their desks, and jump up and down for 30 seconds, and check their pulses again to determine the difference in heart rate. Explain to students that a pluse check will determine heart rate. Breathing hard does not mean they are working hard.

Class Activity

Apply Invite a guest speaker, such as a doctor, to the class to talk about body image. Ask the speaker to discuss self-esteem, self perceptions, advertising, and stereotypes.

Assess

Worksheets

A reproducible quiz for Section 3 is provided in the Teacher Classroom Resources.

Close

Evaluate Collect videos showing a variety of athletic activities. Show the class a 30 second spot from each video. Ask students to write down whether the activity is aerobic or anaerobic.

SECTION 4 — Gaining Flexibility

Focus

Vocabulary Activity

Vocabulary worksheets are provided in the Teacher Classroom Resources.

Teach and Apply

Class Activity

Apply Lead a discussion asking students to suggest 5 to 10 questions for a fitness questionnaire. Then, ask students to interview 5 to 10 people using the questionnaire. Sample questions may include:

1. Do you exercise? If so, how often? If not, is there a reason?

2. Do you think exercise is important? Why or why not?

3. Do you know the difference between aerobic and anaerobic exercise?

4. Why is flexibility important?

5. How much exercise do you get in a typical week?

Ask students not to share the names of the people they interviewed. After completing the interviews, ask students to share their findings with the class. Ask: Were you surprised by their findings? Were people exercising more or less than they had anticipated?

Assess

Worksheets

A reproducible quiz for Section 4 is provided in the Teacher Classroom Resources.

Close

Apply Be sensitive to students who may not wish to perform any activity in front of the class. Ask a student to perform a sit-and-reach exercise for the class. The student should sit on the floor with his legs extended, knees slightly bent. Place the zero end of a yardstick against one heel so that it extends out in front of the student. With his hands together, the student should stretch as far as is comfortable toward the yardstick. Have another student record the number of inches the student stretches. Repeat for each student who wishes to participate. Ask students to set flexibility goals for themselves and develop plans to reach their goals. Give the students a chance to retest themselves in two weeks to see if their flexibility has improved.

SECTION 5 — Gaining Muscle Strength and Endurance

Focus

Vocabulary Activity

Vocabulary worksheets are provided in the Teacher Classroom Resources.

Teach and Apply

Class Activity

Discuss Ask students to describe steroid use might be a short-term method of self-esteem building. Ask why some people might choose to use steroids rather than use a long-term method like exercise. Ask students to consider the health effects of steroid use. Are health effects that could shorten your life worth the risk?

Evaluate Lead a class discussion asking students to describe how steroid use may lead to improved athletic performance. Ask students to describe the side effects of steroid use.

Assess

Worksheets

A reproducible quiz for Section 5 is provided in the Teacher Classroom Resources.

Close

Comprehend Have students bring to class one article from a magazine or newspaper that pertains to the information presented in this section. Have the students present the article orally to the class.

SECTION 6

Preventing Sports Injuries and Heat Stroke

Focus

Vocabulary Activity

Vocabulary worksheets are provided in the Teacher Classroom Resources.

Teach and Apply

Class Activity

Apply Ask students for examples of athletic injuries. What do they think caused the injury? What could have been done to prevent the injury?

Guest Speaker

Discuss Ask a sports medicine professional or registered dietitian to visit the class to talk about the effects of various foods on athletes. Ask students to prepare questions such as:

a. Are there some foods that are better than others for athletes to eat?

b. Are there different food requirements for different athletic endeavors?

c. How would you change this nutritional information if it was to be given to a non-athlete?

Assess

Worksheets

A reproducible quiz for Section 6 is provided in the Teacher Classroom Resources.

Reproducible Chapter Tests A and B are provided in the Teacher Classroom Resources.

Close

Apply Ask students for a resource list for preventive methods or treatments for athletic injuries. For example: fitness club, fitness director of a company, nurse, doctor, athletic trainer.

Go Online

To find supplemental information for your class, visit the following Web site to find additional Internet resources. As with all Web sites, check the site first to be sure the information is appropriate for your students.

KidsHealth:

kidshealth.org/parent/nutrition_fit/fitness/
fitness_13_18.html

CHAPTER 10 Your Body: An Owner's Manual

Objectives

- Discuss ways to keep teeth healthy and breath fresh.
- Discuss the importance of clean hair and nails.
- Identify ways to care for eyes and ears.
- Discuss personal cleanliness.
- Demonstrate correct posture.
- Determine when it is appropriate to get medical help.
- Discuss the importance of getting the proper amount of sleep.

Features

- *Consumer Skills Activity:* Advertisement Techniques (page 272)
- *Applying Health Skills:* Decision Making (page 282)
- *Q&A:* Our Need For Sleep (pages 284–285)

Introduction

Teaching Support

Fast Files

- *Vocabulary:* Learning Vocabulary, Fill in the Blanks
- *Study Outline*
- *Reading Cloze*
- *Reteaching Activities:* Completion, Personal Cleanliness Facts and Fallacies
- *Enrichment Activities:* Straighten Up!
- *Cooperative Learning Activity:* Just Ducky or Pure Quackery
- *Career Briefs:* Dental Hygienists
- *Life Choice Inventory:* Are Your Immunizations Up to Date?
- *Handouts:* Some Terms Used on Cosmetic Labels, Personal Care Products Shopping Analysis
- *Quizzes:* Sections 1–4
- *Tests:* Chapter 10 Test A, Chapter 10 Test B

Multimedia Support

- *ExamView® Assessment Suite*
- Online Learning Center

Chapter Preview Activity

Divide the class into small groups and have students list all the strategies that they use to maintain healthy bodies. Have them record these on chart paper. Allow each group to share and discuss their lists with the entire class.

Bulletin Board Ideas

Divide the bulletin board into two sides. On the left-hand side, post advertisements for products (or the actual products) truly needed for personal hygiene. Examples may include: toothbrush, toothpaste, comb, soap, deodorant, shampoo. On the right-hand side, post advertisements, labels, or actual products of the numerous items people use in their hygiene routine. Examples of these can include: teeth whiteners, lotions, make-up, hair styling products, special hair brushes, colognes and perfumes, and so on. As a possible activity, students could bring in the advertisements of the products they use.

Planning Guide

Not Enough Time?

Here are some suggestions to ensure that you cover the key topics in this chapter.

DAY 1 Assign students to read Sections 1 and 2 prior to class. In class, do the activities listed throughout the sections. Assign students to read Sections 3 and 4 prior to the next class.

DAY 2 In class, do the activities throughout Sections 3 and 4. Conclude with the Section Reviews.

Fact or Fiction?

Answers:

1. True.

2. False. Although cleanliness is important, there are no simple answers to preventing or curing acne.

3. True.

 Writing Paragraphs will vary.

SECTION 1
Healthy Teeth and Fresh Breath

Focus

Vocabulary Activity

Vocabulary worksheets are provided in the Teacher Classroom Resources.

Teach and Apply

Class Activity

Evaluate Ask students to name the teeth and gum products that they buy and use regularly. Do they use a particular brand of toothpaste? Why?

Class Activity

Apply Invite a dentist or dental hygienist to visit the class. Have the speaker share some of the more common dental procedures performed in their office, as well as more extreme procedures, such as root canals and crowns. Ask the speaker to compare the costs and effort of daily dental care, compared to the costs of major dental work that is the result of poor dental care. Invite students to ask the speaker questions.

Group Activity

Research Divide the class into groups of 3–4 students. Have each group research and prepare a presentation about dental procedures, problems, or diseases. Ask students to include information about how good dental hygiene will help avoid dental problems. Students should be encouraged to create videos, oral reports, or podcasts to create their presentations.

Comprehension Check

Apply Use an oversized model of teeth and a toothbrush and the steps illustrated in **Figure 10.2** to demonstrate the steps to cleaning teeth properly. Ask students to volunteer to demonstrate the brushing techniques. Have other students critique the volunteers' techniques.

Assess

Worksheets

Evaluate A reproducible quiz for Section 1 is provided in the Teacher Classroom Resources.

Close

Students should be able to do at least one of the following:

1. Participate in a class discussion on the steps to proper dental care. Have students explain why each step is important.

2. Name and describe in writing two dental problems that can occur from improper care. Tell what procedures or treatments are followed to remedy the problems.

SECTION 2 Personal Cleanliness Concerns

Focus

Vocabulary Activity

Vocabulary worksheets are provided in the Teacher Classroom Resources.

Teach and Apply

Class Activity

Analyze Ask students to volunteer to estimate how much they spend on hair-care products and services monthly. Have them list the products they buy and the services they pay for. Compile the numbers and compute a class average. Discuss the results.

Class Activity

Apply Invite a cosmetologist to your classroom or visit a cosmetology classroom or salon. Have the cosmetologist explain proper hair care procedures. Ask the cosmetologist to speak on proper skin care procedures. Hold a question-and-answer session following the demonstration. Ask the class to share what they observed and learned from the demonstration. Ask the class to share some ideas for better hair and skin care, which they can include in their daily hygiene routines

Group Activity

Apply This chapter outlines the basics of good hygiene. Information is given that helps students realize that these habits improve not only their physical health, but also helps their emotional health. Good personal hygiene habits are important for maintaining good interpersonal relationships.

Have students brainstorm to make a list of the basic items necessary for good personal hygiene. Review each section of the chapter as needed to make sure all areas are included. Discuss with students the cycle that can develop when people have serious difficulties. For example: A man is out of work. The family struggles to maintain their usual lifestyle for as long as possible, but ends up losing their home. The money or facilities for good daily hygiene are not available, and as a result it is embarrassing to go for job interviews. Without work, the family can't reestablish those good hygiene habits, and the cycle continues.

Have students research, organizations in your area that provide help to the homeless or to abused/battered women and children. If possible, have students make a list and bring items from home to put into kits to be donated to those who need them. You may want to have a fundraising event to earn money for the purchase of the items to be donated.

Class Discussion

Discuss Give students the handout entitled "Some Terms Used on Cosmetic Labels." This handout lists some commonly used terms and provides definitions and explanations for students to help them become more informed about products they are buying. Ask students to compare the handout to products they may have at home or have seen in stores. Why would it be beneficial to be familiar with these terms when purchasing cosmetic products?

Assess

Worksheets

A reproducible quiz for Section 2 is provided in the Teacher Classroom Resources.

Close

Recall Utilize the students' displays, reports, collages, and analyses to review. If you have kept cooperative groups the same throughout the series of assignments, assign each group a specific personal care area (hair, skin, and so on) on which to report. The group will compile its resources on that area. Each group will give an oral presentation of its findings.

SECTION 3 — Posture and Image

Focus

Vocabulary Activity

Vocabulary worksheets are provided in the Teacher Classroom Resources.

Teach and Apply

Learning with Visuals

Comprehend Use a model of the back to teach the structure of the vertebrae, names of its parts, and the weight-bearing responsibility of the back. Instruct students on which muscles surround the back area and the physiology of these. Point out the relationship of these to the abdominal muscles, as well. Review the vocabulary terms and encourage students to use the vacabulary to describe the structure of the back to a partner.

Group Activity

Apply Refer students to **Figure 10.10,** page 279. Have students work in pairs to check their standing posture. When a student is standing properly, the partner should be able to draw an imaginary straight line from the ear lobe to the outside of the ankle bone. Students should stand against a wall with their backs pressed against it for this activity.

Exercises to develop lower back and abdominal muscles will help prevent lower back pain. Exercises to develop physical endurance will not only help a person lose weight, but will also give increased energy. In turn, this will help with good posture because physically fit people are less inclined to slouch.

Assess

Worksheets

A reproducible quiz for Section 3 is provided in the Teacher Classroom Resources.

Close

Apply Have students keep a "posture check diary" on a piece of paper in their notebook. Have them mark the number of times during the day that they catch themselves using bad posture. Did they start using better posture after a couple days of trying to notice whether or not they had bad posture?

SECTION 4 — When to Visit a Health Care Provider

Focus

Vocabulary Activity

Vocabulary worksheets are provided in the Teacher Classroom Resources.

Teach and Apply

Pursuing Wellness

Apply Have students choose a health care provider and research that occupation.

Students should report back to class on the educational requirements, the duties, and any other interesting facts they can find about the particular health care provider.

Group Activity

Evaluate Tell students that only about 33 percent of all doctors today are family physicians, general internists, and pediatricians. Only 17 percent of all medical school graduates are choosing to become generalists. In comparison, in England 73 percent of physicians are generalists. Is the trend toward specialists (surgeons, oncologists, dermatologists, and so on) good or bad for the students as patients?

Divide the class into two groups. Have the first group take the position that there should be more general physicians, and have the second group take the opposite position—that more general physicians aren't necessary. Arguments of the first group could include: Most people don't need specialized care; if general physicians had fewer patients they could be more involved, thus helping prevent the need to go to a specialist. Arguments for the second group could include: People with complicated conditions need doctors in that specialty for better care; research into new techniques might slow down if more doctors were only general physicians.

Assess

Worksheet

A reproducible quiz for Section 4 is provided in the Teacher Classroom Resources.

Reproducible Chapter Tests A and B are available in the Teacher Classroom Resources.

Close

Apply Divide the class into pairs. Give each pair the name of one health care provider in your local area. (You may want to contact providers in advance to ask if they would be willing to cooperate.) Have students request a short interview with the providers, to get a "Dos and Don'ts" list for when to see a doctor. Then have each pair make a poster of the "Dos and Don'ts" for classroom display.

Go Online

To find supplemental information to suit your individual class, you may want to visit the following Web site where you can find additional Internet resources to enhance the study of this chapter. As with all Web sites, you should check these out first to be sure the information found there is appropriate for your students.

Choosing a Doctor:

www.ama-assn.org/

This site offers some helpful guidelines to keep in mind when choosing a doctor.

CHAPTER 11 Planning Guide

CHAPTER 11 Drugs as Medicines

Objectives

- Discuss the actions of various medicines.
- Analyze the risks and safety of medicines.
- Discuss over-the-counter (OTC) medicines.
- Discuss prescription medicines.

Features

- *Consumer Skills Activity:* Money and Medicines (page 298)
- *Applying Health Skills:* Accessing Information (page 299)
- *Health Skills:* Taking Medicines Safely (page 300)
- *Q&A:* Caffeine (page 304)

Introduction

Teaching Support

Fast Files

- *Vocabulary:* Learning Vocabulary, Fill in the Blanks, and Word Choice
- *Study Outline*
- *Reading Cloze*
- *Reteaching Activities:* Effects of Medicines, What Are Medicines?
- *Enrichment Activities:* Reading a Label
- *Cooperative Learning Activity:* Over-the-Counter Medicine
- *Career Briefs:* Pharmacists
- *Life Choice Inventory:* How Wisely Do You Choose OTC Medications?
- *Handouts:* How New Drugs Are Discovered, Attitudes About Over-the-Counter Drugs, Analyzing Medicine Use, Caffeine Content of Beverages, Foods and OTC Drugs
- *Teacher Information Sheet:* Food/Drug Interactions
- *Quizzes:* Sections 1–4
- *Tests:* Chapter 11 Test A, Chapter 11 Test B

Multimedia Support

- *ExamView® Assessment Suite*
- Online Learning Center

Chapter Preview Activity

Have students record inventory of the medicine sections of a local drug store. This inventory should include: names of medicines, purpose, active and inactive ingredients, classification (generic or brand name, over-the-counter or prescription), costs, and expiration dates.

Bulletin Board Ideas

Use the Health Skills sidebar, "Taking Medicines Safely," on page 300, as the basis for your bulletin board. Condense some of the longer tips so that each one can be made large enough to be seen easily.

Not Enough Time?

Following are some suggestions to help you make sure that you cover the key topics in this chapter if you have limited time. (Refer to the daily lesson plans in your Teacher Classroom Resources for additional suggestions.)

DAY 1 Assign students Sections 1 and 2 to read prior to class. During class, have students do the Preview Activity and the activities listed throughout Sections 1 and 2. Conclude the class with the Section Reviews.

DAY 2 Before Day 2, have students read Sections 2 and 3. During class, have students do the Preview Activities. Conclude with the Section Reviews. Assign Section 4.

DAY 3 During class, have students do the activities listed throughout Section 4. Have students complete the Chapter Review.

Answers:

1. False. All drug use involves risk.

2. True. This is one of the factors that affect the action of a drug.

3. False. Generic drugs contain the same active ingredients, but may contain different inactive ingredients.

 Writing Paragraphs will vary.

SECTION 1 · The Actions of Drugs

Focus

Vocabulary Activity

Vocabulary worksheets are provided in the Teacher Classroom Resources.

Teach and Apply

Teaching with Visuals

Evaluate Refer students to **Figure 11.2**. Tell students that they should not be frightened

of the list of possible hazards associated with each of these drugs. They were tested extensively before the government permitted their sale. These are potential problems and reactions that take place, which people should be aware of. Following are some additional side effects that you might want to tell students about.

a. Acetaminophen—difficulty in diagnosing overdose because reaction may be delayed for up to a week after taking medication

b. Antacids—possible concealment of ulcer, prevention of certain antibiotics' functioning

c. Aspirin—excessive bleeding during surgery or childbirth

d. Diet pills—nervousness and crabbiness

Have students tell of times when they suffered the side effects of a drug. Were any of the situations frightening or life-threatening? Do students feel that they take the warnings that accompany medicines and drugs seriously enough? Would someone who drove under the effects of an antihistamine be acting as irresponsibly as someone who drove while intoxicated?

Assess

Worksheets

A reproducible quiz for Section 1 is provided in the Teacher Classroom Resources.

Close

Evaluate Students should be able to complete the following:

1. List five ways medicines benefit people.

2. Describe the advantages and disadvantages of aspirin.

3. Describe the factors that influence the effects of drugs.

 **Testing Drugs: Risks and Safety**

Focus

Vocabulary Activity

Vocabulary worksheets are provided in the Teacher Classroom Resources.

Teach and Apply

Pursuing Wellness

Evaluate Incidence of nonfatal poisoning is alarmingly high. Past actions such as the Poison Prevention Packaging Act (PPPA), the annual poison prevention week, the shift to less toxic fuels (natural gas and LP gas) for cooking and heating, and safety standards for products that release combustion byproducts have all helped to reduce the risk of poisoning.

Prescription drugs and some other hazardous materials are sold primarily in child-resistant containers as required by the PPPA. Improvements in child resistant containers should be sought so they can be more readily used by older people than current containers. Have students go home and evaluate how safely their medicines are stored. They should be current in date and out of reach of young children.

Assess

Worksheets

A reproducible quiz for Section 2 is provided in the Teacher Classroom Resources.

Close

Recall Students should be able to answer these questions:

1. What is the function of the FDA?

2. What is a lethal dose?

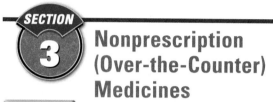 **Nonprescription (Over-the-Counter) Medicines**

Focus

Vocabulary Activity

Vocabulary worksheets are provided in the Teacher Classroom Resources.

Teach and Apply

Class Activity

Evaluate Students should not be in the habit of taking medicine the second they experience discomfort. Ask students what they can do when they have a headache, other than grab a pain reliever. (eat a solid meal, take a short nap, massage their neck) What can they do to relieve a stuffy nose that would not involve medicine? (take a hot bath, breathe steam from a bowl of hot water or from a vaporizer, use saline nasal drops) Why does our society seem to go for the "quick fix," even though it may not be the best one?

Class Activity

Evaluate Give students the handout entitled "Attitudes About Over-the-Counter Drugs." The handout provides students with an opportunity to explore their own attitudes about over-the-counter drugs. Encourage students to give their immediate, honest responses to each question. Ask students the following questions:

1. What has shaped their attitudes and values about over-the-counter drugs?

2. How do their attitudes and values affect their decisions about which medications to purchase or use?

Worksheets

A reproducible quiz for Section 3 is provided in the Teacher Classroom Resources.

Close

Students should be able to answer the following questions:

1. What is the difference between OTC drugs and prescription drugs?

2. What are the advantages of using generic drugs?

SECTION 4 Prescription Medicines

Focus

Vocabulary Activity

Vocabulary worksheets are provided in the Teacher Classroom Resources.

Teach and Apply

Group Activity

Apply Give students an opportunity to practice identifying good health strategies in taking medicines safely. Have students break into groups and present short scenarios, and then decide which of the guidelines applies to each situation.

Class Discussion

Discuss Have students bring in as many caffeine-containing food, beverage, or medicine labels as they can find. Make up a bulletin board showing all of the products they discovered. Ask students these questions: How did they find their products? Are the products ones that are commonly used at home or by the student? How often? Were they aware that all of the products collected contain caffeine? Which ones came as surprises?

Assess

Worksheets

A reproducible quiz for Section 4 is provided in the Teacher Classroom Resources.

Reproducible Test A and B Chapter 11 are provided in the Teacher Classroom Resources.

Close

Recall Students should be able to answer the following questions:

1. List three reasons prescription drugs are not freely available.

2. List five questions one should ask the doctor before taking a prescribed medicine.

3. List 10 guidelines to follow when taking medicine.

Go Online

To find supplemental information to suit your individual class, you may want to visit the following Web sites, where you can find additional Internet resources to enhance the study of this chapter. As with all Web sites, you should check these out first to be sure the information found there is appropriate for your students.

Nonprescription Medicines—What's Right for You?

www.nmafaculty.org

Problem-Free Prescriptions:

www.cigna.com

These sites have information for making informed decisions regarding medication.

CHAPTER 12 — Planning Guide

CHAPTER 12 Drugs of Abuse

Objectives	Features
• Define drug use, abuse, and misuse. • Explore society's views of drug use and abuse. • Learn the consequences of drug abuse. • Practice refusal skills in situations involving drug and alcohol abuse. • Differentiate between physical and psychological addiction. • Learn the effects of drug addiction.	• *Consumer Skills Activity:* Look-Alikes (page 328) • *What Teens Think:* How Has Drug Abuse Affected Your School or Community? (page 331) • *Applying Health Skills:* Accessing Information (page 334) • *Q&A:* Refusing Drugs (pages 338–339)

Introduction
Teaching Support
Fast Files
- *Vocabulary:* Learning Vocabulary, Fill in the Blanks
- *Study Outline*
- *Reading Cloze*
- *Reteaching Activities:* All About Marijuana, All About Cocaine, Kinds of Drugs
- *Enrichment Activities:* Making Healthy Decisions
- *Cooperative Learning Activity:* Party Situations, Strengthen Your Refusal Skills
- *Career Briefs:* Human Services Workers
- *Life Choice Inventory:* Is Any Drug or Medicine a Problem for You?
- *Handouts:* Attitudes About Drug Abuse, Mini Glossary of Drug Abuse Terms
- *Teacher Information Sheet:* Stopping Drug Addiction, Federal Trafficking Penalties

- *Quizzes:* Sections 1–7
- *Tests:* Chapter 12 Test A, Chapter 12 Test B

Multimedia Support
- *ExamView®* Assessment Suite
- Online Learning Center

Introducing Chapter 12
Chapter Preview Activity

Invite a judge or lawyer to visit your class and explain how drug abuse affects all aspects of our society. This should introduce the chapter as well as establish why students should learn how they can help on an individual level. Also, have students brainstorm a list of why students take drugs. Follow up by reading current event articles related to crime or death as a result of drug abuse.

Not Enough Time?

Following are some suggestions to help ensure that you cover the key topics in this chapter.

DAY 1 Before class, have students read Sections 1 and 2. During class, complete the activities throughout Sections 1 and 2. Assign students Section 3 to read for homework.

DAY 2 During class, have students do the activities throughout Section 3. Assign students Section 4 to read for homework.

DAY 3 During class, have students develop a drug-free plan for their futures. Discuss the drug categories and the effects of drugs, using Figure 12.6. Assign Section 5 as reading homework.

DAY 4 During class, ask students to brainstorm a list of OTC drugs that they may have at home that could affect driving. Lead a discussion about sober driving. Have students answer the Section 5 review questions. Ask students Sections 6 and 7 to read for homework.

DAY 5 During class, have students complete the activities throughout Sections 6 and 7. Assign the Chapter Review.

Bulletin Board Ideas

Create a bulletin board with creative ideas for "just saying 'no' to drugs." Use pictures of students in your classes or pictures of people in advertisements. Use speech balloons for each statement of drug refusal, and make it look like each person has a different way of saying "no" to drugs. Make some of the statements humorous and others more serious. Ask students for permission before putting their pictures on the bulletin board.

Answers:

1. False. Psychological addictions can be as powerful as physical ones.

2. False. Smoking marijuana is associated with harmful health effects similar to tobacco use.

3. False. People rarely recover from drug dependency on their own.

Writing Answers will vary.

SECTION 1 — Drug Abuse Defined

Focus

Vocabulary Activity

Vocabulary worksheets are provided in the Teacher Classroom Resources.

Teach and Apply

Pursuing Wellness

Comprehend Ask students what influence *family* can have on wellness. To prompt discussion, have students consider:

1. The methods family members use to deal with stress.

2. The amount of tobacco, alcohol, and drugs used in their families.

3. Methods used by their families to have fun.

4. The use of, or failure to use, devices such as seat belts that indicate a practice of safe living.

The *community* also influences personal wellness. Have students think of specific examples of the following:

1. Hotline availability for drugs or teen pregnancy

2. Community commitment to drug-free teen activities

3. Recreation programs for teens

4. Active community involvement in DARE or similar programs

Assess

Worksheets

A reproducible quiz for Section 1 is provided in the Teacher Classroom Resources.

Close

Apply Have students describe, in a few short paragraphs, the different ways in which drugs are abused in our society.

SECTION 2 — Why Do People Abuse Drugs?

Focus

Vocabulary Activity

Vocabulary worksheets are provided in the Teacher Classroom Resources.

Teach and Apply

Class Activity

Evaluate Ask students to give examples of appropriate drug use. (Two examples are taking aspirin for a headache or antibiotics prescribed by a doctor—both according to directions given on the bottle.) Then ask students to give examples of drug misuse.

The examples should simply identify some abused drugs to show the differences between drug use and misuse. Seek examples involving both medicines and illegal drugs (like taking too many painkillers for the purpose of an emotional high, or smoking marijuana).

Class Discussion

Discuss Ask students if they agree that people with high self-esteem are less likely to abuse drugs. Remind students that success does not always equal high self-esteem, as can be seen in the drug abuse of otherwise successful and famous people.

Class Activity

Evaluate Ask students to identify different mental and emotional reasons for abusing drugs. Ask students what they believe is the most common of these reasons. Do students think that there are different motivations for trying drugs for the first time and for not ending the drug abuse?

Class Activity

Evaluate Have students write a few short paragraphs explaining their answers to the following situation: One of your friends asks you to do cocaine. What is your reply to the persistent invitations? Invite volunteers to share their paragraphs with the class.

Pursuing Wellness

Apply Ask students to complete the worksheet in the Teacher Classroom Resources entitled "Attitudes about Drug Abuse." This will help them evaluate their present attitudes about drugs. Be sure they realize that there are no right or wrong answers to the worksheet.

Assess

Worksheets

A reproducible quiz for Section 2 is provided in the Teacher Classroom Resources.

Close

Analyze Have students think of songs about drug and/or alcohol abuse. Write the song titles or lyrics on the board. Is the abuse of drugs and alcohol "put down" in the songs or glorified? Is taking drugs shown to be mysterious or "cool"? Discuss.

 SECTION 3 Addiction

Focus

Vocabulary Activity

Vocabulary worksheets are provided in the Teacher Classroom Resources.

Teach and Apply

Group Activity

Apply Have students develop a list of ten activities that give them a natural high. Tell them that what one person enjoys, another may not like at all. Sometimes friendships between two people are based on activities that both enjoy, such as playing a particular sport. Interests like this can help students "fit in" with a group whose members enjoy doing the same kinds of things.

Have students read their lists. Write on the board the suggestions that come up most frequently. Ask students who enjoy each activity to raise their hands as you read each aloud. Tell them to look around the room to notice the other people who share the same interests.

Class Activity

Apply Ask students to review **Figure 12.4**, The Spiral That Leads to Physical Addiction. Ask students to explain in their own words what happens at each point. As students explain the figure, check for understanding of terms such as euphoria, dysphoria, tolerance, elevated drug doses, withdrawal, and addiction.

Comprehension Check

Analyze Have students write a paragraph explaining the difference between physical addiction and psychological addiction. Invite volunteers to read their paragraphs to the class.

Assess

Worksheets

A reproducible quiz for Section 3 is provided in the Teacher Classroom Resources.

Close

Recall Before moving on to the next section, check to be sure that students are able to:

1. Describe both physical and psychological addiction.

2. List ways to stimulate endorphin release in their own minds without drug use.

 **SECTION 4** Commonly Abused Drugs

Focus

Vocabulary Activity

Vocabulary worksheets are provided in the Teacher Classroom Resources.

Teach and Apply

Background Information: Drug Education Programs

A quality school health education program should provide factual information about the harmful effects of drugs, support and strengthen students' resistance to using drugs, carry out collaborative drug-abuse prevention efforts with parents and other community members, and be supported by strong school policies, as well as services for confidential identification, assessment, referral to treatment, and support groups (often provided through a student assistance program) for drug users.

Traditionally, alcohol and other drug education programs have focused on junior and senior high school students. However, as indicated by statistics for the average age of first use of the gateway drugs, prevention must also be directed to elementary school students. It is particularly crucial to prevent or at least delay the use of alcohol and other drugs by children and teens because rapid growth can amplify the physiological and psychological effects.

Class Activity

Evaluate Divide the class into two sides. Have the first side argue that the only way to stop drug use and abuse is to arrest all the dealers. (If there are no more drugs to buy, no one else will start.) Have the other group argue that more money should be spent on education about drug abuse. (If no one would buy the drugs, there would be no more dealers.) Give extra credit to the side that presents the best case.

Comprehension Check

Discuss Ask students what the word *empathy* means. What does it mean to be empathetic to someone? (trying to put oneself in someone else's shoes; seeing the world from another's point of view) Then have students tell you what qualities a good listener has (maintains eye contact, blocks out distractions, and so on).

Class Discussion

Discuss Have students discuss the safety and purity of drugs of abuse compared with that of medicines. Ask students why drugs of abuse are unsafe and impure.
(No FDA approval, greed motivates additions of unknown substances, no consumer protection)

Class Activity

Evaluate Ask students to review **Figure 12.6**. This figure will provide students with important supplemental information, such as street names and medical uses of drugs. To familiarize students with the figure, ask the following questions:

1. How many different classes of drugs are included in the table and what are the names of those classes?

   Six: narcotics, depressants, stimulants, hallucinogens (psychedelics), inhalants, cannabis

2. Do all of the drugs have a medical use?

   No, most of the hallucinogens do not

3. Which classes of drugs potentially can cause death?

   All but cannabis

Group Activity

Analyze Divide the class into six groups. Have each group research and create a presentation on one of the following drug classes: narcotics, depressants, stimulants, hallucinogens, inhalants, and cannabis. Encourage students to be creative and use visual aids, create video presentations, podcasts, or public service announcements.

Class Discussion

Evaluate Ask students if any of their thoughts on marijuana and its dangers are different after reading the marijuana section. Did they consider it a harmless drug, used just for recreational use? How will this section help them say "no" to marijuana if they are ever offered it?

Class Activity

Evaluate Have students develop a drug-free plan to follow for life. Students should write a list of goals they want to accomplish and the role drug and alcohol abuse will play in their lives. They should develop a plan with alternative activities to help them stay away from drug and alcohol abuse. Have students include a plan for social interaction, coping with stress, and developing and improving self-esteem without using drugs. Ask volunteers to share their plans.

Assess

Worksheets

A reproducible quiz for Section 4 is provided in the Teacher Classroom Resources.

Close

Synthesize Assign students to choose three types of drugs. Then have them write essays describing how the drugs would adversely affect their lives if they abused them.

Drugs and Driving

Focus

Vocabulary Activity

Vocabulary worksheets are provided in the Teacher Classroom Resources.

Teach and Apply

Group Activity

Evaluate Have students investigate how different drugs affect the nervous system and a person's judgment. Have different groups research marijuana, alcohol, over-the-counter (OTC) medications, and amphetamines.

Class Discussion

Discuss Have students read What Teens Think on page 331. Ask students if they believe drugs have affected their own school or community. Ask them to think about ways they can fight drug abuse and encourage others to do so. Have volunteers share their ideas.

Class Activity

Apply Invite a member of the police department to talk to the class about the dangers of driving under the influence of drugs. Ask students if they feel differently about driving under the influence of drugs.

Class Activity

Evaluate Ask students to conduct research on the number of traffic accidents caused by someone who has abused a substance. Ask students to write a one page report presenting their findings. In the report they should include an evaluation of why abusing drugs is just as likely as alcohol abuse to lead to traffic accidents. Remind students that someone under the influence of drugs is just as likely as someone who abuses alcohol to make poor judgments that could lead to a traffic accident.

Assess

Worksheets

A reproducible quiz is provided in the Teacher Classroom Resources.

Close

Evaluate Have students write a paragraph describing how drugs can affect driving.

Making Behavior Changes

Focus

Vocabulary Activity

Vocabulary worksheets are provided in the Teacher Classroom Resources.

Teach and Apply

Group Activity

Apply Have the students participate in a round-table discussion on drug prevention programs. An excellent premise would be having the students describe an ideal program and what treatment methods they would use. Have them discuss such issues as intervention and peer counseling. Design an informational brochure describing your program to the public.

Class Activity

Apply Have students write an essay about how they would help a friend if he or she admitted a drug problem to them and asked for their help. Encourage students to use their textbook as a reference source to help them develop their essays.

Class Discussion

Discuss Ask students how they might help someone who abuses drugs who does not want to quit or acknowledge that there is a problem. Evaluate and discuss the students' answers. Remind students that a person must first admit to the problem and want help.

Class Discussion

Describe Ask students if they can think of reasons why a person who has a problem with drugs cannot just give up using drugs. Why can't a drug abuser use willpower to stop taking the drug? Have students think of things in their own lives (a favorite video game, friend, dessert, or television program) that would be hard to give up if someone asked them to. Remind students that none of these things has the same type of physical and psychological effect as does drug abuse.

Class Activity

Role Play Divide students into groups of three or four, with two students playing the part of friends and one or two students encouraging them to try a drug. The students who are friends should use refusal skills to say no to drugs using material they have learned in this chapter. Give each student a chance to practice refusal skills in this exercise.

Assess

Worksheets

A reproducible quiz for Section 6 is provided in the Teacher Classroom Resources.

Close

Apply Have students take the Life Choice Inventory, provided in the Teacher Classroom Resources. Even though they might not abuse drugs, these questions might be answered for a family member or friend, or they might have relevance to other compulsive behaviors such as gambling, overeating, or shopping.

SECTION 7
Helping Someone Else Kick the Habit

Focus

Vocabulary Activity

Vocabulary worksheets are provided in the Teacher Classroom Resources.

Teach and Apply

Group Activity

Apply Assign students a role-play. One student's job is to show disapproval of another student's drug abuse problem. Enforce the rules, however, that they cannot blame and they cannot judge the individual. The drug abuser is to try to justify the drug habit. Invite the class to interact and help both.

Class Activity

Evaluate Ask students to write a paragraph explaining how they would help a friend who is abusing drugs. Students should include showing disapproval, making information available, and making sure the drug abuser knows where to seek help. Invite volunteers to share their paragraphs with the class.

Assess

Worksheets

A reproducible quiz is provided in the Teacher Classroom Resources.

A reproducible chapter test is provided in the Teacher Classroom Resources.

Close

Evaluate Have the class list negative consequences of drug abuse. Have several students share their lists. Ask students the following questions: Do you want to prevent these things from happening to you? Why or why not? Do you feel the need to protect your family members and friends from these things? Why or why not? What things might stand in your way as you try to protect family and friends from situations involving drug abuse?

Apply Ask for volunteers to participate in a role-playing scenario in which you ask each of the students to use some illegal drugs. When they refuse, have them give their reasons for refusing. Try to focus on valid arguments to combat peer pressure. Show students how to use refusal skills and still keep their friends by following these steps:

1. Be direct, friendly, and confident in refusing.

2. List the health and legal consequences.

3. Offer a fun alternative that will not get you in trouble.

4. If they refuse your alternative, leave an open invitation and walk away.

Another option is to divide the class into groups to role-play. Give them the following scenario and have the groups develop skits using their refusal skills. "You are walking down the street with a group of your friends. One of them pulls out and lights up a marijuana cigarette and offers it to you."

Go Online

To find supplemental information to suit your individual class, you may want to visit the following Web site, where you can find additional Internet resources to enhance the study of this chapter. As with all Web sites, you should check this out first to be sure the information found there is appropriate for your students.

Web of Addictions

www.well.com/user/woa/

The Web of Addictions is a jam-packed site for information on all types of addictions. There are fact sheets as well as links to other sites.

CHAPTER 13   Alcohol: Use and Abuse

Objectives	Features
• Define moderation in drinking. • Identify health effects of moderate drinking. • Identify long-term effects of excessive drinking. • Identify the role of alcohol in auto accidents and other violent situations. • Identify costs of alcoholism. • Demonstrate refusal skills to refuse alcoholic beverages.	• *Consumer Skills Activity:* How Alcohol is Advertised (page 347) • *Applying Health Skills:* Analyzing Influences (page 348) • *Health Skills:* How Not to Enable (page 361) • *Health Skills:* How to Host a Party Without Alcohol (page 363) • *Q&A:* Alcoholism, the Disease (pages 365–366)

Introduction

Teaching Support

Fast Files

- *Vocabulary:* Learning Vocabulary, Fill in the Missing Term
- *Study Outline*
- *Reading Cloze*
- *Reteaching Activities:* The Facts About Alcohol, Alcohol and the Human Body
- *Enrichment Activities:* Alcohol Awareness Designs, Alcoholism in the Family
- *Cooperative Learning Activity:* You Be the Judge and Jury
- *Career Briefs:* Social Workers
- *Life Choice Inventory:* Does Someone You Know Have A Drinking Problem?
- *Handouts:* Thinking About Drinking, Test Your Knowledge, Classify Your Drinking Behavior, Blood Alcohol Concentration by Number of Drinks and Body Weight, The Disguises of Alcoholism, Characteristics of Alcoholism, Attitudes About Drunk Driving, The Progression of Alcoholism, Myths About Alcoholism, Family Roles in Dysfunctional Families
- *Teacher Information Sheet:* Withdrawal From Alcohol, The Family Dynamics of Alcohol Abuse
- *Quizzes:* Sections 1–5
- *Tests:* Chapter 13 Test A, Chapter 13 Test B

Multimedia Support

- *ExamView® Assessment Suite*
- Online Learning Center

Chapter Preview Activity

The Life Choice Inventory, available in the Teacher Classroom Resources, is an excellent activity to begin this chapter. Students can answer for themselves or for a friend they are concerned about. Another effective activity for beginning the chapter is to discuss the Consumer Skills Activity, "Advertisements for Alcohol," on page 347. Discuss some of the most popular ads, shows, and entertainers that influence our thoughts on alcohol.

Not Enough Time?

Following are some suggestions to help you make sure that you cover the key topics in this chapter if you have limited time.

 DAY 1 Assign students Sections 1 and 2 to read prior to class. At the beginning of class, do the Fact or Fiction? on page 343 to evaluate students' comprehension of the information.

 DAY 2 Discuss Section 3 and use the Writing Critically activity in the Section 3 Review as a role-play activity.

DAY 3 Assign students Sections 4 and 5 to read prior to class. Close the lesson on alcohol by using the activities provided throughout Sections 4 and 5.

Bulletin Board Ideas

On one side of the bulletin board, pin up advertisements for alcoholic beverages—from beer to wine to hard liquor. On the other side of the bulletin board, pin up pictures that reflect the dangerous consequence of alcohol use and abuse—newspaper pictures of car accidents; illustrations of damaged livers from a medical journal; a picture of a man or woman sporting a "beer belly;" a person looking like they are suffering from a hangover. Title the bulletin board something like "The Myth and the Reality."

Fact or Fiction?

Answers:

1. True.

2. False. Alcohol is not digested. It is immediately absorbed into the blood.

3. False. Coffee can wake up, but not sober up, a person who is drunk.

 Writing Paragraphs will vary.

SECTION 1 — Why Do People Drink?

Focus

Vocabulary Activity

Vocabulary worksheets are provided in the Teacher Classroom Resources.

Teach and Apply

Group Activity

Apply Select from the following or devise your own scenarios based on the needs of your students: **(1)** The "Skills for Moderation" list from Section 1, page 349; **(2)** The Writing Critically activity from Section Reviews in Sections 2–5; **(3)** Suggestions for dealing with someone who is intoxicated, from "When a Friend Drinks Too Much," Section 3, page 357; **(4)** Refusal skills in the "Making the Healthy Choice" section, Section 5, page 363; and **(5)** Making Decisions about Health from the Chapter Review.

Divide the class into groups and have them discuss the role-play situation. They can then decide on the best way to handle a certain set of circumstances before presenting the role-play. Ask students to think of situations they have been in and to evaluate whether or not they could have made different choices in how to handle themselves.

Life Choice Inventory

Ask students to complete the Life Choice Inventory found in the Teachers Classroom Resources or the Online Learning Center.

Assess

Worksheets

A reproducible quiz for Section 1 is provided in the Teacher Classroom Resources.

Class Discussion

Discuss Ask students if they have ever been around someone who has had too much to drink and acted in unpredictable, irrational ways. Remind students not to use any names. How did this person's behavior make them feel? Embarrassed? Uncomfortable? Fearful? Remind students that with increasing doses of alcohol, behavior becomes unpredictable and judgment becomes seriously impaired. Not only can a person put themselves in danger, but they can endanger those around them.

Close

Recall Before proceeding to Section 2, the students should be able to answer these questions:

1. What impact can alcohol abuse have on your life?

2. Why is abstinence from alcohol as a teenager and moderate use of alcohol as an adult important?

3. What are some signs that alcohol is becoming a problem for an individual?

SECTION 2 Effects of Alcohol

Focus

Vocabulary Activity

Vocabulary worksheets are provided in the Teacher Classroom Resources.

Teach and Apply

Learning with Visuals

Apply To demonstrate the effects of alcohol in the brain, mix a cup of pure alcohol with a cup of water. Point out to the students that the mixture measures less than two cups because the alcohol absorbs the water. Alcohol has the same effect on the liquid in the brain. After a night of excessive drinking, blood vessels and their associated nerves expand and stretch causing the headache pain associated with a hangover.

Assess

Worksheets

A reproducible quiz for Section 2 is provided in the Teacher Classroom Resources.

Close

Recall Before going to the next section make sure that students can explain the following:

1. Alcohol is toxic to the brain and liver and has immediate effects on all body systems, behaviors, and perceptions.

2. The liver is the organ that processes alcohol at a rate of 1 ounce per hour.

3. Hangovers are the result of dehydration and the formation of formaldehyde in the body.

4. Alcohol has many long-term effects, including fetal alcohol syndrome.

SECTION 3 Accidents and Alcohol

Focus

Vocabulary Activity

Vocabulary worksheets are provided in the Teacher Classroom Resources.

Teach and Apply

Pursuing Wellness

Apply Have students contact or visit offices of organizations in their community that have programs to help alcoholics, such as Alateen and Students Against Destructive Decisions (SADD). Ask students to pick up brochures that provide information about alcoholism or the organization's programs. Display the brochures in the classroom.

Class Activity

Apply Write the following situation on the board:

You are at a party that your parents or guardian told you that you could not attend. Your ride to the party has been drinking and you do not have money to take public transportation.

Ask students what they would do in this situation. Is it better to risk injury or death than to tell your family the truth and ask for help? Discuss each student's response.

Assess

Worksheets

A reproducible quiz for Section 3 is provided in the Teacher Classroom Resources.

Close

Recall Before proceeding to the next section, students should be able to:

1. Write the definitions of DWI and DUI.

2. Connect alcohol use and abuse with accidents and violence.

SECTION 4
The Way Back: Strategies for Recovery

Focus

Vocabulary Activity

Vocabulary worksheets are provided in the Teacher Classroom Resources.

Teach and Apply

Class Discussion

Discuss Distribute the handout entitled "The Progression of Alcoholism". This handout shows the behavior that occurs in five stages of developing alcoholism. Discussing the behaviors listed on the handout will help increase student interest in Section 4.

Comprehension Check

Comprehend Write the word *enabling* on the board. Ask students to give definitions. Then ask the following questions:

1. How do family members enable parents who are alcohol abusers? (They call work and make excuses, clean up after them, accept their apologies, and cover up for their problem.)

2. How do teens enable their friends who are problem drinkers or alcohol abusers? (They let them copy homework, lie for them, and drink with them.)

3. What is the number-one way teens enable their friends? (The "code of silence." They keep their mouths shut even though they know there is a problem. They know facts and conceal them from adults. Teen alcoholics rely heavily on the unspoken "code of silence.") Use this activity to lead in to a discussion of the Health Skills sidebar "How Not to Enable," on page 361.

Assess

Worksheets

A reproducible quiz for Section 4 is provided in the Teacher Classroom Resources.

Close

Recall Before going to the next section, students should be able to explain in their own words that:

1. Many people are victims of alcoholism in some way.

2. Only the alcohol addict can take the first step to recovery, but it is up to others to show compassion without enabling.

3. The goal of a recovering alcohol addict is to enjoy life without alcohol.

SECTION 5

How to Refuse Drinks

Focus

Vocabulary Activity

Vocabulary worksheets are provided in the Teacher Classroom Resources.

Teach and Apply

Class Activity

Apply Divide students into three groups, with equal numbers of males and females in each group. Ask them to draw a line down the middle of a sheet of paper. On one side, they are to list all the things that could be done to have fun at an alcohol-free party. On the other side, they are to list the things nondrinkers need to remember or can do if criticized or pressured by drinkers. Once they have developed a list they can all agree on, give each group two pieces of poster board. Ask the groups to use markers to transfer their lists onto the poster pieces. Display the posters on the wall.

Class Activity

Describe Have students brainstorm positive, drug- and alcohol-free activities that would be fun at a party. Some examples might include karaoke, video game parties, dancing, movies, or game nights. Discuss students' ideas.

Assess

Worksheets

A reproducible quiz for Section 5 is provided in the Teacher Classroom Resources.

Reproducible Chapter Tests A and B are also provided in the Teacher Classroom Resources.

Close

Recall Before going to the next chapter, students should know:

1. No amount of alcohol is legal for people younger than the legal drinking age.

2. For adults, drinking within the acceptable limits of the law or abstinence is a personal choice.

3. They should expect others to respect their choice of abstinence.

Go Online

To find supplemental information to suit your individual class, you may want to visit the following Web site, where you can find additional Internet resources to enhance the study of this chapter. As with all Web sites, you should check these out first to be sure the information found there is appropriate for your students.

Al-Anon and Alateen

www.al-anon.alateen.org/

Al-Anon's purpose is to help families of alcoholics by practicing the Twelve Steps, by welcoming and giving comfort to families of alcoholics, and by giving understanding and encouragement to the alcoholic.

Planning Guide

CHAPTER 14 Tobacco

Objectives

- Identify reasons why some people may use tobacco.
- Understand advertising's role in teen tobacco use.
- Recognize tobacco as a gateway drug.
- Identify health effects of smoking.
- Determine the risks of passive smoke.
- Identify health risks of using smokeless tobacco
- Identify strategies to live a smoke-free life.

Features

- **What Teens Think:** Why Do Some Teens Think Smoking Is Cool? (page 374)
- **Consumer Skills Activity:** Tobacco as a Gateway Drug (page 375)
- **Health Skills:** Giving Up Smoking (page 391)
- **Applying Health Skills:** Refusal Skills (page 392)
- **Q&A:** How Can I Help Someone Quit Smoking? (pages 395–396)

Introduction
Teaching Support
Fast Files

- *Vocabulary:* Learning Vocabulary, Fill in the Missing Term
- *Study Outline*
- *Reading Cloze*
- *Reteaching Activities:* Tobacco and Disease, True or False
- *Enrichment Activities:* Fact and Fantasy, Keep Them Going in Circles, Concerned Students
- *Career Briefs:* Respiratory Therapists
- *Life Choice Inventory:* What Motivates a Smoker?
- *Handouts:* Smokers and Their Smoking Habits, Smoking Facts, Analyzing Advertisements for Tobacco, International Smoking, Public Health Objectives
- *Quizzes:* Sections 1–5
- *Tests:* Chapter 14 Test A, Chapter 14 Test B

Multimedia Support
- *ExamView® Assessment Suite*
- Online Learning Center

Introducing Chapter 14
Chapter Preview Activity

To get students thinking about how their life choices and behaviors affect their lives, ask them to write a paragraph describing how they plan to spend the last 20 years of their lives, or how they would like to live after they retire. When they have completed this part of the assignment, ask them to turn their papers over and write how smoking would affect their retirement plans. Remind students that smoking may cut as many as 18 years from their lives. Smoking or other tobacco use causes lung diseases. It also increases the likelihood of developing heart disease and cancer. They now have two years of retirement to write about. This will help students realize how devastating the smoking habit can be to them and to their plans.

Not Enough Time?

The following are some suggestions to help you make sure that you cover the key topics in this chapter if you have limited time.

 DAY 1 Assign students the chapter to read prior to class. Ask students to answer the Section 2 Review questions on page 385 and the Section 3 Review questions on page 387. Next, assign the Section 4 Review questions on page 389. After students have completed the section review questions, go over their answers aloud. If re-teaching activities are needed, choose some of the activities that are provided.

DAY 2 Assign students Sections 1 and 5 Review questions to answer on pages 376 and 394. The additional activities in the review will provide reinforcement for these sections.

Bulletin Board Ideas

Re-create the table in **Figure 14.7** on page 381. You might also want to show pictures of blackened lungs, people who have to use a personal oxygen device, and other effects of tobacco on the human body. Contrast these with anti-smoking advertisements.

 Fact or Fiction?

Answers:

1. False. The main reason for continuing to smoke is addiction to nicotine.

2. True

3. True

 Writing Paragraphs will vary.

Why People Use Tobacco

Focus

Vocabulary Activity

Vocabulary worksheets are provided in the Teacher Classroom Resources.

Teach and Apply

Group Activity

Synthesize Tell students that most all adult smokers began smoking before the age of 18. What does this say about the effectiveness of the cigarette ad campaigns targeted toward teenagers? Do students think any of the new advertising regulations will make a difference in the number of teens who start smoking?

Class Activity

Analyze To help students understand why smoking is such a controversial issue, what the effects of smoking are on their health, and what the dangers are to themselves and others, you may want to stage a debate. The topic for the debate is: Are the rules imposed by the government effective at stopping young people from smoking?

Divide the class into two teams: one side will defend the "yes" position, the other will defend the "no" position. Allow at least one week for students to research the issue. Each side should have the same amount of time to present its position, then each side should have an equal amount of time for rebuttal.

Possible sources of information may include the school library or media center, the school nurse, teachers in the science department, the public library, public health clinics, the American Cancer Society, the American Lung Association, the Tobacco Institute, and the Internet. Students may also wish to interview people who smoke or who have quit smoking.

Suggested points of argument:

1. Are the current laws tough enough to prevent young people from smoking?

2. Can or should the laws be made tougher or more restricting?

3. Should tobacco products be labeled as controlled substances?

4. Will higher tobacco product prices be a deterrent in preventing young people from starting to smoke?

Assess

Worksheets

A reproducible quiz for Section 1 is provided in the Teacher Classroom Resources.

Close

Apply To show mastery of the information in the first section, students are to develop a plan for the following assignment. "The president just named you as the new surgeon general. Your first assignment is to significantly lower the number of teens starting to smoke in America. Which reasons for smoking do you attack first, and how?" After giving students time to draw up their plans, ask them to present short oral summaries of their plans to the class.

SECTION 2 — Health Effects of Smoking

Focus

Vocabulary Activity

Vocabulary worksheets are provided in the Teacher Classroom Resources.

Teach and Apply

Class Activity

Evaluate Invite a doctor or nurse to speak to the class about the effects of smoking seen daily in the clinic. Ask the speaker to focus the message on the irreversible damage and the end result caused by this bad habit. Also, ask the speaker to talk about how smoking affects a fetus.

Learning with Visuals

Apply Perform an experiment using a collecting device (smoking machine) to show the amount of tar a smoker inhales. You can obtain the needed information and material from the American Cancer Society.

Comprehension Check

Comprehend Using lung cancer as an example, tell students that if they smoke they are at least seven times more likely to develop lung cancer than if they do not smoke. Depending on how much they smoke, they could be as many as 15 times more likely to develop lung cancer.

Class Activity

Apply The American Cancer Society can identify former cancer patients to speak to classes. Some have obvious physical impairments, such as no larynx, as a result of surgery for cancer. Some may be willing to speak to classes about their experiences and their attitude toward smoking.

Assess

Worksheets

A reproducible quiz for Section 2 is provided in the Teacher Classroom Resources.

Close

Apply Have students draw a picture of a smoker. They are to show and label as many affected body parts as they can. This will show comprehension of the material learned in Section 2.

SECTION 3 Passive Smoking

Focus

Vocabulary Activity

Vocabulary worksheets are provided in the Teacher Classroom Resources.

Teach and Apply

Group Activity

Apply Form groups of three or four students to write an article entitled "Survivor's Guide to Living around Smokers." Each group is to come up with ten tips for protecting health in an environment of smokers. Tips might relate to survival in smoke-filled washrooms, homes, workplaces, cars, and so on. Combine all tips and turn in the article to the school newspaper for possible publication.

Class Activity

Apply Ask two volunteers to role play. One student will is a smoker lighting up a cigarette in a car. The other is a passenger, a nonsmoker, who does not want the car to smell like smoke. How does each justify his or her feelings to the other? Ask for volunteers to analyze their arguments.

Assess

Worksheets

A reproducible quiz for Section 3 is provided in the Teacher Classroom Resources.

Close

Apply Ask students to write a letter to a friend that smokes. The letter should explain how smoking causes health risks as well as creates other undesirable effects.

SECTION 4 Smokeless Tobacco

Focus

Vocabulary Activity

Vocabulary worksheets are provided in the Teacher Classroom Resources.

Teach and Apply

Class Activity

Evaluate The use of smokeless tobacco is prevalent in the sport of baseball. It is not uncommon to see professional ball players with a wad of tobacco in their cheek during a game. How is this a mixed message? (Athletes, who are supposed to be in prime physical condition, are using something that can cause great physical harm.)

Class Activity

Evaluate Tell students they have been asked to serve on a panel of experts that will devise a plan to discourage the use of smokeless tobacco in the general public, as well as among teens. What incentives and deterrents can students think of to discourage its use? Encourage students to share their ideas.

Assess

Worksheets

A reproducible quiz for Section 4 is provided in the Teacher Classroom Resources.

Close

Apply Ask students to write essays explaining how they would answer their 10-year-old brother if he asked them to buy him some snuff. What would they tell him about the effects of smokeless tobacco?

SECTION 5 The Decision to Quit

Focus

Vocabulary Activity

Vocabulary worksheets are provided in the Teacher Classroom Resources.

Teach and Apply

Comprehension Check

Comprehend Ask students spend the weekend trying to stop a habit or addiction that they have. Some examples of habits would be biting nails, eating candy, or chewing gum. On Monday, have students give a short oral report explaining how they did. Ask if it was as easy as they had thought it would be. Explain that a chemical addiction would be tougher to give up because it is both physically and psychologically addictive.

Life Choice Inventory

Ask students to complete the Life Choice Inventory found in the Teacher Classroom Resources or the Online Learning Center.

Assess

Worksheet

A reproducible quiz for Section 5 is provided in the Teacher Classroom Resources.

Reproducible Chapter 14 Tests A and B are also provided in the Teacher Classroom Resources.

Close

Apply In order to show that students have mastered the material in Section 5, have each of them write a letter to a friend or relative who smokes. Have them include why the person should stop smoking and what products can help the person stop. Students should explain that they disapprove of the habit, not the person, and that they would support any attempts to quit. This will give students a chance to use all the information learned from this section.

Go Online

To find supplemental information to suit your individual class, you may want to visit the following Web sites, where you can find additional Internet resources to enhance the study of this chapter. As with all Web sites, you should check these out first to be sure the information found there is appropriate for your students.

QuitNet
www.quitnet.org

Quit4Life
www.quit4life.com

Campaign for Tobacco-Free Kids
www.tobaccofreekids.org

QuitNet gives suggestions to personal quit programs. Quit4Life is an interactive site following four teens through their steps from addiction to recovery.

CHAPTER 15   Infectious Diseases

Objectives

- Identify diseases caused by bacteria and viruses.
- Learn about the body's defenses against disease.
- Identify ways people can protect themselves against disease.
- Determine how foodborne illness can be avoided.

Features

- *Applying Health Skills:* Practicing Healthful Behaviors (page 410)
- *Consumer Skills Activity:* Is It a Cold or Is It Flu? (page 412)
- *Health Skills:* How to Avoid Infections (page 413)
- *Q&A:* Mononucleosis—The Kissing Disease (page 415)

Introduction

Teaching Support

Fast Files

- *Vocabulary:* Learning Vocabulary, Infectious Disease Puzzle
- *Study Outline*
- *Reading Cloze*
- *Reteaching Activities:* Word Choice, Understanding Infectious Disease, Bacteria vs. Virus
- *Enrichment Activities:* Food Poisoning, Famous Contributors, The Course of a Disease, Public Service Messages
- *Career Briefs:* Clinical Laboratory Technologists and Technicians
- *Life Choice Inventory:* How Well Do You Protect Yourself Against Infectious Disease?
- *Teacher Information Sheets:* How Fever Works, Disease Information—Symptoms, Transmission, and Control
- *Handouts:* The First Vaccine, Researching Infectious Diseases, Immunization Schedule, U.S. Public Health Service Objectives for the Nation, Microbes at a Picnic, Answers for Teachers for Handout 20: Microbes at a Picnic
- *Quizzes:* Sections 1–4
- *Tests:* Chapter 15 Test A, Chapter 15 Test B

Multimedia Support

- *ExamView® Assessment Suite*
- Online Learning Center

Introducing Chapter 15

Chapter Preview Activity

Ask students how many of them have had chicken pox. Explain that chicken pox is caused by a virus and that most people get this disease only once. Ask the students why someone might never get chicken pox. Then tell students that some people do get this infectious disease twice. Why might this happen? (Shingles can occur later in life.) Ask students at what age they think most people become infected. Why do they suppose people tend to get the disease at that age? Also tell students that a chicken pox vaccination is available now, so chicken pox might just become a disease of the past, like mumps and measles.

Ask students what the term *incubation* means and explain that for chicken pox it lasts 12 to 19 days. Review some symptoms. Explain that treatments might include an anti-itching lotion. Health care providers might also suggest cutting the infected person's fingernails. Discuss why this might be necessary.

 Not Enough Time?

If you have limited time for this chapter, the following are some suggestions to help you make sure you cover the main objectives.

DAY 1 Before class, have students read Sections 1 and 2. Also assign the Life Choice Inventory, "How Well Do You Protect Yourself Against Infectious Diseases?" and the Fact or Fiction? activity. During class have students do activities for Sections 1 and 2.

DAY 2 Before class, have students read Sections 3 and 4; the Consumer Skills Activity, "Is It a Cold or Is It Flu?" on page 412 and the Q&A section, "Mononucleosis—The Kissing Disease" on page 415. During class have students do the activities provided throughout Sections 3 and 4.

Bulletin Board Ideas

Re-create the Health Skills sidebar, "How to Avoid Infections" (page 413) on the bulletin board. If you are artistic, draw a person suited up in a protective suit with a gas mask, or look for an advertisement with something like this. Position the strategies around the figure.

Answers:
1. True.
2. False. Antibiotics are useful against bacteria but useless against viruses.

3. False. Fevers are part of the body's defense against infection, and low fevers are not dangerous.

 Writing Paragraphs will vary.

SECTION 1 — Microbes and Illness

Focus

Vocabulary Activity
Vocabulary worksheets are provided in the Teacher Classroom Resources.

Teach and Apply

Comprehension Check
Comprehend Make sure students know the difference between microbes and pathogens. Do all pathogens cause disease? (Yes) Do all microbes cause disease? (No) Are all microbes pathogens? (No) Are all pathogens microbes? (Yes)

Class Activity
Apply Ask students to tell about the last time they took antibiotics. Did they take the medication for the entire amount of time prescribed by their doctor, or did they stop once they started to feel a little better? Remind them that doing this only causes stronger, more resilient bacteria to grow, and the next bacterial infection may not be so easy to treat.

Assess

Worksheets
A reproducible quiz for Section 1 is provided in the Teacher Classroom Resources.

Close

Ask volunteers to close their books and name the different types of pathogens identified in Section 1 and some common infectious diseases they cause.

 SECTION 2 Defenses Against Infectious Diseases

Focus

Vocabulary Activity

Vocabulary worksheets are provided in the Teacher Classroom Resources.

Teach and Apply

Group Activity

Apply Have students research one infectious disease from the past, with details on how it spread through the world and affected history.

Class Activity

Analyze Ask students to list ways the school district attempts to provide protection against infectious diseases. Encourage students to include help provided by custodial crews, cafeteria staff, bus drivers, teachers, school nurses, and administrators. Discuss the students' lists. Ask students what they can do to protect themselves and others from infectious diseases at school.

Assess

Worksheets

A reproducible quiz for Section 2 is provided in the Teacher Classroom Resources.

Close

Recall Before going on to the next lesson, students should be able to answer the following:

1. How does a good public health system reduce the spread of infectious diseases?

2. Explain the ways diseases are spread.

3. Describe how a vaccine works.

Discuss the answers to these questions in class.

 SECTION 3 The Body's Defenses

Focus

Vocabulary Activity

Vocabulary worksheets are provided in the Teacher Classroom Resources.

Teach and Apply

Group Activity

Synthesize Divide the class into groups of four. Assign each member of each group a letter (A, B, C, or D). After everyone has been assigned a letter, instruct each letter group to meet. Assign the A group to Section 1, the B group to Section 2, the C group to Section 3, and the D group to Section 4. Have the groups read their section together, complete the questions at the end of the section, and come up with a brief plan of how to explain it to their original groups. Have each group come up with a chart or poster that will help them teach their section to their original groups.

After the letter groups have completed their sections, have them return to their original groups and share their ideas and findings with the other members of their group. By doing this, all members of the group will be given information about the chapter in a relatively short period of time.

Worksheets

A reproducible quiz for Section 3 is provided in the Teacher Classroom Resources.

Close

Have students close their books, name the five stages in the course of a disease, and give a brief description of each.

Taking Action

Focus

Vocabulary Activity

Vocabulary worksheets are provided in the Teacher Classroom Resources.

Teach and Apply

Group Activity

Apply Have students create a comic strip style bulletin board or set of posters. They should find a way to visually or graphically represent each of the 11 listed strategies in the Health Skills sidebar on page 413. Remind them that they must find a way to get and keep people's attention if they want to get their message across.

Group Activity

Apply Divide the class into groups of 3–4 students. Have each group write short radio-style public service announcements that can be broadcast over the school's public address system. One or more of the 11 strategies should be included in each announcement. Again, remind students that they must get and keep the attention of their intended audience if they want their message to get through.

Background Information: E. coli and Salmonella

Tell students that up to 20 percent of raw meats sold in U.S. supermarkets may have the *E. coli* bacteria, and that 3 percent may have *Salmonella*. Tell students this is why it is important that all poultry be cooked thoroughly and kept from contact with any other foods.

Pursuing Wellness

Discuss the following with students.

1. How many students get flu shots? Do they seem to help?

2. Do some students seem to catch more colds than others? Why?

3. Here are reasons why some people might catch colds more frequently than others: not wearing warm clothes, not keeping dry, being around people who are infected, not getting enough sleep, being overly stressed, not eating properly, and not washing at appropriate times. Do students think any of these reasons are stronger factors than the others? If so, which ones?

4. How do students treat their cold or flu? Do they go to the doctor, use over-the-counter medicines, use home remedies, or wait it out?

5. What recommendations would students give for avoiding colds or flu?

Assess

Worksheets

A reproducible quiz for Section 4 is provided in the Teacher Classroom Resources.

Reproducible Chapter 15 Tests A and B are also provided in the Teacher Classroom Resources.

CHAPTER 15 Planning Guide

Close

Recall Students should be able to answer the following questions:

1. What are some ways to prevent infections?

2. What are the symptoms of food poisoning?

3. What are some ways to protect yourself from food poisoning?

Go Online

To find supplemental information to suit your individual class, you may want to visit the following Web sites, where you can find additional Internet resources to enhance the study of this chapter. As with all Web sites, you should check these out first to be sure the information found there is appropriate for your students.

National Immunization Program

www.cdc.gov/vaccines/

Infections and Immunizations

www.drreddy.com/shots/

CHAPTER 16 Planning Guide

CHAPTER 16 Sexually Transmitted Diseases

Objectives	Features
<ul><li>Identify symptoms and characteristics of common sexually transmitted diseases.</li><li>Discuss HIV and AIDS</li><li>Identify strategies to prevent sexually transmitted diseases.</li></ul>	<ul><li>**Consumer Skills Activity:** Techniques Used to Sell STD Treatments (page 426)</li><li>**Health Skills:** Avoiding Contracting STDs (page 441)</li><li>**What Teens Think:** Would Your Behavior Toward a Classmate Change if That Person Contracted AIDS? (page 442)</li><li>**Q&A:** Alcohol, Drug Abuse, and STDs (pages 444–445)</li></ul>

Introduction

Teaching Support

Fast Files

- *Vocabulary:* Learning Vocabulary, Avoiding STDs Puzzle
- *Study Outline*
- *Reading Cloze*
- *Reteaching Activities:* Understanding AIDS and Other STDs, Word Choice, Multiple Choice, Common Sexually Transmitted Diseases
- *Enrichment Activities:* Getting the Word Out, Role Play
- *Career Briefs:* Physicians
- *Handouts:* U.S. Public Health Services Objectives for the Nation
- *Quizzes:* Sections 1–3
- *Tests:* Chapter 16 Test A, Chapter 16 Test B

Multimedia Support

- *ExamView® Assessment Suite*
- *Online Learning Center*

Introducing Chapter 16

Chapter Preview Activity

Students may have false beliefs about how STDs are transmitted. To help student learn the truth, use the Fact or Fiction as a pre-test on STDs. This is a safe way for students to uncover their own false beliefs without revealing them to classmates. The Fact or Fiction? feature can also be used by students at the end of this chapter to check their understanding and prepare them for the final test. An extension of this activity might be to have students give the Fact or Fiction? statements to others, such as family members and students in other classes, to determine the most common myths believed by these groups of people.

 Not Enough Time?

The following are some suggestions to help ensure that you cover the key topics in this chapter.

DAY 1 Before class, have students read Section 1. During class, begin the Fact or Fiction? pre-test, then do the activities provided throughout Section 1.

DAY 2 Continue with the activities provided in Section 1. Assign Sections 2 and 3 for homework.

DAY 3 Begin class with a discussion of AIDS and a few student responses to the Preview Activity. After ten minutes of discussion, use the Q&A section to explain how AIDS attacks the body. Allow time for questions and discussion as well as opportunities for reteaching material as needed.

DAY 4 Allow time for further questions and discussion. Have students complete the Chapter Review.

Bulletin Board Ideas

Re-create **Figure 16.2**, found on pages 422–423. Condense the information so that you can make it large enough to read easily.

Fact or Fiction?

Answers:
1. False. Birth control pills do not protect a woman against any form of sexually transmitted disease.
2. False. Asking potential partners about past sexual experiences does not ensure that you will learn the truth about their STD status.
3. False. Condoms may provide an effective barrier to bodily fluids, but they sometimes fail to protect against STDs.

Writing Paragraphs will vary.

Focus

Vocabulary Activity

Vocabulary worksheets are provided in the Teacher Classroom Resources.

Teach and Apply

Group Activity

Evaluate Divide the class into small groups. Ask each group to debate whether tests for STDs should be a standard part of an examination by a physician. Have a spokesperson from each group share the pros and cons with the class. Students should emphasize the point that regular checkups are important because symptoms of an STD are not always visible. The complications caused by these illnesses can only be avoided if health care providers know the person is infected.

Learning with Visuals

Synthesize Refer to **Figure 16.2** on page 422, or the bulletin board chart you recreated from this figure. This chart contains a great deal of information about the most common STDs. Its primary value is as a reference for students as they work through the chapter. Students should be aware that the information has been condensed and that they can learn much more about the individual diseases from the text explanations and descriptions. One of the things you'll want to do with this chart is to focus students' attention on the preventive measures available for the different STDs. While specific measures are given for each disease, abstinence is always mentioned first.

Pursuing Wellness

Apply Ask students to create a list of clinics, hospitals, and public health facilities in the area that provide diagnosis and treatment of STDs. If possible, obtain information concerning the cost of various diagnostic tests and the cost of treatment.

Background Information: Syphilis

Many historians and anthropologists believe that Christopher Columbus and his men introduced syphilis to Europe upon their return from America, where they had been infected. In the year 1500, an epidemic of syphilis erupted in Europe. European physicians said it was a disease that they had never seen before. However, other experts say that syphilis had been in Europe since ancient times but had been confused with leprosy. Researchers have examined skeletons, both in Europe and the Americas, looking for signs of syphilis. While interpretations vary, the consensus seems to be that no definite effects of syphilis can be found among the remains of early Europeans.

Class Activity

Analyze Have students research sexually transmitted viruses linked to cancer. Some STDs to consider researching are: hepatitis, herpes, and HPV. Ask students to also research ways to prevent cancer by preventing these STDs.

Comprehension Check

Discuss Have students review **Figure 16.2**. Then, have students take out a sheet of paper and list the STDs that are curable on one side of the paper and those that are not on the other. Discuss the following questions:

1. What do the curable diseases have in common?

2. What do the incurable diseases have in common?

   The curable diseases are caused by bacteria or parasites and respond to antibiotics, but the incurable ones are caused by viruses—AIDS, herpes, genital warts—for which there are no cures.

Assess

Worksheets

A reproducible quiz for Section 1 is provided in the Teacher Classroom Resources.

Close

Analyze Have students explore why females tend to have fewer symptoms of certain STDs than males. Discuss anatomical differences that make it much easier for a male to see his genitals, as well as any sores or discharge, than it is for a female, whose organs are on the inside of her body. For this reason, what should a male do once he discovers he has an STD? (He should tell his partner to be treated.) What might be the result if he remains silent?

SECTION 2 — HIV/AIDS

Focus

Vocabulary Activity

Vocabulary worksheets are provided in the Teacher Classroom Resources.

Teach and Apply

Class Activity

Recall Ask students what STD they read about earlier in this chapter that resembles AIDS. (Syphilis) How is AIDS similar to syphilis? (People often do not experience symptoms right away or are not aware of the symptoms. People can remain in good health for many years after contracting the disease. Toward the end, serious damage is done to the body, and death occurs.) **What are the differences?** (AIDS is caused by a virus, while syphilis is caused by bacteria. There is a cure for syphilis now; there is no cure for AIDS. While the duration of the disease varies a great deal for both diseases, AIDS does seem to kill more quickly than syphilis.)

Group Activity

Evaluate Have groups of students research different treatments and combination treatments to extend the life and health of people with AIDS. One treatment to consider is protease inhibitors. Protease inhibitors, a group of medicines to treat AIDS symptoms, have proven to be effective at slowing the progression of AIDS. Although AIDS patients remain HIV-positive and suffer symptoms when the medication is stopped, they show remarkable improvement while taking the protease inhibitors.

Class Activity

Apply This activity will help students understand how quickly HIV can spread, and that there is no real way of identifying a person with HIV.

Without any preparation, ask students to stand and face the center of the room. Walk to the center of the class and shake hands with the three students closest to you. Ask those three to shake hands with three more students each, and pass on the instruction to shake hands with still another three. Give the students about one minute, then interrupt the activity and ask all students who did not shake hands with anyone to remain standing, while those who did shake hands should sit down. Point out that the people who are standing are the only ones who did not have contact with your initial handshake. AIDS and other STDs can travel as rapidly as the handshake did. People with STDs often appear healthy, so there is no real way of identifying them in advance.

Class Discussion

Evaluate Write the words *safe sex* on the board and ask students whether they believe there is such a thing as safe sex. Remind students that condoms can fail due to leaks or breaks. Discuss.

Assess

Worksheets

A reproducible quiz for Section 2 is provided in the Teacher Classroom Resources.

Close

Recall Instruct students to write three true statements describing the progress of AIDS in the body and three true statements describing how AIDS is spread. Statements can be written on cards and then exchanged at random. If students receive statements that do not seem correct, they should raise their hands and read them out loud. The class will then decide if the statements are true or false. Collect the cards to evaluate students' understanding at the end of this section.

SECTION 3
Strategies to Prevent Sexually Transmitted Diseases

Focus

Vocabulary Activity

Vocabulary worksheets are provided in the Teacher Classroom Resources.

Teach and Apply

Group Activity

Apply Since refusal skills are a big part of practicing abstinence, have two students role-play a situation in which a teen is pressuring his or her boyfriend or girlfriend to have sex. Abstinence is important to the teen being pressured. What should he or she do in this situation?

Class Activity

Apply Lead a class discussion about a person's responsibility in notifying partners about being infected with an STD. Tell students that according to a University of Southern California study, the more sexual partners an HIV-infected male has had prior to discovering his infection, the less likely he is to try to notify them of the risk.

Class Activity

Apply There is general agreement that the topic of STDs can be embarrassing and is usually avoided in conversation. As a result, too many young people are unaware of the dangers they may be facing. The "What Teens Think" feature on page 442 gives students the opportunity to read other teens' opinions regarding the question, "Would your behavior toward a classmate change if that person contracted AIDS? If so, how would it change?"

Give your students the opportunity to share their opinions on this question. You may divide the class into small groups to give more students the chance to brainstorm. Ask students to share ideas on what they think could or should be done to better inform teens about the risks of STDs and AIDS.

Comprehension Check

Recall *Mutually monogamous* is a term that may sound confusing to students. Monogamous is defined in the Glossary. Ask students to define mutually. (having to do with both parties; same for both people involved) Students should see that it is not enough for one person to be monogamous to avoid contracting an STD; both must be.

Assess

Worksheets

A reproducible quiz for Section 3 is provided in the Teacher Classroom Resources.

Close

Apply Have each student write a paragraph detailing his or her official plan to avoid AIDS and STDs. Tell them that during sexual activity is not the time to come up with a clear plan of action for avoiding STDs.

Go Online

To find supplemental information to suit your individual class, you may want to visit the following Web sites, where you can find additional Internet resources to enhance the study of this chapter. As with all Web sites, you should check these out first to be sure the information found there is appropriate for your students.

An Introduction to STDs

www.cdc.gov/STD/

HIV InSite

www.hivinsite.ucsf.edu/

These sites are well organized and easy to understand. They each offer comprehensive information on key HIV, AIDS, or STD topics.

CHAPTER 17 Planning Guide

CHAPTER 17 Lifestyle Diseases

Objectives

- Identify the difference between infectious disease and lifestyle disease.
- Distinguish between type 1 and type 2 diabetes.
- Identify dangers involved with diabetes.
- Identify three key methods of controlling diabetes.
- Learn the relationship between atherosclerosis and cardiovascular disease.
- Identify causes and symptoms of heart attack and stroke.
- Identify lifestyle factors that can be controlled to reduce the risks of CVD.
- Distinguish between different types of cancers.
- Identify controllable cancer risks.
- Identify strategies for early detection and treatment.

Features

- *Health Skills:* Reducing the Risk of CVD (page 468)
- *Applying Health Skills:* Advocacy (page 471)
- *Health Skills:* Helping a Friend with Cancer (page 483)
- *Consumer Skills Activity:* Being Careful (page 486)
- *Q&A:* Diet for Disease Prevention (pages 488–489)

Introduction

Teaching Support

Fast Files

- *Vocabulary:* Learning Vocabulary, Fill in the Blanks
- *Study Outline*
- *Reading Cloze*
- *Reteaching Activities:* Heart Parts and Blood Flow; What is CVD?; Warning Signs of Diabetes, Heart Attack, Stroke, and Cancer; Reducing Your Risk of Diabetes, Heart Attack, Stroke, and Cancer; Paragraph Completion—Cancer

- *Enrichment Activities:* Taking Control of My Heart Goals, When a Friend Has Cancer, The Average American and Diabetes
- *Career Briefs:* Radiologic Technologists
- *Life Choice Inventory:* How Healthy is Your Heart?
- *Handouts:* Diabetes, Heart Disease, Stroke, Cancer Scenarios; Practical Tips for Teens with Diabetes; U.S. Public Health Service Objectives for the Nation; Factors Beyond People's Control; Medical Tests
- *Quizzes:* Sections 1–8 Quizzes
- *Tests:* Chapter 17 Test A, Chapter 17 Test B

Multimedia Support

- *ExamView® Assessment Suite*
- Online Learning Center

Chapter Preview Activity

Have students review the definition of "lifestyle diseases" in Chapter 1 and list all of their behaviors and those of their parents that they feel might increase the possibility of developing a lifestyle disease. (Answers will vary.) Now have the students imagine giving up these habits or behaviors. How would their lives change physically, financially, and mentally? Discuss their answers.

Bulletin Board Ideas

The American Heart Association (AHA) is a rich resource for posters and other educational information on the heart and heart disease. It can be reached by calling 1-800-AHA-USA1. This will route you to the closest AHA office. Contact the AHA for current posters to use for bulletin board displays for this unit.

 **Not Enough Time?**

The following are some suggestions to help ensure that you cover the key topics in Chapter 17 if your teaching time is limited.

DAY 1 Before class, have students read Sections 1 and 2. During class complete the Chapter Preview Activity. Discuss Sections 1 and 2 with students.

DAY 2 Before class, have students read Sections 3 and 4. Have students complete the activities provided throughout Sections 3 and 4. For both sections, use the Section Reviews to evaluate students' understanding of the material.

DAY 3 Before class, have students read Sections 5 and 6. During class do the activities located throughout Sections 5 and 6.

DAY 4 Before class, have students read Sections 7 and 8. During class do the activities provided for Sections 7 and 8 and the Section Reviews and the Chapter Review.

 Fact **or Fiction?**

Answers:

1. True.
2. False. Of the two types of diabetes, type 2 is largely preventable by controlling body fat.
3. True.

 Writing Paragraphs will vary.

SECTION 1 **First Facts**

Focus

Vocabulary Activity

Vocabulary worksheets are provided in the Teacher Classroom Resources.

Teach and Apply

Group Activity

Synthesize Many lifestyle diseases such as type 2 diabetes, cardiovascular disease, and cancer tend occur more often later in life, and many teens think of them as diseases that only affect old people. Today, diseases such as type 2 diabetes are occurring more frequently in teens and pre-teens. Also, the evidence of the start of heart disease has been detected in those as young as 13 years of age. To emphasize the fact that many young people may have misconceptions about lifestyle diseases and their causes, cures, and effects, you may want to have students conduct a survey of other teens. The goal of the survey is to determine teen's beliefs about who is affected by lifestyle diseases. Students should conduct the surveys and chart the results.

The survey should include information from each section of the chapter and have 10 to 20 questions. (An alternative would be to have students use the Fact or Fiction? questions at the beginning of the chapter as the basis for the survey.) Assign each student a set number of surveys to give. When the surveys have been completed, you may want to divide the class into groups to tabulate the results. Data can then be charted or graphed in several ways: by the total number of correct and incorrect answers for each question; by the total number of correct and incorrect answers by gender; by the total number of correct and incorrect answers by age; and so on. Students can present their findings in a bar graph, a double bar graph, or a line graph. You may decide to use other categories or methods.

Assess

Worksheets

A reproducible quiz for Section 1 is provided in the Teacher Classroom Resources.

Close

Apply Have each student write down two lifestyle changes they could make to improve their long-term health. Emphasize the concept that people who adopt healthy habits when they are young lower their risk of lifestyle diseases when they are older. Then have them write down the single strongest factor that prevents them from making these changes and how they will overcome it.

SECTION
2

Diabetes

Focus

Vocabulary Activity

Vocabulary worksheets are provided in the Teacher Classroom Resources.

Teach and Apply

Group Activity

Apply Have pairs of students write and enact a mock interview about the symptoms, causes, and treatment of type 2 diabetes. One student might pose as a physician while the other poses as the interviewer. The interviewer should ask questions about the common causes of type 2 diabetes, what is the most common age of onset, and how the disease is affecting young people. Ask selected pairs to perform their interview for the class.

Assess

Worksheets

A reproducible quiz for Section 2 is provided in the Teacher Classroom Resources.

Close

Recall Ask students to write a paragraph describing diabetes and its treatment using the following terms: pancreas, insulin, glucose, type 1, type 2, diet, medication, and exercise.

SECTION
3

Cardiovascular Disease (CVD)

Focus

Vocabulary Activity

Vocabulary worksheets are provided in the Teacher Classroom Resources.

Background Information

Explain to students that high blood pressure places additional strain on the heart, causing it to becomes larger and the muscle wall thickens especially in the left ventricle. Research indicates that an enlarged left ventricle reflects advancing heart and artery disease. This heart abnormality can be detected by a test that compares the mass of the left ventricle to the other portions of the heart. This comparison produces a score known as the *left ventricle mass index.*

Learning With Visuals

Apply Ask a student to draw a diagram of the heart on the board. Ask other students, one at a time, to add to, correct, or delete from the picture, and label all of the structures as the diagram progresses. Labeling should include the left atrium, right atrium, left ventricle, right ventricle, aorta, inferior and superior venae cavae, septum, pulmonary artery, pulmonary vein, and valve locations. Use arrows to indicate the flow of blood into, through, and out of the heart, to the lungs, back to the heart, and out to the body. Use two chalk colors for arrows, heart chambers, and blood vessels to differentiate oxygenated and deoxygenated blood flow. Check each correct item as the diagram progresses.

Learning With Visuals

Apply Create a blood vessel out of a loosely rolled piece of poster board. Line the inside with a cloth that has a rough surface. Obtain as many ping-pong balls a possible. Attach a small square of Velcro to each ball. Allow the students to demonstrate blood clots (a thrombus and an embolus) by rolling balls inside the tube. Ask students to identify which configurations of the ping-pong balls represent a thrombus, a thrombosis, an embolus, and an embolism. (Refer students to pages 460–461.)

This may be done in groups of two to four students, one group at a time, or simultaneously if you are able to construct more than one blood vessel model. This activity can also be demonstrated by the teacher or a few students.

Assess

Worksheets

A reproducible quiz for Section 3 is provided in the Teacher Classroom Resources.

Close

Comprehend Select five to ten vocabulary terms from the section and list them on the board. Then ask students to write a paragraph on CVD—what it is and how it can affect a person's life—using the vocabulary words. Read some of the paragraphs to the class when completed and have the class evaluate the accuracy and completeness of the paragraphs.

SECTION 4 Heart Attack and Stroke

Focus

Vocabulary Activity

Vocabulary worksheets are provided in the Teacher Classroom Resources.

Teach and Apply

Class Discussion

Discuss Discuss the warning signs of a stroke or heart attack with students. Ask students if they would know what to do in the event of a stroke or heart attack (see **Figure 17.9** on page 463). Remind students that if they believe someone may be having a heart attack or stroke to call 911 and get help immediately.

Comprehension Check

Recall Stroke was defined earlier in the chapter on page 460. Ask students to define it here.

Learning With Visuals

Apply Have students pick one condition, heart attack or stroke, and create a poster showing some of the warning signs. Each poster should include the instruction to call 911. Hang the posters in the classroom or on a bulletin board.

Assess

Worksheets

A reproducible quiz for Section 4 is provided in the Teacher Classroom Resources.

 SECTION 5 Reducing the Risks of CVD

Focus

Vocabulary Activity

Vocabulary worksheets are provided in the Teacher Classroom Resources.

Teach and Apply

Pursuing Wellness

Apply Have students write a letter to the editor of their school or local newspaper in which they advocate the importance of making healthful lifestyle choices to reduce the risk of cardiovascular disease. Suggest that students focus their letters on one lifestyle choice and describe how this behavior reduces the risk of CVD. Review letters and encourage students to submit them for publication.

Assess

Worksheets

A reproducible quiz for Section 5 is provided in the Teacher Classroom Resources.

Close

Recall Before going on to the next section, students should be able to:

1. List six risk factors of CVD.

2. Mark each of the risk factors as controllable or uncontrollable.

3. List five ways to reduce the risk of CVD and give an example of how to accomplish each of these.

4. List ten healthy food choices they can make to reduce the risk of CVD.

 SECTION 6 Cancer

Vocabulary Activity

Vocabulary worksheets are provided in the Teacher Classroom Resources.

Teach and Apply

Comprehension Check

Describe Ask students to describe what happens inside the body when cancer grows. Students should respond that cancer develops when cells begin to reproduce in an out of control fashion, and begin killing off healthy cells. Write *benign* and *malignant* on the board and point out to the students that they are opposite in meaning. Tumors can be either malignant or benign. Benign tumors are not cancerous, while malignant tumors show that cancer is spreading.

Pursuing Wellness

Apply Have students pick a type of cancer and write a public service announcement informing listeners about the number of people affected each year, risk factors, symptoms, and screening methods for early detection. Students should present their public service announcement to the class.

Assess

Worksheets

A reproducible quiz for section 6 is provided in the Teacher Classroom Resources.

Close

Recall Students should be able to answer these questions:

1. What is the difference between a cancerous tumor and a benign tumor?

2. What are some common carcinogens?

3. What is the difference between a promoter and an initiator?

4. What are the different types of cancer?

5. What are the steps in the development of cancer?

SECTION 7 Controllable Cancer Risks

Focus

Vocabulary Activity

Vocabulary worksheets are provided in the Teacher Classroom Resources.

Teach and Apply

Class Discussion

Dicuss Remind students that people who use smokeless tobacco are still at risk for cancer. Have students describe the health risks involved with using smokeless tobacco or cigarettes.

Background Information: Vitamins

As enrichment, you may want to tell students that the mixture of vitamins in fruits and vegetables may also block the progress of certain cancers. For example, the vitamin C in oranges may stop the formation of certain carcinogens and the vitamin A in vegetables and fruits such as sweet potatoes and peaches is important in preventing cancer in the body's external and internal linings. The fibers of plant foods, such as whole grains, fruits, and vegetables, may play roles as well.

Assess

Worksheets

A reproducible quiz for Section 7 is provided in the Teacher Classroom Resources.

Close

Recall Before going on to the next section, students should be able to answer these questions:

1. How can you cut down on the amount of exposure to radiation (UV rays) from the sun?

2. What are some risk factors for melanoma?

3. How do diet and exercise play a role in cancer prevention?

Discuss the answers to these questions in class.

SECTION
8

Early Detection and Treatment

Focus

Vocabulary Activity

Vocabulary worksheets are provided in the Teacher Classroom Resources.

Teach and Apply

Comprehension Check

Comprehend After students have looked at **Figure 17.20** on page 482, have them close their books and see how much of the information from the figure they can generate. Begin by having them list the six types of cancers that most often cause death in people aged 15 to 34. Then see how many symptoms they can remember for each disease. Finally, write the text statistics for survival on the board and see if they can match those to the proper types of cancer.

Class Activity

Recall Have students create a game show type of activity. Students earn points by answering questions correctly that are related to lifestyle diseases. The categories of questions should be Stroke, Reducing the Risk of CVD, Cancer, Cancer Risks that People Can Control, and Early Detection and Treatment. Each student should write one question. Have each student write his or her name on the slip of paper with the question. Students are not allowed to answer their own question.

To play the game, divide your class into three or four equal teams. One team picks a category and point value and that team has one minute to answer the question. If they answer correctly, they will receive the points from that category. If they do not answer cor-

rectly, any of the other teams may answer. The person who raises their hand first gets the first chance to answer.

Assess

Worksheets

A reproducible quiz for Section 8 is provided in the Teacher Classroom Resources.

Close

Students should be able to answer these questions:

1. What are the eight warning signs of cancer?

2. What are some protective factors and preventable risk factors for cancer?

3. What body organs can be self-examined for early cancer detection?

4. Name the basic types of cancer treatments.

5. List some of the major side effects of chemotherapy or radiation.

6. List the two ways cancer treatments destroy cancer cells.

Discuss the answers to these questions in class.

Go Online

To find supplemental information to suit your individual class, you may want to visit the following Web sites where you can find additional Internet resources to enhance the study of this chapter. As with all Web sites, you should check these out first to be sure the information found there is appropriate for your students.

The National Heart, Lung, and Blood Institute

www.nhlbi.nih.gov

Wellness, Inc.

www.wellness-inc.com/

Information, including research and educational activities as well as links to other sites, is fairly extensive.

CHAPTER 18 Dating, Commitment, and Marriage

Objectives	Features
• Distinguish between mature love and infatuation. • Identify the stages of a healthy relationship. • Identify steps to develop a healthy intimate relationship. • Learn to work through conflict or break-ups.	• *Health Skills:* Meeting New People (page 499) • *Consumer Skills Activity:* Love and Sex in Advertisements (page 503) • *Health Skills:* Developing a Healthy Intimate Relationship (page 505) • *Applying Health Skills:* Stress Management (page 507) • *Q&A:* Sexual Violence Prevention (pages 510–511)

Introduction
Teaching Support
Fast Files
- *Vocabulary*: Learning Vocabulary
- *Study Outline*
- *Reading Cloze*
- *Reteaching Activities*: Conflict Resolution
- *Enrichment Activities*: "Stop," The Advice Column, Choices in Marriage, Controversial/Difficult Relationships
- *Career Briefs*: Physician Assistants
- *Life Choice Inventory*: Will the Marriage Work?
- *Handouts*: What Is Your Capacity for Intimacy?, Myths and Truths about Healthy Relationships, Attributes I Consider Important in a Prospective Partner, Writing a Marriage Contract
- *Teacher Information Sheets:* Relationship Compatibility: The Myers-Briggs Type Indicator
- *Quizzes*: Sections 1–2

- *Tests*: Chapter 24 Test A, Chapter 24 Test B

Multimedia Support
- *ExamView® Assessment Suite*
- Online Learning Center

Introducing Chapter 18
Chapter Preview Activity

Students may have difficult questions about the material in this chapter. Establish an environment that allows students to ask questions and state their opinions freely, and remind students that if they have questions they do not want to ask in class, to talk to you or another adult after the class. Use the Fact or Fiction? questions to open the discussion. You may want to add the following:

1. Distrust is never a part of mature, loving relationships.

2. Beginning a relationship with someone who is on the rebound is asking for trouble.

3. If a couple has been in a close relationship for a year, continuing abstinence will ruin the relationship.

4. If a girl is dressed seductively, she's just "asking" for sexual attention.

Ask students to answer the questions honestly, then discuss in class. As you discuss each question, ask how many said *true* and how many said *false*. Then ask students to volunteer the reasons for their answers. When you are finished, tell the students that these topics will be covered in this chapter and that they should check their answers again at the end of the chapter to see if their opinions have changed.

 Not Enough Time?

The following are some suggestions to help ensure that you cover the key topics in this chapter.

 DAY 1 Before class, have students read Sections 1 and 2. During class do the activities located throughout Sections 1 and 2 to initiate a discussion on relationships.

 DAY 2 Begin a discussion on the major points of Section 2. The discussion should cover the important factors necessary for a successful relationship. Assign the Q&A section to be read for the following day.

 DAY 3 Invite a guest speaker to talk to the class. Be sure the person is prepared to give facts and guidelines for rape prevention. Alternatively, have a marriage counselor come in to discuss major divorce-causing issues and how to increase the chance of having a successful marriage.

 Fact or Fiction?

Answers:

1. False. You can tell when love is real because it develops slowly through the conscious choices of both partners.
2. True.
3. False. Couples in a healthy, intimate relationship maintain separate interests as well as shared ones.

 **Writing** Paragraphs will vary.

SECTION 1 Infatuation or Mature Love?

Focus

Vocabulary Activity

Vocabulary worksheets are provided in the Teacher Classroom Resources.

Teach and Apply

Class Activity

Evaluate This activity promotes listening skills and encourages students to voice their opinions. Before class list five to seven statements on the board:

1. "Love at first sight" can really happen.

2. Physical intimacy makes a relationship last.

3. Teens don't really know how to be in a mature, loving relationship.

4. The most important qualities necessary in a healthy relationship are _____.

5. Someone in a relationship with a chemically-dependent person should _____.

6. In order to love someone else, you must first love yourself.

7. There are more advantages than disadvantages to sexual abstinence in a relationship.

8. There is no such thing as healthy conflict in a relationship.

9. Marriage means _____.

Show students a small sponge ball; then tell them this activity is based on listening to each other's opinions. Explain that only the person holding the ball can speak. When that person is done, the ball will be passed to someone whose hand is raised. The first student will choose a topic and agree or disagree with it. The class will stay on that topic until all who want to speak about it have had the chance. The topic may then be changed. Remind students to use "I" messages when providing their point of view, and that anyone who attacks the viewpoint of another student will lose their turn to speak.

Assess

Worksheets

A reproducible quiz for Section 1 is provided in the Teacher Classroom Resources.

Close

Evaluate Ask the students to write an essay describing a perfect relationship. They must include the qualities *they* deem to be of a high priority and also what they expect each person to bring into this ideal relationship.

SECTION 2
How to Develop a Healthy Relationship

Focus

Vocabulary Activity

Vocabulary worksheets are provided in the Teacher Classroom Resources.

Teach and Apply

Class Activity

Analyze In your supplementary material, you will find a detailed explanation of the Meyers-Briggs Type Indicator and how the four basic temperaments used in this assessment relate to compatibility and relationships. You may find this information useful to present prior to discussing compatibility with the students.

Group Activity

Evaluate Write these four categories across the top of the board: *Infatuation, In Like, Dependency, In Love*. Divide the class into four groups, each with an equal number of boys and girls. Ask the groups to brainstorm the qualities that describe each category of relationship. Once the groups are finished, go over the categories by asking a spokesperson from each group to take turns giving *one* quality. As one group speaks, check the other three groups to see if they agree. Be sure you have your own prepared list of qualities of which you want the students to be aware. Derive your *Infatuation* and *In Love* lists from **Figures 18.2.**

Group Activity

Analyze Ask students to apply what they have learned by analyzing some of their own feelings about dating, commitment, and marriage. Bring in several copies of the fairy tale Cinderella. Discuss the way the relationship between Cinderella and the Prince develops. Ask students to imagine themselves as the main characters: boys become the Prince, girls become Cinderella. How would they feel if they met someone in such a way? Can they imagine what life might be like after the carriage carries off the happy couple? Ask your students to write the sequel by putting themselves into the story. After five, ten, or twenty years, how are Cinderella and the Prince doing?

Class Activity

Describe An alternative assignment could include asking students to rewrite or update fairy tales, possibly by writing new endings. They might also be required to use the vocabulary words and terms for this chapter: love, infatuation, mature love, intimacy, date, sexual intercourse, external pressures, internal pressures, thrill-seekers, marriage.

Assess

Worksheets

A reproducible quiz for Section 2 is provided in the Teacher Classroom Resources.

Reproducible Chapter Tests A and B are also provided in the Teacher Classroom Resources.

Close

Make sure that students understand the difference between serious dating and marriage. Ask students whether they think a serious dating relationship is the same thing as being married? What are some of the similarities? What are the differences? You may want to prompt students by asking: What financial considerations are associated with dating? How does that change when a couple marries? What other differences exist?

Go Online

To find supplemental information to suit your class, you may want to visit the following Web site, where you can find additional Internet resources to enhance the study of this chapter. As with all Web sites, you should check these out first to be sure the information found there is appropriate for your students.

Safe Surf

www.safeflorida.net/safesurf

This Web site is sponsored by the Florida Attorney General Office to emphasize the need for cyber safety. Many teens are turning to the Internet for social networking, this site gives valuable information about staying safe on the Internet.

CHAPTER 19 · Planning Guide

CHAPTER 19 Family Life

Objectives

- Recognize the nature of the family.
- Understand the life stages of a family.
- Identify the importance of effective communication and getting along with others.
- Identify changes that come with family problems.
- Identify the change in the family's role in society.

Features

- *Health Skills:* Meeting New People (page 499)
- *Consumer Skills Activity:* The Marketing of the Family (page 522)
- *Health Skills:* The Essence of Conflict Resolution (page 526)
- *Q&A:* Parents as People (pages 538–539)

Introduction

Teaching Support

Fast Files

- *Vocabulary:* Learning Key Terms, Break the Code
- *Study Outline*
- *Reading Cloze*
- *Reteaching Activities:* Family Matching, Reviewing the Chapter
- *Enrichment Activities:* Family Scenes, Emotional Family Health, Assertive Communication
- *Career Briefs:* Preschool Teachers and Child-Care Workers
- *Handouts:* Emotional Upset Following Separation and Divorce, Negative Rules and Negative Messages Commonly Heard in Alcoholic and Other Troubled Families, Family Roles in Dysfunctional Families
- *Quizzes:* Sections 1–4
- *Tests:* Chapter 19 Test A, Chapter 19 Test B

Multimedia Support

- *ExamView® Assessment Suite*
- Online Learning Center

Introducing Chapter 19

Chapter Preview Activity

Ask each student to answer the following on a sheet of paper:

1. What is the definition of family?

2. What is an ideal family?—either a description or perhaps the name of a fictional family.

3. Have students share their definitions of family. How close are their definitions to one another's? What crucial information do most definitions share? Discuss the students' responses to the other questions.

CHAPTER 19 Planning Guide

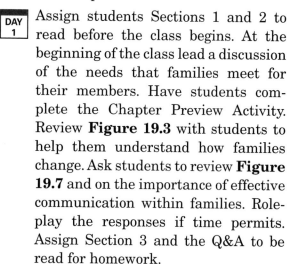

Not Enough Time?

The following are some suggestions to help you ensure that you cover the key topics in this chapter.

DAY 1 Assign students Sections 1 and 2 to read before the class begins. At the beginning of the class lead a discussion of the needs that families meet for their members. Have students complete the Chapter Preview Activity. Review **Figure 19.3** with students to help them understand how families change. Ask students to review **Figure 19.7** and on the importance of effective communication within families. Role-play the responses if time permits. Assign Section 3 and the Q&A to be read for homework.

DAY 2 Define *dysfunctional family* and discuss **Figure 19.9**. Go over **Figure 19.11** to help students compare the characteristics of functional and dysfunctional families. Finish up with a brief discussion of how modern families are changing.

Bulletin Board Ideas

Prepare a family collage for the bulletin board using one of the following themes:

1. Your students' families. Have your students bring in pictures of families from magazines and other media to post on the board as a collage. Remind students that some families may include grandparents or other family members, or some families may be made up of one parent or two parents who are not living together. Some families with children who are adopted may represent several cultures and races.

2. Families in other cultures. Create a collage of pictures showing families in many different cultures around the world.

Fact or Fiction?

Answers:

1. True.

2. False. Parents want to think of their children as honest and trustworthy but may learn to distrust them in response to dishonesty.

3. True.

Writing Paragraphs will vary.

SECTION 1 The Nature of the Family

Focus

Vocabulary Activity

Vocabulary worksheets are provided in the Teacher Classroom Resources.

Teach and Apply

Class Activity

Apply Ask students to think of three ways in which a family can shape a child. Student responses can be positive or negative. If students provide negative ways that a family can shape a child, remind students that each one of us has the ability to shape our own lives as we grow into adulthood.

Comprehension Check

Comprehend Review "A Glossary of Types of Families" (**Figure 19.2**) with students. Ask students to write their own definitions for each of the terms, and then compare their definitions with those in the glossary.

Class Activity

Analyze Have students research the origins of their surname. Learning about the origins of their surname may teach them a little about their genealogy, or their family's culture. They may be able to find information from an Internet search, or students might interview an older family member.

Students may be interested in family names when they discover the meanings that lie behind them. They can easily see that names with *son* or *sen* at the end carry the meaning "son of" (e.g., Anderson, Petersen). Endings that mean "son of" in other languages include *ez* (Spanish), *tse* (Chinese), *wicz* (Polish), and *ov* (Russian and other Slavic languages). Some examples would be Rodriguez (son of Rodrigo) and Ivanov (son of Ivan).

Many last names are associated with a person's line of work, such as Carpenter, Farmer, Baker, Miller, and Smith (blacksmith). Characteristics of a person often lead to the use of other names, such as Young, Black, Long, White, and Little.

Tell students that different cultures have different rules for family names. In English-speaking countries, most children take the last name of their father. Some countries use both the mother's and father's name (this custom is growing in the U.S.). A Spanish surname, for example, would consist of the father's family name followed by the mother's family name (e.g., Teresa Perez Gutierrez).

Assess

Worksheets

A reproducible quiz for Section 1 is provided in the Teacher Classroom Resources.

Close

Recall With their books closed, ask students to write out as many ways as they can remember in which families mold members and meet their needs. Have them number these ways in order of importance. Have students compare their lists.

SECTION 2 — Getting Along with Others

Focus

Vocabulary Activity

Vocabulary worksheets are provided in the Teacher Classroom Resources.

Teach and Apply

Pursuing Wellness

Evaluate Remind students that the following traits are shared by physically and mentally healthy people: expressing emotions appropriately; feeling that life is meaningful; living according to values; managing stress; maintaining personal health; having satisfying relationships with family and friends; avoiding risky behaviors; practicing safety; and having fun. Ask what influence *family* can have on wellness. Lead a class discussion, asking students to respond to the following:

1. Methods family members use to deal with stress

2. Use of tobacco, alcohol, and drugs in their families

3. Ways their families have fun

4. Use of devices like seat belts as an indication of practicing safe living

Then, ask students to provide examples of how the *community* influences personal wellness. Some prompts may include:

1. Hotline availability for drugs or teen pregnancy

2. Community commitment to chemical-free teen activities

3. Strong codes of conduct for athletes

4. Recreation programs for teens

5. Active community involvement in DARE or similar programs

SECTION 3 — Families with Problems

Class Activity

Evaluate Ask students to describe how the traditional family is similar or different from a blended family, a family with adopted children, or a single parent family.

Group Activity

Evaluate Select two typical television families: one from the 1950s or 60s, one current. You can use comedies or dramas. If possible, show one or two episodes in class. Ask students to list the types of problems faced by each of the two families. What constituted a family crisis in the ideal TV family of the 50s and 60s? How about in today's TV families? What sorts of problems confronted the TV children of 50 years ago? What about today's TV children? How do siblings relate to one another in the two time periods? How do parents relate to one another and to their children? What conclusions can students draw about the changes taking place in families over the past 50 years? Remember that while the TV families do not necessarily present an accurate picture of family life in either time period, they do give insight into changes in what is considered a healthy, functioning family.

Assess

Worksheets

A reproducible quiz for Section 2 is provided in the Teacher Classroom Resources.

Close

Recall Refer to the list of qualities of a strong family that was developed by the class early in the section. Have the class review the list. What changes would they make to the list now, in terms of qualities listed and order of importance?

Focus

Vocabulary Activity

Vocabulary worksheets are provided in the Teacher Classroom Resources.

Teach and Apply

Class Activity

Evaluate Lead a class discussion that focuses on qualities of strong families. Tell students that the qualities listed below are often observed in healthy families and can serve as goals for their own families.

1. *Commitment*—Family members demonstrate commitment to promoting each other's happiness and welfare.

2. *Appreciation*—Family members appreciate one another and contribute to each other's self-esteem.

3. *Good communication patterns*—Strong families talk to each other, and their members are good listeners.

4. *Desire to spend time together*—Even with individual time commitments, members desire each other's company.

5. *A strong value system*—Family members generally agree on basic issues.

6. *Ability to deal with crises and stress in a positive manner*—Strong families are resilient and capable of bouncing back from adversity.

Have students relate this list to what they have learned in the previous two sections.

Class Discussion

Discuss Divorce affects all of the children in a family. These effects may last into adulthood and can reduce self-esteem.

Remind students that the children are not to blame for a divorce. Divorce occurs because the relationship between the two adults has ended. Children cannot prevent a divorce. Even though children are not responsible for divorce, they do have rights regarding the divorce.

Ask your students to consider what rights children may have before, during, and after a divorce. The following list will get them started:

1. Children should have the right to have their questions answered about the divorce.

2. Children should be spared from hearing negative comments from one parent about the other.

3. Children should have the right to see their noncustodial parent and grandparents.

4. Children should have the right to be children and not be expected to take on adult roles following a divorce.

Class Activity

Analyze Lead a class discussion about the number of families in the U.S. that include a stepparent. Today, at least one-third of all children in the U.S. are expected to live in a stepfamily before they reach age 18. Ask students to write an essay describing how the media may have created an image of stepparents as being wicked or mean.

Comprehension Check

Comprehend You may want to break up the term *dysfunctional*. Tell students that *dys-* means *bad* and *function* means *to perform*. *Dysfunctional*, then, means "performing badly;" thus, a dysfunctional family is one that is not performing right, or isn't working correctly.

Comprehension Check

Comprehend You may want to discuss the term *passive abuse* with students, since the word *abuse* is so much more commonly associated with physical abuse. The idea that *not doing* something or withholding something is abuse may be difficult for some students to comprehend. Have students make a list of both physical and psychological things that are so essential that withholding them could be considered abuse. Discuss these in class.

Assess

Worksheets

A reproducible quiz for Section 3 is provided in the Teacher Classroom Resources.

Close

Evaluate Have students list the characteristics of a dysfunctional family. They should put a star next to the characteristics they personally feel would be the most difficult to cope with and explain why.

SECTION 4 · Society's Support of Families

Focus

Vocabulary Activity

Vocabulary worksheets are provided in the Teacher Classroom Resources.

Teach and Apply

Group Activity

Analyze A significant portion of the public policy debate surrounding the abuse of children is the question of the "place of family." Is the family a private or a public institution? Are families able to live private lives, unaffected by public opinion, or does the public sector have the right to impose certain standards on family life?

Ask your students to debate the issue of community responsibility for child abuse and neglect. Remind students to avoid providing personal details if they are uncomfortable talking about their families. If your school has a debate team, you may wish to invite it to participate in the discussion of this issue.

Here are two possible topics for students to debate:

1. *Family as a public institution*: The community has the responsibility and right to step inside the family to insure the safety and well-being of children.

2. *Family as a private institution*: The family has the right to treat children as they see fit.

As a conclusion to the debate, you may invite a representative of the local Child Protective Services to discuss government procedures for identifying and reporting child abuse in your community. If it is possible to identify someone from a community organization that advocates family sovereignty and limited government intervention, invite that person to offer the opposing viewpoint.

Group Activity

Evaluate Divide the class into small groups. Have each group write out as many of the issues facing families today as they can remember. Students should determine reasons why these issues develop and possible solutions. Evaluate and discuss the solutions as a class.

Assess

Worksheets

A reproducible quiz for Section 4 is provided in the Teacher Classroom Resources.

Assess

Evaluate Refer the class to the section titled "Today's Problems" on page 536. Have students decide which problems are most prevalent. Divide the class into groups, one group for each problem the class cited as most immediate. Have each group determine reasons why this is a problem and develop possible solutions. Evaluate the solutions as a class.

Go Online

To find supplemental information to suit your class, visit the following Web sites, where you can find additional Internet resources to enhance the study of this chapter. Check all Internet sites to make sure the content is appropriate for students.

Family Resource Online
www.familyresource.com/

family.com
family.go.com/

Family Resource Online is a nonprofit organization. The site provides families with current information, online resources, and provides a forum for raising concerns about the family.

CHAPTER 20 From Conception through Parenting

Objectives

- Identify teen parenting risks.
- Determine factors to consider when making a responsible decision about having children.
- Understand the menstrual cycle.
- Understand that the health habits of both parents prior to pregnancy can affect the health of the baby.
- Identify the three stages of gestation and the fetal development that occurs during each.
- Identify health issues that can be caused by congenital abnormalities.
- Learn the stages of childbirth.
- Identify elements of parenting.

Features

- **Applying Health Skills:** Decision Making (page 547)
- **Health Skills:** How to Keep a Pregnancy Safe (page 562)
- **Q&A:** Drinking Alcohol During Pregnancy (pages 570–571)

Introduction

Teaching Support

Fast Files

- *Vocabulary*: Learning Vocabulary, Fill in the Blanks
- *Study Outline*
- *Reading Cloze*
- *Reteaching Activities*: Conception and Pregnancy, Reproduction and Conception, Risk Factor Match
- *Enrichment Activities*: Teenage Pregnancy, Lourde's Pregnancy
- *Career Briefs*: Registered Nurses
- *Life Choice Inventory*: Are You Ready to Have a Child?
- *Handouts:* Reproductive System Labeling, Tests During Pregnancy, Effects of Potentially Harmful

Substances on the Fetus, The Parenting Process, Breast Milk versus Formula, General Guidelines for Parenting, U.S. Public Health Service Objectives for the Nation, Effects of Malnutrition During Critical Periods of Development

- *Teacher Information Sheets:* Body Changes Associated with Pregnancy, The Importance of Four Nutrients During Pregnancy, Phenylketonuria, How Bonding Takes Place
- *Quizzes*: Sections 1–8
- *Tests*: Chapter 20 Test A, Chapter 20 Test B

Multimedia Support

- *ExamView® Assessment Suite*
- Online Learning Center

DAY 3
On Day 3 discuss Sections 7 and 8. Finish Section and Chapter Assessments.

Introducing Chapter 20

Chapter Preview Activity

These activities will give the students an idea of how much is involved in being a parent.

1. Have each student write an anonymous short essay entitled, "As a parent I will. . ."

2. Shuffle, redistribute the papers, and have them read aloud.

3. At the end of the chapter, have the students write the same essay again. As these essays are read to the class, ask the students to note the differences between the first set and the second set.

Bulletin Board Ideas

1. Have students bring in pictures showing the progression from a couple dating to getting married and becoming parents. Add new pictures as each section of the chapter is completed to show the growth and development of the child and of the family.

 Not Enough Time?

The following are some suggestions to help ensure that you cover the key topics in this chapter.

DAY 1
Assign students Sections 1, 2, and 3, the Fact or Fiction?, and the Life Choice Inventory to read and complete prior to class. During class have students do the Chapter Preview Activity to introduce the chapter. Assign Sections 4, 5, and 6 to be read prior to Day 2.

DAY 2
On Day 2 have the students brainstorm ideas of dos and don'ts for males and females prior to childbearing. The lists should include any lifestyle behaviors that could possibly benefit or harm their future children. Complete the Preview Activity. Assign Sections 7 and 8 to be read prior to Day 3.

 **Fact** **or Fiction?**

Answers:

1. True.

2. False. Women who are not pregnant may miss periods due to other factors, and a pregnant woman may have vaginal bleeding.

3. True.

Writing Paragraphs will vary.

SECTION

1

The Responsibilities of Pregnancy

Focus

Vocabulary Activity

Vocabulary worksheets are provided in the Teacher Classroom Resources.

Teach and Apply

Comprehension Check

Comprehend Read this statement: The younger people are when they have children, the more having children will change their lives. Can students think of any reasons why this would be so? Ask them to express the meaning of the sentence in their own words to make sure they understand.

Ask students if they have younger siblings. What changes occurred in their lives as a result of having a younger sister or brother?

Class Discussion

Discuss Ask students if they have younger siblings, or other younger family members. What changes occurred in their lives and in the lives of their families after the birth of their younger family members? Were some of the changes difficult to manage? Encourage volunteers to share their ideas and opinions. Explain to students that the birth of a new baby causes many changes to take place within families. Many times these changes can be challenging.

Assess

Worksheets

A reproducible quiz for Section 1 is provided in the Teacher Classroom Resources.

Close

Apply Assign students the task of writing an editorial listing some of the reasons why teens should not become parents. Students should include some of the factors listed in the section.

SECTION 2 Deciding to Bear or Adopt Children

Vocabulary Activity

Vocabulary worksheets are provided in the Teacher Classroom Resources.

Teach and Apply

Class Activity

Apply Divide the class into small groups. Ask the groups to analyze the reasons why some families choose to adopt children while other parents may bear children. Have students select a recorder and a spokesperson for each group. The recorder is responsible for the group's written work. The spokesperson will share the group's responses with the entire class.

Have students discuss the reasons why parents may choose to adopt. What are some ways that having children, either through natural methods or adoption, can positively impact the family?

Class Activity

Evaluate Distribute the Life Choice Inventory entitled Are You Ready to Have a Child?, located in the Teacher Classroom Resources or the Online Learning Center. Ask students to think about each question before writing a response. Student responses are personal; however, you may want to ask the class if the Life Choice Inventory changed their perceptions of bearing children.

Assess

Worksheets

A reproducible quiz for Section 2 is provided in the Teacher Classroom Resources.

Close

Evaluate Instruct the students to list the problems associated with becoming a teen parent. Have them compare their lists and discuss any differences.

SECTION 3 Reproduction

Focus

Vocabulary Activity

Vocabulary worksheets are provided in the Teacher Classroom Resources.

Teach and Apply

Pursuing Wellness

Evaluate Have students research in vitro fertilization, as they may have questions about it while studying the process of fertilization.

In vitro fertilization is a technique in which eggs and sperm are collected and then combined in a medical laboratory. Eggs that are successfully fertilized are then placed into a mother's fallopian tubes or uterus. The term *in vitro* literally means "in glass," and refers to the fact that the eggs and sperm are combined outside the mother's body. The first in vitro fertilization that resulted in a live birth was performed in 1978.

Comprehension Check

Discuss To monitor comprehension, ask students how long the egg can live (12–24 hours). How long can sperm live? (up to three days) Can intercourse a few days before ovulation produce pregnancy? (Yes) Can intercourse two days after ovulation produce pregnancy? (No, the egg would no longer be alive) Remind students that for many females, it can be difficult to determine the exact time of ovulation. Therefore, it is important to practice abstinence, or use contraceptive methods that protect against pregnancy as well as STDs.

Assess

Worksheets

A reproducible quiz for Section 3 is provided in the Teacher Classroom Resources.

Close

Discuss Ask students to write any questions they have about childbirth, reproduction, or heredity on index cards. Ask students to read their questions aloud, and ask other students to provide answers. Correct any information that students provide to answer their classmate's questions.

SECTION 4 — Pregnancy

Focus

Vocabulary Activity

Vocabulary worksheets are provided in the Teacher Classroom Resources.

Teach and Apply

Learning with Visuals

Apply Discuss the differences among the various home pregnancy tests. Ask students to conduct research on the Internet to learn the accuracy rates, ease of use, and cost for each test.

Class Activity

Comprehend Ask students how the health of both parents affects the fetus. Prompt students by asking if substance abuse can affect the fetus. Do they know that the use of drugs by the parents prior to conception could harm the infant? What about the diet of the parents?

Pursuing Wellness

Apply Many communities have a number of organizations that can provide you with a guest speakers on topics related to teen pregnancy. Suggestions for speakers include the following:

1. *Social worker*: Ask a local human services professional who deals with adoption or child protection to discuss the effects of teen pregnancy on the child.

2. *Medical professional*: It's beneficial to have students understand the physical effects of pregnancy and birth on teen girls. Nutrition and prenatal care could also be included in this discussion.

3. *Teen pregnancy hotline director*: Workers at the hotline may be able to offer relevant information to your students.

4. *Teen parents*: The best information about teen pregnancy and parenthood comes from teens who have experienced it. You will want to have both mothers and fathers participate in the discussion. Include recent parents and those who have matured and can look back on the experience.

Assess

Worksheets

A reproducible quiz for Section 4 is provided in the Teacher Classroom Resources.

Close

Analyze Ask students to prepare a two-minute speech summarizing the characteristics of a healthy lifestyle prior to beginning a pregnancy. Tell them to make three main points during their presentation.

SECTION 5 Fetal Development

Focus

Vocabulary Activity

Vocabulary worksheets are provided in the Teacher Classroom Resources.

Teach and Apply

Pursuing Wellness

Apply Assign each student a lifestyle habit that can be harmful during pregnancy. Instruct students to research the effects that the lifestyle habit can have on the fetus and infants. Students should name specific disorders and complications that could result from the lifestyle habits of one or both parents. They may wish to include information they secure from interviews. Have the students write a report using their own research and present the report to the class.

Class Activity

Apply Ask students to go to MyPyramid.gov to conduct research on a healthy eating plan for a female who is pregnant or who is trying to become pregnant. Ask students to develop a healthy eating plan for one day.

Assess

Worksheets

A reproducible quiz for Section 5 is provided in the Teacher Classroom Resources.

Close

Evaluate Have the students complete a creative writing assignment describing how a sperm or an egg meet and form to create a zygote or fetus. Students should demonstrate knowledge of the conception process and stages of pregnancy.

SECTION 6 Birth Defects and Other Problems

Focus

Vocabulary Activity

Vocabulary worksheets are provided in the Teacher Classroom Resources.

Teach and Apply

Class Activity

Apply Ask students to conduct research at the library or on the Internet to learn about one type of birth defect. Students should prepare a pamphlet listing some of the characteristics of that birth defect. They should also describe any treatments that are available.

Assess

Worksheets

A reproducible quiz for Section 6 is provided in the Teacher Classroom Resources.

Close

Evaluate Have the students construct charts listing inherited problems in a newborn, problems not genetic in nature, and problems caused by drug or alcohol use during pregnancy. Assign each student one of the topic areas. Students are to find at least one specific disorder associated with that type of problem and prepare an informational chart regarding that disorder. Display the chart in the classroom. Allow time for the students to view the charts and record notes on every disorder charted.

SECTION 7 Childbirth

Focus

Vocabulary Activity

Vocabulary worksheets are provided in the Teacher Classroom Resources.

Teach and Apply

Learning with Visuals

Apply Divide the class into groups and ask students to conduct research at the library or on the Internet to find information describing the birthing process. Check to make sure that the information comes from a reputable source. Ask each group to prepare a poster, pamphlet, or model describing the steps of the birth process. Be sure to name specific body parts that are involved.

Assess

A reproducible quiz for Section 7 is provided in the Teacher Classroom Resources.

Close

Synthesize Have the students write a summary describing some of the problems that may occur during pregnancy or during childbirth. Ask students to list ways that some of the problems may be avoided, and to list treatments for infants born with birth defects.

SECTION 8 The Elements of Parenting

Focus

Vocabulary Activity

Vocabulary worksheets are provided in the Teacher Classroom Resources.

Teach and Apply

Class Activity
Apply Ask students to write a letter to the editor encouraging the local government to consider providing parenting classes in the community. Suggest that students use statistics related to child abuse and neglect to urge legislators to provide resources for new parents.

Class Activity

Analyze Under your direction, have students discuss the advantages and disadvantages of breastfeeding and formula feeding. Divide the class into two teams: one for breastfeeding, and one for formula feeding. Have each team research and study their issues and prepare to debate the opposing team. Distribute the handout entitled Breast Milk vs. Formula as a reference source for each team.

Assess

A reproducible quiz for Section 8 is provided in the Teacher Classroom Resources.

Reproducible Chapter 20 Tests A and B are also provided in the Teacher Classroom Resources.

Close

Recall Ask students to describe what parents or other caregivers should provide to teens and children. Remind students of the basic human needs such as food and shelter that need to be met. Lead a discussion on the responsibilities of parents and other caregivers.

Go Online

To find supplemental information to suit your individual class, you may want to visit the following Web sites, where you can find additional Internet resources to enhance the study of this chapter. As with all Web sites, you should check these out first to be sure the information found there is appropriate for your students.

National Parenting Center

www.tnpc.com/

Kids Health

kidshealth.org/parent/

Shaken Baby Alliance

www.shakenbaby.com

These sites are parenting information and advice resource centers providing articles and product reviews, and information about common illnesses and ways to prevent them, specific health conditions, behavior and development, nutrition, and more.

CHAPTER
21

CHAPTER 21 Understanding Sexuality

Objectives	Features
• Discuss the nature of sex and sexuality. • Discuss sexual activity. • Dispel sexual myths. • Discuss sexual orientation.	• **Consumer Skills Activity:** Medicinal Enhancements (page 584) • **Q&A:** What About Me? Am I Missing Out? (pages 588–589)

Introduction
Teaching Support
Fast Files
- *Vocabulary*: Learning Vocabulary, Break the Code
- *Study Outline*
- *Reading Cloze*
- *Reteaching Activities*: Myth Busters
- *Handouts*: Attitudes About Sexuality, Effects of Drugs on Sexual Functioning
- *Quizzes*: Sections 1–4
- *Tests*: Chapter 21 Test A, Chapter 21 Test B

Multimedia Support
- *ExamView®Assessment Suite*
- Online Learning Center

Introducing Chapter 21
Chapter Preview Activity

1. Have students list their sources of sexual information. Have them rank the list in two ways: from most to least reliable, and from most to least accessible. The list might include friends, magazines, parents, teachers, books, TV, movies, and church. Compare the students' lists and their rankings.

2. Another possibility for an introductory activity is for the students to brainstorm, either as a class or in small groups, 101 ways to show love without having sex.

3. Have each student interview family members or other caregivers to learn about dating customs when they were the student's age. As a class, develop a list of interview questions to be used. Share these interviews as oral reports or make a class book of interviews. This is a good long-term project and can be effective at strengthening school and community ties.

 Not Enough Time?

The following are some suggestions to help ensure that you cover the key topics in the chapter.

DAY 1 Before class, have students read Sections 1 and 2. During class have students complete the Chapter Preview Activity.

DAY 2 Before class, have students read Sections 3 and 4. During class complete the activities located throughout the chapter.

Bulletin Board Ideas

To go along with the third point in the Chapter Preview, have each student bring in photographs of what they perceive to be a typical date during a certain period of time. For example, what was a typical date during the 1900s, 1950s, etc. Display the photographs prominently in the classroom.

Fact or Fiction?

Answers:

1. False. Sexuality is part of a person's total personality from birth to death, with or without sexual activity.

2. True.

3. False. If you tried to identify "the homosexual lifestyle," you could not do it.

 Writing Paragraphs will vary.

SECTION 1 — The Nature of Sex and Sexuality

Focus

Vocabulary Activity

Vocabulary worksheets are provided in the Teacher Classroom Resources.

Teach and Apply

Comprehension Check

Comprehend If students do not see the difference between the terms *sex* and *sexuality,* refer them to the definitions in the section. You could also tell them that sexuality is broader and more complex than sex. Sexuality involves not only sex, but what we do sexually and who we are sexually.

Class Activity

Evaluate Distribute the handout entitled "Attitudes About Sexuality." Encourage students to answer the questions honestly and as fully as they can. Have volunteers discuss their overall thoughts and feelings about the questionnaire.

Assess

Worksheets

A reproducible quiz for Section 1 is provided in the Teacher Classroom Resources.

Close

Apply Have students name one or two of their favorite celebrities. Ask students to provide reasons why they like the celebrity. Ask students how much of the person's image they know is real, and how much might be created by the media. Ask students how they can really know how celebrities really behave to others? How can they be sure that the person would be a good partner?

SECTION 2 — Sexual Activity

Focus

Vocabulary Activity

Vocabulary worksheets are provided in the Teacher Classroom Resources.

Teach and Apply

Learning with Visuals

Apply Cut out a large variety of magazine photographs of a variety of attractive, well-dressed men and women. Have students rank the photographs from most attractive to least attractive. See if boys as a group and girls as a group can guess the order the other group will choose. Discuss the fact that different people have different opinions about what constitutes an attractive person.

Group Activity

Apply Have students brainstorm a variety of activities for couples that encourage affection, but not sexual intimacy. Discuss the concept that some dates are more likely than others to lead to sexual activity, such as watching a movie when parents aren't home as opposed to going to a movie theater.

CHAPTER 21

Class Activity

Evaluate Have students research and write a paper in which they compare the sexual and dating customs of the past to current customs. Have students state how they think the differences have hurt or improved society, and how sexual myths have influenced both past and current dating customs.

Assess

Worksheets

A reproducible quiz for Section 2 is provided in the Teacher Classroom Resources.

Close

Analyze Have students engage in a series of debates on the following topics:

1. Sexual tension can be controlled.
2. The mind, not the feelings, should control sexual activity.
3. Date activities do not influence sexual activity.
4. The female is responsible for controlling the date, so if it gets out of control, it is her fault.

SECTION 3 Sexual Myths

Focus

Vocabulary Activity

Vocabulary worksheets are provided in the Teacher Classroom Resources.

Teach and Apply

Class Discussion

Discuss Ask students to define the term *myth*. List some common myths on the board, not necessarily related to sex. Ask students why they think myths occur. Do they think that some myths can be dangerous? Examples of some dangerous myths might be:

- Marijuana is not as addictive as cocaine or "harder" drugs.
- Club drugs such as ecstasy, GHB, and rohypnol are not dangerous or addictive.
- A person cannot get pregnant the first time they have sex.
- You can't get STDs from giving or receiving oral sex.
- Masturbation is a sign of physical or mental problems.
- If you love your girlfriend or boyfriend, you should want to have sex with them.

Pursuing Wellness

Apply Ask students to keep a private journal. Encourage them to record their reactions to the material and information presented. They should also record questions that may arise, especially if they are too embarrassed to ask the question in class. That way they can go back, find the question, and ask it of an adult they feel comfortable with. You may want to give students an opportunity to reflect and write for the last few minutes of each class session.

Encourage students to think about what they are learning and apply it to their lives. Remind them that making decisions before they are in a sexual situation gives them control, rather than leaving themselves vulnerable in the "heat of the moment."

Assess

Worksheets

A reproducible quiz is provided in the Teacher Classroom Resources.

Comprehend Write the vocabulary terms relating to the first three sections on the board. Number the words. Have student volunteers roll a die and define the word that corresponds to the number they rolled. As the game progresses, words must be correctly used in a sentence, spelled, or used as the basis of a question you develop.

SECTION 4 — Sexual Orientations

Focus

Vocabulary Activity

Vocabulary worksheets are provided in the Teacher Classroom Resources.

Teach and Apply

Learning with Visuals

Apply Get magazine photos of attractive and unattractive men, women, boys, girls, and adults of all ages. Write a one-paragraph imaginary biography for each individual. Ask students to include an equal number of good and bad personality traits. The biography should also describe the person's education, family, and age. Then, ask students to exchange pictures and biographies. Ask that student to write a summary describing why they would or would not like to date or be a friend to the person in the picture.

Class Discussion

Discuss After reading the Q&A section, encourage a class discussion about sexual messages. Ask students the following questions:

1. Why would a person ask someone he or she loves to do something against that person's personal values?

2. Give one emotional reason to practice abstinence.

3. Give one physical reason to practice abstinence.

Have volunteers share their thoughts and ideas.

Class Activity

Evaluate Have students write down two things they have learned in Section 4. On the same paper, ask students to write any questions they might have. Try to get the answers for any questions they may ask.

Assess

Worksheets

A reproducible quiz for Section 4 is provided in the Teacher Classroom Resources. Reproducible Chapter Tests A and B are provided in the Teacher Classroom Resources.

Close

Lead a class discussion on the topic of sexual preferences. Ask students whether having knowing someone or having a friend who is homosexual automatically means that the student is also homosexual. Remind students that our culture values acceptance of many lifestyle choices.

Go Online

To find supplemental information to suit your individual class, you may want to visit the following Web sites, where you can find additional Internet resources to enhance the study of this chapter. As with all Web sites, you should check these out first to be sure the information found there is appropriate for your students.

Teen HealthFX

www.teenhealthfx.com/answers/
Sexuality/index.php

TeenHealthFX.com is a project funded by Atlantic Health's Morristown Memorial Hospital and Overlook Hospital. The site is maintained with input from teenagers and support from community leaders.

CHAPTER 22 Planning Guide

CHAPTER 22 Preventing Pregnancy and STDs

Objectives

- Identify contraceptive methods.
- Determine reliable sources to get information about contraception methods.
- Identify ineffective contraception methods.
- Understand sterilization.
- Discuss options to consider when unintended pregnancy occurs.

Features

- *Health Skills:* Avoiding Pregnancy (page 599)
- *Q&A:* Why People Don't Use Contraception (pages 618–619)

Introduction

Teaching Support

Fast Files

- *Vocabulary:* Learning Vocabulary, Fill in the Blanks
- *Study Outline*
- *Reading Cloze*
- *Reteaching Activities:* Matching, Degrees of Effectiveness, Condom Catch-up
- *Enrichment Activities:* Birth Control, The Pill Story, Adrianna's Situation
- *Handouts:* Teen Pregnancy, STD, and AIDS Statistics; Pregnancy Scenarios; Sample Welfare Expenses; Community Resources; Abstinence vs. Sexual Intercourse; Conflicting Views on Abortion; U.S. Public Health Service Objectives for the Nation
- *Teacher Information Sheet:* Family Planning, Depo-Provera, Abortion, Choices Diagram
- *Quizzes:* Sections 1–5
- *Tests:* Chapter 22 Test A, Chapter 22 Test B

Multimedia Support

- *ExamView® Assessment Suite*
- Online Learning Center

Introducing Chapter 22

Chapter Preview Activity

Without mentioning to students that you will be discussing abstinence, start with this activity. Ask students to provide examples of attributes the ideal contraceptive would have. Students may come up with qualities such as:

1. Either sex can use it.

2. It prevents sexually transmitted diseases (STDs).

3. It is 100 percent effective.

4. It is free.

5. It is readily available.

6. It is biodegradable.

7. It has no side effects.

8. It is easy to use.

Write all of their responses on the board. Once the list has been completed, ask students if any one method can accomplish everything on the list. If students respond 'no', remind them that abstinence from sexual activity is the only way to avoid an unintended pregnancy and STDs

 **Not Enough Time?**

Here are some suggestions to ensure that you cover the key topics in this chapter.

DAY 1 Assign the chapter to be read before class. During class, complete the Chapter Preview Activity.

DAY 2 Using the information given in Section 2, discuss the different contraceptives, their effectiveness, and how they work. Choose activities from the section that best fit your students' needs for understanding.

DAY 3 Begin with a discussion of Section 3. Use the activities throughout the chapter that best fit your students' needs.

Bulletin Board Ideas

Have students create a bulletin board display out of photographs of the various methods of contraception. Under each method, list the pros and cons of use, such as effectiveness, prescription, ease of use, ability to stop the spread of STDs, etc.

Have students create a bulletin board listing the names of all the STDs they know of at this time. As they read the chapter, ask students to add new information to the bulletin board, along with the way the STD is transmitted, the short- and long-term health effects, and treatments for the STD.

Fact or Fiction?

Answers:

1. False. No contraceptive method is perfect. To obtain the advantages of one method, a person must be willing to put up with its disadvantages.

2. False. Condoms are prone to failure, but abstinence always prevents sexually transmitted diseases.

3. False. A woman who isn't taking the pill may be using another form of birth control, such as condoms or a diaphragm. The term *birth control* refers to all contraceptive methods, including the pill.

Writing Paragraphs will vary.

SECTION 1 Choosing Contraception and STD Protection

Focus

Vocabulary Activity

Vocabulary worksheets are provided in the Teacher Classroom Resources.

Teach and Apply

Class Activity

Evaluate Remind students that the fact they are studying this information does not mean that they are being advised to become sexually active. The text has stressed, from page one, the need for each person to make his or her own choices; the purpose of the text is to provide information to help people make wiser, better informed choices. This text has also presented a strong case for abstinence in several chapters prior to this one.

Comprehension Check

Comprehend Ask students to look at the definition of contraception in the chapter. Then ask them to explain the difference between the terms *contraception* and *birth control*. Contraception is any method used to prevent conception. Birth control is any method of preventing birth. Birth control, therefore, is a broader term and includes such things as abortion, which is not included as part of contraception.

Learning with Visuals

Analyze Ask students if they realize that the odds of becoming pregnant were as high as Figure 22.1 on page 594 shows them to be. Did they think they were higher?

Class Activity

Evaluate Have students imagine that a couple has decided to engage in sexual activity. Ask students the following questions:

1. What will determine whether or not the couple will use reliable contraception?

2. Who is responsible for providing contraception?

3. What type of contraception will be used?

Encourage volunteers to share their thoughts and ideas.

Class Discussion

Discuss Ask students why they think contraception is a controversial topic. What attitudes do they have about contraception? What ideas are conveyed through the media? What values and ideas about contraception are learned from their family? Encourage students to share their thoughts and to ask questions about contraception if they feel comfortable doing so.

Class Activity

Analyze Distribute the handout entitled Community Resources, located in the Teacher Classroom Resources. This handout provides guidelines to help students locate and organize information regarding counseling services available in their community. Encourage students to research the internet for additional information regarding local organizations and services available to them. Have volunteers report their findings.

Assess

Worksheets

A reproducible quiz for Section 1 is provided in the Teacher Classroom Resources.

Close

Analyze Tell students that one million teens become pregnant each year. That is one in every ten American teen girls. Other countries that are similar to the United States in standard of living and education don't have the high pregnancy rates we do. Only 1 in 30 Swedish teens and fewer than 1 in 20 British, Canadian, or French teens becomes pregnant. Ask students why they think this is so.

SECTION 2

Contraceptive Methods

Focus

Vocabulary Activity

Vocabulary worksheets are provided in the Teacher Classroom Resources.

Teach and Apply

Comprehension Check

Recall You may want to refer back to the Chapter 20 discussion of ovulation before students read the explanation of how oral contraceptives work.

Comprehension Check

Comprehend Review the term *oral contraceptives*. Ask students to define the term. If necessary, remind students that this category of contraceptives is called oral contraceptives because it refers to the mouth. Tell students that oral contraceptives are those that are taken orally, through the mouth. Encourage students to review the vocabulary for Section 2, and point out any words they find especially difficult to understand. Review the definitions as needed.

Group Activity

Evaluate Organize students into small groups. Have each group conduct research on the history of one birth control method. Ask students to prepare a presentation, with each person taking part in the presentation. Presentations should provide the history of the method, how it is used, and any side effects associated with the method.

Pursuing Wellness

Evaluate Tell students that taking pills is not the only way to introduce progestins into the body. Some contraceptive devices, such as intrauterine devices or vaginal rings, release the drug directly into the uterus or vagina. Women can also receive a shot of progestins that lasts for three months. Have students research alternative birth control options.

Class Activity

Evaluate You may want to discuss with students some major drawbacks to condom use. One of the chief drawbacks is that the condom must be put on after the man has been aroused, but before he enters the woman. This necessary interruption in sexual intercourse is the major reason for users neglecting or "forgetting" to put on a condom. Also, some men complain that sensation is dulled by the condom. The use of condoms made of animal tissue will help remedy this problem, but as the text states, animal tissue condoms (such as the lambskin condom) will not prevent STDs.

Group Activity

Evaluate Have students research the effectiveness of condom usage. You may share the following information about condom use from the *University of California at Berkeley Wellness Letter* with your students.

Condom breakage is more common than most people realize. According to a study of 98 males who use condoms, 50 percent said they had had a condom break. Of those 50 percent, 30 percent had failed to tell their partners of the breakage at least one time.

They gave the following reasons for failing to tell:

- They didn't want to interrupt intercourse.
- They didn't want to take responsibility for the break.
- They didn't want their partner to become anxious about the break.

If a partner doesn't know that the condom broke, they won't be able to seek medical testing for pregnancy or STDs.

Comprehension Check

Comprehend You may want to tell students that fertility awareness methods, such as the rhythm method, require education, training, and planning. Other types of fertility awareness methods are the basal body temperature method, the mucus (also called the Billings or ovulation) method, and the sympto-thermal method.

Assess

Worksheets

A reproducible quiz for Section 2 is provided in the Teacher Classroom Resources.

Close

Recall Before class, prepare slips of paper, each with one contraceptive method on it. You will need to have two or three slips with the same method to accommodate a class of 30 students. Fold the slips and put them in a box. Have each student draw out one. The assignment is to describe on paper how the method picked works and how it is correctly used. You may want to put a diagram of the male and female reproductive systems on the board or on an overhead projector to aid students. Collect the papers and check for understanding.

SECTION 3 — Methods Not Recommended for Contraception

Focus

Vocabulary Activity

Vocabulary worksheets are provided in the Teacher Classroom Resources.

Teach and Apply

Class Activity

Evaluate Brainstorm with the class about the myths they have heard about contraception. Make a list on the board. Students will respond with statements such as these: You can't get pregnant the first time you have sex. You can't get pregnant if you drink ice water after sex. A male won't be able to get a female pregnant if he sits in a hot or cold bath before sex. You can't get pregnant if you have sex standing up. A female can't get pregnant during her period. A male can't get someone pregnant if he wears a rubber band around his penis during sex.

Discuss with students why these myths are untrue. Why do students think the myths persist? Why do some people still believe them?

Comprehension Check

Recall Review with students the forms of contraception that do not work by having them list them on a piece of paper. Have the students also explain why the methods are ineffective. Have students share their lists with the class. Discuss the answers.

Assess

Worksheets

A reproducible quiz for Section 3 is provided in the Teacher Classroom Resources.

Close

Analyze Ask students the following questions: If a sexually active teen decides not to use a contraceptive device or uses a method that is not recommended to achieve birth control, what conclusions might be drawn about that person? What might be some outcomes of the decision? Answers will vary. List them on the board and discuss.

SECTION 4 — Sterilization

Focus

Vocabulary Activity

Vocabulary worksheets are provided in the Teacher Classroom Resources.

Teach and Apply

Comprehension Check

Comprehend Why can a male who has had a vasectomy still cause a pregnancy for about six weeks after the operation? Explain to students that a supply of living sperm is still stored in the male reproductive tract. This is the reason a man can still cause a pregnancy for about six weeks after a vasectomy.

Class Activity

Analyze Discuss with students the permanent solution of sterilization. Ask students if they think it would be wise for a young adult to choose a permanent method of birth control. Should a teen be provided with that choice?

Assess

Worksheets

A reproducible quiz for Section 4 is provided in the Teacher Classroom Resources.

Close

Evaluate Ask students if they believe that teens should have access to contraception. Should teens be encouraged to wait to begin sexual activity? Is it fair to tease teens who have decided to wait to begin sexual activity? Remind students to be courteous of other opinions.

SECTION 5 Contraceptive Failure

Focus

Vocabulary Activity

Vocabulary worksheets are provided in the Teacher Classroom Resources.

Teach and Apply

Group Activity

Evaluate Write *Abortion* on one side of the board and *Adoption* on the other. Divide each side of the board into two parts. Label one section *Pros* and one *Cons* for each of the two sides.

Have students brainstorm the pros and cons of each choice and write their responses in the appropriate place. Discuss.

Assess

Worksheets

A reproducible quiz for Section 5 is provided in the Teacher Classroom Resources. Reproducible Chapter Tests A and B are provided in the Teacher Classroom Resources.

Close

Comprehend Make sure that students understand that both adoption and abortion are possible choices for unwanted pregnancies, but one must take time to consider the options to best suit their situation.

Go Online

To find supplemental information to suit your individual class, you may want to visit the following Web sites, where you can find additional Internet resources to enhance the study of this chapter. As with all Web sites, you should check these out first to be sure the information found there is appropriate for your students.

MayoClinic

www.mayoclinic.com/

American Public Health Association

www.apha.org/

CHAPTER 23 Mature Life, Aging, and Death

Objectives	Features
• Learn realistic expectations for successfully aging. • Identify physical, emotional, and social changes that occur as one ages.	• *Consumer Skills Activity:* Longevity Products (page 629) • *What Teens Think:* What Makes Your Favorite Senior Citizen Your Favorite? (page 632) • *Q&A:* Learning From Older People (pages 638–639)

Introduction

Teaching Support

Fast Files

- *Vocabulary:* Learning Vocabulary, Match the Definition
- *Study Outline*
- *Reading Cloze*
- *Reteaching Activities:* Helping Grandma
- *Enrichment Activities:* The Dilemma of Death, What's Your Opinion?
- *Career Briefs:* Homemaker-Home Health Aides
- *Teacher Information Sheets:* Anti-Aging Strategies; Nutrition, Aging, and Disease; Malnutrition Among the Elderly; Food and Assistance Programs for Older People; Selecting Institutional Care for Older People; Stages of Grief;
- *Quizzes:* Sections 1–3
- *Tests:* Chapter 23 Test A, Chapter 23 Test B

Multimedia Support

- *ExamView® Assessment Suite*
- Online Learning Center

Introducing Chapter 23

Chapter Preview Activity

Take a class poll on the following statements. Have students indicate whether they agree or disagree with each one. Allow volunteers to share their opinions.

1. TV accurately portrays how elderly people behave and look.

2. People over the age of 65 should not be allowed to drive.

3. Elderly people are boring.

4. Elderly people are unable to make important decisions.

5. It's stimulating to talk with elderly people.

6. Most elderly people are forgetful.

7. Elderly people should be able to work until they no longer want to do so.

8. Most elderly people should be in nursing homes.

9. Younger people can benefit from the experience of the elderly.

10. Elderly people are no longer productive members of society.

After discussing the students' feelings, ask them why they think they feel the way they do about the elderly. Ask them if they have any suggestions for getting to know elderly people better and finding out what they are really like.

 **Not Enough Time?**

Here are some suggestions to ensure that you cover the key topics in this chapter.

DAY 1 Assign Section 1 to be read prior to class. During class have students complete the Chapter Preview Activity.

DAY 2 Assign Section 2 to be read prior to class. During class have students complete the activities provided throughout Section 2.

DAY 3 Assign Section 3 and the Q&A section to be read prior to class. During class have students complete the activities provided throughout Section 3.

Bulletin Board Ideas

Have the students bring in photographs of older adults who are active and appear to be happy. Arrange the bulletin board in order of the age of the photograph's subject. Discuss with the class similarities and differences between individuals of approximately the same age.

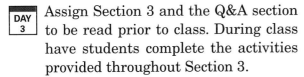 **Fact or Fiction?**

Answers:

1. False. The happiest people are those who have lived through at least one major life tragedy.

2. False. The human life span has not changed, but the life expectancy has increased steadily over the past years.

3. False. Less than one-third of older adults spend any time in a nursing home.

 **Writing** Paragraphs will vary.

 **SECTION 1**

Expectations and Successful Aging

Focus

Vocabulary Activity

Vocabulary worksheets are provided in the Teacher Classroom Resources.

Teach and Apply

Class Activity

Evaluate Have the students brainstorm words and thoughts that come to mind when you say the words *aging*, *death*, and *dying*. Count the positive responses and the negative responses. Are their ideas about these concepts primarily negative or positive? If they are negative, ask them what they can do to change these feelings.

Class Discussion

Discuss Tell students the elderly can face stereotypes in our society. The term age discrimination is used to identify prejudices facing elderly adults. Ask students to describe what aging means to them. Check for negative and positive descriptions that indicate an aging stereotype, such as weak, frail, patient, or caring. Discuss.

Class Activity

Evaluate Divide the class into small groups. Have each group discuss and answer each of the following questions. If time is limited, assign one or two questions to each group. Have each group present their findings to the class.

1. Does development continue after age 60 or is this period of life marked only by decline? Give examples.

2. What does your community do to promote full and active lives for the elderly?

3. What jobs are available for the elderly?

4. Have elderly relatives, neighbors, or friends had a positive impact on your life? How?

5. What can you do to make a difference in the life of the elderly?

Assess

Worksheets

A reproducible quiz for Section 1 is provided in the Teacher Classroom Resources.

Close

Recall Have students list the characteristics of people who age successfully. If they miss any, make sure to add them to the list.

SECTION 2
The Aging Process

Focus

Vocabulary Activity

Vocabulary worksheets are provided in the Teacher Classroom Resources.

Teach and Apply

Comprehension Check

Comprehension Put these three terms on the board: *life span*, *life expectancy*, and *longevity*. Ask the students to define them and explain the differences between them. Discuss which of the three has changed over time and which remains the same.

Group Activity

Evaluate Point out to students the possibility of the human life expectancy increasing in the years to come. People who are 100 years old today were born in the early 1900s. Have groups of students think about the difficulties those people may have had to deal with in terms of living conditions, lack of medicines, and lack of knowledge regarding things such as nutrition and disease. Then have the students think about the conditions in which today's newborns will grow up and mature with regard to those same areas. It could be that the life expectancy will increase simply due to these changes and conditions.

Comprehension Check

Recall Have students review **Figure 23.4**. Ask students to list behaviors they can practice or avoid in order to slow or prevent the changes that have checkmarks in the middle column. For example, smoking excessive alcohol consumption, and other drug abuse ages the skin. Have volunteers share their lists with the class. Discuss.

Assess

Worksheets

A reproducible quiz for Section 2 is provided in the Teacher Classroom Resources.

Close

Apply Have students develop a service project for a local nursing home or for local senior citizens. They may want to do one of the following: develop a pen pal system for elderly people with no relatives or visitors; plan a holiday party for the elderly; or hold a spring clean-up day for senior citizens who need help with their yards and windows.

SECTION 3 Dying

Focus

Vocabulary Activity

Vocabulary worksheets are provided in the Teacher Classroom Resources.

Teach and Apply

Apply Rent a copy of a movie such as "Young At Heart," which shows the elderly performing rock and roll songs in prisons and other venues throughout the world, and show part of the film in class. Lead a class discussion asking students if the film changed their idea about what the elderly can and cannot do. Did the film help them think of the elderly in a new way? If so, how?

Class Activity

Apply Have students read the Q&A section on pages 638–639. Have students list ways they could lend support to family or friends that have lost a loved one. Encourage volunteers to share their thoughts and ideas with the class.

Class Activity

Evaluate On a sheet of paper, ask students to write a letter to themselves telling what they hope to accomplish in the next year. They are to put the letter in an envelope, self-address it, and stamp it. Tell them they will receive the letter in one year to see their progress on those goals. (You will have to remember to mail the letters back to the students in one year.)

Assess

Worksheets

A reproducible quiz for Section 3 is provided in the Teacher Classroom Resources. Reproducible Chapter Tests A and B are provided in the Teacher Classroom Resources.

Close

Apply Have students write a list of things that they would like to accomplish if a doctor said they only had one month to live. What types of things would be most important to do? What unfinished business would they finish?

Go Online

To find supplemental information to suit your individual class, you may want to visit the following Web sites, where you can find additional Internet resources to enhance the study of this chapter. As with all Web sites, you should check these out first to be sure the information found there is appropriate for your students.

National Institute on Aging

www.nih.gov/nia/

Before I Die

www.thirteen.org/bid/

The National Institute on Aging site contains information on promoting healthy aging, including biomedical, social, and behavioral research and public education. The Before I Die site is a well-designed and informative site, discussing personal concerns and issues about death and dying through a wealth of personal stories, an interactive discussion forum, and thought-provoking essays.

CHAPTER 24 Accident and Injury Prevention

Objectives	Features
• Identify techniques for auto safety. • Identify outdoor safety skills. • Demonstrate skills to prevent fire and burns. • Demonstrate skills to prevent accidents and falls. • Identify safety preparedness skills. • Determine safe and reliable techniques for caring for children.	• *Health Skills:* How to Avoid Alcohol-Related Driving Accidents (page 648) • *Applying Health Skills:* Refusal Skills (page 649) • *Health Skills:* Water Rescue Techniques (page 652) • *Health Skills:* Tips for Babysitters (page 662) • *Q&A:* Fire Prevention and Escape (page 664)

Introduction

Teaching Support

Fast Files

- *Vocabulary:* Learning Vocabulary
- *Study Outline*
- *Reading Cloze*
- *Reteaching Activities:* Concept Matching, Responses to a Natural Disaster
- *Enrichment Activities:* Accident Prevention, Baby-Sitting Safety, Ask the Professional, Teens and Car Accidents
- *Career Briefs:* Firefighting Occupations
- *Life Choice Inventory:* How Safety-Conscious Are You?
- *Handouts:* Household Fire Safety Checklist
- *Quizzes:* Sections 1–6
- *Tests:* Chapter 24 Test A, Chapter 24 Test B

Multimedia Support

- *ExamView® Assessment Suite*
- Online Learning Center

Chapter Preview Activity

Talk with your students about disasters that can possibly occur in your community. Talk about why you need to prepare for these events. Calmly explain the potential dangers, and plan to share responsibilities and work together as a team. Make sure every student knows his or her particular responsibilities. Designate an alternate in case a person is not there at the time.

Bulletin Board Ideas

Prepare a bulletin board to list emergency and safety agencies and their phone numbers (some possibilities are listed at the end of this activity). Have the students choose, or you can assign students to either visit or call one of the following organizations to find out what educational safety programs are available in your community. Match each section in this chapter with an agency. Some possibilities include:

- A safety commission.
- The American Heart Association.
- The American Red Cross.
- A fire marshal.
- A hospital.
- A sheriff's department.
- The U.S. Coast Guard.
- The U.S. Forest Service.
- The state wildlife and game commission.
- The state division of parks and recreation.

 Not Enough Time?

Here are some suggestions to ensure that you cover the key topics.

 DAY 1 Assign students the chapter to read prior to class. During class do the Preview Activity to promote awareness and to stimulate thought about safety in students' own activities.

 DAY 2 Because this chapter is so diverse, select one or two sections to emphasize depending on the needs of your students. For example, if most of your students drive and have a high rate of accidents, select one or two activities from Section 1. Conclude the class with the Section Review.

 DAY 3 Divide the class into the same number of groups as remaining sections you want to teach. Assign each group one of these sections along with your choice of activity for that section. Allow groups half of the class time to prepare a five-minute class presentation to be given during the remainder of class. This should highlight key points of the chapter for the benefit of the entire class.

 Fact or Fiction?

Answers:
1. False. One out of every three, not ten, people suffer an injury each year.
2. False. Skill is important, but attitude is equally important in preventing accidents on the road.
3. True.

 Writing Paragraphs will vary.

 SECTION 1 **Highway Accidents**

Focus

Vocabulary Activity

Vocabulary worksheets are provided in the Teacher Classroom Resources.

Teach and Apply

Life Choice Inventory

Ask students to complete the Life Choice Inventory found in the Teacher Classroom Resources or the Online Learning Center.

Class Activity

Evaluate Ask students if they have ever witnessed any of the driving behaviors described in the Health Skills sidebar on page 648. Ask students to recount the situation, then ask if they reported that driver to the police. Why or why not?

Assess

Worksheets

A reproducible quiz for Section 1 is provided in the Teacher Classroom Resources.

Close

Recall Before going on to the next lesson, students should be able to do the following:

a. Name the four necessary aspects of defensive driving.

b. List four responsibilities of a driver in preventing accidents.

c. Identify four guidelines for recognizing driving under the influence of alcohol or drugs.

d. Name two automobile safety features that ensure driver protection.

e. Name four things that affect insurance rates for teenagers.

SECTION 2 — Safety for Outdoor Activities

Focus

Vocabulary Activity

Vocabulary worksheets are provided in the Teacher Classroom Resources.

Teach and Apply

Group Activity

Apply Divide the class into four groups. Ask each group to select an outdoor activity, such as hiking, biking, swimming, etc. Ask students to prepare a checklist of items to be included in a safety kit for that activity. Have students share their lists with the class, and remind students to update the lists as they read the material in this section.

Class Activity

Analyze Ask students to research local organizations or areas where swimming instruction is offered. Ask students who know how to swim to talk about how long it took them to learn, how difficult it was, and how much fun they have swimming.

Assess

Worksheets

A reproducible quiz for Section 2 is provided in the Teacher Classroom Resources.

Close

Apply Collect newspaper articles about various recreational accidents. Ask students to pick one and identify the following:

1. The hazard

2. The unsafe act, habit or behavior

3. The attitude

4. The possible preventive measures

SECTION 3 — Fire and Burn Safety

Focus

Vocabulary Activity

Vocabulary worksheets are provided in the Teacher Classroom Resources.

Teach and Apply

Learning with Visuals

Ask students to turn to **Figure 24.6** on page 655 of the textbook. The symbols in the last row describe the type of fire that the extinguisher should not be used to put out. Ask students which three symbols they would look for if a grease fire occurred in their kitchen. An electrical fire? An ordinary fire?

Class Activity

Evaluate Ask students to think about possible fire hazards in their home or at school. What can students do at home to decrease the risk of a fire? What can students do at school to decrease the risk of a fire? Invite volunteers to share their thoughts and ideas with the class.

Assess

Worksheets

A reproducible quiz for Section 3 is provided in the Teacher Classroom Resources.

Close

Recall Have students identify the three classes of fire extinguishers and either draw the symbols or name the use(s) for each one. Discuss where fire extinguishers are located around the school.

SECTION 4 Falls and Other Accidents

Focus

Vocabulary Activity

Vocabulary worksheets are provided in the Teacher Classroom Resources.

Teach and Apply

Class Activity

Evaluate Ask students if they think that posting a list of precautions somewhere in their home would help prevent accidents. Where would they post the list? Have students customize a list of home safety precautions to post in their homes.

Ask students to think for a few minutes about the types of accidents, that have occurred in their homes. What were the causes of these accidents? Could they have been prevented? What can family members do to prevent a recurrence of this type of accident?

Class Activity

Apply Divide the class into groups of three or four students. Have each member of the group write an individual safety checklist and emergency evacuation plan for their own home. The checklist should include a list of possible hazards that exist and what needs to be done to correct the situation. The emergency evacuation plan should include an escape route, detailed locations of fire extinguishers, and a designated meeting place for all members to go to after leaving the house. Have each student share their plans with the other members of the group.

Assess

Worksheets

A reproducible quiz for Section 4 is provided in the Teacher Classroom Resources.

Close

Apply Ask students to conduct research on the Internet for any new items to add to the list of precautions found in this section that would further help to reduce accidents, injuries, and possible death. Ask students to explain why they believe any new items should be added to the list. What makes the student believe the item does what it is advertised to do? How did they evaluate the product's effectiveness? For extra credit, have students make posters to illustrate these ideas and display them in your room or hallway.

SECTION 5 Preparedness for Disasters

Focus

Vocabulary Activity

Vocabulary worksheets are provided in the Teacher Classroom Resources.

Learning with Visuals

Apply Organize students into groups and have each group prepare a video or script describing how to react to a natural disaster that may occur in the area of the country where the school is located. Students should be encouraged to use their creativity to present the information as a documentary, with students playing the roles of disaster survivors. Remind students to make sure that the videos make clear points about the actions that people should take during a natural disaster.

Class Activity

Discuss Ask students to name the types of natural disasters that can occur in your location (earthquakes, floods, forest fires, hurricanes, tornadoes, etc.) Ask students to list items that their families can collect in a kit before a natural disaster occurs that would be useful. Items may include water, canned food, medicines, clothing, blankets or sleeping bags, etc. Remind students that the power may be out for a few days after a natural disaster. Would a cell phone charger using a hand crank or solar power be useful? What about an emergency radio? Then ask students what they would do if they were not at home when a natural disaster occurred. Does their family have a plan for getting in touch with each other if a natural disaster occurs? Tell students that their families can develop a phone tree, where one member calls another member, then that member calls someone else.

Assess

Worksheets

A reproducible quiz for Section 5 is provided in the Teacher Classroom Resources.

Close

Apply Have students find out from a variety of local resources (civil defense, fire department, and so on) how different areas of their community would be evacuated if necessary. To receive extra credit, students should obtain a street map of their community and clearly mark the evacuation routes. Display one in your classroom and post others throughout your school.

SECTION 6 **Care of Others: Child Care**

Focus

Vocabulary Activity

Vocabulary worksheets are provided in the Teacher Classroom Resources.

Teach and Apply

Class Activity

Evaluate Ask how many students are responsible for younger children from time to time, either in paid babysitting situations or in taking care of younger siblings. Ask students if they feel that they know enough about how to protect the young children they are watching. How often do they check on the children? Have any accidents or injuries ever occurred while they were responsible for the children? How did they react? Discuss the suggestions for babysitters in the Health Skills sidebar on page 662. Do any of the students have any other suggestions?

Group Activity

Describe Divide students into groups of three or four. Ask each group to brainstorm and come up with one slogan that reminds parents and others who take care of young children of safety precautions they should remember. Then ask each group to develop a radio or video public service announcement script that uses the slogan.

Assess

Worksheets

A reproducible quiz for Section 6 is provided in the Teacher Classroom Resources.

Reproducible Chapter Tests A and B are provided in the Teacher Classroom Resources.

Close

Apply Have students take a visual trip around the classroom. Have them look for the various safety problems discussed in the chapter. If a young child were to enter the classroom, what would be some hazards that could endanger the child's safety? Discuss this as a class and point out ways the classroom could be made safer.

Go Online

To find supplemental information to suit your individual class, you may want to visit the following Web sites, where you can find additional Internet resources to enhance the study of this chapter. As with all Web sites, you should check these out first to be sure the information found there is appropriate for your students.

American Red Cross

www.redcross.org

Ready.gov

www.ready.gov

CHAPTER 25 Planning Guide

CHAPTER 25 Emergency Measures

Objectives

- Identify items that should be in a first-aid kit.
- Identify actions to take in offering first aid.
- Demonstrate understanding of how to give CPR.
- Demonstrate understanding of techniques to care for choking and severe bleeding.
- Identify and understand how to perform other first aid procedures including burns, broken bones, and poisoning.

Features

- **Health Skills:** Reducing Disease Risks (page 673)
- **Health Skills:** First Aid for Shock (page 674)
- **Health Skills:** Summary of Emergency Actions (page 675)
- **Applying Health Skills:** Stress Management (page 688)
- **Health Skills:** Splinting a Broken Bone (page 692)
- **Q&A:** Herbs and Folk Remedies

Introduction

Teaching Support

Fast Files

- *Vocabulary:* Learning Vocabulary, Fill in the Blanks
- *Study Outline*
- *Reading Cloze*
- *Reteaching Activities:* First Actions First; Airway, Breathing, Circulation, Severe Bleeding, Shock; Down to Basics and Beyond
- *Enrichment Activities:* Investigation of Alternative Healing Methods; Help! There's Been An Accident
- *Career Briefs:* Emergency Medical Technicians
- *Life Choice Inventory:* How Well Prepared for Emergencies Are You?
- *Handouts:* Snakebite Kits: No Substitute for Knowledge; Selected First-Aid Measures
- *Quizzes:* Sections 1–4

- *Tests:* Chapter 25 Test A, Chapter 25 Test B

Multimedia Support

- *ExamView® Assessment Suite*
- Online Learning Center

Introducing Chapter 25

Chapter Preview Activity

Contact your community's local emergency response provider and ask whether a paramedic or member of the fire department can visit your school. In many communities, the local fire department will offer free CPR training, even to teens. Ask the emergency medical technicians (EMTs) to explain to students the nature of their work, the most frequent type of call they respond to, what their response time is, how citizens contact their local fire and rescue services, and how well the community deals with the emergency situations before rescue arrives.

Not Enough Time?

Here are some suggestions to ensure that you cover the key topics in this chapter.

DAY 1 On Day 1 read aloud Chapter 25 as a class. Pick several students to read the various sections. At the end of each section, discuss the key points.

DAY 2 On Day 2 do the Chapter Preview Activity, ask students to conduct research on local emergency service providers. Students should ask how to contact emergency personnel, what types of services are provided, what types of training are provided to the public, and whether there is a minimum age limit for those who register for trainings. Ask students to prepare a summary to present to the class.

DAY 3 On Day 3 have students score themselves using the Life Choice Inventory, "How Well Prepared for Emergencies Are You?" Students may then determine how well prepared they are to respond to a medical emergency.

Bulletin Board Ideas

Post the CPR and first-aid steps on the most prominent bulletin board along with a schedule of classes for each.

Fact or Fiction?

Answers:

1. False. To be of real help and not make things worse, the rescuer should apply the principles gained through a first-aid class taught by a qualified instructor.

2. False. The first thing to do in an emergency is to inspect the scene to determine what happened. Move the victim only if the scene presents immediate danger.

3. False. A person in a state of shock is experiencing a physical reaction to injury. Shock is a dangerous condition, and first-aid treatment is recommended.

Writing Paragraphs will vary.

SECTION 1 — Providing First Aid

Focus

Vocabulary Activity

Vocabulary worksheets are provided in the Teacher Classroom Resources.

Teach and Apply

Class Activity

Evaluate Can students name which of the items listed in **Figure 25.2** are contained in their home medicine chests? After discussing this in class, have students inspect their home medicine chests and use **Figure 25.2** to determine whether they have the standard supplies recommended. Discuss their results.

Comprehension Check

Comprehend After students have read the explanations in Step 1 on pages 672–675, have them close their books and, as a group, see how many of the procedures they can remember. Some key points are:

a. Get someone to call for help.

b. Assess the danger—don't put yourself in jeopardy.

c. Determine if anyone else can help.

d. Avoid moving the injured party, or move the person as little as possible.

e. Help the person who needs it most, first.

f. Get information from the patient, if possible.

g. Look for clues to what happened.

SECTION 2 Cardiopulmonary Resuscitation (CPR)

Comprehension Check

Recall Have students list the signs and symptoms of shock on the board. Invite students to explain how to reduce the risk of shock, using the information from the Health Skills sidebar on page 674.

Class Activity

Apply Tell students to imagine they are rescuers at an accident scene. Have students create a scenario and write the report they would give on the phone to rescue personnel when calling to report the accident. Students should include information listed under "Step 2: Calling For Help". Invite volunteers to share their scenarios and reports.

Assess

Worksheets

A reproducible quiz for Section 1 is provided in the Teacher Classroom Resources.

Close

Recall Before beginning the next lesson, students should be able to answer these questions:

1. What two self-protective items should always be available to minimize the risk of contracting AIDS and other communicable diseases when administering first aid?

2. Explain the use of these two self-protective items when administering first aid. How are they used and for what purpose?

Focus

Vocabulary Activity

Vocabulary worksheets are provided in the Teacher Classroom Resources.

Teach and Apply

Class Activity

Analyze Have students investigate the Good Samaritan laws in your state. (A Good Samaritan law is one that protects people who help others in emergencies from being sued for accidentally doing the wrong thing or not doing the right thing.)

Get a copy of your state's Good Samaritan laws, read it for your students, and discuss the degree of protection afforded to the rescuer. Ask students for examples of what might constitute gross negligence or willful misconduct.

Class Activity

Evaluate Have students review the material in Chapter 6 on the cardiovascular system. Then tell them that CPR is a lifesaving technique. No one should attempt to administer CPR without training. A mannequin—not a person—should be used during CPR practice sessions. A formal training course is offered by the American Heart Association (AHA) and the American Red Cross.

Assess

Worksheets

A reproducible quiz for Section 2 is provided in the Teacher Classroom Resources.

Close

Recall Before going on to the next section, students should be able to answer the following questions:

1. What are five measures you should take when dealing with a suspected heart attack victim?

2. Who should administer CPR?

3. When should CPR be started?

4. How long does a victim have before brain damage or death may occur if breathing and pulse have ceased?

Discuss the answers to these questions in class.

SECTION 3 Choking and Severe Bleeding

Focus

Vocabulary Activity

Vocabulary worksheets are provided in the Teacher Classroom Resources.

Teach and Apply

Comprehension Check

Comprehend Ask students why they should not hit a person who is chocking on the back. (It may cause the lodged particle to move deeper into the passageway.) Emphasize to students that they should place their fists firmly against the victim's abdomen before thrusting upward to perform the Heimlich Maneuver. Also make sure that all students know the location of the abdomen. They must start the movement below the rib cage.

Comprehension Check

Comprehend Impress upon students the importance of controlling external bleeding. This is second only to the maintenance of air passages and the restoration of breathing. Ask students how to control external bleeding.

Class Activity

Discuss Remind students that it's easier to prevent an accident than to manage one after it has occurred. Have the class brainstorm ways they can live more safely.

Assess

Worksheets

A reproducible quiz for Section 3 is provided in the Teacher Classroom Resources.

Close

Recall At the end of this section, students should be able to recall techniques for the Heimlich maneuver and how to control severe bleeding.

SECTION 4 Other First-Aid Procedures

Focus

Vocabulary Activity

Vocabulary worksheets are provided in the Teacher Classroom Resources.

Teach and Apply

Learning with Visuals

Apply Obtain posters and pamphlets about sunburn from your local American Cancer Society. Display these in the classroom and discuss the information given in them. Continue the discussion by asking the following questions:

1. What degree is sunburn?

2. What causes sunburn? What are some ways to prevent sunburn from occurring?

3. How should you decide what sunscreen to buy? What should you look for on the sunscreen bottle?

Comprehension Check

Comprehend Have the students make two columns on a piece of paper and label one column "Do" and the other column "Don't." Have students go back through the text and list all the things to do when caring for burns in general (not for the specific degrees of burns). They should then list all the things not to do (for example: do monitor breathing; don't remove burned clothing). Have students add to their own papers the items shared by the class that were not on their lists.

Background Information

Eye Injuries Incorrect handling of even a minor eye injury can lead to permanent damage. Eye injuries are best treated by specialists. Only superficial foreign bodies should be removed, and then always using thoroughly cleansed hands and sterile materials.

Tears are the body's attempt at removing foreign particles, but rubbing the eye can cause damage by scratching the delicate eye tissue or lodging the particle deeper in the eye.

If a particle is loose in the eye, flush the eye with clean water while holding the eyelids apart. Sometimes a particle lodged under the upper eyelid can be removed by drawing the upper eyelid over the lower eyelid so that the lower lashes wipe the inside of the upper lid. Remember, however, that this method can also introduce particles into the eye.

If something is embedded in an eye, it should only be treated by a doctor or eye specialist. The best course of action is to apply a loose bandage to *both* eyes. This will help prevent the injured eye from moving. Keep the victim lying down and transport the person in that position.

Comprehension Check

Apply On the board list as many activities as possible that could cause hypothermia. Have the students pick five and write down precautions that could be taken for each activity to prevent hypothermia.

Life Choice Inventory

Apply Ask students to complete the Life Choice Inventory found in the Teacher Classroom Resources or the Online Learning Center.

Comprehension Check

Recall Write the word *frostbite* on the board. Make two columns labeled "Do" and "Don't." Fill each column with the dos and don'ts of treating a frostbite victim.

Comprehension Check

Recall Hyperthermia treatments are varied. Students may try sponging the victim's bare skin with cool water, applying cool packs, or placing the victim in a tub of cool water until the temperature is sufficiently lowered. They also can try fanning the victim to create a cooling draft, or moving the person into an air-conditioned space.

Comprehension Check

Describe Ask students what to do to treat a sprain. Remind students of the *rest, ice, compression,* and *elevation* procedure for treating sprains and other minor injuries.

Assess

Worksheets

A reproducible quiz for Section 6 is provided in the Teacher Classroom Resources.

Reproducible Chapter Tests A and B are provided in the Teacher Classroom Resources.

Close

Apply Divide the class into groups of five. Ask group members to describe a scene from a television show in which someone was injured. Each group should produce a two-paragraph report describing the incident and what rescue personnel did to treat the victim. Groups can then share their findings with the class.

To find supplemental information to suit your individual class, you may want to visit the following Web sites, where you can find additional Internet resources to enhance the study of this chapter. As with all Web sites, you should check these out first to be sure the information found there is appropriate for your students.

Your First Aid Kit

www.survival-center.com/firstaid/kit.htm

This is an excellent resource for which items you should carry in a well stocked first-aid kit.

American Heart Association CPR Guide www.americanheart.org

The American Heart Association establishes the standards for education in CPR training nationwide. It gives basic pointers on CPR and information on how to find classes for CPR certification.

CHAPTER 26 Planning Guide

Objectives	Features
• Identify ways human behaviors affect the world's air, water and, living things—and vice versa. • Determine the impact that consumption has on the world. • Identify ways individuals as well as the government can help curb the effects of pollution. • Identify lifestyle choices individuals can make to promote a healthy environment.	• *Applying Health Skills:* Communication Skills (page 703) • *What Teens Think:* Should We Be Doing More to Protect Our Environment? If So, What Should We Be Doing? (page 716) • *Q&A:* Voluntary Simplicity (pages 724–725)

Introduction

Teaching Support

Fast Files

- *Vocabulary:* Learning Vocabulary, Fill in the Blanks
- *Study Outline*
- *Reading Cloze*
- *Reteaching Activities:* You and Your Environment, Helping the Environment
- *Enrichment Activities:* Environmental Problems, Caring for the Environment, Protecting the Environment, Clean Up the Environment: A Group Project
- *Career Briefs:* Foresters and Conservation Scientists
- *Life Choice Inventory:* How Well Do You Care for the Environment?
- *Handouts:* Living A Simpler Lifestyle; Lifestyle Choices Affect the Environment and Health; Sound Intensities and Their Effects; Some Ways to Reduce, Reuse, and Recycle; Home Appliances and Global Warming; Energy Used by Appliances; Using Nontoxic Products in the Home; U. S. Public Health Service Objectives for the Nation; Resource Use in the United States and China Compared
- *Quizzes:* Sections 1–6
- *Tests:* Chapter 26 Test A, Chapter 26 Test B

Multimedia Support

- *ExamView® Assessment Suite*
- Online Learning Center

Introducing Chapter 26

Chapter Preview Activity

Ask students to list all of the products that they used this morning to get ready for school. Ask if they created any waste. If so, can this waste be recycled? Tell students that not only do people need to be aware of the items they purchase that cause waste, they also need to recognize that some waste can be recycled.

Not Enough Time?

Here are some suggestions to ensure that you cover the key topics in this chapter.

DAY 1 Complete the Chapter Preview Activity. Have students do the Life Choice Inventory. Assign students Sections 1 and 2 to read for homework.

DAY 2 Have students complete the activities provided for Sections 1 and 2.

DAY 3 Have students read Sections 3 and 4 prior to class. Have students complete the Preview Activity. Have students complete the activities provided for Sections 3 and 4.

DAY 4 Have students read Sections 5 and 6 prior to class. During class do a selection of the activities provided throughout Sections 5 and 6.

Bulletin Board Ideas

Have students bring in a variety of packaging that can be recycled, as well as some that cannot. Have students help you sort through the items and place each in its proper pile for recycling. Have students find places that will accept each type of item to be recycled. Then have students highlight these places on a map of your community, using different highlighter colors for each type of recyclable material. Make a key below the map that shows the colors on the map and which materials correspond. Display the map where it can be easily seen by all students.

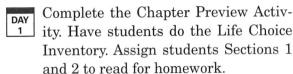

Answers:
1. True.
2. False. Refrigerators, hot water heaters, heaters, and air conditioners use more energy, because they are on all the time.
3. True.

 Writing Paragraphs will vary.

The Environment and You

Focus

Vocabulary Activity

Vocabulary worksheets are provided in the Teacher Classroom Resources.

Teach and Apply

Comprehension Check

Comprehend Ask students to define *environment* in a way that suggests they are separate from the environment. Then ask them to explain how a person and the environment are part of a single system. The environment supplies material making up the body; the environment provides energy; materials and energy flow through our bodies from the environment and back into the environment.

Class Activity

Analyze Distribute the Life Choice Inventory for Chapter 26. Have students read the scoring directions and complete the inventory. Have volunteers compare their scores. Were students surprised by their scores? Why or why not?

Assess

Worksheets

A reproducible quiz for Section 1 is provided in the Teacher Classroom Resources.

Close

Apply Walk with students around your school campus. After returning to the classroom, have students make two lists: one list will include choices people at the school have made to benefit the environment (example: recycling bin for aluminum cans); the second list will include choices people have made that will damage the environment (example: litter on the ground instead of in the trash cans).

Encourage students to keep their lists and use the information they gain in this chapter to develop ideas that will help change the damaging choices into beneficial choices.

SECTION 2 The Impact of Pollution

Focus

Vocabulary Activity

Vocabulary worksheets are provided in the Teacher Classroom Resources.

Teach and Apply

Group Activity

Evaluate Ask students to answer the question, "In what ways might your choice of food and clothing as a consumer affect the environment?" Discuss.

Comprehension Check

Comprehend The text identifies ten trends that are having a negative effect on our environment. Have the students study the list on pages 704–705, close their books, and practice writing the problems until they can list all ten. For extra credit they should be able to write a sentence explaining or describing something about the problem to indicate that they understand its meaning.

Class Activity

Apply Have students research community service projects aimed at protecting or cleaning up the local environment. Encourage students to create a service group or club at school to promote recycling or another environmental project. Have students create a plan for their service group and present their plan to the school principal for approval.

Assess

Worksheets

A reproducible quiz for Section 2 is provided in the Teacher Classroom Resources.

Close

Apply Bring in an item from the grocery store. Have students write the steps involved in getting this item to the shelf of the store for purchase. Have them tell how these steps affect our environment.

SECTION 3 Shopping

Focus

Vocabulary Activity

Vocabulary worksheets are provided in the Teacher Classroom Resources.

Teach and Apply

Background Information: Recycling

Point out to students that many products labeled "green" or "recyclable" are, in practice, neither. Many plastic items fall into this category. Plastic containers of all sorts are now printed with recycling symbols. Recycling centers, however, may only be able to handle certain kinds of plastics. The other plastics, even though they bear the symbol, are actually throwaway types. Another scam is using the recycling label on paper products that actually contain no paper that has been through human hands.

Learning with Visuals

Apply Have the students create a poster with an abbreviated version of the list on page 710. Tell students to present this information to their family and to evaluate what types of products they purchase. They can hang the poster on their refrigerators at home as a reminder to choose green products.

Comprehension Check

Comprehend Have students research the recycling policy for your school cafeteria. Can they suggest improvements to make it more efficient?

If there is no recycling program, research the possibility of starting one in your school. Ask for help from the school administration and school board, if necessary.

Assess

Worksheets

A reproducible quiz for Section 3 is provided in the Teacher Classroom Resources.

Close

Evaluate Start a discussion with a statement such as, "People are more important than the environment or a bunch of trees. If we save trees, then people will die of starvation."

SECTION 4 — Home Energy Use

Focus

Vocabulary Activity

Vocabulary worksheets are provided in the Teacher Classroom Resources.

Teach and Apply

Class Activity

Evaluate Have students think of a time when the electricity went out in their homes. Ask students what they had to go without during that time and what they did for entertainment. Find out whether students think they could live with fewer appliances. Ask them how they would prepare for another power outage if they knew in advance that it would happen. Have them imagine what life might be like if energy were rationed.

Class Activity

Apply Ask students to conduct research at the library or on the Internet to learn of ways their families can make their homes more energy-efficient. Ask about alternative sources of energy, how well they work, and the cost of installation and regular use.

Group Activity

Apply After reading the chapter, ask students to research other ways to save energy in the home. Turning off lights in empty rooms, closing doors when the air condition is on, closing refrigerator doors, and not running tap water while brushing your teeth are examples of ways to safe energy. There are several measures you can use to save water-heating energy. You can set the heater at 120 degrees Fahrenheit, no hotter. You can put it on a timer. You can wrap it in a blanket for insulation (and wrap the pipes carrying the hot water). You can also install heat-trapping devices at the inlets to keep heat from creeping along the lines when the water is standing. When buying a water heater, people can choose smaller, instant-type heaters, and gas or solar heaters, rather than electric.

Assess

Worksheets

A reproducible quiz for Section 4 is provided in the Teacher Classroom Resources.

Close

Recall Ask students to list the different types of energy and tell why each is important in our attempts to conserve energy resources, or make posters with environmental slogans to be displayed around the school.

Water Use and Garbage

Focus

Vocabulary Activity

Vocabulary worksheets are provided in the Teacher Classroom Resources.

Teach and Apply

Class Activity

Evaluate The first part of this section gives several suggestions for conserving water. Ask students what strategies they use to conserve water. Are they similar to the ones discussed in the chapter? What else can you do?

Class Activity

Apply Have students tell you what type of containers they carry their lunches in. Multiply the percentage of the types of containers in your class by the entire student body to represent how much energy might be wasted each day in one school in the form of containers. Discuss how habits can be changed to save energy.

Assess

Worksheets

A reproducible quiz for Section 5 is provided in the Teacher Classroom Resources.

Close

Apply Have students brainstorm environmental slogans. You might want to buy T-shirt paints and tell students to bring a T-shirt to class to decorate with their environmental slogan.

 **Hunger and the Environment**

Focus

Vocabulary Activity

Vocabulary worksheets are provided in the Teacher Classroom Resources.

Teach and Apply

Class Activity

Evaluate Have students write a short paragraph describing all the things that improve their quality of life and are taken for granted. Pick some things to which a person who is poor, homeless, or hungry would probably not have access. Compare lists in class and discuss what other possibilities could be included.

Comprehension Check

Comprehend The beginning of Section 6 contains numerous facts and examples of worldwide problems resulting from hunger and poverty. Have students reread this information and pick the one fact or example that makes the greatest impression on them. Have each student state which piece of information they picked and why.

Group Activity

Analyze Before students read the part of Section 6 entitled "Poverty, Hunger, and Overpopulation" on page 722, ask them if they think couples in poverty would be more or less likely to have large families. Ask for reasons for their opinions. They will probably be surprised that poverty and hunger actually encourage larger families. Why is that?

Assess

Worksheets

A reproducible quiz for Section 6 is provided in the Teacher Classroom Resources.

Reproducible Chapter Tests A and B are provided in the Teacher Classroom Resources.

Close

Apply

1. Have students brainstorm a list of ways they can help alleviate local hunger problems. Discuss with students ways that they could go about accomplishing these tasks.

2. Have students draw an illustration showing poverty and starvation as they imagine it. Tell them that their artwork should represent some of the feelings the people living in that situation might be experiencing.

Go Online

To find supplemental information to suit your individual class, you may want to visit the following Web sites, where you can find additional Internet resources to enhance the study of this chapter. As with all Web sites, you should check these out first to be sure the information found there is appropriate for your students.

The Internet Consumer Recycling Guide www.obviously.com/recycle/

This site contains useful information on how to recycle postconsumer waste. It covers everything from home to garden to business to industrial waste.

United States Environmental Protection Agency—Office of Water

www.epa.gov/ow/

This is a very informative site regarding water use, including discussions of how to protect our water resources.

CHAPTER 27 Planning Guide

CHAPTER 27 The Consumer and the Health Care System

Objectives

- Learn the different approaches to health care.
- Determine the best health insurance to fit individual needs.
- Identify ways to research and select a credible medical provider.

Features

- **Health Skills:** Tips for Emergency Room Visits (page 736)
- **Health Skills:** Selecting and Using Medical Care Facilities (page 737)
- **Health Skills:** Choosing a Health Care Provider (page 741)
- **Consumer Skills Activity:** Genuine and Fake Credentials (page 742)
- **Q&A:** Health Claims (pages 744–745)

Introduction

Teaching Support

Fast Files

- *Vocabulary:* Learning Vocabulary, Fill in the Blanks
- *Study Outline*
- *Reading Cloze*
- *Reteaching Activities:* How Will I Pay for My Health Care?, Making an Informed Decision About Your Physician
- *Enrichment Activities:* Fee (Fi Fo Fum), Who Can Help?, Health Care Expectations. What's Your Opinion?
- *Career Briefs:* Insurance Agents and Brokers
- *Handouts:* Health Care Delivery, Past, and Present/Future; Guidelines for Chapter Project; Advertising of Drugs
- *Quizzes:* Sections 1–3
- *Tests:* Chapter 27 Test A, Chapter 27 Test B

Multimedia Support

- *ExamView® Assessment Suite*
- Online Learning Center

Introducing Chapter 27

Chapter Preview Activity

Have students conduct research to find listings of various medical services and health care providers. Students should make a list of the categories of doctors advertising on the Internet or other sources.

 Not Enough Time?

Here are some suggestions to ensure that you cover the key topics in this chapter.

 On the day prior to beginning Chapter 27, ask students to read the chapter so they will be ready to discuss it in class. On Day 1, start with the Chapter Preview Activity. Review payment options and availability of resources in your community. Evaluate with the Section Reviews.

 On Day 2 begin by reviewing Section 3. Discuss health resources in your community. Close the class with the Section and Chapter Reviews.

Bulletin Board Ideas

List as many health care providers as you can on a bulletin board where everyone can see. Discuss with the students why there are so many options for health care. Tell students that doctors may specialize in different areas of medicine. You might suggest that students bring in pictures of their doctors or health care providers to put faces to the types of providers.

Answers:

1. False. You may need as many as five different kinds of insurance. Even then, specific medical needs might not be covered.

2. True.

3. True.

 Writing Paragraphs will vary.

SECTION 1 — Paying for Health Care

Focus

Vocabulary Activity

Vocabulary worksheets are provided in the Teacher Classroom Resources.

Teach and Apply

Comprehension Check

Comprehend Ask students to compare HMO plans to other types of health insurance. Students should see that belonging to an HMO is the same as buying any other type of health insurance. You pay premiums for your health insurance whether you use any of the benefits or not. You pay a monthly fee to the HMO whether you use it or not. Other health insurance policies do not cover preventive care, but HMO plans usually do.

Assess

Worksheets

A reproducible quiz for Section 1 is provided in the Teacher Classroom Resources.

Close

Analyze. Have students conduct research in the library or on the Internet to learn about different types of health insurance plans. Have students compare two plans from the same company, and write a one-page report showing the benefits and drawbacks of each plan. Students should include the cost of each plan, if possible.

SECTION 2 — Our Health Care System

Focus

Vocabulary Activity

Vocabulary worksheets are provided in the Teacher Classroom Resources.

Teach and Apply

Class Activity

Analyze Ask students if they think the fact that people live longer increases or decreases the cost of health insurance. Students might think that people are living longer and must be healthier, causing insurance rates to go down. However, the opposite is true. Because people live longer, they need care for longer periods of time later in life.

Group Activity

Synthesize Ask students to conduct research and create a list of several different types of health care facilities and their primary functions. Students should write a two-page paper briefly describing the functions of their chosen facility.

Pursuing Wellness

Analyze Ask students to pretend that they are adults with a spouse and two young children. Assign an income level to students, the health status of their family, and whether they live in a community with considerable or few resources. Ask them to determine the family's health care needs and options. Then ask students to choose a plan that is affordable and covers the family's needs. Review the options and choices in class.

Assess

Worksheets

A reproducible quiz for Section 2 is provided in the Teacher Classroom Resources.

Close

Recall Have students create a brochure that discuss the problems and advantages of our health care system (refer to Figure 27.3 on page 738).

SECTION 3

Choosing Health Care Providers

Focus

Vocabulary Activity

Vocabulary worksheets are provided in the Teacher Classroom Resources.

Teach and Apply

Group Activity

Apply Have students research different kinds of health care careers and report to the class. They should include information such as training or schooling, job outlook, employment practices, working conditions, earnings, and general advantages and disadvantages.

Comprehension Check

Describe Ask students to define the term *diagnosis*. Diagnosis means the use of scientific and skillful methods to establish the nature of a person's illness. Ask students to name some of the questions they should ask a doctor when they are diagnosed with an illness.

Assess

Worksheets

A reproducible quiz for Section 3 is provided in the Teacher Classroom Resources.

Reproducible Chapter Tests A and B are provided in the Teacher Classroom Resources.

Close

Discuss Ask students to summarize ways that they can be good health care consumers. What information should they look for when considering health care purchases? What questions should they ask? What organizations can they contact to obtain detailed information on health care products and services?

G⊙ Online

To find supplemental information to suit your individual class, you may want to visit the following Web sites, where you can find additional Internet resources to enhance the study of this chapter. As with all Web sites, you should check these out first to be sure the information found there is appropriate for your students.

Institute for Health Freedom
www.ForHealthFreedom.org/
This site is devoted to educating people about the ability to choose their own medical care.

Agency for Health Care Research and Quality www.ahcpr.gov/
As an agency of the United States Department of Health and Human Services, this site describes research being conducted to find ways to reduce costs and help consumers be better informed about health care choices.

HEALTH
Making Life Choices

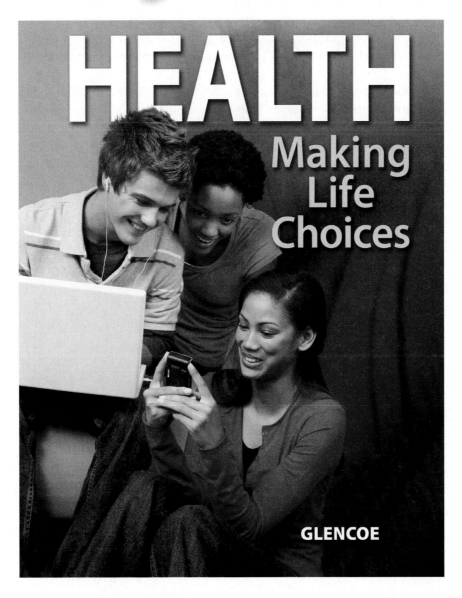

HEALTH
Making Life Choices

GLENCOE

Frances Sizer Webb   **Linda Kelly DeBruyne**

 Glencoe

About the Authors

Frances Sizer Webb, MS, RD, FADA, received an Associate of Arts in Nursing from Miami-Dade Community College in 1977; she attended Florida State University's College of Human Sciences where, in 1980, she received her BS, and in 1982, her MS in nutrition. She has counseled clients in the University's stress-reduction clinic and served as consultant to schools and alcoholism programs in Florida. Among her writings are the textbooks *Nutrition: Concepts and Controversies,* now entering its twelfth edition; *Life Choices: Health Concepts and Strategies; Essential Life Choices;* and *The Fitness Triad: Motivation, Training, and Nutrition.* She has published in *Shape* magazine, in the newsletter *Healthline,* and in the *Journal of Chemical Senses.* She is vice-president and a founding member of Nutrition and Health Associates, an information resource center in Tallahassee, Florida, now entering its twenty-fifth year. She now devotes full time to writing and lecturing on topics in health and nutrition. In her free time, she actively supports *ECHO,* a Tallahassee-based resource that provides emergency food, clothing, job readiness training, and other assistance to people in crisis.

Linda Kelly DeBruyne, MS, RD, received her BS in 1980 and her MS in 1982 in nutrition and food science at the Florida State University. She is also a founding member of Nutrition and Health Associates, where her specialty areas are fitness and life-cycle nutrition. Her other textbooks are *Life Span Nutrition: Conception through Life; The Fitness Triad: Motivation, Training, and Nutrition; Nutrition for Health and Healthcare,* and *Nutrition and Diet Therapy.* She also serves as consultant to a group of Tallahassee pediatricians for whom she teaches infant nutrition classes to parents. She is a member of the American Dietetic Association.

Glencoe

The McGraw-Hill Companies

Printed in the United States of America.

Send all inquiries to:
Glencoe/McGraw-Hill
21600 Oxnard Street, Suite 500
Woodland Hills, CA 91367

ISBN:	978-0-07-880043-6	(Student Edition)
MHID:	0-07-880043-9	(Student Edition)
ISBN:	978-0-07-880735-0	(Teacher Annotated Edition)
MHID:	0-07-880735-2	(Teacher Annotated Edition)

1 2 3 4 5 6 7 8 9 027/043 13 12 11 10 09 08

Health Specialist Reviewers

Elizabeth M. Casparian, Ph.D.
HiTOPS
Princeton, NJ

Judy Chiasson, Ph.D.
Los Angeles Unified School District
Los Angeles, CA

Nora Gelperin, M.Ed.
Rutgers University
Piscataway, NJ

Susan Haas, M.D.
Boston Medical Center
Boston, MA

Mary Krueger, Ph.D.
Bowling Green State University
Bowling Green, OH

Susan Milstein, Ed.D.
Montgomery College
Rockville, MD

Ismael Nuño, M.D.
University of Southern California, Keck School of Medicine
Los Angeles, CA

Martha R. Roper, M.A.
Parkway South High School
Manchester, MO

Teacher Reviewers

Joel R. Barton, III, Ph.D.
Lamar University
Beaumont, TX

Cheryl Bower
Newberg High School
Newberg, OR

Terry Collins
Oxnard High School
Oxnard, CA

Charlene Cook
Goshen High School
Goshen, IN

Sue Couch, Ed.D.
Texas Tech University
Lubbock, TX

Deneise Crace
Meridian High School
Meridian, ID

Marge Danielson, M.S., MFCC
Thousand Oaks, CA

Paul Dean
Pine Bluff High School
Pine Bluff, AR

Thomas Dolde
Connellsville Area High School
Connellsville, PA

Joleen Eiklenborg
Education Service Center
Waco, TX

Rick Ford
Carter High School
Strawberry Plains, TN

Ira Gibel
Oceanside High School
Oceanside, NY

Lillian Goodman, R.N., M.Ed.
Los Angeles Unified School District
Los Angeles, CA

Paige Harbough, M.D.
Tallahassee, FL

Rhonda Helgerson
Del Rio High School
Del Rio, TX

Dee Herman
Northside High School
Fort Wayne, IN

Jeff Herring, M.S., LMFT
Tallahassee, FL

Dr. Gay James
Southwest Texas State University
San Marcos, TX

Elaine Jones
Kenwood Academy
Chicago, IL

Nancy Kidd
Oshkosh North High School
Oshkosh, WI

Patricia Kosiba
P.D. Schreiber High School
Port Washington, NY

Roxanna Laycox
West Carrollton High School
West Carrollton, OH

Contributors

Charles Lee Libby
East Central High School
San Antonio, TX

John Markham
Northbrook High School
Houston, TX

Carol Martin
Pekin Community High School
Pekin, IL

Sandy Mayon
Robert E. Lee High School
Baytown, TX

Tim McCormick
Wheeling Park High School
Wheeling, WV

Judith McGuire
Boone County High School
Florence, KY

Ron Meurer
West Mesa High School
Albuquerque, NM

Bruce Miller
Heritage High School
Broadlands, IL

Timothy Mitchell
Bellaire High School
Bellaire, TX

Betzy Nelson
Orange Park High School
Orange Park, FL

Peter Olson
South Carroll High School
Sykesville, MD

Don Rogers
Richmond High School
Richmond, IN

Kathleen Schaefer
Gates Chili High School
Rochester, NY

Dr. Roger Shipley
Texas Woman's University
Denton, TX

Michael Smith
Wilson High School
Long Beach, CA

Marlene Snyder
Sharon High School
Sharon, PA

Elaine Stover, M.A.
Thousand Oaks, CA

Steven Sykes
Harrison Central High School
Gulfport, MS

Linda Troolin
East High School
Duluth, MN

Lori Turner
Northport, AL

Todd Urbanek
Boswell High School
Fort Worth, TX

Laura Van Dellen
Bell High School
Los Angeles, CA

Tara Wah, M.D.
Tallahassee, FL

Glenda Warner
Ferncreek High School
Louisville, KY

Dennis Weisz
Sioux City West High School
Sioux City, IA

Connie Wood
Orange Park High School
Orange Park, FL

Jim Wussow
Plano Independent School
District
Plano, TX

Contents in Brief

Table of Contents

Unit 3 **Your Physical Health**

Table of Contents

Table of Contents

Table of Contents

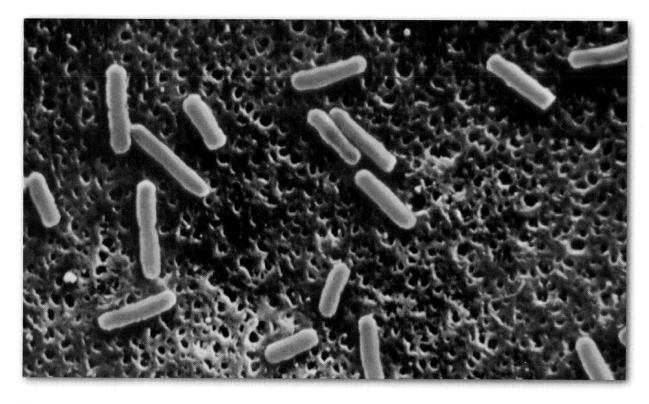

Table of Contents

Feature Contents

APPLYING Health Skills

Feature Contents

Consumer SKILLS ACTIVITY

What Teens THINK

Feature Contents

Feature Contents

Health Skills

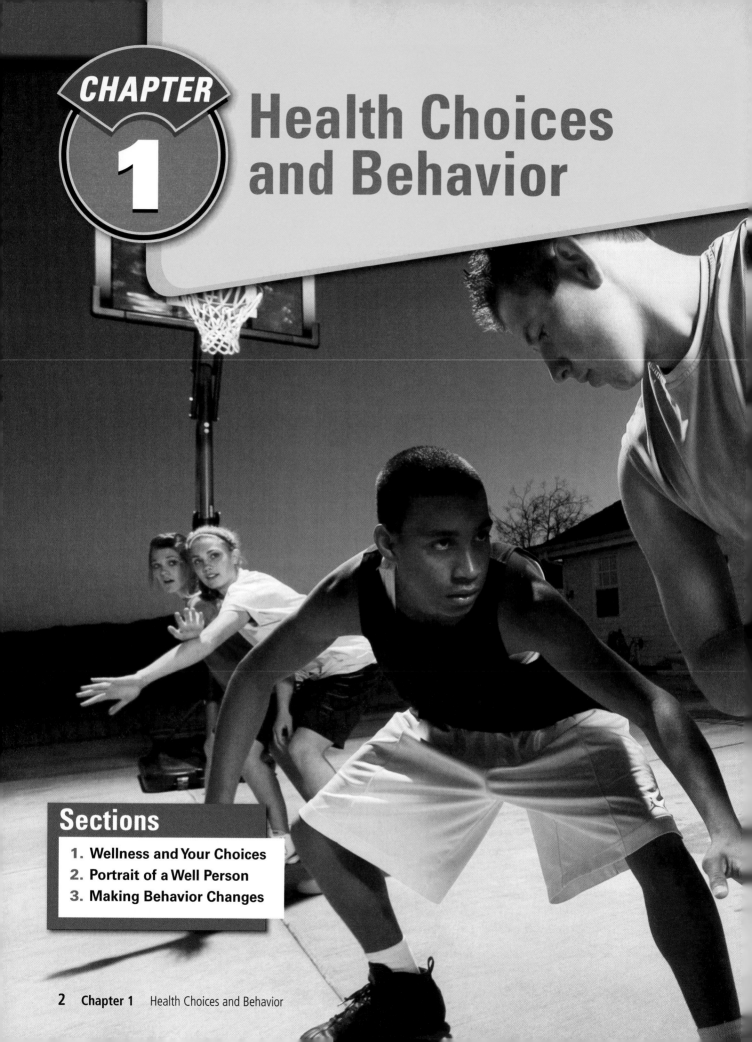

CHAPTER 1

Health Choices and Behavior

Sections

1. Wellness and Your Choices
2. Portrait of a Well Person
3. Making Behavior Changes

This book is about enjoying life. It challenges you to learn about and to explore emotional health, nutrition, and disease prevention, to name a few. The book aims to help you move forward in all these areas with confidence.

This is an ambitious goal, especially since everyone already has at least some experience in, and knowledge about, these subject areas. Most schoolwork ensures that people learn the basics of language and mathematics. However, by using these basics, people can also learn the essential life-management skills, the skills that help a person to realize his or her potential to be well and enjoy life. If you apply yourself as you read and study this book, you can fill in important gaps in your own knowledge. You can also grow more successful at taking care of yourself.

Fact or Fiction?

What Do You Think?
Is each statement true or false? If you think it's false, explain what's true.

1. People make hundreds of choices every day that affect their health.
2. The way adults contract most diseases is by catching them from somebody else.
3. Accidents are among the major causes of death for teens.

 Writing Think about the choices you make every day. Why are these choices so important to your personal health? Write a paragraph about how the choices you make can affect your health.

(Answers on page 23)

Go Online
Visit **glencoe.com** and complete the Life Choice Inventory for Chapter 1.

SECTION 1

Wellness and Your Choices

You make hundreds of choices every day—what to eat, whom to be friends with, how active to be, when to sleep, and more. In making these daily choices, you affect your **health**, *freedom from physical disease, poor physical condition, social maladjustment, and other negative states,* whether you mean to or not. Today's choices will either improve you or harm you. Plus, their effects will multiply over time. Today's choices, repeated for a week, will have seven times the impact. Repeated every day for a year, they will have 365 times the effect on your health. Over years, the effects accumulate still further.

Today's choices affect not only your physical health, but also your **wellness**—*maximum well-being, the top of the range of health states.* Consider, first, your physical health.

Vocabulary

health
wellness
chronological age
physiological age
centenarians

Welcome to
Making Life Choices

Today's Choices

✔ *Be physically active*

✔ *Relax*

✔ *Eat healthfully*

✔ *Drink water*

✔ *Brush and floss teeth*

✔ *Stay smoke-free*

✔ *Stay alcohol-free*

✔ *Stay drug-free*

✔ *Take safety precautions*

✔ *Enjoy life*

■ **Figure 1.1** *Making healthy lifestyle choices today will enable you to live a happier, more healthful life. What do you do to stay in good health?*

Caption Answer: Sample answer: "I ride my bike to school."

Physical Health Yesterday and Today

MAIN IDEA ▶ The leading causes of death have changed over time.

If you use the information presented in this book, you can make choices today that will improve your chances of living a long, healthy life. In the past, many children and teens, as well as older people, died helplessly of infectious diseases, diseases that are caused by infecting organisms and can be passed from person to person. These diseases were poorly understood and unpreventable. Today, however, that happens less often. Some infectious diseases do still threaten young people in our society and must be taken seriously. Their causes are known, though, and the great majority of these diseases are preventable. A later chapter shows how to prevent infectious diseases.

Daily Choices Affect Your Health

Lifestyle choices are daily choices of how to treat the body and mind. People who consistently make poor lifestyle choices, on a daily basis, can expect to suffer from lifestyle diseases, diseases that are made likely by the neglect of the body. Lifestyle diseases that may be caused by neglect include heart disease, lung disease, cancer, diabetes and liver disease.

Figure 1.2 contrasts the major causes of death from more than a century ago with those today. It shows that while people used to "catch" most of their deadly diseases from disease agents ("germs"), they now are more likely to "contract" diseases because of the ways they choose to live.

| Figure 1.2 | The Leading Causes of Death |

The lists to the right show, in order, the leading causes of death for the whole U.S. population. For teens today, accidents are the leading cause of death.

1890s
Flu
Pneumonia
Tuberculosis
Digestive diseases
Bronchitis
Scarlet fever
Stroke
Kidney disease

2000s
Heart disease
Cancer
Stroke
Chronic lung disease
Pneumonia/flu
Diabetes
Other accidents
Motor vehicle accidents
Suicide
Kidney failure

Figure 1.3

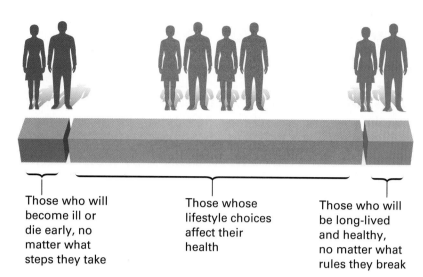

Lifestyle Choices Made Today Affect Health in Later Life

The vast majority of people affect their health by the choices they make. Only a few people with excellent health habits have their lives cut short by disease. Only a few people who ignore all health warnings have long lives and remain healthy.

Those who will become ill or die early, no matter what steps they take

Those whose lifestyle choices affect their health

Those who will be long-lived and healthy, no matter what rules they break

When people do not follow a healthy lifestyle they are likely to suffer from lifestyle diseases. The choice to smoke, for example, is a major cause of lung disease. Poor choices in nutrition and physical activity can make heart disease and diabetes likely. **Figure 1.3** shows that the majority of people affect their own health by the choices they make.

Family Medical History and Environment

Making good choices throughout your life can have a positive effect on your health as you get older. That means eating a healthy diet most of the time, maintaining a healthy weight, getting regular exercise, avoiding tobacco and other substances. However, some people may do all the right things and still get a disease such as heart disease, lung disease, liver disease, diabetes, or cancer. That's because the behavior isn't solely responsible for the development of disease. Two factors besides people's own choices that can cause these diseases are heredity and the environment.

Heredity In some people the tendency to develop certain diseases may be common within a family. Family members may carry a gene that makes it more likely that a person in that family will get diseases such as cancer. Being a member of such a family doesn't mean that a person is certain to get a disease. It does mean that a person may be more likely to get a disease. However, eating a healthy diet, exercising regularly, avoiding tobacco and other substances can still reduce the person's risk, even if they have a family history for certain diseases.

Environment The other cause is factors in the environment. This includes infectious diseases and also diseases caused by pollution of the air, water, and food. You will learn more about how the environment affects health in Chapter 26. The environment you live in plays an important role in your health. Environmental impacts include physical, social, and cultural environmental factors.

- Physical environment refers to the place where you live. In cities, several environmental factors can impact your health. These include air pollution, the availability of safe places to play, access to parks and other recreational facilities, and access to medical care.

- Social environment refers to the people around you, including your family and friends. If your parents live an active, healthy lifestyle, chances are that you will too. Having friends who encourage you to play sports or engage in fitness-related activities will also impact your health.

- Cultural environment refers to the beliefs and customs that your family practices. Your family's culture can impact the food you eat, whether or not exercise, and other aspects of your life.

The Power of Taking Control

The more you learn, the more control you can gain. **Figure 1.5** on page 8 shows that your wellness can exist anywhere along a line, from maximum wellness on the one end to total failure to function (death) on the other.

Where would you like to be on this line? If you read the figure, you'll see that it also shows how your choices affect your position on the wellness line.

When people understand that they have some control over their health, they realize that the responsibility for their health is also theirs. Taking responsibility lays the foundation for lifelong health. It is central to wellness, as **Figure 1.6** on page 10 demonstrates.

Class Activity.
Analyze:

- Organize students into groups of two or three.

- Ask each group to develop a list of questions to determine how changes in society over the past 40 to 50 years have led to lifestyle changes. Ask each group to interview one senior citizen, using the questions the group wrote.

- Each group should then write a two-page essay describing how the changes in society have impacted health.

■ **Figure 1.4** *People who live long lives often say they have made healthy decisions such as staying physically active, eating nutritious foods, not smoking, and many others. What changes can you make now so you can live a longer, more healthful life?*

Caption Answer: I can exercise with friends, and I can choose to eat healthier foods.

Figure 1.5   **The Wellness Line**

How well do you meet your needs? The arrow below shows that no matter how well you maintain your health today, you may still be able to improve it in the future. Likewise, a person who is well today can slip down in the scale in the future by not maintaining health-promoting habits.

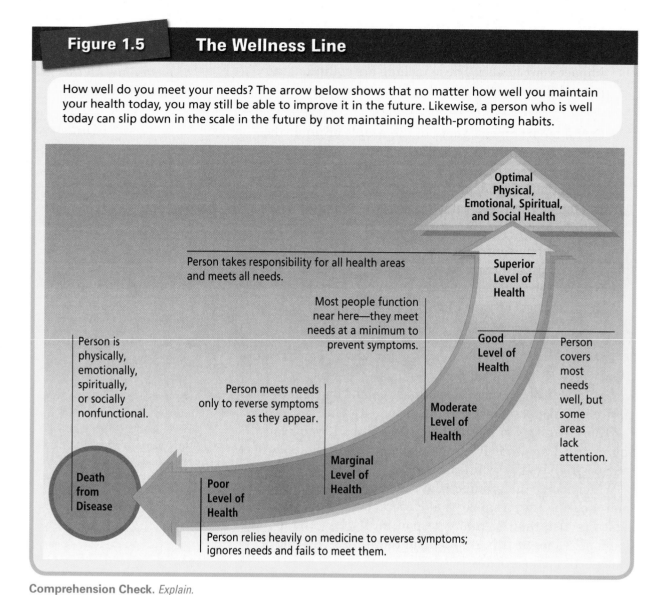

Comprehension Check. *Explain.* Explain to students that a *continuum* is something that changes gradually from one end to the other. A continuum cannot be divided into two halves (good and bad). Health is shown on a continuum because you can't separate people into two groups and say the people on one side have good health and the people on the other side have bad health. Health and wellness are matters of degree.

Age: A Matter of Definition

MAIN IDEA ▶ Lifestyle choices affect overall health and even the length of life.

As fine, strong, and young as you are right now, you already carry within you the older person you will become. Will that person, at 30, 60, or 90 years of age, be healthy and strong too? You can determine the answer to that question. Of course, chance may change your plans. Accidents or diseases may occur. You can influence your health, even in terms of how old you will be.

"Wait a minute," you may say. "When I've lived 60 years, I'll be 60 years old. No one can change that." That's true, but only on the calendar. Your **chronological age**—*age as measured in years from date of birth*—after 60 years will indeed be 60, but what about your **physiological age**, *age as estimated from the body's health and probable life expectancy?*

► Objectives
- State possible options in a situation involving a health-related decision.
- Apply decision-making skills to make a health-promoting decision.

All Work and No Play

Miguel works after school for several hours three days a week. It's the first time he has worked during the school year. He's managing to keep up with his schoolwork and maintain his good grades. Some of Miguel's friends are starting a running club to stay fit, and they want Miguel to join them. They plan to meet two weekdays after school and on Saturday afternoons.

Miguel would like to join the club. He wants to stay fit and also spend more time with his friends. Right now, he isn't getting much exercise, and he mainly sees his friends just at school. On the other hand, Miguel doesn't want to give up his job or let his grades slip. He's having a hard time deciding what to do.

► Identify the Problem
1. What decision is Miguel trying to make?

► Form an Action Plan
2. List two of Miguel's options, and state possible outcomes of each option.
3. What does Miguel value, and how does each option fit with his values?
4. Which option do you think would be better for Miguel's health? If he decides on this option, how could he tell whether he made the right decision?

► What Did You Learn?
5. Think of a recent health-related decision that you made. How did your values influence the option you chose?

Two scientists have shown that people can dramatically alter their physiological age. These scientists studied nearly 7,000 adults in California and noted that some people seemed younger, and others older, than their years. To find out what made the difference, the scientists focused on the lifestyle habits of the people they were studying. Certain practices seemed to have the most impact on the condition of these people's body systems—that is, on their physiological age. The five factors were:

- Get eight to nine hours of sleep each night.
- Eat regular, nutritious meals, including breakfast.
- Engage in regular physical activity.
- Avoid the use of tobacco, alcohol, and other drugs.
- Maintain a healthy weight.

Applying Health Skills:

1. Miguel is trying to decide whether to join his friends' running club.
2. Not join the club and to join the club. Not joining the club may lead to lowered fitness and spending less time with friends. Joining the club and running only when he has the time will lead to greater fitness and spending more time with friends.
3. Miguel values his job, good grades, staying fit, and his friends. Not joining the club fits with his first two values. Joining the club but running only when he has time fits with all four values.
4. Joining the club and running would maintain Miguel's health. If he joins the club, and can keep working and not let his grades slip, he has made the right decision.
5. Answers will vary.

Personal Responsibility is Central to Wellness

These four areas of wellness are made up of many other health components. For example, the health of the environment contributes to both physical and social wellness; fitness contributes to physical and mental/emotional wellness.

Worksheets: A reproducible quiz for Section 1 is provided in the Teacher Classroom Resources.

Lifelong health habits also affect the length of life. Evidence comes from the study of **centenarians,** *people who have reached the age of 100 years old or older.* Scientists are curious to know how these people's lifestyles differ from those of people who died earlier in life. Often, the same factors turn up. Centenarians are usually well nourished, but not overweight. They usually are nonsmokers and don't abuse alcohol or other drugs. They maintain regular patterns of eating and sleeping. Above all, they are usually physically active.

SECTION 1 Review

1. Chronological age is a person's age measured in years from date of birth. Physiological age is an estimated age based on the body's health and probable life expectancy.

2. A lifestyle disease is a disease caused by neglect of the body.

3. Although there are still some life-threatening infectious diseases, doctors today know the causes of theses diseases and the majority of cases are preventable.

4. Possible answers: Heart disease, lung diseases, cancer, diabetes, liver disease

5. Answers will vary.

Reviewing the Vocabulary

Review the vocabulary on page 4. Then answer these questions.

1. Define *chronological age.*
2. What is a *lifestyle disease*?

Reviewing the Facts

3. Analyze. Explain why infectious diseases of today do less harm than they did 100 years ago.
4. Recall. List three examples of lifestyle diseases described in this section.

Writing Critically

5. Personal. Describe choices you can make now that will enhance your future wellness.

For more vocabulary practice, play the eFlashcards game at **glencoe.com.**

Portrait of a Well Person

Wellness expresses itself in all parts of your life: not only physical, but also mental/emotional, spiritual, and social health. To show you what high goals you can aim for in your own life, the next sections describe a superbly well person. The descriptions are roughly in the order of the chapters to come.

Mental/Emotional and Spiritual Health

MAIN IDEA ▶ Mental/emotional and spiritual health are a part of wellness.

A well person works on developing many mental/emotional and spiritual strengths. Among other things, the person:

- Maintains a strong sense of self.
- Is willing to accept new ideas and try new behaviors.
- Handles setbacks without loss of self-esteem.
- Is aware of emotions, and manages and expresses them appropriately.
- Recognizes emotional problems in self or others, and seeks help when needed.
- Feels that life has meaning.
- Successfully manages stress with skill and enjoyment, not letting it become overwhelming.

Preview Activity.
Analyze:

- Divide the class into three groups. Assign each group one category of health: Physical, Social, Mental/Emotional, and Spiritual.

- Give the groups five minutes to develop a list of qualities for their aspect of health.

- After the groups have developed their lists, lead a class discussion, asking students to share their ideas. Point out to students how the three aspects of health are related.

■ **Figure 1.7** *Wellness is expressed by your physical, mental/emotional, spiritual, and social health. What can you do to have good mental/ emotional and spiritual health?*

Caption Answer: Maintain a strong sense of self.

Understanding Health News

A news reader who had stopped eating butter years ago to improve his heart's health complained after reading this headline: Margarine Fat as Bad as Butter for Heart Health. "Do you mean that I could have been eating butter all these years? That's it. I quit. No more health changes for me."

The reader's response is quite understandable. Behavior changes take effort to make and are hard to continue. When science appears to change its advice, it is difficult to know what is really true.

Many people are confused by today's health news, and especially by information from the Internet. They can learn how to read health news and to judge information on science and reporting.

Many Studies, Not Single Findings

In science, the findings of a single study never prove or disprove anything. Many studies on the same topic are needed to confirm or disprove a finding. Each study contributes to the whole picture. It takes many studies to tell the story. News media, however, report every study as if it solved a mystery. The excitement of a "breakthrough" in the headlines makes for interesting reading, and sells more magazines and newspapers.

To spot exaggerations of science, watch for phrases like these: "Now we know...," "The answer has been found...," "This study proves...," "The truth is...," or "In a startling finding..." Real scientific reporting never uses such phrases, but instead sounds like this: "Our finding supports the idea...," "The possibility is raised...," or "More research will help to reveal..."

Readers seeking simple answers to complex health problems often believe headlines, and try to apply them right away. It is better to read the whole story with an educated eye. In the end, use common sense.

Internet Know-How

Information on the Internet should be read in the same ways as news. Many false reports there appear to be reliable. Sites with addresses ending in ".gov" are often reliable because government agencies approve their content.

Use a Critical Eye

When a headline tries to shock you with a new "answer" to a health question, or the Internet tries to convince you something is true, read the whole story critically. It could indeed be a breakthrough; however, it could be a story to sell newspapers and magazines, not to offer balanced health information.

 Writing

1. Why are many studies needed to confirm or disprove a scientific finding?
2. Why do you think people are so anxious to believe news media reports about scientific "breakthroughs"?

You might wonder if spiritual health means belonging to any particular religious organization. It could, but it doesn't have to. It does mean having a feeling of purpose and a sense of values in life.

Physical Health and Preventive Care

A well person also values physical health and works to maintain it. Among other things, the person:

- Gets eight to nine hours of sleep each night.
- Eats nutritious foods.
- Maintains an appropriate weight.
- Works to achieve and maintain physical activity.
- Does not use any drugs, including alcohol and tobacco.
- Takes preventive measures for personal safety.
- Takes measures to prevent infectious diseases.
- Analyzes health information and products.
- When necessary, uses the health care system wisely.

Social Health

A well person realizes that other people and groups are an important part of life. The person also:

- Develops supportive friendships.
- Effectively resolves conflicts.
- Socializes well with others without the influence of alcohol or other drugs.
- Develops and maintains psychological intimacy with others.
- Can form a successful long-term partnership.
- Understands and accepts his or her sexuality.
- Understands the risks of sexually transmitted diseases and pregnancy and takes responsibility for his or her own behavior.
- Continues growing, learning, and facing new challenges throughout life.
- Knows what is involved in facing death (one's own or someone else's) and accepts grief in all of its stages.
- Relates to the larger environment (home, community, world) and takes a share of the responsibility for it.

Figure 1.8 on page 14 sums up all that has been said so far. Outside factors affect health, but daily decisions do too. The descriptions given here not only define wellness but imply actions to achieve it. The Health Skills sidebars throughout this book are about taking action—they suggest what to do.

Health Skills

Reading Health News

Read a health news article, and answer the following questions:

- What type of language does the writer use? Health news should suggest the experimental nature of science.
- Does the report mention other studies?
- What methods did researchers use to perform the study? Methods should be described in detail.
- Who is doing the reporting? Good reporters often have a science background.
- Is the finding meaningful? Can you apply it to yourself?

Figure 1.8

The Factors That Affect Health

Heredity, environment, and available health care affect your health. Daily choices do too.

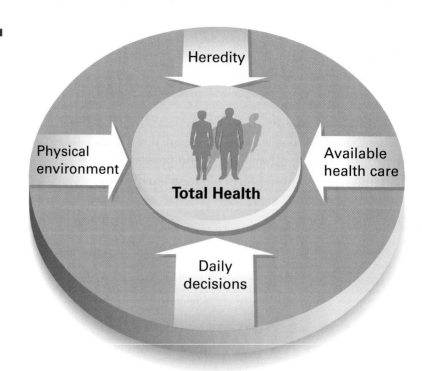

Heredity

Physical environment

Total Health

Available health care

Daily decisions

Worksheets: A reproducible quiz for Section 2 is provided in the Teacher Classroom Resources.

1. Physical health, mental/emotional health, spiritual health, and social health

2. A well person maintains a strong sense of self, is willing to accept new ideas and try new behaviors, and handles setbacks without loss of self-esteem, maintains an appropriate weight, avoids the use of tobacco, alcohol, and other illegal drugs, and takes preventive measures to maintain personal safety, develops supportive friendships, and effectively resolves conflicts.

3. What type of language does the writer use? Does the report mention other studies? What methods did researchers use to perform the study? Who is doing the reporting? How meaningful is the finding?

4. Heredity, environment, and available health care all affect your health.

5. Answers will vary.

6. Answers will vary.

SECTION 2 Review

Reviewing the Facts

1. **Recall.** Wellness expresses itself in four parts of your life. Name these four parts.
2. **List.** List at least three components of:
   a. Mental/emotional and spiritual health.
   b. Physical health.
   c. Social health.
3. **Describe.** What are some questions you should ask yourself when reading articles on health news?
4. **Recall.** Other than daily choices, what factors affect your health?

Writing Critically

5. **Personal.** Recall how you have been tempted or influenced by others to do things that are not healthy. How would engaging in unhealthy behaviors affect your wellness?
6. **Explain.** Write a paragraph to explain how the four parts of wellness, mental/emotional, spiritual, physical, and social health, is expressed in your life.

Go Online

For more information on health careers, visit Career Corner at **glencoe.com**.

Making Behavior Changes

Health knowledge is of little value if people only use it to get As on their health tests. Its true value lies in people's use of it to guide their behavior. Since you are reading a whole book on your choices and your health, you will learn facts that will make you want to improve your health behavior. In order to do that, you will need **motivation**, *the force that moves people to act.*

Motivation to Change Behaviors

__MAIN IDEA__ ▶ Obstacles to change arise in competence, confidence, and motivation.

Motivation that comes naturally is from instincts, or human **drives**, *motivations that are not learned.* Drives are strong motivators that make you take the actions necessary to meet your needs for food, water, and safety. Drives can also be involved in situations with other people, such as aggression and the need to protect your family. Learned motivation is also powerful. The desires for possessions and achievements are two types of learned motivations.

If you want to change, will you do it? The next section describes how awareness leads to action.

Vocabulary

motivation
drives
self-efficacy
commitment
will

Preview Activity.
Discuss:

- Lead a class discussion asking students about motivation. Ask: What motivates you to try and get good grades? Why do you exercise? Why do you choose the foods you eat?

- Write students' answers on the board.

- When reviewing all the answers, remind students that many times, we are motivated to take action that will lead to a future reward. For example, exercising regularly may help a student make the team, but it can also help that student maintain lifelong fitness.

- Remind students that the habits they establish today will help determine their future health.

■ **Figure 1.9** *The motivation to succeed helps you to meet your goals. How has someone in your life helped or motivated you?*

Caption Answer: Sample answer: "My aunt likes to talk to me about different career choices."

Figure 1.10   Stages of Behavior Change

Stages of Behavior Change	Actions to Take
Before Awareness: People in this stage have no intention to change; they see no problem with their behavior.	Collect information; learn about your current behaviors and how a change might benefit you.
Awareness: People in this stage admit that change may be needed; they weigh the costs and benefits of both changing and not changing.	Commit to making a change and set a date to start.
Preparation: People in this stage are getting ready to make a change; they are taking some first steps, such as setting goals.	Write out a plan for change; state the actions you will take. Set small-step goals. Tell others about your plan to change.
Action: People in this stage are using time and energy to make a change; the person is following guidelines for healthy behavior.	Make room in your life for your new behavior. Expect and recognize lapses as a normal part of the process.

Class Activity

Discuss:

Ask the students to quickly list five things that they'd like to change about themselves. (The changes must be possible.) Then ask them to put a "+" next to each one that they know how to change. Tell them to put another "+" next to the ones they *really, really* want to change; then another "+" next to the ones they definitely will change, and finally another "+" next to those they are already changing.

> "*Well begun is half done.*"
>
> —Horace
> (65–8 B.C.)
> Roman poet and satirist

From Awareness to Action

How does a person go about changing a health behavior? This question is important because even people who want to improve their health may fail to do so. The steps that often successfully lead to behavior change are listed below. These steps don't always appear in the same order. However, they always seem to appear.

Obstacles to Change

It is not uncommon for a person to want to change a behavior but to have trouble following through. Obstacles can occur everywhere. Often, just when people reach part of their goal, they lapse into old behaviors. This can happen several times before a new behavior becomes permanent.

Obstacles often arise in these three general areas:

- **Competence**—The person lacks needed knowledge or skill to make the change.

- **Confidence**—The person possesses the needed knowledge and skills but believes that making the change is beyond the scope of his or her ability, or that the problem lies outside the realm of personal control.

- **Motivation**—The person possesses both competence and confidence, but lacks sufficient reason to change.

Competence The first obstacle, competence, is by far the easiest to correct. For example, a student who eats no vegetables but would like to start needs to learn how to prepare vegetables. She can talk to someone who cooks, or read a cookbook to find out. Her skills will improve as she tries out recipes.

Confidence When a task seems too large to accomplish, a person's confidence can lessen. If a student sets a goal such as, "I will consume all the vegetables I need," she might eventually think, "I'll never be able to eat all those vegetables—what's the use of trying?"

Instead, she should set a small, specific goal, such as, "I will purchase carrot sticks tomorrow and eat them for my snacks this week." This small task is easily accomplished, and she may feel empowered to attempt more small changes to meet her goal. A later section tells how, exactly, to set goals.

Two other things affect confidence. One is a high sense of **self-efficacy**, that is, *the belief in one's ability to take action and successfully change a behavior*. To boost self-efficacy, it helps to develop a strong internal locus of control, which means the source of responsibility for life's events. An internal locus of control identifies personal behaviors as the driving force, and predicts successful behavior change. A person with an external locus of control blames chance, fate, or some other external factor, and predicts less success. Most people's attitude falls somewhere in between. This means that the individual believes that personal behaviors can control life's events. Otherwise, people feel helpless against outside forces, believing that luck or fate accounts for life's events. The more you believe in yourself and your ability to change things for the better, the more likely it is that you will succeed in doing so.

■ **Figure 1.11** *Permanent changes take effort and determination. How has determination helped you reach a goal?*

Caption Answer: Answers will vary. Students may say that determination helped them stay focused on their goal.

Motivation The toughest obstacle to overcome, however, is a lack of motivation. For example, everyone likes the idea of being a top musician, a world-class athlete, or even a popular author. Without the motivation to practice playing your instrument, or to spend hours training, or even spend your free time writing, it will be difficult to meet that goal. The motivation that is required to become a musician, athlete, or author is the same type of motivation that's needed to meet a goal such as maintaining a healthy weight, exercising regularly, or staying positive when you face difficulties in life.

The student described earlier in this section, may have both competence and confidence. She still will not make a change unless she has the motivation to do so. This student may have learned in health class that making it a habit to eat more vegetables each day will help her maintain throughout the lifespan. The student may think, however, "I'm healthy now—why should I bother to eat more vegetables?" Motivation is shaped by four factors and results when the reward she expects from a change outweighs its costs. These four factors are:

- The value of the reward. (How big is the reward?)
- Its timing. (How soon will the reward come? How soon will the price have to be paid?)
- The costs. (What will be the risks or consequences of seeking the reward?)
- Its probability. (How likely is the reward, and how certain the price?)

Action: Setting Goals

MAIN IDEA ▶ In taking action to change behavior, it helps to set goals.

To succeed in achieving your goals, it's best to start small. Set short-term goals, one at a time. Suppose a person decides to start exercising regularly, get a part-time job, volunteer for a local charity, go to religious services every day, spend at least two added hours each day on homework, and . . . That person might feel overwhelmed. All these changes are possible, but not all at once. After only a few days, the person will be exhausted and will give it all up.

Experts suggest that one way to begin goal setting is to write down some areas you would like to work on. Then pick a goal to work on first. Perhaps you'd like to choose the goal that you know you could accomplish most quickly or the one that would bring you the most benefits. Maybe you'd start with a goal that just "feels right." The Health Skills sidebar, "Steps to Goal Setting," will start you on your way.

Steps to Goal Setting

1. When setting goals, think about what you want to accomplish, and to develop short-term goals. Identify your goal. Write it down in general terms.

2. State three or more specific behaviors that will help you achieve your goal. Write them down.

3. Identify steps you'll have to take to get ready.

4. Commit to a specific time to get your plan under way.

5. Set up a chart on which you can measure your progress in units.

6. Plan rewards for yourself that fit the goal you've chosen.

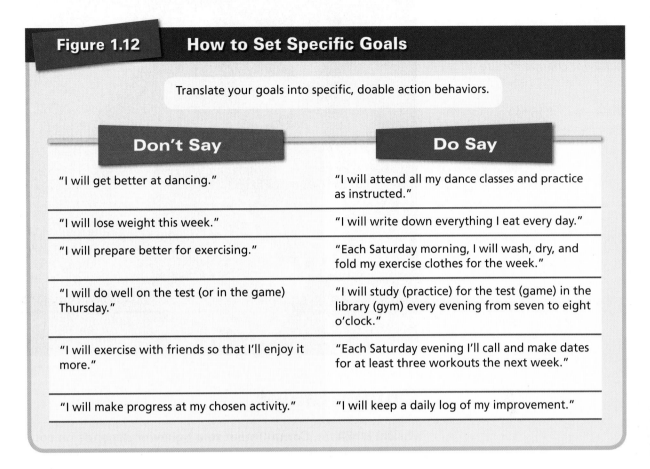

Figure 1.12   How to Set Specific Goals

Translate your goals into specific, doable action behaviors.

Don't Say	Do Say
"I will get better at dancing."	"I will attend all my dance classes and practice as instructed."
"I will lose weight this week."	"I will write down everything I eat every day."
"I will prepare better for exercising."	"Each Saturday morning, I will wash, dry, and fold my exercise clothes for the week."
"I will do well on the test (or in the game) Thursday."	"I will study (practice) for the test (game) in the library (gym) every evening from seven to eight o'clock."
"I will exercise with friends so that I'll enjoy it more."	"Each Saturday evening I'll call and make dates for at least three workouts the next week."
"I will make progress at my chosen activity."	"I will keep a daily log of my improvement."

Figure 1.12 gives examples of how to make your goals specific.

Here is one example on applying the Health Skills steps:

1. My goal: I'd like to get in shape.
2. Three behaviors that will help me achieve my goal are:
   a. I'll save $3 a week so that I can buy some hand weights.
   b. I'll read a good book on fitness.
   c. I'll join a walking club.
3. Preparation:
   a. I'll keep the money in my top drawer.
   b. I'll borrow the book from the library.
   c. I'll clean up my walking shoes.
4. My time commitment: I'll start on Tuesday, and I'll continue saving and walking for a month.
5. How I'll measure my progress:
   a. I'll record how far I walk each day.
   b. I'll graph my distances over a month.
6. My first reward: When I've collected $12 and walked for a month, I'll buy my hand weights.

Meaningful, specific plans like these can carry you through the difficult times in a behavior-change program. A vague desire to improve is not enough. You must translate that desire into specific actions. It's okay to state a goal in general terms. However, be sure to translate it into specific, doable action behaviors.

■ **Figure 1.13** *It takes determination to maintain a behavior change for life. What is the "Rule of Three?"*

Caption Answer: Trying a new behavior three times for at least three days.

Commitment

MAIN IDEA ▶ Commitment to a behavior depends on continued rewards from it.

To change a behavior, a person has to make a **commitment**, *a decision adhered to for the long term; a promise kept.* Commitment is a step in which the **will**—*a person's intent, which leads to action*—is involved. Sometimes, even after what seems to be a firm commitment to changed behavior, a person slips back. Why? Once you have made a change, you will maintain it only if you continue to feel rewarded by the change.

Having Determination

Try to use the "Rule of Three," or committing to trying a new behavior three times or for at least three days. This way, you aren't just impulsively trying a new behavior, only to abandon it later. You are making the effort to install and maintain a behavior change for life. You are willing to put in the necessary effort and practice for a permanent change. Now, imagine you have a friend named Amy, who wants to go on a crash diet to lose weight, but who doesn't want to change any of her habits permanently. Amy has bought some diet pills to cut her appetite long enough to lose 10 pounds. She has no plans to change any of her eating habits, so she's going to regain the 10 pounds, plus some. You should have no trouble predicting which person will gain health and fitness: you will. Amy's weight will go up and down like a yo-yo. She will continue to lose and gain on a frustrating cycle.

The Changed Self-Image

It is also important to change the way you think of yourself. Sometimes a behavior slips back because a person's self-image is slow to change. Sometimes people have to do some psychological work along with their physical work in order to change. A person who gives up smoking has to imagine, and really see, herself as a confirmed ex-smoker. A person who takes up swimming every day has to adopt a new identity: "I am a swimmer." In short, the person needs:

- A changed self-image.
- A sense of self-efficacy.
- High self-esteem.

People who believe in their own ability to take action and perform new tasks, that is, people with a strong sense of self-efficacy, most often succeed in changing their own behavior. A person's will and a healthy self-esteem help too.

Worksheets: A reproducible quiz for Section 3 is provided in the Teacher Classroom Resources.

SECTION 3 Review

Reviewing the Vocabulary

Review the vocabulary on page 15. Then answer these questions.

1. What is *self-efficacy*?
2. What does *commitment* mean?

Reviewing the Facts

3. **Analyze.** What are three areas that may become obstacles to making behavioral changes?
4. **Recall.** What are two factors that affect confidence?
5. **List.** List the six steps for setting goals.
6. **Evaluate.** When setting goals, why is it important to start with smaller, short-term goals instead of making a lot of changes all at once?

Writing Critically

7. **Personal.** List a behavior that you would like to change in your life. How would you go about changing this behavior—what steps would you follow and why?

For fitness and health tips, visit the Fitness Zone at **glencoe.com**.

1. Self-efficacy is the belief in your ability to take action and to successfully change a behavior
2. A commitment is a pledge or decision for the long term.
3. Competence, Confidence, And Motivation
4. Self-efficacy And Locus Of Control
5. Identify your goal. State three or more specific behaviors that will help you achieve your goal. Identify steps you'll have to take to get ready. Commit to a specific time to get your plan under way. Set up a chart to measure your progress. Plan rewards for yourself that fit the goal you have chosen.
6. By making smaller, short-term goals you are less likely to give up on your larger goals.
7. Answers will vary.

Reviewing Vocabulary

Use the vocabulary terms listed below to complete the following statements.

infectious diseases
chronological age
lifestyle choices
will
health
motivation
life-management skills
commitment

1. Age measured in years from date of birth is_____.

2. Types of diseases that are caused by infecting organisms and can be passed from person to person are called _____.

3. A person's intent, which leads to action, is called _____.

4. Decisions made daily that have to do with how a person treats his or her body and mind are called _____.

5. The force that moves people to act is _____.

6. A range of states with physical, mental/emotional, spiritual, and social components is called _____.

7. The set of skills that help a person realize his or her potential to be well and enjoy life is known as _____.

8. A decision adhered to for the long term is called a _____.

Recalling Key Facts and Ideas

Section 1

9. **Name.** The two causes, besides people's own choices, that bring on lifestyle diseases.

10. **Explain.** What decisions can you make about your environment to maintain or improve your health?

11. **List.** List five lifestyle practices that greatly contribute to a healthful lifestyle.

Section 2

12. **Name.** Name five of the seven characteristics of mental/emotional and spiritual health.

13. **Identify.** Name five characteristics of physical health and preventive care.

14. **List.** List five ways a person can be socially healthy.

Section 3

15. **Name.** Name one of three obstacles to changing behaviors and give an example of how to overcome it.

16. **Recall.** What are the six steps in goal setting?

17. **Explain.** How does high self-esteem enhance behavior changes?

18. **Analyze.** What must a person continue to feel in order to maintain a change in his or her behavior?

Writing Critically

19. **Personal.** After reading this chapter, are you satisfied with your health? What can you do to change the negative areas into positive ones? If all your areas are positive, what will you do to keep them positive?

1. Chronological age **2.** Infectious diseases **3.** Will **4.** Lifestyle choices **5.** Motivation **6.** Wellness **7.** Self-efficacy **8.** Commitment **9.** Heredity and environment. **10.** Keep your community clean and decide which customs to follow. **11.** Get adequate sleep, eat nutritious meals, get regular physical activity, maintain a healthy weight, avoid tobacco, alcohol, and drug use. **12.** Maintain a strong sense of self, accept new ideas, handle setbacks, manage and

20. **Descriptive.** Explain what the health and wellness line is. Where do you think you are on that line right now? List five things you could do to move toward the positive end, and five things you could avoid doing to stay away from the negative end.

21. **Expository.** Many Americans are concerned with the treatment of diseases, but they neglect disease prevention. Discuss some of the barriers people might face in disease prevention. How can we promote prevention instead of waiting until treatment is needed? How would or could you do this in your school?

Activities

22. Keep a daily activity log of health choices you make. After a week write down changes you can make to improve your wellness. What do you need to do more? What should you do less?

23. Imagine a couple that fits the definition of wellness. What characteristics do you think they have? Brainstorm with your classmates to develop a complete picture of them.

24. You are asked to speak at a local elementary school about the importance of wellness. List some of the main points you would stress to the students. How would you help the students understand the importance of maintaining wellness throughout their lives? Since these students are younger than you, you may need to devise interesting and unique approaches to get their attention and get your points across.

Making Decisions about Health

25. Imagine that a friend of yours has told you that she has developed some friendships that she is now afraid will lead to trouble. The new friends are engaging in some risky behaviors; some smoke and drink, and a few take drugs. Your friend says that she sees trouble ahead, but at the same time, she is enjoying the thrill of these new and somewhat dangerous activities. She wants advice on how to change her behavior before it's too late. Based on what you have learned in this chapter, what can you tell your friend?

Go Online

For more vocabulary practice, play the True/False game at **glencoe.com**.

Fact or Fiction?

Answers

1. True.
2. False. Today most of the leading causes of death are primarily related to lifestyle, not infectious diseases.
3. True.

 Writing Paragraphs will vary.

express emotions appropriately **13.** Answers will vary.
14. Develops healthy relationships, resolves conflict
15. Answers will vary. **16.** Identify the goal, state behaviors to achieve the goal, identify the steps of the goal, commit to the

goal, measure progress, and reward yourself. **17.** Answers will vary. **18.** Continuous rewards **19–25.** Answers will vary.

CHAPTER 2

Emotional Health

Sections

1. Self-Knowledge
2. Relating to Others
3. Making Decisions and Solving Problems
4. Finding a Place in Society

Possessing good **emotional health**, *the state of being free of mental disturbances that limit functioning*, means that you seek, value, and maintain good relationships. Your relationships with your family, friends, teachers and other adults, and even with your community are a key part of total wellness. People with good emotional health are able to accomplish the following:

- Develop close personal relationships
- Receive support from others
- Contribute to society

How do you know if you are emotionally healthy? How can you improve your emotional health? This chapter provides information that will help you answer these questions.

Fact or Fiction?

What Do You Think?
Is each statement true or false? If you think it's false, explain what's true.

1. Emotional health is not related to physical health.
2. Once a person adopts values, they remain firmly fixed for a lifetime.
3. It is best to reject illogical or unpleasant feelings.

 Writing Why do you think emotional health is so important to your overall health? Why is it important to maintain a healthy relationship with yourself and others? Write a paragraph explaining why you think emotional health is important.

(Answers on page 49)

Visit **glencoe.com** and complete the Life Choice Inventory for Chapter 2.

Self-Knowledge

One of the most important relationships in your life is the relationship you have with yourself. The point is to develop a relationship with yourself that pleases you. Then when asked, you can honestly reply, "This is the way I am, and I feel okay about it." This doesn't mean you should stop changing. You may want to improve yourself in a lot of ways; most people do. But you can still say, "This is the way I am—I am a person with faults and virtues, I am learning and growing, and I like myself."

Vocabulary

emotional health
thoughts
cortex
values
emotion
status
emotional intelligence
resentment
suppress
confrontation

Self-Confidence

MAIN IDEA ▶ A first step toward emotional health is getting to know yourself.

Self-confidence is attractive. It's attractive to friends, to dating partners, to teachers, to everyone. The emotional warmth, energy, and enthusiasm that seem to radiate from a confident person set up a sort of chain reaction. Before long the people around that person start to feel good too. Who wouldn't like someone who made them feel that way? Being self-confident is not the same as being conceited. A person who is conceited has a falsely high opinion of himself for traits that are imaginary or greatly exaggerated.

■ **Figure 2.1** *One of the most important relationships in your life is the relationship you have with yourself. How can you have a better relationship with yourself?*

Caption Answer: Learn what values are important to you.

In contrast, a person who is confident may be smart, or tough, or attractive, or rich, or may not be. In any case the confident person feels okay about her traits without exaggerating them. When you are with confident people, you feel that they are comfortable with themselves.

How Can I Be More Self-Confident?

Self-confidence starts with self-knowledge, which is learned by going through experiences.

Self-knowledge begins when you ask yourself, "Who am I?" You may answer this question by just saying your name: "I am Leslie Owens." You may add that you are a young man or woman, an important aspect of yourself. You may go on to describe other outward traits, such as your height, weight, age, occupation, and race. Beneath these surface traits, though, who are you, really?

To become acquainted with yourself, you must learn about and manage three parts of your private, internal world—your thoughts, values, and emotions (feelings). Once you've discovered how you function in these areas, you can judge which parts serve you well and which you wish to change, now or later.

Thoughts, values, and emotions also play roles in the decisions you make. We all know what it's like to face a decision in which feelings pull us one way and values another. The process of making a decision involves weighing and evaluating what you think is true, what you believe is right, and how you feel about the situation. The best decisions from an emotional health point of view are those that are in line with all three aspects of the self.

Thoughts

MAIN IDEA ▶ Thoughts help you gather information about yourself and the world.

Your **thoughts**, *those mental processes of which a person is always conscious*, take place in *the outermost layer of your brain,* or **cortex**. Your thoughts are conscious; you are always aware of them. They help you to gather information about yourself and your world, and to make sense of it.

Your thoughts shape your actions. If you think destructive, negative thoughts, you will act in destructive, negative ways. If you think constructive, positive thoughts, you will act in constructive, positive ways. In general, negative thoughts breed more negative thoughts, and can lead a person to think badly of everything. On the other hand, a person can acquire peace of mind, reduced stress, and improved health through simply learning to think positively.

Health Skills

Thinking Positively

You can change negative thoughts into positive ones. Try to:

1. **Recognize your own negative thoughts.** Pay close attention to identify the negative messages you are sending yourself.

2. **Stop the negative thoughts.** Force yourself to think of something else to block out negative self-talk.

3. **Replace negative with positive thoughts.** Your own positive traits are the best source for your positive-thought statements. Ask a parent or a guidance counselor to help you identify some positive statements.

Class Activity

Analyze: Family plays a major role in developing a person's value system. Have the students discuss values with their parents or other trusted adults. Students should then write a one-page report, answering the following questions:

1. What values are most important to you?

2. Can you describe how your values changed as you were growing up?

3. Have your values been much different from your parents' or those of an adult you are close to? If so, how?

4. What values, if any, are unique to your generation?

5. Are you happy with your values? How would you change them?

Values

MAIN IDEA ▶ Learning to manage and live by your values is an important part of emotional health.

Your **values**, *what a person thinks of as right and wrong, or sees as important*, are your rules for behavior. Values can be thought of as life's steering wheel because they guide the direction your life takes. You learn your first values from your family. You learn such statements as "We work hard," "We believe in education," or "We stick together."

A person's values change from time to time. Working them out remains a lifelong task. The teen years are a time when most people struggle to balance the values of their parents with those they observe in peers. Some teens reject their parents' values for a while. However, most return to them as proven rules for living.

Why Are Values Important to Me?

Your values guide you in assigning positive and negative weights to behaviors. For example, you may value sports and reading positively, but babysitting a sibling and cleaning your room negatively (or the reverse). The weights that you assign then guide your thinking and actions.

Values are both conscious and unconscious. Sometimes you can state them in words, but many times they guide your behavior without your awareness. People who know themselves well are keenly aware of their values. That awareness helps them to choose their behaviors without confusion. For example, a student who values honesty and is conscious of this value will choose without hesitation not to cheat on exams. Another student may have the same values but may not be aware of them. This student may suffer emotional distress in trying to decide whether or not to cheat.

Personal Values

You can discover your own values by stating your beliefs. For example, you might say, "I believe it is best to be honest." This means you value honesty. Then, to discover how strong your values are, you can ask some questions about them. For each value that you state, ask the following questions:

- Would I be willing to state this value to others? For example, I am an honest person. I do not cheat on tests.

- How faithfully will I stand by this value when it is challenged, or when acting according to the value brings negative consequences? For example, your best friend did not study for a test and wants you to share your answers. If you refuse, your friend might be angry with you and will spend time with other friends.

- Do I act consistently and repeatedly in line with this value? For example, even though you know your friend will be angry with you and may ignore you for a while, you refuse to share your answers during the test. The value you place on honesty is very strong; you are honest even when it's hard to be honest, or when it's tempting to cheat.

APPLYING Health Skills

Advocacy

➤ Objectives
- Demonstrate the use of "I" messages to express emotions in a healthful way.
- Demonstrate skills for communicating effectively.

When Best Friends Disagree

Marissa and Julia have been best friends ever since kindergarten. Now, in high school, Marissa has been hanging out with a guy named Dave and his friends. Dave and his friends smoke cigarettes and often skip school. Marissa thinks they're the most popular people in school and doesn't understand why Julia won't hang out with them. Recently, Julia argued with Marissa. She feels that Marissa's new friends may be a bad influence on her. Julia doesn't want to lose Marissa as a best friend and doesn't want Marissa to be influenced by Dave's group. She does not want to hang out with Dave's group but doesn't know what to do. She wonders how to respond to Marissa.

➤ Identify the Problem
1. Describe Julia's situation.

➤ Form an Action Plan
2. Using "I" messages, write a short dialogue in which Julia tells Marissa how she feels.
3. What questions might Julia and Marissa ask one another to eliminate misunderstandings and help resolve the conflict?

➤ What Did You Learn?
4. If you had a friend who started hanging out with the wrong crowd and spent less and less time with you, what would you say to them? How would you say it?

Applying Health Skills:

1. Julia does not want to hang out with Dave's group. She wants to tell Marissa that she's worried about her and doesn't want to lose their friendship.

2. Julia might say: "I am concerned about losing our friendship. I'd rather us hang out alone than with Dave's group."

3. Questions should help Julia and Marissa see the conflict from the other person's perspective and eliminate misunderstandings.

4. Answers will vary.

■ Figure 2.2 *Being aware of your values can help you choose your behaviors without confusion. What values are important to you?*

Caption Answer: Honesty, schoolwork, family.

When two values conflict with each other, decisions and actions become difficult. At such points you may struggle to decide:

- Should I have fun (value: enjoying life) or study (value: good grades)?
- Should I tell my friend a true but unpleasant fact (value: honesty) or keep quiet to protect the friend's feelings (value: friendship)?

Values keep on changing. One of the skills to develop in moving through life is to learn when to change to new values and when to stick by old ones.

Emotions

MAIN IDEA ▶ Recognizing, accepting, and expressing feelings are important to emotional health.

An **emotion** is *a feeling that occurs in response to an event as experienced by an individual.* Some emotions are probably present in humans from birth, such as affection, anger, and fear. Others, such as envy and prejudice, are learned. The terms "emotions" and "feelings" are often used to mean the same thing.

The emotions you feel in response to an event often depend on earlier experiences of the same kind. The experience of hearing the front door open, for example, may bring on the emotions of fear, happiness, or interest, depending on what you are expecting. Failing to reach a goal may arouse a mixture of emotions, including impatience, anger, and irritation. Losing a loved one (the experience of grief) brings a series of emotions, including both anger and sorrow. Even when emotions seem unreasonable, they are not wrong. All emotions are acceptable and healthy.

It is acceptable to feel emotions. Feeling emotions is natural. Everyone feels emotions such as happiness, sadness, anger, and frustration during their lifetimes. Most of us feel all those emotions several times a day. It's not wrong to feel these or any emotions. It may be wrong, however, to act on some of these emotions in ways that hurt yourself and others. It may not be acceptable to act on all emotions, but learning how to manage your emotions is possible. Sometimes you may hold back an emotion for a moment (for example, if you got upset at your parents for setting a curfew). However, it is usually best to face the emotion as soon as possible. You might calm down and then try to talk to your parents. Emotions can build up, making it difficult for a person to function. Generally, people who are aware of their feelings and who express them appropriately are more emotionally healthy than people who ignore them.

Emotions vs. Actions

People may fear some emotions because the emotions could lead to unacceptable behaviors. It helps to keep in mind the difference between emotions and actions. Some actions are not acceptable, of course, but emotions toward them arise naturally. Emotions can build up, making it difficult for a person to function. Some psychologists now use the term **emotional intelligence**, *the ability to recognize and appropriately express one's emotions in a way that enhances living*, to describe people who can express their emotions well.

Emotions are not always a reliable guide to action. More appropriate than to act on each emotion is to wait it out or express it in ways that are harmless to yourself and others.

Consumer SKILLS ACTIVITY

"Added-value" Advertising

Do you know anyone who always has to have the latest gadget or fashion item? Advertisers wish everyone felt this way. They use all sorts of techniques to convince you that you need what they are selling. One technique is to imply that self-worth depends on your owning their product. Cars, sneakers, jeans, sports equipment, and many other products are sold by way of the concept of "added value." Advertisers convey that the products themselves are worthwhile. Cars deliver you where you need to go, sneakers cover and protect your feet, jeans clothe you, and sports equipment may help you become more fit.

Beyond these functions advertisers suggest that their brand names also have an added value. You must have a certain basketball shoe or jacket to prove to others that you are worthwhile. Some people may even begin to feel unworthy if they do not possess the "in" brands, even if the brand they own is just as high in quality as the popular brand.

What happens to such people when their possessions are no longer trendy? They scramble to replace them with the latest added-value items, because without them they feel diminished in **status**, *a person's standing or rank in relation to others, many times falsely based on wealth, power, or influence.* Only people who value themselves for their own internal worth are protected from this effect. Their sense of worth is based on substance, not on symbols.

Writing

1. What sorts of products can you think of that sellers try to tie to people's values?
2. What sorts of visual images are used in television and magazine ads to make the connection between a product and a certain status?
3. Why do some people spend money on products that are promoted in this way?

When you can do the following, you have developed emotional health:

- Recognize all kinds of emotions in yourself.
- Admit that you have different kinds of emotions.
- Express all kinds of emotions in acceptable ways.

Expressing Emotions

Expressing emotions can be done physically and verbally. That means doing something: speaking, writing, crying, shouting, laughing, or otherwise acting out emotions. Calmly saying "I'm angry" may not fully express the feeling of anger.

A person who feels anger but cannot express it holds it inside and instead builds **resentment**, *anger that has built up due to failure to express it*. It is healthier to admit and to express anger in appropriate ways, such as physical activity, than to **suppress** it, *to hold back or restrain*, and be consumed inwardly by resentment. When managed assertively, a **confrontation**, a showdown; *an interaction in which one person expresses feelings to another*, can be a constructive conversation to help resolve a person's strong emotions.

Managing Your Emotions

Learning to express emotions in healthful ways will help you better cope with your feelings. To deal with an emotion, you should:

1. **Recognize it.** What am I feeling?

2. **Own it.** Accept that you feel it.

3. **Verbalize it.** Express it in words to yourself or someone else. For example, "I'm angry," or "I'm frustrated."

4. **Express it physically.** Engage in physical activity to express emotions. For example, go running or take a walk.

If a negative emotion persists or returns, think about who you can talk to for help with dealing with your negative feelings.

Worksheets: Vocabulary worksheets are available in your Teacher Classroom Resources.

A reproducible quiz for Section 1 is available in the Teacher Classroom Resources.

SECTION 1 Review

Reviewing the Vocabulary

Review the vocabulary on page 26. Then answer these questions.

1. What is *emotional health*?
2. Define *thoughts*.
3. What is *status*?

Reviewing the Facts

4. **Analyze.** What is the difference between values and emotions?
5. **Evaluate.** What is the danger of negative thinking?
6. **Describe.** Where do you learn your first values?
7. **Explain.** What happens when emotions build up and are not dealt with?

Writing Critically

8. **Personal.** To gain self-knowledge, you need to be aware of your strengths and weaknesses. Knowing your strengths builds your self-esteem. Knowing your weaknesses helps you form a realistic self-concept. Take a personal inventory by making two lists—one that includes at least ten strengths, and one that includes at least ten weaknesses. List ways you can improve your weaknesses and build on your strengths.

For more vocabulary practice, play the Concentration game at **glencoe.com**.

1. Emotional health is the state of being free of mental disturbances that limit functioning; also the state of having developed healthy perceptions and responses to other people and life events, based on thoughts, emotions and values. It is also called mental health.

2. Thoughts are those mental processes of which a person is always conscious.

3. Status is a person's standing or rank in relation to others, many times falsely based on wealth, power, or influence.

4. Values are what a person thinks of as right or wrong. Emotions are feelings that occur in response to an event.

5. Negative thinking can affect your self-confidence.

6. From your family

7. Resentment can build.

8. Answers will vary.

Relating to Others

Recall that the emotionally healthy person functions well in three areas—in relation to self, to others, and to society. So far, this chapter has been devoted to one of the most important relationships in anyone's life—the relationship with self. Now, what about relationships with others?

People who value themselves, because they are confident and happy, attract other people into friendships. A person's friends can form a strong **support system**, *a network of individuals or groups with which one identifies and exchanges emotional support*, which can be a great help in times of need. The members of your support system may be family members, neighbors, school friends, members of a sports team, people in a religious organization, a **mentor**, *a wise person who gives advice or assistance,* or an advisor, or a therapy or self-help group. You will learn some basic skills for getting along with others in this chapter. You'll learn more about peer groups in the next chapter.

Vocabulary

- support system
- mentor
- conflict
- violence
- feud
- tolerance
- communication
- assertive
- passive
- aggressive
- mediator

Dealing with Conflicts

MAIN IDEA ▶ Assertive communication and conflict resolution strategies can often prevent the escalation of conflicts.

Every day, people must deal with **conflict**, *a struggle or opposition between people, especially when people compete for something in the belief that only one can have what he or she wants, at the expense of the other*. Whether you are at home, at school, at work, or out with friends, small situations

■ **Figure 2.4** *The feud between the Hatfields and McCoys offers an example of what can happen when conflicts go unresolved. What strategies an you use to resolve a conflict?*

Caption Answer: Be honest and assertive, use "I" messages, and put yourself in the other's shoes.

occur and are settled without a fuss. Someone accidentally bumps into someone else, who good-naturedly steps aside. Sometimes, however, conflict can occur. The difference lies in people's reactions to annoyance. The question to ask, therefore, is not whether you will experience conflicts, but how to handle them when they come up.

It's important to learn how to mange your emotions when conflict arises. If you don't stay calm, the conflict could lead to **violence**, *brutal physical force intended to damage or injure another*. On the other hand, if you ignore the conflict, it may get worse.

A true tale shows the outcome of conflict handled badly. Two families, the Hatfields and the McCoys, lived in the mountains on opposite banks of the river that separates eastern Kentucky and West Virginia. Some claim the theft of a hog started it all, but whatever the first event, it ignited a forty-year **feud**, a *bitter, continuing hostility, often involving groups of people*, that ravaged the two families, then their counties, and finally even their states. Incredibly, the U.S. Supreme Court finally had to step in to resolve the forty-year conflict.

Viewing the "Enemy"

If you think a feud like the one between the Hatfields and the McCoys could never happen today, you are mistaken. The story demonstrates a dangerous change that occurs in the minds of people in conflict. At some point, they begin to view one another as "enemies" and start searching for evidence of one another's villainy. The Hatfields were missing a pig, someone reported seeing an extra pig at the McCoy's place, the Hatfields retaliated, both sides heard rumors of other crimes, and the shooting started. Examples more likely today are these:

- Tomika thinks that Tom lied. Now Tomika is waiting to catch Tom in another lie.
- Tom thinks Tomika has spread a rumor about him. Now, whenever he sees her talking to another person, Tom imagines that Tomika is gossiping about him.
- Tom can see none of the good things that Tomika does. Tomika notices only bad things about Tom.

Problems quickly multiply. People embroiled in conflict stop communicating. Soon, they hate one another on vague, general principles. Then others "pick sides," and more people become involved. You may know of examples like these:

- Your friends hate your "enemy's" friends.
- Members of this group don't speak with members of that group.
- People in his family cannot become friends with people in her family.

Health Skills

How to Resolve Conflicts

When you find yourself in conflict with another person:

- Be honest and assertive.
- Use only "I" messages ("I don't like it when…") rather than "you" statements ("Why don't you…").
- Repeat what the other person said in your own words. Wait for agreement.
- Ask, don't guess. Wait silently for the whole answer.
- Put yourself in the other's shoes; show respect; say that you wish to be friends.
- Use humor. Laughter relieves stress.
- Choose a mutually good time and place to discuss issues.
- Ask for one or two changes that will end the conflict. Be open to change yourself.
- Both people should feel like winners—in terms of closeness, friendship, and self-esteem.

If you fail, try again with a **mediator**, *a neutral third person who helps two people in conflict.*

Analyze: Five conflict resolution strategies are presented in Figure 2.6 on page 37. Students may judge themselves and others based on the values they assign to the various methods. For example, a person who walks away from a fight could be viewed as "chicken" or "cool." Ask students to identify and analyze how they feel about using each of the methods. Read each statement below to students, and have them write their feelings about each.

1. A person who gives in when conflict arises is cooperative.

2. A person who walks away is afraid.

3. A person who does nothing saves the other person's feelings.

4. A person who fights dirty usually wins.

5. A person who tries to understand the other's point of view can meet his or her own needs by doing so.

Trust or **tolerance**, *accommodation and acceptance of differences between oneself and others*, can be forever lost—unless someone stops the conflict. Luckily, most conflicts can end happily. Resolving a conflict takes courage and work, but it can be done, as the next section describes.

Strategies for Resolving Conflicts

Conflicts, if well-handled, can end constructively. People who resolve their disagreements with others are motivated to make things better. All sorts of ideas, innovations, and inventions have sprung from what were, at first, uncomfortable situations. With the right attitude, people can break down barriers and create more trust—essential for resolving conflict. Both parties should adjust their attitudes to do the following:

- **Desire a resolution**. Have a genuine desire to solve the problem.

- **Strive for a win-win outcome.** Know that if each person helps meet the other's needs, everyone's needs can be satisfied.

- **Honor the relationship.** Desire to maintain or improve the friendship, partnership, or community.

- **Be flexible but firm.** Be flexible on how needs are met; be firm that one's needs *will* be met.

- **Be sincerely apologetic** when appropriate.

- **Show courage.** Have courage to face the problem even while feeling threatened or afraid of hurting others' feelings.

- **Be open-minded.** Be willing to brainstorm and listen to all ideas for new solutions, even if the ideas are later discarded.

■ **Figure 2.5** *Being honest and tolerant can help you resolve conflicts constructively. Why is it good to be tolerant of others' feelings?*

Caption Answer: Being tolerant of others can help establish trust so conflicts can be solved.

Figure 2.6 — Five Conflict-Resolution Strategies—Pros and Cons

Strategy	Traits	Good Uses	Cautions
1. Giving in	One person yields to the other person's wishes.	Use when issues are not critical to your needs. Use as a way to negotiate an unimportant item in exchange for something you truly want and need.	Your needs may be overlooked. If you give in too quickly, you may feel cheated, angry, manipulated, or resentful and so perpetuate the conflict.
2. Walking away	One party physically or psychologically leaves the conflict.	Use when your or another's anger rises. Use when you need time to think about other options that are open to you.	The conflict may continue unresolved, and may worsen if not addressed. A mediator can sometimes help to get problem solving back on track.
3. Doing nothing	Both sides ignore the problem.	Use when time will cure the problem—for example, when one party is leaving town soon, or when classes will soon change. Use when the problem feels unimportant to both parties.	Hostility can silently grow worse. The parties may feel stress and discomfort in each other's presence.
4. Fighting dirty	One party attempts to "win" by lying, manipulating (pouting or crying), threatening, blaming, and calling names.	None.	Fighting dirty clouds issues and worsens conflicts.
5. Constructive problem solving	Both parties understand that they have much to gain by resolving the conflict, and they work toward solutions.	Use when both parties are competing for the same resources. The more important the issue, the more urgently you need to solve the problem.	Both people must be willing to compromise to an acceptable solution. Both parties must also agree to follow the ground rules and attitudes presented in this chapter.

With the attitudes described above, people can approach resolving their conflicts. Some methods of resolving conflicts are shown in **Figure 2.6**. Some work better than others, but all are shown for comparison. The Health Skills sidebar on page 35 gives details about one method that usually works best: constructive problem solving. To use it effectively, the parties express their wants and needs, but at the same time respect the feelings of other people.

Assertive, Not Aggressive, Communication

Of great importance during a conflict is your style of **communication**, *a two-way exchange of ideas or thoughts*. You have to perform a sort of balancing act between getting what you want and meeting the needs of others. The happy center between the extremes of never speaking out and verbally attacking others is assertive behavior, rather than passive or aggressive behavior.

Class Activity

Define:

- Define assertive, passive, and aggressive behaviors, then have students work in groups to come up with examples of the difference between assertive and aggressive behavior.
- Then give groups the following situations and ask them to tell how an aggressive person and an assertive person would react:
  1. A fellow worker is not doing his fair share of the work;
  2. A classmate is disrupting class, making it hard for others to concentrate; and
  3. A brother or sister is spending too much time listening to your radio in your room. (See figure 2.7 on page 38.)

Class Activity

Analyze: Give students some situations in which they can role play assertiveness. Some possible situations are: someone cuts in front of the lunch line or someone walks into the room and changes the TV channel while you're already watching something. Monitor the role plays, pointing out the advantages of assertive behavior versus aggressive or passive behavior.

Being **assertive** means *to possess the characteristic of appropriately expressing feelings, wants, and needs while respecting those of others.* On the other hand, **passive** behavior is *not expressing feelings appropriately,* while **aggressive** behavior means *to be overly demanding of others.* Assertiveness does not come naturally to many people. However, assertiveness has great value when problems must be worked out.

In **Figure 2.7**, three conflict situations are described in which people are behaving nonassertively (passively or aggressively). The people will not succeed in getting what they want. Decide how each person could resolve the conflict by using assertive responses.

In the first example, Sarah is passive. She simply does not speak up for herself. In the second, Mom makes it clear to James that she feels overworked, tired, and grumpy. However, she doesn't say what she wants him to do about it. In the third example, Ken tells his little sister what their father had told her to do, which is assertive. However, he then goes on to insult her, which is aggressive and hurtful.

By contrast, notice how the appropriate, assertive responses differ in tone and content. They each express a single, specific, concrete request of the moment. Assertive statements are like that: "Please wash the dishes." "Please pay me the five dollars you owe me." Also, they speak of the action they want, not of the person. The person spoken to knows exactly what to do and does not have to feel attacked. Use the strategies in "Making Your Wishes Known" Health Skills sidebar on page 39 to help you develop assertive behavior.

Figure 2.7 — Nonassertive vs. Assertive Responses

Situation	Nonassertive responses	Assertive Responses
A person steps in front of Sarah, who has been standing in line for an hour.	*Sarah:* "Well, excuse me!" *or* *Sarah:* Says nothing aloud; mutters "Some people…"	*Sarah:* "Excuse me. I was here first. The end of the line is back there."
James comes home, pours some juice, sits down, and flips on the television.	*James's mom:* "I sure wish I could rest like that at the end of the day. But no, I have to cook dinner, bathe the baby, wash up—I'm tired, too."	*James's mom:* "Would you please cook dinner while I bathe the baby?
Ken notices that his little sister hasn't cleaned up her room even though their father told her to do so earlier.	*Ken:* "Sis, Dad told you to clean up your room. What's the matter with you? You're the laziest child I ever saw."	*Ken:* "Dad told you to clean up your room. Now do it." (And he sees that she does.)

■ Figure 2.8 *A mediator can help resolve conflicts by listening to each party's wants and needs and proposing solutions. How does a mediator help to solve conflicts?*

Caption Answer: A mediator listens to both sides without taking sides so a solution can be found.

Assertiveness is the key to getting cooperation and resolving conflicts. It makes it easier, not harder, for people to get along with you.

The Mediator's Role

Sometimes the help of a neutral third party can move people in conflict closer to resolution. In the Hatfield and McCoy story, a mediator—in this case, the U.S. Supreme Court—stepped in to help separate real issues from imaginary ones. A mediator can be a guidance counselor, teacher, friend, or anyone who can offer a clear perspective.

A mediator meets with both parties, but stays neutral (that is, doesn't take sides). This gives each party time to tell its version of what happened, with no interruptions. The mediator then helps to identify the facts and issues that are common to both parties. Many times, a mediator can help the arguing parties to respect each other, to wait while the other talks, and to tell the truth. Once everyone agrees on the same set of facts, solutions become possible. In some high schools, trained students act as "peer mediators" to help settle conflicts among their fellow students.

Forming New Relationships

MAIN IDEA ▶ Rejection is a risk of forming new friendships, but the risk is worth taking.

Some people may fear trying to make new friends. Reaching out to other people usually does not lead to rejection. To get started, though, you have to be willing to risk rejection and to handle it if it occurs.

Health Skills

Making Your Wishes Known

To confront someone, express yourself assertively but not aggressively.

1. Ask yourself, "Does this bother me every time it happens, or is it an isolated incident?" If it happens often, mention it.

2. Make feeling statements about yourself, not judgment statements about the other person.

3. Pair a resentment with an appreciation: "I appreciate (this), but resent (that)."

4. Focus on the one incident that bothers you. Don't discuss other issues that have made you mad for months.

5. Be specific. Identify the behavior you want. Don't just complain.

What most often happens when you reach out is that the other person is pleased to be approached. At best, a rewarding relationship has a chance to form. For those who may be shy, a few suggestions can help. Think of the word SOFTEN to remind you of what to do during actual conversations with new people:

S Smile
O Open posture
F Forward lean
T Touch
E Eye Contact
N Nod

Some other helpful hints include: tell of your own feelings. People always find feelings interesting; ask about the other person's feelings. People like you to be interested in them; and listen closely. People love to be listened to. Friends can reinforce your values and motivate you, which in turn, can promote all aspects of your health.

Reviewing the Vocabulary

Review the vocabulary on page 34. Then answer these questions.

1. Define *mediator*.

2. What is a *support system*?

Reviewing the Facts

3. Identify. In addition to friends, what other people can be part of a support system?

4. List. What are some strategies for resolving conflicts?

5 Analyze. What happens if you are a passive communicator?

6. Describe. What is a mediator's role?

Writing Critically

7. Explain. Look over the Health Skills sidebar "Making Your Wishes Known," on page 39. Which strategies listed are you skilled in using? Which strategies listed do you need to improve on? How could you go about making each improvement?

For more information on health careers, visit Career Corner at **glencoe.com**.

Making Decisions and Solving Problems

Some decisions—what should I wear today?—are easy to make. Others are more weighty, such as, for example, "How can I tell my parents I don't want to be the person they want me to be?" In tackling tough decisions, it helps to follow a plan. One such plan is described below. The discussion that follows offers help with the steps.

Making Decisions

MAIN IDEA ▶ Problems can be solved by making decisions and taking action.

Your Values

The decisions you make reflect your personal values and the values of your family. For example, you may value being fit and healthy. The decisions you make will reflect this value. If you value relationships with your family and friends, you will make choices that reflect honesty, caring, and respect.

Because values are first learned from your family, talk with family members first if a decision is troubling you. Because their values are similar to your own, they can provide feedback if you are confronted with a difficult decision.

The Decision-Making Process

Have you thought about what goes into making a decision? One good strategy to use is called the HELP strategy:

H (Healthful) Does this choice present any health risks?

E (Ethical) Does this choice reflect your personal values?

L (Legal) Does this choice violate local, state, or federal laws?

P (Parent Approval) Would this choice be approved by your parents or guardians?

The HELP strategy provides useful questions that will help guide you through the decision-making process. The process begins by naming the problem.

Name the Problem The first step, *naming the problem*, may seem simple, but it may not be. Pinpointing the problem of what to wear usually is simple enough. Some problems, though, are so complex that they require years to figure out ("How can I improve my relationship with my parents?"). Whatever the problem is, the first step is to put it into words. Then you can begin seeking a solution.

Preview Activity:

- Brainstorm with students typical problems that teens encounter. (Little or no money for social activities, people have been spreading rumors, etc.)

- Divide the class into small groups. Have each group use the decision-making process to arrive at possible solutions to one of the problems. Then have them rank-order the proposed solutions.

- Discuss the results with the class. Each group can write its solutions on construction paper to hold up when explaining to the class.

Describe the Problem's Parts Breaking a problem up into parts will make it more manageable. Say, for example, that you feel you don't fit in with your peers. Stated that way, the problem seems impossible to solve. Stated in its smallest units, though, it may look like this:

- I like to discuss world events. The group likes gossip.
- The group spends more money than I can afford to spend.

When you think about these smaller components, you can deal with them one by one. If they arouse emotions such as resentment, anger, or embarrassment, this may be a sign that the group's values are not in line with your own. This realization may help you to think up solutions that will meet your needs.

Brainstorm The brainstorming step involves thinking up many different solutions to the problem. During this step, don't try to solve the problem. Instead, exercise your imagination, and tap your creativity. This can be fun—and funny.

Brainstorming for the problem just described can bring out possibilities such as seeking other friendships, joining a club for people with more common interests, taking a class dealing in world events, and so on. Some ideas may be impractical. Some may be pure fantasy: move to another state; don't leave the house for a year; call the president of the United States. Writing down even impractical solutions is valuable, though. It could just be that a combination of answers is best. It helps to view them all.

Think About Each Solution In thinking about each solution, judge it based on your own values and feelings. Use the HELP strategy to guide your choices. Imagine and list the probable outcomes, both positive and negative. Compare the ideas. Then rank them in order from best to worst.

Consider the practicality of each solution. For example, a person who wanted to socialize with a group of friends but who had money problems might consider helping the group plan some affordable but enjoyable activities, such as a pot-luck dinner or a hike.

By helping plan activities, the person could assist the group without spending money. Then the person could participate because the activities would be low in cost.

Choose a Solution and Act on It Once you have thought all possible solutions through, you can pick one that fits your values and your personal circumstances. Try it out. Then answer the following questions to evaluate the solution:

- Did the solution produce the results you expected?
- How did the solution fit with your feelings and values?
- Did the solution fail to meet your needs in any significant way?

Evaluate the Outcome If the solution seems satisfactory, the decision was a good one. If the solution seems less than ideal, you can usually adjust it. In that case, you begin the process of deciding all over again.

Comprehension Check: Without using the book, have students name the six steps in the decision-making process.

Worksheets: A reproducible quiz for Section 3 is available in the Teacher Classroom Resources.

SECTION 3 Review

Reviewing the Facts
1. **List.** List the six steps for making decisions.
2. **Explain.** Why is the first step in the process so important?
3. **Synthesize.** Why should you be sure to brainstorm all the possible solutions to a problem?
4. **Describe.** What are three questions you can use in the evaluating process?

Writing Critically
5. **Expository.** Imagine you are a mediator for two friends at school who are having a conflict. Explain strategies to help them resolve the conflict.

For fitness and health tips, visit the Fitness Zone at **glencoe.com**.

1. Name the problem, describe the problem's parts, brainstorm, think about each solution, choose a solution and act on it, and evaluate the outcome.

2. Before you can make a decision you have to decide what the problem is. Some problems are easy; however, some are very complex.

3. All solutions, however impractical, can be valuable. Sometimes a combination of ideas is best.

4. Did the solution produce the results you expected? How did the solution fit with your feelings and values? Did the solution fail to meet your needs in any significant way?

5. Answers will vary.

Finding a Place in Society

You and the other people with whom you have relationships fit into your environment—your society. Your society may consist of the community you live in, your school, and your ethnic or religious group as well as other groups. Societies have sets of values and expectations of their own that they impose on their members.

Vocabulary

alienation
ostracism
nonconformist

Different Societies, Different Values

MAIN IDEA ▶ Each person must work out a relationship with society that is rewarding.

Preview Activity: Assign students an essay in which they describe how they know they are accepted by a group or society.

Our society has traditionally held values devoted to action and achievement in high regard Not all societies uphold the same values for their members. Furthermore, in our society and many others, no law forces people to live by the values of the majority. However, if they don't go along, they lose approval and support. People whose values differ from society's may experience **alienation** and **ostracism**. Alienation is *withdrawing from others because of differences that cannot be resolved*, while ostracism is *rejection and exclusion from society*. A person who doesn't fit in is a **nonconformist**, *a person who does not share society's values and therefore behaves in unconventional ways*.

Each of us must determine our relationship with the larger world according to his or her personal goals and values. Another may choose to live with a subgroup in society whose values differ from the majority's values.

■ **Figure 2.10** *Our values and expectations are part of a greater relationship with society. What can happen if people do not hold the same values as their society?*

Caption Answer: They can feel like they do not fit in.

Finding a Career

For most people, an important part of finding a place in society is to discover a fitting job or career. Some experts believe that rewarding work is the single most important aspect of adult life relating to well-being. Many people who are unhappy at work wish they had explored more options, through courses and summer jobs, before specializing in one field. Such people may decide to change careers later in life. They may find it worth all the effort to finally be in the right career.

If you are uncertain about a career, you might try some volunteer work with a variety of industries. For example, some veterinarians may appreciate your help in their offices a few hours a week. A local theater might need people to usher the attending crowds. A hospital, nursing home, or other health care facility might welcome some after-school help.

SECTION 4 Review

Reviewing the Vocabulary
Review the vocabulary on page 44. Then answer these questions.
1. Define *alienation*.
2. What is *ostracism*?

Reviewing the Facts
3. **Explain.** What elements make up society?
4. **Analyze.** What are the disadvantages of having values that differ from society's values?
5. **List.** Give some suggestions to a teen who is unsure about a future career.

Writing Critically
6. **Descriptive.** Your school is a type of self-contained society. The school staff has a set of values and expectations they impose on you. Which values and expectations do you accept? Are there any you reject? Give an example of a values confrontation you have experienced in school and how you handled it.

For more vocabulary practice, play the eFlashcards game at **glencoe.com**.

Class Activity
Discuss: Have students list as many reasons as they can think of why it's important that a job or career fit in with their values. Some of the reasons that students should list include: so that you feel good about your job or career, so that you enjoy the job or career, so that family, friends, and society approve of your job or career. Then, ask students what the consequences might be for someone who chooses a job or career that goes against his or her values. You may prompt students that a vegetarian may feel that a job in a fast food restaurant goes against their values.

Worksheets: A reproducible quiz for Section 4 is provided in the Teacher Classroom Resources.

Reproducible Study Outline and Reading Cloze worksheets for Chapter 2 are available in the Teacher Classroom Resources.

1. Alienation is withdrawing from others because of differences that cannot be resolved.
2. Ostracism is rejection and exclusion from society.
3. Societies have sets of values and expectations that are imposed on its members.
4. People may lose support and approval and may experience alienation and ostracism from society.
5. Try to volunteer your time within a variety of industries: a hospital, veterinary clinic, a theater, or a museum.
6. Answers will vary.

Teens and Violence

 Understand and Apply Read the conversation below, and then complete the writing exercise that follows.

The violent crime, a crime that involves threat or uses force, including assault, murder, rape, or robbery, associated with some groups of teens today triggers fear in almost everyone. In most communities the overall rate of murders and assaults has declined recently, but younger criminals are now committing a larger portion of these crimes, especially in lower income neighborhoods.

Q: I often hear about teens and crime. How are teens connected with crime?

A: Most often, reports about teens and crime focus on teenage criminals. They may fail to report that teens are crime's most frequent victims. Teens suffer the effects of violent crime and theft at a rate of about twice that of adults.

Statistics show that some teens carry weapons to school, at least occasionally. to protect themselves from fellow students. Other teens feel forced to cut classes or whole days of school to avoid violent classmates. These situations occur on a daily basis. In contrast, the tragic, mass school shootings that receive so much attention in the news occur only rarely.

Q: Who is committing all these violent crimes?

A: Older teens and young adults (18 to 24 years of age) commit the most murders. From the mid 1990s to the present, however, murders committed by this age group have declined. In fact, murders overall have recently reached new low levels.

Q: I only hear of a few teens on the news who commit violence. Where do regular kids fit into the picture?

A: The majority of teens do not commit violent crimes. For example, three out of five teens volunteer at least a few hours every week for worthy causes. Overall, teen criminals constitute a small group of "repeat offenders." Teens in this minority are usually male and have long-standing social problems.

Unfortunately, these offenders often victimize other teens as their targets. This bullying creates an atmosphere of fear that keeps other teens constantly under stress. A newer form of bullying is cyberbullying. Cyberbullies send false or misleading messages to others as a way to create fear and intimidate other. Some experts have expressed concern about the lasting psychological damage to adolescents who are affected by bullies.

Class Discussion. *Analyze*: Ask students to list the impact of violence crime on their family, their school, their community, and on themselves. Remind students not to give personal details of any crimes they may have witnessed or for which they have been a victim. Then, ask students whether they fear crime in their daily lives, and to describe some of the reasons for crime in their community. Have students brainstorm ideas that could reduce crime in their communities, and have the class write a letter to the city council or other local government, listing some of their ideas.

Q: What causes so much violence in our society?

A: One theory blames the legal system. The theory says our society is too soft on criminals. The theory points to the need for more police and longer jail times for offenders. This may sound like a simple solution, but the problems of crime and violence are complex. The United States imprisons more of its citizens for longer times than most other developed nations, yet its teen crime rate continues to climb higher.

Drug and alcohol abuse encourage delinquency. A majority of teen males arrested for crimes such as assault, burglary, or grand larceny test positive for drugs.

Some people blame the violent themes in music lyrics, television or music videos, and other media. Studies show that children who watch violence on television become more aggressive and insensitive to violence in real life. Some teens imitate the role models they see in the media.

Q: I think someone needs to take control and protect teens from violence. What can we do to help?

A: Sometimes, if enough people stand together on an issue, they can change things. Some strategies people use to prevent violence include:

- Providing positive, caring adult role models for young people who have none.
- Teaching young people social skills, such as how to maintain self-control, how to form friendships, how to communicate and interact with others in positive ways, and how to resist peer pressure.

- Using students to teach their peers about violence prevention.
- Providing recreation, student work, or volunteer activities for young people so they have the chance to spend time in structured, purposeful environments.

Learn and use the conflict-resolution strategies offered earlier in this chapter. In addition, you can take an honest look at your friends. If they often fight or carry weapons, take yourself out of their crowd and find other buddies.

Q: In my school, we have lock-ins, lockouts, drug tests, metal detectors—they even tell us that we can't wear certain kinds of clothes and makeup! What's the point of all these rules?

A: Rules and restrictions reflect a schools' attempts to establish a safe zone, so that their students can learn. In districts with high rates of crime, testing and "zero tolerance" for drugs, guns, and knives have reduced violence. Banning certain gang-related clothing or cosmetics is also believed to help. Peer mediation programs, mentioned in the chapter, also help end arguments that could otherwise lead to fights.

Programs that foster parent-child relationships, community involvement, religion or spirituality, promotion of peace, protection of the environment, improving literacy, or commitment to stamping out inequality can be life-enhancing. Seek out these groups and become involved.

 Writing Research one of the community organizations in your area devoted to fighting crime. Write a report detailing your findings.

Reviewing Vocabulary

Use the vocabulary terms listed below to complete the following statements.

resentment

status

emotion

emotional health

1. The state of being free of mental disturbances that limit functioning is _____.
2. A(n) _____ is a feeling that occurs in response to an event.
3. Anger that has built up due to a failure of expression is _____.

Recalling Key Facts and Ideas

Section 1

4. **Recall.** Which relationship supports you throughout your life?

5. **List.** List three benefits of positive thinking.

6. **Describe.** Describe how to change a negative thought into a positive one.

7. **Identify.** What is the advantage of being aware of your values?

8. **Name.** What three questions can you ask yourself about how strong your values are?

9. **Explain.** Why are all emotions considered acceptable?

Section 2

10. **Recall.** What are the problems with passive and aggressive behaviors?

11. **Explain.** Why does assertive behavior improve your relationships with people?

12. **Name.** What is the most common fear people have when meeting someone new?

13. **Identify.** What is the SOFTEN technique?

Section 3

14. **Recall.** What are the six steps you should follow when faced with making a decision?

Section 4

15. **Name.** What are some examples of a society to which you might belong?

16. **Explain.** What are the advantages of having a career you enjoy?

Writing Critically

17. **Explain.** Think back over your recent experiences and identify a situation in which you did not act assertively.

   a. Write a description of the experience. Include the reason for the conflict as you perceive it, the verbal interchange that occurred, and the outcome of the situation.

   b. Analyze your behavior. According to the definitions provided in Section 2, were your responses passive or aggressive?

   c. Write a revised version of the incident in which you act assertively. Describe the feelings you would probably experience after such an exchange.

1. Emotional health 2. Emotion 3. Resentment 4. Your relationship with yourself. 5. Peace of mind, reduced stress, and improved health.. 6. Recognize your negative thoughts, stop the negative thoughts, replace the negative thoughts with positive thoughts. 7. Awareness helps you choose your behaviors without confusion. 8. Would I be willing to state this value to others? How faithfully will I stand by this value when it is challenged? Do I act consistently and repeatedly in line with this value? 9. Emotions are a natural part of us. 10. They are not expressed appropriately. 11. You are able

18. **Personal.** Maintaining emotional health is easier for a person with a strong, well-developed support system than for someone who remains isolated from others. Examine how extensive your support system is by making a list of all your supports. Be sure to include people you have relationships with in all areas of your life. Which people on your list would you consider to be the most valuable supports? Are you satisfied with the support system you have developed for yourself? Describe any changes or improvements you would like to make.

Activities

19. Create a collage of magazine illustrations of different emotions.

20. Make a list of activities in your school and community that enhance emotional health. Suggest other activities the school could offer.

21. Devise a list of community resources for people seeking help for emotional problems. Provide the name, address, and phone number of each agency.

22. Write a short report on how school has affected your emotional health in the past year.

23. Keep an emotion diary for two days. List the emotions you felt, the situations that prompted them, and the outlets you used to deal with them.

24. Select a popular song that depicts a particular emotion. Discuss the music and lyrics that portray emotion.

Making Decisions about Health

25. You have just been treated unfairly and are uptight and tense. You return to your room where you pace around, shaking your head, with many unsaid remarks still running through your thoughts. Several times you start to pick up the phone, but there's no one you want to bother with your problems. Several times you start toward the door, but there's no place you want to go, feeling so uptight. Finally, you settle down, still angry, and try to do some home work, but you end the day with a knot in your stomach. Describe how you could have handled this situation to reduce your distress.

Go Online

For more vocabulary practice, play the True/False game at **glencoe.com**.

Fact or Fiction?

Answers

1. False. Emotional health is closely tied to physical health.
2. False. Once a person adopts values, that person continues to test those values and can change them when necessary.
3. False. It is best to face and deal with all feelings as promptly as possible, even those that seem illogical or unpleasant.

Writing Paragraphs will vary.

to express your emotions while respecting those of other people. **12.** Rejection **13.** It is a technique to remind you of what to do during a conversation with new people. Smile, Open posture, Forward lean, Touch, Eye contact, Nod. **14.** Name the problem. Describe the problem's parts. Brainstorm.

Think about each solution. Choose a solution and act on it. Evaluate the outcome. **15.** Community, school, religious group **16.** You will be happier and healthier if you have a career you enjoy. **17–25.** Answers will vary.

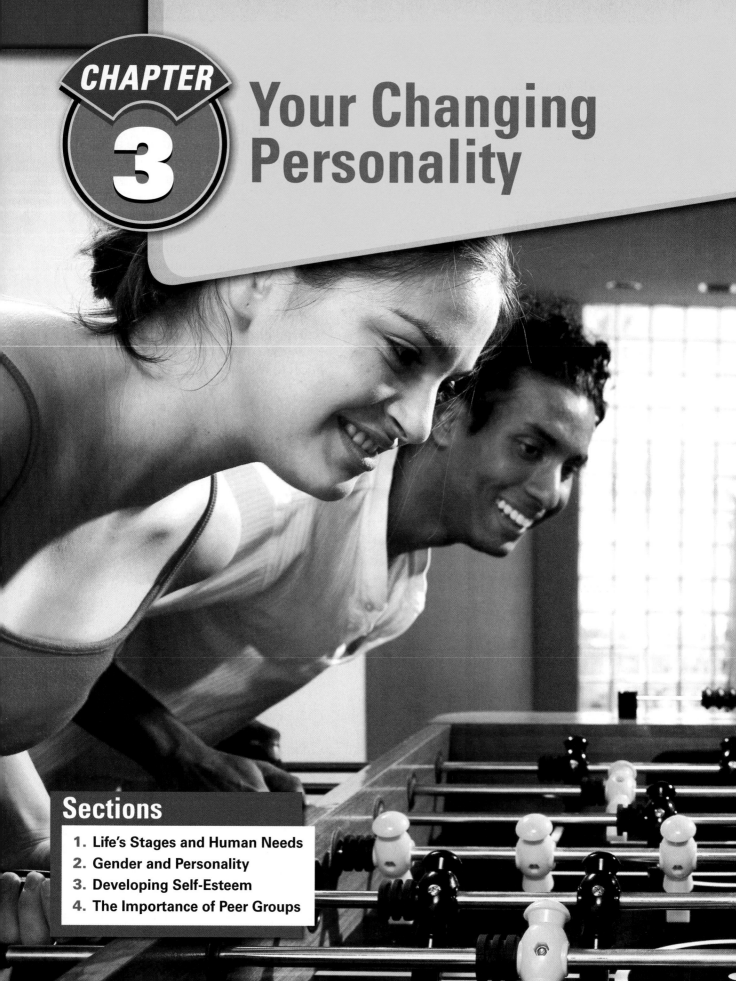

CHAPTER 3

Your Changing Personality

Sections

1. Life's Stages and Human Needs
2. Gender and Personality
3. Developing Self-Esteem
4. The Importance of Peer Groups

You may overhear someone say, "Leticia is so great to be around" or "I really like playing soccer with Mike." In each case, the speaker is reacting to Leticia's or Mike's personalities. Your **personality**, *the characteristics of a person that are apparent to others*, is a large part of how people see the total "you," on the outside. There is much more to you than what's seen from the outside. Your personality, the way you think, feel, and behave, defines you to others.

Personalities are not fixed for life. Each person has certain tendencies, which remain the same. Personalities can keep changing through life, however. A baby may be born shy, but the future child, teen, or adult can become outgoing. You are continually adapting your personality to fit the picture you have of who you really are, your **self-image**, *the characteristics that a person sees in himself or herself*. This chapter explains some influences that affect personality. It also guides you in developing a healthy self-image.

Fact or Fiction?

What Do You Think?
Is each statement true or false? If you think it's false, explain what's true.

1. One of the most important tasks of the teen years is to work out an individual identity.
2. Human beings need the respect of others even more than they need shelter.
3. People who imagine themselves as more successful than they are need to stop dreaming.

 Writing How might a friend or a family member describe you? Write a paragraph about your own personality traits. What are some things that influence someone's personality?

(Answers on page 77)

 Online

Visit **glencoe.com** and complete the Life Choice Inventory for Chapter 3.

Life's Stages and Human Needs

Changes that occur in people's lives can affect their personalities. For example, making the transition from middle school to high school might help a shy youngster discover a more outgoing confident, nature. In this section you will learn about two personality theories that may help you better understand your own development, behavior, and self-image.

Erikson's Eight Stages of Life

MAIN IDEA ▶ Erikson's theory divides the human life span into eight stages.

In **psychology**, *the scientific study of behavior and the mind*, the pioneer thinker Erik Erikson has described how people become who they are. Erikson's widely accepted theory states that people move through eight stages in the course of their lives. In each stage they learn important things about themselves and about the world.

■ **Figure 3.1** *Early in life, children's gender roles are shaped by society. How many stages of life make up Erikson's theory?*

Caption Answer: Eight

Figure 3.2 **Eight Stages of Life According to Erikson**

The numbered paragraphs describe the tasks that a healthy person will master at each stage.

1. **Infancy (0 to 1)** To learn trust. The infant learns that needs are met. (If neglected or abused, the infant learns distrust that can last a lifetime.)

2. **Toddler stage (1 to 2)** To learn independence. The toddler learns self-will. (If unable to complete this development, the adult may remain dependent and feel inadequate.)

3. **Preschool age (3 to 5)** To learn initiative (the ability to think and act without being told to do so). The child explores with curiosity and imagination. (If discouraged in this development, the adult may avoid leadership and risks.)

4. **School age (6 to 12)** To develop industriousness (earnest, steady effort). The child has confidence to pursue self-chosen goals. (If this development fails, the adult will lack social confidence and will perform poorly.)

5. **Adolescence (13 to 20)** To develop an identity. The teens develops a strong sense of self, goals, and timing and learns how to fit into the social circle—as leader, follower, female, male. The adolescent picks out role models and grows with confidence. (The failure of this development produces a confused person without a secure sense of direction.)

6. **Young adulthood (21 to 40)** To develop intimacy (close, personal relationships). The young adult can commit to love, to work, and to a social group. (Failure leads to avoidance of intimacy, misuse of sexuality, isolation, and destructiveness.)

7. **Adulthood (41 to 60)** To develop generativity (giving yourself and your talents to others). The mature adult moves through life with confidence, taking pride in accomplishments. (The negative side of this is stagnation, self-involvement, and failure to encourage others.)

8. **Older adulthood (61 and older)** To retain ego integrity (satisfaction with life). The person feels fulfilled and faces death with serenity. (The adult who has not moved positively through earlier stages experiences isolation, despair, and fears of death.)

- Remind students that the negative words we say to each other can be as destructive and damaging as a physical attack, and the effects are often more long lasting.

- Ask students to write every positive comment they hear about themselves or someone else during the next 24 hours.. Also have them write every negative comment they hear.

Stimulate class discussion by asking:

- Where were most negative comments made—directly to the person or behind that person's back?

- How do you feel about negative comments you learn are directed to you?

- Emphasize that making positive comments helps students develop self-esteem for themselves as well as others. Encourage them to make positive comments as often as possible.

Each stage ideally consists of positive development, and each builds on the one before it. For example, the one-year-old learns basic trust as an infant. He then can progress toward becoming independent in the next year. The eight stages are shown in **Figure 3.2** on page 53. No one, however, moves perfectly through all of the stages.

The path of development, according to Erikson, might go like this: If, as an infant, toddler, and preschooler, you received mostly approval from the adults in your life, you progressed confidently from one stage to the next. By the time you started school, you were sure of your ability to master new tasks. As a result, you worked with confidence and persistence through the school years, even in the face of frustrations.

By the end of the teen years, the successful person has achieved a positive sense of identity. From there, the teen moves to the first stage of adulthood—the stage of building a mature, intimate relationship with another person.

A Teen's New Experiences

MAIN IDEA ▶ People develop their identities and their ability to reason during the teen years.

The teen years can be an exciting time for discovering your identity. To develop an identity means to partially move away from what is known and to explore the unknown.

New Ideas and New Groups

Teens try out new ideas, develop new words, and give new meanings to old phrases. Clothes, music, and art are other areas in which teens use their imaginations to explore and search for their identities.

New Ways of Thinking

Teens are also developing a new way of thinking. Children think only in concrete terms, relying on past experiences to predict the future. Teens, though, begin to think in more abstract terms. They can imagine what might happen "if this" or "should that" be the case.

Teens can consider **variables**, *changeable factors that affect outcomes*, and use logic to make predictions of what might happen. They can plan to achieve desired outcomes, and they spend hours exploring "what ifs." The hours teens spend with others permit them to practice reasoning, a skill that gives them a great advantage in working out relationships with others. Thinking develops considerably during adolescence.

New Emotions

Many teens may feel the ups and downs of different emotions. For example, one minute you might feel like a total success and a few minutes later, like a failure. These ups and downs are normal and lead to the development of an identity. At times almost anything they try may seem a possible way to pattern their lives.

A person who emerges from the teen years feeling "okay" can move on to adult tasks without difficulty. The less fortunate teen who feels a sense of self-doubt and failure may have difficulty performing the tasks of adulthood.

Human Needs According to Maslow

MAIN IDEA ▶ **Personality develops in stages throughout life.**

Erikson saw life's tasks as associated with age groups. The psychologist Abraham Maslow, in contrast, described them as a **hierarchy**, *a ranking system in which each thing is placed above or below others*. This is like a ladder of human **needs**, *urgent wants for necessary things*, that people ofall ages experience at different times. He linked these needs to life's accomplishments.

Comprehension Check
Ask students to explain a basic difference between Erikson and Maslow. (Erikson's theory says tasks progress primarily by age; Maslow's says they develop by needs.)

Worksheets: Vocabulary worksheets are provided in the Teacher Classroom Resources.

Figure 3.3   Maslow's Hierarchy of Needs

SELF-ACTUALIZATION NEEDS

ESTEEM

LOVE

SAFETY

PHYSIOLOGICAL NEEDS

A Ladder of Needs

According to Maslow, people will first try to meet their basic needs before they can begin to think about "higher" needs (see **Figure 3.3**). Most basic are needs related to survival—needs for food, clothing, and shelter (physiological needs). Next are the needs to feel physically safe and secure (safety needs). If safe and secure, people can fulfill their needs to be loved and to feel emotionally secure (love needs). If those needs are met, people can try to get in touch with their needs for respect and esteem. Given that, they can seek to achieve the ultimate need: **self-actualization**. This is *the realization of one's full potential:* becoming "all that they can be."

Traits of Self-Actualization

Maslow believed that all self-actualizing people share some traits in common. Such people:

- Accept themselves and others, and accept imperfections.
- Are self-motivated, rather than externally motivated.
- Are problem solvers, rather than complainers.
- Have a strong set of values by which they live, and are sensitive to ethical issues.
- Believe in the power of people, holding that most are basically good.
- Are at peace with themselves and their world.

Service to Others

Like all people, teens share the common need for respect and the esteem of others. Many people say that some of their best experiences as teens involved some sort of service to others. To be helpful, especially to those who really need help, fills a need to feel important and to be appreciated by others. Being helpful enhances self-esteem.

Performing needed service to others helps also in the development of identity. Teens who work together during disasters to assist other people may develop part of their identities in the process. Other teens who volunteer in the community may find that this experience adds to self-understanding and identity.

A Lifetime of Needs

No one ever arrives at the point of being completely finished with any level of needs. As soon as one is met, another takes its place. This gives us something to work on, which is itself a need we all seem to have.

Worksheets: A reproducible quiz for Section 1 is provided in the Teacher Classroom Resources.

SECTION 1 Review

Reviewing the Vocabulary

Review the vocabulary on page 52. Then answer these questions.

1. What is the difference between personality and self-image?
2. Define self-actualization.
3. Write a sentence using needs.
4. _____ is the scientific study of behavior and the mind.
5. Define variables.
6. A ranking system in which each thing is placed above or below others is called a _____.

Reviewing the Facts

7. **Explain.** How does the thinking of teens differ from children's thinking?
8. **Describe.** What are some of the extremes in emotions that teens may feel?
9. **List.** What are some of the most basic human needs according to Maslow?

Writing Critically

10. **Personal.** List in order Maslow's hierarchy of needs. Identify what your specific needs are in each of Maslow's major categories. Make a list of some steps you could take that you believe would help to bring you closer to self-actualization.

Go Online

For more vocabulary practice, play the True/False game at **glencoe.com.**

1. Personality is the characteristics of a person that are apparent to others. Self-image is the characteristics that a person sees in himself or herself.

2. The reaching of one's full potential according to Maslow's hierarchy of needs.

3. Everyone has basic needs for survival.

4. Psychology

5. Variables are changeable factors that affect outcomes.

6. Hierarchy

7. Children rely on past experiences to predict the future. Teenagers have the intellectual ability imagine what might happen "if this" or "should that" be the case.

8. Teens may feel successful one minute and failure the next.

9. Food, clothing, shelter

10. Answers will vary.

Gender and Personality

Two parts of human development undergo rapid change during the teen years. One is the development of physical characteristics. Another, which goes along with the physical changes, is the development of gender identity—a personality with maleness or femaleness.

Physical Maturation

MAIN IDEA ▶ Adolescence is a time of rapid physical and mental change.

Children grow and mature physically from birth to adulthood. However, not until some time around the early teen years do they enter the period of sexual maturation called **adolescence**, *the period of growth from the beginning of puberty to full maturity.* The beginning of adolescence is marked by **puberty**. Puberty is *the period of life in which a person becomes physically capable of reproduction.* During these years, nature seems in a hurry to complete the final details needed for full adulthood. The adolescent growth spurt is a time of rapid growth and change (see **Figure 3.6**).

Vocabulary

- adolescence
- puberty
- gender
- gender roles
- gender identity
- femininity
- masculinity
- stereotypes
- sexual harassment

■ **Figure 3.5** *Parents who teach their children to value working hard will raise teens who are motivated to succeed. Name two changes that occur during the teen years?*

Caption Answer: Physical characteristics and gender identity

Preview Activity:

- Tell students that humans have male and female gender roles.

- Ask students to make a list, using one- or two-word answers, of personality traits they feel are considered feminine and masculine.

- Students might identify some traits as both masculine and feminine. Lead a class discussion about how gender roles shape our society.

Figure 3.6 **Physical Changes of Adolescence**

Females

Growth
Rapid gains peak around age 12, then growth slows to a stop at maturity.

Hair
Hair grows on underarm and genital areas, and other body hair may grow coarser and longer.

Skin
Acne may develop.

Body shape and composition
Hips widen, fat deposits collect, and breasts develop.

Hormonal changes
Ovaries produce more estrogen and progesterone.

Reproductive organs
Uterus and ovaries enlarge; genitals enlarge; ovum ripening begins; monthly menstruation begins.

Males

Growth
Rapid gains peak around age 14, then growth slows to a stop at maturity.

Hair
Hairline of forehead begins to move upward (recede). Hair grows on face, in underarms, and around genitals. Other body hair grows coarser and longer.

Skin
Acne may develop.

Body shape and composition
Muscle tissue develops.

Hormonal changes
Testicles produce more testosterone. Reproductive organs (penis and testicles) enlarge; sperm production begins.

For some, the changes occur faster than the individuals can adjust to them. For others, the changes come so slowly that they fear being left behind. The teen years soon pass; you then join society's adults as an equal.

The Adolescent Growth Spurt

During adolescence, individual growth rates vary tremendously. Generally, girls begin an intensive growth spurt by age 10 or 11, while boys arrive at this time of rapid growth at 12 or 13. Two healthy, normal adolescents of the same age may vary in height by a foot.

Class Activity

Key Passage: Hormonal changes also lead to increased growth as a teen's adult body develops. Ask students which of the following continue to change after adolescence, and which do not: thoughts, emotions, spiritual beliefs, and physical growth. (physical growth slows.)

As they grow toward adulthood, girls naturally develop more body fat than boys do. This fat is needed for breast formation and other normal development. In contrast to girls, boys naturally develop more muscle tissue. As is true in girls, this tissue grows in response to hormones.

Hormones and Other Changes

The hormonal changes of adolescence greatly affect every organ, including the brain. The release of hormones also result in mood changes.

Hormonal changes also lead to increased growth as a teen's adult body develops. Some teens feel awkward during this stage. As the body improves in coordination, movements requiring control and skill become possible.

As boys and girls grow into young men and women, their social relationships also change. They must develop new ways of relating to their peers and work out new rules to govern their relationships. Physical maturity, however, does not mean the end of growth and change. Mental, emotional, and spiritual growth and change can continue for a lifetime.

Gender Identity

MAIN IDEA ▶ Each person adopts characteristics that go with that person's gender.

Your personality is affected by your **gender**, *the classification of being male or female*. Your gender helps mold your behaviors and your self-image.

Gender Roles

The male or female roles people play are known as their **gender roles**, *roles assigned by society to people of each gender*. A person's inherited genes play a part in the development of a person's gender role. Society's expectations are powerful in molding these roles. Each society creates rules as to how it expects males or females to act. Not everyone adopts all of society's gender roles. In fact, if enough people find them a bad fit, the roles themselves may change. The parts of the male or female role that a person adopts and lives by become that person's **gender identity**, *that part of a person's self-image that is determined by the person's gender*.

A Lifetime of Influence

Society responds even to its newest members according to its gender expectations. People can be overheard saying when observing a newborn boy, "Look how big and strong he is!" If the baby is a girl, they might say, "She's so tiny and delicate!" Actually, newborns differ in size, strength, and activity not according to gender but according to their heredity.

Toddlers begin to demonstrate their gender identity before they can even talk. Two-year-olds show real understanding of these roles. Young teens, with their newly maturing sexual bodies, often exaggerate these roles. They want to make sure that those around them are aware of their **femininity**, *traits, including biological and social traits, associated with being female*, or **masculinity**, *traits, including biological and social traits, associated with being male*.

What If the Roles Don't Fit?

Accepting all of society's gender roles is not always easy or even desirable. People are individuals. Roles that may fit one person perfectly may not fit another. If everyone accepted roles without question, societies would never change. **Stereotypes**, *fixed pictures of how everyone in a group is thought to be; ideas that do not recognize anyone's individuality*, may harm individual development. No one is treated fairly when allowed only a limited space in which to grow toward personhood.

It takes generations to replace old gender stereotypes completely. Some that you may see changing during your lifetime are these:

- Men are active and independent; women are passive and dependent.

- Men hide their emotions; women show their emotions.

- Men discipline their children; women nurture them.

- A man's success is seen in his earnings or status; a woman's success is measured by the man she marries.

Evidence that confining old roles are breaking down can be seen all around us. High-ranking political offices are now open to and held by women. The nursing profession has welcomed men into the field. These are just two of many examples.

Sexual Harassment

The process of breaking down old gender stereotypes has not been easy. Strong female figures in politics and the military, for example, have been verbally or even physically attacked for being too aggressive or outspoken—traits that their attackers identify as male. Similarly, men who do not embrace traditionally masculine characteristics have been ridiculed.

■ **Figure 3.8** *Gender identity is important, but even more so is the full realization of a person's potential. Why is it more important to try to realize your potential rather than to choose a career based on gender identity?*

Caption Answer: If you are good at something, it does not matter if you are a male or female.

Today, both men and women are speaking out against sexual harassment that was once endured silently. **Sexual harassment** is the *unwanted sexual attention, often from someone in power*. Sexual harassment is illegal. It shouldn't be ignored. If you experience it, tell the person to stop. If it doesn't stop, report it to school officials, your parents or guardian, or another trusted adult.

Worksheets: A reproducible quiz for Section 2 is provided in the Teacher Classroom Resources.

SECTION 2 Review

Reviewing the Vocabulary

Review the vocabulary on page 58. Then answer these questions.

1. The classification of being male or female is called your _____.
2. Define *adolescence*.
3. What is the difference between a person's *gender identity* and *gender role*?
4. _____ means traits, including biological and social traits, associated with being male.
5. Define *stereotypes*.
6. Unwanted sexual attention, often from someone in power, that makes the victim feel uncomfortable or threatened is called _____.

Reviewing the Facts

7. **Recall.** At approximately what age do adolescent girls begin a growth spurt?
8. **List.** List some changes that occur due to increased levels of hormones during puberty.
9. **Describe.** Name some common gender stereotypes.

Writing Critically

10. **Explain.** What do you think are some of the most common things boys and girls your age worry about most as their bodies show physical changes?

For more information on health careers, visit Career Corner at **glencoe.com**.

1. Gender
2. The period of growth from the beginning of puberty to full maturity. Timing of adolescence varies from person to person.
3. Gender identity is the part of a person's self-image that is determined by gender. A gender role is assigned by society to people of each gender.
4. Masculinity
5. Fixed pictures of how everyone in a group is thought to be.
6. Sexual harassment
7. Age 10–11
8. Changes in mood, coordination and movement
9. Men are active, and independent. Women are passive and dependent.
10. Answers will vary.

Developing Self-Esteem

People who know and like themselves are emotionally healthy. Not only do they have a strong sense of self-efficacy for accomplishing tasks, as described in Chapter 1, but they also have a high **self-esteem**, *the value a person attaches to his or her self-image*.

People with high self-esteem do not think they are perfect. In fact, they know they are not, but they like themselves anyway. They not only cherish the positive sides of themselves, they have learned to accept their flaws.

Actions to Promote Positive Self-Esteem

MAIN IDEA ▶ To develop high self-esteem, use positive self-talk to turn ideas about what you'd like to be into realities.

Many factors can benefit your self-image, such as friends who value and respect you, regular physical activity, and being involved in community activities. Another factor is replacing negative self-talk with positive self-talk. **Positive self-talk** is *the practice of making affirming statements to oneself*. Positive self-talk gives you power—that is, it increases your feelings of self-esteem.

Vocabulary

self-esteem
positive self-talk
body image

Preview Activity: Write the words *self-image, self-esteem,* and *value* on the board. Ask students for a definition of each. (Self-image: the characteristics a person sees in him or herself; Self-esteem: The value a person attaches to his or her self-image; Value: relative worth, importance, degree of excellence.) Ask students how self-image and value affect self-esteem.

■ **Figure 3.9** *Volunteer activities can help increase a person's self-esteem. What factors can benefit your self-image?*

Caption Answer: Having friends who value and respect you, regular physical activity, community activities

You give yourself the power to become the person you want to become and to do the things you want to do when positive ideas replace self-defeating messages. To practice positive self-talk, repeat to yourself an idea that you wish to become a reality. For example, a person who wishes to feel less anxious might think or say aloud, "I can relax when under stress." A person who wishes to feel less lonely might think, "I can be alone without being lonely" or "I like people, and they like me" or "I accept myself and I can change myself if I choose to." The Health Skills sidebar, "Improving Self-Esteem," lists some positive actions for developing a more successful you.

You can also help yourself to succeed at whatever task you undertake, or to develop whatever quality you desire, by mentally seeing yourself already there. Imagining a successful outcome in advance helps people battle diseases, win athletic contests, and overcome emotional problems.

Positive Body Image

A positive body image contributes to self-esteem. **Body image** is *the way a person thinks his or her body looks*. Unfortunately, some teens may feel unhappy with their body type. They may compare their bodies to those of models, athletes, or actors. As you might guess, a negative body image and the intense pressure from society for a sexier appearance make many people easy prey for advertisers who want to take advantage of consumers.

During adolescence, both males and females mature at different rates. It is important not to compare your body to others. Each person matures normally on their own timetable, and each deserves respect and acceptance. Some are early to mature, some are later, but all eventually arrive.

Some teens might try and change their body type by trying a fad diet. Your physical health will benefit most through eating healthfully and engaging in physical activity. Chapters 7 through 9 go into more detail on nutrition and physical activity.

Self-Acceptance

MAIN IDEA ▶ Enjoy your accomplishments and view yourself as a worthwhile and valuable person.

Another way to acquire a positive view of your inner self is to appreciate your own uniqueness. Many unhappy people compare themselves with others and rate themselves lowly by comparison. Learn to see yourself as special and unique—as a person who is worthwhile and valuable.

Instead of making comparisons between yourself and others, celebrate the strengths you see in others and also those you know you possess. Believe in yourself.

Health Skills

Improving Self-Esteem

These actions can bolster your self-esteem and improve your self-image:

1. Write positive statements about yourself.
2. Find activities related to your goals.
3. Be grateful for what you have.
4. Practice positive self-talk.
5. Search for books and movies with positive themes.
6. Find friends who believe in you.
7. Support others. Be a positive friend.
8. Refuse to think negatively about yourself or others.
9. Celebrate your successes.
10. Give and receive appropriate affection—hugs, for example.

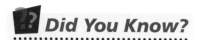

APPLYING Health Skills

Communication Skills

➤ **Objectives**
- Create a clear, organized message to assert feelings.
- Describe assertive body language and tone of voice.
- Demonstrate effective communication skills.

New Girl in School

The students that Shanae hang out with say mean things about a new girl in school. The girl is from another state and talks and dresses differently than Shanae and her friends. Shanae sometimes laughs at the things her friends say, even if some of these remarks make her feel uncomfortable. Shanae doesn't join in and put the new girl down, but she also hasn't asked her friends to stop. She would like to be more assertive and speak her mind, but she can't seem to find the courage. Shanae feels guilty for not speaking up and defending the new girl. She feels that she's always been a good friend. She tries to accept new students at school. It's starting to have a negative effect on her self-esteem.

➤ **Identify the Problem**
1. Why would Shanae like to be more assertive?

➤ **Form an Action Plan**
2. Write a clear, organized message that Shanae could make to express her feelings to her friends. Use "I" messages.
3. Describe the body language and tone of voice that Shanae should use to assert her feelings when she makes the statement.
4. What reasons might Shanae give for asking her friends to stop saying mean things about the new girl?

➤ **What Did You Learn?**
5. If a friend of yours was making cruel remarks about another student, what would you say to the friend to stop the remarks? How would you say it so your friend knew that you really meant it?

1. Shanae wants to be more assertive. She should tell her friends how she feels about their remarks and ask them to stop. Being passive is making her feel guilty and negatively affecting her self-esteem.

2. Shanae might state, "I think the new girl would feel really hurt by the things you are saying. It makes me feel uncomfortable when you say those things. I would feel better if you would stop talking about her like that."

3. Shanae should sit or stand up straight and look her friends directly in the eye when she makes the statement. She should speak in a clear, steady voice without hesitation. She should act serious but not pushy or angry.

4. Shanae might remind her friends that just because the new girl talks and dresses differently, it doesn't mean she is a bad person or deserves to have her feelings hurt. Shanae also might describe how she would feel if she were in the new girl's position.

5. Answers will vary. Sample answer: I felt the remarks were unkind and unnecessary. I would also say that they made me feel uncomfortable. I would say it in a serious tone of voice while looking my friend directly in the eye.

Part of developing self-esteem is to value who you are, and not just what you do. Society often focuses on achievements such as how much money people make, how many awards they win, the grades they earn, and the like. While these all are worthy goals, stay aware that they do not define the worth of a person. People who link their inner selves too tightly with outer accomplishments easily fall into the trap of defining themselves by their deeds. Then, when they fail or make mistakes, they think of themselves as failures or mistakes. They don't realize that the mistake is what they did, not what they are.

Know that you are unique and worthwhile aside from your achievements and accomplishments. You are important in spite of your failures and mistakes. Once you've developed high self-esteem, achievements and accomplishments follow naturally.

SECTION 3 Review

Reviewing the Vocabulary
Review the vocabulary on page 64. Then answer these questions.
1. Define *self-esteem*.
2. What is *positive self-talk*?
3. _____ is the way a person thinks their body looks.

Reviewing the Facts
4. List. List two qualities of people who have high self-esteem.
5. Analyze. What is to be gained by using positive self-talk?
6. Explain. Why is a negative body image so common in our society?

Writing Critically
7. Descriptive. List ten things about yourself and your life that you really like. Then, beside each item you listed, write one way you can use these things you like to help others feel more positive about themselves. For example, if you think you have a nice smile, smile at friends and others more often.

Go Online
For fitness and health tips, visit the Fitness Zone at **glencoe.com.**

1. The value a person attaches to his or her self-image

2. The practice of making affirming statements about oneself, helpful in building self-esteem

3. Body image

4. They know and like themselves; they do not think they are perfect, but accept their own flaws.

5. Positive self-talk can improve your self-esteem.

6. There is intense pressure from society to have a "sexier appearance."

7. Answers will vary.

The Importance of Peer Groups

So far, this chapter has emphasized the individual. However, an important part of normal development in the teen years is an association with peer groups. A **peer group** is simply *a group of friends similar to yourself in age and stage of life*. For many adolescents, peer groups are a positive influence on development. Peer groups help to bridge the gap between the dependent state of childhood and the independent state of full adulthood.

Peer groups can be a negative influence if they pressure you to engage in harmful activities. They might apply **peer pressure**, *the internal pressure one feels to behave as a peer group does, in order to gain its members' approval*. Often members of a peer group will form a **clique**, *a peer group that rejects newcomers and judges both their members and nonmembers harshly*. Teens sometimes ignore their own values just to fit in with the crowd.

Peer groups operate in the same way as many organizations. Each has a set of rules and expects certain behaviors from its members. For example, if the crowd expects sophisticated, "cool," or snobbish behavior, students who act otherwise may be treated with hostility. Cliques, especially, take a rigid stance, rejecting new people and new ideas.

Vocabulary

- peer group
- peer pressure
- clique
- deviant
- gangs
- cults
- refusal skills

Preview Activity:

- Remind students that individual positive development is very important. A normal teen's development includes associating with peer groups.

- Discuss this as a class. Ask for a definition of the term *peer group*. Ask them for the names of some peer groups they have been associated with since starting school.

- Discuss in class the reasons they enjoyed these peer groups and stress that sometimes we outgrow certain peer groups and go on to others.

■ **Figure 3.10** *To find their identity, teens often experiment with different styles. Why are peer groups important?*

Caption Answer: They help us develop our identity.

Most peer groups, though, provide their members with a sense of belonging. A circle of friends offers a place to share ideas, interests, and opinions. These friends also provide support and strength. It's easier to be confident when you know others are on your side. Belonging to a wide variety of groups may help teens learn to get along with many kinds of people. The Health Skills sidebar on this page offers tips for making new friends.

The Formation of Peer Groups

MAIN IDEA ▶ Belonging to many peer groups can be a positive influence on development.

For most teens, peers become important in providing clues to each individual's identity. By observing the reactions of their peers, young teens learn valuable lessons about their own tendencies and how they interact with others.

Some peer groups of young teens are easy to identify. They talk alike, dress alike, and do everything together. These tight groups help young people to find their places in the larger society. Within these groups, young teens begin to develop their identities. By the late teen years, associations with peers usually loosen to become less demanding. They still remain important, however, and can evolve into more mature friendships that may last throughout life. Many teens, however, move to different peer groups as they get older and develop new interests.

Some teens hesitate getting into new groups. Shyness is really a fear that if other people knew the person within, rejection would follow. Shy people can get over these fears by seeking comfortable settings in which to meet with others, and by realizing that many other people feel the same way.

The Value of Peer Groups

MAIN IDEA ▶ Peer groups can help teens feel a sense of belonging.

An important function of peer groups is to help lessen teens' natural fears. Young people often feel an exaggerated sense of uniqueness— "I'm the only one who feels this way." or "Everyone is looking at me. I must look awful!" These extreme feelings are natural, but are not based on reality. Most people feel the same emotions as other people from time to time. As for the judging stares from the crowd—those people are all thinking about themselves and probably believing that everyone is staring at them.

Health Skills

Making New Friends

The three Cs that are essential to making friends: communication, cooperation, and compromise:

1. **Communication.** Learn to listen well. In your own words, repeat to the speaker what you think you heard.

2. **Cooperation.** Be a good team player, Develop an open mind and a willingness to help others.

3. **Compromise.** Be willing to give up something to reach an acceptable solution. Don't compromise your beliefs or values though.

CAMERA SURVEILLANCE

GRAFFITI PUNISHED TO THE FULL EXTENT OF THE LAW

Caption Answer:: Communities can enforce curfews, establish neighborhood watch programs, and after-school programs.

Class Activity

Discuss:

- On the left side of the board or an overhead transparency, write *Constructive Outcomes*. On the right, write the words *Destructive Outcomes*.

- Now have the students tell you all the constructive or good outcomes that can be experienced from being connected to peer groups. List their answers under Constructive Outcomes.

- Do the same thing for Destructive Outcomes, listing all the negative outcomes that can be experienced from being connected to peer groups.

- Have a class discussion of your lists. Are there any trends that can be seen? What are the long-term benefits and negative consequences of belonging to a peer group?

Peer groups provide a shelter from these extremes. Numbers also provide safety and a degree of anonymity in which each person can try out a newly emerging identity.

Finally, peer groups can help teens through tough times. It's natural to share feelings with others. For example, suppose a student whose parents were divorcing was constantly upset. She talked about her feelings to some friends and was surprised to learn how many had gone through similar experiences. As she listened to their stories, she came to realize that although her pain was significant, it was not permanent. She also found that talking with others made her feel better. It helped to know that she wasn't alone.

Parents Are Primary Influences

MAIN IDEA ▶ **Parents remain the primary influencers in the lives of many teens.**

Although parents may fear that peer group values will replace parents' values, research shows otherwise. Along with a search for independence, most teens maintain strong relationships with their parents and permanently adopt many parental values.

In general, teens adopt their parents' values on issues that matter—family, religion, work, morals, standards, and the like. Teens most often adopt peer values concerning style and taste—dress, music, clothes, cars, and so forth. Teens also may turn to peers for opinions on issues their parents may hesitate to discuss—sexuality, drugs, birth control, and dating. In this way, teens tend to blend family values with new values they've worked out for themselves. However, most teens typically develop a set of values similar to those of their parents.

Deviant Peer Groups—Gangs and Cults

MAIN IDEA ▶ Gangs and cults may meet a person's need to belong, but they do not provide a positive peer group experience.

A teen's needs to develop an identity and to belong to a group are strong. These needs are so strong, in fact, that teens can be led astray by groups that are not beneficial. **Deviant** groups, groups *outside the normal system*, may provide an identity and meet a person's need to belong, but they do so at a high price. A positive-minded peer group may help a student stay in school. A deviant group, however, may influence the person to drop out.

Gangs

Gangs are *groups that exist largely to express aggression against other groups*. Gangs enforce their rules within their group by their own authority. They remain outside of the larger society. A gang may require its members to commit serious crimes, take or sell illegal drugs, or take part in other dangerous or harmful activities. Gang activities are mostly related to obtaining money in illegal ways for the benefit of high-ranking gang members.

What Teens Think
Discuss:

a. Do students feel that they encounter a lot of peer pressure? How often?

b. Do they agree with Jordan H. that peer pressure is anything that causes you to "stray from your uniqueness"?

c. We usually think of peer pressure as being negative. Can students cite positive examples, such as the one given by Sean N.?

What Teens THINK

What Experiences Have You Had with Peer Pressure?

People are pressuring people to be on the same side of an issue as themselves. They have made me feel like a fool because I wouldn't take a side or because I disagreed with them.

—Carrie Z., 16, Oregon

Experiences involving peer pressure occur every day. It has to do with more than drugs and alcohol. Peer pressure is anything that tries to make you stray from your uniqueness. I try all the time to remember who I am, and not to do something just because someone else is doing it.

—Jordan H., 17, Florida

I've been peer pressured to study more! Once, my friends and I were studying for a test. I had been invited to a party that night and suggested we all go. My friends convinced me that it was better for us to stay home studying. We all did really well on the test the next day. So, sometimes peer pressure is good.

—Sean N., 17, Maryland

Sometimes when I go to a party with my friends, it can be hard to say no if someone tries to give me alcohol. But I stop and think about what I value most in life and that makes it easier to say "no thanks!"

—Alicia W., 16, Ohio

Figure 3.12 *Practicing refusal skills can empower you to make good decisions. What are some refusal skills you can use to refuse peer pressure?*

Caption Answer: Listen to your feelings and values, ask for help from a trusted adult, stand up for yourself.

Health Skills

Practicing Your Refusal Skills

These skills will help you refuse peer pressure:

1. Sort out feelings and identify them accurately.
2. Judge persuasion tactics against your beliefs and values.
3. Use effective communication skills to turn them to your way of thinking.
4. Be assertive.
5. Take wise actions such as walking away.
6. Ask for help from parents or school authorities if someone suggests something dangerous or illegal.

Gang members often try to conform to their group. They often dress alike, talk alike, and use special symbols to identify themselves. A member may struggle mentally and physically to develop a reputation within the gang. A gang can become a dangerous substitute for other important groups such as family or community.

Cults

Cults are *groups of people who share intense admiration or adoration of a particular person or principle.* Some cults a group that monitors "mind control" cults, hundreds of such organizations are active today. Some of them have enormous scope and power.

Cults may disguise themselves as a group offering peace or contentment. In reality, though, they may exist for the sole purpose of amassing money for themselves. People who are drawn into cults are often convinced—through guilt, brainwashing, threats, or even legal actions—to hand over their worldly goods, and to work for the profit of the cult while living in poverty.

When people join groups that step outside of the rules of the larger society, they do not have many close friendships or a limited social network. Sometimes they face rejection and punishment from the majority. The people most drawn to such groups seem to be those who fail to fit in successfully with peer groups during young life, and for whom the larger society has little to offer as adults.

Peers are important. Make sure you choose them with care. People who get involved with deviant groups often find it difficult to get themselves out again. The Health Skills sidebar, "Practicing Your Refusal Skills," and the Q&A section offer tips on how to stand up to unwanted peer pressure.

Class Activity

Discuss: How can gang involvement cause problems with friendships? Ask students, "What would you do if a close friend joined a gang, and you didn't want to join? What are some of the consequences of joining a gang?"

SECTION 4 Review

Reviewing the Vocabulary

Review the vocabulary on page 68. Then answer these questions.

1. Define *peer group*.
2. What is a *clique*?
3. What are *gangs*?
4. The internal pressure one feels to behave as a peer group does, in order to gain its members' approval, is called ____.
5. ____ means outside the normal system.
6. Groups of people who share intense admiration or adoration of a particular person or principle are called ____.
7. Define *refusal skills*.

Reviewing the Facts

8. **Explain.** What changes occur in peer groups from early teens to late teens?
9. **Analyze.** What are some functions of peer groups?
10. **Describe.** What is the advantage of belonging to a wide variety of peer groups?

Writing Critically

11. **Narrative.** Relate a positive personal experience with peer pressure. What did you gain?
    a. Describe a negative personal experience with peer pressure. If you had this situation to live over again, how would you do it?
    b. Has it become easier or harder to resist peer pressure as you have gotten older? Why do you think this is so?

For more vocabulary practice, play the eFlashcards game at **glencoe.com**.

1. A group of friends who are similar in age and stage of life.
2. A peer group that rejects newcomers and judges both their members and nonmembers harshly
3. Groups that exist largely to express aggression against other groups
4. Peer pressure
5. Deviant
6. Cults
7. A set of social strategies that enable people to competently resist the pressure by others to engage in dangerous or otherwise undesirable behaviors
8. Early teen peer groups tend to dress alike and talk alike. By the late teen years, peer groups become less demanding.
9. Peer groups offer support and strength and may build confidence.
10. By belonging to a wide variety of groups, teens learn to get along with many kinds of people.
11. Answers will vary.

Dealing with Peer Pressure

 Understand and Apply Read the conversation below, then complete the writing exercise that follows.

Each day presents teens with new choices to weigh against personal values. Which choices are right? Which are wrong? While many choices lead to productive and positive experiences, other paths lead to destructive lifestyles that can set a negative course that lasts a lifetime. Teens don't make these choices alone. They are influenced by the behaviors of their peer groups

Q: When people talk about peer pressure, they usually say that your friends are pushing you to do things you don't want to do. Are peers usually a bad influence?

A: Not always. In fact, a positive peer group can encourage individuals to achieve things they never thought possible. Group values can give individuals the strength to say no to temptations. A peer group can be a major influence in a student's decision to excel in school, for example.

Some groups are mostly negative, though. They exploit the inborn human need to belong, especially in teens who lack either the strong self-esteem or the skills needed to refuse peer pressure. Many teens are willing to pay an enormous personal price for approval from almost anyone else.

Q: How can teens fight the urge to do self-destructive things in order to fit in?

A: Most important is to first decide for yourself, away from the group, what you will or will not do. In other words, the first person to say no to is yourself. Then, be prepared to say no to others.

Q: How, exactly, can I say no without losing friends?

A: **Refusal skills** can help. They are *a set of social strategies that enable people to competently resist the pressure by others to engage in dangerous or otherwise undesirable behaviors.* With rehearsal and repetition, you can use these skills to handle almost any sort of uncomfortable situation, including refusal to engage in behaviors that are not true to your values. A person who wants to use refusal skills must practice using them until they feel natural even when peer interactions get sticky. Try practicing these skills with a friend. Rehearsal means that you should think of imaginary situations and then figure out ways to apply one or more skills to each situation. Repetition means using the skills every time an opportunity to do so arises.

■ **Figure 3.13** *A peer group that values achievement can help motivate its members to stay in school. What can you do to movtivate your friends or classmates?*

Caption Answer: I can help friend study for tests, I can cheer them on in sports

Q: **Does peer pressure disappear as people mature?**

A: People encounter the most peer pressure during early adolescence, but even adults experience some peer pressure. It expresses itself in adults in many forms of prejudice and bigotry, including racism, sexism, ageism, and others.

Q: **I want to join a new peer group. What can I do to make an impression?**

A: Like it or not, first impressions are lasting in people's minds. People who do not know you may judge you on the surface only—just by the way you project yourself. Imagine this: You are invited to share a meal with someone's family. You want to impress them, but you arrive sloppily dressed, chew with your mouth open, make a mess at the table, and belch loudly as you finish your meal. How would they view you?

Q: **Do you mean that to be part of a social group, I have to memorize a bunch of rules about which fork to use?**

A: How you present yourself has more to do with honoring others in small ways and treating them as you'd like to be treated. Little rules do exist, but these are just refinements. In the situation described above, you desire acceptance by people who have other customs. It's up to you to observe how they do things, and do your best to show respect for them. How you conduct yourself can influence someone's impression of you.

Keep in mind, too, that the most important person in your life is you. Taking care of that person will ease the way to desired friendships and help you make right decisions.

 Writing Write a journal entry that describes a time you encountered peer pressure and how you handled it. What strategies or refusal skills did you use? Were the skills effective? You may keep your entries private.

CHAPTER 3 Review

Reviewing Vocabulary

Use the vocabulary terms listed below to complete the following statements.

body image

peer pressure

personality

puberty

1. The characteristics of a person that are apparent to others is known as _____.

2. _____ is the period of life in which a person becomes physically capable of reproduction.

3. The way a person thinks his or her body looks is called _____.

4. _____ is the internal pressure one feels to behave as a peer group does, in order to gain its members' approval.

Recalling Key Facts and Ideas

Section 1

5. **Recall.** According to Erikson, during what age span should a person develop industriousness?

6. **List.** List Maslow's hierarchy of needs.

7. **Explain.** Why is it especially beneficial for teens to be helpful to those who really need help?

Section 2

8. **Recall.** When do adolescent males usually begin a growth spurt?

9. **Explain.** What is the main difference between females and males body composition?

10. **List.** List two changes that have occurred in gender roles over the years.

Section 3

11. **Identify.** What are some qualities of a person with high self-esteem?

12. **List.** List four strategies for improving self-esteem.

Section 4

13. **Identify.** What are some benefits peer groups provide?

14. **Name.** Give some suggestions for ways to stand up to unwanted peer pressure.

Writing Critically

15. **Descriptive.** Describe how labels can influence a person's self-esteem.

16. **Descriptive.** Many times people do not like the way others see them. Fortunately, you have the ability to change your personality and self-esteem if you so choose. List four labels you would like to have attached to you and describe how you could best achieve them.

Activities

17. Write a description of the person you think you will be ten years from now. What are you like? What is your lifestyle like?

18. Analyze ads in magazines to determine if gender sterotypes are used to sell the product. Write a brief report describing your findings and include a copy of the ad in your report.

1. Personality 2. Puberty 3. Body image 4. Peer pressure
5. Ages 6–12 6. Physiological, safety, love, esteem, and self-actualization needs 7. Being helpful fulfills a need to feel important and to be appreciated by others. 8. Ages 12–13

9. Females develop more body fat for breast formation and other development than do males. Males develop more muscle tissue. 10. Political offices are now held by women, the nursing profession includes men. 11. A person with high

19. Give yourself a boost! Write a letter to yourself convincing you of your worth as a person. Tell why you are special and include all your good points, talents, and skills.

20. Transfer your interpretation of Maslow's hierarchy of needs onto a poster by using pictures from magazines or your own original illustrations to portray each need.

21. Make a list of ten events that took place in one particular day. Evaluate each in relation to how it affected your self-esteem. Clearly state if the event increased, lowered, or had no effect on your self-esteem.

22. Watch television for two hours. List the commercials that appeal to gender identity and contain stereotypical gender roles. Write a one-sentence description of how each commercial used this theme.

23. Make three columns on a sheet of paper. Label the columns from left to right, "Positive," "Stages," and "Negative." In the center column, list each of Erikson's eight stages. In the left column, summarize the positive side of each stage. In the right column, summarize the negative side of each stage. Share your answers with the class if you are comfortable doing so.

Making Decisions About Health

24. Look through the magazines and cut out pictures showing the people pictured at different developmental phases. Keep a copy of Erikson's theory with you as you look through magazines. Create an album describing what it is about each picture that makes you associate it with a certain developmental level.

25. You have a friend who has been hanging out with a gang and beginning to feel uneasy about it. The gang members are pressuring her into doing things that make her uncomfortable. She wants to leave the gang, but she worries: Will my friends be angry? I don't really have many friends outside the gang. If I leave the gang, who will be my friend? How much longer can I keep my gang membership a secret from my parents? She's confused and is unable to make a decision. What advice would you offer your friend.

Go Online

For fitness and health tips, visit the Fitness Zone at **glencoe.com**.

Fact or Fiction?

Answers
1. True.
2. False. Human beings first need the essentials for survival—food, clothing, and shelter. Then they become free to notice other needs.
3. False. People who imagine themselves as more successful than they are may be taking an important first step toward a more successful future.

 Writing Paragraphs will vary.

self-esteem does not think they are perfect, they accept their flaws. **12.** Write out positive statement about yourself; Find activities that are related to your goals and join in; Be grateful; Seek out books and movies with positive themes. **13.** Peer groups provide support, strength, and confidence. **14.** Ask for help from authorities; use communication skills; stand up for yourself assertively. **15–25.** Answers will vary.

CHAPTER 4

Stress and Stress Management

Sections

1. Stress and Stressors
2. Stress and Your Body
3. The Stress Response
4. Managing Stress

Chapter Preview

You probably hear and use the word stress every day. **Stress** is *the effect of physical and psychological demands on a person.* When you say "I'm under stress," you might mean that you have three major tests this week. You might mean that you're nervous about a big game or that you're low on money and don't have a job. You can probably think of dozens of other situations that make you feel stressed.

There are stress-management techniques, however, that can help you manage daily stress. They include:

- Planning ahead

- Thinking positively

- Practicing relaxation responses

In this chapter, you'll learn more about the effects of stress on your body and your mind. You'll also learn about ways to deal with the stress in your own life.

Fact or Fiction?

What Do You Think?

Is each statement true or false? If you think it's false, explain what's true.

1. The same event may be very stressful for one person and not at all stressful for another person.
2. You cannot change the way you react to stress.
3. Prolonged stress increases a person's risk of becoming ill.

 Writing How do you know you're under stress? What changes do you notice in your body? Write a paragraph describing your own symptoms of stress.

(Answers on page 105)

Go Online

Visit **glencoe.com** and complete the Life Choice Inventory for Chapter 4.

SECTION 1

Stress and Stressors

Almost everyone feels the effects of stress. An argument with a friend, a lower-than-expected test grade, or a minor auto accident causes stress that can damage the body. However, positive events can also cause stress. Receiving an award or moving from the junior varsity to the varsity team may also be stressful events.

Kinds of Stress

MAIN IDEA ▶ Everyone faces stress. A stressor is anything that requires you to cope with, or adapt to, a situation.

Sometimes stress, especially negative stress, seems to go on and on. **Chronic stress**, *unrelieved stress that continues to tax a person's resources to the point of exhaustion*, can damage body systems in a number of ways. The heart and blood vessels often suffer the most damage from stress. Some people who have not learned to deal with stress may look for relief in self-destructive behaviors, such as using alcohol or other drugs. These substances cause stress themselves, and they worsen both the stress, and its effects.

You may have noticed some effects of another kind of stress, the short-term kind that arises when a problem suddenly demands to be solved. **Acute stress** is *a temporary bout of stress that causes alertness or alarm, which prompts a person to deal with a specific event*. This sort of stress may bring you new energy. You may be amazed at all you can accomplish. If the stress continues, though, it becomes chronic. Energy gives way to exhaustion, and you may become sick. Students often push hard to study for tests and complete assignments toward the end of the grading period. Then, when they relax in the break that follows, they become ill.

Too often, people ignore their stress. Many don't take steps to manage their stress until they suffer stress-related health problems. You do not have to wait. You can take action as soon as you notice signs indicating too much stress. Cold hands and feet are among the first signs. **Figure 4.1** lists other signs of stress.

All stress is a response to a **stressor**, *a physical or psychological demand that requires a person to adapt to a situation*. It's important to be able to **adapt**, *to change or adjust in order to accommodate new conditions*. Physical stressors include all physical conditions, such as air temperature, intensity of lighting, bacteria, injuries, or radiation. Psychological stressors include life-changing events, both desirable and undesirable.

Vocabulary

stress
chronic stress
acute stress
stressor
adapt
perception

Preview Activity
Discuss:

- Write the word *stressor* on the board and define the word to the class. (anything that requires a person to cope with, or adapt to, a situation) Have students list stressors that exist in their lives.

- Compare how commonly the stressors given exist among teens.

- Discuss ways in which teens deal with these stressors.

- Have students list some more effective ways of dealing with the situations if their methods seem ineffective.

Comprehension Check:
Acute means sharp, intense. This is in direct contrast to *chronic*, which is not so intense but lasts much longer.

Feeling stress is a natural part of life. Often, situations associated with stress are unavoidable. How much the stress affects you, however, depends in part on your perception of it.

Figure 4.1 — Signs of Stress

Physical Signs	Psychological Signs
• Pounding of the heart; rise in blood pressure	• Anxiety, irritability, tension, or depression
• Rapid, shallow breathing	• Impulsive behavior and emotional instability; an overpowering urge to cry or run and hide
• Dryness of the throat and mouth	• Lowered self-esteem; thoughts or conversations related to failure
• Raised body temperature; blushing; sweating	• Excessive worry; insecurity; concern about other people's opinions
• Feelings of weakness, dizziness, or faintness	• Reduced ability to communicate with others
• Dilated pupils; trembling, nervous tics	• Increased awkwardness in social situations
• Grinding teeth during sleep; sleeplessness	• Excessive boredom; unexplained dissatisfaction with normal conditions
• Restlessness; an inability to keep still	• Feelings of isolation; confusion
• High pitched, nervous laughter, speech difficulties	• Avoidance of activities, omission of play
• Loss of appetite; unintended weight loss; excessive appetite; sudden weight gain	• Irrational fears (phobias) about specific things; nightmares
• Increased use of substances (tobacco; legally prescribed drugs such as tranquilizers or amphetamines; alcohol; other drugs)	• Inability to organize oneself; tendency to become distraught over minor matters
• Frequent illnesses, accident proneness	• Inability to concentrate or reach decisions
	• Loss of energy; loss of spontaneous joy
	• Feelings of powerlessness; mistrust of others

Figure 4.2 **Psychological Stressors for High School Students**

People ranked these events according to how stressful they perceived them to be. Identify the events below that you have experienced in the past year. Use the number system to determine how many stress points you are experiencing. Then consider your score below.

Life Event	Stress Points
• Death of parent	199
• Divorce of parents	98
• Death of a close family member (other than parent)	92
• Breakup with boyfriend/girlfriend	79
• Expulsion from school	79
• Major personal injury or illness	77
• Death of a close friend	70
• Getting a job	62
• Money troubles	61
• Dating	57
• Addition of a new family member	57
• Change in finance	56
• Major illness of family member or close friend	56
• Failing grades at school	54
• Change in number of arguments with peers	51
• Parent beginning or stopping work	46
• Peer difficulties	45
• Loss or death of loved pet	44
• Change in responsibilities at home or school	43
• Brother or sister leaving home	42
• Moving away	41
• School beginning or ending	38
• Trouble with parent	38
• Outstanding personal achievement	37
• Change in schools	35
• Christmas or other major holiday	30
• Change in recreation	29
• Trouble with teachers/principal	29
• Change in personal appearance	27
• Change in social activities (joining new group)	27
• Change in eating habits	27
• Change in sleeping habits	26
• Vacation	25
• Traffic tickets or other minor violations of the law	22

Over 200: Urgent need of intelligent stress management.
150–199: Careful stress management indicated.
100–149: Stressful life; keep tabs on your mental health.
Under 100: No present cause for concern about stress.

Your answers are personal and private. Share them with others only if you are comfortable doing so.

The Stressors of High School

MAIN IDEA ▶ All high school students face many stressors.

During the high school years, teens must adapt to a variety of changes. In fact, high school is often considered one of the most stressful periods of life. Many of the changes high school students face seem positive, and others seem negative. All kinds of change, however, can be stressors.

A group of researchers studied the effects of life changes on high school students. They found that, when students faced more than one change at a time, their grade point averages dropped. So did their scores on a test of self-esteem. Students who handled changes one at a time were less affected by stress. If you are experiencing many changes or stressors listed in **Figure 4.2**, try focusing on them one at a time. That will help reduce your level of stress and protect your self-esteem.

> " *The greatest weapon against stress is our ability to choose one thought over another.* "
>
> —William James
> (1842–1910)
> Psychologist and philosopher

The Perception of a Stressor

MAIN IDEA ▶ An event may be more or less stressful, depending on how you perceive that event.

Your reaction to an experience depends largely on your **perception**, *a meaning given to an event based on an individual's previous experience or understanding of it.* Your perception of any event is not quite like anyone else's, because your life experiences are unique to you. Your life experiences shape your perceptions.

For example, you and a friend might be together during a powerful thunderstorm. Your friend might be afraid while you enjoy watch the rain come down. You and your friend react to the storm based on your perceptions of thunderstorms.

Figure 4.3 demonstrates how your perception affects the way you respond to events.

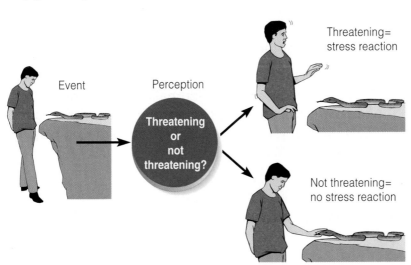

Event   Perception

Threatening or not threatening?

Threatening= stress reaction

Not threatening= no stress reaction

Figure 4.3

Perceptions and Stressors

To produce stress, and event must be perceived as threatening.

For example, suppose you see a snake at your feet. You may have one of these reactions, or you might have a completely different reaction.

- "Snakes are dangerous!" You feel fear.
- "Snakes are beautiful!" You feel joy.
- "I'm trying to learn more about snakes." You feel interest.

Obviously, the snake encounter is more or less stressful, depending on your perception of snakes. In the same way, a student who feels well prepared for a test experiences less stress than a classmate who forgot to study. Many events and experiences—family interactions, schoolwork, relationships, and more—have the potential to cause stress.

Worksheets: A reproducible quiz for Section 1 is provided in the Teacher Classroom Resources.

SECTION 1 Review

Reviewing the Vocabulary
Review the vocabulary on page 80. Then answer these questions.

1. What is a *stressor*?
2. What is the difference between *chronic stress* and *acute stress*?
3. What does *adapt* mean?

Reviewing the Facts
4. Evaluate. Why is it important to recognize the physical signs of stress?
5. Synthesize. How can acute stress become chronic stress?
6. Analyze. What might make a student feel stressed about a test, even though that student has prepared thoroughly for the test?

Writing Critically
7. Personal. Write a private journal entry, describing your own stress and explaining which stressors seem most difficult for you. Also include strategies to help you manage this stress.

Go Online

For more vocabulary practice, play the Flashcards game at **glencoe.com**.

1. A stressor is a physical or psychological demand that requires a person to adapt to a situation.

2. Chronic stress continues to tax a person's resources to the point of exhaustion. Acute stress is temporary.

3. To change or adjust in order to accommodate new conditions

4. Sample answer: Stress can damage body systems in different ways.

5. If the stress is ignored or if people don't take steps to relieve their stress.

6. If the student perceives that he or she hasn't prepared enough

7. Journal entries should be confidential.

Stress and Your Body

Playing basketball, taking an exam, and buying a new car all affect your body in about the same way. Physically, your heart beats faster and your lungs breathe more quickly. This is your body's way to act — physically, in the case of basketball, and psychologically, in the case of the exam or car purchase. All changes stimulate you this way to some degree. They require you to change in some physical way—that is, to adapt. Environmental changes, such as changes in the temperature or the noise level around you, require your body to adapt. So do all psychological events, both desirable and undesirable. All the body's systems, especially the nervous system, the hormone system, and the immune system, are affected by stress.

The Nervous System

MAIN IDEA ▶ The nervous system responds to challenges by producing reactions that restore normal body conditions.

The **nervous system** is *the body system that manages the body's activities by sending and receiving messages between the brain, spinal cord, and nerves.* The nervous system plays a key role in how your body deals wtih stress. A stressful event may be a psychological challenge, such as an exam, or a physical challenge, such as cold weather. Whatever the challenge, the responses of the nervous system are always similar. The nervous system always produces a set of reactions to restore normal conditions inside the body. For example, consider the body's responses to cold weather.

Vocabulary

nervous system
hormonal system
hormone
gland
stress hormones
immune system
immunity

■ **Figure 4.4** *It's important to understand the effects of stress on the body. What happens to your heart when you get "stressed out?"*

Caption Answer: It beats faster.

Preview Activity
Discuss: Ask students to think back to the last really stressful event they experienced at school. Have them identify each of the physical and psychological responses they had to the event. Ask students to share and compare their responses.

Comprehension Check
Ask students to describe how the nervous system responds to stress. Provide prompts, such as: What happens when you are afraid? Cold? Nervous about a test?

■ **Figure 4.5** *Extremes in temperature and physical activity are physical stressors to which the body must adapt to survive. Which body system reponds when you are exposed to extremes in temperature?*

Caption Answer: The nervous system responds to extremes in temperature.

When you go outside in cold weather, nerves in your skin act as a thermometer, sending "cold" messages to the spinal cord and brain. The central nervous system reacts to these messages and signals the smallest blood vessels, closest to the skin's surface, to shut down. This action forces your blood to circulate deeper in your tissues, where its heat will be conserved. The system also signals the muscles just under the skin surface to contract, forming goose bumps. All muscle contractions, even goose bumps, produce heat as a by-product. If these measures do not raise your body temperature enough, the nerves signal your large muscle groups to shiver. The shivering, or contractions, of these large muscles produces still more heat.

Now let's say you come in and sit by a fire and drink hot cocoa. You are warm, and you no longer need the body's heat-producing activity. At this point, the nervous system signals the skin surface capillaries to open up again, the goose bumps to subside, and the muscles to relax. The nervous system is now helping to keep you from getting too warm.

The Hormonal System

MAIN IDEA ▶ The hormonal system consists of glands that produce hormones.

The **hormonal system**, *a system of glands that control body functions in cooperation with the nervous system,* works with the nervous system to maintain communication among body organs. The two systems complement each other in helping the body adapt to changes in the environment.

A **hormone** is *a chemical that serves as a messenger.* Each hormone is released by a gland and travels in the blood stream to one or more target organs, where it brings about responses. A **gland** is *an organ that secrets one or more hormones in response to information about changing body conditions.* Then they release hormones into the bloodstream to control those conditions. However, only the hormone's target organs respond.

Consumer Skills Activity:

1. Stress uses up protein from muscle and other lean tissue, calcium from the skeleton, and vitamins and minerals from every cell of the body. Stress vitamins seem to be a quick and easy way to provide the body with the nutrients it is lacking.

2. They can't provide all of the nutrients and substances that the body needs. They can't take the place of nourishing food. There are no quick fixes.

3. Eat well-balanced meals all the time so that your body is prepared when the crisis hits.

Consumer

SKILLS ACTIVITY

Claims for "Stress Vitamins"

People often wonder whether any particular diet can protect against the ill effects of stress. Stress does drain the body of its nutrients. It uses up protein from muscle and other lean tissue, calcium from the skeleton, and vitamins and minerals from every cell of the body. Yet most people cannot eat during crises or cannot digest their food, because the stress response shuts down digestive activity in favor of muscular activity. Going without food and nutrients further stresses the body.

To store the needed nutrients ahead of time, you need to eat foods that contain those nutrients. Proper nutrition can build up your defenses.

However, products advertised as "stress vitamins" are not the best choice. They simply cannot provide all the nutrients and other substances that the body needs. If you cannot eat for a long time, you probably do need vitamins, but you need minerals as well. It may help a little to take a vitamin-mineral preparation that supplies a balanced assortment of nutrients, not in "megadoses" but in the amounts needed daily. Even the best pills can't take the place of nourishing food. It's still important to eat as well as possible. There are no quick-fix pills that will make you strong in a crisis.

 Writing

1. In what ways can stress drain the body of its nutrients? Why are stress vitamins popular?
2. Why are stress vitamins not the best choice for supplying the needs of the body under stress?
3. How should a person prepare nutritionally for times of stress?

■ **Figure 4.6** *During times of stress, physical changes can take a toll on the body. How does stress affect the immune system?*

Caption Answer: Stress lowers the immune system's ability to protect the body.

Like the nervous system, the hormone system is active during times of stress. It sends messages from one body part to another to try and maintain normal functioning while the body deals with the stressor. *The hormones that control the body's response to stress* are called the **stress hormones**. The two most important stress hormones are epinephrine, also called *adrenaline*, and norepinephrine, also called *noradrenaline*. They regulate the body's activities during emergencies and when the body is in a period of stress.

The Immune System

MAIN IDEA ▶ The immune system is the body's main defense against disease. Unrelieved stress can weaken the immune system.

The cells, tissues, and organs that protect the body from disease comprise the **immune system**. The immune system includes white blood cells, bone marrow, thymus gland, and spleen. Many organs, tissues, and glands function within the immune system. The main cells of **immunity**, *the body's capacity for identifying, destroying, and disposing of disease-causing agents*, are the white blood cells. These are made in the bone marrow and travel to other glands, where they mature. White blood cells make antibodies, the body's main ammunition against infections. All the body's tissues work together to provide immunity. All the body's fluids connect the parts of the immune system so that they act as one system.

The activity of the immune system is lower than normal during times of stress. However, between periods of stress, the immune system recovers quickly. Short periods of stress, followed by periods of relief from stress, can strengthen the immune system. Long periods of unrelieved stress, however, can reduce the number of white blood cells or reduce the effectiveness of white blood cells. This makes a person likely to suffer diseases.

The physical changes that take place in your body during times of stress can take a toll on your body. Some of the physical effects of stress include:

- Headache.
- A weakened immune system.
- High blood pressure.
- Digestive disorders.

Worksheets: A reproducible quiz for Section 2 is provided in the Teacher Classroom Resources.

SECTION 2 Review

Reviewing the Vocabulary

Review the vocabulary on page 85. Then answer these questions.

1. What is the *nervous system*?

2. What is a *hormone*?

3. Which system protects the body from disease?

Reviewing the Facts

4. Analyze. Explain what makes cold weather a stressor.

5. Synthesize. What might happen if production of the stress hormones were blocked?

6. Analyze. Why can chronic stress increase a person's risk of disease?

Writing Critically

7. Persuasive. How would you persuade a person you care about to reduce the stress in his or her life? What reasons would you give? What facts would you explain? Write one persuasive paragraph that might convince your reader to reduce and manage stress.

For more information on health careers, visit Career Corner at **glencoe.com.**

1. A network that manages the body's activities by sending and receiving messages between the brain, spinal cord, and nerves

2. A chemical that serves as a messenger

3. The immune system

4. Extremes in temperature are physical stressors to which the body must adapt.

5. The body would not be able to adapt to changes because the stress response would be affected.

6. Chronic stress, or long periods of stress, can reduce the number of white blood cells, compromising the immune system.

7. Paragraphs will vary.

SECTION 3

The Stress Response

A little stress can be beneficial. However, too much stress, unrelieved, can be exhausting and harmful. Consider what causes stress, both physical and psychological, and what it does to you.

Stages of the Stress Response

MAIN IDEA ► The stress response occurs in three stages: alarm, resistance, and recovery or exhaustion.

The body's response to a demand or stressor is called the **stress response**. Whatever the stressor that triggers it, the stress response has three phases: alarm, resistance, and recovery or exhaustion.

Alarm

The first phase of the stress response, in which you recognize that you are facing a change or a challenge is **alarm**. The body releases the stress hormones, which activate the nerves in all systems.

Resistance

The second phase of the stress response is resistance. **Resistance** is *when the body mobilizes its resources to withstand the effects of stress.* The stress hormones continue to flow, causing muscles to contract and other body functions to shut down. During the resistance phase, your resources are mobilized. These resources are your attention, your strength, and fuels. You can use your resources until they run out or wear out. Then you need to replace or repair them.

Vocabulary

stress response
alarm
resistance
recovery
exhaustion

Preview Activity
Discuss:

- Ask students to describe what happens to their bodies when they feel stressed. Answers may include that their heart beats faster, breathing speeds up, muscles tense.

- Explain that stress causes physical as well as mental/emotional changes.

| Figure 4.7 | Stress Ending in Recovery or Exhaustion |

Exhaustion sets in when resistance is required for too long a period of time.

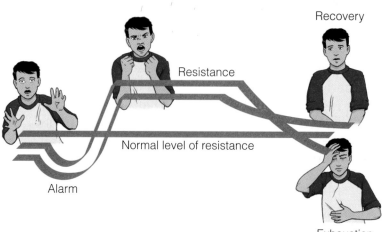

Recovery or Exhaustion

The third phase of the stress response is one of two opposite states, recovery or exhaustion. **Figure 4.7** shows both. **Recovery**, a healthy third phase of the stress response, *occurs when the body returns to normal.* Before your resources run out, you deal with the source of stress or it goes away, and you recover. Then your stress hormone levels drop to normal, your body systems slow down, your muscles relax, and you become ready for the next stressful event.

If stress continues without a break and your body stays in overdrive for too long, your resistance breaks down. **Exhaustion**, *a harmful third phase of the stress response,* is when stress exceeds the body's ability to recover. Then recovery is delayed or becomes impossible.

It stress continues and your body becomes exhausted, you can become sick. Stress, however, can make you stronger if you successfully recover from a bout with stress. Just as your muscles grow stronger with repeated use, so does your stress resistance. However, you must have periods of rest to build that strength.

Physical Reactions to the Stress Response

MAIN IDEA ▶ Each stage of the stress response involves physical reactions.

The first stage in the stress response is alarm. Every organ responds to the alarm. Some of the changes are:

- Your heart rate speeds up.
- The pupils of your eyes widen, enhancing vision.
- Your muscles tense.
- Fuels, such as fat, are released from storage so they can be used by the muscles.
- The blood flow to your skin is reduced to protect against blood loss in case of injury.
- The blood flow to your digestive organs is reduced.
- The blood flow to your muscles and brain increases.
- Your immune system shuts down temporarily to free up energy.

The second stage of the stress response, resistance, puts your body into an unbalanced state. Your muscles flex while body functions, such as digestion and immune defenses shut down. This unbalanced state helps your body deal with an emergency. Later, when the danger has passed, your body functions become balanced once again. This is the recovery stage of the stress response.

Class Activity

Analyze. Ask students to think of three or four situations in which they were very tired, without knowing why. Can they think of stressful situations that might have preceded their periods of exhaustion?

For me, the most stressful thing is school. Because school is a central part of my life, it can be very hard to balance other things such as after-school activities or hanging out with friends. Some days the homework can take hours to finish, and when I have after-school activities in the way, it takes even longer. This creates another problem that a lot of teens face—lack of sleep. Not getting enough sleep can be very stressful on the body. It seems like I can never catch up, which produces even more stress.

—Alexandra C., 15,
California

My home environment causes the most stress in my life. This involves my siblings, parents, and after-school activities. It seems the days get shorter and shorter. I never seem to have enough time to do everything. There is much pressure to be mature and responsible at home. When you're with your friends you can relax and be yourself, but at home there is a specific format you feel you must follow. Also, when you're home you have more time to think about your current problems, and they all come together at once.

—Anand M., 16,
New York

The most stress in teens, I think is the pressure they get from school. The students that have goals in life and try to become something probably have the most stress because they are trying the hardest.

—Terence M., 15,
New Mexico

I believe that it is peer pressure. Peer pressure is the thing that causes stress for so many other matters. For instance, with school, people try to fit in so they go to a party instead of doing their homework. That causes stress at school. Then at home, they try to be "cool" so they stay out late, come and argue with their parents. That causes stress in the home. Peer pressure causes stress with students themselves, with students and school, and with students and their parents.

—Saundra D. 16,
West Virginia

I would have to pick violence. My family was raised under violence. We lived in and around the projects. There were drug sellers, drunks, fights, and shooting every week. I would worry where I was and who I was with.

—Jordan H., 15,
Massachusetts

The thing that causes the most stress for me is my schedule. I have enough trouble keeping up with my homework, after-school sports, and part-time job, finding any time to spend with my friends can be impossible. I am always staying up late studying when my friends are watching TV, playing computer games, or surfing the net.

—Franklin L., 17,
Virginia

School definitely causes the most stress in my life. Starting high school was so stressful. There are so many rules and things to worry about. Everyone is so concerned about being cool. You have to worry about your clothes, your hair, who likes you, who doesn't. Then there are your grades, getting into college, and your future to worry about. It all makes me so stressed out.

—Carlotta. J. 15.,
Texas

Digestive system activity and immune defenses can resume. Normal functioning help keep you running smoothly during peaceful times. Stress resistance gets you through emergencies.

Prolonged stress, however, can make diseases of the heart and arteries likely. During a stressful period, fat is released into the bloodstream. This fat serves to fuel the muscles, but it may not be used up if no physical action occurs. When this fat remains in the bloodstream, it tends to collect along artery walls, damaging them. In this way, psychological stress can contribute to the development of heart disease.

If a period of stress leads to recovery and to a greater ability to respond to the next stressor, then it can benefit you. On the other hand, if it leaves you drained and less able to respond the next time, it can harm your physical health. It's important to learn how you can manage stressors and make your stressful experiences beneficial.

Worksheets: A reproducible quiz for Section 2 is provided in the Teacher Classroom Resources.

SECTION 3 Review

Reviewing the Vocabulary
Review the vocabulary on page 90. Then answer these questions.
1. What are the three phases of the stress response?
2. What happens during the second phase of the stress response?
3. What is the major difference between recovery and exhaustion?

Reviewing the Facts
4. **Explain.** Explain which diseases are likely if a person undergoes prolonged stress.
5. **Synthesize.** What is likely to happen to a person who faces a series of major stressors, one after the other?
6. **Evaluate.** Do you think it's healthy to try to increase stressors and stress? Why or why not?
7. **Descriptive.** Think of a situation in which a character in a book or movie faced a major stressor. Write a paragraph describing the phases of the stress response for that character. Describe each phase of the stress response, and clarify whether the response ended in recovery or exhaustion.

1. Alarm, Resistance, Recovery or Exhaustion

2. The body mobilizes its resources to withstand the effects of stress.

3. Recovery is what happens when the body returns to normal and exhaustion is what happens when stress exceeds the body's ability to recover.

4. Prolonged stress can make diseases of the heart and arteries likely.

5. A person's resistance will break down and exhaustion will occur.

6. No, because too much stress can be draining and reduces one's ability to respond to the other stressors.

7. Paragraphs will vary.

Go Online

For more vocabulary practice, play the Concentration game at **glencoe.com**.

Managing Stress

Stress is part of everyone's life. Teens deal with a variety of stressors, including those shown in **Figure 4.8**. However, stress can be managed. Strategies for managing stress include being physically active, relaxing, managing your time, using coping devices, and changing perceptions.

Vocabulary

relaxation response
progressive muscle
  relaxation
coping devices
displacement
venting
defense mechanisms

Physical Activity

MAIN IDEA ▶ Physical activity strengthens stress resistance. It can ease muscle tension and help the body recover.

Physical activity can relieve anxiety and bring temporary relief. It keeps the body strong and strengthens your immune system between times of stress. During stress, physical activity plays a special role. If you experience anxiety or fear, your body is ready to be physically active, but it doesn't act.

Figure 4.8

Stressors in the Lives of Students

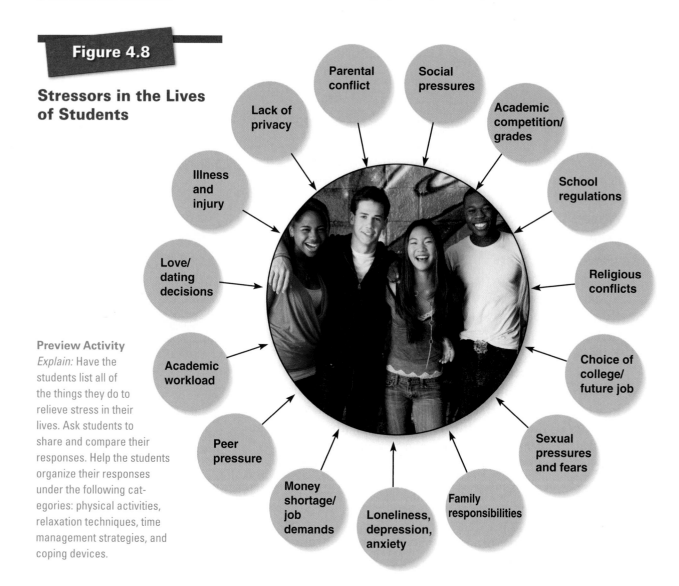

Parental conflict

Social pressures

Lack of privacy

Academic competition/ grades

Illness and injury

School regulations

Love/ dating decisions

Religious conflicts

Academic workload

Choice of college/ future job

Peer pressure

Sexual pressures and fears

Money shortage/ job demands

Loneliness, depression, anxiety

Family responsibilities

Preview Activity

Explain: Have the students list all of the things they do to relieve stress in their lives. Ask students to share and compare their responses. Help the students organize their responses under the following categories: physical activities, relaxation techniques, time management strategies, and coping devices.

Now your muscles are tense and can't relax. Your blood is rich with fuels that are building up and can damage your heart. You are in a state of high alert with no relief in sight. This state drains your reserves, exhausts you mentally, and lowers your resistance to diseases of all kinds. It's time to work out.

Relaxation

MAIN IDEA ▶ The relaxation response is the opposite of the stress response. The relaxation response can be learned.

The exact opposite of the stress response is the **relaxation response**. This is *the body's ability to reduce blood pressure, slow the pulse, quiet anxiety, and release tension.* Relaxation permits your body to recover from the effects of stress. You can learn to relax, even in the middle of a stressful situation. You can relax anywhere, at any time.

Muscle Relaxation

One way to relax is to use **progressive muscle relaxation**, *a technique of learning to relax by focusing on relaxing each muscle group in turn.* This involves lying flat and then locating and relaxing each group of muscles, beginning at either the head or the feet. People who have never tried this are surprised to discover the tightness they may have in the muscles of the upper back and neck or the face. Fifteen different sets of muscles in the face alone can become tense. Some people learn that the only thing preventing them from relaxing is that their shoulders are hunched up. Others find that they clench their jaws or that they are squint or frown without knowing it.

With practice, you can learn to relax your muscles whenever you think of it, not just when you have time to lie still. Professional mountain climbers train themselves to relax selective muscles while climbing. Each time they take a step, they have to tense one leg while relaxing the other leg. That way, they rest throughout the climb, and they can reach the summit without becoming exhausted. Students may not have physical mountains to climb, but they do face mental mountains.

Other Ways to Relax

Remember, by practicing relaxation you can reverse your body's natural responses to stress. Everyone needs to find ways to relax that work for them. For some people, engaging in a game of pickup basketball may be relaxing. For others, relaxation is found in reading a book, or taking a walk, or even listening to music. The Health Skills sidebar offers other ways to manage stress.

Class Activity

Organize: Contact your local hospital's wellness center. Ask them if they have an exercise specialist who could demonstrate exercises students can do to relax their necks, shoulders, arms, legs, and stomachs while sitting at their desks. These exercises are easy to do and can be done by the students at any time to help ease stress. Spend class time over a period of a week doing these exercises for five minutes at the beginning of each class session.

Health Skills

Managing Stress

To manage stress:

1. Maintain strong personal wellness.
2. Get regular physical activity.
3. Cultivate high self-esteem
4. View stressors as opportunities for growth.
5. Manage time wisely.
6. Recognize warning signs of stress early.
7. Release tension by crying, laughing, talking with friends, or relaxing.
8. Identify which stressors you can control.
9. If stress becomes unmanageable, seek outside help.

Organize: Not having enough time in the day to complete their activities is a common source of stress for teenagers. The best way students can respond to such stress is to develop effective time management strategies.

- Ask students to create a time management chart. In the first column of the chart, have them list their school, home, work, and social activities.

- In the second column they should record the amount of time spent in each of the four activity areas.

- In column three they should write what they can do, if anything, to reduce the amount of time spent on each activity area.

- In the fourth column, have students include what they would do with the free time they have now created for themselves.

■ **Figure 4.9** *It's important to manage your time. How can managing your time benefit you?*

Caption Answer: I can have time to spend with my friends.

Time Management

MAIN IDEA ▶ **Wise time management helps control stress.**

Efficient time management can also help you to minimize stress. Time is similar to financial income. You receive certain amounts of it at regular intervals. In the case of time, you receive 24 hours each day.

Managing time wisely helps you plan ahead and enjoy the present. When your friends call on a Sunday to invite you out, you don't want to be caught with no money on hand, no clean clothes, and no studying done for the big exam on Monday. That is an avoidable stress. Planning ahead can prevent it.

The best way to manage your time is to make a time budget. Follow these steps to create your own weekly time schedule (see **Figure 4.10**):

- Draw a grid that lists the days of the week across the top. List blocks of time, such as each hour from waking to bedtime, down the left side.

- Fill in your set appointments, such as class meetings.

- Add study time, waking and travel time, time for physical activities, chores, and mealtimes.

- Add times for recreation and relaxation.

- Make a list of special plans for the week.

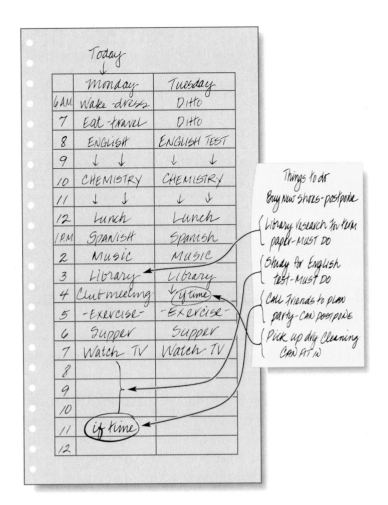

Figure 4.10

Time Management

Managing your time more efficiently can help you better deal with stressors.

Class Activity

Analyze:

- Have students plan one weekday of their time for a full 24 hours, from midnight to midnight. Ask them to include all the things they must do, and all the things they would like to do for the day. Require them to account for every half hour of the day.

- Discuss how time management can help to reduce stress.

- Ask students to explore time management and whether it would work for them. If students think it would be effective, the activity can be extended so students plan out a schedule for a week or even a month.

To schedule a long-term assignment, such as a big report, start by identifying all the tasks of the project. Work backward from the due date and schedule tasks.

Part of wise time management is knowing when you have too many commitments. Identify your limits and learn to say no.

Coping Devices

MAIN IDEA ▶ Coping devices help you deal with stress.

When you face several major stressors, you may not be able to handle them all at once. Temporary measures that can get you through hard times are **coping devices** are *safe, short-term methods of managing stress, such as displacement or venting.*

Displacement

One coping device is **displacement**, *transferring the energy of suffering into something else.* This is using the emotional energy to do tasks or other activities. For example, if you are anxious about an upcoming test and you've finished studying, do something around the house.

Class Activity

Explain:

- Have students suggest positive coping devices for dealing with stress. List them on the board.

- Then ask students to suggest negative examples of coping devices and list these beside the positive examples.

- Discuss how negative coping devices can create more stress.

APPLYING Health Skills

Stress Management

Applying Health Skills:

1. Deonte is worried about his dad's health. He is also concerned that he won't have enough time to complete his school project because of all the other commitments on his time. These concerns are causing him stress.

2. Deonte could use a planner to record all his activities. Then he could schedule project tasks by working backward from the project deadline. If Deonte thinks he needs more time to complete the project, he could look for ways to gain extra time.

3. Students' planners should include all of Deonte's routine activities, as well as time to work on his project and meet with the group. Students may or may not think that Deonte will have enough time to complete his project, depending on their estimates of the amount of time required for his activities. If students think Deonte needs extra time, a good option might be for him to ask for one Saturday off to meet with the group.

4. Answers may vary. Sample answer: I would identify and drop low-priority activities to gain extra time to work on my project. For example, I might stay home on weekends to work on my project instead of going out with friends. I would also try to identify "wasted" time, such as time spent texting my friends after school. Instead, I would use the time to work on my project.

➤ Objectives
- Identify the relationship between time and stress.
- Demonstrate how to apply time-management tips to reduce stress.

Stressed Out Over Time

Deonte's dad was diagnosed with cancer last month. Deonte is really worried about his dad. He also has more responsibilities around the house now that his dad is sick. He has to make sure his little brother finishes his homework, and has to make sure dinner is ready. Tuesdays and Thursdays he works at a supermarket for three hours after school. Mondays and Wednesdays he picks his little brother up from school.

One of Deonte's teachers just assigned a project that requires group work with a few of his classmates for a project. He's worried that he won't have the time to meet with his group and wonders how he will complete the project. The deadline is two weeks away, but it's already causing him stress.

➤ Identify the Problem
1. What is causing Deonte stress?

➤ Form an Action Plan
2. How could Deonte apply time-management tips to solve his problem?
3. Create and fill in a two-week planner for Deonte. Use the information given above and your own estimates of the time needed for other activities, such as sleeping, eating, and homework. Schedule Deonte's project by breaking it into smaller tasks and adding deadlines to the planner. Do you think Deonte will have enough time to complete his project? If not, how could he gain extra time?

➤ What Did You Learn?
4. If you needed more time to complete a project, what would you do to gain extra time?

Venting

Another way of coping is **venting**, *the act of verbally expressing one's feelings,* "letting off steam" by talking. This helps to relieve pain. You may have heard of the expression and, sometimes, a friend can provide suggestions for managing the stressors. After venting, people can often go on to work directly on solving a stressful problem. Talking about problems is a very effective way of handling stress.

Some coping devices can have negative effects especially when overused. They are useful only for short periods and only because they prevent a worse thing from happening: complete breakdown. These are sometimes known as defense mechanism. **Defense mechanisms** are *automatic, subconscious reactions to emotional injury.* People unconsciously use these defense mechanisms in cases of serious stress.

- **Denial** is the refusal to admit that something unpleasant or painful has occurred. "No, I don't believe it."

- **Fantasy** involves imagining, in the face of a painful or unpleasant situation, that something positive has happened instead. "She didn't really die. She's just gone on vacation."

- **Projection** is the belief, in the face of an unpleasant or painful situation you have caused, that it is another person's fault. "The teacher asked the wrong questions on the exam."

- **Rationalization** is the justification of an unreasonable action or attitude by manufacturing reasons for it. "I couldn't prevent the accident, because I had to pay attention to something else."

- **Regression** involves using inappropriate, childish ways of dealing with painful realities.

- **Selective forgetting** is a memory lapse concerning an experience or piece of news too painful to bear.

- **Withdrawal** involves avoiding people and activities to avoid pain.

Coping devices, including defense mechanisms, help people survive bad periods of stress. They are especially useful when the stress is unexpected and severe, like the sudden death of a loved one.

Stressors often seem to be out of your control. You might not be able to prevent an automobile accident, a losing streak in sports, or the problems caused by difficult relationships. You do, however, have control over your assessment of those events. Remember that it is your perception of an event, more than the event itself, that causes the stress response in your body.

Class Activity

Describe:

- Have students identify positive and negative coping devices. (Positive coping devices are displacement and venting; negative coping devices are defense mechanisms such as denial, fantasy, projection, regression).

- Ask students to explain the main differences between positive and negative coping devices. (Positive coping devices help relieve stress while negative coping devices ignore the stress.)

- For their own consideration, not for class discussion, ask the students if they ever use defense mechanisms, and, if so, what stressors trigger their use? Can the students think of more positive ways to deal with the stressors?

■ **Figure 4.11** *Challenges are a part of life. How can you control the stress you experience from challenges?*

Caption Answer: By changing your perception of challenges, you can reduce the stress you experience from them.

Class Activity
Describe:

• Tell students that people who grow up in cultures other than their own must adapt to dramatic changes in language, dress, values, and social customs. These people can experience *acculturative stress*, which is marked by confusion, anxiety, hostility, depression, alienation, and physical illness.

• Four common methods of adapting to this stress are: **a.** *integration*—maintaining old cultural identity, but participating in a new culture; **b.** *separation*—maintaining old identity and avoiding contact with new culture; **c.** *assimilation*—adapting to the new culture and having contact with its members; **d.** marginalization—rejecting the old culture; but also suffering rejection by members of the new culture.

Changed Perceptions

MAIN IDEA ▶ **Changing your perception of events can reduce the stress those events cause you.**

Knowing that stress is a result of your own thinking, you can reassess a situation in ways that reduce its power to cause you stress. Suppose you hit another car while driving, and your car is in bad shape. You might immediately begin listing all of your fears about potential consequences—your parents' anger, your lost transportation, your lost investment, and the threat of being unable to meet obligations. All of these fears are the result of a negative focus. What if, though, you consciously directed your focus toward the positive—no one was hurt or killed, the other driver was at fault for the accident, your car can be repaired. Turning your focus to these more positive assessments short-circuits much of the unnecessary stress you might otherwise feel.

Daily hassles can be major contributors to stress levels. For example, waking up late on the day of a test is not in itself stressful, but your thoughts can make it so. You can think, "This is horrible! I should have gone to bed earlier! My class has started... I'll never make it on time... I'll fail my class!" The late start to your day resulted in negative self-talk that causes a stress response.

How can you reassess the daily hassles? One way is to focus on other things. While getting ready to go to school, tell yourself that you studied for the last two weeks and you are prepared. Make a decision to test your alarm clock the following day.

Keeping a "stress log" is another tool you can use to help change your perceptions. Try noting stressful moments and recording your thoughts at the time. Later, review your log. Look for unrealistic reactions that consistently cause you stress. Then you can work on changing negative attitudes or false beliefs.

Worksheets: A reproducible quiz for Section 4 is provided in the Teacher Classroom Resources.

SECTION 4 Review

Reviewing the Vocabulary

Review the vocabulary on page 94. Then answer these questions.

1. What is the opposite of the stress response?

2. What is *progressive muscle relaxation*?

3. What are *defense mechanisms*?

Reviewing the Facts

4. Synthesize. Explain how physical activity can help a person manage stress.

5. Explain. Describe how time management can help minimize stress.

6. Analyze. How are displacement and venting alike? How are they different?

Writing Critically

7. Narrative. Write a short narrative with two characters. Show one of the characters using a coping device, such as venting, to manage stress. Show how the coping device helps, and tell what the two characters do next.

For more information on health careers, visit Career Corner at **glencoe.com**.

1. The relaxation response

2. A technique of learning to relax by focusing on relaxing each muscle group in turn

3. Automatic subconscious reactions to emotional injury

4. Muscles can relax, which helps relieve anxiety and brings temporary relief.

5. By planning efficiently, a person can plan ahead and not get overwhelmed.

6. They are both short-term ways to handle stress. Displacement is the transferring into something else, and venting is letting off "steam" by talking.

7. Narratives will vary.

Q&A Healing and the Placebo Effect

 Understand and Apply Read the conversation below, and then complete the writing exercise that follows.

Norman Cousins, an author and political journalist, had an unusual experience with stress. Cousins took an especially stressful trip overseas and returned home exhausted. A week later, he found himself hardly able to stand up. When he was diagnosed with a serious disease, he chose a remarkable road to recovery.

Q: What happened to Mr. Cousins?

A: In the hospital, Cousins was diagnosed with a serious disease of the connective tissue of the spine. The physicians predicted that his spine would weaken until he was paralyzed. Stress and exhaustion had led to disease. The disease was expected to be totally disabling and, eventually, to cause Cousins' death.

Lying in his hospital bed, Cousins considered what he already knew about stress, diseases, and cures. It occurred to him that if negative emotional experiences could harm the body, then positive emotional experiences might restore health. To his way of thinking, the most positive emotional experiences would be "hope, faith, laughter, confidence, and the will to live."

Cousins considered the hospital an unpleasant environment. He checked out and, with his physician's approval, moved into a hotel room. There he could be equally well taken care of. Each day, he watched comedy films and had funny stories read to him.

He had spent weeks with hardly any sleep and was in severe pain, but now he made a wonderful discovery. After a hearty laugh, he could relax and sleep soundly for an hour or two at a time.

The laughter, relaxation, and sleep brought about a healing that no medical attention could have achieved. In time, Cousins recovered completely. He recounted his experiences in his best-selling book, *Anatomy of an Illness as Perceived by the Patient: Reflections on Healing and Regeneration.*

Q: Well, how do you suppose he did it? What accounts for his recovery?

A: That's a good question. Most people, including Cousins himself, agreed that it was certainly due, at least in part, to the placebo effect. A placebo is a substance with no ingredients that can either harm or hurt a patient. This substance is labeled "medicine" and used for its psychological effect. The placebo effect is the healing that occurs in people given such medication.

Q: How common is the placebo effect?

A: It is not unusual for experiments using placebos to record a benefit in 30 to 60 percent of subjects. That is, people given only distilled water or sugar pills will recover about half the time, as completely as if they had received a powerful medication.

When given with encouragement ("This will make you better"), placebos are often very effective. In some cases, people who are given placebos recover, even though they would not have recovered without the placebos. In other words, the placebo effect is valuable as a weapon against illness.

Q: Are you telling me that my physician may give me fake medicine?

A: No, that would be against medical ethics. The point is that your response, even to the real drug, may be aided by your faith in the treatment.

Q: Does this mean I shouldn't see a doctor when I get sick?

A: No, not at all. You do need to see a doctor. Pick the most competent, well-qualified health-care provider you can, so that your faith in him or her will help you get well.

Q: How does the placebo effect work?

A: No one knows for sure. Part of the effect may come from the relaxation that brings relief from anxiety. The patient wonders what is wrong, feels helpless, and worries so much that symptoms become worse. Then the patient goes to a trusted expert. The expert names the disease. The patient feels reassured. The expert prescribes a treatment, and the patient relaxes. Both stress and the symptoms begin to disappear.

The placebo effect can actually be measured. Blood pressure falls. Pulse rate slows. The patient gets well, whatever treatment has been prescribed. Faith heals.

Q: Does the placebo effect work for pain?

A: Yes. People who are in pain often experience relief when they are given placebos. It is thought that placebo treatments stimulate the brain to produce natural pain-relieving chemicals. Those chemicals relieve pain even more powerfully than the drug morphine.

Q: Do you suppose that traditional healers work their cures the same way?

A: Probably so. Don't forget that the body often heals itself, given time. Frequently, all that healers have to do is to wait out the course of the illness. If they can offer reassurance and confidence, they provide support that is as important as any chemical or physical procedure might be. In fact, health-care providers in training are taught not only to manage their clients' medical care, but also to dole out liberal doses of TLC, tender loving care.

Some fascinating stories are told about healing in the hospital. Just physically touching people has been shown to hasten healing. Researchers are experimenting to find out how and why it works.

Q: It sounds like you're also talking about the healing effect of love.

A: You might be right. Anything that makes people feel cared for helps them to produce their own internal *tranquilizers* and strengthens their bodies. As Dr. Francis Weld Peabody of Harvard University put it, "The secret of the care of the patient is in caring for the patient."

 Writing Write a paragraph describing what the placebo effect is and include how it works.

Reviewing Vocabulary

Use the vocabulary terms listed below to complete the following statements.

stressor
hormone
stress response
coping device

1. A chemical that serves as a messenger in the body is a _____.
2. A demand that requires the body to adapt is a _____.
3. A temporary, nonharmful way of dealing with stress is a _____.
4. The three-stage reaction the body makes to stress is the _____.

Recalling Key Facts and Ideas

Section 1

5. Identify three physical and three psychological stressors.
6. Describe how multiple stressors affect high school students.

Section 2

7. Name two hormones that react to stressors.
8. Explain how short periods of stress followed by relief affect the immune system.

Section 3

9. Identify ways that stress can make you stronger.

10. Describe what causes the body to go into exhaustion rather than recovery.
11. Name the parts of the body that experience reduced circulation and what parts experience increased circulation during the stress response.
12. Describe the phase of stress resistance called an *unbalanced state*.

Section 4

13. Explain why is physical activity considered an excellent stress-management technique.
14. Name ways you can change the way you react to stress so that events are less stressful.
15. Explain why time management is helpful in reducing stress.
16. Describe which defense mechanism you are using when you blame someone else for your own problems.
17. Describe what you should do if stress becomes so overwhelming that it affects your ability to function.

Writing Critically

18. Develop a personal plan for improved stress management. List three negative coping strategies that you tend to use. Describe how you can benefit from using a positive coping strategy in each situation.
19. Describe in your own words why some people do not believe that stress has any effect on a person's mental health. Do you agree or disagree with this thought? Why do you feel the way you do?

1. Hormone 2. Stressor 3. Coping device 4. Stress response 5. Answers will vary. 6. Students' grades and their self-esteem can be affected. 7. Epinephrine, norepinephrine 8. They make the immune system stronger. 9. A person can better handle the next round of stress. But there must be rest times between the times of stress to build strength. 10. The body's resistance breaks down. 11. Circulation to the brain and muscles is increased, while circulation to the

Activities

20. Keep a journal for three consecutive days in which you record any stressful situations you encounter. Each time you make an entry, include the following information:
    a. Describe the situation.
    b. Identify the stressor.
    c. Tell how you felt.
    d. Explain what you did to reduce the stress.

21. Create a collage on poster board. Divide the poster in half. On one side place pictures that depict teenage stressors and on the other side place pictures of positive stress outlets.

22. Make a chart on which you keep track of the way you manage your time, hour by hour, for two full days. Do you think you managed your time well? How could you change the way you spend your time in order to reduce stress?

23. Cut out magazine and newspaper photos to create a collage of people experiencing stress. Mount the photos on poster board. On the poster board, identify the indicators (clenched jaw, tears, yelling, and so on) in the photos that make you think the people are experiencing stress. Now draw a stick figure that represents you. Draw in (or write in) the indicators that you display when you are under stress. If you can, ask a friend or family member to help you identify the indicators you display when you are under stress.

24. Have a partner trace your outline from the waist up onto a large sheet of paper. Draw in any significant items that will identify the drawing as you. On your head, write five things you are good at doing. On your heart, write five hopes or goals that you want to achieve in your lifetime. On your shoulders, list five things you are not good at doing. On your arms, list five coping skills that you use to handle stress. On your bellybutton, write five things that make you angry. On your stomach, write five things that worry or upset you.

Making Decisions About Health

25. Imagine that last year, Sarah experienced a tremendous amount of stress during final exam time. She doesn't want to find herself in the same position this year. Final exams are one month away and she is already beginning to worry. Design an effective stress-management plan that Sarah can follow to help reduce her stress level.

For more vocabulary practice, play the True/False game at **glencoe.com**.

Fact or Fiction?

Answers

1. True. People react to stressors in different ways.
2. False. You can change the way you perceive a stressor.
3. True. Prolonged stress can weaken the immune system.

Writing Paragraphs will vary but should include physical symptoms of stress.

skin and digestive system is reduced. **12.** It is a state that favors muscular activity while it shuts down other necessary functions, such as digestion. **13.** It relieves anxiety and brings temporary relief. **14.** Learn to manage stress. **15.** Because not having enough time to accomplish activities is a common source of stress. **16.** Projection **17.** Seek outside help. **18.–25.** Answers will vary.

Mental and Emotional Problems

Sections

Everyone faces problems with emotions some of the time. Most people are able to deal with difficult emotions when they come up, but in some cases, emotional or mental problems can be serious enough to interfere with daily life. Dealing with problems of this sort can make people feel alone and ashamed. However, even people with serious mental disorders can learn to overcome them or cope with them with professional help. Mental health professionals, such as counselors, psychologists, and psychiatrists, are available in your community's schools, clinics, and hospitals.

Many teens with mental health problems are reluctant to seek help because they do not recognize the seriousness of their condition. However, no one should ever feel embarrassed to talk with someone about mental or emotional problems.

Fact or Fiction?

What Do You Think?

Is each statement true or false? If you think it's false, explain what's true.

1. Emotionally healthy people handle life's problems without any help.
2. Anxiety is always a sign of a serious mental problem.
3. Depression is one of the most common mental disorders.

 Writing Think about a time you or a friend felt sad or troubled. Write a paragraph describing some positive things someone can do to feel better during a difficult time.

(Answers on page 129)

Go Online

Visit **glencoe.com** and complete the Life Choice Inventory for Chapter 5.

Coping with Difficult Emotions

On any given day, you may experience a wide variety of emotions, from happiness and excitement to anger and sadness. By themselves, emotions are neither positive nor negative. Feelings such as fear and anger may be unpleasant, but that doesn't make them bad or wrong. Becoming angry or upset as a result of strong emotions may lead to problems with family and friends. Emotions can be managed. Learning how to stop and think about what is causing the emotion is one way of managing strong emotions. It's the way you deal with these emotions that can be good or bad for your health. Learning to handle emotions in a positive way will protect your physical, emotional, and social health.

Vocabulary

- anxiety
- grief
- guilt
- shame

Dealing with Anxiety or Fear

To deal with anxiety or fear, follow these steps:

1. Identify the cause. What do you fear? Write it down.
2. Deal with the cause if you can.
3. If you can't change the cause, let it go.
4. Try to envision a positive outcome. Focus on success.
5. Use any extra energy for physical activity.
6. Practice relaxation techniques.

Fear and Anxiety

MAIN IDEA ▶ In small doses, fear and anxiety can help you meet challenges, but too much anxiety is disabling.

Fear is a normal, instinctive response to a dangerous situation. It triggers the stress response you learned about in Chapter 4, preparing your body to fight against a threat or flee from it. Fear can be healthy when it encourages you to be careful in dangerous situations. Sometimes, however, the things that frighten you are not real or serious threats. For instance, some people might feel an unreasonable amount of fear every time they need to speak in public. This type of fear is called a phobia. Fears like this can hold you back, preventing you from doing your best.

Anxiety, or *an emotional state of high energy that triggers the stress response*, is related to fear. Like fear, anxiety is an emotion that everyone feels sometimes. Common symptoms of anxiety include rapid heart rate and breathing, sweating, trembling, and increased muscle tension.

Anxiety is natural and even helpful in some situations. If you feel anxious while taking a test, for instance, your increased alertness may help you perform better. However, extreme anxiety can hurt your performance, making you feel overwhelmed and causing you to freeze up. Stress management techniques, such as physical activity or deep breathing, can help you cope with anxiety. The Health Skills sidebar offers some suggestions for dealing with ordinary anxiety.

Sadness and Grief

MAIN IDEA ▶ Normal sadness is not the same as depression, a serious mental illness.

Like fear, sadness is a normal reaction to events in your life, such as a bad grade or a breakup with a boyfriend or girlfriend. Sadness can be mild and brief or deep and long-lasting. The deepest form of sadness most people experience is **grief**, *the emotional response to a major loss, such as the death of a loved one*. The Q&A section at the end of this chapter discusses grief in more detail.

People who feel sad may say that they are "depressed," but sadness and depression are not the same thing. Sadness is a normal and temporary emotion, while depression is a serious illness that interferes with a person's daily life. If sadness lasts a long time, a person may become depressed. In that way, sadness may lead to depression.

Anger

MAIN IDEA ▶ Dealing with anger involves recognizing the emotion, addressing the cause, and taking time to cool off.

During your teen years, the increased levels of hormones that your body is producing can cause you to become angry over small things. Learning to manage your anger can keep it from damaging your relationships or, worse, leading to violence.

To control anger, you must first recognize the emotion and identify its cause. This can be tricky. Try to identify the reason why you are angry before reacting. Sometimes we may be angry about one thing, but react to that anger for an entirely different reason. Sometimes you may think something trivial, like having to clean up your room, has caused your anger but when you look deeper, you find that something else, like an argument with a friend, is the true cause. Other times, you may feel stressed if you have a lot of schoolwork to do, or if your schedule is too busy. Everyone needs some time to relax. Once you understand what's causing your anger, you can think about ways to deal with the problem, such as resolving the conflict with your friend.

First, however, give yourself a chance to cool off. If you confront another person while your anger is still intense, you might make matters worse. Some people give themselves a time-out from their anger by counting to ten. Other strategies for calming down when angry include going out for a walk, listening to music, writing your thoughts in a journal, or practicing other healthy behaviors to relieve stress.

■ **Figure 5.1** *Too much anxiety can prevent a person from performing even the most routine tasks. What are some ways you deal with anxiety?*

Caption Answer: I try to relax or go outside and be physically active.

Class Discussion
Discuss: The students' major question as they begin this chapter will probably be "What is an emotional problem?" Focus their attention on the definition —"patterns of thinking or behavior that cause a person significant emotional pain or prevent normal functioning." Ask students to consider the difference between temporary emotional pain and the pains that don't go away.

Guilt and Shame

MAIN IDEA ▶ Guilt can remind you of your values. Shame is harmful and can contribute to serious mental problems.

Guilt is *the normal feeling that arises from the conscience when a person acts against internal values.* Feelings of guilt may prompt you to act according to your values. The best way to deal with appropriate guilt is to admit that you are wrong. Sometimes, however, people feel guilty for things that aren't their fault, such as a parent's divorce. Learn to examine each situation realistically and acknowledge that you are not to blame.

Shame is related to guilt, but it is far more destructive. **Shame** is *a feeling of being inherently unworthy.* Shame means feeling bad about who you are as a person. While guilt makes people want to correct their mistakes, shame makes them feel incapable of doing so. Feelings of shame can be linked to serious mental problems such as depression and eating disorders.

■ **Figure 5.2** *Parents who know the difference between guilt and shame discipline children without damaging their emotional health.* How is guilt different from shame?

Caption Answer: Guilt is about what you do, while shame is about who you are.

Worksheets: A reproducible quiz for Section 1 is provided in the Teacher Classroom Resources.

1. An emotional state of high energy that triggers the stress response.

2. Grief

3. The normal feeling that arises from the conscience when a person acts against internal values.

4. Any three: from Health Skills sidebar on page 108.

5. Uncontrolled anger can damage your relationships or lead to violence.

6. Feelings of guilt can prompt you to act according to your values.

7. Answers will vary.

SECTION 1 Review

Reviewing the Vocabulary
Review the vocabulary on page 108. Then answer these questions.
1. *Anxiety* is _____.
2. The emotional response to a major loss, such as the death of a loved one, is called _____.
3. *Guilt* is _____.

Reviewing the Facts
4. **Identify.** Name three ways for dealing with anxiety.
5. **Evaluate.** What are the dangers of letting anger rage out of control?
6. **Describe.** How can guilt be a useful emotion?

Writing Critically
7. **Descriptive.** Describe a situation in which a person might experience anger, guilt, or shame, and explain how to handle the emotion in a positive way.

Go Online

For more vocabulary practice, play the Concentration Game at **glencoe.com**.

Mental and Emotional Disorders

Everyone experiences difficult or unpleasant emotions from time to time. When emotional problems interfere with daily life, however, this may be a sign of mental illness. The term **mental illness** refers to *disorders of thought, emotion, or behavior that cause distress and reduce a person's ability to function*. Mental illness can interfere with work, personal relationships, and even basic daily tasks such as bathing.

Identifying Mental and Emotional Problems

MAIN IDEA ▶ Mental and emotional problems vary in severity and duration. They can have a variety of causes.

Drawing the line between mental health and mental illness is not always straightforward. Problems with emotions range from mild, temporary depression or anxiety to severe, long-term illnesses that affect a person's sense of reality. A problem severe enough to interfere with daily life means that the person needs professional help. **Figure 5.3** lists some signs of a mental problem that may require professional treatment.

In some ways, the term *mental illness* is misleading, because many mental disorders stem from physical causes. For instance, people with severe depression have major differences in brain chemistry from nondepressed people. Similarly, a person with a physical problem, such as hardening of the arteries in the brain, might experience mental symptoms, such as memory loss or confusion.

Vocabulary

- mental illness
- phobia
- obsessive-compulsive disorder (OCD)
- post-traumatic stress disorder (PTSD)
- depression
- bipolar disorder
- schizophrenia
- eating disorders
- addiction

Preview Activity

Describe: Ask students to write descriptions of situations in which they have experienced anxiety, depression, guilt, shame, or resentment. Ask students to write about an instance when they were able to overcome these feelings. How were they able to overcome these feelings?

Figure 5.3	Warning Signs of Mental Illness

- Sudden, noticeable change in personality
- Inability to cope with problems
- Difficulty performing day-to-day tasks
- Bizarre or unrealistic ideas
- Excessive anxiety
- Prolonged depression or indifference to the world

- Dramatic change in eating or sleeping habits
- Extreme highs or lows in mood
- Excessive anger, hostility, or violent behavior
- Thoughts of suicide or homicide. People with this symptom need immediate help.

Figure 5.4

Specific Phobias

Name	Fear of . . .
Acrophobia	Heights
Aerophobia	Flying
Agoraphobia	Open spaces, public places, or being alone in any situation where escape might be difficult
Arachnophobia	Spiders
Brontophobia	Thunderstorms
Carcinophobia	Cancer
Claustrophobia	Small, closed spaces
Mysophobia	Germs
Necrophobia	Death or anything related to death

Other factors can contribute to mental illness as well. For instance, some people inherit a tendency toward depression. Many times, talking to a close family member, friend, or even a doctor can help ease depression. If depression is long lasting, though, medical help may be needed to ease the depression. It's important to remember that mental health disorders are medical disorders. They should be treated like any other medical disorder. People with mental health disorders do not have a character flaw. These people have a medical disorder. Environmental factors, such as poverty and stress, can also increase the risk of mental illness.

Anxiety Disorders

MAIN IDEA ▶ Anxiety disorders can be severe and disabling.

Unlike ordinary anxiety, which is temporary and relatively mild, anxiety disorders last at least six months and can grow worse without treatment. People with an anxiety disorder experience anxiety most or all of the time. They worry about everything—health, work, money, family—even when there is little or no cause. They have difficulty relaxing, concentrating on tasks, and sleeping. They may also develop physical symptoms, such as headaches, muscle aches, nausea, shortness of breath, and fatigue. People who experience such symptoms for months at a time should seek help from a mental health professional.

Phobias

A **phobia** is *an extreme, irrational fear of an object or situation*. People can develop phobias linked to all sorts of things. **Figure 5.4** lists some of the most common phobias.

People with a phobia may go to extreme lengths to avoid the thing they fear. They may not seek treatment unless their efforts to avoid the thing they fear begin to interfere with daily life. Fortunately, most phobias can be treated through therapy.

Social Anxiety

Social anxiety, or social phobia, is extreme fear or anxiety in the presence of other people. Some people fear only specific social situations, such as speaking in public. Others have more general social anxiety, meaning that they feel nervous whenever they are around people they don't know well. They are afraid of looking foolish or being mocked or criticized by others. In social situations, they may blush, sweat, tremble, and have difficulty speaking.

Social phobia differs from ordinary shyness. Many people feel shy or self-conscious around others from time to time. However, most people are able to get past their feelings of nervousness and make new friends. Social phobia, by contrast, is so extreme that it makes people unable to enjoy social activities—possibly leading them to avoid social settings altogether. People with social phobia often need therapy or medication to overcome their problem. Those who are merely shy, on the other hand, can learn to manage their feelings. The Health Skills sidebar offers some tips.

Obsessive-Compulsive Disorder

People with **obsessive-compulsive disorder** (OCD) have *an uncontrollable fixation on specific thoughts and behaviors.* For example, they may have repeated, unwanted thoughts (obsessions) about germs or dirt. This may lead them to develop irresistible patterns of behavior (compulsions), such as washing their hands over and over again, in an effort to drive the obsessive thoughts away. While healthy people may also perform rituals, such as checking to make sure the stove is off and the door is locked before leaving the house, in people with OCD these repeated behaviors interfere with everyday life. Therapy and medications can be helpful in treating OCD.

Post-Traumatic Stress Disorder

People with **post-traumatic stress disorder** (PTSD) experience *a serious stress reaction in response to a terrifying event.* Events that may trigger PTSD include war, terrorist attacks, bombings, serious accidents, violent crime, natural disasters, and abuse. People with PTSD often have flashbacks, reliving the traumatic event over and over while awake or in nightmares when they sleep. They may become tense and edgy and have trouble sleeping or concentrating on tasks. Some people feel emotionally numb, while others become irritable, aggressive, or even violent.

Comprehension Check
Comprehend:
Give students the following definition of anxiety: an emotional state of high energy, with the stress response as the body's reaction to it. Ask students to explain how fear and anxiety are similar and how they are different.

Health Skills

Overcoming Shyness

Shyness doesn't have to ruin your social life. These tips can help:

1. Start small. Practice interacting with people you know.

2. Rehearse what you want to say. Think of some conversation starters ahead of time.

3. Build your self-esteem. Focus on your strong points. Before you enter a social setting, picture yourself succeeding in it.

4. Be yourself. Don't put on an act to fit in.

5. Never use alcohol or other drugs to relax.

Not every person who lives through a traumatic event develops PTSD, and those who do may not experience symptoms right away. PTSD often arises months or even years after the original event. Some PTSD sufferers recover over time, while others require therapy or medication to help them heal.

Panic Disorder

People with panic disorder experience sudden, unexplained attacks of terror. During a panic attack, they experience physical symptoms such as a pounding heart, shortness of breath, sweating, and dizziness. They may also have chest pain, leading them to believe they are having a heart attack. Panic disorder is disabling and interferes with the ability to live a normal life. Like people with phobias, those with panic disorder often reshape their lives to avoid situations that could bring on an attack. Panic disorder can be treated effectively with medication or therapy.

Mood Disorders

MAIN IDEA ▶ Mood disorders, such as depression and bipolar disorder, involve extremes of emotion.

During your teen years, it is normal to experience mood swings—sudden changes in emotions. For some people, however, emotional highs and lows are so extreme that they interfere with day-to-day life. These people suffer from mood disorders, or mental illnesses that affect a person's emotional state. Common mood disorders include major depression and bipolar disorder.

Class Discussion
Discuss:
Test taking is a common cause of anxiety among students. Ask students to come up with some tips on how to deal with the stress they feel prior to an important test. Some examples may include:

1. Preparation—working hard to prepare for the test.

2. Relaxation—learning self-relaxation techniques.

3. Rehearsal—try to simulate the test situation.

4. Restructuring thoughts—change negative thoughts to positive thoughts.

■ **Figure 5.5** *Occasional sad or blue moods are normal. At what point should you suspect a mood disorder?*

Caption Answer: When emotional problems interfere with day-to-day life.

Figure 5.6 — Symptoms of Depression

Someone who experiences five or more of these symptoms for two weeks or longer may be suffering from depression and should seek professional help.

Emotional	Physical	Social
Persistent feelings of sadness, anxiety, or emptiness	Lack of energy	Withdrawal from family and friends
Anger, restlessness, or irritability	Unexplained weight loss or gain	Loss of interest in favorite activities
Difficulty concentrating	Insomnia (difficulty sleeping)	
Inappropriate feelings of guilt or shame	Difficulty getting up in the morning	
Feelings of indifference to the outside world	Unexplained aches and pains	
Thoughts of death or suicide		

Depression

Although everyone feels sad sometimes, **depression**, *a persistent feeling of apathy, hopelessness, or despair*, is a more serious condition. Depression is one of the most common mental disorders, affecting nearly one out of every ten people each year. Most people with depression first experience symptoms during their teen years.

Depression can cause a variety of physical and mental symptoms. **Figure 5.6** lists some of the most common symptoms. Depression can be difficult to diagnose, because some of these symptoms can also result from other common illnesses, such as flu.

People who experience symptoms of depression for more than a couple of weeks should seek professional help. For most people, depression can be treated effectively with some combination of talk therapy and medication.

Bipolar Disorder

Also known as manic-depressive disorder, **bipolar disorder** involves *extreme highs and lows of emotion*. People with this disorder bounce back and forth between depression, with all its symptoms, and an emotional high known as *mania*. During the manic phase, the sufferer's energy level shoots way up. They sleep less and do everything at top speed. Their moods may swing from euphoric happiness to extreme irritability or aggression. They also tend to have difficulty concentrating and display poor judgment and reckless behavior.

Health Skills

Coping with Minor Depression

People can often ease minor depression by taking these steps:

1. Engage in exercise or other activities you enjoy.
2. Spend time with friends and family.
3. Talk about your feelings with people you trust.
4. Set realistic goals. Break up large tasks into smaller ones.
5. Avoid making life changing decisions.
6. Give yourself time to heal.

In adults, episodes of mania or depression may last for weeks or months. Children and teens more often swing rapidly back and forth between the two. Medication can help calm the unstable moods of bipolar disorder.

Other Disorders

MAIN IDEA ▶ Disorders such as schizophrenia, eating disorders, and substance abuse are mental illnesses that require professional help.

Anxiety disorders and mood disorders are two major categories of mental illness. Other mental illnesses fall into different categories. Psychotic disorders, such as schizophrenia, affect a person's sense of reality. Substance-related disorders involve problems with alcohol or drug abuse. Eating disorders are in a separate category.

Schizophrenia

Schizophrenia is *a severe mental disorder that causes people to lose touch with reality.* People with schizophrenia often have hallucinations, meaning that they see or hear things others are unable to perceive. These experiences often frighten the victim, who becomes fearful, anxious, and withdrawn. People with schizophrenia often have difficulty holding a job or caring for themselves.

Like many mental illnesses, schizophrenia seems to be partly hereditary. Faulty brain chemistry also appears to play a role in the disease. Although people with schizophrenia may be disturbing or even frightening to be around, they do not tend to be violent. The chief danger they pose is to themselves. People with schizophrenia are at a greatly increased risk for suicide. Drugs can often relieve the symptoms of schizophrenia, but they cannot cure the disease.

Eating Disorders

People with **eating disorders** have *extreme, unhealthy eating habits, often related to an obsession with weight or appearance.* Eating disorders tend to show up for the first time during adolescence or young adulthood. Three major types of eating disorders are:

- **Anorexia nervosa,** an extreme fear of weight gain that leads people to starve themselves and exercise excessively; they see themselves as overweight even when they are extremely thin.

- **Bulimia nervosa,** a condition in which people *binge*, or eat large amounts of food, and then *purge*, ridding their bodies of the food by vomiting or taking laxatives.

- **Binge eating disorder,** in which people regularly go on eating binges, but without purging afterwards.

Caption Answer: Binge eating followed by purging

■ **Figure 5.7** *People with anorexia nervosa may see themselves as overweight even if they are very thin. What behaviors are associated with bulimia nervosa?*

Eating disorders can lead to serious health problems. People with these disorders need help from a team of health professionals including medical doctors, mental health professionals, and dietitians. Eating disorders are discussed in more detail in Chapter 8.

Addiction

Substance abuse and addiction are related, but they are not the same. **Addiction** is *a physical or psychological dependence on a particular substance, habit, or behavior.* A person who abuses drugs or alcohol may not be addicted to these substances. However, the continued abuse of these substances may lead to addiction. People can also become addicted to behaviors, such as gambling. A person with an addiction may not be able to stop the behavior without help.

Worksheets: A reproducible quiz for Section 2 is provided in the Teacher Classroom Resources.

SECTION 2 Review

Reviewing the Vocabulary

Review the vocabulary on page 111. Then answer these questions.

1. *Mental illness* is _____.

2. A persistent feeling of apathy, hopelessness, or despair is called _____.

3. Anorexia nervosa, bulimia nervosa, and binge eating disorders are three kinds of _____.

Reviewing the Facts

4. Evaluate. At what point is it important to seek professional help for an emotional problem?

5. Synthesize. What do all anxiety disorders have in common?

6. Describe. How common is depression?

Writing Critically

7. Expository. Write a paragraph explaining why you think most people with depression first experience symptoms during their teen years.

For more information on health careers, visit Career Corner at **glencoe.com**.

1. Disorders of thought, emotion, or behavior that cause distress and reduce a person's ability to function.

2. Depression

3. Eating disorders.

4. When the problem becomes severe enough to interfere with daily life.

5. They last at least six months, and grow worse without treatment.

6. It affects nearly one out of every ten people each year.

7. Answers will vary.

Teens and Suicide

During one average day in the United States, about twelve young people aged 15 to 24 end their own lives. Of these, ten are male and two are female. Far more teens attempt to kill themselves but fail. Only accidents and homicides kill more teens than suicides do.

Many teens who attempt suicide, however, don't really want to die. For them, a suicide attempt may be a way to show how much they are hurting. Suicide can often be prevented if people learn to recognize the factors that put teens at risk and the warning signs of a possible suicide attempt.

Suicide Risk Factors

MAIN IDEA ▷ The major risk factors for teen suicide are depression, other mental disorders, and substance abuse.

Most often, the teens who attempt suicide suffer symptoms of depression, whether or not they have received a diagnosis of the disease. Their deep, relentless feelings of despair may lead them to believe that death offers the only escape from their problems. In reality, of course, things almost always improve with time. With appropriate treatment, depression lifts and thoughts of suicide decrease.

■ **Figure 5.8** *Trained volunteers stand by, ready to take calls from anyone who feels a need to talk about his or her problems. What are two warning signs associated with suicide attempts?*

Caption Answer: Drug or alcohol abuse and withdrawal from family and friends

In addition to depression, several other factors put teens at risk for suicide. They include:

- Substance abuse.
- Other mental disorders.
- A family history of mental illness or suicide.
- Abuse or violence within the family.
- Living in a home where guns are present. Guns are involved in more than half of all suicides.
- Spending time in prison.
- Witnessing the suicidal behavior of others, such as family members, friends, or celebrities.
- Feeling alone or isolated.
- Major life stresses, such as physical illness, the death of a loved one, or the divorce of a parent, in combination with depression.

Preventing Suicide

MAIN IDEA ▶ Anyone talking about suicide should be taken seriously. Share your concerns with a trusted adult.

Suicide is preventable. Most people who attempt suicide do not want to die, but they cannot see any other way out of their problems. By learning to recognize the warning signs of suicide and knowing how to intervene, you may be able to save a life.

Warning Signs

Sometimes, it is possible to spot clues that a teen is planning or thinking about suicide. Perhaps the most important predictor is a previous suicide attempt. However, all the signs listed in **Figure 5.9** on page 120 should be taken seriously. Notice that many of these are also symptoms of depression.

Facts and Myths

Many widespread beliefs about suicide are not true. Buying into these myths can make it harder to prevent a suicide. Myths related to suicide include:

- **"Only young people are at risk."** Suicide is actually most common among people aged 65 and older.
- **"They aren't serious."** Anyone who talks about suicide should be taken seriously. Most people who commit suicide talk about it or give other clear signals beforehand.
- **"There's no way to stop them."** Most people who talk about or attempt suicide are just looking for a way to end their pain. Helping them get the treatment they need can prevent future attempts.

Did You Know?

It's a myth that people who talk about suicide won't really attempt it.

Class Activity

Apply:

Review the warning signs of suicidal behavior. Ask students to work in small groups to create a public service announcement or podcast that emphasizes the importance of recognizing these warning signs. They may want to mention some reasons that a teen may consider suicide.

Figure 5.9 — Signs That May Warn of an Approaching Suicide

- Abrupt changes in personality; aggressive, violent, or impulsive behavior
- Alcohol or drug abuse
- Changes in eating or sleeping habits
- Expressing feelings of depression, hopelessness, or guilt
- Giving away valued possessions; making a will or other final arrangements
- Inability to concentrate
- Loss of interest in favorite activities
- Loss of interest in schoolwork and declining grades
- References to "going away," or phrases such as "I won't be around much longer."
- Repeated attempts to run away from home
- Self-inflicted injuries, such as cutting
- Sudden lifting of depression after deciding on suicide as a "solution" to problems
- Thinking, talking, or writing about death, even in a vague or casual way
- Unusual neglect of personal appearance
- Withdrawal from friends or family

- **"It's dangerous to talk about suicide with them."** Some people are afraid to mention suicide to those who are depressed for fear of "putting ideas in their heads." However, speaking openly about suicide can actually ease a person's mind and reduce the risk of a suicide attempt.

How to Help

If you suspect that someone you know is considering suicide, talk honestly with the person about your concerns. Simply by reaching out, you can reassure the person that he or she is not alone. Acknowledge the person's feelings without making judgments. Try to help him or her see that there are other solutions to his or her problems. Remind your friend that you care about him or her and want to help the friend identify someone who can help solve the problem. Your friend may make you swear to keep your conversation a secret, but this is one promise you should not keep. Tell a trusted adult about your concerns, and make sure your friend gets help. If a friend refuses to talk to you, seek help from an adult immediately.

If the person seems on the verge of making a suicide attempt, you need to take immediate action. Call 911 or your local emergency number. Suicide hotlines, which are listed in the phone book, can also be a useful resource. After making the call, stay with the person until help arrives. Don't leave a suicidal person alone until he or she is in professional hands. If the person threatens you with violence, however, protect your own safety. Leave right away and call 911 from a safe place.

Writing Activity

Compose:

Ask each student to write five phrases that could be used in responding to a suicidal teen who elicits a promise of silence. Samples: "I care about you too much to keep this promise. Let's go talk to my mom together. She'll help." Ask volunteers to share their phrases.

If you do not succeed in preventing a suicide, don't blame yourself for the tragedy. The suicide of a friend or acquaintance is a painful experience, and you may need counseling yourself to deal with your grief. You might also consider joining a support group. Another concern related to teen suicide is cluster suicide. Cluster suicides may occur if the friends of someone who commits suicide decide to try suicide too. It's normal to feel grief and depression if a friend commits suicide. Talk to a friend or trusted adult if these feelings become strong. Remember that suicide is a permanent solution to a temporary problem.

Worksheets: A reproducible quiz for Section 3 is provided in the Teacher Classroom Resources.

SECTION 3 Review

Reviewing the Facts

1. **Explain.** About how many young people in the United States end their own lives during an average day?
2. **Analyze.** What do most teens who commit suicide have in common?
3. **Synthesize.** List three risk factors for suicide that are related to a person's family or home environment.
4. **Identify.** List three myths related to suicide.
5. **Evaluate.** What should you do if a person seems to be on the verge of making a suicide attempt?

Writing Critically

6. **Narrative.** Over the last six months, your friend has stopped doing any homework and is getting poor grades. She has also stopped attending dance class, her favorite activity. In conversation, she often brings up the topic of death. Today, she told you she wants you to have some of her valued personal belongings. Write a dialogue between you and your friend showing how you would respond to this situation.
7. **Descriptive.** People who are feeling depressed often see suicide as the only possible solution to their problems. Their condition may prevent them from seeing other ways to look at their problems. List as many reasons as you can think of for teen depression. Then, for each reason listed, suggest a healthy way to deal with the problem. Name some people who could help teens to recognize other solutions to their problems.

Go Online

For fitness and health tips, visit the Fitness Zone at **glencoe.com.**

1. Twelve
2. They suffer from depression.
3. Any three: Family history of mental illness or suicide; abuse or violence in the family; living in a home where guns are present; death of a family member or divorce of parents.
4. Any three: Only the young are at risk; people who talk about suicide are not serious; suicide cannot be prevented; it's dangerous to mention suicide to someone who is at risk.
5. Call 911, a local emergency number, or a suicide hotline. Stay with the person until help arrives, unless he or she threatens you with violence.
6. Answers will vary.
7. Answers will vary.

SECTION 4

Emotional Healing

Therapy is *any activity or treatment that helps a person cope with a mental or emotional problem.* Many teens seek therapy to help them through troubled periods in their lives, such as divorce in the family or an episode of bullying at school. Seeking help for your problems does not mean that you are "crazy" or "sick;" it just means that you could use a little assistance right now.

Vocabulary

therapy
psychotherapy
behavior therapy
codependent
enabling

Reasons for Seeking Help

MAIN IDEA ▶ People may seek therapy for a variety of reasons. It is important to find a qualified therapist who is a good fit for you.

Teens may seek help for a variety of reasons. Some examples include:

- Depression, anxiety, or just ordinary stress.
- Eating disorders.
- Learning or attention problems that interfere with schoolwork.
- Painful events such as a serious illness, the death of a loved one, or a divorce in the family.
- Substance abuse or other destructive habits.
- Everyday problems like managing anger, coping with peer pressure, or improving self-confidence.

In some cases, however, teens may be reluctant to seek help. They may feel that seeing a mental health professional is a sign that they are too weak to solve their own problems. In fact, asking for help when it is needed means just the opposite—that you are willing to do what it takes to deal with your problems. In particular, those with serious disorders, such as depression, addiction, or eating disorders, should know that these problems will not go away on their own.

Teens may also dislike the idea of discussing their personal problems with a stranger. It may help to understand that therapy is completely private and confidential. Therapists may not reveal anything they hear from their clients to anyone—not even the person's parents. The only exception is for people who might harm themselves or someone else.

 **Did You Know?**

The first step to getting help for an emotional problem is being aware that help is needed.

Types of Therapy

Any activity, from playing softball to writing in a journal, can be a form of therapy. However, those who seek professional help for their problems will most likely experience one-on-one **psychotherapy**, *a type of therapy in which a patient discusses problems with a trained therapist.*

There are other forms of therapy as well. Each type is based on the patient's needs. Family therapy involves members of a family meeting together with a therapist to discuss problems that affect them as a group. Some patients may benefit from group therapy in which several people with similar problems receive support from each other and from a counselor.

Another type of therapy, **behavior therapy**, is *therapy in which a therapist helps a person break an unhealthy pattern of behavior through a system of rewards and desensitization*—a process of confronting and overcoming fears. Behavior therapy is often used to treat depression, anxiety disorders, and phobias.

Finally, there may be times when patients benefit from medications or drug therapy. It involves the use of medications to treat mental illnesses such as depression or obsessive compulsive disorder (OCD).

Seeking Help

If you feel you may need help with a mental or emotional problem, there are several places you can look. Your first step might be to talk to a parent or guardian. Other people who may offer help include teachers, a school guidance counselor, a religious leader, or your doctor. Community health centers may offer therapy or counseling at low cost. You can also check your local phone directory for crisis hotlines or support groups, such as Alcoholics Anonymous.

It's important to choose a therapist you are comfortable with. If you don't feel that you can confide in the therapist, try talking to another therapist. **Figure 5.11** on page 124 list types of mental health professionals who can offer one-on-one therapy. Don't hesitate to consider such factors as the therapist's age, gender, languages spoken, and cultural background. During your first visit, you may want to ask questions, such as:

- How long have you been practicing?
- What are your office hours?
- How much do you charge? Will my insurance cover it?
- Do you work with teens regularly?
- Do you have experience helping people with problems like mine?
- What is your basic approach to treatment?

If you are not satisfied with the answers you get, keep looking until you find someone who is a good fit for you. Remember, too, that you can change therapists at any time if you feel the treatment isn't meeting your needs. Finding the right therapist can be a key to learning to deal with your problems and get the most out of life.

Caption Answer: It can help people express their feelings.

■ **Figure 5.10** *Any activity that has a healing effect can be a form of therapy. How can painting help relieve an emotional problem?*

Figure 5.11   **Mental Health Professionals**

People with these titles are qualified to offer therapy. Any others who claim to provide mental health services may not be trustworthy.

Name	Services	Training
Psychiatrist	Can provide medical and psychiatric evaluations, perform psychotherapy, and prescribe medications	A medical degree (M.D. or D.O.) with at least four more years of specialized training in psychiatry
Psychologist	Perform psychological testing and evaluations, provide psychotherapy, and treat emotional and behavioral problems	A graduate degree (master's degree or doctorate) in psychology. Many states also require licensing for psychologists.
Psychiatric nurse	May assess and treat mental illnesses, perform psychotherapy, and in some states, prescribe medication	College degrees ranging from associate's to doctoral, along with specialized training in hospitals
Social worker	Assess and treat mental illnesses, perform psychotherapy, and help individuals manage problems with mental health and daily life	Typically, a master's degree in social work. In most states, social workers must also pass an examination to be licensed to practice.
Counselor	Provide counseling to individuals, families, and groups	Licensed Professional Counselors have a master's degree in psychology or counseling, plus a license from the state where they practice. However, in some states, people may offer their services as "counselors" without any of these qualifications.

Helping Others

MAIN IDEA ▶ Recognize when it is possible to help a friend and when professional help is necessary.

Class Activity

Recall: Write the titles of the emotional health and suicide prevention professionals listed in Figure 5.11 on a set of index cards. Write their job descriptions on another set of cards. Have the students play a matching game, either with the entire class or in small groups.

You can often help someone who is dealing with an emotional problem. However, the kind of help you can provide depends on the nature of your friend's problem. A friend who is going through a tough time, such as a divorce in the family, may need no more than a sympathetic ear. Listening and offering support can help your friend work through problems or troubling emotions.

Some problems require the help of a trained professional. The untrained person can do more harm than good by saying or suggesting the wrong things. For example, a person who hopes to help may become **codependent**, *focused on the needs of others to the extent that the person's own needs are neglected.* When a codependent prevents a troubled person from facing his or her own problems, this weakens the person.

The term **enabling**, describes this *misguided "helping"* because it allows the problem behavior to continue. Without having to face conse-quences, troubled people have no reason to change.

Caring and support are important to those suffering from more serious mental illness. However, these people also need more help than an untrained friend can provide. A person who shows any of the signs of mental illness should be encouraged to seek professional help. Trying to help a person with a seri-ous illness by yourself may be destructive, both for your friend and for you.

Another way to help those who have been diagnosed with a mental disorder is to talk honestly about their condition. Avoiding the subject may simply make them feel more isolated. Do not judge or label those with a mental illness. Instead, treat them as you would anyone, with consideration and respect.

Comprehension Check
Comprehend:
Tell students to think of the word *enabling* as meaning someone who enables the other person to continue his or her bad habit. Enablers do this by giving the person with the problem money or making excuses for them. Ask students for additional examples of ways in which people can enable others to continue their dependence.

Worksheets: A reproducible quiz for Section 4 is provided in the Teacher Classroom Resources.

SECTION 4 Review

Reviewing the Vocabulary

Review the vocabulary on page 122. Then answer these questions.

1. *Therapy* is _____.
2. A type of therapy in which a patient discusses problems with a trained therapist is called _____.

Reviewing the Facts

3. **Analyze.** Give an example of a condition that might be treated with drug therapy.
4. **Identify.** List three types of professionals who are trained to help people with emotional problems.
5. **Describe.** Name three places you might go to seek help for an emotional problem.
6. **Analyze.** When should a friend be encouraged to seek professional help?

Writing Critically

7. **Persuasive.** Write a script for a one-minute public service announcement about seeking help for mental and emotional problems. Address the reasons teens are reluctant to seek help or focus on places to go for help.

For more vocabulary practice, play the eFlashcards game at **glencoe.com**.

1. Any activity or treatment that helps a person cope with a mental or emotional problem.

2. Psychotherapy

3. Possible answers: depression, OCD.

4. Any three: psychiatrists, psycholo-gists, psychiatric nurses, social workers, counselors.

5. Any three: parents or guardians, teachers, school guidance counselor, religious leader, primary care physician, community health center, crisis hotline, support group

6. You can help a friend who is going through a tough time, but anyone who shows signs of serious mental illness needs professional help.

7. Answers will vary.

Q&A Dealing with Loss and Grief

Understand and Apply Read the conversation below, and then complete the writing exercise that follows.

Grief is the normal response to a death or other major loss, but it is still painful and often overwhelming. Still, grief cannot be avoided. Knowing something about the grieving process helps.

Q: Grief is just awful pain, isn't it? What more is there to know about it?

A: Grief is painful, but it can also produce other emotions. For many people, the first reaction is numbness or disbelief: "This isn't real; this can't be happening." Other emotions often linked to death and loss include:

- **Yearning** for things to return to the way they used to be.

- **Anger**—at the person who has died, at other people, or just at the unfairness of the world in general.

- **Sorrow, depression, or emptiness.** The grieving person may feel as if there is no hope or no reason to go on.

- **Acceptance.** The grieving person may still feel sadness, but is ready to go on with life.

People experiencing grief may also have physical symptoms, such as weakness, nausea, or shortness of breath. They sometimes have trouble sleeping, eating, or working, and they may withdraw from friends. It can help to recognize that all these feelings and symptoms are normal, and that they will pass in time.

Q: This sounds a lot like the way I felt when my parents got divorced. Is it normal to feel grief when no one has died?

A: Yes, people can feel grief in response to many types of painful changes in their lives. In addition to the death of a friend or family member, people may grieve over the loss of a pet, a move that takes them away from friends and family, divorce, job loss, or severe illness.

Q: But why do people grieve? Why do they have to go through all this?

A: People who have been through a severe loss must accept the loss as a reality. Pain is a natural response, and people who are grieving need time to work through the physical and emotional pain associated with the loss. Finally, they must adjust to living with the loss.

Q: How long does that take?

A: There's no simple answer to that question. The grieving process is different for everyone. Most people report that the emotions associated with grief come in waves or cycles. Even when you are feeling good, a sudden rush of memory may bring all the feelings back as if the loss had just occured. This may go on for months or even years.

While feelings of grief can come and go over a long period of time, they will gradually become less intense. Someone whose grief is not at all lessened after four months or longer may actually be suffering from depression and should seek help.

Q: Does that mean there's nothing you can do to feel better until the grieving process runs its course?

A: No, not at all. In fact, there are many things people can do to cope with their grief and ease their pain. Recognizing and respecting the feelings associated with grief is one important step. People need to give themselves permission to mourn. People who are grieving need to understand that their emotions are normal and not try to suppress them.

Reaching out to others is another way to deal with the pain. People who are grieving should seek the company and support of friends and loved ones—both those who have shared the loss and others. Support groups for people who have suffered similar losses can also be a source of comfort. Expressing their feelings about the loss can help people work through the grieving processes toward acceptance.

Another important thing to do at a time of loss is to take care of physical health. People who are grieving should make an effort to eat well, stay active, and get plenty of rest. They should also recognize that their situation puts them at an increased risk of becoming dependent on drugs or alcohol. They should avoid using these substances as a way to escape from their feelings of grief. It won't make the feelings go away and will hurt them more in the long run.

Q: How can I help someone else who is dealing with grief?

A: One of the most helpful things you can do is to give your friend a chance to talk. Let that person share his or her feelings and memories of the deceased. This is an important part of the healing process. Don't

■ **Figure 5.12** *A professional can help you deal with problems by talking through them. What are two ways to find help for an emotional problem?*
Caption Answer: Talk to a parent or seek help from a professional.

try to comfort the person by saying things like, "It was for the best" or "You'll get over it in time." Even if this is true, it belittles the pain the other person is feeling right now. Just listen and show sympathywithout trying to make any sort of judgment.

Another thing you can do for a friend who is coping with a loss is to offer practical help, such as cooking meals or running errands. Don't just ask, "Can I do anything to help?" because the person may be too emotionally drained to think of anything. Instead, make a specific offer, like "Would you like me to pick up a few things for you at the grocery store?" A small favor such as this can be a great help to someone who is feeling overwhelmed by grief.

 Writing Write a paragraph describing how you might console a friend who has recently lost a loved one.

CHAPTER 5 Review

Reviewing Vocabulary

Use the vocabulary terms listed below to complete the following statements.

addiction

anxiety

behavior therapy

depression

phobia

post-traumatic stress disorder

1. A ____ is an extreme, irrational fear of a specific object or situation.

2. People with ____ experience a serious stress reaction in response to a terrifying event.

3. A physical or psychological dependence on a particular substance, habit, or behavior is known as ____.

4. ____ uses a system of rewards and desensitization to help a person break an unhealthy pattern of behavior.

5. ____ is the condition of feeling apathetic, hopeless, and withdrawn from others.

6. ____ is an emotional state of high energy, with the stress response as the body's reaction to it.

Recalling Key Facts and Ideas

Section 1

7. **Explain.** How can fear be a healthy emotion?

8. **List.** List three steps for controlling anger.

9. **Identify.** What is the difference between guilt and shame?

Section 2

10. **List.** List three warning signs of mental illness.

11. **Identify.** What is the difference between social phobia and ordinary shyness?

12. **Recall.** What are the two major symptoms of obsessive-compulsive disorder?

13. **Name.** What are the symptoms of post-traumatic stress disorder?

14. **Describe.** How does bipolar disorder differ from depression?

Section 3

15. **Name.** What are the major risk factors for suicide?

16. **Recall.** What is the most important predictor of a possible suicide?

Section 4

17. **List.** List two reasons why some teens are reluctant to seek help for mental or emotional problems.

18. **Identify.** List two forms of therapy.

Writing Critically

19. **Expository.** Brainstorm a list of terms people use to describe people who suffer from mental or emotional disorders. Circle all the terms on your list that have negative connotations. Then write a paragraph discussing the reasons why people with mental illness are often treated with fear or

1. Phobia 2. Post-traumatic stress disorder 3. Addiction
4. Behavior therapy 5. Depression 6. Anxiety 7. When it encourages you to be careful in dangerous situations.
8. Recognize the emotion and its cause; think about ways to resolve the problem; give yourself time to cool. 9. Guilt: sense

of having done something wrong; Shame: a feeling of being unworthy. 10. Sudden, noticeable change in personality; inability to cope with problems; difficulty performing day-to-day tasks; bizarre or unrealistic ideas. 11. Social phobia makes people unable to enjoy social activities.

disrespect, and suggesting some ways that people could learn to understand and respond to these problems.

20. **Personal.** Think about what you learned from the Q&A section, "Dealing with Loss and Grief." In your own words, describe the process of grieving, as you understand it. Discuss the events that can cause grief, the emotions associated with grief, and ways of coping with it.

Activities

21. Make a chart on poster board that lists six different anxiety disorders discussed in Section 2. Briefly describe the symptoms of each disorder and note the recommended treatment or treatments.

22. Read an article or watch a movie about an individual who struggles with a mental or emotional problem. Write a summary that describes the person's problem and how he or she dealt with it. Include a copy of the article or the name of the movie.

23. Write a script for a public service announcement aimed at teens on one of the following topics:
    - Coping with anxiety
    - Managing anger
    - Recognizing the warning signs of mental illness
    - Overcoming shyness
    - Easing symptoms of depression
    - Facts and myths related to suicide

    As a bonus, make a tape or video recording of your announcement.

24. Use a phone book to look up facilities in your community that provide mental health services. Call five facilities to find out what services they provide. List each facility on a sheet of paper, along with its address, phone number, and services provided.

Making Decisions About Health

25. Suppose you have a friend whose parents have not been getting along with each other for quite a while. They recently told your friend they are getting divorced. Ever since hearing this news, your friend has been having trouble eating, sleeping, and concentrating on schoolwork. What steps would you take to help this friend?

For more vocabulary practice, play the True/False game at **glencoe.com**.

Fact or Fiction?

Answers

1. False. Emotionally healthy people often benefit from professional help, and it is well worth seeking.
2. False. Ordinary anxiety is a normal emotion that everyone experiences from time to time.
3. True.

Writing Paragraphs will vary.

12. Obsessions and compulsions. **13.** Flashbacks, constant anxiety, trouble sleeping. **14.** Involves extreme mania and depression. **15.** Depression, other mental disorders, and substance abuse. **16.** A previous suicide attempt.
17. It is a sign of weakness; Reluctant to discuss their personal problems with a stranger. **18.** Any two: psychotherapy (or talk therapy), family therapy. **19–25.** Answers will vary.

CHAPTER 6

The Human Body and Its Systems

Sections

How does your body do the things it does? How do your legs "know" how to walk? How does food in your stomach nourish your toes? To answer questions like these, you need to understand the body systems and how they work together. **Body systems** are *groups of related organs that work together to perform major body functions.*

Most sections of this chapter are written as a series of questions and answers based on a figure showing one of the body systems. While reading about each system, refer to the figure to see the body parts being discussed. For definitions of many of the body parts named in the figures, turn to the main glossary at the end of the book.

Fact or Fiction?

What Do You Think?

Is each statement true or false? If you think it's false, explain what's true.

1. Once bones have grown to adult size, they gain no more materials, although they may lose some.
2. If the digestive system did not protect itself, it would be digested by its juices.
3. The lungs are equipped with muscles in their walls that draw air in and out of the lungs' chambers.

 Writing Can you list all the body systems? Write down as many as you know.

(Answers on page 159)

Go Online

For fitness and health tips, visit the Fitness Zone at **glencoe.com**.

SECTION 1

The Integrated Body

No one body system can function without help from the other systems. Each system depends on all the others to keep the body working as a whole. The body systems adjust to changing conditions to maintain the internal conditions the body needs. **Homeostasis**, which means "staying the same," is the *maintenance of a stable body environment, achieved as body systems adapt to changing conditions.*

Here is an example of how body systems work together to maintain homeostasis. The kidneys, which are part of the urinary system (see page 146), can sense the amount of water circulating in the blood flowing within the cardiovascular system (page 144). When water levels are too high, the kidneys remove the extra water from the blood and release it from the body as urine. This brings the blood's water content back to normal. When the blood's water content drops too low, by contrast, the kidneys reduce the amount of water in the urine.

This is just one of countless ways your healthy body systems work together to maintain homeostasis. These processes go on every minute of every day, automatically, without your having to do a thing.

Structures Within the Body

MAIN IDEA ▶ The body's cells are organized into tissues and organs that carry out specific tasks.

The body is made up of trillions of microscopic **cells**, *the smallest units in which independent life can exist.* Each of the body's cells is a self-contained, living unit, as seen in **Figure 6.1**. However, each cell works in cooperation with every other cell to support the whole.

Within most human cells is a **nucleus**, *inside a cell, the structure that contains the genes.* Nearly every cell with a nucleus also contains a complete set of **chromosomes**, *slender bodies inside the cell's nucleus which carry the genes.* The chromosomes are made up of **DNA** (deoxyribonucleic acid), *the genetic material of cells which serves as a blueprint for making all of the proteins a cell needs to make exact copies of itself.* The DNA is organized into units called **genes**, *the units of a cell's inheritance, which direct the making of equipment to do the cell's work.*

The human body contains many different kinds of cells, each cell with its own function. For example, the nerve cells produce and send electrical signals throughout the body.

Vocabulary

body systems
homeostasis
cells
nucleus
chromosomes
DNA (deoxyribonucleic acid)
genes
tissues
organs

Figure 6.1 **The Organization of the Body**

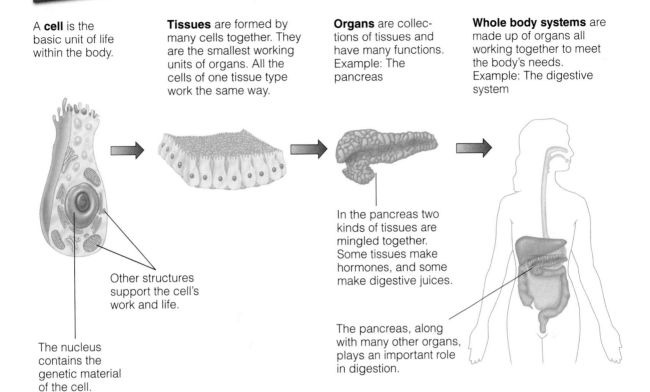

A **cell** is the basic unit of life within the body.

Tissues are formed by many cells together. They are the smallest working units of organs. All the cells of one tissue type work the same way.

Organs are collections of tissues and have many functions. Example: The pancreas

Whole body systems are made up of organs all working together to meet the body's needs. Example: The digestive system

Other structures support the cell's work and life.

The nucleus contains the genetic material of the cell.

In the pancreas two kinds of tissues are mingled together. Some tissues make hormones, and some make digestive juices.

The pancreas, along with many other organs, plays an important role in digestion.

Tissues are *systems of cells working together to perform specific tasks.* For example, muscle tissue contains groups of cells with the ability to contract. Tissues, in turn, are organized into organs. **Organs** are *whole units, made of tissues, that perform specific jobs.* The heart is an organ in which muscle tissues, nerve tissues, and other types of tissue all work together.

Body Systems

MAIN IDEA ▶ Each body system cooperates with other body systems to carry out its functions.

Body systems contain groups of organs that work together to perform various functions within the body. For example, the cardiovascular system (also called the circulatory system) consists of the heart and blood vessels, which work together to deliver blood to the body's tissues. **Figure 6.2** on page 134 presents simple diagrams of various body systems.

No body system is completely independent of the others. Here are some ways in which body systems work together to maintain the body's health:

- The *skeletal* and *muscular systems* work together to enable the body to move.

Comprehension Check
Define: Remind students that all of the parts labeled in the illustrations and discussed in the various sections of this chapter are defined in the glossary.

Figure 6.2 The Integrated Body

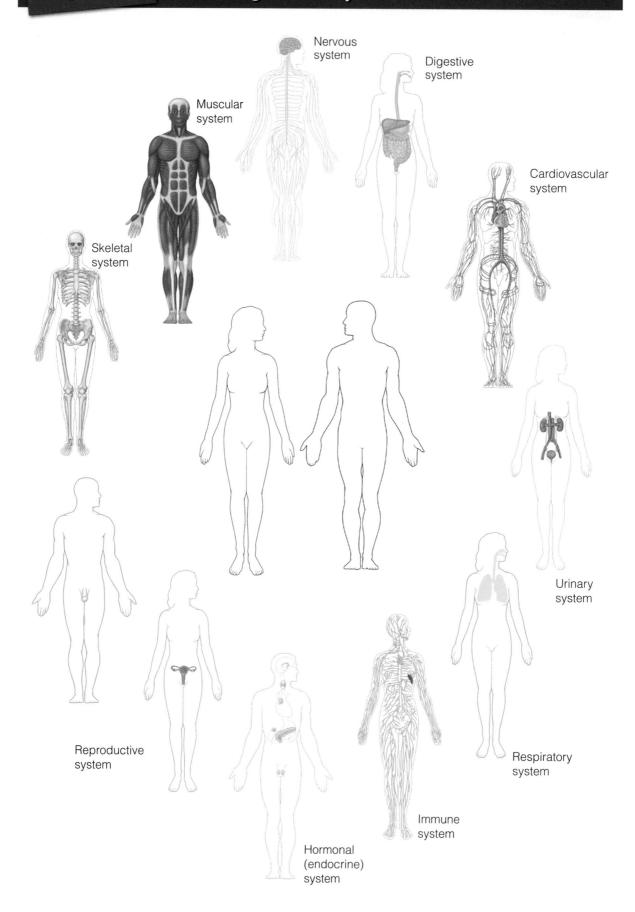

Nervous system

Digestive system

Muscular system

Cardiovascular system

Skeletal system

Urinary system

Reproductive system

Respiratory system

Immune system

Hormonal (endocrine) system

- Messages from the *nervous system* direct the activities of all other body systems.

- The *cardiovascular system* works with the *respiratory* and *digestive systems* to carry oxygen and nutrients to all other systems. It also works with the *urinary system* to remove wastes from the body, and carries messages from the *hormonal system*.

- The *immune system* protects all other body systems from infection.

- The *hormonal system* (also called the *endocrine system*) communicates with many other body systems to direct their activities. The signals it sends to the *reproductive system* regulate sexual development.

Comprehension Check.

Evaluate: Have students choose any body organ and list the many systems that require the function of that organ, or have them choose a system and list the ways in which that system is affected by or affects other systems. For both options, student points are determined by the number of relationships they can list.

Worksheets: A reproducible quiz for Section 1 is provided in the Teacher Classroom Resources.

SECTION 1 Review

Reviewing the Vocabulary

Review the vocabulary on page 132. Then answer these questions.

1. Define *homeostasis*.
2. What is *DNA*?
3. What are *organs*?
4. Define *body systems*.
5. What are *chromosomes*.

Reviewing the Facts

6. **Explain.** How do the kidneys manage the water balance in the body?
7. **Explain.** What are genes?
8. **Analyze.** Explain how two of the body's systems work together.

Writing Critically

9. **Expository.** The body systems can be affected by our health choices. Give at least five specific examples of behaviors that could affect one or more of your body systems.

For more vocabulary practice, play the eFlashcards game at **glencoe.com**.

1. The maintenance of a stable body environment, achieved as body systems adapt to changing conditions.

2. The genetic material of cells which serves as a blueprint for making all of the proteins a cell needs to make exact copies of itself.

3. Whole units, made of tissues, that perform specific jobs.

4. Groups of related organs that work together to perform major body functions.

5. Slender bodies inside the cell's nucleus which carry the genes.

6. When the kidneys detect excess water, they flush the water out of the body as urine.

7. The units of a cell's inheritance, which direct the making of equipment to do the cell's work.

8. The skeletal and muscular systems to enable the body to move.

9. Answers will vary.

SECTION 2

The Skeletal System

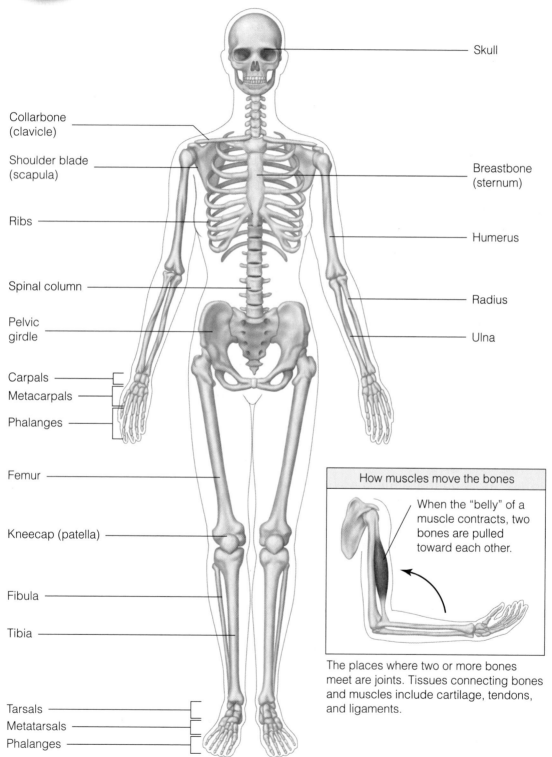

Skull

Collarbone
(clavicle)

Shoulder blade
(scapula)

Breastbone
(sternum)

Ribs

Humerus

Spinal column

Radius

Pelvic
girdle

Ulna

Carpals

Metacarpals

Phalanges

Femur

Kneecap (patella)

Fibula

Tibia

Tarsals

Metatarsals

Phalanges

How muscles move the bones

When the "belly" of a muscle contracts, two bones are pulled toward each other.

The places where two or more bones meet are joints. Tissues connecting bones and muscles include cartilage, tendons, and ligaments.

Without a skeleton, the body would be made entirely of soft tissues. It would have few distinguishing features. It would be easily injured and would find movement difficult, at best.

Bones determine the body's shape. They also protect soft vital organs, such as the brain and kidneys. They allow movement by serving as anchors for the body's muscles, which attach to bones and operate them like levers. In addition, bones store the mineral calcium and release it into the bloodstream when it is needed. Perhaps the most amazing job performed by the bones is manufacturing most of the body's blood cells, without which life would not be possible.

You may think of your bones as nonliving structures, like the concrete supports that hold up a bridge. However, bones are actually made of a mixture of living and nonliving tissue that is even stronger than reinforced concrete. Their strength comes from their structure. Bones are composed of two types of material: calcium salts and protein fibers. Calcium salts are especially hard, while the protein fibers are flexible. The bond between the two types of materials makes bones able to withstand different kinds of forces. A network of blood vessels runs through the bones, bringing nutrients and oxygen to bone cells and picking up stored nutrients to carry to body tissues.

How do bones grow?

Bones are equipped with both bone-building cells and bone-dismantling cells. The human skeleton begins to develop before birth. At first, it is made mostly of the flexible tissue cartilage. Gradually, the bone-building cells add hard deposits of calcium salts and other minerals, making the bones more and more rigid. It takes about 20 years for the skeleton to harden fully. As the bones grow, they need to be reshaped. Bone-dismantling cells break down old structures, while bone-building cells put new ones together.

Once built, do bones ever change?

Even after the skeleton has hardened, the process of dismantling bones continues but the bone-building processes diminish. In addition, the bones are always changing in composition. Each day, they store and release calcium to maintain the level needed in the bloodstream.

As you grow older, the rate at which old bone tissue breaks down begins to exceed the rate at which new bone tissue forms. As a result, the bones become less dense. Many older people develop a condition called osteoporosis, which makes the bones weak and brittle. Having a physically active lifestyle and getting plenty of calcium and vitamin D in the diet can reduce people's risk of developing this condition as they age.

The risk of osteoporosis is greatest in people who do not build up enough bone mass in their youth. Thus, having healthy habits during your teen years can help you maintain strong bones throughout your life. Getting enough calcium in your diet and engaging in regular physical activity are especially important.

How do the bones help the muscles to move the body?

Bones are connected to each other at flexible joints, as shown on the previous page. Muscles pull on these joints to make movement possible. For example, the biceps muscle is attached at one end to the bone of your upper arm. The other end is attached to a bone of your forearm. When you want to reach up to touch your shoulder, the biceps muscle contracts. This pulls the forearm bone upward, bending your arm at the elbow.

Comprehension Check

Analyze: Emphasize that the bones in the skeletal system are alive. Ask students to consider what would happen to the body if the bones were not constantly growing and changing.

SECTION 3

The Muscular System

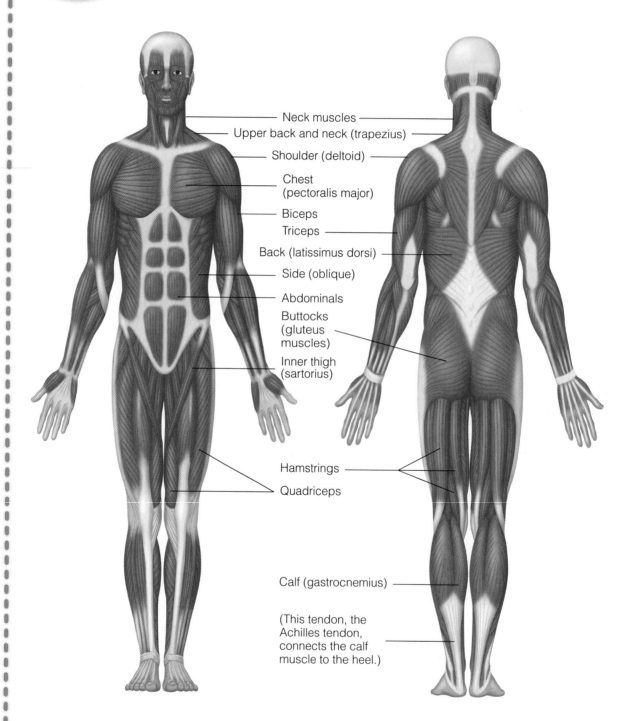

Neck muscles

Upper back and neck (trapezius)

Shoulder (deltoid)

Chest
(pectoralis major)

Biceps

Triceps

Back (latissimus dorsi)

Side (oblique)

Abdominals

Buttocks
(gluteus
muscles)

Inner thigh
(sartorius)

Hamstrings

Quadriceps

Calf (gastrocnemius)

(This tendon, the
Achilles tendon,
connects the calf
muscle to the heel.)

The structure of muscle tissue makes body movement possible. Bundles of muscle fibers form strong muscles that work in pairs to pull the bones back and forth in ways that make it possible to dance, ride a bike, and use sign language. The figure on the previous page shows the main muscle groups. Other muscles, found deep inside the body, control the movements of the heart and the digestive system.

Are all muscles the same?

No, there are several types. The muscles that move your skeleton are under your control. They are called skeletal or voluntary muscles. Seen under a microscope, these muscles have a striped, or *striated* (STRY-ay-ted), appearance.

Other muscles are not under your control, such as those in the walls of the stomach and intestine that move food through the digestive system. These appear smooth under a microscope and are called the involuntary or smooth muscles. The nervous system directs their movements without any conscious effort from you.

A third kind of muscle, called cardiac muscle, is found only in the heart. This type of muscle also moves automatically to squeeze blood out of the heart and through the blood vessels with each heartbeat.

What makes muscles contract?

Muscle cells respond to signals from the nervous system. A part of the brain responsible for movement sends electrical signals through the nerves that cause tiny fibers within the muscle cells to slide closer together so that they overlap. When enough cells receive the signal, the whole muscle contracts.

How do muscles work together to move the body?

The contraction of muscles causes your joints to bend. However, muscles can only pull the bones; they cannot push them back.

Therefore, muscles work in pairs to move the joints. An earlier example explained that when you bend your elbow, the biceps muscle on the front of your arm contracts, pulling the forearm upward. At the same time, the triceps muscle on the back of the arm relaxes. To straighten the elbow, the triceps contracts, pulling the forearm downward, while the biceps relaxes.

Is it true that to strengthen muscles, you must work them until they are sore?

Muscles often feel sore a day or two after a tough workout, especially after doing a new type of exercise. Pushing the muscles past their normal limits causes tiny tears in the muscle tissue. It isn't necessary to work muscles to the point of soreness in order to strengthen them. Even without injury, muscles grow in size and gain in strength after working. Chapter 9 provides details about how to gain muscle size and strength.

Which muscle is the strongest?

That depends on your definition of strength. The hardest-working muscle is definitely the heart, which pumps 2,500 gallons of blood through the veins each day. The largest muscle in the body is the gluteus maximus, the major muscle of the buttocks. The muscle is responsible for keeping the body in an upright position. The muscle that is strongest for its size, however, is the masseter, one of the muscles that works the jaw. It can push teeth closed with a force of up to 200 pounds!

Class Activity
Apply: Have students hold onto the edge of their chairs with legs out straight, feet on the floor, and lower themselves down as far as they can and back to place. Have students list the muscles they worked.

The Nervous System

Top view of the brain

Each half is a hemisphere (cerebrum)

Side view of the brain showing where various functions are located

Motor area (controls voluntary muscle movement)

Visual center (visual messages received)

Eye field (eyes)

Frontal lobes (intellect)

Temporal lobes (hearing and memory)

The central nervous system (CNS) consists of the brain and spinal cord.

The peripheral nervous system (PNS) consists of the nerves.

Cerebellum (coordinates muscle movement)

Spinal cord (receives messages from the body)

Brain

Nerves

Spinal cord

Cutaway side view of the brain showing the center and one hemisphere

Cerebral cortex (outermost layer of the brain)

Midbrain (controls sight, hearing, and some voluntary movements, such as eye movements)

Cerebellum

Brain stem (serves as a bridge connecting the spinal cord and higher areas; controls breathing, heart rate, and sleep)

A person whose cortex is injured by an accident or disabled by a disease such as Alzheimer's may live a long time with an intact brain stem.

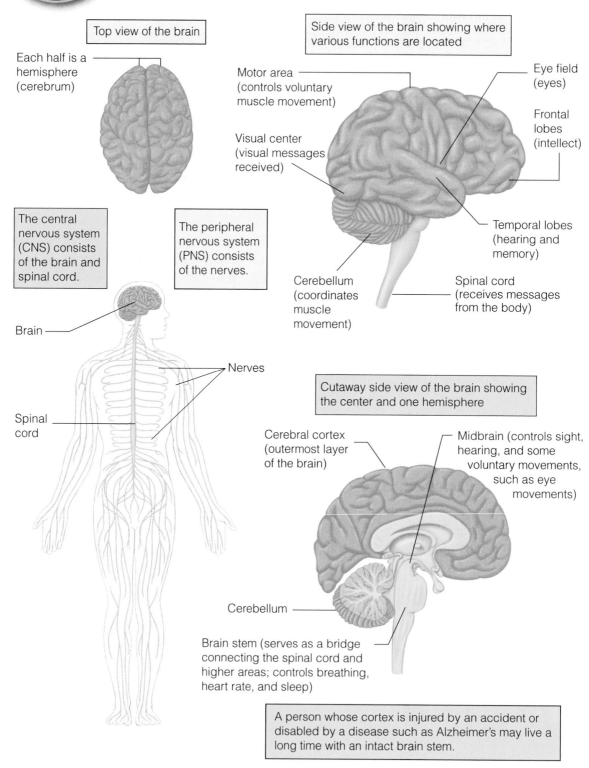

Your central nervous system consists of the brain and spinal cord. The brain is a mass of specialized nerve tissue weighing about three pounds. It controls almost every physical body function, thought, and emotion you experience. The brain receives information about events and conditions around the body and delivers instructions to all other body systems. The instructions travel through the spinal cord which serves as the body's main communication line.

The *peripheral* (per-IH-fer-al) nervous system, the second main part of the nervous system, consists of all the nerves that branch out from the spinal cord to the rest of the body. These nerves carry messages back and forth between the brain and all the tissues of the body.

Do the different brain parts do different things?

The brain divides its work among its various physical parts. In the outer layer, or *cortex*, of the brain's two main hemispheres, conscious thought takes place. The small bulb lying at the base of these hemispheres, the cerebellum, maintains balance and directs muscle movement. The hindbrain leading to the spinal cord controls breathing and other basic body functions.

Within these large brain areas are smaller divisions, each with specific duties. The frontal lobes handle intellectual tasks, such as reading a book. When you talk with friends, a spot on the left side of your brain converts your thoughts into words. When you hear a song on the radio, the hearing center becomes active. If the music creates emotion in you, you can thank your limbic system—a set of structures buried deep within the cerebrum, sometimes called the "emotional brain." Should you dance, your motor area directs your muscle movement.

Does the brain control everything the body does?

Almost, but there are a few exceptions. A *reflex* is a sort of intentional short circuit in the nervous system. Reflexes protect your body from things that could cause harm. One example is the way you jerk your hand away when it touches something hot—even before you realize that it burns. The message from your nerves saying "This is hot!" generates a response as soon as it reaches the spinal cord, instead of traveling all the way to the brain and back. The spinal cord sends back a signal to pull your hand away within a split second.

What keeps harmful substances from entering the brain?

The brain maintains a control system, known as the blood-brain barrier, which blocks out certain chemicals carried by the blood. The barrier keeps out hormones and other substances that could interrupt the brain's work. This keeps the brain's internal chemistry balanced, despite changes in the rest of the body's chemistry. Substances the brain needs, such as glucose, which cells use for fuel, can pass through the barrier by special means.

Although the system blocks out some harmful chemicals, it cannot stop all of them. For example, certain mind-altering drugs can pass freely into brain tissues. Alcohol and barbiturates are two examples.

What if nerve or brain tissues are injured? Do they heal?

For hundreds of years, scientists believed that nerve cells could not regenerate after an injury, as other tissues do. However, modern medicine has discovered that, under the right circumstances, nerve cells can regrow to reconnect a damaged nerve. This process can take anywhere from 6 to 18 months.

Class Activity. *Analyze:* Discuss with students the problems that could arise if we did not have reflexes. Encourage students to share their ideas with the class.

The Digestive System

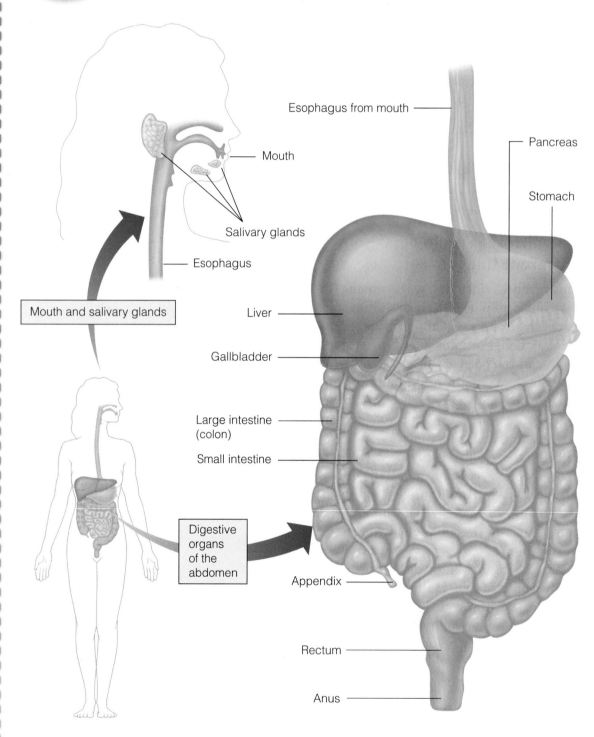

Esophagus from mouth

Mouth

Salivary glands

Esophagus

Mouth and salivary glands

Pancreas

Stomach

Liver

Gallbladder

Large intestine (colon)

Small intestine

Digestive organs of the abdomen

Appendix

Rectum

Anus

The human body is shaped something like a tube, with the digestive tract running through the center to form the hole. The digestive system breaks down the food you eat into nutrients the body can use. It performs three main processes:

- **Digestion.** The stomach breaks down food into a form the body can absorb.

- **Absorption.** In the small intestines, nutrients are absorbed into the blood, which carries them to the body's cells.

- **Elimination.** Material the body cannot use passes through the large intestine and out of the body.

Why doesn't the stomach digest itself?

The powerful acids and juices of the stomach would indeed digest its lining if it weren't for a protective layer of mucus that coats the inside of the stomach. In fact, all along the digestive tract, a special group of cells does nothing but produce and release mucus. The constant flow of mucus forms a barrier that protects the living tissues of the digestive tract from its harsh contents.

What causes indigestion, and what is the best cure?

Indigestion, or upset stomach, can occur for a variety of reasons. Eating too much, especially fatty or spicy foods, can cause discomfort. Eating too quickly can have the same effect. Stress, alcohol, and certain medications can also upset the digestive system.

The best treatment for indigestion is prevention. Avoid foods that have caused problems for you in the past. Eating smaller, more frequent meals and eating more slowly may also help. Exercise regularly, but avoid exercising right after a meal. If you do develop indigestion, you might obtain relief from over-the-counter remedies. However, it's a good idea to consult a physician if you have indigestion often. It could be a symptom of a more serious disease.

What does the appendix do, and why must some people have theirs removed?

The appendix is the little worm-shaped sac that hangs from the lower right side of the large intestine. It seems to have no purpose in digestion. It is notable only if it becomes blocked or inflamed. This condition, called appendicitis, is painful. It is also dangerous, because the sac can burst open, spilling its contents into the abdomen and causing a life-threatening infection. This danger can be prevented by surgically removing an inflamed appendix before it bursts.

Why does my stomach sometimes grumble?

As fluid and gas squeeze past the convoluted folds and turns of the digestive organ tissues, the bubbles produce a gurgling, grumbling sound. The sound may be inconvenient at times, but it is normal, especially when you are hungry.

Why do people "pass gas," and what causes its odor?

Intestinal gas, or flatus (FLAY-tus), is a normal waste product of digestion. The gas consists partly of nitrogen, oxygen, and carbon dioxide from air you swallow while eating, drinking, or chewing gum. Another part is hydrogen and methane, produced when bacteria in the large intestine break down undigested particles of food. The odor, however, comes from trace gases that add up to less than 1 percent of the total volume. Most of these are also produced by bacteria. Foods containing sulfur, such as cauliflower, eggs, and meat, often produce strong odors.

Class Activity

Analyze: Have students research the digestive systems of two other animals and compare and contrast them to the human digestive system.

The Cardiovascular System

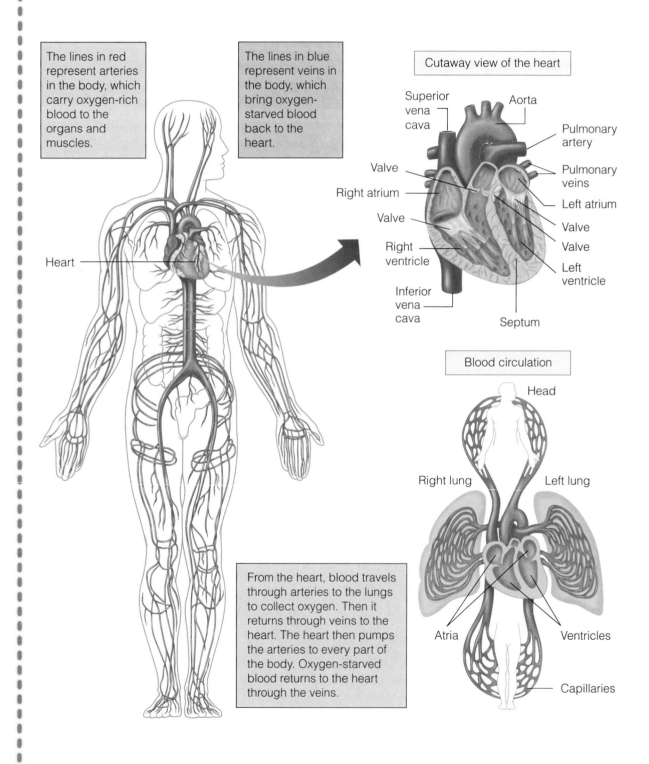

The lines in red represent arteries in the body, which carry oxygen-rich blood to the organs and muscles.

The lines in blue represent veins in the body, which bring oxygen-starved blood back to the heart.

Heart

Cutaway view of the heart

Superior vena cava

Aorta

Pulmonary artery

Valve

Pulmonary veins

Right atrium

Left atrium

Valve

Valve

Right ventricle

Valve

Left ventricle

Inferior vena cava

Septum

Blood circulation

Head

Right lung

Left lung

From the heart, blood travels through arteries to the lungs to collect oxygen. Then it returns through veins to the heart. The heart then pumps the arteries to every part of the body. Oxygen-starved blood returns to the heart through the veins.

Atria

Ventricles

Capillaries

With its vast network of arteries, veins, and capillaries, the cardiovascular system (also known as the circulatory system) transports fluids throughout the body. Each cell in the body depends on this system's life-sustaining work. Cells dump their wastes into the bloodstream and draw out all the nutrients and other chemicals they need to live and function.

How does the heart know how fast to beat?

The heart responds to a small area of its upper right chamber (right atrium), its natural pacemaker. This structure sends an electrical impulse through the heart that causes both atria to contract. The signal then travels through the ventricles, causing them to contract as well.

The pacemaker adjusts the heart rate in response to instructions from the nervous system. During exercise, for instance, it speeds up the heart rate to pump more oxygen-rich blood to the body.

Does the heart ever rest?

In a sense, the heart muscle does rest, or relax, as often as it beats. Each beat, or contraction, of the heart muscle pumps blood out into the blood vessels. Between beats, the heart relaxes, allowing more blood to flow into its chambers.

When the blood picks up wastes from the cells, how does it get rid of them?

Several body systems remove the waste products deposited in the blood. Carbon dioxide, for instance, leaves the body through the lungs. Other waste products from the cell processes are pulled out of the blood by the liver. Still others are filtered out by the kidneys and discarded as urine. Thus, the cardiovascular, respiratory, digestive, and urinary systems all work together on the task of cleansing the blood.

If blood is red, why do the veins under my skin look blue?

Blood outside the body is red because of the enormous number of red blood cells it contains. Take away the red cells, and what's left is not red at all, but a clear, sticky, yellowish liquid. The red cells contain *hemoglobin*, an iron-containing protein that turns bright red whenever it is in contact with oxygen.

As red cells move through the lungs, they pick up oxygen from newly inhaled air. The oxygen binds to the hemoglobin in the cells, giving them a bright red color. As the cells travel through the body, they give up their oxygen to the tissues and replace it with carbon dioxide. Without oxygen, the red cells take on a dark maroon color. When seen through the colorless veins under the skin, however, it appears blue because of the way your skin absorbs light.

What makes a wound stop bleeding?

Blood platelets in the blood form a net, which traps still more platelets and other blood cells. This forms a clot, which plugs the wound until it can heal.

What are blood types?

Human blood is classified into four types. The types are based on the presence or absence of two proteins, called antigens on the surface of the red blood cells. The antigens are designated as A and B. Type A blood contains antigen A and type B contains antigen B. Type AB contains both, and type O contains neither.

Class Activity

Comprehend: Have students use any one of the following terms in a sentence with either "heart" or "cardiovascular system": aorta, carbon dioxide, cells, left atrium, oxygen, right atrium.

The Urinary System

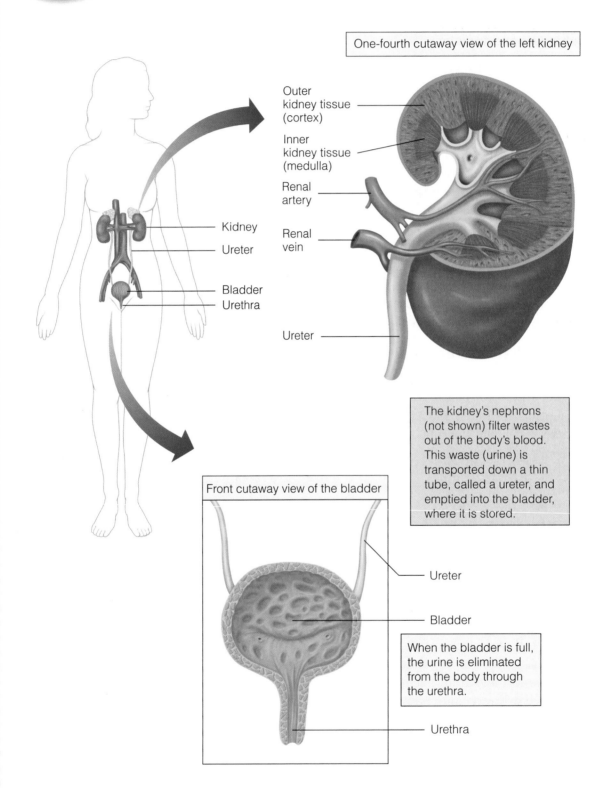

One-fourth cutaway view of the left kidney

Outer kidney tissue (cortex)

Inner kidney tissue (medulla)

Renal artery

Renal vein

Ureter

Kidney

Ureter

Bladder

Urethra

The kidney's nephrons (not shown) filter wastes out of the body's blood. This waste (urine) is transported down a thin tube, called a ureter, and emptied into the bladder, where it is stored.

Front cutaway view of the bladder

Ureter

Bladder

When the bladder is full, the urine is eliminated from the body through the urethra.

Urethra

The task of removing wastes from the blood is the specialty of the urinary system. This process is absolutely essential to life. Without the kidneys' careful monitoring of the blood's composition, toxic wastes would soon build up to harmful levels in the bloodstream.

Among the first signs of kidney failure are confusion, inability to make judgments, and dizziness. Should the situation continue, the person would lose consciousness. These symptoms demonstrate the connection between the functions of the urinary system and the workings of the brain. All body tissues depend entirely on the correct composition of the blood, which the urinary system works to maintain.

How do the kidneys know what's inside the blood vessels?

The kidneys contain a million tiny units, called nephrons. The nephrons draw out fluid from the blood. The kidney can then detect and measure various chemicals in this fluid. It adjusts the levels of water, salts, and other materials in the fluid. Chemicals the body needs, such as sugar and other nutrients, are returned to the blood. Wastes dissolved in water flow out of the kidneys as urine.

How do the kidneys know how much water to put back into the blood, and how much to make into urine?

The water balance of the blood is important. If the kidneys do not remove enough water, the tissues will swell. If they take out too much, the body will become dehydrated. The kidneys have a partner that helps them to perform this balancing act: the pituitary gland in the brain. The brain also monitors changes in the blood composition. When the water level begins to drop, the pituitary sends a hormone to the kidneys, telling them to conserve water. The kidneys do so, and they respond with their own hormone to broadcast the news of the need for water to all the body's tissues. One of the tissues that responds to the kidney's hormone is the brain, which lets you know that you are thirsty. You drink a glass of water, and your blood fluid level is replenished.

How does the bladder know when to empty?

Urine formed in the kidneys carries the blood's waste products down two tubes, called *ureters*, which lead to the bladder. The bladder is the holding tank for urine.

The walls of the bladder stretch and expand as urine collects inside. When the bladder is full nerves in the bladder's walls send a message to the brain. When the person is ready to urinate, the brain signals a ring-shaped muscle at the opening of the urethra called the *sphincter*, to relax. The bladder contracts, and urine flows out of the body through the urethra.

Is the urinary system the same in males as in females?

Males and females have similar urinary systems, except for the urethra. The male urethra is about four times as long as the female urethra. It conducts semen, as well as urine, out of the body. A sphincter muscle inside the body prevents these two functions from happening at the same time.

The female urethra is used for waste disposal only. Because its opening is positioned close to the rectum and the vagina, where bacteria are often found, females are at a higher risk than males for infections of the urinary tract. Urinary tract infections, or UTIs, should always be treated promptly. Left untreated, they may endanger the health of the kidneys.

Comprehension Check
Evaluate: Ask students what symptoms they would expect to signal kidney failure. How do these symptoms illustrate the connection between the functions of the urinary system and the workings of the brain?

The Respiratory System

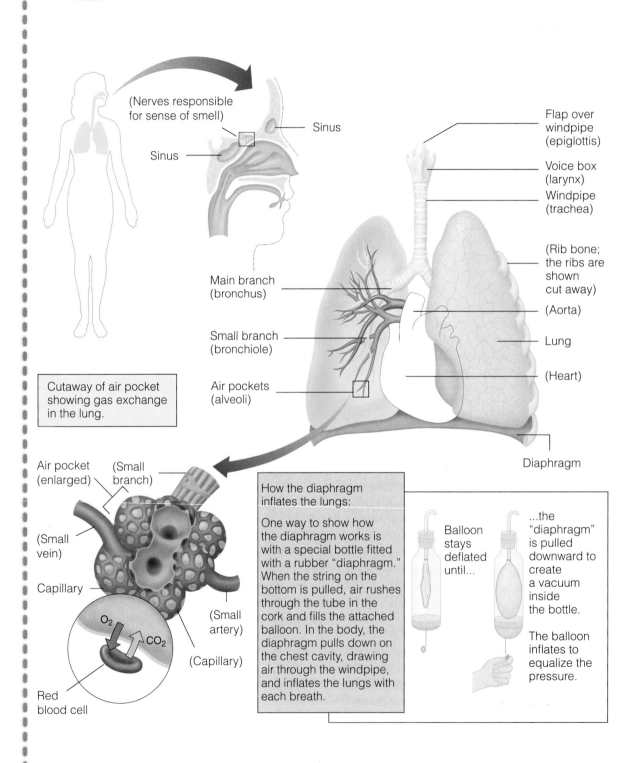

(Nerves responsible for sense of smell)

Sinus

Sinus

Flap over windpipe (epiglottis)

Voice box (larynx)

Windpipe (trachea)

(Rib bone; the ribs are shown cut away)

(Aorta)

Lung

(Heart)

Main branch (bronchus)

Small branch (bronchiole)

Air pockets (alveoli)

Diaphragm

Cutaway of air pocket showing gas exchange in the lung.

Air pocket (enlarged)

(Small branch)

(Small vein)

Capillary

O₂

CO₂

(Small artery)

(Capillary)

Red blood cell

How the diaphragm inflates the lungs:

One way to show how the diaphragm works is with a special bottle fitted with a rubber "diaphragm." When the string on the bottom is pulled, air rushes through the tube in the cork and fills the attached balloon. In the body, the diaphragm pulls down on the chest cavity, drawing air through the windpipe, and inflates the lungs with each breath.

Balloon stays deflated until...

...the "diaphragm" is pulled downward to create a vacuum inside the bottle.

The balloon inflates to equalize the pressure.

Every day, the lungs breathe in and out the amount of air in an average-size classroom. With each inhaled breath, the lungs take in the oxygen that cells need to produce energy. On exhaling, the lungs expel carbon dioxide, the major waste product of the body's fuel use.

The lungs themselves have no muscles to move air in and out of their chambers. Instead, they inflate and deflate thanks to the work of the diaphragm and chest muscles. When someone takes a breath, the diaphragm pulls downward, as demonstrated on the previous page. At the same time, the muscles of the chest pull the ribs outward. The combined effect is to enlarge the chest cavity, lowering the air pressure inside it. As a result, air rushes into the lungs through the windpipe. When the diaphragm and chest muscles relax, the chest contracts and air pressure increases. As a result, air flows out of the lungs.

What determines how fast I breathe?

A brain center that measures your need for oxygen also determines how fast you breathe. It can tell, from the levels of carbon dioxide and oxygen in your blood, how fast you need to exchange these two gases in your lungs. The harder your body is working, the more oxygen you will need, and the faster you will breathe.

Is it best to breathe through your nose?

The nose is superbly designed for breathing. While the mouth pulls air directly from the environment into the lungs, the nasal passageways also warm it and add moisture. In addition, the nose serves as a filter to prevent debris from entering the lungs. Nose hairs filter out large particles, such as dust or fibers, from inhaled air. Any particles that get by this first barrier are likely to be expelled when they trigger the sneeze reflex.

If tiny particles pass by these two defenses, they still must flow over the mucous membranes lining the nasal passageway. These membranes are lined with tiny, waving hairlike structures called *cilia*. The cilia sweep dust and bacteria either out of the nose or into the throat to be swallowed. In the stomach, bacteria and debris are destroyed by acids and digestive enzymes.

What are the sinuses?

Your skull contains eight air spaces called sinuses. Six of them are located in the facial area—behind the nose, over the eyebrows, and in the cheek area. The other two are found just above the throat. The main function of the sinuses is to lighten the weight of the skull. They also play a role in creating the sound of the voice as sound waves resonate inside them.

The sinuses are lined with membranes that produce mucus, which helps trap harmful bacteria. When infection or allergy causes the membranes to swell, though, the passages leading to the sinuses can become blocked. Pressure can build up in the sinuses, causing headaches, congestion, and postnasal drip (mucus dripping down the back of the throat). If bacteria settle into the sinuses, antibiotics may be needed to help the person recover.

What is a hiccup?

A hiccup is an involuntary contraction of the diaphragm, caused by irritation. The sound is made when the sudden contraction of the diaphragm sucks air over the vocal cords. The cords then snap shut, cutting off the air flow and the sound.

Class Activity
Apply:
1. Ask students to quietly sit upright and count the number of breaths they take in one minute.
2. Ask which muscles seem to be involved.
3. Ask students what determines the rate of breathing.

The Immune System

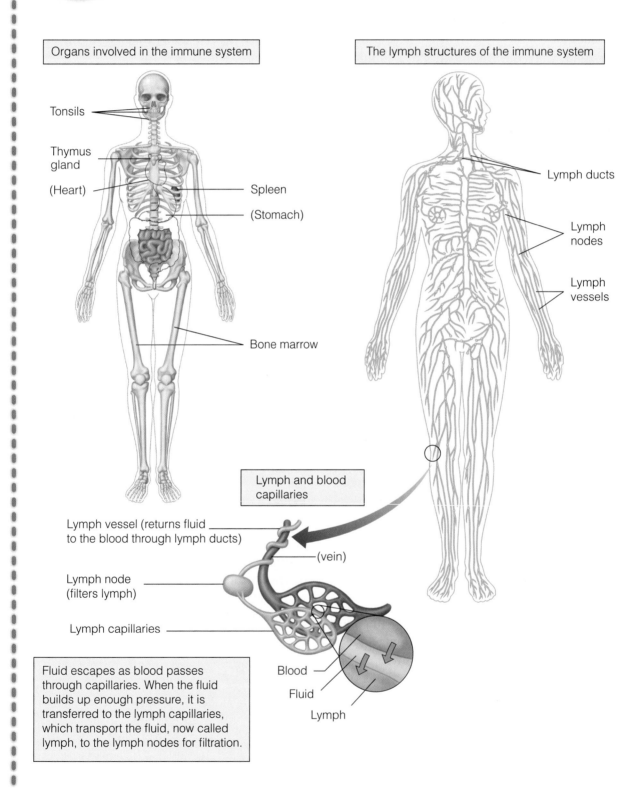

Organs involved in the immune system

Tonsils

Thymus gland

(Heart)

Spleen

(Stomach)

Bone marrow

The lymph structures of the immune system

Lymph ducts

Lymph nodes

Lymph vessels

Lymph and blood capillaries

Lymph vessel (returns fluid to the blood through lymph ducts)

(vein)

Lymph node (filters lymph)

Lymph capillaries

Blood

Fluid

Lymph

Fluid escapes as blood passes through capillaries. When the fluid builds up enough pressure, it is transferred to the lymph capillaries, which transport the fluid, now called lymph, to the lymph nodes for filtration.

Each day, the immune system traps and destroys many invaders in the body, such as bacteria, viruses, and even cells that could start cancers. This system's special cells are busy everywhere in the body. They cluster in areas where invaders are likely to intrude, such as the throat, digestive tract, and groin. The lymphatic system plays a large role in immunity.

What does the lymphatic system do?

The lymphatic system is important in many ways. Like the cardiovascular system, this system moves a fluid, known as lymph, around the body. Special vessels carry this fluid away from the body's tissues so that it does not accumulate and cause swelling. The lymphatic system also helps to transport fats and some vitamins that have been absorbed from food in the digestive tract.

One important function of this system is its role in fighting disease. The lymph nodes act as filters to remove bacteria and viruses from the body. Lymphatic organs also help to maintain the body's fighting force of white blood cells. These cells circulate through the bloodstream, searching for invaders to destroy.

Does the heart pump the lymph around the body?

The lymphatic system does not have a built-in pump the way the cardiovascular system does. Instead, the movement of body muscles helps to squeeze the lymph along the vessels. Lymph vessels contain valves that keep lymph from flowing backward.

What does the thymus gland do?

The main job of the thymus is its role in producing certain white blood cells, known as *T cells* (*T* for *thymus*). T cells are produced in the bone marrow along with other kinds of white blood cells. Then they enter the thymus, which sorts out the cells that can recognize and destroy invaders in the body. Only T cells that pass this test leave the thymus and enter the bloodstream to fight germs.

Is the spleen important for anything?

The spleen is a spongy organ that produces disease-fighting white blood cells. It also filters blood the way the lymph nodes filter lymph and it destroys old, worn-out red blood cells. In addition, the spleen's spongy structure allows it to act as a sort of reserve for the blood supply. If the body needs more blood to carry oxygen to the tissues, the spleen contracts and squeezes blood from its chambers into the bloodstream. The spleen can also produce white blood cells and, in infants and young children, red blood cells.

Why do people with infections get "swollen glands"?

The swellings found in such spots as the jaw, throat, and armpits are not actually "glands" but lymph nodes. While fighting an infection, these nodes often become enlarged and painful to the touch. The swelling generally subsides after the infection clears up.

Can anything damage the immune system?

Various diseases, including AIDS and certain cancers, can affect the immune system so that it does not function properly. Certain medications can also suppress the immune response. Poor nutrition can also prevent the immune system from doing its job.

Class Activity

Comprehend: Write the following terms on the board and tell students to write the correct term as you read the following sentences:

1. The second circulatory system is the _____. (immune system)
2. Lymph nodes filter _____ out of the body. (bacteria)
3. The _____ gland releases cells that can recognize and destroy the invaders. (thymus)
4. Lymph travels through the systems by the squeezing action of _____. (muscles)

The Hormonal System

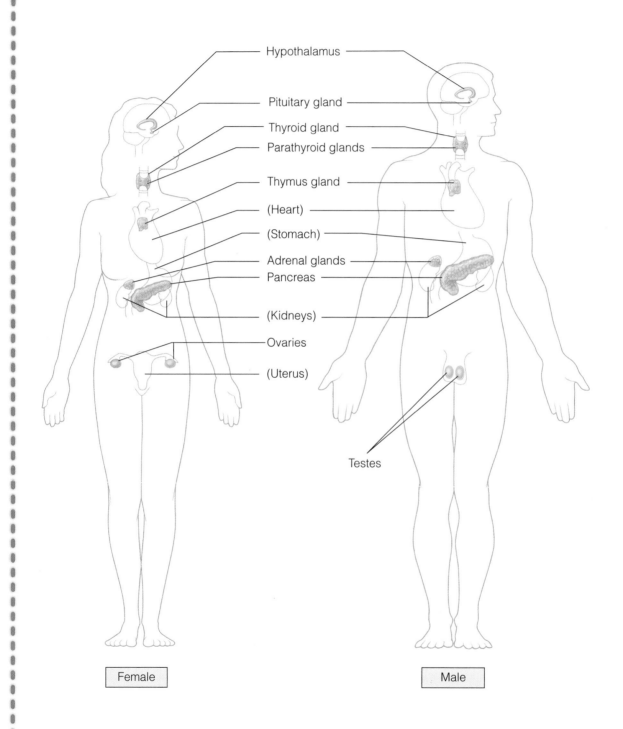

Hypothalamus

Pituitary gland

Thyroid gland

Parathyroid glands

Thymus gland

(Heart)

(Stomach)

Adrenal glands

Pancreas

(Kidneys)

Ovaries

(Uterus)

Testes

Female

Male

Like the nervous system, the hormonal system coordinates body functions by sending and receiving messages. However, while the impulses of the nervous system are electrical, the messages of the hormonal system are chemical—hormones released into the bloodstream. Hormones travel everywhere in the body, but they only become active in tissues that can recognize them.

What functions do hormones control?

Hormones play a role in many body functions, including growth, development, and metabolism. A single hormone can do many jobs in the body. For example, consider growth hormone, produced by the pituitary gland in the brain. This hormone stimulates the growth of bones and other body tissues. Later in life, after growth is complete, growth hormone remains an important regulator of the body's use of protein, as well as its use and storage of fat and carbohydrate.

Does growth hormone cause young teens to grow extra fast?

Growth hormone is produced at a more or less steady rate through the growing years. The rapid growth that often occurs at puberty is triggered by a different hormone. This hormone, released by the brain, causes the body to release other hormones involved in sexual development. These hormones produce the various changes of puberty, and give growth an extra boost—the adolescent growth spurt. They also cause changes in body shape, growth of body hair, and the maturing of reproductive organs (discussed in Sections 11 and 12).

What would happen if a male or a female started producing the hormones of the opposite sex?

In fact, both males and females normally produce both "female" and "male" hormones. The difference is the amounts produced. Males have much higher levels of "male" hormones, or *androgens*. Females have higher levels of "female" hormones, or *estrogens*. Androgens in females play a role in the normal changes of puberty. They are also involved in normal sexual function. The role of estrogens in males is less clear, but they may help to maintain the appropriate amount of body fatness.

Do thyroid problems make people gain or lose body fat?

The thyroid gland, at the front of the throat, produces *thyroxine*, a hormone that regulates the use of fuel in the body. Thyroxine is essential both to feeling energetic and to the maintenance of normal body weight. When the thyroid produces too little thyroxine, the person may gain weight and lack energy. Other symptoms include dry skin and hair and feeling cold most of the time. Taking thyroxine in pill form can treat these symptoms. A person whose thyroxine level is too high may lose weight and feel nervous or irritable. Should weight loss become severe, medical treatment to remove or partly destroy the thyroid can be lifesaving.

How do hormones affect mood?

Many hormones can play a role in how a person feels. For example, when under stress, some may feel irritable or angry. These feelings may be related to the hormones involved in the stress response. Changing levels of sex hormones at puberty can also cause mood swings. Other hormones affect moods in other ways.

Group Activity

Synthesize:

- Divide the class into seven groups.
- Assign each group a gland to research and report on. Students should be able to locate the gland, define its function, describe what would happen without the gland, and tell what systems of the body would be affected.

The Female Reproductive System

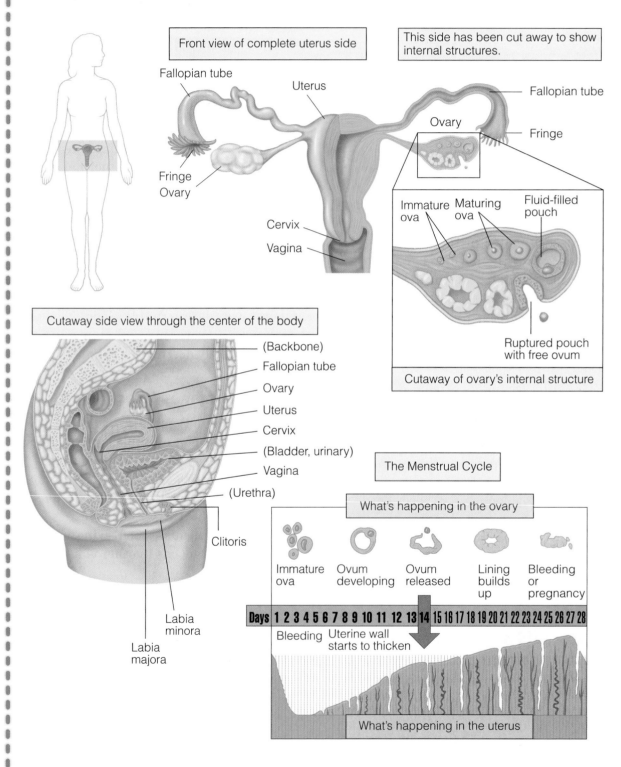

Front view of complete uterus side

This side has been cut away to show internal structures.

Fallopian tube
Uterus
Fallopian tube
Ovary
Fringe
Fringe
Ovary
Cervix
Vagina

Immature ova
Maturing ova
Fluid-filled pouch

Ruptured pouch with free ovum

Cutaway of ovary's internal structure

Cutaway side view through the center of the body

(Backbone)
Fallopian tube
Ovary
Uterus
Cervix
(Bladder, urinary)
Vagina
(Urethra)
Clitoris
Labia minora
Labia majora

The Menstrual Cycle

What's happening in the ovary

Immature ova
Ovum developing
Ovum released
Lining builds up
Bleeding or pregnancy

Days 1 2 3 4 5 6 7 8 9 10 11 12 13 14 15 16 17 18 19 20 21 22 23 24 25 26 27 28

Bleeding
Uterine wall starts to thicken

What's happening in the uterus

The female reproductive system produces the female reproductive cells, the ova. It also supports each fertilized ovum from the beginning of pregnancy through birth. Starting from the ovaries, the ova travel by way of the fallopian tubes to the uterus and vagina.

Each month, one of the ovaries releases an ovum. The monthly timing of this event is triggered by the rise and fall in levels of the female sex hormones. This cyclic ebb and flow is described fully in Chapter 20.

How do the ovaries produce ova?

Although the ovaries release the ova, they don't really make any new ones. All of the cells that will ever become ova are present in the ovaries at birth. A baby girl holds more than half a million of these immature ova in her ovaries. By the time she reaches puberty, a little more than half of those ova remain alive in her ovaries. For the rest of her reproductive life, her body will release roughly one of these ova per month.

What does an ovum look like?

An ovum is a single cell, smaller than the period at the end of this sentence. Unlike most cells, ova possess only half the normal amount of genetic material. Male sperm cells are 10 times smaller than ova, but also contain half the regular amount of genetic material. When the ovum and sperm unite, they form a single cell that possesses a complete set of genetic material.

Where does an ovum become fertilized?

On being swept up by the gentle, beating fingers at the end of a fallopian tube, the ovum starts a journey. Once in the tube, the ovum may meet sperm that are swimming up from the vagina. If they do, one of these sperm may fertilize the egg. Whether this happens or not, the ovum continues through the fallopian tube to the uterus.

Unfertilized ova continue traveling through the cervix and out of the vagina. If the ovum has been fertilized, however, it begins to divide as it travels down the fallopian tube. By the time it reaches the uterus, it has formed a hollow ball of cells called a blastocyst. This ball of cells can attach itself to the lining of the uterus, beginning a pregnancy.

What is menstruation?

Each month, the uterus prepares itself to support a pregnancy. It builds up a thick lining of tissue that can nourish a developing ovum that might implant there. If no ovum implants, the uterus sheds its lining by way of *menstruation*, a period of bleeding that lasts roughly three to seven days. The 28-day cycle shown on the previous page is typical. However, cycle lengths vary among individuals and even in the same female from time to time.

How does an infant fit through the vagina to be born?

The muscular elastic walls of the vagina enable it to expand to form a passageway large enough for an infant. However, the opening to the uterus itself, called the cervix, is normally very narrow. At the time of childbirth, hormones stimulate the uterus to contract and soften the cervix to allow it to temporarily open enough for a baby's head to pass through.

What is a hymen?

In many, but not all, young girls, the vaginal opening is partly or entirely covered by a thin membrane—the hymen. Later in life, this membrane may disintegrate through sexual intercourse, tampon use, or physical activity.

Class Activity
Apply: On a chart or transparency, have students trace the journey of an ovum from the ovaries to the vagina.

The Male Reproductive System

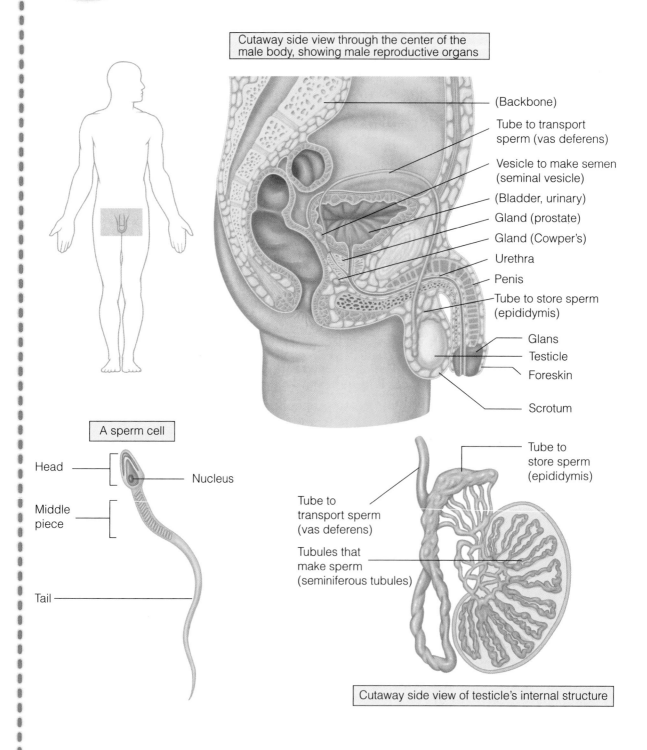

Cutaway side view through the center of the male body, showing male reproductive organs

(Backbone)

Tube to transport sperm (vas deferens)

Vesicle to make semen (seminal vesicle)

(Bladder, urinary)

Gland (prostate)

Gland (Cowper's)

Urethra

Penis

Tube to store sperm (epididymis)

Glans

Testicle

Foreskin

Scrotum

A sperm cell

Head

Nucleus

Middle piece

Tail

Tube to store sperm (epididymis)

Tube to transport sperm (vas deferens)

Tubules that make sperm (seminiferous tubules)

Cutaway side view of testicle's internal structure

The male reproductive system produces, stores, and delivers sperm cells that can fertilize an ovum. The major organs of this system, the penis and testicles, are located on the outside of the body. However, most of the route taken by the sperm cells lies within the abdominal cavity.

Where are the sperm produced, and how do they get to the penis?

Sperm are produced in hundreds of tiny, coiled tubes that lie inside each testicle. These tubes lead into another structure that stores sperm until it is needed. From there, the sperm move through a series of tubes, one leading to another. Ultimately, they leave the body through the urethra, the same passageway that carries urine out of the body.

Why are the testicles outside the body?

It may seem strange that the testicles, which play a vital role in reproduction, are located outside the protection of the abdominal cavity. However, this location serves an important purpose: temperature regulation. To produce sperm, the testicles must stay at about 3 degrees Fahrenheit below normal body temperature. If the testicles were inside the body, its heat would bring sperm production to a halt. The scrotum, the tough sac of skin and muscle tissue that contains the testicles, keeps them at the right temperature. When the testicles become too cool, a muscle contracts to draw them close to the body and warm them with body heat.

What is semen?

Semen is a mixture of sperm and fluids produced by various glands. It contains sugars to nourish the sperm and other fluids that help them move. It also helps to neutralize the acids from urine in the urethra and the slight acidity of the vagina. This is important because acid kills sperm. Muscular contractions (ejaculation) propel semen out of the body.

Can sperm really swim?

Sperm can move through fluid by propelling themselves with their long, whipping tails. On their own, they can move at a rate of about 3 millimeters per hour—not bad for something less than a tenth of a millimeter long.

What is the prostate gland, and why does it cause trouble for older males?

The prostate is one of the glands that produce semen. The urethra runs through the middle of the prostate. In older males, the prostate may become enlarged and partly block off the urethra, resulting in urinary problems. Other problems of the prostate include inflammation (prostatitis) and cancer. It is important for older males to have periodic checkups to make sure that their reproductive organs are healthy.

What is circumcision, and is it medically useful?

A fold of skin called the *foreskin* covers the head of the penis at birth. Circumcision, the surgical removal of the foreskin, is meaningful in some religions. Parents may also choose to have a son circumcised for cultural reasons or because of concerns about hygiene. An uncircumcised penis requires careful cleaning under the foreskin during bathing to prevent infection. There is also some evidence that circumcision may reduce the risk of cancer of the penis later in life. However, like any surgery, circumcision involves some risk. It's up to the parents to decide whether the benefits outweigh the risks. If the procedure is performed, it should be done within two to three weeks after birth.

Class Discussion
Analyze: Discuss the advantages and disadvantages of the location of the male reproductive system outside the body. Then have students write down the major organs of the male reproductive system and locate and describe each.

Reviewing Vocabulary

Use the vocabulary terms listed below to complete the following statements.

chromosomes

cells

tissues

genes

1. The body is made up of trillions of microscopic _____.

2. _____ are threadlike structures that carry all the information needed to make a whole organism.

3. DNA is organized into units called _____ that contain the instructions for making specific chemicals the body needs.

4. Groups of cells working together to perform specific tasks are called _____.

Recalling Key Facts and Ideas

Section 2
5. **List.** List some functions of the bones.

Section 3
6. **Name.** Name three types of muscles present in the body.

Section 4
7. **Describe.** Describe the spinal cord and its part in the central nervous system.

8. **Identify.** Identify the main parts of the brain and their functions.

9. **Recall.** What is the blood-brain barrier and why is it important?

10. **Explain.** How does a reflex action work?

Section 5
11. **List.** List the three major functions of the digestive system.

12. **Name.** Name three possible causes of indigestion.

Section 6
13. **Describe.** Describe the job of the cardiovascular system.

Section 7
14. **Explain.** How do the kidneys cleanse the blood?

15. **Describe.** How do the kidneys maintain the balance of water in the body?

Section 8
16. **Explain.** Why is it better to breathe through the nose rather than the mouth?

17. **List.** List two functions of the sinuses.

Section 9
18. **Explain.** How is the lymphatic system similar to the cardiovascular system?

19. **Describe.** How do white blood cells help fight infection?

Section 10
20. **List.** List one differences between the way the nervous system and the hormonal system control body processes.

Section 11
21. **Explain.** Trace the path of an egg cell after it leaves the ovary.

Section 12
22. **Recall.** Why aren't the testicles located inside the body?

1. Cells 2. Chromosomes 3. Genes 4. Tissues 5. Protect soft organs, allow movement. 6. Skeletal, smooth, cardiac 7. Nerve tissue within the bones of the spine; communication line between the brain and the rest of the body. 8. Cortex, conscious thought; cerebellum, maintains balance and muscle movement; hindbrain controls breathing. 9. Blocks harmful chemicals; admits chemicals the brain needs. 10. Spinal cord sends a message to the muscles to respond to danger. 11. Digestion, absorption, elimination 12. Eating too much, eating too quickly, spicy foods 13. Transports blood, provides nutrients and chemicals to all cells, removes waste.

Writing Critically

23. **Descriptive.** Think about the following statement: "We cannot live life without taking some risks." Do you agree or disagree with this statement? Why? Describe some of the risks people take each day and how these risks can affect their body systems.

Activities

24. Make a diagram that shows how two or more of your body systems work together. For example, you might show how the skeletal and muscular systems work together to move the body, or how the cardiovascular and respiratory systems work together to provide oxygen to cells and remove carbon dioxide. Use the illustrations provided in this chapter of the various body systems to help you draw your diagram. You may choose to make an anatomical drawing, showing the positions of the organs in the body, or a more abstract diagram.

25. Take your pulse for 15 seconds and then multiply it by 4. This is your resting pulse rate. Then do two minutes of continuous exercise. Retake your pulse. Compare the two readings. What is the difference? Retake your pulse every minute until it returns to the resting rate. How long did it take to get back to normal? Compare your results with those of another person in your class. Whose pulse returned to resting rate more quickly?

26. Pick a partner in your class to check your lung capacity. Inhale as deeply as you can and then exhale into a balloon. Compare results with your partner. Which one of you has the larger lung capacity?

27. Write a fictional journal entry describing a day in the life of a specific body system. Describe some of the activities that body system performs from the time a person gets up each day until he or she goes to bed at night.

Making Decisions About Health

28. A friend says to you that she doesn't think it matters what she eats because "it all breaks down into the same stuff anyway." What would you say to this friend about how the foods she eats can affect her various body systems?

Go Online

For more information on health careers, visit Career Corner at **glencoe.com.**

Fact or Fiction?

Answers

1. False. Adult bones are continuously breaking down and building up throughout life.
2. True.
3. False. The lungs fill passively with air when the diaphragm contracts and reduces the air pressure in the chest cavity.

 Writing Answers will vary.

14. Nephrons adjust fluid levels by returning needed materials to the blood. **15.** Pituitary gland alerts the kidneys to remove water or return it to the blood. **16.** Warms air, filters air, adds moisture. **17.** Lighten the skull; creates the sound of the voice. **18.** Moves fluid around the body. **19.** Circulate through the bloodstream to destroy infections. **20.** Nervous system, electrical signals; hormonal system, chemical signals. **21.** Travels from the fallopian tube to the uterus where it implants or leaves the body. **22.** They must stay a few degrees below body temperature. **23–28.** Answers will vary.

CHAPTER 7

Nutrition: The Nutrients

Sections

Each year you probably make thousands of decisions about what you are going to eat. Although each day's food intake may affect your body only slightly, over a period of years the effects of those intakes will significantly influence your health. This is why it's important for you to learn now to make wise food choices. This chapter will explain how the body turns food into the energy it needs to carry out daily tasks. It will also provide you with the tools and information necessary to make healthier food choices.

Fact or Fiction?

What Do You Think?

Is each statement true or false? If you think it's false, explain what's true.

1. To be well nourished is eating the right amount of foods with enough of the right nutrients.
2. All fats are the same, as far as the body is concerned.
3. Most people can easily get enough calcium, because it is found in so many foods.

 Writing Write a paragraph explaining how you can add two healthful choices to your day's food choices.

(Answers on page 199)

Go Online

Visit **glencoe.com** and complete the Life Choice Inventory for Chapter 7.

SECTION 1

Benefits of Nutrition

Good nutrition helps keep your body strong, fit, and healthy. An eating plan that consistently provides all the needed nutrients underlies the health of your whole body.

What Is the Best Food for Me?

MAIN IDEA ▶ Good nutrition promotes growth and helps prevent diseases.

Each day your body breaks down the foods you eat and extracts the nutrients that help body tissue grow. **Nutrients** are *substances in food that the body requires for proper growth, maintenance, and functioning.* Your body uses nutrients to replace some old or damaged muscle, bone, skin, and blood. Therefore, the best food supports normal growth and maintains strong muscles, sound bones, healthy skin, and enough blood to cleanse and nourish all the parts of your body. It also provides enough energy (calories) to fuel your growth and activities. Too much food energy, however, can lead to excess body fat.

The best food choices also reduce your risks of developing illnesses later in life. Your food choices, along with other lifestyle choices, can either increase or decrease your chances of developing lifestyle diseases.

Some people do not obtain enough nutrients from their food. They may develop **nutrient deficiencies**, *too little of one or more nutrients in the diet, one form of malnutrition.* **Malnutrition**, is *the result of serious undernutrition.* Adolescents are sensitive to deficiencies because their nutrient needs are high. A person who does not receive proper nutrition during the teen years may never reach full height, may feel tired, experience mood swings, and suffer pains or discomfort from a lack of nutrients. In short, the teen suffers from **undernutrition**, *too little food energy or too few nutrients to promote growth.* Throughout the United States, undernutrition is not a serious problem. In fact, in the United States, the abundance of food has caused the opposite problem. Many people in the U.S. consume more food than their bodies need for energy.

This threat to people's health is overnutrition. **Overnutrition** means *consuming too much food energy (calories) or excessive amounts of some nutrients.* Many people are overweight, or have daily intakes of salt, harmful fats, cholesterol, and added sugars that may be too high for health. Others eat too few vegetables and too much meat, choices linked to many diseases. Even vitamins and minerals can be poisonous if too many are taken in concentrated form. The key to good nutrition is to eat foods that provide enough, but not too much, energy and nutrients.

Vocabulary

nutrients
nutrient deficiencies
malnutrition
undernutrition
overnutrition

Health Skills

Dietary Guidelines for Americans

1. Eat nutritious foods within your calorie allowance.
2. Balance the foods you eat with at least 60 minutes of physical activity on most days.
3. Eat a balanced diet from all food groups.
4. Keep intakes of saturated fat, trans fat, and cholesterol low.
5. Choose fiber-rich fruits, vegetables, and whole grains often.
6. Limit salt.
7. Avoid illness from foods by keeping foods safe to eat.

SECTION 1 Review

Reviewing the Vocabulary

Review the vocabulary on page 162. Then answer these questions.

1. Define *nutrients*.
2. What are *nutrient deficiencies*?
3. What is the difference between *undernutrition* and *overnutrition*?

Reviewing the Facts

4. **List.** List some benefits of good nutrition.
5. **Recall.** Name three Dietary Guidelines for Americans.

Writing Critically

6. **Describe.** Name some nutrition-related threats to a person's health.
7. **Personal.** Take a look at your diet, and predict what path your health may be likely to follow in the future.

 **Online**

For more vocabulary practice, play the True/False game at **glencoe.com**.

How to Choose Nutritious Foods

The food you eat supplies nutrients, fiber, and other materials. The nutrients fall into six classes: carbohydrate, fat, protein, vitamins, minerals, and water. Altogether, people need enough of about 40 vitamins and minerals along with all the other nutrients. **MyPyramid**, *a diet-planning pattern*, shows what foods fall into each of the five food groups.

The MyPyramid Plan

MAIN IDEA ▶ The MyPyramid plan helps people make balanced, healthy food choices.

Each nutrient has its own unique pattern among foods. It might seem tricky to work them all into the meals you eat. However, people meet their needs for these nutrients from a variety of diets.

Happily, eating healthfully doesn't require giving up favorite foods, although it may require limiting how much of them you choose. Most people's diets just need a little fine-tuning. Eat certain foods more often, and eat other foods less often.

The MyPyramid plan can help you to choose enough nutritious food of each kind to meet your nutrient needs. The six classes of nutrients include:

- **Carbohydrates**. *A class of nutrients that include sugars, starches, and fiber*. Sugar and starches supply four calories per gram. Fiber does not provide calories.

- **Protein**. *A class of nutrients that build body tissue and supply energy*. Proteins form part of every cell in the body. They also provide four calories per gram.

- **Fats**. *An energy source for the body*. They provide nine calories per gram.

- **Vitamins**. *Compounds that are required for growth and proper functioning of the body*. Different vitamins perform different functions.

- **Minerals**. *Elements that perform many functions that keep the body growing and functioning*. Teens often need calcium and iron. Calcium promotes bone growth and strength.

- **Water.** Water is necessary for most body functions. Teen females need about 10 cups of fluid a day, and teen males need about 14 cups each day. About 20 percent of that comes from moisture in food.

Vocabulary

MyPyramid
carbohydrates
proteins
fats
vitamins
minerals
whole foods
whole grains
phytochemicals
fiber

" *Moderation. Small helpings. Sample a little bit of everything. These are the secrets of happiness and good health.* "

—Julia Child
(1912–2004)
American cook, author, and television personality

MyPyramid suggests how much of certain foods in each food group meet the needs of people like you. The MyPyramid plan can also help you to avoid eating too many calories. This plan groups similar foods together based on their nutrient contents. Look at **Figure 7.4** on page 167. The colored stripes of the pyramid represent the five food groups, plus oils—their names are listed along the bottom of the figure:

- Grains
- Vegetables
- Fruits
- Milk
- Proteins

Notice that the stripes are not all the same width. The different widths show which foods you can eat more of, and which foods should be eaten less often.

The Five Food Groups

Figure 7.3 on pages 166–167 lists the five food groups, plus oils, with examples. Once you understand the food groups, you can select foods from each group to provide the nutrients you need to stay healthy.

The food groups contain only **whole foods**, *foods that are close to their farm-fresh state, or those that have benefited from light processing.* One food that processing improves is milk: fat-free milk contributes the same nutrients as whole milk, but its saturated fat is removed. You can find low-fat and fat-free cheese products as well. Another is frozen orange juice: mixed with water, frozen juice equals the nutrition of fresh, but it lasts longer and costs less.

Whole Grains

Whole grains are *grains used in their intact forms, with all of their edible parts included.* Whole-grain foods, such as bread, cereals, rice, and pasta, should be chosen with nutrients in mind. For health, at least half the day's grain foods should be whole grains. Grain choices should be low in added fats and sugars too. Biscuits, cookies, muffins, fried rice, snack crackers, and others may provide more calories from fat and sugar than from the grain itself. These are best saved for occasional treats. Whole grains, including oatmeal, popcorn, brown rice, and whole-grain breads and cereals are best choices.

■ **Figure 7.2** *Fruit provides needed nutrients. What kinds of nutrients are found in apples?*

Caption Answer: Vitamins, minerals, water

Figure 7.3 **The Food Groups**

● Foods lower in calories ● Foods higher in calories

Grains

For carbohydrates, fiber, and vitamins and minerals. Make at least half of grain selections whole grains. 1 ounce grains is the same as 1 slice bread; ½ cup cooked rice, pasta, or cereal; 1 ounce dry pasta or rice; 1 cup ready-to-eat cereal.

● Whole grains (brown rice, oats, wheat), whole-grain low-fat breads, cereals, crackers, pastas, popcorn; enriched bagels, breads, cereals, pastas, pretzels, rice, rolls, tortillas.

● Biscuits, cornbread, doughnuts, muffins, pancakes, pastries, presweetened cereals, taco shells.

Vegetables

For folate, vitamin A, vitamin C, vitamin K, fiber, and other nutrients. Choose a variety of vegetables each day. ½ cup raw or cooked vegetables is the same as ½ cup cooked legumes; ½ cup vegetable juice; 1 cup raw, leafy greens.

● Broccoli, collard greens, romaine lettuce, spinach, carrots, sweet potatoes, squash, black beans, black-eyed peas, soybeans, soy products, corn, green peas, beets, cabbage, cauliflower, celery, cucumbers, green beans, mushrooms, onions, peppers, tomatoes, zucchini.

● Coleslaw, french fries, potato salad.

Fruits

For folate, vitamin A, vitamin C, potassium, and fiber. Choose a variety of fruits and limit fruit juice. ½ cup fruit is the same as ½ cup fresh, frozen, or canned fruit; 1 medium fruit; ¼ cup dried fruit; ½ cup fruit juice.

● Apples, avocados, bananas, blueberries, cherries, grapefruit, grapes, oranges, peaches, pears, pineapples, plums, raspberries, strawberries, watermelon, dried fruit, unsweetened juices.

● Canned or frozen fruit in syrup; juices, punches, ades, and fruit drinks with added sugars; fried plantains.

Milk

For calcium, riboflavin, vitamin B_{12}, magnesium, potassium, and, when fortified, vitamin A and vitamin D. Make fat-free or low-fat choices. Choose other calcium-rich foods if you don't consume milk. 1 cup of milk is the same as 1 cup fat-free milk or yogurt; 1½ ounces fat-free natural cheese; 2 ounces fat-free processed cheese.

● Fat-free milk and fat-free buttermilk, cheeses, cottage cheese, yogurt; fat-free fortified soy milk.

● Reduced-fat milk and whole milk; reduced-fat and whole-milk cheeses, cottage cheese, yogurt; chocolate milk, custard, ice cream, and pudding.

Proteins

For protein, niacin, thiamin, vitamin B₁₂ , iron, and other nutrients. Make lean or low-fat choices. Prepare them with little, or no, added fat. 1 ounce meat is the same as 1 ounce cooked lean meat, poultry, or fish; 1 egg; ¼ cup cooked legumes or tofu; 1 tablespoon peanut butter; ½ ounce nuts or seeds.

● Poultry (no skin), fish, shellfish, beans and peas, eggs, lean meat, fat-trimmed beef, ham, lamb, pork; low-fat tofu, peanut butter, nuts or seeds (flaxseeds, pumpkin seeds, sunflower seeds).

● Bacon; baked beans; fried meat, fish, poultry, eggs, or tofu; refried beans; ground beef; hot dogs; luncheon meats; marbled steaks; poultry with skin; sausages; spare ribs.

Oils

For vitamin E and essential fats; high in calories. Although they are not a food group, small amounts of oils are needed from among these sources.

● Liquid vegetable oils such as canola, corn, flaxseed, nuts, olive, peanut, safflower, sesame, soybean, and sunflower oils; mayonnaise, oil-based salad dressing, soft margarine; avocados, fatty fish, nuts, olives, seeds (flaxseeds, sesame seeds); and shellfish.

Figure 7.4   The MyPyramid Plan

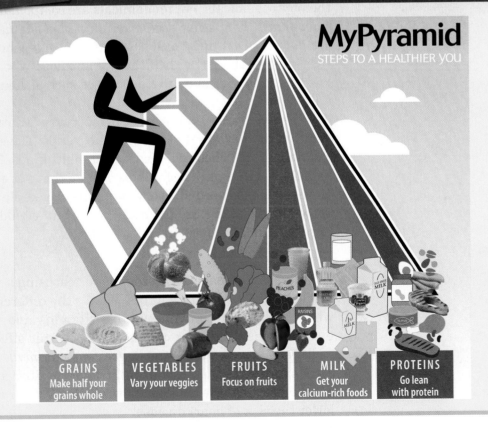

Figure 7.5   **Vary Your Vegetables**

You should vary the types of vegetables in your diet, but still make sure you are eating the daily recommended amounts.

Vegetable subgroups	Examples	Active Female Teen (2,200 calories)	Active Male Teen (3,200 calories)
Dark green	Broccoli, bok choy, collards, romaine lettuce, spinach, turnip greens	3 cups/week	3 cups/week
Orange and deep yellow	Butternut squash, carrots, sweet potatoes	2 cups/week	2½ cups/week
Dry beans and peas	Black beans, lentils, red beans, soy beans, split peas	3 cups/week	3½ cups/week
Starches	Corn, green peas, potatoes, lima beans	6 cups/week	9 cups/week
Other	Cabbages, celery, cucumbers, mushrooms, onions, peppers, tomatoes	7 cups/week	10 cups/week

Vegetables

Vegetables are loaded with nutrients that the body needs every day. Most are low in calories as well. They provide substances that, while not nutrients, are active in the body: the phytochemicals. **Phytochemicals** are *compounds in foods from plants that perform important functions in the body, but are not nutrients*. Research shows that people who eat diets rich in vegetables stay healthier than those who do not. A low-vegetable diet may invite diseases such as heart disease and cancer.

Vegetables are so varied and so important to nutrition and health that they are divided into subgroups. The subgroups can help people choose enough of the right kinds. **Figure 7.5** lists the subgroups of vegetables. Notice that not every kind of vegetable is needed every day. The vegetable amounts shown in the figure are not daily goals, but should be eaten in several smaller portions over *each week*.

Fruits

Figure 7.6 on page 170 recommends choosing a variety of whole fruits, but limiting juices. What's the difference? Both whole fruits and fruit juices offer vitamins and minerals, but only whole fruits or cut-up pieces of fruit offer fiber as well. **Fiber** is *indigestible substances in foods, made mostly of carbohydrate*. Fruit juices have little or no fiber and easily deliver many calories in just a few swallows. Fiber also helps lower the risk of heart disease.

Milk

Milk is especially important to teens because their bones are still growing. Milk and milk products such as yogurt and cheese are rich in calcium and other bone-building nutrients. When choosing milk, yogurt, or cheeses, choose fat-free or low-fat to reduce calories and harmful fats.

Meat and Beans

Choose lean or low-fat meats, fish, and poultry, prepared with little or no fat. Beans and peas, technically vegetables, are also in this group. They contribute protein and iron to the diet, just as meat, fish, and poultry do. Beans are a good protein source for people who do not like to eat meat or for those who eat vegetarian diets. Other foods that are high in protein include foods such as soy. Tofu, a soy product, can be used as a meat replacement.

Applying Health Skills:

1 Carlos lacks energy and wants to make healthier food choices, but he doesn't know how to choose healthy foods.

2. Carlos eats mainly high-fat, high-sugar foods such as French fries and ice cream, and he seldom eats healthy foods such as fruits, vegetables, and milk.

3. The food choices should include whole grains, fruits, vegetables, lean proteins, and low-fat dairy products.

5 Compared with the food choices Carlos usually makes, these food choices are lower in fats and sugars and higher in fiber, protein, vitamins, and minerals.

5. Answers will vary.

APPLYING Health Skills

Practicing Healthful Behaviors

►Objectives
- Evaluate poor food choices and explain why they are unhealthy.
- Use MyPyramid to make healthy food choices.

Fast Food Foul

Carlos loves fast food. He drinks colas and eats French fries, chicken nuggets, or hamburgers almost every day. He also has a sweet tooth, so he usually snacks on cookies, cupcakes, or ice cream. Carlos doesn't care for fruits and vegetables and eats them only a couple of times a week. He also rarely drinks milk. Fortunately, Carlos doesn't have a problem with his weight.

Lately, Carlos has noticed that he can't keep up with his friends on the basketball court. By the time he's ready to quit, they're just getting warmed up. Carlos wonders if his food choices are the problem. Maybe if he ate better he would have more energy. The trouble is he doesn't know how to choose healthy foods.

►Identify the Problem
1. What is Carlos' problem?

►Form an Action Plan
2. Evaluate Carlos' food choices. Why are they unhealthy?
3. Use MyPyramid to select a day's worth of foods that represent healthy choices for a teen. Choose foods for breakfast, lunch, dinner, and two snacks.
4. How do your food choices in answer 3 compare with the food choices Carlos usually makes?

►What Did You Learn
5. Describe the foods you typically choose to eat. How could you make healthier food choices?

Figure 7.6   How Many Servings Per Day?

	Active Female Teen	Active Male Teen
Calories	2,200	3,200
Fruits	2 cups	2½ cups
Vegetables	3 cups	4 cups
Grains	7 ounces	10 ounces
Meat and Beans	6 ounces	7 ounces
Milk	3 cups	3 cups
Oil	6 teaspoons	11 teaspoons
Extras—solid fat and added sugars	290 calories	650 calories

Oils

Although oils are not considered a food group, they provide essential nutrients. Oils should be used sparingly because they are high in calories. Liquid oils in salad dressings, mayonnaise, margarine, and vegetable oils are required in a healthy diet—but in amounts measured in teaspoons per day. Does this mean that fried foods are good for you, then? As you might guess, the answer is "no." The high heat of frying destroys the essential nutrients in the raw oils. Other sources of healthy oils are avocados, nuts, oily fish, and olives. Oils are very high in calories, so these foods can be fattening when eaten in large amounts.

How Much Food from Each Group?

To plan a healthy diet, you must ask yourself, "How much food from each group do I need? Should I eat one apple or three? May I eat ham and eggs for breakfast, a hamburger for lunch, and a pork chop for dinner?" Part of the answer can be found in **Figure 7.6**, which shows the correct amounts of food that an active teen male and female need each day.

The amounts listed above, however, may not be perfect amounts for everyone. The number of recommended calories is based on the needs of 15-year-olds who participate in vigorous activity for 30 to 60 minutes each day. You may be more active or less active. The example teens are of average height and weight, although some people may not fit this description. A taller or more muscular teen needs more food from these categories to meet nutrient needs; a shorter, more slender person needs less. To customize a plan for you, visit **mypyramid.gov**.

Class Activity.

Analyze: Ask students to bring in recipes from home, newspapers, magazines, or the internet. Have them work in pairs to determine what servings from the food pyramid are represented and what other foods are still needed to fill in the rest of the day's requirements.

Controlling Calories

Now that you know how many servings of foods to eat to get enough nutrients, what about controlling calories? The MyPyramid plan can also help develop an eating plan for someone who needs to control his or her calorie intake. The MyPyramid offers flexibility. For example, you can replace milk with low-fat cheese because both supply the same nutrients in about the same amounts. You can choose dried beans and nuts to stand in for meats.

The plan can be applied to different national and cultural foods. By giving careful thought to the principles of the MyPyramid plan, you can develop a diet that meets your needs.

Class Activity

Create: Have students create a poster or presentation in which they show how to trim down their own diets and replace foods that are high in fat or low in nutrients with healthy food choices. Have them list the nutrients that they added to their diets and the unhealthy items that they took out.

Worksheets: A reproducible quiz for Section 2 is provided in the Teacher Classroom Resources.

SECTION 2 Review

Reviewing the Vocabulary

Review the vocabulary on page 164. Then answer these questions.

1. Define *carbohydrate*.

2. What is a *protein*?

3. What is *MyPyramid*?

Reviewing the Facts

4. Explain. What is the best possible way to meet all of the body's nutrient needs?

5. Analyze. How can you avoid consuming large amounts of calories and still meet the body's nutrient needs?

6. List. List two reasons why vegetables are so important to sound nutrition and good health.

Writing Critically

7. Personal. Look at your results from the online Life Choice Inventory. List the areas in which you scored well. List the areas in which you were deficient. List three improvements you could make in your meals and snacks. Were you pleased with your scores? Why or why not?

8. Personal. Write a paragraph on how you can make improvements to your daily eating pattern.

Go Online

For more information on health careers, visit Career Corner at **glencoe.com**.

1. A class of nutrients that includes sugars, starches, and fiber.

2. A class of nutrients that build body tissue and supply energy.

3. A guide that recommends the kinds and amounts of foods to eat each day to meet your nutrition needs.

4. Follow the advice of MyPyramid for your calorie level.

5. Use the MyPyramid plan to choose the right amount of calories and nutrients.

6. Vegetables are full of nutrients and provide phytochemicals.

7. Answers will vary.

8. Answers will vary.

Energy from Food

Three nutrients—carbohydrates, fats, and protein—provide energy the body can use. **Energy** is *the capacity to do work or produce heat.* The body uses energy from these nutrients to grow, to move, and to create heat to maintain a steady temperature.

Energy from Nutrients

MAIN IDEA ▶ The body stores extra energy from the carbohydrates, fats, or proteins you eat as glycogen or body fat.

Carbohydrates supply the body with one of its main fuels, called glucose. **Glucose** is *a simple form of carbohydrate which serves as the body's sugar.* The brain and nervous system depend almost entirely on glucose for energy to think, trigger movement, and send messages between tissues.

Fat supplies the body with another main fuel, **fatty acids**, *building blocks of fat that supply energy fuel for most of the body's cells.* The muscles, including the heart muscle, rely heavily on fatty acids to fuel physical activity and movement.

Protein supplies **amino acids**, *building blocks of protein normally used to build tissues or, under some conditions, burned for energy.* In difficult situations, such as starvation or severe stress, the body can burn amino acids from protein for fuel at a much greater rate than in normal times. In summary:

- **Carbohydrate**—provides energy as glucose.
- **Fat**—provides energy as fatty acids.
- **Protein**—builds working body parts, and can provide energy as amino acids.

Vocabulary

energy
glucose
fatty acids
amino acids
toxin
calories
gram
digestion

■ **Figure 7.7** *For perfect functioning, every nutrient is needed. What kinds of snacks are good choices to stay healthy?*

Caption Answer: Apples, carrots, whole-grain bread

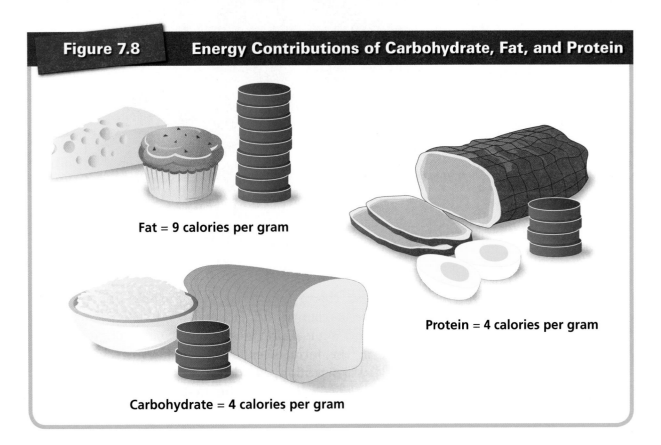

Figure 7.8 | **Energy Contributions of Carbohydrate, Fat, and Protein**

Fat = 9 calories per gram

Protein = 4 calories per gram

Carbohydrate = 4 calories per gram

Alcohol also provides calories, but is not a nutrient. Alcohol does not promote growth, maintenance, or repair of the body. In fact, it is a **toxin** or *poison*: the body can only tolerate it in small quantities.

The term calories is familiar to everyone as a measure of how fattening a food is. A more accurate definition of **calorie** is *a unit used to measure energy*. If you consume more carbohydrate, fat, and protein than you need, these nutrients will be stored in your body, mostly as fat. **Figure 7.8** shows the energy calories contributed by carbohydrate, fat, and protein. Note that calories are listed per gram of fat, carbohydrate, and protein. A **gram** is *a unit of weight, about ¹⁄₂₈ᵗʰ of an ounce*. Vitamins and minerals are often measured in grams or milligrams.

Energy from Food

MAIN IDEA ▶ The best source of energy for the body is a balanced diet.

When you get hungry, what should you eat? One obvious choice might seem to be a candy bar or "energy bar" for quick energy. It is true that the body can quickly raise its blood glucose level from the concentrated sugar in candy. However, a dose of sugar by itself lasts only a short time in the blood. It is quickly used or stored. You'll soon be hungry again, and possibly shaky as well.

> *"If you can stick to basic, healthy eating habits, it will go a long way toward achieving fitness."*
>
> —Abby Wambach
> (1980–)
> Professional soccer player and Olympic gold medalist

Writing Activity
Evaluate: Have students write three reasons to eat a balanced meal rather than a candy bar, when hungry.

■ **Figure 7.9** *A balanced meal. What might you replace to keep this meal balanced?*

Caption Answer: Answers will vary.

A better choice is a meal that provides the right amounts of carbohydrate, fat, and protein. The carbohydrate in the meal provides a quick source of glucose energy in the form of calories. The fat in the meal slows down **digestion**, *the breaking down of food into nutrients the body can use.* This makes the glucose last longer. The protein in the meal helps you feel fuller longer.

SECTION 3 Review

Reviewing the Vocabulary

Review the vocabulary on page 172. Then answer these questions.

1. What are *calories*?

2. Define *digestion*.

3. What are *fatty acids*?

Reviewing the Facts

4. Explain. What is an example of a balanced meal?

5. Analyze. How does the body meet its glucose need if you have not eaten?

6. Synthesize. Why is a balanced meal considered the best source of energy for the body?

Writing Critically

7. Expository. Write a list of ways you can include more fruits and vegetables in a day's meals.

 **Online**

For fitness and health tips, visit the Fitness Zone at **glencoe.com**.

1. Units used to measure energy.
2. The breaking down of food into nutrients the body can use.
3. Building blocks of fat that supply energy fuel for most of the body's cells.
4. A good balance of carbohydrates, fats, proteins. Chicken, rice, broccoli.
5. The body will burn protein instead of glucose for fuel.
6. Carbohydrates provide glucose energy, fat slows down digestion and provides energy, and protein helps the body feel fuller longer.
7. Answers will vary.

The Carbohydrates

Carbohydrates important in the diet are starch, fiber, and sugars. The body digests the starch and sugars from food and converts them into the blood sugar glucose. Fiber passes through the digestive tract without being digested, but it contributes to health in other ways.

Starch

MAIN IDEA ▶ Starch is a main source of energy.

Starch, the main carbohydrate in grains and vegetables, is *the main energy source for people around the world*. Starch serves the human body well. It provides glucose in a form the body uses best. And that's not all that starch does. If the starchy foods you eat are foods like whole-grain breads, potatoes, or whole-grain cereals, then your body receives many of the *other* nutrients (vitamins and minerals) it needs, along with a steady supply of glucose.

The brain needs glucose to perform at its best. Studies of schoolchildren show that those who do not eat breakfast cannot concentrate on school work or pay attention as long as their well-fed peers can. Without breakfast, their bodies run out of glucose. The starch in whole foods such as brown rice, whole-grain breads, cereals, and pasta, potatoes, and beans, as well as the sugars of fruits and vegetables, provide the brain with the glucose it needs to perform at its best.

Storing Glucose as Glycogen

The body stores extra energy in two forms: glucose and fat. **Glycogen** is *the form in which the liver and muscles store glucose*. Fat, as you probably know, is stored mostly under the skin and in the abdomen (belly area) as body fat.

Within seconds after eating carbohydrates, glucose flows into your blood. Your liver and muscle cells gather up all the glucose they can hold and store it as glycogen. If still more glucose flows in, the liver will convert it into fat. Then the fat cells in fat tissue store it.

Using Glycogen for Fuel

The body's stores of glycogen are small, so you must eat regularly to maintain them. The **hypothalamus**, *a brain regulatory center*, sends out a hunger signal when blood glucose levels get too low. If you don't eat, the body starts to use its four or so hours' worth of glycogen (stored in your liver) to provide glucose.

Vocabulary

- starch
- glycogen
- hypothalamus
- sugars
- added sugars
- empty calories

■ **Figure 7.10** *Everyone needs carbohydrates to be at their best. How does your body use carbohydrates?*

Caption Answer: Carbohydrates provide energy to your body.

Comprehension Check

Comprehend: After reading about fiber, ask students to close their books and name diseases that fiber helps prevent. (heart disease, diabetes, cancer) Ask them to explain how fiber does this. (It binds with various materials and carries them out of the body.)

Fiber—Not an Energy Source

MAIN IDEA ▶ Fiber is a plant form of carbohydrate that helps maintain the health of the digestive tract.

Fiber is a carbohydrate, but it is not digestible by human beings. Fiber provides very few calories. However, it helps to maintain the health of the digestive tract. The body needs about 25 grams of fiber each day to remain healthy.

Health Benefits of Fiber

Most types of fiber in foods move through the digestive tract almost unchanged. Fiber aids in digestion by making the digestive tract contents (stools) soft and bulky. Also, fiber binds with cholesterol and carries it out of the body in the stools. Thus it reduces blood cholesterol and the risk of heart disease. Fiber also helps to balance blood glucose and so helps to control the most common form of the disease diabetes. Some fibers bind cancer-causing agents in the digestive tract, reducing the risk of cancer.

Fiber may also help to control body fat. The person who eats fiber-rich foods chews longer and fills up sooner on fewer calories than the person who eats too little fiber. It is hard to eat a diet high in fiber and also gain excess weight.

Sources of Fiber

Plants with their skins and seeds intact are especially rich in fiber. Foods from animals have none. Fiber can be destroyed when foods are refined or overcooked. Apples have more fiber than applesauce. Apple juice has none. Baked potatoes with the skins have more fiber than mashed potatoes. Potato chips have almost none. Each serving of any food listed here provides about 2 grams of fiber:

- Fruits in the natural state with skins, 1 piece; ¾ cup berries; 2 prunes.

- Whole grains, including 1 slice whole-wheat bread or 2 slices cracked-wheat bread; 2 rye crackers or other whole-grain crackers; $\frac{1}{3}$ cup any bran cereal; 1½ cups puffed wheat cereal; 2 cups popped popcorn.

- Vegetables, lightly cooked, ½ cup; 1 cup raw celery; 2 cups lettuce; ½ cup cooked dried beans or peas; 1 large tomato; 1 small potato (with the skin); $\frac{1}{3}$ cup corn.

- Other sources: 2½ teaspoons peanut butter; ¼ cup most nuts; 1 large pickle; 1 tablespoon strawberry jam.

Try choosing foods with high amounts of fiber. Choose whole grains, whole fruits, and whole vegetables most of the time. Eat some of these foods cooked lightly, and eat some raw.

Sugars

MAIN IDEA ► Sugars are naturally found in fruits and milk. They are also added to some foods.

The last type of dietary carbohydrate is the **sugars**, *carbohydrates found both in foods and in the body*. All sugars are chemically similar to the sugar called glucose. They can be converted into glucose in the body. The four sugars most important in human nutrition are:

- **Glucose**, also known as blood sugar or the body's fuel.
- **Fructose**, the natural sugar in fruits and honey.
- **Sucrose**, also known as table sugar.
- **Lactose**, the natural sugar in milk.

In foods, all four sugars are delivered in diluted form mostly from fruits, vegetables, and milk. Some of them also are delivered in concentrated form as sweeteners: table sugar, honey, brown sugar, corn syrup, and molasses. Any ingredient on a food label that ends in –ose, such as fructose or maltose, is a sugar.

Nutrition experts recommend that you consume fruits and vegetables with natural sugars, but they caution you to "avoid consuming too much added sugar." **Added sugars** are *sugars and syrups added to a food for any purpose, such as to add sweetness*.

Consumer Skills Activity:

1. Answers will vary.

Consumer SKILLS ACTIVITY

Liquid or Solid—They're All Added Sugars

The average person in the United States eats about 100 pounds of added sugars each year. Little of this sugar comes from sugar at home. Most comes as corn syrup and other sweeteners added by manufacturers to soft drinks and other sweetened foods and beverages. Many different forms of added sugars used to sweeten foods are named on ingredient lists of food labels, and a wise nutrition-conscious consumer learns to identify them all. Foods high in added sugars are often high in calories and low in nutrients. For example, teens who drink two cans of sugar-sweetened soft drinks each day consume 300 calories a day from sodas alone. At the same time, sodas rob teens of calcium and other nutrients when they take the place of milk in the diet.

 **Writing**

1. If soft drinks are empty calories, what type of sweet beverage would be a more nutritious choice? Please explain.

■ **Figure 7.11** *Sugars may benefit health when they are consumed as fruits or milk. How can too much sugar affect your health?*

Caption Answer: It provides empty calories and not enough nutrients.

Worksheets: A reproducible quiz for Section 4 is provided in the Teacher Classroom Resources.

What's the difference? The answer lies in part with the term **empty calories**, a popular term referring to *foods that contribute much energy (calories) but too little of the nutrients.* When you eat an apple, many of its calories come from its natural sugars. You also consume vitamins, fiber, and minerals. By contrast, a 12-ounce regular cola beverage delivers about 150 calories from sugar without any other nutrients but water. The calories you receive from the cola are considered empty calories.

SECTION 4 Review

Reviewing the Vocabulary

Review the vocabulary on page 175. Then answer these questions.

1. What is *starch*?
2. What are empty calories?
3. Define *hypothalamus*.

Reviewing the Facts

4. Explain. How does fiber benefit the body?
5. Analyze. What dangers are there in consuming a large amount of sugar?
6. List. Give two examples for each: foods high in carbohydrates, foods high in fiber, foods high in sugar.

Writing Critically

7. Personal. Which of your favorite foods provide empty-calories? Which ones do you think are the most nutritious?

Gⓞ Online

For more vocabulary practice, play the eFlashcards game at **glencoe.com**.

1. The main carbohydrate in grains and vegetables
2. Foods that contribute much energy (calories) but too little of the nutrients.
3. A brain regulatory center
4. Maintains the health of the digestive tract and lowers cholesterol
5. Large amounts of sugar promote dental caries and are fattening.
6. Carbohydrates; whole-grain bread, potatoes; Fiber: peas and beans; Sugar: fruit, honey
7. Answers will vary.

The Fats

Fat supplies most of the body's fuel. It also transports fat-soluble vitamins. Some types of fat are essential and important for a healthy nervous system. In food, fat adds to the flavor.

Because fat can be stored, it serves as a reserve supply of energy. Fat is stored in a layer of cells beneath the skin, in many pads in the abdomen, and elsewhere. Body fat also helps to insulate the body and protect it from cold temperatures. Pads of fat also cushion the body organs, protecting them from shocks and bruises. Too much body fat, however, is not healthful.

Forms of Fat

MAIN IDEA ▶ Fat is a major source of fuel for the body. Food fat comes in saturated and unsaturated forms.

The fats you eat come in two forms—saturated fat and unsaturated fat (unsaturated fat includes polyunsaturated fat). **Saturated** fats are *fats associated strongly with heart and artery disease*, while **unsaturated** fats are *fats less associated with heart disease*. **Polyunsaturated** fat is *a type of unsaturated fat especially useful as a replacement for saturated fat in a heart-healthy diet*. For people who are developing heart and artery disease, the most important dietary step to take is to switch from saturated fat to mostly unsaturated fat in foods.

Saturated fats come mainly from animal sources, including meat fats, whole milk, butter, and cream. They tend to be solid at room temperature so the MyPyramid plan calls them "solid fats." A few plant oils, such as coconut oil and palm kernel oil, are also high in saturated fats.

Unsaturated fats come primarily from vegetable oils. They include olive oil, corn oil, and canola oil. These tend to be liquid at room temperature. **Fish oil**, *a polyunsaturated fat from certain fish, thought to be necessary for health*, is an animal fat, but it is polyunsaturated. People who eat enough fatty fish are generally healthier than others because they receive two essential fatty acids that other foods lack.

Some foods high in *unsaturated* fats, including the *polyunsaturated* type, are listed in the margin. Some foods high in *saturated* fats are listed below them.

Another type of fat is called trans fats. **Trans fats** are *a type of fat that forms when polyunsaturated oils are processed*. These trans fats act like saturated fats in the body.

Vocabulary

saturated
unsaturated
polyunsaturated
fish oil
trans fats
cholesterol

⁉ Did You Know?

Unsaturated fat sources:
- Avocados, nuts, seeds, olives, peanut butter.
- Margarine, mayonnaise, salad dressing, oils (liquid types).

Saturated fat sources:
- Bacon, sausage, cold cuts, lunchmeats, hot dogs, hamburgers.
- Butter, coconut and coconut oil, cheeses, palm oil.

Figure 7.12 Fat and Calories

Fat hides calories in food. When you trim fat, you trim calories.

Instead of . . .	Try . . .
Pork chop with ½ inch of fat (352 calories)	Pork chop with fat trimmed off (265 calories)
Baked potato with 1 tablespoon butter and 1 tablespoon sour cream (350 calories)	Baked potato with 1 tablespoon of salsa (225 calories)
Whole milk, 1 cup (150 calories)	Nonfat milk 1 cup (90 calories)

Health Skills

Getting the Saturated Fat Out of Your Diet

To get some of the fat out of your diet:

1. Choose lean meats.
2. Keep portions of meat within MyPyramid guidelines. Get part of your foods from the Protein group from dry beans and nuts.
3. Use canned tuna or salmon for their protein and healthy oils.
4. Eat grilled chicken or turkey.
5. Choose low-fat or nonfat dairy products.
6. Try using olive oil instead of butter and stick margarine.

Another form of fat is **cholesterol**, *a type of fat made by the body from saturated fat*. The body makes some cholesterol from other fats in the body because cells need it to function properly. Too much cholesterol, though, is linked with heart and artery disease. Cholesterol causes deposits to build up along arteries and increases the risk of heart attacks and strokes.

People trying to lower blood cholesterol cannot do so by limiting only their cholesterol intakes. They must also limit their saturated fat intakes.

Why Should I Reduce My Fat Intake?

MAIN IDEA ▶ A diet high in saturated fat is linked to many lifestyle diseases.

More than any other diet factor, a high saturated fat intake contributes to heart disease. Many forms of cancer are also linked to high fat intakes. Other diseases may be, as well, including obesity, gallbladder disease, diabetes, and others. The most important dietary step you can take to prevent diseases is to limit your intake of fats, and especially saturated fat. One more diet-related step is also critical to preventing diseases: keep your weight within a healthy range. The Health Skills sidebar, "Getting the Saturated Fat Out of Your Diet," describes some choices you can make to cut down harmful fat.

Reducing fat intake offers another benefit to people who wish to cut calories. A spoon of fat contains more than twice as many calories as a spoon of sugar or pure protein. By removing the fat from a food, you can drastically cut its calorie count. **Figure 7.12** shows that the single most effective step you can take to reduce the calorie count of a food is to eat it with less fat.

Reading Food Labels

MAIN IDEA ▷ Food labels provide information to help you determine a food's nutritional information.

One of the most helpful tools for the nutrition-conscious person is the food label. Label-readers learn details about the nutrients in foods. The Consumer Skills Activity on page 182 shows a pretzel box label. Notice that the Nutrition Facts panel lists some percentages down the right-hand side. Those percentages reflect how much of a nutrient one serving of that food contributes to the day's need for someone who eats 2,000 calories daily.

The Daily Values were developed for use on food labels. They act as a sort of general average of people's needs for nutrients. They assume that everyone needs to consume either 2,000 or 2,500 calories of food in a day. They also assume everyone is adult, not pregnant, not lactating, not aged, and other assumptions. The Daily Values are therefore limited, but they are useful enough for their purpose in allowing nutrient comparisons among food labels.

The label shown in the Consumer Skills Activity lists fat information as follows:

Amount per Serving	% Daily Value
total fat 3g	*5%*

In a diet of 2,000 calories, a serving of these pretzels would offer just 5 percent of the entire day's allowance for fat. It would take 20 servings of foods like this one to reach the day's fat limits.

$$\frac{\text{3g}}{\substack{\text{(total fat} \\ \text{per serving} \\ \text{of pretzels)}}} \div \underset{\text{(total daily fat)}}{\text{65g}} \times \underset{\substack{\text{(calories per} \\ \text{serving)}}}{\text{110}} = \underset{\text{(total fat Daily Value)}}{\substack{\text{5\% of Daily Value} \\ \text{for fat}}}$$

A label from a can of chili or other meaty item, however, can easily list closer to 20 grams of total fat. In that case, a single serving of that one food contributes about a third of the total fat allowance for the whole day. A day's meals that include such a food should be finished off with low-fat grains, vegetables, fruits, and nonfat milk to keep fat from exceeding the recommended limits.

Food Allergies

Food labels also warn consumers of the six most common food allergy triggers: milk, egg, peanuts, tree nuts, fish, and shellfish. A food allergy should not be confused with a food intolerance, such as lactose intolerance. Food allergies can cause the sudden onset of life-threatening symptoms.

■ **Figure 7.13** *Unsaturated fats come from olive oil, nuts, avocados, olives, and fatty fish. Why are unsaturated fats better than saturated fats?*

Caption Answer: Unsaturated fats are less harmful to the heart.

How to Read a Food Label

Food labels on everything from a package of potato chips to a box of cereal provide consumers with meaningful nutrition facts. Knowing the proper way to read food labels can put you many steps ahead of the average buyer. Here's an example to show you what's on a food label.

Nutrition Facts

Serving Size 30g (about 12 pretzels)
Servings Per Container 30 ✵

Amount Per Serving

Calories 110	Calories from Fat 10 ✵

	% Daily Value*
Total Fat 3g	**5%**
Saturated Fat 0g	**0%**
Trans Fat 0g	**0%**
Cholesterol 0mg	**0%**
Sodium 300mg	**13%**
Total Carbohydrate 23g	**8%**
Dietary Fiber 1g	**4%**
Sugars Less than 1g	
Protein 3g	

Vitamin A	0%	•	Vitamin C	0%
Calcium	0%	•	Iron	4%

* Percent Daily Values are based on a 2,000 ✵ calorie diet. Your daily values may be higher or lower depending on your calorie needs:

		Less Than		
Total Fat	Less Than	65g	80g
Sat Fat	Less Than	20g	25g
Cholesterol	Less Than	300mg	300mg
Sodium	Less Than	2,400mg	2,400mg
Total Carbohydrate		300g	375g
Dietary Fiber		25g	30g

Calories per gram:
Fat 9   •   Carbohydrate 4   •   Protein 4

Serving Size and Servings Per Container Used to calculate the nutrient and calorie content of a food.

Calories This section shows the percentage of calories in each serving that come from fat.

Nutrients The amounts of total fat, saturated fat, trans fat, cholesterol, and sodium per serving, measured in grams (g) or milligrams (mg) are listed here.

Vitamins and Minerals This section shows a few major vitamins and minerals, listed as a percentage of your daily needs.

Footnote This section is the same for every product, providing advice on the amounts of certain nutrients that you should consume each day.

Percent Daily Value Daily Value (DV) of a nutrient is a guide to approximately how much of the nutrient you need each day. Percent Daily Value shows the percentage of the DV a serving of the food will provide. The DV is based on the Reference Daily Intakes, or RDIs, which are established by the FDA. DVs for energy-producing nutrients, by contrast, are based on Daily Reference Values (DRVs), which show how much of each nutrient is recommended for a person who consumes 2,000 calories each day.

Writing

1. Why do you think the percentages of daily values are based on a 2,000 calorie diet?
2. Why do consumers need all this information?

In a food allergy, the immune system responds abnormally to a food material (usually a protein). Food intolerance creates mainly digestive disturbances. Children and teens often suffer from food allergies but may outgrow them. Intolerances tend to worsen with age.

In either case, the person must avoid foods that cause a reaction. This can be tricky because problem foods can sometimes be found in other foods. A person allergic to eggs and peanuts, for example, may not suspect that fried chicken may be coated in egg batter and fried in peanut oil. For this reason, people with a severe food allergy must keep medications close at hand.

Nutrition suffers when people avoid food that provides a key nutrient but do not replace the nutrients from other sources. Teens who must avoid milk should make it a point to consume other calcium-rich foods, listed earlier, each day.

Consumer Skills Activity:

1. The Daily Values are meant as a baseline for use in comparing products and for giving a rough estimate for how much many people need.

2. To compare and choose foods that provide the nutrients they need without overdoing on some nutrients, such as fat, cholesterol, and sodium, and on calories

Worksheets: A reproducible quiz for Section 5 is provided in the Teacher Classroom Resources.

SECTION 5 Review

Reviewing the Vocabulary

Review the vocabulary on page 179. Then answer these questions.

1. What is the difference between *saturated fat* and *unsaturated fat*?
2. A type of fat made by the body from saturated fat is called _____.
3. Fish oil is a _____.

Reviewing the Facts

4. **Explain.** What are the main functions of body fat?
5. **Identify.** Identify two benefits of limiting the amount of fat in your diet.
6. **Recall.** What information is given by the Daily Values on food labels?

Writing Critically

7. **Expository.** Give a few suggestions on how you might best keep your blood cholesterol at a healthy level through your food choices.

Go Online

For more information on health careers, visit Career Corner at **glencoe.com**.

1. Saturated fat mainly comes from animal fats while unsaturated fats mainly come from plant sources.
2. Cholesterol
3. Polyunsaturated fat
4. Body fat is a source of stored energy in body tissues and insulates the body from cold temperatures and cushions body organs from injury.
5. Reduce risk of some health problems such as heart disease and helping to maintain a healthy weight.
6. It provides the percent of fat, carbohydrates, and other nutrients for a 2,000 calorie a day eating plan from a single label serving of that food.
7. Answers will vary.

Proteins

Proteins are the body's machinery—they do the cells' work. The energy to fuel that work comes mainly from carbohydrate and fat. As mentioned earlier, protein donates energy (calories) as well.

Proteins are made of building blocks, the amino acids. A set of 20 different amino acids form proteins. Your body can make some of the amino acids for itself. The other amino acids, **essential amino acids**, are *amino acids that cannot be made by the body;* they must be eaten in foods.

Vocabulary

essential amino acids
vegetarians

Class Activity

Apply: Using Figure 7.15, have students create a vegetarian diet plan for a week. The necessary amino acids must be included. Have students underline sources of protein, circle sources of fiber, put a check mark beside those that provide carbohydrates, and place a dot by those that are high in fat.

Protein in Foods

MAIN IDEA ▶ Protein is made of amino acids and serves as the building material for many body structures.

Protein is found in meats, fish, poultry, eggs, cheese and milk, as well as plant foods such as grains and beans. Other vegetables also provide protein. In fact, a teen receives more than enough daily protein from one egg, three cups of milk, and an assortment of grains and vegetables—without a single serving of meat.

Vegetarians, *people who omit meat, fish, and poultry from their diets*, can easily get enough protein from plant foods alone. **Figure 7.15** lists some high-protein vegetarian food combinations.

Animal proteins supply all of the essential amino acids in the right amounts for building human tissues. Most plant proteins, in contrast, contain limited amounts of certain essential amino acids. To build muscles, make new cell parts, and grow, the body needs all of the essential amino acids. Therefore, single plant proteins alone usually won't serve the need. People who eat only plant foods must eat a variety of them each day to receive the full range of needed amino acids. The food combinations suggested in **Figure 7.15** and others like them provide the full range of essential amino acids, beneficial starch and fiber, and many more nutrients besides.

■ **Figure 7.14** *Milk provides protein as well as many other nutrients. What kinds of foods contain protein?*

Caption Answer: Fish, poultry, beans

Nutrients in Vegetarian Diets

Even though this is a section about protein, other nutrients also need attention in vegetarian diets. People who do not eat any foods from animals cannot get enough vitamin B_{12}. Vitamin B_{12} is found only in meats, poultry, fish, eggs, and milk—foods that come from animals. Vegetarians who eat only foods from plants must rely on vitamin B_{12}–fortified foods such as soy milk or breakfast cereals, or take a supplement.

Two other nutrients that may need attention in vegetarian diets are vitamin D and calcium. Milk is fortified with vitamin D and is calcium-rich, so milk drinkers usually get enough of these nutrients. People who do not drink milk can drink calcium- and vitamin D–fortified soy milk, and eat leafy green vegetables and calcium-fortified foods such as cereals and orange juice.

Iron also deserves attention in vegetarian diets. The iron in foods from plants such as beans, leafy green vegetables, and whole grains is not absorbed as well as the iron in meats and poultry. Fortunately, vitamin C improves iron absorption from beans and leafy vegetables and vegetarians usually eat many vitamin C–rich fruits and vegetables.

Protein Deficiency

A person who does not consume enough protein can become protein deficient. The body wastes away its lean tissues and is left defenseless against diseases. This happens in the U.S. among neglected and homeless children, sick people in hospitals, substance abusers, and others. For most people who eat a normal diet, though, protein deficiency is rarely a problem.

Figure 7.15

Vegetarian Protein Combinations

Choose foods from *two or more* of these groups in a day to obtain needed amino acids:

Grains: Barley, bulgur, cornmeal, oats, pasta, rice, whole-grain breads and other grain products.

Legumes: Dried beans, dried lentils, dried peas, peanuts, soy products.

Seeds and Nuts: Cashews, nut butters, other nuts, sesame seeds, sunflower seeds, walnuts.

Vegetables: Broccoli, leafy greens, other vegetables.

SECTION 6 Review

Worksheets: A reproducible quiz for Section 6 is provided in the Teacher Classroom Resources.

Reviewing the Vocabulary

Review the vocabulary on page 184. Then answer these questions.
1. Define *essential amino acids*.
2. What are *vegetarians*?

Reviewing the Facts

3. **Explain.** What is the function of protein in the body?
4. **Identify.** What foods provide complete protein?
5. **List.** List three nutrients that may need special attention in a vegetarian diet.

Writing Critically

6. **Expository.** How can vegetarians best meet the body's protein needs without consuming animal proteins? Develop your own vegetarian protein combinations.

For fitness and health tips, visit the Fitness Zone at **glencoe.com**.

1. Amino acids that must come from food because they cannot be made by the body.
2. People who omit meat, fish, and poultry from their diet.
3. Protein is part of all body cells. It is used to build and repair body tissue, including muscle.
4. Meats, fish, poultry, milk, cheese, yogurt, and soy protein
5. Vitamin B$_{12}$, iron, Vitamin D, and calcium
6. Answers will vary.

Vitamins

The discovery of vitamins thrilled people around the globe. Whole groups of people had been unable to walk, or to see, or to stop bleeding. Then, like a miracle, they recovered when the missing vitamin was added to their diets. On reading stories like these, people came to believe that vitamins could cure almost anything. Today we see many advertisements for vitamins and supplements. A **supplement** is *a pill, powder, liquid, or the like containing only nutrients*.

Vitamin Safety

MAIN IDEA ▶ Too little or too much of any vitamin or mineral is harmful to health.

The truth is that a vitamin can cure only the disease caused by a deficiency of that vitamin. A **deficiency** is *too little of a nutrient in the body*. Also, an overdose of any vitamin can make people as sick as a deficiency. Some can even cause death.

While vitamins are dangerous in high doses, minerals are even more dangerous. They can cause illness when taken in amounts not far above the recommended levels. A balanced diet of ordinary foods supplies enough, but not too much, of each of the vitamins and minerals. For those who wish to add up the vitamins they take in each day, a guideline exists.

The vitamins fall naturally into two classes—the fat-soluble ones and the water-soluble ones. The **fat-soluble** vitamins are *able to dissolve in fat and tend to remain in the body*. For this reason, the fat-soluble vitamins can build up to dangerous levels if a person takes supplements of them.

The **water-soluble** vitamins are *able to travel in the body's watery fluids and leave the body readily in the urine*. This means that you must be sure to eat foods that provide water-soluble vitamins regularly to replace those that you have lost.

Vitamin A

MAIN IDEA ▶ Vitamin A is important to many body processes.

Vitamin A is well known for its roles in vision. Each year, half a million young children around the world go blind from a lack of vitamin A. One of the earliest signs of vitamin A deficiency is **night blindness**, which is *a slow recovery of vision after flashes of bright light at night*. As vitamin A deficiency grows worse, it leads to permanent blindness.

Vocabulary

supplement
deficiency
fat-soluble
water-soluble
night blindness
beta-carotene
antioxidant
free radicals

Vitamin A also works in other vital ways. Vitamin A helps the body fight infections. It maintains normal, healthy skin and promotes growth. The symptoms of vitamin A deficiency therefore make themselves known not only in the eyes, but throughout the body. Infections quickly occur, the skin becomes dry, and growth slows.

Too Little or Too Much

In countries where food is scarce, protein and vitamin A deficiencies are major nutrition problems. In developed nations such as ours, people who take supplements of vitamin A should be cautious. Vitamin A dissolves into body fat, and can build up to toxic levels. Like vitamin A deficiency, toxicity of the vitamin can affect all the body's tissues. Vitamin A toxicity symptoms include nausea, vomiting, headache, blurred vision, weakness of the bones and muscles, and liver damage.

Beta-carotene

Vitamin A from plants differs chemically from the vitamin A in supplements or fortified foods. The form of vitamin A in plants is beta-carotene, which never causes dangerous build-ups to occur. **Beta-carotene** is *an orange vegetable pigment that the body can change into the active form of vitamin A.* Only vitamin A from supplements or fortified foods poses the threat of toxicity.

Beta-carotene plays a special role as an **antioxidant** nutrient. An antioxidant is a substance that *defends the body against destructive compounds.* These destructive compounds are called **free radicals**. Free radicals are substances that *trigger damaging chain reactions in the cells of the body.* The damage may then promote cancer or heart disease. Beta-carotene takes the brunt of free radical attacks and protects the tissues.

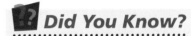

Did You Know?

Foods high in beta-carotene: apricots, broccoli, brussels sprouts, cantaloupe, carrots, leafy greens (bok choy, collards, kale, turnip or mustard greens, spinach), dark green lettuce (leaf lettuce or romaine), pumpkin, winter squash.

■ **Figure 7.16** *Beta-carotene, the plant form of vitamin A, is found abundantly in foods like these. Why is beta-carotene important to your health?*

Caption Answer: It helps defend the body against free radicals. It also turns into vitamin A, an essential vitamin.

Best Sources or Fortified Foods

The best food sources of beta-carotene are dark green vegetables and deep yellow and orange fruits and vegetables. As for vitamin A in foods of animal origin, the richest sources are liver and fish oil, and fortified foods such as milk and milk products. Fast foods such as burgers and fries are poor sources of vitamin A. Many teens' diets lack fruits, vegetables, and milk products, and are therefore low in vitamin A.

Vitamin E

MAIN IDEA ▶ Eating foods rich in vitamin E may help protect against heart disease.

Like beta-carotene, vitamin E is an antioxidant nutrient. People who eat plenty of vitamin E–rich foods have lower rates of heart disease than those who do not eat these foods. No harmful effects are known to arise from eating vitamin E in foods.

The main food sources of vitamin E are raw vegetable oils, such as canola oil, safflower oil, and olive oil, and products such as margarine and salad dressing made from them. Wheat germ oil is particularly vitamin E–rich. Other good sources of vitamin E include unprocessed cereal grains, nuts, fruits, and vegetables. Vitamin E is destroyed by heat and processing, so fried fast foods and processed convenience foods are poor sources of the vitamin.

Thiamin

MAIN IDEA ▶ To get enough thiamin and other nutrients, a teen must eat many servings of nutritious foods each day.

Thiamin is typical of many water-soluble vitamins. It helps the body use energy from other nutrients, such as carbohydrates. Vitamins themselves provide no energy to the body. Instead, thiamin, along with some others, helps to release energy from carbohydrate, fat, and protein.

People with a serious thiamin deficiency can suffer severe symptoms such as paralyzed limbs, loss of muscle tissue, swellings, enlargement of the heart, irregular heartbeat, and ultimately death from heart failure. Extreme deficiencies rarely occur, but a mild lack of thiamin also produces symptoms. These include stomachaches, headaches, fatigue, restlessness, problems sleeping, chest pains, fevers, feelings of anger and aggression, and symptoms often mistaken for mental illness. It takes medical tests to determine the true causes of such common symptoms.

Class Activity

Report: Divide the class into small groups and assign each group a vitamin deficiency to research. Foods that supply the vitamin should be included in the report. Have each group share their findings with the class.

Did You Know?

Mild thiamin deficiencies can be caused by diets low in nutrients and high in calories, sugar, fat, and salt.

Figure 7.17   **Major Roles and Sources of the Vitamins**

Vitamin	What it Does in the Body	Major Sources
Fat-soluble		
Vitamin A	Maintains normal vision and healthy bones, skin, internal linings, and reproductive system; strenghtens resistance to infection	Vitamin A–fortified milk and dairy products; margarine; liver
Beta-carotene	A form of vitamin A and an antioxidant	Dark green vegetables (broccoli, spinach, greens); deep orange fruits and vegetables (cantaloupe, apricots, sweet potatoes, carrots)
Vitamin D	Promotes growth and health of bones	Vitamin D–fortified milk; eggs, liver, sardines, sunlight on the skin
Vitamin E	Protects the body cells from attack by oxygen: an antioxidant	Vegetable oils and shortening; green, leafy vegetables; whole grains; nuts and seeds
Vitamin K	Helps with blood clotting and bone growth	Normal bacteria in the digestive tract; liver; dark green, leafy vegetables; milk
Water-soluble		
Vitamin C	Acts as the "glue" that holds cells together; strengthens blood vessel walls; helps wounds heal; helps bones grow; stengthens resistance to infection but does not cure colds; an antioxidant	Citrus fruits, dark green vegetables; cabbage-like vegetables; strawberries; peppers; potatoes
Thiamin	Helps the body use nutrients for energy	Small amounts in all nutritious foods
Riboflavin	Helps the body use nutrients for energy; supports normal vision; helps keep skin healthy	Milk; yogurt; cottage cheese; dark green vegetables; whole-grain products
Niacin	Helps the body use nutrients for energy; supports normal nervous system functions	Milk; eggs; poultry; fish, whole-grain products; all protein-containing foods
Vitamin B_6	Helps the body use protein and form red blood cells	Green, leafy vegetables; meats, fish, poultry; whole-grain products; beans
Vitamin B_{12}	Helps form new cells	Dark green, leafy vegetables; beans; liver
Folate	Helps form new cells	Dark green, leafy vegetables; beans; liver
Biotin and pantothenic acid	Helps the body use nutrients and energy	Widespread in foods

Note: The names given here are the official names. Other names still commonly used and seen on labels are alphatocopherol for Vitamin E, vitamin B_1 for thiamin, pyridoxine for vitamin B_6, folic acid and folicin for folate, and ascorbic acid for vitamin C.

Folate and Vitamin B₁₂

MAIN IDEA ▷ Folate and vitamin B_{12} illustrate why it is important to eat foods from each of the food groups.

The vitamins folate and vitamin B_{12} work together in the body, but they are found in separate food groups. Folate is found in fresh, leafy green vegetables such as spinach. In contrast, vitamin B_{12} is found only in foods that come from animals—meats and milk. This is why it is important to eat foods from every food group. When you omit one or more entire groups of foods, you miss out on the nutrients that are in those foods. People who eat diets that contain few fruits and vegetables risk folate deficiency. Those who choose diets that omit all meats, eggs, and milk products risk vitamin B_{12} deficiency. Folate deficiency causes anemia, weakened immunity, and abnormal digestion. Vitamin B_{12} deficiency causes anemia and abnormal nerve and muscle function. Most people can obtain all the vitamins they need from the foods they eat. That's why good nutrition requires eating healthy portions from all the food groups..

Worksheets: A reproducible quiz for Section 7 is provided in the Teacher Classroom Resources.

SECTION 7 Review

Reviewing the Vocabulary

Review the vocabulary on page 186. Then answer these questions.

1. The two classes of vitamins are _____ and _____.

2. A powder or pill that contains only nutrients is called a _____.

3. A _____ is a condition in which the body lacks an essential nutrient.

Reviewing the Facts

4. Describe. What is the difference between a *fat-soluble* and a *water-soluble* vitamin?

5. Recall. What are some roles of vitamin A in the body?

6. Identify. What is an example of a vitamin that helps the body use energy from other nutrients?

Writing Critically

7. Personal. Why is it better to obtain the nutrients you need from foods, rather than supplements? Explain.

Go Online

For more vocabulary practice, play the eFlashcards game at **glencoe.com**.

1. Fat-soluble, water-soluble
2. Supplement
3. Deficiency
4. Fat-soluble vitamins dissolve in the body's fats and can be stored in the body. Water-soluble vitamins travel in the body's fluids and the excess is removed in body waste.
5. It helps the body fight infections, helps with night vision, and maintains skin and hormone growth.
6. Thiamin
7. Answers will vary.

Minerals

All minerals, even those present in just tiny amounts, are essential for proper body functioning. A tiny trace of a mineral contains billions of molecules that play vital roles in the health of our bodies.

Calcium

MAIN IDEA ▶ Calcium is needed to form and maintain strong bones.

Calcium is the most abundant mineral in the human body. Most of the body's calcium is stored in the bones and teeth. Milk and milk products are the best food sources of calcium. Children and teens need milk daily to support the growth of their bones. Calcium is not found in many other kinds of foods, however, and low intakes of milk are common.

A deficiency of calcium during childhood, and especially in the teen years, threatens the strength of the bones for the rest of the person's life. **Osteoporosis**, *a disease of gradual bone loss*, can cripple a person in later years.

The obvious way to meet the need for calcium is to drink milk or eat milk products daily, because they are almost the only foods that contain much calcium per serving. **Figure 7.18** shows the amounts of milk that will meet the calcium intake recommendations. A few other foods contain calcium, too: almonds, canned sardines (with the bones), leafy greens, broccoli, and beans. Orange juice sometimes has calcium added to it. This can be valuable for people who are allergic or sensitive to milk.

Iron

MAIN IDEA ▶ Iron carries oxygen in the red blood cells. Meats, fish, poultry, and beans are rich sources of iron.

Iron is present in every living cell and is the body's oxygen carrier. In the red blood cells, iron carries oxygen from the lungs to the tissues. Tissues must have oxygen to produce the energy they need to do their work.

Too Little Iron

Too little iron causes **anemia**, *reduced number or size of the red blood cells*. With too few or too small red blood cells, the person with anemia grows weak and tires quickly. Energy will return, though, after a few weeks of eating the needed iron-rich foods.

Vocabulary

osteoporosis
anemia
electrolytes
salt
hypertension
urine

Figure 7.18

Recommended Daily Calcium Intake

Age	Recommended Daily Intake
Children	2 cups
Teens	3 cups
Adults[a]	2 cups
Pregnant women	3+ cups
Pregnant teens	4+ cups
Older women	3 to 5 cups

[a]Nonfat or low-fat milk is recommended for adults.

■ Figure 7.19 *Teens need the equivalent of three cups of milk each day. Where is most of your body's calcium stored?*

Caption Answer: It is stored in bones and teeth.

Worldwide, as many as half of all people—especially children, teens, and females—suffer from iron deficiency. In the United States iron deficiency may affect about 1 in 10 toddlers, adolescent girls, and young women. Children and teens are prone to iron deficiency because of their rapid growth. Females in their reproductive years are prone to iron deficiency because they lose iron in the blood of menstruation, and pregnancy demands extra iron for the developing infant.

Early Symptoms

People who are low on iron begin to feel tired long before they are diagnosed with iron-deficiency anemia. They do not have the energy to work or play or keep up with the demands of everyday life. Teens who lack iron perform poorly on tests of concentration and memory.

Iron-Rich Foods

Meats, fish, poultry, and beans are rich in iron. Foods that are rich in iron, however, are low in calcium. Any plan for a balanced diet must provide enough of both. **Figure 7.20** lists the minerals important in the diet, what they do in the body, and food sources of each one.

Electrolytes

MAIN IDEA ▶ **Electrolytes help maintain the proper balance of fluids in the body.**

Three minerals—sodium, chloride, and potassium—serve as **electrolytes**, *minerals that dissolve in body fluids and carry electrical charges*. Electrolytes help maintain the proper balance of fluids in the body. This balance

Figure 7.20   Major Roles and Sources of Minerals

Mineral	What It Does in the Body	Major Food Sources
Calcium	Structural material of bones and teeth; helps muscles contract and relax; helps nerves communicate; helps blood to clot	Milk and milk products; small fish with bones; dark green vegetables; beans
Phosphorus	Structural material of bones and teeth; supports energy processes; part of cells' genetic material	All foods that come from animals
Magnesium	Helps builds bones and teeth; helps build protein; helps muscles contract and relax; helps nerves communicate	Nuts; beans; dark green vegetables; seafood; whole grains; chocolate
Sodium	Maintains cell fluids; helps nerves communicate	Salt; soy sauce; processed foods; celery; milk
Potassium	Helps build protein; maintains fluids; helps nerves communicate; helps muscles contract	All nutritious foods; meats; milk and milk products; vegetables; whole grains; beans
Iron	Helps red blood cells carry oxygen; helps tissues use oxygen to release energy; supports normal immunity	Red meats; fish; poultry; shellfish; eggs; beans; dried fruits
Zinc	Helps build genetic material and protein; supports normal immunity; supports growth; helps make sperm; helps wounds heal	Protein-rich foods; meats; fish; poultry; whole grains
Iodine	Part of thyroid hormone needed for growth	Iodized salt; seafood
Selenium	An antioxidant, works with vitamin E	Seafood; meats; vegetables
Copper	Helps make red blood cells; helps build protein; helps the body use iron	Organ meats such as liver; seafood; nuts
Chromium	Helps the body use carbohydrates and fat	Liver; nuts; whole grains; cheese
Fluoride	Helps strengthen bones and teeth	Water; seafood
Manganese	Helps with many processes	Whole grains; fruits; vegetables
Molybdenum	Helps with many processes	Milk; beans

is essential for the cells' work, such as nerve-to-nerve communication, heartbeats and contraction of muscles. When fluid is lost through sweat, blood, or urine, electrolytes are lost. Sometimes too many body fluids and electrolytes are lost, as in heat stroke, severe diarrhea, or blood loss. This is a serious medical emergency that requires expert medical assistance. Electrolyte balances can also occur if you drink too much water too quickly. Drinking large amounts of water over a short period of time dilutes electrolytes. This condition is called *hypotremia*. Most teens, however, do not drink enough water.

Class Activity

Present. Ask students to develop an oral report on a mineral. Remind them to report on deficiencies as well as overdoses of the mineral and the results of each.

Sodium is best known as part of sodium chloride, the most common salt in foods. **Salt** is *a compound made of minerals that, in water, dissolve and form electrolytes*. Sodium chloride is ordinary table salt, a much-loved food seasoning. Because salt is so widespread in foods, people easily meet their need for sodium. For this same reason, however, most people as they age must try consciously to reduce salt intakes to avoid **hypertension** or *high blood pressure*. Details about hypertension and cutting down on salt are presented in Chapter 17.

Water

MAIN IDEA ▷ Water carries materials in the body and provides the needed environment in which human tissues must live.

Water is the major substance of which bodies are made. About 60 percent of your body's weight is water. It is the most vital of nutrients: you can live for many days, weeks, or even months without consuming many other nutrients, but you can live only a few days without water.

Water carries oxygen, nutrients, wastes, and other materials from place to place in the body. It also provides the environment that human tissues require to live. Your body loses water daily in sweat, exhaled breath, and **urine**, *fluid wastes removed from the body by the kidneys*. You must replace all the water you lose, so you need to drink enough fluids in the form of beverages including water. Teen males need to drink about 11 cups of beverages a day; teen females need about 8 cups.

Figure 7.21	Calories and Nutrients in 8-oz Beverages	
Beverage	**Calories**	**Nutrients**
Water	0	May contain minerals
Low-fat or fat-free milk	80	Rich in vitamins and minerals
100% fruit juice	110	Rich in vitamins and minerals
Diet soft drinks	80	None
Regular soft drinks	120	None
Fruit punches	110	Few vitamins and minerals, unless added
Sports drinks and fitness beverages	50	Some electrolytes, if added

A look at **Figure 7.21** shows why teens need to be choosey about their fluids—many types provide too many empty calories. A male teen, for example, who drinks even half of his fluids as fruit punches and sugary soft drinks can pack in an extra 600 calories a day this way. Even 100-percent fruit juices are high in calories. They are also high in nutrients, so juices can fill in for up to half of the day's fruit intake, according to the MyPyramid plan. If you are engaging in physical activity, however, some sports drinks may provide electrolytes the body needs.

Your body is unique. It responds to foods and the nutrients contained in those foods in its own characteristic ways based on its genetic inheritance and its current needs. For example, one person may tend to gain weight and may need to take steps to expend more calories in physical activity or to reduce calorie intake from foods and beverages. Another person may stay thin and may be best advised to increase their calorie intake. Think carefully about your own body and its needs before changing your diet.

■ **Figure 7.22** *Water is the most vital nutrient of all. When should you make sure to drink extra water?*

Caption Answer: All the time. When you are physically active and sweat a lot for other reasons, you need to pay special attention to getting enough.

Worksheets: A reproducible quiz for Section 8 is provided in the Teacher Classroom Resources.

SECTION 8 Review

Reviewing the Vocabulary

Review the vocabulary on page 191. Then answer these questions.
1. Write a sentence using each term.
2. _____ is a disease of gradual bone loss.
3. _____ is a condition in which a reduction in the number and size of red blood cells is seen.

Reviewing the Facts

4. Explain. Where is most of the body's calcium stored?
5. List. List four foods that provide calcium.
6. Identify. What is an important function of electrolytes?

Writing Critically

7. Expository. List all the ingredients and nutrition information that appear on the label of a popular sports drink. List any other label information you feel might encourage you to buy this product. Are you convinced this drink is the right choice? Explain.

For more vocabulary practice, play the Concentration game at **glencoe.com.**

1. Answers will vary.
2. Osteoporosis
3. Anemia
4. Bones and teeth
5. Answers may include: milk, yogurt, calcium-fortified juice and soy milk, leafy greens, broccoli
6. Electrolytes carry electrical charges to help maintain the body's balance of fluids.
7. Answers will vary.

SOS: Selection of Supplements

 Understand and Apply Read the conversation below, and then complete the writing exercise that follows.

Each year, people spend billions of dollars on vitamin pills. After studying nutrition, you may be wondering whether supplements can really help clear up the skin, make glossy hair and strong nails, or help build strong muscles, as many advertisers claim. Read on.

Q: Are there any supplements that can improve my appearance or physique?

A: Nutrients do support human growth and are absolutely necessary for clear skin, glossy hair, strong muscles, and all the rest. People who are already well nourished do not need supplements. Supplements do not improve the physical features of a person who eats well.

Q: Can people get the nutrients they need from food alone?

A: People who haven't learned enough about nutrition think they need supplements as insurance against their own poor food choices. Taking supplements is no guarantee that they will get the particular nutrients they need. It's more likely that they'll get a duplication of the nutrients their food is supplying and still lack the ones they need. The only way to be sure to get the needed assortment of nutrients is to construct a balanced diet from a variety of foods.

Q: Are you saying that no supplement supplies all the nutrients you can get from food?

A: Yes, that's right. Even if you could get all your vitamins and trace minerals from a supplement, there is no way you can package the bulk of protein, fiber, carbohydrate, calcium, and others you need into a pill. No one knows enough, yet, to construct a synthetic substitute for food.

Q: In the chapter I read that fat-soluble vitamins can build up to dangerous levels in the body. How dangerous is this?

A: This can be dangerous. Excess vitamin A, for example, can damage the same body systems that are damaged by vitamin A deficiency. Symptoms such as blurred vision, blood abnormalities, organ damage, bone pain, pressure inside the skull, and fatigue can occur with vitamin A excess. Water-soluble vitamins can be toxic as well, but are less likely to cause such severe symptoms. Minerals, too, can be extremely dangerous and even deadly in high doses.

Q: Do people ever have unusually high nutrient needs that require that they take supplements?

A: No two people have exactly the same nutrient needs. However, an ordinary diet of mixed foods can easily meet the highest of those needs.

In rare instances, genetic defects may alter nutrient needs considerably. However, only 1 person in 10,000 has such a defect. That person needs a diagnosis and treatment by a qualified health care provider.

Q: What about high nutrient needs caused by different lifestyles? I've seen vitamins for stress, for cigarette smokers, for athletes—things like that.

A: Stresses, including smoking, do deplete people's nutrient stores somewhat. However, which supplements to give stressed people is just guesswork on the part of the manufacturers. The way to supply lost nutrients is still to eat well, not to take supplements. Another way is to learn to control stress. People who smoke should give up smoking, not take supplements. As for athletes, they need supplements less than other people, because their bodies require more food to replace the energy they burn off in physical activity. Larger food intakes mean higher nutrient intakes.

Q: Would there ever be a time when I should be taking a vitamin pill?

A: Yes, when a health care provider recommends it, and yes, in at least two other instances:

- When your energy intake is below about 1,500 calories and you can't eat enough food to meet your vitamin needs. (People who can't exercise have this problem.)

- When, for whatever reason, you are going to be eating irregularly for a limited time.

Remember that if vitamins are needed, minerals are needed too. A vitamin pill is not enough. A vitamin-mineral supplement is called for.

Q: When I do need a supplement, what kind should I take? I've heard the organic, natural ones are best.

A: Read the ingredient lists, and buy the one that contains the nutrients you are looking for at the lowest price. When selecting a supplement, look for one that contains no more than the RDA for nutrients. As always, it is best to consult with a doctor before adding any supplements to your diet.

Q: Can taking supplements prevent heart disease or cancer?

A: No. Scientific evidence shows no protection from supplements. Good nutrition can certainly help protect you, however. People who eat poor diets develop more cancer and many other ills than do well-nourished people. You need every nutrient contained in foods, with all the other compounds foods contain, if you really want protection.

Q: Suppose I just want to take a supplement to be sure I get enough nutrients. There's no harm in that, is there?

A: Perhaps not—if you keep the dose low, and if you do not fall into a sense of false security. Pills can never make up for a poorly chosen diet. The right mix of foods is simply indispensable to the health of the body.

 Writing Write a letter to a younger friend or relative who eats a high-fat diet lacking important nutrients. In your letter, explain the health risks and provide examples of a healthful eating plan that your friend or relative could follow.

Reviewing Vocabulary

Use the vocabulary terms listed below to complete the following statements.

trans fats

vegetarians

cholesterol

B vitamins

minerals

1. A high-fat diet, especially from saturated fat, tends to increase the level of _____ in the blood.
2. People known as _____ eliminate meat, poultry, and fish from their diets.
3. Types of fats that form when polyunsaturated oils are processed to make them more solid are called _____.
4. Riboflavin, niacin, and thiamin are examples of _____.
5. Calcium, fluoride, and phosphorus are examples of _____.

Recalling Key Facts and Ideas

Section 1
6. **Explain.** Why do you need to include a wide variety of foods in adequate amounts in your meals and snacks?

Section 2
7. **Analyze.** Plan a meal using the MyPyramid food plan. The foods you choose should help you meet your body's needs and at the same time keep your calorie count down.

Section 3
8. **Explain.** Why is a nutrient-rich meal a better choice for health than eating a candy bar?

Section 4
9. **Explain.** Explain how fiber aids the digestive process.

Section 5
10. **Identify.** Identify three risks related to an eating plan that is high in fat.
11. **List.** List three types of information found on a food label.

Section 6
12. **Explain.** What is the difference between amino acids and essential amino acids?
13. **List.** List four foods that are high in protein but low in saturated fat and calories.

Section 7
14. **Explain.** Explain why excessive amounts of fat-soluble vitamins can be more dangerous than excess amounts of water-soluble vitamins.
15. **Recall.** Why may some teens' diets lack sufficient vitamin A?

Section 8
16. **Name.** What is the most abundant mineral found in the body?
17. **Recall.** What is the major function of iron in the body?

Writing Critically
18. **Personal.** According to research, many Americans do not have adequate eating plans. Discuss some of the barriers people might face in making nutritious food choices. What barriers do you find yourself facing?

1. Cholesterol 2. Vegetarians 3. Trans fats 4. B Vitamins 5. Minerals 6. To make sure you are getting the amount of nutrients your body needs to function properly 7. Answers will vary. 8. It provides energy to fuel your body as well as essential nutrients. 9. It keeps contents moving smoothly through the digestive tract. 10. The development of heart disease, cancer, and diabetes 11. Ingredient list, % Daily Values for nutrients per label serving, calories per label serving 12.

19. **Expository.** What influence does advertising exert on our food choices? Do you see this as having a positive or negative impact on your food choices? Explain why and give some examples.

20. **Personal.** Food product labels are sources of nutrition information. Do you generally read food labels? Why or why not?

Activities

21. Find a recent article from a newspaper or magazine on the topic of nutrition and write a summary. Be sure to include the date, source, and a copy of the article.

22. Analyze the food selections on your favorite restaurant's menu. Does the menu provide a variety of foods, including fruits and vegetables? What changes would you make in the menu in order to make the choices more nutritious?

23. Create a set of healthful meal plans for yourself for a full day. Include breakfast, lunch, dinner, and two snacks. Use the MyPyramid food plan on pages 166–167 as a guide. Be sure to use foods you enjoy when making meal and snack choices. You might also include a food that is new to you. Go easy on empty-calorie foods and make your plan match your energy need.

Making Decisions About Health

24. You have noticed that your friend has a habit of skipping breakfast. Your friend is not at all worried because she has been taking a multivitamin every morning. What would you say to her to let her know your concern? Describe a more effective meal planning strategy for her to follow.

Go Online

For more information on health careers, visit Career Corner at **glencoe.com**.

Fact or Fiction?

Answers

1. True.
2. False. Saturated and trans fats can increase the risk for heart disease, while vegetable oils and fish oils may have heart health benefits in small amounts.
3. False. Low intakes of calcium are common, because few foods contain it in large amounts.

 Writing Paragraphs will vary.

There are about 20 amino acids. Of those, the essential amino acids cannot be made by the body, and the others can be. **13.** Fish, poultry, dry beans (legumes), nuts **14.** Fat-soluble vitamins remain in the body and can build up to harmful levels. **15.** They may not consume enough—or enough variety of—fruits and vegetables. **16.** Calcium **17.** It carries oxygen in blood throughout the body. **18-24.** Answers will vary.

Nutrition: Healthy Body Weight

Sections

Are you pleased with your body weight? Many people think they should weigh more or less than they do. Some may want to lose weight to fit within certain societal standards. Others understand that there is a link between weight and physical health.

People also think they should control their weight. Two false ideas make their task difficult. The first is to focus on *weight*; the second is to focus on *controlling* weight. To put it simply, it isn't your weight you need to control. You need to control the amount of fat in your body in proportion to the lean tissue. Furthermore, it isn't possible to control either one, directly. It is possible only to control your behavior.

Fact or Fiction?

What Do You Think?

Is each statement true or false? If you think it's false, explain what's true.

1. Being underweight presents a risk to health.
2. The dieter who sees a large weight loss on the scale can take this as a sign of success.
3. It is harder to lose a pound than to gain one.

 Writing Think about your daily activities and the foods you eat. Write a paragraph to explain the importance of good nutrition and physical activity. Describe how you incorporate them into your daily life.

(Answers on page 229)

Go Online

Visit **glencoe.com** and complete the Life Choice Inventory for Chapter 8.

SECTION 1

Body Fat Risks

A person who is overweight and has too much body fat is at a higher risk of developing diseases, such as heart disease and diabetes. Excess body fat can also place stress on the muscles, joints, and organs of the body, making it more difficult to engage in physical activity. However, too little body fat can also be harmful to health. A person who is **underweight**, at a *weight too low for health*, may not get enough nutrients to function normally.

Risks of Overweight and Obesity

MAIN IDEA ▶ Both too much and too little body fat may lead to health problems.

Too much body fat, or being overweight, can lead to many health problems. Among those problems are high blood pressure, or hypertension, and type 2 diabetes. These diseases also tend to be passed from one family member to another. If a member of your family has type 2 diabetes or high blood pressure, it's more important that you maintain a healthy weight. Excess body fat also increases the risk of heart disease. Being overweight and having too much fat in the blood can clog the arteries of the heart, leading to a heart attack or a stroke.

Conditions such as breast cancer, diseases of the gallbladder, arthritis, breathing problems, and problems in pregnancy are also caused or made worse by being overweight. The health risks caused by being severely overweight are so serious that it has been declared a disease.

Vocabulary

underweight
obesity

Preview Activity
Discuss: Ask students what they feel is the most important reason ideal weight should be maintained. Write the different responses on the board. Discuss.

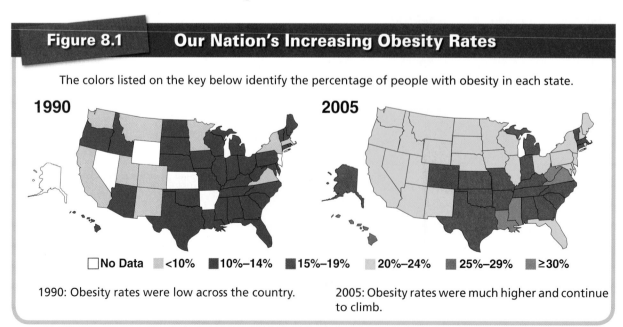

| Figure 8.1 | Our Nation's Increasing Obesity Rates |

The colors listed on the key below identify the percentage of people with obesity in each state.

1990   **2005**

☐ No Data <10% ■ 10%–14% ■ 15%–19% 20%–24% 25%–29% ■ ≥30%

1990: Obesity rates were low across the country.

2005: Obesity rates were much higher and continue to climb.

202 **Chapter 8** Nutrition: Healthy Body Weight

Obesity, or *overfatness to the point of injuring health* has been named as one of the leading health problems among young people in the United States today.

Since the 1980s, more and more of the nation's young people have become obese. Three times as many 12- to 19-year-olds are obese today. At the same time, the nation's obesity rates continue to grow dramatically (see **Figure 8.1**). Rates of diabetes, a serious disease that occurs more frequently among those who are obese, are also dramatically higher among children and adolescents. Among those who are obese, health professionals encourage those people to reduce calorie intake and increase physical activity to lose weight in a healthful way. With healthy weight loss, health risks related to being overweight or obese will decrease.

Some people become chronic dieters, people who frequently diet in unhealthy ways in an attempt to lose weight. More than half of all high school aged females report being "on a diet" even though many may not be overweight. About one quarter of high school males also report that they are dieting. This chapter provides honest information on the benefits of maintaining a healthy body weight. It also helps distinguish between healthy and harmful weight-control strategies.

SECTION 1 Review

Reviewing the Vocabulary
Review the vocabulary on page 202. Then answer these questions.
1. What is *obesity*?
2. Define *underweight*.

Reviewing the Facts
3. **Explain.** Why might being extremely thin pose a health risk?
4. **List.** List four health problems associated with excess body fat.
5. **Describe.** How can excess body fat increase the risk of heart disease?

Writing Critically
6. **Expository.** Some people in our country judge obese people unfairly. Explain how someone can avoid contributing to this social stigma.

For more vocabulary practice, play the True/False game at **glencoe.com**.

1. Obesity is excessive body fat to the point of injuring health.
2. Body weight which may have too little body fat
3. A person likely will not get enough nutrients for energy, growth, or health
4. Heart disease, diabetes, some cancers, and joint stress
5. Obesity is linked to higher blood cholesterol levels, which narrow the arteries.
6. Answers will vary.

The Right Weight for You

Your body's weight reflects its composition—the total mass of its bones, muscles, fat, fluids, and other tissues. The more of any of these you have, the more you weigh. Each type of tissue can vary in quantity and quality. One tissue, body fat, varies the most. Fat is the material in which the body can store the most food energy. Fat responds the most to changes in food intake and physical activity. Fat is usually the target of efforts to control weight.

Measuring Body Fat

MAIN IDEA ▶ Body fatness can be measured with a skin-fold caliper.

Health care professionals prefer to measure body fatness, rather than weight. However, body fatness is hard to measure directly. A **skin-fold test**, *a test of body fatness*, uses a **skin-fold caliper**—*a pinching device that measures the thickness of a fold of skin on the back of the arm, below the shoulder blade, on the side of the waist, or elsewhere*. Skin-fold measures reflect total body fat fairly well, because about half of the body's fat lies beneath the skin. *An informal way of measuring body fatness* is known as the **pinch test**. Use the thumb and forefinger of one hand to pinch the skin and fat at the back of the other arm. Take your fingers away and measure the space between the areas your fingers touched. A skin fold over an inch reflects too much body fat.

Scale Weight

Body *weight*, by itself, says little about body *fatness*. A person with strong muscles and bones may not be overweight, but may seem overweight on the scale. Also, a person who doesn't seem overweight on the scale may have too much body fat for good health. Even so, weight on the scale can help people get an idea of whether they need to lose or gain weight. It can also be useful during weight loss or gain to help track progress.

No simple answer to the question, "How much should I weigh?" exists. Factors such as height, gender, growth rate, and activity level must be considered. One useful measure is the **body mass index** (BMI), *an indicator of overweight or underweight based on a person's weight for height*. **Figure 8.2** presents the calculation for teens, often called *BMI for age*, which takes into account both age and gender. This is because normal body fatness changes during growth and differs between females and males.

Vocabulary

skin-fold test
skin-fold caliper
pinch test
body mass index (BMI)

? Did You Know?

To maintain a healthy weight, burn the same amount of calories as you take in.

Key Passage

Comprehend: Make sure students understand that there is a difference between body fat and weight. Ask them to write the components of the body that make up their total weight. (bones, muscles, fat, fluids, and other tissues)

Figure 8.2   **Calculate Your BMI**

Calculate your BMI by multiplying your weight (pounds) by 703, and then dividing by your height (inches) squared. Here's an example for a 16-year-old boy who weighs 145 pounds and is 69 inches tall:

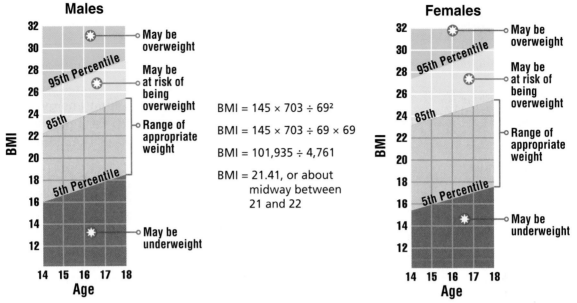

$$BMI = 145 \times 703 \div 69^2$$

$$BMI = 145 \times 703 \div 69 \times 69$$

$$BMI = 101,935 \div 4,761$$

$$BMI = 21.41, \text{ or about midway between 21 and 22}$$

Follow the example to calculate your own BMI. Then look at the BMI chart for your gender and find your age at the bottom. Follow the column up to your BMI range on the left axis of the chart.

Do not be alarmed if you are just slightly over or under the appropriate BMI range. If you are growing normally, and if your skin fold is average, your weight is probably just right.

Worksheets: A reproducible quiz for Section 2 is provided in the Teacher Classroom Resource.

Reviewing the Vocabulary

Review the vocabulary on page 204. Then answer these questions.

1. What is the *body mass index*?

Reviewing the Facts

2. Explain. What is the difference between measuring body weight and body fat?

3. Describe. Describe how to use the pinch test?

Writing Critically

4. Personal. Use the BMI method in **Figure 8.2** to determine your BMI range.

For more information on health careers, visit Career Corner at **glencoe.com**.

1. It is a measure of body weight relative to height.

2. Body weight is your total amount of body weight and body fat is just the amount of fat in your body.

3. Use the thumb and forefinger to pinch the skin and fat at the back of your arm. Take away your fingers and measure the space between the area your fingers touched. If the space measures over an inch, it indicates excess body fat.

4. Answers will vary and should be kept private.

Energy Balance

Suppose you are told by a health care provider that you are overweight or underweight. How did that happen? By having an unbalanced energy budget—that is, by eating either more or less food energy than you used up.

Your Energy Budget

Vocabulary

basal energy
physical activities

MAIN IDEA ▶ The balance between food energy taken in and energy spent determines how much fat a person's body stores in its fat tissues or how much it uses from storage.

Your body fat reflects your energy income and expenses in much the same way as your savings account reflects your money income and expenses. In the case of body fat, though, more is not better.

A day's energy budget (in calories) looks like this:

Food energy taken in (calories)
— Energy spent by the body (calories)

Change in fat stores (calories)

More simply:
Energy in — Energy out = Change in fat

Energy In

"Energy in" is the amount of energy, or calories, you put into your body. An apple brings in 100 calories; a candy bar, 425 calories. For each 3,500 calories you eat over the amount you spend, you store one pound of body fat. The reverse is also true: for every 3,500 calories you spend beyond those you eat, you will use up a pound of body tissue as fuel.

Energy Out: Basal Energy

As for the "energy out" side, the body spends energy in two major ways: to fuel its basal energy needs and to fuel its physical activities. **Basal energy** is *the total of all the energy needed to support the chemical activities of the cells and to sustain life.* **Physical activities** are *movements of the body under the command of the conscious mind.* It is possible to change both of these in order to spend more or less energy in a day.

Basal energy supports the work that goes on in your body all the time. The basal processes include:

- Beating of the heart.
- Inhaling and exhaling of air.
- Maintenance of body temperature.
- Working of the nerves and glands.

These basal processes support life.

Basal energy needs are surprisingly large. A person whose total energy needs are 2,000 calories a day spends 1,200 to 1,400 of them to support basal activities. This means that you use up 1,200 to 1,400 calories a day even if you just sit still and do nothing.

Energy Out: Physical Activity

The number of calories a person spends on a physical activity depends on four factors:

1. *The number and size of the muscles that are working.* The larger the active muscle mass, the more energy needed. For example, using the large muscle groups of the legs and buttocks to walk upstairs takes more energy than lifting books to a shelf with your arms and shoulders.

2. *The total weight of the body parts being moved.* The heavier the body parts, the more energy required to move them. This explains why a 200-pound person uses more energy than a 100-pound person does when both are doing the same activity with equal effort.

"Physical fitness is not only one of the most important keys to a healthy body, it is the basis of dynamic and creative intellectual activity."

—John F. Kennedy
(1917–1963)
Thirty-fifth President
of the United States

What Teens THINK

Do Teens Diet Too Much or Too Little?

Today's society makes everyone feel like they have to be thin and beautiful to be accepted. I'm really tired of seeing what today's society does to today's youth. We are all a bunch of robots trying to be accepted by anyone and everyone who's popular. Who really cares more about your image, you or them? Learn to like yourself the way you are.

—Andrew B., 16,
Minnesota

I believe that the word *diet* is understood incorrectly by most teens. Most teens think of *diets* as short-term ways to lose weight. Really you should make your diet a long-term, lifelong commitment, not a way to fit into a dress for a dance in two weeks. Teens should try to eat foods filled with nutrients and low in fat and calories. Two candy bars and a can of soda just don't do it.

—Joseph B., 16,
Pennsylvania

Most teens diet too much because of society's standards and ways of thinking, which make everyone so self-conscious that they have low self-esteem. I think it happens with more females than males because of the way society pictures them.

—Hannah G., 15,
New Mexico

I think this question cannot be answered about teenagers as a whole. I believe some teens diet too much, some too little, and some just right. The teens who diet too much may become obsessive about exercise and eating, and therefore worry about it constantly. They tend to be thin or regular-sized females. Compulsive dieters can eventually develop anorexia, bulimia, or both. The second type of teen, who diets too little, usually does not care what goes into his body (drugs, alcohol, food, etc.). He eats what and when he pleases and does not exercise regularly. Lastly, there are teens who diet just the right amount. These people eat healthy foods and exercise regularly. They maintain a constant, healthy body weight by living a healthy lifestyle. I think that the opinion of whether teens diet too much or too little depends on the person's point of view and the individual being judged.

—Joy W., 15,
Montana

3. *The length of time of physical activity.* The longer the activity lasts, the more calories are spent.

4. *The amount of effort put into the movement—the activity intensity.* Hard work takes more fuel.

Total Energy Expenditure

A typical breakdown of the total energy spent by a moderately active person (for example, a student who walks from class to class) might look like this:

Energy for basal activities:	1,250
+ Energy for physical activities:	650

Total energy needs: 1,900 calories

The basal energy cannot be changed much. However, it is possible to increase physical activities and spend more calories. Making physical activity a daily habit can also increase your basal energy output over the long term. As lean tissue develops and fat decreases, basal energy output will increase as well.

Worksheets: A reproducible quiz for Section 3 is provided in the Teacher Classroom Resources.

SECTION 3 Review

Reviewing the Vocabulary

Review the vocabulary on page 206. Then answer these questions.

1. Define *basal energy*.

2. What are *physical activities*?

Reviewing the Facts

3. Describe. What happens when you take in more calories than your body expends?

4. Explain. What are the two major ways the body spends energy?

5. Name. Name three factors that determine the number of calories spent on a physical activity.

Writing Critically

6. Personal. Are you satisfied with your body's energy budget? Why or why not?

For fitness and health tips, visit the Fitness Zone at **glencoe.com.**

1. The total of all the energy needed to support the chemical activities of the cells and to sustain life

2. Movements of the body under the command of the conscious mind

3. The excess calories are stored as fat in the body

4. Basal activities and physical activities

5. The number and size of the muscles that are working; the total weight of the body parts being moved; the length of time of physical activity.

6. Answers will vary.

Weight Gain and Weight Loss

You step on the scale and note that you weigh a pound more or less than you did the last time you weighed yourself. This doesn't mean you have gained or lost body fat. Changes in body weight reflect shifts in many different materials—not only fat, but also water, bone minerals, and lean tissues such as muscles.

Fat Tissue, Lean Tissue, and Body Water

MAIN IDEA ▶ To lose weight safely and permanently, a person must lose fat tissue, not lean tissue or water.

A healthy 18-year-old teen, who is about 5 feet 10 inches tall and who weighs 150 pounds, carries about 90 of those pounds as water and 30 as fat. The other 30 pounds are the lean tissues: muscles; organs such as the heart, brain, and liver; and the bones of the skeleton. Stripped of water and fat, then, the person weighs only 30 pounds!

The body's lean tissue is vital to health. When a person who is overweight seeks to lose weight, it should be fat, not this precious lean tissue, that is lost. For someone who wants to gain weight, it is best to gain both lean tissue *and* fat, not just fat.

The type of tissue gained or lost depends on how the weight is gained or lost. Some of the most dramatic weight changes people achieve reflect losses and gains in the body's fluid content, which ideally shouldn't change much at all.

Vocabulary

diuretic
diet pills

Did You Know?

A teen who is 5 feet tall and weighs 100 pounds has only 20 pounds of lean tissue.

■ **Figure 8.3** *The cautious consumer distinguishes between loss of fat and loss of weight. Why is it important to only lose body fat?*

Caption Answer: You don't want to lose lean tissue or muscle.

Relate: Ask students to read pages 209–210 of Section 4 and then consider the following paragraph:

> If dieting is done with physical activity, 95 percent of the weight lost will be fat, and 5 percent will be lean tissue. If dieting is done without physical activity, 75 percent of the weight lost will be fat, and 25 percent will be lean tissue.

Ask students to explain the significance of physical activity as it relates to dieting. Discuss.

Did You Know?

Teens trying to gain weight should try to increase the amount of lean muscle on their bodies, as well as fat.

Yet some people may seek to bring about such weight changes because they like to see quick results. They fail to realize how useless such changes are in changing what really matters—the body's lean and fat tissue.

One dangerous way to lose fluid is to take a **diuretic**, *a drug that causes the body to lose fluids*. Diuretics cause the kidneys to draw extra water from the blood into the urine. Another dangerous weight-loss technique is to exercise heavily in the heat, losing large amounts of fluid in sweat. Both practices are dangerous, and are not recommended.

Most quick—weight-loss diets cause large fluid losses that look like dramatic changes on the scale but are really temporary. Such diets cause little loss of body fat.

Feasting: Weight Gain

MAIN IDEA ▶ The energy from any food can build up in body fat if a person eats more calories than are spent.

When you eat more food than you need, where does it go in your body? An excess of any energy nutrient—carbohydrate, fat, or protein—can be stored as follows:

- Carbohydrate is broken down, absorbed, and changed into glucose. Inside the body, glucose may be stored as glycogen or body fat.

- Fat is broken down mostly to fatty acids and absorbed. Then these may be stored as body fat.

- Protein, too, is broken down to its basic units (amino acids) and absorbed. Inside the body, these may be used to replace lost body protein. Any extra amino acids are changed into body fat and stored.

No matter whether you are eating steak, brownies, or baked beans, if you eat enough of them, the excess will be stored as fat within hours.

■ **Figure 8.4** *It's hard for some young girls to know how thin is too thin. Why is it dangerous to be too thin?*

Caption Answer: The body needs a balance of good nutrition and exercise to be healthy.

Fasting: An Unsafe Weight-Loss Strategy

MAIN IDEA ▶ **Fasting and low-carbohydrate diets are not healthy ways to lose weight.**

When a person stops eating altogether, the body has to draw on its fuel stores to keep going. One of our great advantages is that we can eat a meal, store fuel, and then use it until the next meal. People can store fat and glycogen, but their stores are limited. A person with just average fat stores has enough fat to provide the body with energy for weeks, even when no food at all is eaten (fasting).

By comparison, the body's supply of carbohydrate, stored as glycogen, is small. When too little carbohydrate is taken in, such as when the eater consumes a diet too low in carbohydrates or fails to eat at all, the glycogen stores last for less than a day. While glycogen runs out, the body's demand for the carbohydrate fuel glucose remains strong.

So how does the fasting body get the needed glucose? It begins to convert protein to carbohydrate. In fasting, the body has no external source of protein, and so it takes apart the protein in its own muscles and organs to keep up the supply of glucose needed to feed the brain and nerves.

For this reason, dieters should avoid both fasting and diets too low in carbohydrates. People who follow weight-loss programs that employ fasting or low-carbohydrate diets drop weight quickly, especially at first. This is because they are using up protein from muscles and organs as fuel. Protein contains only half as many calories per pound as fat, so it disappears twice as fast. Furthermore, with each pound of body protein used for fuel, three or four pounds of water are also lost from the body. Because of this, the person who stops eating altogether sees a great change in weight on the scales.

If the body were to continue to feed on itself at this rate, death would occur in about ten days. Instead, the fasting body switches to an emergency route of energy use that allows it to use every possible calorie from its stored fuel. In addition, vital functions slow down to reduce the need for basal fuel. The person slows down mentally, too, and feels too tired to be physically active.

For the person who wants to lose weight, a balanced low-calorie, adequate-carbohydrate diet has in fact been proven to promote the same rate of weight loss and a faster rate of fat loss than a total fast. As a general rule, to lose weight safely and effectively, a person should not consume less than 10 calories per pound of present body weight per day.

Health Skills

Identifying Unsound Weight-Loss Programs

Be cautious of weight-loss programs that:

- Promise weight loss of more than 1 percent of total body weight per week.
- Use diets that are below 1,000 calories per day.
- Use diets that provide less than six ounces of carbohydrates in a day.
- Make people dependent upon special products.
- Do not teach the importance of regular physical activity and behavior modification.
- Misrepresent salespeople as nutritional "counselors."
- Require large sums of money or contracts.

Other Unsafe Weight Loss Strategies

You can judge a good weight-loss diet not by the speed of weight loss but by how well those who use it maintain their new weight. By this standard, fad diets and fasting are neither safe nor effective ways to lose weight. True nutrition experts never recommend them.

Other ways *not* to lose weight are water pills, diet pills, muscle stimulators, and hormones. Diuretics do nothing to reduce fat. They only result in the loss of a few pounds on the scale for half a day. Most over-the-counter **diet pills**, *medications that reduce the appetite or otherwise promote weight loss*, have unintended effects. One pill ingredient, now banned, caused thousands of people to fall ill; hundreds are believed to have died from its effects. Even today's safer pills leave a person with another problem: how to stop taking the pills without gaining more weight back. Muscle stimulators reduce body measurements by making muscles tighter, not by reducing their fat content—and only for an hour or so.

As for hormones, they affect body functions including appetite, but most have proved useless and often hazardous as weight-loss aids. Medical researchers who are studying the appetite-controlling hormones hope to discover new obesity treatments for people.

Consumer SKILLS ACTIVITY

Weight-Loss Schemes

One survey of 29,000 weight-loss programs found fewer than 6 percent of them effective—and 13 percent dangerous. People may respond to this fact with the question, "Can't the government do something about that?" The government tries to find and eliminate fraudulent diet programs. Smaller agencies, however, have too few staff members and too little money to handle the huge number of reported cases.

It is easy to get a product on the market and hard for the government or other groups to remove it. Consumers should remember that if something sounds too good to be true, it probably is. The Health Skills sidebar on page 211, "Identifying Unsound Weight-Loss Programs," offers clues to help you recognize bad weight-loss ideas.

 Writing

1. Do you think it might be worth it to some people to take a risk trying a new diet program for weight loss? If so, why? If not, why not?
2. Under what circumstances might you try one?
3. What might be a better plan?

Today, an alarming number of teens are obese and face serious risks to health. Is weight-loss surgery a reasonable option for them? Experts debate this question. For obese adults, surgery to reduce the size of the stomach often reduces food intake, causes weight loss, reduces disease risks, and lengthens life. To be considered for such surgery, however, a teen must have a very high BMI (40 or greater). Other factors must also be taken into account: growth status, skeletal system maturity, emotional development, family support, and ability to follow dietary instructions, for example. Such surgery can cause both mild and serious problems. Infections, nausea, and vomiting can set in right away. Later on, nutrient deficiencies can damage health, and patients may experience psychological challenges as well.

For all except those with life-threatening obesity, the risks from surgeries and pills outweigh the benefits. Success, as measured by long-term weight maintenance, is seldom achieved by these methods.

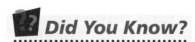

Did You Know?

Physical activity:

- Improve self-esteem and feelings of well-being.

- Help build and maintain bones, muscles, and joints.

- Build endurance and muscle strength.

- Lower risk of heart disease, colon cancer, and type 2 diabetes.

- Help control blood pressure.

- Reduce feelings of depression and anxiety.

SECTION 4 Review

Worksheets: A reproducible quiz for Section 4 is provided in the Teacher Classroom Resources.

Reviewing the Vocabulary

Review the vocabulary on page 209. Then answer these questions.

1. Define *diuretic*.

2. What are *diet pills*?

Reviewing the Facts

3. Explain. Why is it important to lose mostly fat tissue and not water or lean tissue when you diet?

4. Analyze. Where does the body get the glucose it needs when a person has not eaten in a while?

5. List. List four methods that you should not use in attempting to lose weight.

Writing Critically

6. Expository. Why do so many people try dangerous weight loss strategies and invest money thinking they will solve their weight problems? Explain.

Go Online

For more vocabulary practice, play the eFlashcards game at **glencoe.com**.

1. A drug that causes the body to lose fluids

2. Medications that reduce the appetite or otherwise promote weight loss

3. Water and lean tissue are vital to the strength of muscles and organs in the body

4. Proteins in lean tissue break down to become the needed fuel for the body

5. Fad diets, fasting, water pills, diet pills

6. Answers will vary.

Smart Weight-Loss Strategies

With so many weight-loss programs available, what weight-loss program actually works? How can a person lose weight safely and permanently? The secret is a sensible approach that uses diet, physical activity, and behavior changes. It takes a great deal of effort, at first, for a person whose habits have all led to overfatness to adopt the hundred or so new habits that bring about thinness. When people succeed, they do so because they have used the methods described here.

Diet Planning

MAIN IDEA ▶ To design a successful weight-loss diet, design it to last a lifetime. Be realistic and make it adequate.

Before embarking on such a plan, you must learn to distinguish between hunger and appetite. **Hunger** is *the physiological need to eat, experienced as a drive for obtaining food, an unpleasant sensation that demands to be fed*. Most people would name hunger as the reason for eating, and often this is true. The physical need for food is not the only reason people eat, though. Another reason is **appetite**, *the psychological desire to eat, a learned motivation and a positive sensation that accompanies the sight, smell, or thought of food*. Appetite may arise in response to the sight, smell, or thought of food even when you are full. An example of this occurs when a server offers dessert after you've finished eating, and suddenly you desire a piece of cake.

Other factors influence eating too. Some people react to stress by losing their appetites, while others indulge in **stress eating**, *eating in response to stress*. Some eat in response to all sorts of complex human feelings other than hunger or appetite. Sensations such as boredom, depression, or anger can sometimes be lessened for a while by eating. All your reasons for choosing foods contribute to the nature of your diet. All must be recognized, honored, and sometimes, controlled, as you develop your weight-control plan. In weight management, eating becomes a deliberate process, rather than an automatic one.

No plan is magical. You needn't include or avoid any particular food. Don't think of it as a "diet," but rather as an eating plan that you will adopt for life. It must consist of foods that you like or can learn to like, and foods that are available to you. You can see from **Figure 8.5** that even fast foods can undermine weight-loss efforts or support them.

Vocabulary

hunger
appetite
stress eating
behavior modification
lapses

"*While we may not be able to control all that happens to us, we can control what happens inside us.*"

—Ben Franklin
(1706–1790)
Author, inventor, politician, statesman, diplomat

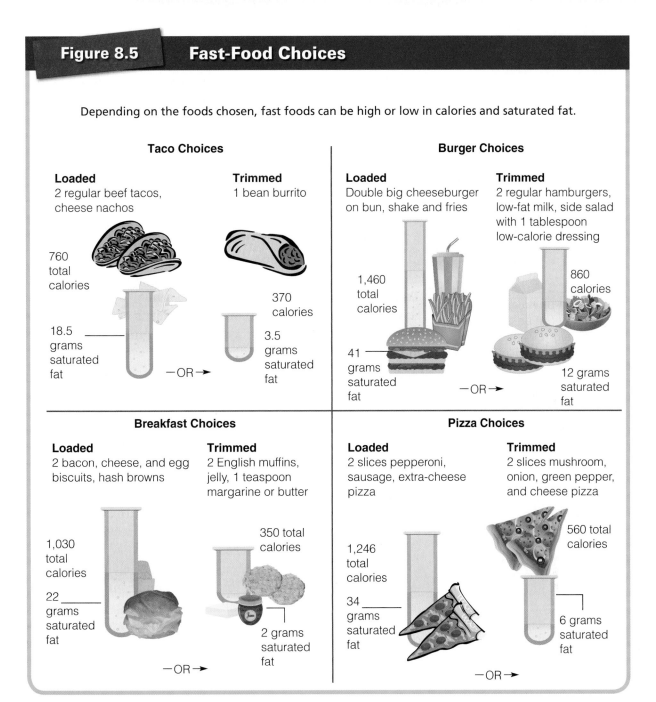

Figure 8.5 — Fast-Food Choices

Depending on the foods chosen, fast foods can be high or low in calories and saturated fat.

Taco Choices

Loaded
2 regular beef tacos, cheese nachos

760 total calories

18.5 grams saturated fat

—OR→

Trimmed
1 bean burrito

370 calories

3.5 grams saturated fat

Burger Choices

Loaded
Double big cheeseburger on bun, shake and fries

1,460 total calories

41 grams saturated fat

—OR→

Trimmed
2 regular hamburgers, low-fat milk, side salad with 1 tablespoon low-calorie dressing

860 calories

12 grams saturated fat

Breakfast Choices

Loaded
2 bacon, cheese, and egg biscuits, hash browns

1,030 total calories

22 grams saturated fat

—OR→

Trimmed
2 English muffins, jelly, 1 teaspoon margarine or butter

350 total calories

2 grams saturated fat

Pizza Choices

Loaded
2 slices pepperoni, sausage, extra-cheese pizza

1,246 total calories

34 grams saturated fat

—OR→

Trimmed
2 slices mushroom, onion, green pepper, and cheese pizza

560 total calories

6 grams saturated fat

Calories and Nutrients

Choose a calorie level you can live with. A shortage of 500 calories a day for seven days is a 3,500-calorie weekly shortage. That is enough to lose a pound of body fat. If you adopt an eating plan rather than a "diet," you will practice positive behaviors while losing weight. You can maintain a healthy weight for the rest of your life. Make your meals meet your nutrient needs. The MyPyramid food plan in Chapter 7 is a good approach to follow.

Most people could lose weight at a reasoable rate following such a plan and meet their nutrient needs. Foods such as fruits, vegetables, and whole grains are much more satisfying too.

■ **Figure 8.6** *Eating sensibly and living a physically active lifestyle are the best ways to control weight. Name some nutritious foods you should eat every day.*

Caption Answer: Fruits, vegetables, whole grains

Crunchy, wholesome foods offer bulk and a feeling of fullness for far fewer calories than refined high-calorie foods. Limit your portions of meats: an ounce of ham contains more calories than an ounce of bread, and many of them are from fat.

Timing of Meals

Three meals a day is standard for our society, but many people choose to eat four or five smaller meals. What is important is to eat regularly and, if at all possible, to eat before you are very hungry. When you do decide to eat, eat the entire meal you have planned for yourself. Then don't eat again until the next meal. Commit to eating breakfast each day, and to eating as many meals with your family as possible. Teens who do so more often maintain a healthy body weight. Save "free" (lowest-calorie) or favorite foods or beverages for a snack at the end of the day, if you need insurance against late-evening hunger. Also, drink plenty of water.

Portion Sizes

Portion sizes greatly influence calorie intakes. The bigger the food servings, serving bowls, utensils, drinking glasses, and dinnerware at a meal, the bigger the portions people consume. As people eat larger servings, their calorie totals increase. Yet, after they've finished, they say they feel about as full as do those who ate less.

The trick seems to be to eat just until satisfied and then to stop because continued eating produces less satisfaction while unneeded calories increase. Almost every dieter needs to measure food in cups and measuring spoons for a while to learn to judge portion sizes. Read labels and compare calories per serving.

Remember, too, that reduced-calorie foods are not calorie-free. Eating a reduced-calorie cookie or two in place of ordinary cookies can save calories; however, eating a large portion still increases your calorie intake.

Other Helpful Hints

At first it may seem as if you have to spend many hours planning and eating your meals. After about three weeks, sticking to your diet plan will be much easier. Reward yourself often, but never with food. Visualize your future self as fit and healthy. Your new eating pattern will become a habit.

Weigh yourself frequently enough to track your progress, but expect your weight to bounce around a bit. Gains or losses of a pound or more in a matter of days disappear quickly. The average is what is real. Don't expect to continue to lose as fast as you do at first. A sizable water loss is common in the first week, but the loss slows down dramatically soon after. If you have been working out lately, your scale weight may show no loss or even a gain.

This may reflect a gain of lean body mass—just what you want, if you want to be healthy. If you slip, don't punish yourself. If you ate an extra 1,000 calories yesterday, don't try to eat 1,000 fewer calories today. Just go back to your plan.

Behavior Modification and Supportive Thinking

MAIN IDEA ▶ Reward yourself for following your weight-loss diet.

Behavior modification means *changing one's choices or actions by manipulating the cues that trigger the actions, the actions themselves, or the consequences of the actions.* It also offers ideas that make sticking with your plan easier. **Figure 8.7** on page 218 offers some of these ideas.

Setting realistic goals can increase weight-loss success. A person who sets an unreasonable goal, and then fails to achieve it, may become discouraged and give up trying to achieve a healthier body. Discouragement can be replaced by true and supportive ways of thinking. For example, instead of setting the goal, "I want to be a size 2 by summer," restate the goal as: "I want to lose 10 percent of my body weight in one year." Give yourself credit for each successful step along the way ("I have lost over 11 pounds, or 6 percent of my body weight—just 6 pounds away from my goal of 10 percent!").

It takes belief in oneself and honoring of oneself to lay the foundation for change. Self-acceptance predicts success, while self-hatred predicts failure. Remember to enjoy your accomplishments and to honor your emerging fit and healthy self.

Physical Activity

MAIN IDEA ▶ Physical activity increases lean tissue, expends energy, and boosts self-esteem.

Some people who want to lose weight dislike the idea of physical activity. Weight loss, to a point, is possible without physical activity. Even if you choose not to be physically active at first, let your mind be open to the idea. As body weight decreases, moving your body becomes easier. You may want to take up an activity or a sport.

Physical activity contributes to weight management by helping to develop the body's lean tissue. It raises the rate of basal energy use. Physical activity also promotes mental health. Looking and feeling healthy boosts self-esteem, self-efficacy, and confidence. High self-efficacy helps a person to stay with a weight-management effort—a beneficial cycle.

Weight loss without activity can have a negative effect.

Did You Know?

Forty-five percent of bone mass is added during the teen years.

Class Discussion

Discuss: Ask students if they have ever given up on a diet plan. How long did they continue the diet before giving up? Can they think of other skills they have learned that took more time? How much time should they be willing to devote to changing their eating habits as compared to learning other new skills? Remind students that goal setting is a great tool to use to change eating habits.

Class Activity

Demonstrate: Fill 1-gallon plastic jugs with water. Ask for volunteers to hold the jugs and walk across the room. Ask how they would feel about physical activity if they had to carry the extra weight with them at all times. Ask students to consider the relationship between being overweight and lacking the energy to exercise. Discuss.

Figure 8.7   Using Behavior Modification for Weight Management

1. **To eliminate inappropriate eating cues:**
   - Let other family members buy, store, and serve their own sweets. When the television shows food commercials, change channels or look away.
   - Stay away from convenience stores.
   - Carry appropriate snacks from home.
   - Avoid vending machines.

2. **To reduce the cues you can not eliminate:**
   - Eat only in one place, in one room.
   - Clear plates directly into the garbage.
   - Create obstacles for eating problem-foods (for example, make it necessary to unwrap, cook, and serve each one separately).
   - Minimize contact with excessive food (serve individual plates, don't put serving dishes on the table, and leave the table when you are finished).
   - Make small portions of food look large (spread food out, and serve it on small plates).
   - Don't deprive yourself (eat regular meals, and don't skip meals).

3. **To strengthen the cues to appropriate eating and physical activity:**
   - Encourage others to eat appropriate food and to be physically active.
   - Keep your favorite appropriate foods in the front of the refrigerator.
   - Learn appropriate portion sizes.
   - Save foods from meals for snacks (and make these your only snacks).
   - Prepare foods attractively.
   - Keep your inline skates (hiking boots, tennis racket) by the door.

4. **To practice the desired eating and physical activity behaviors:**
   - Slow down while you eat (pause for two to three minutes, put down utensils, chew slowly, swallow before reloading the fork, and always use utensils).
   - Leave some food on the plate.
   - Join in physical activity with a group of active people.

5. **To arrange negative consequences of inappropriate eating:**
   - Eat your meals with other people.
   - Ask that others respond neutrally to your deviations (make no comment). This is a negative consequence, because it withholds attention.

6. **To arrange positive consequences of appropriate eating and physical activity behaviors:**
   - Keep records of food intake, physical activity, and weight change.
   - Arrange for rewards (not food) for each behavior change or weight loss.
   - Ask for encouragement from your friends and family.

A person who diets without being physically active loses both lean and fat tissue. If the person then gains weight without being physically active, the gain is mostly fat. Compared with lean tissue, fat tissue burns fewer calories to maintain itself. The person who returns to eating the same amount as before the diet gains body fat, but not lean tissue. This cycle of gaining, losing, and gaining again can leave people more overweight than if they had not dieted at all.

On the other hand, the more lean tissue you develop, and the more calories you spend, the more you can afford to eat. This brings both satisfaction and nutrients.

Physical activity speeds up your body's energy use *permanently*—that is, for as long as you keep your body fit. Physical activity, of course, also spends energy while you are doing it. **Figure 8.9** on page 220 lists energy costs of activities.

If an activity is to help with weight loss, it must be physical. Being moved passively, as by a machine or a massage, does not help. The more muscles you move and the longer and more vigorously you move them, the more calories you spend.

Weight loss is not the only reward to be won from working out. If you incorporate the right kinds of workouts into your schedule, your heart and lungs, as well as your muscles, will become and stay fit.

Weight Maintenance

MAIN IDEA ▶ **People who maintain weight take responsibility for their weight.**

It can be much harder to maintain weight loss than to lose weight. An appropriate calorie intake for maintenance is higher than the level of intake to promote loss, but it still may take effort not to overeat. Those who succeed in maintaining appropriate weight have some key traits in common.

" *Getting my lifelong weight struggle under control has come from a process of treating myself as well as I treat others in every way.* "

—Oprah Winfrey
(1954–)
Emmy Award-winning
talk show host and actress

■ **Figure 8.8** *Whether you are trying to maintain, gain, or lose weight, physical activity is essential for health. What happens to our bodies if we don't do any physical activity?*

Caption Answer: If we do not participate in physical activities, our bodies become unhealthy.

Figure 8.9 Energy Demands of Activities

Activity	Cal/Lb/Min[a]	110	125	150	175	200
		Calories burned per minute				
Aerobic dance (vigorous)	0.062	6.8	7.8	9.3	10.9	12.4
Basketball (vigorous, full court)	0.097	10.7	12.1	14.6	17.0	19.4
Bicycling						
13 miles per hour	0.045	5.0	5.6	6.8	7.9	9.0
19 miles per hour	0.076	8.4	9.5	11.4	13.3	15.2
Canoeing (flat water, moderate pace)	0.045	5.0	5.6	6.8	7.9	9.0
Cross-country skiing (8 miles per hour)	0.104	11.4	13.0	15.6	18.2	20.8
Golf (carrying clubs)	0.045	5.0	5.6	6.8	7.9	9.0
Handball	0.078	8.6	9.8	11.7	13.7	15.6
Horseback riding (trot)	0.052	5.7	6.5	7.8	9.1	10.4
Rowing (vigorous)	0.097	10.7	12.1	14.6	17.0	19.4
Running						
5 miles per hour	0.061	6.7	7.6	9.2	10.7	12.2
7.5 miles per hour	0.094	10.3	11.8	14.1	16.4	18.8
10 miles per hour	0.114	12.5	14.3	17.1	20.0	22.9
Soccer (vigorous)	0.097	10.7	12.1	14.6	17.0	19.4
Studying	0.011	1.2	1.4	1.7	1.9	2.2
Swimming						
20 yards per minute	0.032	3.5	4.0	4.8	5.6	6.4
45 yards per minute	0.058	6.4	7.3	8.7	10.2	11.6
Tennis (beginner)	0.032	3.5	4.0	4.8	5.6	6.4
Walking (brisk pace)						
3.5 miles per hour	0.035	3.9	4.4	5.2	6.1	7.0

[a]Cal/Lb/Min is an abbreviation for calories (cal) per pound (lb) of body weight per minute (min). You can use it to calculate the number of calories you use at your body weight for a minute of activity. To calculate the total number of calories you spend for a longer time, multiply the cal/lb/min factor by your exact weight. Then multiply your answer by the number of minutes you spend on the activity. For example, if you weigh 142 pounds, and you want to know how many calories you spend doing 30 minutes of vigorous aerobic dance: 0.062 cal/lb/min x 142 lb = 8.8 calories per minute. 8.8 cal/min x 30 minutes = 264 total calories spent.

Comprehension Check

Comprehend: Have students use the column in Figure 8.9 that most closely matches their weight to find an estimate of how many calories they will burn for each activity. Have students search the internet for other activities and calculate the calories burned for each activity they find. Invite them to share their findings.

Some of the key traits to successful weight management include taking responsibility for body weight. The responsibility for weight management is not placed on programs, professionals or pills. Feeling confident about maintaining a healthy weight will also result in greater success of weight management.

Anticipating **lapses**, *times of falling back into former habits,* is another normal part of both weight change and weight management.

People who maintain weight have learned to cope with lapses. They identify the triggers that lead to them and they learn to avoid them. For example, a person who unexpectedly overate at a party would forgive the lapse, and continue with his or her program. One action might be to promise to eat a balanced meal before attending the next party and to stay away from the buffet. When normal lapses occur, cope by saying, "I'm doing it again, but I do it less often now. I'm making progress."

Worksheets: A reproducible quiz for Section 5 is provided in the Teacher Classroom Resources.

SECTION 5 Review

Reviewing the Vocabulary

Review the vocabulary on page 214. Then answer these questions.

1. What is *stress eating*?
2. Define *behavior modification*.
3. What is the difference between *hunger* and *appetite*?

Reviewing the Facts

4. **List.** List four recommendations for developing a successful weight-loss program.
5. **Explain.** How can behavior modification be helpful for weight control?
6. **Describe.** What are some advantages of including physical activity in a weight-loss and weight-maintenance program?

Writing Critically

7. **Expository.** A sound program of physical activity is important in losing and maintaining weight and overall health. Choose several activities that you enjoy. Make up a schedule for a week that includes at least one activity for each day. Make note of your body size and how long you do the activity. Calculate the number of calories you'll spend on each activity.

For more vocabulary practice, play the Concentration game at **glencoe.com.**

1. Eating in response to stress

2. Changing one's choices or actions by manipulating the cues that trigger the actions

3. Hunger is the physiological need to eat and appetite is the psychological desire to eat.

4. Choose the appropriate amount of calories, eat regular meals, control portion sizes, take time to plan your meals before you become hungry.

5. It helps you to take actions that can help you stick to your plan.

6. Physical activity allows you to lose fat while retaining lean muscle tissues.

7. Answers will vary.

Smart Weight-Gain Strategies

It is as hard for an underweight person to gain a pound as it is for an overweight person to lose one. Similarly, the person who wants to gain must learn new habits and learn to eat new foods.

Physical Activity and Increased Calories

MAIN IDEA ▶ Healthful weight gain can be achieved by a program of physical activity and increased intake of calories.

An underweight person must decide whether gaining weight is best for health. A thinner person is less likely to suffer from heart disease, for example. For teens who are still growing, it could be that they will gain weight naturally in a year or two—the low weight is temporary. However, if an underweight person is unwell and eats poorly, then learning to eat well in ways that support the body's healthy weight is the best course.

Physical Activity

Physical activity is essential for health. It should continue unless body weight is so low as to be life-threatening. The healthy way to gain weight is to build it up by patient and consistent physical training and, at the same time, to eat enough calories to support the weight gain. If you are not dangerously underweight, adopt an activity program designed to build lean body tissue.

Selecting High-Calorie Foods

In addition to exercising appropriately, you must eat enough calories to support weight gain. If you add 700 to 800 extra calories of nutritious foods a day, you can achieve a healthful weight gain of 1 to 1½ pounds per week.

A person who wants to gain weight often has to learn to eat new foods. No matter how many helpings of boiled carrots you eat, you won't gain weight very fast. Carrots simply do not offer enough calories. A person who can't eat much volume should select high-calorie foods. To gain weight, then:

- Eat an extra 700 to 800 calories per day.
- Use more high-calorie foods such as those listed in Chapter 7.

Vocabulary

anorexia nervosa
bulimia
binge eating disorder (BED)
binge eating

Preview Activity

Analyze: Explain that because so many people struggle with excess weight, it is sometimes hard to relate to the problems associated with being underweight. Give students five minutes to write down the drawbacks that come with being underweight. Discuss the responses as a class.

Also, be aware that most people in the United States are overweight. If you need to gain weight, you may need to take an independent view of the U.S. recommendation to reduce fat and calories. A diet too low in fat might do more harm than good. Be sure that your fats are the unsaturated kinds, however—even thin people can develop heart disease if they eat too much saturated fat. If you don't know which fats are saturated, go back and review Chapter 7.

To increase calorie intake:

- Choose chocolate milk instead of plain milk, peanut butter instead of lean meat, avocados instead of cucumbers, whole-wheat muffins instead of whole-wheat bread.

- Add margarine to cooked vegetables. Use creamy dressings on salads, whipped cream on fruit, sour cream on potatoes, and so forth.

Additional Strategies

Since you need many more calories in a day, you will also need to:

- Eat more often. Make three sandwiches in the morning to eat as snacks between the day's three regular meals.

- Use large plates and bowls, big glasses and utensils, and eat slightly larger portions than usual.

Critical Thinking

Analyze: Ask students to bring in a diet plan from a magazine, internet search, friend or family member. Divide the students into small groups. Each group will then choose one diet and list the positives and negatives of that plan. Invite volunteers to share their findings with the class.

■ **Figure 8.10** *Physical activity helps people achieve and maintain healthy weights. What are some physical activities you do every day?*

Caption Answer: I walk to school.

Analyzing Influences

> ➤ **Objectives**
> - Identify external and internal factors that influence food choices.
> - Analyze whether the factors are positive or negative influences.
> - Create a healthy eating plan to avoid weight gain.

Don't Let Them Eat Cake

When she steps on the scale, Jasmine regrets the pieces of cake, cheeseburgers, and other high-fat foods that she regularly eats. But what can she do? When she sees food ads on TV or goes to fast-food restaurants with friends, she can't resist the temptation to eat such goodies. Besides, she likes fatty foods, and healthy foods such as fish and salads don't appeal to her.

Jasmine wishes she could make wiser food choices. She's 20 pounds over the weight that is normal for her height, and she knows that being overweight is bad for her health. The weight issue is causing her stress, but when she feels stressed out, she heads straight for the kitchen. She relaxes with a piece of cake, a bowl of ice cream, or some other high-fat food. Jasmine is starting to feel trapped in a vicious circle.

➤ **Identify the Problem**

1. What is Jasmine's problem?

➤ **Form an Action Plan**

2. What external factors influence Jasmine to make unhealthy food choices?
3. What internal factors influence Jasmine to make unhealthy food choices?
4. Create a healthy eating plan that Jasmine could follow to avoid gaining more weight.

➤ **What Did You Learn?**

5. What factors influence your food choices? Do you think the factors are positive or negative influences?

Applying Health Skills:

1. Jasmine eats a lot of high-fat foods and is overweight, which is causing her stress. She wishes she could make wiser food choices.

2. External factors include food ads on TV and going to fast food restaurants with friends.

3. Internal factors include a personal preference for fatty foods and eating high-fat foods to relax when she feels stressed out.

4. Answers will vary but should reflect the healthy eating guidelines presented in the chapter.

5. Answers will vary.

Most people who are underweight have simply been too busy to eat enough to gain or maintain weight. In this case:

- Plan ahead what to eat at your mealtimes and snack times.
- Plan time for eating each meal. If you fill up fast, eat the highest-calorie items first. Don't start with soup or salad. Eat meaty appetizers or the main course first.

Most underweight people usually eat small quantities of food. When they begin eating significantly more food, they may feel too full. This feeling is normal, and it passes when the stomach adapts.

For the person who tends to be underweight, maintenance of the new weight is a final challenge. The weight-maintenance methods described on page 219 for the person who tends to gain weight work equally well in this case.

Worksheets: A reproducible quiz for Section 6 is provided in the Teacher Classroom Resources.

SECTION 6 Review

Reviewing the Vocabulary

Review the vocabulary on page 222. Then answer these questions.

1. Define *bulimia*.

2. _____ is repeated binge eating, but not followed by vomiting.

3. A disorder of self-starvation to the extreme is called _____.

Reviewing the Facts

4. Describe. What is the healthiest way to gain weight?

5. Explain. How many extra calories of nutritious food must be added daily to gain 1 to 1 $\frac{1}{2}$ pounds per week if activity levels stay the same?

6. List. Give three recommendations for increasing calorie intake.

Writing Critically

7. Personal. Have you or anyone you know ever had difficulty gaining weight? Explain some of the frustrations involved. How are these problems similar to those of a person who is trying to lose weight? How are they different?

For more vocabulary practice, play the eFlashcards game at **glencoe.com.**

1. Repeated binge eating, usually followed by vomiting
2. Binge eating disorder (BED)
3. Anorexia nervosa
4. Increased calorie intake and physical activity to build lean body mass
5. 700 to 800 extra calories
6. Eat more often, eat slightly larger portions, plan time for eating each meal.
7. Answers will vary.

Eating Disorders

 Understand and Apply Read the conversation below, and then complete the writing exercise that follows.

Many magazines, newspapers, and television screens often display camera-ready women, flaws hidden, and dangerously thin. Acceptance of such unreasonable standards has driven many young women in our society to be obsessed with thinness.

Q: I thought being thin was healthy. Isn't it OK to want to be thin?

A: Being fit is healthy. Being thin may not be. Wanting a healthy body weight is safe and wise. The extreme desire for thinness is linked with three eating disorders: **anorexia nervosa**, *a disorder of self-starvation to the extreme*; **bulimia**, *repeated binge eating usually followed by vomiting*; and **binge eating disorder** (BED), *repeated binge eating, but not followed by vomiting*. Eating disorders are classified as mental illnesses.

Q: What happens to someone who has anorexia nervosa?

A: The story of Julie is typical. Julie is 18 years old. She is a high achiever in school and a fine dancer. She watches her diet with great care, and she exercises and practices ballet daily. She is thin, but she is not satisfied with her weight and is determined to lose more. She is 5 feet 6 inches tall and weighs 85 pounds, but she's still trying to get thinner.

Q: How could she possibly think she's too fat, weighing only 85 pounds?

A: Her self-image is false. When given a self-image test, she drew a picture of herself that was grossly oversized. When asked to draw her best friend, Julie drew a fair likeness.

Q: How can someone get so thin and continue to diet?

A: Julie controls her food intake with great discipline even though she is starving. If she feels that she has slipped and eaten too much, she runs or exercises until she is sure she has burned the excess calories. Her fierce self-control, not lack of hunger, prevents her from eating.

Q: What is happening to her physically, and how serious is this condition?

A: Julie is suffering the physical effects of starvation in all of her body's organs. Her hormone output has become abnormal. Her blood pressure has dropped. Her heart pumps inefficiently. Its muscle has become weak, thin, and small in size. Her heart's rhythms have changed, with a characteristic abnormality appearing on the heart monitor. Sudden stopping of the heart, due to lean tissue loss or mineral deficiencies, causes many sudden deaths among victims of anorexia nervosa.

Q: What happens to someone with bulimia?

A: The case of Sophie is typical of the person with bulimia. Sophie is female, single, in her early twenties, well educated, and close to her ideal body weight. Sophie is a charming, intelligent woman who thinks constantly about food. She sometimes starves herself, and sometimes she engages in **binge eating**, *overeating to an extreme degree*. When she has eaten too much, she makes herself vomit.

Q: If bulimia involves binge eating, why is there also a condition called binge eating disorder?

A: Binge eating disorder (BED) has only recently been identified and named, although people have always suffered its effects. People with BED secretly and destructively binge, just as people with bulimia do, but they do not vomit. Over the years, this behavior leads to severe overweight, a condition that brings many of them to the doorstep of a health professional. People with BED suffer all of the physical and emotional ills of obesity, as described in the chapter, and the guilt and shame of those with bulimia too. The circumstances leading to BED are thought to be the same as those that cause bulimia.

Q. What are the physical effects of bulimia?

A: Swollen hands and feet, bloating, fatigue, headache, nausea, and pain are common. More serious are fluid and electrolyte imbalances caused by vomiting, abnormal heartbeat, and injury to the kidneys. Vomiting causes irritation and infection of the throat, esophagus, and salivary glands; erosion of the teeth; and dental caries (cavities). The esophagus may rupture or tear, as may the stomach. The eyes become red from the pressure of vomiting.

Q: Can a person with anorexia or bulimia be cured?

A: Eating disorders are serious and dangerous illnesses. People with these disorders need help to overcome them. Medical help may involve counseling and nutritional guidance.

Q: What can be done about this situation?

A: One school of thought labels eating disorders as social problems. Perhaps they begin when young people develop low self-esteem and adopt the ideal of some false, "perfect" image as portrayed in the media.

Slowly, society is changing. Women are finding honor and esteem in such traditionally male fields as athletics, science, law, and politics. This has raised all women's self-esteem. Perhaps anorexia nervosa, bulimia, and binge eating disorders will disappear as human roles and ideals change. Prevention may be possible if, early in children's lives, they are nurtured to respect themselves. The best treatments often involve the whole family. The simple concept—to respect and value your own uniqueness—may be lifesaving for a future generation.

 Writing Write a dialogue between two teens. One teen has not been eating and has been losing weight rapidly. The other teen is concerned. Dialogues should reflect how friends can encourage and support someone who has a disorder.

Reviewing Vocabulary

Use the vocabulary terms listed below to complete the following statements.

stress eating

anorexia nervosa

bulimia

1. _____ is eating in response to stress.
2. Repeated binge eating usually followed by vomiting is called _____.
3. _____ is an emotional disorder that results in self-starvation to the extreme.

Recalling Key Facts and Ideas

Section 1
4. **Recall.** Why is it dangerous to have too little body fat?

Section 2
5. **Analyze.** What components make up the sum total of your body weight?
6. **Explain.** Explain why body weight by itself is not an indicator of body fatness.

Section 3
7. **Synthesize.** What happens when a person consumes 3,500 calories more than she spends?
8. **Identify.** What are some examples of basal processes that support life?
9. **Explain.** Why does a 200-pound person expend more energy than a 100-pound person does, doing the same activity with equal effort?

10. **Analyze.** How can you increase your basal energy output over the long term?

Section 4
11. **Explain.** Why is the use of a diuretic considered a dangerous weight-loss method?
12. **Synthesize.** What happens to the excess carbohydrates, fats, and protein a person consumes?
13. **Describe.** In order to lose weight safely and permanently, what must a person lose? What must the person retain?
14. **Analyze.** Why is fasting a dangerous way to lose weight?
15. **Identify.** Identify three dangerous and three sound weight-loss strategies.

Section 5
16. **Analyze.** How is physical activity helpful in weight loss?

Section 6
17. **Identify.** Give two recommendations for a successful and healthy weight-gain program.
18. **Explain.** What are two common behaviors of a person with anorexia nervosa?

Writing Critically

19. **Expository.** Review the Q&A section about eating disorders, and answer the following questions: If you were Julie's friend, what would you say to her about her pattern? What do you feel could have been done to prevent Sophie's bulimic behavior? Why do you think the incidence of eating disorders in our country is steadily increasing?

1. Stress eating **2.** Bulimia **3.** Anorexia nervosa **4.** The body may not be getting enough nutrients. **5.** Bones, muscles, fat, fluids, and other tissues. **6.** Someone with strong muscles and bones may seem heavier, but have little fat; Someone can have a high amount of fat, but not weigh as much. **7.** She will store one pound of body fat. **8.** Beating of the heart, inhaling and exhaling air **9.** The more a person weighs, the more energy it takes to do an activity. **10.** Physical activity builds muscle,

20. **Personal.** Take a close look at your own personal program of eating and physical activity. List four positive and four negative eating habits you have. List four positive and four negative physical activity habits you have. Use MyPyramid as your guide.

Activities

21. Watch television for one hour before dinner. List all the food products that you see advertised during that time. Discuss the possible reasons for airing these commercials at that time.

22. Find three advertisements that seem to encourage teens to be thin. Analyze the techniques used in advertising the products that encourage thinness.

23. Work together as a class to develop a survey on dieting and its problems. First, work in small groups to brainstorm questions to be used on the questionnaire for the survey. Then compile a list of all the questions generated by the groups and, as a class, vote on the questions to be used on the questionnaire. Survey 20 females and 20 males. Make sure the questionnaires are filled out anonymously. Ensure those filling out the questionnaires that their privacy will be protected. Work together as a class to compile the data from the questionnaires. Then try to draw conclusions from the results.

Making Decisions about Health

24. Your friend gets up on a Monday morning determined to start a weight-loss diet. She skips breakfast, and for lunch she has a modest, healthful meal of soup and salad. By mid-afternoon she is famished, but holds off, exerting her strongest will power. At dinner, the smell of food being served is overwhelming. She eats much more than she had intended, and later that evening, still hungry, she indulges in a sweet dessert.

- What errors in planning did your friend make?

- What could she have done to make it easier to practice moderation at dinnertime?

- Describe a more effective meal-planning strategy to help her lose weight.

 **Go Online**

For more vocabulary practice, play the True/False game at **glencoe.com**.

 Fact or Fiction?

Answers

1. True.
2. False. Weight loss may reflect loss of water or lean tissue rather than loss of fat.
3. False. It is as hard for a person who tends to be thin to gain a pound as it is for a person who tends to be fat to lose one.

Writing Answers will vary.

which uses more calories to maintain. **11.** Dehydrates the body **12.** Stored in the body mostly as body fat **13.** Lose body fat; Retain lean muscle tissues. **14.** Energy comes from protein in lean muscle tissues. **15.** Fad diets, fasting, diet pills; eating healthy, exercising, behavior modification **16.** Uses energy; helps burn body fat **17.** Use MyPyramid; do not skip meals. **18.** Undereating; overexercising **19–24.** Answers will vary.

Chapter 8　Review　**229**

CHAPTER 9

Fitness

If you are physically fit, you move with ease and balance. You are strong. You have a healthy body weight and body composition with enough, but not too much, body fat. You have endurance; your energy lasts for hours. You meet normal physical challenges without strain and have energy left over to handle emergencies.

In addition, you are able to meet mental and emotional challenges. Physical fitness supports not only physical work but also mental and emotional endurance. Your confidence is high in all areas of life: social, academic, work, and athletic.

Fitness can be gained through practice. Activities that help you gain fitness are themselves enjoyable, and they quickly lead to improvement.

Fact or Fiction?

What Do You Think?

Is each statement true or false? If you think it's false, explain what's true.

1. When performing stretching exercises, you should feel tightness but no pain.
2. If you feel minor pain in your feet or legs while running, it is best to keep going and try to work through it.
3. You should not stop physical activity to satisfy your thirst.

 Writing Think about the physical activities you enjoy. In what ways have your friends or others influenced you to try a sport or activity? Describe an activity someone has influenced you to try.

(Answers on page 263)

G Online

Visit **glencoe.com** and complete the Life Choice Inventory for Chapter 9.

SECTION 1

Benefits of Fitness

Fitness is the reward of a person who leads a physically active life. The opposite of such a life is a **sedentary** life, which means *physically inactive*. Today's world, full of modern conveniences, enables many people to lead sedentary lives. Elevators, cars, automatic garage openers, remote controls, even moving sidewalks at airports and malls reduce our chances to be physically active.

How Are Americans Doing?

MAIN IDEA ▶ Fitness enables the body to perform at its peak, to meet routine physical demands, to meet sudden challenges, and to withstand stress.

Children, teens, and adults need physical activity to stay healthy. Physical activity reduces the risk of diseases such as obesity and heart disease. It can also help reduce the risk of joint problems later in life. Unfortunately, more than half of the adults in the United States are not active on a regular basis, and 25 percent are completely inactive. Young people (6 to 19 years of age) need at least 60 minutes of physical activity on most days to stay healthy. Surveys show that only about one-third of high school students meet this need.

Vocabulary

sedentary
fitness

Figure 9.1 — Benefits of Physical Activity

Regular physical activity helps protect against these conditions:

Physical

- Acne
- Backaches
- Cancer (colon cancer, breast cancer, and others)
- Diabetes
- Digestive disorders (ulcers, constipation, diarrhea, and others)
- Headaches
- Heart and blood vessel disease (heart attacks and stroke)
- High blood cholesterol and triglycerides, high blood pressure
- Infections (colds, flu, and many others)
- Insomnia (sleep disorders)
- Kidney disease
- Menstrual irregularities, menstrual cramps, and mood swings associated with the menstrual cycle
- Obesity
- Osteoporosis (adult bone loss)

Psychological

- Physically active people experience less anxiety and depression than do sedentary people.
- Fit people deal better with emotionally stressful events than do sedentary people.
- Depressed people who adopt a routine of regular running become as well and stay as well as others who obtain psychotherapy.

Figure 9.2 — Fitness Contributes to All Aspects of Health and Wellness

Physical Fitness

- Makes physical activity easy to perform
- Promotes rest, relaxation, sleep, and healing
- Aids weight control
- Contributes to nutritional health
- Enhances disease resistance (see **Figure 9.1**)
- Strengthens accident resistance

Mental/Emotional & Spiritual Fitness

- Strengthens resistance to depression and anxiety
- Strengthens defenses against stress
- Allows freedom from drug abuse
- Enhances self-esteem
- Enhances ability to learn
- Raises self-confidence
- Instills joy in life
- Inspires courage to face challenges

Social Fitness

- Provides social opportunities
- Enhances intimate relationships
- Strengthens family ties
- Opens the way for social support
- Encourages citizenship
- Enhances energy for productive work

Everyone's capacity to become physically fit differs. Whoever you are, though, you have the ability to improve. This is an important concept in fitness: strive to achieve improvements based on your current fitness level and potential. Do not compare yourself with others or with written sets of standards. Your first goal should be to develop and maintain fitness to support your health. Once you develop a plan, you can set higher goals to challenge and motivate you.

The term **fitness** means *the characteristics of the body that enable it to perform physical activity*. These characteristics include the flexibility of your joints; the strength and endurance of your muscles, including your heart muscle; and a healthy body composition. Add to that definition *the ability to meet routine physical demands, with enough reserve energy to rise to sudden challenges*. This shows even better how fitness relates to everyday life. Ordinary tasks such as carrying heavy suitcases, opening a window, or climbing stairs might strain an unfit person. However, such tasks are easy for one who is fit. Add still one more detail to the definition of fitness: *the body's ability to withstand stress*, including psychological stresses. You can achieve all of these characteristics through regular physical activity.

Physical activity does not simply mean "working out." It includes all kind of activities that you do on a daily basis, such as walking to school, cleaning your room, or playing sports with friends. There are many ways you can incorporate physical activity into your life and enjoy its benefits to your health.

Preview Activity

Discuss: Have students form small groups. Give each group a marker and poster paper. Ask the groups to list the characteristics of a physically fit person and a sedentary person. Compare and discuss the two lists. Ask students to think about the health benefits of being physically fit.

Figure 9.1 on page 232 shows that physical activity helps defend against physical disorders and also helps promote psychological well-being. A fit person benefits in all areas of life (see **Figure 9.2** on the previous page). The most obvious of the benefits are the physical ones. Someone who is physically active, who sleeps soundly, and who eats a healthy diet is one who has every chance to be physically and mentally healthy. Those who are fit feel good.

SECTION 1 Review

Reviewing the Vocabulary
Review the vocabulary on page 232. Then answer these questions.
1. _____ enables the body to perform physical activities.
2. A person who is basically inactive is considered _____.

Reviewing the Facts
3. **Describe.** Describe a physically fit person.
4. **List.** List four benefits of physical activity.

Writing Critically
5. **Expository.** Explain what you think has caused the interest in fitness in our country. What do people have to gain by becoming more physically active?

For more vocabulary practice, play the eFlashcards game at **glencoe.com**.

The Path to Fitness: Conditioning

The path to fitness is physical conditioning, which you can achieve through regular practice or training. **Conditioning** is *the hundreds of small changes that cells make in response to physical activity that make the body more able to do work.*

Even routine daily activities can help condition the body. Small choices you make each day can either add to your fitness or take away from it. The person who chooses to walk upstairs gains more fitness rather than one who rides an elevator, for example. Parking the car a mile from your destination, or getting off the bus several stops early and walking the rest of the way, are both fitness-promoting strategies.

Components of Fitness

MAIN IDEA ▶ The components of fitness are cardiovascular endurance, flexibility, muscle strength, muscle endurance, and body composition.

Five elements of health-related fitness affect your body in different ways. As you become physically fit, you improve the health of your entire body:

- **Cardiovascular endurance** is *the ability of the heart and lungs to sustain effort over a long time.* By maintaining good cardiovascular health, you can run or play sports without tiring.

- **Flexibility** is *the ability to bend joints without injury.* It allows you to touch your toes, or scratch your back. Flexibility can improve your athletic performance and reduce your risk of muscle strain and other injuries.

- **Muscle strength** is *the ability of muscles to work against resistance.* Muscle strength is important for tasks such as lifting, pushing, or jumping.

- **Muscle endurance** is *the ability of muscles to sustain an effort for a long time.* It gives you the power to carry out daily tasks without tiring, such as carrying boxes up and down a flight of stairs.

- **Body composition** is *the proportion of lean tissue as compared with fat tissue in the body.* Having low overall body fat reduces the risk of cardiovascular disease and other diseases associated with being overweight.

Vocabulary

conditioning
cardiovascular endurance
flexibility
muscle strength
muscle endurance
body composition
exercise physiology
overload
progressive overload
   principle
frequency
intensity
duration

Preview Activity
Apply. Ask students keep a diary listing their physical activities for one week. Have them label their activities according to the four components of fitness. Ask students to name examples of the types of exercises needed to each component of fitness.

 **Did You Know?**

Before beginning any fitness program, you should consult a physician.

The only way to get a completely accurate measure of your own fitness is by visiting an exercise physiology laboratory and having measurements taken by a professional. **Exercise physiology** is *the study of how the body works and changes in response to exercise*. However, you can get an estimate of how physically active you are by answering the questions in the Life Choice Inventory for Chapter 9 at **glencoe.com**.

Before starting any activity or fitness evaluation, make sure it is safe for you to undertake a physical activity program. Ordinary physical activity is not hazardous to any healthy person. However, a fitness professional can make sure you start your program at a level high enough to bring about the desired changes, but not so high as to be dangerous.

If, during activity, you become uncomfortable, have trouble breathing, or feel any pain, stop the activity. Consult your health care provider before continuing.

The Overload Principle

MAIN IDEA ► Overload can be used to improve fitness by increasing an activity's frequency, intensity, or duration.

Every day your body works. The stronger and more fit you are, the less you must strain to do that work. **Overload** is *an extra physical demand placed on the body*. Your body responds to overload in a positive way. It gets itself into better shape to meet the extra demand next time.

You can apply overload by using the progressive overload principle in several different ways. The **progressive overload principle** is *the training principle that a body system, in order to improve, must be worked at frequencies, intensities, or durations that increase over time*. You can choose to increase the activity's **frequency**, *the number of activity units per unit of time*. For example, if you enjoy running two days per week, you can increase the number of days per week to three.

You can increase the activity's **intensity**, *the degree of exertion during physical activity*. If you usually run one mile in 8 minutes, you can choose to increase the intensity by running faster, say one mile in 7½ minutes. You can also increase the activity's **duration**, *the length of time spent in each session of physical activity*. If you typically run for 20 minutes, you can increase the duration of your run to 30 minutes.

All three strategies work well, either individually or in any combination. If you enjoy a certain physical activity, do those activities more often. If pressed for time, shorten your workout time, but increase its intensity. Or you can take it easy and work out longer.

Progress Slowly

To safely increase the frequency, intensity, or duration of your activity, work to a point that is only *slightly* beyond what is comfortable. Physical activity should not be painful.

Pain won't help anyone gain fitness, but sustained effort will. A worthwhile goal is to develop a fitness program that you can stick with, year in and year out.

Pushing your body a little beyond its normal level of demand releases hormones that stimulate muscle and bone growth. It also remodels and strengthens the muscles and bones so that next time, the body will meet the more vigorous challenge more easily.

Proceed with Caution

The following tips will also help you when applying the principles of overload:

- Use proper equipment and attire.
- Aim for 60 minutes of physical activity per day.

Goal Setting

➤ Objectives

- Implement strategies and monitor progress in achieving a personal health goal.
- Show how to use the progressive overload principle to reach a fitness goal.

Getting Up to Speed

Rachel wants to go out for the high school cross-country team in the fall. On the first day of summer vacation, she went running with her friend Kiana, who was on the cross-country team last year. Rachel could run only a mile, and it took her nine minutes. Kiana told her that cross-country races cover three miles and the top three runners usually average about seven minutes per mile.

Rachel thinks that she might do well in cross-country because she was a good runner when she was younger. She'd like to finish in the top three at cross-country meets in the fall. That means she has a lot of work to do in the remaining two months of summer vacation. Rachel hopes to get up to speed by September, but she doesn't know how. She needs a plan for reaching her goal.

➤ Identify the Problem

1. What is Rachel's goal? Be specific.

➤ Form an Action Plan

2. How can Rachel use the progressive overload principle to condition for cross-country?
3. Describe how Rachel could set weekly objectives that would help her reach her goal. Objectives should include both distance and speed.
4. How could Rachel check her progress toward her goal?

➤ What Did You Learn?

5. Describe a physical fitness goal you would like to reach. How could you use the progressive overload principle to reach your goal?

Applying Health Skills:

1. Rachel wants to be able to run three miles at an average speed of seven minutes per mile.

2. Over the next two months, Rachel can gradually increase the distance and speed that she runs.

3. Beginning at her current distance and speed of one mile in 9 minutes, Rachel could add ¼ mile to her distance and cut ½ minute per mile from her speed each week.

4. She could run ¼ mile farther each week and check her speed to see if it is ½ minute per mile less than the week before.

5. Answers will vary.

- Listen to your body and if any movement hurts, stop the activity.

- Perform approved activities with proper form.

Strive for balance in your program. Include activities of different kinds to develop all the components of fitness.

Principles of Warm-Up and Cool-Down

MAIN IDEA ▶ Warm-up activities prepare the body for physical activity. Cool-down activities help muscles to relax.

To prepare your body for physical activity and to reduce the risk of injuries, remember to include a warm-up activity before your workout and a cool-down activity afterward. Warm-up activities trigger the release of fuels the body needs for physical work. They also send extra blood through the tissues, warming them and prepare the muscles and connective tissues, so that they will stretch without tearing.

To warm up, take a brisk walk, go for a light jog, or do some easy cycling or other gentle movement, followed by a stretching routine. Another way to warm up is to do a light version of the activity you plan to do intensively later.

> "*Beauty is only skin deep. I think what is really important is finding a balance of mind, body, and spirit.*"
>
> —Jennifer Lopez
> (1969–)
> Actress and musician

Comprehension Check
Comprehend: Have students break up into small groups. Have each group choose a sport or physical activity such as cycling, running, or swimming. Encourage the groups to research warm-up and cool-down activities that would be appropriate for each sport. Have students present their activities to the rest of the class.

A runner may start out walking, break into a jog, and finally, pick up the pace to an outright run. A person who body-builds may start with light weight repetitions. This strategy is thought to best prepare the muscle groups that will be needed to perform the task ahead.

After activity, the body also needs to cool down. A few minutes of light activity after a workout helps relax tight muscles and allows blood to circulate freely, cooling the body. This is also a good time to stretch the muscles. Stretching may help to prevent muscle cramps and soreness that might otherwise occur. Cool-down activities can also help to prevent symptoms—dizziness, for example—that people sometimes feel when they suddenly stop activity.

SECTION 2 Review

Reviewing the Vocabulary

Review the vocabulary on page 235. Then answer these questions.

1. What is the difference between *muscle strength* and *muscle endurance*?

2. _____ is the ability of the heart and lungs to sustain effort over a long time.

3. The _____ states that to improve fitness, one must increase the _____, _____, or _____ of an activity over time.

Reviewing the Facts

4. **List.** What are the five components of fitness?

5. **Explain.** Give some pointers about applying overload in a fitness program.

6. **Analyze.** What is the purpose of warming up before you begin an activity?

Writing Critically

7. **Descriptive.** Think about what physical activities you do during your day. Do you feel your level of activity is good for your overall health? Discuss any changes you feel need to be made in your physical activity level.

For more information on health careers, visit Career Corner at **glencoe.com**.

Gaining Cardiovascular Endurance

Physical activities such as distance running, cycling, or rowing build cardiovascular endurance. These activities increase your heart rate and pump more blood throughout the body. Over time, the heart and lungs adjust to meet the demands made by these activities. The heart and lungs become healthier and work more efficiently.

Aerobic Activity

MAIN IDEA ▶ Cardiovascular training is aerobic and demands oxygen.

The word **aerobic** (air-ROE-bic) refers to *energy-producing processes that use oxygen.* Cardiovascular training, or aerobic activity, demands that the heart and lungs work harder to deliver oxygen to the muscles for as long as the activity lasts. This, in turn, makes the heart and lungs stronger. Not all physical activities, however, are aerobic. The word **anaerobic** refers to *energy-producing processes that do not use oxygen.* Short-term, intense activities such as weight lifting tend to be anaerobic.

Vocabulary
aerobic
anaerobic
pulse rate
target heart rate

■ **Figure 9.6** *Split-second surges of power involve anaerobic work. What is an example of anaerobic activity?*

Caption Answer: An athlete sprinting as fast as he can.

■ **Figure 9.7** *Sustained muscular efforts involve aerobic work. What is an example of aerobic work?*

Caption Answer: A runner who runs at the same pace for a few miles.

Aerobic vs. Anaerobic Work

A way to think of the difference between the two types of activity is to imagine two athletes. The first is a distance runner on an endless stretch of beach. The runner strides steadily across miles of sand. Now imagine you're watching a track meet. A sprinter bursts across the starting line in an explosion of energy. The burst lasts only a few seconds, followed by exhaustion at the finish line.

The distance runner is performing aerobic work, the kind of activity that requires endurance. The ability to continue swimming until you reach the far bank, to continue hiking until you are at camp, or to continue pedalling until you are home reflects aerobic fitness.

The sprinter is performing mostly anaerobic work, which requires strength, agility, and surges of power. The jump of the basketball player, the slam of the tennis serve, and hitting a baseball are all anaerobic work.

Aerobic Work Brings Cardiovascular Benefits

At the start of this chapter, **Figures 9.1** and **9.2** listed some of the health benefits of physical activity. All of the benefits listed there can be credited to cardiovascular fitness. Some of the benefits, such as sound sleep, lean body composition, and improved self-image can also be gained by way of flexibility and strength training. Cardiovascular training promotes all of them, however.

A poorly conditioned cardiovascular system limits a person's ability to perform daily activities even more than a lack of flexibility or muscle strength does. For this reason, cardiovascular endurance is the part of fitness most important to health and life.

Cardiovascular Endurance Training

MAIN IDEA ▶ Cardiovascular endurance increases the heart's size and strength, and makes breathing more efficient.

With cardiovascular endurance training, the blood increases in volume and can carry more oxygen. The heart muscle gains size and strength. The larger, stronger heart pumps more blood with each beat, so fewer beats are necessary to support a given task. The *number of heartbeats per minute*, or **pulse rate**, slows. The muscles that work the lungs gain strength and endurance, and breathing becomes more efficient. Blood moves easily through the body's arteries and veins, and the blood pressure falls. Muscles throughout the body become firmer. **Figure 9.8** shows how the heart, cardiovascular system, and lungs to deliver oxygen to the tissues and carry away the waste product carbon dioxide.

Teacher Support
Explain: **Figure 9.8** shows how the cardiovascular system delivers oxygen to the muscles. Tell students that the person with more fit muscles extracts more oxygen from the inhaled air. The cardiovascular system responds to the demand for oxygen by building up its capacity to deliver oxygen.

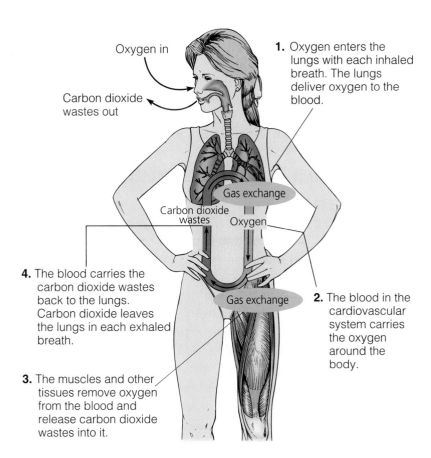

Oxygen in

Carbon dioxide wastes out

1. Oxygen enters the lungs with each inhaled breath. The lungs deliver oxygen to the blood.

Gas exchange

Carbon dioxide wastes   Oxygen

Gas exchange

4. The blood carries the carbon dioxide wastes back to the lungs. Carbon dioxide leaves the lungs in each exhaled breath.

3. The muscles and other tissues remove oxygen from the blood and release carbon dioxide wastes into it.

2. The blood in the cardiovascular system carries the oxygen around the body.

Figure 9.8

Delivery of Oxygen by the Heart and Lungs to the Muscles

The more fit a muscle is, the more oxygen it draws from the blood.

Figure 9.9

How to Take Your Pulse

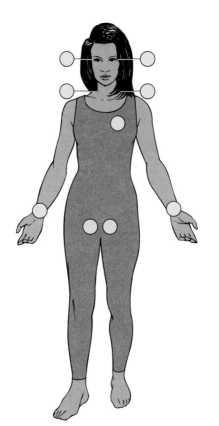

- Use a watch or clock with a second hand. Rest a few minutes to get an accurate measure of your pulse at rest. Place your hand over your heart or your finger firmly over an artery in any pulse location (shown by the yellow circles) that gives a clear rhythm. Start counting your pulse at a convenient second, and continue counting for ten seconds. If a heartbeat occurs exactly on the tenth second, count it as one-half beat. Multiply by 6 to obtain the beats per minute.
- Use only fingers, not your thumb, on the pulse point (the thumb has a pulse of its own).
- Press just firmly enough to feel the pulse. Too much pressure can interfere with the pulse rhythm.

Class Activity

Discuss: Have students write a paragraph describing the life of someone who is fit. Students should also describe a normal day's activities for that person. Ask students to describe the typical day of someone with no cardiovascular endurance. For the last paragraph, have students compare the two lives. Invite students to share their paragraphs. Discuss with students how cardiovascular endurance improves health and quality of life.

A slow resting pulse rate means the cardiovascular system is healthy. The average resting pulse rate for teens and young adults is around 70 beats per minute. However, the rate can be higher or lower. Active people can have resting pulse rates of 50 or even lower. Instructions for taking your pulse are given in **Figure 9.9**.

To improve your pulse rate, do any aerobic activity on most days of the week. A guideline for those who wish to gain fitness is to walk, jog, or run for 20 minutes or more at a rate at which you can talk but not sing. If you are unable to talk, you should slow down. If you can sing, you should speed up.

Activities for Cardiovascular Endurance

MAIN IDEA ▶ Activities that promote cardiovascular endurance raise the heart rate.

To improve cardiovascular endurance, you must work up to a point where you can perform aerobic activity for 20 minutes or more at a session. This means you must raise your heart rate (pulse) for that long. You should increase your heart rate to a level that is quite a bit faster than its resting rate. Athletes call this the **target heart rate**, *the heartbeat rate that will condition a person's cardiovascular system—fast enough to push the heart, but not so fast as to strain it.* You can calculate yours from your age.

To calculate your target heart rate, first subtract your age from 220. The resulting number is close to the absolute *maximum heart rate* for a person your age. You should never exercise at this rate. A rate of about 60 to 85 percent of your maximum heart rate is enough to gain cardiovascular fitness. An intensity below or above this range will either fail to provide benefits or may strain the heart. **Figure 9.10** demonstrates how to find your target range.

When you first work out within your target heart rate range, you may find that even mild activity will push your heart to the target rate. As your cardiovascular fitness improves, you will have to work harder to push your heart to beat this fast. When you can work out at the target heart rate for 20 to 60 minutes, you have arrived at your fitness goal.

Which Activities?

You can develop cardiovascular fitness only if you choose aerobic activity. This activity must:

- Be steady and constant.
- Use large muscle groups, such as legs, buttocks, and abdomen.
- Be uninterrupted and last for more than 20 minutes.

The activities listed in the Teens' Activity Pyramid (**Figure 9.11**) on page 246, all fit this description.

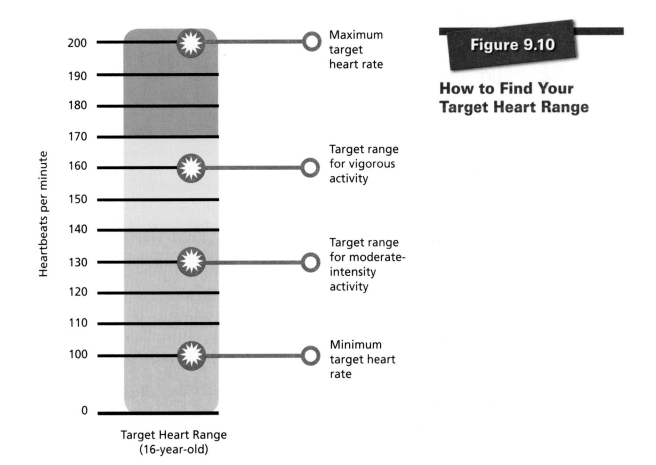

Figure 9.10

How to Find Your Target Heart Range

Heartbeats per minute

200 — Maximum target heart rate
190
180
170
160 — Target range for vigorous activity
150
140
130 — Target range for moderate-intensity activity
120
110
100 — Minimum target heart rate
0

Target Heart Range
(16-year-old)

Figure 9.11

Teens' Activity Pyramid

Set Limits on These
- TV
- Video games
- Watching movies
- Sitting still doing nothing
- Lying down

3–4 Times per Week

Fun Activities
- Baseball, tennis, other sports
- Canoeing, hiking, biking, skating
- Dancing, swimming

Workout Activities
Work on these:
- Cardiovascular endurance
- Flexibility
- Strength

Each Day

Household Chores
- Clean
- Sweep
- Rake
- Mow
- Dig
- Scrub
- Wash car
- Trim

Choosing to Be Active
- Use stairs
- Walk
- Bike
- Join a fitness club
- Stretch often
- Take a fitness class
- Play with children
- Make friends with others who exercise

Class Activity

Evaluate:

Ask students to interview people of different ages who are currently involved in a fitness program. Some questions may include:

- What kind of physical activity do you do?
- How does the program fit with your lifestyle and schedule?
- What motivates you to stick with the fitness program?

Have students analyze the information they collect and draw conclusions about the people who try to remain active.

Walking

Walking is a good physical activity. Strolling along at a pace of 1 or 2 miles per hour might help you to warm up. Striding along at 3.5 to 5 miles per hour, however, will provide a workout for your heart. Walking causes few injuries since its impact on the joint is low.

Running

The challenge, simplicity, freedom, and mental and physical well-being that come with running keep many people running. However, running injuries are common.

A runner hits the ground with a force of about two to three times the weight of the body, hundreds of times per mile. Appropriate running shoes stabilize the feet and cushion the enormous impact of each stride. Most injuries in running result from pushing too hard and too fast, trying to get fit too quickly. To begin a program, start slowly.

Swimming and Cycling

Swimming and cycling strengthen the heart and are almost stress-free for joints and connective tissues. Swimming not only develops cardiovascular endurance, but also develops strength and endurance in the upper body. Cycling develops the lower body while it improves cardiovascular endurance. It also promotes lean body composition. The two activities complement each other in conditioning programs.

Tracking Your Progress

One of the rewards of committing to a regular fitness program is seeing your level of fitness increase over time. You may begin to notice that it takes less time to walk to school, or you may not breathe as hard after climbing stairs.

A fitness journal can help you track your progress. List all of your activities, the length of time you engage in physical activity, how often, and at what level. You should see a noticeable difference if you stick with your fitness program for twelve weeks. Seeing your progress on paper will motivate you to stick to your fitness goals.

SECTION 3 Review

Reviewing the Vocabulary

Review the vocabulary on page 241. Then answer these questions.

1. Your _____ is the number of times your heart beats per minute.

2. Your _____ is fast enough to push the heart, but not so fast as to strain it.

3. What is the difference between *aerobic* and *anaerobic* activity?

4. Write a sentence using each vocabulary term.

Reviewing the Facts

5. Name. Name two aerobic and two anaerobic activities.

6. List. List three effects of cardiovascular endurance training.

7. Identify. Identify three characteristics of activities that promote cardiovascular fitness.

Writing Critically

8. Narrative. Write a letter to yourself from the point of view of your heart. Explain in the letter why it is important to incorporate cardiovascular activities into your life and why it is important to your overall health.

Go Online

For more vocabulary practice, play the True/False game at **glencoe.com**.

1. Pulse rate

2. Target heart rate

3. Aerobic activity uses oxygen and anaerobic activity does not use oxygen.

4. Answers will vary.

5. Aerobic: running and swimming; Anaerobic: sprinting, weight lifting

6. The heart gains size and strength, it requires fewer beats to support tasks, breathing is more efficient.

7. They raise the heart rate, are sustained for 20 minutes or more, and are performed most days of the week.

8. Answers will vary.

Gaining Flexibility

Flexibility allows people to bend and move easily without pain. It reduces the risk of accidents such as falls, and helps prevent lower back pain and injuries to the muscles and joints. Flexibility depends on the elasticity of muscles. **Elasticity** is *the characteristic of a tissue's being easily stretched or bent and able to return to its original size and shape.* Flexibility also depends on **connective tissues**, *fluid, gelatin-like, fibrous, or strap-like materials that bind, support, or protect other body tissues*, and on the health of the joints.

Flexibility

MAIN IDEA ▶ Flexibility depends on the elasticity of the muscles, connective tissues, and the condition of the joints.

Each body joint has its own **range of motion**, *the mobility of a joint;* the direction and the extent to which it bends (see **Figure 9.12**). A joint's range of motion is determined by the shape of its bones, and the placement and condition of its connective tissues. For instance, the knees and elbows limit their movements to two directions. The shoulder joint, however, permits movements in many directions.

Stretching Techniques

Stretching improves flexibility. When you stretch, remember that your goal is to get limber, not to push your joints beyond their range of motion. Warm up first, and then choose easy stretches, and stretch only to the point where you feel tightness but not pain. As you hold the stretch, even the feeling of tightness should gradually ease. If the tightness does not ease, or the stretch becomes painful as you hold it, you are overstretching.

Vocabulary

elasticity
connective tissues
range of motion

Guest Speaker
Apply:
Ask a certified athletic trainer to show the class some stretching activities, and to discuss each activity and its importance. Ask the trainer to share updated information on any changes in traditional stretching activities.

Figure 9.12

Range of Motion of the Hip Joint

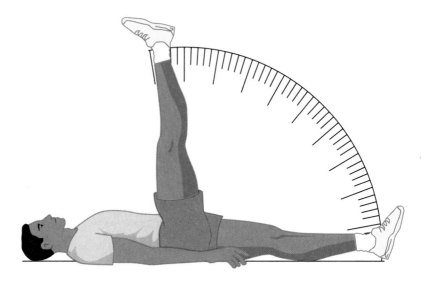

Figure 9.13 Recommended Stretches

Whole-body stretch

Neck stretches

Lower back stretch

Lower back stretches

Calf muscle stretch

Buttocks stretch

Hamstring stretch

Inner thigh stretch

Upper body stretches

Upper back and side stretch

Stretch in smooth motions—do not bounce. Bouncing can easily overstretch or tear a ligament until it can no longer support its joint, making the joint prone to injury. Nerves can overstretch painfully, as well. **Figure 9.13** lists some recommended stretches. **Figure 9.14** on page 250 lists some dangerous stretches.

Figure 9.14   Stretches and Exercises to Avoid

Type of Exercise	Reasons to Avoid
Unsupervised yoga	May cause many types of knee injury
Hurdler's stretch (sit with one leg bent under at the knee, reach for toe of outstretched leg)	May cause knee injury
Toe touching with straight knees	May overstretch tendons and damage major nerves and vertebrae
Deep knee bend; duckwalk (thighs touch heels)	May cause knee injury
Straight-leg lift (lie on back and lift both legs)	Aggravates lower back problems
Hyperextension of the back (arch the back and then let it sag, performed to extremes)	May injure lower back
Toe standing	May damage the foot arch
Straight-leg sit-up	Aggravates lower back problems
Ballet stretch (designed for dancers)	May cause many types of injuries

Worksheets: A reproducible quiz for Section 4 is provided in the Teacher Classroom Resources.

SECTION 4 Review

1. The mobility of a joint; the direction and the extent to which it bends

2. The characteristic of a tissue's being easily stretched or bent and able to return to its original size and shape

3. Fluid, gelatin-like, fibrous, or strap-like materials that bind, support, or protect other body tissues

4. Choose easy stretches, stretch only to the point of feeling tightness, stretch in smooth motions

5. Toe-touching with straight knees; hamstring stretch

6. Answers will vary.

Reviewing the Vocabulary

Review the vocabulary on page 248. Then answer these questions.

1. Define *range of motion*.
2. What is *elasticity*?
3. Define *connective tissues*.

Reviewing the Facts

4. **List.** Give three recommendations for safe stretching.
5. **Name.** Name one stretching exercise to avoid and one safe stretching exercise.

Writing Critically

6. **Expository.** Write a paragraph explaining why it is important to warm up and stretch before physical activity.

For more vocabulary practice, play the Concentration game at **glencoe.com**.

Gaining Muscle Strength and Endurance

Strength is the ability of the muscles to work against **resistance**, *the weight or other opposing force against which muscles must work*. Strong muscles, tendons, ligaments, and bones also best protect the body's internal organs from injury. Muscle endurance is closely related to strength. Muscle endurance is the ability of a muscle to hold a contraction for long periods of time or to contract repeatedly.

Strength Conditioning

MAIN IDEA ▶ Resistance exercises build muscle strength.

Weight training and callisthenics improve muscle strength and endurance. Gaining muscle tissue allows your body to burn energy faster and makes it easier to manage your body weight. **Weight training** is *an activity routine for strength conditioning that uses weights or machines to provide resistance against which the muscles can work*. Weight training can include working with equipment such as free weights and weight machines to provide resistance. **Callisthenics** are *exercise routines for strength conditioning that use the parts of the body as weights*. Callisthenics also provide resistance, and include exercises such as sit-ups, push-ups, and pull-ups.

Setting Goals

Weight training can be an ideal workout for both males and females, and it need not produce big, bulky muscles. Bodybuilders choose to build muscle and follow programs that are designed to do just that. To gain strength without bulk, you can use light weights and more repetitions.

Weight-Training Tips

To develop maximum strength from the smallest number of repetitions, exercise the muscle groups especially slowly. A group of ten repetitions of a particular activity should take about a minute. *A specific number of times to repeat a weight-training exercise* is called a **set**. Performing many sets with lighter weights will increase endurance. Doing fewer sets with heavier weights increases bulk and strength. **Figure 9.15** on the next page shows some examples of activities that build strength and endurance.

Vocabulary

resistance
weight training
callisthenics
set
steroids
human growth hormone
acromegaly

Guest Speaker
Apply.
Invite a certified trainer to visit your classroom or your school's weight room facility. Have the trainer demonstrate muscle strength and endurance routines and invite students to try them as well. Invite students to ask questions they may have about muscle strength and endurance.

Whether the goal is muscle strength, muscle endurance, or improved body composition, weight training every other day seems to produce the best results. However, rest is as important as work. Muscles use the time between workouts to repair small injuries, to replenish fuels, and to build strength for their next workout. Work different muscle groups each day. Give each muscle group a day of rest before working that group again.

Figure 9.15   **Muscle Strength and Endurance Routines**

Triceps extension

Bench press

Upright row

Biceps curl

Stomach crunches

Pull-ups

Pelvic tilt

Back push-ups

Modified back push-ups

Push-ups

Hamstring curl, method 1

Bent-leg lift

Inner thigh lift

Modified push-ups

Hamstring curl, method 2

Quadriceps lift, method 1

Quadriceps lift, method 2

Remember to breathe when you work with weights. Holding your breath puts pressure on the heart and lungs. Exhale as you raise or push the weight away. Inhale as you lower the weight. Also, raise and lower the weight smoothly using your full range of motion. Jerking it up or letting gravity pull it down fails to improve strength and can injure your joints.

Work Muscles Equally

Small muscles fatigue quickly. Therefore, work on strengthening the larger muscle groups first. Make sure to distribute the weight work equally over the arms and legs, using all muscles. Overdeveloped muscles in one part of the body that work in opposition to weak muscles can cause damage. For example, strong back muscles and weak stomach muscles can pull the back out of line, injuring the spine. An overdeveloped muscle that opposes a weak one can also interfere with movement.

Seek Expert Advice

Before starting any exercise program, seek guidance from an experienced, professional trainer who has a reputation for getting results safely. Weight training can cause injury. It's never advisable to work out using heavy weights when you are alone. Ask a friend to join you. Your workout will be safer and more enjoyable.

Consumer Skills Activity:

1. Products are often sold using false or exaggerated claims. It is best to ask a doctor what is needed.

2. They may want to build muscle and strength and are looking for a quick fix.

3. Many people are active and enjoy taking care of their bodies, so the sellers try to sell products to those types of people.

Consumer
SKILLS ACTIVITY

Nutritional Supplements

Most athletes and active people care about their health. They may turn to nutritional and dietary supplements in the hopes of enhancing their fitness programs. Products such as meal replacement bars, protein drinks, and vitamin supplements are readily available to consumers, but may not always work as advertised.

Advertisements for commercial products may claim to build muscles quickly, release special energy, or provide all necessary nutrients in one bar. Most such claims are false, however, or at least greatly exaggerated. Read the food label to learn the product's ingredients. Ask questions regarding the benefits and any effects the product may claim to produce. Discuss supplements with your health care provider, too. A physician can evaluate your needs and recommend any supplements that may be right for you.

 Writing

1. Taking pills and other supplements may seem like a scientific approach to athletics, but why is it good to exercise caution before adding supplements to your diet?

2. Why is it so easy for some people to believe advertising claims for improved athletic performance?

3. What motivates the sellers of such products?

Strength Sought from Steroids and Growth Hormones

MAIN IDEA ▶ Steroids and growth hormones produce dangerous side effects that can damage your body.

Using hormones or other drugs can improve muscle strength and endurance, but these drugs have dangerous side effects and can even cause death. It is unwise to use hormones or other drugs to improve strength. Hormones and drugs that athletes take to gain strength or improve endurance have many dangerous side effects. Despite the hazards, these products often tempt those who want to gain a competitive advantage over others.

The Effects of Steroid Hormones

Males generally develop bulkier muscles than do females, in response to physical activity. This is because males produce larger amounts of certain steroids in their bodies. **Steroids** are *hormones of a certain chemical type that occur naturally in the body, some of which promote muscle growth*. These hormones are also available as drugs that are only safe to use under a doctor's care.

■ **Figure 9.16** *Males generally develop bulkier muscles than females do, in response to physical activity. Why is it important to seek a professional trainer when beginning a weight training program?*

Caption Answer: A professional can help to develop a plan that is safe and effective for you.

■ **Figure 9.17** *Steroids produce dangerous side effects that can harm your body. What health problems arise from steroid use?*

Caption Answer: Steroids can cause changes in blood fats that increase the risk of heart disease, cause liver damage, including cancerous liver tumors.

Like all drugs, steroids can be abused. Some athletes take steroid drugs in the attempt to develop bulky muscles. Athletes struggling to be the best are tempted by the promise of muscles bigger and stronger than those that training alone can produce. Athletes who normally would not be able to compete at high levels can suddenly compete successfully.

The Hidden Price of Steroids

Steroid abuse carries a very high price, however. Steroid abusers experience a sharp change in their blood fats that reflects an increased risk of heart disease. Steroids are also known to interrupt the normal work of the liver; cause cancerous liver tumors, liver rupture, and hemorrhage (bleeding); produce permanent changes in the reproductive system; and alter the structure of the face. In males, steroids cause the testicles to shrink. In females, they cause the growth of excessive body hair, such as mustaches, and cause the breasts to shrink. Steroids can also cause violent behavior, mood swings, depression, and paranoia. The long-term results of steroid use include all of the health problems described above, and can lead to premature death.

 **Did You Know?**

Steroid abuse has been associated with cardiovascular disease, including heart attack and stroke. These heart problems can even occur in athletes under the age of 30.

Human Growth Hormone

Steroids are illegal in competition and can be detected in urine tests. Therefore, some athletes have switched to other unsafe hormones that are not detectable—human growth hormone, for example. **Human growth hormone** is a *non-steroid hormone produced in the body that promotes growth;* it is taken as a drug by athletes to enhance muscle growth. People who take human growth hormone develop symptoms of **acromegaly**, *a disease caused by above-normal levels of human growth hormone.* Symptoms can include a widened jaw line, a widened nose, protruding brow and teeth, and an increased likelihood of death before age 50.

Worksheets: A reproducible quiz for Section 5 is provided in the Teacher Classroom Resources.

SECTION 5 Review

Reviewing the Vocabulary

Review the vocabulary on page 251. Then answer these questions.

1. What is *weight training*?
2. Drugs that are abused by some athletes seeking a shortcut to large muscles are called _____.
3. High doses of _____ can cause a disease known as _____.
4. Strength develops when muscles work against _____.

Reviewing the Facts

5. **List.** What are the two ways people gain muscle strength and endurance?
6. **Explain.** How frequently should weight training be done?
7. **Describe.** What are four dangerous physical side effects of steroid use?

Writing Critically

8. **Expository.** Has anyone you know ever used steroids or any other supplements for fitness? What were the results, both positive and negative?
9. **Narrative.** Set up a personal strength-conditioning program for one week that you would enjoy following. Don't make it too demanding—assume you will add to it as time goes on.

Go Online

For more vocabulary practice, play the True/False game at **glencoe.com**.

---

1. Activity routines for strength conditioning that use weights or machines to provide resistance against which the muscles can work

2. Steroids

3. Human growth hormone, acromegaly

4. Resistance

5. By weight training and callisthenics

6. Every other day

7. Increased risk of heart disease, liver tumors, reproductive damage, and alteration the structure of the face

8. Answers will vary.

9. Answers will vary.

Preventing Sports Injuries and Heat Stroke

Although regular physical activity benefits your health, injuries, while common, are most often preventable. **Shin splints**, *damage to the muscles and connective tissues of the lower front leg from stress*, are caused by improper form, failure to stretch, or inappropriate footwear. **Stress fractures**, *bone damage from repeated physical force that strains the place where ligament is attached to bone*, are caused by repetitive stress of the foot hitting the ground. Athletes who run, play basketball, and perform gymnastics are susceptible to such injuries. **Tennis elbow**, *a painful condition of the arm and joint*, can be attributed to using poor form in playing tennis. These and other injuries can be avoided by doing activities correctly and by building fitness slowly. **Figure 9.18** on page 258 provides a list of injury prevention tips.

Vocabulary

- shin splints
- stress fractures
- tennis elbow
- dehydration
- heat exhaustion
- heat stroke

Injury Prevention

MAIN IDEA ▶ The most important preventive measures are to follow proper form; stop working if you feel pain; and take precautions against dehydration, heat exhaustion, and heat stroke.

Be consistent. An athlete who is inactive for days and then suddenly plays hard invites injury. Vigorous and sudden demands on out-of-condition muscles, ligaments, and tendons lead to sprains. Take on a regular program of fitness to develop the strength that safe play demands. Use proper equipment, such as supportive shoes designed specifically for your sport.

Check the weather and avoid outdoor activities during extreme weather conditions. Layer your clothing in cold weather. Remove layers as you warm up or add layers if the temperature drops. In hot weather, drink fluids before, during, and after physical activity. Avoid prolonged sun exposure and use sunscreen. Wear sunglasses with ultraviolet protection and a wide-brimmed hat to avoid the sun's harmful rays.

Pain during activity is a signal that something is wrong. If the pain continues or gets worse, stop your activity until the pain goes away, or consult a physician. Then try again slowly, increasing your activity level a little at a time.

Class Activity
Evaluate: Ask students to describe injuries such as shin splints, stress fractures, tennis elbow, and other sports injuries. List the injuries on the board. Have students select one of the injuries, and assign them the task of preparing a three-minute presentation on that injury. Encourage students to be creative by using video, podcasts, or skits.

Figure 9.18 Common Injuries and Their Prevention

Injury	Prevention
Achilles tendon pain	Stretch the ankles and calves frequently and gently. When running, avoid or go easy on steep hills. Wear running shoes with a slightly elevated heel.
Ankles/knees: inflamation on outer side of joint	Exercise on flat surface, or change sides often on a sloping surface.
Blisters	Wear socks and shoes that do not rub and slip on the feet.
Cramps	Drink plenty of fluids, eat a balanced diet, increase workload gradually, and stretch often.
Foot pain	Perform calf stretches. Run, dance, or play on firm, springy surfaces. Wear proper shoes.
Lower back pain	Increase the back's workload gradually. Stretch the lower back. Strengthen abdominal muscles.
Pain around or under knee	Build lower body gradually. Use proper equipment and form. If untrained, do not sprint. Slow your pace when cycling or running on hills. Stop at first sensation of pain.
Shin pain	Slow down, and work out on proper surfaces.
Shoulder: inflammation of soft tissues	Build upper body gradually. Don't overtrain.

Class Activity

Synthesize:

Divide students into groups of four or five. Have each group design a poster teaching ways to avoid dehydration, overheating and heat stroke. Display the posters around the room, gym, and school.

Dehydration

Be alert to the dangers of overheating and **dehydration**, *loss of water*. Muscles heat up during physical activity because they are burning fuel. To help control the body's temperature, blood flows through the muscles and carries heat to the skin. Surrounding air and the evaporation of sweat carries the heat away. On humid days, though, sweat does not evaporate and heat builds up. Then the body sweats even more heavily in an attempt to cool itself. Heavy sweating can be extremely dangerous, or even fatal, because severe fluid and electrolyte losses cause cells to stop functioning.

Dehydration interferes with the body's ability to be physically active. Muscle weakness and unusual fatigue on a hot day may mean you need more fluids. However, you do not need salt tablets. These may make dehydration worse, because they pull water from the tissues into the digestive tract. Some people like commercial sports drinks, but these are usually unnecessary. (In the case of endurance athletes, though, who work out for more than 45 minutes without stopping, the sugar in sports drinks may be of some benefit.)

Dangers of Overheating

Overheating progresses through several stages. Early symptoms may include just swelling of the hands and feet or cramps in the legs or other muscles. Without proper cooling and rest, heat exhaustion and heat stroke can occur.

Heat exhaustion is *a serious stage of overheating which can lead to heat stroke*. The symptoms of heat exhaustion are headaches, nausea, chest pains, or diarrhea. These symptoms warn that heat stroke may occur. **Heat stroke** is *a life-threatening condition that results from a buildup of body heat*. Extreme fatigue, intense dizziness, confusion, and loss of consciousness are signs of heat stroke.

The most important preventive steps are to drink enough fluid before and during the activity and wear lightweight clothing that allows sweat to evaporate. If you notice symptoms, stop the activity immediately, seek a cool, shady place, rest, and drink water.

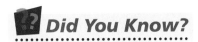

Did You Know?

To avoid heat stroke:
- Rest during times of high humidity, high temperature, or both.
- Limit exposure to any source of heat.
- Wear lightweight, loose-fitting clothing.
- Drink several extra glasses of water before you engage in physical activity.
- During the activity, drink a half cup of cool water every 15 to 20 minutes.
- Listen for your body's distress signals, and if you have to, stop the activity. Take a rest in the shade.

SECTION 6 Review

Reviewing the Vocabulary

Review the vocabulary on page 257. Then answer these questions.

1. How are *dehydration* and *heat exhaustion* related?
2. _____ involve damage to the muscles and connective tissues of the lower front leg due to stress.

Reviewing the Facts

3. **Explain.** Why is it important to be consistent in a fitness program?
4. **Analyze.** How can heat stroke be avoided?
5. **List.** List three steps you can take to prevent injury.

Writing Critically

6. **Expository.** Your friend has begun a fitness program that includes running. While running, he experiences back and leg pain. Use your knowledge gained from studying this section to develop a checklist of things for your friend to consider as causes for his pain, and describe ways in which your friend can avoid injuries in the future.

Go Online

For more vocabulary practice, play the eFlashcards game at glencoe.com.

1. Dehydration is caused by a loss of water and heat exhaustion occurs when the body has severely overheated, due in part, to lack of water.

2. Shin splints

3. Sudden, vigorous demands on the body can lead to injury.

4. By drinking plenty of water before, during, and after physical activity

5. Follow proper form, stop working if you feel pain, and take precautions against dehydration.

6. Answers will vary.

Food for Sports Competition

Understand and Apply Read the conversation below, and then complete the writing exercise that follows.

You may wonder if athletes need special foods or nutrients to help them perform. No supplement or nutrient product has ever been proven helpful in this way. On the other hand, the foods athletes choose at every meal matter greatly. The meals they eat can help or hinder their performance.

Q: I'd like to go out for the track team. Can my diet help me make the team?

A: While the right diet can help you in your efforts, it would be an exaggeration to say that diet alone can help you make the team. Rather, a balanced diet that provides adequate nutrients and fuels can support your efforts. Once these things are in place, dedication and hard work can win you a spot on the team.

Q: I've heard that carbohydrates are the best fuels to support my activity. Why?

A: Yes, carbohydrate fuels are best. "Why" has to do with the way your muscles handle fuels during physical activity. At rest, your body uses a fuel mix of about equal parts of fat and glucose, the body's main form of carbohydrate. In physical work, however, the fuel mix changes. In the early minutes of physical activity, muscles use up large amounts of glucose. They draw this glucose

from their own small supplies that they store as glycogen. Thus, glycogen supplies quickly run out during intense, short-term activities such as sprinting and weight lifting.

During *moderate* activity that continues for longer than 20 minutes or so, the muscles begin to depend more on fat for part of their fuel. Thus, glycogen lasts much longer during such activities as easy jogging, but the muscles still need energy from glucose and they can eventually run out of it.

Q: Okay, but how does carbohydrate in the diet affect physical performance of the muscles?

A: Try to imagine the body packing away into storage some of the glucose molecules from the carbohydrate in potatoes, toast, cereal, beans, or spaghetti. Later, during activity, the body will open up its stores and use those saved glucose molecules for energy. Most diets provide abundant carbohydrate but the body's storage areas are small. To keep them full, you must choose enough carbohydrate-rich foods daily.

In real life, glycogen stores rarely matter much for physically active people such as casual joggers. These people simply do not go long or hard enough to run out of glycogen. For distance runners or other endurance athletes, however, the level of glycogen becomes important in reaching their goals. Thus, high-carbohydrate diets enhance an athlete's endurance by ensuring ample glycogen stores.

Q: What's the best high-carbohydrate food? Candy bars have sugar, and sugar is a form of carbohydrate, right?

A: From the standpoint that candy provides carbohydrate, candy bars might seem, at first glance, to be useful. Before you load up on candy, though, you should know that most candy also contains a lot of fat. In fact, most types contain many more calories of fat than of carbohydrate.

While it provides concentrated sugar and fat for energy, candy provides almost no other nutrients. So consider candy, always, as a treat, not as a food to support health and performance. Whole-grain bread, baked beans, potatoes, and whole-grain or enriched pasta provide carbohydrate as starch, plus many other nutrients.

Q: Is there anything I can do before competition to help me perform my best?

A: On the day of competition, carefully plan your pre-game meal. Eat it three to four hours before the event. The meal should be light (300 to 1,000 calories) and easy to digest. The meal should provide carbohydrate-rich foods such as potatoes, beans, and lentils; whole-grain and enriched pastas and breads; and fruit juices. Not only do these foods supply glucose, but they are quickly absorbed. The juice provides fluids to help guard against dehydration and heat stroke.

Stay away from foods high in fat (such as meat) or foods high in fiber (such as raw vegetables). These require long times for digestion and can cause nausea during physical activity.

Q: Don't athletes need more protein than other people do?

A: Athletes need just slightly more protein than other people do. They use much of the extra to build muscles, and use a little of it for fuel. During physical activity, the muscles use more of certain amino acids for fuel, because these can provide energy in much the same way as glucose.

A balanced diet of regular high-carbohydrate foods provides all of the protein and amino acids that athletes need, and in just the right amounts. However, vegetarian athletes do need to be careful to include generous servings of protein-rich foods such as beans, seeds, whole-grain bread, pasta, and cereals, as well as low-fat milk and milk products in their diets.

Q: Do athletes need more vitamin C than the amount in a regular diet?

A: Like other vitamins, studies show that more vitamin C is not better. Athletes who take vitamins in addition to a healthy diet do not perform any better than those who get enough from food. It's best to try to obtain all your nutrients from food.

A diet consisting of a small glass of orange juice, a baked potato, and a serving of broccoli in a day contains more than the Recommended Dietary Allowance (RDA) for vitamin C from these foods alone.

Q: Are you saying that no supplements have any effects on performance at all?

A: No, that's not quite true. Some concentrated nutrients may hurt an athlete's performance. For example, niacin supplements interfere with the body's release of fat. Without enough fat to use as fuel, the muscles are forced to use extra glycogen in place of fat. This may make the body run out of glycogen sooner. It also makes the work seem more difficult to the exerciser.

 Writing Write a paragraph that explains why carbohydrates are an important part of an athlete's diet.

Reviewing Vocabulary

Select the appropriate key term from the list below.

resistance

sedentary

elasticity

body composition

1. _____ means physically inactive.
2. The proportions of lean tissue as compared with fat tissue in the body is called _____.
3. _____ is the characteristic of a tissue's being easily stretched or bent and able to return to its original size and shape.
4. _____ is a force that opposes another; in fitness, the weight or other opposing force against which muscles must work.

Recalling Key Facts and Ideas

Section 1
5. **List.** List four physical benefits of fitness.

Section 2
6. **Describe.** Offer some pointers for applying the overload principle.

7. **Explain.** Explain the principles of warm-up and cool-down.

Section 3
8. **Analyze.** Why must cardiovascular endurance training involve aerobic activities?

9. **Describe.** How does cardiovascular endurance affect the heart?

10. **Explain.** How long must aerobic activity last to improve cardiovascular endurance?

Section 4
11. **List.** What are some signs and symptoms of overstretching?

12. **Explain.** Why is gentle stretching recommended over bouncing?

Section 5
13. **Describe.** How can you best increase muscle firmness and endurance when weight training?

14. **Analyze.** Why do males generally develop larger muscles than females when they exercise?

Section 6
15. **Explain.** What are the signs of heat stroke?

16. **Analyze.** How can injury best be prevented when you are physically active?

Writing Critically

17. **Expository.** List some of the reasons why being physically fit is especially important in today's world. List some ways to become physically fit at a minimal expense. In your community, what sports activities can you participate in without paying any fees?

18. **Descriptive.** List your personal fitness goals. Make a list of all the physical activities you participate in within a one-week period. Identify which fitness

1. Sedentary 2. Body composition 3. Elasticity 4. Resistance 5. Enables physical activity, helps a person to be able to meet physical demands, to meet sudden challenges, and to withstand stress 6. If you enjoy and activity, do it more often. If you do not have time, increase the intensity.

7. Warm-ups allow the body to lightly use the muscles. Cool-downs provide a chance for the body to relax and stretch 8. Cardiovascular training demands the heart and lungs work harder to provide oxygen. 9. The heart grows in size and strength and can do more work with less effort.

component is promoted by each activity and which activities are anaerobic and aerobic. Will these activities help you to develop all your fitness goals? Now that you have read this chapter, what changes do you think you need to make in your program?

Activities

19. Interview a podiatrist or a doctor whose specialty is sports medicine and write a one-page report on your findings.

20. Write a letter to the President's Council on Physical Fitness to obtain literature about fitness. The address is: President's Council on Physical Fitness and Sports, 200 Independence Avenue, SW, Room 738-H, Washington, D.C. 20201-0004.

21. Visit a local fitness club. Find out about the types of equipment, programs, classes, and instructors the club offers. What is the fee for joining? Overall, would you consider joining this club? Would it be a worthwhile investment? Why or why not?

22. Make a poster of newspaper and magazine advertisements for physical fitness products. Label one half of the poster "Safe and Effective Products" and the other half "Dangerous and Suspicious Products." Place each advertisement under the appropriate title, forming a collage.

23. Write a one-page story about a person who is completely unfit. What would this person be able to do? What wouldn't this person be able to do? What would his or her lifestyle be like? Describe in detail a day in the life of a totally unfit person.

24. Read the following statement: "A sound mind in a sound body is a short but full description of a happy state in this world." (John Locke, 1632–1704) What do you think the author meant by this statement? Do you agree with the statement? Why or why not? Discuss your answers with the rest of your class.

Making Decisions About Health

25. Your classmate considers himself to be in "perfect health." He rarely gets sick, eats right, and is not overweight. His blood cholesterol and blood pressure are within the acceptable range. He insists there is no need for him to participate in any type of physical activity program. Do you agree with your classmate? Why or why not?

For more vocabulary practice, play the True/False game at **glencoe.com**.

Fact or Fiction?

Answers

1. True
2. False. You should stop to avoid serious injury.
3. False. It's best to rehydrate as you go.

Writing Paragraphs will vary.

10. For 20 minutes or more **11.** Pain in the joints and muscles **12.** Bouncing can cause ligaments to tear. **13.** Use light weights with more repetitions. **14.** Males produce hormones called steroids which help to develop larger muscles. **15.** Headaches, nausea, chest pains **16.** Follow proper form, stop

working if you feel pain, take precautions against dehydration. **17–25.** Answers will vary.

CHAPTER 10

Your Body: An Owner's Manual

Sections

1. Healthy Teeth and Fresh Breath
2. Personal Cleanliness Concerns
3. Posture and Image
4. When to Visit a Health Care Provider

The most important aspect of health care is *self-care*. Doing a few simple things for your body can enable you to maintain it and help keep it healthy.

This chapter starts by going over the body head-to-toe and instructs you in some simple self-care techniques. When you keep your teeth, hair, nails, and skin clean, you help reduce the risk of infection. Good self-care practices improve your physical, mental/emotional, and social health. There are times, though, when you must seek out help from a health care provider. The last section tells when you should do so.

Fact or Fiction?

What Do You Think?

Is each statement true or false? If you think it's false, explain what's true.

1. Flossing is more important to the fight against gum disease than is brushing tooth surfaces.
2. People who get acne simply need to keep their faces cleaner.
3. Acne often clears up during summer vacations.

 Writing Think about what you do to take care of your body every day. Write a paragraph describing how you take care of your body and why it is important to your overall health.

(Answers on page 287)

Go Online

Visit **glencoe.com** and complete the Life Choice Inventory for Chapter 10.

Healthy Teeth and Fresh Breath

One of the first things we notice when we meet someone new is his or her smile. A warm, welcoming smile can tell you whether a person is friendly. Healthy teeth and fresh breath can tell you a lot about how the person takes care of him or her self. A person with clean, white teeth and fresh breath spends the time to take care of personal hygiene. Even with the best of dental care, however, it's likely that you will get a few cavities in your lifetime. However, with good dental hygiene, you can minimize the likelihood of developing cavities and gum disease.

Vocabulary

dental plaque
enamel
cavity
dentin
pulp cavity
gum disease

Cavities and Gum Disease

MAIN IDEA ▶ Brushing and flossing teeth properly will prevent tooth decay and gum disease.

Tooth decay can lead to major illness affecting the whole body. Even without decay, teeth that collect food particles and dental plaque create unpleasant mouth odor. **Dental plaque** is *a sticky material on the surface of the teeth*. The bacteria that live in plaque break down food particles and create acid that saturates plaque. This acid dissolves away the **enamel**, *the tooth's tough outer layer*. The person may not feel a cavity forming in its early stages. A **cavity** *is a hole in a tooth caused by decay*. However, as the decay advances into *the tooth's softer, middle layer*, its **dentin**, it eats into nerves. The pain at this stage can be severe. Should the decay infect *the tooth's deepest layer*, its **pulp cavity**, it might kill the tooth. To fix a cavity, a dentist will drill away the damaged part of the tooth surface and replace it with a substance that seals the tooth. **Figure 10.1** shows how cavities form and how sealants work.

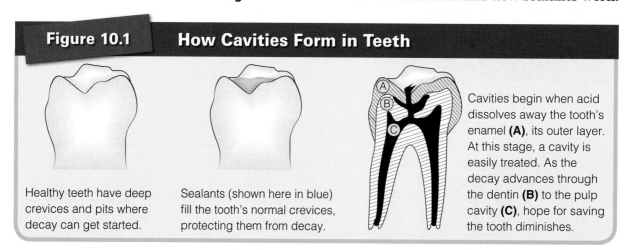

Figure 10.1 **How Cavities Form in Teeth**

Healthy teeth have deep crevices and pits where decay can get started.

Sealants (shown here in blue) fill the tooth's normal crevices, protecting them from decay.

Cavities begin when acid dissolves away the tooth's enamel **(A)**, its outer layer. At this stage, a cavity is easily treated. As the decay advances through the dentin **(B)** to the pulp cavity **(C)**, hope for saving the tooth diminishes.

Gum disease is *the inflammation and degeneration of the pink tissue (gums) that is attached to the teeth and helps to hold them in place*. It causes more tooth loss than tooth decay. Fifty percent of all adults will develop gum disease. An early symptom is gums that bleed easily. Treatment of advanced gum disease often involves the dentist's cutting away diseased gum tissue and scraping the teeth below the gumline. Even then, however, gum disease often returns, especially if the person fails to floss.

Brushing and Flossing

While brushing your teeth, angle the brush at the gum line. Brush tooth surfaces back and forth, not up and down, so as not to push food particles below the gum line. Brushing the gums beneath the gum line will aid in the removal of plaque there.

After brushing, use floss to pull plaque up from below the gum line between the teeth. Use a toothpick or brush to dislodge plaque from below the gum line along the teeth.

If done correctly, brushing the teeth after each meal and flossing once each day can remove food particles and plaque. **Figure 10.2** shows how to get rid of plaque that takes hold at the gumline and beneath it.

In addition to daily cleaning, a professional cleaning about once every six months and a full examination about once a year can go a long way toward helping you keep your teeth for life.

Choosing Foods and Snacks for Dental Health

Choose snacks with care. Sticky, sweet foods and other snacks cling to the teeth and are converted by plaque to make an acid that can cause tooth decay.

Preview Activity

Discuss: Ask the class to respond to the following questions before you have them read this section or do any of the activities:

1. Why would brushing back and forth be better than brushing up and down?

2. What difference does it make how you hold a toothbrush?

Allow time for students to explain their answers; let others make additional comments. Discuss each question thoroughly.

Class Activity

Apply. Use an oversized model of teeth and a toothbrush and the steps illustrated on this page to demonstrate the steps to cleaning teeth properly. Ask two or three volunteers to demonstrate the brushing techniques. Have the other students critique the volunteers' techniques.

Figure 10.2	Brushing and Flossing the Teeth and Gums

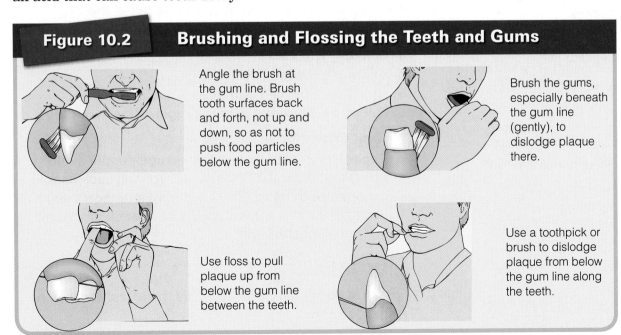

Angle the brush at the gum line. Brush tooth surfaces back and forth, not up and down, so as not to push food particles below the gum line.

Brush the gums, especially beneath the gum line (gently), to dislodge plaque there.

Use floss to pull plaque up from below the gum line between the teeth.

Use a toothpick or brush to dislodge plaque from below the gum line along the teeth.

Some foods are more likely to cause tooth decay than are others. Sugar is one factor, but it's not just the sugar in foods that makes the difference. Other factors, such as fat, fiber, and stickiness matter as well.

These foods are less likely to contribute to tooth decay:

- Milk, cheese, plain yogurt
- Popcorn, toast, hard rolls, pretzels, corn chips, pizza
- Fresh fruits, fruits canned in water, vegetables
- Lean meats, fish, poultry, eggs, beans

These foods contribute to tooth decay. Brush your teeth after finishing them:

- Chocolate milk, ice cream, sweetened yogurt
- Cookies, pies, cakes, cereals, potato chips, crackers
- Dried fruits, fruit canned in syrup or juice, jams, jellies, fruit juices, regular soft drinks
- Peanut butter with added sugar, most luncheon meats
- Candies, sugar-sweetened gum, fudge

Worksheets: A reproducible quiz for Section 1 is provided in the Teacher Classroom Resources.

Reviewing the Vocabulary

Review the vocabulary on page 266. Then answer these questions.

1. The _____ is the deepest chamber of a tooth, which has blood vessels and nerves in it.
2. The tough outer layer of a tooth is called the _____.
3. A _____ is a hole in a tooth caused by decay.

Reviewing the Facts

4. **Explain.** How do cavities form?
5. **Analyze.** How can gum disease be avoided?
6. **Describe.** Describe how to properly floss your teeth.

Writing Critically

7. **Expository.** Why do you think some people avoid going to the dentist? What could you tell such people to convince them to go? How might a person's dental health affect the person's physical, mental/emotional, and social health?

For more vocabulary practice, play the eFlashcards game at **glencoe.com**.

1. Pulp cavity
2. Enamel
3. Cavity
4. Bacteria in plaque break down food particles and create acid, dissolving the outer layer of the tooth.
5. By brushing and flossing regularly and properly
6. Use the floss to pull plaque up from the gum line and in between teeth.
7. Answers will vary.

Personal Cleanliness Concerns

Developing healthy habits not only includes getting enough physical activity and eating a healthful diet, it also includes maintaining your appearance. Along with dental care, the care of your hair, nails, skin, ears, and eyes is important for both appearance and health. Good hygiene helps to maintain your physical health. It can boost self-esteem too.

Care of Hair and Nails

MAIN IDEA ▶ **Cleanliness of hair and nails is important and both are sensitive to malnutrition.**

Each hair strand is a fiber made of long, parallel strands of protein. Hair is a product made in the skin's **follicles**, *vessel-like structures in the skin that contain the oil glands, the muscles that control hair movement, and the roots of hairs* (see **Figure 10.3**). In cross section, a strand of hair may be round (straight hair), oval (curly), or flat (wavy). Hair is a product of living tissue, but is not alive itself.

Hair Products

To keep normal hair looking healthy, keep it clean. Shampoos are all mild detergents, but they vary in their effects.

Shampoos for oily hair have more or stronger detergents. Although some shampoos may contain protein additives that supposedly "repair damage," that is generally an advertising claim. Protein can be added to hair only during its creation. Protein in hair is created within the hair follicles.

Conditioning products coat the hairs, making them slide freely against one another rather than tangling. If hair becomes split or roughened from hot hair dryers, rough brushes, curling irons, or harsh chemicals (such as permanent waves, colorings, or the chlorine in swimming pools), the damaged ends must be trimmed off.

Controlling Dandruff

The scalp is like other skin in that it sheds bits of its thin outer layer each day. Washing removes these bits of skin before they build up and mix with the scalp's oils. Without regular washing, the bits of skin cling together into flakes, called dandruff. If regular washings with ordinary shampoo fail to control flaking, ask a pharmacist for his or her reccommendation for an effective treatment.

Vocabulary

- follicles
- cuticles
- keratin
- acne
- sebum
- pus
- whitehead
- cyst
- blackhead
- comedogenic
- dermatologist
- menstruation
- douches
- menstrual cramps
- premenstrual syndrome (PMS)

Figure 10.3

Skin and Hair Structures

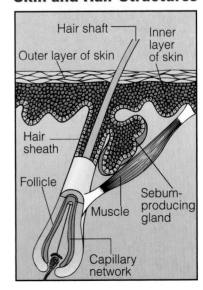

■ Figure 10.4 *To help keep your hair looking healthy, find a shampoo that works for you. What is the cure for damaged hair?*

Caption Answer: The only cure is to trim the damaged hairs.

The Nature of Nails

Like hair, nails grow from a root structure. Under the **cuticles**, *the borders of hardened skin at the bases of fingernails* (see **Figure 10.5**), nail-forming cells bind together protein into sheets that form the nails. *The normal protein of the hair and nails* is called **keratin**. Once formed, nails can no longer accept protein. Biting or clipping nails too short may cause infection. To remain healthy, nails need only be kept clean and trimmed.

Nourishing the Hair and Nails

A healthful diet helps keep hair and nails healthy by providing the nutrients the body needs to grow them. A diet containing too few nutrients can lead to weak, odd-shaped nails. This is because the body conserves nutrients and uses them first for essential functions, such as making immune system cells. Hair loss and changes in fingernails are two early signs of malnutrition. The most effective way to ensure that hair and nails look their best is to nourish the whole body. If the cells that make hair and nails are in top condition, and are given plenty of materials with which to build, the healthiest possible hair and nails are assured.

Figure 10.5

How Fingernails Grow

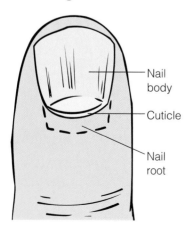

Nail body

Cuticle

Nail root

Help for Acne

MAIN IDEA ▷ Acne results from a buildup of sebum and flakes of skin that get trapped in the skin's ducts.

No one knows why some people get acne and others do not. **Acne** is *a continuing condition of inflamed skin ducts and glands, with a buildup of oils under the skin, forming pimples.* However, acne is known to run in families. If both your parents had acne, it's likely that you will too. The hormones of adolescence also play a role by making the glands in the skin more active.

How Pimples Form

Acne is related to *the skin's natural oil*, called **sebum**. Sebum is made continuously in the deep glands. Sebum normally flows out of the glands to the skin's surface through the tiny ducts around the hairs. In acne, the oil gets stuck below the surface of the skin. Each of the ducts is lined with tissue that normally sheds by scaling and flaking. The oil carries these scales and flakes to the surface of the skin. At times, the scales form a plug, halting the flow of oil and allowing bacteria to migrate down into the duct. The oil and bacteria irritate the skin, causing redness and swelling. **Pus**, *a mixture of fluids and white blood cells that collects around infected areas*, is formed. This is the beginning of a **whitehead**, or *pimple*. A **cyst** may be formed—*an enlarged, deep pimple*. If *an open pimple with dark skin pigments in its opening* is formed, it is called a **blackhead**.

■ **Figure 10.6** *Some over-the-counter acne treatments may help clear up mild acne. How does acne form?*

Caption Answer: When the skin's oil is unable to flow through the ducts, bacteria leaks into surrounding skin.

Bacteria on the skin will not cause acne, but can make acne worse. Also, the color of a blackhead is caused by pigments, not by dirt. Keeping your skin clean will not always reduce the incidence of acne. Squeezing or picking at pimples to try to remove their contents does not help. In fact, it can cause more scars than the acne itself.

Treating Acne

Many simple acne remedies may work to some degree, such as washing frequently, avoiding certain foods and beverages, avoiding **comedogenic**, *acne-causing* cosmetics, or relieving stress. However, everyone responds to treatments differently. What may work for one person may not work for another. The likelihood of developing severe acne will diminish as you get older. Some people, however, will get acne throughout their lives. In some cases of severe acne, a doctor may prescribe antibiotics. Other treatments include those that are applied to the skin.

Consumer SKILLS ACTIVITY

Advertisement Techniques

Some advertisements may use tricky techniques to encourage consumers to purchase their products. One technique is to declare that the product will solve common problems. For example, if you have acne, a television commercial might convince you to buy a product by promising to:

- Clear up your acne.
- Make you popular.
- Make you happy.
- Make you successful.

Other techniques may include loyalty (your family has always used this brand), peer pressure (your friends use the product), a celebrity endorsement (a celebrity appears in an ad for the product), bonus offers (buy the product and receive additional items), personal reports, and opinions from people who have tried products and claim they saw improvement. These and many other selling techniques may tempt people to solve health problems using a particular product. However, consumers should always purchase or use health-related products with care. It is best to read the label (or contact the manufacturer) for a list of ingredients, possible side effects, and any other information that will help you make an informed decision. Your health care provider can also help you decide what products are best for you and your health.

 Writing

1. Have such advertisements worked with you or someone you know?
2. Have you ever bought products because of an advertisement?
3. What are some ways you can make an informed decision when it comes to purchasing a product?

Mild Acne

For mild acne, over-the-counter treatments may work well. Any of the following are effective ingredients:

- Benzoyl peroxide
- Salicylic acid
- Resorcinol
- Sulfur

These ingredients are generally safe and effective. They may have side effects including drying or irritating the skin. Washing carefully twice daily with mild soap helps remove skin-surface bacteria and oil, helps to keep the oil ducts open, and allows topical creams or gels that you might apply reach the skin and pores.

More Severe Acne

If over-the-counter treatments fail to clear acne, see a dermatologist for a prescription medication. A **dermatologist** is *a physician who specializes in treating conditions of the skin.* A dermatologist will examine your skin to try and learn the cause of acne. When developing a treatment plan, a doctor may prescribe certain medications to treat specific problems with the skin. Antibiotic creams or pills can help eliminate bacteria associated with breakouts. One topical cream contains an acid that loosens the plugs that form in the ducts. The oil is then able to flow again so that the ducts will not burst. The skin may clear within a month or so, but it may also be more easily damaged by sunlight and may become dry. These side effects may make the acne look worse at first.

Oral medications are used only for severe acne that scars the skin. Evidence suggests that some oral medications may cause psychological depression in some teens who take them. Other side effects may include irritation and drying of the nose, mouth, and skin. Pregnant females should be aware that some types can cause birth defects.

Acne Prevention

Many people think that certain foods and drinks worsen their acne. Chocolate, cola beverages, fatty or greasy foods, nuts, sugar, and foods or salt containing iodine have all been blamed for worsening acne. It's not proven that these foods worsen acne. If they do seem to affect your skin, however, there's no harm in avoiding them. Stress clearly worsens acne due to the hormones that are secreted in response to it. Vacations from school or other pressures slow secretion of stress hormones and so help to bring relief. The sun, the beach, and swimming also seem to help. However, remember to apply sunscreen on exposed areas of the skin. Use an SPF (sun protection factor) of 15 or higher that blocks both UVA and UVB rays.

Class Activity:
Discuss. How many students have tried over-the-counter acne treatments? What additional remedies have students tried? Which products seem to be most effective? Have students research ingredients such as benzoyl peroxide, salicylic acid, and resorcinol. How do these ingredients treat acne?

Ear Piercing, Body Piercing, and Tattooing

MAIN IDEA ▶ Fashion that requires puncturing the body carries risks of local infections and infectious diseases.

Piercing and tattooing practices have been in existence for thousands of years. Both of these practices require making puncture wounds to the skin. Any wound increases the likelihood of infection from bacteria. Body parts especially prone to bacterial infections are the upper ear, nose, and mouth. Viruses such as hepatitis B and HIV (the virus that causes AIDS) can also spread through the use of unsanitary needles. Oral piercings can damage your mouth and teeth as well. The decision to get a piercing or tattoo can also impact your social health, by limiting job opportunities and relationships.

Eyes and Ears

MAIN IDEA ▶ Care for the eyes and ears should be practiced throughout your lifetime.

Sight and hearing are easy to take for granted. So that your eyes and ears serve you throughout your life, practice a little careful treatment and common sense.

Eyes

The eyelids, brows, lashes, and tears defend against infection and injury. If something does get into the eye and tears don't wash it out, hold the eye open and gently drop plain, clean water or a commercial eyewash into the lower or upper lid. The eyes can be damaged by the sun's ultraviolet rays. When outside, wear sunglasses that protect the eyes from ultraviolet (UV) light. Never look directly into the sun.

Contact lenses, because they are applied directly to the eye, require careful handling. Most must be cleaned thoroughly each day. If left in overnight, they may cause an eye infection. Other types are designed for longer wear, but this should be discussed with the prescribing optometrist (op-TOM-eh-trist; eye doctor).

Some vision problems can be corrected by surgery. Surgery to correct nearsightedness requires that small cuts be made in the eye's clear outer layer, the cornea, to reshape it. Once healed, the eye's new shape allows clearer distance vision, often without glasses. Some people must have repeat surgeries to make small adjustments. Some may require reading glasses at an earlier age than normal. However, most also find the surgery helpful.

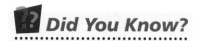

Ears

The ear is composed of three main sections—outer ear, middle ear, and inner ear. Each section has its own unique structure. The outer ear is the visible portion of the ear that channels sound waves into the external auditory canal. This canal leads to the eardrum. The eardrum is a thin membrane that acts as a barrier between the outer and middle ear. The middle ear contains three tiny bones that connect the eardrum to the inner ear. A tiny tube, the eustachian (you-STAY-shun) tube connects the middle ear, which connects to the throat. This tube allows pressure to be equalized on each side of the eardrum when you swallow or yawn. The inner ear consists of spiral passages that aid in hearing as well as controlling your balance.

Care of your ears helps prevent infection and hearing loss. If you suspect an infection, see a health care professional for care. Infections can be treated with antibiotics. Another important aspect of ear care is protecting the ear tissue. Wearing hats in cold weather, and helmets for some sports will protect the ears. Never push anything into the ear canal, even a cotton-tipped swab. Most importantly, avoid exposure to loud noises.

Exposure to loud noises can cause permanent hearing loss later in life. The ears cannot shut out loud noises, which can injure their delicate inner structures and impair hearing (see **Figure 10.7**). Hearing loss caused by noise gets worse with repeated exposures, and damage to the inner ear can be permanent. **Figure 10.8** points out some dangerous noise levels. Try to avoid loud music, wear earplugs in noisy environments such as concerts or sporting events, and move away from loud noises as soon as possible.

Figure 10.8

A Noise Thermometer
This shows the time required to damage hearing at various noise levels.

Decibels

Gunshots, jet engines at take-off — Immediate — 140

125 — Pain threshold

Rock concerts 7 minutes — 120

115 — Baby's cry, jet skis — 15 minutes

Snowmobile in front seat 30 minutes — 110

105 — Helicopter, jackhammer — 1 hour

Stereo headphones 2 hours — 100

95 — Motorcycle, power saw — 4 hours

Lawn mower, truck traffic 8 hours — 90

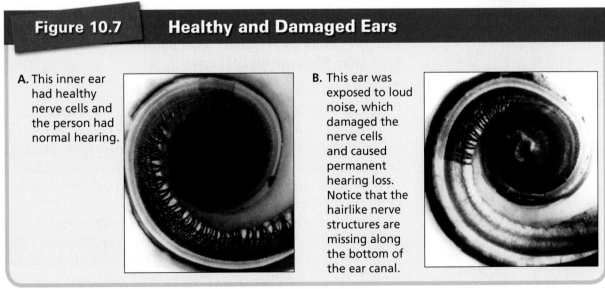

Figure 10.7   Healthy and Damaged Ears

A. This inner ear had healthy nerve cells and the person had normal hearing.

B. This ear was exposed to loud noise, which damaged the nerve cells and caused permanent hearing loss. Notice that the hairlike nerve structures are missing along the bottom of the ear canal.

Avoiding Body Odor

MAIN IDEA ▶ **Cleanliness is the key to freedom from body odor.**

Body odor is caused by the mixture of normal skin bacteria with sweat and skin debris. While no threat to health, unpleasant body odor may impact your social health, causing others to withdraw. This can damage a person's self-esteem.

People who perspire heavily may want to use antiperspirants to reduce the sweat that feeds the bacteria that cause body odor. Antiperspirants and deodorants or colognes are not substitutes for daily bathing, though. Even the most aromatic deodorants and perfumes cannot mask an unpleasant odor.

Male and female external reproductive organs require a careful daily washing to keep them free of infections and odors too. Keep in mind that an unpleasant discharge or bad odor may indicate an infection. If that occurs, see your doctor and have an examination.

Menstrual Concerns

MAIN IDEA ▶ **For health, bodies need only routine cleansing.**

Caring for your reproductive system includes bathing regularly and having regular medical exams. During **menstruation**, *the monthly shedding of the uterine lining in nonpregnant females*, gentle external cleaning is all that is needed. "Personal deodorant" sprays are not needed. Some females also use over-the-counter products for cleansing after menstruation. **Douches**, *preparations sold to cleanse the vagina*, interrupt the vagina's own natural cleaning cycle and may wash bacteria up into the normally bacteria-free areas of the reproductive tract. The vagina can easily become infected with the normal bacteria from the digestive tract. Females should also practice caution when using bathroom tissue. When wiping, females should move the tissue back and away from the vagina. Soiled bathroom tissue should be kept away from the vaginal area.

Feminine Hygiene Products

Many females use tampons to absorb menstrual flow internally. Choose the lowest absorbency needed to control menstrual flow. Change the tampons every four to eight hours, and alternate their use with pads. It is important to change pads and tampons regularly to avoid the development of a rare infection, toxic shock syndrome.

Pads or sanitary napkins are used to collect menstrual flow externally. Pads should be changed every four to eight hours (depending on menstrual flow) to prevent bacterial growth and reduce the risk of toxic shock syndrome.

Menstrual Symptoms

Females who menstruate may experience **menstrual cramps**, normal *contractions of the uterus during and a few days before menstruation,* that may cause pain. Some find relief from the over-the-counter drug ibuprofen. Should cramping become severe, a health care provider should check for problems.

Premenstrual syndrome (PMS) can occur in some females each month before menstruation. **Premenstrual syndrome** includes *symptoms such as physical discomfort, moodiness, and nervousness that occur in some women each month before menstruation.* Such symptoms are normally minor, but can be a problem for some females. PMS often responds to simple remedies such as getting enough rest, physical activity, relaxation, and nourishing food. Reducing intakes of colas, iced tea, and other caffeine sources may help reduce PMS symptoms as well.

" Take responsibility for yourself."

—Tyra Banks
(1973–)
Model, television personality

Worksheets: A reproducible quiz for Section 2 is provided in the Teacher Classroom Resources.

SECTION 2 Review

Reviewing the Vocabulary

Review the vocabulary on page 269. Then answer these questions.

1. A _____ is a physician who specializes in treating conditions of the skin.

2. An enlarged, deep pimple is a _____.

3. _____ is the protein of hair and nails.

4. Define *premenstrual syndrome (PMS).*

Reviewing the Facts

5. Analyze. Why are protein additives in shampoos ineffective in repairing damaged hair?

6. Explain. How does malnutrition affect hair?

7. List. Name two over-the-counter treatment ingredients that are effective for acne.

Writing Critically

8. Expository. Look at several advertisements for skin care products. What techniques are used in the ads to try to get you to use their products? Do you think they are as effective as the ads claim? Explain.

Go Online

For more information on health careers, visit Career Corner at **glencoe.com.**

1. Dermatologist
2. Cyst
3. Keratin
4. Symptoms such as discomfort and moodiness that occur in some females each month before menstruation.
5. Additives do not penetrate the hair follicles.
6. Hair can become dry, brittle, and can fall out.
7. Benzoyl peroxide and salicylic acid

Posture and Image

Proper posture is important to overall health and to the health of your spine. Good posture helps a person look energetic, and helps maintain skeletal health.

The Health of the Spine

MAIN IDEA ▶ Correct posture improves the way a person looks and helps protect the health of the spine.

The way you walk, sit, and sleep greatly affects your skeleton over the years. The bones and cartilage disks of your spine are sensitive. *The delicate, hollow bones of the spine are* called **vertebrae** (VERT-eh-bray) . The **spine** is *a stack of 33 vertebrae that form the backbone and hold the spinal cord, whose nerves enter and exit through spaces between the bones.* The vertebrae are separated by pads, or disks, of cartilage.

Major nerves exit and enter the spaces between vertebrae. If the bones or cartilage disks are damaged, they can bulge out and pinch those nerves (see **Figure 10.9**). The result is that you will feel severe pain in the muscles of the neck, shoulders, back or legs.

Vocabulary

vertebrae
spine

Figure 10.9

The Spinal Column

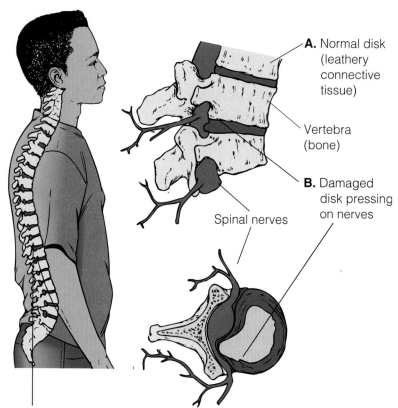

A. Normal disk (leathery connective tissue)

Vertebra (bone)

B. Damaged disk pressing on nerves

Spinal nerves

Normal curve of the spine. When the bones are stacked this way, the disks bear the weight evenly, and the nerves feel the least pressure.

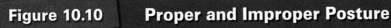

Figure 10.10 **Proper and Improper Posture**

Sleeping

Do not lie flat on your back; this arches the spine too much.

Do not use a high pillow.

Do not sleep face down.

Lie on your back and support your knees.

Lie on your side with knees bent and pillow just high enough to keep your neck straight.

Sitting

Do not leave your lower back unsupported.

Sit straight with back support, knees higher than hips.

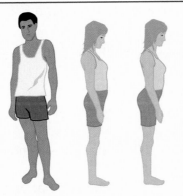

Standing

Do not let your back bend out of its natural curve.

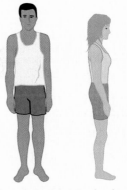

Stand upright, hips tucked, knees slightly bent.

Walking

Do not lean forward or wear high heels.

Lead with chest, toes forward.

Preventing Spinal Damage

Eight out of ten adults have at least one instance of back pain bad enough to seek medical attention. People who do not get enough physical activity are most likely to have back problems. As back and abdominal muscles become weak, the spine tends to become less well supported and slips out of shape. Happily, most back problems are preventable with proper posture and physical activity. Posture dos and don'ts are shown in **Figure 10.10** on page 279. If you experience back pain, consult a physician before participating in strenuous physical activity.

■ **Figure 10.11** *People with good posture seem to radiate energy and high self-esteem. How does good posture relate to high self-esteem?*

Caption Answer: People who walk tall and straight show a positive appearance.

1. Spine, vertebrae
2. The way you walk, sit, and sleep affect your skeleton.
3. People who do not exercise are most at risk for back pain.
4. It arches the spine too much.
5. Good posture promotes good self-esteem.
6. Answers will vary.

Worksheets: A reproducible quiz for Section 3 is provided in the Teacher Classroom Resources.

SECTION 3 Review

Reviewing the Vocabulary
Review the vocabulary on page 278. Then answer these questions.
1. The _____ is made up of the _____, which are hollow bones.

Reviewing the Facts
2. **List.** What three things affect your skeleton over the years?
3. **Describe.** Which people are most at risk for developing back pain?
4. **Explain.** Why is sleeping flat on your back not recommended?
5. **Analyze.** Besides improving the health of the spine, why is good posture important?

Writing Critically
6. **Expository.** Spend a few minutes observing the posture of people as they walk, sit, or stand. What does their posture say about them? Think about your own posture. What does it say about you? Does it need to be improved? If so, how can you go about improving it?

For fitness and health tips, visit the Fitness Zone at **glencoe.com**.

When to Visit a Health Care Provider

Part of caring for yourself involves seeking help from a health care provider when needed. Children and teens need regular medical checkups to make sure they are maturing normally and to receive their immunizations on time.

Checkups and Immunizations

MAIN IDEA ▶ Knowing when to get medical help is an important part of maintaining your health.

Immunizations are *injected or oral doses of medicine that stimulate the immune system to develop the long-term ability to quickly fight off infectious diseases*. **Figure 10.12** provides a list of currently recommended immunizations.

Aside from regular checkups, there may be times when you will need to see a doctor for an illness. If you are unsure whether or not your symptoms warrant a visit to your doctor, the following guidelines can help you determine if medical attention is necessary:

- Temperature above 102 degrees Fahrenheit.
- Any serious accident, injury, or fall.

Vocabulary

immunizations
REM (rapid eye movement)
insomnia

Figure 10.12   Immunization Timetable

Age	Vaccine
Birth	Hepatitis B (Hep B)
2 months	DTP (diphtheria, tetanus, pertussis) HIB (haemophilus influenza, type b), oral polio, Hep B
4 months	DTP, HIB, oral polio
6 months	DTP, HIB
12 months	Tuberculin test, Hep B
15 months	MMR (measles, mumps, rubella), HIB, DTP, oral polio, chicken pox (varicella zoster virus, or VZV)
4 to 6 years	DTP, oral polio, MMR
11 to 12 years	MMR (if not given at age 4 to 6), VZV (if not given at 15 months), Hep B (if not given during infancy)
14 to 16 years	Tetanus-diphtheria toxoid, adult type; booster every ten years or after a contaminated wound if more than five years have passed since the previous injection

Decision Making

➤ Objectives

- Identify personal values that influence a health-related decision.
- Apply the steps of the decision-making process to make a healthy decision.

Blemish Blues

Lately, whenever Jesse looks in a mirror, all he notices are the acne blemishes covering his forehead and chin. He's sure that all the other kids are staring at his skin whenever they talk to him, and it makes him feel self-conscious. He's even too embarrassed by his acne to go to school dances.

Jesse has tried several over-the-counter acne products, including face washes and creams. None of the products have helped. He wonders if a health care provider could treat his acne problem. Maybe there are prescription drugs that would work better than the over-the-counter products he's already tried. On the other hand, Jessie isn't sure that his acne is serious enough to be treated by a professional. What if the health care provider thinks he's overreacting? That would also be embarrassing. Jesse doesn't know what he should do.

➤Identify the Problem

1. What decision is Jesse trying to make?

➤Form an Action Plan

2. What are Jesse's options, and what are the possible outcomes of each option?
3. What values do you think Jesse should consider in making his decision?
4. After Jesse makes his decision, how will he know whether he made the right decision?

➤What Did You Learn?

5. If you were Jesse, what would you decide to do?

Applying Health Skills:

1. Jesse is trying to decide whether to seek help for his acne from a health care provider.

2. Jessie can decide to go or not to go to a health care provider. If he decides to go, the health care provider might be able to treat his acne and clear up his blemishes. If he decides not to go, his acne is unlikely to improve and might become worse.

3. Jesse should consider his health, self-esteem, and happiness.

4. Jesse can monitor his acne and how he feels about it. If his acne clears up and he feels less self-conscious about it, he will know that he made the right decision.

5. Answers will vary.

- Sudden severe pain in the abdomen.
- Breathing difficulty.
- Loss of consciousness, even if brief.
- Severe headache for more than two hours.
- Intense itch.
- Bleeding with unknown cause.
- Faintness; dizziness; abnormal pulse or breathing.
- Sudden loss of mental ability, vision, hearing, touch, or ability to move.
- Any symptoms after taking medication.
- Diarrhea or vomiting for a day or more.
- Noticeable lumps anywhere on the body.
- A change in a mole or freckle.
- Unintended weight loss.

If your illness requires medical attention, be sure to alert your doctor of all symptoms you are experiencing and the length of time you have experienced such symptoms. By having a more complete understanding of your symptoms, your doctor will be able to begin treatment quickly.

Worksheets: A reproducible quiz for Section 4 is provided in the Teacher Classroom Resources.

SECTION 4 Review

Reviewing the Vocabulary
Review the vocabulary on page 281. Then answer these questions.
1. Write a sentence using the term *immunizations*.

Reviewing the Facts
2. List. List some symptoms of illnesses or injuries that indicate the need to seek medical help.

Writing Critically
3. Personal. Check with your parents to find out if your immunizations are up to date. If there are any that are not current, discuss how and when they should be updated.

1. Answers will vary.

2. Temperatures above 102 degrees Fahrenheit, serious accident or injury, breathing difficulty

3. Answers will vary.

For more vocabulary practice, play the Concentration game at **glencoe.com**.

Q&A Our Need for Sleep

Understand and Apply Read the conversation below, and then complete the writing exercise that follows.

This Q&A explores the importance of sleep and tells what is known about its effects on the health of the body.

Q: What exactly does sleep do for me?

A: During sleep, people recover from physical and emotional stresses and injuries. They also dream. We also know that blood pressure falls, breathing and heartbeat slow down, the muscles relax, and the body temperature falls. Most importantly, growth hormone is released at almost no time other than during sleep. Growth hormone provides for growth and renewal of body cells.

At the same time sleep slows your body down, your brain remains hard at work. The brain uses the time to create new memories from the day's events and to form new insights.

Q: If a person is too busy to get enough sleep, can they learn to live with less sleep?

A: People who don't get enough sleep become irritable, can't concentrate, think and learn more slowly, lose focus, and lose coordination. If deprived of sleep long enough, people often feel confused and may begin seeing imaginary things. Other problems with too little sleep include fatigue, reduced ability to work, reduced infection-fighting immunity, and increased risks of heart disease and digestive disorders. Irregular sleep or chronic lack of sleep over years can shorten life.

Q: How much sleep do I really need?

A: People's sleep needs vary. Adults probably need 7 to 8 hours to be well-rested. Children and younger adolescents need 9 or more hours, and babies sleep 16 hours or even more. These differences seem to partly reflect the rate of cell growth, which is fastest in the young and which slows throughout life. In addition, it's not just the quantity of sleep that's important. The quality of sleep matters, too.

Q: I've heard that an hour of sleep before midnight is worth two afterward, but I rarely get to bed before 11 o'clock.

A: The body goes through several sleep stages. First, your body temperature falls and your brain slows its activity. During this stage, your muscles relax, and your heartbeat slows. Minutes later, you enter the second stage of sleep. Brain activity slows more, and your eyes roll from side to side. This stage lasts for about half an hour.

The third and fourth stages of sleep bring very slow brain activity, relaxed muscles, and even breathing. This is the deepest sleep of all. It occurs mostly in the early hours of a night's sleep.

Following these stages, *the periods of sleep in which a person is dreaming,* **REM** sleep, occurs. (REM stands for "rapid eye movement.") The rapid eye movements seem to reflect dreaming, as if the person's eyes were following the actions of the dreams. During REM sleep, your arms and legs are temporarily paralyzed, keeping you from physically acting out your dreams. You cycle several times a night through REM, into other stages of sleep, and back into REM.

Q: I had no idea so much was going on while I was asleep. What do you suppose it's all for?

A: REM sleep seems to be essential to a person's well-being. People deprived of REM sleep become hostile, irritable, and anxious. When sound sleep is again possible, people who have been deprived of REM sleep will experience longer periods of REM to "make up" for what they've missed. This is one reason why sleeping pills may actually harm people. Many of them interfere with this important phase of sleep.

People who drink alcohol, consume caffeine, or smoke cigarettes may also be interrupting their normal sleep patterns without knowing it. Even a single alcoholic drink before bedtime has caused abnormal stoppage of breathing in sleep experiments. Caffeine and nicotine, the drug of tobacco, are both stimulants and can change the brain's activity to prevent normal sleep.

Q: Can I make up for lost sleep by napping or sleeping more on the weekends?

A: Short naps can help by improving alertness, mood, and work performance. But a good night's sleep is essential for full recovery. Sleeping more on the weekends may help relieve some of the sleep "debt" from the week, but will not improve performance during weekdays with too little sleep.

Q: What if I just can't get to sleep?

A: For ordinary **insomnia**, (in-SOM-nee-uh) *sleep abnormalities, including difficulty in falling asleep and wakefulness through the night*, avoid colas or other sources of caffeine late in the day. Be physically active early in the day and not right before going to bed. Schedule a time to relax before trying to sleep. Turn off lights, computers, televisions, and other sleep distracters. Try to keep the temperature in your room cooler than normal. If you often feel sleepy in the day, even if you have slept all night, you may have a sleep disorder that can be treated. Let your parents or the school nurse know about it.

Writing Write a paragraph explaining each stage of the sleep cycle and its importance to your health.

Reviewing Vocabulary

Use the vocabulary terms listed below to complete the following statements.

vertebrae

blackhead

cavity

menstrual cramps

gum disease

keratin

1. A _____ is a hole in the tooth caused by decay.

2. Inflammation and degeneration of the pink tissue that is attached to the teeth and helps to hold them in place is called _____.

3. _____ is the normal protein of hair and nails.

4. A _____ is an open pimple with dark skin pigments.

5. Contractions of the uterus, during and a few days before menstruation, that may cause pain are called _____.

6. The delicate, hollow bones of the spine are _____.

Recalling Key Facts and Ideas

Section 1

7. **Describe.** Describe correct flossing and brushing techniques.

8. **Explain.** Why is it important to floss teeth regularly.

9. **List.** Identify two foods that promote tooth decay and two foods that do not promote tooth decay.

Section 2

10. **Evaluate.** What is the only cure for damaged hair?

11. **Describe.** What happens when oil and bacteria irritate the skin?

12. **Analyze.** Why is it important to avoid loud noises?

Section 3

13. **List.** List one thing correct posture can do for you.

14. **Describe.** How can strong abdominal muscles help you avoid back pain?

Section 4

15. **Explain.** Why do children and teens need to have regular medical check-ups?

16. **List.** List four situations that would require a visit to the doctor.

Writing Critically

17. **Expository.** What are the benefits to the medical profession when people become more involved in self-care? What are some of the specific benefits of practicing self-care? Are there any risks involved in self-care?

18. **Persuasive.** Compare and contrast personal health care today with personal health care in the nineteenth century. Give specific examples.

1. Cavity 2. Gum disease 3. Keratin 4. Blackhead 5. Menstrual cramps 6. Vertebrae 7. Using floss, pull plaque and food particles up from the gum line and in between teeth. 8. Flossing removes plaque and bacteria from under the gumline. 9. Cookies, ice cream; milk, cheese 10. Trimming the ends of the hair. 11. The irritation causes a whitehead, or pimple. 12. Loud noises can harm the eardrum and

Activities

19. Interview a dental hygienist or a dentist about the dental care practices they recommend. Hand in a short report or a tape recording of the interview.

20. Produce an original video commercial or podcast. Use some of the advertising techniques listed on page 272 in the Consumer Skills Activity.

21. Contact some local community health agencies and make a list of educational programs they have available on self-care.

22. Make a poster of the dos and don'ts of personal health care. Try drawing the poster or cut pictures from magazines and newspapers to create a collage.

23. List all the ways to protect eyes to keep them healthy. Identify what occupations and sports commonly use protective eyewear.

24. Write a report on how your life would be different if you could not hear or see.

25. Work with three or four other students to design a bulletin board of strategies for maintaining a healthy body. Use creative ideas. Include drawings, photos from magazines or newspapers, and interesting type to make the bulletin board visually appealing.

26. Talk with an optometrist or ophthalmologist about the types of eye problems they see in teens. What are the most common problems? How do they treat them? What strategies do they have for keeping the eyes in good health? Make a poster with the information you collect from the person interviewed.

Making Decisions About Health

27. You have the feeling that something is wrong with your body. Symptoms seem to come and go and you wonder if you should see a physician. What course of action should you follow?

28. Josh is the drummer for a band that plays rock music. The music is played very loudly. (Josh says, "The louder, the better.") Lately, Josh has been asking people to repeat what they say to him. His grades in class are going down because he misses important points during the discussions and lectures. What do you think is Josh's problem? How can you help him understand that he has a problem? What would you advise Josh to do?

Go Online

For more vocabulary practice, play the True/False game at **glencoe.com**.

Fact or Fiction?

Answers
1. True.
2. False. Although cleanliness is important, there are no simple answers to preventing or curing acne.
3. True.

 Writing Paragraphs will vary.

cause hearing loss. **13.** Correct posture can help your self-esteem. **14.** Strong abdominal muscles help support the spine. **15.** They need to be checked to make sure they are given timely immunizations. **16.** A fever of 102 degrees

Fahrenheit or higher, faintness or dizziness, intense itch, sudden, severe abdominal pain **17–28.** Answers will vary.

Drugs as Medicines

Sections

Chapter Preview

Early in the last century, scientists discovered that certain substances can help prevent, cure, or relieve disease. Called **drugs**, these are *substances taken into the body that change one or more of the body's functions*. Today, people use thousands of different drugs as medicines. **Medicines** are *drugs used to help cure disease, lessen disease severity, relieve symptoms, help with diagnosis, or produce other desired effects*. The health effects of such widespread use of medicines, however, are not always those that people expect.

This chapter presents drugs used as medicines. The Q&A section discusses one of the most common of all drugs—caffeine. The next chapter focuses on drug abuse.

Fact or Fiction?

What Do You Think?

Is each statement true or false? If you think it's false, explain what's true.

1. Prescription medications can be dangerous, but over-the-counter medicines are safe.
2. The action of a drug can depend on whether or not it is taken with meals.
3. Generic drugs are exactly the same as their brand name equivalents, only cheaper.

 Writing Taking responsibility for your health includes making the right choices about taking medicines. Write a list of resources where you can get accurate information about medicines and drugs.

(Answers on page 307)

Go Online

Visit **glencoe.com** and complete the Life Choice Inventory for Chapter 11.

SECTION

1

The Actions of Drugs

People often believe that drugs can cure diseases, but this is not entirely true. Only the body can actually cure diseases. Drugs can only help the body in its efforts. Medicines benefit people in these ways:

- They may help prevent disease (example: vaccines provide immunity from certain diseases).

- They may help in the cure of disease (example: penicillin kills the bacteria that can cause some forms of pneumonia).

- They may make diseases less severe without helping cure them (example: steroid hormones reinforce the body's defense against incurable arthritis).

- They may relieve symptoms (example: aspirin relieves inflammation, aches, and pains).

- They may bring about other desired effects (example: a drug used to treat high blood pressure may also promote hair growth).

Amazing Aspirin

MAIN IDEA ▶ Drugs act by altering body processes, and all drugs have physical side effects.

A familiar, commonly used drug is **aspirin**, *a drug that relieves fever, pain, and inflammation*. Many people take it for headache or fever. It's not addictive, it's readily available, and many people think of it as less powerful than the drugs physicians prescribe. It can, however, have far-reaching chemical effects on the body. All drugs (whether drugs used medically or abused drugs) affect users physically. Their use always involves risks.

Aspirin works by blocking the actions of powerful chemicals. These chemicals exist in all body tissues. They produce fevers, cause the blood to clot, make nerves sensitive to pain, and cause **inflammation**, *pain and swelling caused by irritation*. Aspirin changes these body responses by changing the body's chemistry. Thus aspirin reduces fever and inflammation and prevents the blood from clotting.

Although you may use aspirin to relieve pain and fever, you cannot avoid all of its other effects. For example, a single two-tablet dose of aspirin doubles the bleeding time of wounds. That effect can last from four to seven days. For this reason, it is important not to take aspirin before any kind of surgery.

Vocabulary

drugs
medicines
aspirin
inflammation
side effects
antihistamines
transdermal
tolerance
drug synergy
antagonist

Various pain relievers other than aspirin include:

- acetaminophen (ah-SEET-ah-MIN-o-fen): *a drug that relieves fever and pain.*

- ibuprofen (EYE-byoo-PRO-fen): *a drug that relieves fever, pain, and inflammation.*

- naproxen sodium (na-PROX-en): *a pain reliever that provides longer relief than other common pain relievers.*

- ketoprofen (KEE-toe-PRO-fen): *a drug that relieves fever, pain, and inflammation. Its small pill size eases swallowing for those who have trouble swallowing regular pills.*

All drugs have **side effects**, *effects of drugs other than the desired medical effects.* Some are harmful (see **Figure 11.2** on page 292). For example, many drugs impair driving ability. Cold medicines and **antihistamines**, *drugs that counteract inflammation caused by histamine, one of the chemicals involved in allergic reactions,* can cause drowsiness. Other drugs can slow down a driver's reaction time. If you have any question about a drug's side effects, talk with a pharmacist or other health care provider.

What Factors Can Change the Way a Medicine Works?

MAIN IDEA ▶ The way a drug affects each person depends on several factors.

When you take a drug, many factors work together to determine its effects. Your age, weight, and what method you use to take the drug can modify its effects. For example, drugs taken by mouth must be absorbed through the digestive tract. **Transdermal** drugs that are *absorbed through the skin and into the bloodstream,* or drugs injected into body tissues, go to work right away.

Taking other drugs is one leading factor that affects how medicines work. Other drugs may include alcohol, nicotine (the drug used in tobacco products), drugs of abuse, medicines, herbs, or even vitamins and minerals. Two or more drugs taken at the same time, or drugs taken with herbs or vitamins, can strongly affect one another's actions. They may slow down one another's absorption. They may work against one another in the tissues. One drug may get in the way of the other's breakdown and removal from the body.

A person's history of drug use also affects a medicine's action. This is so important that the next section tells of its effects on the body.

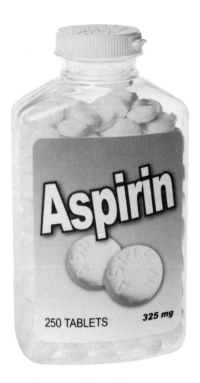

■ **Figure 11.1** *All drugs, including aspirin, have far-reaching chemical effects on the body. What symptoms can be relieved with aspirin?*

Caption Answer: Aspirin reduces fever and inflammation, and prevents blood clots.

Figure 11.2 Side Effects of Commonly Used Medicines

Medicine	Possible Hazard
Acetaminophen	Bloody urine; painful urination; skin rash; yellowing of the eyes or skin (even at normal doses); severe liver damage and death from overdose or chronic low-level excesses
Acid reducers	Fever; diarrhea; headache; anxiety; confusion; depression; dizziness; hallucinations; sleepiness; rarely, severe allergic reactions, heart and liver abnormalities
Antacids	Reduced mineral absorption from food; reduction of effectiveness of other medications; possible worsening of high blood pressure; aggravation of kidney problems
Aspirin	Stomach bleeding; vomiting; worsening of ulcers; enhancement of the action of anticlotting medications; severe allergic reactions in some people; association with Reye's syndrome in children and teens; prolonged bleeding time
Cold medications	Loss of consciousness (if taken with prescription tranquilizers)
Diet pills	Organ damage or death from bleeding of the brain
Ibuprofen	Allergic reactions in some people with aspirin allergy; fluid retention; liver damage similar to that from acetaminophen; enhancement of action of anticlotting medications
Ketoprofen	Stomach ulcers with bleeding
Laxatives	Reduced absorption of minerals from food; creation of dependency
Naproxen sodium	Stomach ulcers with bleeding; kidney damage in the elderly, in people with liver disease, or in those taking other drugs
Toothache medications	Destruction of the still-healthy part of a damaged tooth (for medications that contain clove oil)

Class Discussion

Comprehend: Discuss the statement, "Taking drugs to treat disorders can have several different effects." Have students explain the possible effects and the reasons they may occur.

Previous Drug Use, Other Drug Use

MAIN IDEA ▷ Tolerance to a drug develops when the body gets used to exposure to that drug.

A drug may produce one set of effects when used for just a few days. This same drug, however, may produce an entirely different set of effects when used over weeks, months, or years. Also, taking more than one drug can produce an unintended effect. Taking drugs to treat disorders can have several different effects.

It's important to tell your doctor and pharmacist all of the drugs you are taking so that they can monitor you for the effects of drugs. In some cases, a drug may lose its effectiveness if taken over a long period of time. If your doctor prescribes one drug to you, and you're already taking another drug for another disorder, the combined effect of both drugs may cause an unintended reaction. In other cases, drugs may work against each other, with one drug canceling the effect of another drug.

Tolerance

Often, after taking a drug over a long time, a person will develop a drug **tolerance**, *requiring larger and larger amounts of a drug to produce the same effect*. Tolerance means the body has grown used to being exposed to the drug. The longer the exposure, the better the body becomes at breaking the drug down, and the faster it gets rid of it. Tolerance varies from person to person. When you understand the body's tolerance to a drug, you begin to understand the origins of drug addiction.

Drug Synergy

Drug synergy is *the combined action of two drugs that is greater than the sum of their individual actions*. Sometimes this is beneficial, as when medicines are intended to work together to help cure an illness. Other times, the interactions are dangerous, as when sleeping pills and alcohol are combined. The body gives priority to breaking down the alcohol. Meanwhile, the sleeping medication could build up in the blood to high, or even deadly, levels. Many accidental deaths occur in this way. Many drugs, taken with alcohol, cause dangerous reactions.

Antagonist Drugs

A drug that opposes the action of another drug is called an **antagonist**. They prevent the action of another. Such drugs are often useful in the treatment of accidental overdoses or poisonings. Drugs that block the action of snake venoms are examples of antagonists. Some forms of addiction therapy use antagonist drugs to oppose the effects of the addictive drug.

Factors that Change Medicines' Effects

Several factors can change the way medicines work. When your doctor prescribes medicine to you, ask him or her to describe any factors that may influence how the medicine works. Some of the factors that may change how medicines work include:

- The nature of the drug.
- The form in which it is taken.

Caption Answer: The longer the exposure to the drug, the better the body becomes at breaking down the drug.

■ **Figure 11.3** *It is important to read the side effect information that comes with your medication. What does tolerance mean?*

- The route by which it is taken.
- When it is taken (with or without food).
- Your physical characteristics (age, weight, etc.).
- Other drugs you take.
- Your history of drug use.

SECTION 1 Review

Reviewing the Vocabulary

Review the vocabulary on page 290. Then answer these questions.

1. What are *drugs*?

2. What is the name for drugs used to help cure diseases, lessen disease severity, and relieve symptoms?

3. What is the term for requiring larger and larger doses of a drug to achieve the same effect?

4. Define *inflammation*.

5. What are *antihistamines*?

6. What is *drug synergy*?

Reviewing the Facts

7. Describe. When do drugs become medicines?

8. Analyze. What is an example of a side effect of a single dose of aspirin taken to relieve pain?

9. Identify. Explain a side effect of cold medicines and antihistamines that would affect a person's driving abilities.

Writing Critically

10. Descriptive. Your friend's father has a bad cold with a fever. He sometimes drinks alcohol and smokes, and decides to treat his cold with over-the-counter antihistamines. Write a letter describing why it would be important for him to avoid drinking or smoking when taking drugs as medicine.

For more vocabulary practice, play the Concentration game at **glencoe.com**.

Testing Drugs: Risks and Safety

The Food and Drug Administration (FDA), an agency of the federal government, regulates drugs to be marketed to consumers. The FDA ensures that ingredients in medicines are **safe**, *causing no undue harm*. Medicines also are required to be **effective**, *having the medically intended effect*. The FDA monitors drug companies as they develop new drugs and bring them to market. Then, after the drug is on the market, the FDA continues to check for side effects. Procedures for bringing new medicines to market are constantly reviewed, but approval can still take years.

Do All Drugs Have Risks?

MAIN IDEA ▶ Drugs that carry low risks to health are most helpful in the treatment of disease.

No drug is totally safe for all people at all times at any dose. The safety of any substance depends on how much of it a person consumes. Among the safest drugs are most **antibiotics**, *drugs used to fight bacterial infection*. Antibiotics often work by preventing cell division. Bacteria divide faster than body cells do, so bacteria die off before the person is harmed by the drug. For this reason, the dose and length of treatment have to be just right to wipe out the bacteria and leave the person able to recover.

Vocabulary

- safe
- effective
- antibiotics
- anesthetics
- lethal dose

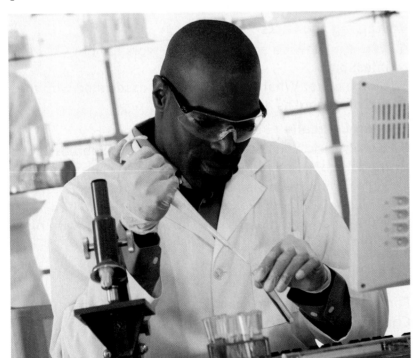

■ **Figure 11.4** *Part of the legal requirement for a drug means that an ingredient will not hurt you and that the ingredient will do what the maker claims it will do. What is the name of the agency responsible for ensuring the safety of medicines on the market?*

Caption Answer: The Food and Drug Administration

Some antibiotics have been overused with disastrous results. A bacterium repeatedly exposed to an antibiotic adapts to the drug's effect and becomes resistant to it. An infection with such an *antibiotic resistant* bacterium can be deadly if no other drugs are available to treat it.

Some drugs are less safe. One example is the drug alcohol, which was once used to kill pain during surgery. Safer **anesthetics** (an-us-THET-icks), *drugs that kill pain, with or without producing loss of consciousness*, were developed which replaced the use of alcohol. The amount of alcohol needed for the anesthetic affect is dangerously close to a **lethal dose**, *the amount of a drug necessary to cause death*. The same comparison is made for other drugs: How close is the effective dose to the lethal dose? Today, better, safer drugs are used for pain management.

Worksheets: A reproducible quiz for Section 2 is provided in the Teacher Classroom Resources.

SECTION 2 Review

Reviewing the Vocabulary
Review the vocabulary on page 295. Then answer these questions.

1. How is a drug described by the FDA if it has the medically intended effect?
2. What are drugs that kill pain, with or without producing loss of consciousness?
3. What is the term for the amount of a drug necessary to produce death?

Reviewing the Facts
4. **Explain.** How do antibiotic drugs work to fight infection?
5. **Synthesize.** What is the major risk associated with the use of alcohol as an anesthetic?

Writing Critically
6. **Expository.** You are going to a party to celebrate your friend's sixteenth birthday. Some students are spreading a rumor that he is planning to drink sixteen shots of alcohol. What do you think could happen to him? Write a paragraph explaining how you would warn him of the risks.

For more information on health careers, visit Career Corner at **glencoe.com**.

Answers (margin):
1. Effective
2. Anesthetics
3. Lethal dose
4. Antibiotics kill bacteria in the body.
5. The amount of alcohol necessary to kill pain can be deadly.
6. Answers will vary.

Nonprescription (Over-the-Counter) Medicines

The FDA divides medicines into two classes. The first is **over-the-counter (OTC) drugs**, *drugs legally available without a prescription*. These drugs are sold without the order of a doctor. The second classification is **prescription drugs**, *drugs legally available only with a physician's order*. You must have written authorization from a doctor to buy these drugs.

How Can People Benefit from OTC Drugs?

MAIN IDEA ▶ OTC drugs are available without a prescription.

Some OTC medicines are used to treat illnesses that are **chronic**, meaning *a disease or condition that develops slowly, shows little change, and lasts a long time*. Many ailments respond to the OTC treatments. Sometimes, though, people buy medicines that are not necessary and may be quite costly. Net sales for OTC medicines are in the many billions of dollars every year.

Vocabulary

over-the-counter (OTC) drugs
prescription drugs
chronic
generic
brand names
active ingredients
inactive ingredients
relapses

■ **Figure 11.5** *When using OTC medicines, follow safety guidelines. Why are some medicines available OTC while others are not?*

Caption Answer: OTC medications are considered safe, apply to most people, and do not cause dangerous side effects.

Unlike prescription drugs, which need a physician's prescription, OTC drugs are readily available. The FDA allows these drugs to be sold as OTC because these drugs are considered to be safe to be used without individual instructions. The instructions are easily understood and apply to most people without causing side effects that would make them dangerous. Sometimes, however, OTC drugs can be used to make other powerful, illegal drugs. Today, some cold remedies which are OTC drugs are stored behind the pharmacists counter to monitor their sales.

Many people, however, use too many OTC medicines too often. Advertisers seeking to sell their products influence people to seek cures for health problems through pills.

Consumer Skills Activity:

1. Answers will vary.
2. Inactive ingredients may affect the way the drug acts in the body.
3. If you want to save money, generic drugs are less expensive.

Consumer
SKILLS ACTIVITY

Money and Medicines

The cost of many medicines is high and getting higher. To save money, you can often use a less expensive alternative. Both OTC drugs and prescription drugs can be sold under **generic** names, *the chemical names for drugs; the names everyone can use,* and **brand names**, *the names companies give to drugs; the names by which they are sold.* Brand names are given to the same medications by companies that make and advertise them. One generic drug may have several brand names.

A generic drug contains the same **active ingredients**, *ingredients in a medicine that produce physical effects on the body,* as the brand name drug. However, it may have different **inactive ingredients**, *ingredients in a medicine for effects other than medical ones.* For example, oils added to lotions may allow them to spread evenly on the skin. Colors may be added to pills to help identify them.

These ingredients may affect the way the drug acts in the body. The next time you need a medication, ask your physi-cian or pharmacist if a generic drug can substitute for a more expensive, brand name drug. If it can, you'll save money and still get the medicine you need.

Consumers may also look for medicine bargains on the Internet. Some reputable online sellers do provide quality drugs at lower prices. Others, though, sell inferior or toxic drugs that look identical to the real thing. No quality control exists for drugs sold online. Serious risks stem from taking useless products while illnesses worsen, or taking toxic products. For now, these risks greatly outweigh any potential savings.

 Writing

1. Why do you think generic drugs cost less than brand name drugs?
2. What dangers might face a sick person who decides to switch to a generic drug without asking a physician?
3. When might a generic drug be preferable to a brand name drug?

For example, a person who has a headache may quickly take a dose of aspirin rather than trying to identify the cause of the headache. Maybe the person's headache is from hunger or tension. Maybe the person needs to rest more, to eat better, to exercise more, or to learn and use stress-reduction techniques.

Pain or discomfort is a signal from your body that something is out of balance. Before heading for the medicine cabinet for every minor ailment, stop and listen to your body. Try to find and relieve the cause of the pain. Instead of taking a tablet for indigestion, try eating more slowly or eating smaller portions. See if that relieves your discomfort.

Some OTC drugs are kept behind the counter. A federal law requires consumers to show identification and sign a log when buying certain OTC drugs. An example is cold medicine that contains pseudoephedrine (sue-doh-ee-FED-rin). This active ingredient opens up the nasal and sinus passages, but it also provides a key ingredient for making an illegal, powerful, and highly addictive drug of abuse. This drug, methamphetamine, is discussed in the next chapter.

How Can I Choose OTC Drugs Wisely?

MAIN IDEA ▶ All OTC drugs carry labels that provide important information to help you use them correctly and safely.

When you need a medicine, how can you tell which medicines to buy? You need to know how to read their labels to find out what's in them. By reading labels of OTC drugs, you can protect yourself against ingredients that may harm you. If you are allergic to the yellow dye tartrazine, for example, you can choose drugs not colored with it. The FDA requires that medicine companies list complete ingredients on labels. A drug label must list approved uses for drugs—that is, conditions against which the drugs have been proved effective. If products have other, unproved claims on their labels, they can be removed from store shelves.

While you're reading the label, check the expiration date. Medicines change with time into other substances that are not effective in treating illnesses. Do not buy medicines if they've passed the date stamped on the label. Throw away medicines you bought earlier, if they've passed their expiration dates. The "Applying Health Skills" feature on the next page shows what else you might find on a medicine label.

Before taking any medication, consult with your doctor and pharmacist to make sure you choose the right OTC drug for your needs.

Health Skills

Taking Medicines Safely

To take medicine safely, follow these guidelines:

1. Read and follow package instructions.

2. Do not share prescription medicine.

3. Do not mix drugs (including OTC, alcohol, herbs, nutrients, and other drugs) without checking first with your doctor or pharmacist.

4. Safely discard medicines that have passed the expiration date.

5. Store drugs in a cool, dark place.

6. Call your physician if the drug isn't doing what you expect it to, or if you develop side effects.

7. Store the drug in its original container.

8. Finish the prescription, even if you feel better right away.

9. Keep all medicines where young children cannot get them.

Accessing Information

➤ **Objectives**
- Identify safety warnings on over-the-counter drug labels.
- Evaluate the reliability of information on how to use over-the-counter drugs safely.

Choosing and Using OTC Drugs

Although over-the-counter (OTC) drugs are relatively safe, you need to read OTC drug labels carefully to choose the best drugs for your symptoms. OTC labels also tell you how to use the drugs safely. Below is a label for a hypothetical OTC drug.

Loradin
Active Ingredient Loratadine
Uses Reduces itchy watery eyes, sneezing, runny nose, itchy nose and throat
Warnings Do not take with alcohol; do not use if you are taking a prescription drug called an MAOI; consult your physician before using if you have high blood pressure, glaucoma, or asthma; may cause drowsiness, headache, and dry mouth.
Purpose Antihistamine
Directions Adults and children over 12 years: 1 capsule every 12 hours; children under 12 years: consult a physician; do not take more than 2 capsules in 24 hours.

➤ **Identify the Problem**
1. Identify a potential safety problem associated with this OTC drug.

➤ **Form an Action Plan**
2. Before purchasing an OTC drug, what information do you need?
3. Is the drug, shown above, safe to give to a six-year-old child?
4. If you are 16 years old, how often and how much of the drug can you safely take?

➤ **What Did You Learn?**
5. Research and compare two pain relievers: one generic and one brand name. Write a paragraph explaining which one you would use and why you would choose it.

Applying Health Skills:

1. Using with alcohol or a prescription drug called an MAOI and using when you have a health problem such as high blood pressure

2. A list of symptoms

3. Consult a physician first.

4. 1 capsule every 12 hours.

5. Answers will vary.

Thinking Twice About Your OTC Drugs

MAIN IDEA ▶ Both OTC and prescription drugs are given two names: generic names and brand names. Drugs have both active and inactive ingredients.

Most OTC drugs help relieve symptoms, but do not cure the illness. A person who is sick and takes OTC drugs should try not to resume normal activities too quickly. It's possible to suffer **relapses**, *illnesses that return after being treated and almost cured*. Relapses can be more severe than the original illnesses.

If OTC medicines don't bring you the relief you seek, it's time to visit your health care provider. Any health care provider can advise you on what actions to take. If you need prescription medicine, you'll need to consult a physician.

SECTION 3 Review

Reviewing the Vocabulary
Review the vocabulary on page 297. Then answer these questions.
1. Explain the differences between active ingredients and inactive ingredients.
2. What are *over-the-counter drugs*?
3. Who gives brand names to drugs?

Reviewing the Facts
4. **Analyze.** What are the benefits of buying generic drugs?
5. **Explain.** What makes over-the-counter drugs safe?
6. **Identify.** List five things you find on a medicine label.

Writing Critically
7. **Narrative.** Angela has a cold and a sore throat. She examines a nighttime cold medicine so she can sleep, something else to take during the day so she won't be drowsy, a cough medicine, nasal spray, and throat gargle. Should she take all of these drugs? Write a dialogue in which Angela discusses with the pharmacist how she might choose the right medicines.

Go Online

For more vocabulary practice, play the eFlashcards game at **glencoe.com**.

1. Active ingredients produce physical effects, inactive ingredients have nonmedical effects.
2. They are available without a doctor's prescription.
3. Companies who advertise and sell drugs give them brand names.
4. They are less expensive alternative drugs.
5. They can be obtained without doctor's order, they are relatively safe, instructions are easily understood.
6. Answers will vary
7. Answers will vary.

Prescription Medicines

As you learned in Section 3, prescription drugs are drugs that are not freely available. You can't buy them over the counter. They can be obtained only if prescribed (ordered) by doctors, because: they may be dangerous and they can easily be misused; the doses must be adjusted to body weight, age, drug use, or other factors; they require guidance to use them correctly and may have complicated directions; and, they can be abused. They can cause addiction or have other serious side effects.

Safe Use of Prescription Drugs

MAIN IDEA ▶ Taking prescription medication safely requires that you follow the medicine's instructions.

Prescription drugs have many uses. For example, for a person whose cells cannot properly use the sugar glucose in the blood, insulin is a life-saving medicine. A person whose heart can no longer use calcium may take a calcium channel blocker, so that his or her heartbeat continues. Prescription medicines can be misused, though. A physician may prescribe these drugs, but the person who takes the drug has a part to play, too, in using them correctly.

Suppose your cold symptoms do not go away, but instead grow worse after two weeks of rest and OTC medication. You begin to wonder if your illness is more serious than a cold. You see a health care professional, who prescribes a medicine for you. Before leaving the doctor's office with your prescription, be sure that you know:

- The name of your condition.
- The name of the prescribed medicine.
- Whether the doctor recommends using a generic version of the drug, if available.

■ **Figure 11.6** *Take care to store medicines properly. What should you know about your prescription before leaving your doctor's office?*

Caption Answer: You should know the name of the medication, how often you need to take it, and its possible side effects.

- How often, how long, and in what doses you should take the medicine.
- Whether to take the medicine with meals or between them.
- What side effects you should look for and report.
- What you should do if you forget to take a dose on time—double the next one, take it late, or leave it out entirely.

Also, be sure that your doctor knows what other medicines you are taking. Sometimes two different drugs may combine to cause unintended effects. Other strategies for taking medications, both OTC and prescription, are summed up in the Health Skills sidebar, "Taking Medicines Safely" on page 300.

Worksheets: A reproducible quiz for Section 4 is provided in the Teacher Classroom Resources.

SECTION 4 Review

Reviewing the Vocabulary

Review the vocabulary on page 302. Then answer these questions.

1. Define *caffeine*.
2. Write a definition for *stimulant*.

Reviewing the Facts

3. **Explain.** List four reasons why prescription drugs can only be obtained with a doctor's order or prescription.
4. **Describe.** What do you need to know about your prescriptions before you take them?
5. **Identify.** The Health Skills sidebar "Taking Medicines Safely" offers guidelines for taking medicines. List five of them.

Writing Critically

6. **Descriptive.** What steps can you take to be sure you are using medicines appropriately? What can you do to improve your own approach to medication? Write a page of guidelines for your family and friends who use over-the-counter drugs to help ensure that they do so safely and effectively.

Go Online

For more vocabulary practice, play the True/False game at **glencoe.com**.

1. A mild stimulant of the central nervous system (brain and spinal cord) found in common foods, beverages, and medicines

2. Any of a wide variety of drugs, including amphetamines, caffeine, and others, that speed up the central nervous system

3. The drug may be dangerous; dose may need to be adjusted; they require directions; they can be abused.

4. The name of the medicine, what dose you need to take, and side effects

5. Students should list five examples from the Health Skills list on p. 299

6. Answers will vary.

Q&A Caffeine

 Understand and Apply Read the conversation below, and then complete the writing exercise that follows.

Young people often use **caffeine**, *a mild stimulant of the central nervous system (brain and spinal cord) found in common foods, beverages, and medicines.* Caffeine is found in cola drinks, chocolate bars, and iced tea. Caffeine in coffee and medications provides an energy boost. Lately, though, some people have been cutting back on their caffeine use because they fear that caffeine may cause harm.

Q: **What exactly does caffeine do?**

A: Caffeine is a **stimulant**, *any of a wide variety of drugs, including amphetamines, caffeine, and others, that speed up the central nervous system.* It peps up the activity of the central nervous system (the brain and spinal cord). Some of its effects help you feel like you're more awake. The effect depends on how much you consume and how much you have used in the past. Most people notice a faster heart rate and feel their muscles tense when they take in the amount contained in two to five cups of brewed coffee. More than this can cause abnormal symptoms.

Q: **What symptoms does caffeine produce?**

A: Caffeine produces signs of stress and prolonged stress can weaken the body. Caffeine also acts as a diuretic—a drug that makes the body lose water through frequent urination. Caffeine also stimulates stomach acid secretion, so it irritates the stomach, especially in a person with ulcers.

The most severe effect of caffeine is fatal poisoning, but that occurs only with huge doses. For example, if a child accidentally ate 30 or so caffeine wake-up pills, emergency treatment would be required.

Q: **How can I tell if I'm getting too much caffeine?**

A: If you take more caffeine than the amount in about five cups of coffee in about an hour's time, your heartbeat may become irregular, and you may feel your heart pounding. You may have trouble sleeping. You may have headaches, trembling, nervousness, and other symptoms of anxiety.

A physician who is unaware of a person's caffeine use may mistakenly prescribe calming tranquilizers or recommend a psychiatrist for symptoms brought on by caffeine. All the person really needs is to cut down on caffeine intake.

Q: **I've heard a friend say, as a joke, "I'm addicted to 'energy drink' colas! I go through withdrawal!" Is caffeine addictive?**

A: Yes caffeine is addictive. Your friend may have built up a tolerance to caffeine by taking in large amounts daily. Many colas contain as much caffeine, ounce for ounce, as coffee.

■ **Figure 11.7** *When choosing beverages, it is best to limit caffeine. Why is it important to limit your caffeine intake?*

Caption Answer: Caffeine can cause headaches and irregular heartbeats if too much is consumed.

If your friend were to suddenly stop drinking these beverages, withdrawal symptoms might start: anxiety, muscle tension, and a headache that no painkiller can relieve. Only caffeine can reverse these symptoms of withdrawal.

Q: Is that why they put caffeine in headache medicines, then?

A: Yes. Someone with a caffeine-withdrawal headache may try plain pain relievers, but these fail to cure the headache. When the person tries an "extra-strength" kind that includes caffeine, the headache disappears. The pills increase the person's caffeine intake even more.

Q: If caffeine is addictive, as you say, is my friend engaging in drug abuse?

A: You may want to read the next chapter and answer that question. If your friend takes caffeine *pills* to avoid withdrawal, then yes, your friend is abusing drugs. However, if your friend drinks only colas, then the caffeine is a food component, not officially a drug. That is why caffeine can be added to soft drinks—it occurs naturally in the kola nut and is an expected part of the product.

Q: Do you think we should all avoid caffeine?

A: Not necessarily. The equivalent of one or two cola beverages or a cup or two of coffee a day is almost certainly safe for any teen or adult. Pregnant females and young children might be wise to do without it, though, just because some questions about caffeine are still unanswered.

Q: What are some alternatives to beverages that contain caffeine?

A: Many sodas are caffeine-free these days. Decaffeinated coffee is one option. (By the way, there is no truth in the rumor that decaffeinated coffee or tea contains dangerous chemicals.) Decaffeinated tea and teas made from mint or other herbs are delicious. Don't forget the best thirst quencher—a glass of water. Also, juice and milk are natural drinks with a health bonus since they provide nutrients your body needs.

 Writing Write a brief paragraph explaining the effects caffeine has on the body. Include reasons to choose beverages that do not contain caffeine.

Reviewing Vocabulary

Use the vocabulary terms listed below to complete the following statements.

ketoprofen

safe

naproxen

over-the-counter drugs

antibiotics

aspirin

acetaminophen

ibuprofen

1. _____ are drugs used to fight bacterial infections.
2. There are five different drugs that are used to relieve fever, pain, and inflammation. They are _____, _____, _____, _____, and _____.
3. A drug that is _____ causes no undue harm.
4. _____ are legally available without a prescription.

Recalling Key Facts and Ideas

Section 1
5. **List.** List three ways in which medicines benefit people.
6. **Explain.** Explain why aspirin must be limited before surgery.
7. **Describe.** Describe the factors that alter a drug's effects on the body.

8. **Identify.** Define tolerance (to a drug).
9. **Explain.** What is the purpose of a drug that acts as an antagonist?

Section 2
10. **Describe.** What must the FDA do in order to approve a new drug?
11. **Explain.** Why are antibiotics among the safest drugs?

Section 3
12. **Recall.** What are OTC drugs?
13. **Identify.** What is the difference between generic drugs and brand name drugs?
14. **Explain.** What is the reason some OTC drugs are kept behind the counter?
15. **Describe.** What does the FDA require to be printed on drug labels?

Section 4
16. **Describe.** What information should you know before leaving the physician's office with your prescription?
17. **Explain.** Why would your physician need to know about any other drugs you are taking before writing a prescription?

Writing Critically

18. **Personal.** Discuss some of the problems people may face from taking aspirin regularly. How can healthier alternatives to aspirin be promoted? How could you publicize this information in your school?
19. **Expository.** Other countries put drugs on the market faster than the United States. Many people go out of the United States to obtain these drugs. Do you think it is safe for many Americans to use drugs from other countries? What possible problems could occur?

1. Antibiotics 2. Acetamenophen, ibuprofen, naproxen sodium, ketoprophen 3. Safe 4. Over-the-counter drugs 5. Prevent disease; cure disease; make disease less severe. 6. Aspirin prevents the blood from clotting. 7. The nature of the drug; the form and route by which it is taken, when it is taken, your age, weight, and expectations, other drugs, history of drug use 8. Requiring larger and larger amounts of a drug to produce the same effect. 9. They prevent the action of another drug. 10. FDA ensures drugs are safe and effective. 11. The body's cells recover quickly

20. Descriptive. On Friday night, Kyle suffered a painful swollen shoulder during the football game. To relieve the pain he took a friend's prescription drug containing codeine. Soon Kyle experienced nausea. What should he do? What should he have done after the injury?

Activities

21. Watch TV for one hour and write down all the advertisements that relate to drugs. How many advertisements are for over-the-counter drugs? What does that tell you about our society and the use of drugs? Take an advertisement that promotes the use of a drug to relieve a health problem and change it to an advertisement that promotes healthful activities instead of drugs, for relief.

22. Bring in one article from a newspaper or magazine about the problem(s) of over-the-counter drug use. Highlight information the class has discussed. Read aloud parts of the article the class has not discussed.

23. Make a video for local elementary schools and high schools showing the effects caffeine has on the body and explain why it's the most widely used over-the-counter drug.

Making Decisions about Health

24. Your friend has been feeling tired and run-down lately. Her hectic schedule, which includes school full time, work part time, and participation on a softball team, leaves no time for adequate rest or proper nutrition. She decides to make a trip to the health food store to see if she can buy something to give her more energy. She spots a bottle that looks interesting. An information sheet nearby promises that the product will give her renewed energy, stamina, and mental alertness. It also promises the product will clean toxins out of her blood. Are such remedies more effective or safer than nonprescription, over-the-counter drugs? Why or why not? What can you say about the reliability of the information presented on the information sheet next to the remedy?

Go Online

For more information on health careers, visit Career Corner at **glencoe.com**.

Fact or Fiction?

Answers
1. False. All drug use involves risk.
2. True. This is one of the factors that affect the action of a drug.
3. False. Generic drugs contain the same active ingredients, but may contain different inactive ingredients.

Writing Paragraphs will vary.

from the antibiotics effects. **12.** They are legally available without a prescription. **13.** They have the same ingredients, generic drugs use the chemical names, and are less expensive. **14.** Some ingredients are regulated by law because of the possibility of abuse. **15.** Truth on all labels, with a listing of approved uses of the drug and conditions for which the drugs have been proven effective. **16.** Name of medicines, how often, how long, and what dose to take. **17.** Because of the possible effects of other drug interactions. **18–24.** Answers will vary.

Chapter 11 Review **307**

CHAPTER 12

Drugs of Abuse

Sections

For many teens, being drug-free means a lot of different things. To be drug-free, avoid those who use drugs. Find friends who don't use drugs. Become a role model for others, and learn how to use refusal skills to resist the pressure to use drugs. Learning how drugs affect the body will help you understand that drugs can have serious consequences to your health.

Drug abuse hurts individuals, families, communities, and society. This chapter begins by defining drug abuse and discussing why some people abuse drugs. The chapter then describes drug addiction, commonly abused drugs, and the dangers of drug abuse and driving. The chapter closes with information about recovery from drug addiction. The Q&A section provides strategies for refusing drugs.

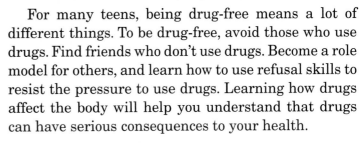

Fact or Fiction?

What Do You Think?

Is each statement true or false? If you think it's false, explain what's true.

1. A physical addiction is more powerful than a psychological addiction.
2. Unlike smoking tobacco, smoking marijuana does not harm health.
3. People usually recover from drug dependency on their own.

 Writing How prepared are you to avoid illegal drug use? Write two responses you might use if someone you know tried to get you to go to a party where drugs will be available.

(Answers on page 341)

Visit **glencoe.com** and complete the Life Choice Inventory for Chapter 12.

Drug Abuse Defined

Definitions of drug abuse vary. Medical experts and the Food and Drug Administration (FDA) have created one set of formal definitions. Society has created another set of definitions. Individual people have created still others, based on their own drug histories and attitudes.

Vocabulary

drug use
drug misuse
drug abuse
recreational drug use

Official Definitions

MAIN IDEA ▶ Drug abuse can damage a person's health and ability to function effectively.

The FDA defines **drug use** as *the taking of a drug for its medically intended purpose, and in the appropriate amount, frequency, strength, and manner.* **Drug misuse** is *the taking of a drug for its medically intended purpose, but not in the appropriate amount, frequency, strength, or manner.* You have learned the importance of following directions when using drugs as medicine. In contrast, **drug abuse** is *the deliberate taking of a drug for anything other than a medical purpose.* Drug abuse can result in damage to a person's health or ability to function. All drugs can be abused, even those prescribed by physicians.

■ **Figure 12.1** *Life is full of natural pleasures, but drug abuse prevents their enjoyment. What effect would drug abuse have on this person's ability to enjoy his sport?*

Caption Answer: This person would not be able to function well enough to enjoy activities.

Society's Definition

MAIN IDEA ► Lawmakers have passed laws related to drug abuse. In our society, the use of mind-altering drugs is illegal.

Some individuals try to define drug abuse differently. Many people who take mind-altering drugs call themselves drug users, not abusers. For example, someone who takes drugs when socializing with friends may consider him or herself a drug user. However, there is no such thing as mere "use" of a drug. People may also use the label **recreational drug use**, *a term made up, to describe their drug use, by people who claim their drug taking produces no harmful social or health effects.* This term is not defined by the FDA.

Class Discussion
Discuss: Have each student create a list of positive and negative consequences that can result from drug use, abuse, misuse, and recreational or social use. Are there more positive or negative consequences? Discuss.

Worksheets: A reproducible quiz for Section 1 is provided in the Teacher Classroom Resources.

SECTION 1 Review

Reviewing the Vocabulary

Review the vocabulary on page 310. Then answer these questions.

1. Define *drug use*.
2. Taking a drug for its medically intended purpose but not in the proper dose is called ____.
3. What is the deliberate taking of a drug for anything other than medical purposes?
4. ____ is a term made up by people who claim their drug taking produces no harmful social or health effects.

Reviewing the Facts

5. **Explain.** What two groups have provided official definitions of drug abuse?
6. **Describe.** Describe how society's views of drug abuse are reflected in its laws.

Writing Critically

7. **Expository.** Using three examples, describe the difference between drug use, misuse, and abuse to an audience of younger students.

 **Online**

For more information on health careers, visit Career Corner at **glencoe.com**

1. Taking a drug for its medically intended purpose
2. Drug misuse
3. Drug abuse
4. Recreational drug use
5. Medical experts and the FDA
6. Society has defined the use of mind-altering drugs as abuse and made it illegal.
7. Answers will vary

Why Do People Abuse Drugs?

Teens face many choices, including whether to try drugs. Those who try them don't realize the extreme risk they are taking. Many factors influence the choices a teen makes about drug use. Some influences can include: peer pressure, family members, role models, media messages, perceptions of drug behavior, and misleading information.

Substance Abuse

MAIN IDEA ▶ People abuse drugs for many reasons, such as the belief that drugs will help relieve problems.

In today's world, drugs are an easy, all-too-available way for people to feel better who are stressed or have other problems. Some people do not know how to cope with their problems in a healthy way. People in physical or emotional pain may seek relief this way too.

Personality

Some people are naturally curious, and may try drugs to experience what they are like. These people may not, however, become chronic drug abusers. Other reasons that people may consider taking drugs include shyness or discomfort in social situations, to relieve tension, or because a person has low self-esteem or a poor self-image.

Peer Pressure

A strong factor that motivates people to abuse drugs is peer pressure. You read about peer pressure in Chapter 3. Among some groups, the desire to fit in socially is strong. Some people are simply risk-takers; they are drawn to dangerous behaviors. While it is important to have friends and status, it is more important to resist the pressure to take or sell drugs. Often, when one or two key people say no, the behavior of a whole group can change. Other reasons people may abuse drugs include:

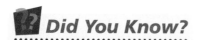

Did You Know?

Peers can influence teens to avoid illegal drug use.

- Values. Teens who lack strong internal values, such as the values of good grades, and high moral standards, often abuse drugs.

- Boredom, or lack of excitement or fun. Some people wrongly believe that taking drugs provides pleasure.

- Escape from life's problems. People who don't feel loved, have no friends, or lack money take drugs as a substitute for what is missing.

Unfortunately, when the drug is gone, the original problems that led to the drug abuse are still there. People cannot escape their problems by taking drugs. It prevents people from recognizing and solving their problems. Once the effect of the drug wears off, the problems remain.

The Nature of the Drug

Some drugs cause feelings of pleasure or **euphoria**, *a sense of great well-being and pleasure brought on by some drugs.* These drugs are among the most likely to be abused. Euphoria is a strong biological motivator, which makes the user want more, and can lead to addiction.

Preventing Drug Abuse

MAIN IDEA ▶ Family support, drug education programs, and legal or social consequences can prevent drug abuse.

The Power of the Family

The best prevention for drug abuse begins at home. Parents greatly influence the values, life goals, and directions of their children. Open communication, positive family relationships, and strong opposition to drug abuse all help to guide teens away from drugs.

The Role of Drug Education

Education about the impact of drugs can prevent drug abuse. Drug education programs that also teach students personal skills, such as refusal skills, also prevent drug abuse.

Consequences from Society

Some teens falsely believe they are protected from prosecution by the authorities if caught with drugs as a **juvenile**, *a legal term meaning a person under age 18, a minor.* They may make easy prey for an adult **drug trafficker**, *a person involved in the transport and sales of illegal drugs.* Regardless of a person's age, harsh punishment awaits those who possess or sell drugs. The punishments range from detention in a juvenile facility to time in jail.

SECTION 2 Review

1 A sense of great well-being and pleasure brought on by some drugs.

2. Juvenile

3. Drug trafficker

4. Any three: curiosity; peer pressure; tension; low self-esteem; lack of values; boredom; escape

5. They produce a feeling of pleasure.

6. Drug education is important but not enough to prevent drug abuse. Programs that also teach refusal skills often prevent drug abuse as well.

7. Answers will vary.

Reviewing the Vocabulary

Review the vocabulary on page 312. Then answer these questions.

1. Define the term *euphoria*.

2. What is the legal term used to describe a person under age 18?

3. A person who transports and sells drugs is known as a _____.

Reviewing the Facts

4. Identify. List three reasons people may abuse drugs.

5. Explain. Drugs that produce euphoria are most likely to be abused. Why?

6. Describe. Describe the importance of drug education in preventing drug abuse.

Writing Critically

7. Persuasive. Entertainers, movies, songs, magazines, and books may portray drug abuse as funny or cool. What can you do to change this image? Write an essay outlining how we as a society can change the media's outlook on drugs.

For more vocabulary practice, play the eFlashcards game at **glencoe.com**.

Addiction

Drug addiction (also called dependence) is *a physical or psychological need for higher and higher doses of a drug.* No one who starts out using a substance intends to become addicted. A person may try a drug for one reason, but becomes addicted.

Drugs and the Brain

MAIN IDEA ▶ Drugs create a "high" by releasing pleasure-producing chemicals in the brain.

Drugs provide a sense of euphoria by imitating the brain's natural way of producing pleasure. The acts of eating, being physically active, and relaxing release **endorphins,** *chemicals in the brain that produce feelings of pleasure in response to a variety of activities.* The lack of these chemicals produces an unpleasant feeling, known as **dysphoria** (dis-FORE-ee-uh), *the unpleasant feelings that occur when endorphins are lacking.*

This pattern encourages people to engage in health-promoting behaviors. These natural chemicals are similar to mind-altering drugs, but there is a key difference. The natural chemicals are produced in response to healthful activities.

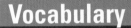

Vocabulary

drug addiction
endorphins
dysphoria
physical addiction
withdrawal
psychological addiction

■ **Figure 12.3** *Some people choose health-promoting activities over those that cause harm. How can physical activities promote a healthy outlook to help teens avoid drug use?*

Caption Answer: Physical activities contribute to healthy self-esteem. People with healthy self-esteem are less likely to do drugs.

Figure 12.4

The Spiral That Leads to Physical Addiction

The craving created by withdrawal, and the need to take higher and higher doses, creates a spiral of physical addiction.

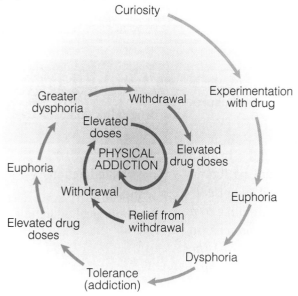

How Does Addiction Set In?

Taking mind-altering drugs produces pleasure with no healthful activity associated with it. At the same time, the brain of the drug taker produces fewer and fewer of its own endorphins. After each round of drug-taking, when the pleasure from the drugs wears off, the person is left with the unpleasant sensation, dysphoria. The person may then use more drugs to chase away the dysphoria, unaware that more discomfort will follow, along with the desire for still more drugs.

When people take drugs to ease dysphoria, they may be headed toward drug addiction. Drug addiction can be either physical or psychological. Most drugs that cause addictions are euphoria-producing drugs, however, a few drugs, including nicotine and caffeine, produce addiction without euphoria.

Physical Addiction

MAIN IDEA ▶ Physical addiction occurs when the body's chemistry adjusts its functioning to the presence of a drug.

Physical addiction, or dependence, causes *a change in the body's chemistry so that without the presence of a substance (drug), normal functioning begins to fail*. The body craves the drug to be able to function normally. As the body begins to clear the drug from the system, then the symptoms of withdrawal begin. **Withdrawal** means *the physical symptoms that occur when an addictive drug is cleared from the body tissues*.

The symptoms of withdrawal may include problems with vision, muscle activity, digestion, brain function, temperature regulation, or many other processes. Withdrawal changes brain patterns, affects mood, and makes the person crave the drug.

Physical addiction also makes the body develop a tolerance to the drug—when the person needs to take higher and higher doses. **Figure 12.4** illustrates the spiral of addiction. The spiral of addiction continues until the person gets medical help to stop using the drugs. Recovery from addiction is described on pages 333–335.

Class Activity

Identify: Explain that one reason drug abusers keep taking drugs is to avoid the withdrawal symptoms. Divide students into groups and have each group research the withdrawal effects of one of the following drugs: marijuana, heroin, methamphetamine, alcohol, and ecstasy. Ask each group present their findings to the class.

Psychological Addiction

MAIN IDEA ▶ The only sure way to escape drug addiction is never to experiment with the drugs that produce it.

Physical addiction always triggers **psychological addiction** or dependence, *mental dependence on a drug, habit, or behavior*. People who never learn to cope with emotional pain may develop psychological addictions to drugs. This happens if people believe they can use drugs to relieve emotional pain. Psychological addictions can be as powerful as physical addictions. The only sure way to escape drug addiction is never to experiment with taking drugs.

> *" Despair is better treated with hope, not dope. "*
>
> —Dr. Richard Asher
> (1912–1969)
> Physician

Worksheets: A reproducible quiz for Section 3 is provided in the Teacher Classroom Resources.

SECTION 3 Review

Reviewing the Vocabulary

Review the vocabulary on page 315. Then answer these questions.

1. What is the name for chemicals in the brain that produce feelings of pleasure in response to a variety of activities?
2. The physical symptoms that occur when a drug to which a person is addicted is cleared from the body tissues are called _____.
3. What is mental dependence on a drug, habit, or behavior called?

Reviewing the Facts

4. **Describe.** What activities do people do that naturally produce endorphins?
5. **Explain.** Describe the effects of physical addiction.
6. **Identify.** List the withdrawal symptoms from physical addiction.

Writing Critically

7. **Narrative.** Your friend Renee has been hanging around a group of teens who use drugs. Write Renee a note explaining the dangers she may face if she is influenced to try drugs.

Go Online

For more vocabulary practice, play the Concentration game at **glencoe.com**.

1. Endorphins
2. Withdrawal
3. Psychological addiction
4. Eating, being physically active, listening to music
5. The body chemistry changes and requires the drug just to function normally.
6. Problems with vision, muscle activity, digestion, brain function, or temperature regulation can occur.
7. Answers will vary.

Commonly Abused Drugs

This section discusses commonly abused drugs. Illegal drugs don't come with warning labels that help you make an informed decision. As they are prepared, illegal drugs may be mixed with unknown substances, even poisons, and can have unexpected effects on your health. **Figure 12.6** on pages 320–323 presents many more details about abused drugs.

Vocabulary

- hallucinations
- amotivational syndrome
- amphetamines
- methamphetamine
- sedatives
- barbiturates
- opium
- opiates
- narcotics
- codeine
- morphine
- heroin
- oxycodone
- hallucinogens
- LSD (lysergic acid diethylamide)
- PCP (phencyclidine hydrochloride)
- peyote
- mescaline
- psilocybin
- look-alikes
- ephedrine
- sudden sniffing death
- club drugs

Marijuana

MAIN IDEA ▶ Marijuana use can cause abnormal heart action, reduced immunity, and lung damage.

Marijuana is the most frequently abused illegal drug in the United States today. Marijuana users smoke it or put it in food. Hashish, a concentrated marijuana resin, is also smoked or sometimes eaten. Among those who use hashish, the risks of abuse are higher, because the taker receives a stronger dose.

■ **Figure 12.5** *Drug tests can detect trace amounts of THC for as long as six months after its use.* *What is the danger in using hashish?*

Caption Answer: Short-term memory loss, irregular heartbeats, altered immune response

The chemicals in marijuana that produce euphoria are all related to the chemical delta-9-tetrahydrocannabinol, or THC, which the plant produces as it grows. When inhaled by smoking, the active chemicals are rapidly absorbed in the lungs. They then travel in the blood to the brain, liver, and kidney, and are released through the urine.

Effects of THC

THC affects brain centers that manage the senses. It alters hearing, touch, taste, and smell, as well as the sense of time, the sense of space, and emotions. THC also produces changes in sleep patterns. THC does have some health benefits. It is sometimes used to fight the intense nausea people suffer when they undergo treatments for cancer and AIDS. It also can reduce eye swelling from the disease glaucoma.

Other Chemicals in Marijuana

In addition to THC, scientists have identified more than 500 different chemicals in marijuana. The different chemicals affect the different experiences people have as a result of using marijuana. Reactions range from a mild euphoria and uncontrollable laughter to **hallucinations**, *false perceptions such as imagined sights, sounds, smells, or other feelings, sometimes brought on by drug abuse, sometimes by mental or physical illness.*

Harmful Health Effects

Despite the euphoria created by using marijuana, its use can have harmful effects on health. Research shows that some of the harmful health effects include:

- Short-term memory loss and a shortened attention span.
- Changes in the heart's action, causing rapid and sometimes irregular heartbeats.
- Altered immune response.
- Reduced hormone levels and sperm count in men.
- Lung damage—bronchitis, emphysema, possibly lung cancer.

Marijuana may also be contaminated with pesticides, poisonous molds, or herbicides. As it is being processed, marijuana may be mixed with other chemicals which can make a user's reaction unpredictable. Another dangerous side effect of marijuana is that it impairs driving ability. Even after a small dose, a person's reaction time and judgment are impaired. Some people respond to long-term marijuana abuse by losing ambition and drive. They suffer from the so-called **amotivational syndrome**, *a loss of ambition and drive characteristic of long-term abusers of marijuana.*

Key Passage

Explain: Tell students that many of the tests that determined the effects of marijuana were performed in the 1960s, when the percentage of THC in marijuana averaged less than .05 percent. Today's marijuana averages about 3.5 percent. Ask students to write a paper explaining how this affects what we know about the effects of today's marijuana.

Figure 12.6 — Abused Drugs and Substances[a]

Drug Name with Selected Generic Names, Brand Names, and Street Names[b]	Medical Use	Physical/ Psychological Dependence
Narcotics		
Opium (paregoric), "O," "black," "dream stick," **Morphine** *Roxanol, Duramorph,* "mister blue," "morpho" **Codeine** *Darvon, Empirin with Codeine, Lomotil, Robitussin A-C, Tylenol with codeine*	Pain reliever, antidiarrheal, cough reliever	Yes/Yes
Heroin (diacetylmorphine), "black tar," "H," "horse," "smack"	No legal use	Yes/Yes
Hydrocodone *Vicodin, Vicoprofen*	Pain reliever	Yes/Yes
Hydromorphone (hydrochloride), *Dilaudid, Demerol* (meperidine hydrochloride)	Pain reliever	Yes/Yes
Methadone hydrochloride *Dolophine*	Pain reliever, heroin substitute	Yes/Yes
Oxycodone hydrochloride *Percocet, Percodan, OxyContin,* "oxy"	Pain reliever	Yes/Yes
Depressants		
Barbiturates (phenobarbital), *Noctec* (chloral hydrate), *Nembutal* (pentobarbital), *Butisol,* "barbies," "downers"	Anesthetic, anticonvulsant, sedative, hypnotic	Yes/Yes
Methaqualone *Quaalude[c],* "ludes,"	Sedative, hypnotic	Yes/Yes
Benzodiazepines *Ativan, Dalmane, Halcion, Klonopin, Librium, Serax, Tranxene, Valium, Xanax*	Anxiety reliever, anticonvulsant, sedative, hypnotic	Yes/Yes
Rohypnol "date rape drug," "rophy," "circles," "Mexican Valium," the "drop drug," "roofies," "rope," "R-2," "roach," "the forget pill"	Not sold or manufactured in the United States	Yes/Unknown
GHB *Gamma hydroxybutyrate,* "liquid ecstasy," "Georgia home boy"	Opiate withdrawal	Yes/Unknown
Stimulants		
Cocaine (cocaine hydrochloride), "base," "coke," "crack," "flake," "rock," "snow"	Local anesthetic	Yes/Yes
Amphetamines *Dexedrine* (dextroamphetamine), *Didrex* (benzphetamine), *Ionamin* (phentermine), *Ritalin* (methylphenidate hydrochloride), *Tenuate* (diethylpropion), *Cylert, Desoxyn, Plegine, Sanorex,* "black beauties," "speed," "uppers," "white crosses"	Control of hyperactivity in children, and sleep disorders	Possible/Yes
Methamphetamine *Desoxyn* (methamphetamine hydrochloride), "crank," "crystal," "ice," "meth"	Diet pill	No/Yes

[a]The most commonly abused drug, alcohol, is given a chapter of its own—Chapter 13.
[b]Generic names appear in parentheses; brand names are italicized; and street names are in quotation marks.
[c]Quaalude is no longer legally sold in the United States.

Usual Method of Administration	Possible Effects	Effects of Overdose	Withdrawal Symptoms
Oral, smoked, injected	Euphoria, drowsiness, respiratory depression, constricted pupils, nausea	Slow and shallow breathing, clammy skin, convulsions, coma, death from sedation of vital functions	Watery eyes, runny nose, restlessness, loss of appetite, irritability, muscle and bone pain, tremors, panic, chills and sweating, cramps, nausea
Injected, sniffed, smoked			
Oral			
Oral, injected			
Oral, injected			
Oral, sniffed, injected			
Oral, injected	Slurred speech, disorientation, drunken behavior without odor of alcohol. For Rohypnol, extreme sleepiness, slurred speech, difficulty walking, confusion, increased irritability, personality changes, memory loss, dizziness, visual disturbances	Shallow respiration, cold and clammy skin, dilated pupils, weak and rapid pulse, coma, possible death	Anxiety, insomnia, tremors, delirium, convulsions, possible death. For Rohypnol and GHB, anxiety, insomnia, tremors, racing pulse, elevated blood pressure, seizures
Oral, injected			
Oral, injected			
Oral			
Oral			
Sniffed, injected, smoked	Increased alertness, excitation, aggression, euphoria, increased pulse rate and blood pressure, insomnia, loss of appetite, reduced athletic endurance, skin lesions. For methamphetamine, extreme aggression, paranoia, hallucinations	Longer, more intense "trip" episodes, psychosis, organ damage, death by accident or suicide. For amphetamine variants, death from heart or kidney failure or from blood clotted in the veins	Apathy, long periods of sleep, irritability, depression, disorientation. For methamphetamine, apathy, long periods of sleep, extreme fatigue, depression, disorientation
Oral, injected			
Ingested, injected, smoked, sniffed			

— continued on page 322

Figure 12.6 **Abused Drugs and Substances**[a] *(continued)*

	Drug Name with Selected Generic Names, Brand Names, and Street Names[b]	Medical Use	Physical/ Psychological Dependence
Hallucinogens (psychedelics)	**Lysergic acid diethylamide,** or **LSD** "acid," "microdot," **Mescaline** and **Peyote** "mesc," "buttons," "cactus"	None	No/Unknown
	Amphetamine variants "MDMA," "ecstasy"	None	Unknown/ Unknown
	Psilocybin and related mushroom species "mushrooms," "shrooms"	None	Unknown/ Yes, rarely
	Phencyclidine hydrochloride "PCP," "angel dust," "dummy dust," "love boat"	None in the United States	Yes/Yes
	Ketamine "K," "special K," "vitamin K"	Pain killer, primarily veterinary use	Yes/Yes
Inhalants	**Hydrocarbon vapors** from many sources, such as plastic cement, gasoline, spray can vapors "glue," "gas," "poppers," *Aspirols, Vaporal,* (amyl nitrite), (butyl nitrite), (nitrous oxide), "laughing gas"	Amyl nitrite relieves heart pain; nitrous oxide relieves anxiety	Yes/Yes
Cannabis	**Marijuana** (delta-9-tetrahydrocannabinol) "Acapulco gold," "dope," "grass," "hashish," "hash," "hashish oil," "hash oil," "pot," "reefer," "sinsemilla," "THC," "Thai sticks," "weed"	Relief of glaucoma and cancer therapy's side effects	Unknown/Yes

[a]The most commonly abused drug, alcohol, is given a chapter of its own—Chapter 13.
[b]Generic names appear in parentheses; brand names are italicized, and street names are in quotation marks.

Usual Method of Administration	Possible Effects	Effects of Overdose	Withdrawal Symptoms
Oral, injected	Illusions and hallucinations, poor perception of time and distance, nausea, vomiting	Longer, more intense "trip" episodes, psychosis, organ damage, death by accident or suicide. For amphetamine variants, death from heart or kidney failure or from blood clotted in the veins	None reported
Oral, injected			
Oral			
Smoked, oral, injected			
Smoked, oral, injected, sniffed			
Sniffed, vapors concentrated and inhaled	Altered sense of time, brief euphoria, nausea, vomiting, dizziness, headache; liver, brain, and kidney cancer	Loss of consciousness, death by suffocation or sudden sniffing death syndrome, cerebral hemorrhage	None reported
Smoked, oral	Euphoria, relaxed inhibitions, increased appetite, memory loss, disoriented behavior	Fatigue, paranoia, possible psychosis	Insomnia, hyperactivity, decreased appetite

The THC from a single marijuana cigarette can linger in the body's fat for a month before being removed in the urine. Drug tests can detect trace amounts of THC for as long as six months after its use.

Amphetamines

MAIN IDEA ▶ Amphetamines and methamphetamines are addictive drugs, because tolerance to them develops quickly.

Amphetamines (am-FETT-ah-meenz) are *powerful, addictive stimulant drugs*. These drugs stimulate the nervous system and so increase activity, block fatigue and hunger, and produce euphoria. When prescribed by doctors, amphetamines are used to treat diseases such as narcolepsy (the inability to stay awake) or, in children, hyperactivity.

People may take amphetamines to combat fatigue, lose weight, or stay awake at night. They may also take amphetamines to reduce the sleepiness brought on by alcohol, marijuana, or sedatives, drugs that have a soothing or tranquilizing effect. Sometimes a daily cycle develops in which people take sedatives to relieve the effects of amphetamines and get rest. Then, the person may take more amphetamines to become alert. As time goes on, the person will need more and more drugs, as the body builds up tolerance in just a few weeks. Those who abuse the drugs may inhale (snort), smoke, or inject them.

Methamphetamine

The most frequently abused of the amphetamines is **methamphetamine**, *a stronger form of amphetamine that is highly addictive, also called speed.* Methamphetamine abuse is a widespread problem partly because the drug can be made cheaply from over-the-counter ingredients. To reduce the availability of some of the over-the-counter ingredients, the federal government requires that pharmacists now stock those medicines with the regulated drugs. Pharmacists track purchases, and only sell a small amount of these drugs to consumers. A recent national survey showed that an estimated 10 million people 12 years of age or older have tried methamphetamine at least once.

How Do People Take Methamphetamine?

Commonly known as "speed" or "meth," the drug is often injected into a vein. A concentrated form of the drug called crystal meth can be smoked or injected. Crystal meth is also known as "ice," "crank," and "glass." Overdoses can occur. People who share needles share infections such as AIDS and hepatitis (a dangerous, often incurable liver infection).

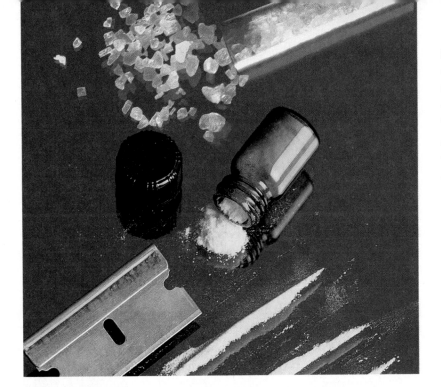

■ **Figure 12.7** *Pure cocaine can cause severe or even fatal results. How does the stress response caused by cocaine affect the body?*

Caption Answer: Cocaine stimulates the nervous system to bring on the stress response.

Cocaine

MAIN IDEA ▷ **Cocaine is a stimulant that produces a short-term, intense high followed by extreme dysphoria.**

The drug cocaine is taken from the leaves of the coca bush. In coca-growing cultures, people chew the leaves to receive small doses of the stimulant in the belief that it will help them to work longer. In other cultures, pure cocaine is usually mixed with other white powders before it is sold.

People may use any of a number of methods to take cocaine. One way is to sniff the powder into the nose. Others are to inject or smoke the drug. Cocaine in its smokable forms ("base," "crack," or "rock") is extremely addictive. The short-lived burst of euphoria from cocaine is mixed with a feeling of being out of control. It is followed by intense dysphoria.

Effects of Cocaine

Cocaine stimulates the nervous system and brings on the stress response—constricted blood vessels, raised blood pressure, widened pupils of the eyes, and increased body temperature. Those who use cocaine feel energized. When cocaine is sniffed it destroys the nasal tissues, leaving a hole internally between the nostrils. Many cocaine abusers suffer chronic fatigue and severe headaches. Cocaine use causes death—usually by heart attack, stroke, or seizure.

Risks to Unborn Babies

Pregnant women who abuse cocaine risk permanent birth defects and death of their infants. Many of these infants are born prematurely, with a low birthweight. Cocaine cuts off the flow of oxygen and nutrients to the fetus, stunting the baby's growth during pregnancy.

Class Activity
Describe: Ask students to make posters of a particular drug. Include street names, effects, side effects, withdrawal symptoms, and punishment for having or selling the drug.

Class Discussion

Discuss: Ask students, "How many of you know in advance what parties or other situations might involve drugs or alcohol?" Ask why it is important to be prepared for such situations. (It can help if students make decisions in advance so they will be less likely to be influenced by peer pressure.)

Addiction

Between 60 and 80 percent of cocaine users reported that they are addicted. They are unable to turn the drug down if offered and unable to limit their abuse of cocaine. A person who is addicted to cocaine loses the ability to work, to play, to keep a job, or to stop abusing the drug.

Sedatives and Barbiturates

MAIN IDEA ▶ Sedatives and barbiturates act as depressants, slowing the body's systems, and causing addiction.

Sedatives are *depressants that slow the body systems.* Some sedatives slow the heart; some act on the brain and nervous system; some do both. They can be dangerous when taken without medical supervision. Some are more addictive and dangerous than others, but none are safe.

Barbiturates are *depressant drugs that slow the activity of the central nervous system.* They slow the heart rate, slow the respiration rate, and lower the blood pressure and body temperature. They too have their medical uses, but they are easily abused. Long-term abuse can cause depression, forgetfulness, reduced sex drive, and many other harmful effects, including addiction.

Opiates

MAIN IDEA ▶ Narcotics are addictive drugs used to relieve pain, and include codeine, heroin, and oxycodone.

A group of drugs from **opium,** *a milky fluid found in the seed pods of the opium poppy,* are known as opiates. **Opiates** are *substances derived from the opium poppy.* They are also known as narcotics. **Narcotics** are *habit-forming drugs that relieve pain and produce sleep when taken in moderate doses.* These drugs are highly addictive.

Codeine, Morphine, and Heroin

Physicians sometimes prescribe **codeine,** *a narcotic drug that is commonly used for suppressing coughs.* **Morphine,** *a narcotic drug that physicians prescribe as a painkiller,* is one of the strongest painkillers in medicine. **Heroin** is *a narcotic drug derived from morphine.* Heroin is the most abused narcotic drug in the United States. It is not used as a medicine because it is so addictive. Some people believe snorting or smoking heroin is "safer" than injecting it. However, as the craving for heroin increases, the abuser may begin injecting the heroin. The costs are often high: dropping out of school, loss of career, loss of family, and also death.

Oxycodone

Oxycodone (ox-ee-KOE-done) is *the narcotic drug in the strong, time-released painkiller called Oxycontin.* The drug is an especially strong, time-released painkiller prescribed for cancer patients or others with severe pain. Abusers either crush the tablets and swallow or snort them, or mix them with water and inject them. Oxycodone is highly addictive and sometimes deadly.

Hallucinogens

MAIN IDEA ▶ Drugs that produce false sensations in the mind, such as vivid and distorted visions, are called hallucinogens.

Hallucinogens (hal-LOO-sin-oh-jens) are *drugs that cause visions and other sensory illusions.* One of the best known of the hallucinogens is **LSD** (lysergic acid diethylamide), *a powerful hallucinogenic drug.* Also called acid, LSD is so powerful that just a tiny drop of solution, ingested with sugar or other food, sends the taker on a mental "trip" of distorted visions that can last for hours. The trip stops when the drug wears off. A person having a bad trip may become irrational and do dangerous things. A person who takes LSD may experience a temporary resurfacing of the drug's effects, called a flashback for many months after the original trip has ended.

PCP

A drug that causes frightening hallucinations and violent tendencies is **PCP** (phencyclidine hydrochloride), *an animal tranquilizer, abused by humans as a hallucinogen.* Users suffer dangerous and unpredictable side effects. PCP causes some users to become so violent that they commit murder or suicide. PCP can give users extraordinary strength, which may lead to injury if the person is restrained while on the drug. Others suffer seizures, coma, and death.

Mescaline and Psilocybin

Some hallucinogenic drugs are made in the tissues of plants. **Peyote** is *a cactus that produces the hallucinogen mescaline.* **Mescaline,** *the hallucinogen produced by the peyote cactus,* produces effects that are comparable to a mild LSD trip, but one accompanied by vomiting, sweating, and painful abdominal cramping. The taking of peyote is part of the religious ceremonies of some Native Americans of the southwestern United States. Another hallucinogen, **psilocybin** (sill-oh-SI-bin), is *a hallucinogen produced by a type of wild mushroom.* Poisoning and death can occur when psilocybin users harvest toxic species.

Inhalants

MAIN IDEA ▶ People who experiment with inhalants risk permanent disability or death.

Three types of chemicals are sometimes inhaled to produce a high. The first type, solvents, consists of liquids that vaporize at room temperature. They include fumes from gasoline, glue, lighter fluid, cleaning fluid, and paint thinner. A second type, aerosols, contains propellants that are added to products such as paint, deodorant, hair spray, fabric protectors, and oil to make them sprayable. A third type, gases, includes those intended for medical use: chloroform, ether, nitrous oxide (laughing gas), and others. Other household or commercial products also contain gases that are inhaled.

Consumer SKILLS ACTIVITY

Look-Alikes

Another group of easily purchased drugs is the so-called **look-alikes**, *combinations of OTC drugs and other chemicals packaged to look like prescription medications or illegal drugs.* Companies that manufacture these drugs combine medicines, such as the potentially dangerous and now banned drug **ephedrine**—*a stimulant added to look-alikes and diet pills, and found in herbs such as ma huang*—with other legal substances to produce pills that look like the illegal drugs that drug abusers crave. One such drug, ephedra, has caused heart attacks, strokes, seizures, and death, especially when combined with caffeine, and has been banned for sale since 2004. Magazines, however, continue to publish ads for other "legal stimulants" suggesting that these drugs produce the same effect as amphetamines, but with one important difference: the pills contain a mix of over-the-counter stimulants, decongestants, caffeine, and other drugs instead of amphetamines.

Abusers of look-alike drugs may take more of these drugs because they tend to be less effective than amphetamines. These abusers can experience sleep disturbances, abnormal heartbeat, and sudden rises in blood pressure. The most dangerous situation is when a taker can't tell the difference between the look-alike and the real thing. When such a person gets some of the real, high-powered drugs and takes the same number of pills, a fatal overdose can result.

Writing

1. Do you think companies should be allowed to advertise "legal stimulants" in magazines? Why or why not?
2. Should look-alikes be legal? Give reasons for your answer.

The effects of inhalants on brain cells are unpredictable. In general, even short-term abuse disrupts vision, impairs judgment, and reduces muscle and reflex control. Many cases of permanent brain and nerve damage have resulted from sniffing inhalants. Many deaths from inhalant abuse are labeled **sudden sniffing death**, *sudden death from heart failure in a person abusing inhalants*. Irregular and rapid heartbeats lead to death within minutes of a session of inhalant abuse. Sudden sniffing death can result from even one session of inhalant use by an otherwise healthy young person.

Club Drugs

MAIN IDEA ▶ Club drugs include a wide variety of drugs such as ecstasy, rohypnol, GHB, and Ketamine.

Club drugs include *a wide variety of drugs abused by young people at dance clubs and all-night dance parties*. Different club drugs have different effects on the body—loss of muscle control, blurred vision, and seizures, to name a few. The most common club drugs include Ecstasy, Rohypnol, GHB, and Ketamine. Methamphetamine and LSD, both described earlier, are also considered club drugs.

Ecstasy

Ecstasy, also called MDMA, is an illegal drug that is both a stimulant and a hallucinogen. Most often taken in tablet or capsule form, the drug produces euphoria and distortions in time and perception.

Ecstasy's popularity is due in part to its deceptive reputation as a "safe" drug among those who take it. In fact, Ecstasy is far from safe. Some who take the drug report rapid heart rate, nausea, muscle cramping, and blurred vision almost immediately. Symptoms of Ecstasy overdoses include high blood pressure, panic attacks, fainting, and in some cases, loss of consciousness. In some people, a rare and unpredictable sharp rise in body temperature is followed by liver, kidney, and heart failure, and finally, death. In animals, even short-term use of the drug produces long-term damage to brain cells. Exactly how Ecstasy affects human brains remains unclear, but those who abuse the drug suffer memory lapses, depression, and confusion. Ecstasy is not a safe drug.

Rohypnol

Rohypnol, also known as "roofies," "roach," and "rope," depresses the central nervous system. It is a colorless, tasteless, and odorless drug known as a "date-rape drug." When mixed with alcohol, Rohypnol incapacitates its victims, leaving them helpless against sexual assault. Victims may not remember what happened to them while they were under the effects of the drug. Rohypnol can be deadly when mixed with alcohol or other drugs.

GHB

Like Rohypnol, GHB (gamma hydroxybutyrate) depresses the central nervous system and has been used by sexual predators to sedate victims. Coma, seizure, and a shut-down of the respiratory system can follow its use. Mixing GHB with alcohol or other drugs greatly enhances the risk of death.

Ketamine

Ketamine, known as "Special K," or "vitamin K," has also been used to commit rape. Ketamine's effects include confusion, hallucinations, excitement, tremors, potentially deadly breathing difficulties, nausea, and heart attack. Ketamine is legally sold as a veterinary medicine.

Worksheets: A reproducible quiz for Section 4 is provided in the Teacher Classroom Resources.

SECTION 4 Review

1. Sudden sniffing death

2. Heroin

3. Powerful, addictive stimulant drugs

4. A stronger form of amphetamine that is highly addictive

5. Combinations of OTC drugs and other chemicals packaged to look like prescription medications or illegal drugs

6. Six months

7. Oxygen and nutrients are cut off; baby's growth is stunted; learning difficulties and socializing problems result.

8. LSD

9. Answers will vary.

Reviewing the Vocabulary

Review the vocabulary on page 318. Then answer these questions.

1. What causes many deaths from inhalant abuse?
2. What is the narcotic drug derived from morphine?
3. Define *amphetamines.*
4. What is *methamphetamine?*
5. Define *look-alikes.*

Reviewing the Facts

6. **Describe.** How long does THC linger in the body?
7. **Analyze.** What are the risks for the unborn baby and the child when the mother uses cocaine?
8. **Identify.** What is one of the best known hallucinogens that causes distorted visions and "trips"?

Writing Critically

9. **Expository.** Reread the Consumer Skills Activity, "Look-Alikes" on page 328. Discuss some of the dangers associated with look-alike drugs.

For more vocabulary practice, play the True/False game at **glencoe.com.**

Drugs and Driving

One more hazard of all the drugs just described is their effect on a person's driving ability. Even when people think they are in control, the effects of drugs can be dangerous and cause many deaths.

Drug Use and Impaired Judgment

MAIN IDEA ▶ Mind-altering drugs, including alcohol, marijuana, and others, slow people's reaction times.

People who are under the influence of drugs are involved in traffic accidents more often than those not on drugs. In tests, alcohol and marijuana impair driving ability for hours after the high from the drug has worn off—even into the next day.

Class Activity.
Discuss: Have students create a list of OTC drugs they have at home that could affect a person's ability to drive. List some examples on the board and discuss the possible outcomes of driving while taking an OTC drug.

What Teens THINK
How Has Drug Abuse Affected Your School or Community?

When the principal or teachers find out that a student has drugs, they call the cops. In our community little kids can't go out and play because of all the drug traffic. There could be a cross-fire shooting or even a dealer trying to sell drugs to them.

—*Shay M., 18,*
New York

Drug abuse is a serious problem in all communities, not just mine. I know of people who have used drugs, and have even sold them. Drugs have become a normal thing. It is common to hear people discussing their plans for the weekend and hear them say they are going to get high, trip, or go out drinking. Because of drug busts in our community, people have stopped, or they have become more aware. You can get drugs as easily as buying a newspaper. They are being sold on every corner.

—*Keith L., 18,*
Florida

Drugs consume the lives of the people who use them to the point where people neglect themselves, their responsibilities, and everything just for a fix. This has lead to chaos in my community. Children have been neglected, and people have been killed. Also, diseases spread easily. Drug abusers do not care about being sterile.

—*Emilee O., 15,*
New Mexico

Drug abuse has changed my community a great deal. When I was younger, it was easier growing up in my neighborhood. People were more concerned for every child. Times have changed. Little ones have to stay in the house. Everywhere you go, people are selling and using drugs. Drug abuse is killing innocent people. Drugs in the community have brought my community down. It seems like the government doesn't care as long as drug abuse stays in the black community.

—*George W., 17,*
California

Although amphetamines speed up the nervous system, they do not improve a user's ability to perform some tasks. Driving and amphetamine use are one example. Heavy amphetamine use allows fatigued people to override their feelings of exhaustion. However, a person's judgment and, therefore, driving ability, decline even though a person thinks he is doing well.

Even many over-the-counter medicines can impair a person's ability to drive. Each year, close to 17,000 needless deaths and untold numbers of injuries could be prevented if people taking drugs or medicines that affect driving would stay away from the wheel.

■ **Figure 12.8** *A person who is too impaired to walk should certainly not drive. What OTC medicines might affect a person's driving abilities?*

Caption Answer: Cough syrup with alcohol

1. They slow reaction times and impair judgment.

2. Yes, each of these has long-lasting effects on driving abilities.

3. Amphetamines cause fatigued drivers to overestimate their abilities even when they are exhausted.

4. Answers will vary.

SECTION 5 Review

Reviewing the Facts

1. **Identify.** List the effects drugs have on driving.
2. **Explain.** Could marijuana and alcohol have an effect on your ability to drive the next day? Explain your answer.
3. **Analyze.** How do amphetamines impair a person's ability to drive?

Writing Critically

4. **Narrative.** Your friend's aunt wants to take you out to her favorite restaurant. She has offered to drive you in her car. Before you go she takes a diet pill. She has been sipping wine most of the afternoon. What are some of the problems that may occur? What will you do to protect yourself from danger? Write a dialogue outlining what you would say to your friend.

For more information on health careers, visit Career Corner at **glencoe.com**.

Kicking the Habit

When people realize they have a drug problem, they have taken one important step: admitting it. Drug addiction is treatable with help. Most drug users need the help of family, friends, and counseling to end their addiction.

Facing the Problem

MAIN IDEA ▶ Admitting a drug problem is the first step to overcoming it.

The first step in solving a drug problem is to admit that you have one. The next step is to seek help.

Getting Help

Rarely do people recover from drugs on their own. **Figure 12.9** lists sources of help. Help comes in many forms including hospitalization and drug-quitting groups. **Narcotics Anonymous** (NA) is *a free, self-help program of addiction recovery*. It uses a 12-step program, promotes personal growth, and leads to the person's helping others to recover. They offer psychological therapy groups, individual psychotherapy, and drug therapy.

An example of drug therapy is the use of **methadone**, *a drug used to treat heroin addiction*. It helps the person through withdrawal. Methadone is an addictive drug, as heroin is. However, it is cheaper, and its effects are milder and longer lasting. Taking a "maintenance" drug such as methadone allows people addicted to heroin to recover socially. That is, they no longer must struggle to buy high-priced illegal drugs to hold off withdrawal.

Vocabulary

Narcotics Anonymous (NA)
methadone

Class Activity
Discuss:

- Explain to the class that groups like NA and others provide a safe place for people with addictions to talk anonymously. Everything said is confidential.

- Lead a class discussion asking students what it means to maintain confidentiality. Why might it be important to not talk about someone else's problem outside the group?

Figure 12.9   Drug-Abuse Agencies

Many agencies stand ready to help teens with drug problems or just to answer questions. You don't have to give your name. A few examples are:

- Covenant House.
- Just Say No International.
- National Cocaine Hotline.
- National Institute on Drug Abuse for Teens.
- Substance Abuse Treatment Facility Locator.

To find these agencies and others:

- Look in your telephone book under Drug Abuse, Drug Addiction, Alcohol Treatment, or Rehabilitation Services.
- Go to the local library, and ask the reference librarian for the addresses and telephone numbers of drug abuse agencies.
- Ask someone you trust—such as your parents, a favorite teacher, or the school guidance counselor— for help in finding a drug abuse agency.

► **Objectives**

- Identify reliable sources of information about drug addiction.
- Find community resources that can help with a health-enhancing decision.

Inhalant Habit

Tasha just heard on the news about a teen dying from inhalant use. Now she's really worried about her close friend Keegan. He's been inhaling glue and paint fumes for the past couple of months, and she thinks he may be hooked. Tasha knows she will have to tell Keegan's parents about it unless he decides to quit. She wants to help Keegan and get a message to him that doing drugs is dangerous.

Tasha thinks that reading about the dangers of inhalants could motivate Keegan to kick the inhalant habit. If he knew help was available in their community, that might motivate him, too. The trouble is, Tasha doesn't know where to look for the information or how to find community resources.

► **Identify the Problem**

1. What information and resources does Tasha want to find?

► **Form an Action Plan**

2. Where might Tasha find the information? List two different places she could look.
3. How can Tasha tell if the information she finds is reliable? What criteria should she use?
4. How might Tasha find community resources to help Keegan? Identify two possible ways she could find the resources.

► **What Did You Learn?**

5. Assume you are in Tasha's position. Locate resources in your community that could help a friend kick a drug habit.

Class Activity

Create: Ask students to write a public service announcement script promoting the idea of obtaining help for addictions. Scripts should include positive messages about the benefits of getting help for an addiction.

Applying Health Skills

1. Information about inhalant use and community resources to help a friend stop using inhalants

2. Internet or medical reference books at the library

3. Online information from government agencies or national drug-abuse organizations; up-to-date reference books

4. Look in the local telephone directory or search the Internet.

5. Answers will vary.

■ **Figure 12.10** *Honest talk helps people face problems. What is the hardest part of getting help for a drug problem?*

Caption Answer: Admitting you have a problem.

Problems Along the Way

When a person first becomes free of the drug, he or she has overcome a big obstacle. When a person successfully breaks free of drug addiction, he or she may need to develop a new support system. Friends who still use drugs may try to convince the person to use drugs again. The person who develops a support system of people who are drug free and makes needed lifestyle changes has the best chance of staying free of drugs.

Worksheets: A reproducible quiz for Section 6 is provided in the Teacher Classroom Resources.

Reviewing the Vocabulary

Review the vocabulary on page 333. Then answer these questions.

1. What is the name of a 12-step program that promotes personal growth and leads to the person's helping others to recover?

2. A drug that is used to treat heroin addiction is _____.

1. Narcotics Anonymous
2. Methadone
3. Admitting that you have a problem
4. Answers should include agencies from **Figure 12.9**
5. Answers will vary.

Reviewing the Facts

3. Discuss. What is the first step in kicking a drug habit?

4. Identify. Name the different agencies that can help people with drug problems.

Writing Critically

5. Personal. What steps can you take to remain drug-free? Create a poem, letter, or diary entry expressing how you could make more healthful choices. What benefits might you gain by making these choices?

For more vocabulary practice, play the Concentration game at **glencoe.com**.

Helping Someone Else Kick the Habit

You may know someone who has a drug problem and feel the need to reach out to that person. First, you may want to take a look at **Figure 12.11** to help you determine whether the person really is a drug abuser.

Signs of Drug Abuse

MAIN IDEA ▶ Recognizing signs of drug abuse can be the first step toward helping a friend or relative to get help.

Concerned friends and relatives need to be aware of the signs of drug abuse. The best way to find out for sure if a person is abusing drugs is to express concern and ask questions. If you care, this is a way to show it.

Another way to show you care about a person with a drug problem is to make the effort to help. You may have to risk confronting the person, taking a stand that goes against your peers, and maybe even losing a friend in the effort to save the person's health or life. Things you can do include:

- Making sure the person knows you don't approve of the drug habit.

- Making available all the information you can gather on the health effects of the drug.

- Making sure the person knows, on choosing to seek help, where to go for it.

Figure 12.11 **Signs of Drug Abuse**

How can you tell whether someone close to you is abusing drugs? Here are some signs to look for:

- Paleness and perspiration
- Dilated pupils
- Runny nose and nosebleeds
- Jitters and hyperactivity
- Ability to go without food or sleep for long periods of time
- Anxiety, anger, or unreasonable suspiciousness
- Loss of memory
- Unexplained increases in energy and talkativeness, followed by lethargy and depression

- Sudden carelessness about personal appearance
- Broken appointments, broken promises, lying
- Inability to explain what happened to money
- Tardiness, unexcused absences, declining grades
- Trouble with the law, family, or school authorities

■ **Figure 12.12** *Offer to help a friend or loved one by listening. Do not judge or blame the person for his or her addiction. What is the key ingredient needed to end addiction?*

Caption Answer: The will to quit

Writing Activity
Evaluate: Ask students to answer the following essay question: A good friend of yours is abusing drugs. How would you help? Students should include showing disapproval, making information available, and making sure the drug abuser knows where to seek help.

Drug addiction does not mean someone is a bad person. Blame is a useless concept. It can make people feel guilty, but it can't help them get better. Drug-addicted people pay heavily enough for past choices. If you want to help, you won't judge and you won't blame.

No amount of effort on your part, however, can supply the key ingredient in someone else's choice to give up drugs: the will to quit. In fact, the toughest job for many people whose lives are affected by drug abusers is to learn to enjoy their own lives. Often they have to learn simply to accept the other person's choice, painful as that may be. Beyond caring, you have to let go. Live your own life as fully as possible while it is yours to live.

Worksheets: A reproducible quiz for Section 7 is provided in the Teacher Classroom Resources.

SECTION 7 Review

Reviewing the Facts

1. **Analyze.** What is the first step to helping someone give up drugs?
2. **Recognize.** List three signs of drug abuse.
3. **Describe.** What are three things you can do to help a person with a drug problem?

Writing Critically

4. **Expository.** There are many agencies that work with drug addictions. How could you help a friend choose the right agency? Write a pamphlet describing the advantages and disadvantages of each of the agencies.

1. Recognizing the signs
2. Any three listed in **Figure 12.11**
3. Make sure the person knows you don't approve; gather information on health effects; be sure the person knows where to go to get help.
4. Answers will vary.

G Online

For more information on health careers, visit Career Corner at **glencoe.com**.

Q&A *Refusing Drugs*

Understand and Apply Read the conversation below, and then complete the writing exercise that follows.

Chapter 3 introduced a set of refusal skills as useful tools for handling all sorts of peer-pressure situations. Many people find those same skills helpful in situations concerning drug abuse. To apply the skills effectively, a primary goal is to develop your confidence in yourself, and let it shine through as you deliver your message.

Q: Is it true that most teens experiment with drugs at least once?

A: By deciding not to use drugs, you protect your health, and become a role model to others. Peer pressure can be intense during the teen years. When the subject of drug use comes up, you may be told that "everybody's doing it." This claim is not true. Most teens never experiment with illegal drugs. Almost 62 percent of high school students have never tried marijuana, and more than 90 percent have never tried cocaine. If someone pressures you to use drugs, then you need to be prepared to commit to be drug free.

Q: What is the first step in how to say no to peer pressure? It's really hard to think quickly.

A: You've already taken the first step—to realize that quickly making a smart decision under pressure is hard. Even harder is making a smart decision while your friends are trying to influence you.

When you speak to peers under pressure, try to sound convincing. This doesn't mean raising your voice, or becoming angry or nasty—far from it. It means calmly expressing your high regard for yourself by choosing your own behaviors, without angering or insulting others in the process.

It helps to keep the consequences of the action firmly in mind. As the chapter mentioned, the law deals out stiff punishment for smoking marijuana and taking other illegal drugs. For minors, alcohol and tobacco are against the law too. Even more important, drugs endanger your well-being.

Q: How do I help make my answer convincing without raising my voice?

A: Be honest and sound firm. Your mind is made up. Give short answers to direct questions to avoid a lot of discussion. The more discussion that occurs, the more you open yourself to pressure from the group. Avoid wishy-washy comments like "I don't think so." Stand straight and proud, look confident and relaxed, and speak convincingly, even if you feel nervous inside. Show that you are in control. Maintain eye contact, and use a steady voice. Smile.

■ Figure 12.13 *Life without drugs has much to offer. Enjoy life with friends and family. What should you do if you suspect a friend or family member is abusing drugs?*

Caption Answer: Express concern and ask questions. Seek professional help if necessary.

Q: But what if my friends don't listen to what I say? What else can I do?

A: One tactic is to walk away. Here is an example:

As you are walking to your car after school, your friends say they are going to someone's house to get high, and they want you along. You quickly act as though you just remembered something and walk away to take care of it. You might call over your shoulder something like, "I need to get home and finish up some things for my parents." If you cannot leave the situation, offer another idea of something to do. "Let's go see a movie or visit a friend." This will allow you to remain in control.

Q: What are some other ways to stay away from drugs?

A: Stay busy and involved. Take up a new hobby. Play a sport or two. Volunteer your time to help those in need. When you are busy and involved in activities you love, you'll meet people who enjoy the same things you do. You'll have fun, and you'll find that drugs have no place in your life.

Be strong, and believe in yourself. Every time you say no, give yourself credit for standing up for yourself and doing what is in your best interest. It takes commitment, skill, and self-confidence to refuse to go along with the crowd. Be proud of your accomplishment.

 Writing Write a dialogue between you and a friend who is thinking about trying an illegal drug. Tell your friend about the consequences of drug use.

Reviewing Vocabulary

Use the vocabulary terms listed below to complete the following statements.

codeine

morphine

dysphoria

amotivational syndrome

1. _____ is a narcotic drug that is commonly used for suppressing coughs.

2. The unpleasant feeling that occurs when endorphins are lacking is called _____.

3. The narcotic drug _____ is prescribed by doctors as a painkiller.

4. A person who loses energy and ambition as a result of marijuana use is said to have _____.

Recalling Key Facts and Ideas

Section 1

5. **Explain.** Explain the difference between drug use, misuse, and abuse.

6. **Recall.** What is the rationale some people use for using the label *recreational drug use*?

Section 2

7. **Name.** Name three factors that lead people to abuse drugs.

Section 3

8. **Explain.** How does the brain produce feelings of pleasure naturally?

9. **Identify.** What is the unpleasant sensation people may feel after taking drugs?

10. **Describe.** Describe the spiral that leads to physical addiction.

Section 4

11. **Explain.** THC affects sensitive brain centers. In what ways does THC affect the body?

12. **Recall.** What is one of the strongest painkillers and why is its use so limited?

13. **Identify.** What is the most often abused narcotic in the United States and why is it illegal?

14. **Name.** What are three types of chemicals inhaled to produce a high?

15. **Explain.** Why is Ecstasy so dangerous to users?

Section 5

16. **Describe.** What happens to the body that impairs driving abilities when mind-altering drugs are used?

17. **Recall.** How long does the driving impairment caused by alcohol or marijuana last?

Section 6

18. **Explain.** Explain how methadone helps in the treatment of drug addiction.

19. **Identify.** What gives a recovering addict the best chance of staying drug-free?

Section 7

20. **Name.** In order to help a drug-addicted person live a drug-free life, what two behaviors should you avoid doing?

21. **Recall.** What is the one key ingredient in someone's choice to give up drugs?

1. Codeine 2. Dysphoria 3. Morphine 4. Amotivational syndrome 5. Drug use is taking a drug for its medically intended purpose. Drug misuse is taking medicinal drugs incorrectly. Drug abuse is the deliberate taking of a drug for other than medical purposes. 6. They claim to suffer no harmful health effects from drug use. 7. Lack of values, boredom, escape 8. Endorphins are produced while eating, being physically active, and listening to music. 9. Dysphoria 10. Drugs change the body's chemistry, causing withdrawal symptoms, requiring more need for the drug in higher and higher doses. 11. THC

Writing Critically

22. Narrative. Suppose a friend who was anxious about getting into college confided in you that she was taking increasingly greater amounts of speed to enable her to study more hours. What advice would you offer your friend? Write a letter to your friend explaining how her actions might jeopardize her college goals.

23. Persuasive. The use of marijuana by young teens is on the rise. Discuss some of the reasons so many more young students are using marijuana. Prepare an essay explaining what you think should be done to solve this problem.

Activities

24. Put together a list of community resources for people seeking help for drug problems. Provide the name, address, and phone number of each agency. Describe the services the agencies provide, the basic costs of their services, and details of services to school-age children and adolescents.

25. Make a video for your class or community about drug abuse. In your video describe the different types of drugs, ways that any drug may be misused, the physical and emotional dangers of drug abuse, and the treatments for various types of drug abuse.

26. Write a public television or radio announcement that describes the physical and emotional dangers of drug abuse. Share these announcements with your local elementary school.

Making Decisions About Health

27. One of your relatives complains of fatigue and depression. The person is also overweight and under a lot of stress at work. The person's health history indicates no regular physical activity routine, and a poor diet. The doctor has run extensive tests and no physical abnormality has turned up, but in hopes of bringing the patient some relief, the doctor reaches for his pad to prescribe a stimulant.

  a. What might be at the root of your relative's complaints?

  b. Why might the prescription of a stimulant for your relative be an unwise decision, given the circumstances?

  c. What might you suggest to your relative so that she may get some relief?

  d. What can you tell your relative about the use of stimulants? What are some of the risks of stimulant use?

Answers

1. False. Psychological addictions can be as powerful as physical ones.
2. False. Smoking marijuana is associated with harmful health effects similar to tobacco use.
3. False. People rarely recover from drug dependency on their own.

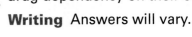

Writing Answers will vary.

---

alters hearing, touch, taste, and smell, **12.** Morphine; because of its addictive properties users need professional help to get through withdrawal **13.** Heroin; because it is so addictive **14.** Solvents, aerosols, gases **15.** Overdoses can cause high blood pressure, panic attacks, heart failure, ometimes death. **16.**

Reaction time is slowed; judgment is affected. **17.** Several hours **18.** It is a maintenance drug that allows addicted people to recover from withdrawal **19.** Support systems, making lifestyle changes **20.** Don't judge or blame the person. **21.** The will to quit **22–27.** Answers will vary.

CHAPTER 13

Alcohol: Use and Abuse

Sections

People who drink give many reasons for using alcohol. Some use it to celebrate, to relax, because they like the taste of alcoholic beverages, or because it's the custom. Some young people may drink because peer pressure encourages it. They may think drinking makes them look grown-up, or think it is a way of rebelling against authority. Sometimes they drink simply because alcohol is available to them. They may not know how to refuse drinks.

It is illegal for teens to use alcohol. Young people are more quickly affected by alcohol addiction than adults. Also, more teens die, or are permanently injured, from alcohol-related traffic accidents each year than from any other cause. As well, a teen's brain is not fully developed, and may be more severely affected by alcohol. Teens who drink alcohol are also more often the ones who abuse other drugs and tobacco and take other types of risks. Drinking alcohol also poses many other threats to your health.

Fact or Fiction?

What Do You Think?

Is each statement true or false? If you think it's false, explain what's true.

1. Alcohol is a drug.
2. In the body, alcohol is digested just as food is.
3. Drinking black coffee can help a drunk person sober up.

 Writing Some teens believe that underage drinking laws are unreasonable. Write a paragraph explaining why you agree or disagree.

(Answers on page 369)

Go Online

Visit **glencoe.com** and complete the Life Choice Inventory for Chapter 13.

Why Do People Drink?

The term **alcohol** refers to *a class of chemical compounds*. One of these compounds is **ethanol**, (or ethyl alcohol), *the active ingredient of alcoholic beverages*. Ethanol is a drug and a toxin (it changes the way a body functions). When alcohol is diluted enough, and taken in small enough quantities, it produces effects on the body that people seek. These effects are achieved at some risk, but many people are unaware of these risks. This lack of knowledge is one reason that alcohol is the most widely used—and abused—drug in our society. Drinking alcohol is legal only for those who are 21 years of age or older. For whatever reasons people drink, they derive drug effects by doing so. Like other addictive drugs, alcohol produces euphoria, changes mood, relieves pain, and releases tension.

Vocabulary

alcohol
ethanol
moderation
alcoholism
proof
drink
binge drinking

Caption Answer: Problem drinkers suffer social, emotional, family, and job-related problems due to alcohol use.

Drinking in Moderation

MAIN IDEA ▶ A moderate drinker differs from a problem drinker in how much the person drinks, the reasons for drinking, and the consequences of the drinking.

Authorities recommend that adults who drink should do so in **moderation**, *an amount of alcohol that causes no harm to health*. This is often described as not more than one drink a day for healthy females, or two drinks a day for healthy males. Just what does this mean? No one exact amount of alcohol per day is moderate for everyone, because people have different tolerance levels. Some people might be able to consume slightly more than one or two drinks a day.

Drinking in moderation may encourage people to relax and be social; in others it leads to problems. Some drinkers suffer from **alcoholism**, *the disease characterized by loss of control over drinking and dependence on alcohol, both of which harm health, family relations, and social and work functioning*. The Life Choice Inventory at **glencoe.com** asks questions that are used to identify alcoholism.

■ **Figure 13.1** *Sometimes others can see the symptoms of a drinking problem more clearly than the person suffering from them. What are symptoms of a problem drinker?*

Females cannot drink nearly as much alcohol as males can without becoming intoxicated. The smaller female body size, smaller volume of blood, and higher percentage of body fat limit the amount of alcohol a female's body can handle. Also, a male's stomach destroys more alcohol than does a female's, so less of what he drinks actually enters into his blood. The point is that females should never try to keep up, drink for drink, with males.

What Is a Drink?

Alcoholic beverages contain a lot of water and other substances, as well as alcohol. Wine and beer have relatively low percentages of alcohol. In contrast, whiskey, vodka, rum, and brandy may contain as much as 50 percent alcohol. *A measure of the percentage of alcohol in alcoholic beverages* is stated as **proof**. Proof equals twice the percentage of alcohol. For example, *100 proof* means 50 percent alcohol, *90 proof* means 45 percent, and so forth.

People measure alcohol in servings. In this way, a standard **drink** is *the amount of a beverage that delivers a half ounce of pure ethanol.* A standard drink may contain:

- 1½ ounces of hard liquor (whiskey, gin, brandy, rum, or vodka).
- 10 ounces of wine cooler.
- 12 ounces of beer.
- 5 ounces of wine.

However, the serving any one person considers to be a drink may not match the standard "drink" that experts use to define moderation. **Figure 13.2** shows the average amount of alcohol contained in different types of alcoholic beverages.

Did You Know?

Teens who drink may suffer by:

- Achieving lower grades.
- Being arrested, losing driving privileges, being fined, or serving a jail or detention sentence.
- Being the victim of a crime, such as rape or assault.
- Being punished or expelled from school.

Figure 13.2 Comparing Beer, Wine, and Spirits

Drink	Alcohol by Volume	Alcohol Content
Beer (12 oz.)	4%	0.5 oz.
Wine (5 oz.)	10%	0.5 oz.
Vodka or Whiskey (1.25 oz.)	40%	0.5 oz.

Figure 13.3 Behaviors of Moderate Drinkers and Problem Drinkers

Moderate Drinkers	Problem Drinkers
They drink slowly (no fast gulping).	They gulp or "chug" their drinks.
They eat before or while drinking.	They drink on an empty stomach.
They respect nondrinkers.	They pressure others to drink.
They know and obey laws related to drinking.	They drink when it is unsafe or unwise to do so.
They avoid drinking alcohol when solving problems or making decisions.	When they have problems to solve, they turn to alcohol.
They do not focus on drinking alcohol—they focus on other activities.	They maintain relationships based solely on alcohol.
They do not view drunkenness as stylish, funny, or acceptable.	They believe drunks are funny or otherwise admirable.
They do not become loud, violent, or otherwise changed by drinking.	When drinking, they may become loud, angry, violent, or silent.
They cause no problems to others by drinking.	They physically or emotionally harm themselves, family members, or others.

Range of Drinking Behaviors

A wide range of drinking patterns fall between not drinking at all and alcoholism. The most danger occurs with excessive alcohol intake and **binge drinking**, *consuming five or more drinks within a few hours' time*. The more a person drinks, the closer to a dangerous extreme the person is. People who drink must monitor and evaluate their own drinking behaviors. It may be difficult, but people who drink must be honest with themselves.

Some of the questions that these people can ask themselves include:

- Does my drinking interfere with my daily life?
- Do I feel bad about things I said or did while drinking?
- Can I resist the desire for an alcoholic beverage?

Drinking behaviors vary from person to person. Some general labels may help people decide whether alcohol is a problem:

- A *moderate drinker* does not drink excessively. The person doesn't behave inappropriately because of alcohol. The person's health is not harmed by alcohol over the long term.
- A *social drinker* drinks only on social occasions. Depending on how alcohol affects the person's life, the person may be a moderate drinker or a problem drinker.

> "*We drink to one another's health and spoil our own.*"
>
> —Jerome K. Jerome
> (1859–1927)
> English humorist

- A *binge drinker* drinks five or more drinks in a short period.

- A *problem drinker*, or an alcohol abuser, suffers social, emotional, family, job-related, or other problems because of alcohol. The person is on the way to alcoholism.

- An *alcohol addict (alcoholic)* has the full-blown disease of alcoholism. The person's problems, caused by alcohol abuse, are out of control.

The list in **Figure 13.3** compares some behaviors of people who drink moderately with behaviors of problem drinkers. However, any alcohol use by teens should be avoided. It is illegal for teens to use alcohol. Most states limit alcohol use to those over age 21.

Consumer SKILLS ACTIVITY

How Alcohol Is Advertised

Ads for alcohol in magazines and on television, the Internet, and other media may target teens and young adults. They imitate ads for soft drinks, using humor, music, friendships, sex appeal, and outdoor adventure. People who drink alcohol in the ads appear fit, healthy, and fun to be around. The message is that to be all these things, you should drink.

In some ads, drinking alcohol is shown as a way to belong to a group. For example, drinking alcohol has become linked with certain sports, partly because famous athletes are paid to wear alcohol logos. Such ads glorify the athletes—and the alcohol that goes with them.

The truth is that alcohol, if abused, can rob people of the very qualities being used to promote it. A person striving for rewarding social relationships won't find friends by losing control, but by developing and maintaining strong relationships. A person seeking sports success will find it not by drinking alcohol, but by faithfully practicing the sport.

Alcohol ads fail to mention any possibility of harm. These ads encourage you to want to drink alcohol. By learning to recognize advertising appeals, you can decide whether you really want what is being offered.

Writing

1. Why do you think that ads may target teens, even though they cannot legally purchase alcohol?

2. Do you feel that athletes, as role models for many young people, should earn money promoting alcohol use?

3. If you were the athlete or the company wanting to pay the athlete to advertise your product, how would you feel about athletes receiving financial rewards to push alcohol?

APPLYING Health Skills

Analyzing Influences

➤ Objectives

- Identify positive and negative influences on teen alcohol use.
- Analyze the roles of media and family on behaviors that affect health.

Looking Up to a Big Brother

Every Friday on her way home from school, Stephanie stops at a supermarket and buys a teen magazine to catch up on her favorite celebrities. She likes the magazine ads, especially the ads for alcohol, almost as much as the stories. The alcohol ads often show cartoon characters or animals such as bears. After buying a magazine, Stephanie hurries home to see her older brother. He usually comes home from college on weekends. Stephanie and her brother are very close, and she has always looked up to him.

When Stephanie arrived home today, her brother was sitting at the kitchen table drinking a beer. He looked very grown-up, sitting there with a beer in front of him, even though he was still in high school just a couple of years ago. Stephanie knows that drinking alcohol isn't healthy for teens, but she was tempted to ask him if she could have a beer, too.

➤ Identify the Problem

1. What unhealthful behavior "tempted" Stephanie?

➤ Form an Action Plan

2. Name two negative influences on Stephanie with regard to alcohol use.
3. What appeals to Stephanie about alcohol ads in teen magazines?
4. Why is her brother's behavior an important influence on Stephanie?

➤ What Did You Learn?

5. What positive and negative influences are there in your life with regard to alcohol use?

Applying Health Skills

1. Stephanie was tempted to drink alcohol.

2. Two negative influences are alcohol ads and her brother's use of alcohol.

3. Cartoon characters and animals such as bears appeal to her.

4. Her brother's behavior is an important influence because Stephanie and her brother are very close and she has always looked up to him.

5. Answers will vary.

Skills for Moderation

Moderate drinkers limit their intake. Among the skills they report they've had to learn are the following:

- "If it's BYOB (bring your own bottle), I take only two drinks with me."
- "If they're serving beer by the pitcher, I still order it by the glass.
- "I drink water or soft drinks if I'm thirsty."
- "I don't accept drinks I don't want."

Assessing Drinking Behaviors

How *much* people drink is not the only question to ask in determining whether people have drinking problems. Other important questions are the *reasons* for their drinking and the *consequences* associated with drinking. The Life Choice Inventory at **glencoe.com** asks questions that are used to identify alcoholism. You can apply these questions to anyone you are concerned about—even yourself.

Worksheets: A reproducible quiz for Section 1 is provided in the Teacher Classroom Resources.

SECTION 1 Review

Reviewing the Vocabulary

Review the vocabulary on page 344. Then answer these questions.

1. Define *proof*.
2. What is *moderation*?
3. Define *binge drinking*.

Reviewing the Facts

4. **Identify.** List three reasons that young people give as to why they drink alcohol.
5. **Analyze.** Give two reasons why alcohol is illegal for teens.
6. **Describe.** List and define the terms used to describe people who drink alcohol.

Writing Critically

7. **Persuasive.** Describe the different ways alcohol is advertised. Write a newspaper editorial outlining your opinions about how alcohol is advertised.

1. A measure of the percentage of alcohol in alcoholic beverages

2. An amount of alcohol that causes no harm to health

3. Consuming five or more drinks within a few hours' time

4. Peer pressure, to look grown up, or to rebel

5. Addiction occurs more quickly and teens are involved in more alcohol-related accidents.

6. Moderate drinker; social drinker; binge drinker; problem drinker; alcoholic. Definitions appear in Figure 13.3, page 346.

7. Answers will vary.

For more vocabulary practice, play the eFlashcards game at **glencoe.com**.

Effects of Alcohol

The drug alcohol has both immediate and long-term effects on the body. These effects depend on the size of the dose of alcohol. As with other drugs, all of alcohol's effects on the body occur when a person drinks it, no matter which effect the drinker is seeking.

Health Effects of Moderate Drinking

MAIN IDEA ▶ Alcohol impairs the central nervous system.

Alcohol can mix with both fatty and watery substances. This means that it can go anywhere in the body. Alcohol affects every cell of the body.

Immediate Effects

Alcohol begins acting on the body the moment a person swallows it. It does not have to be digested. From the stomach and intestines, it moves rapidly into the bloodstream. From the blood, it enters every cell. Within minutes after the first sip of a drink, ethanol is affecting the brain, muscles, nerves, glands, and small blood vessels of the skin. It also passes through the liver.

Vocabulary

intoxication
delirium
tremors
formaldehyde
fetal alcohol syndrome (FAS)

■ **Figure 13.4** *Teens can protect their health by avoiding alcohol use. What are some alcohol-free activities you can enjoy when getting together with friends?*

Caption Answer: Dancing, going to movies, shopping, sports

Alcohol impairs many organs and body functions. Some of these include:

- **Liver** The liver is the organ that changes alcohol into wastes. The liver begins processing alcohol right away, but can handle only about one drink an hour. If a person drinks more than this amount, the excess overflows into the bloodstream.

- **Lungs** The lungs excrete a little ethanol from the bloodstream as a gas exhaled in the breath.

- **Blood vessels** Soon after a few sips of alcohol, the drinker can feel it warming the skin. The central nervous system normally controls the blood vessels of the skin to prevent the body's losing too much heat. Alcohol relaxes these nerves, and the blood vessels of the skin widen. The skin of a person who has been drinking may appear flushed and feel warm.

- **Nerves and brain** Alcohol depresses the action of the nervous system that usually sets limits on behavior. A person slightly under the influence of alcohol will talk or laugh more loudly and gesture more broadly after these controls are gone.

Alcohol is a depressant. Small amounts of alcohol sedate the brain's cerebral cortex (see **Figure 13.5**), where conscious thinking and learning take place. The drinker loses awareness of recent events, insecurities, worries, discomfort, and pain. At the same time, the brain's speech and vision centers are being put to sleep.

Alcohol also disturbs sleep and reduces the ability to learn or to perform mental tasks. In addition, alcohol inhibits awareness and can influence a person to become more emotional. Thus the person expresses love, joy, sorrow, anger, and hatred more easily than before.

Immediate Effects

A moderate drinker may consume no more than one drink a day for a female, or not more than two drinks a day for a male. Some medical research shows that drinking one glass of red wine per day for females and up to two glasses of red wine a day for males may provide some protection from heart disease. However, other studies show that even one drink a day raises the risk of certain types of cancer.

Another immediate effect of alcohol use is how it impairs drivers. It is illegal for young people to drink alcohol. A leading cause of deaths among teens is accidents, homicides, and suicides. Alcohol makes all three much more likely to occur. The likelihood of accidents and homicides increases with alcohol intake. Suicides often occur with psychological depression, and alcohol relates to both.

Figure 13.5

Alcohol's Effects on the Brain

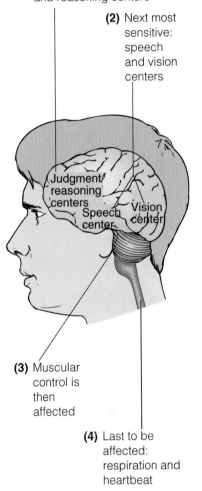

(1) Most sensitive and first to be affected: judgment and reasoning centers

(2) Next most sensitive: speech and vision centers

(3) Muscular control is then affected

(4) Last to be affected: respiration and heartbeat

Class Activity

Explain: Divide the class into groups and give them time to discuss the short-term effects of drinking. Ask each group to create a poster or PowerPoint presentation that explains one immediate effect.

Figure 13.6

**Effects of Various
Blood Alcohol Levels**

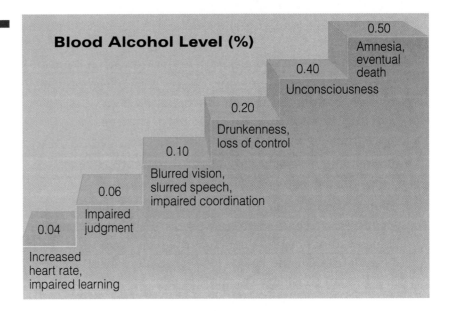

Blood Alcohol Level (%)

0.50 — Amnesia, eventual death

0.40 — Unconsciousness

0.20 — Drunkenness, loss of control

0.10 — Blurred vision, slurred speech, impaired coordination

0.06 — Impaired judgment

0.04 — Increased heart rate, impaired learning

Excessive Drinking

MAIN IDEA ▶ Excessive drinking affects judgment.

With increasing doses of alcohol, behavior becomes more unpredictable. People may act against their own judgment. A person may pick a fight, or may become sexually aggressive or have unplanned, unprotected sexual intercourse. The drinker may attempt a dangerous physical exploit—with painful or even tragic results. The map of the brain in **Figure 13.5** on page 351 shows how the judgment center is impaired by alcohol.

Next, speech, vision, and coordination are disabled. If that person drives a car, it can lead to deadly consequences. Drunk drivers may weave back and forth on the roadway, drive too fast or too slow, and may fall asleep behind the wheel, creating danger for themselves and others on the roadway.

If a person continues to drink, the person can pass out. **Intoxication**, *a state of being poisoned,* is a term often used to mean drunkenness. **Figure 13.6** shows the blood alcohol levels that correspond with progressively greater levels of intoxication.

It is possible to drink enough alcohol fast enough so that alcohol continues to be absorbed after the person passes out. This dangerous situation accounts for the deaths of young people each year who are binge drinking.

The Body's Defenses

The drinker's body is processing alcohol as fast as it can. The throat stings as straight alcohol goes down and triggers the choking reflex. This keeps the drinker from swallowing too much in a gulp. The stomach may reject some of the alcohol dose, causing the drinker to vomit at least part of the dose before it can be absorbed.

Class Activity

Describe: Divide the class into four groups. Assign one of the following systems to each group: circulatory, respiratory, nervous, and muscular. Have each group research the assigned system and then do a class presentation on how alcohol affects that system.

The Role of the Liver

Alcohol entering the stomach and intestines is absorbed rapidly into the bloodstream unless food is present to slow down its absorption. The alcohol then travels directly to the liver, which filters the blood before releasing it to the rest of the body. The liver removes toxic substances from the intestines before they reach other body organs, such as the heart and brain. However, the liver itself can be damaged by alcohol.

Why Do Drinkers Get Hangovers?

The aftereffects of drinking too much alcohol include headache, pain, and nausea, also called hangovers. These symptoms are usually felt in the morning after drinking too much and are a mild form of withdrawal. A much worse form is **delirium**, *a state of mental confusion usually with hallucinations and continual movement*. A drinker may also experience severe **tremors**, *continuous quivering or shaking*. These are warning signs that death may occur. These symptoms require immediate medical treatment.

Hangovers are caused by several factors, such as the amount of alcohol drunk. Dehydration also contributes to a hangover. Alcohol reduces the body's water content, and brain cells lose water too. When brain cells rehydrate the morning after, the nerves hurt as the cells swell back to their normal size. Another cause of hangover is **formaldehyde**, *a substance related to alcohol*. Formaldehyde forms when the body breaks down alcohol. Nothing helps the headache pain and the nausea of a hangover. Time alone is the cure for a hangover.

■ **Figure 13.7** *A hangover is a mild form of alcohol withdrawal. What is the most important factor in the cause of a hangover?*

Caption Answer: The amount of alcohol a person drinks

Figure 13.8

Liver Damage Caused by Alcohol Use

A. Normal liver

B. Liver with excess fat deposits from drinking

C. Liver beyond recovery from years of alcohol abuse

Long-Term Effects of Excessive Drinking

MAIN IDEA ▶ The effects of excessive drinking add up over time, causing severe health damage.

Excessive long-term drinking harms the body systems and organs. It may damage heart, the pancreas, the liver, and the brain.

Liver

The most common disease to occur among abusers of alcohol is liver disease, or cirrhosis. Alcohol causes the liver cells to fill with fat. If the length of time between drinking bouts is not long enough to permit this fat to be removed, then the liver cells die and harden, and lose their function forever, as shown in **Figure 13.8**. When the liver is injured, the whole body suffers. One of the worst effects of liver damage is high blood pressure. High blood pressure increases a person's risk for heart attacks and stroke. Liver damage also weakens the body's defenses against infection.

The liver makes fat from alcohol. This fat collects in the blood vessels and heart muscle, as well as in the liver and other places. Wherever it collects, the fat interferes with function. The fat also collects under the skin at the hips, belly, legs, and other fatty areas. Other times, the alcohol abuser becomes too sick to eat, and alcohol cannot nourish the body. Its toxic effects on muscle and other tissues cause them to wither. The person thus becomes bone thin as the tissues shrink away.

Brain and Other Effects

Nerve and brain tissues are especially sensitive to damage from alcohol. The brain shrinks, even in people who drink only moderately. Excessive drinking over many years can cause major, permanent brain damage affecting vision, memory, learning ability, and other functions.

Alcohol abuse also increases the risk of cancers of the mouth, throat, lungs, liver, pancreas, and rectum. Abusing alcohol causes the pancreas to stop producing insulin. Some people develop diabetes from alcohol abuse.

Other long-term effects of alcohol abuse are: abnormal changes in the blood; kidney, bladder, and gland damage; lung damage leading to flu, pneumonia, or tuberculosis; muscle shrinkage, including the heart muscle; ovary abnormalities and menstrual problems in females; psychological depression and mental illness; skin rashes and sores; stomach and intestinal ulcers; testicle shrinkage and damage; and male sexual problems.

Risks to Unborn Babies

There are severe risks to the fetus when a pregnant female abuses alcohol. **Fetal alcohol syndrome** (FAS) is *a cluster of birth defects, including permanent mental and physical retardation and facial abnormalities seen in children born to mothers who abuse alcohol during pregnancy.* The Q&A section of Chapter 20 describes FAS in more detail.

In short, alcohol abuse damages the health of the person who drinks. It can also harm the health of a fetus, if the drinker is pregnant. Drinking also increases the likelihood of accidents and injuries. Anyone who drinks should ask him or herself if it's worth the risk.

Worksheets: A reproducible quiz for Section 2 is provided in the Teacher Classroom Resources.

SECTION 2 Review

Reviewing the Vocabulary

Review the vocabulary on page 350. Then answer these questions.

1. Define *delirium*.
2. Name the substance made by the body from alcohol that contributes to a hangover.
3. What is *fetal alcohol syndrome*?

Reviewing the Facts

4. Explain. Which cells of the body are affected by alcohol?
5. Synthesize. What are the immediate effects of alcohol to three body systems when a person drinks moderately?

Writing Critically

6. Expository. Steve's parents won't allow him to drink alcohol. They say it's illegal and that it can lead to other drug addictions. Recently, he discovered his parents drinking at a party. They are saying one thing but doing another. The mixed messages he's getting are confusing. What would you tell Steve?

Go Online

For more vocabulary practice, play the Concentration game at **glencoe.com**.

1. A state of mental confusion usually with hallucinations and continual movement.

2. Formaldehyde.

3. A cluster of birth defects, including permanent mental and physical retardation and facial abnormalities seen in children born to mothers who abuse alcohol during pregnancy.

4. All the body's cells are affected.

5. The liver begins to break down alcohol, blood vessels widen and skin feels warm, nerves and brain react and the person loses control.

6. Answers will vary.

Accidents and Alcohol

Drinking slows reactions, impairs coordination, and dulls depth perception. Drinking before and while driving is the single greatest hazard on the road. Of all fatal automobile and motorcycle accidents, about half involve alcohol. There is no better way to display friendship than to prevent a friend from drinking and driving.

Drinking, Driving, Accidents, and Violence

MAIN IDEA ▶ Alcohol use makes auto accidents and other accidents much more likely.

The dangers of drinking and driving are so great that states have passed laws that forbid driving under the influence of alcohol. Under these laws, it is a crime to be **driving while intoxicated** (DWI), *driving with alcohol or any mind-altering substance in the bloodstream.* This is sometimes called driving under the influence (DUI). The alcohol content of the blood is reflected in the alcohol level in a person's breath.

The police use the **breathalyzer test**, *a test of the alcohol level in a person's breath, which reflects the blood level of alcohol.* This test is one method used to measure the blood alcohol level of a person suspected of driving under the influence of alcohol. Intoxication, or under the influence of alcohol, is proved if an adult driver's blood contains 0.08 percent alcohol in most states and 0.10 percent in other states.

■ **Figure 13.9** *You put your health and safety at great risk if you drink and drive, or ride with a driver who's been drinking. What is the blood alcohol limit for driving under the influence in your state?*

Caption Answer: Answers will vary; 0.08 percent to 0.10 percent, or zero tolerance for teens.

To reduce fatal alcohol-related crashes involving drivers under 21, many states have adopted a "zero-tolerance" limit for young drivers—actually, a 0.02 percent blood alcohol limit. It is illegal for people under the age of 21 to drink alcohol.

Special interest groups that advocate on a particular topic, such as MADD (Mothers Against Drunk Driving) and SADD (Students Against Destructive Decisions), support strict laws against drunk driving. People who are involved in these groups may have lost cherished sons, daughters, and friends to alcohol-related accidents.

Not only auto accidents, but drownings, fatal falls, suicide attempts, and abuse of other drugs are all more likely when people drink alcohol. Violent crimes are more likely to occur too. Most are committed by people who drink heavily enough to produce blood alcohol levels from 0.10 to 0.30 percent. With levels higher than that, some people pass out. Under alcohol's influence, however, some people become violent. Violent behavior attributed to the effects of alcohol accounts for one-third to two-thirds of all murders, assaults, rapes, suicides, family violence, and child abuse.

When a Friend Drinks Too Much

MAIN IDEA ▶ Time alone restores a person who is drunk to a sober state.

If a friend drinks alcohol, you can't speed up the recovery process by taking your friend for a walk. Only the passage of time will make your friend **sober**, *free from alcohol's effects and addiction.* Each person's blood is cleared of alcohol at a steady but limited rate.

Writing Activity
Respond: Ask students to write a paragraph explaining how they would react if they found themselves in the following situation: The people you are baby-sitting for come home from a party smelling of alcohol. They are supposed to give you a ride home.

It will not help to give your friend a cup of coffee. Caffeine is a stimulant, but it won't help break down alcohol.

Other suggestions for dealing with someone who is intoxicated are:

- Do show concern.
- Don't respond to emotions brought on by alcohol.
- Do not trust your friend's judgment about further drinking.
- Take your friend's car keys away.

Time is the only cure for a person who drinks too much alcohol. A half pint of alcohol takes ten hours to leave the body. The person who falls asleep after consuming alcohol should lie on their side to avoid choking if vomiting occurs. Don't let the person drive, and never let him or her take a drink for the road.

In the next section, you will learn how people who become addicted to alcohol can get help for their problem.

Worksheets: A reproducible quiz for Section 3 is provided in the Teacher Classroom Resources.

SECTION 3 Review

Reviewing the Vocabulary

Review the vocabulary on page 356. Then answer these questions.

1. What does *DWI* mean?
2. Define *breathalyzer test*.
3. Define *sober*.

Reviewing the Facts

4. Evaluate. What is the single greatest hazard on the road?
5. Explain. What is the legal limit for blood alcohol level for those under 21?
6. Identify. List four suggestions for dealing with someone who is intoxicated.

Writing Critically

7. Narrative. After a party, Tim, who has had two beers, gets into his car to drive home. He claims to feel just fine. What would you do? What other action would you take? Write a dialogue describing what you would say.

 Online

For more information on health careers, visit Career Corner at **glencoe.com**.

1. Driving with alcohol or any mind-altering substance in the bloodstream; sometimes called driving under the influence (DUI)

2. A test of the alcohol level in a person's breath, which reflects the blood level of alcohol

3. Free from alcohol's effects and addiction

4. Drinking before or while driving

5. 0.02 percent, or "zero tolerance"

6. Show concern; don't respond to emotions; don't trust the person's judgment; take away car keys.

7. Answers will vary

The Way Back: Strategies for Recovery

Support groups can be a source of strength. No one is as powerful in helping a person who is recovering from substance abuse as another person who has already traveled that road. The worldwide self-help recovery group Alcoholics Anonymous (AA) works this way. The AA program takes a positive approach—12 steps to recovery and spiritual growth that end in the person's helping others. In AA, thousands of people have helped one another recover from alcoholism.

Costs of Alcoholism

MAIN IDEA ▶ People addicted to alcohol and members of their families suffer financial, physical, and emotional losses.

We know a great deal about the addictive nature of alcohol. We also know a great deal about recovery from alcohol addiction. Some of the struggles to recover from addiction apply only to alcohol. Many, though, apply to all drugs.

Alcohol addiction negatively impacts society. People who are addicted to alcohol place a burden on society by:

- Taking days off work or school.
- Losing or quitting jobs.
- Requiring more hospitalizations.
- Causing accidents or injuring others.
- Engaging the legal system if he or she is arrested.

The true dollar costs of alcoholism, if added up in this way, are huge.

Alcohol addiction also negatively impacts families. The family suffers losses of income and status in the community. They may suffer physical and mental abuse or sometimes death. Both the person with alcoholism and the people close to that person suffer.

However, only the addicted person can stop the cycle of addiction. The day that person admits to having a dependency problem is the first day on a long road to recovery.

You may be wondering why, when faced with all these losses, the addicted person does not simply quit drinking. Addiction to alcohol is powerful. Many times, an alcoholic will not be able to quit without help.

Vocabulary

enable
codependent
denial

" *Water is the only drink for a wise man.* "

—Henry David Thoreau
(1817–1862)
American writer

Did You Know?

Young people who take up alcohol drinking before age 15 are four times as likely to become dependent on alcohol as those who begin drinking at age 21.

Figure 13.11 *Recovery from alcohol addiction takes effort, support, and time, and not everyone makes it. What stages might an alcoholic face on the road to recovery?*

Caption Answer: Denial, bargaining, anger, guilt, acceptance

The addicted person may want to quit drinking and may promise to do so. He or she may drink secretly and then feel guilty and worthless. Those feelings of worthlessness may cause the person to continue drinking. This leads to physical, mental, and emotional deterioration. Finally, one day, the person may admit complete defeat in the face of physical, financial, and emotional losses. This is the point of surrender for many who then seek out helping programs and begin their way back. Others may begin recovery at earlier points.

Recovery from addiction occurs in stages. First, the person has to accept that the problem exists. Then the person must quit using the drug and get help. Then the person must remain alcohol- or drug-free.

The Cost of Enabling

MAIN IDEA ▶ Family members and friends of alcohol-dependent people must live their own lives as best they can.

You may know someone who needs to recover, but is still drinking. If you know someone who drinks excessively, do not enable the person's alcohol abuse. In addiction, to **enable** means *trying to save the addicted person from the consequences of the behavior.* This makes continued alcohol or other drug abuse possible. An enabler is a rescuer—a person who tries to save the alcohol abuser from the consequences of his or her behavior.

Figure 13.12   **Resources for Alcohol-Related Problems**

AL-ANON Family Group Headquarters
(757) 563-1600
1600 Corporate Landing Parkway
Virginia Beach, VA 23454-5617
www.al-anonfamilygroups.org
www.al-anon.alateen.org

Alcoholics Anonymous World Services Office
(212) 870-3400
475 Riverside Drive at West 120th Street
New York, NY 10115
www.alcoholics-anonymous.org

By blocking the consequences of the alcohol abuser's behavior, the enabler prevents the learning that would otherwise take place. Enabling takes many different forms. These include coming up with money for bills, helping make excuses, or doing the other person's work.

A **codependent**, or an *enabler who is a member of the family of, or has a close relationship with, a person addicted to a drug,* may need to seek help to learn how to help the alcohol abuser. Two support groups for codependents, Al-Anon and Alateen, are similar to Alcoholics Anonymous (for people addicted to alcohol). Al-Anon and Alateen help enablers learn how to aid recovery, and how families and friends can best cope with alcoholism in a loved one. Teens, especially, may need help learning how to protect their self-esteem if someone close is an alcoholic. Some children and teens may feel neglected as a result of the alcoholism in the family. They may become overprotective of the parent or other family member who is an alcoholic. Teens and other family members are also more likely to suffer abuse by an alcoholic family member. They also learn that they cannot solve or take responsibility for the alcohol problem of another person.

Figure 13.12 lists resources for people with alcohol-related problems. The Health Skills sidebar, "How Not to Enable," provides rules to prevent enabling.

Recovery

MAIN IDEA ▶ **The road to recovery from alcohol or other drug abuse is long and hard.**

Traveling the road back to life from alcohol addiction may take years. In the beginning of the recovery process, the person doesn't drink or take drugs, but still craves the substance. Only later does the person become sober and begin to enjoy life without the substance.

Health Skills

How Not to Enable

Use these strategies to help a friend with an alcohol problem:

1. Stay concerned. (Give the message, "I care about you.")
2. Be prompt. Speak up after each drinking or drug episode.
3. Avoid attacking the person. (Say, "I worry about you when you drink.")
4. Be specific; name and describe behaviors. Don't judge. (Say, "You fell and broke the lamp.")
5. Act as a mirror—tell what you see. ("Your eyes are red; your hands are shaking.")
6. Don't try to smooth things over. (Say, "Go ahead and cry.")
7. When you are angry, cool off before you talk to the person.

A person giving up alcohol often goes through the same emotional stages as someone who is grieving over the loss of a loved one. One stage is **denial**, *refusal to believe the facts of a circumstance*. A person will refuse to admit that he or she is a problem drinker. Another stage is bargaining. Then comes anger and guilt, and finally, acceptance.

Worksheets: A reproducible quiz for Section 4 is provided in the Teacher Classroom Resources.

SECTION 4 Review

Reviewing the Vocabulary

Review the vocabulary on page 359. Then answer these questions.

1. What is the difference between an *enabler* and a *codependent*?
2. After denial, what four stages of recovery from addiction might a person go through?
3. What is the term meaning "refusal to believe the facts of a circumstance," such as addiction?

Reviewing the Facts

4. **Describe.** What losses does a family suffer when one of its members is addicted to alcohol?
5. **Synthesize.** Describe how an enabler affects a person addicted to alcohol.
6. **Identify.** Name two agencies that help codependents of those with alcohol-related problems.

Writing Critically

7. **Expository.** You have made a date with a very good-looking, popular student at your school. This person likes to have a good time and goes to parties where people drink alcohol. Write a paragraph telling how you would explain the dangers of alcohol to the person before you go out on the date.
8. **Persuasive.** Research agencies in your area that provide services to help those recovering from alcohol. Write a short paragraph describing the agencies and the services they provide. Share your information with your class.

For more vocabulary practice, play the True/False game at **glencoe.com**.

Answers:

1. An enabler tries to save the addicted person from the consequences of the behavior; a codependent is an enabler in the person's family.
2. First bargaining, then anger, guilt, and finally, acceptance
3. Denial
4. Loss of income, status in the community, physical and mental health, and sometimes loss of life
5. By blocking the consequences of the alcohol abuser's behavior, the enabler prevents the person from learning to control his or her drinking.
6. Al-Anon and Alateen
7. Answers will vary.
8. Answers will vary.

How to Refuse Drinks

A problem drinker is someone who drinks in excess. One notable sign that a person is a problem drinker is the occurrence of **blackouts**, *episodes of amnesia regarding periods of time while drinking*. **Amnesia** is *loss of memory*. The person may act normal during a blackout, but later be unable to recall anything about it.

Making the Healthy Choice

MAIN IDEA ▶ Each person has the right to choose not to drink. Expect others to respect your choice.

The only way to be completely protected from alcohol addiction is not to drink at all. Some people who don't like the taste of alcohol may be influenced to use it by friends. Use refusal skills to avoid alcohol use. Remember too, it's illegal for teens to use alcohol. The choice is personal. Those who choose not to drink have every right to make that choice. Unfortunately, some peer groups pressure those in the group who refuse to drink. Some refusal skills you can use are:

- Say no in a firm voice.
- Explain why you are refusing, and suggest alternatives.
- Back up your words with body language.
- Leave the situation if necessary.

Try practicing some useful responses ahead of time, such as: "No thanks, I don't want to. I'm . . . having a soft drink, . . . feeling great and don't want to mess it up."

Benefits of Living Alcohol-Free

Many teens make the commitment to stay alcohol-free. By doing so, they protect their health. Avoiding alcohol will help you with the following:

- **Maintaining a healthy body** You will avoid the damage alcohol can cause to the brain and other vital organs and decrease the risk of being injured in an accident.
- **Making healthy decisions** You will avoid the damage alcohol can cause to the brain and other vital organs and decrease the risk of being injured in an accident.
- **Avoiding risky behaviors** You will reduce the risk of making unhealthy choices, such as drinking and driving.
- **Achieving your goals** Being alcohol free allows you to stay focused on your personal short-term and long-term goals.

Vocabulary

blackouts
amnesia

Health Skills

How to Host a Party Without Alcohol

To host a great party:

1. Tell your friends that alcohol will not be available.
2. Offer interesting nonalcoholic beverages, such as punch or smoothies.
3. Provide plenty of food and snacks.
4. Keep the music low. Loud music makes people anxious.
5. Arrange activities, such as basketball, swimming, or video games, as the focus. Or provide a costume theme.
6. Get your guests involved—ask them to bring and play their favorite music or movies.

■ Figure 13.13 *Your friends can support your decision to stay alcohol-free. How can you use refusal skills to communicate your choice to avoid alcohol?*

Caption Answer: Say no in a firm voice, explain why you are refusing, suggest alternatives, back up your words with body language, leave if necessary.

Worksheets: A reproducible quiz for Section 5 is provided in the Teacher Classroom Resources.

1. Episodes of amnesia regarding periods of time while drinking

2. Amnesia

3. Do not drink at all.

4. Any two: "No thanks, I'm. . . having a soft drink,. . . driving later on, . . not drinking tonight,. . . feeling great and don't want to mess it up."

5. Answers will vary.

Having strategies and goals in place to stay alcohol-free will help you avoid the risks of alcohol use. Remember, it is always your choice to drink alcohol. You can say no when friends encourage you to drink. Practicing refusal skills will help you say no.

SECTION 5 Review

Reviewing the Vocabulary
Review the vocabulary on page 363. Then answer these questions.
1. Define the term *blackouts*.
2. What is the term that describes a loss of memory?

Reviewing the Facts
3. **Explain.** What is the only way to be completely protected against alcohol addiction?
4. **Describe.** What are two useful responses you can use to explain your decision not to drink?

Writing Critically
5. **Persuasive.** Your best friend's parents are addicted to alcohol. Your friend has come to you many times about this problem. You have told her several times to go to the counselor at your school. You want to go to her parents and talk to them, but you don't really know what to say. Design a pamphlet and include facts to back up the information you would like to communicate about alcoholism.

For more information on health careers, visit Career Corner at **glencoe.com**.

Alcoholism, the Disease

 Understand and Apply Read the conversation below, and then complete the writing exercise that follows.

Alcoholism is one of the nation's most serious health problems. Almost two-thirds of all U.S. adults drink. Of these, about one in every ten is addicted to alcohol. The annual cost to the nation, including work time lost to alcohol abuse, is estimated in the tens of billions of dollars. Worse still, the rate of alcoholism is on the rise.

Q: I know people who drink alcohol, but I don't think any of them is addicted.

A: If you know people who drink, chances are that one or more among them, even a teen, is addicted to alcohol or is on the road to addiction. Many people would rather not see the problem of alcohol addiction. In fact, people can choose not to see it. They can convince themselves that it doesn't exist, or that it is a minor problem.

Denial is a major obstacle to recovery from alcohol addiction. An alcoholic may begin to hide his or her drinking from family and friends. If a friend or family member tries to talk about the drinking, the alcoholic may simply refuse to talk about it, or dismiss it as not a real problem. However, these acts of denial are clues that the person knows he or she has may be addicted to alcohol. The alcoholic's denial may convince family and friends that the drinking may be caused by worry or stress, or other health problems—not alcoholism. This creates a situation where the drinking problem may not be acknowledged at all. To deal with alcoholism, everyone must acknowledge it and face it.

Q: Isn't alcoholism easy to recognize? Isn't it drunkenness?

A: No, to be drunk is not the same thing as to be a person with alcoholism. Anybody can get drunk, simply by drinking too much alcohol. However, that does not necessarily reflect alcoholism. It may, but you would have to look at other factors to identify the disease. The key factors are listed in **Figure 13.14**.

Figure 13.14 Alcoholism

The presence of three or more of these conditions is required to make a diagnosis of alcoholism:

- Loss of control over drinking. The person intends to have a drink or two but has nine or ten, or the person tries to quit drinking but fails.
- Continued drinking despite medical, psychological, family, employment, or work problems.
- A great deal of time spent in obtaining and drinking alcohol, or in recovering from drinking.
- Increasing alcohol tolerance. The person needs higher and higher intakes of alcohol to achieve intoxication.
- Withdrawal symptoms. The person who stops drinking experiences anxiety, agitation, increased blood pressure, or seizures.

Many misconceptions attached to the term alcoholism need to be corrected. For example, alcoholism is not related to the kind of beverage drunk. Even wine coolers and beer can produce it. Nor is alcoholism tied to a particular age. As mentioned, even teens can develop it. It is not always obvious. It is easy to hide, even in its advanced stages. People have been amazed to learn that a good friend, whom they thought they knew well, had reached a late stage of alcoholism before they found out about it. The addiction had been developing for years, but friends had no clues.

Q: You have told me what alcoholism is not. Now, please tell me what it is.

A: The American Medical Association (AMA), the American Psychiatric Association (APA), and other authorities define alcoholism as a disease of dependence on alcohol. It is chronic (long-lasting), progressive (gets worse over time), and potentially fatal. It often involves tolerance, physical addiction, and organ damage caused by alcohol.

The path of worsening symptoms is well known. Alcoholism progresses from the first drink to more involvement with alcohol. It progresses to a point where alcohol comes to dominate the person's life, damaging family ties and friendships, work life, and physical health. Alcoholism at its worst typically takes from three to ten years to develop after heavy drinking has begun. For young abusers, less time is required.

Q: How is alcoholism identified?

A: Usually, the person with the problem identifies it by taking a quiz, such as the CAGE questions below:

- **CUT DOWN** Ever felt you should cut down on your drinking?

- **ANNOYED** Ever been annoyed by criticism of your drinking?

- **GUILT** Ever felt bad or guilty about your drinking?

- **EYE OPENER** Ever had a drink to steady your nerves or to get rid of a hangover?

A person with one *yes* answer may have a possible alcohol problem. Someone with more than one is highly likely to have a problem. People with alcoholism try to deny the problem exists. Someone else may see that a person has a problem with alcoholism. However, until the person has accepted that fact, nothing can be done.

Q: What sorts of people suffer from alcoholism?

A: Just as people with diabetes or cancer come in all sizes, shapes, and varieties, so do people with alcoholism. The disease does not respect income, education, social class, or physical attractiveness. The person you most admire is just as likely to be addicted to alcohol as the person you most dislike. All people may be susceptible to alcoholism, but some people's genetic inheritance makes addiction especially likely if they begin drinking alcohol. This means that if one or more of your close relatives has alcoholism, you may have inherited a tendency toward developing it.

It is useful to separate the person from the condition. Think of the person as worthwhile, even though you disapprove of what the person does. Use words that show this attitude. Speak of "the person with alcoholism," not of "the alcoholic." The person is not "an alcoholic" any more than the person with cancer is "a canceric."

Q: Can alcoholism be cured?

A: It is probably not correct to think alcoholism can be cured. However, the disease is treatable, and it can be stopped, as long as the person does not continue using alcohol.

Q: A friend of my brother's drank so much that he passed out. Was that a blackout?

A: No. A person who has had too much to drink may pass out—that just means losing consciousness. A person having a blackout may show no outward signs of it at all. The person acts normal, although he or she is drinking. The next day, however, the person is unable to remember anything that happened beyond a certain time.

Blackouts often mark a turning point for people on their way to alcoholism, because blackouts are scary. When a person admits that his or her life is out of control, he or she may admit the condition. The disease of alcoholism can progress far beyond blackouts, but people can stop drinking at any time along the way.

 Writing Write a paragraph describing the ways to identify signs of alcoholism, and why people may choose to overlook symptoms of the disease.

CHAPTER 13 Review

Reviewing Vocabulary

Use the vocabulary terms listed below to complete the following statements.

fetal alcohol syndrome (FAS)

denial

formaldehyde

moderation

1. _____ is a substance made by the body from alcohol, and it contributes to hangovers.

2. Refusal to believe the facts of a circumstance is called _____.

3. _____ causes no harm to health and the person is in control of drinking.

4. Babies born to mothers who abuse alcohol suffer from _____.

Recalling Key Facts and Ideas

Section 1

5. **Recall.** What is the most widely used and abused drug in our society?

6. **List.** List four reasons that drinkers give as to why they drink alcohol.

7. **Name.** Name five behaviors that are typical of moderate drinkers.

8. **Name.** Name five behaviors that are typical of problem drinkers.

Section 2

9. **Recall.** How much alcohol can the liver handle?

10. **Explain.** How does the body protect itself from toxins?

11. **Name.** What are two symptoms of a hangover?

12. **List.** Excessive drinking over many years can cause severe and permanent brain damage. What are three things most affected by this type of brain damage?

Section 3

13. **Name.** Name three consequences of alcohol abuse in addition to auto accidents.

14. **Recall.** How long does it take for a pint of alcohol to leave the body?

Section 4

15. **Describe.** Describe how alcoholism costs society huge amounts of money.

16. **List.** List the seven strategies to keep from being an enabler.

17. **Explain.** What are the five emotional stages someone has to go through in giving up a drug?

Section 5

18. **Identify.** What are some refusal skills you can use to say no to alcohol use?

19. **List.** List three strategies for giving a great party without alcohol.

Writing Critically

20. **Expository.** Movies and other entertainment media often show an intoxicated person as a funny individual having a great time. But, is this the way it really is? Describe some behaviors of a person under the influence of alcohol that are not funny, agreeable, and friendly. What can be done to change this image?

1. Formaldehyde 2. Denial 3. Moderation 4. Fetal alcohol syndrome (FAS) 5. Alcohol 6. They like the taste, peer pressure, to look grown up, to rebel 7. Answers will vary, should be from table in **Figure 13.3** 8. Answers will vary, should be from table in **Figure 13.3** 9. Only about one drink per hour.

10. Choking reflex, vomiting, liver removes toxins in system 11. Headache, nausea 12. Vision, memory, and learning abilities 13. Answers may include any three: drowning, falls, suicide attempts, abuse of other drugs 14. 10 hours 15. Hospitalization, insurance costs, use of police, ambulance,

21. **Personal.** After reading the Q&A section, "Alcoholism, the Disease," why do you think so many people who are aware of the dangers of alcohol still drink? What did you learn from reading this Q&A section?

Activities

22. Write a report profiling an imaginary person whose behaviors may lead to alcoholism. Include a description of the person's personality and family background.

23. Interview a local law enforcement official about teen drinking. Ask what are the problems. Has raising the legal drinking age to 21 helped alleviate the problems? What does the official think will help stop teens from drinking?

24. Research local agencies or support groups that provide help for alcoholism. What resources do they provide?

25. Write a radio announcement to convince the public not to drink and drive.

26. Identify groups at school or in the community that encourage responsible drinking behavior. A few examples might be Students Against Destructive Decisions (SADD), a safe-ride program, and Mothers Against Drunk Driving (MADD). Call these local agencies and make a poster showing each one's name, address, phone number, and hours of operation. Display these posters around the school.

27. Plan an alcohol-free party. Give the party a clever name. Plan healthful activities and a healthful menu. Design an invitation on a sheet of poster board. Discuss the party you have planned with your class.

Making Decisions About Health

29. Randy and Colleen are both college seniors. Randy is taking Colleen to a dance in his new car. Randy's friends are drinking at a party before the dance. Randy and Colleen decide to drink with them. Randy drinks four beers in one hour and Colleen drinks one glass of champagne.

Randy and Colleen go to the dance for two hours and then go to another party, where they drink and dance for about two hours. Randy has more beers and Colleen has two more drinks. It is getting late and Colleen is nervous because Randy has drunk too much to drive. Colleen is from out of state and doesn't have a current driver's license. What advice would you give Colleen? How should Colleen get home? What should Randy do?

Go Online

For fitness and health tips, visit the Fitness Zone at **glencoe.com**.

Fact or Fiction?

Answers
1. True.
2. False. Alcohol is not digested. It is immediately absorbed into the blood.
3. False. Coffee can wake up, but not sober up, a drunk person.

 Writing Paragraphs will vary.

Tobacco

Sections

Tobacco use continues to be a serious problem for teens as well as adults. The evidence is clear that tobacco use has serious health consequences. Smoking has been linked to lung disease, cancers, and heart disease. Tobacco use is the leading cause of preventable death in the United States. About 90 percent of adult smokers begin smoking as teens. Many teens think they can quit whenever they want; however, quitting is difficult.

In this chapter you will consider reasons why people use tobacco. Then you will read about the health effects of smoking and smokeless tobacco. In the last section you will learn strategies smokers can use to stop using tobacco, and read about ways to help a smoker stop using tobacco.

Fact or Fiction?

What Do You Think?
Is each statement true or false? If you think it's false, explain what's true.

1. After someone has started smoking, enjoyment is the reason he or she continues to smoke.
2. Smoking wrinkles the skin.
3. To live with a smoker is to run the risk of contracting lung cancer.

 Writing Write a paragraph explaining what you know about the addictive properties of tobacco and tobacco products. Then write a question you would like to find the answer to about the effects of smoking as you study this chapter.

(Answers on page 397)

Go Online
Visit **glencoe.com** and complete the Life Choice Inventory for Chapter 14.

Why People Use Tobacco

The tobacco industry uses highly effective advertisements to sell tobacco. Tobacco ads feature young, attractive adults who are role models for teens. It is illegal for tobacco companies to target teens directly, yet their messages still reach the teen audience. The images in the ads are not realistic because smoking ruins people's health. Still, many people are influenced by these advertising techniques. While tobacco advertising prompts teens to start smoking, it is illegal for merchants to sell tobacco products to anyone under the age of 18. In most states, it is a crime for teens to possess tobacco products.

Vocabulary

nicotine
gateway drug

Learning With Visuals
Evaluate: Ask students to collect printed ads for tobacco products. Pass the ads around the classroom. Ask students to choose which ads are "most appealing to adolescents" and why.

Teens and Tobacco Advertising

MAIN IDEA ▶ Tobacco advertising targets teens.

Cigarette companies are required to tell the truth—that smoking harms health—but they often show healthy people smoking. As well as providing mixed messages about the health effects of tobacco use, these companies claim that they do not market their products to minors. Tobacco ads, however, attract young people anyway.

Tobacco companies spend over $26 million a day and almost $10 billion a year on advertisements, both in print and on the Internet, that appeal to young people. They do this to attract young smokers to replace the more than 5 million adult smokers who die each year worldwide from lung cancer and other smoking-related illnesses. The industry knows that a person who doesn't become a smoker during the teen years is most unlikely to take up the habit later on. Almost all adults with smoking habits smoked their first cigarette before age 18.

■ **Figure 14.1** *Many people are quitting smoking successfully. What steps can you take to promote a tobacco-free lifestyle?*

Caption Answer: Answers will vary.

SURGEON GENERAL'S WARNING:
Smoking Causes Lung Cancer,
Heart Disease, Emphysema, And
May Complicate Pregnancy.

UNDERAGE SALE PROHIBITED

SURGEON GENERAL'S WARNING:
Smoking By Pregnant Women May
Result in Fetal Injury, Premature
Birth, And Low Birth Weight.

Statistics on smoking are disturbing. Each day, 4,000 children light up for the first time—some of them only seven or eight years old. When asked, about one in four high school seniors say they smoked during the past month, and many say they smoke cigarettes daily.

Some teens say their reasons for smoking include:

- I'm young now. I can quit later.
- I don't inhale. Smoking can't hurt me.
- Smoking makes me look grown-up.
- I smoke filtered "light" cigarettes. They aren't as harmful.
- My parents (or friends) smoke. Why shouldn't I?
- If I don't spend the money on cigarettes, I'll spend it on something else.
- It keeps me from biting my nails, putting on weight, or being mad or bored or hurt or unhappy.

All of these reasons are unrealistic. However, the new smoker believes them.

Nicotine Addiction

MAIN IDEA ▶ Smoking rapidly causes addiction, especially in teens.

Many times, someone who takes a puff of a cigarette for the first time will feel ill. After just a few tries, however, using tobacco is no longer a choice. Tobacco's active ingredient, **nicotine**, (NICK-oh-teen), is *an addictive drug present in tobacco*. Research shows effects on the brain similar to those of cocaine or heroin.

One tobacco company's memo, made public during a lawsuit, described cigarettes this way: "The cigarette should be conceived not as a product but as a package. The product is nicotine . . . Smoke is beyond question the best vehicle of nicotine and the cigarette the best dispenser of smoke." The memo revealed that tobacco companies were aware of their product's addictive nature.

The director of the FDA once called tobacco use among young people "an epidemic of addiction that has enormous consequences for public health." He went on to say that every year in the United States, "smoking kills more people than AIDS, car accidents, alcohol, homicides, illegal drugs, suicides, and fires *combined*."

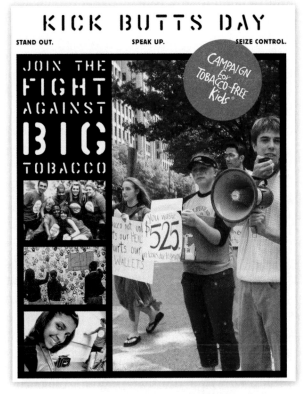

■ **Figure 14.2** *Tobacco ads promote smoking. Ads like this one promote healthy behaviors instead. Name two healthy behaviors you currently practice.*

Caption Answer: Playing sports, volunteering

Nicotine's Harmful Effects

Nicotine has many effects on the body. It affects the body's major organ systems: the nervous system, the cardiovascular system, and the digestive system. It triggers the release of stress hormones, so it speeds up the heart rate and raises blood pressure. It changes brainwave patterns. It calms the nerves, but some people may feel stimulated. It reduces anxiety, reduces feelings of pain, helps the person concentrate, dulls the taste buds, and reduces hunger. Nicotine acts on many different brain centers, so different people respond differently to it. As a result, the reasons why people use tobacco (other than addiction) differ.

The user of tobacco notices the stimulating effects of nicotine immediately. Even more noticeable, however, are the unpleasant effects of withdrawal as the dose wears off. Withdrawal is signaled by a slowed heart rate, lowered blood pressure, nausea, and headache. The person may experience irritability, restlessness, anxiety, drowsiness, inability to concentrate, and a craving for another dose.

What Teens THINK

Why Do Some Teens Think Smoking Is Cool?

I don't smoke, but some of my best friends do. They tell me that they were not pressured by their peers to start smoking. They started because their parents smoke or they saw older teens smoking and thought it looked cool. I don't think it looks cool at all.

—*Jennifer L., 15,*
New Mexico

Many teens see in a lot of movies that the hero of the story is smoking—mainly cigarettes to calm down when they are nervous and cigars when they have reached a goal. Kids may think that if you want to be like this person, you have to smoke. In other situations, one may see older students smoke at school or in other places. They want to imitate them. But to reach that goal, do you have to smoke? The answer is no. If your friends start smoking, do you have to start it too? No. Nobody may tell you what you have to do or not.

—*Jorge S., 17,*
Michigan

For a lot of people smoking simply starts out as a small rebellion. They start smoking to prove that they, not their parents, are in control. The big problem is that the more and more addicted the smoker becomes, the less and less control they have. I think it's wrong to smoke, knowing how addictive it can be.

—*Matthew H., 17,*
Florida

Kids don't smoke because they think it's "cool." They do it because they tried it once and got hooked. Smoking is a waste of money, time, and energy. I choose not to smoke or do drugs because I want to live to be healthy. I have better things to do than waste all my money on something that can end up killing me.

—*Brenda W., 15,*
Illinois

Many users take the next dose of nicotine in order to avoid the withdrawal effects from the last one—a pattern that points to addiction. The addiction becomes so strong that they cannot quit even if they know that their health is suffering in the ways described in the next section.

Consumer Skills Activity:

1. Their illegality for teens, potential for addiction, and the damage they cause to health.

2. They may have "risk-taking" personalities.

Consumer
SKILLS ACTIVITY

Tobacco as a Gateway Drug

Of all the harmful effects of tobacco, one stands out for some teens—tobacco is a gateway drug. This means that users of tobacco are much more likely than nonusers to eventually abuse other drugs, such as alcohol, cocaine, or heroin. Statistics from one U.S. state show that young people who use tobacco products regularly are five times more likely to drink alcohol, eight times more likely to smoke marijuana than those not using tobacco, and three times more likely to take cocaine.

Some people may dismiss the idea of tobacco being a gateway drug. They say that tobacco use does not lead to anything other than more tobacco use. Research shows the opposite to be true. In fact, one U.S. Surgeon General noted that tobacco use among teens should be considered a sign that the teen may be likely to try other high risk behaviors. Of tobacco use, she said, "What is notable about tobacco use is that it consistently occurs early in the sequence of problem behaviors. When a young person starts to smoke or use tobacco, it is a signal, an alarm that he or she may be involved in other risky behaviors."

Why do users of tobacco move on to other drugs? Researchers believe that some teens may have "risk-taking" personalities. These teens may be willing to break the law to purchase tobacco as a minor. A teen may use a fake ID or may be willing to take other risks. In fact, such teens may be attracted to tobacco partly because of the danger it poses. Tobacco may be just the first in a series of risks that they will seek. Their risk-taking tendencies make them likely to commit crimes, cut classes, drive drunk, and have unprotected sexual intercourse, as well as to abuse substances.

Young people may think that smoking a few cigarettes each day won't cause any harm to their health. The trouble is a few cigarettes can lead to smoking an increased number of cigarettes. For some, one illegal and risky behavior can lead to another.

Writing

1. What characteristics do tobacco and other gateway drugs have in common?
2. Why might some teens who use tobacco move on to using other drugs?

Physical addiction is not the only reason people continue to use tobacco, although it is the most important reason. Psychological dependence also plays a role, because nicotine brings both pleasure and reduces pain. People enjoy the behavior itself. It provides an excuse, in a busy routine, to take a break and relax. Important, too, is that it provides a temporary escape from small stresses.

Tobacco is considered a **gateway drug**, *a drug whose abuse is likely to lead to abuse of other, more potent, and dangerous drugs*. The Consumer Skills Activity points out why this makes smoking for teens especially dangerous. Teens often smoke to express their willingness to take risks. For these and many other reasons, people use tobacco, but they pay a tremendous price.

Worksheets:

A reproducible quiz for Section 1 is provided in the Teacher Classroom Resources.

SECTION 1 Review

1. An addictive drug present in tobacco
2. Gateway drug
3. Five million adults
4. Any five from the bulleted list on page 373
5. Nervous system, cardiovascular system, digestive system, hormonal system
6. Answers will vary.

Reviewing the Vocabulary

Review the vocabulary on page 372. Then answer these questions.

1. Define *nicotine*.
2. What is the term for a drug whose abuse is likely to lead to abuse of other, more potent, and dangerous drugs?

Reviewing the Facts

3. **Synthesize.** How many adults die each year from smoking-related diseases?
4. **Explain.** List five statements that describe how smokers try to explain their choice to smoke.
5. **Identify.** Name the major systems of the body that are affected by nicotine.

Writing Critically

6. **Expository.** List the immediate effects nicotine has on the cardiovascular system. How might these affect a person's health?

For more vocabulary practice, play the Concentration game at **glencoe.com**.

Health Effects of Smoking

Any substance, when burned, releases chemicals that are not present in the original raw material. The damage caused by smoking is primarily from the *burning* ingredients of cigarettes.

What's In a Cigarette?

MAIN IDEA ▶ **Smoking releases harmful chemicals that are inhaled by smokers and others.**

More than 4,000 hazardous compounds make their way into the lungs of smokers and into the air that everyone breathes. The most harmful of these are the **tars**, or *chemicals present in tobacco*. Burning tars release many **carcinogens** (car-SIN-oh-gens), *cancer-causing agents*. Carcinogens are known to cause most cases of lung cancer and many cancers of other organs. Smokers who puff 20 to 60 cigarettes per day collect anywhere from ¼ to 1½ pounds of this sticky black tar in their lungs each year. Tars are also the principal cause of **emphysema** (em-fih-ZEE-muh), *a disease of the lungs in which many small, flexible air sacs burst and form a few large, rigid air pockets*. Emphysema is another major disease of the lungs, and can be fatal.

Vocabulary

- tars
- carcinogens
- emphysema
- bronchi
- mucus
- cilia
- bronchitis
- chronic obstructive pulmonary disease (COPD)
- carbon monoxide
- sinuses

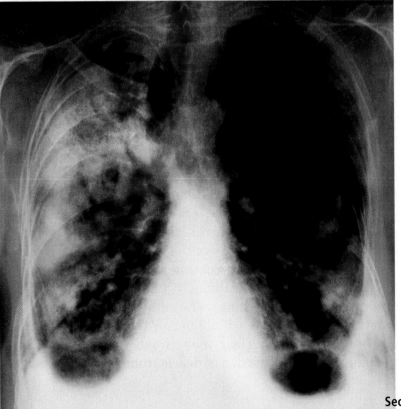

■ **Figure 14.3** *This is a lung from a person who died from a smoking-related lung disease. What diseases of the lungs are caused by smoking?*

Caption Answer: Bronchitis, emphysema, cancers

Figure 14.4

The Lungs

The trachea branches to form the right and left bronchi. These branch again and again, finally ending in tiny passages that pass air into the air sacs (see **Figure 14.5**).

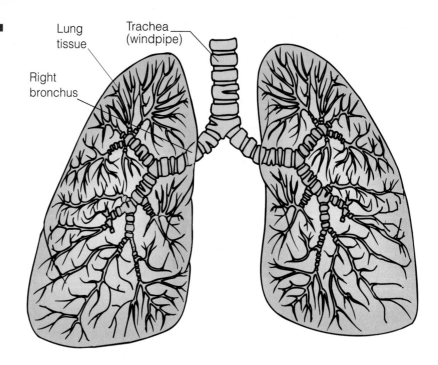

Lung tissue

Trachea (windpipe)

Right bronchus

The Lungs

MAIN IDEA ▶ Smoking cigarettes is linked with health hazards including bronchitis, emphysema, and cancers.

A detailed diagram of the lungs appeared in Chapter 6. **Figure 14.4** serves as a reminder of the lung structures affected by smoking. The lungs receive blood pumped from the heart and add oxygen to it. Then the blood, with its oxygen cargo, returns to the heart to be pumped to all the body's cells. Every cell has to breathe. The lungs provide oxygen to the cells so they can stay alive.

Healthy Lungs

The lungs are large, compared with the heart. They are rich with blood vessels, and they fill the chest. Twelve to fourteen times a minute they draw in air deeply and, like a sponge, soak up oxygen and squeeze out carbon dioxide.

The **bronchi** (BRONK-eye) are *the two main airways in the lungs.* Healthy bronchi are coated with **mucus** (MYOO-cuss), *a slippery secretion produced by cells of the body's linings that protects the surfaces of the lining.* The bronchi also contain **cilia,** *hairlike structures extending from the surface of cells.* Cilia line passageways of the trachea and upper lungs. The waving cilia propel a coating of mucus along to sweep away debris. The mucus catches dirt and bacteria that would otherwise lodge in the lungs. The cilia sweep the mucus in a constant stream to the windpipe and then all the way up to the throat. When you clear your throat, you remove a bit of this mucus with its burden of debris from your air passages.

Smoke Damage to Lungs

Smoking damages the lung tissue in many ways. The tars in cigarette smoke make the mucus abnormally thick. This slows the action of the cilia in sweeping out the mucus. Irritation builds, making the smoker feel like coughing. However, each inhale of a cigarette paralyzes the cilia and numbs the throat for a while, so the smoker experiences *relief* from irritation. As a result, the need to cough feels like a need to smoke.

Bronchitis and Emphysema

Smoking can ultimately lead to one or more chronic diseases of the lungs. These include emphysema or **bronchitis** (bron-KITE-us), *a respiratory disorder with irritation of the bronchi; thickened mucus; and deep, harsh coughing.* Bronchitis is an infection of the bronchi, which become clogged with heavy mucus. The resulting irritation causes deep, harsh coughing and wheezing. Bronchitis is a common illness among smokers.

Emphysema takes longer to develop than bronchitis, and its effects are more life-threatening. Smokers and non-smokers who live in cities with high levels of air pollution are more likely to develop emphysema. So are people who work in coal mines and smokey factories.

The illustration in **Figure 14.5** shows normal lung tissue and lung tissue damaged by emphysema. The normal tissue has many tiny, bubblelike air sacs. A tiny air tube leads to each little sac. As the lung expands, the sac expands and draws air in through the tube. As the lung deflates, the sac gets smaller and squeezes air back out.

> *" The greatest wealth is health.* "
>
> —Virgil
> (70–19 B.C.)
> Roman poet

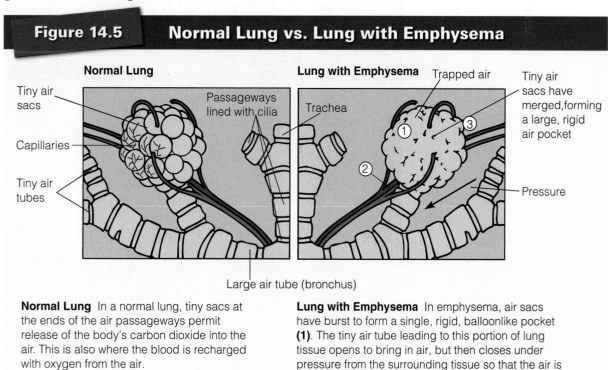

Figure 14.5 Normal Lung vs. Lung with Emphysema

Normal Lung In a normal lung, tiny sacs at the ends of the air passageways permit release of the body's carbon dioxide into the air. This is also where the blood is recharged with oxygen from the air.

Lung with Emphysema In emphysema, air sacs have burst to form a single, rigid, balloonlike pocket **(1)**. The tiny air tube leading to this portion of lung tissue opens to bring in air, but then closes under pressure from the surrounding tissue so that the air is trapped **(2)**. The capillaries are breaking down **(3)**.

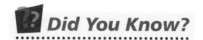 **Did You Know?**

Just 12 hours after smoking a final cigarette, a smoker's carbon monoxide levels in the blood return to normal.

In emphysema, walls between the tiny air sacs break. The sacs balloon out to become large pockets of air with hard, inflexible walls. This is much like what happens when 50 tiny soap bubbles merge to form one big bubble. As the lung expands, the pockets draw air in. As the lung deflates, however, the stiffened tissue around the airways blocks air from escaping. The air trapped in the lungs bursts and tears lung tissue. Lung damage occurs when people can breathe in but cannot breathe out.

A person with emphysema breathes fast—30 times a minute at rest, compared with the normal adult's 20 times. However, due to the emphysema each breath delivers less oxygen. Emphysema ruins the quality of life, and is fatal. Death results from slow suffocation—or from heart failure.

■ **Figure 14.6** *Lung cancer causes more death in women than breast cancer. What other types of cancers can smoking cause?*

Caption Answer: Smoking can cause cancer of the nose, lips, mouth, tongue, throat, and esophagus.

Figure 14.7 The Risks of Smoking

Disease	Smokers Increase Their Risk of Dying by . . .
Lung cancer	7 to 15 times
Throat cancer	5 to 13 times
Oral cancer	3 to 15 times
Esophagus cancer	4 to 5 times
Bladder cancer	2 to 3 times
Pancreatic cancer	2 times
Kidney cancer	1½ times
Heart disease	1½ to 3 times
Emphysema and other chronic airway obstructions (including asthma)	10 to 20 times
Peptic ulcer disease	2 times

Bronchitis, emphysema, and a few other diseases of the lungs are often termed **chronic obstructive pulmonary disease** (COPD), *a term for several diseases that interfere with breathing.* Smoking-related COPD kills an estimated 57,000 people a year in the United States. The surgeon general concludes that "the contribution of cigarette smoking to COPD deaths far outweighs all other factors."

Cancer

Another lung disease—cancer—is much more common in smokers than in nonsmokers. The carcinogens in cigarette smoke can cause lung cancer as well as cancer of the nose, lips, mouth, tongue, throat, and esophagus. Smokers also have higher rates of bladder, pancreas, and kidney cancers (see **Figure 14.7**).

Among women, breast cancer is thought to be the leading cancer killer. In reality, though, lung cancer causes more deaths in women than breast cancer. Women are said to be the victims of an "epidemic of smoking." African Americans suffer the highest rates of lung cancer of any group in the country. Cigarette smoking is the major single, preventable cause of cancer deaths in the United States.

Smoking combined with other risk factors for cancer creates a far greater hazard than smoking by itself. For example, the risk of developing many types of cancer increases sharply among people who smoke and drink alcohol. Exposure to the insulating material asbestos, combined with smoking, adds up to a deadly hazard.

Writing Activity

Comprehend: Have students write their own Surgeon General's warnings to be put on tobacco products. Writing their own warnings should help students better understand the dangers tobacco use.

The Heart and Cardiovascular System

MAIN IDEA ► Smoking places an additional burden on the heart and cardiovascular system.

Smoking causes about one-fifth of all deaths from heart disease and stroke. Smoking burdens the heart in five ways:

- Nicotine speeds up the heart rate. This increases the heart's workload.

- Nicotine raises blood pressure. This too increases the heart's workload and the need for oxygen.

- Smoking reduces the amount of oxygen the blood can carry. When the smoker inhales, **carbon monoxide**, *a deadly gas, formed during the burning of tobacco*, is released into the bloodstream. The carbon monoxide reduces the ability of red blood cells to transport oxygen.

- Nicotine triggers the formation of blood clots. Clots lodge in arteries that feed the heart muscle, which may result in a heart attack. When clots lodge in arteries that feed the brain, a stroke may occur.

The tar and nicotine in tobacco products damages the heart and lungs and can also cause cancer.

■ **Figure 14.8** *A health care professional can easily tell a nonsmoker from a smoker, based on the performance of the lungs and heart. How can smoking cause a heart attack?*

Caption Answer: Nicotine causes the formation of blood clots, and reduces the blood flow to heart arteries.

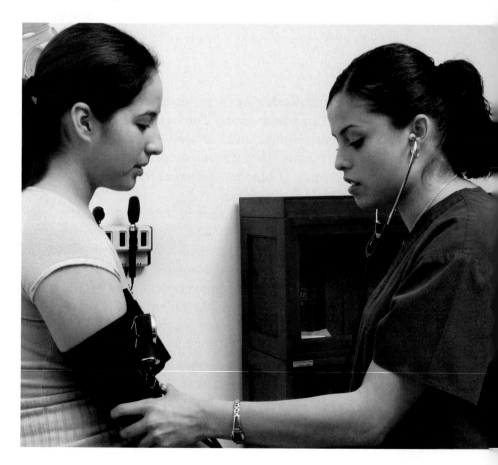

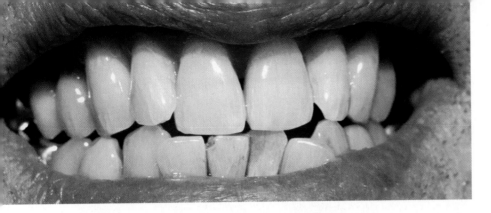

■ **Figure 14.9** *A youthful smile can be destroyed by the yellowing effects of tobacco use. What other effects can smoking have on a person's appearance?*

Caption Answer: Wrinkled skin, bad breath, unpleasant smell on clothes and hair

Other Effects of Tobacco

MAIN IDEA ▶ Tobacco use is the single greatest cause of preventable death in the United States today.

Tobacco use harms every organ in the human body. Smoking and other forms of tobacco use damage the body in the following ways:

- Reduces circulation in the small blood vessels, causing cold hands and feet.

- Causes wrinkling of the skin—especially of the face— graying of the hair, and premature aging.

- Increases the risk of all forms of cancer. The risk of colon cancer is doubled. Pancreatic cancer risk is increased by 70 percent.

- Slows normal growth of lungs in smoking adolescents.

- Increases risks of ulcers, open sores in the lining of the digestive system. Death from ulcers increases among smokers.

- Increases tolerance to drugs, making larger doses needed for illness and pain relief.

- Increases risks of heart attack and stroke in women who take oral contraceptives.

- Limits the supply of oxygen to the fetus. This results in smaller babies, premature births, miscarriages, a doubled risk of birth defects, impaired development in children up to age 11, and early death of infants.

- Causes women to become infertile; results in early menopause and increased bone loss.

- Reduces oxygen supply to the brain, impairing memory.

- Increases the risk of chronic infection of the **sinuses** (SIGN-us-es), *spaces in the bones of the skull*. This can spread to the brain and spinal cord—a life-threatening condition.

- Interferes with the immune response, making colds, flu, and other infections likely.

Discuss: Ask students to describe the physical appearance of someone they know who smoked for years. Ask how long the person smoked and if there were physical symptoms as a result of smoking. Discuss as a class.

- Exposes the chest to radiation. Smoking one pack of cigarettes a day for one year is equal to 250 chest X-rays.

- Makes it likely that men will produce abnormal sperm, resulting in birth defects.

- Causes hearing and vision loss.

- Encourages gum disease.

For some people, the motivation to quit using tobacco products is related to appearance. Smoking causes the skin to age quickly. In addition to wrinkling the skin, smoking causes bad breath and yellows the teeth. The smell of stale smoke clings to the smoker's hair, clothes, home, and car.

Financial Costs and Fire Danger

There is also the cost of tobacco products. Smoking can cost a smoker well over $2,000 a year. A person who saved that could instead take a nice vacation. Finally, there is the danger of fire. Fires started by cigarettes cause some 2,000 deaths and 4,000 injuries a year. Smoking is the single greatest cause of preventable death in the United States today.

Are Any Smoking Products Safe?

MAIN IDEA ▶ Smoking tobacco harms your health.

Among tobacco users, the belief exists that low-tar tobacco products are safer. Low-tar, low-nicotine cigarettes are no better than any other cigarette. Smokers who switch to them often smoke more cigarettes, or inhale more deeply.

Cigar and pipe smoking is just as risky. Cigar and pipe smokers are more likely to develop cancer of the lips and tongue. Pipe smoke contains more tar than cigarette smoke, so pipe smokers may face a higher risk of lung cancer.

The decision to avoid using tobacco products, or quitting smoking, is clearly a healthy decision. The risk of heart attack in both men and women falls rapidly to that of a nonsmoker within a few years. Ten years after quitting, the risk of lung cancer is about half of that for smokers.

SECTION 2 Review

Reviewing the Vocabulary

Review the vocabulary on page 377. Then answer these questions.

1. _____ are cancer-causing agents.
2. Name the two main airways in the lungs.
3. What is a term for several diseases that interfere with breathing, such as bronchitis and emphysema?
4. Define *cilia*.
5. What are *sinuses*?

Reviewing the Facts

6. Explain. What happens to the lungs of a person with emphysema?
7. Identify. List the cancers that are more likely to occur in smokers than in nonsmokers.
8. Describe. In what ways can smoking affect the unborn child of a pregnant woman?

Writing Critically

9. Narrative. The number of women smokers is on the rise. Discuss in a paragraph the most common type of cancer in women today. What steps can be taken to decrease this trend?

For more information on health careers, visit Career Corner at **glencoe.com**.

1. Carcinogens
2. Bronchi
3. Chronic obstructive pulmonary disease (COPD)
4. Hairlike structures extending from the surface of the cells.
5. Spaces in the bones of the skull.
6. The air sacs become rigid and cannot collect air.
7. Colon, pancreas, leukemia
8. Smaller babies, premature births, miscarriages, risk of birth defects, early infant death
9. Answers will vary.

Passive Smoking

Many experts agree that passive smoking can cause disease. Anyone exposed to tobacco smoke is more likely to develop heart and lung disease, as well as cancer.

Health Risks to Others

MAIN IDEA ▶ Passive smoking raises the risks of cancer and heart and lung disease.

Non-smokers who live with tobacco smoke or are exposed to it are passive smokers. Nicotine and other chemicals reach their bloodstream in two ways. **Mainstream smoke** is *the smoke that flows through the cigarette and into the lungs when a smoker inhales*. **Sidestream smoke** is *the smoke that escapes into the air from the burning tip of a cigarette or cigar, or from burning pipe tobacco*. Because mainstream smoke has been exhaled by a smoker, it contains lower concentrations of carcinogens, nicotine, and tar. For this reason, sidestream smoke is more dangerous than mainstream smoke. Together, smoke exhaled from smokers' lungs and sidestream smoke can fill a room. People nearby are exposed to **environmental tobacco smoke** (ETS), *the combination of exhaled mainstream smoke and sidestream smoke that enters the air*. ETS may be inhaled by other people.

ETS Health Risks

Passive smoking raises cancer risks and doubles the risks of heart disease. Nonsmokers who live or work with smokers suffer heart damage. ETS increases allergic symptoms and sinus conditions. It can worsen symptoms of **asthma**, *difficulty breathing, with wheezing sounds from the chest caused by air rushing through narrowed air passages*.

Vocabulary

mainstream smoke
sidestream smoke
environmental tobacco smoke (ETS)
asthma

❓ Did You Know?

Spending one hour in a smoke-filled room presents a nonsmoker with as much carbon monoxide as smoking one cigarette.

Figure 14.11   Carbon Monoxide Sources Compared

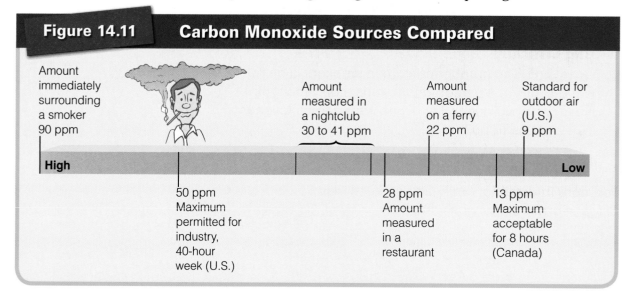

Amount immediately surrounding a smoker 90 ppm

Amount measured in a nightclub 30 to 41 ppm

Amount measured on a ferry 22 ppm

Standard for outdoor air (U.S.) 9 ppm

High   Low

50 ppm Maximum permitted for industry, 40-hour week (U.S.)

28 ppm Amount measured in a restaurant

13 ppm Maximum acceptable for 8 hours (Canada)

ETS causes headaches, dizziness, and nausea. Exposure to it doubles the risk of lung infections. Children suffer permanent lung damage, serious middle ear infections, and asthma attacks. The infant of a woman living with a smoker faces the same risks as an infant born to a mother who smokes.

ETS contains over 40 known carcinogens. One of its gases is carbon monoxide. In a closed room with smokers, a nonsmoker may suffer from the same lack of oxygen in the blood as was described for the smoker. **Figure 14.11** shows that a person exposed to a smoky room may inhale more carbon monoxide than is considered safe. Carbon monoxide has no smell, so you cannot tell if it is present. However, one sign of exposure is yawning.

Smoking Bans

Because of the efforts of nonsmokers' rights associations, most restaurants now ban smoking. Many motels provide nonsmokers' rooms, and a federal law bans smoking on airline flights. Almost every state bans smoking while using public transportation, in hospitals, elevators, schools, libraries, and other public spaces.

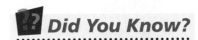
Did You Know?

Passive smoking does about 40 percent as much damage to arteries as smoking does.

Writing Activity:

Have each student write a well-supported essay answer to one of the following questions.

1. What health hazards are presented by passive smoking?
2. What can you do as a non-smoker to avoid passive smoke?

Worksheets:

A reproducible quiz for Section 3 is provided in the Teacher Classroom Resources.

Reviewing the Vocabulary
Review the vocabulary on page 386. Then answer these questions.
1. What is the difference between *mainstream smoke* and *sidestream smoke*?
2. What is the type of smoke that can be inhaled by nonsmokers?

Reviewing the Facts
3. **Evaluate.** What are the health problems associated with passive smoking?
4. **Describe.** How does passive smoking affect allergy and sinus conditions?

Writing Critically
5. **Expository.** Write a description of the portrait of a smoker you'd put on television. Why do you suppose television often glamorizes smokers?

For more vocabulary practice, play the Concentration game at **glencoe.com**.

1. Mainstream smoke goes from the cigarettes to the lungs of a smoker; sidestream smoke goes into the air from a burning cigarette.
2. Environmental tobacco smoke (ETS); exhaled mainstream smoke and sidestream smoke
3. Increases the risk of cancer, heart disease, irritates eyes, causes headaches, dizziness, and nausea
4. It makes them worse.
5. Answers will vary.

Smokeless Tobacco

The dangers of tobacco use are not limited to smoking cigarettes. The nicotine and carcinogens in smokeless tobacco are also absorbed into the blood through the mucous membranes in the mouth or the digestive tract. Smokeless tobacco is as addictive and just as dangerous to your health as smoked tobacco.

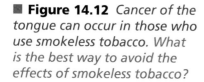

Vocabulary

smokeless tobacco
quid
leukoplakia

Smokeless Tobacco Isn't Safer

MAIN IDEA ▶ Smokeless tobacco contains nicotine.

You've probably seen pictures of baseball players chewing wads of tobacco in the dugout. **Smokeless tobacco** products, *tobacco used for snuff or chewing rather than for smoking,* is just as addictive and harmful to your health as tobacco you smoke. Chewing tobacco held in the cheek in a wad, or **quid**, *a small portion of any form of smokeless tobacco.* The stimulates the release of saliva. The saliva becomes contaminated with tobacco and is spit out.

The use of smokeless tobacco by high school athletes is on the rise. Although the habit carries health risks, as many as one out of three high school athletes has used smokeless tobacco. Smokeless tobacco products produce the same addiction as smoked products, because they also deliver the drug nicotine. Alternatives to using tobacco products include chewing gum or sunflower seeds instead.

■ **Figure 14.12** *Cancer of the tongue can occur in those who use smokeless tobacco. What is the best way to avoid the effects of smokeless tobacco?*

Caption Answer: Do not use tobacco products, choose healthy alternatives to smoking or using smokeless tobacco.

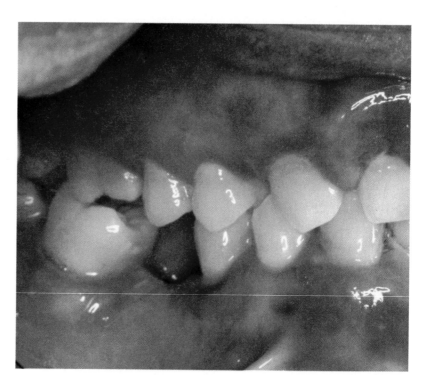

Health Risks of Smokeless Tobacco

Smokeless tobacco is linked to many health problems, from minor mouth sores to cancer. Using snuff is linked to cancerous tumors in the nasal cavity, cheek, gum, and throat. Tobacco chewing brings a greater risk of mouth and throat cancers than does tobacco smoking. More than half of the National League baseball players who use smokeless tobacco have developed mouth sores that lead to cancer. Baseball legend Babe Ruth used snuff and chewing tobacco. He died of throat cancer at age 53.

A sign that a person may be at risk for mouth cancer is **leukoplakia** (loo-koh-PLAKE-ee-uh), *whitish or grayish patches that develop in the mouths of tobacco users.* The patches develop where the quid is held. Leukoplakia may lead to cancer.

Using chewing tobacco and snuff also causes bad breath, brown teeth, and dulled sense of smell and taste. Tobacco chewing damages the gums, wears away the tooth surfaces, and eats away the jawbones.

■ **Figure 14.13** *Laws are in place to protect people from ETS. What would you say if someone lights up a cigarette in a public place?*

Caption Answer: Answers will vary.

Worksheets: A reproducible quiz for Section 4 is provided in the Teacher Classroom Resources.

SECTION 4 Review

Reviewing the Vocabulary
Review the vocabulary on page 388. Then answer these questions.
1. What is the name for tobacco products used for snuff or chewing?
2. What is a *quid*?
3. Describe *leukoplakia*.

Reviewing the Facts
4. **Identify.** List two health problems associated with smokeless tobacco.
5. **Describe.** What are three dental problems that occur with the use of smokeless tobacco?

Writing Critically
6. **Persuasive.** The tobacco industry uses techniques such as showing professional athletes using smokeless tobacco products. Teens look up to these athletes. Write a health advocacy message to compete against advertisers selling smokeless tobacco.

For more information on health careers, visit Career Corner at **glencoe.com**.

1. Smokeless tobacco
2. A small amount of smokeless tobacco
3. Whitish or grayish patches that develop in the mouths of tobacco users
4. Mouth sores, cancers
5. Any three: bad breath, brown teeth, loss of taste and smell, damage to gums, worn teeth and jawbone, loss of teeth
6. Answers will vary.

The Decision to Quit

Tobacco use is declining in the United States. Today many teens are deciding not to start because they don't want to suffer the effects of tobacco use. Of people who still smoke, nine out of ten would like to quit.

How People Quit Smoking

MAIN IDEA ▶ The rewards of a smoke-free life are worth the work.

The tobacco industry seeks to make profits and find new markets for its products. Selling tobacco products is considered by some to be **unethical**, *against the rules of right and wrong, not in line with accepted moral standards*. For a smoker who wants to quit, battling these influences along with the addictive qualities of nicotine may be difficult. A newspaper columnist invited his smoking readers to explain why they continued to smoke. He expected a flood of angry letters scolding him for his strong anti-smoking messages. Instead, most letters referred to the addictive nature of tobacco use.

Vocabulary

unethical

Cooperative Learning

Analyze: Are tobacco companies behaving unethically when their advertisements appeal to young people? Should companies have to give up their right to advertise? Ask students these questions and let them debate the issues.

■ **Figure 14.14** *Today, many teens oppose tobacco use, and are enjoying the benefits of a tobacco-free lifestyle. How can you and your peers benefit from avoiding tobacco use?*

Caption Answer: Answers will vary but should include the health benefits of being tobacco-free.

Preview Activity

Explain: Have students create two lists. One list is reasons to smoke and the other is reasons to stop. Ask students if they have more reasons to start or to stop smoking. Ask them to explain why that might be.

One letter read: "Don't refer to what we do as smoking—refer to it as nicotine addiction. Nobody really likes smoking all that much. It's the nicotine that we get hooked on. I am trying to quit. It is truly the most difficult thing I've ever experienced—and I haven't had an uneventful life. If I give in to the addiction, I know I'll die with a cigarette in my hand."

In other words, people continue smoking because they are hooked. Whenever they try to quit, they face withdrawal: irritability, restlessness, anxiety, and of course, a craving for nicotine. For some people, it may take several weeks for withdrawal symptoms to fade. The Health Skills sidebar, "Giving Up Smoking," provides some tips for the quitter.

Secrets for Success

MAIN IDEA ▶ Smokers must remind themselves again and again of the health benefits of quitting.

Successful quitters believe they can succeed. They know they can resist the urge to smoke. With each success, they gain more confidence and resist more easily. Smokers trying to quit find it useful to discover what they like most about smoking. At **glencoe.com** you will find a Life Choice Inventory to help smokers find out what it is about smoking that is most important to them—stimulation, handling the cigarette, relaxation, or something else.

After discovering what they enjoy most about smoking, a smoker should make a list of activities that will take the place of smoking. For example, smoking may be the way some people relax. To replace this function, such people must find new ways to relax. A long, hot bath or some light stretching may help release tension (see Chapter 4 for more on relaxation, and Chapter 9 for stretching exercises). Other types of smokers should find other activities to replace smoking's functions.

Two Ways to Quit

There are two ways to quit—tapering off or quitting all at once. A way to taper off is to start smoking each day an hour later than the day before. Another is to take up a fitness activity that will replace the smoking. For example, many people take up jogging and notice that smoking limits their performance. This may give them the motivation to quit smoking.

While tapering off works well for some people, most are more successful quitting all at once. This is because the hard part is over more quickly. Weeks after quitting, people have fewer and less intense cravings for cigarettes than those who cut back gradually. Most importantly, a person's health risks will decline and quality of life will improve.

Giving Up Smoking

To give up smoking, smokers must:

1. Ask themselves whether they really want to quit—are they ready to make a change?
2. Believe in their ability to succeed—have self-efficacy.
3. Review the health benefits of quitting smoking.
4. Expect to be challenged.
5. Plan their strategy according to the behavior change method in Chapter 1.
6. Find new ways to relax.
7. Make a list of alternative activities.
8. Make a commitment to themselves.
9. Seek support.
10. Tune in to the immediate rewards.

Applying Health Skills:

1. Jose's friends are pressuring him to smoke cigarettes.

2. Jose should say no firmly and clearly. He should look his friends in the eye, shake his head, and stand up straight to show that he really means it.

3. Jose could explain that he does not want to harm his health or hinder his chances of becoming the captain of the basketball team. He might suggest to his friends that they meet him somewhere else when they are ready to walk home from school or that they play basketball instead of just hanging out after school.

4. Jose should walk away from his friends if they still keep pressuring him.

5. Answers will vary.

The Pleasures of Quitting

At first, quitters are keenly aware of the craving to smoke. They constantly fight the temptation to smoke again. Tuning in to the pleasures of *not* smoking raises the odds in favor of success. Quitters list small and large pleasures:

- I can breathe deep breaths of clean air.
- I'm free from having to carry cigarettes and matches wherever I go.
- My behavior is not a threat to anyone's health. I can look my friends and family members in the eye.
- Food tastes delicious, and I can smell flowers.
- My clothes and hair smell fresh, not like smoke.
- I can walk easily without getting out of breath.
- I can talk on the phone without panicking if my cigarettes are out of reach.

APPLYING Health Skills

Refusal Skills

▶ Objectives

- Demonstrate how to use refusal skills to resist peer pressure.
- State reasons for refusing to smoke and identify healthful alternatives.

Up in Smoke

Several of Jose's friends have started smoking cigarettes. After school, they gather on a corner across from the high school and light up. Jose hangs out with them while they smoke. They all live in the same neighborhood and usually walk home together.

Jose plays on a basketball team at the YMCA and hopes to become team captain next year. He knows smoking is bad for his health and would affect his ability to play ball. He's already seen its effects on some of his teammates. The ones who smoke get winded after just a few minutes of play. Jose's friends keep pressuring him to smoke. He doesn't want to put them down for smoking, so he just shrugs and changes the subject. His friends don't seem to be getting the message because they keep offering him cigarettes.

▶ Identify the Problem

1. What is Jose's problem?

▶ Form an Action Plan

2. Describe how Jose should refuse his friends' offers to smoke, including the body language he should use.

3. What explanation could Jose give for refusing? What alternative activities might he suggest to his friends?

4. What should Jose do if his friends still keep pressuring him?

▶ What Did You Learn?

5. How would you refuse if your friends pressured you to do something you didn't want to do?

■ **Figure 14.15** *Many athletes now recognize the health risks of smokeless tobacco. What are some healthy snacks you can enjoy at game time?*

Caption Answer: Answers will vary but may include chewing gum or sunflower seeds.

- There are no dirty ashtrays around me.
- I have more money to spend on other things.
- That attractive nonsmoker who sits next to me in class has started showing an interest in me.

No matter why people decide to quit, what makes them stick with it is that after only two or three days, they feel better physically, as well as emotionally.

The Fear of Weight Gain

Some smokers are afraid that if they quit, they will gain weight. Some people actually lose weight. However, most quitters do gain—usually about four to five pounds, but sometimes more. Smoking is an oral behavior, and some quitters turn to another oral behavior to take its place—eating. People can prevent weight gain, however, by drinking fluids, snacking on crunchy vegetables, and taking up physical activity. Smokers who do gain a few pounds work to take the weight off. Chapter 8 tells how to manage a healthy weight.

"It is our choices . . . that show what we truly are, far more than our abilities."

—J.K. Rowling
(1965–)
Author

Help for Quitters

MAIN IDEA ▶ There are many different resources to help a person quit smoking.

Classes can help a person quit by helping to identify a smoker's style and then tailoring a quitting plan to each person's needs. Resources include Smokenders, the American Cancer Society, and the American Lung Association.

Nicotine delivery devices, including gum, patches, inhalers, pills, and nasal sprays, are aids available to smokers as stepping stones to freedom from smoking. Both the gum and patches are readily available over the counter. The sprays, pills, and inhalers require a prescription. A dose of nicotine from the gum, patches, inhalers, or sprays equals that in two or three cigarettes. The user must stop smoking and allow the devices to deliver nicotine into their bloodstream instead of tobacco. Nicotine-free pills help curb tobacco cravings and withdrawal symptoms, without nicotine. Side effects are many, though, including shakiness, skin rash, dry mouth, sleeplessness, and, rarely, seizures.

■ **Figure 14.16** *Gum containing nicotine helps some smokers quit. How much nicotine is contained in one dose of nicotine gum or patches?*

Caption Answer: One dose from a patch or piece of nicotine gum contains the same amount of nicotine as two or three cigarettes.

1. Against the rules of right and wrong, not in line with accepted moral standards
2. Irritability, restlessness, anxiety, and a craving for nicotine
3. Taking classes or using gum, patches, sprays, pills, and inhalers
4. Answers will vary.

SECTION 5 Review

Review the vocabulary on page 390. Then answer these questions.

Reviewing the Vocabulary
1. Define the term *unethical*.

Reviewing the Facts
2. Synthesize. Describe the withdrawal symptoms people experience when they quit smoking.
3. Identify. List the different strategies described in this section to help a person quit smoking.

Writing Critically
4. Expository. Learn from a pharmacist or physician how nicotine gum, nicotine patches, nicotine inhalers, and nicotine sprays work, and write a paper explaining what you learned.

 **Online**

For more vocabulary practice, play the eFlashcards game at **glencoe.com**.

How Can I Help Someone Quit Smoking?

 Understand and Apply Read the conversation below, and then complete the writing exercise that follows.

Tough love is the key to helping a smoker quit. If you care about the person, you will not keep quiet about a dangerous habit. Assert yourself. Confront the person. At the same time, show that you care. Talk about the risks of smoking. But realize that smokers can quit only when they are ready.

Q: I'm concerned about my favorite uncle—he smokes. How can I help him to quit?

A: First, you must realize that smokers can quit only when they are ready. Your job, then, is to help your uncle get ready. Always remember, though—this is his challenge, not yours. The key to helping is "tough love." Confront your uncle about his behavior. Assert yourself. Be clear and state that you dislike your uncle's behavior, not him personally.

Q: But I don't want to annoy my uncle, or make him dislike me.

A: Make it clear that you reject his smoking, not him. Talk about the risks of smoking (use information from your textbook), and tell him about the benefits of quitting.

Q: What if he just isn't interested?

A: Try to focus on topics that matter to your uncle. If he enjoys sports, for example, tell him how smoking is known to hurt sports performance. If he loves good food, focus on how smoking reduces the pleasure of tasting delicious flavors.

Q: He often says he knows about the dangers, but he ignores the warnings.

A: You may have to accept that he isn't ready to quit right now. If he continues to smoke, you must protect your own health. Be assertive, not aggressive. Insist, "Please don't smoke around me." Someday your comments, along with those of others, may encourage your uncle to quit for his own sake.

Q: When that day comes, how can I help him?

A: Let him know that you care, and that you respect him for his decision. You might offer to spend time with your uncle, doing things to keep his mind off smoking. Invite him to school functions, such as sporting events or musical or theatrical performances. Ask your parents to invite him to watch a movie with your family, or take a family bike ride, or have a picnic. Remember to show your support for his progress along the way. Many more helpful ideas for quitters and their families and friends are offered by the American Cancer Society.

 Writing Write a short story about a family in which one adult decides to quit tobacco use. Tell how the person takes steps to quit, and describe how the rest of the family is able to offer support and encouragement for the person to succeed.

Reviewing Vocabulary

Use the vocabulary terms listed below to complete the following statements.

emphysema

leukoplakia

nicotine

asthma

1. The addictive drug present in tobacco is _____.
2. A disease that causes flexible air sacs to burst is called _____.
3. _____ consists of whitish or grayish patches in the mouth that may lead to cancers.
4. Difficulty breathing and wheezing sounds from the chest are symptoms of _____.

Recalling Key Facts and Ideas

Section 1
5. **Explain.** Why do tobacco companies spend billions of dollars in advertising every year?
6. **List.** List the withdrawal symptoms people experience as a dose of nicotine wears off.

Section 2
7. **Name.** Name some of the harmful ingredients in cigarettes in addition to nicotine.
8. **Explain.** Explain what tar does to the respiratory tract.

9. **Name.** Name four respiratory problems associated with smoking.
10. **Describe.** Describe why smokers are more susceptible to respiratory infections than nonsmokers.

Section 3
11. **Explain.** What can carbon monoxide do to a passive smoker?
12. **Describe.** Describe the steps that are being taken to protect nonsmokers from sidestream smoke.

Section 4
13. **Explain.** How does using smokeless tobacco damage oral health?
14. **Describe.** Describe why chewing tobacco is not preferable to smoking.

Section 5
15. **Explain.** Explain why smokers sometimes gain weight when they quit smoking.
16. **List.** List the different programs available for smokers who want to quit.
17. **Describe.** How can you influence your peers not to smoke?

Writing Critically

18. **Persuasive.** Some individuals have filed suit against the tobacco industry because family members have died due to smoking. What might be the arguments for each side of the controversy? Which side would you support and why?
19. **Descriptive.** Laws have been passed to prohibit smoking on all domestic airlines. Where else should smoking be prohibited? What action can you take to help prohibit smoking in those places? Why will you take this action?

---

1. Nicotine 2. Emphysema 3. Leukoplakia 4. Asthma
5. To replace the smokers who die from lung cancer
6. Slowed heart rate, lowered blood pressure, nausea, headache 7. Carcinogens, tars, poisons, flavoring agents, moistening agents, ammonia 8. Tars leave a mucus coating,

which slows the cilia and clogs the respiratory system
9. Bronchitis, emphysema, and cancer 10. The irritation and thick mucus damages lung tissues 11. Reduces the amount of oxygen in the blood 12. Laws are passed to prohibit smoking in public places. 13. Causes mouth, tongue, and throat

Activities

20. Smoking causes emphysema. This activity will make you feel like a person who has emphysema. You need a straw to perform this activity. Plug your nose and put the straw in your mouth and breathe through it. Now jog in place for two minutes. Plug your nose and breathe through the straw again. Does breathing through the straw make you feel uncomfortable? In what ways are you uncomfortable? What have you learned about emphysema from this activity?

21. List ten reasons why you would not smoke.

22. Form small groups in your class and go to the elementary school and give a presentation on not smoking. How can you persuade young students not to smoke? What strategies might work best with them? Suggestions include lectures, puppet shows, plays, and admired role models.

23. Find someone you know who smokes. Make charts showing what times of day the person smokes. Use the information to try to help the person quit. Convince the person to replace smoking behaviors with other positive health behaviors. Give rewards for positive progress and penalties for negative smoking behavior.

24. Write to your local chapter of the American Heart Association, Lung Association, or Cancer Society for information about ways to quit smoking. Share the information with the rest of your class.

25. Go to the library and look up ways companies market their cigarettes in our country and other countries. Compare and contrast ways that cigarettes are marketed in several countries.

26. Make a collage of different smoking advertisements found in magazines. Change the advertisements to persuade people not to smoke. Put these collages up around the school.

Making Decisions About Health

27. A middle-aged friend has been a heavy smoker most of her life. The health effects are obvious to you, but not to her. She's short of breath and can walk only a few steps without wheezing. She suffers from frequent colds and her physician has warned her that she's risking severe heart trouble if she continues to smoke. Her doctor has told her family that her life is in danger. Still, she refuses to quit. "I'd rather smoke and die happy," she says, "than live without my habit." What would you do and why?

For more vocabulary practice, play the True/False game at **glencoe.com**.

Fact or Fiction?

Answers

1. False. The main reason for continuing to smoke is addiction to nicotine.
2. True
3. True

 Writing Paragraphs will vary.

cancers, leukoplakia **14.** Chewing tobacco holds a greater risk of mouth and throat cancers than smoking.
15. They turn to eating to substitute the need for a cigarette. **16.** Class through the American Cancer Society, American Lung Association, American Heart Association,

and using nicotine delivery devices **17.** Inform them of the dangers to their health, and the difficulty of quitting once they start and become addicted. **18–27.** Answers will vary.

CHAPTER 15

Infectious Diseases

Sections

1. Microbes and Illness
2. Defenses Against Infectious Diseases
3. The Body's Defenses
4. Taking Action

You are surrounded by millions of **microbes**, *tiny organisms, such as bacteria, yeasts, and viruses, that are too small to be seen with the naked eye*. They are also called *microorganisms*. Microbes are on the surfaces of things you touch, in the air you breathe, on the forks that carry food to your mouth, and on the surfaces of your body.

Most microbes are harmless. Many even perform valuable services, such as decomposing wastes and making nutrients. Others, however, can cause infectious diseases. **Infectious diseases** are *diseases caused and transmitted from person to person, by microorganisms or their toxins.* They are also called *communicable* or *contagious diseases*, or simply *infections*. *Microbes that cause disease* are known as **pathogens**. This chapter focuses on pathogens and offers strategies you can use to protect yourself against infections.

Fact or Fiction?

What Do You Think?
Is each statement true or false? If you think it's false, explain what's true.

1. A hospital is a place where people can easily pick up infectious diseases.
2. Antibiotics are among the few medicines that are effective against viruses.
3. Fevers are dangerous, especially when people have infections.

 Writing Write a paragraph telling what you know about one infectious disease. Then, as you read the chapter, make changes and corrections to the information in your paragraph.

(Answers on page 417)

Go Online

Visit **glencoe.com** and complete the Life Choice Inventory for Chapter 15.

Microbes and Illness

There are two main types of microorganisms that can cause disease. **Bacteria** (singular, bacterium) are *microscopic, single-celled organisms capable of causing disease.* **Viruses** are *organisms that contain only genetic material and protein coats, and that are totally dependent on the cells they infect.* Some bacteria can be beneficial. For example, bacteria found in the digestive tract protects against some disease and helps to digest food. If a person's immune system becomes weakened, though, bacteria may cause illness.

In addition to bacteria and viruses, several other classes of microorganisms can be harmful:

- **Fungi,** living things that absorb and use nutrients of organisms they invade
- **Protozoa** (PRO-toh-ZOH-ah), tiny, animal-like cells, some of which can cause illnesses
- **Worms,** visible parasites that burrow into the blood supplies of victims
- **Parasites,** living things that depend on the bodies of others that they inhabit

Vocabulary

microbes
pathogens
bacteria
viruses
tetanus
tuberculosis (TB)
drug-resistant
Lyme disease
pinworms
head lice

Bacteria

MAIN IDEA ▶ Some bacteria are helpful, but many cause disease in humans.

Bacteria grows and multiplies in warm, dark, moist environments. Bacteria can also thrive inside deep puncture wounds. That is why it's suggested that you seek medical attention for open wounds.

Tetanus

One type of bacterium causes **tetanus**, *a disease caused by a toxin produced by bacteria deep within a wound.* Tetanus is serious and often fatal. Tetanus bacteria produce a poison that causes uncontrollable muscle contractions. When this affects the lungs and heart, tetanus can cause death. A vaccine provides immunity against tetanus.

Tuberculosis

Worldwide, another bacterium that has increased in incidence is **tuberculosis** (TB), *a bacterial infection of the lungs.* TB infects one person every second. It kills millions each year. The World Health Organization (WHO) has declared a global state of emergency for TB, a disease that 20 years ago was thought to be under control. In developing countries, TB causes more than a fourth of all adult deaths.

Caption Answer: When people do not complete the prescribed dose of antibiotic and the bacteria that are left become stronger

■ **Figure 15.1** *New drug-resistant strains of tuberculosis bacteria are causing increased deaths around the world. What causes development of drug-resistant strains of a disease?*

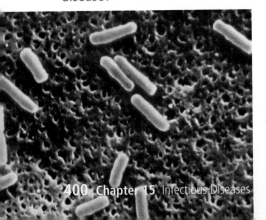

In the United States, new strains of TB are on the rise. These are **drug-resistant**, *pathogens that have lost their sensitivity to particular drugs*. The development of drug-resistant strains may occur because patients fail to complete their prescribed antibiotic therapy. The course of therapy for TB can last up to a year. Some patients, however, do not complete the drug therapy according to the doctor's orders. The remaining bacteria become resistant to the antibiotic used, and the infection becomes a superstrain. Many other drug-resistant diseases now threaten life and health, including malaria, pneumonia, and many sexually transmitted diseases. Scientists hope that future research will bring more effective drugs and treatments.

Lyme Disease

Hikers and others who walk in wooded areas and meadows should protect themselves from **Lyme disease**, *a bacterial infection spread by tiny deer ticks*. The disease often begins with the appearance of a red dot on the skin. Flu-like symptoms may occur. Weeks or months later, the bacteria may cause tissue damage resulting in drooping facial muscles, shooting pains, severe headaches, and an abnormal heartbeat. Severe arthritis and nerve damage may also develop. Antibiotics can cure lyme disease. When walking in wooded areas or meadows, cover exposed skin.

Viruses

MAIN IDEA ▶ Viruses cause diseases by invading cells.

Viruses differ greatly from bacteria. While bacteria are cells, viruses are not. Viruses are genetic material that can invade living cells—even bacteria. By using the cells' equipment, viruses reproduce themselves with astonishing speed. In the living cell, viruses take over the cell's genetic material and force it to reproduce more viruses. The new viruses then move on to infect other cells.

Each year, most people suffer through at least one cold, an upper respiratory tract infection. Some people come down with the flu, or influenza (in-flew-EN-za), a highly contagious respiratory infection caused by any of a variety of viruses.

Once flu and cold symptoms are gone, the virus causing the illness is usually gone. Other viruses, though, can remain in the body long after the symptoms of the initial illness are gone. These viruses can cause disease once again. An example is chicken pox, a usually mild, easily transmitted viral disease causing fever, weakness, and itchy blisters. Shingles is a painful skin condition caused by the reemergence of the chicken pox virus in later life. An adult with shingles can pass the virus to others, who will get chicken pox if they have not previously had it.

■ **Figure 15.2** *Lyme disease is spread by the bite of deer ticks. What are the immediate symptoms of Lyme disease?*

Caption Answer: Headache, joint pain, chills, fever

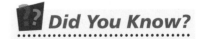

Did You Know?

It is recommended that when you wash your hands that you wash for 15 to 20 seconds. That's about the same time it takes to sing the "Happy Birthday" song twice!

Other Pathogens

MAIN IDEA ▶ Fungi, protozoa, and parasites cause a variety of diseases.

Fungi, protozoa, and parasites can also be pathogens. Fungi include yeasts, which are one-celled fungi; and molds, which are many-celled fungi. Some yeasts and molds can cause disease in humans. Fungi cause a variety of illnesses. Athlete's foot is a fungal infection of the feet, usually transmitted through contact with floors. Other fungi can cause dangerous and incurable lung infections.

Protozoa are single-celled creatures that cause diarrhea and other illnesses. As for worms and other parasites, the most dangerous of those are fairly rare in the United States. Others are common and easily cured. One easily cured parasite, **pinworms**, are *small, visible, white parasitic worms that commonly infect the intestines of young children.* Another is **head lice**, *tiny, but visible, white parasitic insects that burrow into the skin or hairy body areas.*

Worksheets: A reproducible quiz for Section 1 is provided in the Teacher Classroom Resources.

SECTION 1 Review

Reviewing the Vocabulary
Review the vocabulary on page 400. Then answer these questions.
1. What are *pathogens*?
2. Define *microbes*.
3. What is the difference between *bacteria* and *viruses*?

Reviewing the Facts
4. **Identify.** List five types of pathogens.
5. **Evaluate.** Which type of bacterium commonly invades puncture wounds?
6. **Explain.** What are the symptoms of Lyme disease?

Writing Critically
7. **Expository.** List as many reasons as you can think of explaining why children are more susceptible to pathogens than adults. As a teen, are you more or less susceptible to pathogens than when you were a young child? Why do you suppose that this is so?

For more vocabulary practice, play the eFlashcards game at **glencoe.com.**

1. Microbes that cause disease

2. Tiny organisms, such as bacteria, yeasts, and viruses, that are too small to be seen with the naked eye.

3. Bacteria are single-celled organisms that sometimes cause disease. Viruses are organisms that contain genetic material dependent on the cells they infect.

4. Any five: bacteria, viruses, fungi, protozoa, worms, parasites

5. Tetanus

6. Red dot on skin, headache, joint pain, chills, fever, shooting pains, severe headaches, abnormal heartbeats

7. Answers will vary.

Defenses Against Infectious Diseases

Pathogens are around us every day. So why aren't more people ill from infections? As we grow older, our immune system fights infections. Public programs to control infections provide another line of defense.

How Are Diseases Spread?

MAIN IDEA ▶ Public health officials monitor and control the spread of disease.

The spread of disease occurs as a cycle. For example, someone who has a cold may sneeze into the air. Bacteria-laden droplets then circulate, or land on nearby food and objects. Another person breathes in the droplets, or touches a bacteria-laden object and catches the cold. This person then repeats the cycle. Another example of a disease that spreads in this way is **hepatitis**, *a viral infection that causes inflammation of the liver*. If one person eats the same food as, uses the same needles as, or comes in contact with bodily fluids of an infected person, he or she may get hepatitis.

How Are Pathogens Controlled?

Public sanitation efforts provide some protection against infections. Public water supplies are chlorinated and sewage is treated to kill pathogens that could contaminate drinking water. Bacterial infections such as cholera, which causes violent cramping, vomiting, diarrhea, and even death, may be a concern in countries with poor public health systems. In these countries, travelers should avoid drinking local water. They should also avoid eating raw fruits, vegetables, meats, and seafood.

Public pools and other facilities use bleach and other **disinfectants**, *chemicals that kill pathogens on surfaces*. Washing your hands with soap and water will kill bacteria on the surface of your skin. Treating open wounds is a little different. To treat a wound, use an antiseptic ointment or spray that is available over-the-counter in pharmacies.

Public health programs also help control viral diseases. They require that all dogs be vaccinated against **rabies**, *a disease of the central nervous system*. As a result, the number of rabies cases in the United States is very low.

Vocabulary

hepatitis
disinfectants
rabies
vaccine
emerging diseases

Caption Answer: Certain pathogens can be passed to others when food is handled by an infected person.

■ **Figure 15.3** *Health departments inspect public places to be sure they meet standards for sanitary food preparation. Why are restaurants a likely place for people to be exposed to infection?*

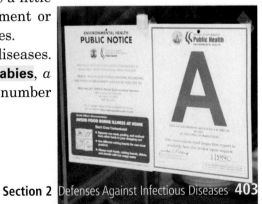

Examples of Infectious Diseases

Pneumonia is a disease caused by a virus or bacterium that infects the lungs.

Polio is a viral infection that produces mild respiratory or digestive symptoms, but may produce permanent paralysis or death.

Measles is a highly contagious viral disease characterized by a rash, high fever, sensitivity to light, and cough and cold symptoms.

Rubella is a viral disease that resembles measles, and can cause serious complications in pregnant females and the fetus.

Mumps is a viral disease that causes swelling of the salivary glands. Mumps can cause swelling in the testicles of males, and may cause sterility.

Worksheets: A reproducible quiz for Section 2 is provided in the Teacher Classroom Resources.

1. Disinfectants

2. A drug made from altered microbes or their poisons injected or given by mouth to produce immunity.

3. Diseases that appear in a population for the first time, or that suddenly re-emerge.

4. To protect against infectious diseases such as cholera

5. By destroying animal and insect carriers of viruses, immunizing pets and people

6. Answers will vary.

Drugs given to humans can prevent disease too. A **vaccine**, is *a drug made from altered microbes or their poisons injected or given by mouth to produce immunity*. Vaccines train the immune system to recognize the disease when it invades the body and prevent it from reproducing.

Controlling Infectious Diseases

The U.S. Public Health Service monitors the outbreak of diseases and works to prevent their spread. Some of the diseases that are monitored closely include some of the diseases listed in **Figure 15.4**.

Emerging Infections

While the public health system can control diseases, they cannot eliminate disease. New **emerging diseases**, are *diseases that appear in the population for the first time, or that suddenly re-emerge*. New diseases, for example, are the bird flu, severe acute respiratory syndrome (SARS), and bovine spongiform encephalopathy (Mad Cow), a disease linked to sick cows. Other diseases may re-emerge suddenly. One example is tuberculosis. This disease was almost eliminated in the United States. However, it re-emerged in recent years, striking people with weakened immune systems.

SECTION 2 Review

Reviewing the Vocabulary

Review the vocabulary on page 403. Then answer these questions.

1. To prevent the spread of infectious agents, you can spread _____ on surfaces.
2. Define *vaccine*.
3. What are *emerging diseases*?

Reviewing the Facts

4. **Analyze.** Why are public water supplies chlorinated?
5. **Synthesize.** How do public health programs control viral diseases?

Writing Critically

6. **Persuasive.** If you were given the task of justifying the need for immunization laws, what would you say? What could be done to encourage people to be vaccinated?

Go Online

For more information on health careers, visit Career Corner at **glencoe.com**.

The Body's Defenses

The body has many barriers against infectious diseases. The skin, membranes, and immune system can block most infectious diseases. When a disease does get past the first barriers, the body can often still fight it off.

Barriers to Diseases

MAIN IDEA ▶ The human body can defend itself against infections.

One way the body controls pathogens is to block their entry into the body. Barriers, such as skin and membranes, prevent the spread of disease. The immune system fights infections that make it past these barriers.

Skin

The skin is one such barrier. It produces salty, acidic sweat, which repels pathogens. It also has one-way pores that let toxins out, but won't let pathogens in. Scientists have also found a natural antibiotic protein that destroys bacteria. They hope to use this strategy to treat infections from bacteria that have developed drug resistance.

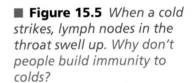

Vocabulary

lymphocytes
thymus gland
T cells
B cells
antibodies
antigens
histamine

■ **Figure 15.5** *When a cold strikes, lymph nodes in the throat swell up. Why don't people build immunity to colds?*

Caption Answer: The pathogens that cause colds are different viruses.

" *Sickness is felt, but health not at all.* "

—Proverb

Figure 15.6

**Antigens and
Antibodies**

1. Body is challenged by
   foreign invaders (antigens).

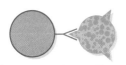

2. Immune system cells record
   shape of invaders.

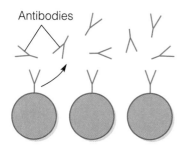

Antibodies

3. Cells use this memory
   record to make antibodies.

4. Later antibodies destroy
   foreign invaders.

5. Memory remains to make
   antibodies faster the next
   time this foreign invader
   attacks.

The Body's Membranes

The membranes lining the body chambers also protect against pathogens. These include a layer of mucus that traps pathogens, cilia that sweep them out, and cells and chemicals that destroy them. Together with the skin, they are the body's first line of defense against diseases.

Components of the Immune System

If a pathogen passes through the body's outer membranes, the immune system takes over. Usually, the immune system can destroy invaders and prevent diseases.

The immune system is located throughout the body. Bone marrow, for example, produces **lymphocytes** (LIM-fo-sites), *white blood cells that are active in immunity*. The **thymus gland**, *an organ of the immune system*, changes some of the lymphocytes into T cells. **T cells** are *lymphocytes that can recognize invaders that cause illness*. The T cells then have the ability to recognize enemies. Other lymphocytes become **B cells**, *lymphocytes that make antibodies*. **Antibodies** are *large protein molecules produced to fight invaders*. The invaders are known as **antigens**, *foreign substances in the body, such as viruses or bacteria, that stimulate the immune system to produce antibodies*. **Figure 15.6** illustrates how the immune system fights infection.

How the Immune System Fights Back

To fight infection, the lymphocytes travel in body fluids. During an infection, they are drawn to the lymph nodes. The swelling you feel on the sides of your neck during a cold are caused by lymphocytes. Another type of swelling is produced by the action of **histamine** (HIST-uh-meen), *a chemical that produces inflammation (swelling and irritation) of tissue*. Histamine inflames the site of attack and attracts defenders to it. During a cold, your nasal passages swell and become inflamed from histamine's action. Antihistamines work by reversing histamine's effects. They relieve the symptoms of unwanted swelling and inflammation from allergy.

T and B cells work as a unit. If one of the T cells detects an enemy, it sends out a chemical message. B cells respond to the message by making antibodies that destroy the invader. Other lymphocytes capture and eliminate the invader. In the background are still other cells that "remember" the invader so that the system can quickly destroy it, should it show up again.

When the immune response ends, only some antibodies and memory cells remain. They carry the history of what has happened. They are responsible for the immunity that follows many infections or immunizations.

You may wonder why people can't develop immunity to colds, flu, or cold sores. The symptoms of colds represent many *different* viruses that cause the same symptoms, each caused by a different pathogen. Also, some flu viruses can hide from immune cells to keep the cells from recognizing them. These viruses can eventually reinfect the person. When the virus becomes active again, the immune system doesn't fully recognize it quickly enough to prevent an outbreak.

The Course of an Illness

MAIN IDEA ▶ Many illnesses follow a predictable course.

Pathogens do break through the body's defenses and produce illness. A person who recognizes the early phases of an infection can take action right away. The five phases are described in **Figure 15.7**.

Antibiotics

When a bacterial infection develops, taking antibiotics can often kill the bacteria. Each type of antibiotic is useful only against certain kinds of bacteria. A health care provider will select the correct drug and dosage. With bacterial numbers controlled, the immune system can overpower and eliminate the pathogens. Antibiotics cannot be used to treat viruses. Antibiotics prevent cell growth, and viruses are not cells. The immune system works to wipe out the virus. All that can be done for most viral infections is to relieve symptoms until the disease runs its course.

Class Activity

Present: Working in pairs, have students select an infectious disease and trace the course of that disease through the five periods (see **Figure 15.7**). Research time will be needed. The final product can be an oral or video presentation, poster, a written report, or podcast.

Figure 15.7	Phases of Illness

Period	Events
1. Incubation	Pathogens multiply in the body. The person may infect others. The immune system may detect the invaders and work to eliminate them. If the immune system is successful, you avoid the disease. If not, then the disease progresses to the next phase.
2. Prodrome	The onset of general symptoms common to many diseases, such as fever, sneezing, and coughing. In this stage, the disease is easily transmitted. The immune system is stepping up its fight.
3. Clinical	The period of symptoms known to be caused by the disease. The immune system is in full battle.
4. Decline	The period when the immune system has almost won the fight against the infection, and symptoms are going away. Memory cells form.
5. Convalescence or death	The period when the body either repairs damage or dies. Upon recovery, the pathogen may or may not remain in the body. If it does, the person may remain a carrier of the disease, able to infect others even if no symptoms are evident. If the body is unable to repair the damage caused by the disease, the person may die.

Figure 15.8   **Fever Guidelines**

Oral temperatures over 102° F: Seek medical attention

Oral temperatures 100° F and less: Do not treat. (If fever persists, see a health-care provider.)

Oral temperatures between 100° and 102° F: Control with acetaminophen or ibuprofen. (Give aspirin only to people over 19 years of age to prevent Reye's syndrome; see Chapter 11.)

Fever

Fever is sometimes feared because it often develops with dangerous diseases. However, fever itself is not an illness and it is far from being an enemy. Fever may actually assist the immune system in its fight against infection. For example, cold viruses thrive and multiply at temperatures between 86 and 95 degrees Fahrenheit, but die off at higher temperatures. Fever also helps to activate the immune system. **Figure 15.8** provides fever guidelines. Aspirin is often taken as a fever reliever. Teens should not take aspirin or any related products (salioylates) because it can put them at risk for Reye's syndrome. Symptoms for Reye's syndrome include disorientation, severe headaches, and coma. Teens with sever fever may be treated with acetaminophen or ibuprofen.

SECTION 3 Review

Worksheets: A reproducible quiz for Section 3 is provided in the Teacher Classroom Resources.

1. Lymphocytes that can recognize invaders that cause illness

2. A chemical that produces inflammation (swelling and irritation) of tissue

3. They provide physical barriers against pathogens.

4. Lymphocytes are changed into T cells to recognize invaders and B cells to make antibodies.

5. Lymph nodes in the throat swell up because histamines inflame the tissues to attack the infection.

6. Answers will vary.

Reviewing the Vocabulary

Review the vocabulary on page 405. Then answer these questions.

1. What are *T cells*?

2. Define *histamine*.

Reviewing the Facts

3. Explain. Why are your skin and internal membranes important in defending against infections?

4. Describe. What role do lymphocytes play when fighting infection?

5. Evaluate. Why does your throat sometimes swell up when you are getting a cold?

Writing Critically

6. Expository. What happens when a person reaches for medicine every time a minor health problem sets in? When is it wise to take medicine, and when is it not wise?

Go Online

For more vocabulary practice, play the Concentration game at **glencoe.com**.

Taking Action

One of the most important steps a person can take to avoid infectious diseases is to keep immunizations current. What more can people do to prevent infections? Resistance to infection can be increased by eating a healthy diet, reducing or eliminating alcohol intake, getting regular physical activity, and reducing or effectively managing stress.

The principles of self-protection against colds and other infections are summarized in the Health Skills sidebar on page 413, "How to Avoid Infections."

Airborne Infections

MAIN IDEA ▶ To minimize the risks of infection you should keep immunizations current, keep your immune system strong, and protect yourself against exposure.

The easiest way to avoid viral and other infections is to remember that pathogens cause disease if they are transferred from a person or an object to you. Millions of pathogens are sprayed into the air when a person fails to cover their nose and mouth while sneezing or coughing.

Vocabulary

food-borne illness
Salmonella
E. coli
botulin toxin
botulism
upper respiratory infection
infectious mononucleosis
epidemic

■ **Figure 15.9** *Covering your nose and mouth while coughing or sneezing is one small thing you can do to prevent passing on airborne infections. What else can you do?*

Caption Answer: Answers may include not touching contaminated surfaces, washing hands regularly with warm water and soap, using disinfectant.

Imagine that the viruses or bacteria are a quart of red paint that has been sprayed all over your classroom, and is still wet. What would happen if you touched the surfaces and then touched your mouth, eyes, or nose? You would have red paint on your face. Bacteria and viruses are transferred in the same way.

To avoid catching a cold or flu, do the following:

- Cover your face if you sneeze or cough.

- Avoid touching contaminated surfaces.

- Always wash yourself, including your hair and your clothes, if you think you've been exposed.

- Always wash your hands with soap and water before handling food and after using the restroom.

This advice holds for cold and flu viruses and for many other pathogens as well.

APPLYING Health Skills

Practicing Healthful Behaviors

➤ Objectives
- Identify behaviors that contribute to the spread of pathogens.
- Describe healthful behaviors that help protect against infections.

Germ Trail

"I think I'm coming down with a cold," Garrett said as he sneezed into his bare hands and then used both hands to push open the door of the classroom.

"I hope I don't get sick," Nicole replied. "I've got a game on Friday night."

Garrett and Nicole took seats next to each other in class. Nicole borrowed a pen from Garrett. As she passed out papers for the teacher, she placed the pen in her mouth.

After class, Garrett and Nicole went to the cafeteria to eat lunch. They didn't wash their hands before eating.

➤ Identify the Problem
1. Identify four behaviors in this scenario that could lead to the spread of pathogens.

➤ Form an Action Plan
2. Describe how Garrett could have reduced the risk of spreading pathogens.
3. Describe how Nicole could have reduced the risk of picking up pathogens.
4. List two other behaviors that could prevent the spread of infections.

➤ What Did You Learn?
5. When you have a cold, what steps can you take to protect the people around you?

Is It a Cold or Is It Flu?

Almost everyone suffers from an **upper respiratory infection**, *an infection of the membranes of the nasal cavities, sinuses, throat, and trachea, but not involving the lungs*, at least once each year. When this happens to you, the most important step is to determine whether you have a common cold. However, what feels like the start of a cold may turn out to be something worse. It could be pneumonia or **infectious mononucleosis**, *a viral infection involving mononucleocytes, a type of white blood cell*. The symptoms vary from mild, cold-like symptoms to high fevers, swollen glands, and spleen and liver enlargement or rupture. It is sometimes called mono.

Influenza, or flu, is almost always caused by a virus. Thus, antibiotics bring no relief. Flu usually spreads as an **epidemic**, *an infection that spreads rapidly through a population, affecting many people at the same time*. Flu often occurs in the spring or fall of the year. It can sweep through a population. Flu symptoms develop one or more days after exposure to the virus. The early symptoms are identical to some of those of a cold. These may include fever and chills, runny nose, sneezing, and nasal congestion. Unlike colds, flu brings a sudden muscle weakness and aches and pains in the arms, legs, and back. A dry, hacking cough, which produces no mucus but which may cause chest pain, is another sign of flu. Flu shots taken in the fall can provide immunity to some kinds of flu. However, flu shots go out of date each year as new strains of virus develop and travel around the globe.

Colds can be viral or bacterial. Symptoms that characterize a cold are a sore throat, watery eyes, hoarseness, and a thick, greenish-yellow nasal discharge. Some people believe that exposure to drafts or having wet feet causes colds. In reality, exposure to infectious pathogens, not wet feet or drafts, will cause a cold. Sometimes, though, a cold or flu turns out to be dangerous. Seek medical attention immediately if any of the following symptoms occur:

- A cold or flu that is accompanied by headache or facial pain (indicating sinus infection)
- A deep cough, wheezing, or shortness of breath (indicating bronchitis or pneumonia)
- A fever of 102 degrees Fahrenheit or above
- Pain in the ears

Colds and flu are usually harmless. Some, though require medical attention. The right treatment can be life-saving.

Writing

1. Why do you think it is important to know that flu and most colds are caused by viruses?
2. Some people see a physician for every sniffle, "just in case." Do you agree or disagree with this course of action? Why?

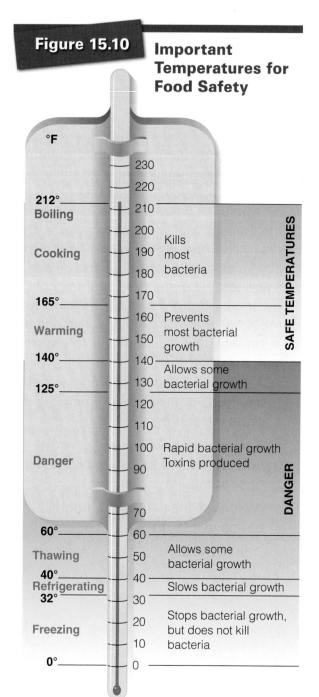

Figure 15.10 Important Temperatures for Food Safety

°F

230
220
212° 210
Boiling
200
Cooking 190 — Kills most bacteria
180
170
165° 160 — Prevents most bacterial growth
Warming 150
140° 140
Allows some bacterial growth
125° 130
120
110
100 — Rapid bacterial growth Toxins produced
Danger 90
70
60° 60
Thawing 50 — Allows some bacterial growth
40° 40
Refrigerating — Slows bacterial growth
32° 30
Freezing 20 — Stops bacterial growth, but does not kill bacteria
10
0° 0

SAFE TEMPERATURES

DANGER

Food Safety

MAIN IDEA ▷ Pathogens growing in foods can make people sick by causing infection or poisoning.

About one-third of people living in the United States are treated for food poisoning each year. Many times, people believe it's the "stomach flu." **Food-borne illness**, *illness caused by pathogens or their toxins consumed in food*, causes most cases of digestive distress and is capable of much worse. Food pathogens make people sick in two ways: by infecting them or by poisoning them.

Food Infection

One food pathogen is the *Salmonella* bacterium, *a common food-borne pathogen causing digestive system infections.* **Salmonella** can infect the digestive tract, causing the symptoms mentioned above. In very old or very young people, or those weakened by illness, *Salmonella* infections can be fatal.

Food Poisoning

Pathogens can also release poisons into food as they multiply. Several fast-food restaurant chains have unknowingly served sandwiches or lettuce toppings containing the **E. coli** (COH-lye) bacteria, *a toxin-producing bacteria that can cause food-borne illness.* An *E. coli* toxin outbreak can make hundreds of people severely ill with bloody diarrhea, severe cramps, dehydration, and kidney damage.

Another dangerous poison can arise in poorly canned food. This is the **botulin toxin**, *a potent poison produced by bacteria in sealed cans, plastic packs, or jars of food.* Without prompt treatment, a person who consumes the botulin toxin may suffer fatal nervous system damage. While rare, symptoms of **botulism**, *the often fatal condition of poisoning with the botulin toxin*, come on fast. The symptoms include double vision, muscle weakness, or difficulty swallowing or breathing after eating canned food. If you or someone you know experiences these, seek medical help right away. Toss out any cans of food that bulge out on top or that appear to be leaking. Never buy a can of food that has been damaged. The seal that keeps the food safe may have been broken.

■ **Figure 15.11** *Correct hand washing prevents illness. What happens to bacteria when you use soapy water to wash?*

Caption Answer: Bacteria becomes dislodged from the skin.

Preventing Food-Borne Illness

MAIN IDEA ▶ Serve and store foods at appropriate temperatures, and keep the kitchen clean.

Most cases of food-borne illness can be prevented. **Figure 15.10** shows important temperatures for food safety. To protect yourself, insist that the food you eat be prepared according to the four simple rules stated below.

Clean

Eat only foods that have been prepared and served on clean surfaces by clean hands. Hand washing with plenty of soap and water prevents the spread of bacteria. Bacteria also live in damp sponges, cutting boards, and other moist surfaces. The best way to safely clean these items is by washing them in a dishwasher. Washing them in hot, soapy water with chlorine bleach added also works.

Separate

Always use separate utensils to prepare different types of foods. Bacteria are easily transferred from meats to raw foods, such as salads, during preparation. For example, if you use a plate to carry raw hamburgers to a grill, be sure to wash that plate before using it to hold the cooked burgers.

Health Skills

How to Avoid Infections

1. Wash hands with soap and water.
2. Use disinfectants on surfaces and objects.
3. Stay current with immunizations.
4. Do not share objects with people who are ill.
5. Wash your hands often throughout the day, especially before eating.
6. Keep away from people who are coughing or sneezing into the air.
7. Select a healthy diet that supports the immune systems health.
8. Exercise regularly.
9. Do not use tobacco or other drugs.
10. Control stress.
11. Get adequate rest.

Cook

Cook foods until they reach an internal temperature that kills pathogens. Most meat and seafood should reach at least 145 degrees Fahrenheit. Ground meat and hamburger should reach at least 160 degrees, and casseroles and stuffing should reach 165 degrees to be safe. Cooked foods should stay above 140 degrees Fahrenheit—piping, steaming hot. Spoiled foods may taste fine, however, they will still make you sick. If the food smells or tastes bad, throw it out.

Chill

Pathogens slow their growth and produce less poison at temperatures below 40 degrees Fahrenheit. Do not eat cold dishes that have been allowed to stand at room temperature for two hours or more—or one hour in hot weather. Cold dishes should be served refrigerator-cold.

Worksheets: A reproducible quiz for Section 4 is provided in the Teacher Classroom Resources.

SECTION 4 Review

Reviewing the Vocabulary

Review the vocabulary on page 409. Then answer these questions.

1. An infection of the membranes of the nasal cavities, sinuses, throat, and trachea, but not involving the lungs is called an _____.
2. A toxin-producing bacteria that can cause food-borne illness is called _____.
3. What is the difference between *Salmonella* and *botulin toxin*?

Reviewing the Facts

4. **Identify.** List four steps a person can take to avoid infectious diseases.
5. **Describe.** What are some common cold symptoms?
6. **Evaluate.** List three food poisoning symptoms that would require a visit to a health care provider.

Writing Critically

7. **Narrative.** Read the Health Skills sidebar on page 413, and honestly ask yourself how well you protect yourself against infectious diseases. What other health practices can you add to the list that would prevent the spread of infection? Name some behaviors you need to change.

For more vocabulary practice, play the True/False game at **glencoe.com**.

Answer sidebar (left margin):

1. Upper respiratory infection
2. *E. coli*
3. *Salmonella* is a food infection, botulin toxin is food poisoning.
4. Any four from the Health Skills sidebar on page 413.
5. Sore throat, watery eyes, hoarseness, thick nasal discharge
6. Double vision, muscle weakness, difficulty swallowing or breathing after eating, bloody diarrhea, severe cramps, dehydration
7. Answers will vary.

Mononucleosis—The Kissing Disease

 Understand and Apply Read the conversation below and then complete the writing exercise that follows.

Infectious mononucleosis, or mono, is a viral disease that resembles an upper respiratory infection. The symptoms, however, are more severe. It is also sometimes called the "kissing disease" because the virus can be spread through saliva. Mononucleosis generally occurs in teens and young adults. The virus that causes the disease remains in your body for life. However, recovery from this viral attack is usually complete, and complications are rare.

Q: Why do they call mono the kissing disease?

A: The name "kissing disease" is related to a theory about activities of the age group most likely to get the disease—15- to 30-year-olds. People in this age range are most active in dating, and mono is thought to be spread through oral contact. Mono sometimes sweeps through a school population as an epidemic, indicating that mono possibly spreads by modes other than kissing.

Q: What are the symptoms?

A: Mono is difficult to diagnose from symptoms alone, because it can imitate so many other conditions. One person may be infected and develop only a mild sniffle. Another may experience weakness, a severe sore throat, fever, swollen glands, an enlarged spleen, and an infected liver with symptoms like those of the dangerous liver infection hepatitis. Mono may come on slowly or quickly. Once the first attack subsides, it can come on again with even more ferocity. Most bouts last from four to six weeks, although some cases can last even longer.

Q: How can physicians tell whether someone has mono?

A: A blood test that takes just minutes can accurately diagnose mono. The test studies the white blood cells known as mononucleocytes, from which the disease gets its name. This test is the only way to distinguish mono from many other infections ranging from colds to hepatitis.

Q: How dangerous is mono?

A: Luckily, few people suffer serious side effects from a case of mono. The spleen may become sensitive and, very rarely, may rupture, requiring surgery. This is why people diagnosed with mono are advised to take it easy. Rest is the best treatment for mono.

Q: After a person recovers from mono, can it come back?

A: The immune system develops immunity to mono after one bout. After full recovery, mono will not strike the same person again.

 Writing Write a description of how the body attacks the virus that causes mononucleosis. Use the correct vocabulary terms in your description.

Reviewing Vocabulary

Use the vocabulary terms listed below to complete the following statements.

hepatitis

Lyme disease

lymphocytes

botulin toxin

1. What is a disease of the liver that is caused by viruses and transmitted by infected needles?

2. _____ is a potent poison produced by bacteria in sealed cans, plastic packs, or jars of food.

3. _____ are white blood cells active in immunity. They include both T cells and B cells.

4. The bacterial infection that is spread by deer ticks is called _____.

Recalling Key Facts and Ideas

Section 1

5. **Explain.** In what type of environment do bacteria grow and multiply best?

6. **List.** Name some precautions you can take against tick bites.

7. **Identify.** Name three diseases caused by viruses.

Section 2

8. **Describe.** Describe how infections spread.

9. **Explain.** How do immunizations prevent the spread of disease?

Section 3

10. **Explain.** How do T and B cells work together to destroy disease-causing invaders?

11. **Describe.** What is the role of the memory cells?

12. **Evaluate.** Why aren't antibiotics effective against viruses?

13. **Analyze.** How does a fever assist the immune system?

Section 4

14. **Identify.** Name one thing that weakens the body's resistance and one thing that strengthens resistance.

15. **Evaluate.** How can you avoid contracting airborne infections?

16. **Describe.** What are some symptoms of *Salmonella* infection?

17. **List.** List four rules that should be followed when preparing food.

Writing Critically

18. **Expository.** In 1979 the U.S. Surgeon General stated that "the health of the people has never been better." Taking into account recent changes in the infectious disease pattern, what kind of statement do you think the Surgeon General might have made in 2000? What statement do you think will be made in five or ten years? Justify your answers.

Activities

19. Find a newspaper or magazine article less than one year old that discusses some aspect of infectious diseases. Write a one-page summary and reaction to the article. Include a copy of the article with the date and source.

1. Hepatitis 2. Botulin toxin 3. Lymphocytes
4. Lyme disease 5. Warm, dark, moist, nutrient-rich environments like the human body 6. Wear high socks, long pants, and tick repellant when hiking or walking in woods 7. Answers will vary. 8. The host contaminates the air, food, or objects near another person who is exposed. 9. A vaccine is made from the pathogen that causes disease, and the immune system recognizes the disease when it invades the body.
10. T cells recognize the invader, and B cells make antibodies to fight the invaders. 11. The memory cells remember the

20. Interview a local public health official to obtain the following information: how the local public health unit keeps track of local incidences of infectious diseases, what the most common infections are in the area, and what reports must be made to higher levels of government. Identify the name of the person interviewed and the agency the person works for.

21. On the left half of a poster board, make a collage of advertisements for cold remedies. On the right half, collage your own non-drug alternatives for treating a cold.

22. Identify some of the community programs in your area that are aimed at preventing disease. List the name, address, and phone number of each program and the services they provide to help reduce the spread of infectious diseases.

23. Choose a foreign country you would like to visit and find out what health precautions are necessary to travel to that country. What vaccines are necessary and why?

24. Choose one of the infectious diseases mentioned in the chapter. Do additional research on the disease you choose. After your research, write a one-page essay on the methods you would use to control or wipe out the disease.

25. Find out more about parasitic worms: flatworms, tapeworms, roundworms, pinworms, and hookworms. How do they invade the human body? How can they be destroyed? What problems and symptoms do they cause? Write down your findings and share the results with the rest of the class.

Making Decisions About Health

26. Your friend has been working part-time after school in a day care center. Since she has been working there, she has had the flu several times and has had many colds. What could you tell your friend about how pathogens are spread? How could she help protect herself from infectious diseases?

27. You're hungry, and cheeseburgers are on the menu of a barbeque party. You notice that the cooked burgers are being served from the same tray as raw burgers. How might this lunch make you sick? What can you do to avoid eating contaminated food? How can you use your communication skills to inform your host without conflict?

Go Online

For a personal health assessment complete the Life Choice Inventory at **glencoe.com.**

Fact or Fiction?

Answers
1. True.
2. False. Antibiotics are useful against bacteria but useless against viruses.
3. False. Fevers are part of the body's defense against infection, and low fevers are not dangerous.

Writing Paragraphs will vary.

pathogen and destroy it if the body is infected again. **12.** Antibodies only prevent cell growth, and viruses are not cells. **13.** Cold viruses die off at high temperatures, and fevers help activate the immune system. **14.** Answers will vary. Alcohol and stress lower resistance; physical activity, nutrition, strengthen resistance. **15.** Avoid people who are coughing or sneezing; wash after contamination. **16.** Abdominal cramps, headache, vomiting, diarrhea, fever **17.** Clean, separate, cook, chill **18–27.** Answers will vary.

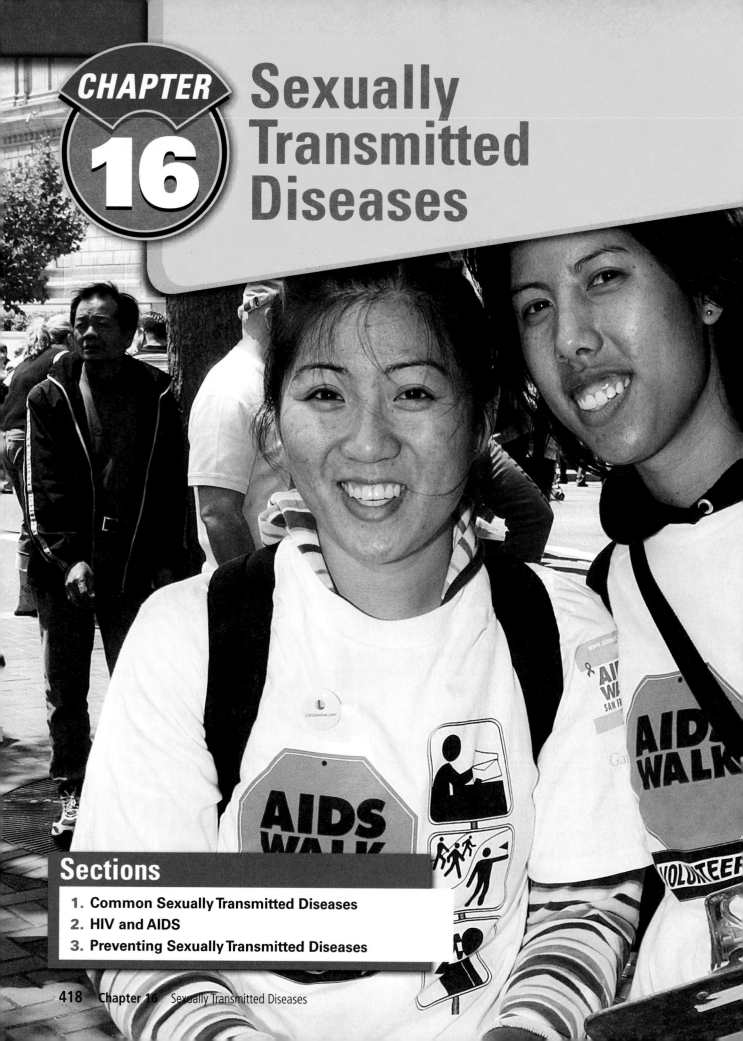

CHAPTER 16

Sexually Transmitted Diseases

Sections

1. Common Sexually Transmitted Diseases
2. HIV and AIDS
3. Preventing Sexually Transmitted Diseases

The pathogens that cause **sexually transmitted diseases** (STDs), *diseases that are transmitted by way of direct sexual contact*, can all be spread from person to person. That is, a person who has sexual relations with someone else who is infected can come down with one or more of these diseases. Sexual relations include any combination of oral, genital, or anal sex through which mucus membranes come into contact. STDs can cause a variety of health problems, like blindness or infertility, and some can cause death.

Some STDs are caused by bacteria. These can be treated with antibiotic drugs. Others are caused by viruses and these cannot be cured. The most threatening virus is the **human immunodeficiency virus** (HIV). This is *the virus that causes AIDS*. **Acquired immune deficiency syndrome** (AIDS) is *a transmissible viral disease of the immune system that creates a severe immune deficiency, and that leaves people defenseless against infections and cancer.*

Fact or Fiction?

What Do You Think?
Is each statement true or false? If you think it's false, explain what's true.

1. Birth control pills protect females against most forms of STDs.
2. A reliable strategy for preventing STDs is to ask potential partners about their past sexual experiences.
3. The use of condoms always protects the user from contracting STDs.

 Writing Write a paragraph to explain how STDs can affect a person's health.

(Answers on page 447)

Go Online

Visit **glencoe.com** and complete the Life Choice Inventory for Chapter 16.

Common Sexually Transmitted Diseases

Many people who suffer the effects of STDs find it difficult to talk about them because they fear embarrassment or social rejection. Meanwhile, the number of curable STD cases in this country far exceeds that of other developed countries. Young people, especially, have a tendency to think they are not at risk; however, they are, and the numbers prove it. Teens account for more than one-fourth of all STD cases reported in the United States each year.

In the U.S., several factors lead to the spread of STDs. The use of alcohol and other drugs can increase the spread of STDs by lowering inhibitions. People who would not engage in sexual behavior with someone else may do so when under the influence of these substances.

In other circumstances, the diagnosis or treatment of STDs may not occur if a person does not have health insurance or does not understand the signs and symptoms of STDs. Some people believe that they can prevent STDs by simply washing themselves after having sexual contact. Others believe that taking birth control pills or other hormonal methods will prevent STDs. Both of these beliefs are myths. Finally, the media play a role in the spread of STDs. Media images that are sexually suggestive often do not include the consequences of that behavior.

Vocabulary

sexually transmitted diseases (STDs)

human immunodeficiency virus (HIV)

acquired immune deficiency syndrome (AIDS)

chlamydia

pelvic inflammatory disease (PID)

gonorrhea

genital herpes

human papillomavirus (HPV)

genital warts

Pap test

syphilis

chancre

latent

fetus

hepatitis B

trichomoniasis

pubic lice

yeast infection

urinary tract infections (UTIs)

jock itch

Caption Answer: Untreated STDs can cause infertility, blindness, and other health problems.

■ **Figure 16.1** *The threat from STDs remains largely unknown because of embarrassment, fear, lack of knowledge, and lack of treatment. If left untreated, how can STDs affect a person's health?*

Sexually Transmitted Diseases

MAIN IDEA ▶ All STDs require medical attention. Some are treatable, but some have no cure.

STDs can affect everyone, regardless of a person's age, educational level, and family income. If a person suspects that he or she may have an STD, it's important to get medical care immediately. In some cases, STDs can be treated and cured. However, even if an STD cannot be cured, medications may be available to lessen the severity of the STD.

The next few sections are arranged to present information about the most widespread STDs first, and to provide some details about their symptoms and available treatments. **Figure 16.2** on pages 422 and 423 briefly describes the most common STDs.

Chlamydia

An STD that threatens the health of millions of people in the United States, but often causes no symptoms, is chlamydia. **Chlamydia** is *an infection of the reproductive tract, with or without symptoms*. Males with this bacterial infection may feel a little burning when urinating or notice a white discharge from the penis. Some may feel pain in the testicles. A few others may develop greatly enlarged lymph glands in the groin. Many males, however, have no symptoms at all.

Females with this infection may have some discharge from the vagina. Most, though, have no symptoms. A few have burning pain when urinating, pain in the lower abdomen, fever, bleeding or pain with sexual intercourse, or irregular menstrual periods.

With or without symptoms, chlamydia can progress to injure the reproductive organs and can be passed on to someone else. This is one reason why regular physical examinations that include STD tests are recommended for anyone who is sexually active. In the United States, experts recommend annual chlamydia screenings for all females who have sexual intercourse up to the age of 26.

In advanced cases, chlamydia spreads to the deeper pelvic structures of females—a condition known as **pelvic inflammatory disease** (PID), *an infection of the fallopian tubes and pelvic cavity in females, causing ectopic pregnancy and miscarriages*. PID can cause sterility in females. Although rare, males may also become sterile if chlamydia spreads to the testicles.

Even in a normal pregnancy, chlamydia can cause premature birth and low birth weight. During birth, the bacteria can infect the lungs or eyes of the newborn baby, causing pneumonia or blindness. Health care providers can prevent these conditions by treating infected pregnant females with antibiotics before delivery.

Class Activity

Analyze: Present students with a story about two teens who have been dating. The female, Tina, has never had sexual intercourse with anyone before and she does not know the sexual history of her boyfriend. Tina thinks they will soon be making a decision about intercourse. Ask students to imagine that Tina has come to them for advice and have them list three pieces of advice they would offer her.

Figure 16.2   **Common Sexually Transmitted Diseases**

	HIV/AIDS (virus)	Chlamydia (bacteria)	Genital Herpes (virus)	Gonorrhea (bacteria)
Symptoms	Swollen lymph glands, diarrhea, pneumonia, weight loss, other infections, night sweats.	In males: usually mild burning during urination. In females: vaginal discharge, abdominal pain, or no symptoms.	Painful, blisterlike sores on or near penis, anus, vagina, cervix, or, less often, the mouth.	Possibly no symptoms; vaginal/penile discharge. In males: painful urination, tender lymph nodes, testicular/abdominal pain, fever. In females: heavy or painful menstruation or painful urination, bleeding after intercourse. Also called "clap," "drip," or "dose."
Treatment or cure	Treatment aimed at curing secondary infections, relieving symptoms, and prolonging life. No cure for AIDS exists.	Antibiotics for both partners simultaneously.	No cure; prescription medication may lessen severity and frequency of outbreaks.	Antibiotics for both partners simultaneously.
Potential complications	Immune system failure, severe illness leading to death, eight to ten years to see signs of infection; infection of infants leads to death.	In females: pelvic inflammatory disease (PID) with abnormal pain, fever, excessive menstrual bleeding, infertility. In males: dangerously enlarged lymph glands of the groin or infection of testicles which leads to sterilization. Infection during birth can cause blindness or illness in newborn.	Recurrence, herpes, eye infection, infection of newborn during birth.	Sterility, PID, arthritis, infection of heart lining, infection of eyes of newborns that leads to blindness.
Prevention measures	Abstinence from sexual intercourse and from use of intravenous drugs; mutual monogamy with uninfected partner; some protection provided by condoms.	Abstinence from sexual intercourse; mutual monogamy with uninfected partner; some protection provided by condoms.	Abstinence from sexual intercourse; mutual monogamy with uninfected partner, some protection provided by condoms only if sores are absent from groin and thighs.	Abstinence from sexual intercourse; mutual monogamy with uninfected partner, some protection provided by condoms.

Hepatitis B (virus)	Human Papillomavirus (virus)	Pubic Lice (parasite)	Syphilis (bacteria)	Trichomoniasis (parasite)
Possibly no symptoms; may have a low-grade fever, nausea, vomiting, fatigue, muscle and joint pain, cough, sore throat, dark urine, jaundice, tender liver.	Often no symptoms. With some varieties, dry, wart-like growths on or near penis, anus, cervix, or vagina. Other varieties cause no outward symptoms, but in a female, create cancerous or precancerous cervical cells that register positive on Pap tests.	Itching; lice in pubic hair; eggs, possibly visible, clinging to hair strands. Also called "crabs."	Primary (3 weeks after exposure): chancre on penis, vagina, rectum, anus, cervix. Secondary (6 weeks after primary): rash on feet and hands; flu-like symptoms, including appetite loss, fever, sore throat, nausea, headache. Tertiary (10 to 20 years later): severe nerve damage.	Possibly no symptoms in males. In females: frothy, thin, greenish discharge; genital itching and pain. Also called "trick."
No cure; treatment aimed at relieving symptoms.	No cure; controlled by removal of growths or abnormal cervical cells.	Prescription or over-the-counter shampoo, lotion, or cream used by both partners simultaneously.	Antibiotics for both partners simultaneously.	Antibiotics for both partners simultaneously.
Chronic liver disease, liver damage (cirrhosis), potential for development of liver cancer.	Recurrence; cervical cancer; penile cancer; possible obstruction of cervix, vagina, anus.	Skin irritation.	Brain damage; heart disease; spinal cord damage; blindness; infection of fetus, causing death or severe retardation.	Bladder and urethra infections; increased risks of PID in females, and of premature birth in pregnant females.
Vaccine is available; abstinence from sexual intercourse and intravenous drug use; mutual monogamy with uninfected partner. Avoidance of tattooing and body piercing.	Abstinence from sexual intercourse; mutual monogamy with uninfected partner; some protection provided by condoms; HPV vaccine available to young females between the ages of 9–26.	Abstinence from sexual intercourse; mutual monogamy with uninfected partner; not sharing towels or bedclothes with others; good personal hygiene; no protection provided by condoms.	Abstinence from sexual intercourse; mutual monogamy with uninfected partner; some protection provided by condoms.	Abstinence from sexual intercourse; mutual monogamy with uninfected partner; some protection provided by condoms.

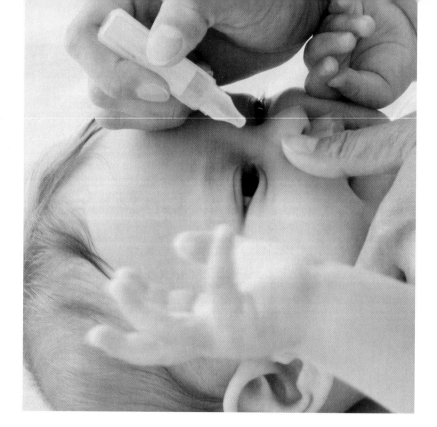

Figure 16.3 *Drops placed in a baby's eyes at birth can help protect the eyes against STD infection. Why do U.S. public health laws require antibiotics to be applied to every infant's eyes immediately following birth?*

Caption Answer: To protect newborns against blindness from gonorrhea and other STDs such as chlamydia and syphilis.

Gonorrhea

As with chlamydia, people infected with **gonorrhea**, *a bacterial STD that attacks many organs of the body when left untreated*, may not feel any symptoms. This allows transmission to other people without knowing it. Again, it is important for people who have sexual partners to be tested for gonorrhea.

Males are more likely to have symptoms of a gonorrhea infection—a thick, pale yellow discharge from the penis, a burning feeling when urinating, and occasional painful swelling in a testicle. Females who have symptoms may notice a yellow-green vaginal discharge and pain when urinating. However, most females have no symptoms at all.

If left untreated, the gonorrhea bacteria can spread all over the body. It attacks the joints, leading to arthritis; attacks the skin, leading to sores and other problems; and attacks the reproductive system, leading to sterility in both males and females. Gonorrhea can also cause PID in females and can infect infants' eyes at birth, a common cause of blindness. To protect babies born in the United States against blindness from gonorrhea, public health laws require that a gonorrhea-killing antibiotic be applied to every infant's eyes within minutes after birth.

Antibiotics are the most effective cure for gonorrhea. However, more and more cases of the disease each year are reported to be resistant to antibiotics. For these cases, combinations of drugs or special antibiotics may be able to wipe out the infection before it can seriously affect the person's health.

Genital Herpes

Another STD, **genital herpes**, is *a common, incurable STD caused by a virus that produces blisters.* Antibiotics cannot cure this STD. The virus causes clumps of painful blisters to appear on the skin. The blisters can occur in several areas of the body, depending on the site of sexual contact:

- On or around the penis
- In and around the vagina
- In the mouth or on the lips
- On the thighs or abdomen
- Around or in the anus.

The sores cause pain, urning, or itching. They closely resemble those of a related condition—cold sores or fever blisters on the mouth. The mouth infection is most often caused by the herpes simplex 1 virus, while the genital infection is usually caused by the herpes simplex 2 virus. A blood test can confirm that a person has been infected.

A person need not have obvious sores to transmit the virus. A female may have internal blisters and can unknowingly transmit the virus to others. It also may be possible for males without active sores to transmit the virus by way of semen. Typically, though, the virus is passed to others by active blisters. After blisters have completely healed, the risk of passing the virus to someone else drops dramatically, but not completely.

With the first outbreak, which occurs 2 to 12 days after acquiring the infection, a person may feel ill with fever, headache, muscle aches, painful urination, and swollen glands. Thereafter, the virus hides in nerve fibers, where it is safe from attack by the body's immune system. Later, the virus can become active again, and cause more sores. Some people experience only one episode in a lifetime. Others suffer outbreaks many times a year for 10 to 15 years or even longer.

Among the rarer, serious effects of herpes are dangerous eye infections that can result from touching the eyes after touching the blisters. The open blisters can also serve as entrances into the body for other microbial infections, including the viruses that cause AIDS or hepatitis.

The newborn baby of a female with herpes is at high risk if blisters are present during the baby's birth. Herpes infections in newborns can cause blindness, severe mental retardation, and even death. Females with severe blisters at the time of delivery may be advised to give birth by Caesarean section rather than take a chance of infecting the newborn.

While not curable, herpes is treatable with an oral antiviral drug that reduces the frequency, duration, and severity of outbreaks. A prescription cream applied to the blisters may shorten an outbreak but this has not been proven through scientific research.

■ **Figure 16.4** *Herpes blisters on the lip. What is the treatment or cure for genital herpes?*

Caption Answer: There is no cure. Treatment includes prescription medication to lessen severity and frequency of outbreaks.

Caption Answer: A person might have a fever, headache, muscle aches, painful urination, and swollen glands.

■ **Figure 16.5** *Herpes blisters. What symptoms may accompany a herpes outbreak?*

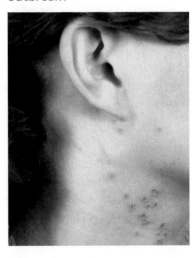

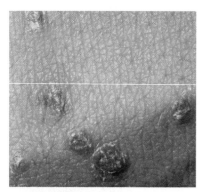

■ Figure 16.6 *Genital warts.*
What viruses can cause genital warts?

Caption Answer:

Human papillomaviruses (HPV)

Consumer Skills Activity:

1. Because without proper treatment, an STD can get worse and may lead to death.

2. Answers will vary.

Human Papillomavirus (HPV) Infection

Another common STD is **human papillomavirus** (HPV), *a group of over 100 related viruses, the effects of which include genital warts and cervical cancer.* Some HPV strains cause no detectable symptoms. Others cause warts on the hands and feet, and **genital warts**, *contagious wart-like growths on infected areas, caused by human papillomaviruses.* Some varieties of HPV cause cervical cancer. The HPV viruses cannot be cured by using medications.

Once in the body, the infection may remain for life. Although there is currently no medical cure for HPV infection, the lesions and warts these viruses cause can be treated. Methods commonly used to treat lesions include freezing that destroys tissue, laser surgery, LEEP (loop electrosurgical excision procedure, the removal of tissue using a hot wire loop), and conventional surgery. In addition, some medications may be used to treat external genital warts. However, even after treatment, the virus remains in the body, and the warts may grow back.

Many sexually active people have the virus, but most never know it. Only 10 percent of people who carry it ever develop the warts that reveal the virus's presence in the body. A female may discover her infection when a routine **Pap test**, *a test for cancer of the cervix,* detects abnormal cervical cells.

Consumer
SKILLS ACTIVITY

Techniques Used to Sell STD Treatments

STDs can be embarrassing. Some people who suspect they might have an STD may feel so embarrassed that they seek treatment outside the medical community. Delaying needed medical attention allows the disease time to progress and to damage the body. Meanwhile, the misuse of antibiotics gives other bacteria present in the body a chance to develop antibiotic resistance.

Especially for STDs such as genital herpes, genital warts, and AIDS—for which no real medical cures exist—fake "cures" are everywhere. The desire for privacy is understandable. Reaching for any hope of a cure is also natural.

Still, only health care professionals have access to reliable diagnostic tests and treatments.

 Writing

1. Why is it important to seek medical treatment for STDs?
2. Why would a person with an STD for which there is no cure be vulnerable to false advertising?

It is not clear whether condoms can prevent transmission of HPV because it can be transmitted during non-vaginal sex, and from the scrotum and/or the vagina.

In 2006, the Food and Drug Administration (FDA) approved a vaccine to prevent infection by four types of HPV, two of which are the most common causes of genital warts and of cervical cancer. The CDC recommends immunization of females between the ages of 9 and 26. The vaccine is given by a series of three shots over a six-month period.

Syphilis

Syphilis is *a bacterial STD that, if untreated, advances from a sore (chancre) to flu-like symptoms, then through a long symptomless period, and later to a final stage of irreversible brain and nerve damage, ending in death.* Syphilis is transmitted by direct contact with a **chancre**, *a hard, painful sore*, during sexual activity. Chancres can occur on the genitals, anus, breast, or mouth. Antibiotics are used to treat this infection.

If a person infected with syphilis allows the chancre stage to pass without treatment, the sore will heal in 3 to 6 weeks, but the infection moves to the next stage. The next stage of syphilis brings swollen glands, a skin rash, patchy hair loss, or flu-like symptoms. If the person fails to seek medical help at this stage, these symptoms, too, clear up by themselves in a few weeks. Untreated, the disease progresses to its **latent** stage, *a temporary period of symptomless advancement of the disease.*

The latent stage of syphilis can last as long as 10 to 20 years. During this stage, the infected person feels well but can transmit the disease to others. With few outward clinical signs, the infection begins to silently attack the internal organs.

In the final stage of syphilis, the infection destroys whole organs. The results are permanent: blindness, deafness, brain damage, skin damage, and heart disease. Without treatment, death is likely. Even in the final stage, a syphilis infection can still be cured and its progression stopped. By that time, however, permanent organ damage may have already occurred.

In pregnant females, syphilis can enter the bloodstream of the **fetus**, *the developing infant from the ninth week after conception until birth*, and may cause severe brain damage or death. For this reason, routine prenatal exams include a test for syphilis.

Hepatitis B

A less common but highly dangerous STD is **hepatitis B**, *a viral STD that causes loss of liver function and severe liver disease.* Once in the body, hepatitis B attacks the liver, causing severe illness. It can lead to incurable liver cancer and death.

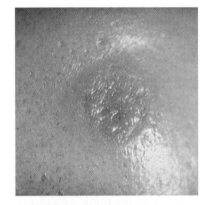

■ **Figure 16.7** *Syphilis is transmitted by direct contact with a chancre during sexual activity. Why is it important to seek medical treatment before syphilis reaches its latent phase?*

Caption Answer: During the latent phase, a person feels well, but can transmit the disease. At this stage, the infection begins to attack the internal organs.

Did You Know?

The open chancre of syphilis also makes a convenient entry port to the bloodstream for HIV, the virus that causes AIDS.

The word *hepatitis* means "inflammation of the liver." Five viruses cause it. The relatively mild one, hepatitis A mentioned in the last chapter, often spreads by way of consuming the virus in contaminated food or water.

Hepatitis B, however, enters the body by way of contact with infected body fluids. This can happen in any of the following ways:

- By having unprotected oral, anal, or vaginal intercourse with an infected person
- By sharing a needle with an infected intravenous drug user
- By receiving a tattoo or having ears or other body parts pierced with unsterilized equipment
- Less likely, by receiving infected blood from a blood transfusion

Once hepatitis B is acquired, there is no cure for it. The virus remains in the body and can possibly infect others throughout life. The key to avoiding the illness, therefore, is prevention. In the United States, it is standard to immunize all children for hepatitis B beginning in infancy.

Trichomoniasis

Trichomoniasis is *an STD caused by a parasite that can cause bladder and urethral infections.* Most often, trichomoniasis is acquired by sexual behaviors such as oral, anal, and vaginal intercourse. In females, this infection causes an unpleasant-smelling, foamy, yellow-green or gray vaginal discharge; abdominal pain; pain when urinating; or itching in the genital area. Most males have no symptoms, although a few have a watery discharge or burning sensation when urinating. Males often unknowingly transmit the disease to their partners. Antibiotics are an effective treatment if both partners are treated at the same time and do not have intercourse until both are cured.

Multiple STDs

A person who has one STD may very well have others. This is of special concern, because one STD may mask another, more dangerous one. Syphilis, for example, is a serious second infection. Its early symptom, the chancre, easily hides, for instance, in a cluster of herpes blisters. If the herpes alone is diagnosed, the syphilis will go untreated and will silently spread through the body. A person who contracts any STD should see a health care provider and request a test for syphilis—and, possibly, for several other STDs. All are likely to be second infections, even **pubic lice**, *an STD caused by tiny parasites that breed in pubic hair and cause intense itching.* The symptoms listed in **Figure 16.8** mean that medical help is needed right away.

Figure 16.8

Common Symptoms of STDs

These symptoms mean that medical help is needed right away:

- Unusual discharge from vagina, penis, or rectum
- Pain or burning while urinating
- Pain in the abdomen (females), testicles (males), or buttocks and legs
- Blisters, open sores, warts, rashes; or swelling in the genital area or sex organs
- Flu-like symptoms; fever, headache, diarrhea, aching muscles, swollen glands
- Bleeding or pain during or after intercourse

Getting Help and Protecting Others

MAIN IDEA ▷ Medical authorities will notify anyone who may have acquired an STD from another person.

A person who suspects that he or she has contracted any STD should see a health-care provider and request testing. The health care provider will test the person for other STDs. This medical help is available anonymously, even for teens. Among possible sources of help are parents, school health services, public health departments, community STD clinics, or the offices of private doctors. Treatments may be free of charge in some clinics. The government requires that identifying information about individuals, such as names, is kept confidential.

A person diagnosed with an STD must notify any sexual partners. Otherwise, the partners may end up passing the disease back and forth several times. Due to some medical confidentiality laws, healthcare providers can only share medical records with a person diagnosed with an STD. Parents may only be able to obtain information directly from the teen and not the health care provider. So fear of punishment by parents should not prevent a teen from receiving care if he or she suspects an STD.

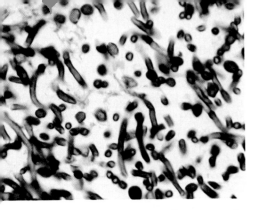

■ **Figure 16.10** *The yeast of candidiasis, magnified over six thousand times. What causes yeast infections?*

Caption Answer: A yeast, candida, that multiplies out of control in the vagina.

Other Infections

MAIN IDEA ▶ Yeast infections and urinary tract infections are not sexually transmitted.

The STDs just described are usually transmitted by sexual contact. Other infections of the genital and urinary organs that are not transmitted by sexual contact are also common. Like STDs, they should be treated right away to maintain the health of the reproductive or urinary tract organs.

Yeast Infections (Candidiasis)

Most females acquire a vaginal yeast infection at some time in life. A **yeast infection** is *an infection caused by a yeast that multiplies out of control in the vagina*. It is sometimes called candidiasis for the type of yeast causing the infection. Yeast may multiply out of control to cause intense itching, burning, irritation, and swelling of the outer genitals and a whitish, lumpy vaginal discharge. A female who is pregnant, takes birth control pills, has diabetes, takes antibiotics, or uses douches is especially likely to develop candidiasis.

Over-the-counter antifungal vaginal inserts and creams relieve symptoms and help cure yeast infections. Although a yeast infection is not an STD, certain STDs such as chlamydia and gonorrhea have similar symptoms. See your doctor for evaluation if over-the-counter products do not eliminate symptoms. If you have never had a yeast infection, it is best to confirm the diagnosis with a physician before seeking over-the-counter treatment. For prevention, wearing loose-fitting cotton—not nylon—underwear or panty hose with cotton panels. Should yeast infections occur frequently or not respond to treatment, a female should see a physician.

Urinary Tract Infections

Other infections, called **urinary tract infections** (UTIs), are *bacterial infections of the urethra that can travel to the bladder and kidneys*. The urethra (the tube through which urine leaves the body) leads to the bladder and makes a convenient route for invading bacteria. Most UTIs cause frequent, urgent, and painful urination, and a strong, persistent urge to urinate with only small amounts of urine actually passing. Some people notice a dull, aching pain above the pubic bone or blood in the urine.

UTIs are easily treated with antibiotics. If left untreated, however, infection of the bladder may progress to a possibly serious infection of the kidneys. People who get frequent UTIs may be able to reduce the frequency by drinking extra fluids; urinating frequently; and for females, wiping from front to back after urination or bowel movements.

 **Did You Know?**

Warning signs of something more serious than a yeast infection:

- Abdominal pain, fever, or a foul-smelling discharge

- No improvement within three days of treatment

- Symptoms recur within two months

Tinea Cruris (Jock Itch)

A fungal infection of the inner thigh and groin, nicknamed **jock itch**, causes intense itching. This condition is common among athletes who sweat heavily and whose clothes stay wet for long periods. The same type of fungus that causes athlete's foot also causes jock itch. Over-the-counter medications usually clear it up. Other preventive measures include staying dry, not sharing towels with others, and not allowing clothing to touch the floor.

Worksheets: A reproducible quiz is provided in the Teacher Classroom Resources.

SECTION 1 Review

Reviewing the Vocabulary

Review the vocabulary on page 420. Then complete the following statements.

1. Diseases that are transmitted by way of direct sexual contact are called _____.
2. A hard, painful sore is called a _____
3. Define *gonorrhea*.
4. An incurable STD caused by a virus that produces blisters is called _____.
5. _____ are bacterial infections of the urethra that can travel to the bladder and kidneys.

Reviewing the Facts

6. **Describe.** Describe the physical problems that can occur in people who are not treated for gonorrhea.
7. **List.** List and identify the areas of the body on which genital herpes blisters occur.
8. **Explain.** What should people do if they are diagnosed with STDs?

Writing Critically

9. **Personal.** Reread the "Common Sexually Transmitted Diseases" chart in **Figure 16.2** on pages 422–423. How serious do you consider the risks associated with STDs as compared with the risks from smoking, drug or alcohol abuse, or other risky behaviors?

Go Online

For more vocabulary practice, play the eFlashcards game at **glencoe.com**

1. Sexually transmitted diseases (STDs)
2. Chancre
3. A bacterial STD that often advances without symptoms to spread through the body, causing problems in many organs.
4. Genital herpes
5. Urinary tract infections (UTIs)
6. The bacteria can spread throughout the body, attacking joints, leading to arthritis, causing sores on the skin, weakening the heart, and causing sterility.
7. Blisters can occur on the penis, in and around the vaginal area, in the mouth or on the lips, on the thighs or abdomen, and around or in the anus.
8. They should notify their sexual partners immediately.
9. Answers will vary.

HIV and AIDS

A disease of enormous concern worldwide is acquired immune deficiency syndrome (AIDS). First observed in the late 1970s, AIDS has spread rapidly to more than 100 countries and every inhabited continent of the globe. **Figure 16.11** shows the advancement of AIDS among U.S. teens ages 13 to 19 and adults. The number of those infected but not yet ill is thought to be ten times greater than the number of people diagnosed with AIDS.

Teens are currently the most rapidly growing group for both infection with HIV and AIDS. In the United States, in every hour of every day and night, one to two teens are infected with HIV.

Vocabulary

Pneumocystis carinii (PCP)
Kaposi's sarcoma
AIDS dementia complex
protease inhibitors
intravenous (IV) drug abuse

HIV Infection and AIDS

MAIN IDEA ▶ HIV is the virus that causes AIDS. A person is diagnosed with AIDS when a specific set of criteria is met.

Infection with HIV and the disease AIDS are not the same thing. A person with an HIV infection may live normally for years with the virus present in the cells of the body. A diagnosis of AIDS comes with the destruction of the immune system and development of the conditions typical of AIDS: a form of pneumonia, fungal infections, and cancers rarely seen in people with a healthy immune system.

Figure 16.11 **U.S. Teen and Adult AIDS Cases Since 1984**

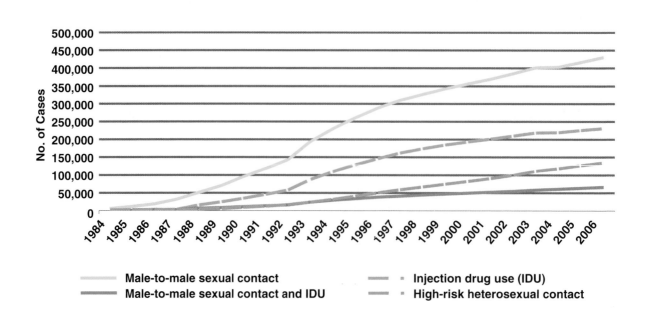

Male-to-male sexual contact
Male-to-male sexual contact and IDU
Injection drug use (IDU)
High-risk heterosexual contact

How HIV Destroys Immunity

HIV attacks the very cells and tissues that provide the body with immunity and disables its defenses. When a person first becomes infected with HIV, the virus incubates in the body for several weeks but causes no symptoms. Then, a period of illness may set in that resembles the flu. If the person is tested for HIV during this time, referred to as the *window period,* the test is likely to turn out negative, because the antibodies detected by the test take several months to form. The infection can still be passed to another person during the window period.

HIV invades the immune system's white blood cells, the T cells. Because it hides inside the cells, it remains safely out of reach of immune defenses. Once inside the T cells, the virus tricks the cells into acting like tiny virus factories. Each cell begins churning out millions of copies of the HIV virus. The new viruses then break free from the "parent" cell to find other T cells to infect.

After months or years of silently infecting T cells and reproducing, the HIV infection begins to destroy immunity. The self-destruction occurs when cells of the immune system find the infected T cells and kill them off as they would any other infected cells. As the T cells are relentlessly attacked and destroyed, the T cell fighting force loses its effectiveness as part of the immune system.

The Disease of AIDS

A diagnosis of AIDS is often first made when a health care provider detects the presence of one of the diseases typical of AIDS. Blood tests reveal low levels of T cells and the presence of HIV genetic material. The first symptoms of AIDS are usually troublesome, but vague. Fatigue, appetite loss, weight loss, and nagging cough are typical. As the disease progresses, AIDS patients typically have persistent yeast infections of the mouth, throat, or vagina.

The disease that first brings most people with AIDS to a physician is called **Pneumocystis carinii** (PCP), *a type of pneumonia characteristic of AIDS.* Other defining diseases include **Kaposi's sarcoma**, *a normally rare skin cancer causing a purplish discoloration of the skin.*

HIV can also make its way to the brain and nervous system, causing **AIDS dementia complex**, *the mental disorder resulting from an attack by HIV on the brain and nerves.* HIV damages the body's tissues, but HIV doesn't kill. People die of the other diseases against which they become defenseless.

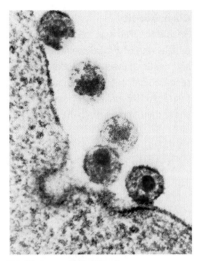

■ **Figure 16.12** *A photomicrograph of the AIDS virus. What is the difference between an HIV infection and the AIDS virus?*

Caption Answer: HIV is the virus that causes AIDS, while AIDS is a diagnosis that comes with the destruction of the immune system.

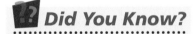 *Did You Know?*

Chapter 15 described the incubation, prodrome, and other typical stages of an illness.

Class Activity

Research: With new treatments, people with HIV/AIDS are living longer and healthier lives. Ask students to research current drug treatments related to HIV and AIDS. Have students share their findings with the class.

Treatment and Life with AIDS

MAIN IDEA ▶ New drugs and drug combinations can help people with AIDS remain healthy.

Many new drug treatments can extend life and health for many AIDS patients. However, the drugs are expensive and therefore unavailable to many people worldwide who need them.

With new treatments of drugs, radiation, and surgery, some people with AIDS are living long, healthy lives. An important first discovery was that antivirus drugs such as AZT (zidovudine) reduce the level of HIV in the blood. The lower the level of HIV in the tissues and blood, the slower the progression of AIDS. Unfortunately, AZT's effects seem to last only about a year, because the virus becomes resistant to the drug.

Combination Treatments

Today, the best medical treatment for HIV infection is a combination of drugs, including those of the AZT drug family, a group known as protease inhibitors, and others. **Protease inhibitors** are *drugs that stop the action of an enzyme which ordinarily helps HIV to reproduce.* The therapy is known as highly active antiretroviral therapy, or HAART (HIV is a member of a group called the *retroviruses*). The therapy consists of giving three drugs that stop HIV reproduction at various stages. HAART gets results: it reduces HIV levels, increases T cells, and prolongs life in 65 to 85 percent of patients using it perfectly.

A key to success with these drugs, however, is the ability of the AIDS patient to stick with a complicated schedule of taking 20 to 50 pills a day, at four-, six-, and eight-hour intervals, around the clock, seven days a week without holidays. Researchers are hopeful that if HAART is used aggressively enough, and started early enough in the course of the infection, that the disease may be controlled completely. In 2006, the FDA approved a once-daily, single-pill treatment for HIV/AIDS. The earlier the therapy begins, the better the chance of preventing irreversible damage to the immune and nervous systems.

The Threat of Resistance

Of great concern to health care providers is the ability of HIV to become resistant to medications. Should a patient taking the HAART medications be prone to forgetting a pill here and there, chances are great that the therapy will soon lose its effectiveness because the virus will become resistant to the drugs. In general, about half of all medical patients fail to take the medications as they are prescribed.

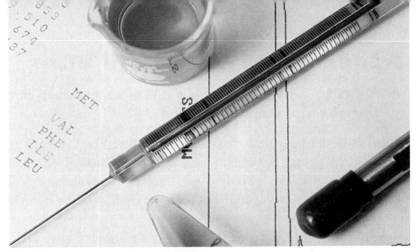

■ **Figure 16.13** *Living with AIDS and treating the infection require strict, daily lifestle changes. What are some current treatments for AIDS?*

Caption Answer: AZT is used to reduce the level of HIV in the blood, and protease inhibitors are used to stop the action of an enzyme which helps HIV reproduce.

Other Concerns

The drugs used to treat HIV infection and AIDS are expensive. Without adequate insurance, few people can afford to buy them. Indeed, this situation applies to the great majority of infected people worldwide. Sadly, most of the world's people with AIDS receive no treatment at all.

Without effective treatments, some people who are infected with HIV sicken and die within six months of infection. Others may live without symptoms for years. Once AIDS symptoms set in, however, most die within two to five years. Researchers are hoping for an effective, inexpensive vaccine to prevent HIV infections and end the epidemic, but such a vaccine is slow in coming.

Living with HIV

A person diagnosed with an HIV infection must accept that he or she has an incurable disease that can be transmitted to others. First the person must accept the diagnosis. Then the person must decide how and whom to tell. Soon follow the losses of finances, changes in sexual activity, health, and some social support. Day-to-day living changes dramatically. The person may face endless medical examinations, begin drug therapies, and adopt strict eating habits to prevent food poisoning and other infections.

The disclosure of HIV infection may result in discrimination concerning housing, employment, child custody, insurance benefits, or potential employment. People who later develop AIDS can expect to lose physical strength, mental sharpness, control of life activities, self-esteem, and later, possibly, life itself.

Many people react to these losses with courage. One young female who believes she contracted HIV as a teen has committed her life to traveling and speaking to teen groups about the disease. Many others may join local education efforts to support those who are newly diagnosed. They work in AIDS food banks, or they answer calls for a help hotline. They may be facing losses, but even so, their self-esteem stays high as they find new, meaningful roles.

Class Activity

Create: Divide the class into small groups. Have each group create a poster, video presentation or podcast that corrects a myth about the transmission of HIV/AIDS. Students may refer to myths other than those listed in the book. Each presentation should present the myth and then supply facts or ideas to debunk that myth.

Transmission of the HIV Virus

MAIN IDEA ▶ HIV can be transmitted in several ways, but not through casual contact.

AIDS is often a fatal disease caused by infection with a virus. HIV is readily transmitted by way of sexual contact or exchange of blood. HIV does not appear to be transmitted through casual contact and is rarely transmitted to health care professionals in the workplace.

People who feel and look healthy can be infected with HIV and can transmit it to others. They can pass on the virus before they develop any signs of illness, during the incubation stage. Often, people who become ill with AIDS in their twenties were infected with the virus when they were teens.

Ways HIV Is NOT Transmitted

HIV is not transmitted by casual contacts such as sharing meals, shaking hands, coughing, or sneezing. It also is not transmitted by mosquitoes or other insects, by saunas, by pools, or by food handled by HIV-infected people. HIV is also not transmitted to people who donate blood using sterilized needles; to those being vaccinated using sterilized needles; or by contact with unbroken, healthy skin. HIV is not transmitted by touching shared objects, such as toilet seats. Intimate sexual activity or contact with blood from an HIV-infected person—not casual contact—can transmit HIV. **Figure 16.14** reviews the ways HIV is transmitted and ways that it is not transmitted.

Sexual Transmission

Most people with HIV acquired their infections by way of sexual intercourse. These people can then pass the virus on to others by way of blood, semen from the penis, fluids of the vagina, or breast milk. Steady sexual contact with people with AIDS presents the greatest risk of contracting HIV.

Figure 16.14 | Ways HIV Is Transmitted and Ways It Is Not Transmitted

HIV is known to be transmitted by:	HIV has NOT been transmitted by:
• Having sex (anal, vaginal, or oral) with someone infected with HIV. • Sharing needles and syringes with someone infected with HIV. • Being exposed (fetus or infant) to HIV before or during birth or through breastfeeding.	• Shaking hands, hugging, or engaging in a casual kiss. • Sitting on a toilet seat, using a drinking fountain, doorknob, dishes, drinking glasses, or food. • Petting or playing with pets. • Receiving a mosquito bite.

Figure 16.15 *HIV-infected mothers who receive drug therapy stand a fifty-fifty chance of protecting their newborns from the virus. How can a mother transmit AIDS to her newborn?*

Caption Answer: A pregnant female can transmit the virus to her infant during pregnancy, at childbirth, or through breastfeeding.

However, it takes just one contact with an infected person to acquire the virus. This means a single sexual encounter can infect a healthy person with HIV.

The presence of STDs can also increase the risk of contracting HIV. The open sores of herpes or syphilis give the HIV virus easy access to the bloodstream. STDs like gonorrhea draw immune cells, such as T cells, to the areas of infection.

Needles

The sharing of needles among people who practice **intravenous (IV) drug abuse**, *the practice of using needles to inject drugs of abuse into the veins*, is the second most common path by which HIV travels from person to person. Programs that allow drug addicts to exchange used needles for sterile ones have reduced the spread of blood-borne illnesses in the United States and other countries. Such programs are controversial in the United States, however, because of fears of encouraging drug abuse. Such a small amount of blood is needed to pass on the virus that even being scratched by an infected needle can transmit AIDS. Unsterilized needles used for any purpose are dangerous, including the needles of acupuncture, tattooing, ear or body piercing, and electrolysis (the removal of hair by inserting an electrically charged needle into the hair follicles).

Pregnancy, Childbirth, Breastfeeding

HIV can be transmitted to infants in three ways. Females who have AIDS or are infected with HIV can infect their offspring during pregnancy, during birth, or by way of breastfeeding. Effective antiviral drugs given to the pregnant female with HIV or AIDS can sometimes protect her infant from being infected. As a rare exception to the rule that breastfeeding is best for babies, new mothers who are HIV-positive are urged not to breastfeed their infants.

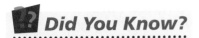
Caption Answer: The virus is transmitted through sexual transmission, sharing needles, pregnancy, childbirth, and breastfeeding.

■ **Figure 16.16** *The AIDS quilt is a tribute to loved ones lost to AIDS. Name the ways in which HIV is transmitted.*

Blood Traces

Only traces of whole cells are needed to convey the virus from person to person. Semen commonly carries HIV, but so can blood—the amount you see sometimes when brushing your teeth, for example. Ordinary kissing poses little danger, especially in people with healthy mouths.

Blood Transfusions and Tissue Transplants

Another way people have acquired HIV infections is by way of blood products used in medical treatments or transplanted tissues or organs. Those who received blood or tissues before 1985 risked being infected with the virus, because medical products were not screened as they have been since that time. Thanks to the advances in screening of potential donors, testing of the donated products, and more accurate tracking of information, today's blood, tissue, and organ supplies are almost always safe to use.

The best protection against acquiring any infection from the office of a health care provider is to notice whether the provider uses precautions such as those listed in the margin. If you find a health care provider who doesn't, leave right away, and report the problem.

The Risk to Health Care Professionals

Young people considering careers in the medical fields often ask about the risk of contracting AIDS in the performance of medical jobs. Very rarely do health care workers contract AIDS by being accidentally stuck with an infected needle. Because the risk is well known, they take every precaution to protect themselves and their patients. Only when health workers become tired, careless, or hurried do accidents happen.

Millions of people have highly rewarding careers in the health care field and remain free of contagious diseases. The chances of dying from almost any other cause are enormous compared with the chance of dying from AIDS acquired by offering routine health care. This is true even for health care providers who specialize in caring for people with AIDS. After all, no one knows better how to stop the spread of disease than a health care professional.

Worksheets: A reproducible quiz for Section 2 is provided in the Teacher Classroom Resources.

SECTION 2 Review

Reviewing the Vocabulary

Review the vocabulary on page 432. Then answer these questions.

1. The mental disorder resulting from an attack by HIV on the brain and nerves is called _____.

2. _____ is a normally rare skin cancer causing a purplish discoloration of the skin, seen commonly among people with AIDS.

3. A type of pneumonia characteristic of AIDS is called _____.

4. _____ are drugs that stop the action of an enzyme which ordinarily helps HIV to reproduce.

5. The practice of using needles to inject drugs of abuse is called _____.

Reviewing the Facts

6. **Explain.** What is the difference between HIV and AIDS?

7. **Describe.** What does the AIDS virus do after it gets into the body?

8. **Recall.** What are the first physical symptoms of AIDS?

9. **Identify.** What is the treatment for AIDS?

Writing Critically

10. Look at **Figure 16.14.** Which items did you already know? Have you heard of other ways AIDS is transmitted or not transmitted? How can we correct misconceptions?

Go Online

For more information on health careers, visit Career Corner at **glencoe.com.**

1. AIDS dementia complex

2. Kaposi's sarcoma

3. Pneumocystis carinii (PCP)

4. Protease inhibitors

5. Intravenous (IV) drug abuse

6. HIV is a virus that lives in the cells of the body. AIDS is the diagnosis that comes with the destruction of the immune system and development of a disease typical of AIDS such as pneumonia, fungal infections, and rare cancers.

7. The virus attacks the immune system's white blood cells, T cells, and tricks the cells into making copies of the virus. The new viruses then go on to find new T cells and copy more and more viruses until the body's immune system cannot function.

8. Fatigue, appetite loss, weight loss, and nagging cough

9. A combination of drugs called protease inhibitors are currently the best treatment.

10. Answers will vary.

Preventing Sexually Transmitted Diseases

Vocabulary

abstinence
monogamous
safer-sex strategies
spermicide

The rest of this chapter gives details about how people must adjust their sex lives to protect themselves from contracting AIDS and other STDs. It describes those practices that *eliminate and reduce* the risk of acquiring a disease through sexual behavior. These behaviors promise that people who follow them consistently will not contract an STD through sexual contact. Total commitment to **abstinence**, *refraining completely from sexual relations with other people*, eliminates the risk of STDs entirely. Commitment to a mutually **monogamous** relationship with an uninfected partner, *having sexual relations with one partner only, excluding all others*, also eliminates the risk of STDs.

The chapter goes on to describe **safer-sex strategies**— *behavior guidelines that reduce STD risk, but that do not reduce the risk to zero*. The Health Skills sidebar, "Avoiding Contracting STDs," summarizes these guidelines.

Eliminating the Risk of STDs

MAIN IDEA ▷ Abstinence and mutual monogamy with an uninfected partner eliminate the risk of STDs.

Only two strategies, if practiced consistently, reduce the risk of sexually acquired infections to zero. Keep in mind, though, that AIDS and other infections of the blood can be passed by nonsexual means. The strategies you are about to study prevent *sexual* transmission only.

■ **Figure 16.17** *Many teens today are committing to abstinence from sexual intercourse. How can teens reduce the risk of STDs?*

Caption Answer: Avoid sexual contact, use latex condoms, do not use alcohol or drugs, avoid high-risk behaviors.

The most effective way to protect against STDs is not to have oral, anal, or vaginal intercourse with other people (abstinence). Limiting sexual relations to one uninfected partner only, who is also monogamous, also provides protection from STDs. Safety here depends on knowing the partner's infection status and on knowing that the partner is monogamous. The problem is that people can have many STDs, including HIV, without knowing it. People who look and feel healthy can be infected. Before using the strategy of mutual monogamy, partners must determine two things:

- The prospective partner's infection status
- The prospective partner's sexual faithfulness

Until the partner's infection status is known, it is not safe to have oral, anal, or vaginal sex.

It's okay to ask about a potential partner's sexual history. Unfortunately, though, some people may be embarrassed to reveal their sexual pasts, and so they may be tempted to lie. Asking about STDs may not be enough. Medical testing, especially for AIDS, is not unreasonable. Both partners must be willing to be tested. Blood tests detect either the antibodies to HIV or the HIV genetic material itself. For privacy, a home test can also reliably detect HIV genetic material. The user scrapes cells from the lining of the mouth and submits them for examination by a laboratory. The results are obtained by way of a recorded phone message, identifiable only by a code from the test package. A parent or pharmacist can help explain the test kit instructions.

A caution about AIDS testing—the blood or cells of people who are newly infected may register as negative for the virus, especially during the early months. That is, if a person was infected just last week, last month, or several months ago, then there is some chance that the person might test negative for the virus today.

Reducing the Risk of STDs

MAIN IDEA ▶ Preventative measures can reduce the risk of transmitting HIV and AIDS.

Some strategies can greatly reduce—but not eliminate—risks of acquiring an STD. With these strategies, the goal is to avoid any exchange of body fluids. Condoms made of latex material (not natural skin) and treated with a **spermicide**, *the compound nonoxynol-9 intended for birth control that also kills or weakens some STD organisms*, if properly used, are effective in reducing the risks of STDs (from 0 to 17 percent failure rate, depending on how they are used). A condom may provide an effective barrier to body fluids, and the spermicide may kill some bacterial cells and weaken some viruses.

Health Skills

Avoiding Contracting STDs

People can completely protect themselves from sexual transmission of STDs by:

1. Practicing sexual abstinence.
2. Having a responsible, mature, mutually monogamous sexual relationship with an uninfected partner.

People can reduce their STD risks by:

1. Avoiding contact with the partner's semen or vaginal fluids and blood.
2. Using latex condoms throughout every sexual act to keep body fluids from being exchanged.
3. Refusing alcohol or other drugs.
4. Avoiding high-risk behaviors, and avoiding relations with others who engage in high-risk behaviors such as drug and alcohol use, and engaging in unprotected sex.

Before choosing condoms for protection, though, people should be aware that some types are more reliable than others and that all types require special care after purchase.

How effective are condoms in preventing STDs such as AIDS? In a few studies, the failure rates in preventing HIV transmission have ranged from 0 to 17 percent, depending on how consistently and effectively the condoms have been used. Of course, even a one percent failure rate can be fatal in the case of AIDS.

Common sense and good judgment are powerful weapons against the transmission of STDs. Chapter 13 made clear that alcohol robs a person of judgment. Other mind-altering drugs do too. The Q&A section that follows makes the point that the person wishing to avoid STDs needs to remain in control of clearheaded thinking.

What Teens THINK

Would Your Behavior Toward a Classmate Change if That Person Contracted AIDS?

If a classmate of mine contracted AIDS, I would not act or behave any differently around them. I'm sure, subconsciously, I would be more careful around them, but I would still treat them as my equal. If I was trusted enough to know about their disease, then I would be mature enough to accept it at face value and move on. I'm sure they wouldn't want any pity or special treatment, anyway. I think it would be bad enough to have AIDS as it is.

—*Emilee O., 15,*
New Mexico

I don't consider myself a biased person, but I do believe that I would probably act differently toward a person who had AIDS. I wouldn't be completely different. For instance, I wouldn't ignore the person by not speaking to him or her or by trying to keep my distance. Instead, I would feel sorry for the person. I would try to be closer to the person. But I must admit that if the person would cut himself or herself, I would probably freak out.

—*Danielia W., 17,*
West Virginia

My behavior toward a student with AIDS wouldn't change, because of the fact that they are people too. You can't get AIDS by touching someone, kissing someone, or even sitting beside them. AIDS is a disease caused by sexual contact or blood transfusion. A person with AIDS would stay my friend, if they already were. Even if they were not my friend, I'd try to make friends with them, to show them I care. AIDS is not a disease that you would want a loved one to have, but regardless of who has it, a caring attitude is important.

—*Natalie L., 15,*
North Carolina

If a classmate contracted AIDS, my behavior toward them would depend on how they had contracted the virus. Our society should put more money into the schools to help teach younger kids about the disease and the responsibility they have to stop the spread of HIV [the AIDS virus]. We need to get rid of the ignorance and the fear.

—*Shaterra M., 17,*
California

Lastly, be aware of groups at high risk for STDs. Avoid becoming sexually involved with:

- Intravenous drug abusers.

- Anyone who has had previous sexual partners and who has not, since then, been tested for STDs.

SECTION 3 Review

Worksheets: A reproducible quiz for Section 3 is provided in the Teacher Classroom Resources.

Reviewing the Vocabulary

Review the vocabulary on page 440. Then answer these questions.

1. Behavior guidelines that reduce STD risk, but that do not reduce the risk to zero, are called _____.

2. _____ means refraining completely from sexual relations with other people.

3. The compound nonoxynol-9, intended for birth control, but which also kills or weakens some STD organisms, is _____.

4. Having sexual relations with one partner only, excluding all others, means a person is _____.

Reviewing the Facts

5. **Recall.** What are the two ways to eliminate the risk of STDs?

6. **Describe.** Describe what two things must be determined before mutual monogamy is effective.

7. **Identify.** What type of condom is most effective against STDs?

Writing Critically

8. **Expository.** Reread the Health Skills sidebar, "Avoiding Contracting STDs," on page 441. How can you be completely protected from STDs? Explain how avoiding alcohol and other drugs may reduce the risks of STDs.

For fitness and health tips, visit the Fitness Zone at **glencoe.com.**

Did You Know?

Never let anyone stick you with a needle, to pierce your ears or skin, to give you a tattoo, or to remove hair, unless you are certain that the needle has been steam-heat sterilized for 15 minutes or is a disposable needle that has never been used.

1. Safer-sex strategies

2. Abstinence

3. Spermicide

4. Monogamous

5. Complete commitment to abstinence or to a monogamous partner who is not infected eliminates the risk of STDs.

6. The prospective partner's infection status and the prospective partner's sexual faithfulness must be determined.

7. A condom made from latex materials and treated with spermicide is most effective.

8. Answers will vary.

Alcohol, Drug Abuse, and STDs

 Understand and Apply Read the conversation below, and then complete the writing exercise that follows.

When Dr. Wah, a respected gynecologist, makes an STD diagnosis in her office she asks the patient, "Had you been drinking alcohol or taking illegal drugs at the time you were exposed to this disease?" More often than not, the answer is yes. Experts would urge young people to take this finding seriously. Strong links exist between teens who experiment with drugs or alcohol and those who acquire an STD.

Q: I know that people who inject drugs can get AIDS and hepatitis from sharing needles. I wouldn't ever inject drugs, so none of this applies to me, right?

A: You are right in saying that sharing needles is extremely risky for the diseases you mention, and you are wise to exclude yourself from the group that does so. The links between substances and STDs, though, go far beyond the danger of injecting drugs. Research finds that those teens who drink alcohol or who smoke crack cocaine are also very likely to contract STDs such as gonorrhea, HPV, herpes, and syphilis, as well as HIV. In other words, people involved with any mind-altering substances are at risk.

Q: That sounds strange. How can drinking or smoking something cause STDs?

A: Of course, these activities don't cause STDs directly. Sexual activity is responsible for passing on the STD-causing microbes. However, people who engage in drug or alcohol abuse often engage in the risky sexual behaviors that make STDs likely.

The reasons why substance abuse and STDs occur together is a topic of debate among health researchers. One school of thought holds that teens who grow up with certain factors in their lives may be more likely to engage in both substance abuse and in risky sexual behaviors. These factors may include:

- An unsupportive, unstable, or abusive home life.
- One or more parents who abuse substances.
- Peer groups who abuse alcohol and other drugs, commit crimes, or are truant from school.
- Poverty and the social disadvantages it brings.
- Inborn personality traits that may make the person prone to taking risks.

A young person with one or more of these factors may begin sexual activities early in life, before having a chance to learn of the health threats from STDs. By adulthood, such a teen may have had more sexual partners than most people do in a lifetime, while being less likely than most to take precautions against STDs. The Health Skills sidebar on page 441 listed those precautions.

Q: **I've seen people make all sorts of dumb decisions when they've been drinking or taking drugs. Does drinking alcohol or abusing drugs make people more careless about STDs?**

A: The observations of physicians like Dr. Wah and of other experts suggest that this is true. The mental effects of drugs and alcohol seem to encourage teens to throw caution to the wind. Many teens who experimented with alcohol or marijuana ended up regretting the result: unplanned and unprotected sexual intercourse that resulted in an STD.

Mind-altering drugs and alcohol reduce a person's ability to make sound judgments. Even a small amount of alcohol, say the amount in one drink, reduces inhibitions and relaxes a person's resolve. A teen who has resolved to abstain from sexual activity but who takes a drink of alcohol or smokes of marijuana, may suddenly lack the judgment necessary to keep that commitment. Risky situations suddenly seem less risky. With more alcohol or drugs, self-control erodes further, until cautious people are likely to take risks they otherwise would not have taken.

An even worse problem is one of addiction. An addiction can strip people of all previous resources. It robs them of money, employment, and other supports. They may be driven to do anything, including having sexual intercourse with strangers, to obtain money to buy the drugs that can hold off the pain of withdrawal. So powerful is the force of addiction that its victims are likely to ignore even the deadly threat of AIDS, if it means that they can get the drug they crave.

Q: **That's interesting. Luckily, those things could never happen to me or my friends. We're too smart to become addicted to drugs or infected by STDs.**

A: Most teens feel just as you do. They think that STDs only infect other people—perhaps only older people, or those who are different from themselves, or those less able to handle life. Yet, the facts suggest otherwise. AIDS today is a leading cause of death among teens, and ten times more teens than those who receive a diagnosis are believed to be HIV-positive.

Teens also make up an enormous proportion of those who are infected with many of the other STDs each year. There are many tragic stories of young adults who lost their health or their ability to bear healthy children as a result of an STD acquired during their teen years. An easy mistake is to think that because you never hear about STDs among your peers, the diseases are absent. However, with or without your awareness of them, STDs are a threat. The best way to avoid that threat is to abstain from sexual intercourse. Avoiding drugs and alcohol is important for all the reasons given in Chapters 12 and 13. Another reason is to help prevent STDs.

 Writing Write a paragraph detailing your personal plan to avoid HIV/AIDS and other STDs.

Reviewing Vocabulary

Use the vocabulary terms listed below to complete the following statements.

acquired immune deficiency syndrome (AIDS)

chlamydia

pelvic inflammatory disease (PID)

human papillomavirus (HPV)

genital warts

hepatitis B

trichomoniasis

AIDS dementia complex

1. An infection of the reproductive tract, with or without symptoms, is known as _____.

2. _____ is an STD caused by a parasite that can cause bladder and urethral infections.

3. _____ is a fatal, transmissible viral disease of the immune system that creates a severe immune deficiency.

4. _____ is any of the over 100 related viruses whose effects include genital warts and cervical cancer.

5. The mental disorder resulting from an attack by HIV on the brain and nerves is called _____.

6. _____ is a viral STD that causes loss of liver function and severe liver disease.

7. _____ is an infection of the fallopian tubes and pelvic cavity in females, causing ectopic pregnancy and pregnancy failures.

8. Contagious wart-like growths on infected areas, caused by HPV viruses, are called _____.

Recalling Key Facts and Ideas

Section 1

9. **List.** List symptoms of the first outbreak of genital herpes.

10. **Describe.** Describe the treatment for human papillomavirus.

11. **Explain.** What is the purpose of a Pap test?

12. **Identify.** Identify the stages of syphilis and the symptoms of each stage.

13. **Recall.** Which females are especially likely to develop a yeast infection (candidiasis)?

Section 2

14. **Describe.** Describe the first symptoms of AIDS.

15. **Identify.** What are the mental symptoms of AIDS?

16. **Describe.** Describe the ways in which HIV is transmitted.

17. **Name.** Name the three additional ways that the HIV is transmitted to infants.

18. **List.** List and identify ways in which HIV is not transmitted.

Section 3

19. **Explain.** What is the most effective way to protect against STDs?

Writing Critically

20. **Expository.** Do you think a school should let the public know if someone with AIDS is going to the school? What would you do if you found out someone with AIDS was in your class? Explain how you would react to being assigned to work with a lab partner with AIDS.

Activities

21. Cut out at least five articles from magazines and newspapers about AIDS research. Write a one-page report on your findings.

1. Chlamydia 2. Trichomoniasis 3. AIDS 4. HPV 5. AIDS dementia complex 6. Hepatitis B 7. PID 8. Genital warts 9. Fever, headache, muscle ache, painful urination, swollen glands 10. Removal of growths or abnormal tissue by surgery

or freezing; applying prescription medication to external growths. 11. To detect cervical cancer 12. First: A chancre appears then disappears in a few weeks; Second: swollen glands, skin rash, hair loss, or flu-like symptoms; Third: no

22. Work with a group of three to five students to prepare a research project on one of the STDs listed in **Figure 16.2**. In addition to the research, your group will be responsible for preparing a 3–5 minute presentation to give to the class. Visual aids should be prepared for use during the talk. You might develop videos, posters, models, podcasts, or drawings to use. The information you present to the class should include the following: cause, symptoms, treatment, complications, and prevention of the STD.

23. Choose one of the STDs described in **Figure 16.2** and prepare a set of flash cards that will teach someone about this disease. Each card will have a question on one side and the answer on the other side. For example, the question could be, "What are three symptoms of chlamydia?" Answer, "Three symptoms are burning during urination, a discharge, and abdominal pain." When the flash cards are finished, use them to work with a partner or group to study STDs.

24. Create a poster or write a newspaper article that influences others to avoid the high-risk behaviors of intravenous drug use and sexual activity. If you create a poster, ask permission to display your poster somewhere around your school. If you write an article, ask to have it published in the school newspaper.

25. Write a dialogue between two people; one thinks he or she has an STD; the other is trying to convince the first to go for testing. In the dialogue, the infected person should give all the reasons for not being tested. The other person should give all the reasons for being tested. If time permits, role-play the dialogue with a partner.

Making Decisions About Health

26. Your friend volunteers at a hospital after school. He has become concerned because he has been asked to help out with some AIDS patients. He is afraid that he'll somehow "catch" AIDS from being around the patients. What advice would you give your friend?

Go Online

For more vocabulary practice, play the Concentration game at **glencoe.com**.

Fact or Fiction?

Answers

1. False. Birth control pills do not protect a female against any form of sexually transmitted disease.
2. False. Asking potential partners about past sexual experiences does not ensure that you will learn the truth about whether or not they are free of STDs.
3. False. Condoms may sometimes fail to protect against STDs.

 Writing Paragraphs will vary.

symptoms for 10-20 years; Fourth: blindness, deafness, brain damage, heart disease **13.** A female who is pregnant, takes birth control pills, has diabetes, takes antibiotics, or uses douches **14.** Fatigue, appetite loss, weight loss, and a nagging cough **15.** Agitation, anxiety, confusion, depression, memory loss, mood swings **16.** Sexual intercourse, intravenous drug abuse **17.** Pregnancy, childbirth, breastfeeding **18.** By shaking hands, coughing, sneezing, sharing meals **19.** Total commitment to abstinence, monogamous relationship with uninfected partner **20–26.** Answers will vary.

CHAPTER 17

Lifestyle Diseases

Sections

The infectious diseases described in the previous two chapters are major health problems. The diseases that we more often face, however, are of a different kind. They are lifestyle diseases, brought on partly by the choices we make each day. This chapter takes a look at three of these diseases:

- Diabetes, both type 1 and type 2
- Cardiovascular disease, including heart attack, heart disease, and stroke
- Cancer

This chapter explains lifestyle disease risk factors, effects on the body, and available medical treatments. Most importantly, it offers suggestions to make healthier choices to reduce the risk of lifestyle diseases.

Fact or Fiction?

What Do You Think?

Is each statement true or false? If you think it's false, explain what's true.

1. Both type 1 and type 2 diabetes affect children and teens.
2. Obesity has no effect on type 2 diabetes and its prevention.
3. Many types of cancer can be prevented by living a lifestyle that includes a healthy diet and regular physical activity.

 Writing Write a letter to your family outlining steps you and your family can take to make healthful choices to avoid lifestyle diseases.

(Answers on page 491)

Go Online

Visit **glencoe.com** and complete the Life Choice Inventory for Chapter 17.

First Facts

Teens often have the mistaken belief that they are not affected by lifestyle diseases. They've heard that these diseases affect only older people—their grandparents or parents, not teens. It is true that older people do contract lifestyle diseases in great numbers. Today, however, more and more children and teens in the United States are overweight or obese, and excess weight, even for teens, often leads to diabetes and hypertension (high blood pressure).

Lifestyle Diseases and Risk Factors

MAIN IDEA ▶ People who adopt healthy habits when young lower their risks of lifestyle diseases later in life.

Lifestyle diseases, or noncommunicable diseases, cannot spread from person to person. For example, you cannot catch diabetes from someone who has this disease. While it is hard to determine who will develop a particular disease, researchers have found that certain risk factors increase a person's chance of developing a disease. Heredity, age, gender, and ethnic group are factors over which people have no control.

Will I Develop a Lifestyle Disease?

Disabling disease is not inevitable. From 1994 through 2004, the death rate from heart disease declined 32 percent. This good news results partly from better medical treatments, and partly from the choices that people make to reduce their risk of heart disease. Even so, heart disease remains the leading killer of adults. Although heart disease is usually diagnosed later in life, the choices young people make influence their health in later life. You can take action now to promote the health of your body before diseases take their toll on your health and quality of life.

Risk Factors for Lifestyle Diseases

Lifestyle diseases tend to have clusters of suspected causes, known as **risk factors**. These are *factors linked with a disease by association but not yet proved to be causes*. Risk factors often include poor diet, physical inactivity, obesity, smoking, alcohol, stress, other diseases, or inherited genetic traits (family history). In many cases, the presence of one risk factor can increase the likelihood of others. For example, lack of physical activity may lead to obesity, high blood pressure, and a high cholesterol level.

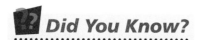

Vocabulary

risk factors

⁉️ Did You Know?

You can take small steps towards a healthy lifestyle to lower your risk for heart disease by:

- Losing excess weight.
- Eating a healthy diet.
- Reducing high blood cholesterol.
- Increasing physical activity.
- Controlling high blood pressure.
- Managing stress.

■ **Figure 17.1** *A family medical history can provide clues to lifestyle changes that might benefit an individual's health. What does family history have to do with health?*

Caption Answer: Genetic tendencies to develop a certain disease can be found in a family medical history.

Family History

Those who inherit a genetic tendency to develop certain diseases benefit most from positive lifestyle changes. A look at your family's medical history can show you which diseases are common in your family. If several close relatives have a disease such as heart disease, high blood pressure, diabetes, or cancer, the family may have a genetic link to the disease.

Worksheets: A reproducible quiz for Section 1 is provided in the Teacher Classroom Resources.

SECTION 1 Review

Reviewing the Vocabulary
Review the vocabulary on page 450. Then answer these questions.
1. Define *risk factors*.

Reviewing the Facts
2. Describe. In what stage of life are lifestyle diseases most often diagnosed?
3. Identify. List seven risk factors for lifestyle diseases.
4. Explain. Which risk factors are under people's control?

Writing Critically
5. Narrative. If you were to discover lifestyle diseases in your family history, what steps could you take to help ensure future good health for yourself?

1. Factors linked with a disease by association but not yet proved to be causes
2. In older adults after years of unhealthful behaviors
3. Poor diet, physical inactivity, obesity, smoking, alcohol, stress, the presence of other diseases, or inherited trait
4. Poor diet, physical inactivity, obesity, smoking, alcohol intake, and stress
5. Answers will vary.

For fitness and health tips, visit the Fitness Zone at **glencoe.com**.

Diabetes

Diabetes, or **diabetes mellitus** (DYE-uh-BEE-teez MEL-ih-tuss), is *a condition of abnormal use of glucose, usually caused by too little insulin or lack of response to insulin*. It is among the top ten killers of adults in the United States. More than 20 million people in the U.S. have diabetes. Diabetes can lead to other serious health problems.

Who Gets Diabetes?

MAIN IDEA ▶ There are two types of diabetes, a disease that has become more common in teens with the rise in obesity.

Diabetes is the leading cause of blindness and kidney failure in the United States. Diabetes can lead to heart disease and stroke as well. In fact, heart disease is the leading cause of diabetes-related deaths. Diabetes comes in two major types: type 1 and type 2. Both are caused by problems in the body's use of its blood sugar, glucose. Type 1 is much less common and most often appears during childhood or adolescence. Most cases of type 2 diabetes occur in overweight middle-aged adults. However, as more children and teens become obese, they increasingly develop type 2 diabetes. **Figure 17.2** shows how diabetes and obesity affect one another. Both types of diabetes produce the same warning signs that can signal their presence (see **Figure 17.3**). Special blood glucose tests confirm the diabetes diagnosis.

Vocabulary

diabetes mellitus

insulin

ketones

diabetic coma

Figure 17.2 **The Obesity-Diabetes Cycle**

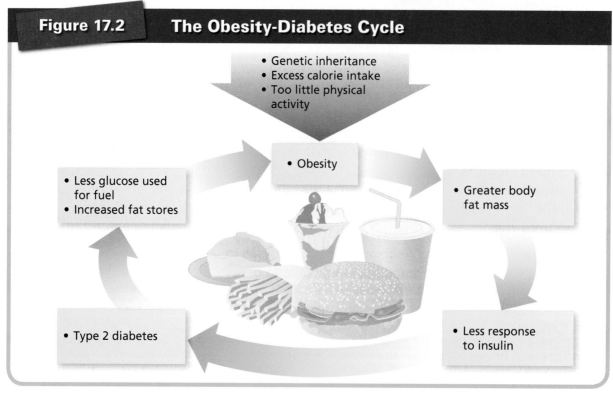

- Genetic inheritance
- Excess calorie intake
- Too little physical activity

- Obesity

- Less glucose used for fuel
- Increased fat stores

- Greater body fat mass

- Type 2 diabetes

- Less response to insulin

Figure 17.3 Warning Signs of Diabetes

- Frequent urination
- Excessive thirst
- Unexplained weight loss
- Increased hunger
- Sudden vision changes, blurred vision

- Tingling or numbness in hands or feet
- Tiredness
- Dry skin
- Slow healing of sores
- More infections than usual

Insulin and the Pancreas

MAIN IDEA ▶ Diabetes occurs when blood glucose levels are not controlled.

Insulin is *a hormone produced by the pancreas and released in response to high blood glucose following a meal*. Insulin promotes the use and storage of glucose by the body's tissues. Insulin is made by the pancreas, and is the key factor in diabetes. Insulin helps glucose be absorbed by the body's cells, which need glucose for energy. Without enough insulin, the glucose level in the blood builds up, even while the body's cells are starving for glucose. Think of insulin as a key that fits a lock in a doorway to a cell. To enter the cell, glucose from the blood must pass through that doorway, which remains locked until opened by insulin. Only insulin can do the job.

When insulin fails to keep blood glucose in check, the kidneys push some of the excess out into the urine. This glucose in the urine draws water out of the blood, increasing the amount of urine produced. This is why frequent urination, thirst, and dehydration are symptoms of diabetes.

Type 1 Diabetes

In type 1 diabetes, the person's own immune system attacks the pancreas and destroys the cells that make insulin. The reason why this happens is not clear. It could be that toxins, allergies, or a virus trigger the attack. A person's family history also plays a role in how the immune system will react. Whatever the cause, the pancreas soon no longer produces enough insulin. Without insulin, each meal brings a large, long-lasting surge of glucose to the bloodstream.

Type 2 Diabetes

A person with type 2 diabetes also has an abnormally high level of glucose in the blood. However, this occurs for a different reason. Instead of too little insulin, the body's cells fail to respond to insulin. The cellular locks have been changed, so to speak, so that insulin cannot open them. Excess fat makes cells less responsive to insulin's effects.

Comprehension Check

Comprehend: Ask students why the body needs insulin. (Insulin is the key that unlocks the body's cells to the entry of glucose, which the cells need for energy.) What two things happen if the insulin cannot deliver glucose to the cells? (The cells starve and glucose builds up in the blood.)

Did You Know?

To help prevent type 2 diabetes and its complications, people should:
- Achieve and maintain healthy body weight.
- Be physically active— at least 60 minutes of regular, moderate-intensity activity on most days. More activity is required for weight control.

Figure 17.4 **Diabetes Types 1 and 2 Compared**

Characteristics	Type 1 Diabetes	Type 2 Diabetes
Prevalence in diabetic population	5 to 10 percent of cases	90 to 95 percent of cases
Age of onset	Childhood, adolescence, young adulthood	Adulthood (45 years of age or older)*
Major defect	Destruction of cells in the pancreas to make insulin; pancreas makes little or no insulin	Body cells resist insulin action; pancreas may make enough insulin but body cells do not respond to it
Insulin therapy required	Always	Sometimes

*Incidence of type 2 diabetes is increasing in children and adolescents; in over 90 percent of cases, it is associated with overweight or obesity and a family history of type 2 diabetes.

Class Activity

Recall: On individual index cards, write the various statements regarding the two types of diabetes from **Figure 17.4**. Then shuffle the cards and read a statement aloud. Have the class state whether it is for type 1 or type 2 diabetes.

Indeed, obesity, or even just modest weight gain, often occurs just before type 2 diabetes sets in. The two types of diabetes are compared in **Figure 17.4.**

Of the two types of diabetes, type 2 is more preventable. It tends to run in families, especially when members of the family are obese. A person's family history can provide a warning of the risk of diabetes. Anyone who is overweight or obese should try to manage their weight to reduce their likelihood of developing diabetes.

What Are the Dangers of Diabetes?

Did You Know?

Diabetes can cause tiny blood vessels in the eyes to become weak. These weak blood vessels can leak blood into the center of the eye, blurring vision. This is called diabetic retinopathy and can lead to permanent blindness.

MAIN IDEA ▷ Low blood glucose levels can cause serious health problems.

Untreated diabetes can cause life-threatening problems. Too little insulin causes severe disturbances in the body's use of energy. When the cells are starved for glucose (even though glucose in the blood remains high), the tissues must use more fats than normal for energy. When this occurs, the fat molecules are not completely broken down. *Fat fragments formed by the tissues during incomplete use of fat for energy* are called **ketones**. When ketones and glucose build up to toxic levels in the blood, the result can be abnormal reflexes, difficulty speaking, seizures, and in some cases, coma. A **diabetic coma** is *loss of consciousness due to uncontrolled diabetes.*

Figure 17.5 — The Destructive Results of Diabetes

Diabetes, especially when poorly controlled, can cause these serious problems:

- Frequent infections
- Impaired circulation
- Disease of the feet and legs that often leads to amputation
- Kidney disease that often requires hospital care or kidney transplant

- Impaired vision or blindness due to cataracts and damaged retinas
- Nerve damage
- Skin damage
- Strokes and heart attacks

Too little blood glucose can be harmful too. When meals are skipped, when too much insulin is given, or when physical activity has used up too much glucose, blood glucose levels can fall dangerously low. Without immediate glucose, the person may suffer shakiness, hunger, sweating, pale skin, rapid heart rate, jerky movements, slurred speech, confusion, or even coma or death. Glucose tablets, candy, or fruit juice are good sources.

Diabetes's long-term effects, while less immediate, can be severe. The damage from uncontrolled diabetes, outlined in **Figure 17.5**, slowly steals the health of the body's organs. Diabetes causes blockage or destruction of small blood vessels that feed organs such as the eyes, heart, and kidneys. It also reduces the blood flow to the legs and feet. Without blood flow through the tissues, they die from lack of oxygen and nourishment. This is why diabetes is named as a risk factor for many other diseases.

Controlling Diabetes

MAIN IDEA ▶ Medication, diet, and physical activity are the three tools for controlling diabetes and its consequences.

Once diabetes is diagnosed, controlling it is essential to maintaining good health. A person with diabetes must balance three lifestyle factors—medication, diet, and physical activity—to avoid the serious health problems mentioned earlier.

Medication

Because the pancreas of a person with type 1 diabetes does not make enough insulin, the person must receive insulin from shots or from an implanted pump at certain times each day. Pills taken by mouth cannot deliver the needed insulin. Insulin is a protein and would be digested before it could be absorbed into the bloodstream. Treatment of type 2 diabetes may involve drugs that help body tissues to use more glucose from the bloodstream.

Group Project

Report: Divide the class into small groups to research some aspect of diabetes. Topics might include the history of diabetes, diabetes and alcohol, diabetes and diet, diabetes and drugs, or recent developments in drugs to treat diabetes. Have students present their findings to the class.

Guest Speaker

Discuss: Invite a registered dietitian to class to discuss diet and lifestyle diseases, as well as the importance of diet in controlling such diseases as diabetes. Have students prepare questions in advance for the dietitian, to encourage class discussion.

Diet

A balanced diet of fresh, high-fiber vegetables, whole grains, low-fat meats and milk products, and other high-nutrient food is best for controlling diabetes. Controlling carbohydrate intake is important, and sugars and sugary foods must be counted as part of the daily carbohydrate intake. The Q&A section on page 488 explains why a healthy diet for protecting against diabetes also helps to control obesity and other lifestyle diseases.

Teens with diabetes often face special problems when making food choices with friends. It may be difficult for a teen with diabetes to say, "No thanks" to a delicious but unhealthy snack. However, with planning, almost any food is acceptable in small amounts. Registered dietitians have tips to make life easier for teens with diabetes.

Physical Activity

Physical activity helps to manage body weight, but also helps the body use blood glucose. Some people with diabetes find that they need less insulin or other drugs when physical activity becomes part of their daily routine.

1. Diabetes mellitus

2. A hormone produced by the pancreas and released in response to high blood glucose.

3. Untreated diabetes can cause a loss of consciousness.

4. Diabetes mellitus

5. Both are caused by problems in the body's use of glucose, or blood sugar. In type 1, the pancreas does not produce enough insulin; in type 2, the pancreas produces insulin, but body cells do not respond to it.

6. Blockage of small blood vessels to the eyes, heart, and kidneys, and blood flow to legs and feet

7. Answers will vary.

Reviewing the Vocabulary

Review the vocabulary on page 452. Then answer these questions.

1. What is the term for abnormal use of glucose in the body?

2. What is *insulin*?

3. What causes a *diabetic coma*?

Reviewing the Facts

4. Identify. What is the leading cause of blindness in the United States?

5. Compare. What is the cause of each type of diabetes?

6. Evaluate. What are the long-term effects of diabetes?

Writing Critically

7. Expository. What advice would you give someone who has diabetes? Write an outline for a brochure explaining signs to watch for and ways to control the onset of diabetes.

For more information on health careers, visit Career Corner at **glencoe.com.**

Cardiovascular Disease (CVD)

The number-one killer of American adults is **cardiovascular disease** (CVD), *a general term for all diseases of the heart and blood vessels*. In the United States, about 1 in 3 people have some form of the disease and it claims the lives of nearly 1 million people each year. CVD develops slowly over a lifetime. Fortunately, however, everyone can take steps to reduce the risks of developing CVD.

The Cardiovascular System

MAIN IDEA ▶ The cardiovascular system is the supply line for nutrients and oxygen and disposes of wastes from tissue.

The body system that provides tissue and cells with all that they need to live is the **cardiovascular system**, *the system of structures that circulate blood and lymph throughout the body*. It is also called the circulatory system. There are three kinds of blood vessels:

- **Arteries** are *blood vessels that carry blood from the heart to the tissues.*

- **Capillaries** are *the smallest blood vessels, which connect the smallest arteries with the smallest veins.* Nourishment and fluid normally trapped in thick-walled arteries and veins can easily pass through the delicate walls of the capillaries.

- **Veins** are *blood vessels that carry waste-containing blood from the tissues back to the heart.*

The Heart's Chambers

The heart, at the center of the cardiovascular system, is almost all muscle. There are four hollow **chambers**, *large, hollow areas that receive incoming blood from the lungs and tissues and pump it out again through arteries*. Heart chambers collect **blood**, *the thick, red fluid that flows through the body's blood vessels and transports gases, nutrients, wastes, and other important substances around the body*. Blood also plays a role in body temperature regulation. Two of the four chambers, the **atria** (singular, atrium), *the two upper chambers of the heart*, pool the blood as it arrives from the body. The **ventricles** are *the two lower chambers of the heart that send blood to the lungs or the tissues*. The heart pumps the equivalent of 4,000 gallons of blood around the body each day, driving this blood with over 85,000 heartbeats.

Vocabulary

cardiovascular disease (CVD)
cardiovascular system
arteries
capillaries
veins
chambers
blood
atria
ventricles
coronary arteries
valves
heart murmur
electrocardiogram
lymph
atherosclerosis
plaques
critical phase
aneurysm
aorta
platelets
heart attack
stroke
thrombus
coronary thrombosis
cerebral thrombosis
embolus
embolism

Figure 17.6

The Heart's Major Arteries

The coronary arteries feed the heart muscle itself. The heart derives no nourishment from the blood inside the chambers.

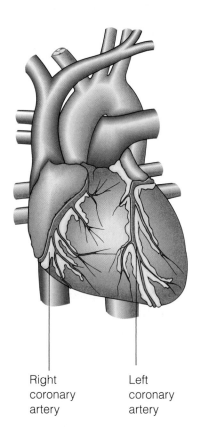

Right coronary artery

Left coronary artery

Coronary Arteries

The heart relies on its own network of vessels for nourishment and blood flow. The **coronary arteries** are *the two arteries that supply blood to the heart muscle.* The coronary arteries branch into capillaries that weave all over the heart's outer surface and feed it with nutrients and oxygen (see **Figure 17.6**). Because the arteries are the lifelines of the heart, any disease affecting the arteries also affects the health of the heart.

The Heart's Valves

You have probably listened to your own or someone else's heartbeat and noticed its two-step rhythm, sometimes called *lubdub.* The first beat ("lub") is the sound made when the atria contract to send the blood they have pooled to the ventricles below them. The second beat ("dub") is the sound made when the powerful ventricles contract to send the blood on its way to the lungs and to the body.

You may wonder why the contraction of the heart muscle should make any sound at all. In reality, it does not. The sound comes from the heart's **valves,** *flaps of tissue that open and close to allow the flow of blood in one direction only.* The heart's valves are located at the entrances and exits of its chambers. Normally, the valves allow blood to flow in only one direction on its way through the heart. If the valves are damaged or unusually shaped, however, some blood will flow backward. This causes a **heart murmur,** *a heart sound that reflects damaged or abnormal heart valves.* Most heart murmurs are harmless, but a physician may order further testing to make sure.

A heart examination includes a physician's listening to the heartbeat and, possibly, an electrocardiogram. An **electrocardiogram** is *a record of the electrical activity of the heart that, if abnormal, may indicate heart disease.*

Capillaries

As blood moves through the smallest vessels, the capillaries, much of its fluid is strained out into the tissue. This fluid is called **lymph,** *the clear fluid that bathes each cell and transfers needed substances and wastes back and forth between the blood and the cells.* Lymph also plays a role in immunity. The fluids flow around the cells of the tissue, providing it with nutrients and oxygen and collecting wastes. Then, the used fluid seeps back into the bloodstream to be carried away for cleaning and renewal. In this way, the tissue is nourished and cleansed.

The next few sections discuss the serious damaging effects of CVD on the body. These diseases can often be postponed or prevented by everyday lifestyle choices.

The Dangers of Atherosclerosis

MAIN IDEA ▶ Atherosclerosis obstructs blood flow and makes blood clots likely.

Disease of the cardiovascular system affects the body's tissues, of course, because the blood nourishes all the tissues. **Atherosclerosis** (ATH-uh-roh-scler-OH-sis) is *a disease characterized by plaques along the inner walls of the arteries*. Also known as hardening of the arteries, it is the most common form of CVD. It begins with an accumulation of soft fatty streaks along the inner walls of all the arteries of the body. These streaks gradually enlarge and become hardened. These **plaques** (PLACKS) are *mounds of fat, mixed with minerals, that build up along artery walls*. Atherosclerosis usually begins at places where the arteries branch or bend because blood flow is disturbed in those areas. Plaques damage the artery walls and make the passageway through the arteries narrower than normal, as **Figure 17.7** shows. Atherosclerosis can cause blockage of arteries that feed critical organs, such as the heart or brain. A **critical phase** is reached *when plaques cover more than half of the inner surfaces of the arteries*.

? Did You Know?

Physical activities, such as taking the stairs, gardening, and walking instead of driving, are as effective as structured gym workouts in improving fitness.

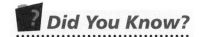

Figure 17.7

The Formation of Plaques in Atherosclerosis

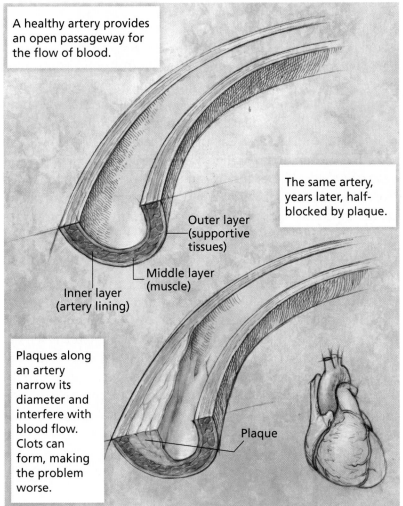

A healthy artery provides an open passageway for the flow of blood.

Outer layer (supportive tissues)

Middle layer (muscle)

Inner layer (artery lining)

The same artery, years later, half-blocked by plaque.

Plaques along an artery narrow its diameter and interfere with blood flow. Clots can form, making the problem worse.

Plaque

Figure 17.8

An Aneurysm and a Hemorrhage

An aneurysm   A hemorrhage

Blood Flow Blockage

When atherosclerosis affects arteries in the heart, the health and strength of the heart are weakened. Blocked blood flow to the heart can cause pain and discomfort in the chest and can lead to a heart attack. Arteries that feed other organs and tissues narrow and harden too, cutting off their supplies of nutrients and oxygen.

When an artery is blocked, the tissue normally supplied by that vessel may be injured or die. For example, blockage of the arteries that supply the kidneys can cause kidney disease or even kidney failure.

Weakened Arteries

Atherosclerosis is a risk factor for **aneurysm** (AN-your-ism), *the ballooning out of an artery wall at a point where it has grown weak.* Plaque can weaken an artery, enabling the artery to balloon out and burst. When this happens in a small artery, it can lead to death of the tissue surrounding it. In a major artery a ruptured aneurysm leads quickly to massive bleeding, or hemorrhage. The **aorta** (ay-OR-tah) is *the largest artery in the body.* Because it moves freshly oxygenated blood from the heart to the tissues, an aneurysm in the aorta can result in death. **Figure 17.8** illustrates an aneurysm and a hemorrhage.

Blood Clots

Some types of plaque are highly likely to rupture. Plaque rupture can cause a blood clot to form within the artery, blocking blood flow. **Platelets** are *the tiny, disk-shaped bodies in the blood that form clots.* Blockage in the arteries of the heart can cause a **heart attack**, *the event in which vessels that feed the heart muscle become blocked, causing tissue death.* In a vessel that feeds the brain, the blockage can cause a **stroke**, *the shutting off of the blood flow to the brain by plaques, a clot, or hemorrhage.* A clot may also break loose, become a traveling clot, and circulate until it reaches an artery too small to allow its passage. The sudden blockage of the vessel causes tissue to die.

Artery Blockages

Atherosclerosis can cause blockage of an artery in three ways:

- The plaques can enlarge enough to block the flow of blood.

- A blood clot can form a **thrombus**, *a stationary clot*. This is called a **coronary thrombosis**—*the closing off of a vessel that feeds the heart muscle by a stationary clot or thrombus*. A **cerebral thrombosis** occurs *when a vessel that feeds the brain is closed by a stationary clot*.

- An **embolus** (EM-bow-luss) is *a clot that breaks loose and travels through the bloodstream*. This *sudden closure of a blood vessel by a traveling blood clot* is called an **embolism**.

Worksheets: A reproducible quiz for Section 3 is provided in the Teacher Classroom Resources.

SECTION 3 Review

Reviewing the Vocabulary

Review the vocabulary on page 457. Then answer these questions.

1. Which body system circulates blood and lymph throughout the body?
2. What are the flaps that allow the body's fluids to flow in one direction only?
3. What is an *aneurysm*?

Reviewing the Facts

4. **Identify.** The equivalent of how many gallons of blood are pumped around the body each day?
5. **Analyze.** How does the heart obtain the nutrients and oxygen it needs?
6. **Evaluate.** What has happened to the arteries of someone diagnosed with atherosclerosis?

Writing Critically

7. **Expository.** Why do people think that cardiovascular disease won't happen to them? How does this thinking cause people to make poor health choices and to continue unhealthy behaviors?

For more vocabulary practice, play the Concentration game at **glencoe.com**.

1. Cardiovascular system or circulatory system
2. Valves
3. The ballooning out of an artery wall at a point where it has grown weak
4. 4,000 gallons
5. Through the coronary arteries.
6. Plaques form along the inner walls of arteries, making the passageways narrower
7. Answers will vary.

Heart Attack and Stroke

Heart attacks are the most common life-threatening events brought on by atherosclerosis. A heart attack occurs when blood flow to the heart becomes so restricted that some of the heart's muscle tissue dies from lack of oxygen. When heart muscle tissue dies, it is replaced by scar tissue that cannot pump efficiently. The remaining muscle tissue must work harder to make up for the loss.

Causes and Warning Signs

MAIN IDEA ▶ **Heart attacks occur when a blockage restricts the amount blood flowing through the heart.**

Reduced oxygen to the heart causes pain. A sudden exertion or emotional upset can bring on **angina** (an-JYE-nuh), *pain in the heart region caused by lack of oxygen.* Angina is not always a symptom of a heart attack, but it can be. A person experiencing angina may misinterpret the pain as indigestion. However, it is important to always take pain seriously. Often, a person has no pain before a first heart attack occurs and so may not be warned of the coming attack. Even medical tests designed to predict future heart attacks often fail to do so. Many heart attack deaths are sudden and unexpected. If you or someone nearby suffers any of the heart attack or stroke symptoms listed in **Figure 17.9**, call 911.

Medical Treatments for Heart Disease

MAIN IDEA ▶ **A person can recover from a minor heart attack with prompt, effective treatment.**

Heart attacks do not always result in death or disability. Treatments of heart attacks and heart disease range from clot-dissolving drugs to heart transplants.

Defibrillation

During a heart attack, **ventricular fibrillation**, *extremely rapid contractions of the heart's lower chambers that lack the power needed to pump blood around the body,* may occur. The heart's lower chambers, the ventricles, contract in rapid spasms. The person quickly loses consciousness, has no pulse, and may die unless a normal heartbeat is restored quickly.

Vocabulary

angina
ventricular fibrillation
pacemaker
coronary artery bypass
 surgery
heart transplant
artificial heart
human gene therapy

Figure 17.9   **Warning Signs of Heart Attack and Stroke**

Heart Attack

Some heart attacks are sudden and intense, but most start slowly, with mild pain or discomfort. Seek help immediately if you experience any of the following symptoms:

- Chest discomfort. A feeling of uncomfortable pressure, fullness, squeezing, or pain in the center of the chest lasting for more than two minutes.

- Discomfort in other areas of the upper body. Pain or discomfort in one or both arms, the back, neck, jaw, or stomach.

- Shortness of breath. May occur with or without chest discomfort.

- Other warning signs. These may include dizziness, fainting, sweats, nausea or lightheadedness. Women are more likely than men to experience shortness of breath, nausea, and back or jaw pain.

If you or someone you are with has chest discomfort, especially with one or more warning signs, do not wait longer than 5 minutes before calling for help. Call 911 or your local emergency number.

Stroke

Contact a physician immediately if you or someone you are with experiences any of the following:

- Sudden, severe headache with no known cause.

- Sudden confusion, trouble speaking, or understanding.

- Sudden trouble seeing in one or both eyes.

- Sudden trouble walking, dizziness, loss of balance or coordination.

- Sudden numbness or weakness. Occurs in the face, arm, or leg, especially on one side of the body.

Any of the above symptoms may be temporary and last only a few minutes, but could indicate an impending stroke. Do not ignore them. Call 911 to get medical help immediately.

Electric shocks, delivered to the chest by a defibrillator, can restart the heart's normal heartbeat. Thousands of portable, computerized defibrillators, called automated external defibrillators or AEDs, are now used in police and emergency vehicles and many public buildings.

Drugs and Surgery

One drug given within a few hours after the onset of a heart attack triggers the clot-dissolving action of the blood and thus stops a heart attack in its tracks, preventing much tissue damage. Other drugs may be used to strengthen and stabilize the heartbeat. A **pacemaker** is *a device that delivers electrical impulses to the heart to regulate the heartbeat.* Pacemakers may be implanted to provide electrical stimulation for a slow heartbeat. Internal defibrillators that look similar to pacemakers can be implanted if a person is a candidate for cardiac arrest. An internal defibrillator performs the same function as a hospital defibrillator or AED by using electrical impulses to regulate the heartbeat.

Class Activity

Describe: Divide the class into groups. Have each group create a public service announcement that describes the warning signs of a heart attack or stroke. Tell them to discuss how to react to these symptoms. Share the public service announcements with other classes.

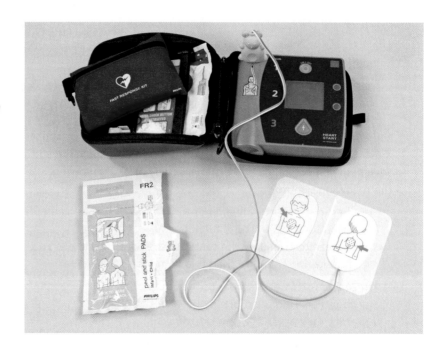

Figure 17.10 *When a person's heart contracts abnormally, a defibrillator can often restore a normal beat. Where have you seen a portable defibrillator device in a public place?*

Caption Answer: Answers will vary but may include hospital, school, shopping mall.

Coronary Artery Bypass Surgery

When the arteries of the heart become blocked, it is necessary to remove or bypass the blockage. **Coronary artery bypass surgery** is *a surgery to provide an alternate route for blood to reach heart tissue, bypassing a blocked coronary artery*. This involves replacing the blocked coronary arteries with sections of the person's own veins. Sometimes a small, metal, mesh tube is placed in the narrowed artery to hold the artery open. In another form of surgery, instruments inserted into the arteries flatten, scrape, or vaporize the plaques to widen the passageways.

Sometimes the heart is so badly damaged that it cannot recover its ability to pump enough blood to meet the needs of body tissues. In such cases, the person's life can often be saved by organ transplant. A **heart transplant** is *the surgical replacement of a diseased heart with a healthy one*. With any transplant, there are always risks. A person who needs a new heart may have to wait years for one to become available. Even then, rejection of the new heart by the body's immune system is a constant threat. Another option is the use of an artificial heart. An **artificial heart** is *a pump designed to fit into the human chest cavity and perform the heart's function of pumping blood around the body*. Artificial hearts are implanted in the body, and have been used for a year or longer.

Although progressive medical techniques exist, blockages can recur, and people may require repeated treatments. **Human gene therapy** is *the use of genetic material to treat, cure, or prevent diseases such as heart disease and cancer*. If research succeeds, physicians may one day treat diseases by replacing defective disease-causing genes with healthy genetic material in a person's cells.

Lifestyle Choices

Today, people are encouraged to make smart lifestyle choices, such as eating a healthy diet and getting regular physical activity. These choices can help prevent or postpone the onset of CVD. Everyday health behaviors are most reliable for preventing—and even sometimes reversing—heart disease.

Stroke

MAIN IDEA ▶ Strokes are blockages or hemorrhages in the vessels that feed the brain.

A stroke, like a heart attack, occurs due to a blockage in an artery. However, in the case of a stroke, the arteries are located in the brain. A stroke can also occur from the bursting of aneurysms (hemorrhage) in the small vessels of the brain. This type of stroke can result from atherosclerosis and can impair a person's functioning.

Causes and Treatments

Stroke is the third leading cause of death in the United States. It is the leading cause of disability in the U.S. Sometimes before a major stroke occurs, a person will experience mini strokes or small strokes. These warn a blockage is forming. A mini stroke may be a warning sign that a more severe stroke could occur.

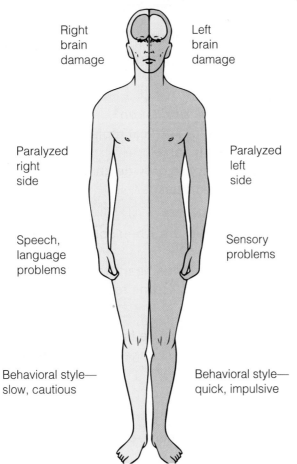

Right brain damage

Left brain damage

Paralyzed right side

Paralyzed left side

Speech, language problems

Sensory problems

Behavioral style—slow, cautious

Behavioral style—quick, impulsive

Figure 17.11

The Effect of Stroke Location

Damage on one side of the brain affects the opposite side of the body.

The impact of a stroke depends on its severity. A minor stroke may have no lasting effect. When a major stroke occurs, a part of the brain is starved for blood and dies. Damage to one side of the brain affects the opposite side of the body. This is illustrated in **Figure 17.11**. Survivors of a severe stroke may lose the ability to talk, walk, form words, or move their arms and/or legs. Sometimes, this damage is permanent. In other cases, they may need to relearn even simple tasks like eating, washing hands, or walking. With the help of doctors, many stroke survivors can recover some functioning.

Like a heart attack, a stroke requires immediate medical attention. Unfortunately, the symptoms of a stroke may be misinterpreted. For two warning signs, slurred speech and trouble walking, a person may look as if they drank alcohol. If there is no smell of alcohol, a stroke should be considered. Medications exist that can stop a stroke as it is occurring. These medications, however, must be given to the person within the first three hours of the beginning of symptoms. Act quickly, should any of the warning signs of stroke occur.

Worksheets: A reproducible quiz for Section 4 is provided in the Teacher Classroom Resources.

SECTION 4 Review

Reviewing the Vocabulary

Review the vocabulary on page 462. Then answer these questions.

1. Define *angina*.

2 What is *ventricular fibrillation*?

3. What is the term for surgical replacement of a diseased heart with a healthy one?

4. What is the surgery to provide an alternate route for blood to reach heart tissue?

Reviewing the Facts

5. Describe. What occurs when someone has a heart attack?

6. Analyze. When might a heart transplant be performed?

7. Explain. Can stroke victims recover fully?

Writing Critically

8. Expository. What lifestyle factors would you suggest a person change to reduce the risk of heart attack or stroke?

For more vocabulary practice, play the True/False game at **glencoe.com**.

1. Pain in the heart region caused by lack of oxygen.

2. Extremely rapid contractions of the heart's lower chambers that lack the power needed to pump blood around the body.

3. Heart transplant

4. Coronary artery bypass surgery

5. Blood flow to the heart is restricted, heart muscle dies.

6. When the heart cannot recover its ability to pump enough blood to meet the needs of body tissues.

7. If the stroke was mild, a survivor may recover full functioning. If the stroke was severe, some functioning may be lost.

8. Answers will vary.

Reducing the Risks of CVD

When people find out they have CVD, they may be surprised. Yet many of their own personal choices—repeated day after day, year after year—may have made the disease almost a certainty. The many risk factors linked to CVD are listed in **Figure 17.12**. Some of the major risk factors for heart disease are age, heredity, gender, smoking, smokeless tobacco, obesity, hypertension, high blood cholesterol, a high-fat diet, physical inactivity, and diabetes. On average, the more risk factors in a person's life, the greater that person's risk of disease. Some risk factors are under personal control and these receive special attention in the next sections.

Smoking and Obesity

MAIN IDEA ▶ Two major factors for CVD that can be controlled through lifestyle choices are smoking and obesity.

Many diseases—not just heart and artery disease—share the same risk factors. Of all the risk factors for cardiovascular disease, some you can control. You cannot control others, such as age, heredity, and gender. Nevertheless, you can be alert and take precautions in other ways. Other major risk factors include smoking, obesity, hypertension, high blood cholesterol, diet, and physical inactivity.

Vocabulary

systolic pressure
diastolic pressure
lipoproteins
low-density lipoproteins (LDLs)
high-density lipoproteins (HDLs)

Figure 17.12   **Risk Factors for Heart and Artery Disease**

- Increasing age
- Gender (being male)
- Family history of premature heart disease*
- High blood LDL cholesterol and/or low HDL cholesterol
- Diabetes

- Obesity (30 percent or more overweight)
- Physical inactivity
- Cigarette smoking
- An "atherosclerosis-promoting" diet (high in saturated fat and low in vegetables, fruit, and whole grains)

* Heart disease or sudden death before age 55 in father, brother, or son. Heart disease or sudden death before age 65 in mother, sister, or daughter.

Smoking

When tobacco smoke enters the lungs, it delivers nicotine into the bloodstream. This triggers the stress response, raises the blood pressure, and increases the heart rate. At the same time, carbon monoxide enters the bloodstream. Carbon monoxide starves the tissues of oxygen. Not only that, but nicotine damages blood vessel cells and makes clot formation likely. This combination of factors greatly increases the risk of heart attacks. To reduce the risk of CVD from smoking, don't smoke. If you do smoke, quit. Even a person who has smoked for years can reduce her risk for heart disease by quitting.

Obesity

Excess body weight raises the risk of heart disease. Obesity increases blood cholesterol levels, blood pressure, and blood glucose. Weight loss in overweight teens lowers blood pressure and improves other risk factors for heart disease. Achieving and maintaining a healthy weight throughout life is critical to reducing the risk of heart disease. Teens who are physically inactive, obese, and have high blood pressure, high blood cholesterol, and diabetes are at the greatest risk of heart disease. Those who also smoke increase their risk.

Hypertension

MAIN IDEA ▶ Lifestyle changes and/or medications can lower blood pressure.

The pressure of the blood against the capillary walls pushes fluids out into the tissues. The term hypertension refers to excess pressure of the blood in the arteries. The higher the blood pressure is above normal, the greater the risk of heart disease. Hypertension has a link to heredity—it runs in African American families. People who are middle-aged or elderly, obese, heavy drinkers, users of oral contraceptives, or suffering from kidney disease or diabetes often develop hypertension.

Know Your Blood Pressure

The most effective step you can take to protect yourself from CVD is to learn whether your blood pressure is high. Even a person who feels healthy may have high blood pressure. Having high blood pressure does not make a person feel sick. That's why the disease is called "the silent killer." Your doctor or other health care professional will take your blood pressure during every visit.

Your blood pressure consists of two numbers: the pressure during contraction of the ventricles of the heart, and the pressure during the relaxation of the ventricles.

Health Skills

Reducing the Risk of CVD

To reduce the risk of CVD:

1. Learn about your heredity.
2. Don't smoke. If you do smoke, stop.
3. Keep your blood pressure below 120/80.
4. Keep your blood cholesterol within the normal range (below 170 milligrams per deciliter for teens).
5. If you have diabetes, keep your blood sugar under control.
6. Be physically active for at least 60 minutes per day on most days of the week.
7. Maintain a healthy body weight.
8. Eat a healthy diet.

Figure 17.13 **How to Interpret Your Blood Pressure**

When the blood pressure is taken, two measures are recorded: the systolic pressure first, and the diastolic pressure second (example: 120/80). In general, for teens, a systolic reading of 120 or higher, or a diastolic reading of 80 or higher, predicts hypertension. Health professionals interpret blood pressure readings using growth chart percentiles and other measures.

120 (Systolic pressure)
—————————————
80 (Diastolic pressure)

The first number is the **systolic pressure** (sis-TOL-ic), *the blood pressure during that part of the heartbeat when the ventricles are contracted and the blood is being pushed out into the arteries*. This is the "dub" of the heartbeat. The second number is the **diastolic pressure** (DYE-as-tol-ic), *the blood pressure during that part of the heartbeat when ventricles are relaxing* (the "lub"). **Figure 17.13** shows what a blood pressure reading means.

Hypertension can usually be controlled by a combination of lifestyle changes and medication. Lifestyle changes include:

- Maintaining a healthy weight.
- Choosing a diet low in salt and saturated fat, and rich in fruits, vegetables, whole grains, and low-fat milk products.
- Getting regular physical activity.

In severe hypertension, or when other factors increase CVD risks, drugs that lower blood pressure can be a life-saving treatment.

High Blood Cholesterol

MAIN IDEA ▶ High blood cholesterol predicts CVD.

Like hypertension, high blood cholesterol has no symptoms to warn of cardiovascular disease. Cholesterol is a type of fat. It is found in foods and is also made and destroyed in the body. Body tissues need some cholesterol, but too much damages them.

Blood cholesterol may be high in some people who are born with the tendency to produce it too fast or destroy it too slowly. Many teens have high blood cholesterol for lifestyle reasons. They eat too much saturated fat, are physically inactive, are obese, or all of these. A blood test can tell you your blood cholesterol level. **Figure 17.14** on page 470 shows how to interpret it.

Comprehension Check
Comprehend: Ask students to explain how high blood cholesterol is connected to cardiovascular disease.

Figure 17.14   Cholesterol Values for Teens

	Total Cholesterol (mg/dL[a])	LDL Cholesterol (mg/dL)
Acceptable	<170	<110
Borderline	170–199	100–129
High	≥200	≥130

[a] Blood cholesterol is measured in milligrams per deciliter of blood.

Did You Know?

One way to remember the difference between LDL and HDL cholesterol is: LDL is bad cholesterol. HDL is good cholesterol.

Comprehension Check

Define: Ask students to write the definitions for low-density lipoproteins and high-density lipoproteins. Explain the function of each.

Cholesterol is a fat that does not mix well in the blood, which is watery. However, proteins mix so well with both watery substances and fats that they can carry fats along with them in the blood. To transfer cholesterol and other fats around the body by way of the bloodstream, the liver wraps the cholesterol and fat with protein in packages called **lipoproteins** (LIP-oh-PRO-teens), *protein and fat clusters that transport fats in the blood.*

Two kinds of lipoproteins carry cholesterol (as well as other fats) around the body. One type, **low-density lipoproteins** (LDL), are *lipoproteins that carry fat and cholesterol from the liver where they are made, to the tissues, where they are used.* LDLs also deposit cholesterol in arteries, forming plaques. The other type, **high-density lipoproteins** (HDL), are *lipoproteins that carry fat and cholesterol away from the tissues (and from plaques) back to the liver for breakdown and removal from the body.*

LDLs carry cholesterol from the liver to the tissue. They are used to make hormones, to build cell membranes, and to make vitamin D. However, harm from cholesterol may also occur. When the tissue has all the cholesterol it needs, LDLs may deposit excess cholesterol along the artery linings, forming plaques. HDLs, on the other hand, work to gather up excess cholesterol from the artery linings and carry it back to the liver to be disposed of.

A rise in LDLs raises a person's risks of developing CVD. High LDL levels are directly related to the development of atherosclerosis. In contrast, raised HDL levels protect against CVD. The thing to remember about the blood level of HDLs is "the higher, the better."

Several factors affect the blood cholesterol level. Some you can control, and some you cannot. For example, females have higher HDL levels than males. Second, nonsmokers have higher HDL levels than smokers. Maintaining appropriate body weight is also helpful. Diet and physical activity also affect blood cholesterol levels.

APPLYING Health Skills

Advocacy

➤ Objectives

- Explain why it is important for teens to have a normal level of blood cholesterol.
- List steps teens can take to help control their blood cholesterol level.

Silent Epidemic

In the United States today, about one-third of young people aged 10 to 19 years have a higher-than-normal level of blood cholesterol. That's about 3 million children and teens. High blood cholesterol doesn't cause any symptoms, so many young people are unaware that they have a problem. However, high blood cholesterol in teens can damage arteries and increase the risk of developing cardiovascular disease in adulthood.

Chances are, about one third of the teens you know have high blood cholesterol. What can they do about it? In most cases, changing their lifestyle can help. They should choose foods that are high in fiber and low in saturated and trans fats. They should also avoid smoking and get regular aerobic exercise, such as running or biking.

➤ Identify the Problem

1. How serious is the problem of high blood cholesterol in U.S. teens today?

➤ Form an Action Plan

2. Why is it dangerous for teens to have high blood cholesterol?
3. What are three lifestyle choices teens can make to help keep their blood cholesterol at a normal level?
4. Which types of fats increase blood cholesterol? What type of exercise helps reduce blood cholesterol?

➤ What Did You Learn?

5. Create a brochure that explains why it is important for teens to have a normal level of blood cholesterol. In your brochure, describe what teens can do to help control their blood cholesterol level.

Applying Health Skills:

1. About one third of U.S. teens today have a higher-than-normal level of blood cholesterol.

2. High blood cholesterol in teens can damage arteries and increase the risk of developing cardiovascular disease in adulthood.

3. They can choose healthy foods, avoid smoking, and exercise regularly.

4. Saturated and trans fats increase blood cholesterol. Aerobic exercise, such as running or biking, helps reduce blood cholesterol.

5. Answers will vary.

■ Figure 17.15 *Dietary fiber helps protect against heart disease. What are some foods that can help keep your heart healthy?*

Caption Answer: Vegetables, fruits, whole grains, low-fat milk, and fish

 **Did You Know?**

Walking, swimming, or other aerobic exercise started gradually and consistently done will greatly improve the physical conditioning of the heart.

Regular physical activity seems to lower LDL and raise HDL cholesterol levels. The role of diet is complex, but it is certain that diet plays a role in the levels of blood cholesterol. Remember that meats contain cholesterol. Other foods may not contain cholesterol, but they trigger the production of cholesterol by the liver. The complexities are worth learning and applying to maintain a healthy heart.

Diet, Cholesterol, and Heart Health

People are often confused about the role of diet in connection with high blood cholesterol. Cholesterol in foods, such as meat or eggs, raises blood cholesterol. However, regular dietary fats—especially saturated fat and trans fat—raise it much more. The key to lowering blood cholesterol is to eat a balanced diet that is low in saturated and trans fats. The fat you do eat should be mostly the unsaturated type. A diet rich in vegetables, fruits, whole grains, and low-fat milk and milk products benefits the heart as well. Lean meats such as chicken and fish are also low in unsaturated fat and contribute to a healthy diet. The role of trans-fats in the development of heart disease has gained much attention. Some cities and states have banned the use of trans-fats in food prepared in restaurants to reduce the impact of heart disease. The American Heart Association recommends cutting the use of trans-fat and notes that eating two servings of fish a week to provide fish oils that benefit the heart.

Physical Inactivity and Emotions

MAIN IDEA ▷ Regular physical activity and controlling emotions reduces the risk of heart disease.

Regular physical activity reduces risk and can even reverse some of the risk factors. Physical activity lowers LDL cholesterol and raises HDL cholesterol. In addition, aerobic activities, such as running, brisk walking, swimming, and cycling, support heart health. For females, lifting light weights can build muscle mass which will speed up fat burning. Light weight lifting will not build bulky muscles. The American Heart Association recommends that teens exercise for at least 60 minutes on most days.

When people get angry, anxious, or depressed, these emotions may affect the heart. While researchers are not exactly sure how this process works, they do know that people who are depressed may not eat healthful foods, or exercise regularly.

Worksheets: A reproducible quiz for Section 5 is provided in the Teacher Classroom Resources.

SECTION 5 Review

Reviewing the Vocabulary

Review the vocabulary on page 467. Then answer these questions.

1. What is the term for blood pressure during that part of the heartbeat when ventricles are relaxing?

2. What are *lipoproteins*?

3. Define high-density lipoproteins.

Reviewing the Facts

4. Describe. List the risk factors for cardiovascular disease.

5. Analyze. What happens in the body after tobacco smoke enters the lungs?

6. Evaluate. What lifestyle strategies help control hypertension?

Writing Critically

7. Expository. What recommendations would you make to someone with high blood cholesterol? Explain the lifestyle changes that can lower the risk for CVD.

For fitness and health tips, visit the Fitness Zone at **glencoe.com**

1. Diastolic pressure

2. Protein and fat clusters that transport fats in the blood.

3. Lipoproteins that carry fat and cholesterol away from the tissues (and from plaques) back to the liver for breakdown and removal from the body.

4. Age, heredity, gender, smoking, obesity, hypertension, high blood cholesterol, a high-fat diet, physical inactivity, and diabetes.

5. Nicotine raises the blood pressure, increases the heart rate, and decreases oxygen to the heart.

6. Regular physical activity, eating a low-fat, healthy diet.

7. Answers will vary.

Cancer

Cancer is *a disease in which abnormal cells multiply out of control, spread into surrounding tissues and other body parts, and disrupt normal functioning of one or more organs.* At one time, the long-term health of someone diagnosed as having cancer was hopeless. Today, battles against cancer can be won. Still, preventing cancer is far preferable to curing it.

Vocabulary

cancer
tumor
malignancy
melanoma
myeloma
lymphomas
leukemias
carcinomas
sarcomas
adenomas
initiator
mutation
promoter
benign
metastasized

Writing Activity

Research: Remind students that cancers are classified by the types of tissue they affect. Ask each student to research one type of cancer, and to write about the cancer, how it develops, the symptoms associated with it, and how it is treated. Allow volunteers to share their information.

Types of Cancers

MAIN IDEA ▶ **Cancers are classified according to the types of tissue they affect.**

Over a hundred diseases are called cancer. Each has its own name and symptoms, depending on its type and location in the body. The suffix "-oma" means **tumor,** *an abnormal mass of tissue that can live and reproduce itself, but performs no service to the body.* A **malignancy** is *a dangerous cancerous growth that sheds cells into body fluids and spreads to new locations to start new cancer colonies.*

Some cancers are named for the body tissues in which they arise. For example, **melanoma** is an expecially dangerous *cancer of the pigmented cells of the skin.* A tumor of the bone marrow is a **myeloma**—*myelos* means "marrow." Other cancers are classified by the tissues or cells they develop from:

- *Cancers that arise in organs of the immune system or the lymph tissues* are **lymphomas** (limf-OH-mahs).
- *Cancers that arise in the blood cell-making tissues of blood-forming organs* are **leukemias** (loo-KEE-me-ahs).
- *Cancers that arise in the skin, body chamber linings, or glands* are **carcinomas** (car-sin-OH-mahs).
- *Cancers that arise in the connective tissue cells, including bones, ligaments, and muscles,* are **sarcomas** (sar-KOH-mahs).
- *Cancers of glandular tissues such as the breast* are **adenomas** (ADD-en-OH-mahs).

How Does Cancer Develop?

Cancer begins with a change in the genes of a normal cell. Cell production increases until it's out of control. The steps in the development of many cancers are thought to be:

1. Exposure to an **initiator**, *a carcinogen, an agent required to start the formation of cancer.*
2. Entry of the initiator into a cell.
3. **Mutation** of the cell, or *a change in a cell's genetic material.*

4. Action of a **promoter**, *a substance that assists in the development of malignant tumors, but does not initiate them on its own.*
5. Rapid multiplication of the cells.
6. Tumor or other malignancy formation.

Cancers can take months or years to develop. By the time a health care provider detects a cancer, the initiator and promoters that caused the cancer can be difficult to trace.

Initiators and promoters work together, an effect shown in **Figure 17.16**. For example, alcohol and tobacco work this way in the development of cancers of the mouth, throat, and esophagus. Alcohol causes these cancers all by itself, but when people drink alcohol and also smoke tobacco, the risk of these cancers grows dramatically. Alcohol and tobacco smoke both initiate and promote these cancers. A person greatly reduces the risk of getting cancer by not using alcohol and tobacco, or by choosing to quit using them.

All of the changes that lead to cancer occur inside the cells. Once started inside the body, cancer can grow and damage any of the body's tissues. Normally, cells divide only when new cells are needed. A cancerous cell, though, does not respond to the command to stop dividing. It divides continuously. The result may be a lump of tissue, or tumor.

Types of Tumors

MAIN IDEA ▶ Cancer can interrupt the functioning of vital organs.

Some tumors are harmless, or **benign** (be-NINE), meaning *noncancerous, not harmful*. A benign tumor is not able to spread from one area to another. It is a well-defined, solid mass contained in an external membrane. A benign tumor poses no threat to the health of the patient. A doctor can either remove the tumor, if it is medically safe to do so, or the doctor can use radiation or other treatments to shrink the tumor.

Cancerous tumors are malignant, which means that they present a threat to health. As a cancerous tumor gains in size, it competes with normal tissues around it for nutrients, oxygen, and space. With time, the cancer interrupts the normal functions of the tissues or organs into which it grows. In cancer of the large intestine, for example, the tumor may block the passage of the intestinal contents. In cancer of the brain, the growing tumor threatens thought processes and control of the body.

In addition to invading surrounding tissue, cancer cells can travel through body fluids to colonize new areas. When a cancer is just beginning, it sheds only a few cells.

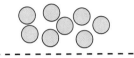

Figure 17.16

Cancer Initiators and Promoters

Initiators and promoters work together to produce many more tumors than initiators alone would produce.

Normal cells

Initiation

Damage to a cell's DNA causes abnormal subdivision

Promotion

Promotion causes multiplication of the damaged cells, resulting in the formation of a tumor

Further tumor development

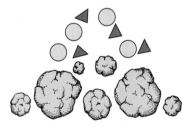

The cancerous tumor releases cells into the bloodstream or lymphatic system

Legend

 Normal cells

 Promoter

 Malignant cell

As it enlarges, however, more and more of these wild cells escape and start new growths in other body parts. At this point, the cancer is said to have **metastasized** (meh-TASS-tuh-sized), *when the cancer cells have migrated from one part of the body to another, and started new growths just like the original tumor.* Cancer causes death when it interrupts the functioning of vital organs, such as the blood-building organs, lungs, or brain.

The immune system works to stop dangerous cancer cells before they lodge in body tissue, but it can catch only a certain number of cancer cells at any one time. When the immune defenses fail, cancer treatment is needed. The success of treatment often depends on whether or not it gets under way before the cancer has metastasized.

SECTION 6 Review

Reviewing the Vocabulary

Review the vocabulary on page 474. Then answer these questions.

1. What is the difference between *melanoma* and *myeloma*?
2. What is an *initiator* in the steps of cancer development?
3. What is a *tumor*?

Reviewing the Facts

4. **Identify.** What are the main classes of cancer?
5. **Analyze.** When does cancer cause death?
6. **Explain.** How does the immune system help fight cancer?

Writing Critically

7. **Persuasive.** To encourage people to seek early medical attention for cancer, the American Cancer Society sometimes asks famous people to appear in public service announcements. Do you think this is an effective technique? What method do you believe would be most likely to sway you, and why?

For a personal health assessment, complete the Life Choice Inventory at **glencoe.com**.

Controllable Cancer Risks

Risks of cancer fall into three categories. Some risks you can control totally—the ones that have to do with your own behavior. Some risks you can control partially, for example, the risks posed by environmental pollutants. Some risks, you cannot control at all. You cannot control your gender, your family medical history, or your age (cancer risk increases with age). This section focuses on the risks you can control.

Tobacco

MAIN IDEA ▶ **Using tobacco products causes cancer.**

The link between smoking and cancer has been proven through scientific research. Smoking causes about 85 percent of all types of lung cancer. In any community of the world, an increase in smoking is followed by a jump in numbers of lung cancer cases. When researchers spread chemicals from tobacco smoke on a patch of living skin, cancer develops at the site.

About a fifth of all cancer deaths are linked to tobacco use. Other cancers that affect other organs also occur due to smoking. Cancer of the larynx (voice box), mouth, esophagus, urinary bladder, kidney, pancreas, and many other organs have all been linked to tobacco use.

Radiation

MAIN IDEA ▶ **X-rays and exposure to the sun increase cancer risks.**

People are exposed to radiation from many sources every day. Whether or not they are affected by it depends on the type of radiation and their length of exposure.

The Sun's Rays

Overexposure to the sun's ultraviolet (UV) rays can cause skin cancer, including melanoma. There are two types of ultraviolet radiation from the sun. **UVA** (ultraviolet A) *passes deep into the skin and can cause long-term skin damage that may lead to cancer and premature aging.* **UVB** (ultraviolet B) *causes sunburn and skin cancer, including melanoma.* More and more of these rays are hitting the earth's surface as pollution from human activity destroys the atmospheric shield (the ozone layer) that used to filter them out.

Vocabulary

UVA
UVB
melanin
sunscreen
sun block

Figure 17.17

Forms of Skin Cancer

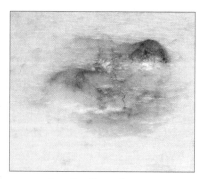

Basal cell carcinoma

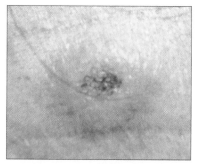

Squamous cell carcinoma

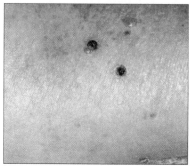

Malignant melanoma

Skin cancers come in several varieties. A major distinction is between the fast-spreading, lethal skin cancer known as melanoma and other, less-threatening surface cancers of the skin. Just one blistering sunburn, if received during the teen years, may be enough to double a person's risk of melanoma. In contrast, working or playing in the sun daily makes people likely to develop the more easily treated forms of skin cancer. **Figure 17.17** shows the different forms of skin cancer.

While no one is immune to the sun's damaging effects, skin color can help predict who is most at risk for cancer. **Melanin** (MELL-eh-nin) is *the protective skin pigment responsible for the tan, brown, or black color of human skin*. It is produced in abundance upon exposure to ultraviolet radiation. When a person is exposed to the sun, the melanin in the skin increases. This causes a sunburn or tan. The increase in melanin, however, does not protect the person from skin cancer.

Fair-skinned people are more likely to develop skin cancer than people with darker skin. However, that does not mean that people with dark skin are completely protected when exposed to the sun. The melanin of dark-skinned people provides limited protection against UV damage. The resulting tan is the body's defense against the dangerous rays—but not against the cancers they cause. Overexposure to the sun also causes wrinkles and ages the skin.

Cancer risks from sunlamps and tanning booths are just as high as those from exposure to sunlight. The Center for Disease Control advises against the use of sunlamps or tanning beds for anyone under the age of 18 because of the increased skin cancer risk.

Sun Protection Products

People can take precautions to avoid dangerous overexposure to the sun. One way is to stay indoors between 10 A.M. and 4 P.M., when the sun's rays are strongest. Sun protection products filter or block ultraviolet radiation and prevent burning. Three main types of products are available for sun exposure:

- Suntan lotion is lotion that may or may not give sunscreen protection.

- **Sunscreen** provides *a partial block against the cancer-causing rays of the sun (gamma radiation)*. The higher the SPF, the less UV rays reach the skin.

- **Sun block** gives *a total block or barricade against the cancer-causing rays of the sun*.

Broad-spectrum sunscreen products offer protection from both UVA and UVB radiation. For the best protection, apply sunscreen 30 minutes before sun exposure and reapply at least every 2 hours.

Did You Know?

Sun facts:
- The strongest sun rays shine from 10 A.M. until 4 P.M.
- Fair-skinned people with blond, red, or light brown hair and blue, green, or gray eyes are most at risk for skin cancer.
- Freckles mean burns are likely.
- By age 18 most people have accumulated most of their lifetime sun exposure. No more exposure is necessary for cancer to develop.
- Medications that increase skin sensitivity to the sun include: acne medications, antidepressants, antihistamines, antibiotics, diuretics, and some pain relievers. Ask a physician or pharmacist whether medication you take has this effect.
- Water, snow, and sand reflect damaging UV rays and increase your chance of sunburn and other damage to the skin and eyes.
- Wear protective clothing such as wide-brimmed hats, long pants and long-sleeved shirts made of tightly-woven fabric to reduce sun exposure.

Water-resistant sunscreens are not waterproof. They still need to be reapplied on a regular basis. All people—even people with dark skin—should use water-resistant sunscreens of at least SPF 15 during sunny or warm weather. To be protected, use a full ounce of product spread on the skin with each application. Enjoy the sun for short times rather than on all-day trips. Take along a big hat. Finally, be aware that UV rays penetrate clouds, so burns are likely even on cool, cloudy days.

X-Ray Radiation

People are exposed to more radiation than just from sunlight. A great deal of background radiation reaches us from the soil, and from the air and water. Human-made radiation comes from medical and dental X-rays and from above-ground nuclear weapons testing anywhere on earth. X-ray examinations are often required for proper medical care. Doses of radiation involved in medical procedures have decreased over the last 20 years. Also, the ability to target radiation more precisely to one part of the body has resulted in less exposure to the rest of the body. However, patients can inform their doctors that they wish to avoid X-rays when possible.

Diet, Body Fat, Physical Activity, and Alcohol

MAIN IDEA ▶ Making healthful choices can reduce cancer risks.

People can take four additional steps to reduce their cancer risks. They can improve their diet, control their body fat, be physically active, and reduce or eliminate alcoholic beverages.

Diet

Four food-related factors link most strongly with high cancer risks:

- High intake of red meat and processed meat
- High intakes of foods that contain large amounts of fat and/or added sugar, fast foods, and sugary drinks
- Low intakes of fruit, non-starchy vegetables, and whole grains
- High intakes of salt-preserved, salted, or salty foods

Details about the foods that make up such a diet are in this chapter's Q&A section, along with answers to questions people ask about additives and supplements.

Body Fat

Being overweight or obese is linked with a number of cancers, including breast (after menopause), colon, esophagus, gallbladder, kidney, pancreas, and uterine cancers. Diet and physical activity influence the amount of fat the body stores. The person who chooses too many high-calorie, fat-rich, or high-sugar foods is likely to gain weight, while someone choosing mostly fruits, vegetables, beans, and whole grains often remains lean. Similarly, physical inactivity, promotes weight gain, while regular physical activity discourages it.

■ **Figure 17.19** *Physical activity can improve your health and reduce the risk of cancer. What physical activities do you enjoy to keep your body healthy?*

Caption Answer: Answers will vary.

Physical Activity

Physical activity protects against cancer too, especially colon cancer. People who fail to work out regularly suffer more constipation than physically active people. The stools contain carcinogenic material. The longer they stay in the colon, the more the chance of their changing the cells of the colon's lining. Physical activity strengthens the muscles used to move the bowels and massages the intestines to help move their contents along. With regular bowel movements, the contents of the stools spend little time in contact with the colon lining.

Alcohol

Alcohol, when consumed in large amounts, leads to poor nutrition, which in turn lowers the body's defenses against cancer. Alcohol may initiate cancer of the breast, colon, esophagus, liver, mouth, throat, and rectum. The type of alcoholic drink does not matter—alcohol itself causes cancer. The more alcohol a person drinks, the greater the risk of cancer.

Worksheets: A reproducible quiz for Section 7 is provided in the Teacher Classroom Resources.

SECTION 7 Review

Reviewing the Vocabulary

Review the vocabulary on page 477. Then answer these questions.

1. Define *UVA* and *UVB*.

2. What is *melanin*?

Reviewing the Facts

3. Identify. What percentage of lung cancer does smoking cause?

4. Explain. What causes skin cancer?

5. Evaluate. What are the four dietary factors that link strongly with high cancer risks?

Writing Critically

6. Descriptive. Do you feel you are doing enough to protect yourself against cancer? Why or why not? List the steps you need to take to reduce your risk of cancer.

Go Online

For more information on health careers, visit Career Corner at **glencoe.com.**

1. UVA passes deep into the skin and can cause long-term skin damage such as premature aging. UVB causes sunburn and skin cancer, including melanoma.

2. The protective skin pigment responsible for the color of human skin.

3. 85 percent

4. Radiation

5. Red meat; high-fat, sugary, fast foods; low intake of fruits, vegetables, and whole grains; high salt intake

6. Answers will vary.

Early Detection and Treatment

The treatment of cancer involves sophisticated equipment, powerful drugs, and specialized medical staff. The detection of common cancers, however, requires mostly routine tests and self-examinations.

Vocabulary

Hodgkin's lymphoma
mammogram
polyps
radiation therapy
chemotherapy

How Is Cancer Detected?

MAIN IDEA ▶ Professional examinations and self-exams can detect early cancers.

Certain cancers are identified as more likely to cause deaths among young people. One example, **Hodgkin's lymphoma**, is *a cancer that attacks people in early life and is treatable with radiation therapy*. **Figure 17.20** lists cancers and symptoms associated with young people. Any of these symptoms should be checked by a doctor immediately.

Figure 17.20 | **Cancers Most Often Causing Deaths in People Ages 15 to 34**

Disease	Early Symptoms	Survival with early diagnosis and prompt treatment[a]
Brain and nervous system cancer	Personality changes; bizarre behavior; headaches; dizziness; balance and walking disturbances; vision changes; nausea, vomiting, or seizures	Poor
Breast cancer	Unusual lump, thickening in, change in contour in, dimple in, or discharge from, the nipple	Excellent (up to 90 percent)
Hodgkin's lymphoma	Swelling of lymph nodes in neck, armpits, or groin; susceptibility to infection	Good (75 percent)
Leukemia	Acts like infection, with fever, lethargy, and other flulike symptoms; may also include bone pain, tendency to bruise or bleed easily, and enlargement of lymph nodes	Poor to good, depending on the type of leukemia
Skin cancer	Unusual discoloration, swellings, sores, or lumps; change in color or appearance of a wart or mole; tenderness, itching, or bleeding from a lump or mole	Excellent (up to 90 percent)
Testicular cancer	Small, hard, painless lump; sudden accumulation of fluid in the scrotum; pain or discomfort in the region between the scrotum and anus	Good to excellent (60 to 90 percent)

[a]The survival rates are estimates based on five years of disease-free survival. For all cancers, survival rates drop dramatically after metastasis.

Cancer "Caution" Signs

Cancer can develop without symptoms, but it is wise to heed all the messages your body sends you, particularly the following warnings:

- Change in bowel or bladder habits, such as diarrhea or constipation
- A sore that does not heal
- Unusual bleeding or discharge
- Thickening or lump that suddenly appears anywhere in the body
- Indigestion or difficulty swallowing
- Obvious change in a wart or mole
- Nagging cough or hoarseness
- Sudden weight loss

To remember this list, recall that the first letters in the warning signs spell the word CAUTIONS. Having one of these symptoms does not necessarily mean that you have cancer. A cold or eating too much might bring about some of them, for example. However, when symptoms last for more than a week, or when they occur more than once, they require the attention of a health care provider.

Medical Exams

A professional can detect a lump in places not easily examined through self-exams. Laboratory tests are important too. The most accurate test for early breast cancer is the **mammogram**, *an X-ray examination of the breast, a screening test for cancer.* Because mammograms involve radiation, which itself can cause cancer, they are used sparingly.

Genetic testing can play a role in identifying inherited traits that make some people likely to develop certain cancers. The hope is that with early warning such people can take action to prevent cancers from getting started.

Recommended tests for females age 18 include a Pap test, a pelvic examination, and a breast examination done by a physician. Males age 18 should have a testicle and prostate examination done by a physician. Both genders need examinations of the thyroid, lymph nodes, mouth and throat, and skin. For early detection of cancer, these tests should continue on schedule throughout life.

A medical professional who sees a person only once a year or so may not notice small changes that would be obvious to a person familiar with his or her own body. Many thousands of cases of cancer have been cured, thanks to early detection through self-exams.

Health Skills

Helping a Friend with Cancer

To help a loved one with cancer:

1. Be there. Spend time with your friend.

2. Let the person talk. Ask the friend if he or she wants to talk about cancer.

3. Make specific offers of help. Ask if you can mow the grass, help with schoolwork, or do any other task that needs to be done—and then do it.

4. Help the friend's family. Offer to stay with your friend for a few hours while they run errands or care for personal needs that may have been neglected.

5. Recognize limitations. Involve your friend in normal activities, but remember that people with cancer tire easily.

6. Be positive. Everyone with cancer needs laughter, hope, and talk of plans for tomorrow.

Figure 17.21   **Breast Self-Examination**

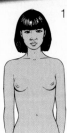

1. Stand before a mirror. Inspect both breasts for anything unusual, such as any discharge from the nipples or puckering, dimpling, or scaling of the skin.

2. Watch closely in the mirror. Clasp hands behind your head, and press hands forward. The purpose of these steps is to find any changes in the shape or contour of your breasts. As you do them, you should be able to feel your chest muscles tighten.

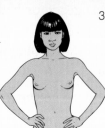

3. Next, press hands firmly on hips and bow slightly toward the mirror as you pull your shoulders and elbows forward.

Steps 4 and 5 of the exam are easy to do in the bath or shower, where fingers glide over soapy skin.

4. Raise your left arm. Use three or four fingers of your right hand to explore your left breast firmly, carefully, and thoroughly. Beginning at the outer edge, press the flat part of your fingers in small circles, moving the circles slowly around the breast. Gradually work toward the nipple. Be sure to cover the entire breast. Pay special attention to the area between the breast and the armpit, including the armpit itself. Feel for any unusual lump or mass under the skin.

5. Gently squeeze the nipple and look for a discharge. Repeat the exam on your right breast.

6. Repeat Steps 4 and 5 lying down. Lie flat on your back with your left arm over your head and a pillow or folded towel under your left shoulder. This position flattens the breast and makes it easier to examine. Use the same circular motion described earlier. Repeat on your right breast.

Breast Self-Exam

Once a month a female should check her breasts for cancer. If you start testing now, while you are young, it will be a habit that will serve you well throughout life. The breast self-exam is easy, especially when done in the shower while the skin is slippery (see **Figure 17.21**).

Lumps in the breast are most often not cancerous. However, they should be checked by a health care provider. You'll soon easily tell the "normal lumpiness" that occurs before the menstrual period from an unusual lump. Many times, a cancerous lump feels like a little pea buried in the breast. Report anything unusual to a health care provider right away.

Testicular Self-Exam

If you are a young male you can help protect yourself from cancer of the testicles through self-examination (see **Figure 17.22**). Although it occurs less frequently than breast cancer, cancer of the testicles can be deadly because it advances rapidly. It most commonly strikes young males between the ages of 15 and 35. Report any large lump, enlargement, or change in shape to a health care provider.

Skin Self-Exam

One more test to perform is a visual check of your entire skin. The more familiar you become with any moles or freckles you may have, the better you will be able to detect changes in them that could mean the start of cancer.

Stand in front of a large mirror, and take a look at your skin. Use a hand mirror to help with the back view. If a mole has changed its shape or color or has begun bleeding, have it checked right away. Always remember to protect your skin from the sun.

Cancer Treatment

MAIN IDEA ▶ Common cancer treatments include surgery, radiation therapy, and chemotherapy.

Cancer treatments destroy cancers in two ways: by removal of the malignant tissue from the body and by destruction of cancer cells within the body. If the cancer has metastasized, surgical removal or destruction of a tumor may not eliminate all the cancer cells. Cancer cure comes when every cancer cell is either removed from the body or wiped out by treatments.

Surgical Treatment

Many cancers are treatable through surgery alone. Removal of a tumor can stop the cancer growth at a site, especially if the cancer is still small. The cure rate drops off, however, as the tumor invades surrounding tissues and metastasizes to other body parts. For example, the large intestine may contain precancerous growths called **polyps**, *tumors that grow on a stem, resembling mushrooms.* Polyps bleed easily, and some have the tendency to become malignant. Removal of polyps protects against cancer. If the polyp begins to invade just a few millimeters into the tissue, however, its surgical removal no longer guarantees complete freedom from cancer at that site.

A small tumor on the skin or other external membrane can sometimes be destroyed by freezing with liquid nitrogen. Such a procedure is often performed in the physician's office and causes little inconvenience or pain.

Radiation Treatment

A treatment for cancer, sometimes used together with surgery, is **radiation therapy**, *the application of cell-destroying radiation to kill cancerous tissues.* Medical professionals use several methods to kill tumors with radiation. A beam may be focused on the area known to be cancerous. Radioactive materials may be implanted in the tumor or, in some cases, injected into the bloodstream. Under the effects of radioactivity, the fast-growing cells of the cancer become disrupted and die off.

Figure 17.22

Testicular Self-Examination

Roll each testicle between the thumb and fingers. The testicles should feel smooth, except for the normal raised organ located on the back of each. Report any hard lump, enlargement, or contour changes to your health-care provider.

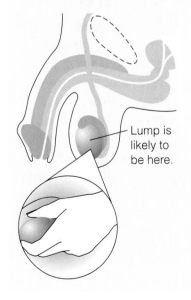

Lump is likely to be here.

Chemotherapy

In addition to surgery and radiation, a third approach is chemical treatments of cancer. **Chemotherapy** is *the administration of drugs that harm the cancer cells, but that do not harm the patient as much as the disease does*. This treatment may cause problems, but does less harm to the patient than the cancer does.

These treatments offer a major advantage when a tumor has metastasized. Once in the body, the drugs seek out and destroy the escaped cancer cells, as well as tumors in all locations. Many drugs are now used against cancer in different ways—to cure, to inhibit cancer growth, to relieve pain, and to allow the person to lead a more normal life. Often, radiation and chemotherapy are used together.

Treatment Side Effects

Both radiation and anticancer drugs that kill cancer tissue also kill normal tissues, although more slowly. Rapidly dividing cells in the body are affected the most. The cells of the digestive tract, for example, normally divide rapidly, so treatments produce diarrhea, nausea, and vomiting. Other side effects are skin damage, hair loss, and fatigue. New blood cells also arise from a rapidly dividing tissue, so people being treated for cancer may develop blood problems.

These are only a few treatments for cancer. Many more have been proven effective. More still are under development. A person who gets cancer has reason to be hopeful about possibilities for a cure.

Being Careful

Not all cancer treatments are effective or medically proven. Misleading cancer treatment claims can be especially troubling because they are aimed at people who are already suffering. For example, cancer treatment products made from shark cartilage and a skin cream marketed as a treatment for skin cancer should be avoided. Although cancer can be frightening, patients and families should consult with medical professionals as to the most effective course of action. Only a licensed doctor who specializes in the treatment of cancer should prescribe medications or suggest treatments for cancer patients.

Writing

1. Why do you think someone with cancer might take chances by trying unproven therapies?
2. What motivates manufacturers to sell medically unproven cancer treatments?

Living with Cancer

People diagnosed with cancer may have difficulty focusing on the areas of their life that support their treatment and recovery. They have fears to cope with. They may need to move emotionally through the stages of grief before they can take part in their own treatments and recoveries.

Some people find ways to face the crisis with courage. They cultivate a sense of humor in the midst of fear. Such people maintain strong family bonds and bonds of friendship throughout the illness. They also have an invaluable asset to recovery—the will to live.

Worksheets: A reproducible quiz for Section 8 is provided in the Teacher Classroom Resources.

SECTION 8 Review

Reviewing the Vocabulary

Review the vocabulary on page 482. Then answer these questions.

1 A _____ is an X-ray examination of the breast.

2. What is the administration of drugs that harm cancer cells but do not harm the patient?

3. What are *polyps*?

Reviewing the Facts

4. Identify. Name two ways to help detect cancer early.

5. Explain. What are the two ways cancer treatments destroy cancer?

6. Describe. What are the three common treatments for cancer?

Writing Critically

7. Descriptive. Look over the Health Skills sidebar "Helping a Friend with Cancer," on page 483. Imagine someone close to you has cancer. Which suggestions on the list would you find easy to follow? What strategies would you add to the list?

Go Online

For more vocabulary practice, play the Concentration game at **glencoe.com**.

1. Mammogram
2. Chemotherapy
3. Tumors that grow on a stem, bleed easily, and tend to become malignant.
4. Medical exams, self exams
5. By removing malignant tissue and by destruction of cancer cells
6. Surgical treatment, radiation, and chemotherapy
7. Answers will vary.

Diet for Disease Prevention

 Understand and Apply Read the conversation below, and then complete the writing exercise that follows.

A U.S. surgeon general said that for Americans who do not smoke or drink excessively, "your choice of diet can influence your long-term health prospects more than any other action you might take." The diet choices associated with good health are well known. A warning: Popular books and magazines, however, make many claims regarding diet and diseases. They know people will buy publications that promise control over lifestyle diseases, and not all of their claims are well founded.

Q: How can diet prevent all of the lifestyle diseases?

A: You are right to say that no diet, by itself, will positively prevent diseases. Some cases of lifestyle diseases will occur no matter what a person eats. However, for most people, food choices greatly alter their risks for developing type 2 diabetes, heart disease, or certain kinds of cancer. Also, the diet that prevents any one lifestyle disease closely resembles a diet to prevent the others. The same diet, well chosen, also boosts the immune system.

Q: What sort of foods do I have to eat to stay healthy?

A: No single food is essential to health, and none has magic powers to prevent disease. You need only apply some general principles when choosing among familiar foods, and to stay physically active.

Q: Saturated and trans fats seem to be big issues. What do they mean when they say to reduce saturated and trans fat intakes?

A: Every legitimate nutrition authority urges Americans to eat less saturated fat and trans fat. With few exceptions, anywhere in the world where people eat diets high in saturated fats from animal products, especially red meats and processed foods, rates of heart disease and cancer are high. Conversely, groups of people who eat diets low in these foods have low rates of diseases. Vegetarians in this country often have low rates of diseases. The reason why may be that they consume little animal fat, no red meat, and few highly processed foods. They choose mostly fruits, vegetables, and whole grains. Trans fat is the product of processing, so processed baked goods, restaurant and fried fast foods, and snack foods such as chips and crackers may contain it.

Q: Do you mean that to be healthy I have to give up meat? I don't care to be a vegetarian.

A: You need not give up meat completely, but most Americans eat dramatically more meat and fewer fruits, vegetables, and whole grains than guidelines suggest. Reducing meat portions has the effect of reducing saturated fat intake. If the meat is replaced with fruits, vegetables, and whole grains, so much the better.

Choosing a healthy diet isn't as simple as omitting one food group from the diet. For instance, even a vegetarian can eat a diet exceptionally high in saturated fat, if it is based on cheese, whole milk, cream, and other fatty dairy products.

Q: Do researchers know which vegetables are best for health?

A: Foods high in phytochemicals include fruits and vegetables rich in vitamin C and vegetables of the cabbage family. These are called cruciferous vegetables. Examples are cabbage, broccoli, and Brussels sprouts. Others may help protect against both heart disease and cancer. Bright orange, yellow, or deep-green–colored vegetables, along with all dark leafy greens, are the ones to choose most often. Garlic; onions; soybeans; other beans; hot peppers; celery; and herbs such as parsley, basil, and oregano are under study as possible disease fighters.

Q: Will supplements provide me with all the nutrients that I would get from fruits or vegetables? It's hard for me to find fresh foods sometimes.

A: Remember, fruits and vegetables contain fluid, phytochemicals, and fibers that supplements do not match. While you should make every effort to eat fresh fruits and vegetables, you can also try dried, frozen, and canned fruits and vegetables. They provide many of the same benefits.

Also, fiber-rich whole-grain cereals, bread, or pasta; brown rice; and beans of any kind have plenty of beneficial protectors against both heart disease and cancers. Oatmeal has become famous for its heart-protecting fiber. Fibers of other whole grains, beans, fruits, and vegetables are just as effective. Many fruits and vegetables in the diet are linked with low rates of cancers.

■ **Figure 17.23** *Foods to fight disease. What kind of vegetables are best for health?*

Caption Answer: Cruciferous vegetables

Of the many foods available for purchase in this country, the simplest, freshest foods are still the best. Vary your choices. Include a wide variety of healthy foods in your diet.

Writing Write a paragraph summarizing the health benefits of eating a variety of fresh, healthful foods.

CHAPTER 17 Review

Reviewing Vocabulary

Use the vocabulary terms listed below to complete the following statements.

atria

high-density lipoproteins

atherosclerosis

ventricles

plaques

low-density lipoproteins

stroke

heart attack

1. _____ are the two upper chambers and _____ are the two lower chambers of the heart.

2. _____ build up in the artery wall and create the disease _____.

3. _____ carry fat and cholesterol from the liver to the tissues; _____ carry fat and cholesterol away from the tissues back to the liver for removal from the body.

4. A _____ is when blood vessels of the heart become blocked. A _____ is when blood flow to the brain is shut off.

Recalling Key Facts and Ideas

Section 1
5. **List.** What risk factors for lifestyle diseases are within a person's control?

Section 2
6. **Explain.** Explain the difference between type 1 diabetes and type 2 diabetes.

Section 3
7. **List.** What are the three tools for controlling diabetes and its consequences?

8. **Identify.** What is the most common form of CVD?

9. **Name.** What is an aneurysm?

Section 4
10. **Describe.** What happens to the heart in a heart attack?

11. **List.** List three medical treatments for heart disease.

12. **Describe.** Describe what difficulties victims of a severe stroke may experience.

Section 5
13. **List.** Name four health strategies for reducing the risk of CVD.

14. **Identify.** What kind of dietary fat raises blood cholesterol?

Section 6
15. **Identify.** What is the number one type of cancer in both males and females?

16. **Explain.** What is a benign tumor?

---

1. Atria; ventricles 2. Plaque; atherosclerosis 3. Low-density lipoproteins; high-density lipoproteins 4. Heart attack; stroke 5. Diet, physical activity, obesity, stress 6. In type 1, the person no longer produces insulin. In type 2, the body may produce insulin, but the body responds abnormally. Type 2 is prevent-

able 7. Medication, balanced diet, physical activity
8. Atherosclerosis 9. Ballooning out of an artery wall
10. Heart muscle tissue dies and scar tissue develop
11. Defibrillators, drugs, and surgery. 12. They lose abilities to do simple tasks. 13. Answers will vary, see Health Skills on

Section 7

17. **List.** Name two cancer-causing factors people can control.

18. **Identify.** What types of cancers are most common in smokers?

Section 8

19. **Explain.** What does CAUTIONS stand for with regard to the warning signs of cancer?

20. **Describe.** When is a person considered to be cured of cancer?

Writing Critically

21. **Persuasive.** Many public places now ban smoking in common areas. Do you think the health benefits justify this restriction? Why or why not? Do you feel that these laws infringe on the rights of the individual? Why or why not? What other restrictions would you place on smoking?

Activities

22. Develop two case histories. In one, describe someone at risk for CVD; in the other, describe someone with hardly any risk for heart disease.

23. Keep a diary of all the lifestyle risk factors for heart disease and cancer to which you are exposed for a full week. Develop a list of ways to avoid these risk factors.

24. Design an educational pamphlet aimed at high school students to inform them about cancer.

Making Decisions About Health

25. Lately, your grandfather has been experiencing sharp chest pains and has felt as though he couldn't breathe when playing actively with his grandchildren. What might your grandfather be experiencing, and what should he do about it?

G℮ Online

For more information on health careers, visit Career Corner at **glencoe.com.**

Fact or Fiction?

Answers

1. True
2. False. Of the two types of diabetes, type 2 is more preventable by controlling body fatness.
3. True

 Writing Paragraphs will vary.

page 468. **14.** Saturated fat **15.** Lung cancer **16.** A tumor that is noncancerous, or non-harmful. **17.** Smoking, radiation, diet, alcohol consumption, physical activity **18.** Lung cancer, larynx, mouth, esophagus, urinary bladder, kidney, pancreas **19.** **C**hange in bowel or bladder habits, **A** sore; **U**nusual bleeding; **T**hickening or lump; Indigestion; **O**bvious change in wart or mole; **N**agging cough; **S**udden weight loss **20.** When every cancer cell is removed or wiped out. **21.–25.** Answers will vary.

CHAPTER 18

Dating, Commitment, and Marriage

Sections

1. **Infatuation or Mature Love?**
2. **How to Develop a Healthy Relationship**

All people need close relationships with others. It is important to share even simple daily life events with someone else. It is important to talk about problems, to voice our opinions, and to hear others' opinions. Loving, close relationships with family and friends are extremely important. During the teen years, you may start thinking about dating. Dating can be a wonderful way to get to know another person. Love relationships are more than infatuation. **Love** is *affection, attachment, devotion*. Such relationships can be fulfilling, but a young person's self-growth and healthy development can be achieved without such a relationship. This chapter looks at these relationships from dating through commitment and marriage.

Fact or Fiction?

What Do You Think?

Is each statement true or false? If you think it's false, explain what's true.

1. You can tell when love is real because it hits you in an instant, whether or not you want to be in love.
2. The best way to learn how to date may not be by dating but by attending social functions.
3. Couples in healthy, intimate relationships spend all their free time together.

 Writing What does love mean to you? Write a list of words or sentences to define what love means to you. During the lesson, refer to your list and make changes to your definition as you learn more about commitment and relationships.

(Answers on page 513)

Go Online

Visit **glencoe.com** and complete the Life Choice Inventory for Chapter 18.

Infatuation or Mature Love?

The first step in learning how to have a strong, close love relationship is learning what one is. "Am I really in love, or is this just infatuation?" **Infatuation** is *the state of being completely carried away by unreasoning passion or attraction.* If you have ever asked yourself this question, you're not alone. Take a look at **Figure 18.2** to find some clues.

Recognizing Infatuation and Love

MAIN IDEA ▶ Infatuation is an all-consuming desire for a partner. Mature love is a strong attachment to someone a person knows very well.

It is natural to feel infatuation at times, especially in the teen years, when the feelings of attraction are brand new. Infatuation can be part of learning about love. Some relationships that begin as infatuation later develop into love. However, relationships built solely on infatuation usually end when the fantasies on which they are built fade away.

Vocabulary

love
infatuation
mature love
intimacy

■ **Figure 18.1** *Mature love takes time to develop, and is based on friendship and sharing. What are three clues that a relationship is based on mature love?*

Caption Answer: It develops gradually with someone who shares interests similar to yours. You enjoy spending time with the other person, but do not feel that you must be with that person during all of your free time.

Figure 18.2 — Is It Love or Just Infatuation?

Infatuation	Mature Love
Usually develops at the beginning of relationship	Develops gradually through learning about the other person
Sexual attraction is central	Warm affection and friendship are central
Characterized by urgency, intensity, sexual desire, and anxiety	Characterized by calmness, peacefulness, empathy, support, and tolerance of partner
Driven by excitement of being involved with a person whose character is not fully known	Driven by deep attachment and extensive knowledge of positive and negative qualities
Extreme absorption in partner	Wanting to be together without obsession
Insecurity, distrust, lack of confidence, feeling of being threatened	Security, trust, confidence, unthreatened feeling
Partner remains unexamined so as not to spoil the dream	Thorough knowledge of partner, mature acceptance of imperfections
Based on fantasy	Based on reality
Consuming, often exhausting	Energizing in a healthy way
Low self-esteem (looking to partner for validation and affirmation of self-worth)	High self-esteem (each person has sense of self-worth with or without partner)
Each needs the other to feel complete	Relationship enhances the self, but person can feel complete without relationship
Discomfort with individual differences	Individually accepted
Each often tears down or criticizes the other	Each brings out best in partner
Partners need to rush things, like sex or marriage; sense of urgency so as not to lose partner	Partners are patient and feel no need to rush events of relationship; sense of security; no fear of losing partner
One is threatened by other's individual growth	Each encourages the other's growth
Relationship not enduring, because it lacks firm foundation	Relationship is enduring, sustaining—based on strong foundation of friendship

Unlike infatuation, **mature love** is *a strong affection for, and a deep attachment to, a person whose character the partner knows well*. The person accepts and tolerates the partner's negative qualities. Mature love involves a *decision* to be devoted to a person. It also requires emotional **intimacy**, *being very close and familiar, as in relationships involving private and personal sharing*. This is not the same thing as physical, sexual intimacy.

Intimacy is probably the most important part of a love relationship. This kind of intimacy builds slowly as two people become close to each other. Two intimate people reveal, a little at a time, the parts of themselves that they don't share with everyone. Both people are open and trusting with each other.

The idea that some things must develop slowly might seem hard to people in our fast-paced society. Most times, therefore, they rush relationships. They may make the mistake of trying to substitute physical, sexual intimacy, which can be available right away, for emotional intimacy, which takes time to grow. Emotional intimacy takes time to develop.

Reviewing the Vocabulary

Review the vocabulary on page 494. Then answer these questions.

1. _____ is affection, attachment, devotion.

2. A strong affection for, and an enduring, deep attachment to, a person whose character the partner knows well is called _____.

Reviewing the Facts

3. Analyze. What is the problem with relationships built solely on infatuation?

4. Explain. Explain why intimacy is so important in a love relationship.

5. Describe. Describe the difference between physical intimacy and psychological intimacy.

Writing Critically

6. Persuasive. After studying **Figure 18.2**, "Is It Love or Just Infatuation?," think of someone you know well. Do you think most of the person's relationships are mature love or infatuation? Why do you think the person's relationships are this way? Do you think the person should change his or her relationships? If so, how?

For more vocabulary practice, play the eFlashcards game at **glencoe.com**.

Answers to Section Review:

1. Love

2. Mature love

3. The relationship usually ends when the fantasies fade away.

4. When people are intimate they share both the good and bad parts about themselves to their partner. They build trust with one another.

5. Physical intimacy means sexual intimacy. Emotional intimacy is when two people share each other's private thoughts and feelings to one another to build a level of trust.

6. Answers will vary.

How to Develop a Healthy Relationship

No two relationships are exactly alike or develop in just the same way. However, healthy relationships have some things in common. Each partner in a healthy relationship must have a positive self-image. Once you feel strong and sure of yourself, you are better able to know what to look for in a partner.

Stages of Healthy Relationships

MAIN IDEA ▶ Healthy intimate relationships grow in stages.

Relationships develop in stages, such as those listed in **Figure 18.3**. They cannot be rushed. Once you find an appropriate partner, do not give in to the temptation to try to "hurry things along" by skipping the early phases of development. These early times provide the foundation of a strong relationship later on. Be patient.

Vocabulary

- date
- sexual intercourse
- external pressures
- internal pressures
- thrill seekers
- marriage
- stranger rape
- date rape

Figure 18.3 — The Stages of a Love Relationship

Love relationships usually follow these stages in their development:

Stage	What Happens
Stage 1: Attraction	Something about the person catches your attention. You are attracted to each other.
Stage 2: Friendship	You and the person enjoy activities together such as movies and concerts. You plan those activities together. During this stage, you explore each other's characteristics. Each is on "best behavior," so commitments are not appropriate yet.
Stage 3: Close friendship	You learn about each other's feelings and values. You begin to discover each other's emotional and spiritual tendencies. At this stage, the relationship may progress or retreat.
Stage 4: Intimate friendship	You both reveal your faults. By this time, each trusts the other's acceptance, because the true self of each—complete with faults—has been seen by the other. The couple may decide to "go steady" or may relax back into being close friends.
Stage 5: Mature love	Each partner continues developing socially, intellectually, emotionally, and spiritually. The degree of closeness of mature love makes conflict likely, but the partners learn to resolve conflict in healthy ways. (The Health Skills sidebar, "How to Resolve Conflicts," presented in Chapter 2 on page 35, describes healthy ways of resolving conflicts.)

What Should I Look For in a Partner?

MAIN IDEA ▶ Some people are available for relationships, but others are not. Choose carefully.

In thinking about a person who interests you, make sure that the person has time and energy available for love. Such people:

- Are not involved in other love relationships.
- Have not just recently broken up with someone else.
- Are open to being in a relationship with you.
- Are free of chemical or psychological addictions.
- Have time to devote to a relationship.
- Respect themselves and others.
- Are close to you geographically—they live in your city or state. Long distance relationships are difficult because the couple is not able to spend enough time together to learn about the other person's likes and dislikes.

■ **Figure 18.4** *When considering whether a person might be compatible with you, observe how the person interacts with others. What are some other things to look for when seeking out someone who is compatible with you?*

Caption Answer: The person is not involved in another love relationship, is open to a relationship with you, and has high self-esteem.

In addition, the person must be compatible with you in terms of basic social values and beliefs. To evaluate these factors, see if you can honestly answer yes to the following questions:

- *Does the person have several close friends?* A person who has learned to keep and enjoy close friendships can put this talent to work in a love relationship.

- *If the relationship ended, would you still want that person as a friend?* Without friendship, the relationship may crumble during times of conflict.

- *Are you happy with the way the person treats other people?* Watch how the person treats others. If the person treats others badly, think about whether you would want to be treated that way. That person may treat you well during the courtship phase of your relationship, but probably will not as you get to know each other better.

Dating

MAIN IDEA ▶ Possibly the best way of learning how to date is through attending social gatherings in a group setting.

During adolescence, teens may find themselves attracted to people they'd thought of only as classmates or friends. This is a good time to develop a set of personal guidelines for healthy dating relationships. To **date** is *to engage in social events designed to allow people to explore their compatibility and to get to know each other*. During the teen years, dating takes on more importance. Not everyone dates, however. Some teens choose not to date because they're shy around people they like. Others may choose not to date because they have other interests or time commitments.

Dating Can Be Fun

While dating may be fun, it is not entirely stress-free. A couple's first date, for example, may lead to thoughts of self-doubt and worry that the person may not like you. Those are normal thoughts and feelings. Don't let them discourage you from dating. Those who date learn how to communicate with many different types of people—a useful skill throughout life.

It is natural to feel nervous when going out with someone for the first time. The best way to ensure that a date will go well is to be open to the possibility that you will be forming a friendship, not a lifelong relationship. Possibly the best way of learning how to date is not through dating at all, but through attending social gatherings in group settings. Read the Health Skills sidebar, "Meeting New People," for some ideas on expanding your possibilities.

Health Skills

Meeting New People

Try these suggestions to meet new people.

1. Join a youth group (try service clubs or a school activity).

2. Take up a hobby, such as dancing or photography.

3. Create a group around a common theme—for example, a foreign language club or a movie group.

4. Learn to play a sport.

5. Volunteer time in your community.

6. Learn to play a musical instrument, and join a school or community band.

7. Get physically fit, get enough sleep, and eat healthfully.

8. Be friendly; reach out to others. Be yourself; don't try to impress anyone.

An especially useful form of dating is a double date or group date, in which two or more couples go out together. This creates a casual and safe environment in which to get to know people. A group of people provides safety and reduces stress. Also, it's important to always let parents or other responsible adults know where you are going, with whom, and when you expect to return home.

Online Friendships

The Internet offers new opportunities to create friendships. It can be a rewarding to meet people in other parts of the world and learn about other cultures. Online friendships, however, can be dangerous. It may be difficult to know if online friends are truthful. Someone who may claim to be a teen may actually be an adult. When communicating online, never reveal any personal information, or pictures of yourself. Never arrange a face-to-face meeting or share your phone number. If an online friend says anything to make you feel uncomfortable, tell a parent or trusted adult immediately.

Commitment and Sexual Pressure

A couple who has dated for a long time may decide to become an exclusive dating couple. The couple agrees to date each other only. Being committed can ease the stress of dating new people. However, it can bring disadvantages as well. While young people who go steady may feel secure, they may also feel tied down. They lose the opportunity to date a variety of others. They also may focus on the growth of the relationship rather than their own growth. If preserving the relationship becomes more important than the emotional health of the individuals, this can diminish self-worth.

■ **Figure 18.5** *Dating is a good way to start getting to know somebody. How can dating improve your social well-being?*

Caption Answer: Dating can help you develop good communication skills.

Some dating situations may increase the likelihood of being pressured to participate in sexual activity. This topic will be discussed at length later in this chapter. Many times teens will fear that if they refuse **sexual intercourse**, *the reproductive act between the sexes*, their partners will find someone else. Unwanted pressure may also include any other sexual activity. Discuss your limits with your dating partner. Clear and honest communication will help your dating partner respect your wishes.

Advantages of Sexual Abstinence

MAIN IDEA ▶ Abstinence from sexual activity helps a new relationship to grow in a healthy way.

Many of the sexual feelings teens experience occur as a result of the body's release of hormones. You don't have control over the feelings caused by your hormones, but you do have complete control over how you respond to them.

By choosing abstinence from sexual activity, you are taking responsibility for your well-being. Abstinence is a deliberate decision to avoid high-risk behaviors, including sexual activity. Many teens choose abstinence because it is the only 100 percent sure way to eliminate health risks associated with sexual activity.

Class Discussion

Discuss: Ask students how engaging in abstinence could promote a healthy intimate relationship rather than detract from it. Encourage all students to share their thoughts openly.

Health Risks

Teenage sexual activity poses health risks. Teens who are sexually active may contract sexually transmitted diseases. The only sure way to prevent sexually transmitted diseases is to abstain from sexual activity.

Teen Pregnancy

Teen pregnancy is another health risk associated with sexual activity. Here are some of the frequent and serious problems resulting from teen pregnancies:

- Interruption of education
- Early marriages with a high likelihood of divorce
- Continuing legal responsibility to support a child
- High risks of poverty
- Low infant survival rates
- Lifetime tendencies toward having more than the average number of children

The costs to society in terms of lost education, lost earning power, and increased need for support of the individuals are staggering. Again, abstinence from sexual intercourse is the only guarantee against teen pregnancy.

■ **Figure 18.6** *A psychologically intimate relationship is most fulfilling. How can abstinence help develop a lasting relationship?*

Caption Answer: Abstinence allows a relationship to grow through psychological intimacy rather than sexual intimacy.

Abstinence Is Freedom

For teens, as for many others, sexual abstinence can reduce worry and can create a feeling of freedom. Abstinence allows teens to grow and develop without interruption by diseases or pregnancy. Abstinence can also allow time for the growth of a healthy intimate relationship.

How to Cope with Sexual Pressures

MAIN IDEA ▶ Pressure to be sexually active arises both internally and externally.

You often hear people talk about the "pressures" to be sexually active. They point to peer pressure, images in movies, popular music, TV, and even pressure from a partner to become sexually active. Another source of pressure comes in the form of product advertisements (see the Consumer Skills

Activity on this page). All of these **external pressures**, *messages from society, peers, and others that pressure people to be sexually active*, can be difficult to deal with.

Even more difficult to deal with are pressures that you put on yourself. Human beings have a natural, biological drive to reproduce. This normal drive creates **internal pressures**, *a person's biological urges toward being sexually active*, that can be hard to deal with. During the teen years these pressures may seem intense as teens' bodies mature, producing more hormones that create these feelings.

Thinking Ahead

The challenge to couples who are not yet mature and committed is to find ways of expressing love and sexual feelings so that both people benefit. Any activity that makes the other person feel loved, and that takes some extra thought or effort on the part of the giver, is satisfying for both people. Think of how you felt the last time a friend gave you a hug, gave you a small gift, did you a favor, or confided in you. The good feelings those gestures brought were a genuine form of love. You can express your love in all sorts of caring ways without having sexual intercourse.

Consumer Skills Activity

1. Answers will vary.

Consumer SKILLS ACTIVITY

Love and Sex in Advertisements

Most people want to be part of special love relationships. Advertisers use this desire for love to help sell their products. Consumers who see the ads on TV, in magazines, or other media, believe if they use the product advertised, they will be loved. They try to make consumers think that certain products can make people more attractive, sexier, more self-confident, and therefore more likely to be loved. Many such ads are aimed directly at teens. A perfume commercial shows physically beautiful people drawn to each other by fragrance. A breath mint is sold as "social insurance." The ads say that you never know when you'll meet someone special, so why take a chance on having less-than-perfect breath?

Buying a product may seem like an easy way to improve one's self. However, the only way to truly become more attractive involves the work of developing healthy self-esteem. With self-esteem, you are willing to meet new people. This helps you expand your social network by making new friends.

 Writing

1. Name some characteristics of people who are influenced by advertisements that promise increased attractiveness. Why do you think people with these characteristics are most likely to be influenced?

Figure 18.7

The STOP Method for Maintaining Sexual Abstinence

S—Stop
Stop the activity that threatens to get out of control. This first step may be difficult but it is critical for remaining in control.

T—Think
Analyze what is happening.
Does your present behavior agree with your values?
Would your parents approve?
Develop in advance a list of questions meaningful to you.

O—Other Activities
If your behavior feels out of control—if it conflicts with your values—direct the energy of the moment into other activities (going out for ice cream or to a movie, for example).

P—Plan
Make the next time easier by planning how to remain in charge. Decide not to plan dates that involve too much time alone (for example, plan to double date or date in public places). Commit to using this method every time you begin to feel out of control.

To express sexual feelings in appropriate ways, it is necessary to decide *in advance* what course of action is right for you. People who approach a situation without a clearly determined plan may find themselves tempted by sexual situations in the thrill of the moment. *People who are especially likely to take chances in exchange for momentary excitement—* **thrill seekers**—must fight especially hard against these temptations.

Other Activities

To cope with the desire that accompanies sexual attraction, try channeling sexual energy into other activities. Instead of using will power to oppose the sexual drive, use it to shift gears to another activity. Dancing, sports, or walking are examples of activities that can release sexual energy. Some people feel that writing, speaking, singing, painting, or other expressive activities can also serve this purpose.

When a situation threatens to get out of control, some find it helpful to say to themselves the word STOP—**S**top, **T**hink, **O**ther activities, **P**lan to abide by their vow of abstinence (see **Figure 18.7**). Sexual intimacy is too important to just let happen. Remember STOP, to give yourself time to think.

Class Discussion

Analyze: Ask students if they believe this STOP strategy could help people abstain from sexual intercourse. Ask them to develop two questions that they would use in the "Think" step. Explain that the questions should help them see that what they're about to do may be something that they would regret later. Write the questions on the board and discuss.

Breaking Up and How to Cope

MAIN IDEA ▶ When coping with a breakup, expect to feel grief.

More often than not, the relationships formed during the teen years do not last. This is true for many reasons. Sometimes partners who are sincere may change and outgrow certain relationships. Most times, breakups are best for both partners, although it may not feel that way at the moment.

While no one really dies of a broken heart, the pain, depression, and stress that can follow breaking up may make people physically ill. Stress weakens the immune system and so can make illness likely. The breakup of a special love relationship can be difficult to cope with.

One thing you can do is to prepare to experience grief—whether for the loss of the loved one, or for loss of a relationship. The Q&A section at the end of Chapter 5 presents the stages of grief. Give yourself the time you need to grieve fully. It is natural and normal to feel intense loneliness and pain. However, those feelings fade with time. A mistake a person may make during this painful time is to quickly seek a new partner. The temptation to do so may be strong, but resist it. You may not have vision clear enough to judge a new partner. Give yourself six months to a year to heal.

People in grief often need affection. Activities and friends can fill the void. When you feel like your old self again, you may be ready for a new relationship.

Commitment

MAIN IDEA ▶ Love requires commitment and working together.

Anyone choosing to have a long-term monogamous relationship makes a commitment to another person. A commitment is a promise to make a long-term choice, in the face of many possible options, with the knowledge that the relationship will not always be perfect. Choosing a life partner is serious. Developing a long-term, intimate bond that truly satisfies both partners involves much more than simply loving each other, the wish to do so, or stating that such a bond exists.

What *does* hold a partnership together? Psychologist Carl Rogers agrees that people should commit to working together through the changes of their relationship. **Figure 18.8** on page 506 shows additional factors. To this list of elements of partnership we would add *independence*. The person who finds ways to meet many of his own needs *outside* the paired relationship

Health Skills

Developing a Healthy Intimate Relationship

To establish a healthy intimate relationship:

1. Learn the difference between a healthy intimate relationship and infatuation.

2. Build your sense of self-worth, or self-esteem.

3. Make sure your partner has time and energy for love. Make sure you do too.

4. Give yourself time to get to know new people socially, intellectually, emotionally, and spiritually.

5. Continue to spend time with other friends. Maintain your identity.

6. Let sexual involvement wait for commitment. Marriage is the highest form of commitment.

7. Know the meaning of commitment.

8. Explore your expectations of marriage.

9. Learn to work through conflict in healthy ways.

Figure 18.8   **Elements of Partnership According to Rogers**

Grow	We see the process of change as necessary and desirable.
Each	We are both doing it.
Commit	We won't back out.
Working	It takes work, and we are willing to work.
Together	It is cooperative—not one for the other, but each with the other.
Changing	We know we cannot keep it as it was in the beginning. We have to take the risk of growing and learning.
Present, currently	It is not just that we promised each other long ago that we would do this. We are doing it now.
Enriching	The rewards are also present. We feel them today.

Caption Answer: Both partners are committed, both partners are willing to work on the relationship, the relationship is cooperative.

■ **Figure 18.9** *In a real marriage, people work things out. Name three elements of a successful partnership.*

will be most successful at pairing. Recall the needs described in Maslow's scheme in Chapter 3. You cannot ask your partner to provide total security—whether emotional, financial, or physical. You must stand on your own feet and provide your own security. You are the only person you will never lose. Understanding and practicing self-sufficiency is a major factor in maintaining healthy, lasting relationships.

Marriage

MAIN IDEA ▶ Marriage is the highest form of commitment in our society.

Did you ever wonder what happened to Cinderella and the Prince after they married? Did they really live happily ever after? At times, every couple has disagreements. A mature couple learns how to resolve problems without harming the relationship before entering into a lifetime commitment. **Marriage** is *the institution that joins a man and a woman by agreement for the purpose of creating and maintaining a family*. The idea that marriage will magically make people happy is probably the most destructive idea that partners can have. Marriage requires good communication, emotional maturity, and sharing a life with someone who has similar values and interests.

APPLYING Health Skills

Stress Management

➤ Objectives

- Apply conflict resolution strategies to a marital conflict.
- Describe a solution to a marital conflict that satisfies both spouses.

A Moving Experience

Barb and Richard Johnson have been married for ten years and have two young children. Barb works outside the home, and Richard works in his home office. Richard's parents live a few blocks away and care for the children during the day.

When Barb came home from work last night, she announced that her employer wants her to take a different job in another city. If she accepts the offer, she will get a raise in pay. Barb is excited about changing jobs, increasing the family income, and moving to a new city. Richard, on the other hand, doesn't want to move. He really likes their current house and living close to his mom and dad. Richard also worries about who would care for their children if they move. The couple argued about the move for more than two hours last night, but they didn't resolve the conflict.

➤ Identify the Problem

1. Why are the Johnsons in conflict?

➤ Form an Action Plan

2. Use "I" messages to state the conflict from each spouse's point of view.
3. What questions could Barb and Richard ask one another to better understand each other's point of view?
4. Describe a solution that might satisfy both Barb and Richard.

➤ What Did You Learn?

5. What did you learn about the importance of good communication in a marriage by trying to resolve this conflict?

Applying Health Skills

1. Barb wants to take a different job in another city but Richard doesn't want to move.

2. Answers will vary, but should include "I" messages from each spouse's perspective.

3. Barb might ask Richard what he loves about their current house and living nearby his parents. Richard might ask Barb why the new job is so appealing.

4. Answers will vary.

5. Answers will vary.

The highest form of commitment between two people in our society is marriage, a relationship based on these ideas:

- The relationship is permanent, or at least permanence is something the partners will work for.
- The partners will be most important to each other. No other relationship with another person will take a higher place.

Marriage is never the end of the story, as in fairy tales. It is the beginning.

Working Through Conflict

MAIN IDEA ▶ Work through conflict by clearly defining and addressing each problem while honoring the other person.

Partners may believe that anger and conflict have no place in a happy, committed relationship and so may hide their negative feelings. In reality, every human relationship has conflicts. How partners handle those conflicts can determine whether the relationship grows or ends.

Even couples in healthy marriages conflict occasionally because no two people will always agree on everything. Some common issues that cause problems in marriages include:

- Differences in spending and saving habits.
- Conflicting loyalties involving family and friends.
- Lack of communication.
- Decisions about having children and arranging child care.

In a successful marriage, both partners respect, trust, and care for each other. Conflicts are resolved fairly without damaging the self-esteem of the other partner.

Writing Activity

Recall and Analyze: Ask students to write about a conflict they have experienced in a relationship. The paper should include the cause of the conflict, how each person reacted, and if it was resolved successfully. The last paragraph should describe how things could have turned out if handled differently.

■ **Figure 18.10** *Every relationship has conflicts. Name some common issues that cause problems in marriage.*

Caption Answer: Differences in spending and saving habits, lack of communication

SECTION 2 Review

Reviewing the Vocabulary

Review the vocabulary on page 497. Then answer these questions.

1. To engage in social events designed to allow people to get to know one another is known as a _____.

2. _____ is the institution that joins a man and woman by agreement for the purpose of creating and maintaining a family.

3. _____ are people who take chances in exchange for momentary excitement.

4. _____ are messages from society, peers, and others that pressure people to have sexual intercourse.

Reviewing the Facts

5. **Identify.** What two things do healthy relationships have in common?

6. **List.** List one advantage and one disadvantage of going steady.

7. **Describe.** Describe the pressures teens face to have sexual intercourse.

8. **Explain.** What is the most destructive idea people have about marriage?

9. **Describe.** What are some common issues that cause problems in marriages?

10. **Explain.** Explain why physical aggression doesn't clear the air.

Writing Critically

11. **Expository.** Your friend, Sally, is thinking about dropping out of high school to get married. What advice would you give Sally? Why would you give her that advice? Would your advice be different if Sally were a male named Jim?

G⊙ Online

For more vocabulary practice, play the Concentration game at **glencoe.com**.

1. Date
2. Marriage
3. Thrill seekers
4. External pressures
5. Each person must have a positive self image, and both partners realize that love develops in stages.
6. It provides relief from the stress of dating new people; however, it may make teens feel tied down.
7. External pressures from peers and others, and internal pressures or biological urges to be sexually active
8. The idea that marriage will magically make you feel happy is very destructive.
9. Differences in spending and saving habits, lack of communication
10. Physical aggression causes the partner to withdraw from conflict rather than resolving the issues.
11. Answers will vary.

Q&A Sexual Violence Prevention

Understand and Apply Read the conversation below, and then complete the writing exercise that follows.

Sexual violence is a serious crime. One of every six females and one in every 33 males have suffered a rape or attempted rape. Other sexual violence, such as touching inappropriately, occurs even more frequently.

Most people know about **stranger rape**—*sexual assault by a stranger.* No less dangerous, and much more common, is **date rape**, *sexual assault by a known person in a dating situation* (also called acquaintance rape).

Q: Isn't stranger rape completely different from date rape?

A: No, both are crimes of sexual violence. The only difference between rape by an unknown attacker and date rape is that in the latter type, the attacker and victim know each other. In both instances, the attacker forces sex on the victim.

Q: How serious is rape?

A: Legally, rape is considered very serious, deserving jail penalties and fines. Rape is also serious physically and emotionally. The rapist may be armed and may kill or injure the victim. The rapist may carry sexually transmitted diseases—even HIV.

Beyond the physical threats, rape is a serious threat to the victim's mental health. Rage, shock, terror, and emotional pain that can last for years are all common in victims of rape.

Q: Are date rapes really rape?

A: Yes, date rape is a crime. With respect to any sexual activity, saying the word "no" means stop. When either partner is uncomfortable and says no, all sexual activity should stop.

Q: Is rape the only kind of sexual violence?

A: No. Significant crimes of sexual violence may not include physical contact. For example, the perpetrator may expose his or her genital organs to a child or other innocent person. Verbal sexual threats are considered sexual abuse, too.

Q: How big a problem is date rape?

A: Date rape is a common form of sexual violence in our society. Compared with the incidence of rape in many other countries, the United States has a high rape frequency.

The social costs of rape are enormous. Not only do victims suffer all the outcomes already mentioned, but courts, jails, and law enforcement systems are straining with the burden of rape prevention and punishment for sex crimes.

Q: What other factors play a role in rape?

A: One theory blames the media. Movies, television, music videos, and romance novels written in this country often suggest that women want to be raped. The media plant the idea that when a woman says no, she will change her mind and say yes if a man overpowers her. This idea is completely false. No normal person wants to be raped, and *no* means *no*.

Q: I remember reading about a connection between drugs, alcohol, and rape. How are these connected?

A: The abuse of drugs or alcohol seriously impairs people's judgment. This results in two effects that make rape more likely. First, alcohol and many drugs reduce inhibitions—even inhibitions against rape in someone considering the idea. Second, drugs and alcohol make people groggy. If a high enough dose is consumed, an extremely dangerous situation occurs when the person passes out. Someone who didn't plan a rape might commit one if a potential victim becomes unconscious from drugs or alcohol.

To protect yourself, don't agree to go out alone with people you don't know well. Accept drinks only from people you know you can trust. Once a drink is opened in a public place, don't let it out of your sight.

Q: How often is rape reported?

A: Sadly, it is likely that fewer than 10 percent of rapes are ever reported. Some rape victims do not report the crimes because they feel ashamed, as though they somehow brought the attack on. It is important to report rape or any type of sexual contact that is unwanted. A person who rapes is a criminal who has behaved in a way that is against the law. It's even less likely that a date rape will be reported. Many times, the person who is raped is reluctant to report the assault. The person may believe that he or she did something to provoke the attack. Date rape is a crime though, and should be reported to the authorities.

If more rapes were reported, more rapists would be convicted. It takes courage, but reporting rapes is important. Even if the victim does not want to press charges against the rapist, the rape should be reported. That way, the statements will be on record in case the victim decides to prosecute later.

Q: How can a woman protect herself from becoming a victim of rape?

A: Avoid putting yourself in a situation where rape may occur. Plan on meeting friends in open, public places. Avoid individual dating until you feel comfortable with a new person. Avoiding drug and alcohol use will help you react appropriately if you feel uncomfortable.

Finally, crimes of sexual violence are serious, both legally and personally. If you experience any sort of sexual violence, report it. If rape occurs, report it and seek medical treatment immediately.

 Writing Write a dialogue between two teens at a party. One teen is trying to persuade the other to go somewhere alone together. The other teen uses refusal skills to avoid the threat of sexual violence.

Reviewing Vocabulary

Use the vocabulary terms listed below to complete the following statements.

date rape

internal pressures

date

stranger rape

infatuation

1. _____ is the state of being completely carried away by unreasoning passion or attraction.

2. _____ means to engage in social events designed to allow people to get to know each other.

3. A person's internal biological urges toward being sexually active are called _____.

4. Sexual assault by a stranger is called _____.

5. _____ is sexual assault by a known person in a dating situation.

Recalling Key Facts and Ideas

Section 1

6. **List.** List five signs of infatuation.

7. **Identify.** List five signs of mature love.

Section 2

8. **List.** List and define the stages of a love relationship.

9. **Identify.** Identify and describe characteristics to look for in a potential partner.

10. **Explain.** How is double dating especially useful when you just begin to date someone new?

11. **Analyze.** It is said that abstinence gives freedom to the people in a relationship. What sorts of freedom does abstinence give?

12. **Describe.** Describe how to establish a healthy intimate relationship.

13. **List.** How are conflicts resolved in a successful marriage?

Writing Critically

14. **Persuasive. Figure 18.8** in this chapter deals with whether a marriage will work. Do you think couples who are going to marry should consider these elements in advance? If so, why? If not, why not?

15. **Expository.** Acquaintance or date rape is a serious problem in society today. Reread the Q&A section on pages 510—511. Why are males getting mixed signals from females? What roles do the media play? What are we being taught about sexual behaviors, and how might misconceptions lead to date rape? Discuss how education might help prevent sexual violence.

Activities

16. Complete the following sentence on a piece of paper: "Love is . . ." Write all of the class members' answers on the board and compare the many ways love is defined. Discuss your response with the rest of your class.

17. Cut out the personal advertisements in the paper. Discuss why you think this is a good way to meet people or why you

1. Infatuation 2. Date 3. Internal pressures 4. Stranger rape 5. Date rape 6. Extreme absorption in another, based on fantasy, all-consuming, discomfort with individual differences, need to rush relationship 7. Develops gradually, driven by deep attachment, wanting to be together without obsession,

energizing in a healthy way, each encourages the other 8. Stage 1: Attraction; Stage 2: Casual friendship; Stage 3: Close friendship; Stage 4: Intimate friendship; Stage 5: Mature love 9. Person is not involved in another love relationship, has time for a relationship, free from chemical or psychologi-

think it is a bad way to meet people. List the pros and cons to share with your class.

18. Write an editorial for your school newspaper on date rape. Be sure to include how to prevent date rape in your paper.

19. Interview two happily married couples: one couple that has been married at least 30 years and another couple that has been married for less than five years. Ask them what the keys are to their happy marriages. Are their lists similar? What conclusions can you draw about happy marriages?

20. Describe the characteristics you consider important, first in a dating situation, then in a marriage partner. Use attributes like looks, personality traits, educational background, age, religious beliefs, ethnic group or race, values (political, ethical), and interests. Are your lists for dates different from your lists for marriage? If so, how and why are they different?

21. Go to your local law enforcement agency and write down the number of rape cases that were reported in your community for the year. Are the numbers surprising to you? Report this to the rest of your class.

22. Write a one-page essay on the perfect relationship. In your essay include qualities and values on which you place high priority and which you would expect the other person to value highly as well. Describe what you would bring to the relationship and what you would expect the other person to bring to the relationship. At the end of your essay, tell whether you think the relationship you described is realistic. Explain why you think the way you do.

Making Decisions about Health

23. Jerome hasn't had a date in a long time. He feels jealous when he hears about his friends' relationships. They aren't all perfect, but at least they provide some companionship. There must be something wrong with Jerome; he's just not the likable type. How might Jerome build up his self-esteem at a time like this? What changes in his attitude might he make and how? What constructive actions could he take to ease his loneliness?

Go Online

For fitness and health tips, visit the Fitness Zone at **glencoe.com**.

Fact or Fiction?

Answers

1. False. You can tell when love is real because it develops slowly through the conscious choices of both partners.
2. True.
3. False. Couples in healthy, intimate relationships maintain separate interests, as well as shared ones.

 Writing Answers will vary.

cal addictions, are open to a relationship with you **10.** Double dating creates a safe, stress-free environment. **11.** Provides the freedom to develop close, emotional intimacy **12.** Learn the difference between infatuation and mature love, build

your self-esteem, make sure you have time to commit to the relationship, get to know new people, maintain your identity. **13.** Clearly define and address each problem while honoring the other person's feelings. **14–23.** Answers will vary.

CHAPTER
19
Family Life

Sections

What is your family like? **Family** is *a group of people who are related by adoption, blood, or marriage, and are committed to each other.* Do you have any **siblings**, *two or more people with one or more parents in common?* Do both your parents live with you? Grandparents? Stepparents? **Stepparents** are *people who marry into a family after a biological parent departs through death or divorce.* What activities do your family members share? What values are important to your family? All of these things and more define the nature of your own unique family.

This chapter begins by describing types of families and the ways in which they meet their members' needs as they change with time. It discusses issues of respect, trust, and communication, which serve as the foundation stones of a healthy family life. The chapter also includes issues that some families may face such as divorce, addiction, codependency, or abuse. The last section covers society's support of the family through changing times.

Fact or Fiction?

What Do You Think?

Is each statement true or false? If you think it's false, explain what's true.

1. A person's values are most powerfully influenced by the values of his or her family.
2. It's natural for parents to distrust their teenage children.
3. People who abuse their own children are most likely to have been abused themselves during childhood.

 Writing Think about the word *family*. Write a paragraph to explain what a family means to you. Make additions and changes to your paragraph as you learn more about families.

(Answers on page 541)

Go Online

Visit **glencoe.com** and complete the Life Choice Inventory for Chapter 19.

The Nature of the Family

When people say the word *family*, what exactly do they mean? After all, families come in all shapes and sizes. **Figure 19.2** on page 517 describes only some of the many possibilities. Wherever people live together, they form some type of family. Families form the building blocks from which each society is made. Without families, societies could not exist.

Family and Development

MAIN IDEA ▶ **Families have far-reaching effects upon their members.**

Families help to mold the personalities of their members. The influence of a child's family reaches far into the future, affecting the rest of that person's life story. Parents, siblings, aunts, uncles, and even babysitters are a child's first teachers. They teach the child about being human, about their values, and about whether or not others are to be loved and trusted. Years later, in adulthood, early family experiences still affect most people's outlooks on themselves and on the world. A child with a supportive, trusting, loving family often grows up secure with a sense of belonging and acceptance.

Vocabulary

family
siblings
stepparents
family identity

Class Activity

Recall: Give students one minute in which to write down all the benefits they can think of that families provide. When the minute is up, have students volunteer the benefits they thought of as you list them on the board. Discuss.

■ **Figure 19.1** *A family's identity is developed through rituals, such as eating meals together. What are some daily rituals you enjoy with your family?*

Caption Answer: My family likes to take walks after dinner.

Lifelong Influences

A person who remembers childhood as a painful time may experience lifelong difficulties, but may never fully understand why. An adult who grew up with an addicted or abusive parent, for example, may choose a series of unsupportive or abusive mates, repeating a familiar but destructive pattern learned during childhood. With the help of therapy or counselors, such a person may come to recognize these choices as part of a destructive pattern. With help, these patterns can be changed.

Triumph over Tragedy

Of course, many children from unsupportive families have overcome difficult childhoods to grow strong and stable, to excel, and to emerge as dependable adults. An important difference between those who overcome an unsupportive childhood and those who do not is a strong belief in their own ability to succeed. They have self-efficacy. This quality lies at the heart of personal change, and seems to be basic to most forms of success in life.

The Benefits of Family

MAIN IDEA ▶ Families provide for many physical and emotional needs of their members.

Why do we need our families? What benefits do they bring us? Our families meet needs that are basic to our existence. Our families provide us with our cultural heritage and traditions. They teach values to the younger generation. In addition, most families meet their members' needs for:

- Affection.
- Food.
- Clothing.
- Safety.
- Security.
- Shelter.

Families also meet the human need for belonging. We need our families, and our families need us.

Meeting the Need for Belonging

People everywhere share a common need to feel as if they are part of a group. Being part of a family creates this feeling. Each family develops a **family identity**, *a unique sense of belonging together as a unit*. Family members participate in the family's ways of doing things.

Figure 19.2

A Glossary of Types of Families

Stepfamily: A family created by remarriage after the death or divorce of a spouse; stepfamilies include a biological or adoptive parent and a stepparent, along with the children of one or both of them; also called *blended* or *combined families*.

Extended family: A family of parents, children, and other relatives, such as grandparents or aunts and uncles. The relatives may live in one household, or they may live close by and share responsibilities, such as childraising.

Foster family: A family formed when a government agency places a child in the temporary care of an adult or couple. The child's own parents may have died or for some reason cannot care for the child.

Married couple: A family consisting of two married adults.

Nontraditional family: A group of people who live together and offer support to one another.

Nuclear family: A mother and father and their natural or adopted children.

Single-parent family: One parent and his or her natural or adopted children.

Class Activity

Analyze: Assign students to groups and ask each group to imagine a society without families. What would that society be like? Have students create a creative presentation such as a skit or video to present their ideas. Discuss each group's presentation.

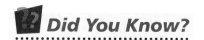

A family identity is maintained by:

- Keeping rituals, such as wishing each other a good night before sleeping, joining together at mealtimes, or hugging when members greet each other.
- Celebrating special occasions and cultural traditions together in the family's chosen ways.
- Learning to compromise and realizing that a family member's attitudes and behaviors affect the nature of the whole family, just as the family affects the individual member.
- Spending time together, and sharing activities and experiences.

Belonging extends beyond our families. Most of us join groups to help meet the need to belong. Circles of friends and social or hobby groups exist for this reason.

Teaching Values

Sometimes, parents formally teach values to their children. They sit them down and talk about the rules. More often, however, older people teach values to young people by the examples they set. Parents who attend religious services with their children convey the value of organized religion. Parents who work to protect the environment offer lessons in valuing the world we live in.

A serious mistake that some adults make is to underestimate the importance of their examples to young people. For example, if an adult tells a child that it is important to be honest, and the adult is caught cheating on his or her taxes, the young person gets the message that cheating is okay. Whether or not the child continues to cheat depends on many factors, of course, including her own tendencies and the values demonstrated by other important adults.

Children learn values from many sources other than their families. Schools, peers, magazines, television, and Internet websites may each convey a set of values, and any of these values may conflict with another. Children and teens who receive information of conflicting values may become confused and wonder which set of values is best for them. In this regard, the most powerful voice is still within the family. Parents and other adult family members can help eliminate confusion.

In addition to meeting the basic needs discussed in this section, many families emphasize spiritual and intellectual schooling. They give instruction in social skills. They may also make sure that everyone has some fun along the way. A healthy family also acts as a refuge from the outside world, a protected place to rest and relax, where members can just be themselves.

Figure 19.3   The Stages and Goals of a Family

Stage	Main Goal
1. Couple without children; creating a family	Develop trust in each other.
2. Family bearing children and rearing newborns, toddlers, and preschoolers.	Develop independence and self-direction in children.
3. Family with schoolchildren.	Develop in children a sense of industry, to allow them to work with steady effort.
4. Family with adolescent children.	Guide adolescent role development, assist identity development in teens.
5. Family with young adults at home or leaving home.	Maintain relationships with children who leave; renew the couple's relationship.
6. Couple without children, moving toward retirement; grandparenting.	Share talents and resources with others; take pride in accomplishments.
7. Aging couple; widows and widowers; grandparenting.	Maintain satisfaction with life; enjoy fulfillment and serenity.

Source: Adapted from E. Janosik and E. Green, Family Life: Process and Practice (Boston: Jones and Bartlett Publishers, 1992), p. 29.

The Life Stages of a Family

MAIN IDEA ▶ Families move through predictable stages.

Few families stay the same from year to year. Instead, they change and evolve in stages with passing time. As children grow, parents must adjust the amount of independence their children receive.

Forming a Family

Most new families form when a couple meets and falls in love. Their story often continues with a lifelong commitment and unfolds as children arrive, grow up, and finally leave home. No one can predict what twists and turns the plot of the family story will take. However, family stories are always interesting. **Figure 19.3** traces a family's progress through some typical stages.

Does your own family fit neatly into one of the stages in **Figure 19.3**? It may or may not. Because you are a teen, your family qualifies for Stage 4. However, you may have brothers or sisters who qualify your family for Stage 2, 3, or 5.

Family Goals

Through the years, a family must constantly seek new ways of meeting the changing needs of its members. Parents of a toddler must provide constant supervision to ensure the child's safety. As the child grows, however, they must loosen

Did You Know?

Sharing family stories is a great way to learn more about you and your family's past. Invite grandparents, aunts, uncles, parents, and others to share a special family story.

their control in order to help the child develop independence and make healthy decisions. The child, in turn, helps to meet the parents' needs for affection and loyalty. Each choice made by a family member contributes to or detracts from how well the family meets the needs of its members.

Family members must also attend to their own needs. For example, adults may save for their retirement (financial goals), teens may volunteer for good causes (spiritual and service goals), and grandparents may make time to be physically active each day (physical fitness goals). Families may have many goals, but meeting the basic ones listed in **Figure 19.3** goes a long way toward supporting the emotional well-being of the family members.

SECTION 1 Review

Reviewing the Vocabulary

Review the vocabulary on page 516. Then answer these questions.

1. Brothers and sisters are _____.
2. A _____ is maintained by families spending time together and celebrating special occasions in the family's chosen way.
3. A group of people who are related by adoption, blood, or marriage, and are committed to each other is called a _____.

Reviewing the Facts

4 List. List three influences a family has on individuals.
5. Explain. What are two main functions of families?
6. Describe. Through what sources do values enter the lives of children?
7. Identify. Identify the seven stages of family life.

Writing Critically

8. Expository. People sometimes join church groups, clubs, or other social groups to meet needs that are not being met by their families. What needs might be met by these groups? How would the groups meet these needs? Are there other ways these needs might be met? If so, what are they?

Go Online

For more vocabulary practice, play the eFlashcards game at **glencoe.com**.

Worksheets: A reproducible quiz for Section 1 is provided in the Teacher Classroom Resources.

1. Siblings
2. Family identity
3. Family
4. They teach the child about being human, about their values, and about whether or not others are to be loved and trusted, among other things.
5. They teach values to the younger generation as well as a sense of belonging.
6. Children learn values through the examples the adults around them set.
7. Couple without children; family bearing children and rearing children; family with schoolchildren; family with adolescent children; family with young adults at home or leaving home; couple without children, moving toward retirement; aging couple.
8. Answers will vary.

Getting Along with Others

Being part of a family isn't always easy. Conflicts are almost certain to arise among people who live close to one another. Common questions may arise such as: Which needs should be given highest priority? Is everyone being honest? Do we trust one another?

Interactions among family members can be more important than you might think. Handling a conflict with a family member can prepare you to handle conflicts with people in the larger world. In a family, you learn to give and take, to communicate your own needs while respecting those of others. These are skills that, once developed, prove invaluable through life—at work, at school, with friends, and eventually, with a future spouse or partner and family. Interactions affect the present too. Each kind word or supportive action by one member uplifts the whole family group. Each negative word or action brings the family down.

Issues of Trust and Honesty

MAIN IDEA ▶ **Being completely honest is the way to gain people's trust. Effective communication is essential to trust.**

There may have been a time when you thought, "How can I get my parents to trust me? They're always checking up on me!" This question may seem unanswerable. In truth, most parents *want* to trust teens. Parents want to think of their children as honest and trustworthy.

Those interested in gaining trust must learn this principle: trust grows in direct proportion to a person's honesty. This principle also operates in reverse: people who are not entirely honest quickly lose the trust of others.

It's difficult to know how to react to someone who hasn't always been honest in the past. When a teen has a history of dishonesty, a parent has no choice but to doubt the teen. How could a parent know whether or not the teen is telling the truth on any one occasion? Dishonesty—that is, intentionally hiding or changing the truth—creates doubt that grow and damages the parent-child relationship.

For example, your brother or sister has agreed to play softball with your team to fill in for an absent player. Game time rolls around, but your sibling doesn't show up. Your teammates are furious, and you must forfeit the game. On your way home, you see your sibling talking and laughing with other friends.

Vocabulary

sibling rivalry

Did You Know?

Four tips for being honest:
1. Never promise more than you can deliver.
2. Allow for emergencies.
3. Let others know what's going on.
4. Plan ahead.

Later, when you ask why your sibling missed the game, he or she replies, "Oh, I felt sick." Would you feel angry? Betrayed? Would you ever fully trust the person again?

Family members will likely forgive one another for such a slip in honesty, especially when the person apologizes and shows regret. Also, family members, or anyone who knows you well, is less likely to judge you for one lapse in judgement. You will be judged by your behavior over a period of time. With time, and with demonstrations of honesty, trust may eventually be restored. This healing of trust requires an honest discussion on the part of everyone.

To establish that you are honest and reliable, never promise more than you can reasonably deliver. If someone asks something unreasonable, don't agree to do it. Instead, explain why it isn't possible. Three other tips to being reliable: make allowances for emergencies, let others know what's going on, and plan ahead.

Consumer SKILLS ACTIVITY

The Marketing of the Family

At some point, you may have seen signs or advertisements that include phrases such as "family restaurant," "Shoes for your family!" or "A toothpaste for the whole family!" Today, advertisers use the word *family* to sell many products. Manufacturers know that just adding the word *family* to advertising slogans attracts consumer attention.

How does mentioning the family increase sales of toothpaste and other products? Most people associate the word *family* with childhood memories. When they read the word on a label, they may subconsciously link the product with love, the freedom of childhood, parental care, and support.

In truth, most people respond to family-based advertising because most have positive mental images about what it means to be part of a family. However, the needs of families are not easily met by simply buying products, even "family" products. Family members need love, communication, and respect.

Writing

1. What do you think of when you hear or see the word "family?"
2. Would seeing the word "family" on a package affect whether or not you would buy the product? Why or why not?

Spending Time Together

MAIN IDEA ▶ Quality time shared among family members benefits their relationships and must be planned ahead of time.

Satisfying family relationships do not "just happen." They take time, commitment, and energy to develop and maintain. Some people hope to meet family members' needs without much effort. However, family relationships do take time and effort. People who make it a point to share time with parents, brothers, sisters, and others in their families find that the results are well worth their efforts.

Why Do Family Members Need to Spend Time Together?

Relationships depend upon time spent together. To know someone well you must share ideas together, enjoy activities together, seek each other's counsel when life gets tough, and share the joys life has to offer. For many people, pressures at work, obligations at school, and social activities take a lot of their time. Finding a good balance between obligations outside of the family and scheduling family time will strengthen family relationships.

TV Time Is Not Family Time

Although watching television may seem like an easy family activity, in reality, it does not generally benefit family relationships. If a television program addresses an important issue, the family may discuss the issue. When the focus is directed to the television, television viewing is a solitary activity.

What is lacking in most families today is quality time, time spent with one another, of sufficient duration to allow a meaningful exchange of ideas. Quality time is the kind of time that bonds family members together and enhances their relationships.

 **Did You Know?**

Here are a few activities that family members enjoy:
- Cooking
- Going to the beach
- Having a picnic
- Hiking in the woods
- Riding bikes
- Visiting relatives

Make your own list. Invite family members to join you in them.

Class Activity

Discuss: Poll your class. How many students have at least one sit-down meal per week with the people in their home? What factors do they think keep people from having meals together? How could these factors be rearranged to promote more family time? Discuss.

Did You Know?

A good way to develop respect within a family is to always knock before opening a closed door. By knocking first, you are respecting the other person's space and privacy.

How Can My Family Find Quality Time?

Quality time is planned. A way to do this is to get everyone together and plan a whole-family event, such as a weekday meal or a Saturday morning walk to the park. The plan can include a special meal that everyone helps to prepare. It can include learning a new game, or making presents for others.

Sharing hobbies with family members is another way to plan quality time. Some families enjoy participating in athletic activities together. Others may enjoy less active pursuits such as cooking, working on cars, and even gardening. Sharing time with family members allows each member to share his or her thoughts. The activities are limited only by imagination.

Spending Time Apart

MAIN IDEA ▶ **Everyone needs time alone to reflect on life and make sense of it.**

As important as time spent with family members is time spent alone. Teens, especially, need some time alone to think, to reflect on who they are, and to imagine who they might become. Alone time can be a sort of quality time in which you get to know yourself. Learn to respect others' need for solitude too.

Teens who spend excessive amounts of time alone, however, may be experiencing depression. A healthy balance among four areas seems ideal for good emotional health: time spent with family, time spent with peers, time spent at school and work, and time spent in solitude. Strive for balance.

■ **Figure 19.5** *It's sometimes surprising to discover how many activities family members can enjoy together. What are some of your favorite family activities?*

Caption Answer: My family likes to take walks after dinner.

Getting Along with Siblings

MAIN IDEA ▶ Conflict-resolution techniques can help siblings resolve problems.

Have you noticed that some people argue more with their brothers and sisters than with their friends or even strangers? Psychologists who study conflicts between siblings say that friction is normal between sisters and brothers. These conflicts are called **sibling rivalry**, *competition among sisters and brothers, often for the attention or affection of parents*.

Sibling Rivalry

Siblings often quarrel because they feel they must compete for the attention of their parents. Even fair and loving parents find it almost impossible to give affection and attention in exactly equal portions. Brothers and sisters should expect that their parents will show different levels of affection to each of their children at times. However, it is important to remember that this does not mean parents favor one child over another. Concentrate on the loving actions and words shown to you. These are yours to keep, and are not lessened by love shown to others.

A family's communication style is the heartbeat of the emotional peace of its members. It drives how and whether family members cooperate with each other. When minor conflicts turn into battles, life can become difficult for everyone.

Acceptance of New Arrivals

The relationship between siblings begins with the entrance of a new child into the family. Acceptance of a new brother or sister can be difficult for the child or other children. Most children have mixed emotions about the newcomer. They may feel excited and proud to become an older brother or sister, but also worry that they might be displaced from the favored position in the family.

Class Activity

Discuss: Ask the students these questions: What are some advantages/disadvantages of being an only child? What are some advantages/disadvantages to having brothers and sisters? How can sibling relationships prepare you for other relationships in life?

 **Did You Know?**

Resolving conflicts with family members will help to develop communication skills that are valuable throughout your life.

Young children, especially, may even fear that they'll be given away, or no longer wanted. Small children can be comforted by parents and older siblings who establish rituals, such as bathing, storytelling, and playing favorite games, that can be continued after the arrival of a new baby. Such attention raises the child's self-esteem and can help with acceptance of new family members. Many good books exist to help families prepare for the arrival of a new baby.

Struggles Among Teens

Older children, and especially teens, have needs that may conflict with those of other family members. Often, issues of control over personal space, privileges, and privacy cause conflicts. Most people develop a sense of ownership over a physical space they consider as theirs. Their sense of ownership also includes their privacy and privileges.

As mentioned, a territory is not always physical space. It may also include rights or possessions, or access to a favorite amusement. For example, two sisters who wear the same size clothing might borrow clothing from one another frequently. Suppose, however, one sister has recently started a part-time job. She now uses some of her earnings to buy clothes for herself and does not want to share the clothes she purchased.

The other sister does not have a job, and often borrows her sister's new clothing without asking. This causes conflicts over personal space and property. A starting point to resolve the conflict might be to discuss the conflict from each person's point of view and then brainstorm as many solutions as possible.

Solving the Conflict

The sisters need only to come up with one solution to which they both agree. For example, the sisters may decide it is okay to borrow clothing if it is returned promptly and cleaned. Or, the other sister may choose to get a part-time job to pay for her own clothes. Many different solutions might work, as long as both agree to abide by it.

Communicating Effectively

MAIN IDEA ▶ Assertive communication helps family members to negotiate with one another.

The secret to communicating effectively is to use an assertive communication style. Teens and their parents often disagree about house rules, chores, and curfews. It's normal for them to discuss the details of their agreements to make these arrangements fit changing circumstances. The more skilled family members become at communicating their wishes, the more likely that differences can be settled to meet everyone's needs.

Health Skills

The Essence of Conflict Resolution

1. Identify the problem.
2. If it is a conflict, then both people must:
   - Desire a resolution.
   - Strive for a solution in which both parties win.
   - Be flexible in how to meet needs.
   - Be *firm* in meeting their own needs.
   - Apologize when appropriate.
3. Brainstorm and keep an open mind.
4. Decide on a solution.
5. Carry out the solution.
6. Evaluate the results, and revise the solution as needed.

Figure 19.7 — Assertive vs. Nonassertive Responses

Situation 1

Devon's father works hard at his construction company all day. He also struggles to keep their home clean and tidy. Devon is sloppy. Today his father comes home to find an all-too-familiar messy trail of newspapers and dirty dishes.

Passive Response	*Devon's dad:* Says nothing; cleans up the mess, making noise in hopes of being heard, but steams inwardly.
Aggressive response	*Devon's dad (yelling):* "What a slob you are, Devon! You always mess up this house! Why can't you be more like your brother?"
Assertive response	*Devon's dad:* "You left a newspaper on the couch and dishes in the sink. Please toss out the papers and wash your dishes." Devon's father watches to make sure that Devon does the chores.

Situation 2

Angela has shared private information with her mother in a conversation that she believed was confidential. Angela is horrified when her mother's friend approaches her and offers unwanted tips on how to handle it.

Passive Response	*Angela:* Vows to keep her secrets from her mother, but still wishes she could tell her some things. This makes Angela feel sad and lonely.
Aggressive response	*Angela (yelling):* "How could you do that to me? You were so mean to tell everyone about my problem. I'll never trust you again!"
Assertive response	*Angela (calmly, but firmly):* "Mom, Mrs. X talked to me about the private conversation I had with you the other day. Please don't repeat our secrets."

Situation 3

Spencer's younger sister, Yvette, eavesdrops on a private phone conversation. She then taunts Spencer with sarcastic jokes about what she heard.

Passive Response	*Spencer:* Ignores the comments; tries to spend as little time as possible in the house with Yvette; misses out on family fun.
Aggressive response	*Spencer (screaming):* "Yvette, you're so annoying! You make me want to hit you!" He listens in on Yvette's telephone conversations to "give her a taste of her own medicine."
Assertive response	*Spencer (forcing himself to stay calm):* "Mom and Dad, please tell Yvette to stop listening in on my phone conversations. I've asked her to stop, but she won't." Then, if it continues, he sticks up for himself by telling his parents again whenever it occurs, until they effectively stop the eavesdropping.

The more you try to meet the needs of the other person, the more that person is likely to try to meet your needs. When daily life becomes hectic, or when family members must deal with their own issues, small differences can explode into big problems. The situations and possible responses in **Figure 19.7** help to clarify how different communication styles can alter a family's interaction.

Class Activity.

Analyze: Have students role-play assertiveness. Possible situations: someone cuts in front of the lunch line, someone walks into the room and changes the TV channel while you're watching something. Point out the advantages of assertive versus aggressive or passive behavior.

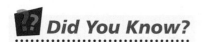
In each of the situations described in **Figure 19.7** on page 527, the responder can choose to be passive, aggressive, or assertive with family members. As you can see from these examples, it is unlikely that a passive reaction will get any response at all. Chances are that the other person won't even know that a problem exists. Aggressive responses are also unlikely to obtain a desired outcome, but are highly likely to provoke a conflict. In each case, the effective response is the assertive one. Assertiveness expresses your needs in a way that doesn't threaten others. Take a deep breath, think about what you are going to say, and discuss the situation clearly and calmly.

SECTION 2 Review

Reviewing the Vocabulary

Review the vocabulary on page 521. Then answer these questions.

1. Competition among sisters and brothers, often for the attention of their parents, is called _____.

Reviewing the Facts

2. **Explain.** For what do family squabbles act as a dress rehearsal?

3. **List.** What two things does quality time do for a family?

4. **Describe.** Why do teens need time alone?

5. **Identify.** What is often the cause of arguments that occur among siblings?

6. **Describe.** What are some things that teens can do to help adults build trust in them?

Writing Critically

7. **Personal.** Reread the Health Skills sidebar, "The Essence of Conflict Resolution" on page 526. Think about the arguments you might have had in the past. How does your behavior during arguments compare to the ground rules given here? What improvements can you make in the way you argue?

For more information on health careers, visit Career Corner at **glencoe.com**.

1. Sibling rivalry

2. Family conflicts can help people prepare for conflicts with others in the world outside of the family.

3. Quality time bonds family members together and enhance their relationships.

4. Teens need time alone to think, to reflect on who they are, and to imagine who they might become.

5. Siblings feel they must compete for their parents' affection.

6. Answers will vary.

7. Answers will vary.

Families with Problems

Sometimes, families experience difficulties beyond those that they can solve themselves. Family members need to seek help for difficult problems. School counselors, mental health counselors, religious leaders, and others can help families in need.

Living Through Divorce

MAIN IDEA ▶ Marriages sometimes end in divorce, causing families to change.

If current trends continue, a little less than half of the marriages formed today will eventually end in divorce. Among children who live with parents, approximately one-fourth live in one-parent families. **Figure 19.8** on page 530 describes some conditions that tend to make divorce likely. Of course, the presence of these factors in a marriage does not mean it will definitely lead to divorce.

In cases where conflict between parents causes extreme anxiety and pain to family members, divorce may prevent further injury. Regardless of the circumstances, however, divorce requires everyone to adjust. Most children eventually adapt to the changes and live normally. Some, however, do not adjust quickly and can experience depression.

Dealing with Hurt Feelings

Both parents and children can feel hurt, lonely, or angry over a divorce, even if the previously intact family unit was destructive. Some children and teens may feel that one or both parents do not love them. Parents are still parents to their children regardless of what else happens or whom else they marry.

In advance of a divorce, parents should tell their children where they will live and with whom. Children need to prepare for changes that affect them including new schools and new friends. Most of all, children need to know that they will be safe and loved.

Parents can help children get through a difficult time by reminding them they are not at fault. Children may find it easier to cope with divorce by discussing their feelings with parents or with other trusted adults.

In some cases, they may want to join a support group for children of divorce. Being part of a group will help a child to know he is not alone.

Vocabulary

grieve
dysfunctional family
active abuse
passive abuse
child abuse
spouse/partner abuse
elder abuse

> "*My balance comes from my family. I have reality around me, and they tell me when I need to calm down, take it down a couple notches. Then they tell me when I do something good.*"
>
> —Beyoncé Knowles (1981–)
> Singer, songwriter

Figure 19.8 — Factors That Often Surround Divorce

These factors are often seen in couples who divorce.
The more factors that apply, the greater the risk of divorce.

Limited income	When money is short, frustration and conflict may grow.
Less commitment to religion	Religious teachings often hold marriage as sacred, and condemn divorce.
Great differences in values and backgrounds	People who have grown up in different social settings possess different values and may think and act in unharmonious ways.
Young age at marriage	Young people may not have matured sufficiently to weather the storms expected in a marriage.
Come from divorced families	People whose parents divorced may be afraid to trust a relationship, and may be quick to discard it. Divorce may also seem familiar and "acceptable" to them.
Short time being married	As time passes, people learn how to better overcome small obstacles and compromise with each other.
Early childbearing	Partners need time to become partners before they become parents.

Source: Adapted from L. Beeghley. *What Does Your Wife Do? Gender and the Transformation of Family Life.* (Boulder, Colo.: Westview Press, 1996).

Allowing Time to Heal

Most children accept divorce eventually. Children of all ages **grieve**, *to feel keen emotional pain and suffering over a loss*, over a parent who has left the family. It is normal to grieve for the family that is gone too.

It takes time to build new families, especially with stepparents. Most of the time, however, new balances of power can be worked out. Teens with good assertiveness skills can express their views. No family is perfect. All families require effort and cooperation to succeed.

Dysfunctional Families

MAIN IDEA ▶ Dysfunctional families fail to provide a solid foundation for normal childhood development.

A family that does not cope effectively with its problems weakens its children by failing to support them. A **dysfunctional family** is *a family with abnormal or impaired ways of coping that injure the self-esteem and emotional health of family members*. Teens who live in dysfunctional families should seek help outside the immediate family. Talking to a trusted adult may help.

Dysfunctional Family Traits

All families face problems sometimes. Families are neither perfectly healthy nor totally unhealthy. Healthy families may behave in unhealthy ways during hard times. However, healthy families do not remain upset. They return to a normal healthy state. Dysfunctional families tend to grow worse. The unhealthy ways of coping grow more frequent and more severe. Dysfunctional families often have members who:

- Have alcoholism or other drug addictions, or long-term mental or physical illnesses.

- Fail to abide by society's laws and values.

- Lack parenting skills or social skills.

- Fail to engage in productive work.

- Engage in **active abuse**—*abuse involving one person's aggression against another.*

- Engage in **passive abuse**—*abuse involving not taking needed actions, such as neglecting to provide food or shelter to a dependent victim.*

With these unhealthy coping methods, families cannot meet their children's emotional needs. This has lasting effects that may stretch into future generations (see **Figure 19.9**).

Parenting in a dysfunctional family may be unpredictable—sometimes loving, warm, caring, interested, and involved, and at other times cold, unavailable, and distant. The more severe the family problem, the greater the potential for emotional damage to the children.

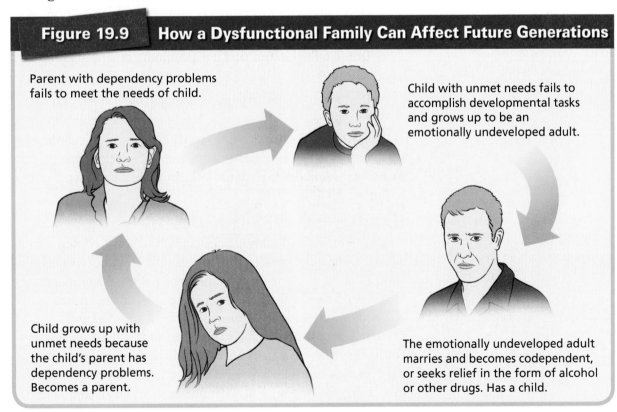

Figure 19.9   How a Dysfunctional Family Can Affect Future Generations

Parent with dependency problems fails to meet the needs of child.

Child with unmet needs fails to accomplish developmental tasks and grows up to be an emotionally undeveloped adult.

Child grows up with unmet needs because the child's parent has dependency problems. Becomes a parent.

The emotionally undeveloped adult marries and becomes codependent, or seeks relief in the form of alcohol or other drugs. Has a child.

■ Figure 19.10 *Divorce requires adjustments on everyone's part. What are some healthy ways to deal with a divorce?*

Caption Answer: Talking to your family or a trusted adult can help a person deal with a divorce in a healthy, positive way.

Dysfunctional families usually have rigid rules such as those listed below:

- **Don't feel**—do not admit to unpleasant feelings such as sadness and anger.

- **Don't talk**—do not discuss problems or unpleasant feelings.

- **Don't trust**—because you cannot trust those who care for you.

In contrast, the functional family shares and accepts feelings, and it strives for a sense of caring, support, and trust. Functional and dysfunctional families are compared further in **Figure 19.11**.

Exaggerated Roles of Children

Children in a dysfunctional family often develop somewhat exaggerated traits in the attempt to supply for themselves forms of support that normal parents would supply. One child may become a sort of hero, accepting much more responsibility than is appropriate for a child. Another may take on the role of scapegoat, accepting the blame for everything that goes wrong. A third role is that of mascot, the one everybody thinks is cute and funny. A fourth role is that of lost child, the one who always needs everyone's help.

In families where people have to play roles, it is difficult for family members to change, grow, or adapt. People who adopt these roles as children often find it helpful during adulthood to discover the causes, work through their difficulties, and no longer take on the role. Others may need more help in the form of therapy to recover completely.

Codependency

MAIN IDEA ▶ Codependent people focus all their energy on helping addicted loved ones and others around them.

Sometimes, a person lives with another person who is addicted to a substance or is dependent in some way. The person may become codependent. Codependency diminishes both the addicted person and the codependent person, so that neither is appreciated, loved, or supported.

People with codependency want to help, but they become so focused on the addicted loved one that they forget to tend to their own needs. If asked "How do you feel?" people with codependency will often respond by saying how other people feel or by saying what they think the asker wants to hear.

Did You Know?

Codependency is the characteristic of being focused on the needs of others to the point of neglecting one's own needs.

Figure 19.11 Traits of a Functional vs. a Dysfunctional Family	
Functional Family	**Dysfunctional Family**
Establishes rules that are appropriate, consistent, and flexible.	Establishes rules for the sake of control; rules are rigid and irrational.
Encourages its members to develop well-rounded personalities.	Assigns rigid roles to each member, such as the hero, the scapegoat, the mascot, and the lost child.
Accepts its problems and strives to solve them.	Has deep, dark secrets that no one may admit to or work on.
Welcomes outsiders into the system.	Resists allowing outsiders to enter the system.
Values and exercises its members' sense of humor. Keeps humor positive.	Expects members to be serious, or uses humor to belittle them.
Honors personal privacy, so members can develop a sense of self.	Permits no personal privacy, so that members have difficulty defining themselves as individuals.
Fosters a "sense of family" so that members may leave and re-enter the system at will.	Enforces loyalty to the family; members may not leave the system.
Allows and resolves conflict between members.	Denies and ignores conflict between members.
Welcomes beneficial changes.	Fights against changes.
Enjoys loyalty and a sense of wholeness.	Has no real unity, is fragmented.

A codependent person suffers deeply, and focuses all attention on the seeming cause of their problems—the addicted partner. A person with codependency issues can change by recognizing the problem and seeking help from a professional.

Family Violence and Abuse

MAIN IDEA ▶ The cycle of abuse can be broken with commitment and effort.

More than three million child abuse cases are reported to the authorities each year. Almost 1,500 children die each year at the hands of their abusers. **Child abuse** is *verbal, psychological, physical, or sexual assault on a child*. Aside from physical abuse, many more children suffer repeated sexual assaults and the constant emotional abuse of unreasonable expectations, humiliation, and unmet needs.

People who abuse children are emotionally unhealthy. They have low self-esteem and little power among adults. Such people may bully those who are weaker. However, it's not just children who suffer from abuse. **Spouse/Partner abuse** is *verbal, psychological, physical, or sexual assault on a spouse or partner*. Spouse and partner violence can happen to anyone regardless of race, age, sexual orientation, religion, or gender. It affects people of all backgrounds and education levels whether married, living together, or even during dating. Abuse can occur in both opposite-sex and same-sex relationships and can happen to intimate partners who are married, living together, or dating. Another type of abuse is called elder abuse. **Elder abuse** is *verbal, psychological, physical, or sexual assault on an older adult*. An estimated one to two million older adults are physically abused each year.

Family violence most often occurs when other problems worsen an existing emotional problem. Very young parents, single parents, those who are unemployed, those who do not manage stress well, and those who have few social contacts are especially likely to abuse their children. Alcohol and other drugs are also strongly linked with child abuse.

The Cycle of Abuse

Most importantly, the cycle of abuse is likely to repeat. People who abuse their own children are most likely to have been abused themselves during their childhoods. Abuse can be passed on from each generation to the next until someone seeks help. A child who is rescued from an abusive situation and who is supported in working through the resulting emotional injuries can recover completely, and can achieve high-level emotional health.

Breaking the Cycle of Abuse

Abuse is a learned behavior and abusers must first recognize that abusing others is wrong. Counseling can help abusers cope with their emotions in healthier ways. Asking for help is a courageous act. Without courage, the violent behavior may increase until it destroys relationships or harms someone. There are government agencies and support groups that exist to protect children and adults from abuse, as well as providing help to abusers. Help can also be provided by contacting a medical professional in your area. All forms of abuse are illegal. Reporting the incident to authorities can help prevent future abuse.

Worksheets: A reproducible quiz for Section 3 is provided in the Teacher Classroom Resources.

SECTION 3 Review

Reviewing the Vocabulary

Review the vocabulary on page 529. Then answer these questions.

1. Abuse involving one person's aggression against another is called _____.

2. _____ is verbal, psychological, physical, or sexual assault on a spouse or partner.

3. Verbal, psychological, physical, or sexual assault on an older adult is called _____.

Reviewing the Facts

4. Describe. When might divorce prevent some injury to a family?

5. Explain. How does a dysfunctional family weaken its children?

6. List. List four roles that children in a dysfunctional family are likely to take on.

Writing Critically

7. Personal. Your friend has shared with you that when her father is drunk, he hits her and her brother. She is afraid to say anything to anyone for fear her father will hit her more. What advice would you give your friend?

Go Online

For health and fitness tips, visit the Fitness Zone at **glencoe.com.**

1. Active abuse

2. Spouse/Partner abuse

3. Elder abuse

4. Divorce may prevent some injury when conflict between parents causes extreme anxiety and pain to family members.

5. A dysfunctional family can lower a child's self-esteem, and does not promote healthy ways of dealing with conflict.

6. Children in a dysfunctional family often develop somewhat exaggerated traits such as being the hero, mascot, scapegoat, or the lost child.

7. Answers will vary.

Society's Support of Families

How can our society best meet the changing needs of its families? For the family to thrive, our nation must commit wholeheartedly to meeting the needs of the family as times and needs change.

The Changing Family

MAIN IDEA ▶ Society has changed in the last 50 years and this has affected the role of the family.

Society has changed dramatically in the last 50 years. In most families today, both parents must work to earn enough money to support the family. Many teens today work, too, and contribute financially to the family.

In the past, the nation depended upon women to perform much of the work involved in keeping a home and rearing children. Today, many women are in the workplace during the day, and many struggle to balance the traditional roles as well.

Today's Problems

Families across society face many common problems. For example, quality day care for very young and very old family members is expensive. **Day care** is *supervision, usually at a facility, for preschool children or older adults who must be supervised during daytime working hours.* This poses real problems for working families. Another related child-care problem is what to do about after-school care for school-aged children while parents are at work.

Vocabulary

day care

⁉ Did You Know?

In 2008, the cost of sending a child to licensed day care for a year exceeded the cost of a year's tuition at many state universities.

Caption Answer: Both parents may work, many teens work part-time.

■ **Figure 19.12** *Day care facilities offer solutions to families who need care for children and older adults. How has the role of the family changed in the last 50 years?*

One solution might be for society to help develop facilities to care for dependent members of the family. Another might be to combine the day care needs of all ages, and allow the able older adults to become involved in caring for the young. Another solution might be for employers to develop flexible work schedules that allow families to care for their members in their own homes.

Conclusion

Family relationships last a lifetime. It is worth every effort to ensure that your own family enjoys a happy, supportive, and functional atmosphere. The support you offer to your family today comes back to you many times over throughout your future.

> " *I wish I could sit here and give you words to describe what my mother means to me. There aren't enough words in the dictionary.* "
>
> —LeBron James
> (1964–)
> NBA basketball player

SECTION 4 Review

Worksheets: A reproducible quiz for Section 4 is provided in the Teacher Classroom Resources.

Reviewing the Vocabulary

Review the vocabulary on page 536. Then answer this question.

1. Write a sentence using the vocabulary term *day care*.

Reviewing the Facts

2. Explain. What must our nation do in order for the family to thrive?

3. Identify. Identify two common problems faced by families across society.

4. List. List three possible solutions for the problems listed in question 3.

Writing Critically

5. Descriptive. You and your partner have been together for a few years and you now have a new baby. You are used to having two incomes to meet all of your financial demands. What will you do? Will one of you stay home with the baby? Or, will you find child care for the baby? Give reasons for your answer.

 **Online**

For more vocabulary practice, play the eFlashcards game at **glencoe.com**.

1. Answers will vary.

2. The United States must commit to meeting the changing needs of the family by offering quality day care programs for young and old, as well as other family-supporting programs.

3. Quality day care is in short supply, and there is a shortage of quality after-school care for school-aged children while parents are at work.

4. Develop facilities to care for dependent members of the family; combine the day care needs of all ages, and allow the able older adults to become involved in caring for the young; employers should develop flexible work schedules that allow families to care for their members in their own homes.

5. Answers will vary.

Parents as People

Understand and Apply Read the conversation below, and then complete the writing exercise that follows.

Some teens may forget that their parents are people with needs, wants, and problems of their own. Teens who strive to meet the needs of their parents maintain their parents' goodwill, gain their trust, and increase the harmony of the whole family. Teens who attempt to understand their parents' points of view can more easily win privileges such as more freedom, an allowance, and so forth.

Q: That sounds interesting. But how can I meet my parents' needs? I'm just a kid!

A: If you think about it, you'll see that meeting your parents' needs isn't too complicated. Parents have simple needs. While simple, though, these needs may not be easy to meet, especially at first. For example, the chapter already made the point that honesty is a major need of parents. A simple (but maybe not easy) way to start meeting parents' needs is to be totally honest with them, so that they can trust you.

Along with honesty, parents need reliability on your part. They need to be able to depend on you to do what you say you'll do. Add courtesy to honesty and reliability, and you have a fairly good start on a universal list of the needs of parents.

Q: Okay. Now how do I go about using that information?

A: Treat your parents as though they were the people you most admire at your school. You wouldn't barge into a conversation and interrupt the people at school, so don't do that to your parents. You'd probably do some extra-nice things for those people at school, so try doing them for your parents.

Also, tell your parents that you love them. This generates warm feelings in almost everyone, including yourself. What many teens have learned is that keeping parents happy is the quickest road to gaining more of what they want at home, and especially to creating a loving home life.

Q: I don't know about that honesty part. I don't think my parents will ever trust me.

A: You may think that you have lost your parents' trust forever, but remember from the chapter, your parents *want* to trust you. If you don't believe it, try this: be totally honest, and tell your parents that you are being honest, for two weeks. Then, when the two weeks is up, observe the changes in your parents' attitudes as they begin to trust you.

Q: How do I know that all of this will work for me? How do I know that my parents will even notice?

A: They'll notice, because parents are people, and people usually respond positively to someone's honesty. For example, suppose you need some money for a school function, say, $18.50. Your parents have only a $20 bill, and offer it to you to cover the costs of the event. Now you are faced with a decision: Should you return the $1.50 that is left?

Absolutely, and here's why. It shows your parents that you are fully responsible in handling their money. This makes them feel great, and it earns you credit for honesty and maturity. Since they know you will spend it wisely, they will be likely to trust you with money in the future.

Q: I guess I've never thought of things from my parents' point of view. So what you are saying is that the more I try to meet my parents' needs, the more they will be able to meet mine?

A: Exactly. Parents of teens face a tough task. They must strike a balance between setting limits on your behavior and allowing you to control your own affairs as you demonstrate readiness to accept responsibility. Parents generally notice your readiness in these three areas:

- You follow the house rules.
- You perform required tasks reliably and consistently.
- You act responsibly at school and elsewhere.

If you want more control over relationships, more privacy, or other items or privileges, then your wisest action is to act in a responsible, positive manner. Take a good, hard, honest look at how you'd grade yourself in the key areas just mentioned. If you can see ways of improving, go ahead and do them.

Q: Give me some examples.

A: Do you turn the television volume up late at night, or do you respect the requests of others for quiet? Do you let your parents know where you are whenever they need you? Is the lawn mowed and the laundry washed, or are your chores piled up? Are your studies under control?

Q: I see what you mean. Maybe if I figure out how to meet my parents' needs, they'll listen to me more.

A: That's right, they very well may. The better you can identify and meet your own parents' needs, the easier your task in convincing them that you are maturing. Try this: study the three examples of readiness listed above, and demonstrate how ready you are to be trusted. Then stand back and watch as your parents react positively, just as other people would.

Of course, you will not be able to influence your parents' every decision, but it's almost a certainty that you will notice a difference in the way you are treated. However, be patient. Remember from the chapter that trust builds over time. So does belief in your maturity. With enough repetition, your parents will be convinced that you are ready to handle whatever life hands you. And, in fact, you will be.

 Writing Write a personal essay about your family. Describe how you interact, and discuss how family members contribute to each other's total health.

Reviewing Vocabulary

Use the vocabulary terms listed below to complete the following statements.

grieve

dysfunctional family

sibling rivalry

family

day care

1. A _____ is a group of people who are related by adoption, blood, or marriage, and are committed to each other.

2. Competition among sisters and brothers, often for the attention or affection of parents, is called _____.

3. To _____ means to feel keen emotional pain and suffering over a loss.

4. A _____ is a family with abnormal or impaired ways of coping that injure the self-esteem and emotional health of family members.

5. Supervision, usually at a facility, for preschool children or older adults who must be supervised during daytime working hours is called _____.

Recalling Key Facts and Ideas

Section 1

6. **Explain.** Who are a child's first teachers?

7. **Describe.** How is a family identity maintained?

8. **Identify.** From what sources do children learn values?

Section 2

9. **List.** List the goals of each family stage.

10. **Identify.** List two secrets to always being honest and reliable.

11. **Explain.** What three things are needed to develop satisfying family relationships?

Section 3

12. **Identify.** List the seven factors that often surround divorce.

13. **Name.** List three rigid rules that a dysfunctional family might have.

14. **Describe.** Describe the characteristics of a codependent person.

Section 4

15. **Analyze.** What are some common problems for families in the United States? What are some possible solutions to these problems?

Writing Critically

16. **Expository.** In what ways are families different from other groups?

17. **Descriptive.** How would you help a friend whose parents are getting a divorce? Make a list of things you would say or actions you would take.

18. **Personal.** How do you think parents should handle conflicts with their teens?

1. Family 2. Sibling rivalry 3. Grieve 4. Dysfunctional family 5. Day care 6. Parents, siblings, aunts, uncles, baby-sitters 7. Keeping rituals, celebrating special occasions together, living with give and take 8. By the examples that adults around them set 9. Develop trust in each other, develop independence and self-direction in children, develop a child's sense of industry, guide adolescent role development, maintain relationship with children who leave home, share talents and resources with others, maintain satisfaction with life. 10. Never promise more than you can deliver, let others

Activities

19. Look through your local telephone book for services and agencies that focus on families. Make a list of your findings. Your list might include such things as day care centers or counseling centers.

20. Work individually and then as a class to compile a list of family traditions. Are there any traditions on your final list that are shared by all members of your class? If so, what are they? Why do you think some traditions are shared by so many?

21. Create a television or radio advertisement about an organization that offers services to families with problems.

22. Survey a number of people to get their opinions of what an ideal family would be like. Analyze the results to find what answers people have in common. Share your results with the rest of the class.

23. Ask an older adult to describe the changes he or she has seen in families over the years. Make a list of the changes and try to determine whether the changes are positive, negative, or neutral.

Making Decisions About Health

24. When Rico started to date, his parents' rule was that he be home by 11 p.m. For six months he was always on time. Then, one Saturday night, he didn't get home until midnight. His parents were furious. For the next several months, they reminded him of the incident.

It was as if his six months of getting home on time hadn't happened. All they could remember was the one time he was late. The situation has caused a lot of resentment and bad feelings between Rico and his parents. What could Rico have done differently? How could his parents have handled the situation differently? What could be done now to correct the situation and restore good feelings between Rico and his parents?

Go Online

For more vocabulary practice, play the True/False game at **glencoe.com**.

Fact or Fiction?

Answers

1. True.
2. False. Parents want to think of their children as honest and trustworthy, but may learn to distrust them in response to dishonesty.
3. True.

 Writing Paragraphs will vary.

know what's going on. **11.** Spending quality time together, good communication, time to be alone **12.** Economic challenges, less commitment to religion, great differences in values and backgrounds, young age at marriage, come from divorced families, short time being married, early childbearing **13.** Don't feel; Don't talk; Don't trust. **14.** Focuses all energy on everyone around them except themselves **15.** Lack of quality day care. **16-24.** Answers will vary.

Sections

When people become parents, their lives are changed forever. At any age, having children greatly impacts the future. In this chapter you will learn about the reproductive process and some basic elements of parenting.

Fact or Fiction?

What Do You Think?

Is each statement true or false? If you think it's false, explain what's true.

1. The lifestyle choices a couple makes in the weeks before pregnancy can affect their future child's development.
2. A missed menstrual period is a sure sign that a female is pregnant.
3. Possibly the single most important task in parenting is to help the child develop positive self-esteem.

 Writing Write a paragraph to explain what it means to be a parent. As you read the chapter, update your paragraph to include new information you learn.

(Answers on page 573)

G⊙ Online

Visit **glencoe.com** and complete the Life Choice Inventory for Chapter 20.

The Responsibilities of Pregnancy

A pregnancy greatly affects people's lives. Many first-time parents cannot imagine the lifestyle changes and responsibilities that await them, both before and after the birth of a baby. Parents must provide protection, food, clothing, shelter, education, and medical care for their children. Parenting also involves fostering emotional growth, instilling values, setting limits, and giving unconditional love. Parents who successfully meet these challenges are often rewarded with some of life's greatest joys.

Teen Parenting Risks

MAIN IDEA ▶ Becoming a parent brings many rewards, but is also hard work.

Teen mothers and fathers face particular challenges and risks. They may become separated from their peer groups, interrupt their educations, and diminish their chances for desired careers. In addition, younger pregnant teens face higher physical risks to both mother and child, as described in later sections.

Did You Know?

Reading to a child at any age will increase their knowledge.

■ **Figure 20.1** *Parenting changes a person's life forever. How does parenting change a person's life?*

Caption Answer: The person must now consider the health and well-being of a child.

■ **Figure 20.2** *Parenting can be both challenging and rewarding. In what ways can teenage parenting be particularly challenging?*

Caption Answer: Teenage parents can become separated from peers and interrupt their education.

The responsibilities of pregnancy affect people in less obvious and less dramatic ways too. Just the fear of pregnancy can damage relationships. Many couples worry and disagree about readiness to bear a child, and they sometimes must make hard choices. When unwanted pregnancies occur, unstable relationships are likely to crumble.

For all of the reasons just named, many teens find that the choice to abstain from sexual activity brings freedoms—from stress, from worry, and from unnecessary complications. The rest of this chapter assumes that pregnancy is an event welcomed with joy by mature, ready, and loving parents.

Cooperative Learning
Analyze and Discuss: Divide your class into male/female pairs. Have each pair research the cost of having a baby, beginning with the hospital bill. Pairs should figure expenses for the necessities a baby needs, including child care. Discuss the findings.

Worksheets: A reproducible quiz for Section 1 is provided in the Teacher Classroom Resources.

SECTION 1 Review

Reviewing the Facts

1. **Explain.** What are some responsibilities that parenting brings?
2. **List.** In what ways is teen pregnancy risky?
3. **Identify.** How does pregnancy affect relationships?
4. **Describe.** What are the freedoms that come from abstaining from sexual activity?

Writing Critically

5. **Narrative.** Paul is 17 years old, and has learned his girlfriend is pregnant. Write him a letter explaining what he will likely experience in the months and years to come with regards to becoming a father. Be realistic, but not harsh.

Go Online

For fitness and health tips, visit the Fitness Zone at **glencoe.com**.

1. Providing protection, food, clothing, shelter, education, and medical care. Instilling values, setting limits, and giving unconditional love.

2. Teen parents may become separated from their peer groups, their educations may be interrupted, and face higher physical risks, both to the mother and the child.

3. Couples can worry or disagree about readiness to bear a child. Sometimes couples have to make difficult choices.

4. Abstinence brings freedom from stress, worry, and unnecessary complications.

5. Answers will vary.

Deciding to Bear or Adopt Children

The decision of whether to have a child is affected by personal beliefs, needs, and wishes. For example, people may base their decisions on childhood memories of a happy family. They may wish to become a parent and to nurture and raise children. Outside pressures—such as a spouse's needs, or parents' or friends' expectations—can also affect these decisions. Finally, people may simply wish to experience being parents. Most decisions, however, should be based on this single question: Am I ready to become a parent? Children are a responsibility for many years.

Responsible Parenting

MAIN IDEA ▶ Prospective parents should think about how children will change their lives.

To get an idea of what it takes to be a parent, you can try the following exercise. Pretend an egg is a baby, and that you are its parent. Don't put it down. Carry it from place to place, even while shopping or showering. Bathe it every day. Keep an eye on it at all times. Sleep with it close by. Set your alarm for 2 A.M., and check the egg. Never let it out of your sight unless you can get another person to agree to tend to it as you are doing. Try this for one week, and you will get some sense of what it would be like to care for a child. Multiply the week by 52 for a year, and then by 18 for the duration of active parenthood. If you find this exercise difficult, remember that rearing a child is more difficult still. An egg requires neither food nor discipline. It does not cry, soil diapers, or get sick.

■ **Figure 20.3** *For parents who are ready to accept the responsibility, babies are a joy. How does a person decide if he or she is ready to become a parent?*

Caption Answer: The person should think about what it would be like to have to feed, protect, and shelter a child for many years.

➤ Objectives
- Apply the decision-making process to a life-changing decision.
- Consider possible outcomes of each option when making a major decision.

Oh, Baby!

Kayla's sister Briana is a college senior who plans to continue her studies by going to medical school. Briana has wanted to become a doctor since she was 10 years old. Last summer, Briana married her boyfriend Todd, who is also a senior in college. Todd has always wanted to become a lawyer, and he plans to go to law school after he graduates.

Lately, Briana and Todd have been talking about having a baby. They love children and are eager to start a family of their own. They know, however, that one of them will have to work, putting any plans for further education on hold. They are trying to decide whether to have a baby now or wait until after they finish their education. Kayla hasn't been asked what she thinks, but she hopes they wait. She worries that they may not have enough time or money to go to medical school or law school if they have a young child now.

➤ Identify the Problem
1. What decision are Briana and Todd trying to make?

➤ Form an Action Plan
2. What are their options? What are possible outcomes of each option?
3. How do their values relate to the decision they are trying to make?
4. What decision does Kayla think Briana and Todd should make? Why?

➤ What Did You Learn?
5. What did you learn from this activity about considering possible outcomes when making a major life decision?

Applying Health Skills:

1. Briana and Todd are trying to decide whether to have a baby now or wait until after they finish their education.

2. They could have a baby now or wait until they complete their education. If they have a baby now, they may not have enough time or money to go to medical school or law school. If they wait, they may be more likely to achieve their career goals. They could have a child in either case.

3. Briana values becoming a doctor, and Todd values becoming a lawyer. Both of them also value having a child. They are eager to start a family, but having a baby now might interfere with the careers they value.

4. Kayla thinks that Briana and Todd should finish their education before having a baby because having a baby now might interfere with their career goals.

5. Answers will vary.

■ **Figure 20.4** *Opening one's home to a foster child can be especially challenging and rewarding. What is the difference between adoption and foster parenthood?*

Caption Answer: Adoption is a legal process of making a child one's own. Foster parenting is not necessarily permanent, but offers the opportunity to care for an older child with special needs.

Some couples decide to start a family by adopting a child. Adoption is the legal process of taking a child of other parents as one's own. People may choose adoption because they want to offer a home to a child or because they are unable to bear a child themselves.

Adoption is not quick. It requires persistence, patience, and the willingness to work with an agency. Such agencies take seriously their job of matching parents and children. Foster parenthood offers an opportunity to care for and provide a home for children who may not be able to stay permanently. Opening a home—and life—to a foster child can be both challenging and rewarding.

Worksheets: A reproducible quiz for Section 2 is provided in the Teacher Classroom Resources.

SECTION 2 Review

1. They can encounter pressure from family, friends' expectations, or spouse's needs.

2. People may choose adoption if they are unable to bear a child on their own or have a desire to open up their home to a child.

3. Answers will vary.

Reviewing the Facts

1. **Identify.** What outside pressures do people encounter while deciding whether or not to have a child?
2. **Explain.** Why might people choose adoption?

Writing Critically

3. **Narrative.** Write a short letter persuading a couple to think about the responsibilities of parenting.

G҈ Online

For more information on health careers, visit Career Corner at **glencoe.com**.

Reproduction

The beginning of a new human being takes place in a single moment. That event is **conception**, *the union of an ovum and a sperm that starts a new individual*. Because many complex events lead up to conception, it may be helpful to review the male and female reproductive systems before proceeding with an explanation of conception. Reread the "Physical Maturation" section in Chapter 3, as well as the sections on the reproductive systems in Chapter 6.

The Menstrual Cycle and Conception

MAIN IDEA ▶ The menstrual cycle prepares the female body for pregnancy. Conception occurs when an ovum and a sperm unite.

Males and females differ in the way they produce reproductive cells. Males produce **sperm**, *the male cells of reproduction*; females produce eggs, or **ova** (singular, *ovum*), *the female cells of reproduction*. In males, a constant flow of the hormone testosterone stimulates sperm cells to mature daily at a steady rate. In the female system, only one (or, rarely, two or three) ova ripen and are released from the ovary each month. This cyclic ripening depends on hormonal changes that occur in a monthly rhythm; this is called the **menstrual cycle**, *the cyclic ripening of an ovum and the preparation of the uterus for pregnancy*.

The Menstrual Cycle

Every 28 days on average, the uterus prepares for a pregnancy. The cycle begins with the building up of the uterine lining (endometrium) with soft tissue and a rich blood supply. At about midcycle, **ovulation** occurs—*the ripening and release of an ovum*.

The ovum is gently swept into the tube leading to the uterus. If the egg encounters sperm cells in the fallopian tube, the egg may become fertilized. If fertilized, it may embed in the prepared uterine lining, beginning a pregnancy.

If the egg is not fertilized, or if the fertilized egg does not embed in the uterine lining, it passes out of the body unnoticed. With no pregnancy, the uterine lining weakens in the two weeks following ovulation, and is eventually shed. This shedding of the uterine lining is called menstruation. Following menstruation, the whole cycle begins anew. The cycle is summarized in **Figure 20.5** on page 550.

Vocabulary

conception
menstrual cycle
sperm
ova
ovulation
fertilization
implantation
fertility awareness method

Figure 20.5

The Menstrual Cycle

The cycle begins with bleeding. The lining of the uterus then begins to thicken to become ready to support pregnancy. If no pregnancy occurs, the lining weakens and is shed in menstrual bleeding to start the cycle again.

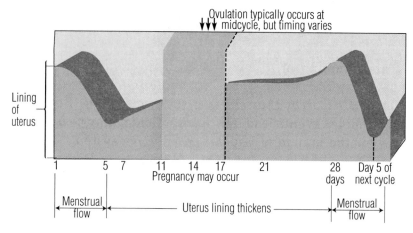

Ovulation typically occurs at midcycle, but timing varies

Lining of uterus

1   5 7   11 14 17   21   28   Day 5 of
                                days   next cycle
         Pregnancy may occur

Menstrual flow | Uterus lining thickens | Menstrual flow

In menstruation, a few tablespoons of blood and fragments of the uterine lining flow from the vagina. Menstruation lasts for four to five days on average. These few days of menstrual flow are only the outward sign of the events that have taken place in the body in the earlier four weeks.

Menstruation normally varies from month to month. It may arrive late or early, with lighter or heavier flows. It may last for a longer or shorter amount of time than expected, though the typical range is 24 to 35 days. Contractions of the uterus—menstrual cramps—are also normal during menstruation. If cramping is uncomfortable, treatment with over-the-counter medicines is usually effective. Should cramping become severe, or should menstrual irregularities become extreme, a health care provider should check for problems.

Conception

Inside the woman's ovary, an ovum becomes ready for **fertilization**, *the joining of an ovum and sperm*. During sexual intercourse, sperm swim up the vagina, through the cervix, through the uterus, and into the fallopian tubes. The ovum, now in the fallopian tubes, powerfully attracts sperm cells to its surface. One sperm finally enters the ovum, triggering an instant change in the ovum's surface so that no more sperm can penetrate (see **Figure 20.6**). The DNA of the two cells unites within the fertilized ovum to produce a zygote, which travels through the remainder of the tube and into the uterus, and implantation occurs. **Implantation** is *the process in which the ovum implants itself in the uterine wall* and begins to develop. About 60 percent of all fertilized ova either fail to implant or dislodge later, to be shed from the body.

For conception to occur, sexual intercourse must take place within a certain time frame. An ovum lives for just 12 to 24 hours, and living sperm must be present during this brief life span if they are to fertilize the ovum. Sperm can live for up to five days within the female reproductive tract, so intercourse within a few days before ovulation can easily lead to conception.

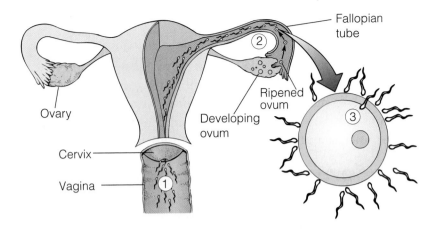

Fallopian tube

Ovary

Ripened ovum

Developing ovum

Cervix

Vagina

① ② ③

Figure 20.6

Fertilization
Sperm **(1)** begin the journey toward a ripened ovum, released earlier from the ovary **(2)**. The sperm work together to weaken the ovum's outer layer, but only one sperm can enter **(3)**. Both sperm and ovum have been greatly enlarged for this illustration.)

A couple who wants to conceive can use the **fertility awareness method**, *a method of charting ovulation*. It is used to help a female determine the time of ovulation by tracking menstrual periods, body temperature, and types of cervical mucus. The couple can then time sexual intercourse to make sure sperm are available at the right time to fertilize the ovum.

Worksheets: A reproducible quiz for Section 3 is provided in the Teacher Classroom Resources.

SECTION 3 Review

Reviewing the Vocabulary

Review the vocabulary on page 549. Then answer these questions.

1. The union of an ovum and a sperm is called _____.
2. Define *mentrual cycle*.
3. The male cells of reproduction are called _____.
4. What is *implantation*?

Reviewing the Facts

5. **Explain.** What is the purpose of the menstrual cycle?
6. **Describe.** What happens to the egg after one sperm penetrates it?
7. **Identify.** How long do sperm live in the female reproductive tract?

Writing Critically

8. **Personal.** Why do you think it is important for females to understand menstruation? Why is it important for males to understand menstruation?

Go Online

For fitness and health tips, visit the Fitness Zone at **glencoe.com**.

1. Conception
2. The cyclic ripening of an ovum and the preparation of the uterus for pregnancy.
3. Sperm
4. The lodging of a fertilized ovum in the wall of the uterus.
5. During the menstrual cycle, the uterus builds a lining where a fertilized egg can thrive. If the egg is not fertilized, the lining is shed and the process begins again. If the egg is fertilized, it will become implanted in the uterine wall.
6. The surface of the egg changes so that no other sperm can penetrate it.
7. Up to five days.
8. Answers will vary.

Pregnancy

Preparation for a healthy pregnancy begins far in advance. Pregnancy and childbearing takes planning and preparation. This involves medical checkups, making sure immunizations are up to date, stopping smoking and other harmful habits, proper nutritional planning, and eliminating medicines.

Concerns Before Pregnancy

MAIN IDEA ▶ Health habits of both parents prior to pregnancy can affect the health of the baby.

Before conception, both parents should be aware that a male's health habits are just as important as the female's. It is recommended that females visit their health care provider to discuss their general health and how it may affect a pregnancy. Doctors will want to review medical history, immunization history, genetic history, and more.

At the time of possible conception, both parents should be free from drugs of all kinds—over-the-counter medications, prescription medications (with the physician's prescription), caffeine, and mind-altering drugs, including alcohol.

Both prospective parents should eat a healthful diet. Nutrition affects the ova and sperm, and good nutrition supports the hormone balance needed for conception. Before pregnancy, a healthy diet would well cover the nutrient needs of the future parents.

■ **Figure 20.7** *Both parents can prepare in advance for a healthy pregnancy. What steps can pregnant females take to help ensure a healthy pregnancy and delivery?*

Caption Answer: Females should take the vitamin folate to lower the risk of birth defects.

A female who chooses a poor diet in order to lose weight or who snacks on candies and high-fat snacks may not receive the nutrients she needs to maintain nutrient stores. She may not know how to choose a good diet, or she may not have enough money to buy nourishing food. If pregnancy is in a female's future, she should develop healthy eating habits now. She should take a daily multivitamin too. She should also be physically active. Then, once pregnancy is confirmed, she can continue eating and exercising as she did before, and her baby will likely be healthy.

Pregnancy Tests

MAIN IDEA ▶ Pregnancy tests will confirm that a child was conceived.

Long before any tests are taken, a female may suspect that she is pregnant. A typical sign is a missed menstrual period. However, periods are missed for many reasons. Vaginal bleeding similar to a period can occur, so regular bleeding does not mean a female is not pregnant. Another sign is that the breasts may become tender and full, and the nipples may darken.

A chemical test can confirm that a female is pregnant. All such tests rely on detecting one of the hormones produced by the placenta. Home pregnancy test kits are available from drugstores without a prescription. Sometimes the results are uncertain. In those cases, a blood test at the doctor's office will provide conclusive results.

Worksheets: A reproducible quiz for Section 4 is provided in the Teacher Classroom Resources.

Reviewing the Facts
1. **Explain.** What health habits should both parents maintain if they are considering beginning a pregnancy?
2. **Describe.** Describe the most likely reasons why women might be poorly nourished in our society.
3. **List.** List two signs of pregnancy in a female's body.

Writing Critically
4. **Expository.** Write a paragraph to explain the importance of good health for parents before conception.

For fitness and health tips, visit the Fitness Zone at **glencoe.com**.

1. Both parents should be free of drugs of all kinds—over-the-counter medications, prescription medications (with the physician's OK), caffeine, and mind-altering drugs, including alcohol. Both parents should also be well nourished.

2. She may not know how to choose a good diet, or she may not have enough money to buy nourishing food.

3. Breast tenderness and darkening of the nipples.

4. Answers will vary.

Fetal Development

Gestation is *the period from the last menstrual period to birth.* In each stage of gestation thereafter, the developing future infant is given a name—first zygote, next embryo, and finally fetus. **Figure 20.8** displays each stage.

Stages of Gestation

MAIN IDEA ▶ There are three stages of gestation, each of which includes important fetal development.

A day after fertilization, the fertilized egg—even while it is still traveling toward the uterus through the fallopian tube—begins to divide. If the first two new cells become detached at this stage, two babies—identical twins—will begin to develop. (In contrast, if two eggs have been released and fertilized at the same time, the two babies will be fraternal twins, not identical twins.)

The fertilized egg, upon its first division, becomes a **zygote**, *the product of the union of ovum and sperm, so termed for two weeks after conception.* After the zygote becomes implanted in the uterine wall, cell division goes on and on. Each new set of cells divides again to create a ball of many smaller cells. These cells sort themselves into three layers that eventually form the various body systems.

From the zygote's outermost layer of cells, the nervous system and skin begin to develop. From the middle layer, the muscles and internal organ systems form. From the innermost layer, the glands and linings of the digestive, respiratory, and urinary tract systems form.

The Embryo

An **embryo**, *the developing infant during the third through the eighth week after conception*, goes through many changes. The number of cells in the embryo doubles approximately every 24 hours. In comparison, this rate slows to only one doubling during the final ten weeks of pregnancy. The embryo's size changes very little. However, the events taking place are of enormous importance.

At ten weeks, the embryo is only a little more than an inch long. However, it already has a complete (although immature) central nervous system and digestive system, a beating heart, well-defined fingers and toes, and the beginnings of facial features. Anything that disrupts the embryo's rapid development at this early stage—when some females do not yet know they are pregnant—alters the structure of the body permanently.

Vocabulary

zygote
gestation
embryo
placenta
amniotic sac
umbilical cord
critical periods
miscarriage
lactation
morning sickness
high-risk pregnancy
prenatal care
low birth weight
premature infant
small for date

The Fetus

The fetus is the developing infant from the ninth week after last menstrual period until birth. The tasks of the fetus are to gain in size and weight. Each organ grows to maturity with its own timing. Each organ has certain **critical periods** during its growth—*periods during development when a body organ is especially sensitive to harmful factors.*

Outside events can affect an organ's critical period. If, during the critical period, an organ's cell division is limited by some factor, that organ will be damaged. Later recovery is impossible. Thus, exposure to a harmful chemical, a nutrient deficiency, or other injury during one stage of development might affect the heart. During another stage, it might affect the developing limbs.

The brain and central nervous system are first to reach maturity in the developing fetus. During its critical period, the fetal brain increases by 250,000 cells a minute. Problems during the brain's critical period can limit brain development permanently. Mental functioning throughout life can be subnormal. Pregnancy, then, is clearly a time for a female to take special care of her health.

The Placenta and Other Structures

MAIN IDEA ▶ The placenta provides nutrients, other materials, oxygen, and waste disposal for the developing fetus.

After implantation, *a new organ that permits exchange of materials between maternal and fetal blood* called the **placenta** grows within the uterus, shown in **Figure 20.9** on page 556. Two other new structures form. One is the **amniotic sac**, *a fluid-filled balloon that houses the developing fetus.* The other is the **umbilical cord**, *a ropelike structure stretching from the fetus's "belly button" to the placenta.* The umbilical cord contains blood vessels that conduct the fetus's blood to and from the placenta.

The placenta is tissue in which fetal and maternal blood flow side by side. The two bloods never mix. The mother's blood delivers nutrients and oxygen to the fetus's blood across the walls of the vessels. Fetal waste products are carried away by the mother's blood, to be excreted by the mother.

The placenta is a highly active organ. It gathers up hormones, nutrients of all descriptions, large proteins such as antibodies, and other needed items and pumps them into the fetal bloodstream. The placenta also releases hormones across a membrane into the maternal blood to maintain pregnancy.

Figure 20.8

Stages of Gestation

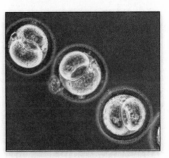

Zygote: From fertilization through week 2

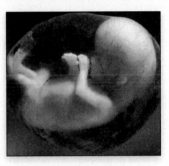

Embryo: From week 3 through week 8

Fetus: From week 9 through the end of pregnancy

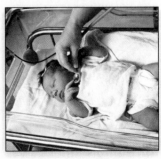

A newborn infant

Figure 20.9

The Placenta

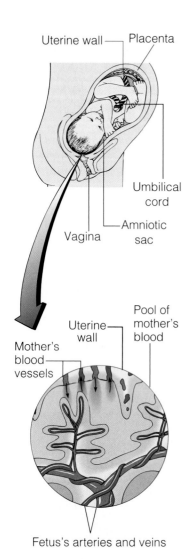

Uterine wall — Placenta

Umbilical cord

Vagina

Amniotic sac

Pool of mother's blood

Uterine wall

Mother's blood vessels

Fetus's arteries and veins

The placenta must develop normally if the future infant is to grow properly. Should the placenta break down, the fetus would be left with no source of nutrients or oxygen. One reason why nutrition before pregnancy is so important is that the placenta is built largely from nutrient stores already in the mother's body at the start of pregnancy.

Miscarriage

MAIN IDEA ▶ A pregnancy may end due to miscarriage.

Not all fertilized eggs develop to become infants. About 10 percent fail to implant in the uterus and are shed without anyone's ever knowing they were there. Of those that implant, about half are shed in **miscarriage**. It is *the expelling of a zygote, embryo, or fetus from the uterus, not induced by medical means.* Miscarriage is the most common complication of early pregnancy. Many times it prevents imperfect embryos from becoming full-term infants.

Most miscarriages take place early, with no other sign than a heavy menstrual flow. A female who experiences a miscarriage late in her pregnancy may feel significant grief at the loss of her unborn child.

Many miscarriages occur because of chromosomal abnormalities or other abnormal types of development. Certain factors such as age, smoking, drugs, caffeine, and weight can increase the risk of miscarriage.

Ectopic Pregnancy

Ectopic pregnancy results when a zygote implants not in the uterus but in the fallopian tube, abdomen, ovary, or cervix. This makes it impossible for the fetus to receive nourishment and grow. An ectopic pregnancy cannot lead to the birth of a healthy fetus. Without diagnosis and treatment, the pregnancy eventually ruptures the tube. This can be fatal to the pregnant female.

Prenatal Care

Prenatal care ensures the health of the female and her baby. Seeing a doctor regularly throughout the pregnancy will provide a new mother with the care and nutritional advice she needs. The doctor will also monitor the development of the fetus.

A doctor is able to confirm normal growth, diagnose if there are any problems caused by the pregnancy, and discuss basic skills for caring for the newborn. An unborn baby receives nourishment from the mother. Pregnant females are encouraged to take prenatal vitamins to ensure the baby receives essential nutrients. A doctor can prescribe the right vitamins to meet the needs of the mother and her growing fetus.

Changes During Pregnancy

MAIN IDEA ▶ Physical and emotional changes occur during pregnancy.

There are many changes that affect a female when she's pregnant. She starts to produce more blood. Her uterus and its supporting muscles increase in size and strength. Her joints become more flexible in preparation for childbirth. Her breasts grow and change in preparation for **lactation**, *the production of milk by the mammary glands of the breasts for the purpose of feeding babies*. The hormones creating all these changes may also affect her brain and change her mood. She may experience constipation, shortness of breath, frequent urination, backaches, or **morning sickness**, *the nausea a pregnant woman may suffer at any time of the day*. Morning sickness results from the many hormones needed to support pregnancy. Sometimes, eating crackers before getting out of bed or snacking on small meals helps to relieve it.

Physical activity may reduce some discomfort, and fitness helps to ensure a quick recovery from childbirth later on. Most types of physical activity are approved, as long as the abdomen is protected against injury. A pregnant female should progress slowly in an exercise routine. If a female is physically active before pregnancy, she should continue as before, so long as she is comfortable doing so.

As pregnancy stretches the skin over a female's abdomen, buttocks, and breasts, the skin's lower layers may begin to painlessly separate, forming scars. The tendency to develop "stretch marks" runs in families. During pregnancy, as at other times, a woman needs to deal healthfully with stress. Studies suggest that stress can cause changes in the nerve cells of embryos. Pregnant females should practice the relaxation techniques described in Chapter 4.

■ **Figure 20.10** *Relaxation is important for the pregnant female and the developing child. List some changes pregnant females experience during pregnancy.*

Caption Answer: Her joints become more flexible in preparation for childbirth. She may experience morning sickness.

Figure 20.11

Example Weight Gain During Pregnancy

Development	Weight Gain
Infant at birth	7½ pounds
Placenta	1 pound
Mother's added blood	4 pounds
Mother's added fluid	4 pounds
Growth of uterus	2½ pounds
Growth of breasts	3 pounds
Fluid to surround infant	2 pounds
Mother's fat stores	7 pounds
Total	31 pounds

Nutrition During Pregnancy

MAIN IDEA ▶ Nutrition in pregnancy is critical to the health of the fetus and the mother.

Class Activity

Plan: Have each student design a one-week menu that is nutritionally sound for a pregnant woman. Students should provide some explanation of the foods they choose. Encourage students to use Chapter 7 as a resource to develop their menus.

An earlier part of this chapter pointed out that malnutrition or obesity before pregnancy can affect the health of a future fetus. During pregnancy, malnutrition not only can reduce the infant's number of brain cells but also can impair every other body organ and system.

A female's nutrient needs during pregnancy are greater than at any other time of life. When the baby is born, its body will contain bones, muscles, blood, and other tissues made from nutrients the mother eats. For a pregnant teen, nutrient needs are extraordinary. This is because the food she eats must supply the nutrients not only to support her growing baby but also her own growth. A diet that includes a variety of foods is the best source of all the needed nutrients.

A female's nutrient needs increase tremendously in pregnancy, but her energy (calorie) needs increase just a little. A pregnant female should not "eat for two." If she does, she will gain unneeded fat and give birth to a fat baby. She needs foods with high nutrient levels but low calorie levels. That means she needs a diet about the same as the one recommended in Chapter 7, but with one more serving of vegetables daily, and one more daily serving of meat or meat alternatives.

Normal weight gain is between 25 and 35 pounds—mostly of lean tissue—during pregnancy. This weight gain supports normal growth of the placenta, the uterus, the breasts, and a 7½-pound baby, as well as an increased blood and fluid volume. **Figure 20.11** shows an example of how a weight gain of 31 pounds is distributed. Pregnant teens should strive for gains at the upper end of the range, because some of the weight gained is that of their own maturing bodies.

Obese women should gain less—about 15 pounds. Their weight gain should not be of fat, but of lean tissue built from nutrient-dense foods.

High-Risk Pregnancies

MAIN IDEA ▶ One common outcome of a high-risk pregnancy is a low-birth-weight baby.

Some pregnancies pose risks to the life and health of the mother and fetus. **Figure 20.12** lists factors that identify a **high-risk pregnancy** or a *pregnancy more likely than others to have problems, such as premature delivery or a low birth weight.* Many of the factors that threaten pregnancy are easy to control once they are discovered. This is why early **prenatal care**, *medical and health care provided during pregnancy*, is so important. Many clues to abnormalities are present in samples of maternal blood or urine.

A pregnant teen is considered at special risk. The demands of pregnancy compete with those of her own growth. Pregnant teens also have more complications during pregnancy, including an increased likelihood to become anemic. Teen mothers are more likely than any other age group to bear premature and low-birth-weight infants. A **low-birth-weight** infant *weighs less than 5½ pounds.*

Figure 20.12 Factors Affecting Pregnancy Outcome

Factor	Effect on Risk
Maternal weight	Too low weight and too high weight increase risk.
Maternal malnutrition	Nutrient deficiencies and overdoses increase risk. Food fads increase risks of malnutrition.
Socioeconomic status	Poverty, lack of family support, and lack of education increase risk.
Lifestyle habits	Smoking, as well as drug and alcohol use and abuse, increases risk.
Age	The youngest and oldest mothers have the greatest risk.

Pregnancies
  Number
  Timing
  Outcomes
  Multiple births
	The more previous pregnancies, the greater the risk.
	The shorter the time between pregnancies, the greater the risk.
	Problems during previous pregnancies increase risk.
	Twins or triplets increase risk.

Maternal blood pressure	High blood pressure increases risk.
Sexually transmitted diseases	Many such infections, including AIDS, can attack the fetus and greatly increase risk.
Chronic diseases	Diabetes, heart and kidney disease, certain genetic disorders, and others increase risk.

1. Gestation
2. Embryo
3. Umbilical cord
4. Lactation
5. Prenatal care
6. Nutrients and oxygen
7. An inch in length, has a complete central nervous system and digestive system, a beating heart, fingers, toes, and the beginnings of facial features
8. More likely to become anemic; more likely to bear premature and low-birth-weight infants.
9. Answers will vary.

Low birth weight can arise from two causes. One is early birth. *When the infant is born early*, it is called a **premature infant** (born before the 37th week). Such babies are the right size for the number of days they have spent in the uterus, and their development is normal. They may be small, but they catch up if given proper care. The other cause of low birth weight is growth failure in the uterus. Low-birth-weight infants may face illnesses such as cerebral palsy, small head size, lung disease, and more. *Babies who are small because of underdevelopment* are called **small for date**. These infants do not catch up as well.

A pregnant female should eat balanced meals. Participating in regular physical activity is also recommended, as is avoiding tobacco, alcohol, and other drugs. Seeing a health care professional throughout a pregnancy can help a mother identify any potential issues and answer questions that may arise.

SECTION 5 Review

Reviewing the Vocabulary

Review the vocabulary on page 554. Then answer these questions.

1. _____ is the period from conception to birth.
2. The developing infant during the third through the eighth week after conception is called an _____.
3. The _____ is the ropelike structure through which the fetus's veins and arteries extend to and from the placenta.
4. The production of milk by the mammary glands for the purpose of feeding babies is called _____.
5. _____ is health care provided during pregnancy.

Reviewing the Facts

6. **Explain.** What does the mother's blood deliver to the fetus?
7. **Describe.** Describe an embryo at eight weeks.
8. **Analyze.** Why is a pregnant teen at special risk?

Writing Critically

9. **Expository.** Why is early prenatal care so important to pregnant teens?

For more vocabulary practice, play the eFlashcards game at **glencoe.com**.

Birth Defects and Other Problems

Although most infants are born healthy, some have congenital abnormalities. **Congenital** means *present from birth*. Some of these conditions are diseases. Others involve abnormally formed body parts, and these are known as **birth defects**, *physical abnormalities present from birth*. Congenital abnormalities can arise from many causes. Two of them, genetic inheritance and exposure to harmful chemicals or radiation before or during the development of the fetus, are discussed here. Others include accidents during childbirth, severe nutrient imbalances, and exposure to excessive heat.

Inherited Problems

MAIN IDEA ▶ Congenital abnormalities can cause health issues for a lifetime.

Certain abnormalities run in families. A **genetic counselor**, *an advisor who predicts and advises on the likelihood that congenital defects will occur in a family*, can advise a family on the odds of bearing a child with a congenital abnormality and help them choose whether to bear or adopt children.

Down Syndrome

A risk more common in pregnancies of older females than younger ones is bearing a child with **Down syndrome**, *an inherited condition of physical deformities and mental retardation*. The condition starts at fertilization, when an error in the transfer of genetic material occurs. The error is then repeated and passed on to every cell of the child's body.

PKU

Many other inherited conditions affect offspring. **PKU** (phenylketonuria) is *a congenital disease causing severe brain damage with mental retardation if left untreated*. This condition is the inherited inability of the cells to handle one of the amino acids (parts of protein). At birth, every baby born in the United States is tested for PKU by the medical attendant so that PKU babies may be given a special diet right away to prevent brain damage.

Many inherited problems can be prevented or controlled with special diets or drugs. Thanks to appropriate prenatal care and tests such as **amniocentesis**, *a test of fetal cells drawn by needle through the female's abdomen,* most babies are born healthy.

Vocabulary

congenital
birth defects
genetic counselor
Down syndrome
PKU (phenylketonuria)
amniocentesis
spina bifida
neural tube defects
sudden infant death
    syndrome (SIDS)

Class Activity
Recall: Ask the class to list any birth defects and inherited problems that they can think of. Write these on the board. The students should make their own lists at the same time at their desks. Ask them to share where they heard about these, and what they know about them.

Figure 20.13

Effects of Drugs on Pregnancy

Amphetamines Possible nervous system damage; behavior abnormalities

Barbiturates Drug withdrawal in the newborn lasting up to six months

Cocaine Uncontrolled jerking motions; paralysis; abnormal behaviors; permanent mental and physical damage

Marijuana Short-term irritability at birth

Opiates (including heroin) Drug withdrawal in the newborn; permanent learning disability (attention-deficit/hyperactivity disorder

Health Skills

How to Keep a Pregnancy Safe

1. Avoid drugs, smoking, and alcohol.
2. Engage in moderate physical activity.
3. Avoid environmental toxins.
4. Skip unnecessary X-rays.
5. Eat healthfully.

Harmful Factors

MAIN IDEA ▶ Pregnant females should avoid several substances to protect the health of the fetus.

Chemicals, radiation, and many other factors cause birth defects. Such factors may damage developing organs directly. They also may act by limiting the supply of oxygen or nutrients to the fetus. Many attack the genetic material of the dividing cells. When the genetic material in a cell of a developing embryo or fetus is damaged, the damage multiplies with every division. The final, completed organ of which those cells are a part remains abnormal throughout life.

Alcohol and Other Drugs

Many drugs, including alcohol, are known to damage developing fetuses. Alcohol abuse can lead to fetal alcohol syndrome. Drugs of abuse also harm developing fetuses. Some are listed in **Figure 20.13**.

Nutrition and Spina Bifida

Very high doses above the medically recommended level of some nutrients can be harmful in pregnancy—especially large doses of vitamins A, B$_6$, C, and D; the mineral iodine; and other minerals. A diet lacking fruits and vegetables can also be harmful. This diet may also lack an important vitamin, folate. Low folate levels jeopardize the nerve development of a fetus. Normal development of the brain, nerves, and spine depends on folate to prevent **spina bifida**, *a birth defect often involving gaps in the bones of the spine, leaving the spinal cord unprotected in those spots,* and other **neural tube defects**, *a group of birth defects caused by interruption of normal development of the neural tube*. These defects range from mild spine abnormalities to serious brain defects causing death shortly after birth.

About half of all neural tube defects are believed to be preventable by an adequate intake of folate before and during early pregnancy. For this reason, all cereals, breads, rice, pasta, and other foods already enriched with other nutrients must now also contain extra folate.

Smoking and SIDS

Smoking is harmful to everyone's health, particularly pregnant females. Smoke contains carbon monoxide, which prevents the full amount of oxygen from getting to the fetus. As a result, low birth weight is possible.

In addition, **sudden infant death syndrome** (SIDS)—*the sudden, unexplained death of an infant*—may be linked to cigarette smoking by a pregnant female or by others in her household during pregnancy. Finally, the surgeon general has warned that maternal cigarette smoking causes death in otherwise healthy fetuses and newborns.

Caffeine

The caffeine in a cola or two is well within safe limits for pregnant females. The Health Skills sidebar, "How to Keep a Pregnancy Safe," sums up the risk factors most important to avoid during pregnancy.

Environmental Hazards

Hazards from environmental contaminants are severe. A female who fears that she may have been exposed to an environmental danger should see a health care specialist to find out what to do. Ordinary household chemicals, such as insecticides or cleaning fluids, should be used with caution.

Pregnant females should avoid eating certain types of fish that are known to contain higher than average levels of mercury. These include shark, swordfish, and king mackerel.

Like chemicals, radiation can harm cells. Radiation passes through cells and disrupts their genetic material. One way a fetus might be exposed to such radiation is through X-rays. If an X-ray examination becomes necessary, the female who knows or suspects that she is pregnant should inform all medical personnel.

Discussion

Discuss: Ask students to come up with some environmental hazards that can pose a threat to pregnant women. Discuss the possible effects.

Worksheets: A reproducible quiz for Section 6 is provided in the Teacher Classroom Resources.

SECTION 6 Review

Reviewing the Vocabulary
Review the vocabulary on page 561. Then answer these questions.
1. _____ means present from birth.
2. Define *Down syndrome*.
3. What is *amniocentesis*.
4. Define *neural tube defects*.

Reviewing the Facts
5. **Identify.** Identify some causes of abnormalities in pregnancy outcomes.
6. **Explain.** Why shouldn't pregnant females smoke?

Writing Critically
7. **Personal.** What can you do to encourage parents to keep pregnancies safe?

 **Online**

For more vocabulary practice, play the Concentration game at **glencoe.com.**

1. Congenital
2. An inherited condition of physical deformities and mental retardation.
3. A test of fetal cells drawn by needle through the female's abdomen.
4. A group of birth defects caused by interruption of normal development of the neural tube.
5. Genetic inheritance and exposure to harmful chemicals or radiation, severe nutrient imbalances, and exposure to excessive heat.
6. Smoking limits the oxygen delivery and nutrients to the fetus. Smoking can cause smaller babies, and other complications.
7. Answers will vary.

Childbirth

As the time for birth nears, conditions become restricted in the uterus. The fetus's head then turns downward and fits snugly into the mother's pelvis. *The sensation a pregnant woman experiences when the fetus settles into the birth position* is called **lightening**. The mother feels relief from the pressure on her stomach, heart, and lungs. She can breathe and eat more easily.

Labor and Delivery

MAIN IDEA ▶ Childbirth progresses in stages. It may be preceded by false labor.

Labor means *contractions of the uterus strong enough to push the fetus through the vagina for delivery*. Mild contractions known as **false labor** are *warm-up contractions that many females experience before the birth process*. These are common throughout late pregnancy. They indicate that the uterus is preparing for the work of labor to follow.

Labor begins as the female's hormones cause her uterus to contract powerfully and rhythmically. Labor proceeds in stages. The first is the **dilation stage**, *the stage of childbirth during which the cervix is opening*. The cervix dilates until the baby's head can pass through. In this stage, the contractions become more powerful and closer together.

Next is the **expulsion stage**, *the stage of childbirth during which the uterine contractions push the infant through the birth canal*. The birth canal is another name for the vagina. **Crowning** occurs; this is *the stage in which the top of the baby's head is first seen*. The amniotic sac breaks (if it has not broken already), and the baby is born. Sometimes the birth attendant performs an **episiotomy**, *a surgical cut made in the vagina during childbirth when the vagina cannot stretch enough without tearing to allow the baby to pass*. *The final stage of childbirth, in which the placenta is expelled* is called the **placental stage**. The *placenta and membranes expelled after the birth of the child* are referred to as **afterbirth**.

Cesarean Delivery

Most births occur as a vaginal delivery. That means the infant is born with the head exiting the vagina first. Sometimes, however, a **breech birth** can occur in which *the infant is born in a position other than the normal headfirst position*. For example, the baby is born feet or buttocks first with the head last. In some cases, the attendant may decide to perform a **cesarean section**, *surgical childbirth in which the infant is lifted through an incision in the woman's abdomen*.

Vocabulary

lightening
labor
false labor
dilation stage
expulsion stage
crowning
episiotomy
placental stage
afterbirth
breech birth
cesarean section
postpartum depression

Classroom Activity

Comprehend: After reading the paragraphs under the heading Labor and Delivery, have the students list the stages of childbirth in the correct order, and give brief explanations of each step.

Some reasons for a cesarian delivery include that the baby is too large to pass safely through the mother's pelvis, the baby is in distress because of the delivery, or the mother is bleeding excessively. Cesarean sections are relatively safe for both mothers and babies. However, recovery for mothers takes longer.

Changes After Delivery

With the birth of her infant, the mother normally loses all the weight of the fetus, the placenta, and the associated fluids in about a week. She is left with the body fat she gained during pregnancy. Breastfeeding can draw on these fat stores and help the female lose weight. Without breastfeeding, many females must manage their calories more carefully to lose the extra weight.

Some females feel depressed or are unable to sleep after giving birth. These discomforts may result from the sharp changes in hormone levels that occur after birth or from exhaustion caused by caring for a newborn baby, who doesn't yet sleep for long stretches. This **postpartum depression** is *the emotional depression a new mother experiences after the birth of an infant.* Spending a few weeks quietly alone with family sometimes helps to ease the adjustments.

Worksheets A reproducible quiz for Section 7 is provided in the Teacher Classroom Resources.

SECTION 7 Review

Reviewing the Vocabulary

Review the vocabulary on page 564. Then answer these questions.

1. Define *lightening*.
2. What is *false labor*?
3. Define *postpartum depression*.

Reviewing the Facts

4. Explain. How will the fetus position itself before birth?
5. List. List the stages of labor.
6. Identify. Why would a cesarean section be necessary?

Writing Critically

7. Persuasive. Gabe and Molly are having their first child. The doctor thinks the baby is too big to be delivered vaginally and suggests a cesarean section. What should Gabe and Molly do?

 **Go Online**

For more information on health careers, visit Career Corner at **glencoe.com**.

1. The sensation a pregnant woman experiences when the fetus settles into the birth position

2. Warm-up contractions that many females experience before the birth process

3. The emotional depression a new mother experiences after the birth of an infant

4. The fetus will turn head-first into the mother's pelvis.

5. First stage: the dilation stage; second stage: the expulsion stage; third stage: the placental stage.

6. If the baby is in the breech position or if the baby is too large

7. Answers will vary.

SECTION 8

The Elements of Parenting

Parenting is a skill that can be learned. While it is true that almost everyone has had a model to follow—that of their own parents—most people would do well to learn more about the needs of children for the various ages. Doing what comes naturally may not always be best for the child. One of the first parenting decisions a couple is called upon to make is how to feed their newborn.

Vocabulary

colostrum
discipline
shaken baby syndrome
fetal alcohol syndrome (FAS)
fetal alcohol effect (FAE)

Caption Answer: Breast milk produces antibodies that protect the baby from diseases.

■ **Figure 20.14** *Both breast milk and infant formula are nourishing foods for growing babies, but experts recommend breastfeeding whenever possible. How does breastfeeding help a growing baby?*

Breastfeeding or Formula Feeding?

MAIN IDEA ▶ Each parent needs to decide if breastfeeding or formula feeding is right for their infant.

A female can choose to feed her infant breast milk or formula. Both will support growth of the infant equally well. However, because breast milk offers additional benefits, the American Academy of Pediatrics recommends breastfeeding for 6 months. Breastfeeding should continue for at least 12 months, even after solid foods are added at about 6 months of age.

566 **Chapter 20** From Conception Through Parenting

The earliest form of breast milk is **colostrum**, *a substance rich in antibodies that protects the infant against diseases.* Glands in the mother's breasts transfer immunity factors such as antibodies from the mother's blood to the colostrum. Later breast milk contains immunity factors too, but the milk of the first few days is richest in them.

Some females should not breast-feed their babies. For example, if a female abuses drugs, the drugs will usually be secreted in her breast milk. Infants who are breast fed by mothers who are addicted to alcohol or drugs may also become addicted. Prescription drugs, however, do not deliver large enough quantities to harm nursing infants. Also, females who test positive for the HIV virus should not breastfeed uninfected babies, because the virus can be passed to the infant through breast milk.

Meeting Children's Needs

MAIN IDEA ▶ Parents must provide for their children's physical, emotional, and social needs.

Every parent has responsibilities to the children in their care. A parent's primary responsibility is to support a child's development. This includes providing for all of their physical, emotional, and social needs.

Physical Needs

Parents must, above all, meet their children's physical needs. From infancy until they are financially able to stand alone, children need food, clothing, play activities, school equipment, the company of other children, transportation to wherever these resources are, and health care. Parenting manuals offer details on these topics.

Every child needs healthy food and physical activity throughout growth. The role of food is easily explained. Infants and children need nutrients, from which they build their bodies.

Physical activity is also important. Children don't get enough exercise just by being children. In fact, the children of today are less fit, fatter, and more disease-prone than at any time in the past. Young children need physical activity. It is up to adults to give them opportunities to obtain it.

Emotional and Social Needs

As for a child's emotional and social needs, refer back to Erickson's stages of development in Chapter 3. This scheme lists the responsibilities of parents. This scheme is also a statement of the tasks for parents. Parents help their children develop trust, autonomy, initiative, and industry. In other words, parents are supposed to nurture and shape the person who will someday be an adult.

■ **Figure 20.15** *Outdoor play benefits everyone. Why is outdoor play essential for a young child's health?*

Caption Answer: Physical activity promotes a healthy body.

 **Did You Know?**

Antibodies and other parts of the immune system were described in Chapter 15.

■ Figure 20.16 *Nutritious foods help a healthy baby grow. Why is it important for babies to receive proper nourishment?*

Caption Answer: Healthy food is necessary to grow strong, healthy bodies.

> "*Love and respect are the most important aspects of parenting, and of all relationships.*"

—Jodie Foster, (1962–)
Academy Award-winning actress, director, and producer

Possibly the single most important task for the parent is to instill in the child a strong sense of self-esteem. As earlier chapters described the feeling that "I am okay, I am worthwhile" helps an individual to be effective in every area of life. This includes relationships with others, work, play, and contributions to the larger society. Also vital is **discipline**, *the shaping of behavior by way of rewards and/or punishments.* Having reasonable limits makes children feel safe and secure.

Some common threads draw together all the theories of child development. Children are not miniature adults. That is, they think and reason in ways unique to children. Children develop in known stages. Each child proceeds through those stages at his or her own pace. The process depends partly on the child's own genetic tendencies and partly on the environment furnished by adults.

Many people have grown up in less-than-ideal family circumstances. In the worst cases, parents whose own childhoods included child abuse, verbal, psychological, physical, or sexual assault on a child, tend to become abusive themselves. This behavior becomes especially likely whenever their own needs are not met. People frustrated by life may discipline with anger, and may inflict injuries such as shaken baby syndrome on young children.

Shaken baby syndrome is *a collection of symptoms resulting from violent shaking of an infant or young child.* It is the most common cause of mortality and long-term disability resulting from intentional head injury. Babysitters may do this too, unless they are warned never to shake a baby. Chapter 19 provided details about dysfunctional families—the kind in which child abuse takes place.

Child abuse is illegal. You can help prevent it. If you ever encounter a suspected case of sexual or other abuse of a child, believe the child. The majority of children's reports of such situations are truthful. Seek expert help, support, and counseling for the child and for the abuser. You can report child abuse without giving your name. Check the "Abuse Registry" in the front of your phone book for a toll-free number.

Worksheets

A reproducible quiz for Section 8 is provided in the Teacher Classroom Resources.

SECTION 8 Review

Reviewing the Vocabulary

Review the vocabulary on page 566. Then answer these questions.

1. _____ is a substance produced by the breasts before they begin producing milk.
2. Verbal, psychological, physical, or sexual assault on a child is called _____.
3. _____ is the shaping of behavior by way of rewards and/or punishments.

Reviewing the Facts

4. **Explain.** Why is breastfeeding a baby in the first few months after birth important to the baby's health?
5. **Identify.** What is possibly the single most important task for the parent?
6. **Analyze.** How can you prevent child abuse?

Writing Critically

7. **Personal.** Your best friend, Kyla, has been psychologically abused all her life. After reading this section, what action would you take to help your friend? Why would you take that action?

Go Online

For fitness and health tips, visit the Fitness Zone at **glencoe.com**.

1. Colostrum
2. Child abuse
3. Discipline
4. Glands in the mother's breasts transfer immunity factors such as antibodies from the mother's blood to the colostrum and breastmilk.
5. Parents must instill in the child a strong sense of self-efficacy and self-esteem.
6. Seek expert help, support, and counseling for the child and for the abuser. You can report child abuse without giving your name.
7. Answers will vary.

Q&A Drinking Alcohol During Pregnancy

 Understand and Apply Read the conversation below, and then complete the writing exercise that follows.

About one in every 1,000 children born in the United States is a victim of **fetal alcohol syndrome**, *a cluster of birth defects, including permanent mental and physical retardation and facial abnormalities, seen in children born to mothers who abuse alcohol during pregnancy.*

Q: How does alcohol affect a baby?

A: When a pregnant female uses alcohol, so does her growing fetus. The alcohol passes through the umbilical cord to the fetus. The fetus breaks down the alcohol more slowly than the female. The alcohol level in the fetus is higher and remains in the bloodstream for a longer period of time than in the pregnant female.

Q: What are the symptoms of fetal alcohol syndrome?

A: At its most severe, FAS involves:

- Retarded physical growth, both before and after birth.
- Damage to the brain and nerves, with mental retardation, poor coordination, and hyperactivity.
- Abnormalities of the face and skull.
- Many major birth defects (defects in major organ systems—heart, ears,

genitals, and urinary system).

In less severe cases of **fetal alcohol effect** (FAE), *a subtle version of FAS, with hidden defects including learning disabilities, behavioral abnormalities, and motor impairments,* the damage is hidden. Parents of a baby with FAE may not suspect any birth defects. Infants born with FAE may suffer from learning disabilities, abnormal behaviors, walking problems, other coordination problems, and more. Ten times as many babies are born with FAE and skeletal and major organ damage.

Q: How much alcohol does a woman have to drink to cause FAS?

A: As few as two drinks a day can cause FAS. The most severe damage is likely to be done in the first month, even before the female is sure she is pregnant. Even if the female stops drinking immediately after she learns that she is pregnant, it may be too late to prevent all the damage.

Females who drink two drinks a day are also more likely to have miscarriages. In one study, females who drank as little as two drinks a week were found to have more miscarriages than nondrinkers. Thus, in some cases, it appears that very small amounts of alcohol can endanger fetuses.

■ **Figure 20.17** *Healthy lifestyle choices during pregnancy are crucial to both the mother and the developing child. Why is it important to maintain a healthy diet during pregnancy?*

Caption Answer: Healthy weight gain is needed to support the growth of the placenta, uterus, breasts, and baby. Weight gain should be lean mass, not extra fat.

Q: What about the timing? Why is the first month so crucial?

A: Oxygen is critical to the development of the fetus's central nervous system. A sudden dose of alcohol can halt the delivery of oxygen to the developing fetus. During the first month of pregnancy, even a few minutes of alcohol exposure and oxygen lack can cause major damage to the rapidly growing brain.

The effects of FAS are severe and lifelong. A person who was exposed to alcohol before birth may respond differently to alcohol in adulthood. That person may also respond differently to some drugs. Learning disabilities also last a lifetime. They are caused by even low levels of alcohol intake.

Not every learning disability is caused by alcohol in pregnancy, but no doubt some are. Some experiments even show ill effects from alcohol consumed before pregnancy occurred. The Journal of the American Medical Association advises females to stop drinking as soon as they plan to become pregnant.

It is important to know, though, that if a female has drunk heavily during the first two-thirds of her pregnancy, she can still prevent some damage by stopping heavy drinking during the last third.

Writing Write a paragraph to summarize the effects of FAS on infants.

Reviewing Vocabulary

Use the vocabulary terms listed below to complete the following statements.

embryo

conception

discipline

crowning

afterbirth

implantation

1. The developing infant during the third through the eighth week after conception is called an _____.
2. _____ is the process in which the ovum implants itself the uterine wall.
3. The placenta and membranes expelled after the birth of a child is called _____.
4. _____ is the union of an ovum and a sperm that starts a new individual.
5. _____ is the stage in which the top of the baby's head is first seen.
6. The shaping of behavior by way of rewards and/or punishments is called _____.

Recalling Key Facts and Ideas

Section 1
7. **Explain.** How might a teenage pregnancy be risky?

Section 2
8. **Identify.** What question should be asked before a couple decides to have a baby?

Section 3
9. **Describe.** What happens to the egg in the female's body after it is fertilized?
10. **Explain.** Explain what happens to the uterine lining when the egg is not fertilized.
11. **Analyze.** What must happen for conception to occur?

Section 4
12. **Analyze.** Why is it important for parents to be well nourished before they start a pregnancy?

Section 5
13. **Explain.** Explain what happens to the fetus if the placenta breaks down.
14. **Name.** Which body systems reach maturity first in the developing fetus?
15. **Describe.** Describe the effects of malnutrition during pregnancy.
16. **Identify.** What is the recommended weight gain for a pregnant female?

Section 6
17. **Name.** What are some factors known to damage developing fetuses?

Section 7
18. **Describe.** Describe what the doctor does when a female has a cesarean section.
19. **Explain.** What happens during the dilation stage of labor?

1. Embryo 2. Implantation 3. Afterbirth 4. Conception 5. Crowning 6. Discipline 7. Interruption of education; increased physical risks to mother and child 8. How would it affect my life if I had a child to raise? 9. DNA unite within the fertilized ovum to produce a zygote. Zygote travels into the uterus; implantation occurs. 10. Uterine lining weakens, and is shed during menstruation. 11. An ovum lives for 12 to 24 hours, and living sperm must arrive during this life span. 12. Nutrition affects the ova and sperm. 13. The fetus would be left with no source of nutrients or oxygen. 14. Brain, central nervous

Section 8

20. **Analyze.** Under what conditions should females not breastfeed their babies?

21. **Describe.** In what ways must parents provide for their children's physical needs?

Writing Critically

22. **Expository.** Reread the Q&A section on page 572 entitled "Drinking Alcohol During Pregnancy." Notice how critical the first month of pregnancy is. Note that most females do not even know they are pregnant in the first month. What can be done to help females who drink alcohol when they might be pregnant? Why do you think so many babies are born with fetal alcohol syndrome? How can we educate females about this problem? What can we do to help the infants born with fetal alcohol syndrome?

Activities

23. Conduct research on the Internet to learn more about adoption. Search for information on the average amount of time it takes to adopt a baby. What type of information is sought from the prospective parents?

24. Create a PowerPoint presentation or brochure describing some healthy behaviors for prospective parents. List behaviors that will protect the health of the infant, and behaviors to avoid.

25. Write a one-page essay on your philosophy of rearing children. What things would you definitely do? What things would you definitely not do? Be sure to tell why you would or would not do the things you list.

Making Decisions About Health

26. Autumn and Jason have been married for only six months and don't feel they're ready to have a baby. They use no contraceptives and try to time sexual intercourse so that they avoid the "dangerous" time of the month, but neither is certain of exactly when that time is. So far, Autumn hasn't gotten pregnant.

    a. What is your opinion of the way Jason and Autumn are dealing with their situation? Why do you feel as you do?

    b. What do you think the outcome of this situation might eventually be and why?

For more vocabulary practice, play the True/False game at **glencoe.com**.

Answers
1. True.
2. False. Nonpregnant women may miss periods because of other factors, and a pregnant woman may have a menstrual period.
3. True.

 Writing Paragraphs will vary.

system. **15.** Malnutrition can break down the placenta, and alter the growth of the fetus during critical periods. **16.** 25 to 35 pounds **17.** Accidents during childbirth, severe nutrient imbalances **18.** Doctor cuts through the mother's abdomen and lifts the baby and placenta out. **19.** Cervix dilates; contractions become stronger and closer together. **20.** Women who abuse drugs, or test positive for the HIV virus should not breastfeed. **21.** Provide healthy food, love, and physical activity. **22–26.** Answers will vary.

CHAPTER 21
Understanding Sexuality

Sections

Sex and sexuality are important issues for everyone. Each plays an important role in all of nature. **Sex** is *a general term often used to mean sexual intercourse*. What does sexuality mean? **Sexuality** means *the quality of being sexual*. It refers to our sexual personality. It is important to look at both sex and sexuality from a medically accurate point of view.

This chapter will explain the nature of sex and sexuality and its importance within a person's life. Section 2 will explore the physical act and stages of sexual intercourse. The chapter will then discuss sexual myths and what determines a person's sexuality. Finally, Section 4 will explore the topic of sexual orientation.

Fact or Fiction?

What Do You Think?

Is each statement true or false? If you think it's false, explain what's true.

1. The term *sexuality* refers to sexual activity, primarily sexual intercourse.
2. At puberty, hormones produced by the body create a drive for reproduction.
3. The brain is the center of sexual response.

 Writing Write a paragraph to define *sexuality*. As you read the chapter, revise your paragraph to include new information.

(Answers on page 591)

Go Online

Visit **glencoe.com** and complete the Life Choice Inventory for Chapter 21.

The Nature of Sex and Sexuality

Sexual behavior plays major roles in human experience. Sexual intercourse ensures that humans reproduce and therefore, ensures that the hereditary materials individuals carry, called genes, are repeatedly shuffled and dealt out in different combinations in every new individual. Sexual relationships also bring joy and intimacy that is very special to the couple.

Human Genetic Inheritance

MAIN IDEA ▷ Sexual intercourse ensures that human beings reproduce.

In the cells of your body, you have genes from your biological parents. Your genes govern physical traits such as your eye color, skin color, and hair color. They also impact nonphysical traits, such as personality type, artistic or musical talent, as well as other traits.

The potential to develop these traits was passed on to you at the moment when you were conceived. Half of them came from each of your biological parents. This mixture of genes, combined with your life experience and personal choices you make, determine what sort of person you will turn out to be.

Vocabulary

sex
sexuality

⁉️ Did You Know?

The genes for human traits are passed down in families from parents to children. For example, if your parents have black hair, then it is likely you and your brothers and sisters will have black hair.

■ **Figure 21.1** *Sexual attraction motivates sexual behavior. Why does attraction between people exist?*

Caption Answer: It is a basic, instinctual urge that can lead to the continuation of life through sexual reproduction or other means.

If someday you decide to have a child, you will pass on a mixture of your mother and father's traits as well as traits from your grandparents. Your child may receive your mother's brown eyes and love of learning, and your father's strong hands and musical ability. Your partner will also pass on a mixed set of traits, some from each of his or her parents. Every child is a brand-new individual, carrying a new combination of genes, and therefore, different physical and nonphysical traits. Sexual reproduction, in short, provides a way to mix inherited traits into new combinations in every generation.

Typically, human cells contain 46 chromosomes. However, the reproductive cells, including the male sperm and the female egg, carry only 23 chromosomes each. When the sperm and egg combine, they create the 46 chromosomes.

To sustain life, all species must reproduce. That is why each person's sexuality has such an influence on the person's life. Attraction leads to the continuation of life through sexual reproduction or other means, such as adoption. It is also linked with the expression of one of the highest forms of human emotion—committed, mature love.

"Love does not consist in gazing at each other, but in looking outward together in the same direction."

— Antoine de Saint-Exupery
(1900–1944)
French novelist

Human Sexuality

MAIN IDEA ▶ Sexuality remains part of who people are from birth to death. It affects many facets of life.

Sexuality is a part of a person's personality. The way you walk, think, and feel, and the ways you talk to and touch others, all are affected by your sexuality. Sexuality affects everyone regardless of age, race, and body type. Your sexuality is greatly influenced by the way you feel about yourself. This means that your thoughts, feelings, values, and self-esteem are all part of your sexuality.

 **Did You Know?**

Levels of chemicals in the brain called dopamine and norepinephrine increase and lead to the excited, elated feeling that so many of us get at the start of a new relationship.

In this book, you have read quite a bit about human sexuality, beginning with puberty, sex roles, and gender identity in Chapter 3. In Chapter 18 you read about love relationships and about the sexual pressures that accompany those relationships. In Chapter 20 you learned about conception and pregnancy. In this chapter, you will read about sexual behaviors, and also about sexual myths and problems. Finally, you will learn about sexual orientation.

SECTION 1 Review

Reviewing the Vocabulary

Review the vocabulary on page 576. Then answer these questions.

1. A general term often used to mean sexual intercouse is _____.

2. _____ is the quality of being sexual.

Reviewing the Facts

3. Describe. What are the two major roles sexual reproduction plays in nature?

4. Identify. What two types of traits do genes govern?

5. Explain. How much of your genetic material was contributed by each of your parents?

Writing Critically

6. Explain. Research online or at the library to learn more about genetics and birth traits. Explain how technology can influence a person's traits.

 **Online**

For more vocabulary practice, play the Concentration game at **glencoe.com.**

Sexual Activity

As you know from reading Chapter 20, people who have developed a healthy intimate relationship may decide to commit to each other. One form of commitment between two people is marriage. Sexual activity and emotional intimacy can add fulfillment to marriage.

Touching, hugging, and kissing are intimate, pleasurable activities. These activities may also satisfy emotional needs, and therefore can be emotionally fulfilling. It is normal and natural in a committed relationship for these activities to sometimes lead to **sexual intercourse**, *the reproductive act between the sexes.* When a couple delays sexual activity for a significant period of time, they give themselves time to develop a committed, loving relationship. Forming an intimate relationship in which the couple have trust and mutual respect for each other takes time. When this occurs, the intimacy that a couple shares can be more fulfilling.

The First Sexual Feelings

MAIN IDEA ▶ Natural curiosity often leads to masturbation, which is a way to satisfy a biological drive.

At an early age boys and girls begin to pay more attention to their appearance. They also enjoy physical sensations, such as rubbing lotions onto the skin, or playing with each other's hair. These are the natural healthy beginnings of sexual feelings and activities.

When young people reach puberty, the hormones produced by their bodies cause teens to think more about their sexual feelings. This sexual tension can become intense at times. One way to release this sexual tension is through **masturbation**, *rubbing or stimulating one's own genitals, usually until orgasm occurs.*

Vocabulary

sexual intercourse
masturbation
orgasm
erection
engorgement
excitement phase
plateau phase
ejaculation
resolution phase

■ **Figure 21.4** *In a truly intimate relationship, closeness and caring are as important as sexual attractiveness. Why is it important to develop emotional intimacy rather than just physical intimacy?*

Caption Answer: Emotional closeness develops into a stronger, more committed relationship.

Medical experts believe that masturbation is healthy and provides a way to release sexual tension and avoid the risks of sexual activity, including pregnancy and STDs. However, some people are opposed to masturbation. They believe it is wrong and harmful. In the past, people were told that masturbation caused pimples, warts, and even excessive hair growth. These are all myths—none of them are true.

It is fairly common for teens to be confused about the desire to masturbate. Some may feel guilty and ashamed because it's something they feel they must hide. They may feel that their parents and other adults do not approve.

Another way our bodies release sexual feelings and tension is through nocturnal emissions. As hormone levels increase, the buildup of pressure may lead to nocturnal emissions. In a male, semen is ejaculated. In a female, the vagina secretes moisture. Nocturnal emissions are natural. They may be accompanied by a dream that is sexual in content, also called a wet dream. Almost all teens, both males and females, experience such dreams from time to time. The **orgasm**, *muscular contractions of the sex organs*, that occurs during a wet dream is the body's normal response for releasing sexual tension and feelings. In males, an orgasm causes the release of semen from the penis and in females, the vagina will secrete moisture as well.

Sexual Intercourse

MAIN IDEA ▶ Sexual stimulation often leads to male erection and female engorgement.

Although it is a simple, physical act, sexual intercourse is also complex. The two people who engage in it bring to it their moods, ideas, self-concepts, feelings about their relationship, and everything else that makes them unique. This section is about the physical events of sexual intercourse.

Sexual stimulation usually results in erection of the penis in males. An **erection** is *the state of a normally soft tissue when it fills with blood and becomes firm*. Fluid moves down the male's urethra, neutralizing the acid left there by urine and creating a safe environment for sperm. Females experience **engorgement**, or *swelling*, of the clitoris and surrounding tissues, and a tipping upward of the uterus. Lubricating fluids begin to flow within the vagina.

During the early phase of the male's erection, a drop or so of fluid leaves the penis. This fluid generally does not contain sperm but can transmit STDs. Sperm can easily travel, even from the outside of the vagina, into the uterus. To prevent pregnancy, any semen must be prevented from touching the vagina.

The Stages of the Sexual Response

MAIN IDEA ▶ The four stages of the sexual response are excitement, plateau, orgasm, and resolution.

The mystery of why a sexual response occurs lies in the human brain. Among the organs that respond to the brain's instructions are the clitoris and vagina in a female, and the penis in a male. For both genders, the four phases of sexual response include excitement, plateau, orgasm, and resolution. Each phase may differ from person to person and may vary in the same person from time to time. A person can stop during any phase of the cycle with no physical harm to the body.

Excitement

The **excitement phase**, *the early state of sexual arousal*, may begin even before physical contact occurs. A loving couple may kiss and then touch one another in ways that feel good. This can lead to erection in the male and engorgement in the female. During this time, the couple can enjoy the emotions of tenderness, love, and gratitude, as well as feelings of sexual pleasure and arousal.

Plateau

If sexual stimulation continues, the partners move into the plateau phase. The **plateau phase** is *the period of intense physical pleasure preceding orgasm*. In this phase the lower third of the vagina constricts, the uterus tilts forward, and the penis enlarges further. The clitoris withdraws under its foreskin as it becomes more sensitive.

Orgasm

With continued stimulation, orgasm occurs. Orgasm is a reflex—an involuntary and pleasurable response that follows stimulation of the genitals. In females, orgasm involves involuntary rhythmic contractions of the clitoris, uterus, the outer portion of the vagina, and the surrounding muscles. In males, it involves muscle contractions in the penis, testicles, anus and surrounding areas as well as ejaculation. **Ejaculation** is *the expelling of semen from the penis, brought about by the involuntary muscular contractions of orgasm*. Orgasm lasts just a few seconds. Sexual intercourse usually ends with the male's orgasm because very soon after ejaculation occurs, the male's erection begins to soften. The female's orgasm can occur prior to, along with, after her partner's, or not at all.

1. Sexual intercourse

2. Masturbation

3. Engorgement

4. Resolution

5. Ejaculation

6. The hormones cause teens to think more about their sexual feelings.

7. Some medical experts believe that masturbation provides a way to release sexual tension without the risk of pregnancy or diseases.

8. Clitoris, vagina, and the penis

9. The four phases are excitement, plateau, orgasm, and resolution.

10. The uterus tilts forward.

11. Answers will vary.

Resolution

In the phase called the **resolution phase**, *the phase of relaxation that follows orgasm*, the physical changes of arousal reverse. Tensed muscles relax. Congested blood vessels and swollen tissues return to normal. In most males, the ability to achieve another erection and orgasm requires some period of time, called the refractory period. This can last for a few minutes to several hours and is completely normal. Some females can experience one orgasm after another.

SECTION 2 Review

Reviewing the Vocabulary

Review the vocabulary on page 579. Then answer these questions.

1. The reproductive act is called _____.

2. _____ is the stimulating of one's own genitals, usually until orgasm occurs.

3. _____ means swelling.

4. The stage of relaxation that follows orgasm is called _____.

5. _____ is the expelling of semen from the penis, brought about by the involuntary muscular contractions of orgasm.

Reviewing the Facts

6. Explain. When young people reach puberty, how can hormones affect sexual feelings?

7. Analyze. What do medical experts believe about masturbation?

8. Name. Which organs respond to the brain's instructions during the sexual response?

9. Identify. What are the four phases of the sexual response?

10. Describe. What happens to the female's body in the plateau phase?

Writing Critically

11. Personal. List some ways that sexual tension can be released without engaging in sexual intercourse.

 **Online**

For more information on health careers, visit Career Corner at **glencoe.com**.

Sexual Myths

Some people may believe that only males and females of certain physical types who are considered attractive by society are desirable. Attractiveness is defined by our culture. Today's idea of an attractive female or male has changed over the past century. While social custom may define attractiveness, it is really self-esteem that determines sexuality. The people with the healthiest sexuality are those with the highest self-esteem, normal body image and comfort with their own sexuality.

What Determines Sexuality?

MAIN IDEA ▶ **It is self-esteem and social skills, not physical makeup, that determines sexuality.**

One widely held sexual myth concerns body measurements. The myth suggests that a male with a large penis makes the best lover. This is false. Most females experience sexual stimulation in the clitoris, an external organ. A larger penis, therefore, does not stimulate a female's clitoris. In addition, the average vagina is only about six inches deep; a penis that is much longer can cause discomfort in a female partner. Also, the brain controls the sexual response. Therefore, what a female thinks about a male is at least as important as any physical aspect of intercourse.

A related myth is that a female with large breasts is more sexually appealing than a female with small breasts. Actually, a female's breast size doesn't affect sexual responsiveness. Sexual responses have much more to do with attitudes and emotional makeup than with physical attributes.

Vocabulary

virgin
monogamous

Did You Know?

It is possible for a female to get pregnant from intercourse during her period, especially if her menstrual cycle is brief or irregular.

■ **Figure 21.5** *People sometimes hold false ideas about sexuality. Give some examples of sexual myths.*

Caption Answer: Once someone has had sexual intercourse, that person is committed to having intercourse again.

Another widely believed sexual myth is sexual intercourse with strangers or acquaintances is the usual and healthy path to commitment. Research reveals that most people who eventually marry meet as friends or co-workers—at school, at a private party, at work, at church, or at other shared activities. They may feel an attraction, but the relationship begins as friendship and grows gradually. They wait and gradually get to know each other before thinking about sex or commitment. In contrast, couples who have sexual intercourse right away usually do not stay together.

A particularly destructive idea is that once a person has had sexual intercourse, that person is committed to having intercourse again with that person and every other partner in the future. Anyone who is no longer a **virgin**, *a term applied to people before their first occasion of sexual intercourse*, may choose abstinence at any time in their lives. The person may change moral or religious beliefs, or may simply decide to wait for the right person or may wish to take a break from worry about pregnancy or spread of infection. For many different reasons, saying no is always an option.

Consumer SKILLS ACTIVITY

Medicinal Enhancements

The idea of a pill or liquid to increase sexual desire has always intrigued people. In reality, no secret compound, no exotic ingredient, and no food or nutrient can enhance sexual desire. Over-the-counter products that claim to do so may be dangerous. They may also interfere with other prescribed drugs that a person is taking. Many contain strong stimulants, hormones, or depressants. The Food and Drug Administration recommends that a person suffering from lack of sexual response should see a doctor to determine if there is a medical reason for the problem. An unusual or unexplained lack of sexual response may signal a need for medical or psychological treatment. Doctors can prescribe certain medications, if necessary, to improve sexual function.

Some causes for reduced sexual response and function include an illness such as cancer; use of alcohol, drugs, or tobacco; excess stress or depression. A lack of interest in sexual behavior could relate to poor communication between partners.

 Writing

1. Advertisements for products that claim to increase sexual desire are generally false. Write a paragraph describing why some people may choose to purchase these products.
2. Name some factors that might decrease a person's sexual response.
3. What is the first thing to do if a person is unable to function sexually?

Another myth is that male ejaculation must occur for a female to become pregnant. The muscular contractions that occur during a female's orgasm may help to speed sperm along her reproductive tract. However, sperm can travel up the tract without female orgasm. Whenever sexual intercourse occurs, with or without orgasm, pregnancy can follow.

Some people try to pressure others into sexual activity by claiming that it is unhealthy to become sexually aroused and then not proceed to orgasm. It may be frustrating, and even physically uncomfortable to experience arousal and engorgement without release, but no harm can be caused to another person's health by saying no to sexual activity, or stopping activity at any point.

For most people, sexual satisfaction is related to the feelings you have for the person. That's why many committed couples choose to remain **monogamous**, *having sexual relations with one partner only, excluding all others*. In a committed relationship, a couple has a lifetime to explore and provide for their partner's likes and dislikes and to explore new ways to express themselves sexually over time. Communication is the true key to satisfying sexual relations.

SECTION 3 Review

Reviewing the Vocabulary
Review the vocabulary on page 583. Then answer these questions.
1. Define *monogamous*.

Reviewing the Facts
2. Identify. What is always an option regarding sexual intercourse?
3. Identify. Name two common sexual myths.
4. Name. What is the true key to satisfying sexual relations?

Writing Critically
5. Expository. There are many myths about sexual intercourse and sexuality in general. How can education change these myths? How would you go about changing these myths?

G⊕ Online

For fitness and health tips, visit the Fitness Zone at **glencoe.com**.

1. Having sexual relations with one partner only, excluding all others

2. Saying no to sexual intercourse is always an option, even if you have had sex in the past.

3. Sexual intercourse with strangers is the usual and healthy path to commitment; once a person has had sex that person is committed to having intercourse again.

4. Communication between partners

5. Answers will vary.

Sexual Orientation

Sexual orientation refers to the gender of persons to whom one is romantically and sexually attracted. A person can be heterosexual, homosexual or bisexual. In the general population, about 90 percent of people are sexually attracted to members of the other sex. These people are **heterosexual**, *feeling sexual desire for persons of the other sex*. Some people, however, are attracted to members of the same sex. These people are **homosexual**, *feeling sexual desire for persons of the same sex*. That is, they are **gay**, *a general term referring to males who are homosexual*, or **lesbian**, *a general term referring to females who are homosexual*.

Origins of Sexual Orientation

MAIN IDEA ▶ Evidence about the origins of sexual orientation does not exist.

In the United States, some people have strong feelings, both positive and negative, about homosexuality. Some religious teachings speak against engaging in homosexual behaviors. Some people may even fear homosexuality. In fact, the word **homophobia** means *an irrational fear and/or hatred of people who are homosexuals*. In some societies and in some groups of our society, however, homosexuality is viewed as a normal expression of sexual orientation.

Evidence about the origins of sexual orientation is just now being gathered. Human sexual orientation is very complex. At this time, scientists cannot say why some people are heterosexual, homosexual, or bisexual. Most people feel they are born with their sexual orientation. The American Psychiatric Association does not consider homosexuality to be an emotional illness to be "cured" by therapy.

Vocabulary

heterosexual
homosexual
gay
lesbian
homophobia
bisexual

Writing Activity

Analyze and Discuss: Ask students to write about why they believe some people might exhibit such strong feelings about the sexual orientation of another person. Discuss the responses.

■ **Figure 21.6** *Some people have strong feelings about homosexuality. Why do some people have strong negative or positive feelings about sexual orientation?*

Caption Answer: Some religious teachings speak against homosexuality, and some people may fear it.

As well as feeling attraction to the opposite sex, or the same sex, some people may be **bisexual**, or *being sexually attracted to members of both sexes*. While we all have feelings for our same-sex friends, those feelings do not necessarily mean that a person is bisexual. Bisexuality is not the same as expressing affection for them by hugging, kissing, or patting on the back. Most people's expressions of such feelings do not imply bisexuality. In early adolescence, it is common for young people to have early sexual experiences with other people—both their own gender and the other gender. Most of these experiences are to satisfy curiosity and do not determine sexual orientation.

Worksheets: A reproducible quiz for Section 4 is provided in the Teacher Classroom Resources.

SECTION 4 Review

Reviewing the Vocabulary

Review the vocabulary on page 586. Then answer these questions.

1. Feeling sexual desire for persons of the other sex is called _____.

2. Feeling sexual desire for persons of the same sex is called _____.

3. _____ is a general term referring to homosexuality, but often referring to homosexual males.

4. _____ is a term referring to homosexual females.

Reviewing the Facts

5. Explain. What does it mean to be homophobic?

6. Describe. What is bisexuality?

Writing Critically

7. Expository. Make a list of all the qualities you would like to have in a partner in a relationship. Put a + by those qualities the person must have. Put a - by the qualities you would like the person to have but could do without. How realistic is your list? Does anyone exist who has all of the qualities you listed? Remember that perfection is not something you're going to find in a partner, any more than your partner will find it in you.

Go Online

For more vocabulary practice, play the eFlashcards game at **glencoe.com**.

1. Heterosexual
2. Homosexual
3. Gay
4. Lesbian
5. A person who is afraid of homosexuals.
6. Sexual attraction to both sexes.
7. Answers will vary.

Q&A What About Me? Am I Missing Out?

Understand and Apply Read the conversation below, and then complete the writing exercise that follows.

Young people hear many conflicting messages about sex. The voices of parents, teachers, and others saying it's best to wait can easily be lost in the sexual messages in magazines, books, advertisements, and movies. Teens who forgo sexual activity may wonder if they are missing out on what life has to offer.

Q: Sometimes I wonder why, if sex is so bad, every magazine I pick up or movie I see is so full of sex. I know that the stories are made up, but they reflect how real-life sexual situations work, don't they?

A: Actually, most people in this society are careful in their choices concerning sexual behavior, while people on TV seem unthinking in the choices they make. The majority of adults value faithfulness to one partner and do not have intercourse with strangers or casual acquaintances. Sexual topics in magazines, on TV, and in film increase sales. Advertisers may not think about the messages they might be sending to young people.

Q: What about love? The characters in stories usually see each other across a room, meet, fall madly in love, become sexually involved, and live happily ever after. Isn't love all that matters?

A: From your description, it sounds as though the characters meet, fall madly into infatuation, and become sexually active. Rarely does true, mature love follow such an encounter. More often, when the partners get to know each other better, the infatuation quickly fades, and the partners lose interest in one another.

People who are looking for a relationship assess every new acquaintance in terms of potential for a partnership. Most people often want mates who are similar to themselves in age, race, education, and social status. The more similar to themselves the new acquaintance seems to be, the more likely they are to assess the new relationship as positive.

Q: My friends all talk about sex and act like it's cool. I'm afraid to say that I'm not doing it. Actually, I don't really want to. But I'm afraid that if my friends find out, they'll think that I'm not popular.

A: Experts suggest that you tell your friends the truth. You may be surprised to find out that your friends feel the same way or that they understand your point of view. Very commonly, teens will say they've engaged in sexual activity when they haven't, just to sound important or grown-up. They may have the same fears that you have, but may talk about sex to put up a smoke screen.

The truth is that fewer teens are having sex than in generations past. More young people are waiting longer too. For them, the pressures of sexual activity are too great. Time spent planning their futures and participating in school activities is more important.

Q: I was once in an uncomfortable situation where I wanted to say no to a date, but I couldn't think fast enough and ended up making the person angry. How can I handle the situation next time?

A: The best attitude is one of self-confidence. It also helps to keep thinking about the consequences, ranging from a lost opportunity for a real relationship to an unwanted pregnancy or a life-threatening disease, such as AIDS.

When you tell your partner your feelings, stay calm. Remember to use "I" messages describing your feelings. Calmly express your high regard for yourself by choosing your own behaviors, without angering or insulting others in the process. It's important to remember, too, that a real friend would not pressure you into doing something that you're not ready to do.

Q: That sounds like it's "easier said than done."

A: Effective communication of your wishes takes effort. You must be honest and sound firm. State clearly that your mind is made up. Give only short answers to direct questions, because there is nothing to discuss or negotiate. Speak convincingly, show that you are in control, maintain eye contact, and use a steady voice.

Here is an example situation and response that may help you practice your responses during uncomfortable situations related to sexuality.

Situation:

While at a party with friends, your partner of a few months says, "It's hot and crowded here. Let's leave and find someplace quieter and less crowded so we can talk."

Responses:

"Yes, it's crowded, but isn't so bad outside. Let's go there and talk."

"Oh, I see my friend over there. I'd like to introduce you to her."

"I'm thirsty. Let's go over there and get a soda."

Try to think of other situations that may occur, and practice some responses you could use in those situations. That way, you'll be more prepared to handle the real thing.

Q: I'd like some help in supporting my decision to postpone sexual activity. I just don't know who to turn to.

A: Talk with friends about your decision to refrain from sexual activity. They should respect your decision and support you in it. They may be glad to have a leader to show them the way as well. If you can, also talk to your parents about your decision, and ask them for their support.

Remember that there's more to life than sex. Develop your skills at school and at home. Enjoy outdoor activities. Fill your days with the company of positive people who support you as you become the person you were meant to be.

 Writing Write a scenario describing how you would handle an uncomfortable situation in which you were being pressured to have sex.

Reviewing Vocabulary

Select the appropriate key term from the list above.

sexual intercourse

sexuality

virgin

erection

excitement phase

engorgement

homophobia

bisexual

1. The quality of being sexual is called _____.

2. _____ is the reproductive act between the sexes.

3. The state of a normal soft tissue when it fills with blood and becomes firm is called _____.

4. The early state of sexual arousal is called _____.

5. A term applied to people before their first occasion of sexual intercourse is _____.

6. _____ is an irrational fear and/or hatred of homosexuals.

7. Being sexually oriented to members of both sexes is called _____.

8. _____ means "swelling".

Recalling Key Facts and Ideas

Section 1
9. **Identify.** What two major roles does sex play in nature?

10. **Name.** What factors have influenced your sexuality?

Section 2
11. **Identify.** What is one form of commitment?

12. **Explain.** Why is sexual intercourse considered a complex act?

13. **Name.** Where do sexual responses begin?

Section 3
14. **Describe.** Describe two myths concerning sexuality.

15. **Explain.** What determines sexuality?

Section 4
16. **List.** Why do some people have strong positive or negative feelings about homosexuality?

Writing Critically

17. Read the Q&A on pages 588–589. Why are topics about sex and sexual behavior so popular on television, in the movies, and in other media? Do the media usually portray real people? Why or why not?

18. Think about the steps for making decisions that were discussed in Chapter 2. (Name the problem, describe it specifically, brainstorm, think about each solution, choose a solution and act on it, and evaluate the outcome.) How could these steps be helpful if someone is faced with a situation in which they are being pressured to have sex?

1. Sexuality 2. Sexual intercourse 3. Erection 4. Excitement-phase 5. Virgin 6. Homophobia 7. Bisexual 8. Engorge-ment 9. It ensures that living things reproduce, and it ensures that genes are shuffled into different combinations in each new individual. 10. Sexuality is influenced by thoughts, feelings, values, and self-concept. 11. Marriage 12. Two people bring to it their own moods, ideas, self-concepts, and feelings about their relationship. 13. In the brain. 14. A woman's

Activities

19. Put together a booklet, presentation, podcast, or video with the following phone numbers: an AIDS hotline, a local youth services organization, a teen talk number, and a crisis pregnancy center. Make these available for everyone at your school to use.

20. Interview your parents or grandparents about dating customs when they were your age. Develop a list of questions with the members of your class. What are the similarities? What are the differences between the dating customs of your grandparents' era and today's customs? Share these interviews as oral reports.

21. What are your rights in a relationship? Do you have the right to make your own decisions? Do you have the right to say no to sex? Make a list of the rights you believe you should have in a relationship. (Remember that the other person would have the same rights.) Work together with the rest of your class to compile a classroom list of relationship rights.

22. Work in groups of four or five classmates to develop a list of ways to say no when a relationship is about to go too far for one or both of the partners. Develop role-plays that use the no answers your group came up with. Then, make a list of alternative activities for the couple so that the situation can be avoided in the future.

Making Decisions About Health

23. Lisa has been in a relationship for several weeks, and the question of sexual intimacy has been raised. She is sexually inexperienced, and even though she cares for the other person and feels a sexual attraction, she has been taught that sex before marriage is wrong. Lisa feels confused, because part of her wants a sexual relationship, but the other part fears that sexual intimacy will lead to loss of respect or rejection. What should Lisa do at this point?

Ge Online

For more vocabulary practice, play the True/False game at **glencoe.com**.

Fact or Fiction?

Answers

1. False. Sexuality is part of a person's total personality with or without sexual activity.
2. True.
3. True.

 Writing Paragraphs will vary.

breast size affects sexual responsiveness, and orgasm must occur before a woman becomes pregnant. **15.** Self-esteem determines sexuality. **16.** Some religious teachings speak against homosexuality, and some people may fear it.

17–23. Answers will vary.

CHAPTER 22

Preventing Pregnancy and STDs

Sections

1. Choosing Contraception and STD Protection
2. Contraceptive Methods
3. Methods Not Recommended for Contraception
4. Sterilization
5. Contraceptive Failure

Chapter Preview

Sexual intercourse, one of the main topics of the previous chapter, can lead to pregnancy. For couples in a committed relationship, who are eager to raise children, pregnancy is a happy event. It can strengthen the couple's relationship and promote their personal growth. For couples who are not yet ready to raise and support children or those who have decided they do not want children, however, pregnancy can be difficult.

Approximately 82 percent of teen pregnancies are unintended. In this chapter you will learn how people can prevent pregnancy. You will also learn that the choice of birth control method can dramatically affect the risk of acquiring a sexually transmitted disease (STD).

Of course, the only guarantee that a pregnancy will not occur is total abstinence from sexual activity.

Fact or Fiction?

What Do You Think?

Is each statement true or false? If you think it's false, explain what's true.

1. People who first obtain all the facts can find the perfect contraceptive method.
2. Condoms are as effective as abstinence in preventing sexually transmitted diseases.
3. If a female is not taking the pill, this means she isn't using birth control.

 Writing Write a paragraph to explain why you think contraception is a controversial topic.

(Answers on page 621)

Go Online

Visit **glencoe.com** and complete the Life Choice Inventory for Chapter 22.

SECTION 1

Choosing Contraception and STD Protection

Vocabulary

contraception
effectiveness
laboratory effectiveness
user effectiveness

" The management of fertility is one of the most important functions of adulthood."

—Germaine Greer
(1939–)
Author

Teens often think that pregnancy is difficult to achieve. For a healthy, sexually active male and female, though, pregnancy occurs easily. Eighty-five percent of sexually active couples who use no birth control become pregnant within one year. As **Figure 22.1** shows, pregnancy is the rule—not the exception—for sexually active people using no contraception. **Contraception** is *any method of preventing conception*.

Contraception

_____

MAIN IDEA ► Various contraceptive methods can prevent conception.

_____

Among sexually active teens, fewer than half report that they always use contraception. Teens also contract STDs at a higher rate than other age groups. While the odds of pregnancy from unprotected sexual intercourse are high, the odds of contracting an STD are higher too.

Not all people see contraception in the same way. Some people's religious beliefs forbid its use. Other people would like everyone worldwide who is sexually active to use it. This chapter does not argue for or against contraception. It takes the position that the choice is personal, and it presents the facts people need to make informed choices.

| Figure 22.1 | The Odds of Pregnancy |

Among ten sexually active couples using no contraception,

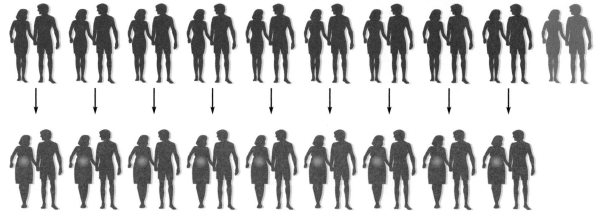

nine become pregnant within one year.

Contraception is not for females only. It is a shared responsibility that accompanies sexual intercourse. No one should ever assume that a partner will take care of protecting against pregnancy or STDs.

Close to a million teens become pregnant each year, but three times that many teens contract an STD. Teens who are sexually active, meaning that the teen is engaging in intercourse, anal sex, or oral sex, should use a condom. This is true even when other birth control methods, such as the pill, is used to prevent pregnancy.

The couple should discuss everything that could happen before deciding to have intercourse. Being concerned about contraception shows a strong commitment to the partner's well-being. Open discussions about contraception not only help the couple find a suitable method, but also may bring them closer together and strengthen their relationship.

Where to Get Help

MAIN IDEA ▷ A health care professional can recommend which contraceptive method is right for you.

Expert advice from a physician, physician's assistant, or nurse practitioner can help a teen who wants to make a decision about contraceptives. Talking to a parent, if possible, can also help. The professional will check for health problems, provide education, and, if one is needed, write a prescription. Student health centers, county health departments, and family planning centers often have reliable printed information sheets. Many provide other contraceptive services at a reasonable cost.

Religious organizations may also provide counseling services. They may address topics of sexuality, pregnancy, and other issues, as well as contraception. Internet sources can also provide reliable information, but teens should do research to make sure the information is reliable. Websites ending in **.gov** are maintained by the government and contain reliable health information.

If you choose to seek outside help, remember that these agencies are made up of individuals, and not every counselor is the right one for every person. If you should feel uncomfortable with one counselor, ask to see someone else. If you don't get the information you are seeking from one type of center, go to another. Do your research before visiting any counseling center that you're unfamiliar with. Check the information that the center distributes against what's available on Websites ending with **.gov** for accuracy. Remember too that no contraceptive method is perfect. Each method will have its own advantages and disadvantages.

Two Kinds of Effectiveness

MAIN IDEA ▶ The effectiveness rating of a contraceptive method depends on how it was studied.

One of the most important aspects of a contraceptive method to consider is its **effectiveness**, *how well a contraceptive method or device prevents pregnancy, expressed as a percentage.* For example, you may hear an expert say that the effectiveness of a contraceptive method is 98.5 percent. Later, you may hear another trusted source say it is only 92 percent effective. Both may be right. The two numbers are different because they are obtained by two different types of scientific studies.

The first expert may be quoting studies that answer the question: How well does this method work in 100 *couples who use it perfectly* for one year? These studies are run in laboratories that permit no mistakes. When this contraceptive method is used perfectly, then its **laboratory effectiveness**, *the percentage of females protected from pregnancy in a year's time under ideal laboratory conditions,* is 98.5 percent.

The second expert is quoting studies of what occurs in real life. These studies answer the question: How many typical users out of 100 become pregnant while using the contraceptive method for one year? The **user effectiveness**, *the percentage of typical female users who are protected,* is 92 percent. In real life, 8 females out of 100 become pregnant because in real life people use methods incorrectly, inconsistently, or the method failed.

Side Effects

MAIN IDEA ▶ Side effects from contraceptives should not be ignored. Some side effects can be deadly.

Side effects from the use of contraceptive methods range from those that are helpful to those that are deadly. Some females say that taking the birth control pill eases the cramping that is associated with their monthly menstrual cycle. Some contraceptive methods, however, can increase the risk of stroke and other serious illnesses. If a female over the age of 35 takes the pill, the risk of stroke increases if she also uses tobacco products. Each person who uses a contraceptive method should talk to a doctor or other health care professional about any side effects.

Worksheets: A reproducible quiz for Section 1 is provided in the Teacher Classroom Resources.

SECTION 1 Review

Reviewing the Vocabulary

Review the vocabulary on page 594. Then answer these questions.

1. The _____ of a contraceptive method is the percentage of females protected from pregnancy in a year's time under ideal laboratory conditions.

2. The _____ is the percentage of typical female users who are protected.

3. How well a contraceptive method or device prevents pregnancy is, in general, called its _____.

4. _____ is any method used to prevent conception.

Reviewing the Facts

5. Describe. What happens in a relationship in which the couple openly communicates about contraception?

6. Recall. Where can teens go to get advice about contraceptives?

Writing Critically

7. Expository. Sarah wants to discuss methods of contraception with her boyfriend, Steve. Steve thinks that contraception is Sarah's responsibility. Write a paragraph explaining why contraception is the responsibility of both individuals.

Go Online

For more vocabulary practice, play the eFlashcards game at **glencoe.com**.

1. Laboratory effectiveness
2. User effectiveness
3. Effectiveness
4. Contraception
5. Open communication shows a strong commitment to the partner's well-being as well as strengthening the relationship.
6. Teens should first talk to a parent or guardian, then seek advice from a doctor.
7. Answers will vary.

Contraceptive Methods

As you read about each contraceptive method, you may notice that some are given more space than others. This is not because they are better methods, but because they are more complex in their actions. Effectiveness and safety are the main factors to consider for each one.

Abstinence

MAIN IDEA ▶ Abstinence is the only method that can be 100 percent effective in preventing pregnancy and STDs.

The safest, most effective contraceptive method to consider is abstinence, refraining completely from sexual relations with other people. Today, teens across the United States are choosing abstinence. Part of the reason is to avoid pregnancy. Also, teens are more aware these days of the threats they face from AIDS, herpes, and other STDs.

When used correctly, abstinence is the most effective contraceptive—100 percent effective. To use abstinence correctly, a couple must remember that a pregnancy can begin if even a single drop of fluid from the penis is deposited near the opening of the vagina. Sperm from this fluid can travel into the vagina and up through the uterus. Therefore, to be 100 percent effective in preventing pregnancy, abstinence must include preventing any contact at all between the man's penis and the female's vagina.

Vocabulary

oral contraceptives
combination pill
estrogen
progesterone
progestin
intrauterine device (IUD)
barrier methods
diaphragm
cervical cap
male condom
female condom

■ **Figure 22.3** *Effectiveness and safety are the main factors to consider when choosing contraception. What are some examples of hormonal methods of contraception?*

Caption Answer: Birth control pill, patch, implants, injections

Abstinence is also 100 percent effective against STDs. Proper use of a latex condom is the next best choice for disease prevention. STDs can be transmitted by any skin-to-skin contact, including intercourse, oral, and anal sex.

The decision to abstain from sexual intercourse can take courage and willpower. Most people who succeed, however, say it is worth the effort. They say they can best focus on their own growth and pursue their own goals without the demands of a sexually intimate relationship. Finally, when they become ready to make a lifelong commitment, they are emotionally ready for a mature relationship.

Hormonal Methods

MAIN IDEA ▶ Hormonal methods of birth control prevent pregnancy by providing hormones that stop ovulation.

Hormonal methods are the most common methods used to prevent pregnancy. Some of those methods include the birth control pill, patch, implants, injections and some intrauterine devices. Hormonal methods, like any birth control method, have side effects.

Oral Contraceptives

Many females choose **oral contraceptives**, *pills that prevent pregnancy by stopping ovulation or by changing conditions in the uterus. They are more popularly known as "the pill."* Several types of birth control pills exist. Each contains a different combination of drugs. The **combination pill** *an oral contraceptive that contains progestin and synthetic estrogen*, uses synthetic versions of **estrogen**, *a hormone that regulates the ovulatory cycle in females*, and progesterone to prevent pregnancy. **Progesterone** is *a hormone secreted in females during that portion of the menstrual cycle in which the uterine lining builds up.* **Progestin**, is *a synthetic version of progesterone used in contraceptives.*

Two new types of birth control pills limit the number of times a female menstruates, or eliminates menstruation. One type of low-dose pill is taken every day of the year and eliminates menstruation. Another type of low-dose pill extends a female's cycle so that she may only menstruate four times a year.

Correct Use of Oral Contraceptives The effectiveness of the pill, as with any type of contraception, depends on regular and correct use. If a female forgets to take her pill for a day or more, she should take the missed pill as soon as she remembers it, get back on her pill schedule, and use a backup method of contraception for the remainder of that pill cycle.

⁇ **Did You Know?**

Some people mistakenly believe the pill to be the only form of birth control. The pill is just one choice among many.

Health Skills

Avoiding Pregnancy

People can completely protect themselves from pregnancy by:

1. Oral contraceptives (prescription).
2. Hormone patches and injections (prescription).
3. Intrauterine devices (IUDs) (prescription).
4. Vaginal spermicides (over-the-counter).
5. Diaphragms (prescription).
6. Cervical caps and contraceptive rings (prescription).
7. Male condoms (over-the-counter).
8. Female condoms (over-the-counter).
9. Fertility awareness method (the rhythm method).
10. Sterilization (surgical procedure).

Emergency Contraception An emergency form of birth control, also called *the morning-after pill*, can prevent pregnancies with 75 to 89 percent effectiveness when used correctly. As its name implies, it is not for everyday use. It consists of two of larger-than-normal doses of the same hormones in regular pills, taken within five days following unprotected sexual intercourse. The method is available over-the-counter to adults. Teens age 17 and younger require a doctor's prescription to purchase the drug.

Side Effects of Oral Contraceptives The side effects of oral contraceptives range from those that help the user to rare, life-threatening conditions. Among those side effects that users report as helpful are regulating menstruation, reducing the severity of cramping, and reducing the likelihood of some forms of cancer. Among the negative side effects, some of the more common, less serious are tenderness of the breasts, mood swings or fatigue, nausea or vomiting, skin conditions, weight gain or loss, a cessation of menstruation, unexpected vaginal bleeding, and a tendency to develop vaginal yeast infections. Rarer side effects are high levels of sugar and fat in the blood, an impaired sex drive, headaches, and fluid retention. Among the most rare and serious side effects are diseases of the heart, kidney, liver, or gallbladder; benign tumors of the uterus; and blood clots that can lodge in vital organs and cause death.

Early symptoms almost always warn a user who is developing any of the serious medical conditions. A female taking oral contraceptives should call her physician if she has:

- Abdominal pain.
- Chest pain.
- Breathlessness.
- Headaches.
- Blurred vision or loss of vision.
- Leg pain.

Females who use birth control pills are advised not to smoke. Smoking increases the risk of heart attack or stroke. The progestin-only pill produces fewer and less severe side effects than the combination pill, so females sometimes switch to it. Of course, the progestin-only pill has possible side effects of its own, including menstrual disorders and, less often, headaches.

Most females who use the pill experience no side effects or very minor side effects. Others who experience minor symptoms may find that they disappear after about three months. Sometimes a switch from one brand of pill to another can bring relief (the female can ask her doctor).

It is important to be aware that depression, which is a relatively common side effect, may take some time to develop.

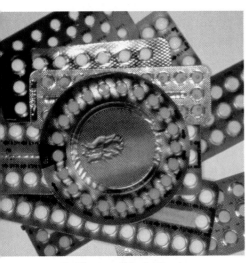

■ **Figure 22.4** *Oral contraceptives. What is the difference between a combination pill and a progestin-only pill?*

Caption Answer: A combination pill contains progestin and synthetic estrogen while a progestin-only pill contains only progestin.

The user may not realize that the depression is caused by taking oral contraceptives. When moodiness, sadness, or irritability is not explained by life events and does not improve after a few months, a pill user should talk to her doctor about the symptoms.

A female who thinks she may be pregnant should not take the pill. Taking it when pregnant increases the risk of birth defects. A female who is using oral contraceptives and decides to become pregnant should switch to another method of contraception for at least two months (some health care providers suggest six months to a year) before she desires to become pregnant.

The Hormone Implants, Patch, and Injection

Progestin, the synthetic hormone of oral contraceptives, can also be delivered by slow-release capsules implanted under the skin. In a simple surgical procedure, a physician implants a thin rod under the skin. These products work by slowly releasing progestin for up to three years. Its effectiveness is about the same as the laboratory effectiveness of progestin-only pills. This method does not protect against HIV or other STDs.

Intrauterine Device (IUD) Another type of device that is placed inside a female's body is the **intrauterine device**, or IUD, (see **Figure 22.5**). The IUD is a *device inserted into the uterus to prevent conception or implantation.* Some IUDs use hormones to prevent pregnancy. Each month after a female completes her menstrual cycle, it's recommended that she check to make sure the IUD is still in place. A tiny nylon thread hangs from the IUD through the cervix into the vagina. If the thread is present, the female will know that the IUD is in place.

The IUD is best suited for females who have had at least one child; are in a stable, mutually monogamous relationship (such as marriage); and have no history of pelvic inflammatory disease (PID).

Pelvic inflammatory disease (PID), which can lead to sterility, has been associated with IUD use. PID may occur if, during insertion of the device, bacteria are introduced into the uterus. Also, a female with an IUD may fail to use condoms to prevent STDs, and STDs often cause PID. An IUD may prevent pregnancy, but it does not prevent STDs.

Vaginal Ring Another type of device that is placed inside a female's vagina is the ring. The ring releases the hormones progestin and estrogen. The walls of a female's vagina keep the ring in place. The ring is worn for three weeks and removed during the menstrual period. A doctor must prescribe the ring. Common side effects can include vaginal infections and irritation, vaginal secretion, headache, weight gain, and nausea. This method does not protect against HIV or other STDs.

Writing Activity
Summarize: Have students research the possible reasons why a female who is using oral contraceptives, should switch over to a different form of contraception for at least a couple of months before becoming pregnant. Ask them to write a summary of the information they gather and allow volunteers to read their summaries aloud.

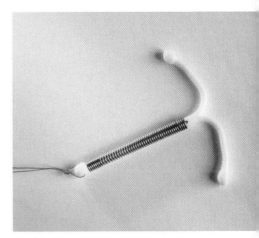

■ **Figure 22.5** *Intrauterine device. How does an IUD prevent pregnancy?*

Caption Answer: Some current IUDs use hormones to prevent pregnancy.

 **Did You Know?**

HPV and other sexually transmitted diseases are discussed in Chapter 16.

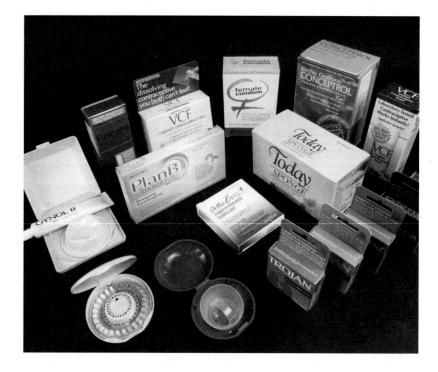

■ **Figure 22.6** *Vaginal spermicides. How should spermicides be used to reduce the risk of pregnancy?*

Caption Answer: Spermicides must be used with other forms of contraception, such as the diaphragm or condoms to greatly reduce the risk of pregnancy.

Group Project

Research: Ask students to work in pairs to research progestin injections. Tell them to gather information on how it works as a method of contraception and why it is not recommended for teens. Students should also be ready to share information about the benefits and possible side effects of the shot. Discuss the findings as a class.

The Patch The patch is worn on the lower abdomen, buttocks, or upper body. Hormones are released through the skin. The patch should be placed on a female's body five days after menstruation begins. It must be replaced once a week for three weeks. During the fourth week, if the patch is not worn, a menstrual period will occur. The patch carries a higher risk for blood clots than oral contraceptives because of the higher levels of estrogen. This method is prescribed by a doctor, and does not protect females from STDs.

It is suggested that the patch be placed on a part of the body that's not easily seen by others. Because the patch may not be easily visible, some females fear that it may fall off. Users of the patch can engage in regular activities. The adhesive on the patch make it unlikely that this form of birth control will fall off.

Injections As an alternative to implants, older females (not teens) can choose to receive a shot of progestin that lasts for three months. Females using this method also need to use condoms for STD prevention.

Barrier Contraception Methods

MAIN IDEA ▶ Barrier contraception methods prevent the sperm from reaching and fertilizing the egg.

Barrier contraception methods are safe and effective ways to prevent pregnancy. These methods work by acting as barriers to keep the sperm from reaching and fertilizing the egg. Some methods, such as male and female condoms may also protect against certain sexually transmitted diseases.

Vaginal Spermicides

Spermicides are chemicals that kill sperm. Spermicides are inserted into the vagina immediately before intercourse. They are available over-the-counter in the forms shown in **Figure 22.6**—foams, creams, gels, sheets, or suppositories. These contraceptives are called **barrier methods**—*contraceptive methods that physically or chemically obstruct the travel of sperm toward the ovum.*

Most spermicides only last a half an hour or so, and therefore must be inserted just prior to each occasion of sexual intercourse. Also, spermicides, when used alone, often fail to prevent pregnancy. The effectiveness of spermicides increases when it's use is combined with another method, such as the diaphragm or condoms. Spermicides may cause irritation in some females. If this occurs, the female should stop using the spermicide, and talk to her doctor.

Spermicides also kill some of the pathogens that cause STDs. Spermicides alone do not kill all viruses, however. The viruses that cause AIDS and herpes are unaffected by spermicides.

Diaphragm or Sponge

The **diaphragm**, another barrier method, is *a dome that fits over the cervix and holds spermicidal cream or jelly against the uterine entrance to block the passage of sperm.* The device is folded into the vagina. Once inside, it springs open to cover the cervix. The diaphragm is shown in **Figure 22.7**. The diaphragm holds spermicide snugly against the entrance of the cervix and bars sperm from entering the uterus. The diaphragm provides a barrier to some STD bacteria that may otherwise invade the uterus. The diaphragm provides no protection against viruses that cause STDs, however, so condoms are still essential.

To work properly, a diaphragm must be custom fitted for each female. A female must be refitted if she gains or loses 10 or more pounds or if she has a child. The user of a diaphragm can insert it up to six hours before intercourse.

If two hours or so have passed before the intercourse occurs the female should apply another dose of spermicide. After intercourse, the female should leave the diaphragm in place for at least six hours and then remove it within 24 hours. To repeat intercourse within the six-hour period during which the diaphragm must remain in place, the female can simply insert an application of spermicide into the vagina. The user should store her diaphragm with care and check it often for holes or other defects by holding it up to a light. It has a limited life span.

Another device, the disposable contraceptive sponge, is available over-the-counter. The sponge is placed inside the female's vagina before intercourse. The spermicides inside the sponge prevent pregnancy.

■ **Figure 22.7** *Diaphragm with spermicide. Why is it important to be fitted for a diaphragm?*

Caption Answer: A diaphragm must be fit to ensure that it is the right size for each female. If a female should gain or lose 10 pounds or has a child, she should be refitted.

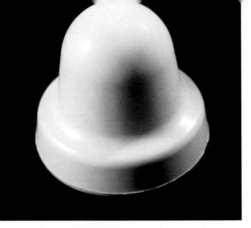

■ Figure 22.8 *Cervical cap.* *What are the similarities between a cervical cap and a diaphragm?*

Caption Answer: They must fit perfectly to prevent the passage of sperm into the uterus and a health care provider chooses the size to fit the user. Like the diaphragm, the cap is used with spermicide and left in place before and after intercourse.

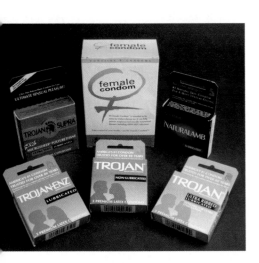

■ Figure 22.9 *Male condoms.* *Why are latex condoms a better choice of condom to use as a contraceptive?*

Caption Answer: Latex condoms offer protection against pregnancy as well as sexually transmitted diseases, such as HIV/AIDS.

Cervical Cap

The **cervical cap**, shown in **Figure 22.8**, is *a rubber cap that fits over the cervix, used with spermicide to prevent conception*. Like the diaphragm, it must fit perfectly to prevent the passage of sperm into the uterus. A health care provider chooses the size to fit the user. Like the diaphragm, the cap is used with spermicide and left in place before and after intercourse. A cervical cap must be prescribed by a doctor. Cervical caps do not prevent infection from STDs.

In a very few instances, the dangerous bacterial poisoning known as toxic shock syndrome (TSS) has been associated with diaphragm and cervical cap use. Teenage girls are its most frequent victims. (More often, toxic shock syndrome has been associated with the use of superabsorbent tampons.) Because of the risk of toxic shock syndrome, it may be wise to avoid using a diaphragm or cap during the menstrual period and always remove it after no more than 24 hours.

Male Condom

Use of a male condom is the only method, aside from sterilization, available to males. The **male condom** is *a sheath worn over the penis during intercourse to contain the semen, to prevent pregnancy, and/or to reduce the risks of sexually transmitted diseases*. Condoms are shown in **Figure 22.9**. Semen collects in the tip of the condom and is discarded with it.

The choice of latex condoms for contraception is best for two reasons. First, latex condoms offer protection against sexually transmitted diseases, such as HIV. As mentioned, females who use another form of contraception against pregnancy must use condoms as well. The pill, patch, injection, and other methods may prevent pregnancy, but they leave people open to sexually transmitted diseases.

The other reason that latex condoms are a wise choice for contraception is that they are superior at preventing pregnancy. Latex condoms with or without spermicide added, if used correctly, can provide pregnancy protection up to 98 percent of the time.

When applying a condom, the user should leave it rolled up as it comes from the wrapper and place it loosely on the tip of the erect penis. The condom is gently and slowly unrolled down to the base of the penis, while the thumb and index finger of one hand hold the condom's tip to create a reservoir for the semen. The condom should not be stretched tightly over the tip of the penis—it could break during intercourse. A condom will slip off a penis that is not fully erect. A man who uses a condom must withdraw from the vagina immediately after ejaculation. Never reuse a condom. Use a new one each time.

The condom must be in place before any contact occurs between the penis and the vagina, to contain the drops of sperm-containing fluid released from the penis before intercourse begins. If the condom is applied too late, its effectiveness drops dramatically. Some condoms are coated with lubricating jelly or powder on the outside to reduce friction in the vagina. Products that provide extra lubrication are sold especially for this purpose. Using petroleum jelly or any oil-containing ("moisturizing") lotion for lubrication can weaken the condom and make it break during intercourse. Instructions for the proper storage of condoms are presented in the next section.

Female Condom

Females need to protect themselves from sexually transmitted diseases, even if their partners refuse to use condoms. So that females can control their own protection, researchers have invented the **female condom**, *a soft, thin plastic tube with two end rings—one to fit over the cervix and one to serve as an anchor outside the entrance to the vagina.* The device is a disposable tubular sack six and a half inches in length (shown in **Figure 22.10**). Flexible plastic rings at each end of the tube hold it in place in the vagina. One ring, at the closed end of the sack, fits over the cervix. The other ring remains outside the vagina to anchor the device in place and to cover parts of the female genital area.

To use the device successfully, the female must be sure that both rings are snugly in place before any contact occurs between penis and vagina. If the internal ring slipped out of place, no extra risk would result, because semen would still not escape from the pouch. Extra risk would occur if the external ring slipped into the vagina. Semen would easily spill over the edges of the condom into the vagina. Using the female condom with spermicide may boost its effectiveness in preventing pregnancy and some STDs.

Condoms and STDs

Abstinence, and restricting sexual activity to contact only with a mutually monogamous, uninfected partner, are the only ways to be 100 percent sure of preventing STDs. Condoms provide some protection against HIV and other STD infections. However, even those experts say that condoms are not perfect.

Judging Effectiveness

Some types of condoms are better than others. Latex condoms manufactured with spermicide applied to them, properly used, are the most effective. The types made of natural skin and lambskin are the least effective. These have pores, as all skin does.

■ **Figure 22.10** *Female condoms. To be most effective, how should a female use the female condom?*

Caption Answer: Using the female condom with spermicide may boost its effectiveness in preventing pregnancy and some STDs.

Class Discussion
Recall: Tell students that latex condoms are more effective in preventing the spread of STDs than any other form of birth control. Ask them to briefly explain why latex condoms provide better protection than other kinds of condoms. Offer bonus points to any student who locates a current study or finding dealing with the effectiveness of latex condoms versus natural skin or lambskin condoms.

The pores are large enough to permit viruses to pass through them. Latex condoms have no pores, and therefore provide a barrier against both bacteria and viruses.

Even latex condoms do not provide complete protection, however. While most people who use them will be protected against STDs most of the time, a certain number of individuals who use condoms, and use them correctly, still become infected with STDs. Just as they may fail to prevent pregnancy occasionally, condoms sometimes fail to prevent STDs, including HIV. Other STDs may still be spread by contact with the thigh, scrotum or other parts of a male or female's body.

Occasionally, but not often, condoms are manufactured with defects. A defective condom may contain a tear that's so small the user cannot see it. Even a condom without tears or tiny holes that does not break may allow secretions to leak over the top. If STD-causing organisms are in a person's secretions, they can infect the partner. Barring abstinence, latex condoms are still the best protection now available against all forms of STDs.

Condoms can vary in quality. Latex condoms made in the U.S. are recommended. Condoms have an expiration date printed on the package, usually abbreviated EXP. Beyond that date, using the condoms is risky. Also, the package should say that the condoms can prevent diseases. Some condoms are just novelties and are useless for disease prevention. Also, look for the words *latex*.

Storing Condoms Heat and light break condoms down. Thus they should be stored in a dark, cool place, such as a closet or drawer. Opening condom packages also requires special care. Use fingers to tear the package open. Don't use teeth, fingernails, scissors, or other sharp objects that may damage the condom. Once the package is open, inspect the condom. If the material sticks to itself or is gummy or brittle, discard it.

Remember that condoms are only a second line of defense against STDs and pregnancy. A person's first and best defense is abstinence from sexual activity or, in the case of STD prevention, mutual monogamy with an uninfected partner.

Fertility Awareness Method

MAIN IDEA ▶ The fertility awareness method is complex to use and has a high failure rate. It requires no drugs or devices.

The fertility awareness method, also called the *rhythm method*, is a method of charting ovulation. It has the highest rate of failure because it is complex to use. The female must track her menstrual cycle and to observe body signs of ovulation, such as body temperature and mucus secretions.

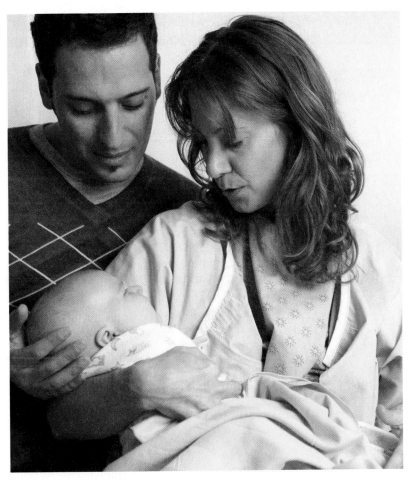

Recognizing these signs is difficult for most females. Once a female does recognize these signs, she should not have sexual intercourse during the few days after she has ovulated.

The fertility awareness method requires no use of equipment. It is available to anyone. However, people who wish to use it must first be trained by health professionals, because its use is complicated. Even the most technical references warn that merely reading about this method is not enough training to ensure that people can use it successfully to prevent conception. People who choose to use it, must go to a health care professional for help in getting started. If used perfectly, the method could be up to 95 percent effective (actual user effectiveness in typical couples is much lower—only about 75 percent).

Another method that requires no equipment is the withdrawal method. With this method, the male removes his penis from the female before ejaculation occurs. Most couples believe that withdrawal is a very effective method. It is very difficult, however, to use this method effectively. For this method to be effective, the female must know when ovulation occurs. Most females do not. Also, a male can remove his penis before ejaculation occurs, and for most males, this proves to be difficult. If a male is successful, some semen may still have been released in the females's vagina.

Did You Know?

The fertility awareness method can be especially helpful to people trying to conceive a child.

Figure 22.12 **Standard Contraceptive Methods Compared for Effectiveness**

Method	Effectiveness (%)		Factors to Consider
	if used perfectly	in typical users	
Abstinence	100	Unknown[a]	Abstinence must be used consistently and perfectly, or effectiveness drops to 0%. Only method that provides 100% protection against STDs.
Oral contraceptives • Combination and Progestin-only pill	99.0	92.0	Users who find it easy to take pills regularly use the method most successfully. No protection against STDs.
Implantable devices Vaginal Ring Patch Injection	99.0 99.7 99.7 99.9	99.0 92.0 92.0 97.0	Implant may be slightly visible. Long-term use is recommended. No protection against STDs.
Intrauterine device (IUD)	99.2	99.4	The device can be expelled without the user's awareness. Pregnancy may occur with the device in place. No protection against STDs.
Vaginal spermicides	82.0	71.0	Users who follow directions exactly use the method most successfully. Slight protection against STDs.
Diaphragm with spermicide	91.0	84.0	Successful use requires proper fit and following instructions. Slight protection against STDs.
Cervical cap with spermicide	91.0	84.0	Successful use requires proper fit and following instructions exactly. Slight protection against STDs.
Male condom (with or without spermicide)	98.0	85.0	High-quality condoms are most protective. Some protection from STDs. Improper use makes failure likely Users must follow directions exactly. Good protection from some STDs. Poor-quality condoms make failure likely..
Female condom	95.0	79.0	High cost. Still proving effectiveness. Good protection against some STDs.
Fertility awareness method	95.0	75.0	Ovulation is unpredictable. A high degree of training, skill, and dedication is required.
Male sterilization	99.9	99.9	Successful, except if the user has intercourse before sperm are absent from semen or if ends of tubes grow together (very unlikely).
Female sterilization (surgical and nonsurgical)	99.5	99.5	Pregnancy is likely only if ends of tubes grow together (very unlikely).

[a]Unknown for those who allow contact between penis and vagina; otherwise provides perfect protection.

All of the methods discussed so far are effective against pregnancy to some degree. **Figure 22.12** on page 608 sums up facts concerning each method's effectiveness.

SECTION 2 Review

Reviewing the Vocabulary

Review the vocabulary on page 598. Then answer these questions.

1. _____ are contraceptive methods that physically or chemically obstruct the travel of sperm toward the ovum.
2. A hormone that, in females, regulates her cycle of ovulation is called _____.
3. _____ is a hormone secreted in females during that portion of the menstrual cycle in which the uterine lining builds up.
4. A(n) _____ is a device inserted into the uterus to prevent conception or implantation.
5. A dome that fits over the cervix and holds spermicidal cream or jelly against the uterine entrance to block the passage of sperm is called a _____.

Reviewing the Facts

6. **List.** List the side effects of taking the pill.
7. **Explain.** How does a diaphragm work?
8. **Describe.** How should male condoms be stored to maintain their effectiveness?

Writing Critically

9. **Expository.** Look at **Figure 22.12**, "Standard Contraceptive Methods Compared for Effectiveness." Explain why there is such a difference between effectiveness rates for typical users and effectiveness rates for people using the methods perfectly. Which methods show the largest differences in percentages? What factors contribute to the large differences?

Go Online

For more information on health careers, visit Career Corner at **glencoe.com**.

1. Barrier methods
2. Estrogen
3. Progesterone
4. Intrauterine device (IUD)
5. Diaphragm
6. Tenderness of the breasts, depression or fatigue, vomiting, skin conditions, weight gain or loss, stopping of menstruation, unexpected vaginal bleeding, tendency to develop vaginal yeast infections.
7. It covers the cervix to prevent sperm from entering the uterus.
8. They should be stored in a dark, cool place such as a closet or drawer.
9. Answers will vary.

Methods Not Recommended for Contraception

People have many false beliefs about contraception and may recommend methods that have high rates of failure. If a couple uses one of these methods and avoids pregnancy, they may believe that the method prevented a pregnancy. As with any health information, do research through reliable sources to determine if the information is accurate.

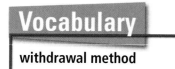
Ineffective Methods

MAIN IDEA ▶ Methods not recommended for contraception include using douches, relying on lactation, or withdrawal.

Ineffective methods of contraception can not only increase the chances of pregnancy, but they can also increase the risk of acquiring STDs. Using douches, misuse of condoms, breastfeeding, and withdrawal, are not recommended methods for contraception.

Douches

Females throughout history have attempted to wash out or kill sperm after intercourse by using douches, preparations sold to cleanse the vagina. Douches of hazardous chemicals, such as turpentine, are extremely damaging to tissues and do not prevent pregnancy. Using douches does not prevent pregnancy. In fact, they may even help the sperm along, because a stream of fluid can wash sperm into the cervix as easily as it can wash them out. Douches cannot prevent or cure STDs, either.

Condom Misuse and Alternatives

Some people have tried to save money on condoms by reusing them or using replacements for them. Once used, a condom is weakened and likely to rupture if used again. Even simply unrolling a new condom before applying it will weaken it and make it likely to break. Covering the penis with plastic kitchen wrap, sandwich bags, or other items is unlikely to prevent semen from spilling into the vagina. Pregnancy and STD transmission can easily occur.

Breastfeeding

Females have also thought, wrongly, that as long as they were breastfeeding their babies, they could not become pregnant. It is true that during lactation (milk production) many females are less likely to ovulate. However, there is no way an individual female can know for sure. Lactation does reduce the total number of children born in a population, but it is not reliable as a contraceptive method for any one female.

Withdrawal Method

A method somewhat better than those just named is the **withdrawal method**, also known as *coitus interruptus*. It is just what it sounds like—*a contraceptive method in which the man withdraws his penis from the vagina before he ejaculates, taking care that his semen is not deposited in, at, or near the vagina.*

Two built-in errors of the method make withdrawal unreliable. First, the male may find it difficult to withdraw his penis when he is near ejaculation. Second, even if he is able to withdraw before ejaculation, he may ejaculate as he is pulling out or might ejaculate before expected. Withdrawal is better than no method at all, but it still allows one female out of five to become pregnant in one year of use. It offers no protection against STDs.

Comprehension Check
Comprehend: Ask students to write a brief explanation as to why the withdrawal method is not a recommended form of birth control or STD prevention.

SECTION 3 Review

Reviewing the Vocabulary

Review the vocabulary on page 610. Then answer these questions.

1. _____ is a technique in sexual intercourse of withdrawing the penis from the vagina just prior to ejaculation.

Reviewing the Facts

2. **Describe.** How can using douches help a female to become pregnant?
3. **Analyze.** Why can't a female use breastfeeding successfully to prevent conception?
4. **Explain.** Why might the withdrawal method of preventing pregnancy fail?

Writing Critically

5. **Expository.** Anna and Rico are engaged to be married. They don't want to have children right away, so they are looking at methods of contraception. Explain the types of contraception that are *not* recommended.

Go Online

For fitness and health tips, visit the Fitness Zone at **glencoe.com**.

1. Withdrawal method

2. Using a douche can help the sperm along because a stream of fluid can wash sperm into the cervix.

3. Many females are less likely to ovulate while breastfeeding, but there is no way an individual female can know for sure.

4. The male finds it difficult to withdraw his penis when he is near ejaculation. Even if he withdrew before ejaculation, live sperm in fluid may already have entered the vagina and may fertilize an ovum.

5. Answers will vary.

Sterilization

Surgical **sterilization**, *the process of permanently interrupting a person's ability to bear children, usually by surgically severing and sealing the vas deferens or the fallopian tubes*. These procedures are a highly effective contraceptive method—in most cases, close to 100 percent effective. Each year, millions of people choose sterilization, and the number is increasing. In fact, sterilization is the leading contraceptive method in the world.

Once chosen, sterilization ends fertility, unless the procedure is reversed. However, the success rates when reversing a sterilization procedure may vary. The choice of sterilization is not generally offered to young adults who may change their mind about having children. The simplest and most common sterilization procedures are **vasectomy**, *surgical cutting and sealing off of each vas deferens to sterilize a man*, and **tubal ligation**, *surgical cutting and sealing off of the fallopian tubes to sterilize a female*.

Vasectomy

MAIN IDEA ► In a vasectomy, a surgeon cuts and seals off each vas deferens in a man to produce sterility.

In a vasectomy, a surgeon makes one or two tiny cuts in the scrotum. The surgeon then severs and seals the tubes (each of which is called a **vas deferens**, *one of the two tubes that conduct sperm from the testicles toward the penis*) through which the sperm travel to become part of the semen. **Figure 22.13** shows how this is done. The procedure takes about half an hour and may be performed under local anesthesia in a physician's office. The incisions are so tiny that vasectomies are called "Band-Aid surgery."

The vasectomized male continues to produce sperm but they are absorbed by his body rather than being released into the semen. The fluid of semen is still present in ejaculation. Only the tiny portion made up by sperm cells is missing. The sperm do not build up or cause any unusual feelings or symptoms. A vasectomy has no effect on the production of the male hormone testosterone or on sexual desire or activity.

A male is not sterile immediately after a vasectomy, because living sperm are still in storage. Usually it takes some weeks to clear them out. Once the sperm are absent from the semen, the chance of pregnancy is practically zero.

Vasectomy permits the male to resume normal activity within a day or so and sexual activity within a few days. Pain is minimal, and side effects are rare.

Vocabulary

sterilization
vasectomy
tubal ligation
vas deferens

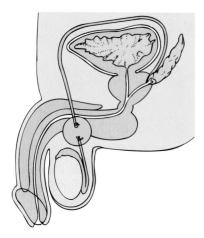

■ **Figure 22.13** *Vasectomy. How does a vasectomy cause sterilization in males?*

Caption Answer: The vas deferens, the tubes through which sperm travel out of the body, are severed and sealed, preventing sperm from becoming part of the male's semen.

Tubal Ligation

MAIN IDEA ▶ In tubal ligation, a surgeon cuts and seals off a female's fallopian tubes, making her sterile.

For a tubal ligation, a surgeon cuts and seals off the fallopian tubes. Sperm traveling up the tubes arrive at a dead end and cannot fertilize the ovum a female might have produced.

Commonly referred to as "tying the tubes," the surgery involves small incisions in the female's abdomen through which the surgeon cuts the fallopian tubes and seals their ends.

The procedure is also slightly more involved than a vasectomy, because the surgeon must cut through abdominal muscle. Still, it leaves only a tiny scar on the abdomen; in the navel; or in cases of surgery through the upper vaginal wall, in the vagina. **Figure 22.14** shows the abdominal operation. The female's hormones, menstrual cycle, and her sex drive remain normal.

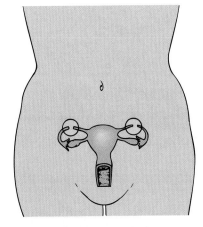

■ **Figure 22.14** *Tubal ligation. Explain how a tubal ligation is performed.*

Caption Answer: The fallopian tubes are severed and sealed, preventing ova from reaching the uterus and being fertilized.

SECTION 4 Review

Reviewing the Vocabulary
Review the vocabulary on page 612. Then answer these questions.

1. A _____ is the surgical cutting and sealing off of each vas deferens to sterilize a man.
2. One of the two tubes that conduct sperm from the testicles toward the penis is called the _____.

Reviewing the Facts
3. **Recall.** How effective is sterilization as a contraceptive method?
4. **Describe.** What happens to the ova after a tubal ligation?

Writing Critically
5. **Expository.** Malcolm and Denise have decided not to have any more children. One of them will become sterile. Why should Malcolm have a vasectomy? Why should Denise to get a tubal ligation?

1. Vasectomy
2. Vas deferens
3. It is nearly 100% effective.
4. The body absorbs them.
5. Answers will vary.

Go Online

For more vocabulary practice, play the Concentration game at **glencoe.com**.

Contraceptive Failure

Unintended pregnancies can occur, even when couples use contraception. All contraceptive methods, with one exception, can fail. A method's failure rate is expressed as an impersonal statistic. In human terms, however, it means that hundreds of couples of all ages are facing unintended pregnancies despite efforts to prevent them. The one exception is, of course, remaining abstinent from sexual activity.

Over 4 million females in the United States alone face unintended pregnancies each year. Considering that each female's fertility lasts 30 years or more, it is clear that nearly every female may face an unintended pregnancy sometime during her life.

Deciding About Abortion

MAIN IDEA ▶ The decision to obtain an abortion should be made with the first trimester of the pregnancy.

Each female facing an unintended pregnancy also faces the decision of whether or not to continue her pregnancy. For some, the choice is really no choice. Some females may have already come to a decision about whether she would consider **abortion**, *a procedure to end a pregnancy before the fetus can live outside the uterus.* Abortion is not a method of contraception. *Contraception* means "to prevent conception." Abortion interrupts a pregnancy that is already under way.

Key Passage
Explain: Ask students to explain how abortion and contraception differ. Have them write a short paper that supports the idea that it is better to consider contraception options early, rather than engaging in sexually risky behavior and then considering their options.

■ **Figure 22.15** *Over four million females in the U.S. face unintended pregnancies each year. Name the only 100% effective contraception.*

Caption Answer: Abstinence

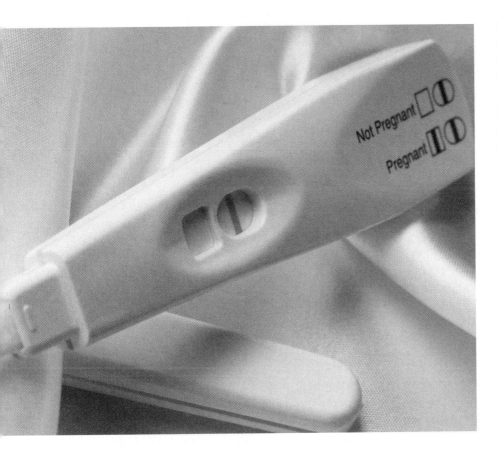

Young people who are risking pregnancy are wise to do some thinking in advance. Otherwise, a female who becomes pregnant unexpectedly must decide. With the help of her partner, counselors, parents, or religious teachers, each person can make a right decision.

A female who suspects that she is pregnant should obtain a pregnancy test. She must choose carefully where to go for the test. Some groups believe that abortion should be available to females and some groups are opposed to abortion. Both groups include extremists who may attempt to influence a pregnant female's decision.

Over-the-counter home pregnancy tests are now available. If a teen takes one of these tests and receives a positive result, that result should always be confirmed by a test provided by a medical professional. Home pregnancy tests check the hormones in a female's urine to determine pregnancy. Accuracy rates range from 80 to 90 percent.

Other locations where pregnancy tests are available include a physician's office; the local health department, which will offer free or low-cost tests without accompanying advice; and specialized clinics. Specialized clinics may also assist and support a female in obtaining an abortion. A religious organization will most likely help support a female in carrying her pregnancy to term and will assist with adoption if she chooses adoption.

Figure 22.17 *Adoption agencies may be able to provide resources, such as prenatal and postnatal medical care. What other groups can offer services to pregnant females?*

Caption Answer: Churches, government agencies and other groups

Chapter 2 said that in making decisions, a person must weigh feelings, judgments, and values. In the case of an unintended pregnancy, all of these may well conflict with one another. Supportive counseling can be a great help in deciding how to handle an unplanned pregnancy. A teen facing an unintended pregnancy may or may not have a strong family support system. Teens in this situation should try to find a trusted adult who can offer advice.

Whatever choice is made, the female must act promptly. Delays increase a female's risks, whether she ultimately has an abortion or continues her pregnancy. If she chooses abortion, the longer she waits, the riskier the procedure becomes. If she continues the pregnancy, the longer prenatal care is delayed, the greater the danger to her health and to that of her fetus.

Abortion Procedures

MAIN IDEA ▶ **Several types of abortion procedures might be available, depending on the length of the pregnancy.**

Abortion methods vary according to the length of the pregnancy. Surgical abortions performed early in pregnancy require little anesthesia and carry minimal risk to the female's health. They are routine for the medical staff. Another way that early pregnancies can be ended nonsurgically is by taking a pill. Normally, the hormone progesterone maintains pregnancy. The drug interferes with the action of progesterone and brings on menstruation and loss of the pregnancy. This drug can only be obtained and taken at a physician's office or clinic.

Adoption

MAIN IDEA ▶ Many organizations provide for the needs of females who carry unplanned pregnancies to term.

Adoption agencies can sometimes find childless couples who are willing to pay some of the expenses of carrying a child to term. Some agencies may directly provide certain needed resources, such as prenatal and postnatal medical care. Churches, government agencies, and other groups may all be of help. Services vary from place to place. They can include free pregnancy testing; group counseling; medical care before, during, and after the birth; housing; adoption services; maternity and infant clothing; food; job training; and day care. Whether a female chooses abortion or continues with her pregnancy, she will be advised to use contraception to avoid another unintended pregnancy.

SECTION 5 Review

Reviewing the Vocabulary
Review the vocabulary on page 614. Then answer these questions.
1. Write a sentence using the vocabulary term.

Reviewing the Facts
2. Recall. How many unintended pregnancies occur in the United States each year?
3. Name. Name possible places a female can get a pregnancy test or help with her decision about an unintended pregnancy.
4. Explain. What is said about the risks of abortions that occur early in pregnancy and abortions that occur later in pregnancy?
5. Describe. How do agencies help support a female who is having a baby that she will give up for adoption?

Writing Critically
6. Expository. Kerri became pregnant in the ninth grade. Kerri didn't know what to do. Explain Kerri's options.

Go Online

For more information on health careers, visit Career Corner at **glencoe.com**.

1. Answers will vary.

2. Over 4 million females in the United States face unintended pregnancies.

3. Physician's office, local health department, abortion clinic, religious organization

4. Females must act promptly. Delays increase the female's risk-because of riskier procedures or danger from lack of prenatal care.

5. They can provide free pregnancy testing; group counseling; medical care before, during, and after the birth

6. Answers will vary.

Q&A

Why People Don't Use Contraception

Understand and Apply Read the conversation below, and then complete the writing exercise that follows.

Many people consciously choose not to use contraception. They may have moral, religious, or personal reasons for this choice. They may want a pregnancy. However, enormous numbers of teen-age girls face unintended pregnancies each year that end in unintended births or abortions. Most of these unplanned pregnancies are not the result of a conscious choice, but of simple failure to use contraception.

Q: Why do people take such chances?

A: Fear and emotional immaturity are two powerful reasons. Teens, especially, may fear discovery and the disapproval of their parents. They may be too embarrassed to purchase condoms or to seek the help of parents or health professionals in obtaining contraceptives. Some may lack information about contraception, or even fail to realize that sexual intercourse leads to pregnancy.

Emotional immaturity can also prevent people from dealing with contraception. An immature person may reject sexuality as part of the person's self-image. The assumption seems to be that sex is great, but nice people don't plan for it—it "just happens."

Young people who confuse sexual activity with love are less likely to use contraception. They trust "love" to be in control, and simply hope for the best. Another group failing to use contraception is made up of people who seem prone to taking chances and risks of all sorts. Such people may smoke tobacco, drink alcohol, take illegal drugs, or commit crimes—and they often engage in risky sexual behaviors.

Q: Has anyone asked teens how they feel about contraception?

A: The attitudes of sexually active teens, when studied, seem sensible enough. They often say that they should postpone sex or usecontraception. However, many teens' behaviors are out of line with their own knowledge and values.

Fewer than half of sexually active teens say they used contraception the last time they had intercourse. The other half say they will not have sex but do so anyway, or they are too embarrassed to obtain contraceptives, or their partners resist using condoms. These teens seem to act as though getting pregnant or catching an STD is as likely as the sky's falling, and that they are equally helpless to prevent any of them.

Q: Does anyone know what makes people decide to use contraception?

A: The more a female owns her own sexuality, the more likely she is to use contraception. The more a couple cares about each other, the more likely they are to protect each other with contraception. The older and more sexually experienced they are, the more likely they are to use it. And the more they see pregnancy prevention as a shared responsibility, the more they will use it.

Q: Do only older partners have such supportive relationships?

A: Not always, but the four characteristics mentioned often come along with maturity. Mature people have had time to get to know themselves and are more able than younger people to understand the role of sexuality in their lives. Also, people in a committed, mature love relationship didn't get there overnight. They gave their love plenty of time to grow naturally without complicating its development with early sexual intimacy.

Genuine concern for the partner is also a mark of maturity. Also, as couples make decisions about when or whether to have a child together, each partner wants to share responsibility for achieving that family goal. Without the shared psychological intimacy of a mature love, sexuality is more likely to be self-centered, and contraception is more likely to be ignored.

Q: Some people I know just don't seem to think about the price they'll pay should pregnancy occur, and so they don't use contraception.

A: That's a common attitude. They may think, "If I have a baby, I'm sure someone will take care of it. The father will marry me; or the mother will take care of it; or my parents will help; or I'll be an adult, then, so somehow it'll be okay." In fact, teens may believe that pregnancy must be all right or else it wouldn't happen. Some think pregnancy is a ticket away from an unhappy home life.

Many teens have no idea of the enormous burden that comes with being a parent. Teens who have jobs may feel that they have lots of money to support a child. However, most teens are not responsible for paying for a home, groceries, insurance, and all the other costs of maintaining a home and family.

Q: I've also heard that contraception lowers the sex drive. Is that true?

A: No, contraception does not reduce the sex drive in people of either gender. In reality, the opposite is often true. With fear of pregnancy removed, people often feel freer to enjoy sexual intercourse.

Sometimes a sexual partner may be resistant to using condoms. Convincing the partner may require being honest and firm. To give in to not using condoms means risking disease or pregnancy, yet a person may fear that insisting on using protection may strain the relationship.

Q: Does sex education help teens make the right choices?

A: Yes, it can help. Between 1988–2004, the U.S. pregnancy rate for teens aged 15–19 decreased from 111 pregnancies per 1,000 teen girls to 72 pregnancies per 1,000 teen girls in 2004. Ideally, parents should be the primary sex educators. However, they sometimes fail to provide the needed information.

To make sure that all children have the information they need, society tries to provide these facts through the schools. In places where meaningful sex education is provided along with wholehearted community support, the numbers of teenage pregnancies drop. Most places in the United States, though, fail to provide such education and support, and so are seeing increased numbers of teenage pregnancies.

Sex education is only part of the solution, though. Research shows that when parents have discussed sex with their teens, those teens are least likely among peers to engage in sexual intercourse early in life and are most likely to use contraceptives later on. Individual families and society as a whole must take responsibility.

 Writing Write a paragraph explaining the reasons why some people fail to use contraception.

Reviewing Vocabulary

Use the vocabulary terms listed below to complete the following statements.

vasectomy

laboratory effectiveness

contraception

oral contraceptives

intrauterine device (IUD)

tubal ligation

1. Any method of preventing conception is called _____.
2. _____ is the percentage of females protected from pregnancy in a year's time under ideal laboratory conditions.
3. Pills that prevent pregnancy by stopping ovulation or by changing conditions in the uterus are called _____.
4. A device inserted into the uterus to prevent conception or implantation is called an _____.
5. _____ is the surgical cutting and sealing off of the fallopian tubes to sterilize a female.
6. Surgical cutting and sealing off of each vas deferens to sterilize a man is called a _____.

Recalling Key Facts and Ideas

Section 1

7. **Recall.** Who is responsible for contraception?
8. **Explain.** What is one of the most important facts to consider about a contraceptive method?

Section 2

9. **Analyze.** Why are teens all over the United States choosing abstinence more often than before?
10. **Recall.** When a female begins using the pill, for how long should she use a backup method of birth control?
11. **Explain.** What should be used to prevent STDs when the pill is being used for contraception?
12. **Name.** Who is the best candidate for an intrauterine device?
13. **Identify.** What is one danger of using a diaphragm or cervical cap during menstruation?
14. **Explain.** Why should a person choose latex condoms over other condoms?
15. **Describe.** Why shouldn't petroleum jelly or moisturizing lotion be used on condoms?
16. **Recall.** What should a female do before using the fertility awareness method of birth control?

Section 3

17. **Describe.** Describe several ineffective methods of birth control.

Section 4

18. **Recall.** How long after a vasectomy does it take a man to become free of sperm?

---

1. Contraception 2. Laboratory effectiveness 3. Oral contraceptives 4. Intrauterine device (IUD) 5. Tubal ligation 6. Vasectomy 7. It is a shared responsibility. 8. Its effectiveness; how well it prevents pregnancies

9. Teens are becoming more aware of how to avoid pregnancy and AIDS, herpes, and other STDs/STIs. 10. One month 11. Condoms 12. A female who has had a child, is in a monogamous relationship (like marriage), and has no history of PID

Section 5

19. **Explain.** Abortion is not a method of contraception. What is it?

20. **Name.** What kinds of services are offered by agencies that help females carry unintended pregnancies to term?

Writing Critically

21. **Expository.** Read the Q&A section, "Why People Don't Use Contraception." What is said about maturity and those who don't use contraceptives? Which couples are likely to use contraceptives? Does sex education help? How?

22. Maria and Joe have been dating steadily for one year. Joe had an illness as an infant, and his doctor told him he is probably sterile. Joe believes that "no harm would be done" by having sex because Maria will not become pregnant. Maria has concerns about premarital sex based on her family and religious values. What is your opinion about what they should do?

Activities

23. Contact a family planning office and ask them to describe the services offered.

24. Contact a crisis pregnancy center and ask about the services offered.

Making Decisions About Health

25. Kelly tried the pill, but it gave her headaches. The IUD she tried gave her cramps. Gels and diaphragms or condoms were too inconvenient. Her monthly cycle is erratic, so natural family planning is out. Now what? What other choices do you think Kelly has? If you were Kelly, what would you do? Why?

26. Jody has never taken time to learn much about birth control. Now when his wife assures him that she'll take care of it, he feels a bit uneasy—will she really take care of it? She's so forgetful. With his heavy schedule at school and a new job, the last thing he needs right now is to become a father. What options do you think Jody has in this situation? If you were in Jody's situation, what would you do? Why?

G℮ Online

For more vocabulary practice, play the True/False game at **glencoe.com**.

Fact or Fiction?

Answers

1. False. No contraceptive method is perfect. To obtain the advantages of one method, a person must be willing to put up with its disadvantages.

2. False. Condoms are prone to failure, but abstinence always prevents sexually transmitted diseases.

3. False. A female who isn't taking the pill may be using another form of birth control, such as condoms or a diaphragm. The term *birth control* refers to all contraceptive methods, including the pill.

Writing Paragraphs will vary.

---

13. Toxic shock syndrome **14.** Protection against STDs/STIs
15. They can weaken the condom, which may cause it to break during intercourse. **16.** A female should be trained by a health professional. **17.** Answers will vary.

18. Several weeks **19.** Interruption of a pregnancy
20–26. Answer will vary.

Sections

1. Expectations and Successful Aging
2. The Aging Process
3. Dying

Why is it important to study the aging process? Research indicates that people who practice healthful behaviors as teens experience better physical health throughout life. Much of the quality of the later years depends on the daily choices a person makes in youth and on the habits as a result of those choices.

Certain factors of aging can be slowed or even prevented by being physically active, maintaining other good health habits, and planning ahead. Adults who have developed lifelong healthful habits, such as eating a healthy diet, exercising, and avoiding alcohol and drugs, continue to stay active and healthy into their later years.

What a person becomes later in life is, to a large extent, whatever that person chooses to become today.

Fact or Fiction?

What Do You Think?

Is each statement true or false? If you think it's false, explain what's true.

1. The happiest people are those who have experienced the fewest tragedies.
2. The human life span has increased steadily over the past 100 years.
3. Most people can expect to spend their later years in nursing homes.

Writing Write a paragraph to describe what aging means to you. As you read the chapter, make additions or revisions to your paragraph based on new information you learn.

(Answers on page 641)

Visit **glencoe.com** and complete the Life Choice Inventory for Chapter 23.

Expectations and Successful Aging

The quality of life in the future tends to become what people expect it to become. Physical health makes a difference, and so does financial security. However, people's expectations also contribute more to their futures than most people realize.

Expectations

Preview Activity

Discuss: Ask students, before they begin to read this chapter, to express their opinions of older adults. Do they enjoy being with older adults? Do they think that older adults tend to have different views than their own on most issues? If so, can they provide some examples? What things can each generation learn from the other?

MAIN IDEA ▶ The views people have on aging can affect the way they live in their later years.

Most people want their later lives to be successful. Some say they want to be like those who have made great intellectual and artistic achievements in their 70s and 80s. They claim they want to model themselves after older people they admire. Such older people are vibrant and happy. They can offer unique wisdom and perspective, having experienced more life than anyone else.

As they get older, people want to be self-sufficient, physically active, socially involved, and clear thinking. They hope to remain fully participating members of society. Many older people report that they are happy and healthy. Such people tend to think positively throughout their lives. They define success by their own values and live accordingly.

■ **Figure 23.1** *A mature life can be one of continued productive activity.* How does living a healthful life in your teen years help you as you become an older adult?

Caption Answer: By exercising and eating a healthy diet as a teen, those habits stay with you during your adult life.

They work toward meaningful goals. They feel their lives have purpose. People who age successfully often display the following characteristics:

- Their lives have meaning and direction.
- They handle life's events with dignity.
- They feel fulfilled.
- They have attained several long-term goals.
- They are pleased with their own growth and development.
- They love and are loved by others.
- They have many friends.
- They are cheerful.
- They accept criticism with grace.
- They have no major fears.

Many of the happiest people have lived through at least one life tragedy. Educational and financial stability also factor into people's happiness. It is important to strike a balance between helping others and a healthy commitment to meeting one's own needs. To be happy as an older adult, begin practicing good physical, emotional, and social health habits now. More people than ever before are living full, healthy lives in their advanced years.

"The years teach much which the days never knew."

—Ralph Waldo Emerson
(1803–1882)
Essayist, philosopher, poet

Worksheets: A reproducible quiz for Section 1 is provided in the Teacher Classroom Resources.

SECTION 1 Review

Reviewing the Facts

1. **Identify.** What are three factors that will contribute to the quality of your future?
2. **Describe.** Identify characteristics of older people who some say they want to be like.
3. **List.** List five of the ten characteristics that people who age successfully display.
4. **Analyze.** If you want to be happy when you are old, what must you begin doing now?

Writing Critically

5. **Narrative.** What are some things you can do now to make the aging process easier? Do you have a negative attitude about the aging process? If so, how can you change your attitude about aging?

For fitness and health tips, visit the Fitness Zone at **glencoe.com.**

1. Expectations, physical health, and financial security

2. They want to model their lives after those people who have made great intellectual and artistic achievements in their 70s and 80s. They want to model themselves after older people they admire.

3. Their lives have meaning and direction, they handle life's events with dignity, they feel fulfilled, they have attained several long-term goals, they love and are loved by others.

4. Begin practicing good physical, emotional, and social health habits.

5. Answers will vary.

SECTION 2

The Aging Process

Although many people believe that aging starts around 40 or 45, aging really begins the moment we are born. Until about age 20, aging takes the form of growth and maturing. Inside the body, the organs and cells age too.

Life Span and Life Expectancy

MAIN IDEA ▶ Aging of the whole body begins at maturity, about age 20. The human life span has not changed, but life expectancy has increased.

Within the different body organs, cells have different aging patterns and life spans. Some blood cells live only three days or so. Most nerve cells last for the person's lifetime. In a healthy older person, each cell lives on to the end of its normal life span in much the same way as in the person's younger years. As the person ages, though, the cells lose some of their function, they collect products not found in younger people's cells, and their cells lose some of their ability to reproduce.

The human **life span** is *the maximum years of life a human being can live*. A person's **life expectancy** is *the average number of years lived by people in a given society*. Life expectancy is determined by your health and the care you receive to maintain health. The human life span is approximately 130 years. Most people, however, do not live this long. In the United States, an average person can expect to live almost 78 years.

Vocabulary

life span
life expectancy
longevity
menopause
hot flashes
arthritis
senility
Alzheimer's disease

■ **Figure 23.2** *Growing old gracefully. Name some things you can do now to maintain good physical health during the aging process.*

Caption Answer: I can eat a healthy diet and exercise regularly.

Figure 23.3 Growing Old Gracefully

1. Maintain appropriate body weight.
2. Obtain regular and adequate sleep.
3. Practice stress-management skills.
4. Limit your time in the sun and use sunscreen protection.
5. See your physician about strategies to fight osteoporosis.
6. Do not smoke. If you do smoke, quit.
7. Expect to enjoy sexual activity with your husband or wife, and learn new ways of enhancing it.
8. Maintain physical fitness.
9. Protect your eyes against sunlight.
10. Be aware that your brain's and nerves' reactions are slowing down. Plan to compensate by being more careful.
11. Use alcohol only moderately, if at all.
12. Take care to prevent accidents.
13. Obtain glasses and hearing aids, if necessary.
14. Maintain adequate nutrition.
15. Stay interested in life, make new friends, and adopt new activities.
16. Drink eight glasses of water a day.
17. Practice your mental skills by solving math problems, reading, writing, imagining, and creating.
18. For adult children of aging parents: provide or obtain the needed care and stimulation for your parents.
19. Make financial plans early to ensure your security.
20. Accept change.
21. Cultivate spiritual health.

Specifically, the life expectancy for Caucasian males in the United States is almost 76 years, and for African American males almost 70 years; for Caucasian females it is almost 81 years, and for African American females about 76 years. Another term referring to length of life is **longevity**—*an individual's length of life.* Some people have extraordinary longevity, perhaps due to genetic inheritance combined with the events of their lives.

People are living longer today than ever before, but the human life span (maximum) has not changed. What has changed over the past 100 years is the life expectancy (average), mainly for two reasons. First, the rate of deaths from diseases and accidents among the very young has declined. Thus, there are fewer young deaths to bring the average down. Second, medical advances are prolonging adults' lives.

Class Activity

Analyze. With books closed, ask students to list the names and qualities of people over the age of 50 who have aged successfully. Ask the students to open their books to page 627 and compare their list to the list, Growing Old Gracefully, in **Figure 23.3**.

Figure 23.4 Changes with Age: Preventable vs. Unavoidable

Certain factors of aging can be slowed or even prevented by being physically active, maintaining other good health habits, and planning ahead. Others are likely unavoidable. However, remember that by maintaining a healthy, well-rounded lifestyle you will age gracefully.

Factor	Can slow or prevent	Cannot prevent
Appearance		
Graying of hair		✔
Balding		✔
Drying and wrinkling of skin	✔	
Nervous System		
Impairment of near vision		✔
Some loss of hearing		✔
Reduced taste and smell		✔
Reduced touch sensitivity		✔
Slowed reactions (reflexes)		✔
Slowed mental function		✔
Mental confusion	✔	
Cardiovascular System		
Increased blood pressure	✔	
Increased resting heart rate	✔	
Decreased oxygen consumption	✔	
Body Composition/ Metabolism		
Increased body fat	✔	
Raised blood cholesterol	✔	
Slowed energy metabolism	✔	

Factor	Can slow or prevent	Cannot prevent
Other Physical Characteristics		
Menopause (females)		✔
Loss of fertility (males)		✔
Loss of elasticity in joints		✔
Loss of flexibility in joints	✔	
Loss of teeth; gum disease	✔	
Bone loss	✔	
Accident/Disease Proneness		
Accidents	✔	
Inherited diseases		✔
Lifestyle diseases	✔	
Psychological/Other		
Reduced self-esteem	✔	
Loss of interest in work	✔	
Depression, loneliness	✔	
Reduced financial status	✔	

Learning with Visuals

Analyze: Show advertisements for anti-aging products to students and ask if they believe any of them. Ask students how great a risk they would take, or how much would they spend, to prevent aging. Use this opportunity to introduce a discussion on how society contributes to a negative view of aging rather than focusing on the positives.

How to Age Gracefully

Although your body will age over time, you can maximize your wellness and enjoyment of life.

One of the most important things to do is to maintain appropriate body weight. Obesity shortens life. Other keys to health maintenance are sound nutrition, including an ample water intake; adequate sleep; regular physical activity; and avoidance of alcohol, tobacco, and other drug abuse.

Much of the quality of the later years depends on the habits formed in youth and the result of those habits. **Figure 23.4** shows some of the physical changes that occur with age.

Dealing with Physical Changes

MAIN IDEA ▶ To stay healthy as you age, accept the physical changes that will occur.

Knowledge helps people deal with the changes that come with age. It is comforting to know that some negative changes of aging are accompanied by positive ones. For example, although it is physically difficult for older people to recover from the effects of stress, they are more capable to recover psychologically. Older people have learned how to bounce back from setbacks. Perhaps this is because they have more life experience and have learned to adjust to life's unexpected events.

Menopause

In females, the later years bring **menopause**, *the years of stopping ovulation and menstruation in a woman.* As the supply of the hormone estrogen is reduced, menstruation stops. Reduced estrogen also causes hot flashes. **Hot flashes** are *sudden waves of feeling hot all over, a symptom related to dilation of blood vessels in the skin, which is common during the transition into menopause.*

Consumer Skills Activity:

1. People often fear aging or fear the loss of a youthful appearance and may look for an alternative.

2. Older adults may fear the future or fear that their medical treatments are not enough, so manufacturers try to offer products they think an older adult might want.

Consumer SKILLS ACTIVITY

Longevity Products

Every person wants to look his or her best, and as people age, they may be apprehensive or nervous about losing a youthful appearance. Many products on the market today promise to restore youth or reverse the aging process.

Manufacturers of many longevity products market to older adults. Consumers should be cautious about any product that claims to make them healthier or increase longevity. Why do manufacturers market to older adults? As people age, they may experience more symptoms and may fear that regular medical treatment is not enough. Fear and uncertainty of the future may cause an older adult to seek alternative treatments not prescribed by a doctor. However, it is always in the best interest of the individual to talk with a doctor about what treatments are best.

 Writing

1. Why are people so open to products that claim to reverse the aging process?
2. Why do some manufacturers market products to older adults?

Caption Answer: Physical activity increases blood flow to the heart, lungs, and other organs, such as the brain.

Class Activity

Evaluate: Have students interview someone age 40 or older who has exercised faithfully over the years. The focus should be on how exercise and proper diet have made the person's life more productive and helped to maintain overall wellness. Ask students to write about what they learned from the interview.

A major surge of bone loss (osteoporosis) takes place at the beginning of menopause. Females whose calcium intakes and physical activity levels have been insufficient to build up the bones before menopause may lose bone material rapidly and develop osteoporosis within a few years. In the younger years, though, prevention is often possible through recommended daily calcium intake from food and plenty of physical activity. Menopause and osteoporosis also set in early in females who smoke.

Males also experience a gradual decline in fertility. Testosterone production gradually decreases, as does sperm production. Hormones and testicular functioning may decrease, as may the desire for sexual activity.

Physical Activity

As people age, their physical abilities change. Older muscles do not build up as quickly as younger ones do, so it takes longer and harder work to condition the muscles. However, even older adults can build and rebuild muscle mass and improve their ability to function.

The more physically active people are, the less likely they are to die of heart and lung diseases. Regular physical activity enhances the quality of life.

As a person ages, the reflexes slow down. The joints may be less flexible than a younger person's. **Arthritis**, *a painful inflammation of the joints caused by infection, body chemistry, injury, or other causes*, is to some extent unavoidable in older people. Weight control and moderate activity, however, help people to withstand its worst effects. Aspirin can help relieve the pain of arthritis. Doctors can also prescribe stronger medications.

Because continued physical activity throughout life helps reduce arthritis, it is important to stay active. Sometimes a pain that an older person believes to be arthritis may instead be caused by joint stiffness from years of inactivity. However, older adults need not work out the same way younger people do. Activities should be adjusted to fit the body's changing abilities.

Dealing with Mental Changes

MAIN IDEA ▶ Some changes in mental sharpness due to aging are preventable.

Changes take place in the brain and nervous system as people age. Research has discovered declines in the areas of: reasoning skill, recall (memory), speed, and senses. These declines, however, are offset by increased wisdom and judgment. People can also adopt strategies to compensate for these declines, such as learning to write things down so that they will not forget or allowing more time for certain tasks.

Senility

The mental confusion called senility is often avoidable. **Senility** is *a general term meaning weakness of mind and body occurring in old age*. Mental confusion in older people has many different causes—and most are preventable. The preventable causes of mental confusion are listed in **Figure 23.6**.

Alzheimer's Disease

Alzheimer's disease, *a brain disease of older people that brings mental confusion, inability to function, and in the final stage, death*, cannot be prevented. The condition appears most often in people over 65 and is a leading cause of death in that age group. It afflicts nearly 50 percent of all those over 85. The disease starts as the loss of memory; it becomes an inability to perform everyday functions, and then leads to the total inability to care for oneself. In the brain, the nerve pathways become tangled and blocked, cutting off the memory functions. Alzheimer's disease is irreversible and progresses from mild confusion to disability and death. The causes are still unknown, and there is currently no cure for the disease.

Figure 23.6

Preventable Causes of Mental Confusion in Older People

Abuse of drugs This includes alcohol abuse and misuse or incompatibility of prescription drugs.

Accidents Falls can cause skull fractures (concussions) or bleeding that puts pressure on the brain, which surgery can relieve.

Dehydration The thirst signal may become faint. As a result, an older person may not drink enough to meet fluid needs.

Depression Depression can slow down the mind in old people, as in the young.

Disease states Diseases present different symtoms in older people than in younger ones. Tuberculosis, diabetes, and even heart attacks can all begin with confusion, rather than with fever or pain.

Not using mental skills People do lose what they don't use. Practicing mental skills brings them back.

Malnutrition Taste enjoyment, digestive secretions, and appetite diminish. Older people eat less, yet nutrient needs remain the same.

Poor vision and hearing Both can cause confusion. Both can be corrected and compensated for.

Class Activity

Discuss: Write the following sentence on the board: "Will you be prepared for your retirement years?" Ask students what needs to be done to prepare for these years. Tell them to cover both financial and mental preparedness. Ask students to share their ideas with the class.

Preparing for Social and Other Changes

MAIN IDEA ▶ An older person must plan for financial, living, and social changes.

Besides physical and mental changes, people who are aging also face financial and social changes. Being aware of these changes will enable people to prepare for the later years of their lives.

Financial planning is essential. Nearly everyone undergoes a change of income in the retirement years. It is important to save for retirement—to have the home paid for or adequate income to pay the rent. It is also crucial to have insurance to cover unexpected medical and other expenses. Begin saving while you are young to have enough money to cover your expenses as you age.

Another way to prepare is to plan for alternative living arrangements, should it become too difficult to stay home.

Figure 23.7, on page 633, describes some possibilities. Less than a third of older adults spend any time in a nursing home. Of those, most spend only about a year there.

Emotional and Social Changes

Financial preparation and deciding where to live as you age will not, however, prevent emotional and social changes. A spouse may become gravely ill. Old friends may move away.

What Teens THINK

What Makes Your Favorite Senior Citizen Your Favorite?

My grandfather is a retired navy shipman with the energy of a teenager. The jokes he tells always make us laugh until we cry, and he has the best war stories. You learn a lot about life by listening to him talk. But above all else, he cares so much about me.

—Erin T., 16, California

My favorite senior citizen is my favorite because they respect me for who I am. They have lived a long time so I can ask advice and they know exactly what I'm talking about. It may not be very up to date, but I can relate it to my life.

—Hannah G., 15, Illinois

My favorite senior citizen is an incredibly supportive fan of high school sports. He has been attending sporting events for many years and has touched the lives of many young people. He is such a special person and means a great deal to me. His children and grandchildren don't live near him, but I am glad he has become an important member of many families here. I hope every child who doesn't have grandparents living close finds a special senior citizen to spend time with and learn from. He constantly tells me how much children mean to him and how he loves to watch our games. He is extremely dear to me—as a fan, a friend, and a grandparent.

—Shannon B., 16, Montana

Figure 23.7 A Glossary of Living Arrangements for Older Adults

Type of Care	Characteristics
Adult day care	Adult day care provides a safe environment for older adults during the daytime hours. A variety of planned programs such as social activities and nutrition, nursing, and rehabilitation services are usually offered.
Alzheimer's care	Most nursing homes and assisted-living facilities offer specialized care to those with memory-impairing diseases such as Alzheimer's and dementia.
Assisted living	Assisted living is for people who choose not to live on their own, but do not require 24-hour care or skilled nursing care. Assisted living provides some help with activities of daily living such as bathing and eating. Most assisted living communities offer meals, housekeeping, emergency call service, planned activities, licensed nurses on staff, and 24-hour caregiver staff.
Continuing care retirement communities	Retirement communities offer a variety of living choices—from private homes to assisted living, and often skilled nursing homes. Residents can live in one place, and as they age, can move to the level of housing or care that they require. Continuing care retirement communities often have requirements such as age, income, and health status to live there.
Independent living	Independent living is for those who do not require personal care or medical care, but choose not to live alone or at home. Most independent living communities offer safety-equipped facilities to make it easier for residents to get around, optional meal plans, recreational activities, and field trips.
In-home care	In-home care offers companion and personal care services to help older adults live at home safely. Services may include fall prevention, medication and fluid reminders, light housekeeping, bathing assistance, and running errands.
Nursing homes	Nursing homes are equipped with medical staff and supplies to offer specialized care for those with illnesses or injuries. Nursing homes offer meals, laundry services, housekeeping, and planned recreational activities.

Children may move away also and may be too busy to stay in touch on a regular basis.

It is important to maintain your personal identity after retirement. People who work full-time often define themselves by their work, such as "I am a doctor, attorney, or teacher." In the retirement years, it is important to discover new ways to define who you are. Many people choose to volunteer their time and give back to their communities, or they may continue to work at a part-time job. In this way, people can maintain a strong sense of self, which will enhance social and emotional health.

Sometimes a person's environment can change as well. A neighborhood or familiar area may no longer exist. Many people try to find new activities or meet new people by attending classes or by joining a social club. Creating a social network will help to relieve any loneliness or anxiety about the person's environment.

Guest Speaker

Discuss: Invite a guest speaker to come in and discuss the physical and mental aspects of aging. Check your local hospitals or social service agencies for the name of a reputable gerontologist. Have students prepare a list of questions for the speaker ahead of time.

Be Happy and Healthy Now

You may think it's unnecessary for a teen to confront the problems of loneliness and loss in later life, but such is not the case. Emotional and social health in the later years is affected by what happens during youth. To be happy when you are older, you need to practice happiness when you are young. Keep reaching out. Maintain a strong social support system so it is easier to gain and maintain friendships at every stage of life. Continue to learn and discover. Cultivate spiritual health too. Find ways to contribute your gifts and to leave something of value to those you care for. Keep working on projects that are meaningful to you. Growing is a lifelong engagement. What a person becomes later in life is, to a large extent, whatever that person chooses to become today.

Worksheets: A reproducible quiz for Section 2 is provided in the Teacher Classroom Resources.

SECTION 2 Review

Reviewing the Vocabulary

Review the vocabulary on page 626. Then answer these questions.

1. _____ is the maximum years of life a human being can live.
2. The average number of years lived by people in a given society is _____.
3. _____ is an individual's length of life.
4. The years of stopping ovulation and menstruation in a woman is called _____.
5. _____ means weakness of mind and body occurring in old age.

Reviewing the Facts

6. **List.** List key principles of maintaining health in the later years.
7. **Analyze.** What might female teens do to avoid osteoporosis later in life?

Writing Critically

8. **Descriptive.** Describe any experiences you've had with people who are senile. What strategies can you recommend to make similar situations as comfortable as possible for everyone involved?

For more information on health careers, visit Career Corner at **glencoe.com.**

Answers (margin)

1. Life span
2. Life expectancy
3. Longevity
4. Menopause
5. Senility
6. The keys to health maintenance are maintaining appropriate body weight, sound nutrition (including ample water intake), regular physical activity, and adequate sleep. Another key to health maintenance is avoidance of alcohol, tobacco, and other drugs.
7. Female teens should get the recommended daily amount of calcium in their diets and be physically active.
8. Answers will vary.

Dying

Imagine you were told today that you had only a few weeks to live. What would you do? Would you change the way you live? Would you take any practical or financial steps? Are there emotional issues you'd wish to work out with parents, brothers or sisters, or friends? What ideas would you pass on to others who will follow you?

Now imagine that someone close to you has only weeks to live. How will you spend your time with that person? What will you say? The value of asking these questions is that they help you realize that time in life is limited—not only for you, but for every other person. Knowing this can help people spend their time today wisely.

Fear of Death

MAIN IDEA ▶ Fear of death is natural, but it can also give more meaning to life.

Many people do not like to think of death. It is natural to fear death. All creatures strive to live. To express your fear and think about death is healthy.

Make the Most of Life

Consider this view: death gives meaning to life! If you knew that you had only a few weeks left to live, that knowledge would give you a good sense of how precious life is. Many people, on learning they are soon to die, report that they enjoy their lives more. Sunsets are more beautiful. Jokes are funnier. Friends are dearer. The way they spend their time becomes more important. They try to make the most of every moment.

The prospect of death or coming close to dying can also cause people to reevaluate their sense of values. Many people, on having near-death experiences, say their lives are changed afterward. A person who might have wanted a career in law may decide that working with disadvantaged children is more important. Other people may not choose a different career, but a changed attitude toward life.

Enjoy the Moment

One of life's great pleasures is to savor each present moment. Even simple things bring great rewards. An orange sunset, a friend's smile, a spring breeze, or the surprise of discovery in a child's eyes can be experienced fully only when we know that our experiences of them are numbered. Acknowledging death helps people cherish their lives rather than simply pass through them.

Vocabulary

living will
brain death
life-support systems
proxy
euthanasia
physician-assisted suicide
terminal illnesses
hospice

" Men do not quit playing because they grow old; they grow old because they quit playing."

—Oliver Wendell Holmes
(1809–1894)
Physician, writer, poet

■ **Figure 23.8** *A living will can let others know how to care for you. Why is it important to prepare for death?*

Caption Answer: So that your wishes are carried out after you are gone

Did You Know?

Contrary to a common misconception, older adults need just as much sleep as younger adults—about seven to nine hours per night.

Comprehension Check

Comprehend: Ask students to explain what a living will is. Tell them to include the definition and the purpose of a living will in their explanation. They should take this opportunity to consider how they would wish to be treated if they could not make the decision for themselves.

Preparation for Death

MAIN IDEA ▶ Preparing for death will make sure your wishes are met and will help your loved ones.

People prepare for death in a few ways. It is advised that people make a will and think about life insurance. These items allow you to make sure a person's family and those that they care about are taken care of in the event of death.

Make a Will

A good time to make a formal will is when you first marry or become a parent. A will is a legal document that ensures that your family or those you care about receive what you want them to have. A person does not have to own a lot of possessions to create a will. When someone dies without having made a will, the state divides up the person's property according to its laws, not by the wishes of the family.

Make Your Wishes Known

Another preparation worth the effort is to decide what you want done if you lose consciousness. In that case, other people will have to decide what will happen to you. You can make your wishes known ahead of time in a living will. A **living will** is *a will that declares a person's wishes regarding treatment, should the person become unable to make decisions.* Such a document states exactly how you want to be treated, should you become unable to decide for yourself. Some people wish to instruct their families to use no life-support systems after **brain death**, *irreversible, total loss of higher brain function*, has occurred. **Life-support systems** is *a term used to refer to mechanical means of supporting life, such as feedings given into a central vein or machines that force air into the lungs.* They may even instruct their families to end life-support if life-support measures have been started.

Other people may request the opposite—that *every measure be taken to save their lives*, regardless of chances for recovery. If you have feelings one way or the other, put them in a living will. Not all states recognize the living will as a legal document, however. In such places a person must name a **proxy**, *a person authorized to act for another*, who then can make decisions concerning medical treatments to prolong life.

A person may not have complete control over what happens in all cases. Some questions about euthanasia and physician-assisted suicide, for example, are still being debated by medical and legal professionals. **Euthanasia** means *allowing a person to die by choosing not to employ life-support equipment or the removal of life-support equipment.* It may be legal in some cases.

Physician-assisted suicide is *suicide of an ill person by way of lethal drugs provided by a physician*. This is not legal in most states.

Another choice people may make is whether to die in a hospital or elsewhere. Many people with **terminal illnesses**, *illnesses that are expected to end in death*, would rather die at home, using a hospice for support. A **hospice** is *a support system for dying people and their families which helps the family let the person die at home with dignity and in comfort*. The purpose is to allow a dying person to choose to stay at home while staff from the hospice help the family to care for the person and to deal with their grief.

Worksheets: A reproducible quiz for Section 3 is provided in the Teacher Classroom Resources.

SECTION 3 Review

Reviewing the Vocabulary

Review the vocabulary on page 635. Then answer these questions.

1. _____ is a will that declares a person's wishes regarding treatment, should the person become unable to make decisions.
2. A person authorized to act for another is called a _____.
3. _____ is a support system for dying people and their families, which helps the family let the person die at home with dignity and in comfort.
4. _____ are illnesses that are expected to end in death.

Reviewing the Facts

5. **Explain.** Why is it natural to fear death?
6. **Analyze.** How do near-death experiences change people's lives?
7. **Describe.** Describe ways in which people should prepare for their death.

Writing Critically

8. **Expository.** Raul's parents are in their mid-40s. Raul wants to talk to them about their will, but death is a subject that is seldom discussed. How can Raul help make it easier for his parents to talk about death without hurting their feelings?

G Online

For health and fitness tips, visit the Fitness Zone at **glencoe.com**.

1. A living will
2. Proxy
3. Hospice
4. Terminal illnesses
5. Because all creatures strive to live
6. People may decide to change a career path, or change their attitudes about life.
7. People can prepare by making a will, creating a living will, and making their wishes known to family members.
8. Answers will vary.

Q&A   Learning From Older People

 Understand and Apply   Read the conversation below, and then complete the writing exercise that follows.

Are you close to an older person in your life? Do you live with a grandparent or visit an older adult neighbor on a regular basis? You may be generations apart from such a person, but each of you has much to offer the other.

Q: My grandmother lives nearby and I go over whenever I can to help her take out her trash or do other chores that she can no longer do. I have never thought about what else I might contribute to her life, or what she could contribute to mine. What might older people like my grandmother offer to teens like me?

A: Older people have knowledge, experience, and wisdom to give to teens. In turn, teens can bring energy, curiosity, and a fresh perspective to older people.

Q: My grandmother loves to tell stories about when she was young and how different life was back then compared with now. I guess if I asked her more questions I could learn a lot. Is that what you mean about older people and their knowledge?

A: Yes, it is. Your curiosity and her knowledge can make a great partnership. As you learn about the time in which your grandmother grew up, you will get a personal look at events you may have heard about in history classes. You will also learn something about your own family history. Your grandmother will be delighted in your interest in her life and how things have changed.

Q: I have an assignment to do an interview for one of my classes. I have been trying to decide whom to interview. Do you think my grandmother would be interested in being the subject of my interview?

A: Of course she would. Your grandmother can help you with your assignment, and you can help her by documenting what she says to share with your family.

Q: I guess there are many things that teens and older people can offer each other. I just had not thought about it much before. What are some other examples?

A: Older people, because they have lived longer, have much more life experience than young people do. Teens may sometimes feel overwhelmed by life's day-to-day pressures—homework, chores, family and friends' expectations. An older person has solved many problems and faced different

■ **Figure 23.9** *To be young at heart is to be young where it counts. Name some ways a person can stay "young at heart."*

Caption Answer: Keep learning throughout life and work on projects that mean a lot to you.

challenges in life and can offer wisdom and advice to teens going through a difficult time. An older person can be a voice of steadiness and calm in the face of life's uncertainty or confusion. An older person can sit down with you, listen, and provide some guidance.

Q: Do you have any other suggestions about what teens can do for older adults?

A: Teens have much to offer to older people. Just as you help your grandmother do some things she can no longer do, you may also be able to teach her some new things that she had not thought about. For example, teens can teach older people new ways to use their computers and keep them up-to-date on the latest advances.

Many older people grew up in a time when there was little or no recycling. They may not recycle simply because they have never done so. Teens can help older people understand the importance of recycling and protecting the environment for future generations.

Some older people may be lonely or bored at times. Teens can simply spend time with them—watching a movie, walking to the park, or just sharing a meal. Teens who share some of their time with older people often discover that they want to do so more often. The companionship works both ways and there is much to be learned from each other.

 Writing Reflect on a time you have spent with a grandparent or an older neighbor or friend. Did you learn anything from his or her life experience? Write a short paragraph describing any stories or advice offered.

Reviewing Vocabulary

Use the vocabulary terms listed below to complete the following statements.

Alzheimer's disease

arthritis

physician-assisted suicide

life-support systems

longevity

1. _____ is an individual's length of life.

2. A painful inflammation of the joints caused by infection, body chemistry, injury, or other causes is called _____.

3. _____ is a brain disease of some older people that brings mental confusion.

4. A term used to refer to mechanical means of supporting life, such as feedings given into a central vein or machines that force air into the lungs, is _____.

5. Suicide of an ill person by way of lethal drugs or other means provided by a physician is called _____.

Recalling Key Facts and Ideas

Section 1

6. **List.** List some characteristics that describe most people who are in their later years.

Section 2

7. **Explain.** After growth is completed, what does aging bring about?

8. **Identify.** What two things have affected life expectancy?

9. **Describe.** Describe strategies to help slow the aging process.

10. **List.** List the areas in the brain and nervous system that are affected by aging.

11. **Analyze.** Why is financial planning so essential for people who are aging?

Section 3

12. **Explain.** How can we view death in a healthy way?

13. **Describe.** What changes occur in many people who learn that they will die soon?

Writing Critically

14. **Personal.** Review the list of preventable versus unavoidable changes with age, **Figure 23.4**, on page 628. You cannot do anything about the unavoidable changes of aging, but you can do something about the preventable changes. What can you do to prevent these changes? Are you practicing these behaviors now? Are your parents and grandparents doing things to prevent or delay some of the changes that come with aging?

15. **Personal.** At what age do you think it is appropriate to make a will? When are you going to make a will? Are you going to make a living will? What are some of the problems relatives of a person who has lost consciousness face when a living will has not been written?

16. **Descriptive.** After reading the Q&A section, "Learning From Older People," on pages 638–639, can you think of some things you can learn from an older adult?

1. Longevity 2. Arthritis 3. Alzheimer's disease 4. Life-support systems 5. Physician-assisted suicide 6. Older adults are physically active, enjoy being social, and offer life experience. 7. Aging brings about changes in the body's cells, and the loss of youthful appearance. 8. There are fewer deaths among the young, and there are a lot of medical advances to prolong lives. 9. Get adequate sleep, drink plenty of water, exercise regularly. 10. Some hearing loss, reduced taste and

Activities

17. Visit a nursing home in your area and adopt a grandparent. Visit and talk with the person for an hour at least once a week for five weeks. Write a report about your experience.

18. Have a class debate on euthanasia. Do you think terminally ill patients should have the right to die? What would you want your family to do if you were terminally ill?

19. Watch television for an hour and write down all the commercials that deal with aging and older adults. What are the products' claims? Do you think the claims are accurate?

20. Find a current magazine or newspaper article about the process of aging or some aspect of this topic (Examples: the effects of alcohol and/or tobacco on the aging process, advancements on slowing down the aging process, and so on). In the article, underline five to ten major points that are made. Using what you learned from **Figure 23.3** in this chapter, "Growing Old Gracefully," compile a list of facts about aging. Then, using the Fact or Fiction feature and other information you can gather, make a list of fallacies about aging. Develop your lists into a poster that can be displayed in the classroom.

Making Decisions About Health

21. Gladys and Sylvia are seniors in high school and are best friends. They have talked about everything together for as long as they can remember. On her way home from school one day, Gladys was in a terrible car accident. She was in a coma and was put on a respirator. The girls had talked about death several times and agreed that they never wanted to be kept alive by a machine. Sylvia went to the hospital every day and talked to Gladys with no change ever taking place. Sylvia told Gladys' parents of their discussion about life-support systems. Sylvia suggested letting Gladys die peacefully. Gladys' parents didn't agree. They felt that as long as Gladys' heart was beating they had a chance for a miracle. They have been keeping Gladys alive for the past six months.

How would you feel if you were Sylvia knowing your best friend didn't want to live like this? What action would you take if you were Sylvia? Why would you take that action? What could Gladys have done to avoid this situation completely?

Go Online

For more vocabulary practice, play the True/False game at **glencoe.com**.

Fact or Fiction?

Answers

1. False. The happiest people include those who have lived through at least one major life tragedy.
2. False. The human life span has not changed, but the life expectancy has increased steadily over past years.
3. False. Less than one-third of older adults spend any time in a nursing home.

Writing Paragraphs will vary.

smell, slowed reactions **11.** Many people retire and need to make sure they have enough to pay for living expenses and emergencies. **12.** Death can help people value life more. **13.** People tend to enjoy life even more and take pleasure in small things. **14-21.** Answers will vary.

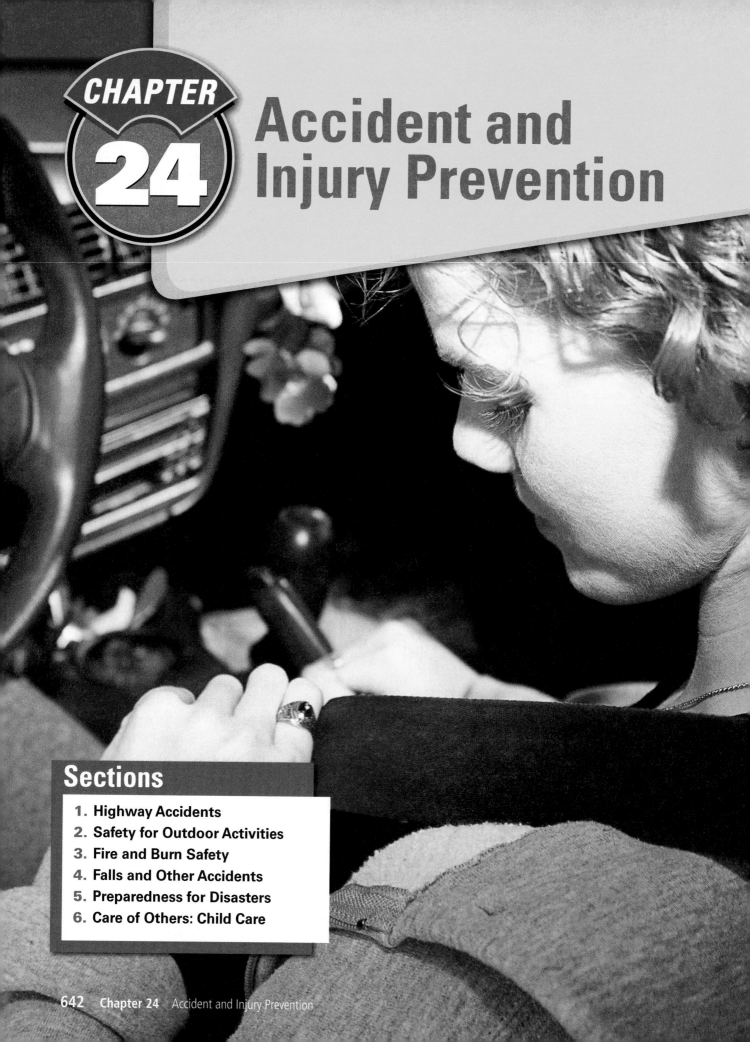

CHAPTER 24

Accident and Injury Prevention

Sections

Being cautious may seem boring, and until accidents happen, they seem unlikely. It is important to learn to be careful enough to avoid getting hurt without losing spontaneity and joy in life.

Although not all accidents and injuries are preventable, many accidents and injuries are preventable with care and preparation. This year, chances are that one out of every three people you know will suffer an injury. Injuries of the kind shown in **Figure 24.2** on page 646 claim more young lives than any disease does.

Relatively little attention has been paid to accidental injuries. Older adults usually die of heart disease or cancer, so those diseases get most of the public's attention. But the leading cause of death among children and teens is accidents and injuries. By answering the questions in the Life Choice Inventory for Chapter 24 at **glencoe.com**, you will learn whether you are skilled in accident prevention or whether you have more to learn.

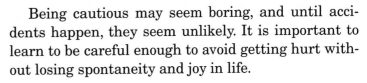

Fact or Fiction?

What Do You Think?

Is each statement true or false? If you think it's false, explain what's true.

1. One out of every ten people suffers an injury every year.
2. The primary characteristic you need to prevent accidents on the road is driving skill.
3. The emergency telephone number in most parts of the United States is 911.

 Writing Write a paragraph to explain what basic safety precautions you take in your daily life.

(Answers on page 667)

Go Online

Visit **glencoe.com** and complete the Life Choice Inventory for Chapter 24.

Highway Accidents

Motor vehicle crashes are the leading cause of death for people between the ages of 15 and 20. Young drivers are twice as likely to be involved in a motor vehicle accident as the rest of the population. This is why auto safety is an important issue for teens.

Auto Safety

MAIN IDEA ▶ Every driver will encounter other drivers on the roadway who are careless.

Knowledge and skill are not enough to prevent car accidents. An equally important aspect of the driver is attitude. Consider the attitudes of two different drivers. One driver might say, "I never have accidents. I'm in control." That person might simply go out and drive, unaware of potential hazards. Another driver might think, "The control is not all in my hands. I need to be aware of other drivers and watch for possible accidents about to happen." A person with this attitude drives defensively.

The most important rule of driving safety is: Pay attention. At least 25 percent of car crashes happen when a driver is distracted. The driver may be drowsy, talking on a cell phone, or just thinking about other things. Reduce or eliminate distractions when you drive by positioning the seat and mirrors and always fasten your safety belt before starting the engine. Make adjustments to the radio or temperature controls before moving.

Vocabulary

head restraints
air bags

■ **Figure 24.1** *Accidents will happen. Name three important aspects of auto safety.*

Caption Answer: Knowledge, skill, and the driver's attitude are all important aspects of auto safety.

Some other examples of items you need to pay attention to while driving include:

- **Other drivers.** Be aware of the cars around you. Make sure other drivers can see you by turning on headlights at night and during bad weather.

- **Road conditions.** Reduce your speed if the road is wet, icy, or covered with snow. Also be cautious while driving on narrow roads, in heavy traffic, or through construction zones.

- **Your physical state.** Never drive when you are tired. Drowsiness can impair your reaction time and judgment. If possible, stop for a snack or a brief stretch. If drowsiness persists, find a safe, well-lit area, pull off the road, and call a family member or friend for assistance.

- **Your emotional state.** Never drive while you are angry or upset. This can also impair your reaction time and judgment. If possible, ask someone else to drive, or if you are alone, pull over to a safe location until you calm down.

"Diligence is a priceless treasure; prudence a protective charm."

—Chinese proverb

The Defensive Driving Attitude

MAIN IDEA ▶ Defensive drivers reduce accidents and save lives.

By driving defensively, you stay alert and take responsibility for your behavior. You watch for potential hazards. A car that is weaving, crossing the center line, making wide turns, or braking without warning may have an impaired driver. If you see such a vehicle, keep a safe distance, or pull over and notify the police.

Knowledge

Driver education courses reduce accidents. As a result, automobile insurance rates are lower for drivers who have taken a driver education course.

Judgment and Attitude

Judgment is just as important in defensive driving as skill. Driving skill is the person's ability to control the vehicle under all road conditions. Driving judgment is the person's ability to recognize a potential accident and to know how to avoid it. The use of both skill and judgment depends on the driver's attitude. Part of the defensive driving attitude is self-defense against injury.

Class Discussion

Analyze and Discuss: Collect newspaper articles detailing all types of vehicle accidents and ask students to choose one, read it, and write an analysis as to the cause(s). They should also suggest possible ways the accidents could have been prevented. Discuss some of the articles with the class.

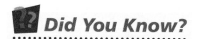
The risk of motor vehicle crashes is higher among 16- to 19-year-olds than among any other age group. In fact, per mile driven, teen drivers ages 16 to 19 are four times more likely than older drivers to crash.

Class Debate

Evaluate: Have a few students call a local car dealership and ask about the current status of air bags in new cars, the additional cost of installation if not factory standard, and the future plans for air bags. Have the students report the information to the class. Allow students to debate which safety features should be standard.

Are Safety Belts Really Necessary?

Defensive drivers buckle their safety belts whenever driving and insist that passengers do the same. Some people claim that safety belts injure people in accidents. They sometimes do, but the injuries are far less severe than not wearing a safety belt at all.

When you are driving at 50 miles an hour, both your car and your body are moving independently at that speed. If the car hits something and stops, your body will continue to move at 50 miles an hour until you hit something. A safety belt slows a person's momentum as the car's momentum decreases. It distributes the force of the impact across the body's strongest parts. Also, it keeps the driver behind the wheel and in control, able to prevent further collisions. Being thrown from the vehicle increases the chances of death by 25 times. Safety belts keep you inside and safe.

Head Restraints and Air Bags

Two other pieces of safety equipment increase safety. **Head restraints**, *high seatbacks or other devices attached to seats in cars at head level*, prevent whiplash neck injuries during accidents. **Air bags**, which are *inflatable pillows designed to inflate upon impact,* stored in the center of the steering wheel of a car or in the dashboard, cushion vehicle interior surfaces and absorb crash energy to protect the head and upper body. Drivers of cars with both front and side airbags often survive crashes that would otherwise prove deadly. For further protection, move the driver's and front passenger's seats as far from the dashboard as possible, without limiting the driver's control of the car.

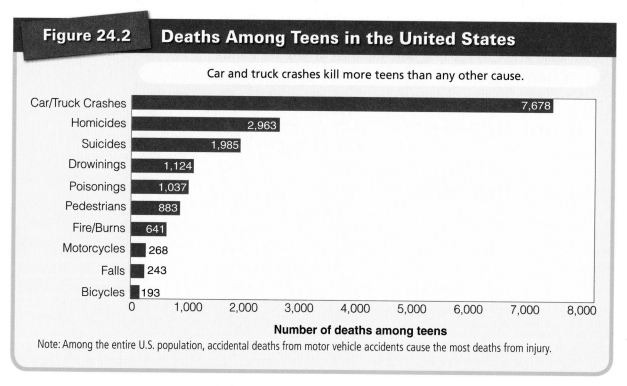

Figure 24.2   Deaths Among Teens in the United States

Car and truck crashes kill more teens than any other cause.

Cause	Number of deaths among teens
Car/Truck Crashes	7,678
Homicides	2,963
Suicides	1,985
Drownings	1,124
Poisonings	1,037
Pedestrians	883
Fire/Burns	641
Motorcycles	268
Falls	243
Bicycles	193

Number of deaths among teens

Note: Among the entire U.S. population, accidental deaths from motor vehicle accidents cause the most deaths from injury.

Figure 24.3   **Proper Child Safety Restraint**

Infants should always ride buckled in a rear-facing infant seat secured into the vehicle's back seat.

Toddlers and preschoolers (older than 1 year and over 20 pounds) may ride buckled into a forward-facing safety seat secured into the back seat.

School-age children who have outgrown their safety seats may ride buckled into a booster seat secured into the back seat.

Older children who have reached 4'9" in height (about 8 to 12 years old) may ride in a regular lap and shoulder belt in the back seat. The front seat is reserved for adults and children older than 13 years.

Air bags, while lifesaving to adults and older children, can pose a hazard for infants and small children. Air bags inflate with a force that can injure the neck of an infant or child. Infants in front- or rear-facing car seats in the front seat are at risk for injury, as are small children in the front, even when buckled into safety belts. Always buckle infants into rear-facing car seats in the back seat, and buckle older children into the back seat too.

The Danger of Alcohol and Drugs

Half of all fatal driving accidents involve alcohol. Many others involve other drugs. The most important steps you can take to protect yourself against car accidents are never to ride with a driver who is under the influence of alcohol or drugs, and never to get behind the wheel if you have been drinking yourself.

Beyond this, the suggestions made in the Health Skills sidebar, "How to Avoid Alcohol-Related Driving Accidents," can help you avoid becoming a victim of someone else's drunk driving.

Other Driving Concerns

Eating, using a cell phone, reading, or engaging in other distractions while driving is dangerous. Be especially careful when driving with friends. Having other teens in the car greatly increases the risk of a crash. The more friends, the greater the risk.

The responsible driver also:

- Keeps the vehicle in good condition—tires, windshield wipers, horn, lights, brakes, wheel alignment, and steering mechanism.

- Wipes or washes all windows before starting the car.

- Wears glasses, if needed.

- Adjusts driving to different driving conditions.

- Obeys traffic signs and all regulations.

- Watches for pedestrians and bicyclists.

- Does not drive after drinking alcohol or after taking drugs or medicines that cause drowsiness, or when emotional, anxious, distracted, irritated, or tired.

If you lose patience with other drivers, use stress-reducing techniques to calm down (see Chapter 4 for details). If you are tired, admit it. Stop and rest.

A professional driver suggests three changes in driving habits that he believes would save lives:

1. Look over your shoulder when changing lanes. Don't rely on mirrors—they distort distance.

2. Keep a safe distance from the car in front of you.

3. After a red light turns green, pause for five seconds before proceeding.

All of these ideas apply equally to motorcyclists. In addition, motorcyclists must use safety techniques specific to them. Helmets should always be worn, whether or not they are required by law.

Health Skills

How to Avoid Alcohol-Related Driving Accidents

To protect yourself from alcohol-related accidents:

1. Don't get into a car with anyone who has been drinking.

2. Watch out for any other driver who:

   - Drives very slowly or fast, swerves, weaves, or straddles the center line.

   - Turns abruptly or illegally. Stops without an apparent reason.

   - Fails to obey traffic signs and signals.

   - Drives with a window down in cold weather.

   - Drives with headlights off after dark.

3. If such a driver is in front of you, stay a safe distance behind.

4. If you are in front, get off the road as soon as possible.

5. Note the license number if you can. Report it to the police.

➤ Objectives

- Show how to use refusal skills to avoid a potentially dangerous situation.
- Explain why honest reasons for a refusal are more effective than dishonest excuses.

Better Safe than Sorry

Luis is 15 years old and has a learner's permit to drive while he completes a driver's education class. His best friend Corey is 16 and got his driver's license two weeks ago. Earlier in the week, Luis accepted a ride from Corey for the first time. During that ride, Luis realized that Corey is a dangerous driver. Corey drove faster than the speed limit and talked on his cell phone most of the time. While Corey was driving and talking on the cell phone, he almost hit another car because he wasn't paying attention to the roadway.

Luis doesn't want to ride with Corey again, until he becomes a safer driver. However, Corey keeps pressuring Luis to ride with him since they live near each other and start school at the same time each day. So far, Luis has made up excuses to get out of riding with Corey. He doesn't want to tell his best friend that he's a bad driver, but his excuses don't seem to be working.

➤ Identify the Problem

1. What is Luis' problem?

➤ Form an Action Plan

2. How should Luis say no to Corey? What body language should Luis use to show that he means what he says?
3. What reasons should Luis give for refusing to ride with Corey?
4. What should Luis do if Corey keeps insisting that he ride with him?

➤ What Did You Learn?

5. Why are honest reasons for a refusal likely to be more convincing than dishonest excuses?

Applying Health Skills:

1. Luis doesn't know what to say to his best friend to get out of riding with him because he is an unsafe driver.

2. Luis should say to Corey, "Thanks for the offer, but I do not want to ride with you." Luis should shake his head no and raise his hand to show that he means what he says.

3. Luis should explain that he does not feel safe riding with Corey because he drives too fast and talks on his cell phone while driving.

4. Luis should walk away from Corey if he keeps insisting.

5. Answers will vary.

Are ATVs and Dirt Bikes Safe?

Riding all-terrain vehicles (ATVs) or off-road motorcycles (dirt bikes) can be fun, but also poses hazards. Tens of thousands of young people (particularly boys under age 16) suffer injuries, and hundreds die in ATV or dirt bike crashes each year. Follow all of the manufacturer's instructions and state laws regarding ATV and dirt bike use. Also, observe all laws regarding the use of the vehicle, and put safety first. Some rules that you should observe may include:

- Always wear a helmet.
- Use good judgment and avoid taking risks.
- Ride the right size vehicle for your age, size, and ability.
- Ride in safe areas—never on roads with cars.
- Do not carry passengers.

Worksheets: A reproducible quiz for Section 1 is provided in the Teacher Classroom Resources.

SECTION 1 Review

Reviewing the Vocabulary

Review the vocabulary on page 644. Then answer these questions.

1. _____ prevent a person's head from snapping back too far when the body is thrown backward in a car.
2. _____ are stored in the center of the car's steering wheel and inflate on impact.
3. Write a sentence using each vocabulary term.

Reviewing the Facts

4. **Name.** What is the number-one killer of young people?
5. **Analyze.** Why are driving skill and driving judgment essential?
6. **Explain.** Why should safety belts always be used?
7. **Identify.** What precautions can minimize ATV and dirt bike risks?

Writing Critically

8. **Expository.** Do you think that every licensed driver should be required to take a driving test every few years? Why, or why not?

For more vocabulary practice, play the eFlashcards game at **glencoe.com**.

1. Head restraints
2. Air bags
3. Answers will vary.
4. Motor vehicle accidents
5. A driver must be able to drive defensively and judge conditions quickly and safely.
6. Safety belts keep you from being thrown from the vehicle in an accident.
7. Riders should wear a helmet, use proper equipment and not carry passengers.
8. Answers will vary.

Safety for Outdoor Activities

Pleasant recreations can turn into hazards when people ignore basic safety issues. A little forethought and straight thinking can make sure that your afternoon of swimming, boating, or other play remains enjoyable.

Drowning

MAIN IDEA ▶ Water safety means learning to swim and never swimming alone.

Every year, nearly 3,000 people die from drowning. Although most drowning incidents involve young children, people of all ages need to be familiar with water safety guidelines. Anyone who enters the water should follow some simple rules to remain safe.

How Can Swimmers Stay Safe?

The most important rule for safety is to know how to swim. Know your limits as a swimmer. If you are a beginner, do not attempt to keep up with skilled swimmers. Stick to shallow areas where your feet can touch the bottom. If you are a strong swimmer, keep an eye on others who are not as skilled. No matter how skilled, you should never swim alone. All swimmers, regardless of skill level, can suffer from muscle cramps or other medical emergencies. Here are additional safety rules for swimming and diving:

- Swim only in designated areas where a lifeguard is present. Obey "No Swimming" and "No Diving" signs.

■ **Figure 24.4** *Moving water is more powerful than it looks; use caution and safety equipment when venturing out in it. What are some things to do to prevent drowning?*

Caption Answer: Learn to swim, never swim alone, and protect pools with fences.

Health Skills

Water Rescue Techniques

You can assist a swimmer who is nearby and in trouble by using these guidelines:

1. If the swimmer is near a dock or in a pool:
   - Lie flat and extend an arm or other object. Pull the person within reach of the edge.
2. If the swimmer is farther away than you can reach:
   - Wade into waist high water. Extend an object so that the person can reach it.
3. If the person fell from a boat:
   - Help the person hang onto the boat or another object.
4. If the person fell through ice:
   - Push a ladder or other long object, tied with a rope at the bottom. If the person is weak, a rescuer can crawl along the ladder to help.

- Protect pools with fences.
- Use extra caution around moving water (rivers, canals, creeks, etc.). Water is more powerful than it looks.
- Supply boats with personal flotation devices (PFDs). Nonswimmers should always wear properly fitting PFDs when on a boat.
- Never play rough in or near the water.
- Swim only when you feel well.
- Do not swim if you have been drinking alcohol or using other drugs or medicines that might make you drowsy.

When diving, never dive where there may be obstructions or where you don't know the depth. Ease in feet-first the first time. Do not overestimate your ability.

It is also wise to have a boat accompany you on a distance swim. Get out of the water when lightning threatens. Even if you are in a boat, go to shore quickly in a storm. Except in emergencies, rely on your own swimming ability, not on inner tubes or floats.

If you see someone in trouble in the water, help by using the techniques described in the Health Skills sidebar, "Water Rescue Techniques." Only a trained lifeguard should attempt rescue by swimming out to the victim. A drowning person can easily overpower a novice and drown them both.

What About Swimming After Eating?

You may have heard that you should not swim until an hour after eating, to prevent stomach cramps. It is not necessarily dangerous to swim with a full stomach, especially if you exercise lightly. However, if you swim hard after eating, you may indeed experience cramps. They are just as likely to occur in your legs or arms as in your stomach. The reason may be that digestion requires energy and oxygen, which are taken from the hard-working muscles. Simply rest while your stomach is full.

Boating Safety

To ensure safe boating activities:
- Make sure the person handling the boat is experienced. Never get into a boat with an operator who has been using alcohol or other drugs.
- Always wear a personal flotation device (PFD) or life jacket. Be sure to wear the proper type for your age, weight, and ability. Do not rely on inner tubes or toys as flotation devices. They are not substitutes for an approved PFD.
- Load the boat properly.
- Keep your weight low in the boat. Sit, don't stand.

- Tell people on shore where you are going and when to expect you back.

- If the boat overturns or fills with water, hang onto it because it will probably still float.

- Plan ahead and check weather reports. If a storm is predicted, do not go into the water. If you are already in the water, head back to shore immediately.

Biking, In-Line Skating, and Skateboarding

Of course, accidents also happen when people are moving fast on land—biking, in-line skating, skateboarding, running, and the like. Here are three guidelines that can help you avoid injury while moving on land:

- **Wear appropriate shoes.** Not only do they protect the feet; they also give stability to the whole body.

- **Use proper gear.** The right-size bike, in-line skates, or skateboard in good condition are safest.

- **Wear a helmet.** Helmets reduce your risk of serious head injuries.

Keep in mind that no one ever has an accident on purpose. It is the unlikely, unexpected event—the one you can't control—against which you are safeguarding yourself.

Avoiding Back Injury

Finally, protect your back. Whenever you bend over, your lower back muscles must lift its weight. To avoid back injury while lifting,

- Plant the feet firmly and slightly apart. Keep your head up.

- Squat—do not lean—forward, keeping the back as straight as possible, and get a firm grip on the object.

- Lift slowly, pushing up with the thigh and leg muscles.

- Do not jerk the object upward or twist your body as you lift.

- To lower an object, reverse this procedure.

Worksheets: A reproducible quiz for Section 2 is provided in the Teacher Classroom Resources.

SECTION 2 Review

Reviewing the Facts

1. **List.** List five ways to reduce the risks of drowning.
2. **Explain.** How might a victim who has fallen through ice be rescued?
3. **Synthesize.** Why might cramps develop if a person swims hard after eating?
4. **Analyze.** Why shouldn't you lift anything by bending over?

Writing Critically

5. **Descriptive.** Describe three instances in which you or someone you know has had accidents on bicycles. Develop some guidelines for cyclists that would help prevent or lessen injuries from accidents.
6. **Persuasive.** Choose an outdoor activity, such as cycling or swimming. Research the activity to develop a "how-to" guide for someone who is a beginner to the sport. Include the proper equipment required, as well as safety information a person would need to know.

For more information on health careers, visit Career Corner at **glencoe.com**.

1. Learn to swim, never swim alone, swim where a lifeguard is present, use a PFD, swim only when you feel well.

2. Push a ladder or other long object, tied with a rope at the bottom rung and secured, out to the victim.

3. Cramps are caused because digestion requires energy and oxygen. Swimming takes a lot of energy and oxygen.

4. Because your lower back must lift its weight. This causes a lot of stress on the lower back.

5. Answers will vary.

6. Answers will vary.

Fire and Burn Safety

Among teens and children, fires and burns rank third, behind motor vehicle deaths and drownings, as a cause of accidental death. Many of those who die are children. The majority of the deaths occur as a result of fires at home.

Preventing Fire and Burns

MAIN IDEA ▶ Many lives are lost to fires each year. Home fires are preventable.

A special class of burns—chemical burns—damages eyes, skin, and lungs without fire. Read the labels of sprays, products that contain gases, and compounds that can burn your skin or hurt your eyes. Follow directions.

Other specifics to prevent fires and burns:

- Install fire extinguishers near dangerous locations.

- Keep a garden hose near a faucet.

- Use chemical fire extinguishers—never water—on electrical fires. Baking soda will safely smother a grease fire, so keep a box handy in the kitchen. (See **Figure 24.6**)

Preview Activity

Analyze: Bring newspaper articles about fires to class. Divide the class into groups and give one article to each group. Ask each group to read their article and determine whether authorities found a cause for the fire. Have groups brainstorm ways the fires could have been prevented.

Figure 24.6   **Common Types of Fire Extinguishers and Fires**

Be sure to have the proper fire extinguishers on hand. Experts recommend one for the kitchen and one for the garage or shop.

If you see these symbols on a fire extinguisher...

ORDINARY **A** COMBUSTIBLES or Class A (paper, wood, cloth)

B LIQUIDS or Class B (flammable liquids, greases)

ELECTRICAL **C** EQUIPMENT  Class C (electrical fires)

follow these instructions:

Use the extinguisher on an ordinary fire of paper, wood, cloth or most plastics.

Use the extinguisher on a flammable liquid such as gasoline or grease fire.

Use the extinguisher on an electrical fire.

If you see these symbols on a fire extinguisher...

follow these instructions:

Do NOT use the extinguisher on an ordinary fire of paper, wood, or cloth.

Do NOT use the extinguisher on a flammable liquid or grease fire.

Do NOT use the extinguisher on an electrical fire.

■ **Figure 24.7** *Keep a safe home, and know what to do in emergencies. What should you use to extinguish an electrical fire?*

Caption Answer: Always use a chemical fire extinguisher on electrical fires.

- Change heating and cooling system filters on schedule, and maintain heating systems.
- Dispose of trash immediately.
- Hang clothes well away from stoves or fireplaces.
- Store matches in a metal container and out of the reach of children.
- Tap water can cause severe scalds. Turn down the temperature setting of the water heater to 120 degrees Fahrenheit, if possible.
- Do not allow anyone to smoke in bed. Provide adequate ashtrays to smokers, or ask them to smoke outside.
- Install home fire detectors.

Finally, if a fire starts, what will you do? Think now, because you need to know ahead of time what action you should take. Carry the emergency telephone number for your area. The telephone number used throughout most of the United States is 911. Memorize the fire department number for your area or keep it in a central location if it's not 911.

SECTION 3 Review

1. Fires and burns
2. Change heating-and-cooling system filters on schedule, and maintain heating systems, dispose of trash immediately, hang clothes well away from stoves or fireplaces, store matches in a metal container and out of the reach of children.
3. 120 degrees Fahrenheit
4. 911
5. Answers will vary.

Reviewing the Facts

1. **Name.** What is the third leading cause of accidental death among children and teens?
2. **List.** Give four recommendations on how to prevent fires and burns.
3. **Recall.** The water heater in your home should not exceed what temperature?
4. **Identify.** What is the emergency help telephone number for most parts of the United States?

Writing Critically

5. **Expository.** Develop a fire escape plan for your home. Figure out two ways to get outside from every room. Designate a place outside where you will all meet.

For fitness and health tips, visit the Fitness Zone at **glencoe.com**.

Falls and Other Accidents

Falls cause many accidental deaths. A fall can result in an injury as minor as a scrape or bruise. However, falls can also result in injuries that cause death. Anticipation and defensive action against falls can prevent them.

How Can I Prevent Falls?

MAIN IDEA ▶ Falls and other accidents at home claim many lives each year.

Most falls happen at home. To prevent slips and trips:

- Wipe up spills.
- Secure small rugs, and corners of large ones. Do not use them at tops and bottoms of staircases.
- Clean up snow in walking areas. Use sand or salt on icy spots.
- Place a safety mat in the bathtub, and install hand-holds on the wall.
- Walk carefully in wet grass, especially with a power mower.
- Clean walking areas and keep the yard free of debris.
- Light stairs and hallways and install handrails.

To prevent falls that occur when climbing or reaching:

- Use a sturdy ladder, placed on level nonslippery ground. Do not stand on furniture or boxes.
- Inspect the ladder before you use it, and have someone steady it as you climb.
- Move the ladder instead of reaching to the side from the top of it.
- Lean a straight ladder at an angle to the wall. The bottom should be placed away from the wall one-quarter of the distance from the base of the ladder to its contact point. Keep your hands free to grip the ladder as you climb.
- Center your body weight.
- Face the ladder when climbing down.
- Hire an expert for roof jobs or those where power wires are nearby.

Caption Answer: Older adults and infants are especially prone to falls and accidents.

■ **Figure 24.8** *Handrails in the bathtub or shower can help prevent falls. What age groups are especially prone to falls and accidents?*

Falls are the leading cause of accidental death and injury to older adults, and balance declines with age. Sudden motions affect balance the most—especially motions involving the head, which is heavy and can pull the whole body off center. Slow down, and move carefully. For infants, falls from tables and bassinets are a frequent cause of injury. Falls into buckets of water, toilets, swimming pools, or other bodies of water can cause death by drowning. Never leave an infant unattended.

Other Accidents

Other accidents can arise from the careless use of tools, toys, guns, and other devices. Work and leisure-time accidents add significantly to the number of deaths and injuries. To prevent them:

- Use sharp objects only for their intended purpose, handle them with care, and keep them out of the reach of children.
- Follow the manufacturer's instructions carefully when using equipment.
- Keep electric appliances, such as hair dryers, away from water, sink basins, and tubs.
- Learn and obey all firearm safety rules.

SECTION 4 Review

Reviewing the Facts

1. **Identify.** Give three recommendations for preventing slips and trips.
2. **List.** List four ways to prevent falls that occur when climbing or reaching.
3. **Recall.** What is the leading cause of accidental death for older adults?
4. **Name.** Name three recommendations for avoiding work and leisure-time accidents.

Writing Critically

5. **Personal.** Look over the lists in this section that specify how to prevent slips, trips, and falls. Which safety precautions do you most often ignore? Discuss why you do not follow these safety tips.

Go Online

For more information on health careers, visit Career Corner at **glencoe.com**.

Preparedness for Disasters

Natural and manmade disasters such as hurricanes, floods, earthquakes, tornadoes, or acts of war or terror, are, for the most part, unexpected. However, there is much people can do to prepare for them. Imagine yourself stuck in your house or in a car, unable to leave the area, having to cope for several days without outside help. What would you wish you had prepared beforehand? What items would you wish you had with you?

Emergency Survival Kit

MAIN IDEA ▶ Natural and manmade disasters occur randomly, so it's important to prepare in advance.

In an emergency, you may need to evacuate your home quickly. You will need supplies to get you through the disaster. An emergency survival kit will ensure you have everything you need until the crisis has passed. These items may include:

- A three-day supply of food and water for your family. Choose foods that are ready-to-eat and shelf-stable. Keep a can opener in your survival kit. Store at least three gallons of water per person. Each person will need one gallon per day.

- A flashlight with extra batteries, and candles and matches.

- A battery–powered radio or television with extra batteries.

- A change of clothing for each family member.

- Sleeping bags, blankets, or other bedding for each family member.

- First-aid supplies and medications.

- Duct tape and plastic sheeting in case it is necessary to seal the windows in your home.

- Copies of important documents such as birth certificates or passports.

- Cash to purchase food and other supplies, or to pay for lodging.

Keep a list of phone numbers for out-of-town family members. Choose a meeting place for your family in case you must evacuate your area.

Class Activity

Comprehend: List the following disasters on the board and have students name precautions for each:

1. Lightning
2. Flood
3. Hurricane
4. Tornado
5. Blizzard
6. Earthquake

Caption Answer: Natural and manmade disasters are unexpected.

■ **Figure 24.9** *Prepare for disasters likely to hit your area. Why should you prepare for disasters?*

■ **Figure 24.10** *Have on hand water to drink and a disaster preparation kit. Why is it important to store drinking water?*

Different geographic areas are prone to different events. Most states provide preparedness routines for events most likely to strike your area. Here are a few additional rules:

- Obey instructions. If told to leave an area, do so.

- In an earthquake, get under a sturdy desk, table, or other furniture, if you can. Do not run outside, where objects may fall on you.

- In storms, stay indoors. When lightning is nearby, keep away from water, plumbing, other metal objects, and all electrical outlets. Do not use the telephone.

- If rising water is a problem or if your home has structural damage from an earthquake, turn off the main power switch. Let an electrician check your home before turning on the power again.

- Afterwards, be aware that electrical power lines may be damaged or down. Keep away from them.

SECTION 5 Review

1. Floods, earthquakes, and storms

2. A flashlight with extra batteries, candles and matches. a battery-powered radio or television with extra batteries. a change of clothing for each family member. sleeping bags, blankets, or other bedding for each family member. first-aid supplies and medications.

3. In an earthquake, get under a sturdy desk, table, or other furniture, if you can. Do not run outside, where objects may fall on you.

4. When lightning is nearby, keep away from water, plumbing, other metal objects, and all electrical outlets. Use only cordless phones or cell phones and only when inside an enclosed building.

5. Answers will vary.

Reviewing the Facts

1. **List.** Give three examples of natural disasters.
2. **Identify.** List six items you should have available in the event of a disaster.
3. **Analyze.** In the event of an earthquake, where should you seek safety?
4. **Explain.** What are some precautions you should take during a lightning storm?

Writing Critically

5. **Descriptive.** Develop a fictitious situation in which you have to prepare for a disaster. Describe the situation you are facing and exactly how you will prepare for it in order to ensure your safety. Discuss the damage that the disaster may cause and how you plan to survive its aftermath.

For fitness and health tips, visit the Fitness Zone at **glencoe.com.**

Care of Others: Child Care

Love and enjoyment of children may come naturally. However, to deliver competent child care, you also have to do some formal learning. Safety precautions are a part of child care.

Home Safety

MAIN IDEA ▶ **Competent child care includes keeping a watchful eye on children.**

Keeping a safe home is a major part of the responsible care of children. Whether you care for younger sisters and brothers or babysit, you should check the home, yard, garage, storage areas, basement, and play areas for hazards to the children's safety. Ask yourself these questions:

1. Are all areas free of hazards that could cause falls, as described in Section 4 of this chapter?
2. Are all areas well defended against fire, as described in Section 3?
3. If there is a pool or other body of water nearby, is it fenced off, so that the children cannot play there unsupervised or accidentally fall in?
4. Are all areas neat and free of trash and bottles?

Fix any areas that are not safe.

Group Project:

Influence: Have students develop safety slogans to put around the home and/or play area to help remind parents and child care providers of safety precautions.

■ **Figure 24.11** *Teens and others who care for children should learn how to handle emergencies. What questions should you ask yourself to determine if an area is safe?*

Caption Answer: Are all areas free of hazards that could cause falls? Are all areas neat and free of trash and bottles?

■ **Figure 24.12** *When adults focus on safety, children can be free to enjoy their play. What are steps you should take if you care for someone's child?*

Caption Answer: Write down phone numbers and location of parents, and keep the child in view at all times.

Health Skills

Tips for Babysitters

Before watching someone else's children:

1. Write down the phone number(s) or address(es) where parents can be reached.

2. Write down one or more neighbors' names and numbers.

3. Write down the telephone numbers of the family doctor, the police department or sheriff, and the fire department.

4. Know how to lock the door(s). Secure all windows.

5. Let no one in unless told in advance that they're coming.

6. Keep an awake child in view at all times. Check a sleeping child every 15 minutes.

Toy Safety

Pay special attention to children's toys:

- Make sure that children do not play with sticks, or with toys or other objects that may break if the children fall. This warning applies to bottles, glasses, and even some plastic toys.

- Do not allow children to play with fireworks.

- Make sure children do not play with or around television sets, electrical devices in the kitchen and bathroom, fans, power tools, household cleaning equipment, sewing machines, lawn tools, and other dangerous objects.

- Do not allow children to play with any guns, including pellet guns, BB guns, and toy guns that look real.

- Even if the home and toys are safe, children should not be left to play unattended.

Prevention of Choking

When feeding children, be aware that they can easily choke on food. To prevent choking, cut food into small pieces. Let children take only small forkfuls of any food. Don't let them speak or laugh with food in their mouths. Make sure they chew each bite thoroughly before attempting to swallow. Take particular care with round pieces of food such as hot dogs, grapes, or cherry tomatoes. Teach children to chew food completely before swallowing. For small children, cut food into tiny pieces. Peanuts should be split open. Popcorn should not be served to small children at all, because it can easily lodge in the throat.

Learn the Heimlich maneuver (abdominal thrust maneuver). If a child does choke, use the maneuver to dislodge the particle from the throat. The next chapter gives a basic description of the maneuver, but you can best learn it in a first-aid course.

When you are babysitting, some additional precautions are in order. See the Health Skills sidebar, "Tips for Babysitters."

■ **Figure 24.13** *Choking poses a real threat: young children easily choke on food. How can you decrease the risk of choking in small children?*

Caption Answer: Cut meat into small pieces; don't let them talk with food in their mouths.

Worksheets: A reproducible quiz for Section 6 is provided in the Teacher Classroom Resources.

Reviewing the Facts

1. **List.** List four precautions you should follow when caring for children in your home.
2. **Explain.** How can children be kept from choking?
3. **Name.** Name five precautions babysitters should take.

Writing Critically

4. **Personal.** In your mind, make a safety inspection of your home. Picture yourself walking from room to room. Evaluate each specific area in terms of potential safety hazards that may exist for infants and small children. List all the safety hazards you discovered. Describe how each can best be remedied.

G☼ **Online**

For more information on health careers, visit Career Corner at **glencoe.com**.

1. Are all areas free of hazards that could cause falls? Are all areas well defended against fire? If there is a pool or other body of water nearby, is it fenced off? Are all areas neat and free of trash and bottles?

2. Food should be cut into small pieces. Let children take only small forkfuls of food. Do not let children talk with food in their mouths.

3. Write down the parents' phone number(s) or address(es). Write down one or more neighbors' names and numbers. Write down the telephone numbers of: the family doctor or pediatrician, the police department or sheriff and the fire department.

4. Answers will vary.

Fire Prevention and Escape

Understand and Apply Read the conversation below, and then complete the writing exercise that follows.

Fires and burns are a leading cause of accidental death in the United States. It is worth studying the guidelines offered here on fire prevention, before you may need them.

Q: What precautions can I take to prevent fires?

A: Good. Many fires are caused by the careless use of fire. Many fires are also caused by smoking in bed. To prevent these fires:

- Don't smoke. If you do, quit. Or . . .
- Dispose of cigarettes and matches safely. Never assume they are out when they might not be.
- Keep matches and lighters out of the reach of children.
- Do not smoke in bed.

Other fires are caused by cooking and heating equipment. Take these precautions:

- Keep cooking and heating equipment clean and in good repair.
- If a gas pilot light or a burner on the stove or oven goes out, ventilate the area before lighting a burner. Do not turn electric switches on or off before the area is ventilated, as switches make a tiny spark when used.

- Turn pot handles on the stove so that you won't knock them when you walk by. Make sure that children cannot reach them.
- Keep the cords of electric cookware on the counter, not dangling.
- Keep portable space heaters out of indoor traffic lanes. Turn them off and unplug them before going to bed. Keep flammable materials away from space heaters.
- Keep cloth (curtains, pot holders, your own loose clothing) and other flammable materials away from cooking surfaces and fires.

Still other fires are caused by liquids. Be sure to:

- Use flammable liquids only as directed.
- Store surplus quantities of flammable liquids outside, in containers designed to hold in fumes as well as fluid.

Q: What if a fire starts? What should I do?

A: Whenever you go into an unfamiliar building, locate the exits, fire escapes, extinguishers, and stairways. In the event of a fire, always use the stairs.

Most importantly, make an escape plan for your home. Figure out two ways to get outside from every room. Involve everyone. Make plans to ensure that people with disabilities can get out. Rehearse. Have a fire drill. Designate a place to meet outside, so that you can be sure everyone is out.

Place fire extinguishers near kitchens and other areas where a fire might start. Should a fire start, you'll have only about 30 seconds in which to use a fire extinguisher safely. After that time is up, you must evacuate the area immediately.

Remove all trash, so fire will not spread across it. Install an outdoor faucet on all sides of the building, and keep hoses nearby. Advance planning is the only effective weapon.

Q: How about installing smoke detectors in homes?

A: All homes should be equipped with properly maintained smoke detectors. Often, by the time people feel the heat or smell the smoke of a fire, it is too late to get out. Most people die in fires because they are unable to breathe, not because they are burned. Once you hear the alarm, you generally have about three minutes to escape.

Smoke detectors should first be placed in sleeping areas. Additional detectors can be placed in other areas. Install fire extinguishers too, but do not put them where the fire is most likely to be. Put them where you can most likely get to them in case of fire. Learn to use them properly. Using water on an electrical or chemical fire can do more harm than good.

Q: Okay, let's say a fire has started. Now what?

A: Because most fatal home fires happen when the occupants are asleep, it is best to sleep with the bedroom door closed. Smoke can be deadly.

If you are alerted to a fire:
1. Roll out of bed, staying low. Heat rises and may overcome you if you stand up.
2. Crawl quickly to the door. Black smoke may interfere with vision, but crawl anyway.
3. Feel the door for heat. If it's cool, open it carefully, but stand behind it. Be ready to slam it shut if smoke or heat rush in. If the door is hot, don't open it. Go some other way.
4. Crawl out quickly. Close doors behind you.
5. Don't go back for pets or possessions.
6. Don't use elevators during fires; use stairs. If trapped on an upper floor, wrap yourself in a blanket, cover your head, hang out a window, and yell. Don't jump unless you absolutely must.
7. Meet your family as prearranged.
8. Call the fire department from a neighbor's phone.

If your clothes catch fire, do not run. Stop, drop, and roll. To help someone else whose clothes have caught on fire, force the same motion if you can. Then smother the person's flaming clothes with a coat or blanket.

 Writing Using information from the Q&A section, create an escape plan for your home. What fire safety precautions are currently in place in your home? What can you do to make your home safer and reduce the risk of fires?

Reviewing Vocabulary

Use the vocabulary terms listed below to complete the following statements.

head restraints

air bags

1. _____ are high seat backs or devices attached to seats in cars, intended to prevent neck and spinal cord injury.

2. Inflatable pillows known as _____ are stored in the steering wheels of cars and are designed to inflate on impact.

3. Write a paragraph using the vocabulary terms from the list above. Underline each term.

Recalling Key Facts and Ideas

Section 1

4. **Identify.** What are the chances that someone you know will suffer an injury this year?

5. **Describe.** Describe the attitude of a defensive driver.

6. **Explain.** Explain why safety belts should be worn by all occupants in a car.

7. **Recall.** What are some ways to avoid alcohol-related accidents?

8. **Name.** Name three changes in driving habits that could save lives.

Section 2

9. **List.** List three safety precautions for diving.

10. **Explain.** If you cannot swim, how can you assist a swimmer who is in trouble?

11. **Name.** Name three tips for safe boating.

Section 3

12. **Recall.** What product should be used to smother a grease fire?

13. **List.** List the three classes of fire extinguishers and the type of fire each is used for.

Section 4

14. **Explain.** Why are falls the leading cause of accidental death and injury for older adults?

15. **Describe.** What are the most common types of falls experienced by infants?

16. **Name.** Give two firearm safety precautions.

Section 5

17. **List.** List at least 5 items you should have on hand to be prepared for disasters.

Section 6

18. **Name.** When babysitting, what phone numbers should you be sure to have in your possession before the parents leave?

Writing Critically

19. **Descriptive.** Describe an emergency situation that you personally experienced or witnessed. Comment on how it felt to be at the scene. Do you ever worry about what to do or whether you would panic in an emergency? Why, or why not? Injuries and deaths during emergencies frequently occur because people panic. How can feelings of panic be reduced? What would help people feel calm in an emergency?

---

1. Head restraints 2. Air bags 3. Answers will vary.
4. One out of three 5. Driver is aware of other drivers and hazards. 6. Slows momentum; keeps drivers and passengers inside of the vehicle. 7. Never ride with someone who has

been drinking. Never drive after consuming alcohol.
8. Change lanes safely, keep safe distances, pause after light turns green. 9. Stay away from obstructions, know the water's depth, do not dive too deep. 10. Lie on the dock, extend an

20. **Expository.** Why do people take unnecessary risks? Discuss why people behave in unsafe ways when they know better. Why do you think most of us think, "It won't happen to me"?

Activities

21. Investigate the different first-aid and lifesaving courses that are available in your community this year. Make a poster and list the dates, locations, and any fees for these courses.

22. Develop a bicycle safety pamphlet. Include illustrations of specific bicycle parts that should be checked periodically, illustrations of hand signals, and information on safety gear. Describe safety precautions to be taken in various traffic and weather conditions.

23. Interview the fire marshal in your area about the most serious problems the fire department faces. Ask what students can do to help promote fire safety.

24. Imagine you are a state legislator who is responsible for establishing laws to curtail drinking and driving. Discuss the laws you would propose regarding: suspending and revoking drivers' licenses, plea bargaining, jail sentences, community service, and fines.

25. Investigate the safety belt laws in your state. What are the laws about securing small children? Are the laws different for front-seat and back-seat passengers? Are there any fines for not wearing a safety belt or for not securing a small child in a car seat? If so, what are they? Write a brief report on your findings.

26. Meet with the school nurse to find out what the most common accidents and injuries are at school. List them and identify ways these accidents could be prevented.

Making Decisions About Health

27. Describe how each of the following situations could best be handled:

- Your car breaks down on a deserted road at night and you are alone.

- One of the children you are babysitting has just fallen and received a cut that may require stitches.

- Your friend is drunk and offers you a ride home.

- The smoke detector in your home has just gone off and woken you from a sound sleep.

For more vocabulary practice, play the True/False game at **glencoe.com**.

Fact or Fiction?

Answers

1. False. One out of every three, not ten, people suffers an injury each year.
2. False. Skill is important, but attitude is equally important in preventing accidents on the road.
3. True.

Writing Paragraphs will vary.

object; pull the victim within reach. **11.** Load properly, sit down, give people your itinerary. **12.** Baking soda **13.** Class A: ordinary combustibles; Class B: flammable liquids; Class C: electrical equipment **14.** Older adults lose balance. **15.** Falls from tables, bassinets, or into bodies of water. **16.** Learn and obey firearm safety rules. **17.** Clean water, flashlight, candles, radio, food **18.** Location of parents, doctor, police and fire departments **19–27.** Answers will vary.

CHAPTER 25

Emergency Measures

Sections

1. **Providing First Aid**
2. **Cardiopulmonary Resuscitation (CPR)**
3. **Choking and Severe Bleeding**
4. **Other First-Aid Procedures**

Chapter Preview

In an emergency, fast, effective action can save a life, perhaps your own. Many people die needlessly after accidents each year because no one nearby knows how to help effectively. This chapter presents some basic emergency measures. However, understand that reading alone cannot adequately prepare you to be of real help in an emergency. Also, attempts to help without the right knowledge can many times do more harm than good.

Take a class from a qualified instructor who teaches **first aid**, literally, "help given first"—*medical help given immediately in an emergency, before the victim is transported to a hospital or treatment center*. This chapter's task is to make you aware that emergencies do arise, and that your actions can make a difference. The Life Choice Inventory will show you the basics you need in order to be really helpful in emergencies.

Fact or Fiction?

What Do You Think?
Is each statement true or false? If you think it's false, explain what's true.

1. To be of real help in an emergency, a person needs mainly to keep a level head and use common sense.
2. The first thing to do in an emergency is to move the victim away from the scene to prevent further upset.
3. A person in a state of shock is experiencing a normal and common emotional reaction that will soon pass on its own.

 Writing Think of a time when you or someone who was with you suffered an injury. Write a paragraph describing how you responded to the injury.

(Answers on page 697)

Go Online
Visit **glencoe.com** and complete the Life Choice Inventory for Chapter 25.

SECTION 1

Providing First Aid

When an emergency arises, many bystanders will try to provide first aid. Before starting first-aid, though, the most important thing to do is call for help. Calling 911 in most communities in the United States will connect you with an emergency dispatcher, a person who answers calls and relays messages to the proper emergency provider. In the United States, emergency dispatchers, emergency room personnel, and poison control center personnel provide **emergency medical service** (EMS). An EMS team is *a team of people who are trained to respond in emergencies, and who can be contacted through a single dispatcher*.

Vocabulary

first aid
emergency medical service
   (EMS)
shock

Class Activity

Apply: Ask each student to assemble a first-aid kit for their car, bicycle, or backpack, using the list of standard supplies for a first aid kit in this chapter. Have the students put their medicine kit in a convenient receptacle such as a plastic box or coffee can, appropriately labeled.

The First-Aid Kit

MAIN IDEA ▶ A first-aid kit will provide you with basic equipment to manage some emergencies.

A well-stocked first-aid kit will provide you with the supplies to handle some emergencies. In the case of any emergency, however, it's important to first call 911 and provide the dispatcher with the name of the victim, a description of what has happened, and the exact location. **Figures 25.1** and **25.2** show some of the supplies that should be included in first-aid kits to be used outside the home and in the home. Before you use any of the techniques described in this section, you should take an accredited first-aid course. The American Red Cross and other organizations offer basic first-aid classes. Check for classes in your area on the Internet. The American Red Cross also maintains lists of items that should be included in first-aid kits. Two of the most important items to keep are disposable gloves and antiseptic hand cleaner.

| Figure 25.1 | Products Preventing the Spread of Disease During First Aid |

Use disposable rubber gloves to avoid contact with blood or body fluids.

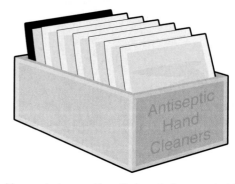

Use waterless antiseptic hand cleaners to kill germs before and after giving care.

Figure 25.2 **Standard Supplies for a First-Aid Kit**

Assemble one first-aid kit for your home and one for your car.

Item	Purpose
For disease prevention	
Disposable rubber gloves	To protect you from disease when you assist a bleeding person
Antiseptic hand cleansers or waterless alcohol-based hand sanitizers	To remove infectious organisms from your hands
Bandages and dressings	
Ace bandages, 3-inch	To wrap and hold sterile dressings or splints in place
Rolled white gauze bandages, 2- and 3-inch widths	To wrap and hold sterile dressings or splints in place
Ready-to-apply sterile first-aid dressings, individually packaged, various sizes	To apply directly to open wounds or burns
Triangular bandages, 36 × 36 inches	To fold diagonally, as slings for fractured or broken arms or shoulders; to hold dressings in place; to make into folded compresses
Rolls of sticky tape, 2- and 3-inch widths	To be cut to size for simple wounds
Adhesive bandages, various widths and shapes	To cover minor cuts and scrapes
Medicines	
Aspirin or aspirin substitute[a]	To relieve pain
Antiseptic cream or petroleum jelly	To prevent bandages from sticking to minor wounds; to reduce chance of infection by some disease-causing organisms
Liquid antiseptic	To cleanse skin surfaces in cases of minor wounds
Calamine lotion	To relieve itching from insect bites or exposure to skin irritants
Antacid	To relieve upset stomach
Activated charcoal[b]	To treat certain cases of poisoning if told to do so
Miscellaneous	
Adhesive tape	To fasten bandages or dressings
Large safety pins	To fasten bandages or slings
Tweezers	To remove splinters or insect stingers
Blunt-tipped scissors	To cut lengths of bandages, adhesive tape, and the like
Thermometer(s)	To take rectal or oral temperature
Hypoallergenic soap	To cleanse wounds
Absorbent cotton, paper tissues	To wipe and cleanse wounds
Chemically activated cold pack	To prevent or reduce swelling
Small flashlight (and extra batteries)	To improve visibility after dark

[a]Reye's syndrome is a rare and potentially life-threatening condition linked to aspirin use during chicken pox or flu. Children and teens should never take aspirin. They should be treated with an aspirin substitute such as acetaminophen.

[b]You should have these supplies on hand so that when you call for help in an emergency, you can use them as directed.

" *A timid person is frightened before a danger, and a coward during the time, and a courageous person afterwards.* **"**

—John Paul Richter (1763–1825) German writer

 **Did You Know?**

Call for help, then proceed. Calls to 911 are free, even from pay phones.

When offering first aid, make sure that you protect yourself before helping the person. For example, do not approach a person who is lying unconscious in a puddle of water with live electrical lines nearby. Call 911 and wait for help. Likewise, if you encounter a person along the side of a road who has been involved in an accident, check the scene first. If approaching the person jeopardizes your safety, wait for emergency medical personnel.

First Actions

MAIN IDEA ▶ The three steps in offering first aid will help the injured person and keep you safe.

When emergency strikes, what should you do? Take a moment to think clearly and take these three actions:

Step 1: Survey the scene for safety and information, and inspect the victim swiftly. Help only if there are immediate threats to life.

Step 2: Call 911 for help.

Step 3: Inspect the victim more closely.

The sections that follow describe each of these three actions.

Step 1: Survey of Scene and Victims

In surveying the scene quickly, you should ask yourself:

- Is it safe?
- What has happened?
- Are there victims? How many?

Get someone to call 911 right away if you can.

As for yourself, don't rush in. Look around. Is it safe? Are hazards present, such as fire, fumes, fast traffic, live electrical wires, or fast-moving water? If hazards are present, do not attempt a rescue.

As you survey the scene, look at the people around you. Are other victims nearby? Who can help by controlling crowds, or by directing traffic? Ask others to help.

Do Not Move Most Victims Assume that every accident victim has an injured neck or spine. Further injury to the spinal cord can cause permanent paralysis or death. Tell the injured person not to move.

The only exception to this rule is if you must move someone away from fire, water, poisonous gas, or other dangers to save a life *and* if you can do so safely.

If you must move someone, and can do so safely, continue assuming that the spine may be injured. Move the person the shortest possible distance. Keep the head and body in line. If possible, pull from the head end, with your hands under the shoulders and the head resting on your arms. Pull the person in a straight line.

If the person is floating in water face down, you must move the person. If it is safe to walk in the water and stand while you do it, roll the person face up as a unit. Then pull the person out of the water just enough to permit you to begin CPR. If several people are injured, first help the one who may have life-threatening injuries, and can benefit from your help.

Talking to the Victim Reassure the person. "I am here to help you." Get information: "What happened?" Caution: "Please don't try to move until help arrives." The responses will help you provide information to the emergency dispatcher.

If the victim cannot speak, look around quickly for clues. For example, should you find an unconscious person lying near a tipped canoe in shallow water, you might suspect that the person had inhaled water or sustained a blow to the head.

Tell the injured person who you are. If he or she can talk, ask for permission to help. If you have been trained by a professional instructor, say so. However, you cannot make the claim of being trained in first aid after simply reading a chapter such as this one.

Did You Know?

Before giving first aid to a conscious person, you must ask for permission from that person.

Health Skills

Reducing Disease Risks

To minimize your contact with someone else's blood or other body fluids:

- Place a barrier between you and the fluid, such as rubber gloves, plastic wrap, or plastic bags.
- Keep your hands away from your own face or any other opening on your body during and after giving help.
- Wash your hands with soap and water after providing help. Wash under nails gently with a soft brush.

Figure 25.4

Signs and Symptoms of Shock

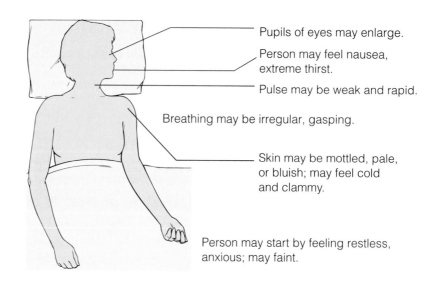

Pupils of eyes may enlarge.

Person may feel nausea, extreme thirst.

Pulse may be weak and rapid.

Breathing may be irregular, gasping.

Skin may be mottled, pale, or bluish; may feel cold and clammy.

Person may start by feeling restless, anxious; may faint.

Health Skills

First Aid for Shock

To reduce the risk of shock:

1. Lay the person flat to aid circulation. Elevate any limb that is bleeding. Raise the feet so that they are slightly higher than the head.

2. Loosen tight clothing.

3. Help the person maintain normal body temperature. For example, if the person appears overly cool or chilled, try to cover the person with blankets.

4. Avoid giving food or liquids to people in shock. Give nothing by mouth, even if the person complains of thirst.

Life-Threatening Conditions In inspecting each victim, you should look for life-threatening conditions including a blocked airway, stopped breathing, and severe breathing. You should also note if the victim is conscious, appears to have any neck or spinal cord injuries, or if the person is in shock. These conditions require immediate help and need to be reported when you call 911.

Concentrate on the victim as you check for life-threatening conditions, and do not let anyone interrupt you. Inspect the victims, allowing just a minute or two for each possible condition.

Checking the Airway and Breathing To check for a blocked airway and for breathing, place your ear and cheek close to the victim's mouth and nose. Look, listen, and use the sensitive skin of your cheek to feel for breathing. Chest movements alone don't mean breathing is occurring. They may just be muscle spasms that mimic breathing.

Severe Bleeding The spurting of blood from a large artery can reduce the body's supply of blood dangerously in just seconds. Respond quickly to stop it as instructed on page 684.

Calling for Help While providing care, keep shouting for help if no one has called yet. If no one responds, then wait to call until after you have controlled airway, breathing, and severe bleeding the best you can.

Other Conditions to Note When the vital conditions are controlled, check or review three other things. Then call 911. To review, here are the three:

- Is the victim conscious?
- Are neck and other spinal injuries a possibility?
- Is the victim in **shock**, *a failure or disruption of the blood circulation, a life-threatening reaction to accidents and injuries?*

In shock, the circulation is disrupted. Shock can cause death. It is very common in accident victims. It can come on fast, or in stages. At first, blood flow to the brain may diminish, causing loss of consciousness. Blood supply to other vital organs may also fail, and the heart itself may fail.

The signs and symptoms of shock are shown in **Figure 25.4**. It demands professional emergency treatment. Call for help. After you've called, take the steps listed in the Health Skills sidebar, "First Aid for Shock" on page 674.

Step 2: Calling for Help

In a serious emergency, it is urgent that someone call 911 as soon as possible. If you are the only one available and you have been trained in first-aid techniques, give first aid first, then call. Stay calm and be prepared to provide information. If you send someone else to make the call, be sure that person knows all the needed information. When you call for help, you must report:

- Your name.
- The location.
- The telephone number you are calling from.
- What has happened.
- How many victims there are.
- How each is hurt.

Step 3: Secondary Survey of Victims

The secondary survey is a head-to-toe survey, and should be swift. You have checked for life-threatening conditions and have called for help. Now you are inspecting the victim for other injuries. These injuries may also require first aid to prevent their getting worse.

Ask the victim about pain. Injured areas usually hurt (although spinal injuries may not). Pain while breathing indicates a problem in the chest or abdomen.

Complete a quick inspection, not more than five minutes in duration. Start with the head and work downward. Look for bumps, bruises, blood, or any odd formations or positions of body parts. As a reminder, if you suspect head, neck, or back injuries, do not move the person except to get him or her out of immediate danger.

Healthy limbs move freely. If you do not suspect neck or back injuries, ask the person to slowly move each joint. For example, a person with a broken collar bone would not be able to shrug the shoulders. Do not lift or try to move the joints for the victim. You may dislocate the ends of a broken bone or worsen other injuries in doing so.

Health Skills

Summary of Emergency Actions

A helper should first take these actions in the order listed:

1. Survey the scene for any danger, such as traffic or toxic gases.
2. Don't help if you are likely to be injured yourself.
3. Do not move anyone at all, except to escape immediate danger.
4. Check quickly for blocked airway, no breathing, and severe bleeding.
5. If any of these are present, quickly take appropriate steps to correct them.
6. Call or have someone else call emergency services for help.
7. Check or recheck for consciousness, spinal injuries, and shock.
8. Inspect the victim again to identify other injuries.
9. Do nothing to worsen injuries and do not rush recovery.
10. Provide first aid for each condition.
11. Maintain the victim's temperature and comfort.

During this close inspection of the victim, keep the person lying quietly until you are certain no serious injury exists. Meanwhile, help maintain the person's body temperature. If a blanket or another type of covering is available, cover the person. Help the victim rest comfortably. Continue to monitor the person's breathing and heartbeat.

SECTION 1 Review

1. Emergency medical service (EMS)

2. Shock

3. First Aid

4. Know how to call for help.

5. Assume that every accident victim has an injured neck or spine.

6. Report your name, where you are, the telephone number you are calling from, what has happened, how many victims there are, and how each is hurt.

7. Answers will vary.

Reviewing the Vocabulary

Review the vocabulary on page 670. Then answer these questions.

1. A team of people who are trained to respond in emergencies, and who can be contacted through a single dispatcher is called ＿＿＿.

2. Failure or disruption of the blood circulation, a life-threatening reaction to accidents and injuries, is called ＿＿＿.

3. ＿＿＿ is literally, "help given first"- medical help given immediately in an emergency, before the victim is transported to a hospital or treatment center.

Reviewing the Facts

4. **Recall.** What is the most important thing to do in an emergency?

5. **Recall.** What should you always assume about an accident victim?

6. **Explain.** What information should you report when you call for help?

Writing Critically

7. **Expository.** Reread the Health Skills sidebar, "Summary of Emergency Actions." Why is it important to follow these steps in order? How can you encourage other people to learn these steps?

 **Go Online**

For more vocabulary practice, play the True/False game at **glencoe.com**.

Cardiopulmonary Resuscitation (CPR)

Someone who has stopped breathing needs help immediately. **Cardiopulmonary resuscitation** (CPR), *a technique of maintaining blood and oxygen flow through the body of a person whose heart and breathing have stopped*, can sustain life until EMS help arrives. This section describes CPR techniques. You must take a CPR course before administering CPR. Methods change and reading alone is not enough.

Vocabulary

Cardiopulmonary
  resuscitation (CPR)

Opening the Airway

MAIN IDEA ▷ Opening the airway is the first step to restoring breathing.

If breathing stops, restoring it is urgent. Within five minutes after breathing stops, death occurs in over 50 percent of people. Almost all others die within ten minutes. Many emergencies can stop a person's breathing: allergic reactions, burns, drug overdoses, poisoning, drownings, and others.

A first step to restoring breathing is opening the airway. Don't move the person unless you must. Moving a person who is injured may cause additional injury. Only move the person if you must to prevent further injury. If you move the person, keep the spine straight. Position the person, and clear the mouth as shown in **Figure 25.5**. The airway may be collapsed shut. Open it without disturbing the neck bones as shown in **Figure 25.6** on page 678.

Figure 25.5	Opening the Airway

Tongue is blocking airway.

If head and neck are flat on the ground, the tongue can block the airway.

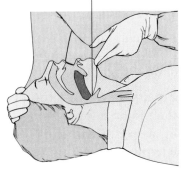

Tongue is out of the way and airway is open.

Hold the forehead, lift the chin, and the tongue will move out of the way.

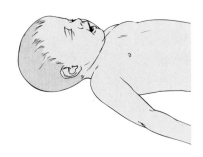

Infant: Tilt the head back. The force of your breath will open the airway.

Figure 25.6   **Preparing to Start Rescue Breathing**

New first aid recommendations are being developed with more information about how to stabilize the head and neck of injured people. Updates like these take place often, making first aid courses essential for helpers.

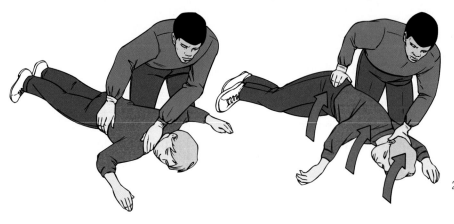

1. If you must roll the person over, keep the spine straight as shown.

2. Use a finger. Be careful. Don't push anything down the throat. Sweep out anything you find in the mouth.

Rescue Breathing

MAIN IDEA ▶ Rescue breathing provides oxygen to someone who has stopped breathing.

Class Discussion

Discuss: Ask students how rescue breathing for adults differs from rescue breathing for children. How is the procedure the same for both? Discuss the ways the treatment of infants and children is unique.

To learn to properly perform the rescue breathing method described here, a person should obtain first-aid training and practice on a model of a victim. An untrained rescuer may cause more injury. Some of the things that might happen are as follows:

- Blowing air into the stomach may cause vomiting. This can block the airway and make breathing impossible.

- Moving the head of someone with a neck injury may cause permanent paralysis.

- The rescuer may not understand when to stop giving assistance. A victim may begin to breathe on his or her own, but weakly. Continued efforts on your part using a different rhythm may shut down the victim's independent breathing.

- Forcing air into a drowning person's lungs when the person is struggling to cough up water may push water into the lungs.

Finally, never use the procedures described for an adult on a child or infant. Using the procedures for an adult on a child or infant can cause harm. The next two figures show how to give breathing assistance to an adult, or to a child or infant, **Figure 25.7**. If you do not feel comfortable performing rescue breathing, begin chest compressions immediately.

Figure 25.7 **Rescue Breathing for Adults and Children or Infants**

Rescue Breathing for an Adult

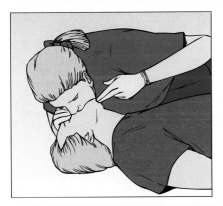

Keep holding the airway open. Pinch the victim's nose closed. Using a CPR breathing barrier or face shield, cover the mouth with your mouth. Blow air into the lungs. You can feel it go down. Let it come out. Blow again. Take a normal (not a deep) breath and give each breath for 1 second. Each breath should make the chest rise. If it doesn't, reposition the head to clear the airway, as in **Figure 25.5**. After two rescue breaths, immediately begin chest compressions, as demonstrated in **Figure 25.8**.

Rescue Breathing for a Child and Infant

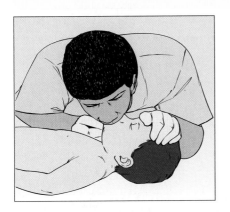

Keep your finger under the chin, lifting slightly. This will help to keep a seal between your lips and the child's face. Using a CPR beathing barrier or face shield, put your mouth over the child's mouth and nose. Give small, slow, gentle breaths. Blow just enough air to make the chest rise. Release, and let the breath be exhaled. Each breath should take 1 second. After two breaths, immediately begin chest compressions, as shown in **Figure 25.8**.

Chest Compressions

MAIN IDEA ▶ Chest compressions keep blood moving in someone who has suffered cardiac arrest.

When a victim's heart stops beating, breathing also ceases. During the first critical few minutes, chest compressions are essential. Never perform chest compressions unless you have taken a training class. An untrained person who attempts chest compressions may even stop a heart that is already beating.

A properly trained helper can assist a person whose heart has stopped. After the helper has:

- Determined the person is unconscious
- Called EMS
- Opened the airway and listened for breathing
- If no breathing, has administered two breaths

Then the helper may begin 30 chest compressions as instructed in the following paragraphs.

 *Did You Know?*

An automated external defibrillator (AED) is a device that can restart a stopped heart. See Chapter 17 for details.

Figure 25.8   **CPR for Adults: Six Steps to Chest Compression**

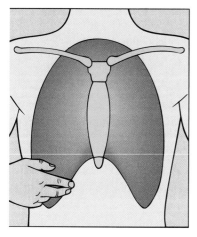

1. Kneeling at victim's side, locate lower edge of rib cage. Follow it up to the notched center.

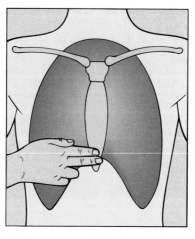

2. Place your middle finger in the notch, index finger above on breastbone.

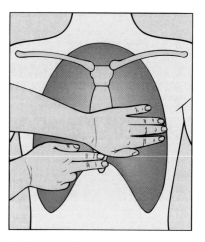

3. Press heel of other hand above index finger on breastbone. Avoid pressing on this part of the breastbone (the xiphoid process)—it breaks easily.

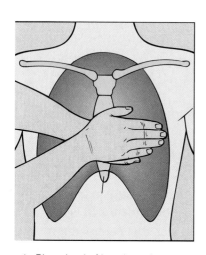

4. Place heel of hand used to find notch on top of other hand. Hold fingers slightly upward, off the victim's chest.

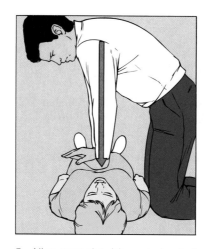

5. Align your shoulder over heel of bottom hand, elbow straight.

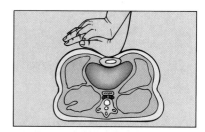
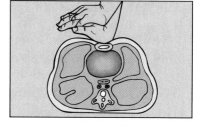

6. Press down to compress victim's chest 1½ to 2 inches, and then release Push hard and push fast. Do not lift your hand away from chest. Repeat 30 compressions and 2 breaths 3 times per minute. All together, the chest compressions and breaths take about one minute.

Starting Chest Compressions

Chest compressions keep the blood circulating to the brain and heart. This allows critical organs to live until professional help arrives. The brain begins to die within just a few minutes after circulation ceases, so start CPR quickly—don't wait.

Warning: a beating but weakened heart can be stopped by chest compression. If you are not sure that a person's heart has stopped, do nothing. When you are sure, follow the steps outlined in **Figure 25.8**. Give 30 chest compressions and two breaths per cycle. Repeat the cycle without stopping until emergency help takes over or the person recovers.

For infants and children, you must be much gentler, and the pace must be faster. **Figure 25.9** shows the key differences. To learn the proper timing of chest compressions it helps to know that, for an adult, 30 compressions should take about 20 seconds. Practice this: Try counting aloud, "one-up-two-up . . . ," while pushing down on the count, and letting up on the "up." Use a stopwatch to time yourself, or have a partner time you.

Did You Know?

Strive for 100 chest compressions per minute. This pace allows blood to fill the heart's chambers between beats and provides enough blood flow to maintain life.

| Figure 25.9 | CPR for Infants and Children |

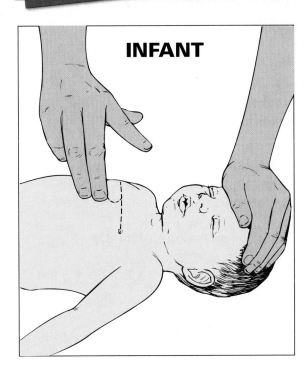

INFANT

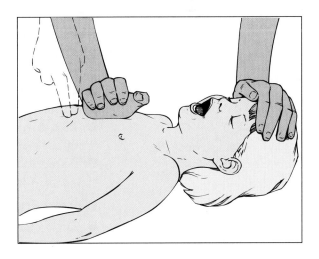

CHILD

Position two fingers as shown on the child's breastbone, about a finger's width below the nipples. Do compressions and give breaths at a rapid pace: 30 compressions, 2 breaths; 30 and 2; 30 and 2; 3 times a minute. At each compression push the chest down about 1/3 to 1/2 the depth of the chest. Keep repeating until heartbeat and breathing resume.

Move two fingers' width above the notch of the ribs, and place the heel of the hand on the breastbone as shown. Keep fingers up (don't touch ribs). Do 30 compressions and give 2 breaths, about 3 times a minute. Make each compression about 1/3 to 1/2 the depth of the chest. Keep repeating until heartbeat and breathing resume.

■ **Figure 25.10** *Chest compressions circulate blood to the brain and heart. What is the ratio of chest compressions to breaths for CPR in adults, children, and infants?*

Caption Answer: 30 chest compressions and 2 breaths

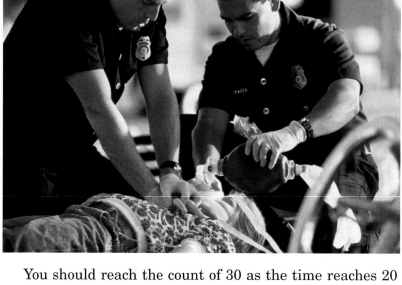

Worksheets: A reproducible quiz for Section 2 is provided in the Teacher Classroom Resources.

You should reach the count of 30 as the time reaches 20 seconds. If the heart resumes beating, check the breathing. If breathing resumes, monitor both heartbeat and breathing until help arrives.

SECTION 2 Review

Review the vocabulary on page 677. Then answer these questions.

Reviewing the Vocabulary
1. What is *cardiopulmonary resuscitation*?

Reviewing the Facts
2. **Describe.** What happens to people who have stopped breathing after five minutes and after ten minutes?
3. **List.** List the emergencies that may stop a person's breathing.
4. **Explain.** What should you be sure of before giving chest compressions?
5. **Explain.** Why do the procedures for CPR differ if the person is a child or infant?

Writing Critically
6. **Descriptive.** Identify the hazards in giving breathing assistance without being trained. What would you do if you had to perform breathing assistance on a family member?

Go Online

For more vocabulary practice, play the Concentration game at **glencoe.com.**

1. A technique of maintaining blood and oxygen flow through the body of a person whose heart and breathing is stopped.

2. Fifty percent of people who stop breathing after five minutes die, and almost all others die after ten minutes.

3. Allergic reactions, burns, drug overdoses, poisoning

4. You must be sure there is no heartbeat present.

5. The pace must be gentler and faster in infants and children.

6. Answers will vary.

Choking and Severe Bleeding

Eating hastily, taking large bites of solid foods, talking, laughing, or breathing hard while eating can invite choking. Choking occurs when food enters and sticks in the air passage to the lungs instead of being swallowed into the stomach. Everyone should learn to give and recognize the universal distress signal for choking shown in **Figure 25.11**.

The Heimlich Maneuver

MAIN IDEA ▶ The Heimlich maneuver can dislodge an object that is preventing breathing.

When someone is choking, you must perform the **Heimlich maneuver** (abdominal thrust maneuver), *a technique of dislodging a particle that is blocking a person's airway*. Perform the Heimlich maneuver immediately. Take the steps below.

First, ask, "Can you make any sound at all?" If the victim makes a sound, air is moving over the vocal cords, which means that some air can get into the lungs. In this case, the person can try bending over, coughing, and other self-help maneuvers before you intervene. Don't hit the victim on the back while the victim is standing or sitting erect. If you do, the particle caught in the throat may lodge deeper in the air passage.

Vocabulary

Heimlich maneuver (abdominal thrust maneuver)

Figure 25.11 **Universal Signal for Choking**

A person giving this signal has a blocked airway and needs help right away.

Figure 25.12 **Unblocking the Airway with the Heimlich Maneuver**

For a person who can stand:

Stand behind the person. Ball up your fist. Rotate your thumb toward the person's stomach. Grasp your fist with your other hand, and position it against the abdomen, just below the rib cage. Squeeze rapidly, inward and upward—one, two, three, four times in rapid succession. The object is to propel air upwards out of the lungs and eject the article from the throat. Repeat, if necessary.

For yourself:

Use the back of a chair or the edge of a table to push against, and perform the same maneuver.

Comprehension Check

Comprehend: Ask students how the Heimlich maneuver should be performed if the victim is large or unconscious. Why would this be more useful than holding them in a standing position?

Figure 25.13

Using Direct Pressure to Control Bleeding

Use sterile gauze or a clean folded cloth to cover the wound. Wear gloves. Use your hand to apply pressure. Bleeding should stop or slow to oozing in under 30 minutes.

If the victim cannot make a sound, this means the airway is blocked. Your next moves are to shout for help and perform the Heimlich maneuver as shown in **Figure 25.12**.

In summary, the steps of the Heimlich Maneuver are:

- Position the person.
- Place your fist above the navel (belly button) as shown.
- Grasp your fist with your other hand.
- Thrust inward and upward four or five times in rapid succession to propel the obstacle out of the throat.

If the person is large or unconscious, you can perform the maneuver while the victim remains lying on his or her back. Kneel with your legs straddling the victim's thighs, and place your fist below the rib cage. Press on your fist with your other hand, quickly and firmly, upward, four times. Be sure to make contact with your fist before the thrust—don't punch, but press suddenly.

If it is you who is choking, you can act as your own rescuer by thrusting your fist into your own abdomen, or thrusting your body forward forcefully against a firmly placed object—the back of a chair, side of a table, or edge of a sink or stove.

Severe Bleeding

MAIN IDEA ▶ To stop severe bleeding, use direct pressure.

Bleeding can be life threatening when arteries or veins have been severed in an injury. If you can't see a wound because of clothing, cut or tear away the clothing. In severe bleeding, the blood will be welling or pulsing out of the wound, and the amount of blood will seem dramatically great.

In almost all cases, bleeding can be controlled by continuous, direct pressure. **Figure 25.13** shows an example of how to apply pressure on a bleeding wound. Don't use a tourniquet (a tight band around a limb) to control bleeding. A tourniquet almost always kills the limb to which it is applied and should be used rarely, if ever. Also, don't try to apply pressure at "pressure points," unless you have been trained in the technique. Constricting an artery at a pressure point can damage the healthy tissue normally fed by that artery.

Elevate the injured part to encourage blood to drain back into the body and to slow the blood flow from it. After bleeding stops, prompt treatment of wounds will be necessary to prevent infection.

Worksheets: A reproducible quiz for Section 3 is provided in the Teacher Classroom Resources.

SECTION 3 Review

Reviewing the Vocabulary

Review the vocabulary on page 683. Then answer these questions.

1. Write a sentence to define *Heimlich maneuver*.

Reviewing the Facts

2. List. List some actions that may cause a person to choke.
3. Describe. Describe the action you would take if you were choking and by yourself.
4. Identify. Identify the hazard in hitting a choking victim on the back while the person is standing or sitting erect.
5. Recall. When is bleeding life threatening?
6. Explain. What should you do after you control bleeding?

Writing Critically

7. Expository. What would you do if a student in the school cafeteria began to choke?
8. Expository. As you're walking home you come across a child who has fallen from a bike. A puddle of blood is beginning to form under the child's arm. What will you do?

Go Online

For more vocabulary practice, play the eFlashcards game at **glencoe.com**.

1. Answers will vary.

2. Eating too quickly, taking large bites, talking, laughing, or breathing hard while eating.

3. Use the back of a chair or edge of a table to push against, and perform the Heimlich maneuver.

4. The food particle caught in the throat may lodge deeper in the air passage.

5. Bleeding can be life threatening when arteries or veins have been severed in an injury.

6. After the bleeding is controlled, prompt treatment of the wound is necessary to prevent infection.

7. Answers will vary.

8. Answers will vary.

Other First-Aid Procedures

First-aid techniques are designed to help the person until EMS arrives. Other emergencies that a rescuer may encounter are burns, normalizing temperature, and dealing with poisonings.

Treating Wounds

MAIN IDEA ▶ **Minor wounds can be treated at home. Major wounds require medical care.**

Treat minor wounds to prevent infection. Major wounds require professional care. Protect yourself from contact with the victim's blood and other body fluids.

Wounds are of four types: scrapes, tears, cuts, and punctures. Each can be mild or serious. Wash mild wounds with soap and water, and keep them clean. If a wound is deeper than the outer layers of the skin, it is serious and requires an evaluation by a health care professional after the first-aid treatments are provided. Medical treatment is a must for any wound that has spurted blood, even if first aid has controlled it. Medical treatment is also necessary for any wound that may have involved muscles, tendons, ligaments, or nerves, bite wounds (animal or human), any heavily contaminated wounds, or any wound that contains soil or object fragments. Objects sticking into the flesh should be left in place when possible until medical help can be obtained.

When providing first aid to bleeding victims, keep your own safety in mind. Serious diseases can be transmitted through contact with an infected person's body fluids—blood, vomit, feces, or urine.

Vocabulary

- hypothermia
- frostbite
- hyperthermia
- fracture
- splint
- herbs
- folk medicine

■ **Figure 25.13** *Treating major wounds requires professional care. What should you keep in mind when treating a victim who is bleeding?*

Caption Answer: Your own safety. Serious diseases can be transmitted by body fluids.

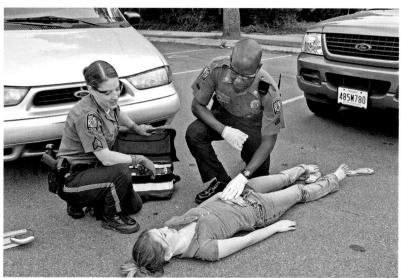

Figure 25.14 **Standard Treatments for Burns**

To treat first-degree burns

- Dip the burned part in cool water, or apply gauze soaked in cool water.
- If exposure to anything unclean is likely, layer dry gauze over the wet gauze to create a barrier to bacteria.
- Never apply grease of any kind to any burn.

To treat second-degree burns

- Treat as described above for first-degree burns, and seek medical treatment. Do not break blisters, remove tissue, or use antiseptic spray, cream, or any other product.
- Elevate burned part.

To treat third-degree burns

- Elevate the burned part, especially the limbs.
- Cover the burn with many layers of dry, sterile gauze.
- Do not apply water unless the area is still burning.
- An ice pack wrapped in a dry towel may be applied on top of the gauze for pain relief.
- Treat for shock, and arrange transportation to an emergency medical facility.
- Do not attempt to remove clothing or debris from the burn.

Burns

MAIN IDEA ▶ All burns require first aid.

Burns are classified by the depth of tissue injury. Proper help for a burn victim depends on whether the burn is of the first, second, or third degree. First-degree burns injure the top layers of skin and appear as redness, with mild swelling and pain. A light sunburn and a mild scald are examples.

Second-degree burns involve deeper tissue damage. They appear red or mottled, develop blisters, swell considerably, and are wet at the surface. A deep sunburn, a flash burn from burning fluid, or a burn from contact with very hot liquid is likely to be a second-degree burn.

Third-degree burns involve deep tissue destruction and have a white or charred appearance. Sometimes third-degree burns will appear to be second degree at first. Flames, ignited clothing, prolonged contact with hot fluids or objects, or electricity can all cause third-degree burns. **Figure 25.14** shows the standard treatments for first-, second-, and third-degree burns.

Class Discussion
Discuss: As a class, discuss precautions that can be taken around the home to prevent burns from happening to family members. Students may relate any specific incidents that occurred to them or their family members.

One key thing to remember about burns is that the skin regulates the body's temperature. When skin is burned, the body can lose heat and grow very cold, very fast. That's why covering a burn victim can be important—but don't cover a person whose clothing is still smoldering. Let the surface reach a neutral temperature, then cover.

Another key: burns on the face may mean that the airway is burned. Look for singed facial hair (eyebrows, mustache). A facial burn may lead to swelling and a blocked airway. Monitor breathing closely in a person who is burned. Never put water on a burn that is caused by a dry powder. Just brush the powder off. A powder may react with water and burn the victim further.

APPLYING Health Skills

Self Management

➤ Objectives

- Explain how to assess whether cuts and burns require professional treatment.
- Identify the correct first-aid procedures for treating minor cuts and burns.

Double Trouble

Twins Megan and Michael had to prepare their own dinner last night because both of their parents were working late. The twins decided to make spaghetti and a salad. While Megan was slicing tomatoes for the salad, she accidentally cut her finger. The cut oozed blood for a few minutes and then stopped bleeding. While watching his sister treat her wound, Michael added the spaghetti to a pot of boiling water without paying attention to what he was doing. He accidentally stuck his finger in the water, burning it. The finger was red and painful for a few hours, but it didn't develop blisters.

Megan and Michael took a first-aid class last year, so they knew what to do when they were injured. They were able to assess their injuries and decide that they did not require professional care. They also knew the correct first-aid procedures for treating the injuries. When you are injured, do you know what to do?

➤ Identify the Problem

1. What injuries did Megan and Michael receive?

➤ Form an Action Plan

2. Why did the twins decide that their injuries did not require professional care?

3. What is the correct first-aid procedure for an injury like Megan's?

4. What is the correct first-aid procedure for an injury like Michael's?

➤ What Did You Learn?

5. Based on this activity, what do you think you should do first when you are injured?

Temperature Extremes

MAIN IDEA ▷ Hypothermia, frostbite, and hyperthermia pose severe health risks if not properly treated.

For the body tissues to function normally, they must be kept at normal temperature—close to 98.6 degrees Fahrenheit. A person whose internal body parts lose heat is at serious risk and needs help fast. Similarly, internal body parts must not be overheated. This, too, poses a serious threat. While hypothermia and hyperthermia can threaten life when allowed to advance unchecked, some simple first-aid measures can, when administered quickly, be life saving. In cases of temperature extremes, call the emergency services immediately. Then proceed as described here.

Hypothermia

Hypothermia, *a condition of too little body heat with abnormally low internal body temperature*, develops when the body loses heat to the environment faster than it can generate heat. Exposure to low temperatures, high winds, and high humidity makes anyone likely to develop hypothermia.

A person with hypothermia may have stiff muscles, with some shivering or trembling; dizziness; weakness; cold skin; problems with coordination; and slowed breathing and heart rate. As hypothermia progresses, the person may become confused and drowsy, may lose muscle coordination, and may stop shivering.

If you suspect hypothermia, call 911 immediately. While waiting for help, move the person to a warm place, taking care to prevent injury. Do not handle the person roughly. Do not attempt to rewarm the person with hot baths, electric blankets, or hot-water bottles. However, do offer warm food or drink to victims who are conscious. If the person is unconscious, don't force fluids or food. Do not raise the feet or legs, for the blood there is cooler than in other parts of the body and can further chill the body's core. Do wrap the person in available covering such as blankets, towels, pillows, scarves, or newspapers.

Frostbite

Another risk of exposure to cold is **frostbite**, *the formation of ice crystals in body parts exposed to temperatures below freezing*. A child busily making a snowman or a teen skiing down a powdered slope may not be aware of frostbite's dangers as they set in. However, the later effects of frostbite—painful injury to the fingers, toes, ears, cheeks, or nose, and possible loss of function—are severe. Some frostbite injuries are so severe as to require surgical removal of the injured part.

Comprehension Check
Comprehend: Ask students to list the symptoms associated with hypothermia and how these symptoms should be treated. Students should be able to explain why hot baths, electric blankets, or hot water bottles should not be used if hypothermia is suspected.

■ **Figure 25.16** *Hypothermia can sneak up on those too busy to notice. What are symptoms of hypothermia?*

Caption Answer: Stiff muscles, shivering or trembling, dizziness, weakness, cold skin, slowed breathing and heart rate.

Frostbite's symptoms include color changes in the skin, usually to white, gray, or blue. The part may feel numb, so the person may have no warning that injury is setting in. Pain can be severe, however, when warmth restores feeling to the previously numb parts.

To prevent this unnecessary destruction of tissue, always handle frostbitten parts gently. Do not rub the affected body part. Remove wet or tight clothing. Cover the affected parts with dry, sterile dressing. Don't pack the area in snow or cold water. The affected tissues need to be gently warmed, so that the ice crystals will slowly melt.

Transport the victim to a hospital. If that is impossible, treat the frostbite as best you can. Move the victim in from the cold. Soak the injured part in comfortably warm (100 degrees Fahrenheit), not hot, water. (If the water is too hot, or if the body part thaws and refreezes, it will die.) Loosely bandage the part by wrapping it lightly with gauze, and seek medical help.

Hyperthermia

Hyperthermia, *a condition of too much body heat with abnormally high internal body temperature*, is likely whenever people are exposed to high temperatures with high humidity. Athletes and exercisers aren't the only ones prone to hyperthermia. Babies, elderly adults, those taking certain medications, and the overweight are especially likely to tolerate heat poorly. **Figure 25.17** describes the symptoms of the two dangerous stages of hyperthermia—heat exhaustion and heat stroke.

Class Discussion

Analyze: Compare and contrast hyperthermia and hypothermia, and their treatments.

Figure 25.17　Symptoms of Hyperthermia

	Hyperthermia (Heat Exhaustion)	Severe Hyperthermia (Heat Stroke)
Skin	Cool, moist, pale or red	Dry, hot, red
Sweating	Heavy sweating	No sweating
Body temperature	Normal or below normal	Very high, possibly to 106 degrees Fahrenheit
Pulse	Faster than normal	Fast and weak
Breathing	Possible deep breathing	Fast, shallow breathing
Other	Dizziness and weakness, headache, nausea	Mental confusion, loss of consciousness, brain damage, death

An overheated person who receives no help may sicken as the body tries to defend itself against the high temperature. In the early stages, the body struggles to cool itself through heavy sweating. Should exposure to the hot conditions continue, though, the body may sweat so much that it begins to run out of fluid with which to make more sweat. As the body loses fluid, it stops sweating, and thereby loses its only defense against overheating further. Then, like an overheating car radiator, the body temperature climbs to the point of damaging all systems, especially the brain.

To prevent damage or death from heat injuries, first call 911 for emergency help. Then cool the person's body by fanning. Apply cold, wet wraps such as wet towels or clothing. Offer the conscious victim a half a cup of plain cool water to drink every 15 minutes or so. Between drinks, lay the person down and treat for shock.

Poisonings, Bites, and Stings

MAIN IDEA ▶ Poisonings and snakebites, and severe allergic reactions demand immediate medical attention.

Any adverse effect on the body from a chemical substance is considered poisoning, from an overdose of drugs to the inhalation of fumes from household products. Poisonings pose difficult problems for those administering first aid, because they vary in symptoms and treatments according to the substance involved. Poisons can enter the body by being eaten or drunk, breathed in, absorbed through the skin, or injected.

Class Discussion

Discuss: Choose a student to read aloud the symptoms of heat exhaustion and another to read aloud the symptoms of heat stroke. Once the symptoms have been read, discuss the differences between the conditions and the treatments for both.

What to Do for Poisonings

The most common household poisonings involve overdoses of aspirin or other over-the-counter pain relievers, eaten by children or taken by mistake by adults. A person who has eaten poison may display any of the symptoms shown in **Figure 25.18** on page 693. In such a case, give nothing by mouth. Quickly call the emergency services. Then call the poison control center. Describe the poisoning.

If the poison involved is an illegal drug, do not try to protect the victim by concealing information. Legal penalties are small when compared with loss of life. Don't hesitate—call. If possible, read aloud over the phone, from the poison container, the information on its label. Follow the instructions given by the poison control experts.

If a poison has been taken by injection, the person may need breathing assistance. It may also be necessary to treat for shock.

Bites and Stings

Bites and stings present a special case of poisoning. Insect bites and stings are especially common. These can be extremely threatening to those who are allergic to them.

The primary threat from most insect bites and stings is allergic reaction to the venom, poison from a living creature, such as a snake or scorpion, which can set in within seconds of the sting. Call 911 immediately if the person has a red, flushed, or swelling face or trouble breathing.

For ordinary stings in nonallergic people, quickly remove any remaining stinger by scraping it out. The longer the stinger remains in the skin, the more venom enters the flesh, so work quickly. Most stinging insects leave no stinger.

Few people are bitten by snakes in the United States each year, and only a handful of those suffer lasting effects or are killed by such bites. Most people receive help promptly. Most snakebites need no first-aid treatment. However, the victim should be kept calm and still, and receive medical help within 30 minutes, just to be sure. Never cut or suck on a snakebite. Never use a snakebite kit that requires cutting into the flesh to treat a bite. Use a kit that applies suction only.

Broken Bones

MAIN IDEA ▶ If you suspect that a bone may be broken, get medical help immediately.

A person with a **fracture**, *a break in a bone*, needs medical treatment. A break in a bone that does not penetrate the skin is called a "closed" break. Open breaks, where the bone end has punctured the skin, may bleed. In the case of an open break, control the bleeding. Remember to use rubber gloves or materials to protect your hands from the blood.

Health Skills

Splinting a Broken Bone

When a bone is broken:

1. Treat the limb in the position in which you found it—don't move it.

2. Place a stick, board, or a splint against the limb. Support an arm from below, a leg from the side.

3. If possible, place the splint so that it holds the joints still, too, both above and below the break.

4. Tie the splint snugly to the limb in several places, leaving the broken area untied. Don't tie it too tightly. A tight splint may cut off circulation.

5. Elevate the part, if possible.

6. Cover exposed bone with moist, sterile dressing.

Neither you nor the injured person may be able to tell whether an injury is a broken bone, a sprain, or a strain. If you suspect a fracture, tie a **splint**—*a stick or board used to support a broken bone to keep its separated parts from moving until it can be set*—to the injured part while waiting for emergency help. The Health Skills sidebar, "Splinting a Broken Bone," on page 692 tells how to do this. Also, if any part of the bone is exposed to the air, keep it moist. Don't try to put it back in place. Just cover it with moist, sterile, or clean dressing.

Splinting techniques vary with injury location, and a first-aid course teaches many splinting techniques. No matter the location, though, the main task remains to keep the injured bone still to prevent further damage.

Figure 25.18

Symptoms of Poisoning

- Burns or injury to tongue or lip area (if the poison was taken by mouth)
- Difficulty breathing
- Pain in the chest or abdomen; diarrhea, nausea, vomiting
- Sweating
- Seizures or loss of consciousness

Worksheets: A reproducible quiz for Section 4 is provided in the Teacher Classroom Resources.

SECTION 4 Review

Reviewing the Vocabulary
Review the vocabulary on page 686. Then answer these questions.

1. If a person has too little body heat, it is called _____.

2. A _____ is a stick or board used to support a broken bone to keep its separated parts from moving until it can be set.

3. A break in a bone is called a _____.

Reviewing the Facts

4. Recall. When is medical treatment necessary for wounds?

5. Describe. Describe characteristics of a third-degree burn.

6. Name. What are the symptoms of frostbite?

7. Explain. How can poisons enter the body?

Writing Critically

8. Descriptive. Look at **Figure 25.14** on page 687. Describe the differences in treatments for the different degrees of burns. Why is it important to know the treatments? What could happen to a person who is treated incorrectly?

G Online

For more information on health careers, visit Career Corner at **glencoe.com**.

1. Hypothermia
2. Splint
3. Fracture
4. If a wound is deeper than the outer layers of the skin
5. Third-degree burns involve deep tissue destruction and have a white or charred appearance.
6. Color changes in the skin, usually to white, gray, or blue; numbness
7. Poisons can enter the body by being eaten, drunk, breathed in, absorbed through the skin, or injected.
8. Answers will vary.

Herbs and Folk Remedies

 Understand and Apply Read the conversation below, and then complete the writing exercise that follows.

Today, many herbs—nonwoody plants or plant parts valued for their flavor, aroma, or medicinal qualities—and other "remedies" are available to consumers. People may wonder if "folk medicine," the use of herbs and other natural substances in the treatment of disease, might offer safer or more "natural" remedies for curing human ills than drugs made in the chemist's laboratory. Even if some do work, the products may not be safe. For this reason, it is necessary to take precautions.

Q: All those warnings make me afraid to try folk medicines. Why do people bother with them?

A: Some people want to return to the olden days. Other people grew up in families that used herbs as medicines and feel comfortable in using them. Still others claim to believe that herbs are safer than refined drugs because they're "natural."

Q: Aren't natural things safe?

A: The word natural does not mean harmless. The natural herbs hemlock and belladonna are two infamous and deadly poisons. The herb sassafras contains a cancer-causing chemical. The herb ma huang contains a stimulant drug, ephedrine, associated with several deaths in the United States. Other herbs, such as witch hazel, are harmless but also useless.

Q: How does ginseng rate as a medicine?

A: The herb ginseng is a plant containing chemicals that have drug effects. In a scientific study, ginseng worked against inflammation (the swelling, heat, and redness of injuries) more effectively than the medical drug hydrocortisone. Ginseng has a wake-up effect like that of caffeine too.

Even if ginseng itself is useful in some cases, the products called ginseng available for sale are rarely effective. Unfortunately, ginseng products vary so widely in contents that it is difficult to determine their effects. Also, real ginseng may cause negative side effects. Insomnia, nervousness, confusion, high blood pressure, and depression make up a condition called ginseng abuse syndrome, a group of symptoms associated with the overuse of ginseng. Ginseng makes a poor drug, because its negative effects occur at about the same dose levels as its drug effects.

Q: Do any herbs work that aren't too dangerous to try?

A: You know of one already—caffeine. Three others are aloe, a tropical plant with widely claimed, but mostly unproved, medical value; chamomile, a plant with flowers that may provide some limited medical value in soothing intestinal and stomach discomforts; and Echinacea, an herb popular for its assumed "anti-infectious" properties and as an all-purpose remedy, especially for colds and allergy. People have used aloe plants for thousands of years to treat burns and skin injuries. For minor kitchen burns and cuts, pluck a leaf and apply the gel from the plant. It relieves pain, and some scientists think it makes minor wounds heal faster. On the other hand, aloe may delay or complicate the healing of severely damaged skin.

Chamomile contains a drug that relieves digestive and menstrual cramping. Whether tea brewed from chamomile flowers has these effects is unknown. This is because the drug doesn't dissolve in water, and only a little of it ends up in a cup of tea. Perhaps the effects of drinking the tea may build up over time.

After thousands of years' use, reports of negative side effects from chamomile tea are almost unknown, except for one: the flowers can cause allergy in people who are sensitive to pollen. If you have hay fever, stay away from chamomile and other herbs as well.

The herb echinacea has been widely sold as a treatment for colds, flu, and related infections. Studies on echinacea did find an effect on the immune system. However, echinacea was of no benefit for those with infections. Because echinacea can affect the immune system, people with immune disorders should not use it. Because it is an herb, it can cause allergic reactions in some people.

Q: What about other folk remedies?

A: One folk remedy worth mentioning is the hormone melatonin, which is a hormone of a gland of the brain, believed to help regulate the body's daily rhythms. It is marketed as a way to reduce jet lag, the ill feelings that follow adjustment to different time zones. Also, some people who have trouble sleeping say it helps them get to sleep.

A kitchen product, meat tenderizer (the kind without seasoning), contains papain, a chemical that breaks down proteins. The stinging venoms of bees and jellyfish are made of protein. Some people find that meat tenderizer kills the pain and reduces the swelling of these stings. To treat a sting, remove the stinger, if any, and apply ice.

Then spread a paste of tenderizer to destroy the painful protein in the venom. Applying vinegar may work too.

Other accurate remedies include these:
- A gargle of warm saltwater can soothe a sore throat and may kill more germs than commercial mouthwashes can.
- A mixture of lemon and honey can soothe a sore throat and may quiet a minor cough.

While these treatments are safe to try, here are some warnings about herbal medicines:
- People can make mistakes in using herbs and mixing different herbs together.
- Different people react differently to the drugs in herbs, just as they do to other drugs. Children and people with certain medical conditions are most sensitive and should not be given any folk medicines.
- Products may claim to promote health, but few do in truth.
- Harmful side effects are common.

 Writing Write a paragraph describing reasons why people should use caution when using herbs or other remedies.

Reviewing Vocabulary

Use the vocabulary terms listed below to complete the following statements.

shock

Heimlich maneuver (abdominal thrust maneuver)

first aid

CPR (cardiopulmonary resuscitation)

hyperthermia

1. Medical help given immediately in an emergency, before the victim is transported to a hospital or treatment center, is called _____.

2. _____ is a technique of maintaining blood and oxygen flow through the body of a person whose heart and breathing have stopped.

3. A technique of dislodging a particle that is blocking a person's airway is called _____.

4. _____ is a condition of too much body heat with abnormally high internal body temperature.

5. A failure or disruption of the blood circulation, a life-threatening reaction to accidents and injuries is called a _____.

Recalling Key Facts and Ideas

Section 1

6. **Name.** What are the two most important self-protective items to keep in a first-aid kit?

7. **Identify.** What are common hazards present when you survey an accident scene?

8. **Recall.** How do you decide who needs treatment first when there are several victims?

9. **Describe.** Describe how you should check a victim's airway.

10. **Explain.** What happens to the blood and other vital organs of a person who goes into shock?

11. **Analyze.** When you do a secondary survey of a victim, what are you looking for?

Section 2

12. **Recall.** How long does it take for a person to die when oxygen is cut off?

13. **Name.** What is one problem that occurs when an untrained person attempts CPR?

Section 3

14. **Explain.** Explain the universal distress signal for choking.

15. **Recall.** If a person is choking but can make a sound, what should a rescuer do?

16. **Recall.** If a person is choking but cannot make a sound, what should a rescuer do?

17. **Explain.** Why shouldn't a tourniquet be used to control bleeding?

Section 4

18. **Recall.** How are burns classified?

19. **Describe.** Describe what a second-degree burn looks like.

20. **Analyze.** What should you be concerned about when a person has a facial burn?

---

1. First Aid 2. Cardiopulmonary resuscitation (CPR) 3. Heimlich Maneuver (abdominal thrust maneuver) 4. Hyperthermia 5. Shock 6. Disposable rubber gloves, antiseptic hand cleaners 7. Fire, fumes, fast traffic, live electrical wires, fast-moving water 8. The person who needs help the most 9. Look, listen, and feel for breathing. 10. Blood flow to the brain may diminish causing loss of consciousness. 11. Bumps, bruises, blood, odd formations or positions of body parts 12. Within five minutes after breathing stops 13. It can be fatal to perform CPR if the heart is already beating. 14. Holding the hands to the throat

21. **Identify.** What temperature should the body be for tissues to function normally?

22. **List.** What are symptoms of hypothermia?

23. **Describe.** What is the treatment for hypothermia?

24. **Explain.** What shouldn't you do when treating for frostbite?

25. **Name.** What is the most common cause of poisoning?

Writing Critically

26. **Personal.** After taking the Life Choice Inventory, how do you feel about your results? What can and will you do to improve your score? If you are already in the excellent range, what will you do to stay in the excellent range?

Activities

27. Make posters on the basics of first aid. Put them up around your school.

28. Make a pamphlet that explains different types of wounds, burns, and broken bones. Explain the first-aid procedures necessary for treating these problems.

29. Interview your principal and see how prepared the school is in case of an emergency. How many teachers are certified in first aid? How many are certified in CPR? Write a report on your findings.

30. Contact the local office of the Red Cross or American Heart Association. Ask for information about CPR and first-aid classes.

    Share the information you gather with the rest of your class.

Making Decisions About Health

31. Imagine you are babysitting and one of the children feels very sick. You feel her forehead and she is burning up. The other two children are fine. What would you do in this situation? How will you take care of the sick child and keep the other two children supervised?

32. You are backpacking on your family vacation, and your mother has slipped off the trail and stumbled down a large embankment. When you go to help her, all her vital signs are good. You think she may be going into shock, though. What action will you take? Why will you take such action?

Go Online

For fitness and health tips, visit the Fitness Zone at **glencoe.com**.

Fact or Fiction?

Answers

1. False. The helper needs to apply training gained through a class in first aid from a qualified instructor.
2. False. Move the victim only if the scene presents immediate danger.
3. False. Shock is a dangerous condition, and first-aid treatment is recommended.

 Writing Paragraphs will vary.

15. Victim should bend over and cough before a rescuer intervenes. **16.** Shout for help, perform the Heimlich maneuver **17.** A tourniquet almost always kills the limb to which it is applied. **18.** By the depth of the tissue damage **19.** Red, develops blisters, swells, and is wet **20.** Airway may be burned. **21.** 98.6 degrees Fahrenheit **22.** Stiff muscles, shivering, dizziness **23.** Move victim to warm place, offer warm food or drink if person is conscious. **24.** Rub the infected area. **25.** Overdoses of aspirin or over-the-counter pain relievers **26–32.** Answers will vary.

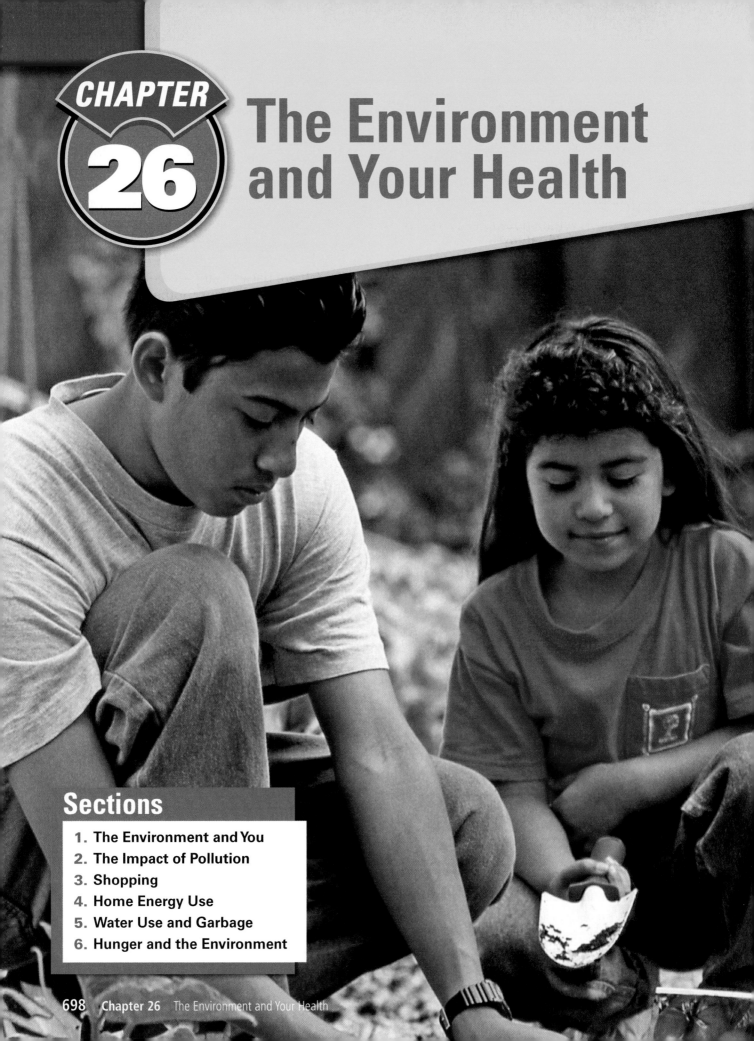

CHAPTER 26

The Environment and Your Health

Sections

1. The Environment and You
2. The Impact of Pollution
3. Shopping
4. Home Energy Use
5. Water Use and Garbage
6. Hunger and the Environment

Ideally, wherever you live, the air is clean, the water is pure, the food is nourishing, and abundant space is open for play. It is true that we can still be healthy without all of these factors. However, a clean environment and plenty of open spaces do provide us with the opportunity to breath clean air, maintain a clean water supply, grow healthy foods, and play in the open.

Many of the things that we enjoy, however, make our environment unhealthy. Automobiles pollute the air. Water may be dirtied by manufacturing processes, and food may be sprayed with pesticides and other chemicals. Finally, open spaces may not be abundant in some areas, such as large cities. These factors affect the health of the earth, which in turn, may affect our health.

Although we may not all be affected by pollution, we all share responsibility in keeping our world healthy. To maintain our own health, we must maintain the health of the world.

Fact or Fiction?

What Do You Think?
Is each statement true or false? If you think it's false, explain what's true.

1. Small groups of people can change the world.
2. The average electric range is one of the most energy-guzzling home appliances.
3. If U.S. consumers used less energy, this would help solve the world's hunger problem.

 Writing Write a paragraph to explain why you think it is important to protect the environment. How does the environment affect your health?

(Answers on page 727)

Visit **glencoe.com** and complete the Life Choice Inventory for Chapter 26.

The Environment and You

We and our environment are really part of a single system. Our **environment** is *everything "outside" the living organism—air, water, soil, other organisms, and forms of radiation.* The environment supplies the materials our bodies are made of and what they need to survive. It also provides forms of energy (especially light and heat energy) that make our lives possible.

Vocabulary

environment

Class Activity
Recall: Have students brainstorm ways the environment can affect our health. Use their responses to introduce topics that will be covered in this chapter.

Caption Answer: Air pollution can cause severe breathing problems. Contaminated water is unsafe to use, and can make people sick, or even die.

■ **Figure 26.1** *Some pollution is visible. However, even air and water that appear clean often contain invisible pollutants. How can polluted air and water affect your health?*

The Impact of the Environment

MAIN IDEA ▷ Human behaviors affect the world's air, water, and living things. In turn, the air, water, and all life on Earth affect human health.

Just as your environment affects you each day, you also affect the environment. Each day of your life, you breathe air, eat food, and leave your wastes. Everything you do impacts the environment.

Many of your activities involve choices. Each day you choose what you eat, how you dispose of your waste, and so forth. To make your choices consciously, you can learn which ones leave the earth better or worse off. It is in your interest to learn this, partly because of the environment's impact on you.

You make choices every day that impact your environment. For example:

- If the air is clean, your lungs can be healthy. If the air is polluted, you may suffer chronic lung diseases.

- If the water is pure, you can drink it without fear. If the water is polluted, it can bring with it all manner of harmful substances, including many that cause cancer.

- If the soil is free of poisons, it will grow food that will sustain you. If it is contaminated, the food may be unwholesome. Some contaminated soil cannot even support plant life, or any kind of living things.

Vast changes are taking place in your environment today. Once your eyes are open, you will see them all around you. When you have become conscious of how your own choices affect the environment, you will also see the effects of the choices of others—and not only the choices of individuals but also those of groups, including industry, agriculture, and government.

You have the right to a healthy environment—the right to clean air, pure water, and safe food. Together with your neighbors, you can demand that other people respect that right. As large as the world's environmental problems may be, they are all caused by people's choices.

Worksheets: A reproducible quiz for Section 1 is provided in the Teacher Classroom Resources.

SECTION 1 Review

Reviewing the Vocabulary
Review the vocabulary on page 700. Then answer these questions.
1. Write a sentence using the vocabulary word *environment*.

Reviewing the Facts
2. Explain. What does your environment do to support your personal health?
3. Analyze. What is the cause of the world's environmental problems and what can solve them?

Writing Critically
4. Personal. Take the Life Choice Inventory that accompanies this chapter at **glencoe.com**. Which environmentally aware choices do you make each day? Which habits do you need to change? Explain your answers.

Go Online

For more vocabulary practice, play the Concentration game at **glencoe.com**.

1. Answers will vary.

2. The environment supplies the materials our bodies are made of and what they need to survive. It also provides forms of energy (especially light and heat energy) that make our lives possible.

3. They are all caused by people's choices. They can also be solved by people's choices.

4. Answers will vary.

The Impact of Pollution

Sometimes people buy and use goods and services without thinking about the effects these products have on our environment. Seldom do we ask ourselves, "What is the cost of this product or service in electricity, gasoline, water, and **pollution**, *contamination of the environment with anything that impairs its ability to support life*?" or "How does my choice of this product or service affect the global environment?" However, the ways our clothes, foods, and toys are produced do affect the global environment. They are even linked to poverty, hunger, and disease of populations on the other side of the world. If we realized the impact of our choices, we might choose differently—yet still enjoy our lives just as much as we do now.

U.S. Consumption

MAIN IDEA ▶ The impact of consumption greatly affects world resources.

The production of goods for U.S. consumers is one of the world's biggest businesses. It involves huge manufacturing efforts that use water and fuel; huge tracts of land to produce raw materials; huge amounts of packaging materials and fuel to make goods ready for market; a huge transportation network. In summary, producing the things you enjoy leads to an enormous consumption of resources and production of pollution.

Choices that are far less harmful to the environment are possible. For example, Floridians can eat carrots grown in Florida. In place of five or six diet sodas in aluminum cans, the consumer might pour soda from one large plastic bottle. Both cans and plastic bottles are recyclable, but producing and recycling the large bottles costs less environmentally.

Many other examples of the impact on the environment will be described in this chapter. The purpose is to make you aware of your choices. A choice one person makes—for example, choosing to eat locally grown vegetables—may appear small in the scheme of things. However, two important benefits come with such choices. First, one person's example, shared with others, is shared again, and so it multiplies. Second, an action taken one time is likely to happen a second and third time, so that a beneficial habit is formed.

Vocabulary

pollution
ozone
air pollution
acid rain
global warming
greenhouse effect
Kyoto Protocol

Class Activity

List: Have students name as many environmental problems as possible. They should name global problems, not just local ones. Discuss.

⁉ Did You Know?

Three rules of the environment:

1. Substances thrown away, flushed, drained, or even burned are still with us and find their way back into our soil, water, and air.

2. Everything we use or consume costs the environment something to produce or run.

3. All things are connected. People and the environment are part of one system.

APPLYING Health Skills

Communication Skills

➤ **Objectives**
- Use communication skills to share important information.
- Explain how to show respect for others when communicating.

Oil and Water Don't Mix

Jamal's health class recently spent a week learning about the effects of the environment on health. The class focused on learning about the health dangers of letting the air and water become polluted. The following Saturday, Jamal saw his neighbor, Mr. Williams, changing the oil in his car. After emptying the oil from his car, Mr. Williams walked to the street and poured the old oil down the sewer. Later that day it rained, and as Jamal learned in his health class, the rain washed the oil into a storm drain, and into the local lake.

Jamal learned in his health class that oil should be kept out of the water supply. He feels that it's important that everyone do their part to help keep the environment clean. He wants to talk to Mr. Williams about his concern. Jamal believes that if Mr. Williams knew about the dangers of disposing old oil by throwing it down a sewer, he would find a healthier way to get rid of the oil. However, Jamal doesn't want to sound disrespectful toward an adult. He's not sure what he should say or how he should say it.

➤ **Identify the Problem**
1. Why is Jamal upset?

➤ **Form an Action Plan**
2. What could Jamal say to Mr. Williams? Write a clear statement that uses "I" messages.
3. What reason should Jamal give for not throwing oil into the sewer?
4. What body language and tone of voice should Jamal use to show respect for Mr. Williams as well as concern for the environment?

➤ **What Did You Learn?**
5. Assume that an adult you know does something to endanger the environment. What would you say to the adult, and how would you say it?

Applying Health Skills:

1. Jamal wants to let his neighbor know that he should clean up oil spills, but he doesn't know what to say or how to say it to avoid sounding disrespectful.

2. Jamal could say, "I noticed that some oil from your car was washed into the storm drain. I recently learned that it's very important to clean up spilled oil."

3. Jamal should give the reason that oil spills can pollute the water supply and cause cancer and other health problems.

4. Jamal should use a polite but serious tone of voice. He should stand straight to show that he means what he says, but he should avoid pointing his finger or using other body language that might seem disrespectful.

5. Answers will vary.

■ **Figure 26.2** *Protecting the environment is another way of protecting your health. What are some ways you can take care of your environment at home?*

Caption Answer: I can recycle plastic and aluminum cans, and store foods in reusable containers.

World Environmental Problems

MAIN IDEA ▶ Damage to land, air, and water can endanger our health and well-being.

Today, we are much more aware of our impact on the earth. Information on the impact of damage to the environment has created an urgency to take steps to protect the planet. A sense of individual control is needed for people to take action.

Current Global Problems

At the present time, all of the following trends are taking place at once:

- Hunger, poverty, and population growth. Every 60 seconds, 106 people die in the world, but in that same 60 seconds, 253 are born to replace them. Most of the earth's new residents are born into poverty.

- Losses of land to produce food. Land to produce food is becoming more salty, eroding, and being paved over. Still, each year, the world's farmers must feed about 77 million more people than the year before.

- Accelerating fossil fuel use. Fossil fuel is coal, oil, and natural gas, which all come from the fossilized remains of plant life of earlier times. Fuel use is accelerating, along with pollution of air, soil, and water; global warming; and depletion of **ozone**, *a substance created when certain types of energy, such as the sun's ultraviolet rays, react with oxygen.*

- Increasing **air pollution**, *contamination of the air with gases or particles not normally found there.* Air quality is diminishing all over the globe. Acids in the air are causing **acid rain**, *rain that carries acid air pollutants.*

- Droughts, floods, and **global warming**, *warming of the planet, a trend that threatens life on Earth.* The **greenhouse effect**, *the heat-trapping effect of the glass in a greenhouse*, is taking place. Levels of heat-trapping carbon dioxide in the atmosphere are now much higher than 200 years ago, and they continue to climb. As a result, the earth is experiencing a massive warming trend. This is changing the climate, causing heat waves, droughts, fires, severe storms, and floods that destroy crops and force people from their homes. Warmer temperatures also bring greater numbers of infectious diseases, such as malaria.

- Ozone loss from the outer atmosphere. The ozone layer, a layer of ozone in the earth's atmosphere that protects living things on Earth from harmful ultraviolet radiation from the sun, is growing thinner. This is permitting harmful radiation from the sun to warm the earth, which melts polar ice caps and threatens the world's coastlines. It also increases skin cancers in people.

- Water shortages. The world's supplies of freshwater are dwindling and becoming polluted.

- Forests and deserts. Forests are shrinking. Deserts worldwide are increasing in size, and new ones are forming.

- Ocean and lake pollution/overfishing. Ocean and lake pollution is killing fish. Overfishing is rapidly depleting those that remain. Polluting chemicals in the water, such as the metal mercury, are making many species unsafe to eat.

- Extinctions of species. Vast extinctions of animals and plants are taking place—some 140 species each day—50,000 each year. Many kinds of whales, birds, giant mammals, colorful butterflies, and thousands of others will never again be seen.

The global problems that need to be solved are all related. Their causes overlap, and so do their solutions. That means that any action a person takes to help solve one problem will help solve many others.

Did You Know?

The average molecule of food eaten in this country travels 1,300 miles before the consumer swallows it.

- To drive a semitrailer 1,300 miles requires about 250 gallons of gas.

- 250 gallons of gas burned as fuel releases 2 ½ tons of carbon dioxide. Carbon dioxide accumulation in the atmosphere is warming up the globe.

- The consumer who drinks a typical can of diet soda obtains from it one calorie of food energy. To manufacture the can, however, costs 800 calories in fuel, pollutes the soil at the mining site with toxic materials, and uses more water than the soda that ends up in the can.

How Can We Fix These Problems?

Despite the magnitude of these disasters, there is much that people can do to help slow, stop, and even reverse these processes and restore a livable world. Each of us can choose what products to buy and what foods to eat. Groups of people can lobby legislators to write laws that protect the environment, demand that the laws be enforced, and insist that corporations and governments honor their principles.

Once aware of their impacts, if people choose to change their actions, two kinds of ripple effect, the effect seen when a pebble is thrown into a pond and waves radiate out from it, can follow. One is the ripple effect that takes place in each person's own mind, as one level of awareness leads to another. First, a person learns how to improve the immediate surroundings. Soon, however, the person learns how to reach much farther. The other kind of ripple effect is the effect on people who hear and see what the person is doing. A word of awareness dropped into another's ear may start a ripple there that grows into a wave. Students often start such waves as they learn of current events and start trying to change them.

Sustainable Choices

The task for consumers is to become aware of their impacts, and to find sustainable ways of doing things. Sustainable is a term used to describe the use of resources at such a rate that the earth can keep on replacing them. Sustainable choices often benefit the health of the human body while also benefiting the environment. Bicycling or walking instead of driving not only keeps the rider fit, but also reduces pollution. Eating a diet of mostly foods from plants benefits health too. People's health depends upon healthy surroundings, for the two are closely connected.

What Can Governments Do to Help?

Governments can change things too, and their degree of commitment to doing so matters greatly. Uniting the world's leaders has proved difficult, however. Many of the world's leaders signed the **Kyoto Protocol**, *an agreement signed by many of the world's leaders in 1997, that spells out the degree of reduction in carbon dioxide emission required of each nation by the year 2012.* However, U.S. leaders found the agreement faulty. Treaties of this kind aim to reduce pollution, particularly carbon dioxide gas, known to speed up global warming. By whatever means, it is now urgent that world governments come together to set more sustainable policies for human activities.

SECTION 2 Review

Reviewing the Vocabulary

Review the vocabulary on page 702. Then answer these questions.

1. _____ is the contamination of the air with gases or particles not normally found there.

2. The outer atmosphere that protects living things on Earth from harmful ultraviolet radiation from the sun is called the _____.

3. _____ is rain that carries acid air pollutants.

Reviewing the Facts

4. Recall. What is involved in the production of goods for U.S. consumers?

5. Name. Name some global trends that are taking place.

6. Describe. Describe how the ripple effect works.

Writing Critically

7. Descriptive. Choose one environmental problem, and describe how it contributes to others and how others contribute to it. Explain how, if you helped solve one problem, you would be helping solve all the others.

Go Online

For more vocabulary practice, play the eFlashcards game at **glencoe.com**.

Did You Know?

The U.S. rate of carbon dioxide release measures twice as high as the next highest releaser among the world's nations.

Group Activity

Create: Divide your class into groups of three or four students. Instruct each group to create a poster that promotes protecting the environment. Examples may include reasons to recycle paper, aluminum, plastic, and glass. After groups have completed their posters, have them displayed in various locations throughout the halls of the school.

Worksheets: A reproducible quiz for Section 2 is provided in the Teacher Classroom Resources.

1. Pollution

2. Ozone

3. Acid rain

4. It involves huge manufacturing efforts that use water and fuel, land to produce raw materials, huge amounts of packaging materials, and fuel to make goods ready for market.

5. Losses of land to produce food, increasing air pollution, water shortages, extinction of species.

6. A ripple effect occurs when one person chooses to change her actions, and another person sees or hears about the action and changes as well, and it continues to reach a greater number of people.

7. Answers will vary.

SECTION 3

Shopping

Shopping involves trips to stores, choices of goods once you are at the store, package choices, and choices of bags in which to carry things home. Let's consider the shopping trips first.

Shopping Trips

MAIN IDEA ▶ Automobiles are the world's single largest cause of air pollution.

In 2010, an estimated 1 *billion* cars are in use worldwide. Every year, tens of millions more are being added. Motor vehicles are the world's single largest source of air pollution. They harm children, the elderly, and people with lung problems; reduce crop yields; cause acid rain; damage forests; and produce major amounts of carbon dioxide which causes global-warming. Transporting oil to provide gasoline for cars is a major cause of oil spills that harm ocean life.

Fuels made from renewable resources, such as corn or sugarcane, help to solve some problems but may contribute to others. A switch to these renewable "biofuels" eliminates oil spills and certain pollutants, and reduces dependence on foreign oil supplies. However, growing enough corn, sugar cane, or other crops to make biofuel uses *non*renewable oil-based fertilizers and pesticides, competes with food crops for farmable land, and requires farm equipment that runs on oil-based diesel fuel. Biofuels also release carbon dioxide into the atmosphere.

Vocabulary

recyclable
biodegradable
dioxins
ecosystems

⁉️ Did You Know?

Brazil is a world leader in using renewable biofuels from crops to run vehicles.

■ **Figure 26.4** *Shopping without a car can be a pleasure. Besides helping the environment, how can walking benefit you?*

Caption Answer: Walking can increase your physical activity and help you stay fit.

Alternatives to the use of private cars includes carpools, mass transit, walking, bicycling, or other forms of transportation. Cities are also combining homes, workplaces, and retail stores in neighborhoods and providing sidewalks and bike paths.

We can all help protect the environment by limiting our shopping trips to once a week. When choosing a car, look for the most fuel-efficient model you can find.

On each trip take along your own shopping bags—either retail bags you received with other purchases or canvas or net bags you can reuse indefinitely. They save pollution in another way, as shown later.

Choose Green Products

MAIN IDEA ▶ To benefit the environment, buy only products that you need, that produce little pollution, and that are responsibly packaged.

From the point of view of the environment, the ideal product is a truly "green" product. A product is "green"—that is, most environmentally harmless—if it earns a "yes" answer to each of these questions:

1. Is it necessary, and not frivolous?
2. Is it durable and reusable? If not, then is it **recyclable**, *made of material that can be used over again*? Is it **biodegradable**, *able to decompose*? If it is disposable, that is, intended to be used once and then thrown away, avoid it.
3. Does it release only safe substances during production or does it release persistent toxins, the opposite of biodegradable—unable to decompose or to be converted by living organisms into harmless wastes? During use? When it is thrown away?
4. Does it consume minimal energy and resources during production, use, and disposal?
5. Is it made from recycled materials or renewable resources?
6. Is it minimally and responsibly packaged? (Does the packaging material meet the same criteria as the product?)

On Question 2, you may wonder why recyclable is second best. The reason is that only about half of recyclable material is saved during recycling. The other half becomes waste. If the material is recycled again, another half is lost, and so on.

Many Web sites discuss products that meet the green definition, but use caution for those selling only their own products. Many ordinary products, produced responsibly, qualify as green.

Did You Know?

In one year, a typical student who drives 10 miles to the store each day in a car getting 25 miles to the gallon:

- Uses about 146 gallons of gasoline.
- Releases about 2,774 pounds of carbon dioxide into the air (each gallon of gas releases 19 pounds of carbon dioxide).
- Spends over $584 on gasoline just for shopping (at $4.00 per gallon).

Another student who drives just 5 miles each day in a car getting 50 miles to the gallon, over one year.

- Uses about 37 gallons of gas.
- Releases about 700 pounds of carbon dioxide into the air.
- Spends only about $148 for gas to take the same number of shopping trips.

Figure 26.5

Products to Benefit the Earth

Each of the products recommended benefits the environment:

- Compact fluorescent lightbulbs.
- Cloth or net shopping bags.
- Cloth dishcloths, napkins, and towels.
- Dishes, cups, glasses, and tableware to replace the disposable versions.
- Flow-reducing showerheads and other water-conservation devices.
- Energy-efficient appliances.
- A good-quality bicycle
- Recycled paper products with a high post-consumer (paper used by a consumer and then recycled) waste content (rather than paper made from new trees).

■ **Figure 26.6** *Non-toxic cleaners are just as effective as those that harm the environment. What are dioxins?*

Caption Answer: Dioxins are deadly pollutants formed when chlorine bleach reacts with other compounds.

Unfortunately, many products are labeled "green" that really are not. Beware of misleading "green" labels on products. **Figure 26.5** lists products that truly benefit the earth.

Many of the products we use in our homes contain or release toxins. If used as directed, these products may not harm us. However, the processes used to manufacture them may pollute the environment. Furthermore, when we dispose of them or their containers, they may again cause harm.

A prime example is chlorine bleach. It works well as a disinfectant, because it kills living cells. That same quality, however, makes it deadly when it goes down the drain. Where strong chlorine concentrations run into waterways, they kill all life—from tiny creatures at the bottom of the **food chain**, *the sequence in which living things depend on other living things for food*, on up to fish and fish-eating birds. (**Figure 26.7** on page 711 shows the workings of a food chain.) Also, chlorine combines with naturally occurring ammonia to produce deadly **dioxins**, *deadly pollutants formed when chlorine bleach reacts with other compounds*. People using safer, non-chlorine products find that they work just as well.

Refillable spray bottles are economical and better for the planet than aerosol cans. Aerosol propellants destroy the ozone layer. Simple cleaning solutions like white vinegar can substitute for harsh products. If you need insecticide, research to find one that is less polluting. Informed customers can save money and also help the environment.

Also, when choosing new appliances, computers, and other electrical gadgets, first ask yourself whether the item is one you truly need. If so, then look for an Energy Star seal on the label before you buy. This U.S. government seal (shown in **Figure 26.8**) identifies products ranked highest for energy efficiency.

Figure 26.7   **How a Food Chain Works**

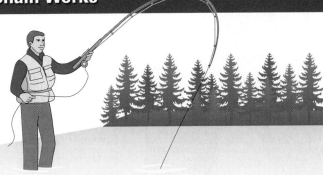

Level 4: A 150-pound person consumes 100 pounds of fish in a year.

Level 3: 100 pounds of fish consume a few tons of plant-eating fish during their lifetime.

Level 2: A few tons of plant-eating fish consume several tons of tiny organisms during their lifetime.

Level 1: Several tons of tiny organisms have become contaminated with toxic chemicals. These chemicals become more concentrated in the bodies of the fish that consume them. One person may ingest the same amount of the contaminant as was present in the organisms.

Foods

MAIN IDEA ▷ Eat more plant foods and buy locally grown foods when possible.

Nutritionists and environmentalists both urge people to eat less meat and more vegetable-based foods. The health benefits of a diet high in grains and vegetables, and low in meats and meat fats, are well known and were presented in Chapters 7 and 8 of this book.

The Impact of Meat

Eating less meat makes sense environmentally too. Growing meat animals by feeding them grain uses more land than does growing grain to feed directly to people. Meat animals also use more water; pollute waterways more; and in general, destroy more native vegetation and wildlife than most plants (there are significant exceptions, however). Furthermore, more fossil fuels are needed just to grow the feed for animals—to run tractors, harvest grain, and transport it. The growing of feed pollutes the environment with fertilizers and pesticides. Wastes from the animals themselves pollute it further.

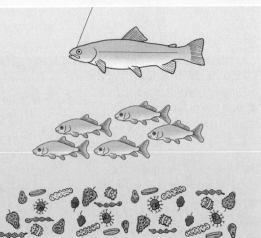

■ **Figure 26.8** *Money isn't all you're saving. What does the Energy Star logo mean?*

Caption Answer: It means the product ranks highest for energy efficiency.

> " *The twentieth century will be remembered chiefly, not as an age of political conflicts and technical inventions, but as an age in which human society dared to think of the health of the whole human race as a practical objective.* "
>
> —Arnold Toynbee
> (1889–1975)
> British historian

Meat and the Rain Forest

The rain forests are the earth's most threatened **ecosystems**, *systems of land, plants, and animals that have existed together for thousands or millions of years and that are interdependent.* They are home to many tribes of native people and many species of plants and animals that are in danger of being wiped out. Rain forests suffer enormous losses because people continue to convert them to beef ranches and other farms. This practice is unsustainable because rain forest soil is thin and wears out within only a few years when used this way. To keep growing beef, for example, ranchers must keep moving their cattle, clearing more rain forest as they go. However, the forest can't grow back on the ruined soil. Each pound of beef produced this way results in the loss of 200 square feet of rain forest—permanently.

Local Foods

In general, buy foods grown as close to home as possible. Locally grown foods may cost more, but they have traveled the shortest distance to the market, and so have required little fossil fuel for packaging, labeling, refrigeration, transportation, and marketing.

Packages and Shopping Bags

MAIN IDEA ▶ Reject unnecessary packaging, including paper and plastic bags.

The products we buy come in a multitude of packages. It costs energy and resources to make packages, and it may cost land or cause pollution to dispose of them too. In general, the packages that are best for the environment are no packages. Next best are minimal, reusable, or recyclable ones.

Carry everything home in a nonpolluting, nonwasteful way. This applies not only to food but also to clothing, books, household items, cosmetics, and everything else you shop for. Reject one-time-use paper or plastic bags that have to be thrown away.

Paper Bags

Paper is made from a renewable resource—trees. However, trees are being cut in this country faster than they are being grown. Environmentalists fear that the nation's forests are not being managed sustainably. Every 700 paper bags not used represent one 15- to 20-year-old tree that need not be cut down.

Furthermore, in the making of paper, pulp mills use chemicals that contaminate waterways with pollutants. Such pollution has been so large and so destructive that it has destroyed whole bays and fisheries.

Plastic Bags

Plastic bags, like most plastics, are a petroleum product. When thrown away, plastics last for years or decades. They create masses of refuse that clog landfills. Some plastics are labeled "degradable," but few really do degrade fully to pure, simple compounds that nature can recycle. Some plastics are recyclable. This makes them preferable to other plastics, but still not perfect, since recycling is only partially efficient.

Reusable Bags

The best choice is to carry reusable shopping bags to the store and refuse all others. Failing in this, ask for plastic bags if they are recyclable—and be sure to recycle them. The third choice is paper bags, and last is nonrecyclable plastic.

SECTION 3 Review

Reviewing the Vocabulary

Review the vocabulary on page 708. Then answer these questions.

1. _____ means able to decompose.
2. _____ means made of material that can be used over again.
3. Deadly pollutants formed when chlorine bleach reacts with other compounds are called _____.
4. _____ are systems of land, plants, and animals that have existed together for thousands or millions of years and that are interdependent.

Reviewing the Facts

5. Describe. How does automobile pollution harm people's health and their environment?
6. Identify. What are the effects of chlorine bleach on our environment?
7. Explain. How does eating less meat make sense environmentally?

Writing Critically

8. Expository. Review **Figure 26.6** on page 710. What can you do to replace products that you use at home with these products?

Go Online

For fitness and health tips, visit the Fitness Zone at glencoe.com.

1. Biodegradable
2. Recyclable
3. Dioxins
4. Ecosystems
5. They harm people with lung problems, children and the elderly, reduce crop yields, cause acid rain, damage forests, and produce major amounts of carbon dioxide.
6. Chlorine kills life at the bottom of the food chain, up to fish and fish-eating birds.
7. Meat animals use more water, pollute waterways, and destroy more vegetation and wildlife.
8. Answers will vary.

Home Energy Use

Home energy use has many environmental implications. A naive consumer might respond to such a statement by saying, "I don't use any fossil fuels in my home. My home is all electric." However, electricity is most often generated by burning fossil fuels—only at the power plant, rather than at the site of use. An all-electric home produces air pollutants and global-warming gases just as if the homeowner were burning fossil fuels at home.

Are Some Cooking Methods Better Than Others?

MAIN IDEA ▷ Cutting foods up, pressure cooking, and microwaving are energy-efficient ways to cook foods.

An example of an environmentally sound way to prepare foods is to cut foods into bite-sized pieces, and then stir-fry them fast in small amounts of oil. This uses little fuel, so it pollutes only a little.

Other ways to cook foods quickly are to use the pressure cooker or the microwave oven. The pressure cooker can tenderize pounds of meat in half the normal cooking time, or cook a potful of potatoes in five minutes. The microwave can cook small portions quickly or warm whole plates of leftovers (which saves using several burners on the stove and washing up the pots afterward).

Vocabulary

active solar

?? Did You Know?

About 10 percent of the nation's electricity is produced by power plants that capture the energy of flowing water—hydroelectric plants. A smaller percentage is generated by nuclear power plants or wind power.

■ **Figure 26.10** *Microwave cooking is quick, efficient, and saves energy. What other cooking methods are quick, efficient, and use less energy?*

Caption Answer: Stir-frying and using a pressure cooker are fast and energy efficient.

The conventional oven, in contrast, is a fuel waster, especially when the entire oven is heated just to bake a potato. Instead, when using the oven, cook many items on both racks, using all the heated space. Don't peek often. Each door opening drops the oven temperature by 25 to 50 degrees Fahrenheit.

Power Tools and Appliances

MAIN IDEA ▶ Use power tools and appliances efficiently, and replace them when possible with energy-efficient models.

A tour around the home reveals many appliances, large and small, that people use to cook, to clean, to heat and cool their homes, and to entertain themselves. All of these appliances run on energy from fossil fuels, with pollution and global warming as byproducts.

The fewer appliances you use and the shorter the times you use them, the better for the environment. Realizing this, many consumers today are returning to "old-fashioned" ways of doing things. They dry clothes on a clothesline in the sun; trim yard greenery with hand tools; and rake the refuse with rakes rather than using electric clothes dryers, weed whackers, hedge trimmers, and leaf blowers.

Solar Power

MAIN IDEA ▶ Solar energy saves resources and reduces electric bills.

People who use solar energy reduce their demand for energy from more polluting sources. Sunlight is free and does not pollute. The average U.S. home creates approximately 13,000 pounds of greenhouse gases from electricity use per year. More and more U.S. families are using solar energy to meet most of their homes' electricity needs. In an **active solar** home, which means *using photovoltaic panels to generate electricity from sunlight*, the sun's light strikes photovoltaic (PV) panels, panels that convert light into electricity, on the roof. These convert the light energy to electrical energy, which is stored in a battery. Having a battery permits the use of a DC (direct current) refrigerator, rather than an AC (alternating current) refrigerator. No fossil fuel is used to run a DC refrigerator operated this way.

When considering solar power, the high initial cost of PV panels, the battery, and the DC refrigerator prevents most people from using them. For those who do use solar power, it becomes possible to meet most of a home's electrical needs with solar energy, thus reducing utility bills to only a few dollars a month. The savings in utilities pay back the initial investment within about seven years. From that point on, energy is virtually free—compliments of the sun.

Did You Know?

The most energy-guzzling home appliances:
- Refrigerators (because they run all the time).
- Hot-water heaters (these run many hours per day).
- Heaters and air conditioners (these also run many hours per day).

Look for energy efficiency when choosing these appliances. You'll save money and reduce pollution too.

■ **Figure 26.11** *Photovoltaic panels capture the sun's energy and convert it into electrical power. Why is solar power a good energy alternative?*

Caption Answer: Solar power is free, reliable, and pollution free.

What Teens THINK

Should We Be Doing More to Protect Our Environment? If So, What Should We Be Doing?

Yes, I think that everyone should be doing more. I see many kids throw their lunch bags away on the lawns or parking lot, as if they don't care about anything or respect others. My grandfather always taught me to put garbage where it belongs, and to respect and enjoy nature by taking care of it. And I have seen the devastating effects of lack of care. Almost every time I go hiking into the mountains I come back with a garbage bag full of other people's junk. Why can't people think of the future and clean up after themselves? It only takes a little effort to make a big difference.

—Elichai F., 19,
Montana

I think I should be doing more for the environment. I already recycle newspaper through the local pickup, and put my note paper in the collection bins at school, but I don't go out of my way to recycle aluminum cans, which aren't picked up with the plastic and newspaper. After all, I have to live here for another 50-odd years; I want to have a good home planet for myself and my nieces and nephews.

—Katye B., 14,
North Carolina

I should probably be doing more to protect my environment because I am not very aware of the environment. I should be recycling more and doing more community service projects to reduce litter. I should help people be more aware also so they can protect the environment. I help a little bit by walking everywhere and hardly ever riding in the car. In some ways I am very conscious of what waste products I use. For example, I would never use styrofoam and I cut up all my plastic six-pack holders. Most of all I don't smoke.

—Hannah G., 15,
New Mexico

Lack of concern bothers me most. Unless other people start worrying about and trying to help our environment, the problems facing us will multiply. Too many people don't believe that one person can make a difference. Other people take the environment for granted. Mother Nature has a lot to take care of; it's time we learned to clean up the messes we have made.

Michelle P., 15,
Florida

Do Lightbulbs Matter?

MAIN IDEA ▶ Replace incandescent light-bulbs with compact fluorescent (CF) bulbs to save energy.

An ordinary 75-watt incandescent light-bulb burns for about 2,500 hours, gives off considerable heat, and demands fuel whose carbon dioxide output amounts to 200 pounds or so over the lifetime of the bulb. Energy- and pollution-conscious people are replacing these lightbulbs with 22-watt, high-efficiency compact fluorescent (CF) bulbs such as those shown in **Figure 26.12**. One CF bulb can match the light output of the incandescent bulb it replaces, but it uses one-fourth the energy to do so. The CF bulbs also last ten or more times as long. Each CF bulb used in place of a succession of "regular" lightbulbs keeps a ton of carbon dioxide out of the air.

■ **Figure 26.12** *Energy-efficient lightbulbs can replace incandescent bulbs. What are some benefits of using energy-efficient lightbulbs?*

Caption Answer: They use one-fourth the energy, last longer, and create less carbon dioxide.

SECTION 4 Review

Worksheets: A reproducible quiz for Section 4 is provided in the Teacher Classroom Resources.

Reviewing the Vocabulary
Review the vocabulary on page 714. Then answer these questions.
1. _____ means using photovoltaic panels to generate electricity from sunlight.

Reviewing the Facts
2. **List.** List three ways to save energy while cooking.
3. **Name.** Name three "old-fashioned" ways of doing things that are better for the environment.
4. **Identify.** What three household appliances use the most energy?

Writing Critically
5. **Persuasive.** This section deals with conserving energy at home. Do your parents follow these procedures? If not, how can you persuade your parents to conserve energy at home? What arguments can you make for energy conservation?

For more vocabulary practice, play the eFlashcards game at **glencoe.com**.

1. Active solar
2. Stir-frying, using a pressure cooker, and using a microwave.
3. Dry clothes on a clothesline, trim yard greenery with hand tools, use rakes for raking leaves.
4. Refrigerators, hot-water heaters, heaters and air conditioners
5. Answers will vary.

Water Use and Garbage

Where water is abundant and inexpensive, people use it freely. It is really not free, though. We all pay for water purification, monitoring, and cleanup through our taxes.

Vocabulary

compost

Water Conservation and Recycling Garbage

MAIN IDEA ▶ Use water-conserving habits and devices. Recycle trash and compost plant scraps.

Conscious of water's true worth, people become more inclined to conserve it. There are many ways to do so. A running faucet uses as much as 3 to 5 gallons of water a minute. Therefore, leaky faucets must be repaired immediately. Just at the bathroom sink, you can save many gallons by turning the faucet off while brushing your teeth. Install a water-saving washer on a faucet to deliver a stream of water with a reduced flow per minute. A dishwasher uses less water than does washing dishes by hand (just load it full, for maximum efficiency). Try reusing clean water. After boiling an egg, for example, let the water cool, and then use it to water the houseplants or in the outdoor garden if you have one.

How Can Trash Turn into Treasure?

As for trash, an average American household of four people produces about 100 pounds a week. Today, our nation is running out of landfill space in which to dispose of all this trash. In addition to the lack of landfill space, every item thrown away is a resource lost. An aluminum can could be used to make a new aluminum can. A plastic bottle could become part of a new carpet.

■ **Figure 26.13** *Compost is a natural, recycled fertilizer. Why are natural fertilizers preferable to synthetic fertilizers?*

Caption Answer: They recycle natural materials, they add nutrients to the soil, and they add texture to the soil.

In the United States, about 70 percent of all the metal mined is used only once and then discarded. The ideal community recycles everything—paper, cardboard, glass, cans, plastic—and permits no materials to be sold that cannot be recycled.

Compost

Other garbage—vegetable scraps, fruit peelings, leftover plant-based foods, leaves, and grass cuttings—are biodegradable. They will form **compost**, *rotted vegetable matter, used as fertilizer,* as it is in nature, to fertilize growing things. Natural fertilizers such as compost and manure are environmentally preferable to synthetic fertilizers. They require no mining; they recycle natural materials rather than wasting them; and they add needed texture, as well as nutrients, to the soil.

SECTION 5 Review

Reviewing the Vocabulary

Review the vocabulary on page 718. Then answer these questions.

1. Rotted vegetable matter used as fertilizer is called _____.
2. Write a sentence using the vocabulary term.

Reviewing the Facts

3. **Recall.** How much water can you save by turning the water off while brushing your teeth?
4. **Identify.** How much trash is produced per week by an average American household of four?
5. **Explain.** What is said about all metal mined in the United States?
6. **Describe.** Describe what the ideal community recycles.

Writing Critically

7. **Expository.** Landfills are a national concern. People are producing more trash each year, and our nation is running out of landfill space. What do you think should be done about this problem?

Go Online

For more vocabulary practice play the True/False game at **glencoe.com.**

1. Compost
2. Answers will vary.
3. You can save three to five gallons of water per minute by turning the faucet off while brushing your teeth.
4. One hundred pounds of trash per week.
5. 70 percent of all metal mined in the U.S. is used once and then thrown away.
6. Communities recycle lawn debris and make their own compost piles.
7. Answers will vary.

Hunger and the Environment

As the 20th century was drawing to a close, four in every ten of the world's people were experiencing the chronic, painful hunger that arises when no food is available. Many more lacked the vitamins and minerals needed to support health and growth. At the same time, the population was continuing to grow, and the world's reserves of stored food had dropped to lower levels than ever before.

How Many People Go Hungry

MAIN IDEA ▶ Poverty is a major cause of disease, starvation, and death.

Over 4.5 half million households in the United States—representing 3.5 million children and almost 8 million adults—sometimes go without food because they lack money to buy it. Many millions more cannot afford to buy the nutritious food they need, and so choose cheaper, less nutritious foods. Not only the disadvantaged—migrant workers, unemployed minorities, and some elderly—are hungry. Also, displaced farm families and families whose adults work at minimum-wage jobs live with uncertainty about food.

> **"** There is no finer investment for any community than putting milk into babies. Healthy citizens are the greatest asset any country can have. **"**
>
> —Winston Churchill
> (1874–1965)
> British statesman,
> Prime Minister

■ **Figure 26.14** *Feeding the hungry—in the United States. How can teens help reduce poverty in the United States?*

Caption Answer: Teens can volunteer their time working at food banks, or volunteer with community organizations.

Only a minority of the poor in the United States are on welfare. Most are working people. The most compelling single reason for their hunger is poverty.

Over 850 million people, mostly women and children, around the globe are also suffering from extreme hunger. Most are drastically underweight. Half a million children go blind every year because of vitamin deficiencies.

Tens of thousands of people die each day as a result of undernutrition. Millions of children die each year from the disease of poverty. Death takes one child every 2 seconds—15 have died in the 30 seconds it may take you to read this paragraph. Poverty, infection, and malnutrition are the killers that cut life short in dozens of developing countries.

Of the world's 6 billion population, one-fifth have no land and no possessions at all. They survive on less than $1 a day. They lack water that is safe to drink, and they cannot read or write. The average U.S. housecat eats twice as much protein each day, and the yearly cost of keeping that cat is greater than the annual income of the one-fifth world population earning $1 a day.

The Environment and Poverty

MAIN IDEA ▶ Environmental degradation causes hunger and contributes indirectly by worsening the effect of poverty.

Many environmental causes contribute to poverty and hunger. Population growth contributes, for the more mouths there are to feed, the worse poverty and hunger become. As more people need homes, the land best suited for producing food may be taken to build houses. Pollution caused by more and more fossil fuel use worsens the health problems and misery of the poor. Water shortages force the poor from their homes, too, and create further hardship. The world's poorest people live in the world's most damaged and harmful environments.

Three steps to environmental correction:

1. **Recognition.** People must first recognize that a problem exists.
2. **Outrage.** People must refuse to accept the unacceptable.
3. **Advocacy.** People must join together to make the necessary changes.

Poverty, Hunger, and Overpopulation

MAIN IDEA ▶ All things are connected.

Strange as it may seem, poverty and hunger encourage people to bear more children. A family in poverty depends on its children to farm the land for food, to haul water, and to make the adults secure in their old age. To complicate things, poverty costs many young lives, so parents must bear many children to ensure that a few will survive to adulthood.

Reducing Population

To help reduce population growth, it is first necessary to help relieve poverty and hunger. When people have better access to health care and education, the death rate falls. As more family members survive, families become willing to risk having smaller numbers of children. Then the birth rate falls.

The Present Threat

The growth of the world's population is slowing, but still continuing to grow. This is threatening the world's capacity to produce adequate food in the future. The activities of billions of human beings on the earth's limited surface are seriously and adversely affecting the planet. We are wiping out many varieties of plant life, heating up the climate, using up fresh water supplies, and destroying the protective ozone layer that shields life from the sun's damaging rays. In short, human beings are overstraining the earth's ability to support life.

■ **Figure 26.16** *Public health programs provide many children with the food they need. What happens when people have better access to health care and education?*

Caption Answer: The death rate falls.

Population control is one of the world's most pressing needs. Until the nations of the world solve the population problem, they can neither succeed in supporting the lives of people already born, nor remedy the planet's galloping destruction. Of the 77 million people being added to the population each year, most are being added in the poorest areas of the world. Population growth worsens environmental damage, poverty, and hunger.

Conclusion

Consumers in the United States and other wealthy nations could help substantially to slow and reverse the downward trends described here by altering their choices. If we were willing to use fewer goods, use fewer resources, create less pollution, and consume less energy, this would go a long way toward remedying global environmental problems. It would also help solve the hunger problem—indirectly, but it would help a lot.

To many people, the preservation of the health of the Earth matters not just for people's sake, but for the sake of wildlife as well. The earth's preservation is a moral responsibility. It concerns us at a deep, spiritual level.

> " *This we know. The earth does not belong to man; man belongs to the earth. This we know. All things are connected like the blood which unites one family. All things are connected. Whatever befalls the earth befalls the sons of the earth. Man did not weave the web of life, he is merely a strand in it. Whatever he does to the web, he does to himself.* "
>
> —Chief Seattle
> (c. 1786 – 1866)
> Leader of the Suquamish and Duwamish Native American tribes

SECTION 6 Review

Worksheets: A reproducible quiz for Section 6 is provided in the Teacher Classroom Resources.

Reviewing the Facts

1. **Identify.** How many people in the United States are chronically hungry?
2. **List.** List at least four environmental causes that contribute to poverty and hunger.
3. **Explain.** How does poverty and hunger encourage people to bear more children?

Writing Critically

4. **Expository.** This section described how we as U.S. consumers could slow and reverse the downward trends of global environmental problems. What are the steps to resolve these problems? Would the steps also help solve the hunger problems? Explain your answer.

 **Online**

For more information on health careers, visit Career Corner at **glencoe.com**.

1. 3.5 million children, almost 8 million adults

2. Population growth, land development, pollution, and water shortages

3. A family in poverty depends on its children to farm land for food, haul water, and to make adults secure in their old age.

4. Answers will vary.

Q&A Voluntary Simplicity

Understand and Apply Read the conversation below, and then answer the questions that follow.

The problems of the environment and the world's growing population may appear so great that they seem solvable only by political leaders. However, consider this: you can change the world. Perhaps most fitting for a book about personal choices is to describe some of the things one person can do. After all, a society is the sum of its people. As we go, so goes our world.

Q: I'm just a kid. I can't have any effect on the way the world goes. In fact, when I think about it, I feel overwhelmed, depressed, and pessimistic.

A: Thoughtful people of all ages feel just as you do at times and are tempted to give up. Optimism is important, though, and many people are working to develop it. They know that optimism gives them energy and makes their efforts to shape the world's future more effective.

Q: How do I develop optimism?

A: By living your own life. Don't try to solve all the world's problems. Mentally draw a small circle around yourself. Work to better yourself through education, spiritual growth, and physical health. Work, too, to better the small world within the circle around yourself.

Q: That sounds simple enough, but I don't see how it will help anything. In fact, it almost sounds selfish.

A: It will help, though. Every move you make leaves the world a better or worse place. Your actions have a ripple effect, often far beyond what you may think. Tending to the lives nearest you, including your own, is your first responsibility.

Your second responsibility is to make sure you can answer yes to the following question: If everyone lived as I do, would the young children of today grow up in a better world?

Those who study the future are convinced that the hope of the world lies in everyone's adopting a simple lifestyle. Many experts agree that the simplification of our lives can benefit all of the world's people.

Q: Are you saying that everybody needs to live in poverty? I can't see how my being poor would help anyone. Besides, wealthy people would never agree.

A: No, the suggestion is not that everyone become poor. It is said that poverty is repressive, and simplicity is liberating. Poverty gives people a sense of helplessness, but simplicity gives them creativity. In other words, to become poor would solve nothing.

Poverty hinders personal growth, but simplicity opens the way to it. You are also right that few people would willingly give up their wealth, even if it would help. What is suggested has nothing to do with wealth. It is a lifestyle—a commitment to live more simply in view of the world's limited resources.

Think in terms of *elegance*, not poverty. Streamlined things, that have no unnecessary frills, are elegant. Life is too. Don't carry extra baggage around. It only burdens you.

Q: What does living a life of voluntary simplicity involve?

A: Such a life involves a thousand small decisions, like the ones that were presented in the chapter. The chapter described ways to reduce consumption of goods, energy and water use, and the throwing away of trash and garbage. Everything you do, you can do simply, with little cost or even a benefit to the earth, or you can do it complexly, with a high cost and no benefit. Together, all the things you do add up to your personal style.

To live simply, it isn't necessary to make every choice the chapter suggested. Some choices may not be right for you. Some choices may be your own original ones, and they may be better ideas than anyone else has yet dreamed up.

Voluntary is a key word, just as *simplicity* is. Each individual must look within to discover a personal sense of what actions are appropriate. Each person needs to find a balance—a path, suitable for that individual, that leads between the extremes of poverty and self-indulgence.

Q: I'm not ready to apply the ideas in the chapter yet. I still have to gain my education and prepare for life. I'll wait and begin to live simply when I'm ready.

A: Some of the chapter ideas may have to wait. However, you have already begun your life, and in some ways it is already beneficial to the earth. Improving yourself is the first step toward improving the world—remember the ripple effect. Learn all you can. Work on your education, and on your emotional and spiritual growth. You will then be better equipped to participate in the world community.

Q: Do you really think that if everyone made choices like these, it would help the state of the world?

A: Yes. Every agency that has studied the future has reached the same conclusion: voluntary simplicity can work. It does not mean living primitively. Most people prefer beauty and ease to ugliness and discomfort. Voluntary simplicity does mean seeking a life free of distractions, clutter, and self-importance—a life that includes self-discipline.

 Writing Write a paragraph describing how you can make choices to help the environment.

Reviewing Vocabulary

Use the vocabulary terms listed below to complete the following statements.

environment
sustainable
acid rain
ozone
pollution

1. Everything "outside" the living organism—air, water, soil, other organisms, and forms of radiation—is called _____.

2. _____ is rain that carries acid air pollutants.

3. A term used to describe the use of resources at such a rate that the earth can keep on replacing them is _____.

4. Contamination of the environment with anything that impairs its ability to support life is called _____.

5. _____ is a substance created when certain types of energy, such as the sun's ultraviolet rays, react with oxygen.

Recalling Key Facts and Ideas

Section 1
6. **Explain.** What can happen to your body when the water you drink is polluted?

Section 2
7. **List.** List three global environmental problems.

8. **Explain.** How can you help slow, stop, or even reverse the global environmental problems?

9. **Describe.** Describe how sustainable choices you make are beneficial to the environment and also to your health.

Section 3
10. **Identify.** What is the single largest source of air pollution?

11. **Recall.** How often should you shop? What other tips are given about shopping?

12. **Explain.** How long do plastics last?

Section 4
13. **Recall.** How many families are now using solar energy?

14. **Explain.** What keeps most people from using solar energy.

15. **Name.** Among kitchen appliances, which is the biggest energy user?

16. **Analyze.** What can you do to save energy while using lightbulbs?

Section 5
17. **Explain.** What can a recycled plastic water bottle become?

18. **Recall.** What materials can be piled up together with some soil and decompose naturally?

19. **Describe.** Describe why natural fertilizers are better for the environment than synthetic fertilizers.

Section 6
20. **Recall.** How many children go blind each year from vitamin deficiencies?

21. **Explain.** In what ways are we overstraining the earth's ability to support life?

1. Environment 2. Acid rain 3. Sustainable 4. Pollution 5. Ozone 6. You can ingest harmful chemicals including many that cause cancer. 7. Hunger, poverty, and population growth 8. Purchase eco-friendly products, lobby legislators to write laws to protect the environment. 9. Riding a bicycle can keep your body fit and reduce pollution, eating mostly plant products can benefit your health as well as cutting down on fuels to produce other food sources. 10. Automobile pollution 11. Once a week. Share rides with friends, carpool, walk or ride a bicycle. 12. Years or decades. 13. More than

Writing Critically

22. Personal. Read the Q&A section on page 724–725, "Voluntary Simplicity." What suggestions are given to protect the earth? How can you simplify your life? What will happen to our environment if nobody changes?

Activities

23. Visit a local health care clinic. Find out how many people have come in due to hunger. What health problems do victims of hunger have? Share your findings with the rest of the class in an oral report.

24. Contact a hunger relief organization in your area. What will your donations actually do for hungry people? How much money goes directly to the people who need it for food? How much money goes to the organization that is helping?

25. Make posters on ways we can recycle products in our homes. Post these around school.

26. Write an editorial in your school newspaper about how our lifestyle choices affect our environment and our health. In your editorial, challenge students to change habits to help the environment and their health.

27. Design a pamphlet that explains how to use nontoxic products to clean our homes. Make copies available to all students.

28. Visit the local wastewater treatment plant. How does the plant dispose of waste products? Write a one-page report about your trip and the process the plant goes through each day.

29. Make a video or podcast about the ten different global environmental problems described in this chapter. For each problem listed, come up with a solution. Share your work with the rest of the class.

Making Decisions About Health

30. Hunger is a major problem in the world. What can you do about the hunger problem? Will you concentrate your efforts on the United States or on other countries? Why?

31. Garbage is a major problem for our environment. Recycling can help control this problem. How could you make everyone in the world recycle? What laws would you pass? How would you enforce these laws?

 **Go Online**

For more vocabulary practice, play the Concentration game at **glencoe.com**.

Fact or Fiction?

Answers
1. True.
2. False. Refrigerators, hot-water heaters, and heaters and air conditioners use more energy, because they are on all the time.
3. True.

 Writing Paragraphs will vary.

20,000 **14.** High initial costs **15.** Refrigerators **16.** Use a compact fluorescent bulb. It uses one-fourth the energy of a regular bulb. **17.** It can be recycled into carpet. **18.** Leaves, grass clippings, yard materials **19.** Natural fertilizers do not require mining and recycle natural materials. **20.** Five

hundred thousand **21.** Overpopulation, overuse of land, pollution, use of fossil fuels **22–31.** Answers will vary.

The Consumer and the Health Care System

Sections

1. **Paying for Health Care**
2. **Our Health Care System**
3. **Choosing Health Care Providers**

No doubt you have been a consumer of the **health care system**, *the total of all health care providers and medical treatment facilities that work together to provide medical care to the population.* Virtually everyone who attends public school must be immunized, and many teens have been treated for the flu or broken bones. When you need the health care system, nothing else can take its place. At present, your parents, your guardians, or other adults probably attempt to get you the treatment you need at a cost your family can afford. By the time you leave home, though, you will need to know how to find your own way around in the system. This chapter invites you to learn to use the health care system to best support your health.

Fact or Fiction?

What Do You Think?
Is each statement true or false? If you think it's false, explain what's true.

1. If you have medical and surgical insurance, you are probably covered for the costs of most medical treatments you might need.
2. Some operations are often recommended when they are not necessary, so it pays to get a second opinion before having surgery.
3. Anyone can adopt the title "doctor," but there are penalties for falsely claiming to be a medical doctor (M.D.) with a degree from a particular school.

 Writing Write a paragraph to explain why community and public health are important.

(Answers on page 745)

Visit **glencoe.com** and complete the Life Choice Inventory for Chapter 27.

Paying for Health Care

You may not have considered how you would pay for medical treatment unless you or someone you love has been injured or has become seriously ill. Modern health care can be very expensive. Most people need to develop a plan in order to pay for medical treatments and emergencies.

Approaches to Health Care

MAIN IDEA ▶ Approaches to health care include the unprepared approach, insurance, and the managed care approach.

Let us suppose you have three health problems this year. You get a severe sore throat; you break your arm; and you develop a heart condition (even though you may be young), but you will not have any symptoms for 15 years. How these events will affect you physically and financially depends on the choices you make.

No Plan

Suppose you have no health insurance. When your sore throat strikes, you try to live with it. Then it becomes so painful that you have to go to the hospital emergency room. There, you have to pay $100 in advance, and are given some medicine. You miss a week of classes or work. When you break your arm, you again rush to the hospital and learn that they will not set your arm in a cast until you have again paid in advance—this time, $500. Your total cost of treatment for the year: $600, a week of missed classes or work, and failure to detect your advancing heart condition.

Insurance and Private Physician Plan

The second approach, the insurance approach, provides a different outcome. You pay $50 a month for insurance. These premiums are regular payments made to an insurance company to cover the costs of unforeseen events such as medical emergencies. When your sore throat worsens, you go to a doctor. You show your insurance card and receive treatment. The same thing happens when you break your arm. The total cost for your care is still the same ($600 for the year), but you do not pay the costs when you seek the care.

An advantage to the insurance approach is that you establish a relationship with a doctor who knows your medical history. A doctor who sees you routinely may be able to detect the symptoms of heart disease that were mentioned earlier

Vocabulary

health care system
managed care
health maintenance
  organization (HMO)
prepayment plan
fee-for-service system

Class Discussion

Discuss: Ask students to create a list of reasons why those without an insurance plan are often forced to go without care. Discuss the long-term consequences of this.

in this section. The doctor may diagnose the condition and provide treatment before it becomes life threatening. In this way, having health insurance protects your health.

Having health insurance, however, does not guarantee that your doctor will be able to diagnose every medical problem you may have. Preventive exams are not usually covered under this type of plan. A visit to a doctor for a preventive medical exam may result in an extra office visit fee that your insurance may not cover.

Managed Care Plan

Still another option is to join a **managed care** plan, which is *a system providing health care based on a prepaid basis.* One example of a managed care plan is a **health maintenance organization** (HMO), *a group of physicians who practice together and who treat people's health problems under a prepayment plan.* The HMO charges you a fee each month that is slightly higher than insurance—say, $75 ($900 for the year). For this you receive many services without paying extra for them. The routine physical examination to catch your heart disease is usually paid for by the plan.

Comprehension Check

Explain: Ask students to explain how a managed care plan works. Their explanation should include one example of a managed care plan. Students may also wish to include experiences they may have had with a managed care plan in their paper.

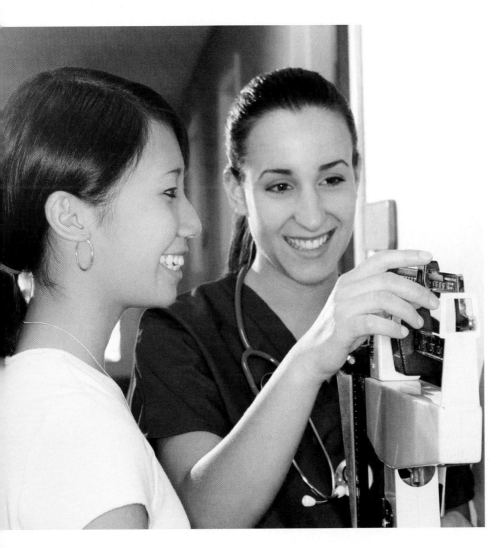

■ **Figure 27.1** *Health care providers such as physicians, physician's assistants, andmore practitioners come in many forms. Why is access to medical care so important?*

Caption Answer: Everyone needs access to medical care for overall wellness.

The key difference between a managed care plan and other health care providers is in how they are paid. An HMO offers a **prepayment plan**, *a system of payment for health care in which the clients pay a fixed fee every month, regardless of how many services they receive.* Other health care providers charge for each service as you receive it. Their method of payment is described as a **fee-for-service system**, *a system of paying for health care in which clients pay individual fees for the services they receive.*

The health care industry has developed a quality "report card" for grading how well a plan meets the medical needs of clients. Consumers who know what to look for in a plan can make informed choices.

Worksheets: A reproducible quiz for Section 1 is provided in the Teacher Classroom Resources.

SECTION 1 Review

Reviewing the Vocabulary

Review the vocabulary on page 730. Then answer these questions.

1. The total of all health care providers and medical treatment facilities that work together to provide medical care to the population is called a _____.
2. What is *managed care*?
3. A _____ is a group of physicians who practice together and who treat people's health problems under a prepayment plan.

Reviewing the Facts

4. **Identify.** What are the three health care approaches listed in this section?
5. **List.** List three benefits of a managed care plan.

Writing Critically

6. **Personal.** Your family has just moved to a little town from a big city. Your family used to belong to an HMO, but the little town does not have one. How will you choose the best care?

For more vocabulary practice, play the True/False game at **glencoe.com**.

1. A second assessment of a diagnosis and treatment plan by another health care provider, usually on the request of a client, to double-check the validity of the original plan

2. A system of providing health care based on a prepaid basis

3. Health maintenance organization (HMO)

4. No insurance plan, insurance plan, and managed care plan

5. You can receive services without paying extra, you would not hesitate to get prompt medical attention, most fees are paid, it pays for physical exams.

6. Answers will vary.

Our Health Care System

Medical care is expensive. A serious illness may easily require treatments costing more than the average family makes in a year. The insurance system is devised to help people avoid being wiped out financially by serious illness.

What Kind of Health Insurance Is Best?

MAIN IDEA ▶ Insurance can pay for many things, but it is no substitute for careful financial planning.

"I'm sorry, but your insurance policy doesn't cover this. Pay in advance please." People can avoid the pain of lack of insurance coverage if they shop for health insurance. The five types of personal health care insurance are:

1. **Hospitalization insurance.** Insurance to pay the cost of a hospital stay.

2. **Surgical insurance.** Insurance to pay the surgeon's fees.

3. **Medical insurance.** Insurance to pay physicians' fees, lab fees, and fees for prescription medications.

4. **Major medical insurance.** Insurance to pay high bills not covered by other insurance.

5. **Disability insurance.** Insurance to replace lost income if a person should be unable to work due to a long illness.

The different types of insurance cover each of these: accidents, hospitalization, surgery, physician services, medicines, pregnancy, and disabilities that might prevent your working. Read each policy you are considering, and think about your needs. For example, if a person plans to start a family soon, insurance should cover those costs.

If you have a healthy lifestyle, you may be charged lower insurance rates than others. Insurance companies know that they are more likely to have to pay large medical bills for people who smoke, who are obese, who use alcohol, who fail to exercise, who don't wear safety belts, and whose blood cholesterol and blood pressure are high.

Special groups of people may be covered by Medicare and Medicaid. **Medicare**, *hospitalization insurance for people who are receiving Social Security benefits*, pays hospital expenses for senior citizens. **Medicaid** is *hospitalization and surgical insurance available for people who qualify as needy*.

Vocabulary

Medicare
Medicaid
second opinion

" *Be careful about reading health books. You could die of a misprint.* "

— Mark Twain
(1835–1910)
American writer

Figure 27.2   Community Health Agencies

These and many other agencies are dedicated to improving the health of people in the United States.

National Level

- The Food and Drug Administration enforces laws intended to ensure pure, well-labeled food, and safe and effective drugs.
- The Centers for Disease Control and Prevention runs research and programs to prevent and halt disease epidemics.
- The National Institutes of Health conducts research that yields national health statistics.
- Medicare and Medicaid help meet the medical needs of the elderly and low-income citizens.
- Private research groups, such as the American Heart Association and the National Safety Council, focus on discovering more about diseases, safety, and health.

Local Level

- School clinics may provide care by nurses, first aid, pregnancy prevention, substance abuse prevention, or other services each community deems are needed for its students.
- Public Health Departments provide immunizations, family planning services, maternal and child services, health worker training, addiction recovery programs, and mental illness services, among others.
- Hospitals, clinics, and physicians provide medical testing, screening, and treatments.

Community Medical Resources

MAIN IDEA ▶ Choose a health care facility that best meets your needs.

A goal of the health care system is to meet the needs of people within their own communities. Many agencies—both government-run and private, voluntary types—work together to achieve this goal. The Food and Drug Administration (FDA) is a watchdog agency that checks up on the manufacturers of foods and drugs. **Figure 27.2** briefly describes a few of the many resources working together to meet the nation's health needs.

Some aspects of health care are better provided at the local level, because communities' needs differ. A large city may need to provide more services for urban low-income groups, while a farming community may have entirely different needs.

Among the private providers of health services, medical facilities have different strengths and weaknesses. The Health Skills sidebar, "Selecting and Using Medical Care Facilities," can help you make that choice.

Smart strategies can also help you save money. For example, if possible, try to see a health care professional during office hours—do not go to a hospital emergency room. Emergency rooms always cost extra. The Health Skills sidebar, "Tips for Emergency Room Visits," offers a few suggestions to make your visit easier.

Health Skills

Tips for Emergency Room Visits

When you must go to an emergency room:

1. Call your doctor first. State who you are, what the problem is, and where you are going.

2. Take identification and your insurance card with you.

3. Know your own medical history and what medicines you are taking.

Getting a Second Opinion

Seek a second opinion before allowing any test or surgery. A **second opinion** is *a second assessment of a diagnosis and treatment plan by another health care provider, usually on the request of a client, to double-check the validity of the original plan.* Some operations are overperformed. That is, they are often recommended when they are not medically necessary. Insurance may cover the cost of a second opinion. If the two opinions differ, consider getting a third.

As many as 90 percent of hospital bills contain errors. Read through your bills to check that you have not been overcharged. If you question any charge, ask for an itemized list of services you received, and send it to your insurance company. The insurance company may be able to get the charges reduced.

Problems Affecting Our Health Care System

MAIN IDEA ▶ The U.S. health care system is a high-cost system.

While our medical system suffers some problems, it also has advantages appreciated by people all over the world (listed in **Figure 27.3** on page 736). Not all nations' health care systems operate as the U.S. system does. For example, Canada has a national program of insurance that offers basic health care to more than 99 percent of its citizens. Canadians, however, lack the advanced technology that is available under the U.S. system.

High costs may be the worst problem in our system. There seems to be no limit on how high costs can go, and high costs prevent some people of limited income from receiving the care they need. The development of modern hospital technology adds to the high cost of medical care.

New technologies open other possibilities. With advanced technology, health care providers can offer patients better care, specialized care, and more efficient communication between doctors and patients. New communications technology, for example, now makes possible a sort of "video clinic." An expert at, say, the University of Chicago sets up a video conference call with a clinic in Kentucky or California that has a patient with specialized problems. Over two-way video cameras, the expert and patient view and speak with each other. The expert observes tests, monitors heartbeat and other vital signs, and offers a diagnosis and a treatment plan.

Health Skills

Selecting and Using Medical Care Facilities

When selecting and using medical care facilities:

1. Know what facilities are available and their specialties.
2. Avoid emergency room visits.
3. Get a second or third opinion.
4. Consider alternatives to hospital tests and surgery.
5. Use the hospital on weekdays; avoid weekends.
6. Ask about each facility's policy on payment.
7. Find out the physician's and hospital's ways of handling insurance claims. They may file the claims, or you may have to.
8. Protest if the bill is in error.
9. Be willing to go out of state, if necessary, for specialized medical care.

Figure 27.3 **Problems and Advantages of Our Health Care System**

The problems of our health care system are real, but many overlook its important advantages. Here is a list of some of its problems that need solving and some of its advantages worth protecting.

Problems	Advantages
Insurance problems of the sick Insurance companies can cancel a policy or charge unaffordable fees, should someone develop a disease with treatment involving unusually high costs. (AIDS is such a disease.)	**Access to life-saving technology** The U.S. health care system supports research and technology, and offers many new technologically advanced treatments that people from around the globe come to receive.
Malpractice suits The legal system allows too many high-dollar awards and frivolous lawsuits against physicians and hospitals, driving up health care costs.	**Access to physicians** Patients can speak directly to physicians by phone, and make emergency appointments. Also, patients can ask questions and receive advice. In some other health care systems, physicians may see up to 100 patients a day.
Job lock Often, when a person changes jobs, that person must also change his insurance carrier. A person who becomes ill under one policy may be turned down for coverage of that illness on a new policy. Some sick people feel locked into a job for fear of losing their insurance coverage.	**Confidentiality and privacy** In the United States, the Health Insurance Portability and Accountability Act (HIPAA) protects a patient's medical records. A patient's medical information can not be released without consent.
Uninsured citizens Some 20% of the population has no insurance, and may be denied some forms of health care. Some emergency rooms must treat them anyway. The emergency rooms raise other prices to cover these costs, or try to recover them from tax money.	**Equitable treatment options** Treatment is available to all who can afford it. Some other systems limit treatment given to elderly or terminally ill patients.
Tax unfairness Large employers can deduct 100% of their insurance expenses from their income taxes. Self-employed and unemployed people can deduct only a fraction or no insurance expenses, and so effectively pay double for health coverage.	**Local treatment facilities** Most communities have access to most procedures, so that a diagnosis of a serious condition normally doesn't require long-distance travel for treatment. In other countries, certain hospitals perform only certain procedures.
Overuse of the system People who feel they are "spending the insurance company's money" have no reason to be frugal about their health care spending.	**Quick access to care** Once a diagnosis is made, treatment is swift. In other countries, sick people often wait months or even years for treatment, even if they need surgery and are in pain.

While health care in the United States is costly, its advantages far outweigh its disadvantages. Patients can choose from a variety of insurance plans that meet their needs. Community health agencies at the local and national levels offer many health care options to people within their own neighborhoods. However, any healthcare system is only as good as the people who provide health care. The next section discusses how to choose health care providers.

Worksheets: A reproducible quiz for Section 2 is provided in the Teacher Classroom Resources.

SECTION 2 Review

Reviewing the Vocabulary

Review the vocabulary on page 733. Then answer these questions.

1. Define *second opinion*.
2. _____ is hospitalization insurance for people who are receiving Social Security.
3. Hospitalization and surgical insurance available for people who qualify as needy is called _____.

Reviewing the Facts

4. List. List the five types of insurance related to your personal health.
5. Recall. Who is eligible for Medicare?
6. Explain. Explain the role of the Food and Drug Administration in helping to meet people's health needs.
7. Describe. List and describe what to do when selecting and using medical care facilities.
8. Name. Name a problem with Canada's health care system.
9. Identify. What is the backbone of a health care system?

Writing Critically

10. Expository. Alberto was out on a bike ride when his front tire hit a rock and threw him off the bike. He landed hard on his wrist. A friend drove him to the emergency room for treatment. At the hospital, Alberto was told he had to pay $400 up front in order to receive treatment. What could Alberto have done in advance to prevent this from happening?

Go Online

For more information on health careers, visit Career Corner at **glencoe.com**.

1. A second assessment of a diagnosis and treatment plan by another health care provider, usually on the request of a client, to double-check the validity of the original plan
2. Medicare
3. Medicaid
4. Hospitalization insurance, surgical insurance, medical insurance, major medical insurance, disability insurance
5. Senior citizens who also receive Social Security are eligible for Medicare.
6. The FDA checks up on manufacturers of foods and drugs so they are safe
7. Know what facilities are available and what their specialties are, avoid emergency room visits, get a second or third opinion, ask about policies on payment.
8. Canada lacks advanced medical technology.
9. The people who provide health care are the backbone of any health-care system.
10. Answers will vary.

Choosing Health Care Providers

A person who gets sick usually will think in terms of "going to the doctor"—but what is a doctor? Anyone can be called "doctor," but not all are trained the same way, and some are even dishonest. This section attempts to sort out who's who in the health care world.

Vocabulary

history
physical examination
integrative therapies

The Health Care Provider

MAIN IDEA ▶ Select your health care provider with care. Research a doctor's credentials closely.

The health care provider most people think of is the medical doctor, or M.D. This is as it should be, for medical school training equips the M.D. to handle many kinds of medical problems. This book refers to such a person as the doctor or physician.

Consumer
SKILLS ACTIVITY

Genuine and Fake Credentials

Most degrees listed next to health care providers' names show that the person completed the training to truly provide help to those who need it. However, not everyone who has a doctor's diploma earned a medical degree. Some organizations that call themselves colleges or universities simply sell official-looking diplomas by mail.

To find out whether a college or university is for real, a person must do some research. The university should be **accredited**, or *approved*, by a professional group (for example, the American Medical Association, for physicians).

Watch out, though. There are also fake professional groups and fake licenses to practice. For every true symbol of legal right to practice, there is a counterfeit that copies it.

If you can apply to an institution for a degree, a diploma, or a license to practice—and get it—then you have uncovered a fraud.

 Writing

1. Why is it important for clients to be certain of their health care providers' credentials?
2. If a person with a bogus degree applied for membership in a real professional group, what do you think would happen? Why?
3. If you were suspicious of someone's credentials, how would you check on them?

Kinds of Doctors

A long course of education leads to the M.D. degree and to the license to practice medicine. Another type of doctor, the osteopath (D.O.), takes the same course of training as an M.D., but in a school of osteopathy, which specializes in the muscles and skeleton.

A physician is licensed to provide medical care under his or her own authority. Other professionals who can provide care independently are the nurse practitioner (N.P. or R.N.P.) and the physician's assistant (P.A.).

Many people seek services from a chiropractor (doctor of chiropractic, or D.C.). Not everyone realizes that this person, although called "doctor," has not received the same medical training as an M.D. Chiropractors can relieve pain (especially from pressure on nerves). However, other medical services, such as diagnosing illnesses and prescribing treatments for them, are the exclusive domain of the M.D.

What Can I Expect at an Appointment?

Once you have found a qualified health care provider, call the person's office. Ask the questions listed in the Health Skills sidebar, "Choosing a Health Care Provider." Before your appointment, write down your questions and take them with you. Also, write down answers as you talk to the professional.

A health care provider will take a thorough **history**—*an interview in which a health care professional asks about past experiences.* The medical history provides your doctor with information to make a diagnosis.

Also expect a thorough **physical examination**, *an examination of the body to gather information about its general condition or to make a diagnosis.* Expect to be told the diagnosis and the treatment options. Your doctor may be able to give you a diagnosis at the end of your visit, or he or she may need to wait for test results to provide a diagnosis.

Complementary or Integrative Therapies

MAIN IDEA ▶ The use of integrative therapies is not yet fully supported by science.

Another approach to medical care are the so-called **integrative therapies**, *approaches to medical diagnosis and treatment that are not fully accepted by the established medical community.* A person seeking an integrative therapy for a headache, for example, might be advised to chew a few fresh leaves of the herb feverfew, or to receive a massage or acupuncture. Medical doctors who employ some alternative therapies with standard medical treatments are said to practice *complementary medicine.*

Health Skills

Choosing a Health Care Provider

When choosing a health care provider:

1. Ask the American Medical Association or people you trust for recommendations.

2. Look for provider's membership in the American College of Physicians or the American College of Surgeons.

3. Ask these questions:
   - What are the fees for office visits? Other visits?
   - Will you accept my insurance as complete payment for the care you provide?
   - What are your office hours?

4. Try one appointment, and notice how it goes.

5. Expect to be listened to.

6. Expect a thorough history and physical examination.

Consumer Skills Activity:

1. client's health would be at risk if their health-care provider did not have proper education and training.

2. Answers will vary.

3. You can check for recommendations and credentials through the American Medical Association.

One of every three people is estimated to use an integrative therapy each year for everything from headaches to cancer. While some techniques offered by alternative therapies, such as stress reduction to lower blood pressure do seem to work, others are unproven. By definition, an alternative therapy:

- Is not taught by most medical schools in the United States.

- Is not reimbursable by most health insurance providers in the United States.

- Is not well supported by scientific tests establishing safety and effectiveness.

Figure 27.4	Integrative Therapy Terms
Therapy	**Description**
Acupuncture	A method of piercing of the skin with needles at points believed to relieve pain or illnesses.
Aroma therapy	A technique that uses oil extracts from plants and flowers (usually applied by massage or baths) to enhance physical, psychological, and spiritual health.
Ayurveda	A traditional hindu system of herbs, diet, meditation, massage, and yoga believed to improve the body's disease-fighting capacity.
Bioelectromagnetic medicine	The use of electrical or magnetic energy to stimulate bone repair, wound healing, and tissue regeneration.
Biofeedback	The use of machines that detect and convey information about heart rate, blood pressure, brain or nerve activity, and muscle tension, to enable a person to learn how it feels to relax, and so slow the pulse and lower blood pressure.
Herbal medicine	The use of plants to treat disease or improve health.
Homeopathic medicine	The use of plants to treat disease or improve health.
Hypnotherapy	The use of hypnosis and the power of suggestion to change behaviors, relieve pain, and heal.
Massage therapy	A method of kneading the muscles to reduce tension, help blood circulate, and improve joint mobility; believed to promote healing.
Naturopathic medicine	A mixture of traditional and alternative therapies.

*These therapies are currently under study by the National Institutes of Health (NIH). The NIH endorses the use of acupuncture as effective against nausea following surgery and chemotherapy, during pregnancy, and following dental surgery.

In the future, some integrative therapies may well be proven useful in disease prevention and cure. Cancer radiation therapy, for example, was once considered unconventional, but now is often central to the treatment of many cancers. Some medical schools are beginning to teach some of these approaches to health. However, view these therapies cautiously.

Keep an open mind as you read about the alternative therapies listed in **Figure 27.4** on page 740. However, exercise caution too. The Office of Alternative Medicine explores unconventional medical practices. The therapies under study by the NIH are marked with an asterisk (*) in **Figure 27.4**.

SECTION 3 Review

Reviewing the Vocabulary

Review the vocabulary on page 738. Then answer these questions.

1. Define *history*.

2. What are *integrative therapies*?

3. Define *physical examination*.

Reviewing the Facts

4. Recall. Counting the years of college, medical school, internship, and residency, how long does a doctor stay in school altogether?

5. Describe. What services can chiropractors offer?

6. List. List six questions you should ask a physician before your visit.

Writing Critically

7. Personal. After rereading the Consumer Skills Activity how would you feel about being treated by a fraud? What can you do to help control this problem? What could your school do to help in this area? How about your community?

 Online

For fitness and health tips, visit the Fitness Zone at **glencoe.com**.

1. An interview in which a health care professional asks about past experiences

2. Approaches to medical diagnosis and treatment that are not fully accepted by the established medical community

3. An examination of the body to gather information about its general condition or to make a diagnosis

4. Ten years

5. Chiropractors can relieve pain , especially from pressure on the nerves.

6. What are the fees for office visits, will you accept my insurance as complete payment, what are your office hours, can I obtain advice my phone, do you recommend I have periodic checkups, who handles the calls when you are not around.

7. Answers will vary.

 Understand and Apply Read the conversation below, and then complete the writing exercise that follows.

All through this course you have been asked to take responsibility for your own habits and choices. Once you leave the classroom, you will still be put to the test in the larger world. Unfortunately, not everyone who claims to have your health in mind has pure motivations. How can you know what to believe and to apply to your life, and what to discount?

Q: I like trying new health care products, and I think people should give new methods a chance. But how can I know whom to trust?

A: You are wise to question sources of new products and schemes. Not all sources are equally valid, although all may claim that their statements are facts. Take, for example, advertisements in which actors, dressed as scientists or physicians, appear on television, on the Internet, or in magazines making solemn statements about "research." When you look closely, you often find little or no evidence to back up their claims. To find the truth, you need skill in sifting the valid health information from the invalid claims.

Q: How can I tell the difference between valid and invalid claims?

A: Ideally, when you first saw the claim for a product or service, you would have time to research it thoroughly. You would find out the credentials of the person making the claim, check out the evidence on which the claim was made, ask where the evidence was published, and analyze the style in which it

■ **Figure 27.5** *Not all sources of information are valid. How can you tell if a health claim is valid?*

Caption Answer: Research it by checking the credentials of the person making the claim, check the evidence, ask where the evidence was published.

Figure 27.6   Red Flags of Health Claims

Be cautious of health claims that:

- **Seem too good to be true.** Present simple answers to complex problems; say what people want to hear.
- **Create suspicions about food supply or medical drugs.** Urge distrust of current medical methods or suspicion about food. Sell "alternatives" profiting the seller.
- **Include testimonials.** Include histories of people claiming to have been "healed" or "made younger" by the product or treatment.
- **Use false credentials.** Use titles such as "doctor" or "university," but have simply created or bought the titles.
- **Cite unpublished studies.** Cite studies that are not published and so cannot be evaluated.
- **Use persecution claims.** Claim that the medical community "is after" them. Try to convince you that doctors "want to keep you ill" so you'll keep paying for office visits.
- **Ask you to simply trust the claim.** Ask you to trust that what is being said is true.

- **Seem motivated by profits.** Make a profit from your believing the claim.
- **State the claim is a paid advertisement.** Have claims that look scientific but that are made by a paid advertiser. Look for the words advertisement, probably in tiny print, on the page.
- **Cite questionable or unreliable publications.** Cite studies that are published, but in newsletters or magazines that publish misinformation.
- **Use logic without proof.** Make a reasonable case for the claim, but offer no science to back it up.

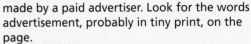

was stated. Remember, just being famous does not qualify a person to make a health claim. A poet's words on physical fitness may sound beautiful, but the words of a trainer of Olympic athletes are probably more accurate. A famed heart surgeon knows hearts, but a family therapist is qualified to speak on love. When someone speaks on health, size up that person's training, education, skill, credentials, and reputation in the field.

Q: That sounds complicated. How can I know how to judge the person making claims?

A: It can be complicated and time consuming to check someone out completely. For most purposes, though, you can answer this most critical question: If the person or organization making the claim stands to profit by selling you something you would not otherwise buy, the claim is probably false. It can be as simple as that. Remember, though, that if you take shortcuts in checking credentials, you do so at your own risk. Study **Figure 27.6** for some tips on how to detect health care fraud. If you detect any of the red flags listed there, it is best to walk away.

Writing Write a paragraph explaining why it is important to check the credentials of a health care provider.

Reviewing Vocabulary

Use the vocabulary terms listed below to complete the following statements.

integrative therapies
managed care
fee-for-service system
Medicare
history
health maintenance organization (HMO)

1. A system providing health care based on a prepaid basis is called _____.

2. A system of paying for health care in which clients pay individual fees for the services they receive is called _____.

3. _____ is a group of physicians who practice together and who treat people's health problems under a payment plan.

4. Hospitalization insurance for people who are receiving Social Security benefits is called _____.

5. An interview in which a health care professional asks about past experiences is called a _____.

6. _____ are approaches to medical diagnosis and treatment that are not fully accepted by the established medical community.

Recalling Key Facts and Ideas

Section 1

7. **Describe.** Describe what a health care provider does beyond treatment.

8. **Identify.** Which of the three approaches to health care is the most risky and why?

Section 2

9. **Recall.** What people can receive Medicaid insurance?

10. **Identify.** Who must pay costs not covered by insurance?

11. **Explain.** What drives our insurance premiums up higher than they should be?

12. **List.** List five hints for emergency room visits.

13. **Describe.** What should you do before an operation?

14. **Analyze.** If you have questions about your hospital bill, what should you do?

Section 3

15. **Recall.** What is the first step in selecting a health care provider?

16. **Describe.** Describe what tests you should expect during a physical examination.

17. **Explain.** Why is it important to give the physician your medical history?

Writing Critically

18. **Expository.** Marie has been looking for medical insurance. She has discovered that most insurance companies require that you have a physical examination before they sell you a policy. She is a smoker, uses alcohol, and is obese. She cannot find an insurance company that will cover her. Most premiums are too expensive for her. What can Marie do? Why is it necessary for her to have insurance? What will happen to her family if she gets sick without insurance? What can her family do? What would you do? Why would you take that action if you were in this situation?

1. Managed care 2. Fee-for-service system 3. Managed care 4. Medicare 5. History 6. Integrative therapies 7. Give a routine physical examinations that detect problems before they start. 8. No health care plan because you cannot afford to be unprepared for emergencies. 9. People who receive public assistance 10. The client is responsible. 11. Malpractice insurance 12. Call your regular doctor first, have only one person go with you, take identification and insurance information, know

Activities

19. Divide into groups and interview local insurance agents. Compare prices and coverage from two companies on:

    a. Medical insurance
    b. Hospitalization insurance
    c. Surgical insurance
    d. Major medical insurance
    e. Disability insurance

    Report your findings to the other groups.

20. Make a video about the different kinds of disability insurance policies available and the benefits of long-term coverage as opposed to term coverage. How do insurance companies encourage you to purchase a policy? What are some of the advertising quirks they use? Put these in your video.

21. Have a class debate on the health and medical care system of the United States versus Canada's health care system. What are some positive and negative aspects of each? Combine the good qualities of both and make up your own health care system.

22. Write or call the American College of Physicians and the American College of Surgeons. Have them send you a list of all the physicians in your area who are members of their associations. Report your findings in your school newspaper.

23. Do research to find out about the following types of health care facilities and the services they provide. Write a full description:
    • Birthing center
    • Convalescent home
    • Extended care center
    • Health center
    • Nursing home
    • Teaching hospital

• Trauma center
• Walk-in emergency center

24. Choose a health care career and talk with someone in that career. Write about the training or schooling, job outlook, employment practices, working conditions, earnings, advantages, and disadvantages of the career. Share the information you gather with the rest of your class.

Making Decisions About Health

25. You have had a medical emergency and had to spend a few days in the hospital. On admitting you, the desk clerk asks for your insurance and you present your card. Now you are checking out, and you have to stop by the cashier's office. The cashier tells you that your insurance does not cover the expenses you have just incurred. You are expected to pay $1,000 in fees within the next 90 days. Describe how you would handle this situation based on this chapter.

 **Go Online**

For more vocabulary practice, play the Concentration game at **glencoe.com**.

 **Fact or Fiction?**

Answers

1. False. You may need as many as five different kinds of insurance. Even then, specific medical needs might not be covered.
2. True.
3. True.

 Writing Paragraphs will vary.

---

your medical history and medications you are taking. **13.** Get a second opinion; operations are often not medically necessary. **14.** Send an itemized list of charges to your insurance company. **15.** Ask the American Medical Association or people you trust for recommendations. **16.** Blood and urine analysis or a chest X-ray exam. **17.** A history provides 70 percent of the information needed for an accurate diagnosis. **18–25.** Answers will vary.

Glossary/Glosario

A

abortion: a procedure to end a pregnancy before the fetus can live outside the uterus.

abstinence: refraining completely from sexual relations with other people.

accredited: approved.

acid rain: rain that carries acid air pollutants.

acne: a continuing condition of inflamed skin ducts and glands, with a buildup of oils under the skin, forming pimples.

acquired immune deficiency syndrome (AIDS): a transmissible viral disease of the immune system that creates a severe immune deficiency, and that leaves people defenseless against infections and cancer.

acromegaly (ack-ro-MEG-a-lee): a disease caused by above-normal levels of human growth hormone.

active abuse: abuse involving one person's aggression against another.

active ingredients: ingredients in a medicine that produce physical effects on the body.

active solar: using photovoltaic panels to generate electricity from sunlight.

acute stress: a temporary bout of stress that causes alertness or alarm, which prompts a person to deal with a specific event.

adapt: to change or adjust in order to accommodate new conditions.

added sugars: sugars and syrups added to a food for any purpose, such as to add sweetness.

addiction: a physical or psychological dependence on a particular substance, habit, or behavior.

aborto: procedimiento para poner término al embarazo antes de que el feto pueda vivir fuera del útero.

abstinencia: abstenerse totalmente de tener relaciones sexuales con otras personas.

acreditado: aprobado.

lluvia ácida: una lluvia que contiene contaminantes de aire ácido.

acné: una condición prolongada de inflamación de los poros y glándulas de la piel con una acumulación de aceites bajo la piel que causa granos pequeños.

síndrome de inmunodeficiencia adquirida (SIDA): una enfermedad viral fatal transmisible del sistema inmunológico que crea una deficiencia severa de inmunidad, la cual deja a las personas sin defensas contra las infecciones y el cáncer.

acromegalia: una enfermedad causada por niveles que sobrepasan los niveles normales de la hormona de crecimiento humano.

abuso activo: el abuso que involucra la agresión de una persona contra la otra.

ingredientes activos: los ingredientes en una medicina que producen efectos físicos en el cuerpo.

solar activo: la utilizacíon de paneles fotovoltágicos para generar electricidad de la luz solar.

estrés agudo: un incidente temporal de estrés que causa la vigilancia o la alarma para impulsar a la persona a enfrentar un evento especifico.

adaptarse: cambiar o ajustarse a fin de acomodarse a nuevas condiciones.

azúcares addicionales: los azúcares y los jarabes puesto en un alimento para cualquier razón, como agregar el dulzor.

adicción: una dependencia física o psicológica por una sustancia, hábito o comportamiento.

adenomas: cancers of glandular tissues such as the breast.

adolescence: the period of growth from the beginning of puberty to full maturity.

aerobic (air-ROE-bic): energy-producing processes that use oxygen.

afterbirth: the placenta and membranes expelled after the birth of a child.

aggressive: to be overly demanding of others.

AIDS dementia complex: the mental disorder resulting from an attack by HIV on the brain and nerves.

air bags: inflatable pillows designed to inflate upon impact.

air pollution: contamination of the air with gases or particles not normally found there.

alarm: the first phase of the stress response, in which you recognize that you are facing a change or challenge.

alcohol: a class of chemical compounds.

alcoholism: the disease characterized by loss of control over drinking and dependence on alcohol, both of which harm health, family relations, and social and work functioning.

alienation: withdrawing from others because of differences that cannot be resolved.

Alzheimer's disease: a brain disease of older people that brings mental confusion, inability to function, and in the final stage, death.

amino acids: building blocks of protein normally used to build tissues or, under some conditions, burned for energy.

amnesia: loss of memory.

amniocentesis (am-nee-oh-cen-TEE-sis): a test of fetal cells drawn by needle through the female's abdomen.

amniotic sac: a fluid-filled balloon that houses the developing fetus.

adenomas: cánceres de tejidos glandulares tales como el pecho.

adolescencia: el período de crecimiento entre el inicio de la pubertad y la plena madurez.

aeróbico: procesos de producción de energía que utilizan oxígeno.

secundinas: la placenta y las membranas expulsadas después del nacimiento de un bebé.

agresivo: ser demasiado exigente con otros.

complejo de demencia por SIDA: el desorden mental resultante de un ataque de VIH sobre el cerebro y los nervios.

almohadas inflables: almohadas inflables, diseñadas para inflarse por impacto.

contaminación ambiental: la contaminación del aire por gases o partículas que normalmente no se encuentran en éste.

alarma: la primera fase de la respuesta al estrés, en la cual reconoces que estás enfrentando un cambio o desafío.

alcohol: una clase de compuestos químicos.

alcoholismo: una enfermedad caracterizada por una pérdida de control sobre la bebida y dependencia en el alcohol, ambos de los cuales causan daño a la salud, las relaciones familiares y el desempeño social y laboral.

enajenación: separarse de otros debido a diferencias que no se pueden resolver.

enfermedad de Alzheimer: una enfermedad del cerebro en algunas personas ancianas que se manifiesta en confusión mental; incapacidad para actuar; y en las fases finales, la muerte.

aminoácidos: formas de proteína generalmente utilizados para construir tejidos, o bajo ciertas condiciones, quemar para obtener energía.

amnesia: pérdida de memoria.

amniocentesis: un examen de las células fetales obtenidas mediante la inserción de una aguja a través del abdomen de la mujer.

bolsa amniótica: la "bolsa de agua" en el útero, en el cual flota el feto.

Glossary/Glosario

amotivational syndrome: loss of ambition and drive characteristic of long-term abusers of marijuana.

amphetamines (am-FETT-ah-meenz): powerful, addictive stimulant drugs.

anaerobic (AN-air-ROE-bic): energy-producing processes that do not use oxygen.

anemia: reduced number or size of the red blood cells.

anesthetics (an-us-THET-icks): drugs that kill pain, with or without producing loss of consciousness.

aneurysm (AN-your-ism): the ballooning out of an artery wall at a point where it has grown weak.

angina: pain in the heart region caused by lack of oxygen.

anorexia nervosa: a disorder of self-starvation to the extreme.

antagonist: a drug that opposes the action of another drug.

antibiotics: drugs used to fight bacterial infection.

antibodies: large protein molecules produced to fight invaders.

antigens: foreign substances in the body, such as viruses or bacteria, that stimulate the immune system to produce antibodies.

antihistamines: drugs that counteract inflammation caused by histamine, one of the chemicals involved in allergic reactions.

antioxidant: a substance that defends the body against destructive compounds.

anxiety: an emotional state of high energy that triggers the stress response.

aorta (ay-OR-tah): the largest artery in the body.

appetite: the psychological desire to eat, a learned motivation and a positive sensation that accompanies the sight, smell, or thought of food.

síndrome amotivacional: la pérdida de ambición o ganas; una característica de los que abusan de la marihuana a largo plazo.

anfetaminas: fármacos estimulantes poderosamente adictivos.

anaeróbico: procesos de producción de energía que no utilizan oxígeno.

anemia: la reducción en el número o tamaño de los glóbulos rojos.

anestésicos: fármacos que eliminan el dolor, con o sin la pérdida de conciencia.

aneurisma: la formación de una bolsa en la pared arterial en un punto en el cual se ha debilitado.

angina: un dolor en la región del corazón causado por la falta de oxígeno.

anorexia nerviosa: un desorden de autoinanición extrema.

antagonista: un fármaco que se contrapone a la acción de otro fármaco.

antibióticos: fármacos utilizados para combatir la infección bacteriana.

anticuerpos: grandes moléculas de proteína producidas para combatir tejidos extraños.

antígenos: sustancias extrañas en el cuerpo, tales como virus o bacteria, que estimulan al sistema inmunológico a producir anticuerpos.

antihistamínico: fármacos que contrarrestan la inflamación causada por la histamina, una de las sustancias químicas que participan en las reacciones alérgicas.

antioxidante: una sustancia que defiende al cuerpo contra elementos destructivos.

ansiedad: un estado emocional de alta energía con que provóca una respuesta de estrés.

aorta: la arteria más grande del cuerpo.

apetito: el deseo psicológico de comer, una motivación aprendida y una sensación positiva que se produce al ver, oler o pensar en comida.

acquired immune deficiency syndrome (AIDS): a transmissable viral disease of the immune system that creates a severe immune deficiency and that leaves people defenseless against infection and cancer..

arteries: blood vessels that carry blood from the heart to the tissues.

arthritis: a painful inflammation of the joints caused by infection, body chemistry, injury, or other causes.

artificial heart: a pump designed to fit into the human chest cavity and perform the heart's function of pumping blood around the body.

aspirin: a drug that relieves fever, pain, and inflammation.

assertive: to possess the characteristic of appropriately expressing feelings, wants, and needs while respecting those of others.

asthma: difficulty breathing, with wheezing sounds from the chest caused by air rushing through narrowed air passages.

atherosclerosis (ATH-uh-roh-scler-OH-sis): a disease characterized by plaques along the inner walls of the arteries.

atria: (singular, atrium) the two upper chambers of the heart.

síndrome de inmunodeficiencia adquirida (SIDA): una enfermedad viral transmisible del sistema inmune que crea una deficiencia inmune severa y que deja la persona indefensa contra la infección y el cáncer.

arterias: los vasos sanguíneos que transportan la sangre desde el corazón a los tejidos.

artritis: una dolorosa inflamación de las articulaciones causada por infección, el organismo, lesiones u otras causas.

corazón artificial: una bomba diseñada para encajar en la cavidad pectoral del cuerpo humano y realizar la función de bombeo de la sangre a todo el cuerpo.

aspirina: un fármaco que alivia la fiebre y la inflamación.

asertivo: poseer la característica de expresar apropiadamente sus sentimientos y necesidades mientras que respeta los de otros.

asma: dificultad para respirar, produciendo un sonido sibilante desde el pecho causado por el paso del aire a través de conductos respiratorios que se han reducido en tamaño.

arteriosclerosis: una enfermedad caracterizada por placas a lo largo de las paredes interiores de las arterias.

aurículas cardiacas: (singular, atrio) los dos compartimientos superiores del corazón.

B

B cells: lymphocytes that make antibodies.

bacteria: microscopic, single-celled organisms capable of causing disease.

barbiturates: depressant drugs that slow the activity of the central nervous system.

barrier methods: contraceptive methods that physically or chemically obstruct the travel of sperm toward the ovum.

basal energy: the total of all the energy needed to support the chemical activities of the cells and to sustain life.

células B: los linfocitos que producen los anticuerpos.

bacteria: organismos unicelulares microscópicos capaces de causar enfermedades.

barbitúricos: fármacos depresivos que reducen la actividad del sistema nervioso central.

métodos de barrera: método anticonceptivo que física o químicamente obstruyen el desplazamiento de la esperma hacia el óvulo.

energía basal: la suma de la energía necesaria para mantener las actividades químicas de las células y para mantener la vida.

Glossary/Glosario

behavior modification: changing one's choices or actions by manipulating the cues that trigger the actions, the actions themselves, or the consequences of the actions.

behavior therapy: therapy in which a therapist helps a person break from an unhealthy pattern of behavior through a system of rewards and desensitization.

benign (be-NINE): noncancerous, not harmful.

beta-carotene: an orange vegetable pigment that the body can change into the active form of vitamin A.

binge drinking: consuming five or more drinks within a few hours' time.

binge eating: overeating to an extreme degree.

binge eating disorder (BED): repeated binge eating, but not followed by vomiting.

biodegradable: able to decompose.

bipolar disorder: extreme highs and lows of emotion.

birth defects: physical abnormalities present from birth.

bisexual: being sexually attracted to members of both sexes.

blackhead: an open pimple with dark skin pigments in its opening.

blackouts: episodes of amnesia regarding periods of time while drinking.

blood: the thick, red fluid that flows through the body's blood vessels and transports gases, nutrients, wastes, and other important substances around the body.

body composition: the proportion of lean tissue as compared with fat tissue in the body.

body image: the way a person thinks his or her body looks.

body mass index (BMI): an indicator of overweight or underweight based on a person's weight for height.

modificación de la conducta: un cambio de las decisiones o acciones de la persona mediante el manejo de señales que causan las acciones, las acciones en sí, o las consecuencias de las acciones.

terapia de conducta: la terapia en la que un terapeuta ayuda a una persona a parar la conducta poco sano por un sistema de recompensas y desensibilizacíon.

benigno: no canceroso, no dañino.

beta-caroteno: un pigmento vegetal color naranja que el cuerpo puede convertir a una forma activa de la vitamina A.

borrachera: consumiendo cinco o más bebidas alcohólicas dentro de tiempo de algunas horas.

ingesta excesiva de alimentos: comer en exceso a un grado extremo.

trastorno de ingesta excesiva de alimentos: ingesta repetida de grandes cantidades de alimentos, pero no seguido por vómitos.

biodegradable: que se puede descomponer.

trastorno bipolar: los extremos de la emoción alta y baja.

defectos de nacimiento: anormalidades físicas presentes desde el nacimiento.

bisexual: atracción sexual por miembros de ambos sexos.

puntos negros: una espinilla abierta con pigmentación oscura en la abertura.

desmayo: episodios de amnesia durante períodos de tiempo mientras se bebe.

sangre: el líquido espeso y rojo que fluye a través de los vasos sanguíneos del cuerpo y transporta gases, nutrientes, desechos y otras sustancias importantes a través del cuerpo.

composición corporal: la proporcion de tejido magro en comparación de los tejidos adiposos del cuerpo.

imagen corporal: la manera en que una persona piensa que su cuerpo luce.

índice de masa corporal (IMC): un indicador de peso excesivo o insuficiente basado en el peso y la altura de una persona.

body systems: groups of related organs that work together to perform major body functions.

botulin toxin: a potent poison produced by bacteria in sealed cans, plastic packs, or jars of food.

botulism: the often fatal condition of poisoning with the botulin toxin.

brain death: irreversible, total loss of higher brain function.

brand names: the names companies give to drugs.

breathalyzer test: a test of the alcohol level in a person's breath, which reflects the blood level of alcohol.

breech birth: a birth in which the infant is born in a position other than the normal headfirst position.

bronchi (BRONK-eye): the two main airways in the lungs.

bronchitis: a respiratory disorder with irritation of the bronchi; thickened mucus; and deep, harsh coughing.

bulimia: repeated binge eating usually followed by vomiting.

sistemas corporales: grupos de órganos relacionados que trabajan en conjunto para realizar las principales funciones del organismo.

toxina botulínica: un veneno potente producido por bacteria en latas cerradas, envases de plástico o frascos de alimentos.

botulismo: la condición, a menudo fatal, de envenenamiento por la toxina botulínica.

muerte cerebral: la pérdida total e irreversible de las funciones cerebrales superiores.

nombres comerciales: los nombres que las empresas dan a los fármacos.

prueba del alcoholímetro: la medición del nivel de alcohol en el aliento de la persona, lo cual refleja el nivel de alcohol en la sangre.

parto de nalgas: un parto en el cual el lactante nace en una posición diferente a la normal de cabeza primero.

bronquios: los dos conductos respiratorios principales en los pulmones.

bronquitis: un trastorno respiratorio con irritación de los bronquios, mucosa espesa y una tos profunda y ronca.

bulimia: la ingesta insaciable de alimentos, generalmente seguido por vómitos.

C
---

caffeine: a mild stimulant of the central nervous system (brain and spinal cord) found in common foods, beverages, and medicines.

calisthenics: exercise routines for strength conditioning that use the parts of the body as weights.

calorie: units used to measure energy.

cancer: a disease in which abnormal cells multiply out of control, spread into surrounding tissues and other body parts, and disrupt normal functioning of one or more organs.

capillaries: the smallest blood vessels, which connect the smallest arteries with the smallest veins.

cafeína: un estimulante leve del sistema nervioso central (cerebro y médula espinal) encontrado en alimentos comunes, bebidas y medicinas.

calistenia: rutinas de ejercicios para acondicionamiento de la resistencia que utiliza las partes del cuerpo como pesas.

caloría: la unidad utilizada para medir la energía.

cáncer: una enfermedad en la cual las células anormales se multiplican sin control, se esparcen a los tejidos vecinos y a otras partes del organismo y perturban el funcionamiento normal de uno o más órganos.

capilares: los vasos sanguíneos más pequeños, los cuales conectan las arterias más pequeñas con las venas más pequeñas.

Glossary/Glosario

carbohydrates: a class of nutrients that include sugars, starches, and fiber.

carbon monoxide: a deadly gas, formed during the burning of tobacco.

carcinogens: cancer-causing agents.

carcinomas: cancers that arise in the skin, body chamber linings, or glands.

cardiopulmonary resuscitation (CPR): a technique of maintaining blood and oxygen flow through the body of a person whose heart and breathing have stopped.

cardiovascular disease (CVD): a general term for all diseases of the heart and blood vessels.

cardiovascular endurance: the ability of the heart and lungs to sustain effort over a long time.

cardiovascular system: the system of structures that circulate blood and lymph throughout the body.

cavity: a hole in a tooth caused by decay.

cells: the smallest units in which independent life can exist.

centenarians: people who have reached the age of 100 years old or older.

cerebral thrombosis: when a vessel that feeds the brain is closed by a stationary clot.

cervical cap: a rubber cap that fits over the cervix, used with spermicide to prevent conception.

cesarean (si-ZAIR-ee-un) section: surgical childbirth in which the infant is lifted through an incision in the woman's abdomen.

chambers: large, hollow areas that receive incoming blood from the lungs and tissues and pump it out again through arteries.

chancre (SHANG-ker): a hard, painful sore.

chemotherapy: the administration of drugs that harm cancer cells, but that do not harm the patient as much as the disease does.

carbohidratos: una clase de nutrientes que incluye el azúcar, el almidón y la fibra.

monóxido de carbono: un gas letal creado durante al quemar tabaco.

carcinógenos: los agentes que causan cáncer.

carcinomas: tipos de cáncer que surgen en la piel, en el revestimiento de las cámaras del cuerpo o en las glándulas.

resucitación cardiopulmonar (RCP): una técnica para mantener el flujo de la sangre y el oxígeno a través del cuerpo de una persona cuyo corazón y respiración se ha detenido.

enfermedad cardiovascular: un término general utilizado para todas las enfermedades del corazón y los vasos sanguíneos.

resistencia cardiovascular: la habilidad del corazón y los pulmones para soportar el esfuerzo durante un tiempo prolongado.

sistema cardiovascular: el sistema de estructura que hace circular la sangre y línfas a través de todo el cuerpo.

carie: el orificio en un diente causado por la descomposición.

células: las unidades más pequeñas en las cuales puede existir la vida independiente.

centenarios: personas que han alcanzado la edad de 100 años o más.

trombosis cerebral: la obstrucción total de un vaso que alimenta el cerebro por un coágulo estacionario.

tapa cervical: tapa de caucho, utilizada con espermicida, que encaja sobre la cérvix para prevenir la concepción.

parto por cesárea: parto quirúrgico, en el cual el bebé se extrae a través de un corte realizado en el abdomen de la mujer.

cámaras: cavidades grandes y huecas del corazón que reciban la sangre que llega de los pulmones y los tejidos y la envían hacia fuera nuevamente.

chancro: una lesión dolorsa y dura.

quimioterapia: la administración de fármacos que dañan las células del cáncer, pero que no dañan al paciente tanto como la enfermedad.

child abuse: verbal, psychological, physical, or sexual assault on a child.

chlamydia (cla-MID-ee-uh): an infection of the reproductive tract, with or without symptoms.

cholesterol: a type of fat made by the body from saturated fat.

chromosomes: slender bodies inside the cell's nucleus which carry the genes.

chronic: a disease or condition that develops slowly, shows little change, and lasts a long time.

chronic obstructive pulmonary disease (COPD): a term for several diseases that interfere with breathing.

chronic stress: unrelieved stress that continues to tax a person's resources to the point of exhaustion.

chronological age: age as measured in years from date of birth.

cilia: hairlike structures extending from the surface of cells.

clique: a peer group that rejects newcomers and judges both their members and nonmembers harshly.

club drugs: a wide variety of drugs abused by young people at dance clubs and all-night dance parties.

codeine: a narcotic drug that is commonly used for suppressing coughs.

codependent: focused on the needs of others to the extent that the person's own needs are neglected.

colostrum (co-LAHS-trum): a substance rich in antibodies that protects the infant against diseases.

combination pill: an oral contraceptive that contains progestin and synthetic estrogen.

comedogenic: acne-causing.

commitment: a decision adhered to for the long term.

communication: a two-way exchange of ideas or thoughts.

abuso infantil: agresión verbal, física o sexual contra un niño(a).

chlamydia: una enfermedad del tracto reproductivo, con o sin síntomas.

colesterol: un tipo de grasa fabricado por el cuerpo de grasas saturadas.

cromosomas: cuerpos delgados dentro del núcleo de la célula, los cuales contienen los genes.

crónico: una enfermedad o condición que se desarrolla lentamente, muestra poco cambio y dura mucho tiempo.

enfermedad pulmonar obstructiva crónica (EPOC): un término para varias enfermedades que interfieren con la respiración.

estrés crónico: un estrés sin alivio que continúa usando exageradamente la energía de una persona hasta que se quede agotado.

edad cronológica: la edad medida en años desde la fecha del nacimiento.

cilios: estructuras de tipo velloso que se extienden desde la superficie de células.

pandilla: un grupo de compañeros que rechazan a los recién llegados y que juzga duramente tanto a los miembros como a los no miembros.

drogas de moda: una gran variedad de drogas abusadas por jovenes en moda y bailes.

codeína: un fármaco narcótico utilizado comúnmente para suprimir la tos.

codependiente: estár tan enfocada en las necesidades de otros que desatiende sus propias necesidades.

calostro: una sustancia rico en anticuerpos que protege al bebé contra enfermedades.

píldora combinada: anticonceptivo oral que contiene progestina y estrógeno sintético.

comedogénico: que produce acné.

compromiso: una decisión que se mantiene a largo plazo.

comunicación: un intercambio de ideas o pensamientos.

compost: rotted vegetable matter, used as fertilizer.

conception: the union of an ovum and a sperm that starts a new individual.

conditioning: the hundreds of small changes that cells make in response to physical activity that make the body more able to do work.

conflict: a struggle or opposition between people, especially when people compete for something in the belief that only one can have what he or she wants, at the expense of the other.

confrontation: an interaction in which one person expresses feelings to another.

congenital (con-JEN-ih-tal): present from birth.

connective tissues: fluid, gelatin-like, fibrous, or strap-like materials that bind, support, or protect other body tissues.

contraception: any method of preventing conception.

coping devices: safe, short-term methods of managing stress, such as displacement or venting.

coronary arteries: the two arteries that supply blood to the heart muscle.

coronary artery bypass surgery: a surgery to provide an alternate route for blood to reach heart tissue, bypassing a blocked coronary artery.

coronary thrombosis: the closing off of a vessel that feeds the heart muscle by a stationary clot or thrombus.

cortex: the outermost layer of your brain.

critical periods: periods during development when a body organ is especially sensitive to harmful factors.

critical phase: when plaques cover more than half of the inner surfaces of the arteries.

abono: una materia vegetal descompuesta utilizada como fertilizante.

concepción: la unión de un óvulo y un espermatozoide que genera un nuevo individuo.

condicionamiento: pequeños cambios que las células realizan en respuesta a la actividad física que hacen posible que el cuerpo esté más propenso a trabajar.

conflicto: una lucha u oposición entre personas, especialmente cuando las personas compiten por algo en la creencia que solamente una de ellas puede tener lo que él o ella desea, a costa de la otra.

enfrentamiento: una interacción en la cual una persona expresa sus sentimientos a otra.

congénito: presente desde el nacimiento.

tejidos conjuntivos: materiales de consistencia fluida, gelatinosa, fibrosa o de bandas que ligan, sostienen o protegen otros tejidos del organismo.

anticonceptivos: cualquier método para prevenir la concepción.

métodos de sobrellevar el afrontamiento: métodos seguros y breves que ayudan manejar el estrés, tales como el desplazamiento o la ventilación.

arterias coronarias: las dos arterias que suministran sangre al músculo del corazón.

cirugía de derivación coronaria: cirugía para proporcionar una ruta alterna para que la sangre pueda llegar a los tejidos del corazón, evitando pasar por una arteria coronaria obstruida.

trombosis coronaria: la obstrucción de un vaso que alimenta el músculo del corazón por un coágulo estacionario o trombo.

corteza: la capa externa del cerebro.

períodos críticos: los períodos durante el desarrollo cuando uno de los órganos del cuerpo se encuentra especialmente susceptible a factores dañinos.

fase crítica: cuando las placas cubren más de la mitad de las superficies internas de las arterias.

crowning: the stage in which the top of the baby's head is first seen.

cruciferous vegetables: vegetables of the cabbage family.

cults: groups of people who share intense admiration or adoration of a particular person or principle.

cuticles: the borders of hardened skin at the bases of fingernails.

cyst: an enlarged, deep pimple.

coronamiento: el momento en que la parte superior de la cabeza del bebé se ve por primera vez.

vegetales crucíferos: vegetales de la familia de la repollo.

sectas: grupos de personas que comparten una intensa admiración o adoración por una persona o principio en particular.

cutículas: los bordes de piel endurecida en la base de las uñas.

quiste: una espinilla abultada y profunda.

D

---

date: to engage in social events designed to allow people to explore their compatibility and get to know each other.

date rape: sexual assault by a known person in a dating situation.

day care: supervision, usually at a facility, for preschool children or older adults who must be supervised during daytime working hours.

defense mechanisms: automatic, subconscious reactions to emotional injury.

deficiency: too little of a nutrient in the body.

dehydration: loss of water.

delirium: a state of mental confusion usually with hallucinations and continual movement.

denial: refusal to believe the facts of a circumstance.

dental plaque: a sticky material on the surface of the teeth.

dentin: the tooth's softer, middle layer.

depression: a persistent feeling of apathy, hopelessness, or despair.

dermatologist: a physician who specializes in treating conditions of the skin.

deviant: outside the normal system.

cita: la participación en eventos sociales diseñados para permitir que las personas se conozcan unos a otros.

violación por novio o conocido: agresión sexual por una persona conocida en una situación de una cita.

guardería: supervisión, generalmente en un establecimiento, para niños en edad preescolar o adultos mayores que deben estar bajo supervisión durante las horas de trabajo diario.

mecanismos de defensa: reacciones automáticas y subconscientes ante el daño emocional.

deficiencia: la falta de un nutriente en el cuerpo.

deshidratación: la pérdida de agua.

delirio: un estado de confusión mental generalmente con alucinaciones y movimiento continuo.

negación: no poder creer los hechos de una circunstancia.

placa dental: la acumulación de un material pegajoso sobre la superficie de los dientes.

dentina: la capa intermedia blanda del diente.

depresión: un sentimiento persistente de la apatía, desesperanza, o desespera.

dermatólogo: un médico que se especializa en el tratamiento de enfermedades de la piel.

desviado: fuera del sistema normal.

diabetes mellitus: a condition of abnormal use of glucose, usually caused by too little insulin or lack of response to insulin.

diabetic coma: a loss of consciousness due to uncontrolled diabetes.

diaphragm: a dome that fits over the cervix and holds spermicidal cream or jelly against the uterine entrance to block the passage of sperm.

diastolic pressure: the blood pressure during that part of the heartbeat when ventricles are relaxing.

diet pills: medications that reduce the appetite or otherwise promote weight loss.

digestion: the breaking down of food into nutrients the body can use.

dilation stage: the stage of childbirth during which the cervix is opening.

dioxins: deadly pollutants formed when chlorine bleach reacts with other compounds.

discipline: the shaping of behavior by way of rewards and/or punishments.

disinfectants: chemicals that kill pathogens on surfaces.

displacement: transferring the energy of suffering into something else.

diuretic: a drug that causes the body to lose fluids.

DNA (deoxyribonucleic acid): the genetic material of cells which serves as a blueprint for making all of the proteins a cell needs to make exact copies of itself.

douches: preparations sold to cleanse the vagina.

Down syndrome: an inherited condition of physical deformities and mental retardation.

drink: the amount of a beverage that delivers a half ounce of pure ethanol.

drives: motivations that are not learned.

diabetes mellitus: una condición de uso anormal de la glucosa, generalmente causado por muy poca insulina o la falta de respuesta a la insulina.

coma diabético: la pérdida del conocimiento debido a una diabetes no controlada.

diafragma: domo que se coloca sobre la cérvix y contiene crema o jalea espermicida para bloquear el ingreso de la esperma.

presión diastólica: la presión sanguínea durante la parte del latido del corazón cuando los ventrículos están relajados.

pastillas para adelgazar: aquellos medicamentos que suprimen el apetito o de alguna manera promueven la pérdida de peso.

digestión: el proceso por el cual el cuerpo convierte los alimentos en nutrientes que el cuerpo puede utilizar.

nivel de dilatación: la etapa durante el parto en que la cérvix se está abriendo.

dioxinas: contaminantes letales que se forman cuando el cloro reacciona con otros compuestos.

disciplina: la formación del comportamiento mediante recompensas y/o castigos.

desinfectantes: compuestos químicos que matan los patógenos en la superficie.

desplazamiento: la transferencia de la energía del sufrimiento hacía otra cosa.

diurético: un fármaco que causa que el cuerpo pierda líquido.

ADN (ácido desoxirribonucleico): el material genético de las células que sirve de programa para elaborar todas las proteínas que la célula necesita para efectuar copias exactas de sí misma.

ducha vaginal: preparados que se venden para limpiar la vagina.

síndrome de Down: una condición congénita de deformación física y retardo mental.

bebida: la cantidad de una bebida que suministra una media onza de etanol puro.

impulsos: motivaciones que no son aprendidas.

driving while intoxicated (DWI): driving with alcohol or any mind-altering substance in the bloodstream.

drug abuse: the deliberate taking of a drug for anything other than a medical purpose.

drug addiction: a physical or psychological need for higher and higher doses of a drug.

drug misuse: the taking of a drug for its medically intended purpose, but not in the appropriate amount, frequency, strength, or manner.

drug-resistant: pathogens that have lost their sensitivity to particular drugs.

drugs: substances taken into the body that change one or more of the body's functions.

drug synergy: the combined action of two drugs that is greater than the sum of their individual actions.

drug trafficker: a person involved in the transport and sales of illegal drugs.

drug use: the taking of a drug for its medically intended purpose, and in the appropriate amount, frequency, strength, and manner.

duration: the length of time spent in each session of physical activity.

dysfunctional family: a family with abnormal or impaired ways of coping that injure the self-esteem and emotional health of family members.

dysphoria: unpleasant feelings that occur when endorphins are lacking.

conducir en estado de embriaguez: (DWI por sus siglos en Ingles) conducir un vehículo bajo la influencia de alcohol o cualquier sustancia en la circulación sanguínea que altera la mente.

abuso de las drogas: la ingesta deliberada de una droga por un propósito no medicinal.

drogadicción: una necesidad física o psicológica de una droga en dosis cada vez más altas.

mal uso de una droga: el uso de un fármaco para el propósito medicinal para el cual fue diseñado, pero no en la dosis, frecuencia, concentración o forma adecuada.

resistente a la droga: un término que describe los patógenos que han perdido su sensibilidad a ciertos fármacos.

drogas: sustancias que cuando ingresan al cuerpo cambian una o más de las funciones del cuerpo.

sinergia farmacológica: la acción combinada de dos fármacos que es mejor de la acción de cualquiera de las drogas por sí sola.

narcotraficante: una persona que está involucrada en el transporte y venta de drogas ilegales.

uso de drogas: el uso de un fármaco para el propósito medicinal para el cual fue diseñado, en la dosis, frecuencia, concentración o forma adecuada.

duración: la cantidad de tiempo que se pasa en cada sesión de ejercicio.

familia disfuncional: una familia con formas de afrontamiento anormales o deterioradas que dañan la autoestima y la salud emocional de los miembros de la familia.

disforia: un sentimiento desagradable que ocurre cuando hay falta de endorfina.

E

E. coli: a toxin-producing bacteria that can cause food-borne illness.

eating disorders: extreme, unhealthy eating habits, often related to an obsession with weight or appearance.

E. coli: una bacteria que produce toxinas y que puede causor la enfermedad alimenticia.

trastornos alimentarios: la ingesta anormal de alimentos originado por causa de una obsesión con el peso o la apariencia.

effective: having the medically intended effect.

eficaz: tener el efecto medicinal propuesto.

effectiveness: how well a contraceptive method or device prevents pregnancy, expressed as a percentage.

efectividad: la efectividad con que un método o elemento anticonceptivo evita el embarazo, expresado en porcentajes.

ejaculation: the expelling of semen from the penis, brought about by the involuntary muscular contractions of orgasm.

eyaculación: la expulsión de semen por el pene, ocasionado por las contracciones musculares involuntarias del orgasmo.

elasticity: the characteristic of a tissue's being easily stretched or bent and able to return to its original size and shape.

elasticidad: la característica de un tejido para estirarse o doblarse y luego tener la capacidad de volver a su tamaño y forma original.

elder abuse: verbal, psychological, physical, or sexual assault on an older adult.

abuso del adulto mayor: la agresión verbal, física o sexual contra una persona de edad.

electrocardiogram: a record of the electrical activity of the heart that, if abnormal, may indicate heart disease.

electrocardiograma: registro de la actividad eléctrica del corazón que, si es anormal, podría indicar enfermedades cardiacas.

electrolytes: minerals that dissolve in body fluids and carry electrical charges.

electrolitos: minerales que se devuelven en líquidos de cuerpo y que llevan cargas eléctricas.

embolism: sudden closure of a blood vessel by a traveling blood clot.

embolismo: la obstrucción repentina de un vaso sanguíneo por un coágulo de sangre no estacionario.

embolus: a clot that breaks loose and travels through the bloodstream.

émbolo: un coágulo que se desprende y viaja a través de la corriente sanguínea.

embryo: the developing infant during the third through eighth week after conception.

embrión: el bebé en desarrollo durante la tercera a la octava semana posterior a la concepción.

emergency medical service (EMS): a team of people who are trained to respond in emergencies, and who can be contacted through a single dispatcher.

servicios médicos de emergencias (SME): un equipo de personas entrenadas para responder a emergencias y que puede ser contactado a través de un solo despachador.

emerging diseases: diseases that appear in the population for the first time, or that suddenly re-emerge.

enfermedades emergentes: las enfermedades que parecen en la población por primera vez, o que vuelven de repente.

emotion: a feeling that occurs in response to an event as experienced by an individual.

emoción: el sentimiento que ocurre en respuesta a un evento experimentado por un individuo.

emotional health: the state of being free of mental disturbances that limit functioning.

salud emocional: el estado de estar libre de trastornos mentales que limitan las funciones.

emotional intelligence (EQ): the ability to recognize and appropriately express one's emotions in a way that enhances living.

inteligencia emocional (IE): la capacidad de reconocer y de expresar apropiadamente las emociones de si mismo en una manera que mejora la vida.

emphysema: a disease of the lungs in which many small, flexible air sacs burst and form a few large, rigid air pockets.

empty calories: foods that contribute much energy (calories) but too little of the nutrients.

enabling: misguided "helping."

enamel: the tooth's tough outer layer.

endorphins: chemicals in the brain that produce feelings of pleasure in response to a variety of activities.

energy: the capacity to do work or produce heat.

engorgement: swelling.

environment: everything "outside" the living organism—air, water, soil, other organisms, and forms of radiation.

environmental tobacco smoke (ETS): the combination of exhaled mainstream smoke and sidestream smoke that enters the air.

ephedrine: a stimulant added to look-alikes and diet pills, and found in herbs such as ma huang.

epidemic: an infection that spreads rapidly through a population, affecting many people at the same time.

episiotomy: a surgical cut made in the vagina during childbirth when the vagina cannot stretch enough without tearing to allow the baby to pass.

erection: the state of a normally soft tissue when it fills with blood and becomes firm.

essential amino acids: amino acids that cannot be made by the body.

estrogen: a hormone that regulates the ovulatory cycle in females.

ethanol: the active ingredient of alcoholic beverages.

euphoria: a sense of great well-being and pleasure brought on by some drugs.

euthanasia: allowing a person to die by choosing not to employ life-support equipment or the removal of life-support equipment.

enfisema: una enfermedad de los pulmones en la cual muchos de los pequeños y flexibles sacos de aire se revientan y forman algunas bolsas de aire grandes y rígidas.

calorías vacías: los alimentos que aportan mucha energía (calorías) y pocos nutrientes.

facilitar: "ayuda" mal guiada.

esmalte: la capa dura exterior del diente.

endorfínas: los elementos químicos del cerebro que producen sentimientos de placer en respuesta a una serie de actividades.

energía: la capacidad de trabajar o producir calor.

congestionamiento: hinchazón.

ambiente: todo lo que queda "fuera" de los organismos vivientes - el aire, agua, tierra, otros organismos y formas de radiación.

humo ambiental de cigarro (AHC): la combinación del humo principal exhalado y el humo indirecto que ingresa al air.

efedrina: un estimulante que se agrega a las pastillas para adelgazar y que se encuentra en yerbas tales como el ma huang.

epidemia: una infección que se esparce rápidamente a través de la población, afectando a muchas personas a la vez.

episiotomía: un corte quirúrgico hecho en la vagina durante el parto cuando la vagina no puede expandirse lo suficiente sin desgarrarse para permitir el paso del bebé.

erección: el estado en el cual un tejido generalmente blando, se llena de sangre y se pone firme.

aminoácidos esenciales: aminoácidos que no pueden ser elaborados por el organismo.

estrógeno: una hormona que, en la mujer, regula el ciclo de ovulación.

etanol: el ingrediente activo en bebidas alcohólicas.

euforia: una sensación de inmenso bienestar y placer que dan ciertas drogas.

eutanasia: permitir que una persona muera al elegir no utilizar equipos de soporte vital o el retiro de los equipos de soporte vital.

Glossary/Glosario

excitement phase: the early state of sexual arousal.

exercise physiology: the study of how the body works and changes in response to exercise.

exhaustion: a harmful third phase of the stress response.

expulsion stage: the stage of childbirth during which the uterine contractions push the infant through the birth canal.

external pressures: messages from society, peers, and others that pressure people to be sexually active.

excitación: se utiliza para describir una fase del coito, la fase inicial.

fisiología del ejercicio: el estudio del funcionamiento y los cambios experimentados por el cuerpo en respuesta al ejercicio.

agotamiento: la tercera etapa dañina de la respuesta al estrés.

fase de expulsión: la fase, durante el parto en la cual las contracciones uterinas impulsan al bebé a través del canal del parto.

presiones externas: los mensajes provenientes de la sociedad, los compañeros y otros, que presiona a las personas a tener relaciones sexuales.

F

false labor: warm-up contractions that many experience before the birth process.

family: a group of people who are related by adoption, blood, or marriage, and are committed to each other.

family identity: a unique sense of belonging together as a unit.

fats: an energy source for the body.

fat-soluble: able to dissolve in fat and tending to remain in the body.

fatty acids: building blocks of fat that supply energy fuel for most of the body's cells.

fee-for-service system: a system of paying for health care in which clients pay individual fees for the services they receive.

female condom: a soft, thin plastic tube with two end rings—one to fit over the cervix and one to serve as an anchor outside the entrance to the vagina.

femininity: traits, including biological and social traits, associated with being female.

fertility awareness method: a method of charting ovulation.

parto falso: las contracciones preliminares experimentadas por muchas mujeres antes de que se inicie el trabajo de parto.

familia: un grupo de personas que se relacionan entre sí por adopción, sangre o matrimonio y están comprometidas entre sí.

identidad familiar: un sentido único de pertenecer juntos como una unidad.

grasas: una fuente de energía para el cuerpo.

soluble en grasa: capaz de disolver en la grasa y quedarse en el cuerpo.

ácidos grasos: formas de grasa que suministran energía calórica a la mayoría de las células del cuerpo.

sistema de pago por visita: el sistema para el pago de los servicios de salud en el cual los clientes pagan tarifas individuales por los servicios que reciben.

condón femenino: un tubo de plástico suave y delgado con dos anillos en los extremos—uno que encaja sobre la cérvix y uno que sirve como ancla fuera de la entrada a la vagina.

feminidad: las características, incluyendo características biológicas y sociales, asociadas con el hecho de ser mujer.

métodos anticonceptivos de abstinencia en días fértiles: un método de graficar la ovulación.

fertilization: the joining of an ovum and a sperm.

fetal alcohol effect (FAE): a subtle version of fetal alcohol syndrome (FAS), with hidden defects including learning disabilities, behavioral abnormalities, and motor impairments.

fetal alcohol syndrome (FAS): a cluster of birth defects including permanent mental and physical retardation and facial abnormalities seen in children born to mothers who abuse alcohol during pregnancy.

fetus: the developing infant from the ninth week after the last menstrual period until birth.

feud: a bitter, continuing hostility, often involving groups of people.

fiber: indigestible substances in foods, made mostly of carbohydrate.

first aid: medical help given before the person is transported to the hospital or treatment center.

fish oil: a polyunstaturated fat from certain fish, thought to be necessary for health.

fitness: the characteristics of the body that enable it to perform physical activity.

flexibility: the ability to bend joints without injury.

follicles: vessel-like structures in the skin that contain the oil glands, the muscles that control hair movement and the roots of hairs.

food-borne illness: illness caused by pathogens or their toxins consumed in food.

formaldehyde: a substance related to alcohol.

fracture: a break in a bone.

free radicals: substances that trigger damaging chain reactions in the cells of the body.

fertilización: la unión de un óvulo con un espermatozoide.

efecto de alcoholismo fetal (EAF): una versión más sutil del síndrome de alcoholismo fetal (SAF), con efectos ocultos, incluyendo discapacidad de aprendizaje, anormalidades del comportamiento y deficiencias motoras.

síndrome de alcoholismo fetal (SAF): un grupo de defectos de nacimiento, incluyendo el retardo permanente mental y físico y las anormalidades faciales, que se observa en niños cuyas madres han abusado del alcohol durante el embarazo.

feto: el bebé en desarrollo desde la novena semana posterior a la concepción hasta el nacimiento.

pelea: una hostilidad amarga, de continuación, implicando a menudo a los grupos de personas.

fibra: sustancias no digeribles en los alimentos, compuestos generalmente de carbohidratos.

primeros auxilios: asistencia médica dada de inmediato antes que la víctima sea transportada a un hospital.

aceite de pez: una grasa poliinsaturada de cierto pez, considerado necesario para la salud.

estado físico: las características del cuerpo que le permiten realizar actividad física.

flexibilidad: la habilidad de doblar las articulaciones sin sufrir daños.

folículos: estructuras de la piel similares a vasos que contienen las glándulas sebáceas, los músculos que controlan el movimiento del cabello y las raíces del cabello.

enfermedades de origin alimenticio: las enfermedades causados por patógenos o sus toxinas que son consumidos en el alimento.

formaldehído: una sustancia relacionada con el alcohol.

fractura: una rotura en un hueso.

radicales libres: substances que provocan las reacciones perjudiciales en las células del cuerpo.

frequency: the number of activity units per unit of time.

frostbite: the formation of ice crystals in body parts exposed to temperatures below freezing.

frecuencia: el número de unidades de actividad por unidad de tiempo.

congelación: la formación de cristales de hielo en partes del cuerpo expuestas a temperaturas por debajo del nivel de congelación.

G

gangs: groups that exist largely to express aggression against other groups.

pandillas: grupos que tienen como objetivo principal expresar su agresión hacia otros grupos.

gateway drug: a drug whose abuse is likely to lead to abuse of other, more potent and dangerous drugs.

droga de entrada: una droga cuyo abuso es probable que conduzca al abuso de otras drogas más potentes y peligrosas.

gay: a general term referring to males who are homosexual.

homosexual: término general que se refiere a la homosexualidad, pero a menudo en referencia a hombres homosexuales.

gender: the classification of being male or female.

género: la clasificación de ser masculino o femenino.

gender identity: that part of a person's self-image that is determined by the person's gender.

identidad de género: esa parte de la autoimagen de una persona que está determinada por el sexo de la misma.

gender roles: roles assigned by society to people of each gender.

funciónes del género: los roles asignados por la sociedad a personas de cada sexo.

generic: the chemical names for drugs.

nombres genéricos: los nombres químicos de las drogas.

genes: the units of a cell's inheritance, which direct the making of equipment to do the cell's work.

genes: unidades de herencia de una célula que dirigen la elaboración del equipo que ejecuta el trabajo de una célula.

genetic counselor: an advisor who predicts and advises on the likelihood that congenital defects will occur in a family.

consejero genético: un consejero que predice y aconseja sobre la posibilidad de la ocurrencia de defectos congénitos en una familia.

genital herpes: a common, incurable STD caused by a virus that produces blisters.

herpes genital: una enfermedad común e incurable, transmitida sexualmente y causada por un virus que produce ampollas.

genital warts: contagious wartlike growths on infected areas, caused by human papilloma viruses.

verrugas genitales: formaciones contagiosas similares a las verrugas en las áreas infectadas, causadas por el virus del papiloma humano.

gestation: the period from the last menstrual period to birth.

gestación: el período comprendido desde la concepción hasta el nacimiento.

gland: an organ of the body that secretes one or more hormones in response to information about changing body conditions.

glándula: un órgano del cuerpo que secreta una o más hormonas en respuesta a la información sobre condiciones cambiantes del cuerpo.

global warming: warming of the planet, a trend that threatens life on Earth.

calentamiento global: el calentamiento del planeta, una tendencia que amenaza la vida sobre la tierra.

glucose: a simple form of carbohydrate which serves as the body's sugar.

glucosa: una forma simple de carbohidrato que sirve como el azúcar del cuerpo.

glycogen: the form in which the liver and muscles store glucose.

glicógeno: la forma en que el hígado y los músculos almacenan la glucosa.

gonorrhea: a bacterial STD that attacks many organs of the body when left untreated.

gonorrea: un ETS bacteriano que ataca muchos órganos del cuerpo sin tratarlo inmediatamente.

gram: a unit of weight, about $1/28^{th}$ of an ounce.

gramo: una unidad del peso, acerca de $1/28$ de una onza.

greenhouse effect: the heat-trapping effect of the glass in a greenhouse.

efecto invernadero: el efecto de conservación del calor efectuado por el vidrio de un invernadero.

grief: the emotional response to a major loss, such as the death of a loved one.

dolor: la reacción emocional a una pérdida inmensa, tal como la muerte de un querido.

grieve: to feel keen emotional pain and suffering over a loss.

lamentar: sentir un profundo dolor y sufrimiento emocional por una pérdida.

guilt: the normal feeling that arises from the conscience when a person acts against internal values.

culpabilidad: el sentimiento normal que surge de la conciencia cuando una persona actúa en contra de sus valores internos.

gum disease: the inflammation and degeneration of the pink tissue (gums) that is attached to the teeth and helps to hold them in place.

enfermedad de las encías: inflamación y degeneración del tejido rosado (encías) que está fijado a los dientes y ayuda a mantenerlos en su lugar.

H

hallucinations: false perceptions such as imagined sights, sounds, smells, or other feelings, sometimes brought on by drug abuse, sometimes by mental or physical illness.

alucinaciones: falsas percepciones, tales como vistas imaginadas, sonidos, olores, u otras sensaciones que ocurran después del uso ilícito de drogas, a veces por enfermedad mental o física.

hallucinogens: drugs that cause visions and other sensory illusions.

alucinógenos: drogas que pueden causar visiones y otras ilusiones sensoriales.

head lice: tiny, but visible, white parasitic insects that burrow into the skin or hairy body areas.

piojos: parásitos blancos pequeñísimos, pero visibles, que se introducen en las áreas de la piel o del cabello.

head restraints: high seatbacks or other devices attached to seats in cars at head level.

apoyo para la cabeza: asientos con respaldos altos u otros artefactos fijados a los asientos de los automóviles al nivel de la cabeza.

health: freedom from physical disease, poor physical condition, social maladjustment, and other negative states.

salud: libre de enfermedades físicas, condiciones físicas deficientes, desajuste social y otros estados negativos.

Glossary/Glosario

health care system: the total of all health-care providers and medical treatment facilities that work together to provide medical care to the population.

health maintenance organization (HMO): a group of physicians who practice together and who treat people's health problems under a prepayment plan.

heart attack: the event in which vessels that feed the heart muscle become blocked, causing tissue death.

heart murmur: a heart sound that reflects damaged or abnormal heart valves.

heart transplant: the surgical replacement of a diseased heart with a healthy one.

heat exhaustion: a serious stage of overheating which can lead to heat stroke.

heat stroke: a life-threatening condition that results from a buildup of body heat.

Heimlich maneuver: a technique of dislodging a particle that is blocking a person's airway.

hepatitis: a viral infection that causes inflammation of the liver.

hepatitis B: a viral STD that causes loss of liver function and severe liver disease.

heroin: a narcotic drug derived from morphine.

heterosexual: feeling sexual desire for persons of the other sex.

hierarchy: a ranking system in which each thing is placed above or below others.

high-density lipoproteins (HDLs): lipoproteins that carry fat and cholesterol away from the tissues (and from plaques) back to the liver for breakdown and removal from the body.

sistema de atención de salud: el conjunto de todos los proveedores de atención a la salud y centros de atención médica que trabajan unidos para dar atención médica a la población.

organización de mantenimiento de la salud: un grupo de médicos que trabajan juntos y que tratan los problemas de salud de otras personas bajo un plan de prepagos.

ataque al corazón: el evento en el cual los vasos que alimentan el músculo del corazón se obstruyen, causando la muerte del tejido.

murmullo cardíaco: un sonido del corazón que refleja que las válvulas del corazón están dañadas o anormales.

transplante de corazón: el reemplazo quirúrgico de un corazón enfermo por uno saludable.

agotamiento por calor: una seria etapa del sobre calentamiento que puede resultar en un golpe de calor.

insolación: una condición que amenaza la vida y que resulta como consecuencia de una acumulación de la temperatura corporal.

Maniobra de Heimlich: una técnica usada para desalojar lo que obstruye el conducto de aire de una persona.

hepatitis: una infeción viral que causa inflamación del hígado.

hepatitis B: una enfermedad viral transmisible por contacto sexual que ocasiona la pérdida de las funciones del hígado y enfermedad severa del hígado.

heroína: una droga narcótica obtenida de la morfina.

heterosexual: atracción sexual por miembros del sexo opuesto.

jerarquía: un sistema de clasificación en el cual cada cosa está colocada sobre o debajo de otras.

lipoproteínas de alta densidad (HDL): las lipoproteínas que transportan grasa y colesterol desde los tejidos (y desde las placas) hacía el hígado para su descomposición y eliminación del organismo.

high-risk pregnancy: a pregnancy more likely than others to have problems, such as premature delivery or a low birth weight.

histamine: a chemical that produces inflammation (swelling and irritation) of tissue.

history: an interview in which a health care professional asks about past experiences.

Hodgkin's lymphoma: a cancer that attacks people in early life and is treatable with radiation therapy.

homeostasis: the maintenance of a stable body environment, achieved as body systems adapt to changing conditions.

homophobia: an irrational fear and/or hatred of people who are homosexuals.

homosexual: feeling sexual desire for persons of the same sex.

hormonal system: the system of glands that control body functions in cooperation with the nervous system.

hormone: a chemical that serves as a messenger.

hospice: a support system for dying people and their families which helps the family let the person die at home with dignity and in comfort.

hot flashes: sudden waves of feeling hot all over, a symptom related to dilation of blood vessels in the skin, which is common during the transition into menopause.

human gene therapy: the use of genetic material to treat, cure, or prevent diseases such as heart disease and cancer.

human growth hormone: a nonsteroid hormone produced in the body that promotes growth.

human immunodeficiency virus (HIV): an abbreviation for human immunodeficiency virus, the virus that causes AIDS.

embarazo de alto riesgo: un embarazo con mayores probabilidades que otros de sufrir complicaciones, tales como un parto prematuro o un bajo peso de nacimiento.

histamina: una sustancia química que produce inflamación (hinchazón e irritación) de los tejidos.

historial médico: una entrevista en la cual un profesional del cuidado médico pregunta por experiencias anteriores.

linfoma de Hodgkin: un linfoma que ataca a las personas de temprana edad y es tratable con radioterapia.

homeostasis: el mantenimiento de un medio ambiente estable dentro del organismo que se logra cuando los sistemas corpóreos se adaptan a condiciones cambiantes.

homofobia: temor irracional y/o odio de los homosexuales.

homosexual: feeling sexual desire for persons of the same sex.

sistema hormonal: el sistema de glándulas que controlan las funciones del organismo en cooperación con el sistema nervioso.

hormona: una sustancia química que sirve como mensajero.

hospicio: un sistema de apoyo para personas en estado terminal y a sus familias, que ayuda a la familia para que deje que la persona muera en su hogar con dignidad y comodidad.

bochornos: sensación transitoria y súbita que se siente por todo el cuerpo, un síntoma relacionado con la dilatación de los vasos sanguíneos en la piel, lo cual es común durante la transición hacia la menopausia.

terapia de genes humanas: el uso de material genético para tratar, curar, o prevenir enfermedades tales como enfermedades cardíacas y el cáncer.

hormona humana del crecimiento: una hormona no esteroide producida en el cuerpo que promueve el crecimiento.

VIH: una abreviatura para el virus de inmunodeficiencia humana, el virus que causa el SIDA.

Glossary/Glosario

human papillomavirus (HPV): a group of over 100 related viruses, the effects of which include genital warts and cervical cancer.

virus del papiloma humano: cualquiera de más de 100 virus cuyos efectos incluyen las verrugas genitales y el cáncer cervical.

hunger: the physiological need to eat, experienced as a drive for obtaining food, an unpleasant sensation that demands to be fed.

hambre: la necesidad psicológica de comer, experimentada como un impulso de obtener alimento. Una sensación desagradable que exige alivio.

hypertension: high blood pressure.

hipertensión: presión arterial alta.

hyperthermia: a condition of too much body heat with abnormally high internal body temperature.

hipertermia: una condición de demasiado calor corporal con una temperatura corporal interna anormalmente alta.

hypothalamus: a brain regulatory center.

hipotálamo: un centro regulador del cerebro.

hypothermia: a condition of too little body heat with abnormally low internal body temperature.

hipotermia: una condición de calor corporal demasiada baja con temperatura del cuerpo interna anormalmente baja.

I

immune system: the cells, tissues, and organs that protect the body from disease.

sistema inmunológico: las células, tejidos y órganos que protegen al cuerpo de las enfermedades.

immunity: the body's capacity for identifying, destroying, and disposing of disease-causing agents.

inmunidad: la capacidad del organismo para identificar, destruir y eliminar los agentes que causan enfermedades.

immunizations: injected or oral doses of medicine that stimulate the immune system to develop the long-term ability to quickly fight off infectious diseases.

inmunización: una dosis inyectada u oral de medicina que estimula el sistema inmunológico para desarrollar la habilidad a largo plazo de combatir rápidamente las enfermedades infecciosas.

implantation: the process in which the ovum implants itself in the uterine wall.

implantación: la inserción de un óvulo fertilizado en la pared del útero.

inactive ingredients: ingredients in a medicine for effects other than medical ones.

ingredientes inactivos: los ingredientes en una medicina que tienen efectos diferentes de los efectos medicos.

infatuation: the state of being completely carried away by unreasoning passion or attraction.

infatuación: el estado de dejarse llevar completamente por una pasión o atracción irracional.

infectious diseases: diseases caused and transmitted from person to person, by microorganisms or their toxins.

enfermedades infecciosas: las enfermedades que son causadas y transmitidas de persona a persona, por microorganismos o sus toxinas.

infectious mononucleosis: a viral infection involving mononucleocytes, a type of white blood cell.

mononucleosis infecciosa: una infección viral que involucra mononucleocitos, un tipo de glóbulo blanco.

inflammation: pain and swelling caused by irritation.

inflamación: el dolor e hinchazón causada por la irritación.

initiator: a carcinogen, an agent required to start the formation of cancer.

insomnia: sleep abnormalities, including difficulty in falling asleep and wakefulness through the night.

insulin: a hormone produced by the pancreas and released in response to high blood glucose following a meal.

integrative therapies: approaches to medical diagnosis and treatment that are not fully accepted by the established medical community.

intensity: the degree of exertion during physical activity.

internal pressures: a person's biological urges toward being sexually active.

intimacy: being very close and familiar, as in relationships involving private and personal sharing.

intoxication: a state of being poisoned.

intrauterine device (IUD): a device inserted into the uterus to prevent conception or implantation.

intravenous (IV) drug abuse: the practice of using needles to inject drugs of abuse into the veins.

iniciador: un carcinógeno, agente necesario para iniciar la formación del cáncer.

insomnio: anormalidades del sueño, incluyendo dificultad para conciliar el sueño y desvelo durante la noche.

insulina: una hormona producida por el páncreas y liberada en respuesta a un aumento en el nivel de glucosa en la sangre después de una comida.

terapias alternativas: enfoques al diagnóstico y tratamiento médico que no son totalmente aceptados por la comunidad médica tradicional.

intensidad: el grado de esfuerzo mientras se ejecuta un ejercicio.

presiones internas: los impulsos biológicos de una persona que la impulsa a tener relaciones sexuales.

intimidad: estado de cercanía o proximidad, como en las relaciones que involucra el compartir lo privado y lo personal.

intoxicación: se refiere al estado de envenenamiento.

dispositivo intrauterino (DIU): elemento que se inserta en el útero para prevenir la concepción o implantación.

abuso de drogas intravenoso (IV): la práctica de utilizar agujas para inyectar drogas de abuso en las venas.

J

jock itch: a fungal infection of the inner thigh and groin.

juvenile: a legal term meaning a person under age 18, a minor.

prurito del jockey: una infección fúngica de la ingle y el muslo interno.

menor de edad: término legal que significa que una persona es menor de 18 años de edad; un menor de edad.

K

Kaposi's sarcoma: a normally rare skin cancer causing a purplish discoloration of the skin.

keratin: the normal protein of the hair and nails.

sarcoma de Kaposi: una rara forma de cáncer de la piel que causa una decoloración púrpura de la piel.

queratina: la proteína normal del cabello y las uñas.

ketones: fat fragments formed by the tissues during incomplete use of fat for energy.

Kyoto Protocol: an agreement signed by many of the world's leaders in 1997 that spells out the degree of reduction in carbon dioxide emission required of each nation by the year 2012.

cetonas: fragmentos formados por los tejidos durante el uso incompleto de grasa para obtener energía.

Protocolo de Kyoto: acuerdo firmado por muchos de los líderes mundiales en 1997 que fija el grado de reducción de las emisiones de monóxido de carbono en cada nación para el año 2012.

L

---

labor: contractions of the uterus strong enough to push the fetus through the vagina for delivery.

trabajo de parto: las contracciones del útero de intensidad suficiente como para impulsar el feto a través de la vagina para su nacimiento.

laboratory effectiveness: the percentage of females protected from pregnancy in a year's time under ideal laboratory conditions.

eficacia del laboratorio: el porcentaje de las hembras protegidas contra embarazo en un año debajo de condiciones ideales de laboratorio.

lactation: the production of milk by the mammary glands of the breasts for the purpose of feeding babies.

lactación: la producción de leche por las glándulas mamarias en las mamas para el propósito de alimentar a los bebés.

lapses: times of falling back into former habits.

lapsos: períodos de retroceso a hábitos antiguos.

latent: a temporary period of symptomless advancement of the disease.

latente: un período temporal sin síntomas mientras que una enfermedad avanza.

lesbian: a general term referring to females who are homosexual.

lesbiana: término general utilizado para referirse a las mujeres homosexuales.

lethal dose: the amount of a drug necessary to cause death.

dosis letal: la cantidad de droga necesaria para causar la muerte.

leukemias (loo-KEE-me-ahs): cancers that arise in the blood cell-making tissues of blood-forming organs.

leucemias: tipos de cáncer que surgen en los tejidos que fabrican glóbulos rojos.

leukoplakia (loo-koh-PLAKE-ee-uh): whitish or grayish patches that develop in the mouths of tobacco users.

leucoplaquia: unas manchas blancuzcas o grisáceas que se desarrollan en las bocas de los consumidores de tabaco.

life expectancy: the average number of years lived by people in a given society.

expectativa de vida: el número promedio de años vividos por la gente en una sociedad en particular.

life span: the maximum years of life a human being can live.

duración de vida: el número máximo de años que un ser humano puede llegar a vivir.

life-support systems: a term used to refer to mechanical means of supporting life, such as feedings given into a central vein or machines that force air into the lungs.

sistemas de soporte vital: término utilizado para referirse a los medios mecánicos utilizados para prolongar la vida, tales como la alimentación suministrada por una vena central o máquinas que fuerzan aire a los pulmones.

lightening: the sensation a pregnant woman experiences when the fetus settles into the birth position.

lipoproteins (LIP-oh-PRO-teens): protein and fat clusters that transport fats in the blood.

living will: a will that declares a person's wishes regarding treatment, should the person become unable to make decisions.

longevity: an individual's length of life.

look-alikes: combinations of OTC drugs and other chemicals packaged to look like prescription medications or illegal drugs.

love: affection, attachment, devotion.

low birth weight: weighs less than 5½ pounds.

low-density lipoproteins (LDLs): lipoproteins that carry fat and cholesterol from the liver where they are made, to the tissues where they are used.

LSD (lysergic acid diethylamide): a powerful hallucinogenic drug.

Lyme disease: a bacterial infection spread by tiny deer ticks.

lymph: the clear fluid that bathes each cell and transfers needed substances and wastes back and forth between the blood and the cells.

lymphocytes (LIM-fo-sites): white blood cells that are active in immunity.

lymphomas (limf-OH-mahs): cancers that arise in organs of the immune system or the lymph tissues.

liviandad: la sensación que una mujer embarazada experimenta cuando el feto se asienta en la posición de nacimiento.

lipoproteínas: grupos de proteínas y grasa que transportan grasa a la sangre.

testamento vital: testamento en que se declara los deseos de una persona respecto del tratamiento en caso de que la persona se encuentre incapacitada para tomar decisiones.

longevidad: la duración de vida de un individuo.

similares: combinaciones de fármacos de venta sin receta y otras sustancias químicas envasadas para parecer medicinas de prescripción o drogas ilegales.

amor: afecto, apego, devoción.

bajo peso de nacimiento: pesa menos de 5½ libras.

lipoproteínas de baja densidad (LDL): lipoproteínas que transportan grasa y colesterol desde el hígado donde se fabrican, a los tejidos donde se utilizan.

LSD: una poderosa droga alucinógena.

enfermedad de Lyme: una infección bacteriana propaganda por pequeñas garrapatas de venados.

linfa: el líquido transparente que baña cada célula y transfiere sustancias necesarias y desechos en una y otra dirección entre la sangre y las células.

linfocitos: glóbulos blancos, que participan activamente en la inmunidad.

linfomas: tipo de cáncer que surge en los órganos del sistema inmunológico y de los tejidas linfas.

M

---

mainstream smoke: the smoke that flows through the cigarette and into the lungs when a smoker inhales.

male condom: a sheath worn around the penis during intercourse to contain the semen.

humo principal: el humo que fluye a través del cigarrillo hasta los pulmones cuando el fumador inhala.

condón masculino: una envoltura usada alrededor del pene durante el acto sexual para contener el semen.

malignancy: a dangerous cancerous growth that sheds cells into body fluids and spreads to new locations to start new cancer colonies.

malnutrition: the result of serious undernutrition.

mammogram: an X-ray examination of the breast, a screening test for cancer.

marriage: the institution that joins a man and a woman by agreement for the purpose of creating and maintaining a family.

masculinity: traits, including biological and social traits, associated with being male.

masturbation: rubbing or stimulating one's own genitals, usually until orgasm occurs.

mature love: a strong affection for, deep attachment to, a person whose character the partner knows well.

mediator: a neutral third person who helps two people in conflict.

Medicaid: hospitalization and surgical insurance available for people who qualify as needy.

Medicare: hospitalization insurance for people who are receiving Social Security benefits.

medicines: drugs used to help cure disease, lessen disease severity, relieve symptoms, help with diagnosis, or produce other desired effects.

melanin (MELL-eh-nin): the protective skin pigment responsible for the tan, brown, or black color of human skin.

melanoma: a cancer of the pigmented cells of the skin.

menopause: the years of stopping ovulation and menstruation in a woman.

menstrual cramps: contractions of the uterus during and a few days before menstruation.

malignidad: un peligroso tumor canceroso que desprende células en los fluidos corporales y se esparce a nuevas ubicaciones para iniciar nuevas colonias cancerosas.

malnutrición: los resultados desnutrición.

mamograma: radiografía de la mama, una prueba de descarte para el cáncer.

matrimonio: la institución que une a un hombre y a una mujer por medio de un contrato con el propósito de crear y preservar una familia.

masculinidad: las características, incluyendo las biológicas y sociales, asociadas con el sexo masculino.

masturbación: el frotamiento o estimulación de sus propios genitales, generalmente hasta alcanzar el orgasmo.

amor maduro: un fuerte afecto para, un profundo cariño hacia una persona cuyo carácter el compañero conoce bien.

mediador: una tercera persona neutral que ayuda a dos personas en conflicto.

Medicaid: un seguro de hospitalización y de cirugía para personas que califican como necesitadas.

Medicare: un seguro de hospitalización para personas que reciben los beneficios del Seguro Social.

medicamentos: drogas utilizadas para ayudar a curar enfermedades, disminuir la gravedad de la enfermedad, aliviar los síntomas, ayudar con su diagnosis, o producir otros efectos deseados.

melanina: el pigmento protector de la piel responsable por el color bronceado, marrón o negro de la piel humana.

melanoma: un cáncer de las células pigmentadas de la piel.

menopausia: los años en que se detiene la ovulación y menstruación en la mujer.

calambres menstruales: las contracciones del útero durante y unos días antes de la menstruación.

menstrual cycle: the cyclic ripening of an ovum and the preparation of the uterus for pregnancy.

menstruation: the monthly shedding of the uterine lining in nonpregnant females.

mental illness: disorders of thought, emotion, or behavior that cause distress and reduce a person's ability to function.

mentor: a wise person who gives advice and assistance.

mescaline: the hallucinogen produced by the peyote cactus.

metastasized (meh-TASS-tuh-sized): when the cancer cells have migrated from one part of the body to another, and started new growths just like the original tumor.

methadone: a drug used to treat heroin addiction.

methamphetamine: a stronger form of amphetamine that is highly addictive, also called speed.

microbes: tiny organisms, such as bacteria, yeasts, and viruses, that are too small to be seen with the naked eye.

minerals: elements that perform many functions that keep the body growing and fuctioning.

misscarriage: the expelling of a zygote, embryo, or fetus from the uterus, not induced by medical means.

moderation: an amount of alcohol that causes no harm to health.

monogamous: having sexual relations with one partner only, excluding all others.

morning sickness: the nausea a pregnant woman may suffer at any time of the day.

morphine: a narcotic drug that physicians prescribe as a painkiller.

motivation: the force that moves people to act.

mucus: a slippery secretion produced by cells of the body's linings that protects the surfaces of the lining.

ciclo menstrual: la maduración cíclica de un óvulo y la preparación del útero para el embarazo.

menstruación: la descarga mensual del endómetro del útero en mujeres no embarazadas.

enfermedad mental: los desordenes de los pensamientos, de la emoción, o de la conducta que causa la angustia y que reduce la capacidad de una persona para funcionar.

mentor: una persona sabia que da consejos y ayuda.

mezcalina: el alucinógeno producido por el cacto peyote.

metastizado: cuando las células cancerígenas han migrado desde una parte del cuerpo hacia otra y han iniciado nuevos tumores iguales al tumor original.

metadona: una droga usada para tratar la adicción.

metanfetamina: una forma sumamente adictiva y más fuerte de la anfetamina; también se llama "speed".

microbios: pequeños organismos, tales como bacteria, levadura y virus que son demasiado pequeños para ser observados a simple vista.

minerales: elementos que realizan muchas funcionas para ayudar el cuerpo crece y funciona.

expulsión espontáneo: la expulsión de un cigoto, de un embrión, o de un feto del útero, no inducido por medios médicos.

moderación: una cantidad de alcohol que no causa daño a la salud.

monógamo: tener relaciones sexuales con una sola pareja, excluyendo a todos los demás.

nauseas matinales: las nauseas que una mujer embarazada puede experimentar en cualquier momento del día.

morfina: una droga narcótica que los médicos prescriben como analgésico.

motivación: la fuerza que mueve a las personas a actuar.

moco: una secreción resbalosa producida por las células del revestimiento del organismo que protege la superficie del revestimiento.

muscle endurance: the ability of muscles to sustain an effort for a long time.

capacidad muscular: la capacidad de los músculos para soportar un esfuerzo por un largo tiempo.

muscle strength: the ability of muscles to work against resistance.

fuerza muscular: la capacidad de los músculos para trabajar contra la resistencia.

mutation: a change in a cell's genetic material.

mutación: un cambio en el material genético de la célula.

myeloma: a tumor of the bone marrow.

mieloma: un tumor en las células de la médula ósea.

MyPyramid: a diet-planning pattern.

MiPirámide: una guía para planear su dienta.

N

---

narcotics: habit-forming drugs that relieve pain and produce sleep when taken in moderate doses.

narcóticos: drogas adictivas que alivian el dolor y producen sueño cuando se toman en dosis moderadas.

Narcotics Anonymous (NA): a free, self-help program of addiction recovery.

Narcóticos Anónimos (NA): un grupo de auto ayuda, libre de costo, para la recuperación de la adicción.

needs: urgent wants for necessary things.

necesidades: deseos urgentes de cosas necesarias.

nervous system: the body system that manages the body's activities by sending and receiving messages between the brain, spinal cord, and nerves.

sistema nervioso: el sistema del cuerpo que maneja las actividades del cuerpo por enviar y recibir mensajes entre el cerebro, la médula espinal, y los nervios.

neural tube defects: a group of birth defects caused by interruption of normal development of the neural tube.

defectos del tubo neural: un grupo de defectos de nacimiento causados por la interrupción del desarrollo normal del tubo neural.

nicotine: an addictive drug present in tobacco.

nicotina: una droga adictiva presente en el tabaco.

night blindness: the slow recovery of vision after flashes of bright light at night.

ceguera nocturna: la recuperación lenta de la visión después de destellos de luz brillante.

nonconformist: a person who does not share society's values and therefore behaves in unconventional ways.

noconformista: una persona que no comparte los valores de la sociedad y por lo tanto se comporta en forma no convencional.

nucleus: inside a cell, the structure that contains the genes.

núcleo: en el interior de una oélula, la estructura que contiene los genes.

nutrient deficiencies: too little of one or more nutrients in the diet, one form of malnutrition.

deficiencias de nutrientes: muy poco de uno o más nutrients en la dieta. Una forma de la malnutrición.

nutrients: substances in food that the body requires for proper growth, maintenance, and functioning.

nutrientes: compuestos presentes en los alimentos que el organismo necesita para crecer, mantenerse y funcionar apropiadamente.

O

obesity: overfatness to the point of injuring health.

obsessive-compulsive disorder: an uncontrollable fixation on specific thoughts and behaviors.

opiates: substances derived from the opium poppy.

opium: a milky fluid found in the seed pods of the opium poppy.

oral contraceptives: pills that prevent pregnancy by stopping ovulation or by changing conditions in the uterus.

organs: whole units, made of tissues, that perform specific jobs.

orgasm: muscular contractions of the sex organs.

osteoporosis: a disease of gradual bone loss.

ostracism: rejection and exclusion from society.

ova (singular, ovum): the female cells of reproduction.

overload: an extra physical demand placed on the body.

overnutrition: consuming too much food energy (calories) or excessive amounts of some nutrients.

over-the-counter (OTC) drugs: drugs legally available without a prescription.

ovulation: the ripening and release of an ovum.

oxycodone: a narcotic drug in the strong, time-released painkiller called OxyContin.

ozone: a substance created when certain types of energy, such as the sun's ultraviolet rays, react with oxygen.

obesidad: sobrepeso al punto de ser dañino para la salud.

trastorno obsesivo compulsivo: una fijación irrefrenable en pensamientos y conductas específicos.

opiáceos: un grupo de drogas que se derivan de la amapola del opio.

opio: un líquido lechoso que se encuentra en las vainas de la amapola de opio.

contraceptivo oral: píldoras que previenen el embarazo inhibiendo la ovulación o cambiando las condiciones en el útero.

órganos: unidades completas compuestas de tejidos que realizan tareas específicas.

orgasmo: contracciones musculares de los órganos sexuales.

osteoporosis: una enfermedad que causa la pérdida gradual de hueso.

ostracismo: rechazo y exclusión de la sociedad.

óvulos (singular óvulo): las células femeninas de reproducción.

sobrecarga: una exigencia física adicional puesta sobre el cuerpo.

sobrenutrición: ingesta excesiva de energía alimentaria o de nutrientes.

fármacos de venta sin receta: fármacos disponibles legalmente sin receta.

ovulación: la maduración y liberación de un óvulo.

oxicodona: el narcótico en il analgésico fuerte que se llama OxyContin.

ozono: una sustancia que se crea cuando ciertos tipos de energía, tales como los rayos ultravioleta del sol reaccionan con el oxígeno. Cuando tiene lugar esta reacción a una gran distancia sobre la.

Glossary/Glosario

P

---

pacemaker: a device that delivers electrical impulses to the heart to regulate the heartbeat.

Pap test: a test for cancer of the cervix.

passive: not expressing feelings appropriately.

passive abuse: abuse involving not taking needed actions, such as neglecting to provide food or shelter to a dependent victim.

pathogens: microbes that cause disease.

PCP (phencyclidine hydrochloride): an animal tranquilizer, abused by humans as a hallucinogen.

peer group: a groups of friends who are similar to yourself in age and stage of life.

peer pressure: the internal pressure one feels to behave as a peer group does, in order to gain its members' approval.

pelvic inflammatory disease (PID): an infection of the fallopian tubes and pelvic cavity in females, causing ectopic pregnancy and miscarriages.

perception: a meaning given to an event based on a person's previous experience or understanding of it.

personality: the characteristics of a person that are apparent to others.

peyote: a cactus that produces the hallucinogen mescaline.

phobia: an extreme, irrational fear of an object or situation.

physical activities: movements of the body under the command of the conscious mind.

physical addiction: a change in the body's chemistry so that without the presence of a substance (drug), normal functioning begins to fail.

marcapasos: un aparato que suministra impulsos eléctricos al corazón para regular los latidos.

método de papanicolau: un examen para cáncer cervical.

pasivo: no expresar sus sentimientos apropiadamente.

abuso pasivo: mal trato que involucra no tomar las acciones necesarias, como el descuido en proveer comida o amparo a una víctima dependiente.

patógenos: microbios que causan enfermedad.

PCP: un tranquilizante animal, abusado por los seres humanos como alucinógeno.

grupos de pares: un grupo de amigos similares a usted mismo en edad y etapa de la vida.

presión de pares: la presión interna que se experimenta para comportarse de la forma en que lo hace el grupo de pares, para ganarse la aprobación de sus miembros.

enfermedad de inflamación pélvica: una infección de las trompas de Falopio y la cavidad pélvica en las mujeres, que causa embarazo ectópico y abortos.

percepción: el significado dado a un evento basado en la experiencia o comprensión previa del individuo.

personalidad: las características de una persona que son evidentes para otros.

peyote: cacto que produce el alucinógeno mezcalina.

fobia: un miedo extremo e irracional a un objeto o situación.

actividades físicas: los movimientos del cuerpo que son controlados por la mente consciente.

adicción física: un cambio en la química del organismo que hace que en la ausencia de dosis cada vez mayores de determinada sustancia (droga), su funcionamiento normal empiece a fallar.

physical examination: an examination of the body to gather information about its general condition or to make a diagnosis.

physician-assisted suicide: suicide of an ill person by way of lethal drugs provided by a physician.

physiological age: age as estimated from the body's health and probable life expectancy.

phytochemicals: compounds in foods from plants that perform important functions in the body, but are not nutrients.

pinch test: an informal way of measuring body fatness.

pinworms: small, visible, white parasitic worms that commonly infect the intestines of young children.

PKU (phenylketonuria): a congenital disease causing severe brain damage with mental retardation if left untreated.

placenta: a new organ that permits exchange of materials between maternal and fetal blood.

placental stage: the final stage of childbirth, in which the placenta is expelled.

plaques: mounds of fat, mixed with minerals, that build up along artery walls.

plateau phase: the period of intense physical pleasure preceding orgasm.

platelets: tiny, disk-shaped bodies in the blood that form clots.

Pneumocystis carinii (PCP): a type of pneumonia characteristic of AIDS.

pollution: contamination of the environment with anything that impairs its ability to support life.

polyps: tumors that grow on a stem, resembling mushrooms.

polyunsaturated: a type of unsaturated fat especially useful as a replacement for saturated fat in a heart-healthy diet.

examen físico: un examen del cuerpo para recopilar información acerca de su condición general o para hacer un diagnóstico.

suicidio asistido por un médico: el suicido de una persona enferma mediante drogas letales suministrados por un médico.

edad fisiológica: la edad estimada de acuerdo al estado de salud del cuepro y la esperanza de vida probable.

fitoquímicos: substancias en alimentos de plantas que realizan funcionas importantes en el cuerpo, pero no son alimentos nutritivos.

prueba del pellizco: una manera informal de medir la grasa corporal.

lombriz intestinal: lombrices parasíticas blancas, pequeñas y visibles que comúnmente infectan los intestinos de niños de corta edad.

fenilcetonuria: una enfermedad congénita que ocasiona daño cerebral severo con retraso mental si se deja sin tratamiento.

placenta: un órgano neuvo que permite el intercambio de materiales entre la sangre de la madre y la sangre del feto.

período placentario del parto: la etapa final del parto, en la cual se expulsa la placenta.

placas: montículos de grasa mezclada con minerales que se acumulan a lo largo de las paredes de las arterias.

altiplano: el período de placer físico intenso que precede al orgasmo.

plaquetas: pequeños cuerpos en forma de disco encontrados en la sangre, una parte importante de la formación de coágulos.

neumonía carinii pneumocystis: la neumonía característica del SIDA.

contaminación: contaminación del medio ambiente con cualquier cosa que perjudique su habilidad de mantener la vida.

pólipos: tumores que crecen en un tallo, asemejándose a los hongos.

poliinsaturado: tipo de grasa no saturada especialmente útil como sustituto de la grasa saturada en una dieta saludable para el corazón.

Glossary/Glosario

positive self-talk: the practice of making affirming statements to oneself.

postpartum depression: the emotional depression a new mother experiences after the birth of an infant.

post-traumatic stress disorder (PTSD): a serious stress reaction in response to a terrifying event.

premature infant: when the infant is born early.

premenstrual syndrome (PMS): symptoms such as physical discomfort, moodiness, and nervousness that occur in some women each month before menstruation.

prenatal care: medical and health care provided during pregnancy.

prepayment plan: a system of payment for health care in which the clients pay a fixed fee every month.

prescription drugs: drugs legally available only with a physician's order.

progesterone: a hormone secreted in females during that portion of the menstrual cycle in which the uterine lining builds up.

progestin: a synthetic version of progesterone used in contraceptives.

progressive muscle relaxation: a technique of learning to relax by focusing on relaxing each muscle group in turn.

progressive overload principle: the training principle that a body system, in order to improve, must be worked at frequencies, intensities, or durations that increase over time.

promoter: a substance that assists in the development of malignant tumors, but does not initiate them on its own.

proof: a measure of the percentage of alcohol in alcoholic beverages.

protease inhibitors: drugs that stop the action of an enzyme which ordinarily helps HIV to reproduce.

autoplática positiva: la práctica de formularse aseveraciones positivas a sí mismo.

depresión pos parto: la depresión emocional que experimenta una nueva madre después del nacimiento del bebé.

trastorno de estrés pos traumático: una reacción grave del estrés en respuesta a un acontecimiento terrible.

lactante prematuro: cuando un bebé nace antes de la fecha de nacimiento que esperaban los padres..

síndrome premenstrual (SPM): síntomas tales como incomodidad física, mal genio y nerviosismo que experimentan algunas mujeres cada mes antes de la menstruación.

cuidado prenatal: los cuidados médicos y sanitarios proporcionados durante el embarazo.

plan de prepago: un sistema de pago por atención de salud en la cual los clientes pagan una tarifa fija cada mes.

drogas de prescripción: aquellos fármacos que solamente están legalmente disponibles con la receta de un médico.

progesterona: hormona secretada por las mujeres durante la parte del ciclo menstrual en que el revestimiento uterino se acumula.

progestina: versión sintética de la progesterona utilizada en los anticonceptivos.

relajamiento muscular progresivo: la técnica de aprender a relajarse enfocándose en relajar los grupos de músculos del cuerpo de uno en uno.

principio de sobrecarga progresiva: el principio de entrenamiento basado en que un sistema corporal, para poder mejorar, tiene que ser trabajado en frecuencias, intensidades o duraciones que aumentan con el tiempo.

promotor: la sustancia que ayuda al desarrollo de tumores malignos, pero que no los inicia por sí sola.

graduación: la medida del porcentaje de alcohol de las bebidas alcohólicas.

inhibidores de la proteasa: fármacos que detienen la acción de la enzima que generalmente ayuda a que el VIH se reproduzca.

proteins: a class of nutrients that build body tissue and supply energy.

proxy: a person authorized to act for another.

psilocybin (sill-oh-SI-bin): a hallucinogen produced by a type of wild mushroom.

psychological addiction: mental dependence on a drug, habit, or behavior.

psychology: the scientific study of behavior and the mind.

psychotherapy: a type of therapy in which a patient discusses problems with a trained therapist.

puberty: the period of life in which a person becomes physically capable of reproduction.

pubic lice: an STD caused by tiny parasites that breed in pubic hair and cause intense itching.

pulp cavity: a tooth's deepest chamber layer.

pulse rate: the number of heartbeats per minute.

pus: a mixture of fluids and white blood cells that collects around infected areas.

proteína: tipo de nutriente que elabora los tejidos del cuerpo y que proporciona energía.

representante: una persona autorizada para actuar a nombre de otra.

psilocibin: un alucinógeno producido por un tipo de hongo silvestre.

adicción psicológica: la dependencia mental de una droga, hábito o conducta.

psicología: el estudio científico de la conducta y la mente.

psicoterapia: un tipo de la terapia en la que un paciente discute los problemas con un terapeuta entrenado.

pubertad: el período de la vida en el cual la persona se vuelve físicamente capaz de reproducir.

ladillas: una enfermedad de transmisión sexual causada por pequeños parásitos que se reproducen en el vello público y causan una picazón intensa.

cavidad de la pulpa dental: la cámara más profunda del diente.

pulso: el número de latidos por minuto del corazón.

pus: una mezcla de líquidos y glóbulos blancos que se juntan alrededor de zonas infectadas.

Q

quid: a small portion of any form of smokeless tobacco.

mascada: una pequeña porción de cualquier forma de tabaco para mascar.

R

rabies: a disease of the central nervous system.

radiation therapy: the application of cell-destroying radiation to kill cancerous tissues.

range of motion: the mobility of a joint.

recovery: when the body returns to normal.

rabia: una enfermedad del sistema nervioso central.

radioterapia: la aplicación de radiación que destruye las células para destruir el tejido canceroso.

arco de movilidad: la movilidad de una articulación.

recuperación: cuando el cuerpo vuelve a su estado normal.

recreational drug use: a term made up, to describe their drug use, by people who claim their drug taking produces no harmful social or health effects.

uso de fármacos para fines recreativos: un término ideado por las personas para describir su consumo de drogas afirmando que su consumo no produce efectos nocivos para su salud o la sociedad.

recyclable: made of material that can be used over again.

reciclable: elaborado con materiales que pueden ser utilizados nuevamente.

refusal skills: a set of social strategies that enable people to competently resist the pressure of others to engage in dangerous or otherwise undesirable behaviors.

tecnicas de rechazo: un conjunto de estrategias sociales que permiten que las personas resistan de manera eficaz la presión de sus pares para involucrarse en conductas peligrosas o indeseables.

relapses: illnesses that return after being treated and almost cured.

recidiva: enfermedades que reaparecen después de ser tratadas y prácticamente curadas.

relaxation response: the body's ability to reduce blood pressure, slow the pulse, quiet anxiety, and release tension.

respuesta de relajación: la capacidad del cuerpo para reducir la tension, aflojar el pulso, calmarse la ansiedad, y soltar el estrés.

REM (rapid eye movement): the periods of sleep in which a person is dreaming.

MOR (movimiento ocular rápido): los períodos del sueño en que una persona sueña.

resentment: anger that has built up due to failure to express it.

resentimiento: cólera que ha aumentado a causa de no expresarlo.

resistance (in fitness): the weight or other opposing force against which muscles must work.

resistencia (en los ejercicios): el peso u otra fuerza opuesta contra cual los músculos deben trabajar.

resistance (in stress): when the body mobilizes its resources to withstand the effects of the stress.

resistencia (en el estrés): cuándo el cuerpo moviliza sus recursos para resistir a los efectos del estrés.

resolution phase: the phase of relaxation that follows orgasm.

resolución: la fase de relajación que sigue al orgasmo.

risk factors: factors linked with a disease by association but not yet proved to be causes.

factores de riesgo: factores relacionados con una enfermedad por asociación que aun no se ha demostrado su relación de causalidad con esta.

S

safe: causing no undue harm.

seguro: que no causa daño excesivo.

safer-sex strategies: behavior guidelines that reduce STD risk, but that do not reduce the risk to zero.

prácticas sexuales seguras: las pautas del comportamiento para reducir el riesgo de contraer enfermedades de transmisión sexual, pero que no reducen el riesgo a cero.

Salmonella: a common food-borne pathogen causing digestive system infections.

Salmonella: un patógeno transmitido por vía alimentaria que produce infeccione.

salt: a compound made of minerals that, in water, dissolve and form electrolytes.

al: un compuesto de minerales que disueltos en agua forman electrolitos.

sarcomas: cancers that arise in the connective tissue cells, including bones, ligaments, and muscles.

saturated: fats associated strongly with heart and artery disease.

schizophrenia: a severe mental disorder that causes people to lose touch with reality.

sebum (SEE-bum): the skin's natural oil.

second opinion: a second assessment of a diagnosis and treatment plan by another health care provider, usually on the request of a client, to double-check the validity of the original plan.

sedatives: depressants that slow the body systems.

sedentary: physically inactive.

self-actualization: the realization of one's full potential.

self-efficacy: the belief in one's ability to take action and sucessfully change a behavior.

self-esteem: the value a person attaches to his or her self-image.

self-image: the characteristics that a person sees in himself or herself.

senility: a general term meaning weakness of mind and body occurring in old age.

set: a specific number of times to repeat a weight-training exercise.

sex: a general term often used to mean sexual intercourse.

sexual harassment: unwanted sexual attention, often from someone in power.

sexual intercourse: the reproductive act between the sexes.

sexuality: the quality of being sexual.

sexually transmitted diseases (STDs): diseases that are transmitted by way of direct sexual contact.

shaken baby syndrome: a collection of symptoms resulting from violent shaking of an infant or young child.

sarcomas: tipos de cáncer que se producen en las células del tejido conectivo, incluyendo los huesos, ligamentos y músculos.

saturado: grasas asociadas con las enfermedades del corazón y las arterias.

esquizofrenia: una enfermedad mental de perdida del contacto con la realidad.

sebo: la grasa natural de la piel.

segunda opinión: una segunda valoración de un diagnóstico y plan terapéutico realizado por otro proveedor de salud, generalmente a pedido del paciente, a fin de verificar la validez del plan terapéutico inicial.

sedantes: depresores que aflojan los sistemas del cuerpo.

sedentario: físicamente inactivo.

autorrealización: la máxima realización del propio potencial.

autoeficacia: tomar medidas y combiar exitosamente una conducta.

autoestima: el valor que da una persona a su autoimagen.

autoimagen: las características que una persona ve en sí misma.

senilidad: un término general asociado al estado de vigor reducido de la mente y el cuerpo que ocurre con el envejecimiento.

conjunto: el número específico de veces que se debe repetir un ejercicio de levantamiento de pesas.

sexo: un término general utilizado para referirse al relación sexual.

acoso sexual: la atención sexual indeseada, frecuentemente por parte de alguien con poder.

relación sexual: el acto de reproducción entre los sexos.

sexualidad: la cualidad de ser sexual.

enfermedades de transmisión sexual (ETS): aquellas enfermedades que son transmitidas por vía del contacto sexual directo.

síndrome del niño maltratado: una colección de síntomas resultando de la sacudida violenta de un bebé o niño joven.

Glossary/Glosario

shame: a feeling of being inherently unworthy.

shin splints: damage to the muscles and connective tissues of the lower front leg from stress.

shock: failure or disruption of the blood circulation, a life-threatening reaction to accidents and injuries.

sibling rivalry: competition among sisters and brothers, often for the attention or affection of parents.

siblings: two or more people with one or more parents in common.

side effects: effects of drugs other than the desired medical effects.

sidestream smoke: the smoke that escapes into the air from the burning tip of a cigarette or cigar, or from burning pipe tobacco.

sinuses: spaces in the bones of the skull.

skin-fold caliper: a pinching device that measures the thickness of a fold of skin on the back of the arm, below the shoulder blade, on the side of the waist, or elsewhere.

skin-fold test: a test of body fatness.

small for date: babies who are small because of underdevelopment.

smokeless tobacco: tobacco used for snuff or chewing rather than for smoking.

sober: free of alcohol's effects and addiction.

sperm: the male cells of reproduction.

spermicide: the compound nonoxynol-9, intended for birth control, that also kills or weakens some STD organisms.

spina (SPY-nah or SPEE-nah) bifida (BIFF-ih-duh): a birth defect often involving gaps in the bones of the spine, leaving the spinal cord unprotected in those spots.

spine: a stack of 33 vertebrae that form the backbone and hold the spinal cord, whose nerves enter and exit through spaces between the bones.

vergüenza: un sentimiento de ser intrínsecamente indigno.

desgarros a la espinilla: daño a los músculos y tejido conectivo de la parte anterior inferior de la pierna producida por el estrés.

shock: la falla o interrupción de la circulación sanguínea, una reacción a accidentes y lesiones que amenaza la vida.

rivalidad entre hermanos: la competencia entre hermanos y hermanas, con frecuencia para atraer la atención o afecto de los padres.

hermanos: dos o más personas con uno o más padres en común.

efectos secundarios: efectos de los fármacos distintos a los efectos médicos deseados.

humo indirecto: el humo que se escapa al aire de un cigarrillo, puro o pipa encendidos.

senos nasales: espacios en los huesos del cráneo.

adipómetro: un instrumento que mide el debajo del omíplato, en el lado de la cintura, o en otra parte.

pliegue cutáneo: una medida de la gordura del cuerpo.

pequeño para la edad gestacional: un bebé subdesarrollado para su edad gestacional.

tabaco sin humo: tabaco utilizado para aspirar o masticar en lugar de fumarlo.

sobrio: libre de los efectos del tabaco y de adicción a este.

semen: las células masculinas de reproducción.

espermicida: el compuesto nonoynol -9, destinado al control natal que también permite destruir o debilitar algunos organismos ETS.

espina bífida: un defecto de nacimiento que con frecuencia presenta huecos entre los huesos que deja al descubierto la médula espinal en aquellos puntos.

espina: conjunto de 33 vertebras que forman la columna vertebral y sostienen la médula espinal, cuyos nervios ingresan y egresan a través de los espacios entre los huesos.

splint: a stick or board used to support a broken bone to keep its separated parts from moving until it can be set.

spouse/partner abuse: verbal, psychological, physical, or sexual assault on a spouse or partner.

starch: the main energy source for people around the world.

status: a person's standing or rank in relation to others, many times falsely based on wealth, power, or influence.

stepparents: people who marry into a family after a biological parent departs through death or divorce.

stereotypes: fixed pictures of how everyone in a group is thought to be.

sterilization: the process of permanently interrupting a person's ability to bear children, usually by surgically severing and sealing the vas deferens or the fallopian tubes.

steroids: hormones of a certain chemical type that occur naturally in the body, some of which promote muscle growth.

stimulant: any of a wide variety of drugs, including amphetamines, caffeine, and others, that speed up the central nervous system.

stranger rape: sexual assault by a stranger.

stress: the effect of physical and psychological demands on a person.

stress eating: eating in response to stress.

stress fractures: bone damage from repeated physical force that strains the place where ligament is attached to bone.

stress hormones: the hormones that control the body's reponse to stress.

stressor: a physical or psychological demand that reqires a person to adapt to a situation.

férula: tablilla o pala utilizado para apoyar un hueso quebrado y evitar que sus fragmentos se muevan hasta que sane.

abuso del cónyuge: la agresión verbal, psicológica, física o sexual del cónyuge.

almidón: fuente principal de sustento para todo ser humano.

posición social: la situación o categoría de una persona en relación a otras, a menudo basada equivocadamente en la riqueza, el poder o la influencia.

padrastro, madrastra: una persona que se casa integrándose una familia luego de que uno de los padres biológicos la abandona por muerte o divorcio.

estereotipo: la generalización sobre la forma de ser de los miembros de un grupo.

esterilización: proceso de interrumpir en forma permanente la habilidad de procrear de la persona, generalmente mediante el corte y sellado quirúrgico del conducto deferente o de las Trompas de Falopio.

esteroides: hormonas de un tipo químico específico que se produce en forma natural en el cuerpo, algunas de las cuales estimulan el desarrollo muscular.

estimulantes: cualquiera de una amplia variedad de fármacos, incluyendo las anfetaminas, la cafeína y otros que aceleran el sistema nervioso central.

violación por extraños: la agresión sexual por un extraño.

estrés: el efecto de las exigencias físicas y sicológicas sobre una persona.

comer por estrés: comer en respuesta al estrés.

fractura por sobrecarga: daño óseo por una fuerza física repetida que estira la unión de los ligamentos a los huesos.

hormonas del estrés: las hormonas que controlan la reacción del cuerpo al estrés.

factores estresantes: una demanda física o psicológica que requiere a una persona para adaptar a una situación.

Glossary/Glosario

stress response: the body's response to a demand or stressor.

respuesta al estrés: la reacción del corpa ante una exigencia o factor estresante.

stroke: the shutting off of the blood flow to the brain by plaques, a clot, or hemorrhage.

ataque apopléjico: la interrupción del flujo sanguíneo al cerebro por placas, un coágulo o una hemorragia.

sudden infant death syndrome (SIDS): the sudden unexplained death of an infant.

síndrome de muerte súbita: muerte sin explicación de un bebé.

sudden sniffing death: sudden death from heart failure in a person abusing inhalants.

síndrome de muerte súbita por inhalación: muerte repentina, generalmente por insuficiencia cardíaca, de una persona abusando de inhalantes.

sugars: carbohydrates found both in foods and in the body.

azúcares: carbohidratos que se encuentran tanto en los alimentos como en el cuerpo.

sun block: a total block or barricade against the cancer-causing rays of the sun.

bloqueador solar: bloqueador total de los rayos solares cancerígenos.

sunscreen: a partial block against the cancer-causing rays of the sun (gamma radiation).

pantalla solar: bloqueador parcial de los rayos solares cancerígenos (radiación gamma).

supplement: a pill, powder, liquid, or the like containing only nutrients.

suplemento: una píldora, polvo, líquido o similar que contiene nutrientes solamente.

support system: a network of individuals or groups with which one identifies and exchanges emotional support.

sistema de apoyo: una red de individuos o grupos con los cuales uno se identifica e intercambia apoyo emocional.

suppress: to hold back or restrain.

suprimir: reprimir o contener.

syphilis: a bacterial sexually transmitted disease that, if untreated, advances from a sore (chancre) to flulike symptoms, then through a long symptomless period, and later to a final stage of irreversible brain and nerve damage, ending in death.

sífilis: una enfermedad bacteriana de transmisión sexual que, si no es tratada, avanza de una llaga (chancro) a los síntomas como la gripe, entonces con un largo periodo de sin síntomas, y mas adelante a un estadio final del daño irreversible del cerebro y del nervio, terminando en muerte.

systolic pressure: the blood pressure during that part of the heartbeat when the ventricles are contracted and the blood is being pushed out into the arteries.

presión sistólica: la presión sanguínea durante aquella parte del latido del corazón cuando los ventrículos se contraen y la sangre es impulsada dentro de las arterias.

T

T cells: lymphocytes that can recognize invaders that cause illness.

células T: linfocitos que pueden reconocer a los invasores que causan enfermedades.

target heart rate: the heartbeat rate that will condition a person's cardiovascular system—fast enough to push the heart, but not so fast as to strain it.

frecuencia cardíaca objetivo: la frecuencia cardíaca que condicionará el sistema cardiovascular de una persona—lo suficientemente rápido para acelerar el corazón pero no tan rápido como para sobreexcitarlo.

tars: chemicals present in tobacco.

alquitrán: sustancias químicas que se encuentran en el tabaco.

tennis elbow: a painful condition of the arm and joint.

terminal illnesses: illnesses that are expected to end in death.

tetanus: a disease caused by a toxin produced by bacteria deep within a wound.

therapy: any activity or treatment that helps a person cope with a mental or emotional problem.

thoughts: those mental processes of which a person is always conscious.

thrill seekers: people who are especially likely to take chances in exchange for momentary excitement.

thrombus: a stationary clot.

thymus gland: an organ of the immune system.

tissues: systems of cells working together to perform specific tasks.

tolerance: accommodation and acceptance of differenes between oneself and others.

tolerance (in drug use): requiring larger and larger amounts of a drug to produce the same effect.

toxin: poison.

transdermal: absorbed through the skin and into the bloodstream.

trans fats: a type of fat that forms when poly-unsaturated oils are processed.

tremors: continuous quivering or shaking.

trichomoniasis (trick-oh-mo-NEYE-uh-sis): an STD caused by a parasite that can cause bladder and urethral infections.

tubal ligation: surgical cutting and sealing off of the fallopian tubes to sterilize a female.

tuberculosis: a bacterial infection of the lungs.

tumor: an abnormal mass of tissue that can live and reproduce itself, but performs no service to the body.

codo de tenista: una lesión dolorosa del brazo y articulaciones.

enfermedades terminales: enfermedades que se espera terminen en la muerte.

tétanos: una enfermedad causada por una toxina elaborada por bacteria que se encuentra en la parte profunda de una herida.

terapia: cualquier actividad o tratamiento que ayuda a una persona para tratar un problema mental o emocional.

pensamientos: aquellos procesos mentales de los cuales una persona siempre está consciente.

buscadores de emociones: aquellas personas que son particularmente propensas a tomar riesgos a cambio de una excitación momentánea.

trombo: un coágulo estacionario.

glándula del timo: un órgano del sistema inmunológico.

tejidos: sistemas de células que trabajan unidas para realizar tareas específicas.

tolerancia: acomodar y aceptar las diferencias entre sí mismo y otros.

tolerencia (en el uso de drogas): reguirir las cantidades más grande para producir el mismo efecto.

toxina: un veneno.

transdérmico: se absorbe a través de la piel y hacia la corriente sanguínea.

ácidos grasos trane: un tipo de grasa que forma cuando los aceites poliinsaturados son procesados.

temblores: temblores o estremecimientos continuos.

tricomoniasis: una enfermedad de transmisión sexual causada por un parásito que causa infecciones de la vejiga y de la uretra.

ligado de trompas: corte y sellado quirúrgico de las trompas de falopio para esterilizar a las mujeres.

tuburculosis: una infección bacteriana de los pulmones.

tumor: una masa anormal de tejido que puede vivir y reproducirse, pero que no realiza ningún servicio para el organismo.

U

umbilical cord: a ropelike structure stretching from the fetus's "belly button" to the placenta.

cordón umbilical: la estructura en forma de cuerda a través de la cual se extienden las venas y arterias del feto hacia y desde la placenta.

undernutrition: too little food energy or too few nutrients to promote growth.

desnutrición: muy poca energía alimentaria o muy pocos nutrientes para estimular el crecimiento.

underweight: weight too low for health.

bajo peso: un peso bajo el peso normal saludable.

unethical: against the rules of right and wrong, not in line with accepted moral standards.

no ético: en contra de las reglas de lo correcto e incorrecto. En disconformidad con los estándares aceptables de moral.

unsaturated: fats less associated with heart disease.

no saturada: grasas que son menos asociadas con enfermedades del corazón.

upper respiratory infection: an infection of the membranes of the nasal cavities, sinuses, throat, and trachea, but not involving the lungs.

infección de las vías respiratorias superiores: una infección de las membranas de las cavidades nasales, los senos nasales, la garganta y la traquea, pero que no compromete a los pulmones.

urinary tract infections (UTIs): bacterial infections of the urethra that can travel into the bladder and kidneys.

infección de los conductos urinarios: una infección bacteriana de la uretra que puede trasladarse a la vejiga y a los riñones. No es una enfermedad de transmisión sexual.

urine: fluid wastes removed from the body by the kidneys.

orina: los desechos líquidos eliminados del organismo por los riñones.

user effectiveness: the percentage of typical female users who are protected.

efectvidad de consumo: el porcentaje de los consumidoras femeninos típicas quienes se protegen.

UVA (ultraviolet A): passes deep into the skin and can cause long-term skin damage that may lead to cancer and premature aging.

UVA (ultravioleta A): las luces ultravioletas que pasen profundamente en la piel y pueden causar el daño de largo plazo de la piel que puede llevar al cáncer y al envejecimiento prematuro.

UVB (ultraviolet B): causes sunburn and skin cancer, including melanoma.

UVB (ultravioleta B): la luces ultravioletas que causan la bronceadura y el cáncer de piel, incluyendo melanoma.

V

vaccine: a drug made from altered microbes or their poisons injected or given by mouth to produce immunity.

vacuna: una droga fabricada de microbios alterados o de sus venenos, inyectada o administrada por vía oral para producir inmunidad.

values: what the person thinks of as right and wrong, or sees as important.

valves: flaps of tissue that open and close to allow the flow of blood in one direction only.

variables: changeable factors that affect outcomes.

vas deferens: one of the two tubes that conduct sperm from the testicles toward the penis.

vasectomy: surgical cutting and sealing off of each vas deferens to sterilize a man.

vegetarians: people who omit meat, fish, and poultry from their diets.

veins: blood vessels that carry waste-containing blood from the tissues back to the heart.

venting: the act of verbally expressing one's feelings.

ventricles: the two lower chambers of the heart that send blood to the lungs or the tissues.

ventricular fibrillation: extremely rapid contractions of the heart's lower chambers that lack the power needed to pump blood around the body.

vertebrae (singular, vertebra): the delicate, hollow bones of the spine.

violence: brutal physical force intended to damage or injure another.

virgin: a term applied to people before their first occasion of sexual intercourse.

viruses: organisms that contain only genetic material and protein coats, and that are totally dependent on the cells they infect.

vitamins: compounds that are required for growth and proper functioning of the body.

valores: lo que una persona considera como correcto o incorrecto, o lo que considera importante.

válvulas: pliegues de tejido que se abren y cierran para permitir el flujo de sangre en una sola dirección.

variables: hechos que cambian y afectan el resultado.

conducto diferente: uno de los dos conductos que transporta la esperma desde los testículos hacia el pene.

vasectomía: corte y sellado quirúrgico de cada uno de los conductos deferentes para esterilizar a los hombres.

vegetarianos: aquellas personas que se abstienen de la carne, pescado y ave en sus dietas.

venas: los vasos sanguíneos que transportan la sangre que contiene desechos desde los tejidos hacia el corazón.

desahogarse: expresar verbalmente sus sentimientos.

ventrículos: las dos cámaras inferiores del corazón que despachan la sangre a los pulmones y los tejidos.

fibrilación ventricular: las contracciones extremadamente rápidas de los compartimientos bajo del corazón que carecen la energía necesaria para bombear sangre alrededor del cuerpo.

vértebras (singular, vértebra): los delicados huesos huecos de la espina dorsal.

violencia: el uso de la fuerza física bruta con la intención de dañar o lastimar a alguien.

virgen: término dado a las personas antes de su primer coito.

virus: organismos que solo contienen material genético y capas de proteína y que dependen totalmente de las células que infectan.

vitaminas: nutrientes que son necesarios para el crecimiento y funcionamiento adecuado del organismo.

Glossary/Glosario

water-soluble: able to travel in the body's watery fluids and leave the body readily in the urine.

soluble en agua: capaz de disolverse en los líquidos aguados del cuerpo y dejar el cuerpo en la orina.

weight training: an activity routine for strength conditioning that use weights or machines to provide resistance against which the muscles can work.

levantamiento de pesas: rutinas de ejercicios para condicionar la fuerza que utiliza pesas o máquinas para proporcionar resistencia contra la cual pueden trabajar los músculos.

wellness: maximum well-being, the top of the range of health states.

bienestar: el bienestar máximo, el rango superior de los estados de salud.

whitehead: pimple.

punto blanco: una espinilla.

whole foods: foods that are close to their farm-fresh state, or those that have benefited from light processing.

alimentos integrales: alimentos que son cercanos a la naturaleza, con el menor procesado posible.

whole grains: grains used in their intact forms, with all of their edible parts included.

granos integrales: los granos en sus formas intactas, con todos sus partes comestibles incluidas.

will: a person's intent, which leads to action.

voluntad: la intención de una persona, que conlleva a la acción.

withdrawal: the physical symptoms that occur when an addictive drug is cleared from the body tissues.

supresión: los síntomas físicos que ocurren cuando una droga a la cual una persona es adicta se elimina de los tejidos del organismo.

withdrawal method: contraceptive method in which the man withdraws his penis from the vagina before he ejaculates, taking care that his semen is not deposited in, at, or near the vagina.

método de retiro: el método anticonceptivo en el cual el hombre se retira el pene de la vagina antes de que él eyacule, tomando cuidado que su semen no está depositado en, por o acerca a la vagina.

yeast infection (candidiasis): an infection caused by a yeast that multiplies out of control in the vagina.

infección por levadura (candidiasis): una infección causada por una levadura que se multiplica fuera de control en la vagina.

zygote: the product of the union of ovum and sperm, so termed for two weeks after conception.

cigocito: el producto de la unión del óvulo y el espermatozoide, denominado así durante las dos semanas posteriores a la concepción.

Index

Index

Index

Index

Index

Index

Index

Photo Credits

Larry Bray/Jupiterimages; **598** Sean Justice/Corbis/Jupiterimages; **600** Phototake Inc./Alamy; **601** Imagebroker/Alamy; **602** Christopher Kerrigan; **603** Visuals Unlimited/Corbis; **604b** Christopher Kerrigan; **604t** Custom Medical Stock; **605** McGraw-Hill Companies Inc.; **622-623** Corbis/Jupiterimages; **624** Benelux/Zefa/Corbis; **626** Corbis/Jupiterimages; **630** Comstock Images/ Jupiterimages; **636** Corbis; **639** Jose Luis Pelaez/Getty Images; **642-643** Diane MacDonald/Getty Images; **644** Royalty Free/Corbis; **647tr** Imagebroker/Alamy; **647br** ImageSource/Jupiterimages; **647tl** Philip Kaake; **647bl** Radius Images/Alamy; **651** Javier Pierini/Getty Images; **656** S. Wanke/PhotoLink; **657** Jeff Greenberg/Alamy; **659** Leo Dennis Productions/Jupiterimages; **660** Roger Ressmeyer/Corbis; **668-669** Steve Liss/Time Life/Getty Images; **682** Bruce Ayres/Getty; **698-699** David Young-Wolff/PhotoEdit Inc.; **700bl** Kent Knudson/PhotoLink; 700br Robert Landau; **704** Mixa Co./Alamy; **708** UpperCut Images/Getty Images; **711** MShields Photos/Alamy; **712** Jupiterimages; **714** Anderson Ross/Getty Images; **716** Russel Illig/Photodisc/Getty Images; **717** Jupiterimages; **718** Paul Glendell/Alamy; **720** Jeff Greenberg/PhotoEdit; **721** Bruce Liron/Alamy; **722** Photodisc/Getty Images; **728-729** Masterfile; **731** Jim Craigmyle/Corbis; **742** Jim Craigmyle/Corbis